The
Editorials of
David Lawrence

General Dwight D. Eisenhower being interviewed by David Lawrence and other members of the staff in the conference room of U.S.News & World Report, January, 1950.

The
Editorials of
David Lawrence

IN SIX VOLUMES

Volume V

The Eisenhower Years

January 23, 1953—January 16, 1961

BOOKS by U.S.NEWS & WORLD REPORT

Contents

The Eisenhower Years

1953-1960

Republican candidate Dwight D. Eisenhower is cheered by his supporters as he arrives at party headquarters in New York's Commodore Hotel, November 4, 1952, to watch returns from the election which made him the first Republican President in 20 years.

The Eisenhower Years *by Albert L. Warner*

*(This review, written by a member of the staff of
U.S.News & World Report, provides a historical background
for the editorials which follow.)*

In a chaotic world of wide-ranging turbulence, President Dwight D. Eisenhower steered his country through one crisis after another. Serious problems or critical dangers touched Korea, Formosa and Vietnam in the Far East; Iran, Suez and Lebanon in the Middle East; Berlin and Trieste in Europe and Guatemala and Cuba in the Western Hemisphere, near the United States.

Anti-Soviet uprisings in Hungary and Poland and ruthless display of Russian force to put them down also featured the confused world scene. On top of this was the rivalry between Russia and the United States in the development of missiles, and twice came the Soviet threat to use rockets against opponents in the cases of the Suez and Cuba.

Russia's launching of the first man-made satellite, Sputnik, took the rivalry into space. It was followed by the American creation of NASA, the National Aeronautics and Space Administration, which was to lead much later to the first landing of men on the moon.

In the perils of the time, Eisenhower and his Secretary of State John Foster Dulles established a ring of alliances around the Sino-Russian Communist perimeter as a means of defense against forceful Communist expansion. NATO was extended as the Western defense in Europe and a contribution of a German force was accepted.

The death of Josef Stalin confronted the U.S. with a new Soviet leadership scarcely more tractable.

Through the crises of his eight years in the White House, Eisenhower maintained the United States out of war although, with resolute firmness, it several times came to the "brink," as Dulles put it.

In domestic policies, the Eisenhower aim was to summon private initiative in the building of the economy and to keep a reasonably balanced federal budget. On the whole, it was a period of prosperity for the United States with income up, wages rising faster than the relatively small degree of inflation.

Government reorganization brought establishment of the Department of Health, Education and Welfare. The big interstate highway program was put under way, the federal role in education significantly extended, national parks improved, the St. Lawrence Seaway authorized, internal security arrangements in the Federal Government tightened, and a series of civil-rights acts initiated while the Supreme Court declared school segregation unconstitutional.

Although subjected to criticism, especially at the end of his Administration, Eisenhower maintained a great personal popularity, perhaps as the figure of a kind and wise father. On his White House desk was a Latin motto which, translated, read: "Gently in manner, strongly in deed."

Three illnesses marked his two terms but did not deter his resumption of the heavy loads of office.

Eisenhower believed in enforcing the law even when that course ran him into controversy. To uphold the courts on school desegregation, he ordered federal troops into Little Rock, Arkansas. To support his conception of international law and justice, he accepted criticism at home and from two principal allies, Britain and France, when he vigorously opposed their use of force against Egypt at the Suez Canal.

As he took office in 1953, Eisenhower, in his state-of-the-union message, pledged, in the cause of peace, to deter aggression. He ordered the American fleet to stop patrolling the Formosa Straits to protect Red China. The fleet had had the dual purpose of protecting Chiang Kai-shek on Formosa and of preventing him from attacking Red China. The Red Chinese were then fighting the U.S. in Korea. The Eisenhower order had no practical significance but it upset British and French officials who wanted no widening of hostilities in the Far East.

The President also served notice that the Korean War had better end or it would be extended beyond Korea. Indirectly, he let Moscow know that, if a reasonable truce in Korea could not be made, the use of atomic weapons would have to be considered. The truce was signed July 27, 1953, but it brought an uneasy peace which was broken for years thereafter in aggressive incidents perpetrated by the North Korean Communists. American troops could not be fully withdrawn.

In Iran, Premier Mossadegh seemed to be leading his country into the Soviet orbit. Eisenhower's concern was relieved by the Iranian Army revolt upholding the Shah. American economic aid was immediately volunteered. Finding a way to get out of the oil dispute, a consortium reached agreement to buy Iran's oil.

President Eisenhower listens as Secretary of State, John Foster Dulles, speaking from The White House, reports to the nation on the Middle East Crisis following Egyptian seizure of the Suez Canal.

Congressional leaders and Atomic Energy Commission officials look on as President Eisenhower signs the Atomic Energy Bill, August 30, 1954. The bill made private enterprise a partner in the development of atomic energy for peaceful purposes.

Foreign Ministers
Vyacheslav Molotov (left)
of the Soviet Union and
Chou En Lai of Com-
munist China arrive in
Geneva, April 24, 1954,
for the Four Power
Conference on Korea
and Indo-China.

Troubles in Vietnam continued all through the Eisenhower years but the involvement of U.S. armed forces was avoided. Eisenhower found that Red China used the end of active Korean fighting to increase its aid to Communist Vietnamese under Ho Chi Minh who were challenging French control.

Eisenhower continually pressed the French for a renunciation of their status as a colony owner in Indo-China but without clear-cut success. The President saw the disadvantage of having the United States lumped with a colonial power but he also believed that Communist victory with Red China behind it and in league with Russia would endanger Laos, Cambodia, Thailand, Malaya and even Burma and East Pakistan as well as threaten Formosa, Indonesia and the Philippines.

By the spring of 1954, the isolated French fortress at Dien Bien Phu, a position which Eisenhower had always termed a bad strategic mistake, was in critical danger. Its surrender could mean the end of the French in Vietnam. Vice President Richard M. Nixon publicly proposed the possibility of sending in U.S. troops against Communist expansion. Some military opinion in Washington favored a U.S. air strike. Eisenhower doubted the effectiveness of such air intervention and was against the use of American ground forces, particularly if the United States was without allies. The President feared a drain on American resources and the absence of free world unanimity. The three service chiefs recommended against a U.S. air strike although Chief of Staff Admiral Arthur W. Radford was for more action.

At the Geneva conference, France agreed to withdraw its troops,

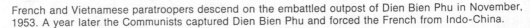

French and Vietnamese paratroopers descend on the embattled outpost of Dien Bien Phu in November, 1953. A year later the Communists captured Dien Bien Phu and forced the French from Indo-China.

Delegates of Britain, France, Russia and the United States assemble with Asian representatives for the last session of the Four Power Conference in Geneva, July 20, 1954. The next day a formal cease-fire pact was signed, partitioning Vietnam and neutralizing Laos and Cambodia.

autonomy was decreed for Laos and Cambodia and Vietnam was partitioned, with elections to come in two years. The United States declined to associate itself with these arrangements but showed it would not use force to disturb this settlement. Refugees going from north to south in Vietnam were aided. Thereafter, economic assistance and a small number of military advisers went to South Vietnam.

To discourage a further Communist push in this area, the Southeast Asia Defense Treaty was signed in September, 1954. Defense treaties were also signed with the Chinese Nationalists on Formosa, with South Korea and Japan.

Dulles also promoted the Central Treaty Organization (CENTO), but the U.S. did not sign this Middle East Defense Treaty. Before long, the signers began to fall apart. Critics have condemned the effectiveness of these defense alliances and the spending of American money on arms aid among allies who did not always remain stable. Question was also raised as to whether the treaties were provocative and perhaps placed signers in more danger. Eisenhower was convinced they retarded Communist expansion.

In the spring of 1955, Formosa and the off-shore islands controlled by the Nationalists became a crisis point. When the Red Chinese began shelling Nationalist islands, Eisenhower received congressional authority to defend Formosa and the Pescadores. The Tachen Islands were evacuated. Eisenhower was determined that no more peoples would be lost to Communist aggression; there would be no more Munichs.

In 1958, Red Chinese bombing of Quemoy and Matsu brought another crisis. When the United States Navy escorted Nationalist supply ships, the threat died away.

British tanks patrol the banks of the Suez Canal near Port Said after the Anglo-French invasion of Egypt in November, 1956.

One of the gravest crises was at the Suez Canal, scene of so much periodical strife. Beginning in 1953, Egypt pressured Britain out of its 1.5-billion-dollar military base where it had extensive defense shops and 80,000 troops. In 1956, the United States was sympathetic toward giving Premier Nasser of Egypt aid to build a huge Aswan Dam on the Nile. But Nasser stalled on accepting American conditions and bargained with Russia for aid. The U.S. withdrew from the project. Nasser denounced this country, and a few days later seized the Suez Canal from its British and French investors and operators and nationalized it.

The aroused British and French wanted the U.S. to participate in vigorous protest and consideration of counteraction. Eisenhower held back, opposed to the use of force and recognizing the right of a nation to expropriate foreign holdings within its territory if appropriate compensation were paid. But he recognized the ruthlessness of Nasser's action and the danger to Western Europe if shut off from Mideastern oil.

An American plan for international supervision of canal operations was rejected by Nasser and by Russia behind him. At this point, in October, riots broke out in Polish cities against the Communist regime and a far-reaching democratic revolt began in Hungary, threatening to remove the nation completely from the Soviet Russian orbit. Russian troops in numbers suppressed the uprisings without mercy.

At about the same time, Egypt, Syria and Jordan announced a military agreement which directly threatened Israel. On October 29, Israel took the initiative in retaliating with strikes which went through Egyptian territory

Russian tanks patrol a major intersection in Budapest after crushing the Hungarian rebellion in October, 1956.

American Marines in landing craft move through the streets of Beirut after being sent to Lebanon to protect the pro-Western government from a Communist take-over.

to the Suez. The next day, France and Britain issued an unanswered ultimatum to Egypt and then struck with planes and landed troops at the Suez. The United States went to the U.N., which ordered a cease-fire—accepted along with the Eisenhower proposal for a U.N. force to oversee the peace. Britain and France had shown in the military action something of a weakness, military and financial.

As to Hungary, the United States demanded that Russia remove its troops, but the answer was no.

Critics accused the Eisenhower Administration of deserting its allies. But Eisenhower, who had not been consulted before they attacked Egypt, was firmly against use of force and deemed their action a violation of international law. He did warn Russia when it threatened to use rockets. As to Hungary, he found no way to give it physical help, surrounded as it was by Communist satellites and neutral Austria. The British-French action at Suez was said by some to have encouraged the Soviet action in Hungary, but Eisenhower did not agree; Russia would have been ruthless, regardless.

In these years, several peaceful agreements were reached without display of force. Russia and the West agreed on a peace treaty with a neutral Austria. Italy and Yugoslavia agreed on the disposition of Trieste. Berlin was preserved in the same uneasy isolation behind Communist lines in Germany. A firm Western stand stopped Russia from turning over its powers in Berlin to the East German Government with the implied threat of a blockade of West Berlin.

But in Lebanon in May, 1958, an increase of Nasser and Communist influence in the adjoining Arab states touched off a rebellion. Eisenhower granted a request from the President of Lebanon for aid to preserve his Government. American Marines were landed. Order was restored and the troops withdrawn.

In the Western Hemisphere, Washington was concerned over the establishment of a pro-Communist Government in Guatemala in May, 1954. A vessel with arms from Communist territory in Europe arrived. The crisis was resolved by the local overthrow of the pro-Communist Government.

The really dangerous Communist invasion of the Western Hemisphere came with the rise of Fidel Castro to power in January, 1959. He was grossly misinterpreted in the United States at first as a democratic liberator of Cuba from a dictator. He was soon executing his opponents, denouncing the United States, seizing all American business firms and establishing economic and military ties with Soviet Russia. Later, he was to acknowledge that he was a Communist. The United States applied economic sanctions, said it would fight to defend the U.S. base at Guantanamo, ordered the fleet to prevent any Communist-led invasion of Guatemala and Nicaragua and broke off diplomatic relations with Cuba January 3, 1961. Eisenhower also quietly ordered the training of Cuban refugees in Guatemala for a possible landing in Cuba.

In domestic affairs, in his first state-of-the-union message in 1953,

Cuban revolutionary leader Fidel Castro parades triumphantly through the streets of Havana, December 16, 1959, after ousting dictator Fulgencio Batista.

Eisenhower showed determination to promote private initiative and enterprise. He ended price and wage controls which had been revived in the Korean War and sought a balanced budget and tax reductions.

The Administration successfully fought the Bricker constitutional amendment which would have limited presidential power in making treaties and executive agreements. The Department of Health, Education and Welfare was created with a woman, Mrs. Oveta Culp Hobby, as Secretary.

During the first Eisenhower term, new farm and housing legislation was enacted, the Air Force Academy established and 32.5 billion dollars authorized for a huge federal highway program to be financed by new gasoline and other highway-user taxes.

A Communist-control act was passed. The Civil Service Commission reported that 2,611 security risks had been dismissed from federal positions in 13 months.

In the period of McCarthyism, which grew partly out of past reluctance in Washington officialdom to acknowledge presence of disloyalty and espionage in the Government, Eisenhower was antagonistic to the extreme and reckless charges made by Senator Joseph R. McCarthy. But he deemed it wise not to give further publicity to the Senator by White House intervention overtly and rather to let McCarthy destroy himself. That was the result when members of the Senate on December 2, 1954, condemned their colleague by a vote of 67 to 22.

Sen. Joseph McCarthy of Wisconsin (right center) and aide Roy Cohn confront Robert T. B. Stevens (far left) and General Robert Young during the Army-McCarthy hearings in April, 1954. McCarthy's conduct during the controversial hearings led to his formal censure by the Senate.

Dr. J. Robert Oppenheimer (left), designer of the first atomic bomb, after being told on June 2, 1954, that he had been removed permanently as an Atomic Energy Commission consultant because of alleged Communist sympathies and his refusal, on grounds of conscience, to work on the hydrogen bomb. Seen below is an explosion over the Pacific.

A case which stirred continuing interest was that of Dr. J. Robert Oppenheimer, war-time head of the Los Alamos atomic laboratory and still a consultant of the Atomic Energy Commission when he was the subject of an adverse FBI report. Oppenheimer refused to resign. Eisenhower appointed a three-man board to hear charges, giving Oppenheimer the right to testify and his counsel the right to cross-examine. Oppenheimer was charged with hiring Communists and aiding Communist causes and with opposing the H-bomb project even after President Truman had ordered work started on it. It turned out Russia had also been developing it.

The investigating committee cleared Oppenheimer as "loyal" but decided, too, against his reinstatement as an AEC consultant. The AEC, in a four-to-one decision, upheld these findings.

Eisenhower thought that the scientist's opposition to the H-bomb was simply a matter of conscience but he agreed with the board that the defendant had shown "character deficiencies" in repeated falsehoods to security officers about Communists he had known.

In the election campaign of 1956, Eisenhower was an easy victor over Adlai E. Stevenson in a landslide electoral and popular vote, the winner by 9.5 million votes.

The Russian launching of the first man-made space satellite, Sputnik, caused a feeling of dismay in the United States that we might be behind in science and defense. Eisenhower thought the cause was a lag in missile development from 1945 to 1953. Concentrated attention to the challenge came with the creation of NASA and the National Defense Education Act advancing federal aid to colleges.

Soviet Premier Nikita Khrushchev in his Kremlin office (above) holding the model of a Russian moon landing craft he later presented to President Eisenhower at the White House (left) during his visit to the United States in September, 1959.

Armed paratroopers stand
guard outside Central High
School in Little Rock, Arkansas,
after being sent by President
Eisenhower to enforce a
Federal integration order in
1957.

Governor George C. Wallace
stands in the door of the
University of Alabama at Tus-
caloosa in an effort to prevent
Deputy Attorney General
Nicholas Katzenbach from
forcing the enrollment of two
black students at the all-white
school, June 11, 1963.

Pilot Francis Gary Powers (left) and his lawyer look at a model of the U-2 plane during hearings before the Senate Armed Services Committee, March 6, 1962. Powers was shot down and captured while on a U-2 reconnaissance mission over Russia, May 1, 1960.

The Administration sought to keep pace in the field of civil rights with the rising aspirations of Negroes. When the Supreme Court ended school segregation, Eisenhower took the position that the law as now construed should be upheld. He ordered immediate desegregation of the District of Columbia schools. While Negroes were boycotting the Montgomery, Alabama, buses because of discrimination in seating, the Administration moved toward civil-rights legislation. It proposed a civil-rights division in the Justice Department, a bipartisan civil-rights commission, protection of voting rights and authority to the Justice Department to intervene in civil discrimination cases. The bill was passed in weakened form in 1957. A stiff civil-rights voting act came in 1960. Meanwhile, in September, 1957, Eisenhower used 500 paratroopers to uphold the court order for the entry of Negro children into a high school at Little Rock, Arkansas.

In May, 1960, came the historic U-2 incident, a high-flying American spy plane brought down by Russian fire deep within Russia. In the international hubbub ensuing when Eisenhower took personal responsibility, the outcries of Russia's Nikita Khrushchev broke up a summit conference. The President decided to be straightforward. Spying by both sides was well-known and Russia had been even more aggressive. At a previous summit, Eisenhower's proposal for open skies, mutual surveillance and exchange of information on all military installations and movements had been rejected by Russia.

With Eisenhower's blessing, Vice President Nixon campaigned in 1960 for the Presidency against Senator John F. Kennedy. The latter was elected by a margin of only 112,881 votes.

Through tumultuous foreign and domestic developments, Eisenhower had steered the country with peace and a high degree of prosperity and an eye to social needs. His personal popularity stayed with him.

The
Editorials of
David Lawrence

The Eisenhower Years

January 23, 1953—January 16, 1961

INAUGURATING CHARACTER

JANUARY 23, 1953

WHEN THE MAN who has been elected President by the American people stands on the steps of the Capitol to be inaugurated, he takes an oath set forth verbatim in the Constitution ever since 1787. The Article reads:

"Before he enter on the execution of his office he shall take the following oath or affirmation:

" 'I do solemnly swear (or affirm) that I will faithfully execute the office of President of the United States, and will, to the best of my ability, preserve, protect, and defend the Constitution of the United States'."

These are fateful words. They permit of no mental reservation.

The oath does not mean that a President may tell members of Congress to pass laws which are admittedly of doubtful constitutionality, relying on a "packed" Supreme Court to decide them his way.

The oath does not mean that powers never granted to the President by the Constitution—namely, to seize private property without a law authorizing the action—can be usurped by the Executive.

The oath does not mean that a President may consider himself under no obligation to cooperate with committees of the Congress to preserve the Constitution, especially when subversive influences are engaged in infiltration in a period of emergency.

The oath does not mean that political friendships are to be given preference over the solemn obligation to select men best qualified for important posts notwithstanding the pressures of politicians inside or outside of Congress.

The oath does not mean that, when a war breaks out unexpectedly and our armed forces are promptly ordered to defend American interests, the President may decide not to ask Congress for specific ratification of his action even though the Constitution provides literally that only Congress may declare a state of war.

The oath does not mean that a President shall rationalize a full-fledged war as a "police action" and take refuge in so-called precedents involving minor military skirmishes in our history when the operation at hand involves casualties of troops larger by far than most of the wars in American history.

The oath does not mean that a President can condone subversion or dishonesty in his entourage. For the measure of his fidelity to the Constitution is the diligence with which he cleans up such wrongdoing without demands from the outside.

What does the oath really mean?

It is not merely a legal definition of duty or a pledge to perform a specified set of duties enumerated in our charter—the Constitution. It is a covenant of conscience. It is an affirmation of character. It is a confession of faith and, above all, a public commitment to a course of honesty.

Countless circumstances arise in the term of any President when the choice is between personal predilection or loyalty to a party or friend and the duty set forth in the Constitution itself. No matter what the pain or political injury, there can be no hesitation as to which decision to make or which action to take where the oath prods the conscience of a President.

The Constitution wisely inserts in the oath the phrase "to the best of my ability." This is a recognition of the limits of human fallibility and error. But the words do not mean: "I shall enforce the Constitution and the laws of the land in the best interest of my party or of the faction of individuals who have given me my office."

Nor does the phrase permit a rationalization which might say: "I will enforce the clauses of the Constitution in accordance with my own judgment as to how they should be interpreted."

The obligation is to follow the plain words of the Constitution. And where there is ambiguity or conflicting decisions of the courts, the President's duty is to rely on the honest judgment of competent legal advisers. This does not mean that the legal advisers shall be instructed to find ways and means of circumventing the words of the Constitution.

Dwight Eisenhower is a man of integrity. He has commanded American troops on the battlefield. He was the trustee under the Constitution for millions of American citizens engaged in defending our freedom against the tyranny of the totalitarian.

Dwight Eisenhower can bring to the Presidency what it has lacked in some recent Administrations, Republican and Democratic—character and honesty. For what profiteth a man that he shall win the plaudits of party or faction if he loses his soul!

The American people are expecting the inaugural oath to be fulfilled by Dwight Eisenhower in the spirit and high purpose which our forefathers intended when they put those simple words into the Constitution of the United States.

We are this week inaugurating character in the White House.

THE NEW RESPONSIBILITY

JANUARY 30, 1953

HAS ONE MAN assumed responsibility for the welfare of the nation? There is a tendency after the inauguration of a President to sit back and adopt the attitude that, once he is installed in office, the rest is up to him alone or to his Cabinet.

It is an oversimplification to say that a new Administration or a triumphant party in Congress has been given the full responsibility for government. The responsibility in a real sense extends to the people as well.

For the people are in truth a part of the governing process. They alone can affirm or repudiate an Administration. They are, therefore, the most vital influence in the operation of government from day to day.

Through the flow of news of what an Administration or a Congress does, the people become informed, and no leadership can succeed without the supporting reaction of the people.

The people usually are tolerant and patient with a new Administration. They allow for errors of inexperience and for honest mistakes of judgment. They give a new Administration plenty of time to find itself.

The political writers call this the "honeymoon" period, when all is sweetness and harmony. The implication of the phrase is that "honeymoons" are of short duration and that in politics the President and majority of his own party in Congress sooner or later start squabbling. This has happened so often in recent years that one forgets the periods when the "honeymoon" lasted through a whole term. A conspicuous instance of this was the "Era of Good Feeling," as they called it, during the entire Administration of Monroe.

There are, of course, many opportunities for a difference of opinion between the executive and legislative branches of the Government and many occasions no doubt when cleavages will occur inside the majority party. But these will be short-lived if a President has the support of the nation.

The key, therefore, is public opinion. As long as it is united behind a President, his leadership rather than that of anybody in Congress is decisive.

For the people are a constantly sitting jury. They pass judgment from day to day on the acts of the Administration.

To exercise such an important judgment, it is necessary that a people be well informed. George Washington in his farewell address said:

"In proportion as the structure of a government gives force to public opinion, it is essential that public opinion should be enlightened."

Public opinion nowadays is formulated by many different media of news—the newspapers, periodicals, newsreels, radio and television. No other country in the world has such comprehensive or such prompt coverage of news.

The most important medium of communication today, however, remains as it was at the beginning of our republic—word-of-mouth conversation and oral discussion of public affairs. Here is where the informed citizen plays his part. It is leadership in the local community, in the neighborhood, in the circle of friends which in the aggregate forms public opinion.

The first prerequisite is confidence in the new leader of our Government. To an extraordinary degree the people have absolute confidence in President Eisenhower. They do not expect him to be a perfectionist but to grapple as best he can with the problems of his office in a disinterested, honest and forthright manner, beholden to no one—not even to party doctrine if his conscience points to the need for reversal.

Though the ways of government, and particularly Congress, may occasionally present hurdles, the man who planned the Normandy invasion and executed the greatest military responsibility given to any man in history is not likely to have stage fright as he surveys the Washington scene.

It is a job that requires the giving of commands, and Dwight Eisenhower is a man who knows how to give them without arrogance or imperiousness. He has a kind heart and a generous personality, but he will not tolerate laxity of any sort from anyone no matter how politically obligated he might have been to such a person. Mr. Eisenhower's respect for the flag and the Constitution are inborn. To him the Presidency is an office of public trust, and he is never likely to forget that he is the trustee of the people.

The new President, however, cannot know what the people are thinking unless they participate in the process of government. They can do so by becoming informed and by informing others. We are too much in the habit of delegating government to our representatives in Washington and then paying intermittent attention to their efforts. We must instead write them our applause when they are right and our criticism when they are wrong.

Above all, we must know what our Government is doing and express our opinions when we have the facts necessary to form a helpful judgment. For the "new responsibility" extends to us all.

PLAIN TALK

FEBRUARY 6, 1953

WITH CHARACTERISTIC ABILITY to penetrate quickly to the core of a controversy, President Eisenhower has sent his Secretary of State, John Foster Dulles, to have a heart-to-heart talk with the leaders of the European governments. He decided not to wait for the various foreign ministers and premiers to string out a series of visits to America over the next several months.

The taxpayers of the United States have been pouring billions of dollars into Europe and have supported several divisions of American troops there in the belief that this was one way to help to defend Europe against a possible Soviet attack.

But it turns out that the Europeans have formed some misconceptions. Instead of uniting into an effective alliance, they have come to regard American economic aid as a sort of "boondoggle" and American troops as a permanent garrison.

The United States has looked to Europe to make an effective defense plan in which Germany, France, Britain and Italy would join forces. If the American people have been mistaken in that assumption, it is high time the air was cleared and an alternative policy formulated. Secretary Dulles, in his remarkably frank speech last week—which is printed in full text on pages 105-107 of this issue—says:

"The United States has made a big investment in Western Europe on the theory that there could be unity there. Of the 40 billion dollars which we have sent abroad since the end of the Second World War, almost 30 billions have gone into Western Europe.

"If, however, there were no chance, and that I just refuse to believe, but if it appeared there were no chance of getting effective unity, and if in particular France, Germany and England should go their separate ways, then certainly it would be necessary to give a little re-thinking to America's own foreign policy in relation to Western Europe."

Here is a historic pronouncement of transcendent importance to the world of 1953. The United States wants allies but will not bear all the burdens of an alliance without the fulfillment of a commensurate responsibility by the other powers of Europe.

Our alliance with Britain has been sagging. Britain wants to trade with the countries behind the Iron Curtain and, in due time, to admit Red China into the United Nations and hand Formosa to the Communists. The British are selling rubber—a strategic material—to the Communists at the rate of 98 million dollars a year while our boys are being killed and wounded in Korea. The British press keeps criticizing our policy of support for Chiang Kai-shek as if this were military and economic help to a particular personality instead of₁to a cause that may some day light the fires of liberty and freedom on the mainland of China and free the people there from the totalitarianism of the Communists.

Britain, moreover, doesn't want any part in the European Defense Army. France doesn't like the idea either, because the Germans are in it. The German socialists want neither a national army nor a European Defense Army for fear of antagonizing the Soviet and delaying a return of East Germany to the fold.

It's truly a mess. It is reminiscent of the bickerings between allies preceding World War II and of the way Hitler moved forward to pick off the allies one by one as they stood there in tragic disunity.

Stalin is doing the same thing now by infiltration. European socialists—in France, in Germany and in Britain—talk the same line as the Communists. They give the impression that America has some ulterior selfish purpose in giving military and economic aid to Europe—to make profits and bolster a war-made prosperity. The slogan of the Democrats in the last campaign—"You never had it so good"—made a deep impression on "left wing" writers in Europe.

Such an illusion sooner or later must be dispelled. That's what Secretary Dulles has gone to Europe to do.

We have been dragged into two world wars because European diplomats failed miserably to weld together the proper alliances which would have produced a real equilibrium of defense power. We are threatened again now with the same failures of British and French diplomacy.

Are we to be dragged into a third world war because of similar mistakes? Are we to be confronted soon in America with a resentful tide of isolationism as political capital is made in both the Democratic and Republican parties out of the fact that Europe not only frustrates our positive policies in Asia but prevents us from being of real help in the defense of Europe?

American public opinion may become reluctant to pour out more troops and money due to Europe's unwillingness to face the facts of international life. We had thought we were part of an effective world alliance against imperialism. But evidently we are not.

It's a time to build an effective alliance. It's a time for plain talk.

TOWARD VICTORY

FEBRUARY 13, 1953

AMERICA HAS JUST TAKEN the first steps toward winning the "cold war." The entire international situation has been moved off dead center by these decisive actions:

1. We have exerted our leadership in Europe. Through the timely visit of John Foster Dulles, Secretary of State—who in one week talked frankly and comprehensively to the heads of the British, French, Italian and German governments—the crucial job of really unifying our allies for the defense of the European community has been begun.

2. We have exerted our leadership in Asia. Restrictions previously imposed by our Navy on the outward movement of the forces of the recognized government of China, whose capital is on Formosa, have been eliminated. Moral support has been extended dramatically to the Nationalist Government in a manner that cannot but impress the people of Asia with the fact that the United States is irrevocably opposed to the Communist Government of China.

3. We have exerted our world leadership by a challenge to Soviet Russia. Moscow has been notified that the agreements made by our previous Administrations at Yalta, Teheran, Cairo and Potsdam will be terminated soon by a formal resolution to be passed by the Congress of the United States. This is the direct outgrowth of the failure of Soviet Russia to live up to those contracts. This step reopens many questions relating to territories and rights which the Soviets thought they had acquired out of the war, and it puts on the negotiating table anew subjects which the Communists have been salting away as "gains." It means a demand for the early return of East Germany now occupied by Soviet armies. It recovers for us a lost leverage in negotiating real agreements for world peace.

4. Leadership within the United States has been asserted. Now not only has a bipartisan policy been pledged, but already through consultation with Democratic as well as Republican leaders—before taking the action ordered in and around Formosa—this pledge has been fulfilled. The "state of the union" message to both houses of Congress last week is the first time since June 1950 that the Congress has ever received from the White House a formal communication on the Korean War. This is evidence of a genuine partnership between the executive and legislative branches of our Government.

In the "cold war," the two principals are not engaged in hostilities against each other and are not likely to be. Soviet Russia feeds weapons and supplies and staff officers to her allies without committing her own troops to action. That's the privilege now of the United States also with respect to aid of all kinds to her own allies.

Our policies, moreover, are in consonance with the letter and the spirit of U. N. pronouncements. For, on February 1, 1951, Communist China was declared by the U. N. to be an "aggressor."

In a broad sense, release of Chiang Kai-shek's forces eventually to bomb the north-south railway on the mainland of China from the air, or to raid the coastal islands from the sea, or to intercept the freighters of any nation carrying contraband cargos of war materials to Communist China are all proper military operations for the Nationalist Government of China. There is no intention on our part to send American troops to the mainland of China at any time.

As a psychological step, the decision to "deneutralize" Formosa will have significance throughout the entire world.

For we have at one fell swoop changed the entire complexion of things in Asia. It is not Chiang Kai-shek, the personality, that we are supporting but a free government.

Just as the withdrawal of support of the Nationalist Government at critical times in the last two years by the previous Administration in Washington served to weaken the Government of Chiang Kai-shek and to strengthen the Communist armies, so, conversely, extending our moral support to the Nationalist Government is a boost to all freedom-loving Chinese. They may some day desire to choose a new leader in place of Chiang Kai-shek, but, no matter who their leader is, they deserve the moral support of America in their fight against Communist tyranny.

With resoluteness and firmness America under President Eisenhower has set out to win the peace without involving our country in a third world war.

We hope to reduce the drain on our manpower and the strain on our economic system, and to get relief from tension. It will require courage and straight thinking. One sentence in the "state of the union" message of the President tells the whole story:

"There is—in world affairs—a steady course to be followed between an assertion of strength that is truculent, and a confession of helplessness that is cowardly."

We are not helpless, and we shall not be cowardly. We have started to move—and let the Kremlin do the guessing now!

WE ARE AT WAR

FEBRUARY 20, 1953

IT IS TIME to face facts in the world and to stop deceiving ourselves and especially the mothers and fathers of the boys being killed or wounded in Korea.

We are calling up 50,000 American boys every month through the draft and sending most of them to Korea. This is a realistic fact.

We are ordering 350,000 Americans to stand by in Korea while Communist shells endanger the lives of many of them. This is a realistic fact.

We are depriving the American field commanders in Korea of the right to strike back at the enemy in any way that will compel a truce. This is a realistic fact.

We are permitting arms and ammunition and the materials which can be manufactured into munitions to be shipped to our enemy, the Communist Chinese. Some allied governments are more concerned about the money-making of their citizens than the lives of our troops. This trade with the enemy is a realistic fact.

We are acting as the military "agent" of the United Nations and, as such, are empowered to conduct military operations against the Communist Chinese, but the American commanders in Korea are prohibited from bombing the bases in Communist Chinese territory from which enemy planes and supplies are coming to the battle front. This is a realistic fact.

For the truth is we are at war with the Chinese Communist Government which, as a faction in China, has assumed the status of belligerent against the United Nations.

The United Nations, by resolution on February 1, 1951, formally declared the Communist Chinese Government an "aggressor" in Korea. This means that war was in reality declared by the United Nations against the Communist Chinese Government at Peiping.

A blockade is, of course, an "act of war," but acts of war are being committed every day on the ridges of Korea against U. N. troops by soldiers under orders from the Chinese Communist Government.

New instructions should now be issued by the United Nations Assembly to the American commander to employ his naval and air power fully to blockade Chinese Communist ports. It goes without saying that no U. N. member should then attempt to resist that blockade.

Rebuttals are heard that such a course would bring the risk of a larger war. That is a counsel of fear. Acceptance of such reasoning would logically require the immediate dissolution of the NATO Army in Europe and the abandonment of the European Defense Army. For what else does the planned mobilization of these armies, on the very threshold of Soviet Russia, mean except that we are all taking a "calculated risk"?

But if the U. N. wishes to backtrack now in the Far East, if governments like that of Great Britain regret the step they took in June 1950, and if it is intended by other members of the U. N. to let American boys wither in Korea while the hands of our commanders are tied behind their backs, it is time to say so frankly.

For then America would have to do some "re-thinking." Maybe the American Government will be obliged to concede, for history's sake, that its own troops have been frustrated because the U. N. was unwilling to pursue the war to victory. Twice—according to General Van Fleet and General Almond—we could have won in Korea, as these commanders now testify. But the allied diplomats, acting through our State Department in Washington, held us back and we were not permitted to strike at the opportune time.

If aggression is eventually to be rewarded by admitting Red China to the U. N.—as so many of the members of the House of Commons in Britain seem to favor as an ultimate step—then the President of the United States should write a letter of apology to the parents of every American boy killed or wounded in Korea. He should arrange for the prompt withdrawal of all American forces as soon as the South Korean divisions are prepared to take over. If an adverse U. N. attitude persists, the United States could fix a target date of possibly two years by which time the withdrawal of all American troops from European countries would be completed. For, when the principle of collective security is nullified by the U. N. itself, there is no further point in keeping large bodies of American troops anywhere outside continental United States.

President Eisenhower as a last resort should attend the opening session of the United Nations' Assembly next week in New York and place the American viewpoint before that body. He should still plead for adherence to the principle of collective security. He should request that all members of the U. N. sever relations at once with the Communist Chinese Government because of its acts of aggression in Korea. He should ask that a naval blockade be imposed on Communist China. He should demand an end to trading with the enemy.

Neither the "cold war" nor any other war will be won by a cringing mood among our allies, even as American youth are ordered day after day to stand up to enemy fire on the "Heartbreak Ridges" of the Korean Peninsula. It's time for all of us to face facts.

WHY TAXES MUST BE CUT

FEBRUARY 27, 1953

TAXES CAN BE CUT, and they will be cut—provided Congress and the country understand why they must be cut.

For 20 years the psychology in government has been based on the fallacious theory that the executive branch determines whatever sums it wishes to spend—not necessarily what ought to be spent. Then the citizens are expected to pay taxes and also lend their savings to meet the budget.

Today that psychology is being reversed. The executive branch of the Government is being warned by a set of tragic facts which have been undermining the stability of our whole economy that the only sums which should be spent are those which the total of estimated tax collections will permit.

This is a change the American people voted for in the last election.

To say that a reduction of taxes is demanded merely because individuals or corporations will thereby have increased sums left over after taxes is to miss the entire point of the controversy.

For the real purpose of a tax reduction today is to restore the basic economic health of our country.

The crisis we face is this: The strongest industrial nation in the world is in danger of a destructive depression growing out of fiscal errors in the past and the reckless use of the taxing power.

It should have been obvious long before this that collapse is in store for a government which spends more than it takes in every year and yet increases tax rates on the theory that the sources of taxation are limitless. It is fundamentally wrong to assume that a private-enterprise economy can survive any such drain.

When the taxing power is abused and the public debt is constantly increased, confidence in the monetary unit is shaken. The American dollar today is relatively stronger than any other currency in the world, but this is merely another way of saying that a man with one broken leg is better off than a man with two broken legs.

If the American dollar goes down, all the other currencies will drop even more precipitately.

The most important bulwark of the free world today is a sound dollar. But a sound dollar means not just a balanced budget. It calls for a surplus in the Treasury and a decreasing tax load.

Taxes are burdensome on every class but mostly on the persons of lowest incomes. The solution is not to be found just in changing the individual tax rates to give relief to certain income groups. It must come by cutting down the tax costs imbedded in the prices of goods everybody has to buy.

This is because taxes are reflected in our high price level of today. In one way or another, taxes have been added to manufacturing and distribution costs so that the purchasing power of the dollar has been cut in half in the last 20 years. The resultant demands for higher and higher wages have produced spirals which have added to the whole strain.

America has been on the verge of an economic collapse due to the unsoundness of the dollar, the virtual exhaustion of the taxing power, and the mounting increases in national debt.

The Eisenhower Administration takes over at a time when the preceding Administration has left a legacy of near bankruptcy. Another four years of spending without cutting appropriations and reducing taxes would have broken down the entire American industrial machine. The American people wisely called a halt.

Today we see in the headlines a series of contradictory statements about tax reduction. It is being said that taxes cannot be reduced until the budget is balanced. This puts the cart before the horse. Actually the budget must not only be balanced but a surplus provided, and this can best be accomplished by first limiting the tax intake. Then—after the amount available for spending is carefully estimated—is the time to make an equitable allocation of the tax fund.

There are no "must" items or sacred items in any budget except those directly concerned with survival. We should reduce our expense for military defense to the minimum of national safety and then cut any or all other items no matter how long they have existed or how deeply they are rooted in the budgets of past years.

This is a painful process. But we must prepare for a period of "austerity" in government spending. Almost every item proposed for the federal budget can be justified as "necessary" by some agency of government or by some interested group. Political and even local business support can be brought to bear to retain or increase certain appropriations. But the answer is to take a look at the grim alternative—the hardships that will come to everybody if the entire business structure breaks down and unemployment ensues.

The whole defense of the free world will suffer if the American dollar collapses.

The budget can be cut because it must be cut and because taxes must be reduced. It's the way to a stronger America.

TO A BEWILDERED RUSSIAN

MARCH 6, 1953

DEAR BEWILDERED RUSSIAN:

It must be puzzling to you to figure out what is happening in the United States, just as it is to us sometimes to try to understand what is going on in Soviet Russia.

You are being told, for example, by your newspapers that the Eisenhower Administration is just a bunch of "capitalists" without concern for the common people. You can hardly be blamed for getting that impression, because over here that is exactly what the leaders of the defeated political party—the Democrats—are saying. Just the other day the chairman of the Democratic National Committee said in a speech that "big business" has taken over in Washington, and he implied, as do so many of your newspapers, that "big business" hasn't been good for the American people.

To be frank with you, it must be admitted that some persons in that same Democratic Party are antagonistic to capitalism and really prefer state socialism, but do not call it by that name.

The system that has built up our individual strength is based on the right of the individual to earn a living and make as much money as his talents or his capacity for invention or his creativeness will bring, and then to conserve these savings as "capital" and hire them out so as to earn interest or dividends, and thus attain real security for old age.

The other system—the New Deal or Fair Deal—calls for confiscation of savings or capital by heavy taxation. It induces the Government constantly to rob Peter to pay Paul and to allocate the people's savings at will for projects often described erroneously as "in the public interest." But such policies mean wasteful spending and huge deficits. They reduce the purchasing power of the dollar, weaken the economic structure, impair incentive, and, if unabated, could destroy capitalism, which is what some of its sponsors desire. The American people, by an overwhelming majority at the polls, have just repudiated that dangerous theory of government.

Now don't misunderstand us—capitalism has faults. But, with all its faults, capitalism has given the people of America a higher standard of living than any other system the world has ever known. This "big business" you read about has brought the prices of automobiles to within the reach of the workingman—and if you could see the crowded parking areas outside our factories on week days and the cars on our roads on Sundays, you would know what we mean.

Likewise, the housewife has an electric washing machine, and she has many another household convenience that has reduced the drudgery of housework or added to the comforts of living. All this has come about because "big business" is efficient and knows how to organize our mechanical skills and assembly lines to get products down to reasonable prices for all.

Don't be misled into thinking any small group of rich persons own our big enterprises. Approximately 500,000 men and women, most of whom work for a living, own General Motors, 250,000 own General Electric, and more than 1,000,000 own the American Telephone and Telegraph Company. All these citizens, and others like them, have put their own "capital"—their savings—into companies of this kind. That's what "capitalism" means to us. It assures expansion. It means work for all who wish to work. It brings good wages, good food, good houses, and good clothes. You, too, can have these things, and we'll be glad to show you how.

To begin with, the state is not the master here but the servant of all of us. We pick our rulers in free elections in America and turn them out of office when they don't suit us. You can do the same if you really believe in the dignity of the individual, if you really see through the fallacies of a state socialism that has brought you organized tyranny. You will find that the friendship of the American people is yours for the asking any time you want to put into operation a real republic. By this we mean a representative system devoted to the ideals of a Judeo-Christian tradition—a system of human rights wherein the individual has duties and obligations but none that is imposed except through a government of his own choosing.

Maybe, as history has proved so often, you are not as bewildered as you seem but will, in your own time and in your own way, emancipate yourselves and not only save your country but other peoples. For the only threat to peace in the world today comes from rulers who, in the guise of an idealistic Communism, have enslaved whole nations.

We Americans are not forgetting that war means death for your sons and ours. There is a better way. It may mean sacrifices by a few martyrs now, but eventually it means liberation for the many.

The "better way" is through the uniting of minds—the combining of your moral force and ours—so that hundreds of millions of people will determine at the same moment to act together to accomplish what military force by itself can never achieve.

Yours, for a reawakened and responsible individualism—the only answer to the evils of Communism.

STALINISM IS MORTAL, TOO

MARCH 13, 1953

"The boast of heraldry, the pomp of pow'r,
And all that beauty, all that wealth e'r gave,
Await alike th' inevitable hour:
The paths of glory lead but to the grave."

The wistful words of Thomas Gray's elegy are reflected in the sadness of the Soviet people over the loss of Stalin, the hero who saved them from the armies of the Nazi invader. They have been taught through propaganda to regard him as an immortal, a superman who along with Lenin steered the nation from the miserable years of Czardom to the "better life."

Our perspective is different. We see only the cruel tyrant whose command has condemned millions to concentration camps and death, whose evil genius has directed an army of agents as they have carried on a worldwide intrigue inside free nations.

We see only the man who, more than any other person in the world, has been responsible for our 130,000 casualties in Korea.

We see only the man who has persecuted people for their religious beliefs—Catholics, Protestants, Jews.

We see only the master mind which has sought to extoll materialism and the doctrine of "might makes right" as above the spiritual motivation of mortal life.

What a commentary on personal power and the misguided ambitions of men! What a disillusionment to those who have believed that man-made rule, even for a single nation, is either durable or permanent!

The whole world today conjectures what the future will bring. Will Malenkov and his group carry on with devilish pride a continuing vice? Will it be a new leadership less certain of its aims and goals, hesitating as it surveys the scene at home and abroad, and then making expedient concessions as it gains time to consolidate wavering elements within the Soviet empire? Will there, perhaps, arise in Russia someday a great hero who will truly bring peace to the world?

We must not assume that the death of one evil man will suddenly transform his eleven evil comrades in the Politburo into virtuous men.

This is no time for us to allow policies of principle to falter in a complacent reliance on wishful thinking.

This is the time to reassert our principles—to call on peoples behind the Iron Curtain to join us in the great revolution we have achieved already. It is a revolution that has carried us from the slavery of the individual to emancipation and freedom—to a standard of living unsurpassed throughout all history.

This is the time to urge peoples who have lost their liberties to strive to regain them with our help.

This is the time to tell them that freedom to produce and to conserve the fruits of their toil, freedom to worship, and freedom to think and to speak are freedoms available to them. For America and the rest of the peoples of the world await eagerly the emergence of a free Soviet republic.

This is the time to re-emphasize the brotherhood of man under God. A good start toward that objective was made by President Eisenhower last week in his message of sympathy and hope to the Russian people.

This is the time to build our physical and moral armament strongly and not to be swayed by an assumption that the evil of the Kremlin will vanish as suddenly as Stalin has passed from the scene.

For it is Stalinism which has been the cult of the misguided rulers of Soviet Russia—a philosophy born of a supposedly idealistic Communism but which has led to compulsion and inevitably to slavery.

It is Stalinism as a "superior" type of Communism which has succeeded in winning the support of groping minorities in various parts of a troubled world. Stalinism not only has reared its menacing authority inside the Soviet Union but by its tactics has hypnotized peoples and their governments on this side of the Iron Curtain as well. It is a myth of strength which has dominated supporters and foes alike.

Playing on the fear of bloodshed, Stalinism has used the technique of the "cold war" to wring from the free world—beguiled and tragically deceived—tactical advantages. It has been the most successful bluff ever made against obviously stronger nations.

Stalin is dead. And Stalinism is mortal, too. It cannot long survive in a climate of free men when they show a readiness to make every sacrifice for their cause.

We should now, therefore, proclaim anew our principles and our philosophy, reaffirm our purposes and utter our solemn warning—that Stalinist imperialism has too long disturbed the peace of the world and that the forces of freedom are unafraid. We are unafraid because we depend for our eternal strength not on one man or group of men but on the power of free minds guided by a conscience which recognizes the spiritual influence of Almighty God. The pages of history record that this influence has been growing steadily greater as, again and again, the material power of temporal rulers has been brought to an ignominious end.

The paths of evil, too, "lead but to the grave."

THE HIT-AND-RUN 'ALLY'

MARCH 20, 1953

SOVIET RUSSIA is supposed to be our "ally." This is set forth in the four-power agreement made in 1945, when the territory of conquered Germany was marked off into "zones." These were to be occupied by the military forces of the United States, Great Britain, France and Russia until a peace treaty with Germany could be signed.

But guns in fighter planes of Soviet Russia—our "ally"—opened fire last week and shot down an American plane and then a British plane. Six British airmen were killed.

All these planes were close to the border of two "zones." Soviet Russia and her satellite, Czechoslovakia, insist that their boundaries had been violated.

If we are still "allies," then there must be some friendly way to handle occasional crossings of the border by jet planes traveling at a speed of 600 miles per hour at a high altitude and with no means of knowing every minute just where the boundary really is.

Nations which are true friends should have no difficulty devising a system of signals to avoid clashes.

But are we "true friends," or have we become "enemies"?

There is nothing in any existing wartime agreement which gives any partner or ally the right to fire on the forces of another ally.

We should inquire of Moscow if the use of military forces now to attack the airplanes of her wartime partners means that the alliance entered into during World War II has been broken and that all agreements made thereunder are now to be considered abrogated.

So far as the American and British military units are concerned, they now are in West Germany as a result of an understanding with the free government at Bonn. Neither East Germany nor Czechoslovakia—whose territories were used as bases for the planes that attacked our airmen last week—have free governments today. Free elections—the best proof of the independence of governments—have not been held anywhere that Soviet troops have been stationed. The puppet governments of East Germany and Czechoslovakia are operating under the duress of Soviet Russia.

The way is opened now, therefore, to a reconsideration of all the wartime agreements and to a demand that all their provisions be fulfilled.

If, however, we are no longer "allies," does the Soviet Government intend to arrogate to itself the right to cross into West Germany at any time and to permit its satellite air forces to cross into an American or British zone and open fire at will on our airplanes?

Such hit-and-run behavior by airplanes of Soviet Russia and her satellites would be expected of enemies. It is not characteristic of friends.

If the Soviet regime reveals by its deeds that it must be considered an enemy, then all diplomatic relations with Moscow should be severed, Soviet representatives should be expelled from the United Nations, and an embargo should be imposed not only on all trade but on all money flowing to Soviet agents in the Western world.

The commanders, moreover, of American and British air forces in Europe must be instructed not merely to return the fire but, under international law, to apply the doctrine of "hot pursuit" so as to drop bombs on any air bases from which the enemy airplanes may be emerging in their hit-and-run attacks.

It would appear that the episodes in Germany last week are not unrelated to what has been happening in the Far East. There the alliance of U. N. members has shown itself timid and hesitant. We should not remain stagnant any longer. We should warn the Soviet Government that, unless it ceases to send munitions over the trans-Siberian railroad to Korea to be used against U. N. troops, it may become necessary for U. N. air forces to bomb that railroad.

There comes a time in a crisis when to falter, to appease, to cringe is to invite a major war. By standing firm now, we will avoid such a war. For the Soviet people, when they know the purpose of their rulers—to involve them in a war—will not support another conflict in which they are again to make heavy sacrifices.

We should tell the Soviet people plainly that, if the Moscow Government persists in its aggression, there will be no alternative but to defend ourselves.

We must be resolute now in thwarting any hostile purpose manifested by the Soviet Union. Otherwise, we shall be the tragic victims of an all-out attack some day by the Hitlers of the Kremlin, who will venture to risk large-scale war because they will have misconstrued our reiterated pleas for peace as cowardice.

It has been said, again and again, by those diplomats who know the Soviet temperament that military force is the only language the Communist Government understands. If so, clear and unmistakable warning should be given now that our military force may have to be used without limit to render ineffective the Soviet supply lines to Communist armies in Korea and to resist any further aggression by the Soviet in Europe.

TAX 'REFORM'—MORE REVENUE

MARCH 27, 1953

PRESIDENT EISENHOWER said last week that, while he doesn't want to see revenues lowered, he doesn't object to tax "reform."

But in that single phrase "tax reform" lies the key to America's fiscal dilemma.

For when the President rightly pointed out that continuing deficits would mean a "cheapening" of the dollar, he might have been reminded that the mere imposition of taxes doesn't guarantee that a budget will be balanced. There is no more certain way to "cheapen" the dollar and cause a lack of confidence in the monetary unit of a nation than to maintain a system of taxation which, having reached the saturation point, begins to bring in less and less revenue.

The task is threefold:

1. To reduce federal expenditures.

2. To revise the tax system so as to increase receipts. This involves some upward and some downward changes in tax rates as well as finding new sources of taxation.

3. To attain a surplus so as to begin paying off the national debt.

Primarily what America must have is a sound economic situation, or else the tax yield will never be enough to balance the budget.

Under the New Deal and Fair Deal, the idea was to use tax "reform" for punitive purposes. The feeling of class hatred was so deep that a "soak the rich" slogan was the basis for confiscatory rates on personal incomes.

Basically the principle of "capacity to pay" is sound, but it never should go to the extreme of destroying incentive or penalizing success. Curiously enough, while the New Deal and Fair Deal imposed high taxes on individual incomes, the tax policies of the Democratic Administrations always favored big corporations.

No better proof of this can be cited than the recent report of the Senate Small Business Committee under the chairmanship of Senator Sparkman, Democrat, of Alabama. In that report—concurred in by Republicans and Democrats—is the following passage:

"Our tax policies seem to contradict implicitly or explicitly the Government's operations in other fields. While Congress passes laws and appropriates funds for the strengthening and administration of antitrust and antimerger laws, present-day taxes seem to be prime motivators in erecting obstacles to healthy competition.

"The owners of small enterprises with uneven earnings records who are paying out a major share of their profits in the form of personal- or corporate-income taxes inevitably are favorably inclined to accept offers to sell out to their larger competitors."

Unquestionably the "excess profits" tax helps big business and penalizes small business. That's one reason why this form of tax, which expires on June 30, should not be re-enacted. At least in the First World War period the excess-profits law provided that no business need pay any higher rate than a competitor, but even this provision does not remove all the inequities.

The President says that, when the present excess-profits-tax law expires, he wants another form of tax to take its place so that revenues will not be reduced.

There is a way to increase receipts by revising our tax system. It can be done by stimulating rather than strangling business expansion. Thus the same Senate Committee says of the surtax and excess-profits taxes:

"Up to 70 per cent of all earnings can be taxed by the Federal Government, and for many firms, of each additional dollar of profit, 82 cents goes to the Federal Government. Many witnesses stated that they were unable or unwilling to take the necessary business risks to expand their business when over 80 per cent of their increased earnings were earmarked for the Director of Internal Revenue."

Among the suggestions made by the Senate Committee is to allow "flexible depreciation policies" so as to contribute "to a healthier operation of our competitive economy," because when business firms "are released from some of the crushing burden of present taxes, they will be likely to modernize and expand their plants."

Tax "reform" is long overdue. A revision of the administrative provisions of our tax laws has not been made in many years. Many of the present provisions are outmoded and unfair.

If Congress could give attention not only to the inequities in business taxes but in personal taxes as well, Treasury receipts would increase substantially as a result of the enlarged volume of transactions throughout our whole economic system.

It's the way to a healthy economy and a sound dollar.

Certain sales taxes may have to be imposed and others eliminated.

Certain income-tax rates can be revised downward.

The problem is not to be solved by a general tax cut or a general tax rise. The time has come for the application of sound principles to a selective system of taxation that has only one object—the collection of more revenue through an expanded economy.

MR. BOHLEN AS A SYMBOL

APRIL 3, 1953

THE SENATE of the United States has written a tragic chapter in American history.

It has failed by resolution to repudiate the Yalta Conference and its iniquities.

It has failed in voting on a nomination for Ambassador to the Soviet Union to reject the philosophy of Charles E. Bohlen, who, upon being selected for that post, publicly testified in support of the evil agreements made at Yalta, where he served as an adviser. He says the agreements were all right at the time—only their subsequent violation and interpretation by the Soviet Union were wrong.

But the facts show otherwise. This comment is not a case of hindsight. Within a few days after the official announcement of the Yalta agreement had been issued to the world in February 1945, there began in this magazine a series of four editorials denouncing the abandonment of principle and flagrant disregard of the pledges of the Atlantic Charter. This Charter was the heart of American idealism—it was for this that American boys were asked to give their lives.

In one of those editorials, the writer said:

"Yalta has changed the face of modern history.

"From an era in which collective security has been the primary objective, the pendulum has swung now to an era in which all the major nations are to be above the law prescribed for the smaller nations.

"Surrender No. 1 at Yalta was acquiescence in the seizure of Latvia, Estonia and Lithuania by Stalin in 1940 when he was a partner of Hitler.

"Surrender No. 2 was the ratification of a deal made in 1943 between Stalin and Churchill to take away from Poland—an ally—one third of her territory.

"Surrender No. 3 was the acceptance of Stalin's demand, first raised at the Dumbarton Oaks Conference, that Russia reserve a power of veto over the Security Council of the proposed United Nations Charter."

In the February 23, 1945, issue the writer said:

"Many of us will still believe that the President's position at the Crimea Conference should have been that which we took earlier in this war, namely, that peace settlements must await the day of victory and that the peace conference must be free from any previous commitments or pledges on territorial questions made in secret or otherwise.

"Russia could not quit the war against Germany if decision on her territorial demands were deferred any more than we could turn from the fight against Hitler because we failed to persuade Russia to wait for the awards of a peace conference, at which all interests, including the people of Poland, would have had a chance to be heard through a government of their own choosing, as specifically provided for in the Atlantic Charter, which says:

" 'They (Russia, Britain, the United States, etc.) desire to see no territorial changes that do not accord with the freely expressed wishes of the peoples concerned.'

"We cannot concede that Russia is winning this war alone against Germany and so deserves everything she asks for. If American lives had not been sacrificed on the Western Front and if we had not supplied airplanes and other materials under lend-lease, Russia could not have mounted her offensives. The American viewpoint has back of it moral right as well as sacrifices of our manpower thousands of miles away from continental United States.

"For American idealism was defeated at Yalta. American constitutionalism was scorned at Yalta, and the pledges given in the Atlantic Charter that no nation—neither Russia, nor Britain nor any other country—will seek 'territorial aggrandizement' were flagrantly violated at Yalta."

Again in another editorial—written immediately after the results of the secret sessions at Yalta became public—the writer said:

"Sooner or later appeasement must end, and Yalta was the place to end it. Russia would have respected us for it and a mere deferment of the Polish question to the peace conference—or its adjudication even before that time by a special international commission at which all interests, including those of Poland, could be heard, and the United Nations could sit in judgment—would never have caused a break in the present alliance between Russia, Britain and the United States. If this partnership is founded on any such frail basis, then, indeed, we are in for trouble ahead and we must appease and appease and appease . . .

"We simply have been outmaneuvered and outbluffed, and we on this side of the Atlantic already have begun to sacrifice our ideals and principles down the long painful road of rationalized surrender."

In another editorial at the time the writer said:

"Where is the courage to challenge the compromises and the appeasements that mean not yet the unconditional surrender of our enemies but already the unconditional surrender of our souls and our consciences to the old, old doctrine that 'might makes right'?"

Will this Congress—or another Congress yet to be elected—give the American answer?

COLLECTIVE APPEASEMENT

APRIL 10, 1953

Is the West about to appease the East?

Is principle to be cravenly abandoned?

Is the main objective of the war in Korea to be surrendered just to accept a "cease fire" agreement whose main terms provide an opportunity for a military buildup by the Communists?

Under the authority of a United Nations resolution in the summer of 1950, the forces of this country and fifteen allies started to turn back the aggressor in Korea —the armies of a puppet government controlled by Soviet Russia.

After having driven the aggressor back in four months to the Yalu River, the U. N. forces were attacked by the armies of Red China.

The United Nations then declared Red China's Government an aggressor, but never has had the courage to declare the Soviet Government the true aggressor.

The United Nations troops were never permitted to put maximum military power into the fray. Enemy bases and supply depots in Manchuria—Red China territory—were never subjected to U. N. air operations. But tens of thousands of casualties were incurred by the United States and her allies because munitions came daily from these arsenals above the Korean border.

And now the Western statesmen reveal a humiliating eagerness to grasp at the straws that the enemy thrusts forth—straws that mean merely that the Communists have condescended to allow the Western countries to beg for peace once more. The Soviet Union and Red China, like conquerors, call the tune.

And what does the new era of "talk" mean? Simply that, when a "cease fire" comes, the peoples of the West are expected to be so overwhelmed with rejoicing that they will forget what the war was about.

The truce terms, moreover, provide that, while no additional troops beyond the number already there may be sent by the U. N. command direct to Korea, the Communists may continue to build airfields in North Korea. Also Soviet Russia and Red China may continue to send jet planes and munitions and soldiers to the sanctuary just above the North Korean boundary—the adjacent territory of one of the belligerents in the war.

With a one-sided armistice agreement signed up, the U. N. will then convene the "political" conference to discuss outstanding issues.

The U. N. resolution of October 1950 called upon its military forces to attain the unification of Korea as an independent, sovereign state. Is hapless Korea to remain divided while the bickering in the new "political" conference goes on endlessly? "Unification" to the Communists means only a government they can control.

The U. N. is influenced to no small extent by Great Britain's diplomacy, which is ready to support the admission of Red China into the United Nations once the fighting has ceased.

How then are the aggressors to be punished? Will not the aggressors actually be rewarded? How can the West argue persuasively that it has "repelled aggression" when the military line at which the armistice is fixed is about what it was in June 1950 and when the aggressors now dictate the terms of "peace"?

Is this the great cause for which our youth gave their lives?

Is this a vindication of the principle of "collective security" which has been proclaimed as the "glorious" mission of the United Nations in Korea?

As long as all nations make equal sacrifices in a common cause, as long as our troops when ordered into action are not required to fight a "sit down" war but a war to win victory, the principle of collective security is sound. It collapses, however, when members of the international organization which orders our sons into action maintain trade with the enemy and only now, after nearly three years of pleading, seem to understand what fidelity to an alliance means.

The new proposals from the Communists are part of a clever ruse to elicit concessions in Europe—to squelch the movement for a European Defense Army and to retard the development of NATO's military forces by dangling a spurious "peace" before the eyes of the Western peoples.

Today the U. N. seems ready to indulge in collective appeasement. The Russian maneuvers are hailed as the beginning of an era of sweetness and light on the part of the racketeers in the Kremlin whose crimes against humanity are legion. One wonders whether this isn't the start of the cycle that will bring us World War III. For when disillusionment comes, passions will run high and an enlarged war will appear as the inevitable alternative.

"Peace at any price" has always been a fatal formula in international disputes. Will the West repudiate that concept by putting a time limit on the "talks" and by dictating the terms of settlement in Asia and Europe? Or will the West fall again before the blandishments of an aggressor who offers minor points in exchange for larger conquests—an aggressor who throughout the last seven years has made a mockery of the word "peace"?

WANTED: A COMPASS

APRIL 17, 1953

IN WHAT A SORRY STATE do we find ourselves today as we drift from crisis to crisis not knowing what the enemy may do and always seeking to contrive for ourselves a new formula to meet each contingency.

Our leaders spend anxious hours trying to guess what the next move of Communist Russia may be, trying to evaluate the personality characteristics of Malenkov or the behavior of evil men in the Kremlin.

If the lives of the great statesmen of history teach in common a single lesson, it is that nations must steer by a compass. That compass is Principle. We cannot chart a new course every time a new problem arises. To forsake Principle for the opportunism of Expediency is to start a nation on the road to self-destruction.

There is but one course America should follow in meeting the so-called "peace offensive" of the Communists. It is the course guided by Principle.

It was on a great Principle that just thirty-six years ago this month America charted a fateful course. We entered the First World War to assure our national safety as against the threat of a totalitarian government. We thought in 1919 after the First World War that we had made the world safe for democracy. But twenty years later the totalitarian government of Hitler dispelled that illusion and we went to war a second time to carry out the same mission.

At this critical time the voice of history calls out to us the immortal words of President Woodrow Wilson—the great Principle proclaimed on the night of April 2, 1917 to a joint session of Congress:

"Self-governed nations do not fill their neighbor states with spies or set the course of intrigue to bring about some critical posture of affairs which will give them an opportunity to strike and make conquest.

"Such designs can be successfully worked out only under cover and where no one has the right to ask questions. Cunningly contrived plans of deception or aggression, carried, it may be, from generation to generation, can be worked out and kept from the light only within the privacy of courts or behind the carefully guarded confidences of a narrow and privileged class. They are happily impossible where public opinion commands and insists upon full information concerning all the nation's affairs.

"A steadfast concert for peace can never be maintained except by a partnership of democratic nations.

"No autocratic government could be trusted to keep faith within it or observe its covenants. It must be a league of honor, a partnership of opinion. . .

"We are accepting this challenge of hostile purpose because we know that in such a (German) government, following such methods, we can never have a friend; and that in the presence of its organized power, always lying in wait to accomplish we know not what purpose, there can be no assured security for the democratic governments of the world. . .

"We are glad, now that we see the facts with no veil of false pretense about them, to fight thus for the ultimate peace of the world and for the liberation of its peoples, the German peoples included: for the rights of nations great and small and the privilege of men everywhere to choose their way of life and of obedience.

"The world must be made safe for democracy."

When we substitute the words "Russian Government" and "Russian peoples" for "German Government" and "German peoples," the foregoing passages read as if they were spoken to us today.

The job is still unfinished. The world in 1953 is less safe for democracy than it was in either 1919 or 1945. The Principle that has twice guided us must continue to guide us. We may be able this time to achieve our objective by the building up of moral power and physical power—by external pressure rather than by a third world war. With modern methods of communicating ideas to vast numbers of people instantly, we may be able to advance the cause of freedom—to start the movements toward self-liberation in all the countries behind the Iron Curtain without actually engaging in large-scale hostilities, though we must never leave any doubt anywhere as to our readiness to go to war if necessary to assure our national safety.

For the Principle in simple terms is that America is not safe, no democracy is safe, as long as there exists in the world any powerful nation controlled by a dictatorship—as long as any regime prevents the peaceful purposes of the people from being expressed through freely elected representatives.

This is the great cause of freedom for which Americans and the peoples allied with us must suffer unbalanced budgets and, if need be, sacrifices of human lives.

This is the Principle that survives the ephemeral events of today and tomorrow.

This is the compass by which President Eisenhower can steer the Ship of State along the true course that must inevitably bring us to the haven of safety—not an uneasy, temporary peace between armed camps but permanent peace in a world made safe at last for democratic governments.

THE EISENHOWER COMPASS

APRIL 24, 1953

THE greatest address of our times on international affairs was delivered last week by President Eisenhower before the American Society of Newspaper Editors.

A compass for the world to steer by has been put before the peoples and governments of every country—a charter for all mankind.

In essence, the President of the United States has reaffirmed the principles of the Atlantic Charter, which was signed from 1942 to 1945 not only by the United States but by 46 other governments, including the Government of the Soviet Union.

The Eisenhower Charter focuses attention on Principle. It points to self-government and free elections as the cornerstone of peace. It places the responsibility for the present tension on the attempt at domination "by a single, unbridled, aggressive power."

The core of the address is in these five precepts:

"First. No people on earth can be held—as a *people*—to be an enemy, for all humanity shares the common hunger for peace and fellowship and justice.

"Second. No nation's security and well-being can be lastingly achieved in isolation, but only in effective cooperation with fellow-nations.

"Third. Any nation's right to a form of government and an economic system of its own choosing is *inalienable*.

"Fourth. Any nation's attempt to dictate to other nations their form of government is *indefensible*.

"Fifth. A nation's hope of lasting peace cannot be firmly based upon any race in armaments, but rather upon just relations and honest understanding with all other nations." (The italics are those of the President.)

The President thus invited the people of the Soviet Union to take part in the ways of the free world. He went further—he emphasized that our European Recovery Program of economic aid is still open to the peoples of the East as well as the West. He said that the peoples of the free world might well invest a substantial part of their savings from a reduction of armaments in a "fund for world aid and reconstruction."

But this can happen, Mr. Eisenhower reminds us, only in "a world that begins to witness the rebirth of trust among nations." Then he turns to the compass—the charter—and points the way for the Soviet Union. He calls for deeds, not "mere rhetoric," and proposes the following concrete "deeds" to be fulfilled:

1. The immediate cessation of hostilities and "the prompt initiation of political discussions leading to the holding of free elections in a united Korea." This dis-poses of all the recent talk about a "divided Korea." His demand is for "not merely an expedient truce in Korea but genuine peace in Asia."

2. An end to the attacks on the security of Indochina and Malaya.

3. Conclusion of a treaty with Austria "which will free that country from economic exploitation and from occupation by foreign troops."

4. An end to "the present unnatural division of Europe" and the establishment of "a free and united Germany, with a government based upon free and secret elections."

The key to it all is self-government—the right of every people, including the Soviet people, to choose their own form of government.

Then the President asks the Soviet Union, which has denied its own people the right to choose their own form of government "by free and secret elections," whether the Moscow rulers at least are "prepared to allow other nations, including those of Eastern Europe, the free choice of their own forms of government and the right to associate freely with other nations in a world-wide community of law."

The words of the appeal for peace are unequivocal. They are accompanied, moreover, by a stern warning that the policies of the Kremlin for eight years have "instilled in the free nations—and let none doubt this—the unshakeable conviction that, as long as there persists a threat to freedom, they must, at *any* cost, remain armed, strong and ready for any risk of war."

There, in plain-spoken sentences, the Kremlin is told it can have peace—or it can lead the world to war. We are ready in either instance. We shall not be intimidated. We shall not appease.

We are ready, too, to serve "the *needs*, rather than the *fears*, of the world." Thus did Dwight Eisenhower speak the heart and mind of America.

The responsibility for war—if it comes—will not be ours.

The responsibility for peace—if it comes—will be that of a self-governing people in the Soviet Union which, though still fettered, can exercise in an inexorable way the moral power and pressure that 200 million people can exert when they know the truth. The Eisenhower speech is a document whose words must inevitably penetrate the Iron Curtain and someday furnish the basis for a true peace.

MURDER OF THOUSANDS

MAY 1, 1953

WHETHER 6,000 or 8,000 is the figure finally fixed as the number of those Americans "missing in action" in Korea who were murdered on the march or starved to death in the prison camps, the fact remains that the lives of many thousands of our youth have been lost in an ordeal of torture rarely paralleled in history.

It is ironic to recall now all the pious utterances from Moscow and Peiping in recent months about "Geneva conventions" and about the meticulous regard by the Communists for the wishes of prisoners as to repatriation. What nonsense the barbarians in Moscow and Peiping have been prating—as the truth now comes out that Americans taken prisoner in 1950 and 1951 had their hands tied behind their backs when they were shot down on their forced marches or shoved over steep embankments after they became too exhausted to walk.

Is this the kind of human relations which the Red China Government sanctions? Is this the government to which our British friends and Premier Nehru of India and ·other supposed allies on our side ask us to give China's seat of permanent membership on the Security Council of the United Nations?

Are the cruel men in the Kremlin and in Peiping now to be taken to our bosoms in a peace "negotiation" and given the right to sit down with us as equals? If we do so, we will not have "repelled aggression"—we will have appeased aggression. Self-respect would seem to require that we lay down our terms—as we have done before after a war—and demand their acceptance. There should be no palaver with the exponents of bestiality.

The tragedy of it all is that the truth has so long been suppressed. The Truman Administration knew the facts about these atrocities many months ago. Why wasn't the information given officially to the American people? Was there a fear that Americans everywhere would react instantly and demand that we fight the war without further handicap to our own troops in Korea, that we let our airplanes bomb the bases from which enemy supplies were coming, and that our ships be ordered to blockade the ports of the world from which strategic materials were being sent to aid the enemy?

The American people are entitled now to all the facts about this indefensible act of censorship if only to teach a lesson for the future in handling the news of what happens to our own soldiers in war.

The Truman Administration repeatedly refused to face the facts of war in Korea. Not only were field commanders restricted from using maximum military power, but the Pentagon bungled and we didn't give our troops the ammunition they needed. It turns out also that American public opinion was prevented from functioning by a refusal to give the people the facts. No dictatorship could have been more absolute.

The cry even today in some quarters that all the atrocity news should be withheld from publication lest it upset the "peace negotiations" reflects the pussyfoot approach that has prevailed in Washington ever since the Korean war broke out. It is to be noted that the British Commonwealth headquarters in Korea last week clamped a news censorship on the reports coming from their own returning prisoners. Presumably the people of Great Britain are not to be told that their youth are among those mistreated by the barbaric enemy.

It is to be noted, incidentally, that Great Britain is the headquarters of the appeasement movement which now seeks peace at any price in Korea. With due respect to the sincere intentions of our British friends, the record shows that the British people have suffered more in the last half-century through appeasement than through the policies of firmness which in a preceding century characterized a glorious Britain.

The whole story of privation and death inflicted on prisoners taken by the Communist enemy will in due time be unfolded completely. The moral force of the civilized nations of the world should be exerted in denouncing the barbarism and in demanding the punishment of the military commanders who engaged in these criminal acts. No recognition should be extended to any government in China unless chosen by the people and until complete satisfaction has been given for the murder of the several thousand Americans by troops under the control of the Communist regime.

Soviet Russia should be asked, moreover, at the bar of world opinion in the United Nations to answer for the acts of her allies in crime. This is the very time to press the point, when Moscow and Peiping are trying to mask their cruel record by a pretense of humaneness in the offer to exchange sick and wounded prisoners.

There can be no basic friendship or enduring peace with any Communist governments that do not disavow the crimes committed in their behalf in Korea.

The Communist governments can demonstrate their good faith—if they have any—only by punishing every one of the war criminals who had a part in the massacre of unarmed, helpless American boys.

FIVE DEFENSE DEPARTMENTS

MAY 8, 1953

THE WORD "PENTAGON"—from the Greek, meaning "five sides"—is coming into its own. There may now be five departments of defense:

1. The Army—responsible to the Secretary of the Army.

2. The Navy—responsible to the Secretary of the Navy.

3. The Air Force—responsible to the Secretary of the Air Force.

4. The Joint Staff—responsible to the Chairman of the Joint Chiefs of Staff.

5. The so-called "Department of Defense"—responsible to the Secretary of Defense.

Each of these departments, under a new plan just promulgated, is to have a substantial personnel. Six more Assistant Secretaries of Defense are to be created. Authority is to be widely diffused.

The net effect of the proposed changes is to create a hodge-podge of responsibilities and a dangerous confusion.

The Joint Chiefs of Staff—which is supposed to be the principal military advisory body—is to be relegated to an unimportant and incidental place in the whole complex structure of the defense establishment.

The Chairman of the Joint Chiefs is to be made the boss of a big staff of Army, Navy, and Air Force personnel divorced from the Chiefs of Staff themselves. The "Chairman" alone is to fix tenure and approve the selections in the new department. This means that he becomes the principal military chief of the Government and, unless his subordinate personnel give him the advice he wants, they can be fired. The Joint Chiefs, who are the operating heads of the three services, would have no authority over the men who are to become the real makers of military policy.

Under the guise of "civilian control," a plan has been hatched which puts America into the hands of a "Chief of a General Staff." This is the plan that Goering had. This is the plan under which Hitler lost. This is the plan that various militaristic gentlemen in our midst have been trying for several years to foist on our Government. They now apparently have found a civilian commission gullible enough not only to recommend the "General Staff" plan but to argue that such a plan is not contemplated.

Despite all the rhetoric about direct "channels of command" and about giving the three civilian secretaries more say, a unified commander in a theater of operations hereafter is to report directly to the Secretary of Defense, thus by-passing his own service chief. Actually, this means he will report to the new Commander-in-Chief of our Armed Forces—whose title is to be "Chairman of the Joint Chiefs of Staff."

There are some euphemistic words in the document about how important the Joint Chiefs are to be and how they are not a "command body" and hence must have time to give military advice. But the effect of the plan is to deprive them of any voice in determining the use to be made of their own forces, although each retains the title of chief of his own service.

What is worse is that the Secretary of Defense, under the proposed program, is to be given authority to "transfer" at any time any "personnel" anywhere within the Department of Defense. He could wipe out the identity of the Army or the Air Force or the Navy or the Marine Corps overnight by putting most of their personnel under any chieftain he selected. He can even delegate to any Assistant Secretary or "any employee" any function or duty or power that he holds as Secretary of Defense.

The whole plan violates the letter and the spirit of the National Security Act. Congress, under the Constitution, is supposed to make the laws regulating the armed forces. Congress cannot abdicate by giving a Cabinet officer authority to do as he pleases with the missions, purposes and functioning of the armed services. There are certain stipulations which Congress put into law so as to maintain the identity and spirit of each of the armed services. Such stipulations now could be wiped out by a stroke of the pen by the Secretary of Defense. It already is announced that he is to revise the "Key West Agreement" and thus rearrange the method of setting up unified commands in the field, without giving a voice to the armed-service chiefs who entered into that contract.

Congress never intended the "Chairman of the Joint Chiefs" to be a military boss. It purposely deprived him of a vote in the Joint Chiefs. Also Congress never gave and never intended to give the Secretary of Defense a military staff. Now he takes over the entire "Joint Staff," with all personnel—about 200 officers—and the Joint Chiefs lose that Staff from any control.

Unless the plan is rejected in Congress by either house within 60 days, America is to be given the Hitler system of a "Chief of General Staff" to do as he pleases with the armed services, thus reversing the entire tradition of American military history. The plan should be defeated.

'INNATE COWARDICE OF HUMANITY'

MAY 15, 1953

EVERY NOW AND THEN our Department of State issues a volume disclosing, for historical purposes, hitherto confidential messages exchanged fifteen years or more ago between the United States and its Ambassadors and Ministers in various countries. Last week a thick volume was released that reveals what happened in diplomacy during the year 1935.

In one of these communications, the American Minister to Switzerland, Hugh R. Wilson, sent in an analysis of the personality of Mussolini. It was based on a conversation which Wilson had with Eduard Benes, then Minister for Foreign Affairs and later ill-fated President of Czechoslovakia.

"Mussolini and Benes," said the message, "have known each other well since 1918. Mussolini (according to Benes) won his way to the front and kept control of Italy through one thing only—his conviction of the innate cowardice of humanity."

Delving through these records of what our embassies in Europe were reporting in that eventful year 1935, one is struck with the parallel between the vacillating positions taken by European governments then and the vacillating attitudes of today.

If one substitutes for "Ethiopia" the name "Korea," the language of those reports reflects a startling similarity to the dispatches we have been reading in the press during the last few years.

For in 1935 Mussolini, by a flagrant act of aggression, invaded Ethiopia. The League of Nations discussed at length the imposing of an economic embargo and then left it to each nation to decide if and when restrictions on the export of oil, steel and copper should be put into effect. The economic embargo against Italy, however, never materialized because of various excuses in London and Paris that such an embargo could not be made effective unless all nations agreed. Then, as now, the materialistic interest was too influential.

The wobbling of Premier Laval in Paris irritated Britain. It will be recalled that the "fifth column" was active in France in those days and there was no "McCarthyism" to expose the subversives. Eleven years later Laval was executed as a traitor because he had collaborated with the Nazis during the war.

Hugh Wilson, after a talk with Anthony Eden, then active in the British Foreign Office as a special envoy, reports on Laval's dilatory tactics:

"Eden also spoke ironically of the apparent desire of the French to bargain . . . Eden felt strongly that it would be incredible to pay a price to France to induce France to carry out its obligations under the Covenant (of the League of Nations)."

And so went the bickering, and so developed the disunity which induced Mussolini and Hitler to believe that the free nations would never get together.

The American Ambassador to Turkey, Robert P. Skinner, an experienced Foreign Service officer, wrote to Washington on March 28, 1935:

"If appearances count for anything we are getting nearer and nearer to a general European war. Protracted discussions based on legalistic considerations seem only to embitter the situation."

Indecision, long-drawn-out palavering, irresoluteness, wavering by the Western Allies, including the United States, all added up to a passive acquiescence in act after act of aggression.

The Allies finally had to order military resistance to the invasion of Poland in 1939 to convince Hitler and Mussolini that the free governments were not cowardly. Individual valor had to be demonstrated at a terrific cost of human life to refute the impression of cowardice which an indecisive diplomacy had created.

While the U. N. intervention in Korea in 1950 should have taught the aggressors a lesson, the Allied disunity on Far Eastern policies since then has nullified the value of our repelling action. It has proved no deterrent to Communist aggression in Southeast Asia. It may, indeed, have encouraged the aggressor.

Today it is "the innate cowardice" of governments that keeps the free nations from imposing a complete embargo on all trade with the Communist countries—the way to clear up the world situation. Legalistic considerations are offered as excuses for failure to act. London unashamedly defends as "legal" her export of strategic materials like rubber to Soviet Russia.

The "warmongers" of today are those "peace at any price" groups and factions who are unaware that their tactics are constantly telling Moscow and Peiping that they can count on the disunity of the Western Allies.

This in 1935 was the certain road to war.

This today is the certain road to another large-scale war within four or five years. It will come unless the free world recognizes now that all the governments on this side of the Iron Curtain must unite wholeheartedly behind policies of firmness. They must reject weak-kneed expediency and be willing to sacrifice together in vindication of the principle of collective security. Only then will the Communists be dissuaded from pursuing their course of aggression.

AS MOSCOW MIGHT WRITE IT—

MAY 22, 1953

Dear American Comrade:

Things are going well here in Moscow. The world situation continues to grow better and better from our viewpoint. We are making gains everywhere.

Our friend Nehru has just announced that, notwithstanding the 1951 embargo resolution of the United Nations, India will continue to send war materials to our ally, China. England gets around it by sending her rubber to the Soviet Union, and we ship it to China for her armies in Korea. The English are clever.

We are progressing in Korea. The imperialist nations are begging us for a truce. We will let them have one only when they surrender on the prisoner question. Then America surely will have to accept the new Churchill-Attlee proposal to welcome Communist China into the U. N. just as soon as the Korean armistice is signed. This will complete our glorious victory in Korea. We can then turn to Southeast Asia.

We are making progress in Egypt. Our campaign there to stir up trouble with the British is succeeding. Naguib wants to demonstrate Egypt's independence and drive the British out of the Suez Canal Zone. When Egypt has achieved this, we shall move in more strongly and take care of Naguib and control the Suez.

The reports from Iran are favorable. We have reduced that country to economic chaos. Things are ripe for our Tudeh Party to take over soon.

We are progressing nicely in Guatemala, Argentina and Bolivia.

But our best reports come from England. Be sure to read carefully the speech last week of former Prime Minister Attlee, leader of the Socialist Labor Party. He is doing a great work for us. Not only is he driving a wedge between England and America but he is trying to make it appear that Dulles and Eisenhower are not working together. You, of course, are familiar with this tactic. Some influential American newspapers are pursuing the same idea. Help it along!

The drive against McCarthy in America looks to us here as if it is going splendidly. We are glad *The Daily Worker* in New York is devoting more and more space to the dispatches telling of attacks on McCarthy. We notice that gullible "liberals" in America are rising more vehemently than ever to attack McCarthy. These "liberals" are, of course, our worst enemies—they believe in individual freedom. But, as long as they do our work now, play along with them. We'll take care of them later. Meanwhile, give conspicuous attention to all their attacks on McCarthy, Jenner, McCarran,

Velde, etc. Keep things stirring. Certain newspapers in England, France and Germany are taking up the crusade, too. We must destroy McCarthy!

As we survey the world situation, we seem to be gaining advantages on every front in the "cold war." We have not sacrificed a single regiment of our troops. We have scared the Western Allies so that they now deploy their military strength all over the whole world. The United States, of course, is beginning to feel the financial strain. With our propaganda we are getting across everywhere the idea that only America wants to fight—it's only America's warmongering that prevents peace. Attlee helped this idea along by his speech. So did Laborite John Hynd with his attack in Parliament on General Harrison, when he said the American negotiator at Panmunjom was too aggressive. Let's keep up this drive to get British politicians to take over the Korean truce negotiations and cut out the Americans.

We are, in fact, getting stronger inside the Socialist Labor Party in Britain. Our Communist comrades are getting more and more influence, too, inside the political parties on the Continent. We are making excellent progress with the West German Socialists. Through our comrades in France, we will prevent ratification of the European Defense Treaty. NATO is on the rocks.

Our peace offensive has succeeded beyond our dreams. Churchill is in his dotage and wants to make a "hero" of himself, so he talks about "personal meetings" of the top rulers. We shall welcome him and flatter him. But we shall yield nothing. Why should we? We are winning the "cold war."

How easy it is for us! We give up a few wounded prisoners in Korea—and people all over the world think peace is here.

Keep in touch with our comrades in all countries where there are nationalistic movements. The Americans are suckers for the "national aspiration" theme. They'll help us in Tunisia and generally in Africa. We shall drive the French out of Southeast Asia, as we have eliminated the Dutch. Soon we shall control Malaya, Burma, Thailand, India, Indonesia, the Philippines, and Japan.

Let's keep up this cry about "underprivileged" nations. It will appeal to Americans. They will never perceive our tactic—to break up the big countries into a lot of little ones so we can infiltrate them all and take over more easily. This is our century—this is our chance to put "nationalism" to work for us.

Yours for the Communist cause! Hail Malenkov!

NEVER A BALANCED BUDGET?

MAY 29, 1953

FOR SEVERAL MONTHS the American people have been told that there would be no tax reduction until and unless a balanced budget was "in sight."

President Eisenhower now proposes that the Government shall deprive itself of 3 billion dollars of revenue by a reduction in personal income taxes effective next January. Yet he gives facts and figures pointing to continuing deficits of substantial size in the budgets of the next two fiscal years ending June 30, 1955.

Nothing in the President's message to Congress last week, moreover, gave the slightest hint as to when, if ever, the budget is to be balanced.

In fact, the message emphasizes a set of circumstances in world affairs which points up realistically the unpleasant fact that a balanced budget is improbable for many years to come.

The sooner the American people realize what is happening to their fiscal affairs, the sooner they will insist that the Administration come to grips with the main problem.

For the main issue is not which taxes shall be repealed or replaced, or what unexpended balances shall be curtailed, or what domestic expenditures shall be trimmed.

The main issue is when the United States will adopt a foreign policy consistent with its resources and its taxing power.

If America is to continue indefinitely with a "defend the whole world" premise as the basis of our armament planning, then there never will be a balanced budget in our lifetime.

The President says the Communists have made a coldly calculated move to try to drive America into insolvency by forcing us into larger and larger military expenditures. But he proposes nevertheless that six months hence taxes which yield a total of 5 billions a year shall be repealed. He suggests, to be sure, as a replacement that at least 2 billions in revenue be provided from other types of taxes. But the net of it is to indicate a series of annual budget deficits. Words of attempted reassurance have since been given to the press by the Secretary of the Treasury, who looks for a balancing of the budget in the fiscal year ending June 30, 1955, provided that business continues at the present high level and provided world tension eases. But there is really no balanced budget in sight today and taxes are being reduced anyway.

Nor is there any consistency in a message which tells us first that we are living not just in a year of peril but in "an age of peril" and then promises more tax reductions in six months—as if the Soviets are suddenly going to relieve us of our anxieties in 180 days. There is no evidence either that the President may be planning to abandon our "defend the whole world" policy. On the contrary, the message itself outlines the same long-range policy of global defense that led to the unbalancing of the Truman budgets.

The time has come for the Eisenhower Administration to make a major change in world policy no matter how annoyed some of our friends in allied countries may become. It is they, not we, who are willing to trust the Communists in Asia and to reward aggression by inviting Red China into the U. N. Security Council. If our allies feel so sure they can trust the Communists not to commit further acts of aggression in Asia, they should be willing now to trust them also to be peaceful in Europe.

In any event, a policy of "America for America" is just as realistic now as the policy of "Britain for Britain." The idealistic principle of collective security broke down when our allies broke faith with us on the conduct of the war in Korea. The British are still arguing that they must trade with Soviet Russia and Red China to take care of their commercial losses. Can they object logically if the American taxpayer now consults his material interests, too?

America must remain solvent. We cannot afford a "defend the whole world" program. We must take the calculated risk of placing on European countries themselves the maximum responsibility for their own defense and economic development. America has poured more than 29 billion dollars into Western Europe from 1945 to date. That is evidence of our generosity and our altruism. But the outlays never have been and never will be enough to satisfy Europe. We cannot keep up this pace without going broke.

It is not tax policy that needs our main attention. It is foreign policy which is breaking our backs. If budgets are to continue unbalanced, inflation will intensify. The sound dollar then will vanish, even as the prospect of a balanced budget for the Eisenhower Administration seems now to be vanishing amidst confusing estimates by the Executive and constant bickerings in Congress as to the size of our armament program. For how can the budget ever be balanced if we are to keep on appropriating vast sums each year in an effort to attain highly imaginary goals or to meet the never-ending military requirements of an "age of peril"?

REALISM FROM MR. TAFT

JUNE 5, 1953

SENATOR TAFT, with characteristic forthrightness, brushes aside all the tricks of verbiage by which the impression has been given heretofore that the United Nations itself has "repelled aggression" in Korea. He calls our coalition there a military alliance and argues that we might as well concede that the U. N. cannot, under its present set-up, be "an effective means to prevent aggression."

Contrary to some interpretations by the press and radio last week, Mr. Taft did not call for a "go it alone" policy. Rather he argues that our allies are about to "go it alone" and that it is time for us to realize that our alliance in the Far East has broken down and that something ought to be done to strengthen it or, by a revision of the Charter, to reconstruct the U. N.

Mr. Taft notes that the Security Council of the U. N. —without the concurrence of Soviet Russia—ordered resistance in the Korean war and that, because all five permanent members did not cast an affirmative vote, this step was of doubtful legality. Certainly if it is the U. N. which has been fighting the war in Korea, the recent truce proposals should have first been submitted to the Security Council. The Council, however, has never since June 1950 had before it any matter concerned with the operation or ending of the Korean war.

Next it is plain that, as Mr. Taft says, the North Atlantic Treaty Organization is a deviation from the U. N. and is a full-fledged, old-time military alliance. Technically it doesn't violate the Charter of the U. N., but it is a fact that one group of members is arming against another group of members.

Senator Taft says "no one should be shocked" at his suggestion that "we might as well abandon any idea of working with the United Nations in the East and reserve to ourselves a completely free hand." He points out that this is exactly what a number of nations, including ourselves, have done in setting up NATO.

Now this doesn't mean that Senator Taft favors no alliances in the Far East. He voted for the Pacific pacts that bind us to the Philippines and to Australia and New Zealand—regional pacts that exclude both Britain and France. Senator Taft, therefore, would agree with every word of what President Eisenhower told the press last week about the value of cooperative rather than isolated effort in the world of today. The Ohio Senator merely suggests that we might as well throw off the pretense of acting in the Far East for a cumbersome, disunited United Nations. He says: "Recent events in France and England indicate that they are more than anxious to settle with Russia, and resume as much trade as possible, which means that as long as Russia talks nicely, the whole military alliance against Russia is weak, even though military preparations behind the lines continue unabated.

"Secretary Dulles has tried to reassure the Iron Curtain nations that we are not going to make a deal with Russia giving the Communists a zone of influence over all the Iron Curtain countries. It seems clear that Mr. Churchill and the French Administration would be willing to assign that zone of influence gladly and abandon the Poles, the Czechs, the Hungarians and the Rumanians to the tender mercies of Soviet Russia in return for some cutting of armaments, freer trade and promises to behave in the future."

The colloquy two weeks ago in the House of Commons, moreover, showed that Prime Minister Churchill intends to support Mr. Attlee's proposal that, as soon as the fighting ceases in Korea, Red China should be admitted to the Security Council of the U. N. Resenting this proposed move, the Senate Appropriations Committee voted last week to forbid any money to be spent by America for the U. N. if Red China or any other country with armed forces fighting against ours in Korea should be admitted to the Security Council. If Red China goes in, we would go out.

The vote was 20 to 3, which shows that nearly all the Democrats as well as Republicans believe in an American policy and reject the proposed British policy which would amount to a reward for the aggressors.

It would be a grave mistake if any Europeans or Americans, because of hasty or superficial reading of what Mr. Taft said, should misrepresent his position as "isolationism." He states that he believes in the U. N. as a means of persuasion and for other useful purposes (see text on pages 98-99). He has voted for the support of NATO. But he doesn't believe in sitting by and letting America get buffeted about by allies who now propose to abandon the objectives for which the troops in Korea have been making their sacrifices.

Though there will rightly be differences with Senator Taft on certain points, especially as to the military defense of Europe, his main thesis—that we should face the realism of our times—is wholesome and will be helpful in forging a strong alliance. For our allies must inevitably perceive that their failure to support wholeheartedly the American effort and purpose in the Far East can be as fatal to the principle of collective security in Europe as it has been in Asia.

WHAT IS 'AMERICAN'?

JUNE 12, 1953

THERE IS A TENDENCY nowadays in "liberal" precincts to belittle a manifestation of patriotic feeling as "nationalism." Last week an editorial in an Eastern newspaper of prominence denounced as a "piece of chauvinism" the passage by the Senate of a bill to forbid the display of the United Nations flag in a position equal to or superior to the flag of the United States.

There seems to have been cultivated the impression that the U. N. is a sort of superstate and not, as intended, a free association of equal and sovereign states. Hence, it is implied that a higher allegiance is owed to the flag of the U. N. than to the Stars and Stripes.

There is an impatience, moreover, with any criticism of the policies of our allies. Mere expressions of dissent are summarily condemned as "isolationism."

The same intolerance crops up among "liberals" generally when they deride as "reactionary" all opposition to government ownership or to policies that threaten confiscation of private businesses. They call "illiberal" anyone who stands for the right of Congress to expose the disloyal in our midst.

Isn't it "American" to demand that our institutions be not undermined again by Communist sympathizers at White House desks or at important desks in the Treasury Department, in the State Department, and in the National Labor Relations Board—as the testimony before congressional committees has revealed? Or is it "American" to say that those who have been aiding the Communists have been just a handful—that the secret of the atom bomb was, after all, stolen by only one spy—such a "small percent"?

Isn't it "American" to insist that the individual shall not again become the victim of a national policy that has handed out the savings of the vast majority of our people to privileged minorities in a "giveaway" of billions of dollars for political ends?

Isn't it "American" to declare that, since the United States has given 40 billion dollars to foreign countries in the past few years, there should be a reciprocal obligation on their part at least to team with us in matters of international policy so that our burdens may not grow bigger and that our troops may not be always expected to do the major job, as in Korea?

Just what is "American," after all?

The answer is simple. This country was founded on the principle of individual liberty as against the encroachments of autocratic government. Our struggle for independence was won on a great principle—the right of free men to govern themselves.

America has always had a deep sympathy, therefore, for other nations striving to gain their freedom from tyranny. But let us be consistent—we should be no less interested in the unification and independence of Korea than in the independence of the Philippines. We should be no less sympathetic to the right of the people of China to be free from domination by Moscow than we are to the right of self-government for the peoples of India or Pakistan.

Our hearts go out to all oppressed peoples now enslaved behind the Iron Curtain. But we cannot help them by the sword. They must show signs of a willingness to throw off the yoke before they can be given even material aid by us. Nor can we bolster up free governments abroad by dollars alone.

We help those who help themselves—that's "American." But at the same time we cannot be expected to arm and defend the whole world in a military sense. We believe in international cooperation and in the usefulness of international organizations. Our moral support and our economic power in cooperation with our allies—still largely unused as an instrument of pressure in behalf of enslaved peoples—can do much more than military force can do in the present military situation.

It is "American" to be generous, altruistic, idealistic. It is "American" to help others. But it is not "American" to feed American boys to the cannon of an unscrupulous enemy and forbid to our troops the use of maximum force in return. It is not in keeping with the American tradition to accept defeat, as we apparently are doing in Korea, or to condone the policies of a group of Munich-like politicians in Europe who trifle with the patriotism and spirit of our youth.

It is "American" to fight under our flag—when national authority calls us to the colors—but it is not "American" to ask our youth to fight under a U. N. flag that stands for hypocrisy, vacillation and surrender of principle. It is "American" to question the materialism of our allies when they trade with the enemy. It is not "American" to rationalize European "isolationism" as commendable and yet to denounce as "disunity" pleas such as Senator Taft has made for a realistic alliance.

It is "American" to give aid to other nations. But it is also "American" to remind the world that our good nature has limits. These limits were symbolized by that challenge to European systems which appeared on the flags of some of our thirteen original colonies: "Don't Tread on Me."

IS WORLD WAR III NOW INEVITABLE?

JUNE 19, 1953

HISTORY TELLS US that every Munich, every appeasement, every compromise with evil men bent on aggression has eventually led to bloody conflict.

Conversely, firmness in a balance-of-power diplomacy has given the world long periods of peace broken only when leaders have let down their guard and chosen short-sighted policies of political expediency.

In the years just before World War I, British diplomacy vacillated. By the spring of 1914, the Foreign Secretary, Sir Edward Grey, found himself striving desperately at the last moment to avert a war that was slowly but surely emerging out of the political appeasements of the past. Germany thought England wouldn't or couldn't help France. So the Kaiser took the chance, and in August 1914 his armies drove toward France.

Back in the spring of 1939, Molotov was sitting in Moscow playing a game of intended alliance with London and Paris while secretly negotiating a mutual security pact with Hitler. This assured Nazi Germany that, for a while at least, it would not be fighting a two-front war—against both Russia and France.

The documents obtained from Germany after the war, however, reveal that the military strength of the Nazis had been grossly overestimated by the Allies and that psychological factors—a belief that Britain would not fight—caused Hitler in September 1939 to take the chance he did when he attacked Poland.

America, too, failed the world in the 1930's, under Republican and Democratic Administrations, by vacillation declining to make clear that the United States would come to the aid of countries which were the victims of aggression. Hitler took advantage of this aloofness and never regarded seriously the messages of diplomatic concern which came to him from President Roosevelt in 1939—too late to be respected and giving no hint that they would be backed up by military force.

What are we telling Soviet Russia today? We are saying that we are unable or unwilling to fight for victory when we have already committed our armies to battle for nearly three years. The story of the Korean truce agreement is the story of a Far Eastern Munich. Substitute the Republic of Korea for Czechoslovakia as the expendable country, and the parallel begins to emerge. Substitute Korea for hapless Poland at the Yalta Conference, and the analogy is complete.

When the North Korean army invaded South Korea in June 1950 and the United States decided to get the authorization of the U. N. to intervene, all the world was notified that aggression would be resisted. Many of us applauded this as an epochal step that might well prevent World War III. It was a notice to the Communists that the free world would fight back.

But Moscow saw in the continuance of British recognition of Red China the beginnings of a rift between America and Britain on Far Eastern policy. When the aggression by North Korean forces was repelled by General MacArthur, Moscow ordered another aggression. The Communist Chinese armies in overwhelming numbers came down from the Yalu River and in December 1950 forced the U. N. troops back to the 38th parallel. According to the Moscow and Peiping viewpoints, "the U. N. aggression" was repulsed.

On October 7, 1950, the U. N., by resolution, had declared that its armies were in Korea to repel aggression and "to establish peace throughout Korea." Always there was the objective of unification by the military means being employed at that time. Otherwise, why didn't the U. N. order a stop before our forces crossed the 38th parallel in early October 1950 and call then for a truce? By January 1951, the Truman Administration, under pressure from our allies, refused to allow maximum military power to be used to win. Suddenly in June 1951 the Secretary of State, Dean Acheson, announced that a truce would be accepted in and around the 38th parallel and that unification of Korea was now only a "political" objective. The Soviets caught the hint and almost immediately Ambassador Malik at the U. N. made a public suggestion that truce talks should be begun. Military defeat for the U. N. was apparent.

Then Moscow tested out the Allies by a long series of sessions at Kaesong and Panmunjom which had for their object a wearing down of the patience of the U. N. members. Coincidentally, friends of Moscow, like India, began to build up an appeasement policy inside the U. N. An artificial issue was trumped up relating solely to the return of prisoners of war. In and of themselves, the differences on this point were not irreconcilable as shown by the agreement made last week. But the argument, deliberately prolonged by the Communists, served a basic purpose—to divert attention from the real issue, which was the continued presence of Communist Chinese on Korean territory.

To say that Communist aggression now has been repelled is to fly in the face of the facts. In June 1950, the North Korean army stood on the 38th parallel. Today the armies of Red China—formally declared by the U. N. to be an aggressor—stand 900,000 strong on the battle line only a few miles north of the 38th parallel, as they threaten the security of South Korea.

Not all the blame rests on our European allies, though the British have favored a "peace at any price" because they feared American military, industrial and financial resources would be diverted to Asia instead of Europe.

American politics played a part in the fiasco. When Dwight Eisenhower conducted his political campaign in 1952, he showed firmness toward the Korean situation—he said he would not agree to a truce with dishonor, he would not appease. Then came the election and inauguration. The Administration's advisers took a look at Korea and a look at our unbalanced budget and a look at the campaign pledge that had been interpreted widely as a promise to end the Korean war. The decision evidently was made to liquidate the whole affair promptly and go along with the British viewpoint.

This was a short-sighted decision. It was taken in privacy. No opportunity was given the American people to debate the issue because the intermittent negotiations of the last 60 days have been conducted in the strictest secrecy. Even our South Korean ally was excluded from the crucial stages, being given copies of our proposals a few minutes before an important session with the enemy envoys.

At no time was the Korean Republic permitted to be a party to the negotiations at Panmunjom. Only "observers" were allowed. Yet the North Korean puppet government was permitted to play a principal role as a party to the truce negotiations. This was not fair treatment for our South Korean ally, which has done most of the fighting and suffered the greatest number of casualties.

If history is a guide—and it has been almost unerring in its lessons—the Administration will find that in the not-far-distant future the aggressor at Moscow will move on toward other areas. Already the news dispatches tell of the unprecedented quantities of ammunition and artillery which have been moved into Indochina in recent weeks to support Communist armies which are fighting the French there.

President Eisenhower, who has a personal admiration for Churchill and has followed his leadership before, has yielded now to the Prime Minister's many personal messages in the last few weeks urging him to accept a truce and forget unification of Korea as a military objective.

Throughout the political campaign Mr. Eisenhower was telling the voters that our troops could come home from Korea in a year or two—just as soon as new divisions of the Republic of Korea were trained and armed.

What do we face today? A reluctant, disillusioned, disappointed Korean Republic whose troops occupy 70 per cent of the front line and whose President has been protesting in vain to our Government, publicly and privately, for more than two years against any truce while the Communist Chinese armies remained on Korean soil. Last week there were newspaper editorials in America demanding that the Korean leaders be coerced into signing the truce. Must we now keep American troops in Korea to police the South Korean army?

The President in an address last week, speaking of our allies and the United Nations, said:

"This essential, indispensable unity means compromise—always within a clearly defined, clearly understood framework of principle."

Must we compromise with evil men in the Kremlin who have stirred up millions of people against us?

Is it within the "framework of principle" to compromise with a government that has demonstrated by military aggression its disregard for all principles of morality?

Must we abandon our ally—South Korea—and tell all Asia that the alliance of free peoples is just tired of fighting and that, if you palaver long enough in a so-called "negotiation," the United States and Britain will finally give in because their governments believe in appeasement? Even now, before a truce agreement is signed, Britain publicly advocates that the Red China Government be admitted soon to the U. N., notwithstanding the Chinese aggression that has cost tens of thousands of casualties on our side.

How far away is the fateful day when the Soviets overreach themselves—when they misconstrue our disinclination in 1953 to pursue military objectives as cowardice and when they challenge us in a way that we cannot ignore? We will then have to fight World War III, just as we fought World War II and World War I, to convince the aggressors that appeasement didn't mean cowardice after all and that we cannot tolerate further acts of palpable aggression.

There is still time to prevent World War III. But it will not be prevented if we become conformists, if we swallow an official line and listen to "the easy way out" which some of our allies in Europe, for reasons of convenience and expediency, are urging on us now. There must be full and free discussion.

The Korean truce is a Far Eastern Munich. For the armistice agreement is really the peace agreement. The U. N. is committed now by President Eisenhower's statement that force will not be employed again in any effort to reunite divided countries. And does anybody believe the Communists will be persuaded by peaceful means to give up what they hold today?

We are acquiescing in a retreat by the United Nations from the resolutions it has formally adopted.

Do our leaders really think all this means peace? Or are we stumbling slowly but surely into the biggest war in all history?

THE ONLY WAY OUT

JUNE 26, 1953

THE WHOLE WORLD has witnessed in the East German revolts of the last few days the exercise of the greatest power known to man—the power of mass action by peoples.

No atomic weapon can rival it because even the hand that would order the bomb dropped on another country can be paralyzed by the command of a peace-seeking people—the final source of authority.

The premise that 200,000,000 persons in Soviet Russia can at any moment overthrow the small group of evil men who rule them has been established by the precedents of history.

Nobody thought that in the midst of war the despotic and all-powerful government of the Russian Czar could be overthrown, but an almost bloodless revolution in 1917 drove him from his throne—and the Czar's own troops looked on with acquiescence.

Nobody thought the Imperial German Government in Berlin, supposedly supported by a well-disciplined people and the Prussian militarists, could be upset in a matter of hours during a war in which patriotism was at fever heat, but a mutiny of sailors at Kiel touched off revolution in 1918—and the Kaiser fled into exile.

What is this power—this sudden panic of courage which seizes a populace that has long been suffering under oppressive rule? It is merely the concerted will of a vast number of human beings who want their liberty, their freedom, their emancipation from tyranny.

Now is the time to lift high the torch of hope —of liberation for the oppressed peoples of Europe. When they begin to rebel, they must look for moral, if not physical, support to the nations of the world which want them to attain their freedom.

To implement the idea of "liberation" requires imagination. There are persons, even in the Western world, here and abroad, who for partisan reasons have belittled it as dangerous and foolhardy.

This is a species of reactionary thinking which has typified our policies and those of our allies in recent years—always fear, always timidity, always frustration, and finally appeasement of the enemy.

Now is the time for the free governments of the world to speak out and encourage the peoples in Soviet Russia and the satellite countries—to tell them we shall assist with food, with farm machinery and with economic measures when they establish a free government.

For, if peace comes, the world will be spared many billions of dollars of expenditure for armament. As President Eisenhower so wisely said in his speech of April 16 before the American Society of Newspaper Editors, we would gladly spend some of those same billions in a world war against poverty, malnutrition and disease.

The significance of what is happening in East Germany and in other countries under Soviet domination is that, without the aid of foreign armies, thousands of people have stood up defiantly before the military force of their oppressors. The outbursts may be quelled temporarily but, once the people really feel their power, the urge to resist will grow. Revolutionary inspiration spreads like wildfire. Eventually the Soviet troops will hesitate to continue to shoot down unarmed persons. Russian soldiers, too, want liberty.

This is the time to be firm and not to weaken, as some of our allies are doing with their speeches that propose the admission of Red China into the United Nations. Rather we should be talking of expelling the Moscow Government from the U. N. because of its perfidy. For the Soviet Government has publicly told the United Nations Assembly that it has been supplying arms and ammunition to Red China—formally declared by the U. N. in 1951 to be an aggressor. How can we overlook that crime of aiding aggression?

Every step we take to dignify and build up the prestige of the Moscow clique as a legitimate government— when we know it is a menace to world peace and that there are many nationalities in the Soviet Union which do not feel such a government is representative of them —tends to postpone the day when the masses can rise up in revolt.

There should be no four-power meeting with Malenkov. There's trouble behind the Iron Curtain and we must not build up even temporarily the stature of a totalitarian government and thereby discourage the aspirations of the people for freedom.

With all the censorship and the devices of suppression, ideas do penetrate the heaviest curtain of secrecy. The power of an idea is infinite—and the peoples of Soviet Russia and the neighboring states must be told that the people of the West are with them in the heartfelt hope that they can soon rise up en masse to recover their rights. This is a propitious moment in history. The peoples in all Iron· Curtain countries should be apprised that we and our allies will be ready to give them the moral help and the economic help they need. Military help from the outside will be unnecessary when revolution from within is astir.

It is the only way out—the only way to real peace.

THE DEATH OF THE U. N.

JULY 3, 1953

THE UNITED NATIONS as an organization designed to enforce peace in the world has come to a humiliating end.

Like its predecessor—the League of Nations—it has been killed by statesmen faithless to the ideals they had once professed.

The Korean war was in our times the acid test of the power of an international organization to operate as a military alliance against aggressors.

When the showdown came, one set of members was arming against another set in Europe. Other members were claiming to be "neutral" in Asia. Still others were deliberately furnishing the aggressors with arms to help kill the soldiers of other states resisting aggression.

The U. N. lacked the moral courage to denounce Soviet Russia for aiding the common enemy—the Communist Chinese and North Korean Communist armies.

No more flagrant example of the decay of international morality could be cited than the concerted behavior of the note-writers in the foreign offices of Great Britain, France, the United States, Canada and India in their recent assault on the little government of Korea. What was its crime? It refused to keep its own brothers from the North in further bondage while the Communists were to send in their agents to "brainwash" those same prisoners—all this under the auspices of a commission of five countries, with the deciding vote held by a pro-Communist government, calling itself "neutral." Was it so ignoble on the part of Korea—not even a U. N. member—to assert its sovereign right as an ally to act against such palpable trickery?

How can the smaller nations of the world ever look again to the larger nations for justice when, with a might-makes-right flourish, the major powers ignored the protest of the Republic of Korea, which had lost 200,000 soldiers in battle and more than 1,000,000 civilians in the ravages of war?

What, then, has the U. N. accomplished? It has failed to discipline the principal aggressors. It has succeeded only in bullying the principal victim of aggression—forcing it to choose between a dishonorable armistice and national suicide.

It is the merest sophistry to pretend that the U. N. intervened in Korea in June 1950 solely to repel aggression at the 38th parallel. The record shows that the U. N. authorized the crossing of the 38th parallel by its military forces, and then a few days later—on October 7, 1950—adopted a resolution declaring that "the United Nations armed forces" must take "all appropriate steps" to "ensure conditions of stability throughout Korea."

Let us concede that the U. N. subsequently met defeat on the battlefields of Korea, when Soviet Russia sent the armies of Communist China into the fray—a defeat imposed by the timidity of the U. N. alliance which refused to allow maximum military power to be used at a crucial moment against the enemy.

Let us concede that this alliance was afraid of Soviet Russia and an enlarged war.

Would it not have been the better part of candor to say so frankly in a formal resolution repealing the previous objective, rather than to claim—nearly three years later—that the U. N. never intended to unify Korea by military means?

The United States is desirous, to be sure, of helping to enforce world peace, sending men and money to foreign lands to achieve that objective. But let us do it with allies who are ready to make the same sacrifices we are willing to make.

Let us resurrect the U. N. only as a forum for international debate, but not as an instrument of collective security. For we have learned now to our sorrow that by a system of majority voting we cannot expect anything but collective insecurity.

Alliances are necessary. We cannot go it alone. But let us not become constricted in a strait jacket of international parliamentarism wherein the lives of our own citizens are of so much less concern to other nations than they are to us.

Our duty is to preserve this nation's independence—to maintain our rightful sovereignty and to make alliances which impose specific obligations not merely on ourselves but on nations capable of reciprocal action.

The U. N. is dead—it was killed by the Korean war. May real alliances emerge as a substitute now to enforce peace!

Methods of enforcing peace can no longer be left to the votes of an all-inclusive international organization which fails to differentiate between friend and foe. Let us forsake an organization which in the name of freedom squelches the aspirations of small nations when they seek emancipation from imperialists as well as from aggressors. This is the American tradition born July 4, 1776. May God give us the courage to preserve the basic principles of the American faith as we see unmoral diplomacy writing, with deceptive phrases, equivocations and quibbles, the inglorious epitaph of the United Nations!

IDEA POWER

JULY 10, 1953

BERLIN, JULY 2—Eighteen Russian soldiers died in front of Soviet firing squads for refusing to shoot anti-Communist Germans during the June 17 riots . . . the executed soldiers not only refused to fire on anti-Communists who broke into the Magdeburg Prison to free political prisoners, but also refused to arrest Germans who convinced them they were merely trying to better their living conditions.

This news item tells a story of human sympathy and human understanding. It is a story of the power of an idea.

The idea is brotherhood. Man instinctively does not wish to kill his fellow man. Real brothers do not threaten one another with death.

The greatest need of the world today is a mobilization of moral force that will make no compromises with evil men but will seek to deprive dictatorship of its authority. This can be done through the concerted will of the peoples themselves.

The first step toward the application of such a force is to distinguish between a dictatorship government and the greater power of the people to emancipate themselves.

Can liberation be accelerated? Is it a matter of physical intervention—of arms to be furnished? President Eisenhower last week told his press conference that military intervention by us is not desirable now in Eastern Europe but that moral help—the holding out of hope by the rest of us to oppressed peoples that at the opportune time we will serve them—is very necessary.

There are definite and tangible things we can do. An idea buttressed by the faith of a free people has a power more penetrating than any physical weapon.

Ideas push back "iron curtains." Ideas invigorate and inspire downtrodden peoples. Ideas spread like prairie fires across stricken lands where poverty stalks and despotism rules the food supply.

The simple idea of human freedom is likely to be taken for granted by most of us. We assume it is a widely known idea. Relatively few peoples in the world, however, have actually experienced it.

Freedom to work, freedom to earn, freedom to save, freedom to acquire food, clothing, and shelter for one's family, freedom to enjoy the blessings and comforts of one's own home and community—can we convey the facts about these attributes of a genuine republic to the peoples who do not have those freedoms? And need we be hesitant to point out that the free world stands ready to pledge a start toward those very things that hundreds of millions of persons yearn for—raw materials, farm implements, tractors, tools, motors and the know-how to build great industrial enterprises?

These are the material things that make up idea power in action.

But there are other things of the spirit—even more magnetic.

Peoples from the beginning of time have looked to their Creator with humble obedience and immutable hope. They recognize the common bond. It is a bond that places human sympathy above all else, no matter what the language or the locale.

What more powerful way than through the spiritual idea to reach the hearts and minds of the peoples behind the Iron Curtain?

Theoretical? Yes—but so have been most of the ideas that have moved mountains in human history.

Practical? Yes—ideas travel from small to large groups, from key individuals to millions of others by word of mouth. Ideas have wings.

Idea power—the ideology of Communism—has caught the minds of millions who see in its promises something better than they have had—a hope. But millions of persons to their sorrow already have discovered that Communism is only a trap to enslave them.

Democracy is a better idea. It is a brotherhood of mutual help in which government is the servant and not the master.

Our leaders then must speak for us to the peoples behind the Iron Curtain—articulating an old faith in new messages.

Why should not the President of the United States begin a series of weekly addresses by radio and by printed leaflets to the people of all countries now under Soviet dictatorship, telling them the true meaning of our friendship, our interest in them, our hopes for them, and above all our faith in the brotherhood and dignity of human beings?

With an immemorial belief in the power of God to help those who begin to help each other, we can speak to the people of Soviet Russia. We can welcome them to a society of free peoples, which itself will be immeasurably strengthened by the addition of their spirit of heroism and the record of their sacrifices for human liberty.

For it is they—the peoples of Soviet Russia inspired by the power of a single idea—who can give to the entire world an era of enduring peace.

AFTER SIX MONTHS

JULY 17, 1953

THE AMERICAN PEOPLE in the last election voted for a fundamental change—but at the end of six months they cannot be said to have experienced it.

They may not get this change for another year or more—and with respect to some major policies, they may not get it at all.

No single aspect of the new Administration's perplexities demonstrates more vividly this continuity of the Truman decisions than the budget situation now ahead of us for at least two years. As a consequence, taxes that the Truman Congress ordered repealed are being extended, and the Democrats eagerly assist in embarrassing their opponents by voting to retain those high taxes. Deficits are bigger than before. Budgets remain unbalanced—all because both sets of politicians are afraid to cut expenses.

Instead of making a clean break with the extravagances and misguided policies of spending in the last Administration, the President and his associates find themselves disbursing virtually as much tax money as heretofore and for the very purposes which the American people repudiated in the last election—namely, economic and military aid abroad beyond the capacity of our taxpayers to pay.

Foreign aid is still based on the illusion and impertinence that the Europeans have to be bribed to refrain from embracing Communism.

America, moreover, is still wedded to a defense program which assumes it is our obligation to police the world while our major allies fail to do the rearming so vital to their own defense.

With military policy, foreign policy, fiscal policy and economic policy intermingled in the "Washington mess," it is not surprising that the Eisenhower Administration has not begun to function on its own.

It is incumbent upon the President, however, to begin soon to give the people an Administration covering at least four factors that influenced the electorate last autumn in its negative verdict against the Democratic Administration. The people asked for:

1. Integrity in public office.
2. An end to "soft" or "pinkish" policies toward Communist doctrines or Communist infiltration in the United States.
3. An honorable termination of the Korean war.
4. Reduction of taxes.

On the matter of appointments to office and improper influence in governmental decisions, there is every indication that the new Administration has heeded the warnings of the election.

On the question of anti-Communism, the Eisenhower Administration is tending toward the "soft" side. It is fumbling the anti-Communist problem as did the Truman Administration.

Mr. Eisenhower himself, for instance, by his speech at Dartmouth University gave exaggerated importance to alleged "book burning" and reflected on his own Department of State. This is climaxed now by the President's further mistake in making it possible to use taxpayer's money to pay for books on topics other than Communism, but written by past or future traitors to the United States Government. Such books, it is now stipulated in a new official order, are entitled to the prestige of a government stamp of approval. No matter what crimes their authors may have committed, their books—even by an Alger Hiss or the Rosenbergs—it is now ordered, must not be barred from Government library shelves abroad. The Congress will surely find it necessary at an early date to correct such a naive attitude by prohibiting in the forthcoming appropriation bill the use of taxpayers' money to advertise such examples of American "culture."

On the question of Korea, the Eisenhower Administration has concurred in the Truman terms as written in the proposed armistice and has bitterly criticized the South Korean Government for hesitating to sign. Yet the Chinese Government at Peiping escapes responsibility for signing the document as a belligerent, although Red China was formally declared by a United Nations resolution in February 1951 to be an aggressor in Korea. The Red China Government is not to be bound by the armistice—for it does not acknowledge any control over the 1,000,000 "Chinese volunteer" troops now in Korea. The Truman Administration from the outset avoided making an issue of it.

So, in a sense, it's a Truman-Eisenhower Administration which has been in power for six months. The American people hope that before long the present Administration will cease to be a mere extension of the Truman Administration. For the majority of the voters want a Republican Administration that is 100 per cent against Communist infiltration, that will re-establish the honor and prestige of the United States in the Far East, and that will comply with the demand of the American people for lower taxes.

Everything, of course, cannot be done in six months—but it is only twelve months before the next congressional-election campaign will be under way.

THE KEY TO PEACE

JULY 24, 1953

THERE IS A STRIKING PARAGRAPH in the latest note sent by the Government of the United States to the Moscow regime. It relates particularly to the future of Germany, but it applies with equal logic to the future of the peoples of Soviet Russia.

The United States, after consulting with its allies, has proposed a conference of the Foreign Ministers of this country, Great Britain, France and Soviet Russia to discuss the "necessary guarantees for freedom of movement, freedom of action for political parties, freedom of the press, and the enjoyment of the basic freedoms by all Germans before, during and after elections."

It is proposed, moreover, that a "free all-German Government" be established "with freedom of action in internal and external affairs."

The very same words could be and should be employed in a proclamation that commends the identical principles to all the peoples of Soviet Russia.

What the governments of the United States, Great Britain, and France should be calling for first is a new government to arise in Soviet Russia based on the "enjoyment of the basic freedoms" and "freedom of action in internal and external affairs."

Then, and only then, can Germany be unified and its political independence guaranteed. Indeed, without such a government in Moscow, there can be no real peace anywhere else in the world, but only a continuance of the international tension which has already caused so much hardship and loss of lives and treasure on both sides of the Iron Curtain.

The recent "purges" in the Soviet regime and in the zones under its control illustrate the shakiness of the police state and how a reign of terror makes it impossible for millions of innocent persons to be assured of the guarantees of "life, liberty and the pursuit of happiness."

There can be no assurance of peace for Europe as a whole or for us in America or for the peoples of Asia as long as a regime dominated by evil men holds power in Moscow.

Lest some observers jump to the conclusion—as did unimaginative partisans during our last presidential campaign—that to accomplish this means a war of "liberation" by the sword, involving this country and others in a general war, it must be said immediately that no such procedure is necessary or desirable.

Moral force is the most powerful weapon known to man. It can penetrate the Iron Curtain. It can reach the 200,000,000 persons who are for the moment under the discipline of a minority—the Communist Party—and stimulate them to recover their own sovereignty.

Moral force works most effectively when it is exerted by nations or individuals who have the courage of their convictions—who are ready to speak resolutely and act firmly to encourage others to follow in their own behalf the road that leads to freedom.

It makes no sense for the governments of the free world to be negotiating or bargaining with the representatives of a gangster government. It makes no sense at any time to compromise with unscrupulous men—conspirators against human liberty.

This is the occasion for the governments of Britain, France and America to take their stand for basic principles of self-determination and free elections and to address to the peoples of Soviet Russia messages that underline the true objective of the free world—namely, that until all governments are free, there can be no peace.

The mere existence of a dictatorship government in a powerful country which can at any moment launch a war of aggression is itself a threat to the peace of the entire world and should be so recognized in a formal declaration of the rights of man.

Who can, for instance, be sure, if peace is patched up with a gangster regime—and the prestige of the ruling group is enhanced internally by reason of the respectability of the other governments which attach signatures to such a document—that the breathing spell between appeasement and the outbreak of war will not be brief? That was our tragic experience between November 1938 and September 1939.

Who doubts, on the other hand, that—if tomorrow a revolution occurred in Moscow and a people's republic emerged therefrom with a legislature really free to act in response to the will of the people—there would be no further threat to world peace from the direction of Soviet Russia?

The certain way—the key to peace—is every day now to insist on the establishment of a free Russia.

The cooperation of the free world will mean more in the way of tangible benefits to the peoples of the Soviet Union than all the Malenkovs and Berias have or ever could achieve for them.

It is time we began addressing ourselves not to such evil men in Moscow or their envoys, but directly to the peoples of Soviet Russia who, like ourselves, want—more than anything else in the world today—an enduring peace.

WHAT DO WE 'SIGN'?

JULY 31, 1953

IN SIGNING the truce in Korea, why do we sign alone? Why do not the two principal enemies—the Communist Chinese Government and the Soviet Government—also sign?

What we are saying by our signature is that we have not achieved military victory and that we have not conquered the enemy.

We are saying by our signature that the Republic of Korea will not be unified by military force—and we imply that we now can obtain by a "political conference" what military force could not obtain for us on the battlefield. If so, why did we use military force at all? What answer shall we make to the next of kin of the 25,000 American dead and to the 115,000 other casualties who have lived to see their sacrifice ignored?

We are saying by our signature that the words of the U. N. resolution of October 7, 1950, were hollow and meaningless—for we have not ensured "conditions of stability throughout Korea," as then pledged.

We are saying by our signature that the words of the resolution of the U. N. on February 1, 1951, denouncing the Government of Communist China as an "aggressor" were hollow and meaningless, too. For, ironically enough, the "aggressor" wasn't even required to sign the truce. The signature of the enemy General in his capacity as commander of 1,000,000 Chinese "volunteers" was deemed sufficient. Yet these "volunteers," of course, have been fighting for nearly three years now as an organized army, aided and supported by munitions from the governments of Red China and Soviet Russia.

We are saying by our signature that, when war breaks out in Asia, we of America supply 95 per cent of the troops and the money, but when it comes to fighting that war we submit our strategy, the area of combat and the weapons to be used to a veto by a group of nations who do not bear the same sacrifice.

We are saying by our signature that we are agreeing to a "cease fire" in behalf of the United Nations—an organization many of whose members have been strengthening the enemy with economic force. Last week a United States Senate Subcommittee established through a well-documented report—uncontradicted by our Department of State—that trade with Communist China by our so-called allies has actually been increasing and has exceeded 2 billion dollars during the Korean war, and that a strategic commodity like natural rubber has been shipped in larger quantity than before by the United Kingdom to Soviet Russia, from whence it was sent to Communist factories to make tires for trucks and planes to carry guns and shells to kill American boys.

We are saying by our signature that we are willing through three years of fighting to pay in human blood while our allies give us doubletalk about the legalistic difference between "strategic" and "non-strategic" goods. The great British Government, which has refused throughout the last three years to ban shipments of rubber to Soviet Russia, historically never made such an unrealistic definition of "contraband" or overlooked before the doctrine of ultimate destination when its Navy was enforcing a blockade.

On March 29, 1953, our Secretary of Defense, Charles E. Wilson, wrote to a Senate Committee:

"The Department is convinced that any goods, or any services, reaching or serving these areas (China and North Korea) increase the capabilities of the Communist forces in Asia not only to continue, but even to intensify and extend the present areas of aggression."

How can we, in the face of that pronouncement, now expect a just settlement out of a "political conference" dominated by members of the U. N. who have proved faithless to us during the war?

Notwithstanding all this, the Congress of the United States this very week is being asked in the name of our own security to keep on furnishing financial aid in the billions to our so-called allies. At what time and after how much expenditure can we be sure that our allies will become faithful to us?

What does the "enemy" sign? What does the "enemy" agree to? Nothing but the *status quo*—a divided Korea as it was in 1945, as it was in 1950, and as it is today. And it will so remain because our President now has publicly proclaimed in advance that military force will not be used to unify Korea.

Thus our military leverage is gone. Our economic leverage is gone. Our moral leverage is gone.

We are saying by our signature that, unless Syngman Rhee indefinitely and interminably agrees to observe the line that now divides his country, he will be guilty of "aggressive action." Yet the Communists are free of any obligation to agree at the peace table to a unified Korea. There is no provision in the armistice agreement that limits the duration of the "political conference."

We have signed away our honor at Panmunjom.

When principle goes by the boards, nations, like governments, begin to decay and the end result is that the aggressor becomes further emboldened until finally he engulfs the whole world in war.

THE FAITH THAT MEN LIVE BY

AUGUST 7, 1953

How often have we observed lately that governments seem to be ready nowadays to forsake principle, in the short-sighted belief that any settlement—any surrender—is preferable to war and hence presents the only way to peace.

On the eve of the "political conference" of U. N. members which is to meet soon to consider questions growing out of the Korean war, we find our own allies already telling the enemy publicly—through the press and parliamentary debate—that we on our side must in effect yield to their demands and trade the honor of a sacred principle for the promise of an illusory peace.

The American people are anxious for peace—but not with dishonor. The people everywhere are sturdier than their governmental spokesmen. But in these days when governmental authority considers itself obligated to manipulate national thought, the people cannot always get at the truth—they are confused by the legalistic quibbles and the deceptive phrases about "collective security" and war prevention which come to them from spokesmen for peace at any price.

Hundreds of millions of people, on the other side of the Iron Curtain, who should know in their hearts that we have no hostile intent toward them, are being taught to believe that we are plotting their destruction. And now spokesmen for our own allies bolster that impression by accusing America of wanting more war for war's sake, even as they themselves repudiate the basic aim of the U. N. itself—to outlaw the aggressor and punish him for his crimes.

The peoples on both sides of the Iron Curtain are bewildered—they lack the leadership that a great faith could give them.

The millions of people who live in bondage under despotism waver between continued life in poverty and hunger and a willingness to make the supreme sacrifice for freedom. They need guidance.

The millions who live amid freedom's great comforts and liberties are reluctant to give up their ease in order to help make the world safe from attack by reckless autocracy which again has broken the peace. They, too, need guidance.

We as individuals cannot act alone—we must look to national leadership to resolve our doubts—to lead us to organized action.

Where, to be sure, is there leadership among the so-called major powers during these fateful times?

We turn to Soviet Russia—regarded as our potential enemy. Malenkov, reared in Communist tyranny, offers no hope. The struggle for succession in Moscow is still going on. The people there look askance at the passing scene. They want leadership for peace.

Britain's Prime Minister, a matchless leader in his day, is ill—clinging to a post he should long ago have relinquished. His successor is about to be chosen.

France has had a new Premier every few months since 1945. Her cabinets—ever changing—give her a dynasty of confusion. A Communist bloc holds the balance of power in the French Parliament.

Italy's man at the helm—De Gasperi—was only last week voted out by his legislature. A Communist bloc here, too, holds the balance of power in parliament and is now demanding posts in the Cabinet.

Germany is a divided country. Adenauer is a strong man but the cross currents of selfish group interests make his hold on the parliament very weak—and he faces a crucial election next autumn.

President Eisenhower may in time make a great leader, but he has yet to learn how to translate the basic desires of the American people into policies that will take them out of the morass—policies that will be acclaimed by the peoples of other lands and cause their stumbling statesmen to walk erect along the pathways of principle. The great moments of history, when Woodrow Wilson inspired and led the entire world with his idealism, are now a fleeting memory.

In this leaderless world of today it is public opinion alone which can make and sway policy. Successful leadership in government, of course, depends on an understanding of the true will of the people. And to understand and obey this sovereign force, he who would lead must not accept policies of day-by-day expediency or listen to pragmatic outcries for "peace at any price." To do so is to fail to sense the fundamental craving of the common man everywhere for peace with honor.

Why do our leaders lack the courage to act on principle—to risk the supposed unpopularity of the harder way? Is it because these leaders mistakenly believe nobody is witness to their weakness—their avoidance of plain duty? Why do leaders think the people are willing to pay any price for peace?

We give no answer when we point hopefully to the fruits of a coming negotiation wherein we are to surrender our ideals three months before the gavel calls the conference to order. We give no answer when in our cringing mood we point to the horrors of a possible war as the only alternative to surrender.

The answer lies deeper—in the souls of leaders who do not know their own peoples. That's why they really fear the risks of leadership.

The world today would not be in turmoil if governments everywhere were commanded by men of faith.

What an opportunity for the truly honest conscience of a nation to be projected today into international policy! If leaders only dared to speak what is in the hearts and minds of the people! What would they say?

We must affirm boldly the truth—no period of peace lasts very long if based on injustice or on a compromise with evil.

We can conquer the foes of peace—dictators—only by refusing to yield to their terms no matter how long the wait—for we must look to the peoples of these dictator countries who some day, if we stand aloof now, will overthrow their present rulers.

But what of our allies? Western Europe today manifests toward America a curious contempt — not a spirit which should be uniting us all in thanksgiving that we, the givers, and they, the recipients, can go forward together to improve the lot of man. No, the voices from abroad, especially Attlee and the Laborites in the British Parliament, are strident and at times even cruel, though we have sacrificed thousands of American youth in the cause of world peace, only to be defeated on the battlefield by a selfish trade which our allies maintained with the dictators—the Communist aggressors.

The ink is hardly dry on the truce agreement in Korea—yet the parliaments of Europe are already counting profits from an enlarged trade with the aggressors who have not been brought to the bars of justice.

How can we, in these moments of discord, reassert truth and restore the power of the human spirit in those precincts where crass materialism is eating away like a cancer the moral fibre of statesmen who were once the leaders of thought in the world?

When will governments adopt the faith that man in the ordinary walks of life lives by? When will governments give their peoples the leadership that appeals to the nobler instincts of the common man? On being asked to serve, the citizen responds with a spirit of

EISENHOWER

MALENKOV

ADENAUER

CHURCHILL

LANIEL

DE GASPERI

Photos: Harris & Ewing, Sovfoto, United Press

sacrifice which only a God-given faith in the rightness of his cause can inspire. How fine this instinct—how simple this faith!

We must take care not to betray that faith. We cannot constantly offer up the sons of America on the altars of today's expediency and expect our youth to enter tomorrow's big war with the zeal of an undiminished patriotism.

For what valor does the defeatism of our allies now instill in the American boys about to don their uniforms? Where shall the spirit and morale come from that moulds a fighting army?

Man-made law has the authority to draft our sons and they obey its summons. But we cannot respect the compromises and inequities whose political immorality is reflected in the glib phrases of today's "diplomacy." For in the double-talk of the hour—reported in dispatches from Europe—we are being asked to take unto our bosom the very governments, the very leaders who only yesterday massacred and tortured our sons by the thousands in disregard of the accepted code for the treatment of prisoners of war.

To the people of China and Soviet Russia we can wholeheartedly extend the hands of friendship, but their rulers should pay the penalty for their crimes against humanity.

The higher law pronounces sentence upon them. The law of truth and morality—which rises above the hypocrisies of statutory law and foreign office pronouncements—calls for the removal from power of those criminals in Moscow and Peiping who were responsible for the Korean war.

Food packages for the hungry, charity for the indigent, embargoes on war materials, withdrawal of diplomatic recognition, expulsion from the U. N. of all aggressors—these are the weapons of moral force which courageous nations can apply in concert without killing innocent people in Soviet Russia or elsewhere.

We must put our faith in the power to ostracize evil men from human society. We cannot condone the unmoral.

For only in the moral and natural law of a Divine Providence is to be found the faith that men must live by.

TO THE UNRETURNED PRISONERS:

AUGUST 14, 1953

Dear Americans of a Bygone Age:

The word comes that 2,000 of you were murdered by the Communists during the winter of 1950 to 1951 in North Korea.

The word comes that maybe 2,000 or more of you are still alive, but that the Communists do not yet acknowledge your existence.

The word comes from hundreds who have just come back that some of you were beaten and starved and that you experienced terrible torture.

You were marching in agony during the last months of 1950 and the early months of 1951. You had won a smashing victory over the North Korean aggressors when the Chinese Communist armies intervened. Your America became hesitant then and asked the advice of other governments allied with us. Should we pursue the enemy to his bases, we inquired, and knock out his sources of supply? This was a curious question to ask when authority had already been delegated by the various governments to a supreme commander to conduct effective military operations.

You did not know that the answer which came back was a craven message of fear—fear that to support you would involve us in an "enlarged war." You might rightfully ask why you were ordered to go to the mainland of Asia in the first place, if not to defeat and punish the aggressor.

You might ask why we did not fear an enlarged war in June 1950. The truth is we knew all along and still know that Soviet Russia cannot conduct a two-front war effectively and particularly would never risk war in Asia and Europe because of the tenuous hold by the Communist Government on the Red Army. Thus were we and our allies bluffed into defeatism.

You may ask what did happen. President Truman fired General MacArthur in April 1951 and announced publicly in May 1951, through Secretary of State Acheson, that we were through—we would sign an armistice with the enemy and would be satisfied to let our armies stay in and around the 38th Parallel where the aggression began. The Communists accepted our pleas for truce talks and there ensued months and months of diversionary argument about "repatriating" the prisoners who didn't want to go back to the Communists. But we heard very little about how we were to be assured of the safe return of our own men who were taken prisoner or about punishment for those guilty of mistreating our soldiers.

We in America until this last week did not know of the brutality experienced by Americans who were prisoners. We did not know until General Mark Clark, Far Eastern Commander, revealed publicly that there may be 2,000 or 3,000 of you still alive and about to be used for ransom. Either we give in now to the Communist demands at the "political conference" or, it seems, you will not be released.

We still do not know what happened to all Americans captured during the Korean war. We know there are 8,075 missing—aside from the 3,313 who are on the official list of those to be returned. If 2,000 or 3,000 more are alive, at least 5,000 are still unaccounted for.

Can we really sit down at a peace table with barbarians guilty of such war crimes? You wouldn't think so. But we who live in the so-called "free world" are already witnessing a clamor in the British Parliament that the barbaric government of Red China be admitted to the United Nations.

You didn't know that, during all the time you were suffering, money was more important to some of our allies than your lives. Strategic materials were shipped to Soviet Russia—admittedly the nation that supplied Red China with her munitions for the Korean war.

You may ask what has happened to the so-called "free world"—has it become just a victim of materialism, or is it just afraid?

The answer is that moral force and morality are at low ebb. We could have won the Korean war, we could still win it. But we must learn again how to stand firmly for the right. Today the people behind the Iron Curtain are looking to us—for food and help. Only a minority of voices among us have pleaded right along for a positive policy that will liberate the enslaved without war and without the killing of innocent people by our own military forces—a policy that must ignore barbarian governments and must deal only with peoples.

If we could only get the vast majority in the free world to demand a policy that severs diplomatic relations with all governments under Communist control in Europe and Asia and appeals to their peoples to overthrow those governments, all war criminals responsible for the crimes committed against them as well as against you would in due time be punished and we would see a new era of peace in the world.

Meanwhile, you will not be forgotten—you cannot be forgotten as long as the conscience of man keeps reminding us of the difference between inhumanity and humaneness, between barbarism and civilization, between cowardice and bravery.

THE GAME OF BLUFF

AUGUST 28, 1953

Terror over the invention of a new weapon of great destructiveness is not new to the world.

Mere fear, however, of the new horrors of war has never prevented the next war from breaking out. President Wilson, speaking at Denver in September 1919, just after World War I, said:

"Stop for a moment to think about the next war, if there should be one. I do not hesitate to say that the war we have just been through, though it was shot through with terror of every kind, is not to be compared with the war we would have to face next time. There were destructive gases, there were methods of explosive destruction unheard of even during this war, which were just ready for use when the war ended— great projectiles that guided themselves and shot into the heavens, went for a hundred miles and more and then burst tons of explosives upon helpless cities, something to which the guns with which the Germans bombarded Paris from a distance were not comparable. What the Germans used were toys as compared with what would be used in the next war. Ask any soldier if he wants to go through a hell like that again. The soldiers know what the next war would be. They know what the inventions were that were just about to be used for the absolute destruction of mankind."

The inventive mind of man has never been paralyzed by the creation of destructive weapons. Against the submarine, we devised the sound detector and the depth bomb and techniques of spotting from airplanes launched from aircraft carriers. We also have now the proximity fuse and the guided missile as a counter-attack against hostile planes.

Thus the principle of interception is already being applied successfully in a limited way.

The time is near at hand when hostile planes can be detected at long distances and destroyed before they approach their targets.

What we are witnessing at the moment is a gigantic game of bluff.

The objective of the Soviets is to neutralize the use of the atom bomb and the H-bomb.

For if, along with poison gas and germ warfare, both sides agree not to use the new bombs, the advantage from a military viewpoint in Europe and Asia will go to the Communists. They will feel free to pursue their political infiltration and even their aggression. For they will not be afraid of an allied army or conventional operations of war. They have more troops in the field in Europe than we and our allies combined.

Naturally the Soviets had a reason for proclaiming to the world that they have the H-bomb. They want to persuade gullible Americans, including some short-sighted scientists, to make all our secrets available. We may expect, therefore, to see an immediate renewal of the Soviet drive for full publicity of atom information by us on the specious theory that everything vital is already known or can be ascertained in due time anyway. This is illusory doctrine, and it is to be hoped that our Government will not fall for that kind of bluff.

It is Soviet Russia which is afraid of the H-bomb. We have a long lead in such weapons.

But the Kremlin is even more afraid of something else—our ideas. Once these are communicated effectively to the people of Soviet Russia, the movement to eliminate the gangsters in Moscow will gain irresistible momentum. For it's the pen that might order the H-bomb dropped which can and must be stayed.

The strongest possible defense against war in the meantime is not only a powerful army, navy and air force but a really cohesive international alliance in the free world.

The biggest danger we all face today is in Europe, where the cry of "neutralism" has been raised and where fixed land bases for our airplanes may at any time be taken from us by an internal change in countries which could then readily adopt a policy of "neutrality" as between the United States and Soviet Russia. We need more floating bases—aircraft carriers that can cover the seven seas without regard to political upheavals in Europe or Asia.

Today the Communists have as their ally the British Labor Party, which can exercise enough influence to weaken any firm stand taken by the Conservative Government. In France and Italy, Communist blocs hold the balance of power.

We need resolute allies—not cringing partners. We have the weapons and the industrial strength to hold the Soviet regime at bay and prevent a war. But we must not provoke a war. Wars are not provoked just by military attack. They can be provoked by manifestations of weakness and dissension among allies.

That's the way to bring on war. When actually attacked, the British people and the French people and the Italian people will, of course, join us in resisting the enemy. How much better it would be to stand together now so that, in the present game of bluff, the Communists will not dare to make the miscalculation that Hitler did!

TRAITORS IN OUR MIDST

SEPTEMBER 4, 1953

THE REPORT ON SOVIET ESPIONAGE issued unanimously by the Internal Security Subcommittee of the Senate Judiciary Committee—published in this magazine in full text last week—is a sensational document.

For the first time, a comprehensive narrative is presented, with sworn testimony, giving names and details of two Soviet spy rings which have existed inside the Government of the United States. Hinting that there are two more spy rings in the Government not yet exposed, the Committee report says:

"In general, the Communists who infiltrated our Government worked behind the scenes—guiding research and preparing memoranda on which basic American policies were set, writing speeches for Cabinet officers, influencing congressional investigations, drafting laws, manipulating administrative reorganizations—always serving the interest of their Soviet superiors . . .

"This penetration has extended from the lower ranks to top-level policy and operating positions in our Government."

Soviet henchmen inside our own Government, the report says, influenced labor policy, agriculture policy, Treasury policy, foreign policy—especially the acquisition of China by the Communists.

The Committee names the departments and agencies where the Communists had men planted—the White House, the Department of State, the Treasury, the National Labor Relations Board, the International Monetary Fund, and even committees of Congress.

But, it will be asked, what steps were taken to eradicate the traitors, and who took them?

First of all, the Federal Bureau of Investigation sent a secret memorandum in November 1945 to President Truman and other high officials calling attention to 80 individuals named by an ex-Communist as being "connected with the Soviet espionage organization either in Washington or in New York."

The FBI stated at the time that 37 of these individuals had been identified as employees of the Government. Among those identified was Alger Hiss. The memorandum said the FBI also had interviewed a former code clerk in the Russian Embassy in Canada who had deserted the Russians and had revealed that in May 1945 the Russians had as an agent in the United States an assistant to the Secretary of State.

Why didn't the Democratic Administration do something about these FBI reports? Why did President Truman in 1948—three years after the FBI had distributed the secret memorandum—call the whole agitation by congressional committees a "red herring," particularly when the name of Alger Hiss first came into the headlines?

The FBI itself cannot remove anybody from a Government post. It cannot prosecute anybody. Action must be authorized by the President or the Attorney General. Senator McCarthy, when he began his crusade early in 1950, made that very point. The Wisconsin Senator is not a member of the Senate Subcommittee on Internal Security, but his main contention is certainly sustained in the Subcommittee's report, which says:

"It is the function of the Federal Bureau of Investigation to uncover and compile security information and make it available, without evaluation and without recommendation, to the proper executive agencies. The Federal Bureau of Investigation cannot expose and cannot force action once it has reported the results of its investigation. This fact is basic in the understanding of the function performed by a congressional committee."

But if the last Democratic Administration was deceived or fooled, what explanation can be made of the persistent attitude of leading Democrats and so-called "liberals" today who keep sniping away at those members of the Senate and House who have helped to expose Communist activities inside the Government?

If the Democratic Party as a whole is ever to regain the public confidence which it lost on the anti-Communist issue in the last presidential election, it must show more zeal in Congress than it has lately in ferreting out Communist agents and influences in America. It will not suffice to try to smear Senator McCarthy.

Indeed, why are the efforts to get at and spread the truth about the worst conspiracy in the history of the United States met with false cries about "witch hunts" and "hysteria" and an "age of fear"? Only the guilty need have any fear.

The report of the Senate Subcommittee deserves the widest circulation. Every patriotic citizen should urge his local newspaper to reprint it. Every patriotic organization should reprint it. Every student in our colleges should be asked to read it, and so should every editor, clergyman, lawyer, and everybody else who influences thought in the community.

Only by a nationwide campaign of education can the hidden traitors be forced into the open and further treason prevented.

Our first line of defense is inside America.

TO OUR BRITISH FRIENDS

SEPTEMBER 11, 1953

THERE IS EVERY REASON why the American and British peoples should remain friendly—for they have the same ideals and the same concepts of individual freedom.

Whatever estrangement has developed lately is the direct consequence of misunderstandings that can and must be removed.

Twice American armies have gone to Europe to help save the cause of freedom, and on each occasion have come back with renewed admiration for the courage and fighting spirit of the British people.

The British and American peoples believe in free debate.

Let us begin with the kind of news the American people have been reading. Here, for example, is a London dispatch of last week by the United Press, dated September 2, concerning the political party which holds almost 50 per cent of the seats in the British Parliament:

"Rank-and-file members of the British Labor Party took a loud and bitter anti-American stand today.

"The agenda for the annual Party conference was sprinkled with strong resolutions criticizing U. S. foreign policy and indicating that 'anti-Americanism' may be the only issue to reunite the Party.

"Most resolutions demanded a neutral foreign and economic policy. They came almost traditionally, however, from the most vocal left-wing sections of the Party. The resolutions are almost certain to be watered down by the Party leadership and the more conservative trade unions. The conservative unions will hold the balance of power at the Party conference to be held at Margate, England, September 28 to October 2.

"The rank-and-file demand included a Big Five meeting, with Communist China attending, admission of the Chinese Reds to the United Nations, full trade with Communist nations, disarmament, a neutral Germany and 'independence' from the United States.

"Not a single resolution criticized Russia. A few were even plainly Communistic, although the Party prides itself on rooting out Reds.

"Even though Party leaders succeed in toning down the resolutions at the convention, a basic disagreement with American policy in trade and in the Far East will remain."

After reading that dispatch, the American people read on September 3 another dispatch by the United Press from London:

"A strike called by the Communist-led electrical trades union today affected the Harwell atomic energy station, Britain's main atomic-research center, and the London docks."

Rightly or wrongly, many people on this side of the Atlantic believe that the British Government, under Labor Party rule, was lax in dealing with the infiltration attempted by the Communists in Britain. The careless way by which Klaus Fuchs, the spy, was "cleared" by the British Government for entrance to American atomic-energy projects has not been forgotten. Likewise, in recent months Messrs. Maclean and Burgess, two officials of the British Foreign Office—one of them familiar with some atomic-energy matters—have fled behind the Iron Curtain, though it was known for a long time among their friends in London that they were active Communists.

It has been suggested that, instead of denouncing Senator McCarthy for crimes he never committed and for the alleged loss of liberties by American citizens that neither he nor anyone else has taken away from any innocent person, the British might better develop a McCarthy who, using British methods of procedure, can at least stir up as much awareness of the menace of infiltration as the American people have today.

But it is in the realm of foreign policy that most of the misunderstanding prevails. The American people today despise Communists as much as the British despised Nazis. The Communists are the same under the skin—cruel, ruthless, deceitful and fomenting the same "fifth column" treachery that the Nazis used in undermining France in the '30s. To suggest to America today the admission of Red China to the Security Council of the U. N. evokes the same bitter reaction as the British would have had to a proposal by us in 1944 that the British and ourselves forget the indignities we both had suffered and begin to "do business with Hitler."

Surely our British friends must know that Americans have no real desire to exercise "world leadership" but prefer to be left to pursue their own ways on this continent. Yet no nation can today "go it alone." We need each other. Principles are safer to follow for the long run than expediency of the moment.

We believe the issue is the same as it was after Munich. Secretary Dulles, in a speech before the American Legion last week, made it very clear that you cannot appease aggressors. Let us examine all the facts objectively—and may we hope that the British and ourselves eventually will agree that there can be no compromise at any time with evil men. In this way we will avert a third world war.

A VICTORY FOR MORAL FORCE

SEPTEMBER 18, 1953

AMERICA HAS WON TO HER SIDE a sturdy ally—the people of Germany.

The defense of the free world has been made stronger as against the evil men in the Kremlin.

These are the great consequences of the election in which Chancellor Adenauer and his party achieved such an extraordinary triumph last week.

The influence of this event—the most significant since the close of World War II—will be felt for many years to come in the policies of governments on both sides of the Iron Curtain.

For it has been demonstrated anew that the key to world peace is in the hands of peoples.

Without coercion or intimidation, the voters of Germany came to understand the fundamental issues. They responded unequivocally and with an instinctive support for the ideals of the free world.

This was the working of moral force—persuasion based on facts and reason, instead of coercion. The German electorate, operating under freedom of speech and a free press and radio, heard and read everything—Soviet propaganda and the Western viewpoint—and the voters in West Germany took note especially of the food parcels sent to their brethren in East Germany by America.

What a remarkable thing it is that a people—only lately conquered by invading armies, their factories and their homes bombed by airplanes which had wrought daily destruction—should emerge now without enmity in their hearts toward their conquerors and take their place alongside of other free peoples!

Indeed, in the recent campaign the German militarism which gave birth to Hitlerism was widely denounced by both major parties. When the ballots were counted, neither the new Nazis nor the Communists had polled enough votes to get the minimum recognition as a party in the German legislature.

The election result corroborates what many Americans have always felt about the moral fibre of the German people. It is not unlike that of the free nations, despite the fact that during a period of postwar economic depression the Nazi leaders were able to mislead the masses and to impose a dictatorship which deprived the people of the right of free expression.

German emigrants who have come to America for decades have proved that they are the same as any other Americans in their desire for freedom and liberty. It is a myth to assume that there is something inherently bellicose in the German character. The militarism which swept Germany before 1914 and which was revived by Hitler in 1933 is not a phenomenon confined to any one nation or any particular period in history.

The Weimar Republic in Germany after World War I should have succeeded. Had it been assisted at the opportune moment by the other nations, there never would have been a second world war.

France and America, working together now, can perform an incalculable service in giving to the new Republic of Germany under the Adenauer leadership the moral support which the Western allies failed to give the Weimar Republic in the 1920s.

The Soviet, of course, will count on the Communist Party in France to disrupt, if it can, any government that cooperates with Germany. From the United States the hand of friendship which has been proffered by Democratic and Republican Administrations since the close of the last war will continue to be extended in the hope of carrying forward in Germany the triumph of moral force that has just been recorded at the polls. We put our trust in the German people—and our faith has been vindicated.

The Germans are a virile nation. They can and will build a strong economy. They want an alliance with the United States and with all other nations that seek a common objective—an end to war. The opposition to rearmament, for example, inside Germany has been vehement—it has come from a people disillusioned by Hitlerism. But the realism of the hour bids the Germans to rearm, and they will do so reluctantly. If France does not accept a European Defense Army, the alternative ultimately will be a German national army with all the risks implied in a possible revival of intense nationalism.

For Germany cannot be expected to stand defenseless in the center of Europe—menaced by a blackmailing Moscow which holds as hostages 18 million Germans in East Germany. Unification of all Germany is much more likely to come if West Germany rearms than if it were to stay unarmed. That's why the majority in the election last week approved a policy of rearmament—but as an integral part of an alliance of free peoples.

Germany cannot long be denied a rightful place as an equal in the family of nations.

The cause of peace has been advanced by the German elections. In the heart of Europe an ally has been reared, an ally with spirit and patriotism based on the strongest moral force the world has ever known—democracy and freedom.

'APOLOGIES' TO AL CAPONE?

SEPTEMBER 25, 1953

MAYBE WE OWE AN APOLOGY to the late Al Capone, or to his memory, or to his brethren in gangland who still appear every now and then in Chicago or on the waterfront of New York City.

Maybe we should "negotiate" with the gangsters and racketeers who remain in our midst today and "search for settlements." Maybe we should have said to the Capone gang:

"After all, what we want is peaceful co-existence. We won't let a little matter of income-tax cheating or machine-gun massacres stand in the way. Let one gang take North Chicago, and the other South Chicago. There is room for both of you."

The analogy has only to be stated to reveal the parallelism that exists today with the appeasers in the world who still want to "negotiate" with the gangster governments in Moscow and Peiping.

Last week Adlai Stevenson, presidential candidate of the Democratic Party in 1952, made at Chicago a report to the nation after a world-wide journey. The text of his speech and the address by the Secretary of State, John Foster Dulles, before the United Nations last week commenting on some of the same points, are both printed in this issue.

There are some curious contradictions in Mr. Stevenson's advice to his countrymen. First he says:

"Will Red China yield at the conference table what it fought to prevent on the battlefield? It would seem to me unlikely if we adopt arbitrary positions in advance and our room for maneuver and negotiation is limited. I hope our leaders will not be prisoners of domestic political propaganda or hobbled by inflexibility."

"Personally I am skeptical of Red China's intentions, but when we search for settlements we have to search, and when we negotiate we have to have something to negotiate with as well as for. Many of our friends think China wants peace and trade above all, as they themselves do. With so much at stake in Asia—the unification of Korea, Formosa, peace and security in Indochina—it would seem to me that we owe it to ourselves as well as to our friends at least to find out, if we can, what Communist China's ultimate intentions are."

How many more thousands of Americans must be killed and wounded in Asia and how many more Frenchmen must be killed and wounded in Indochina to find out what Red China's "intentions" are? How many more resolutions must be adopted by the United Nations declaring Red China an aggressor before the appeasers in America and in India and in other parts of the world will become convinced what the intentions of gangsters really are in the world of today?

Mr. Stevenson would "negotiate" with Communist Russia. Yet he shows his own skepticism about the practicality of it when he says there is "no certain evidence that the softer music from Moscow reflects any basic change in the Soviet design of world domination," and he adds:

"If the Soviet Union rejects assurances of nonaggression, if the Red Army will not withdraw behind its borders, if an Austrian peace treaty and German unification are impossible except on the Soviet's terms, then we will at least have cleared the air. We will have resolved the uncertainties of many about Soviet sincerity and intentions, and we will have clearly fixed the responsibility for the present state of insecurity and fear."

Should there be any doubt anywhere today as to the responsibility for the present insecurity in the world? Are we not already familiar with the emptiness of Soviet assurances or the insincerity of their pledges? How much more fog and smog must we encounter before we all agree that the air is thick with Communist lawlessness?

What kind of "maneuvering" and "negotiation" is feasible—even if it were desirable—when so many of our "allies" proclaim to the enemy in advance that they want Red China admitted to the U. N.?

There can be no compromise at any time with evil. There can be no appeasement of gangsters. There can be no "peaceful co-existence" with a barbarian who knows no code of honor and applies only torture and unspeakable cruelties to those who fall into his hands.

The *New York Times* rightly declared last week that the question is not one of legalism or expediency but is based "on moral grounds that are matters of principle," and that American opposition to the admittance of Red China to the U. N. is the 'sober judgment of the overwhelming majority of the people of the United States" —and "not a view of only a few shrill propagandists or some mythical 'China Lobby.'"

Let us reaffirm our moral principle. Let us not be deluded into the belief that gangsterism can be the subject of treaties or agreements or "negotiation." We can and must ostracize the gangster governments. We must embargo their trade. We must talk directly to the people of Soviet Russia. We must meanwhile build up our military defenses so as to be sure of our own security.

There should be no compromise with the Capone-like gang on the international front.

WITHDRAW FROM KOREA!

OCTOBER 2, 1953

THE LOGIC OF EVENTS demands that the United States prepare to withdraw all American troops from Korea and turn the task over to the military forces of those members of the United Nations which to date have not done their full duty in that area.

For a stalemate is now certain.

Soviet Russia does not intend to agree to the unification of Korea, and the United Nations does not intend to use force to bring about such unification.

Lester Pearson, the Canadian Secretary of State for External Affairs, says that the 16 nations which sent forces to Korea did so only "to repel aggression." He went on to say to the U. N. General Assembly last week:

"So far as the Canadian Government is concerned, we will not support any military action in Korea that is not United Nations action and we would be opposed to any attempt to interpret existing United Nations objectives as including unification of Korea by force."

Mr. Pearson is saying the same thing that President Eisenhower wrote in his first letter to Syngman Rhee on June 6, 1953, when he declared further measures of force would not be used to attain unification.

But the significance of Mr. Pearson's declaration is that he makes it now—after evidence of gross violations of the armistice agreement and the Communist failure to return all prisoners as pledged. What it amounts to is that the Communist side is being notified publicly that it is under no compulsion of military force to make a peace agreement.

What leverage, then, is there left, if any? Mr. Pearson puts it this way:

"If the Communist side, or anyone else, by obstruction and inadmissible demands make a peaceful solution impossible, then the responsibility will be made clear, and the United Nations, at least, will have done its duty."

How many times does the air have to be "cleared"? How many resolutions adopted by the same United Nations must be dishonored and discarded before the world learns from the United Nations where the responsibility is for the Communist aggression in Korea?

One wonders what the United Nations meant in its October 7, 1950, resolution, when, after it had authorized the U. N. forces to cross the 38th Parallel, it told General MacArthur to "ensure conditions of stability throughout Korea." One wonders what the United Nations meant also when, on February 1, 1951, it declared Red China an "aggressor."

The responsibility has already been plainly fixed. It is simple duty which is being evaded and avoided.

If there is to be a stalemate of years in Korea—and that's the outlook now—the United States should not be expected to do the guard duty hereafter. The burden should be transferred to other countries in the United Nations.

India, for example, has an immense quantity of unused manpower. Here is a nation which is supposed to be a "neutral" in the Korean dispute—though just how a U. N. member nation can be "neutral" when the U. N. declares a belligerent like Red China to be an aggressor is a little difficult for the Western mind to fathom. But Indian troops are already on guard duty in Korea and these could be augmented.

For if the U. N. intends to continue to be an instrument "to repel aggression" it should maintain a substantial military force at the armistice line in Korea to keep the peace.

Why should American sons be drafted hereafter to maintain a stalemate indefinitely? We have sacrificed more than 30,000 lives and have suffered more than 100,000 casualties already. If there is to be no fighting but a "peaceful co-existence" on the Korean armistice line, let the other members of the United Nations now send their troops there and pay for the military upkeep, too.

There are nations in the U. N. which want to start trading with Red China and to lift present restrictions on the shipment of strategic materials. They cry out that it is essential to trade as a means of livelihood. If materialism is to be the rule, then the United States should pay heed to its own tax dollars and let the expense of Korea be borne by those who trade with Red China and the countries behind the Iron Curtain. It's a fair swap.

But, above all, if our own Government concurs with the views of the other members of the U. N. and does not intend to resume the fighting, no matter how futile the "political conference" turns out to be, then it is time for the United States to arrange for the gradual withdrawal of its own forces.

If, however, the other members of the U. N. do not want to do guard duty, then they should not object to letting the Republic of Korea do it as the designated agent of the United Nations. After all, the Korean Republic was established originally by the U. N., and its new army will soon be strong enough to "ensure conditions of stability throughout Korea."

HOW LONG—HOW LONG?

OCTOBER 9, 1953

MUST AMERICA REMAIN under arms for decades to come—her youth drafted annually and her troops stationed permanently in 49 countries of the world?

The outlook today is for years and years of tension.

The Soviet strategy is becoming clear—the Communists have not the slightest intention of listening to the cringing pleas for "negotiation" which are emanating from the various governments of the free world and which are being echoed in behalf of the Democratic Party here in America by Messrs. Truman, Acheson and Stevenson.

We have said we will never fight unless attacked—and the Soviets have no intention of attacking us directly. So why shouldn't they stand pat and continue their "cold war" tactics? They are convinced we are begging for peace because we are telling everybody we are afraid of war.

From England and France come recurrent cries for "conferences" or "Big Four meetings" to "negotiate" a settlement. This implies that the Communists really want to make a deal or would honor any future agreements when they now are deliberately violating existing agreements. In truth, the Communists have little to gain from any "negotiation," as they see it, except to emphasize still more to their own peoples that successful Communist propaganda about the H-bomb has scared the whole world into submissiveness and has seemingly paralyzed all counter-planning.

Is the free world to sit on its haunches, telling everybody, including the enemy, that it is frightened? What will happen inside France, Italy, Germany and Great Britain if the President of the United States embarks on the dubious adventure of "telling all" to the American people—emphasizing in nationwide broadcasts what the hydrogen bomb can do to us in America? Will not the peoples of Europe then cry out, "O, Communism, where is thy sting?" Will they not be eager to appease the enemy and surrender their principles rather than face the bombs which our President will be describing as something that could do untold damage to us but which could even more quickly be dropped on European cities?

There is one thing more horrible than war—a living death under slavery. Pacifism, which has always been based on an abhorrence of war, has never been the answer. Nor is defeatism the answer today.

The real way to peace—the only way today—lies through an alliance with an emancipated people in Soviet Russia. It must come through the overthrow of the Kremlin and all the gangster governments by their own peoples. We must definitely encourage such action.

Today we have no policy that can begin to accomplish that objective for even the far-distant future. We sit in the United Nations with lawless governments that should be expelled for violating the Charter, which explicitly prohibits acts of military aggression against any state. We continue to give the Communist leaders prestige inside Russia by meeting with them in the U. N. and by constantly offering to "negotiate" with them. We accept criminals as equals at the U. N.—as capable of honest negotiation when the plain facts tell us otherwise.

What a travesty on modern courage! We seem to be afraid even to speak directly to the peoples of the Iron Curtain countries and to declare frankly and boldly that peace for them, as well as for us, lies in asserting their will fearlessly.

We have never said out loud what financial or economic aid we can give them to help stabilize their economic systems and to improve their standard of living. In short, we have done little to advance the positive policies that can lead to the overthrow of the governments at Moscow and Peiping.

We should first of all ostracize the lawless regimes of Soviet Russia and Red China. We should mobilize the moral force of mankind in a denunciation of such governments. We should next cut off all trade with them and wherever necessary buy from or subsidize the producers in all those countries allied with us which may be damaged by such an embargo. All diplomatic relations with Moscow and Peiping should be severed. When free governments arise in Russia and China that are responsive to the will of the people, we can settle existing disputes amicably and equitably.

How long—how long before the Government of the United States, in full association with its partners overseas, begins to map out a long-range policy to deal with the menace of Communist imperialism?

The answer lies within ourselves. As long as we are dominated by fear, we shall pay the penalty of indecision and weakness.

The sooner we face up to the simple fact that we must concentrate on winning as allies the peoples of Soviet Russia and the other enslaved peoples of Europe and Asia, the quicker our ingenuity and resourcefulness will be stimulated to achieve for mankind—without recourse to war—the greatest victory of all times.

'IT COULD BE HEAVEN'

OCTOBER 23, 1953

THE AUTUMN SEASON with its enchanting beauty is all around us. As one travels the back roads of the countryside, the thought comes again and again: "There must be millions and millions of square miles like these in the world—just as beautiful, just as peaceful. This could be heaven if—"

But the world's troubles grow. Apprehension is increasing. Friction multiplies and the air is filled with threats of destructive war. Thoughtful people everywhere grope for solutions. Some would appease the wicked—and postpone the day of reckoning. Others would find some new formula like a supra-national state in which presumably all the lions and the lambs, upon reading the admonishing phrases of a new charter, would lie down together in submissive tranquility.

Will a solution come someday through a world state in which each nation gives up its sovereignty—or will it come through the more intensive development of the very opposite, namely, the individuality of each state?

The theory has often been advanced that a collective alliance of states, whether imposed by force or by a voluntary union prompted by a common fear, is a better system than reliance by isolated nationalities on their own efforts. But there is a vast difference between a federation of independent nations and a permanent alliance which seeks to create a super-state.

What the extreme advocates of a supra-national government fail to grasp, of course, is that free government is never imposed from the top down. It must come from the bottom, from the will of individuals at the grass roots—and not just in one country but everywhere. Our attention might better be directed today at winning converts to national freedom in other lands than in urging other peoples to accept an international mechanism theoretically based on equality but actually based on dominion by the powerful.

As long as might makes right in the world, each nation will jealously guard its sovereignty. The main effort, therefore, must be to apply moral force to arrest the tendency to abuse sovereign power.

Peace in the world can come only from the will of the people to make all governments free. There is no menace to other nations from countries where public opinion is free to assert itself. President Eisenhower last week told the Inter-Parliamentary Union:

"Representative government is an expression of faith that free people can govern themselves. Consequently, since public opinion in a free country is the power and the force that gives validity to every pro-posal, the nearer we can come to bringing together the public opinions of nations rather than merely their governmental representatives, the greater significance and the greater importance should apply to such a meeting."

The sooner we diagnose the source of the infection, the earlier we will cope with the epidemic of evil itself. The source is the individual. National misbehavior cannot happen unless there is individual acquiescence. Persons who are willing indefinitely to accept slavery are not willing to pay the price of liberty. The story of liberty, like the story of a nation's emancipation, begins with the individual.

Where the citizen cares only for creature comforts and cares nothing for the things of the spirit, there ensues a deterioration and finally the decay of all human values. Where the inspiration to serve the cause of freedom comes from the Higher realm, the willingness to sacrifice even life, if need be, becomes a dominant passion. Bravery on the battlefield is not incompatible with Christian ethics. For the Christian doctrine does not condone the suicide of the state—pacifism.

Since it is to the individual that the world must look for the evolution of peace among nations, it is to the individual in those foreign lands where despotism holds sway that the picture of freedom must be constantly portrayed. For in all the wide spaces of the earth where the autumn leaves are manifesting their many-colored beauties, there is "enough for everybody's need but not enough for everybody's greed."

The world is still taught by example. The virtues of a responsible individualism are expressed in the life of free America and in the life of peoples in free lands across the seas. Less emphasis on the subtraction of sovereignty and more emphasis on the great good that can come to the world from a growth in individual responsibility must inevitably bring mutual respect and better understanding among nations.

We can federate at times in the common interest but we cannot amalgamate. We should instead strengthen the idea of a national spirit. We can do so without erecting new barriers of excessive pride or extreme nationalism. A partnership of free peoples needs no pact between them to prevent aggression.

And when we recognize that individual responsibility is the key to national policy everywhere, the whole world will begin to enjoy the blessings of these many bountiful lands, and we will perceive that even in mortal days there can be a heaven on earth.

THE ENGINE STALLS—

OCTOBER 30, 1953

WE HEAR ON EVERY SIDE inquiries about the business outlook: Will there be a recession? Will it be mild or severe? Will there be much unemployment? How long will the slowdown last?

Even as we ask such questions, we are aware that the business mechanism of America is far too complex to be measured at any given moment by a yardstick that will at once apply to all industries and to all parts of the country simultaneously. There are, however, certain basic trends in the past which can aid to some extent in determining what the future holds for us.

We can look back at the way the American economy wrestled with a postwar readjustment from the autumn of 1945 to the summer of 1950. We saw then the virtual elimination of overtime in large industries, and yet the steady rise of base pay. We saw production starting to catch up with the shortages occasioned by four years of war controls.

Then came the Korean war in the summer of 1950. It meant a return of a wartime economy, with new controls and new taxes. Shortages developed as restrictions on production of civilian goods were imposed, and demand again exceeded the supply. Production facilities—new plants and new equipment—were increased. Credit was expanded and consumption of goods then rose once more.

Now, with the armistice in Korea in the summer of 1953 and the abandonment of Government controls, supply once more has been catching up with demand. We are beginning to produce an excess. Under such circumstances, the economic engine stalls—and pauses until there's another push on the starter.

There have been many occasions in the past 80 to 90 years of our economic history when the domestic mechanism has had to slow down for a while to absorb its own production rate. Such readjustments have varied in severity—but they have never been entirely painless. Someone always is hurt.

It has become trite to say America's fundamental situation is sound—but that's only a way of observing that an economic depression of 1929-33 proportions can be warded off in the next decade by achieving now a proper balance of economic forces within the nation and avoiding a psychological pessimism that keeps the engine stalled longer than necessary.

There are signs of an approach to an economic balance in the world. The symptoms are to be found in the universally expressed desire of all nations to increase their trade with one another. The talk about the removal of trade barriers is much more a signal of a returning normalcy than we perhaps realize. This doesn't mean that a larger interchange of goods and services will necessarily result from a reduction in tariffs—for such a policy could bring disaster with consequent unemployment in many of our domestic industries. But it does mean that the traders of the world are groping for a solution. This ought not to be considered as the affair of one nation either, extensive though our markets here at home may appear to our friends abroad. They, too, have tariffs and quota restrictions. Trade must be encouraged everywhere—not just between America and the rest of the world.

We cannot expect, moreover, to tear up the economic structures of a continent by a world war and find a ready means of quickly putting them together again in a few years afterwards. It takes a longer time.

We shall for many years more be required to spend somewhere around 30 to 40 billions of dollars a year for defense. This is a worrisome fact—for it isn't the way to build a sound economy. Nor is it healthy for the Government to be required always to support farm prices or industrial prices as against foreign competition. What may be unhealthy in theory, however, becomes necessary in fact as a piece of political realism. The Eisenhower Administration knows it must continue to use some of the instruments whereby the Government, ever since the Hoover Administration, has intervened in the economic life of the country—or else suffer defeat at the polls in 1954. Pressure groups, shifting their votes from one party to the other, hold the balance of power in politics.

It is a time to resist inflationary pressures and to get the engine started at a steady though slower velocity in order that the laws of supply and demand may operate again and prices may be adjusted accordingly. For America after each economic setback has always made her greatest progress in reconstruction by cutting costs, by technological improvements, and by increased productivity of labor, so that prices are at least kept from climbing further upward.

America can and will come through the present readjustment, possibly in a matter of months. The Eisenhower Administration, of course, cannot regulate every detail of the economic mechanism but, by a wise tax policy and a prudent handling of the credit apparatus, it can provide a climate in which business can move steadily on to a larger and larger national income and a stabilized economy.

PROTECTING THE CITIZEN

NOVEMBER 6, 1953

INTERVENTION BY THE GOVERNMENT in the economic life of the nation is sometimes referred to by speakers or writers of today as if it were a comparatively recent development.

Yet the principle is as old as the American Republic. It was recognized when, upon the recommendation of Alexander Hamilton, the Congress, in order to protect "infant industries," imposed the first tariff on goods from foreign countries. It was recognized further when large areas of public lands were granted by the Government a century ago to the railroads to enable them to build a transportation system for the nation.

It was emphasized in 1887 with the establishment of an Interstate Commerce Commission to regulate railroad rates, and in 1890 with the passage of the Sherman Antitrust Law to assure free competition. Indeed, the principle of governmental intervention has been gradually extended into various fields by legislation over the last 50 years.

Thus, in 1926, with the adoption by a Republican Congress of a law to make collective bargaining a legal requirement as between railroads and labor unions, the way was opened for a Democratic Congress to pass the Wagner Labor Relations Act in 1935. The Supreme Court, moreover, when upholding the Wagner law in 1937, based its decision primarily on the collective-bargaining precedent established in 1930 when it declared the Railway Labor Act constitutional as a regulation of commerce.

In an emergency, in time of disaster or violent depression, the grant of relief either by Government loan or gift goes beyond the function of mere regulation. It goes directly to the aid of the distressed. The assumption here, however, is that this is temporary and not permanent. For paternalism would inevitably break down our whole system of individual initiative.

It is a strange commentary on the lack of understanding of the principle of governmental intervention that some persons who for years have favored a protective tariff have been slow to recognize the right .of the farmer to be protected against the disorderly marketing forces which would compel him to sell his product when speculation may have depressed the prices.

Efforts of the Republican Congresses in the 1920's— seeking, either by McNary-Haugen bills or by a Federal Farm Board, to achieve orderly marketing and prevent the collapse of farm prices—testify historically to the acceptance of the principle of governmental intervention in agriculture. Support of farm prices is today recognized as analogous to a protective tariff.

But, in saying this, it must be noted that the manufacturer who marks up his price almost to the very top of the tariff wall, because he is sure no competitor from abroad can challenge him, is abusing the principle just as much as the farm group which demands a rigid price support irrespective of the marketing conditions of the future. It is in both instances a disregard of the public interest—the consumers.

In still another field—banking—Congress for decades past has maintained a system of supervision through audits and periodic examination designed to protect the citizen. The Aldrich-Vreeland Currency Act of 1908, during a Republican Administration, followed as it was by the Federal Reserve Act of 1913 during a Democratic Administration, applied even further the principle of governmental intervention to the banking system. Today monetary and credit regulation are accepted as a proper exercise of the federal function.

When depression became worldwide and America began to be vitally affected, the Hoover Administration in 1932 established with congressional authorization a system of intermediate credit—direct lending by the Government—known as the Reconstruction Finance Corporation. The purpose was to conserve in an emergency the assets of soundly managed properties.

Governmental intervention to regulate conflicting interests or to prevent such groups from impinging on the public interest is, of course, a vastly different approach from asking the Government to guarantee employment or wages or profits.

Both political parties have long accepted as essential to our way of life the principle of governmental intervention in our economic system, either as a stimulus or as a monitor of economic forces, in the public interest. But the federal function must not be abused and special privileges granted to favored groups under the catch-all phrase—"general welfare." We must guard against proposals for government operation of natural resources or government control of industry, agriculture and labor. That is the road to state socialism.

Reliance on individual initiative and resourcefulness is still the key to the success of the American economic system. It has provided the highest standard of living in the world. It has outdistanced all other economic systems. And our industrial power, derived from private enterprise, is still the best protection for the citizens of our country in this atomic age.

MIXED VOICES

NOVEMBER 13, 1953

OUT OF THE VARIETY of local contests at the polls last week, no trend on national issues can be clearly discerned as between political parties.

A victory for the Democratic organization of Senator Byrd in Virginia against a Republican Party augmented by a substantial number of New Dealers—who supported Stevenson a year ago but who voted for the Republican nominee for Governor this time—gives us no real evidence of the relative strength of the two parties. New Dealism, as expounded by the Republican nominee for Governor, was repudiated under the auspices of the Democratic state organization in Virginia.

A victory for Tammany Hall in New York City, bringing back to power a political machine with the worst record of corruption in American history, is not evidence of a trend on policies in either party nationally. For, if the political factions against Tammany had entered into a fusion, they would have triumphed. The two anti-Tammany nominees who lost received a combined total in excess of the vote of the Tammany candidate for mayor who won.

The successful Democratic nominee for Governor in New Jersey said publicly on the day after election that the Eisenhower policies were not in any way an issue—that it was wholly a local contest. Scandals inside the State Republican organization drove many Republican voters into the Democratic camp.

Both in New Jersey and in New York the Republicans retained the same control of the Legislatures that they had—no national trend here.

So far as city machines are concerned, the Republicans made big gains in Chicago and also in Philadelphia. These victories can have some bearing on organizing the vote for future contests, but they reveal no cleavages on national issues.

We are left, therefore, with only one national trend —failure of Republicans to vote.

The election statistics show that Democrats went to the polls proportionately in greater numbers this time than did the Republicans.

Thus, in the recent special election for Congress in Wisconsin—which the Democrats won—only 25 per cent of the Republicans who voted in 1952 were in evidence, whereas the Democratic vote was 60 per cent of its 1952 total.

In New Jersey's special election for Congress last week, the Democrats brought out 68,793 votes, as against 67,159 a year ago—a gain of 1,634. The Republicans, on the other hand, polled only 66,796 as against their 121,252 for Congressman last year.

Why did the Republican vote fall off so substantially with no corresponding gain for the Democrats?

Do voters who stay at home do so out of protest?

The late Senator Taft was sure that the stay-at-home voters were indifferent, uninformed, and only to a small extent a protest. Thus, in 1948 Truman carried Ohio by 7,000 over Dewey, while a large Republican vote stayed at home. But two years later Senator Taft put on a militant campaign and won re-election by 430,000.

Voters have to be convinced that their ballots will make a difference. Conservative Republicans do not feel it worthwhile to go to the polls to choose between a New Deal Republican and a New Deal Democrat.

Yet it is also probable that if the Administration followed only ultra-conservative policies, it would alienate "independents" who swing from party to party on specific policies.

All this apparently is why President Eisenhower wants to avoid extremes in either case and travel politically in the middle of the road.

The President inherited "a Washington mess." It will not be straightened out overnight. The people are impatient for tax reduction and an end to the continuous drain on their youth for military service. They are still opposed to Communism and corruption in Government. They expect the Administration to maintain prosperity on the farm and in factory, yet they don't want to see unsound measures adopted that can bring on a ruinous inflation.

Dwight Eisenhower is learning his job. He is a completely honest, unselfish and faithful public servant. He has been pushed from side to side by conflicting advisers, most of whom have not given weight to obvious political currents. They assumed there was plenty of time to "plan" and to appoint commissions of study—and that the "doing" could come later.

The Administration now may be stimulated to move ahead more rapidly to the "doing" stage. For it is apparent that the main job is to keep the Republican voters of 1952 convinced that the change they sought at the polls last year will be consummated. It will require patience. Meanwhile, the Administration might well tell the public more about the true state of the Government on January 20 last and about the pernicious policies that were driving us rapidly to the brink of bankruptcy. The Eisenhower Administration's "Operation Candor" on the political front is long overdue.

WHO IS GUILTY?

NOVEMBER 27, 1953

THE CHARGE made by Attorney General Brownell on November 6 in a speech in Chicago reads as follows:

"The failure of our predecessors to defend the Government from Communist infiltration left the new Administration a necessary but very difficult task.

"We are now confronted with this problem, not because there was any real lack of information available to our predecessors as to the identity of the Communists in Government, but because of the unwillingness of the non-Communists in responsible positions to face the facts and a persistent delusion that Communism in the Government of the United States was only a 'red herring.' As an illustration I will give you the case of Harry Dexter White . . .

"He (White) smuggled secret documents to Russian agents for transmission to Moscow. Harry Dexter White was known to be a Communist spy by the very people who appointed him to the most sensitive and important position he ever held in Government service."

Immediately after that speech was printed in the newspapers, Mr. Truman said that White had been "fired" just as soon as he was found to be disloyal.

In a nationwide broadcast on November 16 Mr. Truman withdrew that comment as an "error"—but omitted to answer many essential questions. Indeed, on all of this he said he was unwilling to permit a congressional committee to examine him either by subpoena or in response to an "invitation." He chose to tell only what he wanted to tell.

So we are compelled to look at the record as it was made by Mr. Truman in his public comments—which were not under oath—and by Attorney General Brownell and J. Edgar Hoover, Director of the Federal Bureau of Investigation, who testified under oath last week before the Senate Internal Security Subcommittee. The episode raises these questions:

1. Did Mr. Truman know in February 1946 whether or not Harry Dexter White was a Russian spy? He must have known. He admits giving consideration to a withdrawal of White's commission as U. S. Director of the International Monetary Fund but decided on further surveillance. The testimony of Mr. Byrnes and the FBI Director shows that Mr. Truman was reluctant to issue the commission to White but was persuaded not to withdraw it by somebody as yet undisclosed.

2. Was the plan which Mr. Truman decided upon approved in any way by the FBI Director? No. Mr. Hoover testified that promoting White to the International Monetary Fund, on whose premises the FBI could not even enter, actually "hampered" surveillance and that other members of the Soviet spy ring closely associated with White in our Government were allowed to go with him to the Monetary Fund.

3. Was Mr. Truman guilty of bad judgment, stupidity, or what? The answer as given by Mr. Brownell in his Chicago speech should suffice: "The manner in which the established facts concerning White's disloyalty were disregarded is typical of the blindness which afflicted the former Administration on this matter."

4. Was White "proved" at any time while he was alive to be a Russian spy? Not in the sense that he could be convicted under existing espionage laws, which practically require an affidavit from the enemy as "proof." Also evidence obtained by local police through wire-tapping cannot at present be used in federal court cases. But, as the FBI Director pointed out in his testimony, the President did not need technical proof to dismiss an employe who was a bad security risk. He needed only to satisfy himself of the authenticity of information given him from official sources.

5. Was the FBI information as given to Mr. Truman reliable? The FBI Director testified that he got information from 30 different sources which indicated that White was "a valuable adjunct to an underground Soviet espionage organization operating in Washington, D. C." Seven FBI reports on White were sent to Mr. Truman between November 8, 1945 and July 24, 1946.

6. Why did Mr. Truman on April 30, 1946, write to White when he resigned as Assistant Secretary of the Treasury that, in the new position, "you will add distinction to your already distinguished career with the Treasury"? And why did Mr. Truman on April 7, 1947, write a letter to White stating that "with sincere regret and considerable reluctance" he was accepting White's resignation from the Monetary Fund? And why did Mr. Truman, in that same letter, write White that he (Mr. Truman) "will feel free to call upon you from time to time for assistance in dealing with the problems we will be continually facing"? Mr. Truman either forgot the episode of February 1946 or whoever prepared the letters and whoever got Mr. Truman to sign them failed in their duty.

It was "blindness" of which Mr. Truman and his staff were guilty. The Democratic Administration was blind to the Communist menace in many departments of the Government where information was repeatedly filched by enemy agents. That's the only verdict that can be rendered at this time on the available facts.

TALKATHON NO. 3

DECEMBER 11, 1953

WE TALKED FOR MONTHS AND MONTHS at Panmunjom—and then laid down our arms, credulously hoping it would mean an agreement later to unify Korea and secure the withdrawal of Chinese Communist armies from Korean territory.

We have been talking ever since the truce was signed only about the time and place and the membership of the proposed peace conference. Concurrently, the Communists have been building new airfields in North Korea and bringing in scores of Russian-type jet planes to threaten our troops and terrorize the Korean people. This build-up is, of course, a violation of the armistice terms, but we still talk at Panmunjom.

We have agreed, moreover, to talk about European problems at a four-power conference of Foreign Ministers at Berlin. This third series of talks may last for months and months, too. We have had only 289 "talks" in the last few years with the Soviets on the Austrian problem.

Morality in diplomacy is at a low ebb. Dishonesty and hypocrisy are condoned. The illusion seems to be that there is some magic way by which those who tell falsehoods to the world can be suddenly converted to truth-telling and sincerity merely by listening to the eloquent words of an Old World statesman.

Deals with gangsters never work out. Neither Mr. Churchill nor anyone else can negotiate an agreement with Soviet Russia today that would be worth the paper it is written on. Until there is a free government in Russia, there can be no durable peace.

If talk is futile, is war the only alternative? Not at all. Military strength can produce a balance of power in the world—can deter an enemy who is uncertain of his own capability in a war with the other side. But nothing will deter even an enemy of inferior strength if the alliance which faces it is weak and decadent.

The free world alliance is frail. It lacks not only military solidarity and strength, but it lacks moral courage.

Despite the recent caution uttered by Secretary of State John Foster Dulles about the importance of overseas bases for our airplanes—and hence the need for catering to our European allies—the fact remains that a sudden attack by atom bombs on the United States direct from Russia would mean a negotiation until permission could be obtained, as now required by agreement between the Attlee Government and the Truman Administration, before our planes could take off from bases in Great Britain with atom bombs. It might mean a debate in the British Parliament. Meanwhile, many American cities would have been hit and perhaps destroyed.

We may, on the other hand, face another Pearl Harbor—an attack without warning in the Pacific. Atom bombs could be dropped on aircraft plants on our own Pacific Coast by planes flown from bases in Communist China or North Korea. Once this attack came, the Soviets might naively declare that this was only the act of "Chinese volunteers" and that Moscow was really "neutral." Would our European allies vote then to let us use their bases against Soviet Russia, or would they insist that, since Europe itself had not been attacked, it would be better for them to remain neutral?

Is there any assurance, moreover, that the European parliaments, which can be infiltrated any day by a Communist bloc, will not suddenly vote to prohibit us from using their bases?

The plain lesson of today for the American people is to build more intercontinental bombers for our Air Force that can deliver a death blow on our enemies from our own territory and construct at once as many big aircraft carriers as we can for our Navy. This would enable us instantly—if we are attacked—to reach the enemy heartland without depending on overseas bases.

Only in this way can we prevent our country from being blackmailed into surrendering our principles merely to get the theoretical use of bases from which we may never be allowed to fly our planes.

America must look to her own defenses first and rely only secondarily on the use of overseas bases. We must not stay in the sorry position in which the Secretary of State, in his formal statement last week, inadvertently put this country when he virtually conceded that even the unmoral trading with the enemy by the Europeans during the Korean war must be overlooked as we cravenly seek the right to a continued use of overseas airbases.

It is time to consider the safety of the United States as primary and as of the highest priority. No other policy can now be regarded as dependable after the startling revelation by the Secretary of State concerning the price we evidently are being asked to pay to keep overseas bases. No membership in any alliance is worthy of American honor if it is built on the sacrifice of moral principle.

THE BIG ILLUSION

DECEMBER 18, 1953

NO FINER EXAMPLE of American idealism has been presented to the world in our times than the address delivered last week by President Eisenhower before the United Nations General Assembly. It won approval instantly from governments throughout the world, with the exception of the Communist governments at Moscow and Peiping.

But the illusion in the address was its euphemistic premise—that the present government in Moscow is a decent, respectable agent of the people of Soviet Russia, a government worthy of trust, a government capable of negotiating agreements that would be honored by the Soviets.

The simple truth is that the government at Moscow is an unmoral instrument, possessing for the moment the power to mislead hundreds of millions of persons behind the Iron Curtain.

It is often argued that we might as well talk and confer with the Soviet Government, and then, if the Communists spurn our proposals, we will at least know—and the world will know—who is obstructing peace.

What a naive approach! It is as if we haven't had countless pieces of evidence for several years now that the leopard doesn't change its spots. Actually, by our continued conferences we are building up the prestige of the Malenkov government inside Russia. By treating it as an equal, we glorify its standing and strengthen its internal position.

What advantage is there in acting as if the other person were not a criminal—imagining the devil to be a person of innate virtue and of good conscience? Are criminals rehabilitated before or after they have served a term of ostracism imposed by the other members of society?

The fact is that evil is not redressed or eradicated by ignoring its existence. When there are gangsters in the city, we do not "negotiate" with them. There can be no "peaceful coexistence" with criminals. No churchman that we can recall ever rose to defend "coexistence" when some citizens argued that red-light districts in our cities should remain because they were segregated and hence did not hurt the main residence districts.

"Peaceful coexistence" as a slogan in the world situation today is a mockery. It is only an alibi for moral cowardice.

Significantly enough, the President in his speech pointed to the danger of a "surprise aggression." He was certainly not referring to any government in the free world. He wisely served warning that the immense atomic power of America would be swiftly and resolutely used in retaliation if such an aggression occurred. He told the people of Soviet Russia what a terrible fate awaited them if their rulers ever chose to make the awful mistake of starting an aggressive war.

These words, however, by themselves can at this time do little more than assist our propaganda campaign as against the Communist propaganda in the "cold war." Sooner or later we must face squarely the big illusion. We must recognize that it is impossible to continue diplomatic relations with a gangster government in Moscow. The people of Soviet Russia must be told in unequivocal language that the peoples of the rest of the world are waiting for them to set up a free government.

For, while it is axiomatic that neither this country nor any international organization should tell a sovereign people what form of government they shall have, it is also fundamental that any form of government which is a menace to world peace cannot earn the respect or recognition that is customarily accorded a decent, civilized government representing a free people. Minor dictatorships here and there in the world are at times disregarded as local phenomena, but when any dictatorship becomes a threat to world peace, its impact is no longer just internal, but external. It then becomes properly a matter of international concern.

We must stop deluding ourselves with the idea of "negotiating" with criminals. We must instead exalt morality. For we cannot end tension merely by making a deal with the unmoral and the unscrupulous.

The time has come to ostracize the unmoral governments that threaten world peace. The first step should be the expulsion of the Soviet Government from the United Nations, followed by the cutting off of all communication and all trade by the free world with the governments at Moscow and Peiping. We can well afford to subsidize those on our side who are financially damaged. It would cost only a fraction of the billions we spend annually on armament.

This is the only policy that presents an effective alternative to war.

We must look, therefore, to peoples—not dictatorship governments—to stay the hand that would drop an atom bomb among human beings anywhere in the world. And when all peoples are represented by governments chosen in free elections, the Eisenhower plan to pool atomic knowledge for peaceful purposes will become practical, and the world can then begin to enjoy an era of enduring peace.

CHRISTMAS 1953—A SURVEY

DECEMBER 25, 1953

As we survey the world today, we find that men entrusted with leadership in several countries called "free" have begun to worship false idols. They are becoming believers in a complacent materialism whose only answer to evil is a suppliant plea for "peaceful co-existence" with evil.

Men who profess a belief in the fundamentals of Christianity or who proclaim fidelity to the Ten Commandments would, for expediency's sake, grasp the blood-stained hands of those rulers in the world who have ordered the murder of tens of thousands, who have tortured countless human beings, and who have stolen the property of their fellow men. The talk is mostly of ways to gloss over misdeeds—not to insure punishment for crime.

Men in leadership positions have become disciples of defeatism and futility. Challenged by despots, our spokesmen vacillate when moral principle is at stake and convey to the enemy an attitude of craven fear.

Men in government, in a misguided effort to prove their peaceful purpose, are inducing miscalculation by evil governments and unwittingly tempting them to continue aggression in the mistaken belief that our defense will be neither vigorous nor resolute.

Men in Congress, in Parliament, in the clergy, in the press, in business and in the collegiate world are in larger and larger numbers calling upon us to appease wicked governments, notwithstanding that such regimes have violated every law of mankind.

Men in government are compromising truth by hypocritically proclaiming a cause of idealism which they do not uphold. Having only a few months ago extolled an armistice agreement in Korea, they now tolerate its flagrant violation.

Men in commerce are asking their governments to protect "trade" with countries whose governments are engaged in a war against their own troops.

Men in diplomacy are using words of camouflage and transparent dishonesty and calling it "negotiation."

Men in high posts abroad are showing such eagerness for "deals" and surrenders that the cry "warmonger" is expressed whenever there is dissent from a policy of appeasement.

Men in government in our own and allied countries have been summoning the youth of today to military service but have failed to permit maximum power to be used to pursue the enemy that attacks them.

Men on the platform, on radio and television forums and in the press are preaching hate against those fellow men of zeal who seek to ferret out traitors in our midst.

Men called "intellectuals" are refusing to aid their own government in the detection of crime and quibble about constitutional rights, though their plain duty to society is to assist in punishing enemies from within or without the state.

Men in high places are depending on armament alone as a deterrent to possible aggression by gangster governments and are failing to use the great power of moral force to encourage peoples to liberate themselves by overthrowing such evil governments.

Millions of righteous men and women everywhere whose lives are dedicated to the principles of Christianity are looking hopefully to men in high places to lead them. These trustful people have always borne the burden and made the sacrifices. Will they be betrayed?

Almighty God, may the prayers of mankind in this Christmas season bring the misguided to repentance. May they be forgiven and, having seen the error of their way, seek from Thee the guidance that can come only with an obedience to truth and morality.

Almighty God, may the misguided learn that the ways of materialism are of no avail to quiet a troubled conscience. May the misguided perceive that wealth, creature comforts and even the joy of living must be sacrificed, if need be, to uphold the God-given standards of honesty and unselfishness which centuries of experience have taught us are the only standards that can bring happiness to man.

Almighty God, may courage be given to us all to arrest the deteriorating influences of modern life—to revive among us the moral courage that will turn back those currents of decadence which now threaten to engulf us on every side.

Almighty God, may there be enshrined in our hearts the glorious valor that has made men in the past not afraid to die. May those of our youth who have been recently fighting so valiantly in Korea be vindicated by the fearless acts of those of us who make national and international policy.

May we be given, O Lord, the inspiration not to forsake those who have just made the supreme sacrifice for us. May we never forget also the dead of two world wars who sleep beneath those millions of white crosses in our midst and in so many lands across the seas. For they had faith. May we emulate their faith in the hours of crisis that will confront us tomorrow.

This is our Christmas prayer.

1954

WHO IS FOOLING WHOM?

JANUARY 1, 1954

THE SOVIET NOTE in reply to President Eisenhower's proposal to establish an international pool of atomic materials for peaceful uses is a masterpiece of deceptive propaganda.

With characteristic optimism, some officials in Paris, London and Washington, on reading the first news bulletins, expressed satisfaction that something important had been achieved. But from a reading of the full text which came later, it was apparent that the Soviet Government was playing the same old theme song.

Just why there should be such outbursts of joy among any officials in the free world the moment the Soviets say they will "talk" is inexplicable. For several years now, the Communists not only have shown themselves willing to talk but anxious to use every such occasion to twist words to their propaganda advantage.

The text of the Soviet note reveals an air of innocence and virtue, a professed devotion to the cause of peace, a supposedly deep aversion to anything aggressive, and an eloquent plea for a ban on weapons of mass destruction. So confident are the Communist notewriters of their ability to fool the rest of the world that the Soviet Government brazenly protests it doesn't believe in military blocs or alliances or military bases for itself on neighboring territories. Blandly the Soviet Government writes as if no such things have happened as the aggression in Korea, or the infiltration of other countries by subversive agents of Moscow, or the military domination of such countries as East Germany, Rumania, Bulgaria, Czechoslovakia, Poland and Communist China. We are asked to put out of our minds the fact that the Red Army has its battalions stationed in every one of those supposedly sovereign and independent countries.

The transparent insincerity and hypocrisy of the Soviet note nevertheless does not conceal the concern of the Kremlin that America has a huge stockpile of atomic weapons and a productive capacity which can increase the output from year to year.

The Soviets naturally complain that the proposal to allocate atomic ingredients for peaceful purposes, as made by President Eisenhower, does not "tie the hands" of the major countries and prevent them from continuing to manufacture atomic weapons of war. What the Soviets would like the free world to do, of course, is to demolish its stockpile and stop all production of such weapons while the Communist regime—which has never been willing to agree to any effective system of international inspection—goes on building atomic armaments to catch up with the United States.

The American Government, on its part, announces a willingness to keep on talking with the Soviets, either publicly by more notes or privately through diplomatic channels. But it is evident that Moscow—as a condition prerequisite to any final agreement—wants Red China admitted immediately to the United Nations and demands the scrapping at once of such alliances as the North Atlantic Treaty and the European Defense Community agreement.

These mischievous provisions of the note show that the Soviet Government is still counting on dissension among the allies. Certainly as long as the London Government openly advocates admission of Red China to the United Nations and as long as the Communist bloc in the French Parliament can keep the European Defense Community proposal from being ratified, the Moscow notewriters need not worry.

The United States Government, meanwhile, is entrapping itself in endless conversations with the Communists. The prevalent theory in Washington is that it is necessary to keep up indefinitely such an exchange of views. The excuse is offered that somehow there is in all this an advance toward peace.

Actually, this is wishful thinking. Various officials and influential newspapers in Europe are fooling their people, too. They are victims of a delusion that by mere talk or "negotiation" peace can be achieved. It is being mistakenly assumed that the Soviet Government really has been or is interested in conceding something fundamental when it is under no compulsion whatsoever to concede anything. On the contrary, the longer the palaver goes on, the more confident the Communists are that the leaders of the free world will grow weary and surrender point after point.

Thus is waged the battle of attrition of men's minds. It is a kind of "brainwashing" by reiteration.

Moral principle unfortunately has weakened already on our side, as shown by the readiness of the governments of Britain, the United States and France to negotiate and make deals with gangster governments.

Sooner or later it must dawn on our statesmen that they have no leverage at all except economic pressure and moral ostracism to compel the Soviets to behave decently, and that to enter into any agreement with the Communists to ban existing weapons would be to commit suicide.

The Soviets in the long run cannot fool the American people. It is important that the leaders of the free world shall not try to fool their own people, either.

'STATE OF THE UNION'—IN MOSCOW

JANUARY 8, 1954

WHOEVER "BRIEFS" Premier Malenkov might well be saying to him something like this:

"Things have gone well for us in 1953. We have made sensational progress toward winning the 'cold war.' We are on the road to bigger achievements—and all this without losing the life of a single Soviet soldier.

"First, in the Far East, our noble ally, Communist China, has one million men in North Korea at the 38th Parallel. Hitherto we were dependent on only a weak North Korean Army. We are also integrating North Korea into the Manchurian economy. There will, of course, be no unification of Korea.

"We are planning to infiltrate South Korea. We are counting on the British to keep the Americans from helping Syngman Rhee and, if he starts any attacks, he will get no help from the West, and then we will walk in.

"We are making some progress in Japan. The Communist Party is already stirring up trouble between America and Japan. We are optimistic that we can prevent the rearmament of Japan.

"In India, things are going very well for us indeed. Prime Minister Nehru, with his 'neutralism,' is really on our side.

"We are gaining also in Indonesia and in Indochina. It is true the Western countries threatened us with retaliatory action if the armies of our allies became active in Indochina after the Korean truce. But their words are empty. They will do nothing about it. For we have a strong following in the French Parliament and can count on them to force a French surrender in Indochina.

"Our strength in Parliament is enough, too, to keep France from ratifying the European Defense Treaty. As long as we can keep Germany divided—and France will help us to do this—we need not be concerned too much about any threat from West Germany.

"As for Great Britain, the Prime Minister knows he has a narrow majority in Parliament, and our Labor Party friends are constantly harassing him because of his dependence on United States policy. It is important to humor Churchill and to invite him to more conferences. This flatters him and helps divide the West.

"We are still stirring up trouble in Iran, in Egypt and in Morocco and Tunisia. Our reports show real progress in our 'anti-colonialism' campaigns.

"In Latin America we are making more headway than ever before. We have infiltrated many of the countries there. Our setback in British Guiana is temporary. We now have complete control in Guatemala. We are pushing extreme reforms there and fighting American investments—all this is good nationalistic activity. Besides, we now have in Guatemala a good base for all our agents in Central America and South America and a distributing center for our espionage funds.

"As for the United States, we are doing well there, too. Many people in America sympathize with our socialistic doctrines—although they don't agree with our 'methods.' Senator McCarthy is being beaten down gradually by a counter-crusade about 'civil liberties' and 'witch hunts.' Already the Americans are seriously considering new restrictions upon congressional committees which will permit us to delay and obstruct investigations just as we did by our tactics in Judge Medina's court when 11 of our comrades were tried.

"America is facing a depression. Shortly she will have to cut down on money for Europe and this will give us a chance to bring about trade with the Western countries and thereby we can get the machinery, the rubber and other raw materials we need so badly for our armament program. Then in 1956 we will be invincible.

"If our proposals to outlaw the use of atomic weapons succeed, this will give us freedom to use conventional military forces inside Europe at our pleasure. American ground forces are being diminished as reliance is placed on atomic weapons, the use of which will surely be prohibited.

"The West is weak-kneed. It has talked loudly about maintaining an embargo on trade until after a Korean peace settlement. But, even without a peace conference, British businessmen are coming to us begging for orders, and the British Government has announced its sympathy with the resumption of such trade.

"We must be very careful, however, about those Americans. Some of them are not so easily deceived and may demand stern measures. The thing to do is to start some more four-power or even 16-power conferences so as to talk on and on. The United Nations furnishes a splendid forum to carry on more and more debates.

"All this gives the newspapers a chance to print headlines about peace being 'just around the corner.' Or, if they eventually become wise to this maneuver, let's release a few of the American prisoners we have on hand. If we dole out just a few each month, that's enough to get headlines and editorials in various American and British newspapers about how peaceful we are and about the new climate for peace that we are bringing to the world and how 'tension is being relaxed.'

"All in all, things are going well for us everywhere—here's to another year of victories in the 'cold war,' Comrade Malenkov!"

'SOMETHING FOR EVERYBODY'

JANUARY 15, 1954

THERE'S A SOMETHING-FOR-EVERYBODY flavor about President Eisenhower's address to Congress on the "state of the union." It is reminiscent of the days of the New Deal, or of its historical ancestor, the Roman Senate, which, in order to retain popular support, pampered the people with "bread and circuses."

Mr. Eisenhower's message is an omnibus of promises. Most of them unfortunately will go unfulfilled, either because of ideological strife at home or the behavior of evil forces abroad.

Everybody wants lower taxes, more social security benefits, higher farm prices, lower living costs, better schools, better health facilities, intelligent use of natural resources, equitable labor-management laws, more and better highways, better defense for less money— all this and a balanced budget, too.

Everybody wants peace in the world, untroubled by threats of war, either cold or hot.

Everybody wants a "stronger America" and a well-organized Europe militarily, and more self-reliance there, and less economic aid from us.

But, unfortunately, we live in an everyday world of practicality and realism. Facts must be faced. Otherwise we will endanger our safety and, when disillusioned, we will lose faith in those leaders who have indulged in wishful thinking.

The President's message must be read carefully to extract the real meaning of some of his implicit, if not paradoxical, statements. He says:

"There has been in fact a great strategic change in the world during the past year. That precious intangible, the initiative, is becoming ours. Our policy, not limited to mere reaction against crises provoked by others, is free to develop along lines of our choice not only abroad, but also at home."

The President also says confidently that our armament is deterring aggression and that "our international and defense policies" will enable us "to negotiate from a position of strength." But apparently we have been unable for several months now to "negotiate" even the fixing of the time and place and the composition of a Korean peace conference.

Can it be said that the "initiative" is ours when announcement is made in Washington that America, by secret agreement with our allies, has been for five months relaxing the embargo on certain strategic articles vitally needed by the Communists and that we have apparently done this without obtaining any concessions in return?

Can it be said that we have taken the "initiative" when hundreds of American boys captured in Korea still languish in Soviet jails even though the armistice agreement solemnly pledged their return?

Can it be said, moreover, that the presence of 1,000,-000 Communist Chinese soldiers in North Korea, or the stepped-up war in Indochina, or the attempt to seize the government in British Guiana, or the successful infiltration of the government of Guatemala by the Communists, or the steady weaning-away from our side of India, Indonesia and powerful elements in the Middle East, represent victories for us or for Soviet Russia during 1953?

The President speaks about our "massive capability to strike back" at Communist aggression and of "our great and growing number of nuclear weapons." This doesn't sound as if limitation of armament or the outlawing of atomic warfare was near at hand. We apparently are in for decades of heavy spending for armament unless the President's hint about "signs that tyranny is in trouble" behind the Iron Curtain means a revolution is to be expected.

Along with all the promises of bigger and better social welfare programs than the predecessor administrations gave us, the President does say in one breath that "reduced spending will move the new budget closer to a balance" and then in another breath declares: "I find it necessary to renew my request for an increase in the statutory debt limit."

Maybe a clue to the fulfillment of our hopes is to be found in the simple and incontrovertible truth that Mr. Eisenhower expressed in the concluding section of his message, when he said:

"A Government can sincerely strive for peace, as ours is striving, and ask its people to make sacrifices for the sake of peace. But no Government can place peace in the hearts of foreign rulers."

To this it might be suggested that our Government had better forget about trying to influence or deal with evil rulers and concentrate instead on plans to reach the peoples behind the Iron Curtain.

For we can place thoughts of peace in the hearts of the peoples now living within the Communist empire.

They can liberate the world.

Then we can afford a something-for-everybody program as the billions spent for the sword are turned into the plowshares of constructive rather than destructive enterprise.

Then and then only will there be peace.

CLEARING THE AIR

JANUARY 22, 1954

THE PUSSY-FOOT POLICY adopted by the Truman Administration at the behest of some of our hesitant and overcautious allies has been reversed at last.

Hereafter, when there is a war, the United States will fight it with maximum power—no holds barred. There will be no ban on the use of the atom bomb and no ban on the hydrogen bomb.

In fighting the Korean war—the third largest in our history against a foreign enemy—it was the advocacy of such a policy that led to the dismissal of General MacArthur by President Truman.

The courageous and realistic decision to revive the traditional American objective of striving for victory when we are compelled to fight an enemy was revealed last week by the Secretary of State, John Foster Dulles. His splendid address is printed in full beginning on page 56 of this issue.

Under the announced policy, Soviet Russia is put on direct notice that, so far as the United States is concerned, any military attack will be resisted instantly and without reservation. There are to be no "privileged sanctuaries" anywhere on the territory of the enemy.

An epochal change has been made in our historic strategy in war. For it means reliance on atomic weapons rather than on conventional forces alone. All three services are essential, but air power will be primary—the air power that will carry bombs from the overseas bases of the U. S. Air Force and from the decks of the Navy's big carriers.

Such an interpretation of our new strategy, however, should not be oversimplified. If a war comes, more military force of every kind will be needed than is being authorized today as a "deterrent to aggression." The present objective, of course, is simply to make a "hot war" improbable by setting up the deterrent strength of a massive retaliatory power.

No group of sane men at the head of any government will dare to challenge by force the determined policy of the United States. Only a misguided group of statesmen among our allies would seek to weaken our resolve.

The question then arises: Will Communist Russia and Red China now turn toward an intensification of the "cold war"?

There are many observers who think "World War III Russian Style" has been in progress for some time and that there never has been any intention on the part of the Kremlin to bring on a large-scale military conflict. If this thesis is accepted, the tactics of the Com-munists in the "cold war" thus far seem logical from their standpoint. It is less costly for them. They seek to infiltrate and conquer certain Western countries from within. They have been taking advantage of local friction and provoking local troubles everywhere. The Korean adventure was a miscalculation based on the public statement of Secretary Acheson in January, 1950, that the United States would not defend Korea.

It is conceivable, of course, that the Kremlin may push things too far or make another miscalculation. When matters get beyond control in local areas, a full-fledged war can break out. So the warning from the United States demands self-restraint by the Communists everywhere lest they bring on a big war.

Meanwhile, what should American policy in the "cold war" be? Shall we now build up the Soviet strength by allowing essential materials to be traded in, so that the Communist totalitarian state will grow stronger? Shall we supply consumer goods and reduce the causes of discontent among enemy peoples as against their own government? Or is it our duty to wage the "cold war" relentlessly with the knowledge that the economic embargoes we already have imposed have been pinching the enemy and should, therefore, be strengthened instead of weakened?

It is the long-range view in world affairs which has just been advocated by our Secretary of State. He says we must make policies for the long haul and not just for isolated emergencies. This means we must base our policy on enduring principle.

We cannot, therefore, recognize any government that is the puppet of the Kremlin.

We must not strengthen any Communist regimes by furnishing them the necessary sinews of war or the means of building up their domestic economies.

We must carry on our offense and defense in the "cold war" with all the energies we can mobilize.

We must use moral force more effectively than in the past. We must encourage the peoples behind the Iron Curtain to strive for liberation.

The President and the Secretary of State have come a long way in clearing the air about the policy to be pursued in the event of a military attack upon us.

What was announced last week relates directly to a "hot war."

Now it is desirable to clear the air about what we intend to do in a "cold war."

For sometimes, as happened in 1914 and 1939, "local" wars turn into major wars.

LET THE PEOPLE RULE

JANUARY 29, 1954

THE DEBATE over the proposed amendment to the Constitution sponsored by Senator Bricker of Ohio has revealed some curious contradictions.

Thus, it is contended by opponents of the Amendment that the President should have full power to sign treaties whether or not they modify rights reserved to the people under the Constitution. It is argued also that the President shall be the sole judge of whether or not an executive agreement with a foreign government should be formally submitted to the Senate for approval or disapproval. It is urged, moreover, that the Congress—the people's elected representatives—must not "interfere" in the conduct of foreign affairs.

The wording of the Amendment, on the other hand, would empower Congress "to regulate all executive and other agreements with any foreign power or international organization." This would give Congress authority over negotiations by the Executive, but no check is provided against arbitrary negation by Congress.

There can be no doubt that some flagrant abuses of presidential power in foreign affairs have developed in recent years. The real question is whether the proposed Amendment goes to the root of the problem.

We know that a President of the United States, Franklin D. Roosevelt, made agreements with foreign governments at Yalta which changed the whole course of modern history—and he never submitted them to the Senate for ratification. Plainly the wording of the Bricker Amendment would not compel a President to submit such agreements to the Senate.

We know also that, when the United States joined the United Nations, it did not intend to surrender any of its sovereignty. Yet the third largest war in American history against a foreign enemy was fought at the command of a President of the United States, Harry S. Truman, in pursuance of a resolution adopted by the United Nations Security Council. Our military forces —which, under the Constitution, can only engage in war at the behest of Congress—were unable to attack all parts of the enemy territory or to apply maximum power to win the war because no declaration of war on China was submitted to Congress and because other members of the U. N. objected to such a step.

Plainly the Bricker Amendment would not correct this abuse of power, either.

The truth is that the American people do not have continuous control of their Executive because the Presidency is subject to a check by the people only once in four years.

Our next-door neighbor—Canada—has developed a stable system of government in which the treaty-making power is delegated to the Prime Minister under a written constitution. But he, in turn, must get explicit approval of all his acts from the national legislature or he can assume he has approval if Parliament fails to challenge him on specific questions. Freedom of action is bestowed on the leader of a parliamentary government, but the people can remove him from office overnight if he oversteps the bounds.

The Bricker Amendment would specify that no treaty can be valid unless it is within the Constitution, and the proposal also says:

"A treaty shall become effective as internal law in the United States only through legislation which would be valid in the absence of a treaty."

But who is to determine whether a treaty is "valid" or whether an internal law has been adopted by Congress that is constitutional? Only a concrete case by private citizens in the courts, presenting proper issues, can lead to a decision on the question of the validity of a treaty. Would not foreign governments be compelled to wait a long time, perhaps years, for such a determination before being sure that the United States could constitutionally fulfill its pledges?

There is only one certain way to prevent recent abuses. It is to amend the Constitution so that a Congress or a President can be required to go before the people at any time if a difference of opinion on a major issue arises between the Chief Executive and the majority in Congress.

The Constitution should be amended to require that all executive agreements and treaties must be submitted to both Houses of Congress for approval within three months after they are consummated, unless Congress votes to extend the period.

If a treaty or agreement is rejected by as much as a two-thirds vote, the President should resign and his successor be chosen by Congress.

The President, on the other hand, should have the right to challenge the action of Congress. If he fails to get a two-thirds vote of ratification, and wants to carry the issue to the people, a special election should be called at the request of the President to hold Congress immediately accountable.

Let us veer away from the concept of one-man government, one-man dictatorship in foreign affairs, and one-man control of the destinies of our youth without legal sanction by our Congress. Let the people rule.

THE CHANCE OF A LIFETIME

FEBRUARY 5, 1954

AMERICA is on the threshold of a big change. The opportunity that presents itself is to change from a war-stimulated economy to an incentive system of private rather than government spending. The role of government would not be paternalism, but a role of direct encouragement to individual enterprise.

Such a transition, however, can be effected only by the cooperation of both parties in Congress.

For in the next 120 days the crucial decision must be made—whether to continue indefinitely on a zig-zag course that leads to State Socialism, or to take the straight road toward the goals of prosperity unlimited and the highest standard of living ever achieved for the American people.

America, to be sure, has not yet recovered from the effects of the 1929-1933 depression caused by the economic convulsions of World War I. Unemployment totals, it will be recalled, were reduced to negligible amounts only when World War II broke out. The wartime economy—which was resumed when the aggression of 1950 occurred in Korea—has brought a deceptive cycle of high wages and reduced purchasing power of the dollar, high profits but a lower net income after taxation, and a dependence on war or threat of war for the "prosperity" of an illusory inflation.

President Eisenhower's formula—described in his Economic Report to Congress which begins on page 44 of this issue—calls for a healthy capitalism, as opposed to the Socialism that feeds solely on the power of the state. The Eisenhower program calls on the Government not to own businesses, not to control them, not to dispense special privilege, not to compete with private enterprise, but by a revision of tax laws to give the American investor a chance to share in the fruits of American progress. It is a program not of public ownership, but of popular ownership.

Demagoguery, however, can sabotage this program. Voices have been heard in Congress already arguing that raising of personal exemptions from $600 to $700—which means a tax saving of less than a dollar a week per taxpayer but which would cost the Treasury 2.3 billion dollars annually in revenue—is a better plan than to give investors a chance to earn more money and workers to get higher wage scales.

Superficially it sounds politically alluring for these critics to cry out that the Eisenhower program "helps the rich" or that this is "the kind of prosperity that is supposed to trickle down from the top." But actually this is the jargon of the anti-capitalists. It can be heard at any time, all the way from Moscow to Peiping.

The basic test of any plan for economic betterment is how many jobs are created and what job security is provided for the future. We heard in the 1930's a lot about how made-work on "leaf-raking" projects was designed to increase the purchasing power of individuals and relieve unemployment. But the New Deal turned a deaf ear to those who argued for a stimulus to heavy-goods industries by which millions of jobs would be created to last long after the leaves were raked.

Do the demagogues in Congress want the United States to prosper, or do they seek political advantage out of human misery? Do they themselves wish to be charged at the polls next autumn with having blocked business recovery and expansion for America?

The Eisenhower plan calls for a revised system of tax credits for businesses, large and small, to help pay for new plants and equipment as they wear out. A company with obsolete machines, the cost of which is being deducted in twenty years, could buy new equipment now if the allowances could be spread over ten years instead. It could mean more efficient production and lower prices to the public. Incentive tax laws can bring us the biggest expansion in construction and manufacturing that America has ever known.

But such expansion must be financed privately—by shareholders and not by the Government. Too long has debt increase, with a bigger and bigger load of interest charges, been the only source of new capital, and this only to a relatively few businesses which could earn, after taxes, enough to pay off such debt.

The real need in America has been to encourage risk capital. In order for business to get this in abundance, the investor must be encouraged to put his money in shares. Hence the President's plan to eliminate double taxation of dividends is the most far-sighted reform that could be made to attract investors and thus help America finance new plants and equipment.

The President has recommended various proposals to use government funds to help refinance mortgages for homes and buildings and to encourage the construction of new units of large-scale housing. There are innumerable ways by which private funds can be utilized, with proper governmental encouragement, to bring about a prospering America.

Will Congress in the next 120 days vote these programs? Never before have our legislators been faced with such a responsibility for decision. America stands at the crossroads. It's the chance of a lifetime.

AN ERA OF STABILITY

FEBRUARY 12, 1954

So ACCUSTOMED have we become in recent years to an upward curve in everything—in sales, in profits, in wages, and in production costs—that we lose sight of the changing value of the dollar.

Throughout history peoples have failed to discern and have often been deceived by the changing value of their monetary unit.

We see it happening with wages. Many an individual today gets more dollars than he received in 1939, but the dollars do not buy as much as they did then. The spiral is unending. When prices go up there is pressure for higher wage levels. This in turn pushes up costs and then prices rise, and in the end many persons are worse off than before.

So the period we have just entered—a period of readjustment—shows the first real progress toward stability that the nation has made in twenty years.

Incalculable benefits are being bestowed already on the economic community. Wage rates have not been pressed upwards in recent months but have remained fairly stable. Such increases as have been granted are moderate. The amount of money that might have been added to production costs by reason of a normal upward rise of wages in the last few months cannot be estimated as yet, but undoubtedly the saving on the expense side is very large.

Similarly the fact that prices are not being raised generally and that businesses have experienced a period of relative stability in prices is another constructive result of the current readjustment.

This is not to say that we must accept hereafter a stagnant economy. For, with our growth of population and improved means of production, we shall expand sales volume more and more in the years to come. Wage levels will go up gradually. As demand comes to be measured more accurately and there is no such panicky accumulation of goods as occurs when a war emergency causes sudden shortages, the economic system will function more evenly and the country will grow progressively more prosperous for all concerned.

The present recession or readjustment, with 2.4 millions unemployed, is no mysterious malady that has affected the business health of the country. It can be readily diagnosed. Moderate declines from the preceding year's figures such as are now being experienced have occurred before. Thus in 1921, three years after the close of World War I, we felt the impact of a recession. It was a time when the economic system had just about filled the pent-up demands of the war period.

We then went along on an even keel for several years after 1922, and it was not until 1929 that Europe began to feel the full force of the economic convulsions of World War I. The collapse came everywhere as bank and business failures swept through Europe.

Recovery started throughout the world in the summer of 1932. But the American people in November of that year made the mistake of switching administrations in the middle of the depression. Widespread rumors of the incoming administration's plan to tinker with the gold value of the monetary unit disturbed markets everywhere and brought on in March 1933 perhaps the worst panic in our history—an event chargeable to the refusal of the then President-elect, Franklin D. Roosevelt, to cooperate from November 1932 to March 1933 with the Hoover Administration so as to avoid the breakdown of our banking system.

From March 1933 to September 1939, when World War II broke out, unemployment was by no means eliminated. Under the New Deal, unemployment was cut only from an average of 12.8 millions in 1933 to an average of 9.5 millions in 1939, when armament orders from abroad started to give jobs to the unemployed.

America continued on a war economy until 1946. In the postwar years our business system struggled through a painful readjustment, with the peak of unemployment averaging 3.7 millions in 1950. Then came the Korean war and another cycle of inflation.

The nation is confronted now with the necessity of substituting private spending for government spending as military appropriations decrease steadily and we face a long period of tension rather than a global war.

The Eisenhower Administration, therefore, has taken the first steps toward stabilization of the value of the dollar.

We must construct a stable base before the American economy can be expanded. We must find, with new machinery and methods, a way to produce efficiently at gradually descending prices.

We must view the present readjustment as the forerunner of what may prove to be a more satisfactory decade ahead than we have experienced since inflation, starting in 1940, began to reduce the purchasing power of the dollar until it will buy only 52.1 cents' worth of goods today as compared with the 1935-39 average.

The rise in the value of the dollar will benefit not only the people of the United States but the peoples of other countries with which we trade. Stability is the key to a new prosperity.

DO WE MEAN WHAT WE SAY?

FEBRUARY 19, 1954

WHEN THE KOREAN ARMISTICE was signed, the United States warned the Communists that the truce would be valueless if the Reds used their military strength to step up the war in Indochina. Solemn words came at the time from President Eisenhower and Secretary Dulles.

But now, when the Executive decides to send to Indochina only 200 American mechanics to supplement 125 who have been there for a year and announces that the purpose is to aid the French airmen in handling the B-26 bombers which we have loaned to them, there are adverse repercussions in Congress and in the press.

Certainly anybody who reads the news dispatches from Washington can tell that Congress is cold toward sending American boys to aid the French in Indochina. Fears are openly expressed that the dispatch of the 200 mechanics now may be followed later by larger contingents of American troops.

Granting that the problem is one of joint responsibility on the part of both the executive and the legislative branches, it would seem to have been the better part of wisdom for the President to have consulted leaders of both parties in Congress and to have gotten an agreement on the extent to which America should come to the aid of the French in Indochina.

If the legislators had been made fully aware in advance of just what the implications were in sending American mechanics to Indochina, there would have been no need to telegraph through the press to Moscow all the details of the American debate, with its unfortunate differences of opinion. In a "hot war," such as is going on in Southeast Asia, why should news of military movements be published at all? Such a violation of security would never have been permitted in World War II.

Everybody familiar with the delicate issues that have arisen in Indochina knows that factors are present which could lead to a large-scale war. If we can checkmate the Communists there by giving timely aid to the French, we certainly should do so.

Unhappily the French themselves are not sure what should be done in the Indochina situation. Influenced by the American decision to get out of Korea with a truce that did not attain victory, French opinion veers to the same sort of "solution" as an expedient way out of it all.

It isn't generally realized that the taxpayers of the United States are financing the French defense in Indochina and that it is costing us about a billion dollars a year. So we have a deep interest in finding out whether an appeasement in Indochina, coupled with the recent appeasement in Korea, will not ultimately result in such "loss of face" for the United States and its European allies throughout Asia as to make that continent hereafter a source of more and more complications for America.

Plainly the Indochina situation is at the moment the hot spot and spearhead of the Communist strategy in the "cold war." America cannot speak to the world with divided councils. Congress and the President ought to get together, so the world will know we mean what we say. If a liquidation of the war is decided upon by the French, the United States should insist that all further East-West trade negotiations with Moscow be suspended until Communist aid to the rebels in Indochina is withdrawn.

Even assuming that it is a desirable thing to trade in nonstrategic materials with the Communist countries—which certainly seems doubtful—it can hardly be argued that concessions by our side should be made without exacting corresponding concessions from the Communists. East-West trade should be resumed only when Moscow and Peiping stop all the wars in Asia and only when all Americans now held prisoner by the Communists are returned to us.

The worst mistake we could possibly make would be to let the Communists think we are no longer concerned with what they do to consolidate the gains they have achieved by aggressive action in Asia. Since the United Nations has been proved to be ineffective as an instrument for the enforcement of peace in the world, the task must rest squarely on the major powers. If we mean what we say about Indochina, Congress and the President should at the earliest moment proclaim that purpose in unequivocal terms. World War I and World War II would never have been initiated if Berlin had not miscalculated twice on what British policy would be and on whether America would enter each of the two wars on the side of the Western Allies.

There should be no room left for doubt and no chance for miscalculation by Moscow as to what will happen if Red Chinese armies now invade Indochina.

We must be firm and help to win a smaller conflict and thus avoid a larger one later. For, if we manifest weakness now in military and diplomatic policies, this inevitably will bring on the large war nobody wants.

It's time to say what we mean and to make sure the Communists know we mean what we say.

—AND SO THEY TALKED

FEBRUARY 26, 1954

THE BERLIN CONFERENCE ended about as was expected—with a decision to keep on talking at a subsequent conference two months hence.

The vital issues, however, in both Asia and Europe remain unsettled. Germany is to be kept divided. Soviet Russia is to continue to maintain occupation armies in East Germany. Austria is to remain enslaved. There isn't the slightest sign of a common ground for negotiating the settlement of European problems. As for the Korean mess, American armies are bogged down indefinitely on the mainland of Asia with no prospect of any change for years to come.

Two things were significant at Berlin. One was the undiminished arrogance of the Communist regime in its utter defiance of the Western world. The other was the splendid solidarity shown by the governments of Great Britain, France and the United States.

It might be asked just why the Communists are so indifferent to the pleas of the Western Allies for some sort of peace settlement. The answer would appear to be that the West has thrown away virtually all its leverage for negotiation. President Truman in December 1950 refused to order the bombing of Manchurian bases which were supplying the Red Chinese armies in their attack on American troops in Korea. President Eisenhower in June 1953—even before the armistice was signed—announced that Red China's armies would not be forced by any military action on our part to give up the fruits of their aggression in North Korea. Red China remains in possession of North Korea today.

Moscow knows, therefore, that the "cold war" can be prosecuted vigorously without much risk. So more and more pressure by the Communists can be anticipated in Indochina as the game of blackmail goes on, with its demands for concessions in East-West trade in exchange for the release of a few prisoners now unlawfully held anyhow.

We seem to be ready to increase trade with Soviet Russia as the line between strategic and non-strategic goods is being gradually relaxed, especially in Britain. There is a tendency on the part of the West to acquiesce in a prolonged period of tension on the theory that the only alternative is war.

But is that the only alternative? Is the true power of moral force to be ignored in the battle which, if courageously waged, can convert peoples behind the Iron Curtain to the cause of freedom?

Last week Senator Paul Douglas of Illinois, Democrat, proposed in a Senate resolution that the United States withdraw diplomatic recognition from the governments of all the satellites of Soviet Russia. He proposed, moreover, that the United Nations expel those governments.

This is a sensible approach but does not go far enough. We should withdraw recognition also from Soviet Russia, which not only has flagrantly violated the recognition agreement made with us in 1933 but has broken the spirit as well as the letter of the United Nations Charter. We must show the peoples in the Soviet orbit by unmistakable acts that the Western world will be behind them in their struggle for emancipation from slavery.

Sooner or later the Western Allies will have to accept the premise that nothing is to be gained by continuing, through international meetings, to enhance the prestige of the leaders of the Moscow regime at home. To carry on relations with an immoral government as an equal is in itself dishonorable. We can no longer afford to give the impression to the Soviet nation and the satellite peoples that we are putting the stamp of approval on dictatorship governments.

Repeatedly in recent years the Communists have inspired their followers to demand conferences at a high level. Many fine people on the Western side who haven't the slightest sympathy with Communist objectives have felt that these meetings should be held because, it was argued, even if nothing tangible were accomplished, the talks would "clear the air."

The air has been "cleared" many times since 1945 by conferences with the Soviet representatives which result in no agreements. One wonders how many more such futile international conferences there must be and how many more months must be given over to frustrating parleys before it will become apparent to the Western world that the Soviet gangsters regard the West as craven and weak and suppliant every time we enter another conference.

Sooner or later there must be a counteroffensive. The best way to achieve it is to embargo all trade with the East, compensate those in the West who are damaged thereby, and sever diplomatic relations with all Communist governments until such time as there emerge in their place free governments which will agree to a rule of reason rather than a rule of force in the world.

A policy of moral ostracism of evil governments, firmly pursued, will maintain our honor and inspire oppressed peoples to take those steps which eventually must bring them freedom and independence.

THERE'S NO SUBSTITUTE FOR VICTORY

MARCH 5, 1954

ONCE AGAIN the western world faces a critical decision: Shall we accept a stalemate in Indochina and lose all of Asia by making another truce as in Korea? Shall we find ourselves again giving way to the aggressor? Or shall we go on to victory in Indochina no matter how long it takes to do the job?

Influenced by our own decision not to fight the war with maximum power in Korea, many French leaders now say the precedent applies to their war in Indochina and that any way out through a truce and a "political conference" is preferable to further fighting. "Peace at any price" is the fatal doctrine that dominates too much of the western world today.

When the Korean armistice was signed, we were told that the Communists would know that we had "repelled aggression." We said through our official spokesmen that we would not tolerate diversion of military strength by the Communists from Korea to Indochina.

But the facts are that, by being relieved of the war strain in Korea, the Communists have actually stepped up their supplies to the Communist armies in Indochina. The West has procrastinated—and the Communists know now that our threat was an empty one.

Official observers have repeatedly reported to the American Government that the prevailing view throughout Asia is that we lost in Korea. The peoples of Asia are waiting anxiously now to see if the gains achieved by the Communists in Korea will be consolidated further by a surrender in Indochina.

We in this country may gloss over the facts and wishfully persuade ourselves that we have settled something in Korea. But the other peoples in Asia see the large Communist armies of Red China firmly entrenched in North Korea where they had not encroached before June 1950. And no "political conference" at Geneva will oust them, either.

Why are the peoples of Asia who are our friends losing hope?

They see Soviet Russia, which has acknowledged publicly that she furnished arms and ammunition to the Red armies in Korea, taking a seat as an "inviting" power at Geneva.

They see Prime Minister Churchill only last week announcing that trade restrictions with Soviet Russia, Poland and Hungary were being relaxed and stating that he will ask the American Government's agreement to further relaxation.

They read Washington dispatches saying that members of Congress will concur. Yet Soviet Russia and other Iron Curtain countries sent direct to Red China over the Trans-Siberian Railroad 75 per cent of the supplies for the Korean war.

They see American politicians rejoicing over the ending of the fighting in Korea as an "achievement" and members of Congress protesting against the possible use of American military forces in Indochina.

They see the western world cowed and frightened— begging the Communists in conference after conference to give by "negotiation" what they have refused to give on the battlefield.

"There is no substitute for victory" is the phrase used by General MacArthur when he sought permission to bomb the bases in Red China from which planes were coming to attack American soldiers and supplies were being transported to help the Red China armies.

The cry went up from the Trumanites that, if we bombed Manchuria, there would be a third world war. This cry didn't go up, however, when we intervened in Korea in June 1950. A calculated risk had to be taken then, and it should have been taken in December 1950 when General MacArthur wanted to use maximum power to defeat the enemy. Every piece of evidence available to us, as well as the facts of Soviet history, showed that Stalin would never fight a two-front war. Certainly if Russia had intervened in the Far East, she would have opened herself to attack in Europe.

France has argued that she could not build up an army to help defend Europe through the North Atlantic Treaty Organization and still carry on what has become a large-sized war in Southeast Asia. So the United States has been furnishing a billion dollars a year to support the French military operation.

Our side can win the war in Indochina. There are native troops in abundance to fight for freedom. They can be trained as the South Korean Army has been trained—by American military missions. They can be given the benefit of American naval and air power to help blockade the coast of China.

We will need, however, faithful cooperation by our allies, and a strict embargo so that Red China will not be aided by supplies furnished by the West.

A truce now such as Nehru of India is proposing merely means entrenching the Communists in the greater part of Asia.

Our allies in Asia—Indonesia, Thailand, Pakistan, the Philippines and Japan—will become dispirited and discouraged if we appease the Communists again.

There is, indeed, no substitute for victory.

THE FOUR-PARTY SYSTEM

MARCH 12, 1954

WE MUST SEEK OUT the true causes of party dishar-mony in America. For it is bringing us an era of utter irresponsibility in government. We are threat-ened with a spirit of factionalism that can force eco-nomic chaos and a disintegration of our national unity.

Party solidarity has broken down because leader-ship within both major parties has failed. Differences of opinion are not composed, as they used to be, through a sensible appreciation of the need for party unity. In-stead differences are accentuated and seem to be ac-cepted as irreconcilable. There is no party discipline.

When a party is in the minority in Congress nowa-days, it sometimes votes as a unit on procedural ques-tions and even presents a semblance of uniformity on certain issues if only to confound the majority party. But essentially the two big parties are split and for all practical purposes, instead of control by two parties, we have a four-party system.

On the civil rights issue, for example, the Southern Democrats will not go along with their Northern breth-ren. There are Republicans, particularly from the West, who will be found voting with the Southern Democrats in an adherence to States' rights.

Likewise, on the matter of federal or State priority in the use of the police power to govern the relations be-tween labor unions and management, a substantial number of Southern Democrats often unite temporar-ily with Northern Republicans to prevent a federal po-lice power from being established that would super-sede the States' control of local functions.

Just as Big Business has been tamed by governmental power and kept within competitive limits and subject to vigilant observation, so also is Big Unionism being examined now to determine whether federal or State regulation or both shall curb the excesses enjoyed by a privileged group that seeks a monopolistic status.

There are many questions of the hour on which the two major parties do not divide as parties but on which there is a natural coalition of groups within both parties to achieve temporary majorities.

Is this a good thing for America? Every piece of evidence from our political history says it is not. Parties are more serviceable instruments of our de-mocracy when they are cohesive and unified.

But how is party unity to be attained? Nearly a half-century ago, we were arguing on the tariff issue that only the President could lead his party because its members in Congress saw issues through sectional eyes and because the Chief Executive alone had a na-tional viewpoint. But, precisely because the tasks of the Presidency are now so complex and include such a variety of powers delegated by Congress, the White House is no longer the only place to look for political leadership. It must be sought in the Congress as well.

No parliamentary government in any democracy in the world accepts the leadership of the executive with-out the full participation of the entire legislative body in the making of decisions.

There is something manifestly wrong with the pres-ent system. What is wrong is the failure of the Pres-ident and the legislative membership in the present era to thresh out their differences in lengthy confer-ences such as are held in Great Britain when the par-ties work out their programs. With us a party platform, drafted in the pressure of a convention wherein the chief business is to select a presidential candidate, is expected once in four years to furnish guidance for the party in Congress.

The time has come for the Republican Party to call a conference in which all its members in Con-gress will have an equal chance to argue for the policies they believe should be adopted. When the debate has been concluded, a set of principles should be voted on. Continued membership in the party should depend on the willingness of those who accept the party confer-ence to abide by a majority vote of the participants. Without party discipline there can be no unity.

The Democratic Party should tackle the problem in the same way. Too long has its Northern wing turned a deaf ear to the wishes of the Southern wing.

These party conferences should vie with each other in presenting programs which truly seek the maxi-mum good for the nation.

Splinter parties have broken down European parlia-ments. We are headed for the same fate in America un-less we can learn to iron out our differences within a party. This does not mean dictatorship by the man in the White House or by the man who was the standard bearer for the losing party in the previous election. It should mean common counsel and an honest effort to work out the program that can benefit the nation and hence deserve the support of the voters themselves.

Parties can be restored to their original strength in America by a renewed devotion to principles pro-claimed not just in a presidential year but before each congressional election. It is the road away from legislative chaos. It is the road to party harmony and responsible government.

THE MISSING U. N.

MARCH 19, 1954

HOW NAIVE are the American people—or rather how naive are the speakers who think the public credulously accepts misleading statements about the true position of the United Nations in the world today?

Mrs. Franklin D. Roosevelt and a host of other well-meaning persons are going up and down the country in community after community telling the people to put their faith in the United Nations as an effective organization for the enforcement of world peace.

But the United Nations actually has failed so utterly to live up to its original purposes and to the solemn words of its Charter that a statement of the truth would do far more toward building faith in any remodeled organization of the future than pious claims which ignore the facts of international life.

Thus it was the Security Council of the United Nations which sent American troops into Korea in June 1950. Our troops engaged in that war by reason of an "executive agreement" which was never submitted to either house of Congress for approval.

For more than three years the words "United Nations command" have been used in official documents and in reports to the United Nations. The fiction has been maintained that an army subject to United Nations instructions was fighting in Korea. The American Government at the outset was designated as "agent" for the U. N., and never has the "United Nations" been omitted from the phraseology of all communications and reports bearing on the Korean war.

Yet when the conference between the "United Nations command" and the Communists at Panmunjom broke down recently and no political conference was arranged for—as stipulated by the armistice—the United Nations dropped out of the whole thing.

No armistice agreements or peace proposals have ever been submitted to the Security Council of the United Nations. Hence the unit which authorized the bloodshed had ceased to have a hand in endeavoring to consummate the peace agreement. The U. N. has abandoned in a practical sense the job of representing the more than 79,000 persons, including 31,500 Americans, who gave their lives in the fight against the Communist armies.

Today the "United Nations" has no part in calling the Geneva conference starting April 26. This meeting is an improvised substitute for the "political conference" which the armistice agreement asked in vain to be called not later than October 28, 1953.

The Geneva conference is really a group of principals in a war theoretically fought by the "United Nations." Soviet Russia—having acknowledged that it sent arms and ammunition to the Communist Chinese Government, which was declared an aggressor by the United Nations Assembly—is not in any way being brought to book or punished for its violation of the Charter. Instead Russia now is given prestige as an "inviting power" at Geneva and, as such, invites the North Korean and Red Chinese governments to participate. This is the hypocrisy of the hour.

Here, therefore, is a multi-power conference outside the United Nations, owing no allegiance as a conference to the United Nations itself. When the meeting is over, the members of the U. N. who participated in the Geneva affair will, of course, file with the U. N. a report of what happened—a routine act without significance, as the die will have been cast anyway.

The facts about the failure of the U. N. have never been faced by any of the statesmen of the world except the late Senator Taft, who a year ago pointed out that, in setting up the North Atlantic Treaty Organization to maintain the peace of Europe, several of the important members had by-passed the U. N. and that dependence must be placed hereafter on alliances of free nations for special purposes.

It is often argued that the U. N. is a handy forum—a debating society. It is, of course, an instrument for discussion through which moral force can be mobilized. But the sooner the apologists for the U. N. concede that the U. N. has failed as an enforcement body and that, in and of itself, the organization cannot be used for collective security in a military sense, the sooner will be dispelled the illusions being spread across this country about the nature of the "United Nations."

Preparations are being made now to revise the Charter of the U. N. Morality cannot be legislated. To amend only the form and ignore the substance is to fail to meet the issue. There is no use revising the Charter until there is a moral code observed by the members. There can be no substitute for good faith and an allegiance to solemnly given pledges.

It is the character of some of the members rather than the phraseology of the Charter which needs revision. There is no room in any collective-security system for the faithless and the treasonable. The U. N. will begin to thrive when it expels from its membership unmoral governments and establishes an alliance of nations that are truly free.

THE REAL ISSUE

MARCH 26, 1954

THE REAL ISSUE before the American people today must not be obscured or beclouded by extraneous controversies that fill the headlines nowadays.

The real issue is not whether a Senator, provoked by the non-cooperation of a witness, loses his temper and makes extreme statements while trying to investigate the red tape which bestowed on Communists certificates of honor from the U.S. Army.

The real issue is not whether a member of a congressional committee staff asked the Army to give another staff member, who had been drafted, passes for week ends so that he could complete his reports for the Senate subcommittee. Nor is the real issue whether staff members of a Senate committee or civilian officials of the Army used improper pressure in connection with the episode.

The time has come to differentiate between the petty disputes of the hour and fundamental issues.

The real issue confronting the nation today is whether the savings of the American people shall be confiscated by unscrupulous politicians who abstractly denounce the philosophy of Communism and then concretely accept its doctrines of organized thievery.

For the Communist propaganda is aimed at the destruction of the capitalist system—the system of free enterprise—the system of private savings invested in the industries and businesses of America.

Whoever hides behind the front of so-called "liberalism" and votes to destroy the system of private enterprise through tax laws that penalize the successful and the thrifty is paying homage to the doctrine of national socialism—the precursor of Communism.

The Communists have long aimed to pit class against class, to sow suspicions between employers and the workers, and to make every businessman appear as an exploiter of his fellow man.

Coincidentally, this same line is pursued by the "left wing" in America which, with labor-union support, has captured the Democratic Party's leadership.

Listen, some nights, to the regular broadcasts by commentators sponsored by the funds of labor unions and you will hear the language of class war, designed to divide America and to spread hate and to make it appear that the men who have had the genius to create jobs in this country are the enemies of the workers.

The real issue that means more to America than the petty squabbles of the day came to a head last week in the House of Representatives. Only by the narrow margin of 6 votes out of 414 was America saved from proposals that would have prevented an incentive system of taxation from being adopted and that would instead have demoralized the capitalistic system by discouraging future investment in American enterprises.

A handful of Democrats voted with an almost solid Republican membership to reject the political conspiracy which would have forced the unbalancing of the budget by many billions of dollars.

The solvency of America is as essential to our life as the preservation of the free enterprise system. Those who would destroy the system of private capital and investment will continue to use these political stratagems to dupe the Democratic leadership and a few timid Republicans in schemes that mean a raid on the Treasury and a breakdown of the integrity of the dollar, leading almost certainly to public bankruptcy.

The vote by almost the entire membership of the Democratic Party in the House last week for unsound proposals is regrettable. Must it be said hereafter that only the Republican Party is dedicated to the task of preserving private capitalism?

Will it be charged on the stump now that, in addition to softness toward Communists in the last 20 years, various spokesmen for the Democratic Party openly espouse class warfare as a means to a partisan end?

Surely the great party of Jefferson and Jackson and Wilson has never before succumbed so completely to the "redistribution of wealth" fakery of the demagogue which, if adopted, can only result in a wide distribution of poverty.

The real issue is whether the Democratic Party in Congress is going to embrace the Communist philosophy of anti-capitalism. The test will come when the tax bill is before the Senate and in countless other proposals before Congress that seek to make the state master of the individual and ultimately to confiscate the savings of the thrifty.

For the real issue is whether little by little the Government shall impose a philosophy that destroys the economic system by a steady process of creeping socialism and Communist poison, or whether we shall have prudent fiscal policies and incentive taxation to keep America the most powerful industrial nation in the world, with the highest standard of living known to man.

Let the extraneous issues be dealt with, of course, but let them not befog or draw a red herring across the real issue—the preservation of private initiative against the confiscationists who are the twin brothers of the Communists.

KEEP THE CHURCHES OUT OF POLITICS

APRIL 2, 1954

CHRISTIANITY is the dominant religion of America, but the basic principle of our constitutional system is to keep Church and State separate.

Lately some of the national church organizations have begun to meddle in politics. If the trend is not arrested, it can only lead to a loss of faith in churches and in clergymen who profess to teach Christianity.

It has become commonplace to pick up the Monday morning newspapers and read sermons vehemently attacking persons who are conspicuous in the political polemics of our day. The press associations eagerly transmit to newspapers from coast to coast the invectives of partisan spleen that come from the pulpits. Some clergymen seem more interested in making headlines than in making Christians obedient to Christian principles in their everyday life.

It is a truism of our times that politics would be cleaner and the controversies in governmental affairs which cause so much emotional furore would be dissolved if men who became protagonists would surrender themselves to the will of God and be guided in paths of truth and human love.

For the decay in present-day morals and the deterioration of moral principle in governments throughout the world is perhaps due to the fact that many clergymen have been grossly negligent in their devotion to spiritual tasks. They have been diverted from their real duty. They have not fulfilled their true mission. They have become controversialists themselves—infected by the poison of pride and egotism.

Soon laymen in America will be asking each other: "Are you attending a pro-McCarthy or anti-McCarthy church these days?" Soon other laymen will be asking: "Is yours a Republican or Democratic Party pulpit?"

How much faith, how much confidence can there be in any clergy which allows itself to become an integral part of the factional strife of the political world?

As citizens, clergymen may express themselves on anything they please. But in speaking for Protestant, Catholic or Jewish churches, they ought not to intrude in politics or take sides on political questions —that is, if they expect to retain the confidence of their congregations.

A case in point is the National Council of Churches of Christ in the U.S.A., which has just issued a statement demanding that Congress adopt certain rules and regulations, which the National Council would prescribe, with reference to the handling of congressional investigations. The phraseology of the document is copied in large part from the language of political spokesmen who are making partisan use of such proposals. Granted that there is need for such reforms, why does the National Council feel that laymen are incompetent to fight that battle and that the prestige of such a big church organization must be dragged into the mire of partisan politics? For the conduct of congressional inquiries is a political football these days.

This manifesto declares that congressional committees are usurping "powers not granted to Congress by the Constitution and failing to concentrate on the primary task of collecting information for purposes of new legislation." Yet nowhere in all the decisions of the Supreme Court of the United States has Congress been told that the Constitution requires its investigating committees to limit themselves to collecting information for new legislation. Would the Teapot Dome scandal or the perjury by Alger Hiss or the many cases of corruption by individuals in Government have been uncovered if there had not been constitutional authority for such probes by the legislative branch of the Government and its committees?

The manifesto, moreover, still clings to the illusion that, when persons suspected of Communist affiliations or connections have been investigated by congressional committees, this is merely an attempt to castigate them for their "personal economic and political beliefs," and not for their possible relationship to the Communist conspiracy. The FBI and the various U. S. District Attorneys have been confronted in the courts with the same line of defense by Communists who have been convicted of participating in a conspiracy to overthrow the Government of the United States by violence.

All these pronouncements by national church organizations can have only one object and purpose— to use the dignity and spiritual power of the church as an agency to draw church members into a political force which shall mobilize public opinion on a question of governmental procedures.

Is it advisable for large church organizations, as such, to enter the political field? Wouldn't it be better if they taught us more about Christian philosophy and inspired us by their example to settle the conflicts within everyday America by reason instead of by emotion, by truth instead of by slander, by the governing rules of a God-given conscience?

This is the time of all times for clergymen to teach Christianity and not to become sinners themselves in the unmoral precincts of present-day politics.

H-BOMB HYSTERIA

APRIL 9, 1954

MANY OF THE COMMENTS both here and abroad on the latest tests showing the fantastic power of the H-bomb unite in a common plea. It is that every effort now must be made to prevent further wars—as if the decision on such a desirable objective is solely in the hands of the United States.

Perspective will be lost in the current hysteria and little progress made toward achieving a durable peace if the emphasis is continually placed on destructive weapons instead of on the facts relating to the power of decision by the Soviet Government, which can conceivably take the initiative in ordering those new weapons to be used in a war of aggression. For the heart of the unsolved problem is not how to convince the free world that peace is better than war but how an effective restraint can be imposed on a small number of evil men in Moscow who temporarily have captured control of a large population.

America may have all the peaceful instincts and desires of a saint and yet find herself face to face with the devil, who, when he has a sufficient arsenal, may try to force frightened nations to do his bidding.

The question is not novel just because the latest weapons are of novel strength. The British people, who faced so courageously the terrible bombardment during World War II by Nazi rockets and block-buster bombs, know what terror can be like and how, despite the underground shelters, thousands of lives of civilians were lost. Terrorizing the non-combatant population did not win the last war. Destruction of certain industrial plants of Germany by selective bombing was the decisive factor, along with pressure by our troops on armies whose vital supply lines were being pounded to pieces.

Everyone knows today that the United States would not be experimenting with the hydrogen bomb if the Communists had not stolen scientific secrets from us and begun testing the same type of bombs themselves. Whether we like it or not, we are in the midst of an armament race such as has preceded nearly every great war. Because our enemy arms to the hilt, we too arm to the hilt. It's a familiar story.

But there is another part of the story which needs to be told and retold. It is the failure of some peace-loving nations in the past to be realistic—to spend the necessary money and make the necessary sacrifices to rearm and to be resolute instead of wobbly in the critical stages of diplomacy. Thus, the British and French were singularly short-sighted when they let Hitler build up his military strength from 1933 to 1939. They even sold him munitions and raw materials with which to make weapons up to the last few months before World War II broke out. We also failed for a long time to embargo the export of munitions to Japan.

Today—this very week—Britain is demanding that the United States agree to relax restrictions on trade with the Communist countries. The usual quibbles that the commodities are not "strategic" are being advanced. Soviet Russia and her satellites, of course, need consumer goods. The captive peoples are restless and might revolt if they can't buy consumer goods. So the free world is about to help out the totalitarian government by permitting it to acquire consumer goods which are "nonstrategic" and thus enable her to concentrate her energies and her factories on making munitions of war. This can only aid the Communist regime by strengthening the Kremlin's hold on the people.

Plainly our policy should be to drive a wedge between the Communist Government in Moscow and the people. We should be striving earnestly to win to our side the people behind the Iron Curtain. We should never assist in strengthening the prestige of the Communist Government at home.

If, moreover, as a consequence of the news of the H-bomb tests, a frightened America and her frightened allies manifest weaknesses, we may unwittingly encourage the aggressor. His miscalculation as to our true willingness to resist in the local conflicts of the "cold war" could bring on the big war we dread so much.

We must not diminish by one iota our readiness to fight if need be. We cannot accept pacifism or non-resistance. We can hold out the hand of friendship to all the peoples behind the Iron Curtain and tell them again and again that their rulers have refused to cooperate in a program of peace and have declined repeatedly to agree to submit to a system of international inspection. This we have offered through the United Nations as a means of controlling, if not eliminating, the use of massive weapons of war.

Now is the time of all times to be diligent in the use of moral force. It can exercise incalculable influence over the minds of human beings everywhere. For today it is not the production of the big bomb which is the key to it all. Primarily the key is to be found in the minds of the people of the Soviet Empire, who need to be persuaded that they have no enemies anywhere in the world today except among the unscrupulous men in the Kremlin itself.

A "UNITED WILL"

APRIL 16, 1954

MORE THAN A MERE DECLARATION of words is being sought by Secretary of State John Foster Dulles as he urges Great Britain and France to join the United States in a solid front against Communist aggression in Indo-China.

What Mr. Dulles is asking for is not a formula or chart of military operations but a dramatic manifestation by the three allies of a spirit of resolution to check the growing Red menace in Southeast Asia.

This is a crisis for the whole world. The issue of war or peace may turn on what the three allies do about Southeast Asia.

This is, moreover, a particular crisis for the United States. It could be a turning point that might bring back isolationism in America. For certainly, if America is deserted on the Indo-China question, there would be no sense in "going it alone" there. There would be every reason also to pull in from all distant areas of the world lest our troops be exposed and left in the lurch by irresolute allies unwilling to stand firm when the chips are down.

Conversely, this is an opportunity for the free world. If France can emerge from her factionalism and if London, which sees the situation far more clearly than does Paris, can persuade the French leaders to realize that this is a chance for a common front which can change the whole course of history, then the initiative taken by Secretary Dulles will not have been in vain. America believes in collective security, but this means faithful, not faithless, allies.

We can dismiss as irrelevant the newspaper comments from abroad that Mr. Dulles should have waited till the Geneva conference before asking for a declaration with respect to the future in Indo-China. On the contrary, it is as important to have France and Britain and America clear the air ahead of Geneva as it was important for the heads of these same three governments to meet in Bermuda last December in order to collaborate on the positions to be taken at the subsequent Berlin conference.

What is needed now is a statement of purpose that is unequivocal and unmistakable. It is the will to resist aggression which must be clearly proclaimed. Secretary Dulles knows that "united action" is a logical sequel to a "united will," but it is important to tell the Communists that this "united will" does exist—or doesn't it?

Again and again in world history the aggressor has miscalculated what the defenders would do. Two world wars have shown the tragic result of failure on the part of the democracies to make known in advance, and in explicit terms, their will to resist aggressors. Let us not make that mistake today. For weakness now by us and a miscalculation of that weakness by the Communists could conceivably bring the third world war which everybody, including the Soviet people, wants to avoid. It may be too late if the situation in Southeast Asia is bungled.

Just as there have been comments from Paris that a statement of "united will" might better await the outcome of the Geneva conference, there have been comments from Administration leaders of our Senate that appropriations for foreign aid could also better await the outcome of the Geneva conference. These are pointed warnings across the seas, and they reveal a sad case of misunderstanding between allies, which the visit of Mr. Dulles with the British and French premiers must resolve.

France is torn with political dissension. Britain has her internal friction, too, with partisans willing to place party above country. But the times are much too serious for such squabbling. It is the fate of Europe which hangs in the balance. Will the politicians in London and Paris involuntarily drive America out of Europe's councils and bring about the very estrangement which Moscow has been so assiduously seeking to achieve?

American public opinion up to now has assumed that Europe wants American aid as a means of self-protection. But if British and French politicians don't really want that protection and if they do not mind alienating American public opinion, they can accomplish that purpose by an attitude of defeatism on the question of Southeast Asia.

For, if it isn't important to keep all of Asia—and particularly the rubber and tin areas—from falling into the hands of the Communists, then Americans generally will begin to feel they had better concentrate on continental defense here and let Europe worry along as best she can.

This country cannot afford indefinitely to send troops and planes and money to build up air bases in countries that at a critical moment will not show the will to resist.

It is better to develop a "united will" now than to try desperately at the last moment to transform a coalition of dispirited allies into an effective military alliance.

A HISTORIC DECISION

APRIL 23, 1954

THERE ARE GREAT MOMENTS IN HISTORY when the simple words of a government declaration seem so natural an expression of purpose that their transcendent significance is not always immediately apparent.

Such is the nature of the pronouncement issued by President Eisenhower last week telling the world that the United States is definitely committed to the defense of all of free Europe.

Germany is not a member of the North Atlantic Treaty Organization, the object of which has been to warn Soviet Russia against any attack on the fourteen countries in the Organization. These are Great Britain, France, Belgium, Luxembourg, Holland, Norway, Denmark, Iceland, Portugal, Italy, Greece, Turkey, Canada and the United States.

The language of this treaty—ratified by our Senate—makes it clear that the United States, for example, is bound to regard an attack on any one of the other thirteen countries as the same thing as an attack on this country. This is realistic alertness in an airplane and atomic age.

But up to now there has been no provision as to what the United States and other countries like Great Britain and France would do if Soviet Russia attacked Germany. It was to assure a united defense against such an attack that the European Defense Community idea has been advanced, and Germany has ratified it.

With France reluctant to sign the European Defense Community agreement or to admit Germany to the North Atlantic Treaty Organization, because of a fear that it would mean the rearmament of Germany, the major powers have had to grope for a satisfactory formula to overcome those objections. The Eisenhower statement, therefore, is intended as a reassurance to France, some of whose politicians have insisted that America's motive in pressing for ratification of the European Defense Community pact—of which America and Britain are not signatories—is merely to build up a defense organization that will make it possible some day for those two countries to withdraw from the North Atlantic Treaty Organization.

So the President reaffirms in unmistakable phrases America's conviction that the defense of Europe in its entirety is essential to ward off possible aggression against the United States. A similar pronouncement has just been made by Great Britain. The President declares:

"In consonance with its policy of full and continuing support for the maintenance of the integrity and unity of the European Defense Community, the United States will regard any action from whatever quarter which threatens that integrity or unity as a threat to the security of the United States. In such event, the United States will consult in accordance with the provisions of Article 4 of the North Atlantic Treaty.

"In accordance with the basic interest of the United States in the North Atlantic Treaty, as expressed at the time of ratification, the treaty was regarded as of indefinite duration rather than for any definite number of years. The United States calls attention to the fact that for it to cease to be a party to the North Atlantic Treaty would appear to be quite contrary to our security interests when there is established on the continent of Europe the solid core of unity which the European Defense Community will provide."

What this means is that, as long as there is unity, America will help with troops against any outside attack. But it goes without saying that, if Germany and France were to become involved in a war against each other at some future date, the "unity" would be destroyed and the United States would have a free hand to make whatever decision circumstances may require.

The President's declaration also says:

"The United States will continue to maintain in Europe, including Germany, such units of its armed forces as may be necessary and appropriate to contribute its fair share of the forces needed for the joint defense of the North Atlantic area while a threat to that area exists, and will continue to deploy such forces in accordance with agreed North Atlantic strategy for the defense of this area."

This is not a program without flexibility. It permits America to determine the extent of her participation if there should be any one-sidedness and it permits a re-examination of the nature of or effectiveness of the defense which the Europeans themselves will have built up. For there are times when the countries themselves with foreign troops on their soil want them to leave their territory.

The historic statement by the President ties together all the threads of the European Defense Community proposal and the North Atlantic Treaty.

The United States is committed to collective security and asks only that all other members of the alliance faithfully honor their obligations when a big crisis comes. Such an attitude now can deter the aggressor, and Secretary Dulles by his visit to Europe has consummated a constructive policy for peace.

PEACE AT GENEVA IF—

MAY 7, 1954

AT GENEVA

THERE CAN BE PEACE in the world, and it can be made here at Geneva.

But it can come only if America and her allies acquire a self-disciplined unity and a resoluteness which the free world has not shown since World War II.

For the secret of victory lies in a united front that does not consist solely of the high-sounding phrases of diplomacy but also of concrete acts by leaders of all parties in every one of the free countries. Such acts must culminate in a determination to fight whenever and wherever necessary—to repel with arms the invasion of the enemy—and to check by moral force his infiltration of our ranks. We must take steps to frustrate those same fifth-column tactics which brought the downfall of France in 1940 and which are being manifested now within nearly all the free countries.

It is evident that the Soviets think they have captured substantial segments of the public opinion of the Western countries. They believe that, because we shun war and are horrified at the destruction which atomic warfare can bring, we have been anesthetized by our fears and will supinely accept almost any encroachment imposed upon us.

Twice in this modern age the free countries have been forced to go to war to prove they were not cowards. What a terrible price we have had to pay in human casualties and in disrupted economic life just because dictatorship regimes misconstrued the diversity of view and the peaceful intentions of our peoples as indicative of a nonresistant pacifism!

The key to peace is not here at all but in the public opinion of each of the Western countries.

The big news of this conference is in the revelation of the confident tactics of the Soviets. They are convinced they have enough influence with British public opinion to keep the British Government from taking a firm stand in favor of the unification of Korea or the emancipation of Indo-China from Communist military pressure. They are convinced also that they have France in the hollow of their hands and that, even though Foreign Minister Bidault is desperately trying here to go along with the American point of view, he will be commanded to do otherwise when critical decisions are to be made or else the cabinet in Paris of which he is a member will be overthrown through the skillful maneuvers of the Communist Party bloc inside the French Parliament.

There is only one language that the Soviet rulers understand, and that is the language of a united alliance against them. Unfortunately, such an alliance exists today in name only. Yet anyone who knows the bravery of British and French soldiers in past history and the deep-seated patriotism and love of freedom by the British and French peoples cannot for a moment assume that, when the call comes to defend a great cause, they would not respond courageously.

But why cannot that unified purpose be expressed now? Why must partisan leaders needle the administrations in power and force them to say publicly things that make the Soviets believe the free countries will never fight? Why is it that we and our allies do not articulate our courage at all times, especially during a big conference like the one here in Geneva?

It would be tremendously impressive if Representatives Rayburn and McCormack of the Democratic Party leadership in the House and Senators Lyndon Johnson and Russell of the Democratic Party leadership in the Senate walked down the center aisles with their respective colleagues of the Republican leadership and in unison said to Europe and Moscow:

"We stand together as Americans. We are ready as Americans to shed our blood once more in the cause of freedom, for we cannot as Americans accept tyranny as a way of life nor live happily in a world rendered unsafe for democratic institutions by the acts of aggressor governments. We know that war is horrible, but we shall not be intimidated and, if attacked, there will be massive retaliation. So, instead, let us solve our problems by peaceful means. Let the military forces of the aggressor governments retire behind their boundaries and give evidence of good faith as against recurrent aggression."

It would be impressive if similar statements came from leaders in the French and British Parliaments.

Secretary Dulles has expressed here with brilliant logic and with a firmness of which every American can be proud the practical idealism of the United States. For we seek no colonies or selfish advantage and we have no imperialistic designs anywhere. We are concerned only with the enforcement of world peace. We will not intervene in Indo-China or anywhere else alone. We will march only at the side of free men upholding the principle of collective action as a means of achieving collective security.

For genuine unity on our side is the only force—physical and moral—which the Soviets must and will respect. It is the way to peace.

AMERICAN POWER ABROAD

MAY 14, 1954

AT GENEVA

To UNDERSTAND THE FORCES that can bring peace to the world, it is necessary to analyze the impact of American power abroad.

The influence America has internationally today is not so much related to the fact that we live under a system of free institutions, however much this may evoke worldwide admiration. Our influence stems primarily at this time from our economic and military strength. The rise and fall of our prestige abroad will be affected largely by how we use that great economic and military power.

So deep is the dependence of Europe on who holds the purse strings in the United States that it is perhaps natural for Europeans to want to see—as some of them privately and discreetly admit nowadays—the return of the New Deal or Fair Deal in America because they think it would mean a more generous flow of funds to Europe.

This is why it is so important that a bipartisan unity be established in the Congress of the United States so that America's world policy can make progress instead of being slowed down by the coming congressional campaign. It ought really be made clear to our European friends that Democrats and Republicans think alike as Americans.

For American power abroad has not yet been exerted to the point of maximum influence. We are portrayed here as being either meddlesome and impertinent or else selfishly nationalist. There seems to be no middle ground among the critics. Actually the United States is concerned with the affairs of Europe and Asia only in the sense that it wants to use its industrial and military resources to assure and guarantee an era of peace. We seek no territory, no colonies and no preferential advantages for our citizens.

It must not be assumed from this emphasis on economic and military factors that moral force is any less important. On the contrary, what the spokesmen of the United States say publicly, what the press of our country says every day and what positions we assume in our diplomacy can be the strongest influences of all in bringing to our side the whole-hearted concurrence of allied peoples in all parts of the world.

Sympathizing as we do with the passion of individuals everywhere for liberty and freedom, America's moral power is enhanced when it encourages self-determination and independence for all struggling nationalities.

But we must be consistent. We cannot reproach the French for being too slow about giving independence to the small states in Indo-China and remain silent about the various states and nationalities which make up the Soviet Union and are equally deserving of their independence. We must, moreover, never fail to advocate the restoration of the independence of the Baltic States as well as of Poland, Czechoslovakia, Hungary, Bulgaria and Rumania. We must continue to urge the reunion of East Germany with West Germany. These are goals to which, with renewed vigor, our moral force must be dedicated.

We have been groping under the past and present Administrations for the formulation of such a policy. It would seem opportune for the President to set forth the basic principles so all the world may know these truths:

First, we are ready—at whatever sacrifice necessary—to use our physical power to guarantee as against outside attack the territorial integrity as well as the political independence of all nations whose governments rest on the consent of the governed.

Second, we are ready to furnish economic aid and military support to the people of Soviet Russia and China in a system of collective security provided the peoples there are liberated and can become masters of their own government through free elections.

Third, we stand ready to contribute our share of the manpower needed for a system of collective action but we believe that the primary responsibility for protecting the nations of Europe and the nations of Asia, respectively, must rest on their own manpower.

Fourth, we look askance at those free nations which make "neutralism" their policy while the potential invader threatens the safety of sister nations.

Fifth, we must all stand together as free governments to protect ourselves internally against elements of infiltration—the "fifth columns" such as sabotaged France in 1940. We must pool our information to protect free governments against the machinations of subversive elements on our soil financed and directed by autocratic governments hostile to us.

Sixth, we must organize effectively our economic power and refuse to sell strategic goods to any country dominated by the governments of potential aggressors.

We must in short mobilize our industrial, our military and our moral power abroad so that we can win to our side all the free peoples in an effective system of collective security.

OUTMANEUVERING THE KREMLIN

MAY 21, 1954

AT GENEVA

ANYBODY WHO THINKS a conference of 19 nations nowadays is actually a negotiation would be promptly disillusioned by a few days' observation here.

For the instances where, across the luncheon or dinner table, there is an opportunity on the part of the topmost delegates to fathom the mind of the Soviet representatives are few indeed, and these usually reveal not the slightest interest in the "give and take" of real negotiations. From the Soviet viewpoint, it is all "take" and no "give."

Nothing that has happened in the world has affected the Soviet intransigeance. The Moscow delegation has come here for the sole purpose of probing the weaknesses of the allies and perhaps driving a deeper wedge between them.

Accordingly, what is the countermaneuver and how are we in the Western world faring? First of all, a "united will" among our allies is a hope and an aspiration but not a reality. Its absence is conspicuous and the Soviets know the frustrations on our side. There is no use blaming individuals who happen at the moment to head the British or the French government. They have their hands tied by a faltering, defeatist public opinion which, though it is not yet admitted, actually is dangerously near a surrender and farther away than ever before from a willingness to fight a war, if need be, to uphold a moral principle.

But are we in the United States any different? We, too, shrink from any demonstrations of military force lest they lead to war, and we have already condemned war as a futile instrument that cannot bring real peace after an armistice is signed. Yet we go on appropriating vast sums for national defense on the assumption that it is not safe to be without modern weapons and well-equipped forces and that, if we are compelled to fight, we must be able to defend ourselves.

This raises the question of whether disunited allies who manifest their weaknesses on the policy front do not create precisely the conditions which bring on the very war we do not want. Appeasement encourages the aggressor to encroach too far and then war comes because it is too late to apply the influences of reason.

Are we, therefore, utilizing the strongest moral power we can exert without actually resorting to war?

Threats are, to be sure, unwise and ultimatums are a thing of the past. There is only one strategy that the United States can wisely pursue at the moment—and that is, with unremitting fervor, to express its point of view in the court of world opinion. We must bring to our side the people of all other countries, including those behind the Iron Curtain.

Will this have any effect? How do we reach people who are forbidden to hear radio broadcasts or to read uncensored newspapers? These are barriers indeed, but they are by no means insurmountable. Truth does penetrate if we can present the truth in unison.

Our immediate task is not on the other side of the Iron Curtain but on this side. For, surprising as it may seem, we have not convinced the public opinion of the allied countries as to the rightness of our cause or the sincerity of our purpose in America. There is a disposition, even among some Americans who live overseas, to disparage the idealism of America and to believe the fantastic stories that America's sole reason for the Marshall Plan was to bolster a weakened economy back home or to maintain full employment.

Plainly the bickerings between our political partisans are a handicap but not because, as is sometimes argued, American "prestige" abroad is thereby injured. Europeans are not familiar with our institutions and care little about the news of the eccentric controversies which get big headlines in our own newspapers. They care primarily about American action that affects them directly. Just now there is little appreciation of American unselfishness and a tendency to believe the Communist propaganda which charges that we are out to conquer the world by military means.

Our duty is clear. Our spokesmen must by day and by night answer the vilifying charges made in Europe and Asia against American purposes and ideals. We must get fair treatment for our case in the press in Europe, where unfortunately the other side has already begun to use the same weapons of subsidy and corruption as the Nazis used with the French press in the years immediately preceding World War II.

Confident that we are in the right, we must take our stand on principle. We must espouse the cause of collective action. We must rebuild and strengthen the United Nations. We must speak out in the U. N. forum again and again. We must refute promptly the slanders against us that appear in the European press.

We must first of all, however, have unity on foreign policy in America and, if we can do this and achieve unity with our allies, we can speak to the whole world with a good chance of having our views prevail. That's the best way to outmaneuver the Kremlin.

WHY ARE THE COMMUNISTS DEFIANT?

MAY 28, 1954

AT GENEVA

THE ISSUE OF PEACE or war for the world is wrapped up in the answer to this question: "What makes the Communists defiant?" It is but another way of asking what is the source of the intransigeance which they have exhibited at the Geneva Conference.

The attitude of the Communist negotiators at every conference or discussion or negotiation since 1945 has been in the main the same. Minor concessions on inconsequential matters have been made, but these serve only to emphasize what has not been conceded.

Some consciousness of strength must actuate the Communists to express publicly their contempt for the Western nations and to carry on simultaneously their steady encroachment on the smaller countries of the free world. What is back of it all?

Winston Churchill said repeatedly during the years immediately after World War II that it was our possession of the atomic bomb which deterred the Soviets from starting a third world war. Military men, inside and outside of government in America and Europe, said that, by refusing to demobilize her armies in Europe, Soviet Russia achieved a potential superiority. This presumably enabled the Communists to act with arrogance. But nevertheless this continued after the democracies began, through NATO and other steps, to reinforce their military position in Europe.

Within the last five years the Soviets have exploded an atom bomb and conducted tests of the hydrogen bomb. There is every reason to believe that we have a numerical superiority in atomic weapons. But still the Soviets show no signs of reasonableness in any negotiations on any issue of real importance. Such an adamant attitude can be rationalized only on the theory that the Soviets feel, if a war broke out, they could win.

What is the basis for such confidence? It must be that they are sure we will not throw the first bomb, and there may be good reasons why they themselves plan never to throw one either. Given a conventional setup in a military sense, therefore, the Western countries are at a serious disadvantage. They do not have enough manpower in Europe to defend themselves against the numerically greater number of divisions in the Red Army. It is asserted again and again that our side will use all weapons in our arsenal, but the Soviets probably do not believe it.

The Communists, moreover, may be assuming that America is not going to be able to launch any bombs from bases in Britain or France because of the prospect that "neutralist" sentiment will stay the hand of any British or French Cabinet which might be asked to sanction such a step. The British and French peoples are fearful that America may engage in atomic warfare and involve them unnecessarily.

The biggest source of reliance for the Soviets must be the conviction that the democracies will surrender area after area without a fight—that they will give in to almost any demand rather than risk the fury of another world war. The Communists are encouraged in this belief by the disunity of the allies and by their hesitancy to face facts.

Just as Hitler was convinced that Britain and France wouldn't wage an all-out war in 1939 and that he could add Poland to his list of conquered countries, so the Soviets, looking about in Asia as well as Europe, see the extent of their own influence widening all the time without any really serious resistance. Our stand in Korea would have been impressive if we had allowed our Air Force to bomb bases in Manchuria and to destroy the lines of supply from China to Korea and if our Navy had been allowed to blockade the China Coast, as our Joint Chiefs of Staff recommended. But our European allies vetoed that plan in the autumn of 1950.

So the Soviet rulers are playing here the same game that Hitler played and that, to a somewhat lesser extent, the Japanese war lords played in their negotiations with us in the summer and autumn of 1941. The Communists lead from strength, and they will continue to do so until the Western countries have a plan for united action that looks militarily as if it could be effective whenever the challenge comes. As Secretary of State Dulles says, we must be ready to take the risks of peace or we will find ourselves in war.

There is no substitute for military strength when dealing with a ruthless and intransigeant foe. The test is here now in the Indo-China situation. The peoples of Soviet Russia and the satellite states will be emboldened to throw off the Communist yoke only if they are sure we are strong enough to checkmate the Kremlin's march.

Moral force—the attempt to win away the peoples of Soviet Russia and China from the Moscow clique and the Peiping clique, respectively—must go hand in hand with the build-up of our military power in Europe and Asia. Then and only then will it be possible for international conferences to succeed in settling disputes between the East and the West.

THE FRANCE WE DON'T KNOW

JUNE 4, 1954

AT PARIS

WE IN AMERICA are inclined to think of France as one of the major powers of the world. We speak of the "Big Three" whenever the foreign ministers of France, Great Britain and the United States get together, and an impression is conveyed in the press that France is on a par with us—capable of contributing to the Western Alliance virtually equal military strength.

But this is not a realistic picture. It is time to face facts, not only for the good of France but for the good of America.

Do we in the United States really understand the France that only nine years ago was liberated from a five-year military domination by a conquering enemy? Do we know what five years of military occupation by a foreign army does to a nation? Do we know what it means to lose in two world wars more than two millions of the nation's finest men, with millions more hobbling along the streets the rest of their lives and with hardly a family untouched by the casualty lists?

The seven-year war in Indo-China has been a big load to carry. It has strained an already over-extended budget. Death on the battlefield has taken a heavy toll of officers—the equivalent each year of an entire graduating class at the French West Point. The flower of the regular French Army—40 per cent of the non-commissioned officers and 25 per cent of the commissioned officers—is being risked now in Indo-China. Yet the pressure to furnish troops for the North Atlantic Treaty Organization and now for the European Defense Community continues. It presupposes a reorganized France, fully capable of taking such responsibilities in her stride.

What we little realize in America is that our own territory has not been invaded and that bombs have not destroyed our factories and our homes and that the task of reconstructing a war-torn country is not a mere matter of handing out billions of dollars to rebuild heavy industries.

The social structure of a nation is not remade overnight, nor is human nature suddenly transformed because American money is forthcoming to sustain a weak economy. Workers, underpaid and now formed into powerful labor unions, listen to Communist harangues and become the innocent tools of the Communists, whose infiltration is by no means underestimated here.

The Communist strength at the polls is gradually diminishing as economic conditions improve. There is no fondness for Communism or for Soviet imperialism among the masses of the French people or even among the majority of the leaders of political parties. But there is enough Communist influence among the trade unions and enough Communist members in Parliament to enable the dissident groups to throw monkey wrenches into the machinery and to exploit the economic and political weaknesses of the French nation.

Is the spirit of the people defeatist? On the contrary, there is a basic faith that France will right herself some day. There is among the people a significant dissatisfaction with the quality of the French Cabinets since the war and a feeling that the men in public life have not risen to the challenges of postwar France.

As in all countries just emerging from a war era, there is a floundering and a perplexity, and it is not reduced by American insistence on greater effort by the French in preparing militarily for a third world war or for a more intensified campaign in Indo-China.

We of America must find, besides France, more allies—friendly countries in Asia and Europe. For the same dependence as before cannot be placed on French manpower.

But, above all, it is even more necessary to invigorate the French people with new hope, and this can come by a deeper sympathy and a better understanding of French problems. We have only to remember that, following the War Between the States in our own country 90 years ago, the reconstruction was slow and painful and that only in the last 15 years has the South in an economic sense come back into its own.

Then there is also the question of pride. A nation which has enjoyed the glory that the French people have known is slow to acknowledge that it is no longer a major power. For France today is largely dependent on the help she can get from her friends. Also, in the midst of her struggle for an economic equilibrium, France is finding herself pressed by world opinion and by Communist sabotage to give up colonies and foreign possessions, with all the commercial ties and benefits which have accrued in past years.

These are tough times for France. But her spirit has not been squelched. As the soldiers parade by and the crowds cheer, there is still the fervor and the love of country that made the French poilu fight so bravely alongside American doughboys in World War I. The heroism of De Castries is but a flicker now of the France that was, but it can grow into the flames of a renewed patriotism if the battalions of freedom must march again.

THE ENGLAND WE DON'T KNOW

JUNE 11, 1954

AT LONDON

NO NATION CAN UNDERSTAND the privations of another unless there has been an identical experience. Americans cannot possibly know what has been the residual influence of the four years of Nazi bombing of London and other British cities and towns. In that psychological experience lies the key to present-day manifestations of British policy.

Two peoples with a common language and culture can disagree vehemently and yet never veer from their basic faith in each other. There have been irritations between our two countries in recent years which have been aggravated by careless reporting and unfortunate resentments in the realm of official intercourse.

But Britain at heart is as American as her Prime Minister, whose father was a Briton but whose mother was born in the United States. There is in England a fear on the part of the people that another war will come by accident and that maybe America, with her great military power, will be goaded into a general conflict or will find herself unable to withstand the commitments of a developing crisis.

The people of Britain don't want any more war.

A nation which has suffered setbacks in her economy due to two costly wars does not look complacently on a rising military budget for a third war. The demand is growing—and it is justified—for more social reforms and for an improved standard of living. Postwar controls have lasted here 14 years and food rationing ends on July 4 next. The mere thought of the return of such restrictions is enough to strike discouragement in the hearts of the people.

The British nation will continue to exert upon either a Conservative or a Labor Party Government the most effective restraints that an alert public opinion can apply. But let it not be assumed that Britain will not march at our side if a real crisis comes. Here, as an example, is an editorial published last week in the London *Daily Telegraph,* a staunch supporter of the Churchill Government. Under the title "American Ideals and Practice," it says:

"In his speech at Columbia University, President Eisenhower restated the ideals on which American foreign policy rests. In general, America seeks the rebirth of trust between nations. In particular, she seeks honourable peace in Korea, freedom and unity for Germany and for Austria, security for Indo-China and Southeast Asia, and international control of atomic energy.

"For those with the will to see, the working out of these ideals in the day-to-day conduct of American affairs is plain enough. Yet suspicion of American methods, and to a lesser extent of American motives, persists. Such parts of this suspicion as have no rational foundation cannot be rationally refuted. In this category, we can distinguish envy, which resents America's inheritance of Europe's former position, or an irrational fear, which sees in every American gift the bait for servitude . . .

"Much publicized 'divergences' from America mostly arise from differences of expression and of conventions and not from fundamental differences of thought. In the first place, while expecting America to show infinite patience with all the vagaries of public opinion in other lands, we tend to forget that America has an influential public opinion of her own to contend with. For instance, despite the expressed views of American experts that Indo-China is not yet ready for independence, American public opinion demands that independence be one of the prerequisites of American intervention. Here we see America's mistrust of colonialism still active in an age when America herself, with scant logic, is accused of colonial ambitions.

"Again, we tend to suppose that every remark of any member of the Administration or service chief in some way commits the Administration. In fact, policymaking goes on in public, and individual statements are little more than contributions to a symposium. Furthermore, accustomed as we are to the Delphic pronouncements of European statesmen, we tend to read into the remarks of American statesmen more than was actually said.

"For instance, asked if he thought that Southeast Asia could be defended without Indo-China, Mr. Dulles said he did. This was widely construed as meaning that he thought Indo-China of no importance. Yet, he meant nothing of the sort. In the same way, Mr. Dulles's belief that Geneva will fail is often regarded as a hope that it will fail. Words to most Americans mean nothing more nor less than they say.

"If we are to work harmoniously with America (and the peace of the world depends on this) we must not only recognise the nobility of America's intentions but the natural limitations on her power to execute them. To ignore these, as we sometimes do, is to court disaster. Furthermore, if we are to reconcile our two policies in the Far East, we must also recognise that we have no monopoly of moderation and good sense. And let us remember above all that friendship needs to be kept in constant repair."

THE AMERICA THEY DON'T KNOW

JUNE 18, 1954

ON RETURNING FROM EUROPE, a contrast is to be observed in the attitude of people here and abroad toward the possibility of a general war.

Europeans show much less fear of an invasion by the Red armies than might be expected of those who live next door to Soviet Russia. When asked about this seeming complacency, the answer usually given by officials is that Americans should not be deceived by outward appearances and that the danger is fully recognized.

But what is strangest of all is the rather widespread idea abroad that, if a general war comes, America in some way may be responsible for its outbreak. This curious impression deserves careful analysis, for it is related to many of the misunderstandings that crop up between the United States and our allies.

To the American who knows his own country, its traditions, its record of unselfish participation in two world wars, nothing could be more preposterous than to hear that the Government of the United States might precipitate a general war. But among some members of the British and French Parliaments, for example, including various officials in the Foreign Offices, there is a tendency to assume that the United States may suddenly react to some "local war" situation in a manner calculated to bring on the big war.

Perhaps the best illustration of this is in what occurred when an American commanded the U. N. forces in Korea. The European concept was that the troops should stop at the 38th parallel in repelling aggression. The MacArthur idea of using maximum military power was viewed as likely to precipitate a world war.

But it would be wrong to assume that the Europeans came to this conclusion on their own. Many Democratic Senators and the Truman Administration itself accused General MacArthur of wanting to bring on a third world war. When the Republican Administration came into power in Washington, it was assumed for a while that there would be a vigorous resumption of the fighting in Korea. Hence, there was a sigh of relief in Europe when the armistice was negotiated early in the Eisenhower Administration.

Looking back over what has happened since, if the allies had stood firmly together in 1950 on military strategy, the free world today would not be facing a crisis in Indo-China.

A wave of fear is now sweeping Europe. It has come as a consequence of the dispatches reporting that the United States has been giving serious consideration to the idea of intervening in Indo-China. To many Europeans this means the possible start of a world war. Yet the only reason the subject has been given consideration in Washington has been because an ally—France—requested it.

On top of all this is the frequent publicity given to the A-bomb and H-bomb tests. The demand for more data about the superbombs may be a natural curiosity on the part of some scientists, but the overeagerness of others to have a lot of public discussion about the bombs is misconstrued abroad as the equivalent of "sword rattling" or what Secretary of Defense Wilson recently called "bomb rattling."

What Europeans do not seem to understand is that the people of America believe there is in the world a real menace, known as "Communist imperialism," which has already caused this country to appropriate vast sums not only for its own defense but for the defense of European and Asian allies.

It is incomprehensible that any European who knows anything at all about America should think of us as "war mongers." Yet that very term—which has been insidiously introduced in the press of Europe—has taken hold there among persons who haven't the slightest idea that they are swallowing the Communist line.

What Europeans didn't take into account is our long history of isolation and aloofness. They forget that we were drawn into two world wars and had nothing to do with the start of either one. They seem unaware also of our great concern for their safety. They do not realize that the true American instinct would be to withdraw from Europe and Asia and let the other countries defend themselves—except that we do not believe our allies have the strength to defend themselves. In the long run we would be fighting on our own shores against an enemy-dominated Europe and Asia, whose bases would be used for guided missiles and intercontinental bombing.

If we do at times speak bluntly, it is because we do not like diplomatic doubletalk or attempts to appease an enemy who misconstrues acts of conciliation for cowardice. We recall that vacillation in diplomacy has encouraged aggressors to start two world wars.

There is much that Europe should know about America. Important as it is to send our messages through the air and by other media of communication to the peoples of Soviet Russia and the satellite countries, it would seem of equal importance to tell the peoples of allied countries more about the ideals and disinterested purposes of the people of the United States.

SURRENDER?

JULY 2, 1954

THE BIG DECISION before the Western powers in Europe is not just to surrender to the Communist aggression in Indo-China—but how to do it gracefully.

For it is apparent now that our European allies have rejected the idea of resisting by military force the march of the aggressor in Southeast Asia and are ready finally to appease the enemy.

The new Prime Minister of France dislikes appeasement but feels that French public opinion demands it.

The Prime Minister of Great Britain, faced with the rising political power of his opposition in Parliament, evidently assumes that he also must stand for peace at almost any price.

So the British Foreign Secretary comes forth with a speech recommending a non-aggression pact with Soviet Russia such as was adopted at Locarno in 1925 and was torn into shreds later by Hitler, when it suited his purpose. What is significant is that Britain seems ready to recede from the doctrine of military pressure as a deterrent force and prefers to trust to the tender mercies of the Kremlin to refrain from precipitating a world war.

Mr. Eden has said again what Mr. Truman and Mr. Acheson said so often in their speeches about the fear of a general war. Every time such a fear is expressed as the basic motive for appeasement, the enemy construes the statement as a sign of weakness—namely, that the West will do almost anything to prevent a war, even perhaps surrender in advance.

So the governments of Britain and France are today, in effect, begging the enemy to be cooperative—to set up a pattern that will save their faces.

Reading some of the speeches delivered in the House of Commons last week, one would imagine the menace of Communist imperialism was wholly theoretical rather than real and that the United States alone has been disturbed by this supposed bugaboo.

The infiltration by Communist imperialists around the world cannot be brushed aside merely by ignoring it. The events in Guatemala—at our own back door—dramatically confirm the inroads made by the Communist agents who have also been stirring up trouble for Britain in Iran and Egypt and Malaya and for France in Tunisia and Morocco, as well as in Indo-China.

Are the British and French statesmen blind to realities? Not at all. They know as well as anybody in this country that the Communists are evil and they knew that Hitler and his Nazi techniques were evil, too. But they felt compelled to try appeasement at Munich in 1938, and they are trying it again today. It is a policy of desperation.

Can it stay the hand of the enemy now even though it didn't stop World War II fifteen years ago? Wishful thinking prevails at present throughout Europe, where the horror of another war has implanted itself so deeply that it is not unfair to say that there are many Frenchmen who, on being asked to choose between a military occupation by the Communists and a world war, would gladly choose survival through surrender rather than death in a war.

Pacifism and non-resistance have become widespread since the news of what the H-bomb can do has been publicized. Diplomacy no longer can operate in London and Paris as in the past on the confident assumption that peoples would fight for their freedom and independence and die rather than become slaves.

In the face of such a trend, the Communists have only to intensify their infiltration tactics to take over free governments in Europe, one by one, as they see victory ahead in the worldwide campaign for their ideology.

America alone stands unconvinced that surrender and appeasement are necessary. There are, to be sure, even some Americans who call their own government a "war monger" and who exert the pressures of criticism upon those of us who plead for old-fashioned American courage. But, fortunately, their cringing philosophy is not dominant. The true "war mongers" today are the appeasers who unwittingly encourage the same miscalculation by the enemy as has twice before brought on world wars.

Our allies are privileged, of course, to assume the calculated risks of a policy of pacifism and appeasement. They could be right. But the risks of such a policy being wrong are too great for America to take.

What then should America do? We should firmly stand our ground, even if we are the last citadel in the world—the nation that refuses to be beguiled by the wiles of the Communist aggressor.

While it may be painful to say, "I told you so" if World War III some day calls us to rescue our misguided allies from their policies of appeasement and surrender, it is necessary that we do not try, by threatening withdrawal of economic or military aid, to coerce our friends abroad. We must rearm ourselves to the utmost even as we anxiously watch the gradual processes of surrender in the shell-shocked, fatigued and distraught countries that once held morality and honor so high in the councils of the leading powers of the world.

THE EUROPE WE DON'T KNOW

JULY 9, 1954

Report on Impressions Derived
From a Recent Trip to Europe

I WENT TO GENEVA with the primary idea of finding out, if I could, whether there was any kind of "give" in the East-West situation—whether the Russians could be dealt with on any reasonable basis. Could the diplomats from our side sit down, for instance, and, in the parlance of business, "make a deal," even though the word "deal" has an unfortunate connotation? Could there be a basis of "give and take," notwithstanding the tension in the world? Was there anything that would lead us to believe, if we conceded "X," maybe they would concede "Y"?

International meetings are unique in that they encourage the interplay of powerful influences. Delegations from 19 nations fraternized at Geneva, as did members of the press from many countries. And two sets of adversaries sat down together formally and informally for several weeks. There were opportunities to fathom the other fellow's mind and to learn whether there was any resiliency in his point of view.

Nothing is all-black or all-white, so oversimplification is sometimes a temptation. As a result of my studies, I wouldn't say there is no "give" at all in the situation, nor would I say there is any reasonable hope of reaching any kind of agreement in the near future.

The Perspective of Time

In order to understand that sort of paradoxical statement, the background of European affairs has to be carefully considered. The European mind—not just the Soviet mind—functions differently than ours. We are a relatively new nation, we are successful in industrial achievements, we feel the pulse of our progress every minute, and we want things to happen quickly.

Europe, on the other hand, has seen the ups and downs of international policy through the centuries and is a little bit more complacent and less impulsive than we are. Therefore, time makes a difference. We, on our part, would like to settle this whole international situation in a month or two—or in a year perhaps. The perspective over there is more likely to be 10 years, 20 years or 50 years.

Perhaps the most disconcerting impression that I derived from my recent visit abroad was the confirmation of what I found two years ago—the weakness of both Britain and France morale-wise and on the economic side. This has a decided bearing on what our attitude should be toward Europe. It raises the big question of what and how much we should do when our friends are in trouble.

Sometimes people in America say: "Well, we paid a lot of money to keep those countries on our side, and they haven't stayed bought."

This is an affront to the peoples of Europe. For the situation there in respect to the will to fight hasn't much to do with dollars. The dollars we have sent abroad were important. They are still important. They have to do with the complex economic mechanism which has to put each country on a sound basis so that there will be employment—any kind of equilibrium at all. But the basic factors that give a nation its spirit are psychological, and not merely economic, though they both contribute to the mood of the times.

We little realize that World War I took out of France and Great Britain the flower of the manhood of their respective countries. We little realize, also, that the Second World War took away much of the replacement and that the generations which are there today—outwardly trying to make believe they are as strong as before—actually have a lessened morale which is noticeable. The "glories" of a great past are swept aside in a tidal wave of cynicism that is perhaps a characteristic effect of the bombings suffered in the last war.

The truth is there are no first-class powers in the world today except the United States and Soviet Russia. This must be said not in a spirit of pride so far as we are concerned, but more in the spirit of tragedy.

If you look that fact in the face, the conclusion is inescapable that, while you cannot always get as much cooperation from allies as you wish, you cannot afford, on the other hand, to lose them or take the kind of position that will make them more and more dispirited and depressed.

Why Russia Is Confident

As for the Soviets, a very pragmatic philosophy governs their behavior. They see themselves militarily stronger than any of the other countries. They know they are stronger than Germany because they have a

76

substantial part of its territory. They might not be so self-confident if Germany were unified. The Communists, however, do hold 20,000,000 Germans in East Germany as hostages, and the prewar German domestic market is seriously impaired.

Britain, of course, is not the empire it was. Its dominions have more economic independence than before. The old days of an English monopoly in empire trade are gone. New competition for the British has arisen in Asia where India and neighboring countries are trying to live their own lives.

The Soviets, seeing the picture of a fluctuating Western Alliance—seeing particularly the military weaknesses—have come to feel that they are on top now, and they are determined to have their way in both Europe and Asia.

What Is "Communist Imperialism"?

It is a little bit puzzling sometimes to analyze what the Russian objectives may be, because we ourselves have a tendency to oversimplify, and lots of us have emphasized only the phrase, "Communist imperialism." But this is really a combination of the old Russian imperialism and Communist dogmatism. The Kremlin wants everything that the Czars wanted from the Arctic to the Mediterranean and from the Middle East to the Pacific. But this imperialism now includes a crusade for worldwide Communism which, under the guise of offering more opportunities for the average man in a classless society, would destroy every free government that stands in the way of Communist ambitions. We see, therefore, Soviet influence spreading out in a number of satellite countries in Europe and Asia through the use of a new weapon—propaganda and subversion.

We hear often the theory that all this is only a "battle of ideas" in the world. That's an oversimplification, too. When you look at the millions of people who live in Asia, at their poverty and their illiteracy and their lack of the means of internal communication that we possess, and you hear some of our friends saying, "You have to meet this with ideas," it should be asked, "Who is going to read about these ideas and how are they going to be distributed?"

The only thing that can influence Asia profoundly today is an improvement in its economic condition. This the Asian people will not get from the Soviet Government. The Communists may keep on promising the moon, but they never yet have improved the economic conditions of any neighboring country in their orbit.

It is not, therefore, a battle of ideas alone. It is a battle between good and evil, between imperialism and freedom, between starvation and survival. But behind it all is the intrigue and political infiltration which de-

ceives the people in backward countries as well as their bewildered leaders.

The Communists have captivated many of the intellectuals in these areas, and those people will not be converted by some high-sounding words on our part about how we are going to meet these ideas with ideas.

Neutralizing the Super-bombs

This battle will require not only ingenuity on the idea side, but it must necessarily have a material or economic as well as a military support. You must, of course, bring moral force to bear as well, and this means psychological factors. But basically military force is the most essential of all. It is vital for self-protection. Let me illustrate:

Many of us think that the next world war is going to be an atomic war. This has been dinned into our ears for many months now, and the news reports of civil-defense rehearsals underline the prospect. But suppose it is not an atomic war. It may very well be a non-atomic war, or a war mostly with conventional weapons.

The Soviets know we have a bigger quantity of bombs and atomic material than they have. Suppose they announce that they would never drop an atomic bomb on United States territory or anywhere else, for that matter—even after a war starts—unless an atomic bomb were first thrown at them. Suppose, also, they say that, if an atomic bomb or an H-bomb is dropped on Soviet territory by the United States, they will drop an H-bomb on London, Paris and Rome and on other big cities of our allies?

Such an announcement in advance of a war would almost insure the neutrality of our allies in Europe in their present state of mind, unless we agreed to the proposal not to use the super-bomb. For our allies want to avoid an atomic war, and you cannot convince some people that death by bombs is to be preferred to survival under any kind of system, even the Communist system.

This is a practical, realistic phase of the matter which I do not think we have taken into account. The French people lived for four years under the Nazi occupation and survived, and hence the idea of a Communist occupation does not evoke half the terror for them as the mere talk of destruction by atomic bombs seems to convey today.

So you have the possibility that—not by agreement, but by neutralization or by mutual self-restraint, as in the case of poison gas or germ warfare—neither side will use super-bombs. It is significant that the most powerful propaganda unleashed by the Soviet Government all over the world in recent months has been a demand that the H-bomb be outlawed. The motive is apparent.

Our military men are insistent that if a war starts we will use every weapon in the arsenal. But they do not decide these policies. Political leaders in London and Paris and Washington make those decisions. Safety requires that we prepare, therefore, for every contingency, including the prospect that we may be forced to fight alone if France and Britain are neutral and including also the possibility that—if we want to keep our European allies—we might find it expedient to agree, from a political rather than a military standpoint, to the neutralization of the super-bombs.

This means that ground warfare may predominate. The question then arises whether we have adequate military power for a war fought along these lines. Where are we going to get additional manpower? There must be more allies and more contributions from our present allies if we are to have enough manpower. We must seek more allies in Asia as well as in Europe.

Manpower on Our Side

If you look at a military map nowadays and note where our allied forces are stationed, you will see there is a defense ring around the Soviet Union. Starting in the Far East we have a good army in South Korea consisting of 300,000 or more Koreans well equipped and well trained. This Korean Army is helping to hold in check a million Red Chinese in North Korea.

We have Nationalist Chinese allies on Formosa— 400,000 to 500,000 trained soldiers—who are holding another million Red Chinese in fixed positions across the straits on the mainland. There is in the Philippines an army allied with us and we can count on additional forces in Australia and New Zealand. Japan is a big potential. In Southeast Asia there are the beginnings of a build-up of more military power and more alliances.

We have staunch armies allied with us in Pakistan, in Greece and Turkey and in Yugoslavia. We have the NATO armies in Europe, with a line drawn from Norway at the Arctic Circle, down through Germany— another big potential—to the Mediterranean, where big naval fleets are concentrated nowadays.

But there must be a further mobilization of ground troops across Asia and the Near East. Let us not overlook Africa as a source of manpower. The record of its soldiers in both world wars was outstanding.

I believe, of course, in the "new look" and everything it implies by way of an assumption that we must be prepared to fight an atomic war. But, in addition to that, we must have some sure means of fighting a conventional war if political considerations in the world force us into that kind of dilemma. It involves larger appropriations and more expenditures in order to build and equip bigger armies, but we can meet them if we must.

Manpower can be found abroad. There are lots of places in this world where many young men imbued with a national spirit will serve in an army and take the necessary training. That is true particularly in Asia, where millions and millions of persons starve to death every year. The old-fashioned method of building armies should not be abandoned in this shaky world. We must prepare for the unexpected. The memory of the kind of war we had to fight in Korea is recent enough to make us realize that the enemy does not always fight a war the way you expect him to fight it.

So far as making deals are concerned, or negotiating with the Soviet Union, that time will not come until there is military strength on our side, not necessarily of a threatening but of a balancing nature. We know that the Soviets are impressed by military strength.

But we must not neglect coincidentally to set in motion psychological influences that can affect masses of people. Nobody knows how far we can penetrate into the Soviet backyard with psychological programs until we try them. Yet, at the same time, I think we have been all too tolerant of what the other fellow has been doing in our backyard. We discovered suddenly a few weeks ago that he had been sending shipments of munitions to Guatemala and stirring up neighboring countries. We seemed surprised, as if this was a new thing. But that is what the Communists have been doing in all parts of the world with other forms of penetration, not necessarily munitions.

The Smokescreen of "Colonialism"

The Communists are fomenting trouble on every continent. While it is true that nationalism has a great deal of momentum on its own in all the colonial areas where disturbances have occurred, this momentum has been accelerated by the infiltration of the Communists. A lot of the talk about independence and colonialism is a smokescreen because, as important as it is to give peoples their freedom, it is more important that they shall be able to keep it when they get it.

What good would it do to give the three states of Indo-China—Laos, Cambodia and Vietnam—complete independence tomorrow and cut them off from all ties with the French Union if the next day the Soviet Government were to move in and take over, not necessarily with troops but by the tactics of subversive infiltration at which they are so adept? The Communists would then control those helpless governments, just as completely as they do the governments of Czechoslovakia, Bulgaria, Rumania and Poland.

So far as our own Government's foreign policy is concerned, we have been subjected to a great deal of criticism. There is a tendency abroad among some Americans always to blame their own government. Much of this is political because the repercussions of partisan speeches from the United States do reach foreign countries, too.

I said to some of my American friends abroad: "What's wrong? We have been trying to do our job in the world. We have no desire for colonies. We don't want any territory. We are guided primarily by the wishes of our allies. We propose plan after plan, and often they say they don't want to do it that way. All we can do is ask them, and they can tell us what they want. We have not been bludgeoning anybody. The plan for the European Defense Army, for example, was entirely a French concept. Then when we took it up and supported it, we were accused of trying to force something on the French."

We have not been at fault in our policy toward Europe. There has been a consistent and persistent effort on the part of our Government since 1945 to do in Europe what an enlightened leadership would naturally seek to do in a postwar era. We have made mistakes—particularly in Asia, and they were serious mistakes. That story is a tragic one. But we have steered the right course in Europe.

Now as to the billions of dollars which the United States has spent abroad, some of it has been wasted, but I believe the bulk of it has been used constructively. For we have managed to maintain a kind of economic equilibrium in Britain and France and Italy. We have saved Greece and Turkey for the free world. It has cost a great deal, but it has been worthwhile. The disintegration of those countries in an economic sense would, on the other hand, have meant a greater burden for us in the long run.

Views of British and French Premiers

I had the pleasure of lunching with Sir Winston Churchill at 10 Downing Street and we talked for more than an hour on a variety of subjects. Much of what was said about relations with the United States has since been reflected in public statements by the Prime Minister on his recent visit to Washington. From all my talks with various officials in Great Britain, I formed the impression that there is in London no clearer idea as to what should be done in the world than there is anywhere else. There is no exact formula. So much is dependent upon what Russia intends to do. It takes only one side to disturb the peace or to upset the most peaceful intentions of the other side. We are, therefore, feeling our way. But I believe that, despite all the publicity about differences between Great Britain and America, we will stick together.

I spent an hour with M. Mendès-France, now Premier of France. We talked at his home in Paris on every phase of the European situation. His approach is sincere and realistic. He feels that France is weak internationally because it is weak internally. It is true that internal reforms in France have long been neglected. The war in Indo-China, moreover, takes too

much money out of the French budget. America has been helping a good deal, but the portion that the French are spending outside of France is too big for their resources. The new French Premier has a feeling that a domestic reform program of an economic nature, undertaken now, could build a stronger France.

"Quarantining" the Communists

During the two months that I spent in Europe, I found little disagreement with the thesis that the Soviet Union is determined to impose its ideology and its control over the rest of the world.

Sooner or later, some nation or group of nations will have to stand up and stop the march of Communist despotism. I don't believe we actually have to go to war to stop it. But I do believe we will have to make sacrifices and take calculated risks. I do believe we will have to make up our minds to "quarantine" the Communists behind the Iron Curtain.

We must stop the flow of their money to Soviet agents everywhere in the world. They could not have done the things they have done in Guatemala and Egypt and Tunisia and elsewhere except with money supplied from Moscow. If this were a hot war, we certainly would not be trading across the boundary, and there wouldn't be any money coming into countries on our side from Russia either. Soviet gold is flowing across the Iron Curtain boundary right into our own ranks and helping to finance trouble. Someday we must come to the point of saying that this infiltration will have to stop. A lot can be done by counter-measures without going to war.

The possibility of war is discussed abroad on every side. Unfortunately, we are accused by some Europeans and Asians of wanting to make war. I don't mean that we are really thought to be warmongers, but there is a fear that we may be impulsive and get our allies into a war which they want to avoid at all costs.

When the newspapers in the United States were discussing a possible military intervention in Indo-China, the discussion may not have done any harm in America, but the nervousness inside Germany, for example, was noticeable. They said, "If America goes into Indo-China, maybe this is the time Russia will decide to go into Germany."

There is a nervousness in Europe about any move on our part, whether big or little. The H-bomb tests caused shivers of apprehension because the military significance of such tests is well understood. One of the reasons Europeans were so glad the Korean war was over was because they thought there would be more military power available to bolster the defense of Europe.

Our task is, however, global. Our military forces are widely dispersed in both Europe and Asia. It is up to us to bring about a wide dispersal of the Russian forces so they cannot concentrate in Europe.

The only way that wars can be prevented is to prepare to meet all contingencies ahead of time with a balanced force. The time to have prevented World War II was in 1936 when Hitler marched into the Rhineland or in the years when we were discussing the Italian aggression in Ethiopia and the oil sanctions that were never applied by members of the League of Nations against Mussolini.

History Repeats Itself?

We are going through a similar experience now, when a firm attitude can prevent a big war. If in a few years we should have such a war, we will be saying regretfully, "In 1954, at the time of the Indo-China affair, was when we should have been firm and decisive."

Yet American public opinion has looked upon the Indo-China controversy as something remote, though it has a direct meaning for the American people because a wrong policy now can encourage Soviet aggression elsewhere in the world.

The only compass we can steer by is moral principle. We must take the risks that are involved—building up sufficient strength to defend our moral principle, so that the enemy will not have any doubts whatsoever about our intentions.

The Russians have two strategies. One is to win the war without themselves being participants in the fighting, and the other is to win the war with the least amount of fighting.

But today they are rather confident that eventually they will be able to control both France and Italy without a war. They are making a lot of headway. They have in the French Parliament 100 members of the Communist Party who hold the balance of power. They have a substantial strength in Italy. If they can control Italy, they can weaken Yugoslovia.

We should be looking at this whole problem of strategy through Soviet eyes. We in America are fearful that the United States will suffer a sudden attack.

Yet the Soviet mind is working toward capturing Europe, the biggest prize of all. If they can do that and use European resources, they might tackle us a few years later on. They wouldn't, therefore, provoke us first into a retaliatory attack. There is no doubt that a great many of their planes would be intercepted in a war against us. The results from our "massive retaliation" would be terrible for them. Why, then, should they run that risk, particularly when they think they can win on another battlefield? In war you choose your own battlefield if you can, and not the other fellow's.

Patience with Allies

What offsetting moves could we make to prevent the Soviets from moving in on France and Italy? When the battle front is 3,000 miles away, you must do everything to build up that battle front in advance. You must strengthen it in an economic sense as well as in a moral and spiritual sense. You must help to build the morale of your allies, and that means you must be patient with allies. You cannot coerce—you must coax, and convince.

You must show your friends always that you are with them wholeheartedly. Otherwise their situation disintegrates before your eyes.

Europeans, despite everything said to the contrary in speeches or newspapers that criticize us, are well aware of our industrial and military might and look to us for leadership, though reserving the right to disregard that leadership every now and then when their national viewpoints conflict with ours.

It is, to be sure, a trying time for the Western Alliance, but it will be kept together by a common danger, which at present shows no signs of dissolving.

Tension will continue for a long time. Nothing is hopeless, nothing is inevitable, nothing is certain. And all of us have a chance to influence the course of events, notwithstanding the rather discouraging circumstances that constantly beset us.

THE UN'S OPPORTUNITY

JULY 16, 1954

THE UNITED NATIONS has an opportunity to do more toward the establishment of world peace by its debate over the admission of Red China than has been possible in any of the discussions during all the nine years of its existence as an international forum.

No more realistic words have been spoken about the true nature of the U. N. than those of President Eisenhower who last week at his press conference said:

"The United Nations was not established primarily as a supergovernment, clothed with all the authority of supergovernment and of great power to do things. It was, among other things, an attempt to marshal the moral strength of the world in order to preserve peace, to make certain that quarrels were composed through a decent respect for justice and fairness and right, and to see whether we couldn't avoid resort to force."

The U. N. was never intended to be an enforcement body. The one conspicuous instance in which it essayed that role was in 1950 by intervention in Korea. But what did the use of military force in Korea by 16 members of the United Nations prove? It demonstrated that the international organization would not as a whole act in concert to enforce peace and that only certain members would send their troops to back up the ideals and principles of the U. N. Indeed, Soviet Russia defiantly aided the aggressor by sending it munitions.

This series of events confirmed the wisdom of the authors of Article 51 of the Charter of the United Nations which says that any group of nations may organize alliances separately for their common defense without violating the charter itself. Under that article the North Atlantic Treaty Organization was formed and regional alliances like the Organization of American States were brought into lawful being.

So what the Charter really does is to make the United Nations the central forum for the mobilization of moral force in the world. It will not enforce peace by military means and it will not act as a supergovernment attempting to lay down laws for the governing of the affairs of its members. It will continue to be like the League of Nations, a federation of sovereign states.

But having limited its military orbit the fact remains that there are no limitations on the use of moral force. This, indeed, is the key to peace in a distraught world. For with the growing awareness of the futility of military force alone to solve the disputes of the world, the strengthening of the role of moral force becomes of far-reaching importance.

This is not to say that moral force is a complete substitute and that military force should be excluded. On the contrary pacifism and non-resistance are impractical and there comes a time when the combined use of the vehicles of moral force and military force can bring peace to the world—always with the hope that the possession of adequate military defenses against potential aggressors will act as a deterrent and give moral force a chance effectively to influence the minds of the peoples behind aggressor governments.

The debate over admitting Red China to the Security Council of the U. N. is salutary. It is desirable that all points of view be expressed. For the issue is a simple one: shall the moral force of the United Nations be weakened by a willingness to barter admission to the U. N. of Red China in exchange for some material gain such as world trade?

The London *Times* says: "British public opinion looks at the problem of Peiping's admission to the United Nations as one of law and not of morals." Does this mean that we take refuge in legalisms because we do not have the courage to defend moral principles?

The United Nations by formal resolution declared Red China's government an aggressor. Nothing has happened to show that the aggressor has purged himself of his sin and is capable of adhering to the moral standards required of members.

It is not necessary at this time to decide, as the President so wisely has stated, whether the United States should withdraw from the U. N. if Red China is voted in by the majority of other members.

What is important is to let the whole world know now the moral issues and if in the face of these there are governments which wish to disregard moral law and rationalize such disregard on the grounds of expediency then membership in the United Nations will not be worth the paper it is written on. So far as moral force is concerned, the organization itself would fall into disuse without raising the technical issue of America's presence or absence in such a discredited body.

But if the United Nations exhibits a due regard for moral issues, its position will be enhanced throughout the world. The Communist governments will see themselves and their propaganda stymied in the court of world opinion even as the peoples of the Communist countries are encouraged by such a universal display of moral courage.

It is a great opportunity for the United Nations.

"PEACEFUL CO-EXISTENCE"

JULY 23, 1954

"PEACEFUL CO-EXISTENCE" will now become the euphemistic phrase to be substituted for "cold war." Prime Minister Churchill and President Eisenhower have each defined "peaceful co-existence" in their own way. And while they both accept the general principle of a peaceful effort to reduce the tension in the world, they differ somewhat as to how and where the principle shall be applied.

Briefly, "peaceful co-existence" means "live and let live." It could, therefore, mean acceptance of the *status quo* in the world, with an implied pledge not to do anything to disturb the existing hold by the Communists on weaker nations.

On this point, however, the Churchill-Eisenhower declaration, issued after their recent meeting and sometimes called the "Potomac Charter," says:

"As regards formerly sovereign states now in bondage, we will not be a party to any arrangement or treaty which would confirm or prolong their unwilling subordination."

The President, when asked in his press conference the next day for an interpretation of that paragraph, authorized this quotation: "I will not be a party to any treaty that makes anybody a slave."

A concrete situation has just arisen in the Indo-China negotiations which will challenge the validity of those words. Under the proposed "settlement," all foreign troops are to be withdrawn from Cambodia and Laos, while Vietnam is to undergo a military partition such as is already in effect in Korea.

Mr. Eisenhower, it will be recalled, in a letter to Syngman Rhee last year before the Korean armistice was signed, said that the United States would not advocate the use of force to bring about the unification of any of the divided territories of the world—either Germany or Korea.

Now in Indo-China another 10,000,000 people are to be added to those under Communist bondage. But the United States, although not agreeing to any "arrangement" which involves a permanent partition of Vietnam, is nevertheless stymied in any attempts to attain unification except by the persistent application of moral force.

Soon, therefore, we will have three major areas in the world—Germany, Korea and Southeast Asia—where the Communist aggressor, through no legal right of his own but solely through the exercise of military pressure, will have obtained control of large amounts of territory.

"Peaceful co-existence" could mean that the free world is resigned indefinitely to the idea of letting the Communists maintain their control over hundreds of millions of people who live in bondage.

But, on the other hand, the words of the "Potomac Charter" imply also that Great Britain and the United States are obligated to continue unremittingly their efforts to encourage the hopes of the peoples of all the countries behind the Iron Curtain so that some day the millions of slaves will be able to achieve for themselves the emancipation they deserve.

Most vital now for the formulation of policy on all such questions is the unity of the free world. Prime Minister Churchill told the House of Commons last week that, while he does not advocate admission of Red China into the United Nations "at the moment," he does favor such a move perhaps in the next year or so.

"Peaceful co-existence" must not be construed to mean admission of Red China into the United Nations until the government at Peiping has been completely purged of its war crime against the U. N. itself and until free elections have been held in all of China so that a government may arise which is capable of discharging its international obligations.

"Peaceful co-existence" should never mean assent, tacit or otherwise, to the policy of the criminal rulers in Soviet Russia or anywhere else to continue their enslavement of hundreds of millions of persons.

These are not legalistic but moral issues. In some of our cities, for example, there has been at times a tendency to accept the gangster domination of certain districts, thus sanctioning a kind of "peaceful co-existence." But an aroused citizenry has usually in the end refused to tolerate any such partnership with evil. This is the inexorable working of moral law.

For there can be no "co-existence" between slavery and freedom. Abraham Lincoln expressed it aptly nearly 100 years ago when he said that America could not "endure permanently half slave and half free."

So it is with the world of today. Our hearts must go out constantly to the enslaved peoples behind the Iron Curtain. We must pledge ourselves to use every measure short of war to encourage their self-liberation. We must never accept any part of a "co-existence" doctrine which would discourage the millions of persons now in bondage as they look to the free world for moral help and inspiration. There can be no "peaceful co-existence" with Satan.

CONSCIENCE TAKES A HOLIDAY

JULY 30, 1954

ONCE AGAIN, as at Munich in 1938, the democratic governments of Britain and France have compromised their honor and made an abject surrender on the altar of expediency.

For the Geneva agreement on Indo-China is no settlement. It is an appeasement. It is an act of moral cowardice. It will cost the governments who signed it more in prestige throughout the world than they ever will gain by their transparent attempt to glorify what they have just done as a step toward a so-called "peace." Indeed, it may involuntarily bring on in the end the large war that the truce was designed to avoid.

For, despite the soothing words uttered for diplomatic reasons last week by our own officials—who, to their credit, refused to sign the agreement—the fact remains that it is a shameful chapter in the annals of free governments.

On April 28 last, at the opening of the Geneva Conference, Secretary Dulles warned his colleagues as follows:

"Peace is always easy to achieve—by surrender. Unity is also easy to achieve—by surrender. The hard task, the task that confronts us, is to combine peace and unity with freedom."

We have just witnessed the surrender of 12 million persons to Communist rule, with the prospect of another 11 million going the same route in a few months.

Neither peace nor unity nor freedom is in store for the peoples of Indo-China.

For a long time we have heard the specious cry that the real issue in Indo-China was French colonialism, even though the granting of full independence for the three states of Indo-China has actually been under way.

Now these same states must bow to Communist colonialism. As for "independence," they will get the kind of independence that has come to Poland, Czechoslovakia, Bulgaria, Rumania, Hungary, Latvia, Estonia and Lithuania—the living examples of modern slavery.

The Government of France engineered the surrender. The French Parliament is plagued by a bloc of 100 Communists who apparently care more about Soviet Russia than they do about France. They wouldn't even rise in tribute recently to the heroes of Dienbienphu when all the other members stood in respect for the dead.

It was the "left-wing" in Paris which forced the liquidation of the Indo-China war. No Cabinet could stand if it refused to accept defeat in Indo-China.

A "fifth column" brought about the surrender of France in 1940, and "fifth column" influences accomplished the surrender of Indo-China by the French in 1954.

Here is a classic example in which the fate of freedom in the world for millions of innocent persons is decided by the "peace at any price" politicians of one country. America stood ready to aid, even with military force, but the French defeatists wouldn't agree to make the issue international, as it was in Korea. Even though this had been done, it might have been futile. For a veto by France against the use of maximum military power by the Allied commanders would have been in effect, and American lives might have been wantonly sacrificed. It is pertinent to recall that the obstinate refusal of the British and French governments in 1950 to let General MacArthur bomb bases in Manchuria led in 1953 to the ignominious truce forced upon the United States in Korea.

The American Government in its Indo-China policy has been consistent and honorable throughout, but it could not itself veto a unilateral decision of the French Cabinet.

Political expediency rules the day. "Peace at any price" has been substituted in Europe for honorable persistence in behalf of the moral law of mankind.

This can only embolden the aggressors and cause them to risk a try at further encroachment.

It can only weaken confidence everywhere in the leadership of the Western Alliance.

It can only drive into the orbit of the Communist coalition those smaller countries of Asia whose co-operation in the defense of that area against Communist aggression is so vitally important.

It can only stimulate Moscow to complete the wreckage at Paris of the European Defense Community.

It can only cause many millions of Americans to lose faith in the sincerity of the British and French governments and to urge an "agonizing reappraisal" of American foreign policy.

It can only cause many of us to wonder whether American troops now based overseas may be subjected to a sudden jeopardy by a fateful turn in the policies of some volatile French Cabinet of the future.

It can only cause a political upheaval inside West Germany, where a movement to appease Soviet Russia is already under way.

For tragedy inevitably follows tragedy when moral principle is abandoned and conscience takes a holiday.

A GREAT LAW

AUGUST 6, 1954

FOR THREE-QUARTERS OF A CENTURY no law has been passed to revise generally the revenue-raising procedures of our Federal Government.

Circumstances have changed substantially in that period, affecting the ways of doing business and the everyday lives of individuals.

Yet antiquated provisions of law have remained on the statute books, piling inequity upon inequity.

What the Congress has just done is to establish principles of fair play as between the Government and the taxpayer. The new law is not perfect—it still fails to cure certain inequities. But it is such a far-reaching improvement upon existing law and does so much to give a square deal to the taxpayer that it must be hailed as one of the most constructive pieces of legislation of our times.

An effort to revise the tax laws has been made again and again without success. Too often the sessions of Congress have concerned themselves with scales of rates, and each time the administrative provisions have been shunted aside.

A vast amount of work has been done on these matters by the tax experts of previous administrations, and the tax authorities have pooled their accumulated experience to make the new law what it is—a balanced application of the principles of fairness and non-discrimination.

It isn't fair, for instance, for a man who has built up a business to find that his heirs will have to sell it to get the money with which to pay estate taxes.

It isn't fair to deny a working mother the benefit of a tax deduction, as a "business expense," for paying someone to take care of her children, when a business can deduct the expense incurred by a salesman in entertaining a customer.

There are thousands of points such as these which are covered in the new law. But there are many more that remain for future action by Congress.

Perhaps the most outstanding characteristic of the new measure is the encouragement it gives the system of private enterprise.

Incentive is the key word in the American system. While the Government needs adequate revenue to pay its expenses, it must not depart from the true function of taxation by trying to apply the socialist doctrine of "share the wealth." In other words, the Government's policy should never be "reform for reform's sake." It should never penalize success or discourage thrift.

Yet some of these very inequities have been foisted upon the taxpayer by the demagogues whose thinking is far closer to Moscow concepts than it is to the principles of free enterprise that have built up the American economic system.

For Communism isn't always just a philosophy tied to the Soviet Government. There are loyal and patriotic Americans who misguidedly would do things by law to communize or socialize the American system in pursuance of a theory of government whose dangerous implications they fail to perceive.

The new law belatedly, for example, recognizes the viciousness of double taxation. For the first time dividends have a partial exemption from tax.

To their discredit, be it said that there were many Democrats in Congress who sought to make a demagogic dispute out of this. They fought the revision as "relief for the rich." But if they make such an issue in the coming campaign, it will not be an unmixed blessing. For the American people ought to become informed at last on the true facts of this controversy.

A man, for example, has an idea, builds a business, creates jobs for others, and his incorporated company pays now a 52 per cent tax on all profits. Then the money which the enterprising head of the business gets out of it himself is taxed over again as "income." This double taxation is unfair, especially since another man who is a lawyer or a doctor or in some other profession pays only one tax.

To raise money to expand a business requires the other fellow's capital—his savings after years of toil. He has already paid taxes on those savings, but he has been taxed a second time on the income from the same money when he risks its investment to help build a business enterprise.

The new law doesn't give much relief on dividend payments, but at least it recognizes the concept that double taxation is unfair. The late President Roosevelt was against this double taxation but he and his party never had the courage to do what President Eisenhower and a Republican Congress have just done.

The new statute should stimulate confidence in business, especially the new clauses liberalizing allowances for the wear and tear of machinery and tools.

These changes will permit the necessary capital to be raised to expand America's plant to meet the needs of a growing population. It is a landmark in legislative progress. For the new tax law is truly a great law.

LEADER OR DICTATOR?

AUGUST 13, 1954

SOME PEOPLE look upon the President of the United States as a kind of boss of the whole Government, with power to order Congress and even the Supreme Court to adopt whatever policies he wishes.

This illusory concept is probably due to the craving for an easy way to achieve legislative discipline in a democracy. Even some prominent citizens not long ago signed a petition asking the President to regulate the activities of committees of Congress and arbitrarily to punish members thereof unless they conformed to standards he would prescribe.

Despite our excellent schools and colleges, there is a widespread lack of understanding of the simplest facts about our constitutional system.

President Eisenhower himself revealed recently that some citizens had written him demanding that he remove a certain Senator from office. This may not be as far-fetched as it sounds, because two Presidents of the United States—Franklin D. Roosevelt and Harry Truman—tried unsuccessfully in party primaries to "purge" Congress of those members who did not vote consistently for some of their legislative proposals.

The people resented the intrusion of a President in their local affairs—his usurpation of the right to tell the voters who should represent them.

Failure to support the party's nominees after a primary election would be an act of political stupidity on the part of any President, and yet Mr. Eisenhower is being importuned to withhold support from any member of Congress whose voting record on public questions is not satisfactory to the White House staff. This is "conformity of thought" with a vengeance.

It may be asked whether the proponents of such a strategy realize that they may be forfeiting to the Democratic Party the control of Congress in the next election. For if the White House rejects a Republican nominee for Senator or declines to endorse someone chosen in a Republican primary to run for a seat in the House of Representatives, this is equivalent to saying that the President would not mind seeing a Democrat elected in that particular State or district. Yet defeat of only two such Republicans could make the difference between Republican and Democratic Party control of the House and Senate. Would Mr. Eisenhower be entitled to the respect of his party if, by any act of omission or commission, he caused his own party to lose control of Congress during the second half of his Administration?

The loss of control means, of course, a loss to the Republicans of all committee chairmanships. The minority leader of the Senate—a Democrat—would then become the majority leader. He certainly would not be sympathetic to the Administration's legislative program.

The school of thought which has been plaguing Mr. Eisenhower to exert "leadership" not only has been arguing for a "strong arm" attitude toward Congress as a whole but has needled him into fights with members of his own party. Persons around him with more zeal than political sense have dragged the President into the position of trying to "purge" such members.

The concept that a President is a leader rather than a dictator is ingrained in America's constitutional system. The Constitution explicitly vests certain powers in the Congress and certain powers in the Presidency. No authority is given the President to select or dismiss any member of Congress, nor has he the right to impose his judgment as to the kind of rules either house should adopt for the performance of its constitutional functions.

No such interference with the freedom of thought of members of a coordinate branch of the government would probably be considered by Dwight Eisenhower if he were being properly briefed on the American political tradition. For he is one of the kindliest and fairest men who ever sat in the White House. But while he concedes his unfamiliarity with "politics," he continues to take advice from a staff which is too often goaded by the so-called "liberal" newspapers and leftist groups. And despite their pleas of disinterestedness, they do not have at heart the future welfare of the Republican Party. Mr. Eisenhower sometimes seems like a prisoner of his inexperience, but this doesn't excuse his failure to consult those who do have experience.

It would be a sad day for America if the totalitarian instinct which somehow creeps into "the end justifies the means" attitudes of many a protagonist today should lead to an acceptance of the dangerous concept that presidential leadership permits the exercise of quasi-dictatorial powers over Congress.

Leadership in ideas and in the advocacy of principles is, of course, a presidential prerogative. But if pressure is further extended by future Executives as they apply the precedents being established nowadays, our Congress could ultimately go the way the Reichstag did under Hitler. The House and Senate must remain independent of any form of coercion by the Executive. The people of each State alone must choose the members of both houses of Congress.

A STRANGE CONTRAST

AUGUST 20, 1954

MESSRS. ATTLEE AND BEVAN of the British Labor Party are hobnobbing these days with the Communist imperialists at Moscow and Peiping.

British labor leaders are forsaking their brethren inside the Communist countries whose trade unions have been suppressed. The slave-labor camps and the suffering of the workers are apparently no longer the concern of British labor chieftains, who are falling for the same deceptive strategy of the aggressor which has led to two world wars.

Labor leaders of the United States take the opposite view. Here are excerpts from a statement just issued by the Executive Council of the American Federation of Labor after a three-day meeting:

"If Moscow were sincere in its revival of this maneuver ['co-existence'], devised by Lenin in 1920 in order to gain time for preparing the final assault on the democracies, it would first of all liquidate its activities aimed against the existence of those with whom it claims to seek 'co-existence.' These fifth column activities, directed by the Kremlin, have but one aim—to subvert, overthrow, and replace the governments with which the U.S.S.R. is supposed to be at peace or even has special treaties of alliance and friendship. These Communist activities are a form of indirect, but nonetheless infernal, Soviet aggression—fatal to the freedom and national independence of big as well as small nations (China, Czechoslovakia). Before there could ever be co-existence, conducive to the peace and well-being of all mankind, the Soviet dictatorship would have to fulfill certain conditions. Let the U.S.S.R. go back to the borders of 1939 (pre-Stalin-Hitler pact). Let the Kremlin accept U.N.-supervised democratic elections in all areas of tension (Germany, Korea). Let Moscow agree to the actual banning of atomic and hydrogen weapons through effective international inspection and control.

"The Executive Council of the American Federation of Labor rejects the notion that the free world must choose between 'co-existence'—the policy of successive or massive appeasement of the Soviet aggressors—and a policy of waging a preventive war against the Moscow-Peiping axis. We sincerely want peace with freedom. We, therefore, reject both of these policies. The policy of 'co-existence' can lead only to another world war—under conditions in which the democracies would, morally, materially, and militarily be far less able to resist, let alone defeat, the Communist enemy.

"Instead of helping the Communist dictatorship to overcome the serious economic and political difficulties now besetting the Soviet orbit, instead of providing these totalitarian aggressors with the commodities and credit they need for strengthening and streamlining their already powerful and dangerous war machines, let the democracies pursue a positive program to aid freedom and peace through building up their own unity and ever greater strength. The Executive Council of the AFL proposes that this program should have among its guiding lines the following measures:

"1. Complete rearmament—military, economic, political and social—adequate enough to discourage and defeat Communist subversion and aggression against the free nations of all continents.

"2. Setting of definite time limits for granting independence to the colonial and semi-colonial peoples, as the U. S. did in the Philippine Islands.

"3. Expansion of purchasing power, productivity and trade, and stabilization of the prices of basic raw materials (rubber, tin, etc.) within the free world.

"4. U.N.-supervised democratic elections in all areas of conflict (Germany, Korea, China, Indo-China) in order to reduce international tension and to enable the peoples of these countries to achieve genuine national re-unification in freedom and to select governments which shall enjoy full sovereignty in their foreign as well as domestic affairs.

"5. Rigid and permanent opposition to admitting into U.N. membership the Mao Tse-tung regime or any other government which (a) has been imposed on a nation by a foreign power; (b) which exercises effective control of the country by denying its people the human rights specified in the U.N. Charter; and (c) which is engaged in, or has been found guilty of, aggression against the U.N.

"6. Bilateral non-aggression and mutual-aid pacts between free nations (U. S. and Republic of Korea, Philippines, Nationalist China) until such time as agreements can be reached for organizing a more inclusive collective-security system.

"7. Negotiations for the settlement of international disputes to be conducted through regular diplomatic channels or through the channels of the U.N. with a view of strengthening the U.N. as an instrument of world peace.

"8. Continuous and increased emphasis on advancing the cause of peace through promoting a genuine disarmament program—a practical program carried out in stages, effectively controlled and inspected internationally on both sides of the Iron Curtain."

WHITE FLAG FOR THE U. N.?

AUGUST 27, 1954

MAYBE THE TIME HAS COME to take the blue—which stands for truth and freedom—out of the United Nations flag and leave it just white.

For white is the symbol of surrender.

White is the color that denotes acquiescence and unwillingness to fight any further—a plea for mercy.

Here are some United Press dispatches of last week that tell how the United Nations has failed to live up to its pretense of honor and courage:

"The Defense Department charged that the Chinese Communists are holding 15 U. S. Air Force fliers as 'political prisoners' in violation of international law and the Korean armistice agreement. The pilots were captured during the Korean war . . .

"The Defense Department said that at the Geneva conference the Communists admitted the imprisonment of the 15 'political prisoners.' Their captivity, the Department said, also had been verified by returned prisoners of war, who report that the Communists said the servicemen will be held 'for use as one of the bargaining points to secure Red admission to the United Nations' . . .

"A Defense official disclosed that negotiations have been conducted through 'third parties' during the past year for the release of the airmen and other Americans being held by the Reds. He said the Communist position, in effect, has been: 'Admit us to the United Nations and we will release your men'."

Yet the armistice which was signed by the United Nations command contained a pledge by the Communists that they would give back "all" prisoners.

These same facts have been known to officialdom for many months.

Yet the British Government, a leading member of the U. N., has been urging admission of Red China into the Security Council of the United Nations.

Also, a delegation of members of the British Parliament have been wining and dining with the officials of the Red China Government these last few days after a visit of similar intimacy at Moscow with the high officials of the Soviet Government.

What hope is there for the future of the United Nations when there is such a flagrant disregard of the pledged word and such an indifference by governments like that of Great Britain to the moral value of a signed agreement? Why should a government that has been declared an aggressor now be allowed to join the United Nations when that organization has not even been able to secure respect for the agreements made in its name at Panmunjom?

On top of all this comes a significant statement made by Lu Shu Chang, trade official of the Red China Government, to British reporters at Peiping who have been accompanying the Attlee-Bevan mission. The Red official said:

"We feel that West Germany, Belgium, France and others seem to be more interested in business with China than is Britain. We have imported steel, other metals, machinery and heavy equipment from them. But many British shipping companies have provided the shipping services to bring these goods to China."

Congressional committees have sought the facts. There is no clear-cut record yet available, however, as to what is or is not being done and who has been providing the shipping.

Another United Press dispatch last week from London reports:

"The Ministry of Transport said that no British ships had carried strategic cargoes to Red China at least since March, 1953, when strict new controls were put into effect."

Does this mean that from June, 1950, to March, 1953 —for almost three years of the Korean war—when our young men were sacrificing their lives, the British Government was not obeying the resolution of the U. N. asking its members to refrain from aiding the aggressors?

Plainly the United Nations has not succeeded in influencing its members to refrain from sending important commodities to Red China, nor has it been able to secure in any other way respect for the agreements made with Red China as an outgrowth of the Korean war.

There's an important lesson in all this for American fathers and mothers. Shall they send their sons abroad again to fight in any more wars—in Europe or in Asia—as long as the United Nations or the alliance of free governments fails to stand up for the rights of those who have already fought under the United Nations flag?

Surrender sometimes appears on the surface to be an easy or expedient way out, but in the long run it means death for nations which sanction it. Will the United Nations acquiesce in what Red China is doing, or will it demand the immediate return of these prisoners under penalty of a united action that will shut off commercial and diplomatic intercourse with gangster governments? The time has come to end double-talk and hypocrisy and to act with courage.

WILL HISTORY REPEAT?

SEPTEMBER 10, 1954

THIRTY-FIVE YEARS AGO the United States Senate at the close of World War I refused to ratify the Versailles Treaty which provided for American entry into the League of Nations.

Also, the French and British asked the United States to join them in a special treaty to defend the frontiers of France against Germany. But this treaty was never even voted upon, though President Wilson submitted it to the Senate in 1919.

The viewpoint of the critics of the League of Nations Covenant was that it created a "super-state" and would bind the United States to meddle in Europe's local wars.

Those of us who espoused the cause of the League felt that the United States had no such legal obligation under the treaty but could decide through its own constitutional processes whether any attack on members of the League involved our own national safety.

Throughout the 1920's a surge of nationalism swept America and, despite the reasons which had led us to enter World War I to help "make the world safe for democracy," there was a regrettable swing in America toward aloofness from European affairs.

The disappointment over America's attitude was widespread in Britain and France. The United States was accused of sabotaging the principle of collective security. To this day there are historians, including Prime Minister Churchill, who feel that the failure of the United States to put her moral and military force behind the League of Nations made that institution too weak to stand up against the aggressions of Mussolini and Hitler before World War II.

Today nationalism in France has defeated the European Defense Community agreement—another effort to establish a system of collective security for continental Europe. The opposition in France has come from many members of Parliament who feel that it would create a "super-state." But there are 100 deputies in the same Parliament belonging to the Communist Party, and without their votes the majority to defeat the project could not have been obtained.

It is quite evident that the Communists in the Chamber of Deputies assisted in exploiting the nationalistic spirit which is as fervent in France today as it is in the colonial areas about which we have been hearing so much lately.

America tried to "go it alone" after World War I but was nevertheless drawn into World War II.

If France tries to "go it alone" now, there will be no collective defense which can effectively stop the aggressor in Europe. Will this not help to bring on World War III?

The suggestion that Germany be permitted to rearm and be given membership in the North Atlantic Treaty Organization is widely advocated. But is French public opinion in its present mood ready to welcome German rearmament in any form? Unfortunately, the opponents of the European Defense Community agreement did not even permit debate in the French Parliament. They killed the proposal on a procedural motion.

What is needed now is full and frank debate throughout France. That's the way democracy must work. The French people are entitled to hear all the arguments pro and con and to decide the issue for themselves in an election which shall choose a new Parliament.

Certainly when the French people discover that the United States cannot possibly afford any longer to take the risk of maintaining several divisions of its troops in a country whose fidelity to the alliance against Soviet Russia is in doubt, they will see the true picture.

It is essential, therefore, that every effort be made to work out a substitute plan for the defense of Europe. The North Atlantic Treaty Organization is an excellent starting point.

Control of the allocation and disposition of all allied troops could still remain in the hands of the Western nations as a group. Germany would not be able to "go it alone" or dominate the alliance. For the North Atlantic Treaty Organization is a federation of equals with a unified command. This in itself should be an assurance to the French people that there could not be a resurgence of German militarism or another threat from Germany to the peace of Europe, without an opportunity to check it in the incipient stages.

Will history now repeat itself? Will we be forced into a third world war because the aggressor is encouraged by the disunity of our allies? Will the French become prey for easy conquest again as they did prior to 1940 when they permitted a "fifth column" to infiltrate the Army and national institutions? France should see plainly now the necessity for outlawing the Communist Party.

The survival of France as a free nation—against enemies from within and without—will be assured only if she accepts wholeheartedly the obligations of a collective-security system.

THE HOPE OF THE WORLD

SEPTEMBER 17, 1954

FEAR AND DESPAIR fill the minds of men.

The evil designs of potential foes compel us to arm in self-defense—in expectation of the big conflict that may come to us at an unknown hour.

The tension goes on and on—and men worry constantly what to do about it.

Governments seem frustrated and without a compass. They steer timidly from shoal to shoal. They offer less and less confidence to their peoples.

Individuals naturally delegate responsibility to governments, but they nevertheless feel uneasy, distrustful—concerned whether the leaders can be depended upon to take the right course that will provide a haven of safety.

The world has always been faced with threats of war, and we glibly say that "innocent peoples" have always been its victims. But are peoples as innocent of guilt as they are presumed to be? Are cabinets and rulers alone responsible for the sequence of events that lead to war?

As populations increase and the actual task of governing the multitude grows in complexity, more and more people tend to abdicate their responsibility and transfer the power of decision to a small group of men—even to a dictator.

Materialism is the main reason for this cancerous growth. It is the key to elections in a democracy and to submissiveness in a police state.

As the crumbs are handed out, dictatorship grows stronger. And in a democracy, as creature comforts increase, government shows less and less inclination to disturb the self-indulgent lives of the voters.

For "prosperity" can anesthetize the spirit of a nation and its morals. It is a paradox whose presence we do not like to concede. But it is true that, as nations enjoy a higher and higher standard of living, they become more interested in preserving their luxuries than in preserving the ideals that made them great.

Nations thus become infected with germs of a decadent morality. They become victims of a selfishness which misconstrues aloofness from international responsibility as the safest form of nationalism.

In an atomic age, nationalism is in itself an incredible phenomenon. It assumes that the hurricanes of evil which sweep the world will avoid particular areas just because we have the windows boarded up.

A-bombs themselves and the planes that can carry them anywhere in the world are mere pieces of metal. More dangerous are the few men who can order the big bombs dropped. And those few are subject to the will of millions of supposedly innocent people. Yet it is they—the so-called "helpless" millions—who can take concerted action. They have the real power to encourage or discourage the plotters of war.

Intercommunication among peoples is feasible. But what shall we communicate to each other? Shall we boast of virtues we do not possess? Can we who are not good inside ourselves inspire goodness in others? We cannot, of course, influence others if we ourselves are indifferent to the welfare or plight of our brethren, in the neighborhood or the country as a whole, or in the world at large.

We acknowledge that Jesus taught by example. But do we as a nation—the most powerful in resources—furnish an example that others could wish to follow? The question should be asked of individuals, too—for nations are no better than the collective acts of their individual citizens.

Are we, in this troubled world, giving to the problems of human society the time and the thought and the sacrifice that will make our nation worthy of a place of leadership in the councils of other nations? And are those citizens of other nations who look with envy at our possessions, or who favor compromise with evil and assume a craven attitude of indifference toward the moral issues of our day, likely to be impressed when we, too, remain passive? May we not expect others to rationalize their programs of peaceful cowardice as logical for them, if we ourselves so soon forget the bravery and sacrifices of the valiant soldiers who not so long ago faced death that we might live?

These are days when peace and freedom are taken for granted—as things we deserve and things we can have for the asking. We pray to the Supreme Being for help—as if prayer is a one-way street. We ask for the blessings of peace, and what do we offer in return? How much do we sacrifice in a world that is still ravaged by disease and poverty and hunger?

When we give of ourselves as a nation—not just dollars but the things of the spirit that draw men together—we shall receive the bountiful rewards of an untroubled conscience.

Yes, this is an age of materialism. And when we transform it into an age of reborn morality, in which the courage of a God-given spirit shall guide us as it did our forefathers, then we will discover anew that the hope of the world is really to be found dormant within our own bosoms—within ourselves.

PRINCIPLES ABOVE PARTY

SEPTEMBER 24, 1954

THIS IS THE PERIOD for meditation by the individual voter on what ballot, if any, to cast in the coming election for members of Congress. There are among our citizens three group attitudes:

First, there are the straight-party voters who regularly cast their ballots for the party of their choice and who do so in every election, irrespective of whether their own party has made a good record in office or offers to put into effect a program of constructive merit if victorious at the polls.

Second, there is the group of so-called "independent" voters who switch from party to party in successive elections. These are, for the most part, "negative" voters dissatisfied with the record of the party in power.

Third, there is the group which doesn't go to the polls regularly, feels no strong allegiance to any party, and often stays at home out of protest against both candidates or both parties.

When it is considered that only 62.7 per cent of the voting population voted in the presidential election of 1952—which was a high percentage, indeed, compared to previous presidential elections—it is clear that about 36 million persons eligible to vote did not vote two years ago. That's more votes than the total that either major party has ever received, including the record of the 1952 election.

The stay-at-home citizen is just as influential in producing the final election result as the one who goes to the polls. For, by withholding his vote—if he happens to be a Republican, for example—he is contributing a half vote to the Democrats.

Again and again it has been proven that, when there is a protest or negative tide running—and there usually is in varying degrees on different issues against the party in power—the stay-at-homes, if persuaded to go to the polls, can sometimes overcome numerically the effect of the "switchers."

Thus, for instance, it would not help the Republican campaign workers very much to concentrate their efforts on converting those who, due to unemployment or a drop in farm income or any other grievances, have decided to switch from the Republican to the Democratic Party. But if, for every one of the bolters, they can find and get to the polls two persons who are satisfied with their economic situation or who approve of what the party in power has done, the damage by protesting voters would be overcome.

The Maine election results reveal that, while there were 93,000 votes polled for Eisenhower in 1952 which did not mark a Republican ballot for Senator in that same election, many of them remained home this time. Senator Margaret Chase Smith, who was re-elected last week on the Republican ticket, had a pro-Eisenhower record in the Senate, is generally called a "liberal" and has voiced severe criticism of Senator McCarthy. She actually got 16,000 fewer votes than when elected six years ago. The Republican vote in last week's election thus dropped from 71.4 in 1948 to 58 per cent. The Democratic Party, on the other hand, increased its vote for Senator by 38,000 as compared with 1948—a gain from 28.6 to 42 per cent.

If this percentage drop for the Republicans occurs nationally in the November elections, affecting States which, unlike Maine, are closely divided between the parties, we shall see the Democratic Party win control of both houses of Congress by comfortable majorities.

What is the average voter to do—shall he vote his protest against the party in power, or shall he judge the whole record on balance and support the incumbent party? Or shall he express his dissent from the leadership of both major parties and stay at home?

The conservative particularly finds himself in a quandary this time because both the Republican and Democratic parties have in them dominant elements which believe in radical doctrines with respect to the use of the federal power. The believer in States' rights, for instance, can find little comfort in either party. The believer in a government of laws and not just of men can find little solace in some of the acts of the present or past Administrations. Nor can a third party be immediately effective, for the record shows that most third parties have not survived.

There is only one rule that can give satisfaction to the voter, and that is to do as his conscience guides him —putting principles above party. It could mean for the independent voter that he casts his ballot for the Administration on the theory that it deserves a further opportunity to carry out its program. Or it could mean— by voting Democratic or by staying at home—the registering of a protest against the party in power for such deviations from its previously-announced principles as have been revealed.

There is yet time for debate on the issues. And voters of all groups, before making up their minds, should examine carefully the pros and cons of the various questions as they are debated for the next few weeks. It's a time to place principles above personalities, and issues above parties.

THE COMMON DANGER

OCTOBER 1, 1954

IS THE FRENCH PARLIAMENT satisfied that there is no menace in Soviet imperialism, no menace to the future of the French people, and that the much-talked-about defense of Europe against the possible march of the Red Army is unnecessary?

American policy has assumed that everybody in Europe recognizes a common danger—the threat from the rulers of the Soviet Union.

By the rejection of the European Defense Community agreement, the French Parliament, however, told the world, in effect, that it does not consider any such danger exists or, if it does, that somehow this is of no acute concern to France.

If we examine the currents of French opinion, as reflected in the vacillation of cabinets heretofore and in the recent vote of the Chamber of Deputies at Paris, we find that there are apparently more deputies who fear that Germany, rather than Soviet Russia, is the real enemy of the future.

The French had better make up their minds as to whence the threat to their national safety comes. For if they fear the military resurgence of Germany in a decade or more, they might better ask themselves how there can arise a remilitarized Germany to attack France again. Even a remilitarized Germany could not operate independently if the forces of all the Allies, including Germany, were integrated in a unified military instrument dependent on supplies coming from abroad.

The real hazard which the French Parliament evidently has not taken into account is that, once American military strategy changes, France will be in greater danger than she is today.

For it is clear that American strategy must change, and change soon, if the French refuse to consider the Communists to be a menace to their security.

The United States, if deprived of the help of France, would have to shift its entire military axis to the Mediterranean and to Spain, Italy, Austria, West Germany, Greece and Turkey as the best way to apply the tactics of "massive retaliation" in defense against a Soviet attack. This, by the way, was Winston Churchill's original concept of wartime strategy—to attack the "soft under belly" of Europe, instead of immediately rescuing France.

The alternative strategy of building a supply line to Belgium, Holland and West Germany is, of course, being considered in combination with the drawing of a defense line in Southern Europe.

The United States cannot be expected to defend nations that do not want to be defended.

If the French Parliament finally assumes the grave responsibility of crossing their country off the military defense map of Europe so far as the Western Allies are concerned, there is nothing the American Government can do to prevent that debacle except to appeal to the French people not to commit suicide.

French officials little realize how far, in just a few weeks, American public opinion has shifted toward an alternative strategy which unhappily does not include the defense of France at all.

The American people are becoming impatient over the haggling at Paris. For many months the French refused to put to a vote the European Defense Community agreement. When this agreement was defeated, it was through the votes of the Communist Party in the Parliament that the victory for Moscow was achieved. Are we to witness now another era of haggling? All sorts of plans are being advanced "in principle" by the French Cabinet. Will it be largely talk and no action? Will there be attempts to delay the consummation of any effective plan? Nothing could suit the Kremlin more.

America considers the Soviet rulers to be the real menace in Europe today, and cannot accept any program which does not include the defense of Germany.

Military policy by the Allies must necessarily be based on an awareness that the Soviet Union is an active aggressor, having in a few years brought about the subjugation of Latvia, Lithuania, Esthonia, Poland, Rumania, Czechoslovakia, Bulgaria and East Germany.

If France, which is only a few hundred miles away from the Soviet Army, isn't afraid and doesn't believe a common danger exists, then obviously America has made a wrong assumption and logically should bring her troops home. But the people of the Low Countries and of Southern Europe as well as Central Europe evidently do fear the Communist aggression, and want American aid to help resist it. So a new defense plan which by-passes France becomes inevitable for those peoples who wish to join with the United States in a common defense against a common danger.

The words of Premier Mendès-France in his interview, on another page of this issue, are reassuring. Will the French Parliament back him up? This is the next source of anxiety as the big conference this week in London tackles a new plan for the defense of Europe.

FORGET IT'S McCARTHY—
REMEMBER THE CONSTITUTION!

OCTOBER 8, 1954

CERTAINLY a Senator is guilty of bad manners when he denounces a witness who is evasive in testifying before a congressional committee.

Certainly a Senator is intemperate when he denounces a fellow Senator who has provoked him.

Certainly a Senator uses poor judgment when he sends bitterly worded replies to letters from a Senate committee which has invited him to testify, even if he regards its hearings as a political smear.

But—and here's the crux of the entire case—not a single statement or charge made in the report issued last week by the committee headed by Senator Watkins of Utah affords constitutional justification for punishing any United States Senator now or hereafter.

The Constitution makes no reference at all to "censure," but specifically says that each house of Congress "may punish its members for disorderly behavior."

Crimes of the mind, however, are not crimes of the hand. Censure cases in the past have primarily concerned physical acts—fist fights in the heat of Senate debate. Neither contemptuous language nor a contemptuous "manner of expression" by a Senator is legal contempt of the Senate.

Drastic treatment in cross-examination of a recalcitrant witness was vigorously defended in 1936 by Senator Hugo Black of Alabama, Democrat, then chairman of a Senate investigating committee and now a Justice of the Supreme Court of the United States. The right to excoriate fellow members off the floor of Congress has always been held to be a prerogative of members of Congress in political campaigning.

If the censure motion is approved by the Senate, the cause of freedom of speech will suffer a setback in the legislatures of the world. It will change the nature of the United States Senate. It will make of it a body in which minority rights hereafter will always be at the mercy of an intolerant majority.

The Watkins report points to an alleged act of impropriety in 1952—a refusal by the Senator in question to accept an "invitation" extended to him by a previous committee to testify on his personal finances. There's nothing in the records to justify the failure of that committee to issue a subpoena, which the same Senator repeatedly had said he would honor.

Also, the Department of Justice and the Internal Revenue Service, under the present and preceding Administrations, have not found any violations of law by the Senator in connection with his personal finances or his use of funds to fight Communism. Has it not been argued often that to ferret out violations of law is primarily an executive and not a legislative function?

The Watkins committee says, however, that an invitation by the previous committee requesting the Senator to testify should have been enough. But is that law, or is it a new code of senatorial etiquette never before proclaimed in the Senate's own rules or precedents?

Back in 1929 and 1930 a demagogue from Alabama, the late Senator Heflin, vilified the Catholic Church, the Pope and the Vatican and Americans of Catholic faith, in tirade after tirade, on the floor of the Senate. No Senator moved a vote of censure.

Likewise, in 1918 in the midst of war, the late Senator La Follette, Sr., made a speech denouncing the war and virtually inciting the populace not to allow their sons to be drafted. A Senate Committee considered censure but refused to recommend it.

Both these instances of contemptuous speech are examples of what the late Justice Oliver Wendell Holmes of the Supreme Court of the United States, a great liberal, meant when he defined the freedom of speech guaranteed in our Constitution as "freedom for the thought we hate."

That's the acid test today, too. Are we true liberals, or are we totalitarians? If we are believers in "a government of laws and not of men," the Watkins report should be rejected by the Senate.

As a substitute motion, the Senate Committee on Rules—which for many months has been taking testimony on the subject of the procedures and methods of congressional investigating committees—should be directed to bring in a report defining what is or is not permissible in examining witnesses and what is or is not the proper procedure in obtaining testimony from Senators or Representatives themselves.

Congressional history is replete with instances of a refusal by members to accept invitations to testify before investigating committees. It is regrettable that the Watkins committee declined to allow the evidence on this point to be introduced into the record.

Let's not legislate retroactively on any Senator. The Constitution says no *ex post facto* law shall be adopted. This means that no statute or rule shall punish any citizen or any member of Congress for any past action which at the time was not a prohibited offense.

Let's forget it's McCarthy, and remember the Constitution!

AN ANSWER TO MR. MOLOTOV

OCTOBER 15, 1954

Molotov, the Communist Minister of Foreign Affairs, has just proposed that all foreign troops be withdrawn from East and West Germany. He says his purpose is to end the occupation which has continued since the close of World War II.

The proposal comes as a countermove to the agreement reached in London recently among the Western allies, when they decided to include Germany in a plan to defend Western Europe against possible aggression by the Communists.

But the Molotov tactic should itself be countered with a demand that the Soviet regime withdraw its armies of occupation also from Poland, Latvia, Estonia, Lithuania, Hungary, Rumania, Czechoslovakia, Bulgaria and Austria.

Thus would the security of Europe be served far more than merely by "neutralizing" a reunited Germany. For what the Soviet Minister, in effect, is proposing is that Germany be made a buffer state. A glance at the map of Europe shows that it would be of little avail to keep Germany disarmed if the big Red armies are mobilized on its frontier.

In fact, there can be no peace of mind in Europe or elsewhere in the world if the Red armies continue in a state of war mobilization.

What is needed is the complete dispersal and reduction to police force size of the Red military organization. This, in turn, would naturally induce a comparable reduction of the military forces in Western Europe. That's the best way to promote limitation of armaments.

For the realistic fact is that withdrawal of Soviet troops from Germany would merely put the Western powers at a military disadvantage. As long as the Red armies are in a state of war mobilization and numerous divisions are kept in Poland, the threat of aggression remains.

Unquestionably the Molotov move was made for propaganda purposes and to wreck the London agreement. But it opens up a way in reply to tell the peoples in the countries under the Communist yoke that the Western democracies have not forgotten them.

Every opportunity that presents itself to encourage the peoples in the oppressed countries should be utilized by the Western allies. The constant talk in London and Paris in favor of "co-existence" means to the enslaved peoples a maintenance of the status quo—a willingness to keep things as they are indefinitely.

But does this not insure building up the power of the Soviet regime? Will it not discourage the peoples in the Balkans, who are bound to feel that liberation has likewise been indefinitely postponed? Must these oppressed peoples continue to endure the tortures of slavery while the West continues to buy temporary immunity from attack and pays a big price in renewed trade so that the Communist regime can strengthen itself internally?

The recent relaxation of restrictions on trade with Soviet Russia are indefensible. Soviet Russia is being permitted to buy commodities on the theory that she has an abundance of some of them anyhow or that she can get them in other ways.

But why should we make things easier for the Communist regime? Why should we permit the industries of Soviet Russia to be relieved of the necessity of producing the consumer goods so badly needed by the Russian people? For if the allies withheld those commodities, the limited amount of manufacturing machinery available inside the Soviet orbit would be unable to meet the demands for munitions of war as well as consumer goods.

The Western allies have a unique chance now, and they should take advantage of it.

Instead of dismissing offhand the Molotov plan as just "old stuff," the Western allies should announce their determination to go ahead with the London conference agreement and still state their readiness to examine the possibilities of withdrawing all troops from Germany. But Soviet Russia should be asked, as a primary condition, to agree to demobilize all her armies and lift her stranglehold on the smaller countries which she has taken over since the war.

If the Communist regime is sincere in its desire to help the cause of peace in Europe by withdrawing troops from Germany, it should as a first step, for example, ratify the Austrian peace treaty, especially since the allies by making concessions finally agreed virtually to the Soviet's own proposal.

To withdraw Red troops, moreover, from occupied areas outside the Soviet Union isn't enough. Free elections must be held immediately. Until the peoples in the Iron Curtain countries, including Soviet Russia itself, are able to express their own free will in elections, there can be no peaceful existence for anybody.

If Mr. Molotov means to give the German people their freedom from foreign rule, the idea is a good one to apply to all those peoples now in Communist bondage. It's a splendid chance to expose the hypocrisy of the Moscow "peace" propaganda.

CENSURE FOR THE SENATE

OCTOBER 22, 1954

A SENSATIONAL REVELATION—disclosing a grave lack of security inside the executive branch of the Government of the United States—has just been made.

Joseph S. Petersen, Jr., a scientist specializing in physics and mathematics, has been arrested and formally charged with having in his possession—outside his office in the Government—secret documents of the highest importance. Our Government knows they were transmitted to a friendly government in Europe. The papers were then passed on to Moscow presumably by an agent planted in one of the offices abroad of that friendly government, which itself is now astounded and embarrassed by what has happened.

For nearly five years—from March 1948 to December 1952—documents of a top-secret nature were taken out of the National Security Agency by Professor Petersen, an employe, and used, as the Department of Justice now charges, with the intent to injure the United States.

The damage done by this leakage is incalculable. An attorney from the Department of Justice told the court that the far-reaching extent of the injury to the United States may not be known for several years.

The National Security Agency—which is not to be confused with the National Security Council—is a "hush-hush" operation wholly inside the Department of Defense. It is under Army jurisdiction. It is engaged in studying ciphers and developing codes. It is vested with the duty of protecting the secret communications of the United States Government.

As a consequence of this laxity, it may be asked, how much has Moscow been reading of our secret messages as they passed in code from Washington to telegraph and radio offices in other countries—messages to and from our embassies and messages containing vital facts about our Army, Navy and Air Force, and about the location of our atom-bomb piles abroad?

The truth is that, despite all the recent debate about running subversives out of the Government, there still are weaknesses in our security system.

Each governmental department or agency is, for example, the final judge of its own security set-up.

There is no over-all check and supervision from the standpoint of efficiency and follow-up.

No government-wide system to evaluate on a professional basis the derogatory information gathered about government personnel has yet been established.

Too much attention has been given to the smoke-screen raised by the "left wingers" about protecting individual rights and too little time has been spent investigating the security techniques of each department.

The Army seems particularly vulnerable. To this day the public doesn't know the truth about the breakdowns of security at Fort Monmouth, N. J., where new radar devices were being developed for use in intercepting enemy bombers.

To this day we don't know who in the Army promoted Dr. Peress to be a major, and who sat on the boards which failed to dismiss him as a security risk.

To this day we don't know why the recommendations made months ago by officers in the Army urging a cleanup at Fort Monmouth were so long disregarded.

It is the duty and responsibility of Congress and particularly of the Senate of the United States to check up on governmental operations of this kind.

Why, therefore, did a Senate committee spend nearly three months on trivialities such as the Cohn-Schine case, when there were serious deficiencies in our whole security system that need to be investigated by that same Permanent Subcommittee on Investigations of the Senate Committee on Government Operations?

The record shows that the Senate itself has been preoccupied with petty controversies over the intemperate remarks and bad manners of a Senator but has allowed a system to remain which lets our topmost secrets fall into the hands of our enemies.

The Senate is to convene in special session on November 8. It has no more important job to do than to insist that its committees be given full information by every government agency as to the procedures in use and the reasons why government personnel who must handle secret documents are not checked and double-checked periodically by a competent board.

The Petersen case is a shocking affair. It brings into disrepute the honor of the Government itself. It is a shameful neglect of the public interest. It is contemptuous of the American people.

Censure in the court of public opinion must be visited upon that large number of Senators who, by their diversionary acts, have actually "obstructed the legislative process." For they have unwittingly blocked the work of the very committee charged with the all-important duty of investigating governmental operations—particularly our security system itself.

The issue is more important than the individual behavior of any Senator. It involves a means of protecting the safety of the United States from the espionage of the Communists—a matter of the highest priority for the American people.

SHALL THE SENATE DESTROY ITSELF?

OCTOBER 29, 1954

In the October 8 issue of U. S. News & World Report, *nineteen pages were devoted to the printing of the full text of the report of the Watkins Committee which gives one side of the controversy over the proposal to censure Senator McCarthy of Wisconsin, Republican. Here is an analysis challenging on constitutional grounds the main points of that report. The viewpoint expressed herein is solely the opinion of this writer after making his own research into the historical practices of the Senate.*

The United States Senate is about to convene in special session to consider a report made by a select committee of six members, headed by Senator Watkins of Utah, Republican. The report recommends that on three points Senator Joseph R. McCarthy of Wisconsin be "censured."

The proposed action is unprecedented in the entire history of the Senate.

There have been three cases in the past in which "censure" has been voted. Two of them involved physical behavior—fist fights on the floor of the Senate—and the third was concerned with the ineligibility of a member of a Senator's own staff to attend executive sessions of the committee over which the Senator in question presided as chairman.

While the Constitution specifically grants to the Senate the power to punish its members for "disorderly behavior," there has been no "censure" ever voted for "disorderly" speeches or statements of individual Senators. Before the Watkins Committee report was submitted, there had never been offered in the Senate such a proposal to curtail freedom of speech.

The Senate, of course, can adopt any new rules that it pleases. But never in the past has the Senate sought by *ex post facto* action to apply retroactively any new rule or code of behavior. To do so violates the spirit as well as the letter of the Constitution. It is not dislike of a man which is the issue, but a procedure that will affect our system of government for generations to come. It is of transcendent importance to the preservation of the

freedom of the Senate itself to examine the basis for the most unusual action now recommended.

One of the startling conclusions of the Watkins Committee reads as follows:

"From an examination and study of all available precedents, the select committee is of the opinion that the Senate has the power, under the circumstances of this case, to elect to censure Senator McCarthy for conduct occurring during his prior term in the Senate, should it deem such conduct censurable."

Usurping "Censure" Power

But no Senator has ever been censured—or punished in any other way—for conduct as a Senator occurring in a prior term. The Committee acknowledges this point, yet proceeds nevertheless to usurp the power to censure as it says:

"While it may be the law that one who is not a Member of the Senate may not be punished for contempt of the Senate at a preceding session, this is no basis for declaring that the Senate may not censure one of its own Members for conduct antedating that session, and no controlling authority or precedent has been cited for such position."

Nor is any "controlling authority or precedent" cited in the report to sustain the Committee's position. For it may be stated with equal positiveness that, since a Senator may not be punished for legal contempt committed at a previous session, he cannot be legally censured either for what he did in a prior term.

The Watkins Committee naively comments that, since the Hennings Committee report containing various charges against Senator McCarthy "was filed on January 2, 1953, and since the new Congress convened the next day, there was not time for action in the prior session." Yet the Hennings Committee had the matter under consideration more than 16 months. Would the Supreme Court of the United States uphold a prosecutor who claimed he "just didn't have time" to bring a case prior to the expiration of the "statute of limitations"?

There are several Senators whose conduct prior to their terms of office has been questioned in their respective States. If the Watkins Committee report is adopted, the Senate will be in duty bound now to follow the new precedent, or else admit the charge that so many people are making—namely, that this is a case of persecution of one Senator who happens to be fighting Communism. For why has the power of "censure" never been invoked in comparable cases against anybody else? Also, why did the Watkins Committee refuse at its hearings to receive evidence on similar conduct by other Senators?

Election Makes Charges Moot

Even more arbitrary is the bold effort of the Watkins Committee to deprive the people of the States of the Union of the right to pass judgment themselves at the polls on political charges made against their Senators.

The Watkins Committee indeed has ruled, in effect, that, when a Senator is elected by the people of a State, the Senate of the United States—entirely apart from an examination of possible fraud or taint in an election—may inquire into the previous behavior of a Senator and "censure" him for any reason which political feeling or prejudice may have inspired.

This is an intolerant position which no fair-minded person in the Senate can justly defend. To accept such a rule is to amend the Constitution itself, and to do so without permitting the people of the States to have a voice in the making of such a change. This recommendation by the Watkins Committee is itself contemptuous of the rights of the American people.

The argument is made by the Committee that the Senate "can pass judgment upon conduct which is injurious to its processes, dignity, and official committees." But it is not explained how any injury to the "processes, dignity, and official committees" of the Senate can be committed by someone prior to the time he was elected for his current term.

Obviously, the occasion for raising such an issue is during the term of the Senator in question, and not when the people of his own State, after hearing the nature of the charges in a political campaign, have nevertheless elected him.

The Watkins Committee is, in fact, contradicted on this point by the very words of the document which played so large a part in bringing about the "censure" proceedings—namely, the report by the Senate Subcommittee on Privileges and Elections, headed by Senator Hennings of Missouri, Democrat. At the end of its final report—the one it filed on January 2, 1953—was this "addendum":

"However, because of a lack of continuity in the Committee membership and delays beyond the control of the present membership of the Committee, its preparation has given us great concern as a number of its aspects have become moot by reason of the 1952 election. Such facts therein as were known to the people of the States particularly affected have been passed upon by the people themselves in the election."

All the important issues in the Hennings Committee report were published in the press before or during the campaign and were passed upon by the people of Wisconsin when they reelected Senator McCarthy in November 1952. Since also the facts themselves relate to incidents which occurred prior to the election, the charges therefore have become moot.

There were two minor incidents which did occur after the November 1952 election and which were properly the subject of examination by the Watkins Committee. One was a refusal by Senator McCarthy of a written invitation to testify sent him on November 21, 1952. Incidentally, this was the first formal invitation to testify ever sent to Mr. McCarthy by instruction of the Hennings Committee during its 16 months of life. The Watkins Committee says in its report that it accepts as a fact that this particular invitation was not personally received by the Wisconsin Senator in time for the meeting date specified. But the Hennings Committee has never explained why it didn't then set another date for a hearing. The other point concerned a "denunciatory" letter written by Senator McCarthy and dated December 1, 1952, in which he charged that the Hennings Committee had impugned his honesty and integrity without evidence to support its charge. He declared, moreover, that the Committee was politically motivated.

But the Watkins Committee concedes that "similar language" was used in Senator McCarthy's letters denouncing the Committee which were published long before the 1952 election in Wisconsin.

McCarthy Credentials Accepted

The Watkins Committee argues repeatedly the right of the Senate to disregard the votes of the people of a sovereign State. It says:

"The reelection of Senator McCarthy in 1952 did not settle these matters. This question is answered in part by our conclusions that the Senate is a continuing body and has power to censure a Senator for conduct occurring during his prior term as a Senator, and in part by the fact that some of the contumacious conduct occurred after his reelection, notably the letter of December 1, 1952. The Senate might have proceeded with this matter in 1953 or earlier in 1954 had the necessary Resolution been proposed.

"Some of the questions, notably the use for private purposes of funds contributed for fighting communism, were not raised until after the election. The people of Wisconsin could pass only upon what was known to them."

The time to have challenged Senator McCarthy on all these issues, however, was on the afternoon of January 3, 1953, as he was about to take the oath of office for his second term in the Senate. He had declared at the time in a public statement that if anybody wished to question his right to take his seat, the time to do it was then. The very members of the Senate who 18 months later proposed "censure" charges were present at the session at which the credentials of Senator McCarthy were offered and accepted by the Senate.

The Senate really knew through the press before January 3, 1953, all the charges, insinuations, and allegations in the case. The enemies of Senator McCarthy had levelled all kinds of accusations at him in that campaign.

Certainly if the Wisconsin Senator were not qualified for admission to a new term, or if there was anything about his conduct that required further examination, it was the duty of the Senate, when it convened at noon on January 3, 1953, to ask him to step aside while it adopted the necessary procedure then and there to settle the question of whether or not he had acted with propriety.

Senator-Elect Not "Continuing" Member

The Watkins Committee pointedly characterizes the Senate as a "continuing body." This, however, can refer, when the Senate reconvenes, only to those Senators whose terms have not expired. The Constitution declares specifically that the six-year term of a Senator shall "end" at noon on January 3rd of the year set for the assembling of each new Congress. By no stretch of legal reasoning can anybody be considered a "continuing" member of the United States Senate whose term has ended or whose credentials as a Senator-elect have not yet been duly accepted by the Senate.

The Watkins Committee holds as a basis of censure in 1954 that the Wisconsin Senator declined to appear in person in 1951 and 1952 before the Hennings Committee to testify on charges made against him. But he did testify on other matters before the same committee on July 3, 1952, and could have been questioned that day on anything the Committee chose to ask him.

The Wisconsin Senator, of course, did answer the Committee again and again in writing, and categorically denied the truth of the specific charges concerning his personal affairs.

The Watkins Committee, moreover, admits that at no time did the Hennings Committee issue a subpoena, but says that a mere written request to testify should have been enough. Is that, however, in accord with precedent? How many cases have there been in which United States Senators who were merely "invited" to testify have declined to do so?

In all fairness, the Senate should make public now the names of those Senators who even in recent months have for various reasons declined to testify before a Senate committee in response to its invitations.

It is argued, of course, that in the case of Senator McCarthy the issue was related to his personal conduct and personal finances. But so far as the Senate is concerned —if these are to be the new rules—it does not matter what the basis for the request happens to be. For the Watkins Committee plainly implies that a United States Senator must respond to an invitation to testify, irrespective of the subject matter under consideration.

Is an "Invitation" Valid?

If it be conceded that the Senate, on the other hand, does have the right to inquire into the behavior of a Senator in a prior term, an examination of the legal circumstances under which the so-called invitations to testify were issued by the Hennings Committee to the Senator from Wisconsin becomes pertinent. The Watkins Committee says:

"It is the opinion of the select committee that a request to appear, such as the letter and telegram from the subcommittee to Senator McCarthy dated November 21, 1952, was sufficient (aside from any question whether Senator McCarthy received them in time) to meet the requirements of the law."

What "law" is the committee talking about? There is no "law" on the subject. The rules of the Senate do not specify anything about response to committee invitations. In fact, there are no rules at all in the Senate covering this subject.

How can it be persuasively argued that the Wisconsin Senator "obstructed the legislative process" when the Senate Subcommittee on Elections and Privileges itself did not exercise its right under the "legislative process" to issue a subpoena?

It is true that, prior to November 1952, the Wisconsin Senator did receive informal invitations, giving him "the opportunity to appear," as a matter of courtesy, before the Senate subcommittee. He made it clear in his replies that he would not appear voluntarily but would obey a subpoena. He did stipulate also that he would appear if he were given by the subcommittee the right to cross-examine witnesses.

The Watkins Committee says on this point:

"He [Senator McCarthy] also stated that he would not appear unless he were given the right to cross-examine witnesses. We feel that this right should have been accorded to him and that upon proper request, either to the Committee on Rules and Administration, of which Senator McCarthy was a member, or to the Senate itself, he could have obtained this right, but that in any event, this cannot be a justification for contemptuous conduct."

Using the same reasoning that the Watkins Committee has employed, why was it necessary for the Senator from Wisconsin to go beyond a simple request to the chairman of a Senate subcommittee when asking for the right to cross-examine? Why was it obligatory for him to adopt any legal process involving the passage of a motion by the Senate itself in order to get the simple right to cross-examine?

Informal Request Works Both Ways

The Watkins Committee cannot have it both ways. It cannot argue the sufficiency of informal requests by the Hennings Committee in one case, inviting Senator McCarthy to testify, and justify in another instance the failure of that same subcommittee to honor an informal request by the Senator from Wisconsin seeking the right to cross-examine.

Since, moreover, the Wisconsin Senator is now held by the Watkins Committee to have been right in his contention that he should have been accorded the opportunity for cross-examining witnesses, was this not a sufficient justification for his declination of the invitation of the Hennings Committee before which he was asked to testify? His request went to the core of the issue—the conditions under which he would be testifying as to his personal affairs if he voluntarily accepted the invitation.

Is it "contemptuous" to ask that your personal rights be safeguarded by a tribunal that has sought to indict you?

The Watkins Committee holds nevertheless that failure to testify was indeed "contemptuous, contumacious, and denunciatory." It carefully refrains from charging the Senator with "legal contempt," but plays on words in an attempt to convey an equivalent meaning.

In this connection, the Watkins Committee speaks of Senator McCarthy's letter denouncing in "harsh terms" the Hennings Committee as "contumacious in its entire form and manner of expression."

Since when are members of the Senate to be deprived of their right off the floor of the Senate to denounce other members of the Senate?

Are we to have political campaigns in which only those persons who are not members of the Senate may denounce the candidates who happen to be Senators?

Are we to have campaigns in which Senators go into other States and speak in criticism of incumbent Senators and then become subject to "censure" under this alleged rule of the Senate? This goes to the heart of the free speech question. For the right to denounce is the right of free speech.

Accusation Without Proof

Evidently the Hennings Committee itself felt no restraint about asking what Senator McCarthy regards as "insulting" questions. They were indeed full of innuendos, impugning the integrity of a fellow-Senator. Yet the Watkins Committee upholds that form of accusation without proof. Its report says on that point:

"It is our opinion that the failure of Senator Mc-

Carthy to explain to the Senate these matters: (1) Whether funds collected to fight communism were diverted to other purposes inuring to his personal advantage; (2) whether certain of his official activities were motivated by self-interest; and (3) whether certain of his activities in senatorial campaigns involved violations of the law; was conduct contumacious toward the Senate and injurious to its effectiveness, dignity, responsibilities, processes, and prestige."

Do not the members of the Watkins Committee know that dozens of members of Congress every year collect funds for public purposes, and not one of them has yet been required to divulge the names of his contributors except in regular election campaigns?

Since when must a Senator answer all the smear accusations filed against him by his critics, especially those charges which vaguely claim, as the Senate Committee phrases it, that "certain of his official activities were motivated by self-interest"?

Where is the rule of the Senate which defines what is or is not "self-interest"?

How many members of the Senate are doing business today with the Government of the United States through their private business connections?

How many members of the Senate vote from time to time on issues in which they have a direct personal interest?

As for the charges that funds collected for a public cause were used for personal purposes, is it not the function and duty of the Department of Justice and the Internal Revenue Service to determine whether there are violations of federal law involved? Subsequent to the time when the Hennings Committee made its report on January 2, 1953, the Department of Justice examined the document, made its own investigation, and then stated publicly that it found no violations of federal law by the Wisconsin Senator.

The Internal Revenue Service, moreover, has thoroughly investigated Senator McCarthy's income tax returns. It did so when the Truman Administration was in power, and likewise examined them again under the Eisenhower Administration. But, according to an article published in the Washington *Evening Star,* last August, before the Watkins Committee made its report, no evidence of any violation of law has been found.

Why didn't the Watkins Committee, with its deference to and professed respect for the jurisdiction of executive agencies, take cognizance of the action of the Internal Revenue Service and the Department of Justice, both of which were concerned with the truth or falsity of these very charges?

The Committee rightly decided that what Senator McCarthy may have said in inviting federal employees to supply him, as the chairman of a congressional committee, with information concerning corruption, Communism or treason in Government, does not furnish ground for "censure."

No "Censure" When Provoked

The Committee rejected also as a basis for "censure" the comment made by the Wisconsin Senator that the Vermont Senator was "senile." The Committee says:

"The remarks of Senator McCarthy concerning Senator Flanders were highly improper. The committee finds, however, that they were induced by Senator Flanders' conduct in respect to Senator McCarthy in the Senate caucus room, and in delivering provocative speeches concerning Senator McCarthy on the Senate floor. For these reasons, the committee concludes the remarks with reference to Senator Flanders do not constitute a basis for censure."

This is the most amazing paragraph in the entire Watkins Committee report. Here it is flatly stated that Senator McCarthy should not be censured for his denunciation of Senator Flanders because the latter had delivered "provocative speeches" concerning the Wisconsin Senator on the Senate floor. But what about the Vermont Senator who furnished the provocation? Logically, is he not subject to a "censure" resolution now?

The Watkins Committee plainly says in this instance that Senator McCarthy is to be absolved from "censure" because he was provoked. Yet, later on it recommends a "censure" count against the Wisconsin Senator because of his statement of January 2, 1953, saying that, in joining with the two Democrats and signing the Hennings Committee report, his fellow-Republican—Senator Hendrickson of New Jersey—was "without brains or guts."

What a petty business to introduce this as a basis for a "censure" resolution, and with what mock dignity, coming as it does from Senators accustomed to the epithets of the stump! Alongside President Truman's letters to the music critic and about the Marines and, in a public speech, his use of "S.O.B."—and he didn't use just the initials either—to characterize a political critic, the language of the Senator from Wisconsin seems to have been rather restrained.

"Unintentional" Provocation

The last "censure" count concerns the treatment of General Zwicker, who was a witness before Senator McCarthy's Committee early in 1954. This was an incident that did occur in the current term of the Senate and hence it is within the proper time limitation. The Watkins Committee declares:

"There is no evidence that General Zwicker was intentionally irritating, evasive, or arrogant."

The testimony of General Zwicker has been printed in full for everybody to read. There are honest differences of opinion as to whether the General was provocative. But the Watkins Committee poses a new problem in mental gymnastics when it says he was not "intentionally" irritating, evasive or arrogant.

Is this to be taken to mean that he actually may have been irritating, evasive or arrogant, but did not intend his remarks to have such an impact? If so, is not what actually happened the best proof? It was obvious to anyone present at the hearing that the Wisconsin Senator was irritated and was provoked into an outburst of temper.

Is the United States Senate to be censorious of all such conduct? If so, it must go back into its own records and begin to appoint committees to investigate the conduct of other Senators who have from time to time either ejected witnesses bodily or else said things even worse than Senator McCarthy ever said.

One member of the present Senate told a recalcitrant witness—a General, too—at a congressional hearing a few years ago that anybody who took the attitude he did about the security procedures under discussion should be taken out and shot.

Several Senators have used profanity in arguing with witnesses.

One Senator last summer made a speech implying in so many words that another Senator was morally delinquent in his personal life.

One Senator only last week in a written statement issued during the heat of the campaign said, with reference to a fellow-Senator who had left his own party, that "when a renegade leaves the camp, he becomes a worse traitor than an enemy spy."

Must not all these Senators now be hauled before the bar of the Senate and "censured" for "contemptuous" language? Or is freedom of speech to be regarded as the late Justice Oliver Wendell Holmes defined it—as "freedom for the thought we hate"?

Whatever motivates the human mind and provokes it to anger is speculatively interesting but hardly constitutes a fit subject for the adoption of a "censure" resolution by the United States Senate. It is beneath the dignity of that body and tends to bring its prestige as a legislative institution into nationwide disrepute.

Whether or not General Zwicker was "intentionally irritating, evasive or arrogant," it is a fact that he did provoke Senator McCarthy. The Senate Committee itself has said in the Flanders case that, where there is provocation, there is no justification for censure, irrespective of what the remarks happen to be. Why doesn't "provocation" therefore constitute grounds for eliminating the "censure" charge growing out of the remarks made by the Wisconsin Senator to General Zwicker?

Contradictions in Findings

The Watkins Committee contradicts itself further on

another point in its findings. Under the heading, "The Law Governing the Treatment of Witnesses before Congressional Committees," the Committee says:

"The law and precedent on this subject has been stated many times."

But in the next paragraph the Committee declares:

"There are no statutes and few court decisions bearing on the subject."

Which statement are we to accept?

There are, of course, no statutes discussing the treatment of witnesses before a Senate committee except in cases of legal contempt. Nor has the Senate ever adopted any "law" or rule on the subject of the treatment of its members as witnesses, other than the legal process which takes effect if there is a refusal to obey a subpoena.

The facts are that General Zwicker himself, in his testimony, admitted he had read in the press that Major Peress had invoked the Fifth Amendment, but told Senator McCarthy at the hearing that he didn't know it was in connection with Communist activities. Yet he previously had informed a Senate committee staff member he knew about the charges of Communist activities by Peress. This was an astonishing contradiction. Small wonder this double-talk produced the impression that the General was evasive. That's why it drew the fire of the Wisconsin Senator.

The real point, however, is that the General failed in all candor to tell the subcommittee of the Senate Committee on Government Operations the procedures in the case in which he himself was a factor. His main excuse was that he was obeying an order.

The Senate of the United States, on the other hand, is not required to conform to any executive order limiting the testimony of subordinates in the Government with respect to governmental operations. The Congress holds the purse strings, and it has the right to command testimony on government procedures.

"A More Drastic Attack" Necessary

No Senator should be "censured" for his persistent effort to get information from an evasive witness during the course of a committee investigation. In the last issue of this magazine an article was reprinted from *Harper's Magazine* in which Hugo Black, then Senator from Alabama—now a Supreme Court Justice—wrote in 1936 of his difficulties in getting information from witnesses. He said that sometimes it is necessary "in the presence of a witness who is deliberately concealing the facts to attempt to shake it out of him with a more drastic attack."

Provocations of Senators and Representatives to anger when they try to cross-examine witnesses are frequent. While these instances are numerous, no case of censure of a Senator who has been the victim of such provocation has been recorded. The Watkins Committee makes this pertinent comment:

"The very paucity of precedents tends to establish the importance placed by the Senate on its machinery of censure.

"Obviously, with such limited precedents the task of this committee in undertaking to determine what is and what is not censurable conduct by a United States Senator was indeed formidable. Individuals differ in their view and sensitivities respecting the propriety or impropriety of many types of conduct. Especially is this true when the conduct and its background present so many complexities and shadings of interpretations. Moreover, it is fairly obvious that conduct may be distasteful and less than proper, and yet not constitute censurable behavior."

If the Watkins Committee had stopped there, it would have been stating the facts as they have been historically established. The Watkins Committee might well have added then that it would propose certain new rules to be adopted and that it would ask the Senate to pass concretely on the phraseology of such rules. This would be orderly procedure.

It is disruptive of orderly procedure, however, to introduce as a basis for "censure" a vaguely worded critique on a "manner of expression" by a Senator or to interject a dogmatic treatise on psychology in order to rule on what is intentional or unintentional "provocation" by a witness. This creates for the future all sorts of doubts and misgivings concerning the true rights of members of the United States Senate.

The Watkins Committee itself recognizes the dilemma in this observation:

". . . we are cognizant that the Senate as a political body imposes a multitude of responsibilities and duties on its Members which create great strains and stresses. We are further aware that individual Senators may, within the bounds of political propriety, adopt different methods of discharging their responsibilities to the people.

"We did not, and clearly could not, undertake here to establish any fixed, comprehensive code of noncensurable conduct for Members of the United States Senate."

Had the Committee been content with that broad statement and proposed that a set of explicit rules be adopted to govern future conduct, it would have been well within its rights. It would have been following the precept of the Supreme Court of the United States, which has again and again ruled that vaguely-written laws are invalid unless "legislative standards" are prescribed for the guidance of those who are to administer the statutes. Had the Watkins Committee prescribed the standards for the future, its report would have been welcomed by everybody as a constructive contribution to the whole subject.

What Conduct Is "Legal"?

Today the country is confused, and so may well be the future members of the Senate as to what is or is not proper conduct from a legal standpoint.

If the Watkins Committee report is adopted, an intolerant majority in the United States Senate will feel it has the right at any time hereafter to wipe out minority dissent by the simple device of "censure." Will a Southerner, for example, who has made speeches denouncing members of the Supreme Court of the United States for their decision on segregation now be eligible for admission to the United States Senate if a majority chooses to decide that "disorderly" words constitute conduct prior to his term sufficient to deny him admission under the "inherent power" doctrine asserted in the Watkins report?

A rule of fear has been proposed by the Watkins Committee. That rule must be summarily rejected by the Senate unless it wishes to apply "thought control" or "conformity of thought" to a free institution which has existed since 1789.

Shall the Senate destroy itself by curtailing the right of free speech?

What did Abraham Lincoln say under somewhat analogous circumstances? During the War Between the States, Postmaster General Blair, whose own home had been burned by Confederate troops, exclaimed that "nothing better could be expected while politicians and cowards have the conduct of military affairs." Secretary of War Stanton wrote President Lincoln backing up the demand of General Halleck that Blair be dismissed from the Cabinet. Mr. Lincoln said in reply:

"Your note . . . enclosing Gen. Halleck's letter . . . relative to offensive remarks supposed to have been made by the postmaster general concerning the military officers on duty about Washington is received. The general's letter in substance demands that if I approve the remarks I shall strike the names of those officers from the rolls; and that if I do not approve them the postmaster general shall be dismissed from the cabinet.

"Whether the remarks were really made I do not know, nor do I suppose such knowledge is necessary to a correct response. If they were made, I do not approve them; and yet, under the circumstances, I would not dismiss a member of the cabinet therefor. I do not consider what may have been hastily said in a moment of vexation at so severe a loss is sufficient ground for so grave a step. Besides this, truth is generally the best vindication against slander. I propose continuing to be myself the judge as to when a member of the cabinet shall be dismissed."

Fundamental Issue of Free Speech

A courageous Senate, free from passion and the proddings of pressure groups, true to the historic principles of liberalism which have governed the American people from the foundation of the Republic, will seek to uphold the highest principles of American jurisprudence.

The Senate, therefore, should table the "censure" resolution and promulgate a rule in an orderly manner prescribing the standards for future conduct of its members. But such rules must be written so as not to prejudice the right of free speech guaranteed by the Constitution of the United States to everybody—including members of the United States Senate itself.

Where are the true liberals in America? Let them stand up and be counted on this fundamental issue of free speech.

THE BATTLE GOES ON

NOVEMBER 5, 1954

AMERICA HAS JUST PASSED through one phase of a tug-of-war between rival ideologies and is about to enter another. For the elections held this week mark merely a temporary realignment of forces in the struggle between those who want to confiscate private savings and those who believe in the right of the individual to conserve the fruits of his toil.

The battle for power is worldwide. It is particularly intense in all the English-speaking democracies.

In Britain, Australia and New Zealand the conservatives for the last three years have had only a bare margin over the socialists. It has been nip and tuck on economic issues.

In this country, while the Democratic Party has a few conservative leaders influential especially in the handling of legislative business in committees, the radical liberals are pressing them on the issue at every turn. With the 1956 election only two years away, these radicals will be tempting their Democratic brethren of the conservative-liberal branch of the party to join them on key roll calls in their main strategy—to put the Republican Administration in a hole politically.

Inside the Republican Party, to be sure, there is division, too. Some of it is due to differences of opinion about the handling of the anti-Communist issue, but there are more penetrating factors than this producing dissension in the Republican Party. For the most part, the discord is due to a tendency by some Eisenhower lieutenants to be lured into the paths of radical liberalism.

The Republican Party, far from being the reactionary or stand-pat institution its opponents on the Democratic side like to have the public believe it to be, is today largely a conservative-liberal party. The Democratic Party, on the other hand, is dominated mainly by a radical-liberal group, primarily of labor leaders who have seized control.

It is sometimes claimed that the Republican Party is opposed to the intervention of the Government in the economic life of the nation. But the principle of intervention has been an accepted fact in American public policy since the foundation of the Republic when tariff protection for "infant industries" was proclaimed by Alexander Hamilton. It is axiomatic that no political party can long remain in power if it is indifferent to the public welfare.

The varying degree of such intervention by the Government—the extent of controls to be exercised by the state in peacetime—is the core of the perennial issue.

For the forces of confiscation seek constantly to attain complete government control of business and the ownership of basic industries. Resisting this trend have been the champions of private enterprise—a system with a record of achievement and industrial progress unparalleled in the world.

The public interest, of course, demands competition and continued enforcement of the antitrust laws so that large business shall not destroy small business. In certain fields where natural monopoly exists, as in electric power, the Government, moreover, must continue to protect against abuse in rate-making. But it is a far cry from proper regulation to the erection and continued ownership by the Government of steam electric plants in direct competition with private industry.

It is, however, primarily in the area of taxation that the tug-of-war is most conspicuous. The pressure constantly exerted by certain labor-union leaderships, which for years accepted the counsel of out-and-out Communists, is for a heavier and heavier tax on success and thrift. The pernicious doctrines of enforced "redistribution of wealth" are being brazenly offered again in free America.

An inflationary trend of many years due to New Deal excesses and wartime expansion—threatening to lead to national insolvency—has been reversed by the Eisenhower Administration. But the dikes will not hold if the politicians interpret this week's election results as a mandate for more and more inflation.

The battle of our political parties for possession of the powers of government is not between the conservative liberals of each of the major parties. For these two groups have much in common and often act in coalition in Congress. The fight is between all conservative liberals and the radicals who would usher in the "welfare state." This would mean a program of confiscation of savings and the gradual destruction of the private-enterprise system by government competition.

The stumping tours and political telecasts of the 1954 campaign are over. The 1956 campaign for Congress and the Presidency begins this week. The real struggle now is transferred to the halls of Congress, where the tug-of-war will be resumed.

America cannot be successfully infiltrated by Communists. But it can be destroyed from within. Its economic vitality can be sapped if the radical liberals—the twin brothers of the Marxist Communists in social and economic philosophy—are permitted to dominate both political parties.

STALEMATE GOVERNMENT

NOVEMBER 12, 1954

IN THE GAME OF CHESS there comes occasionally a stalemate—when neither player can win. The only thing to do is to begin another contest.

The election last week did not provide a clear-cut victory for either party. While the House of Representatives went Democratic, neither party actually won control of the Senate. The actual result is a line-up of 48 Senators who in this or previous elections were chosen as Republicans and 48 Senators who were elected as Democrats. Normally such a tie would be resolved by the vote of the Vice President, who is a Republican.

But it so happens that one Senator—who four years ago and ten years ago was a successful candidate on the legally designated Republican ballot of his State in a primary election and who then accepted the votes of the same party also on a legally designated Republican ballot in the general election—announced a few weeks ago that he would leave his party and vote with the Democrats in the next organization of the Senate. This can give to the Democratic Party control of the Senate, which means the right to appoint committee chairmen and to have a larger ratio of Democrats than Republicans sit on each committee.

Thus one man—not the people of America—will have decided the control of the United States Senate in the next Congress, which begins in January.

This was never contemplated by those who from the earliest days of American history sponsored the concept of party responsibility and party discipline. While members of Congress have veered from one side to the other on concrete issues, never has there been a case in which a Senator has deserted his party on the strictly procedural question of organization.

The episode reveals the glaring weakness of the American constitutional system and underlines the need for the adoption of the Canadian parliamentary system wherein the people vote in or out of power a party as such and hold either major party responsible for both executive and legislative functions.

Today America faces a divided government, an irresponsible government, a stalemate government.

For many years the threat of serious injury to the welfare of the American people, indeed to their safety, has been present in the failure of the Constitution to provide a system that insures responsibility by a single party over both the executive and legislative branches.

It is conceivable that in the midst of war a divided government can do great damage. Such a divided government was voted in during the last two weeks of World War I. It did frustrate American diplomacy in the subsequent two years. It did bring decisions by the Senate which contributed indirectly to the outbreak of World War II. For if a partisan Republican Senate had not rejected the plea of a Democratic Party President and America had joined the League of Nations, as many of us urged at that time, the whole course of world history might have been changed.

Since the people delegate legislative power to the Congress and administrative obligations to the President, it is desirable that both branches should hold office concurrently. A two-year term for members of the House of Representatives, a six-year term for Senators, and a four-year term for the President is illogical. A uniform term of either two years or four years would be a marked improvement.

The seats of two thirds of the Senate members were not voted upon at all last week. The people in many States of the Union were not permitted to have a voice in the selection of the members of the new Senate who now can control or modify its policies.

The trend of events, therefore, reveals more and more the necessity for a revision of the Constitution.

What America needs, what every republic needs, is a system in which the executive and the legislative are elected from the same party and together entrusted with power. What the people need, as has been stated on this page many times before, is a means of continuing in power a party that satisfies public opinion or of turning out promptly a party that has failed to fulfill the wishes of the electorate.

If it be not desired to allow the people an instantaneous check on both the Presidency and the Congress—as is the case in other English-speaking countries—at least there is merit in the idea of a two-year term for both houses and for the President himself, with no limitation on the number of terms to which the Executive could be re-elected.

America today has no satisfactory means of expressing the national will through the combined action of the national legislature and the Executive.

The President ought to be selected by a majority of the members of Congress from its own membership after an election in which the party leaders have explained to the electorate their programs of public policy. This would insure the choice of a President with legislative experience and also the proper coordination of the work of the Congress and the President. That is the way to prevent stalemate government.

THE URGE TO PEACE

NOVEMBER 19, 1954

THERE IS IN AMERICA no urge to go to war. Despite the worldwide propaganda being spread by the Soviets that Americans are "warmongers," there is not the slightest basis of fact in such an insinuation.

Unfortunately, the propaganda is often given an assist by a few American, British and French newspapers of considerable influence in forming world opinion. They keep talking about the existence here in Washington of a "preventive war" group with a "let's-drop-the-bomb" attitude.

What makes those newspapers which indulge in such irresponsible statements so harmful is their reckless accusations which appear regularly attacking high American military officers for the recommendations they must necessarily make in performing their duties as military advisers.

The fact, for example, that the U. S. Joint Chiefs of Staff formally report to the President plans for the defense of Quemoy Island—off the coast of China's mainland—in relation to the protection of Formosa does not mean that such military officers actually want to see America involved in a war or that they are deliberately pushing for a large-scale war.

It is important to note the distinction between advice on military policy and the position which the Department of State or the President may take after a survey of all the factors. The urge to peace inside the Government of the United States is unanimous.

The urge to peace is basic also in the thoughts of the American people. No better example of this point of view can be given than President Eisenhower's calm discussion at his press conference last week of the circumstances surrounding the unwarranted attack on an American B-29 by Soviet planes off the coast of Japan near some Russian-held islands.

Mr. Eisenhower was right in saying it was not a clear-cut incident because the area over which the American plane was flying is a sort of twilight zone, and the jurisdiction over it has been disputed since World War II.

But there was something else that the President said which was overlooked by those who are ready to denounce anyone who urges a firm course toward Soviet Russia. Mr. Eisenhower declared that it would be different if there had been a clear-cut incident. This was the real news of that press conference—a warning that America will not be imposed upon if its planes are attacked while flying over waters that are free to all nations. Significantly, the President mentioned his order that hereafter fighter planes will escort our large planes and will resist attack.

Freedom of the air is as precious to us today as was freedom of the seas in 1917. It may be recalled that on May 7, 1915, a British passenger ship, the *Lusitania,* was sunk by a German submarine. More than a hundred American lives were lost. This started an exchange of notes covering a period of nearly two years, during which assurances were gradually extracted from the Imperial German Government that all passenger ships would thereafter be given due warning.

Then, on January 31, 1917, the Imperial German Government announced that it would engage in unrestricted submarine warfare—against all ships, whether neutral or belligerent, approaching the coast of Europe or entering the Mediterranean.

Aroused by this action, President Wilson ordered diplomatic relations with the Berlin Government severed on February 2, 1917. This was intended as a warning—an act of moral force. Those who today advocate a severance of diplomatic relations with the Soviet Government are actuated by the same motive—to use moral suasion to avoid a war.

Mr. Wilson, moreover, immediately requested Congress to give him authority to arm American merchant ships so that they could defend themselves against submarine attack. The House approved by 403 to 13. But a filibuster developed in the Senate and, when the fixed date for adjournment came on March 4, Mr. Wilson complained bitterly that "a little group of willful men" had endangered the peace of America.

Encouraged by this division, the German navy continued its sinkings and more American lives were lost. On April 2, Mr. Wilson asked Congress for a resolution formally recognizing the existence of a state of war which, he said, had been thrust upon us by the German proclamation of unrestricted submarine warfare.

Four days later—April 6, 1917—the President signed the war resolution, which had been passed by overwhelming vote of both houses.

Thus, it will be noted that, less than five weeks from the time of the filibuster on the proposal to arm American merchant ships, public opinion swung definitely from steps to avoid war to an acceptance of war itself.

Moscow should recognize that this can happen again. There is in America a deep-seated urge not to go to war but to remain at peace. Let not Moscow misconstrue the patience of the American people.

'PEACE-LESS' COEXISTENCE

NOVEMBER 26, 1954

IT IS CHARACTERISTIC of the moral weakness of our times that even a proposal to debate the facts of international life is regarded as "dangerous"—as fostering perhaps a climate of war.

Senator Knowland of California last week called upon the Senate of the United States to study the implications of "peaceful coexistence"—the phrase which seems to have anesthetized so many of the statesmen of the free world.

Mr. Knowland spoke—as Senator Taft often did— not necessarily as the Republican leader of the Senate, but with the deep-seated sense of duty of a representative of a large State. The California Senator's comments were met with an outburst of criticism in the press, though he was, to be sure, joined sympathetically by the Democratic Party leader, Senator Lyndon Johnson.

Is it a phenomenon of our day that Congress must abdicate its position as a coordinate branch of the Government and furnish only "rubber stamp" Senators who blindly follow the Executive?

All that Mr. Knowland really proposed was that the entire field of diplomatic and military policy be surveyed to determine whether America is being duped into accepting the theory of a "stalemate" while Soviet Russia continues her conquest of weaker countries. Are we, in effect, the victims, he asks, of a self-imposed, one-sided truce? Should not our policies be re-examined constantly in the light of Soviet behavior?

Mr. Knowland is a realist who doesn't believe that "peaceful coexistence" is attained by wishful thinking or by issuing agonized pronouncements about the horrors of an atomic war.

But, exclaim some of the other Senators, doesn't Mr. Knowland understand that there is no alternative to "peaceful coexistence" except a terrible war?

The very asking of that question emphasizes the moral bankruptcy of the hour—the inability to perceive that there is and always has been an alternative to war, namely, the concerted use of moral force.

For there are even stronger weapons than atom bombs with which to attain peace in the world. They are the weapons which mean moral ostracism of the aggressor and non-intercourse with the potential enemy. They are weapons which do not destroy peoples but organize their desires for peace in a positive and constructive program of action.

To apply moral force requires courage. Unfortunately, it takes far more courage nowadays merely to sever diplomatic relations with the Soviet Union and to cut off all trade intercourse than it used to take to declare war when an overt act came. The protest which arises from the victims of the terror propaganda of today whenever a non-intercourse policy is suggested is symptomatic of the craven attitude which is fast becoming characteristic of many a government.

Yet why should we furnish materials to build up the enemy's war machine?

Why should we, by our passive acquiescence, lead the rulers in the Kremlin to believe that they may take a chance and commit acts of aggression because we ourselves talk always as if we are frightened? Such moods of frustrated despair could force war upon us some day as an inevitable alternative. And war then would be the product of our own fallacious pacifism.

The hope of the world lies in the emancipation of the people of Soviet Russia and in the liberation of the people of the satellite countries. They can be convinced that the peace of mankind is in their hands. The mere mention, however, of the word "liberation" is greeted by our allies with the specious argument that only military force can achieve such an objective.

The Red Army is an influential segment of the Soviet people. There is today no more affinity inside the Red Army for the despotism of the Kremlin than there was for the Czar who was overthrown in 1917.

We can and must give hope to the peoples behind the Iron Curtain. They regard "peaceful coexistence" as a willingness on our part to condone evil—to forsake the oppressed. Knowing that the Soviets always distort the word "democracy" in describing their own form of government, the enslaved peoples may well wonder why the Western world grasps the phrase "peaceful coexistence" with such enthusiasm.

How shall we convince these peoples that we are not being deceived? Certainly not by accepting the insidious policy of "peaceful coexistence" which is only a means of lulling us into a state of fancied security.

Episode after episode reveals the belligerent purposes of the Communist regime—its words are at times soft-spoken, but its acts are still those of the aggressor, as recent incidents in Indo-China, and particularly the repeated shooting down of our planes, will testify.

Let the debate go on. What discussions do we fear?

The basic desire of everybody is for coexistence. The real question is whether it is to be "peaceful" or "peaceless." We must not adopt a do-nothing attitude. There must be a constant survey and re-survey of the acts as well as the words of the Soviet Union.

SO-CALLED "LIBERALISM"

DECEMBER 3, 1954

THE CONCEPT OF "LIBERALISM" certainly has changed since the days when Alexander Hamilton and his "Federalists" advocated a strong national government and the days when the Jeffersonians and Jacksonians fought all encroachment by government upon the rights of the people.

Nor is the concept of "liberalism" the same as was held during that long period of our history when a strict construction of the Constitution by the Supreme Court meant the safeguarding of those rights of the people never delegated to the national government.

Today it is the so-called "liberal," however, who interprets the Constitution so as to permit the legislature to do any and all things supposedly necessary to achieve a social objective.

The late President Roosevelt, moreover, in 1937 frankly confessed in a public speech the contempt felt by his "liberals" toward the method of amending the Constitution as set forth in the document itself. He boldly proposed instead—as an expedient substitute—that the Constitution be amended thereafter by a Supreme Court packed with his partisans.

But even as the conservatives have tended more and more toward the position of the Jeffersonian Democrats of our early history, so have the so-called "liberals" of today—in both major parties—moved to embrace socialist programs. They have in their legislative proposals revealed a distinct tendency toward the repression of private initiative. Their chief reliance is on government as the boss of our economy. Government by pressure groups is their practice, though time was when "equal justice for all, special privilege for none" was the Jeffersonian axiom.

The so-called "liberal" has not been content to urge public ownership of just one industry, such as electric power, but he reaches out with his proposals for a control of the means of production of other industries, especially agriculture. His goal is state capitalism.

We shall hear more and more in the next few years about public power as the great benefactor of the people's interest, and we shall hear more about the necessity of nationalizing major industries. For one is the precursor of the other.

In the matter of human rights—where the "reactionary" or the "rugged individualist" used to be censured for alleged heartlessness—the so-called "liberal" now is revealing a philosophy of coercion analogous to the tyrannies so common to the history of Europe. His concept of executive power today, for instance, is authoritarian. He would restrict the right of Congress to investigate the operations of the executive agencies. He would deprive Congress of the right of independent judgment in appropriating funds for use abroad. He would ignore the constitutional right of Congress to determine when our armed forces should be ordered into war. He lumps all this together as "foreign policy" and cavalierly rejects the right of Congress to express a different viewpoint. He tends, in short, toward the absolutism of one-man government.

Such a concept was definitely rejected by the elder Senator La Follette and Senator Norris, who are so often extolled by present-day "liberals."

Too often, moreover, we find the so-called "liberal" condemning from the pulpit and from collegiate halls the attempt to ferret out and punish those engaged in a conspiracy to overthrow our government. On this point, J. Edgar Hoover, FBI Director, said in a recent speech:

"Pseudoliberals, who seek to conceal themselves behind the cloak of liberalism, have been beguiled, captivated and perverted because they have not been conscious of the horror, duplicity and godlessness of atheistic Communism. The eager readiness of some in this group to attack everyone and everything related to the efforts to expose the Communist conspiracy in this country is hardly the mark of a true liberal. Indeed, the true liberal is opposed to everything Communism represents, for the very nature of Communism is the antithesis of liberalism."

What America needs today is an awakening to the dangers of so-called "liberalism." For it permeates many of our institutions. It is the residue of the Machiavellian new dealism that rooted itself so deeply in American life for twenty years, beginning with 1933.

The true liberal, on the other hand, wants to see no monopoly, either by trusts or by labor unions or by any other group. He wants only an open partnership between the people and representative government. He wants to see better and better wages for labor, better and better returns for risk capital, and a constitutional use of the functions of the government for the benefit of all the people.

The true liberal seeks measures that will promote the general welfare but never at the expense of a dynamic system of individual enterprise—and never at the expense of freedom of thought or individual liberty. His motto is: Freedom from all tyranny—even that of government.

"PASSIVE RETALIATION"?

DECEMBER 10, 1954

AMERICAN AIRMEN who, according to the terms of the Korean armistice agreement, should have been given their freedom are being held in bondage by the clique which rules Communist China. The Government of the United States has filed its protest for the record.

But what else is our Government going to do about it? Bring it up in the United Nations and make speeches there? Isn't that about all the Communists ever expect us to do? Isn't that why they continue their calculated insults, as our planes are shot down and as American soldiers are held in prison?

Senator Knowland of California has proposed that there be a naval blockade of the China Coast. Secretary of State Dulles answers, in effect, "not now but perhaps later." The President says he will have to ask Congress to authorize it if it is to be done, because he feels a blockade is "an act of war." International law, however, is replete with instances of naval action never considered as an act of war but as a reprisal to protect American lives and property. We have even seized ports in the past. In China, we and our allies in 1900 landed Marines to rescue the personnel of the American and other legations held captive in Peking during the "Boxer" Rebellion.

But what is the United States doing today? The peace-at-any-price elements have risen to denounce any suggestion of a blockade as leading to war, and it is asserted that war must be avoided unless we are directly attacked.

Apparently we are to assume an attitude of passive retaliation with vaguely worded protests and speeches. It is analogous to the doctrine of passive resistance as dramatized by the late Mahatma Gandhi of India. It is a species of pacifism.

Even as the Secretary of State describes the importance of building up our military strength to deter aggression, he couples it with a statement that we never intend to use that military strength unless we are attacked. It is true that we have signed a series of mutual-assistance pacts to defend various countries allied with us in Asia, but it is crystal clear that we do not intend to fight even a "local war" or apply reprisals to secure respect for our rights if such steps might lead to an enlarged conflict. This can be interpreted to mean that we will not use military force at all.

To argue against such a policy always brings forth from the pacifists the cry that "preventive war" is being advocated as an alternative course. Yet a policy of announcing that we will not fight unless directly attacked encourages the Communists to proceed with their aggression in and infiltration of free countries. They know that they will not meet with any "massive retaliation" but merely more conversation, conferences, and "coexistence." This is not a policy to deter aggression. It is a policy that stimulates aggression.

What leverage do we possess short of war?

First, we can threaten to cut off all trade with the Communists. We can offer to compensate allied producers for any financial losses.

Second, we can threaten to sever diplomatic relations with the Government of Soviet Russia—the main culprit—and mobilize the moral force of the world against the Communists.

Third, we can tell the peoples behind the Iron Curtain that we may have to abandon intercourse of any kind—financial and economic—with the Communist governments.

But we or our allies repeatedly announce that we will not adopt such a policy. We forfeit our leverage by constantly telling the enemy what we will not do.

Yet these measures could gradually pave the way for liberation of the oppressed peoples. This policy at least would clarify the whole atmosphere and give the free world a definite goal—a great cause.

To accept "peaceful coexistence" and do nothing in the face of threats to our safety, as the Communists infiltrate the free countries, is the same as saying that we are willing to allow them to get control of each allied government and that we will fight only after the United States has been isolated.

This is the road to an early war. The advocates of peace-at-any-price and appeasement have brought on two world wars. They can bring on a third by encouraging the potential aggressors.

For our policies to date are contradictory and may produce in the minds of the Communists the erroneous belief that they can risk going to almost any lengths in their aggressive acts because we and our allies are paralyzed with fear of an atomic war.

Sooner or later we must face the issue and courageously make it clear that we will really resist further aggression. We must ascertain which allies will go along with us to deter the Communists from picking us off one by one, as Hitler did.

For no war has ever been avoided by a willingness to buy peace at any price—nor by proclaiming through meaningless notes of protest a policy of passive retaliation.

THE CASE FOR SEVERING RELATIONS WITH SOVIET RULERS

DECEMBER 17, 1954

Is it time to break diplomatic relations with Communist Russia? Has U.S. only aided Soviet rulers by recognizing a Government that openly seeks to overthrow this nation?

For 16 years American Presidents avoided relations with the Kremlin. For the last 21 years recognition has been extended.

All through this period official records show agreements violated, hostile acts committed, warnings of Soviet intent to injure U.S. The American Government today is talking of "peaceful coexistence" and still hopes to do business with the Communist rulers of Russia.

What follows is a study of official records—the warnings that began 35 years ago. They read as if they were written yesterday.

I. Why Recognition Was Withheld in the 1920s

To understand what is fundamentally involved in the question of severing diplomatic relations with the Soviet Government, we must re-examine the facts of our own troubled relations with Soviet Russia—the facts in the period prior to the resumption of diplomatic relations with Moscow in 1933.

We must study especially the basis on which recognition was originally extended, and review particularly the solemn agreements and pledges made by the Soviet Union which have since been flagrantly violated.

As we look at the history prior to the initiation of our present diplomatic relations with the present Soviet Government in Moscow we find a remarkable record. It is evident that few people today who discuss the question have ever read the actual documents in the case.

In the first place, 16 years elapsed while this very question of resuming diplomatic relations was argued, not only in the forums of the world, but in the diplomatic correspondence between the United States and various governments, other than Russia.

The first document which it is important to note was a message sent on August 2, 1920, by Bainbridge Colby, Secretary of State in the Democratic Administration of President Woodrow Wilson, to the American Ambassador in Great Britain, Norman Davis. It read in part as follows:

"It is the feeling of the American Government that recognition of the Soviet regime or negotiations with it involves sacrificing moral strength for the sake of material gains, advantages which will prove to be temporary and bought at a very high price. This Government feels

that no permanent and just settlement of Eastern European affairs can be thus attained. The revulsion felt by the civilized world against the tyranny now holding Russia in its power is shared by this Government. This tyranny disregards all principles upon which dealings and relations between nations are founded and is not freely chosen by any considerable part of the people of Russia. A permanent and wise solution of the problem of Russia, it would seem, cannot be reached until there is put into effect *a plan whereby all elements of the Russian people will be represented effectively for the consideration of the reciprocal needs, political and economic, of the different regions which made up Imperial Russia."*

On August 10, 1920, Secretary Colby, in a communication to the Italian Ambassador in Washington, who had inquired on behalf of the Italian Government concerning the views of the United States with respect to the Russian advance into Poland, wrote as follows:

"That the present rulers of Russia do not rule by the will or the consent of any considerable proportion of the Russian people is an incontestable fact. Although nearly two and a half years have passed since they seized the machinery of government, promising to protect the Constituent Assembly against alleged conspiracies against it, they have not yet permitted anything in the nature of a popular election. At the moment when the work of creating a popular representative government based upon universal suffrage was nearing completion the Bolsheviki, although, in number, an inconsiderable minority of the people, by force and cunning seized the powers and machinery of government and have continued to use them with savage oppression to maintain themselves in power.

"Without any desire to interfere in the internal affairs of the Russian people, or to suggest what kind of government they should have, the Government of the United States does express the hope that they will soon find a way to set up a government representing their free will and purpose. When that time comes, the United States will consider the measures of practical assistance which can be taken to promote the restoration of Russia, provided Russia has not taken itself wholly out of the pale of the friendly interest of other nations, by the pillage and oppression of the Poles.

"It is not possible for the Government of the United States to recognize the present rulers of Russia as a government with which the relations common to friendly governments can be maintained. This conviction has nothing to do with any particular political or social structure which the Russian people themselves may see fit to embrace. It rests upon a wholly different set of facts.

"These facts, which none dispute, have convinced the Government of the United States, against its will, that the existing regime in Russia is based upon the negation of every principle of honor and good faith, and every usage and convention, underlying the whole structure of international law; the negation, in short, of every principle upon which it is possible to base harmonious and trustful relations, whether of nations or of individuals.

"The responsible leaders of the regime have frequently and openly boasted that they are willing to sign agreements and undertakings with foreign Powers while not having the slightest intention of observing such undertakings or carrying out such agreements. This attitude, of disregard of obligations voluntarily entered into, they base upon the theory that no compact or agreement made with a non-Bolshevist government can have any moral force for them. They have not only avowed this as a doctrine, but have exemplified it in practice.

"Indeed, upon numerous occasions the responsible spokesmen of this Power, and its official agencies, have declared that it is their understanding that the very existence of Bolshevism in Russia, the maintenance of their own rule, depends, and must continue to depend, upon the occurrence of revolutions in all other great civilized nations, including the United States, which will overthrow and destroy their governments and set up Bolshevist rule in their stead. They have made it quite plain that they intend to use every means, including, of course, diplomatic agencies, to promote such revolutionary movements in other countries.

"It is true that they have in various ways expressed their willingness to give 'assurances' and 'guarantees' that they will not abuse the privileges and immunities of diplomatic agencies by using them for this purpose. In view of their own declaration, already referred to, such assurances and guarantees cannot be very seriously regarded. . . .

"In the view of this Government, there cannot be any common ground upon which it can stand with a Power whose conceptions of international relations are so entirely alien to its own, so utterly repugnant to its moral sense. There can be no mutual confidence or trust, no respect even, if pledges are to be given and agreements made with a cynical repudiation of their obligations already in the mind of one of the parties. We cannot recognize, hold official relations with, or give friendly reception to the agents of a government which is determined and bound to conspire against our institutions; whose diplomats will be the agitators of dangerous revolt; whose spokesmen say that they sign agreements with no intention of keeping them."

The foregoing note was delivered to all embassies and legations of the United States abroad. This was the deliberate opinion of the Department of State under a Democratic Administration.

Let us look now at the viewpoint of the United States Government as expressed in a Republican Ad-

—Harris & Ewing

BAINBRIDGE COLBY, Secretary of State 1920-21

ministration when the Secretary of State was Charles Evans Hughes, who had served previously as an Associate Justice of the Supreme Court of the United States and was later to become Chief Justice of the United States.

Mr. Hughes, on March 21, 1923, addressed a delegation of the Women's Committee for Recognition of Russia. During that address he said:

"As I said to the representatives of your organization a year ago, the fundamental question in the recognition of a government is whether it shows stability and a disposition to discharge international obligations. Stability, of course, is important; stability is essential. Some speak as though stability was all that was necessary. What however would avail mere stability if it were stability in the prosecution of a policy of repudiation and confiscation? In the case of Russia we have a very easy test of a matter of fundamental importance, and that is of good faith in the discharge of international obligations.

"I say that good faith is a matter of essential im-

portance because words are easily spoken. Of what avail is it to speak of assurances, if valid obligations and rights are repudiated and property is conficated? This is not a question of the rich or of the poor. It's a question of principle. . . .

"Here is a simple test. We have in this case no need to speculate, as of what avail are assurances when we find properties taken, without compensation or restoration, obligations repudiated,—properties of all sorts, the investments of one of our great life insurance companies, for example.

"Not only would it be a mistaken policy to give encouragement to repudiation and confiscation, but it is also important to remember that there should be no encouragement to those efforts of the Soviet authorities to visit upon other peoples the disasters that have overwhelmed the Russian people. I wish that I could believe

−Harris & Ewing

CHARLES E. HUGHES, Secretary of State 1921-25

that such efforts had been abandoned. Last November—last November Zinoviev [head of the Communist International] said: 'The eternal in the Russian revolution is the fact that it is the beginning of the world revolution.'

"Lenin, before the last Congress of the Third Internationale, last fall, said that 'the revolutionists of all countries must learn the organization, the planning, the method and the substance of revolutionary work.' 'Then, I am convinced,' he said, 'the outlook of the world revolution will not be good but excellent.'

"And Trotsky, addressing the Fifth Congress of the Russian Communist Youths at Moscow last October—not two years ago, but last October—said this: 'That means, comrades, that revolution is coming in Europe as well as in America, systematically, step by step, stubbornly and with gnashing of teeth in both camps. It will be long protracted, cruel and sanguinary.'

"Now I desire to see evidences of the abandonment of that policy. I desire to see a basis for helpfulness. We want to help. *We are just as anxious in this Department*

and in every branch of the Administration as you can possibly be, to promote peace in the world, to get rid of hatred, to have a spirit of mutual understanding, but the world we desire is a world not threatened with the destructive propaganda of the Soviet authorities, and one in which there will be good faith and the recognition of obligations and a sound basis of international intercourse."

A few months later in the same year, July 9, Samuel Gompers, President of the American Federation of Labor, wrote to Secretary Hughes and asked for an expression of his views on the American position regarding the Russian Soviet power. The labor leader said it had been the consistent contention of the American Federation of Labor "that the Soviet power cannot be recognized because it is an autocracy forced upon the people of Russia without their consent and against their will and maintained in the same manner."

Mr. Gompers added that he could not see where good crops or an improving economic condition, including an acknowledgment of Russia's financial obligations, could change the American position regarding recognition "as long as the principle of tyranny remains."

Mr. Hughes, on July 19, made a lengthy reply in which he said in part:

"The fundamentals of the Russian situation are pretty generally understood in the United States and have made a profound impression upon the thought of our people. We are constantly made aware of this in the Department of State by the various ways in which public opinion makes itself felt in the seat of government. We learn of the hope of America that Russia should have the opportunity of free political expression and that she should be enabled to restore her economic life and regain prosperity and once more to take her place among the nations on the basis of mutual helpfulness and respect.

"There can be no question of the sincere friendliness of the American people toward the Russian people. *And there is for this very reason a strong desire that nothing should be done to place the seal of approval on the tyrannical measures that have been adopted in Russia or to take any action which might retard the gradual reassertion of the Russian people of their right to live in freedom. . . .*

"We are not concerned with the question of the legitimacy of a government as judged by former European standards. We recognize the right of revolution and we do not attempt to determine the internal concerns of other States. . . .

"When there is a question as to the will of the nation it has generally been regarded as a wise precaution to give sufficient time to enable a new regime to prove its stability and the apparent acquiescence of the people in the exercise of the authority it has assured. The application of these familiar principles, in dealing with foreign States, is not in derogation of the democratic ideals cherished by our people, and constitutes no justification of tyranny in any form, but proceeds upon a consideration of the importance of international intercourse and upon the established American principle of non-intervention in the internal concerns of other peoples.

"But while a foreign regime may have securely established itself through the exercise of control and the submission of the people to, or their acquiescence in, its exercise of authority, there still remain other questions to be considered.

"*Recognition is an invitation to intercourse. It is accompanied on the part of the new government by the clearly implied or express promise to fulfill the obligations of intercourse.* These obligations include, among other things, the protection of the persons and property of the citizens of one country lawfully pursuing their business in the territory of the other and abstention from hostile propaganda by the one country in the territory of the other. *In the case of the existing regime in Russia, there has not only been the tyrannical procedure to which you refer, and which has caused the question of the submission or acquiescence of the Russian people to remain an open one, but also a repudiation of the obligations inherent in international intercourse and a defiance of the principles upon which alone it can be conducted. . . .*

"*What is most serious is that there is conclusive evidence that those in control at Moscow have not given up their original purpose of destroying existing governments wherever they can do so throughout the world. Their efforts in this direction have recently been lessened in intensity only by the reduction of the cash resources at their disposal. . . .*

"While this spirit of destruction at home and abroad remains unaltered the question of recognition by our Government of the authorities at Moscow cannot be determined by mere economic considerations or by the establishment in some degree of a more prosperous condition, which of course we should be glad to note, or simply by a consideration of the probable stability of the regime in question.

"There cannot be intercourse among nations any more than among individuals except upon a general assumption of good faith. *We would welcome convincing evidence of a desire of the Russian authorities to observe the fundamental conditions of international intercourse and the abandonment by them of the persistent attempts to subvert the institutions of democracy as maintained in this country and in others.* It may confidently be added that respect by the Moscow regime for the liberties of other peoples will most likely be accompanied by appropriate respect for the essential rights and liberties of the Russian people themselves.

"The sentiment of our people is not deemed to be favorable to the acceptance into political fellowship of this regime so long as it denies the essential basis of intercourse and cherishes, as an ultimate and definite aim, the destruction of the free institutions which we have laboriously built up, containing as they do the necessary assurances of the freedom of labor upon which our prosperity must depend."

The diplomatic documents in the foreign relations of the United States are filled with episodes confirming, incident by incident, the views expressed by Secretary of State Hughes. Operations of the Communist Party throughout the world were the subject of many interesting communications which are printed in the records.

There were even denials by the Russian Government that it was intimately connected with the Communist International, and there was a time when Moscow endeavored to create the impression that it no longer favored international operations by the Communist Party abroad.

II. Misgivings About Recognition in 1933

We come then to the period immediately preceding the recognition of the Soviet Government in 1933. The published documents of our diplomatic history show that, during the period of 16 years in which the United States Government refused to extend recognition, there was no evidence of any important change in the policy of the Soviet Government. But the economic pressure inside Soviet Russia became intense, and it was evident that the Moscow government needed the recognition of the United States in order to carry on trade with this country and other countries. So a determined effort was made by the Communists to try to impress the new Administration in Washington, the Democratic Administration of Franklin D. Roosevelt and the New Deal, that the time had come for recognition and a change.

Notable is the document prepared by Robert F. Kelley, Chief of the Division of Eastern European Affairs in the Department of State, dated July 27, 1933, which was handed to President Roosevelt by the acting Secretary of State on that date.

Having determined to take a chance on recognition and the resumption of diplomatic relations, there was a desire, at the same time, to impose conditions so as to achieve, through the very act of recognition, some of the agreements which it had not been possible to attain before.

The Kelley memorandum said:

"In order that the United States may derive from the recognition of the Soviet government the benefits which normally follow the recognition of a foreign Government, the recognition of the Soviet government should involve the establishment of relations with Russia on a basis which would render possible the maintenance of friendly cooperation between the Governments of the United States and Russia, and the development of trade and intercourse between the two countries.

"The experience of countries which have extended recognition to the Soviet government has shown pretty conclusively, it is believed, that there are serious obstacles in the way of the establishment of the relations with Russia on such a basis, and that so long as these obstacles remain, official relations, established as a result of recognition, tend to become, in view of the extraordinary nature of these obstacles, the source of friction and ill will rather than the mainspring of cooperation and good will.

"It would seem essential, therefore, that every endeavor should be made to remove these obstacles prior to the extension of recognition. Until a substantial basis of mutual understanding and common principles and purposes has been established, official intercourse, with its increased contacts, is bound to lead to friction and rancor.

"Formal diplomatic relations may be established, but the substance of a useful relationship will be lacking, as much for the Russians as for ourselves, unless and until we have cleared up the existing difficulties through mutual agreement and work out a *modus vivendi* for the future."

This document is of transcendent significance. It shows not only the basis on which recognition was extended, but it justifies in every respect the withdrawal now of that recognition through the severance of diplomatic relations because the original conditions became an integral part of the act of recognition.

The Kelley memorandum went on to say:

"*The fundamental obstacle in the way of the establishment with Russia of the relations usual between nations in diplomatic intercourse is the world revolutionary aims and practices of the rulers of that country. It is obvious that, so long as the Communist regime continues to carry on in other countries activities designed to bring about ultimately the overthrow of the Government and institutions of these countries, the establishment of genuine friendly relations between Russia and those countries is out of the question.*

"Even when these activities do not constitute a present menace to the established order, the systematic interference of a foreign power in the domestic affairs of a country constitutes *ipso facto* a source of deep resentment and unavoidable friction. *The persistence of such interference after diplomatic relations have been established leads inevitably either to the rupture of relations—as has taken place in the case of England, China, and Mexico—or to serious tension and the reduction of the existing diplomatic relations to a barren, meaningless relationship—as has taken place at times in the case of France, Germany, Poland, et cetera.*

"It would seem, therefore, that an essential prerequisite to the establishment of harmonious and trustful relations with the Soviet government is the abandonment by the present rulers of Russia of their world revolutionary aims and the discontinuance of their activities designed to bring about the realization of such aims. More specifically and with particular regard to the United States, this prerequisite involves the *abandonment by Moscow of direction, supervision, control, financing, et cetera, through every agency utilized for the purpose of Communist and other related activities in the United States.*"

The memorandum pointed out furthermore that the Soviet Government had been unwilling to observe "certain generally accepted principles governing the conduct of nations towards each other," because it refused to respect the rights of citizens of other States, and that international obligations had been rejected, which the experience of mankind "has demonstrated are vital to the satisfactory development and maintenance of commerce and friendly intercourse between nations."

Cordell Hull, Democrat, who was Secretary of State at the time, requested Judge Walton Moore, Assistant Secretary of State, and William Bullitt, who subse-

quently went to Moscow as the first American Ambassador, to prepare memoranda on the more important "conditions and understandings that might be considered significant in connection with the development of plans for the recognition of the Russian Government."

Mr. Bullitt, in his memorandum, said:

"Whatever method may be used to enter into negotiations with the Soviet Government, it seems essential that formal recognition should not be accorded except as the final act of an agreement covering a number of questions in dispute. Before recognition and before loans, we shall find the Soviet Government relatively amenable. After recognition or loans, we should find the Soviet Government adamant."

Mr. Bullitt wrote that there were three important conditions which in his opinion had to be met before

-Harris & Ewing

CORDELL HULL, Secretary of State 1933-44

recognition could be forthcoming. He outlined these as follows:

"1. Prohibition of Communist propaganda in the United States by the Soviet Government and by the Comintern.

"2. Protection of the civil and religious rights of Americans in Russia which are inadequately protected under current Russian practice (e.g., 'economic espionage').

"3. Agreement by the Soviet Government that the act of recognition shall not be retroactive to the foundation of that government (which is the usual practice), but shall take effect only from the day on which it may be accorded. This is essential to protect both our Government and many citizens and corporations from suits for damages."

The Bullitt memorandum said further:

"There are of course scores of other questions involved in resuming normal relations with Russia. Our position would be strongest, I believe, if all these questions, whether of a legal, economic or financial nature, should be handled as a unit in one global negotiation, the end of which would be signature of the agreements and simultaneous recognition."

Negotiations proceeded, and by an exchange of notes in the latter part of 1933 recognition was formally extended.

The exact language of the exchange of notes is of vital importance to examine now because the documents are equivalent to a treaty which must be honored by both nations if the signatures are to mean anything.

When formal recognition was finally extended on November 16, 1933, the action was taken through an exchange of letters between the Soviet Commissar for Foreign Affairs, Maxim Litvinov (who came to Washington especially for the occasion), and the President of the United States.

The language of the two notes is identical. Mr. Litvinov wrote:

"My dear Mr. President: I have the honor to inform you that coincident with the establishment of diplomatic relations between our two Governments it will be the fixed policy of the Government of the Union of Soviet Socialist Republics:

"1. To respect scrupulously the indisputable right of the United States to order its own life within its own jurisdiction in its own way and to refrain from interfering in any manner in the internal affairs of the United States, its territories or possessions.

"2. *To refrain, and to restrain all persons in government service and all organizations of the Government or under its direct or indirect control, including the organizations in receipt of any financial assistance from it, from any act overt or covert liable in any way whatsoever to injure the tranquility, prosperity, order or security of the whole or any part of the United States, its territories or possessions, and in particular, from any act tending to incite or encourage armed intervention or any agitation or propaganda having as an aim, the violation of the territorial integrity of the United States, its territories or possessions, or the bringing about by force of a change in the political or social order of the whole or any part of the United States, its territories or possessions.*

"3. Not to permit the formation or residence on its territory of any organization or group—and to prevent the activity on its territory of any organization or group, or of representatives or officials of any organization or group—which makes claim to be the Government of, or makes attempt upon the territorial integrity of, the United States, its territories or possessions; not to form, subsidize, support or permit on its territory military organizations or groups having the aim of armed struggle against the United States, its territories or possessions, and to prevent any recruiting on behalf of such organizations and groups.

"4. *Not to permit the formation or residence on its territory of any organization or group—and to prevent the activity on its territory of any organization or group, or of representatives or officials of any organization or group—which has as an aim the overthrow or the preparation for the overthrow of, or the bringing about by force of a change in the political or social order of the whole or any part of* the United States, its territories or possessions."

It is interesting to observe that President Roosevelt in acknowledging receipt of this note in his letter to Mr. Litvinov gave exactly the same assurances as the Soviet had given to us in the numbered paragraphs above.

It is significant, too, that on the same date separate letters were exchanged, on the subject of religious freedom, in which Mr. Roosevelt said to Mr. Litvinov:

"As I have told you in our recent conversations, it is my expectation that after the establishment of normal relations between our two countries many Americans will wish to reside temporarily or permanently within the territory of the Union of Soviet Socialist Republics, and I am deeply concerned that they should enjoy in all respects the same freedom of conscience and religious liberty which they enjoy at home. . . .

−United Press

MAXIM LITVINOV, Soviet Foreign Commissar in 1930s

"The Government of the United States, therefore, will expect that nationals of the United States of America within the territory of the Union of Soviet Socialist Republics will be allowed to conduct without annoyance or molestation of any kind religious services and rites of a ceremonial nature, including baptismal, confirmation, communion, marriage and burial rites, in the English language, or in any other language which is customarily used in the practice of the religious faith to which they belong, in churches, houses, or other buildings appropriate for such service, which they will be given the right and opportunity to lease, erect or maintain in convenient situations. . . .

"We will expect that religious groups or congregations composed of nationals of the United States of America in the territory of the Union of Soviet Socialist Republics will be given the right to have their spiritual needs ministered to by clergymen, priests, rabbis or other ecclesiastical functionaries who are nationals of the United States of America, and that such clergymen, priests, rabbis or other ecclesiastical functionaries will be protected from all disability or persecution and will not be denied entry into the territory of the Soviet Union because of their ecclesiastical status."

Again Mr. Litvinov wrote to President Roosevelt assuring him that the right "to free exercise of liberty of conscience and religious worship" and protection "from all disability or persecution on account of their religious faith or worship" was guaranteed by the fixed policy of the Soviet Union and that it was supported by various laws and regulations existing in the various republics of the Soviet Union.

Almost immediately after the acts of recognition occurred, the Soviet press declared that the United States had been "compelled" to restore diplomatic relations and there began a series of events which showed clearly that those who had had misgivings before were not wrong in their assumptions as to what might happen after diplomatic relations had been resumed.

We find Ambassador Bullitt shortly afterward writing to Secretary of State Hull "in regard to several instances in which the Soviet Government does not seem disposed to carry out understandings between it and the Government of the United States."

We note on August 14, 1934, Mr. Hull writing to Ambassador Bullitt in Moscow as follows:

"Since recognition was accorded the Soviet Government the Department has followed the communist movement in the United States for the purpose of ascertaining whether the propaganda pledges contained in Mr. Litvinov's note to the President of November 16, 1933, are being observed. Furthermore, various individuals and organizations, such as the American Federation of Labor, *have laid before the Department evidence tending to show violations of the pledges.*

"The Department believes that the following transactions, evidence of which seems indisputable, constitute such violations and in particular of the pledge covered by paragraph 4 of Mr. Litvinov's note. . . .

"You should emphasize that, as Mr. Litvinov is certainly aware, the American people are most sensitive with respect to interference from foreign governments in their domestic affairs and that our Government is hopeful that the Soviet Government will take appropriate means to prevent further acts in disregard of the solemn pledges he gave in its behalf."

Ambassador Bullitt reported from Moscow on October 5, 1934, as follows:

"In accordance with the instruction contained in your August 14, I protested today to Litvinov orally and informally with regard to direction from Moscow of the activities of the Communist movement in the United States. I informed Litvinov that if at the Comintern Congress, which is scheduled to take place in the month of January, there should be attacks on the Government of the United States or indications that the Communist movement in the United States is being directed by Moscow the most serious consequences might result; that the Government of the United States was as sensitive as the people of the United States to any interference in our internal affairs by agencies of foreign countries. Litvinov replied that he did not even know that the Comintern Congress would take place and that he was not aware of any activities of this nature. . . .

"I think I might go so far as to intimate to Litvinov verbally that we *might sever diplomatic relations* if the Comintern should be allowed to get out of hand. . . ."

Then on October 8 Secretary of State Hull sent a note to Ambassador Bullitt in which he said:

"Without making any statement to Litvinov that *diplomatic relations might under certain circumstances be severed,* it is highly desirable to give him the impression that in case of a violation of pledges he made when here and failure to agree to that settlement on such reasonable terms as we have proposed, the relations between the two governments will inevitably be less close and friendly than anticipated, and the reason for our government doing many things contemplated may disappear."

Again we find Ambassador Bullitt on July 19, 1935, writing to Secretary of State Hull as follows:

"*Contrary to the comforting belief which the French now cherish, it is my conviction that there has been no*

PRESIDENT FRANKLIN D. ROOSEVELT
—United Press

decrease in the determination of the Soviet Government to produce world revolution. Diplomatic relations with friendly states are not regarded by the Soviet Government as normal friendly relations, but 'armistice' relations, and it is the conviction of the leaders of the Soviet Union that this 'armistice' cannot possibly be ended by a definitive peace but only by renewal of battle. The Soviet Union genuinely desires peace on all fronts at the present time, but this peace is looked upon merely as a happy respite in which future wars may be prepared.

". . . I feel sure that the Department must have received many reports that the Soviet Government has abandoned the idea of world revolution and that the convictions I have expressed above may seem ill founded. I can only say that my own observations, without exception, have convinced me of the accuracy of my statement. *I have yet to converse with a single leader of the Soviet Union who has not expressed his belief in the necessity of world revolution.*"

This was the view of Ambassador Bullitt, who had gone to the Soviet Union with a very friendly attitude toward the regime there, and who had indeed participated in the negotiations leading to the extension of recognition. But he was quickly disillusioned when he came into actual contact with the Russians in Moscow.

Ambassador Bullitt on August 21, 1935, in a message to the Department of State, pointed out how Litvinov's pledges had been violated and describing in detail the meeting of the Communist International, together with the attacks made upon the United States at that meeting. Urging that President Roosevelt make a speech giving utterance to his views concerning the activities of the Communists inside the United States, Mr. Bullitt wrote:

"I venture to suggest that henceforth the law excluding Communists from the United States should be applied rigidly and that you should instruct all American Missions to refuse visas to Soviet citizens unless they present entirely satisfactory evidence that they are not and have never been members of the Communist Party or Communist International, and are not candidates for admission to the Communist Party or Communist International and are not members of the Profintern."

Instead of a speech by the President, a note was sent to the Russian Government on August 25, expressing the protest of the United States. Attention was called to the Litvinov pledge and to its violation at the meeting of the "All World Congress of the Communist International," and the note added:

"The Government of the United States would be lacking in candor if it failed to state frankly that it anticipates the most serious consequences if the Government of the Union of Soviet Socialist Republics is unwilling, or unable, to take *appropriate measures to prevent further acts in disregard of the solemn pledge given by it to the Government of the United States.*"

The Russian Government answered the note on August 27 by saying that it could not take upon itself "obligations of any kind with regard to the Communist International."

Secretary of State Hull on September 1, 1935, issued the following statement to the press:

"The recent note of this Government to the Government of the Soviet Union and the reply of that Government raises the issue whether that Government, *in dis-* *regard of an express agreement entered into at the time of recognition in 1933,* will permit organizations or groups operating on its territory to plan and *direct movements contemplating the overthrow of the political or social order of the United States.* For sixteen years this Government withheld recognition—as did many other Governments—mainly for the reason that the Soviet Government had failed to respect the right of this nation to maintain its own political and social order without interference by organizations conducting in or from Soviet territory activities directed against our institutions.

"In 1933 this Government, observing the serious effects upon peace and prosperity of the many partial or dislocated international relationships throughout the world, took up anew the question whether the United States and the Soviet Union, two of the largest nations, could not find a way to establish more natural and normal relations, which would afford a basis for genuine friendship and collaboration to promote peace and improve material conditions both at home and abroad.

"After various stipulations in writing had first been carefully drafted and agreed upon by representatives of the two governments, recognition was accorded to the Government of the Soviet Union by this Government in November, 1933. One of the most important provisions of the agreement thus reached *was the pledge of the Soviet Government to respect the right of the United States to order its own life within its own jurisdiction in its own way and to refrain from interfering in any manner in the internal affairs of the United States, its territories or possessions.'*

"The essence of this pledge was the obligation assumed by the Soviet Government not to permit persons or groups on its territory to engage in efforts or movements directed toward the overthrow of our institutions. . .

"*In its reply of August 27, 1935, to this Government's note of August 25, 1935, the Soviet Government almost in so many words repudiated the pledge which it gave at the time of recognition . . . If the Soviet Government pursues a policy permitting activities on its territory involving interference in the internal affairs of the United States, instead of 'preventing' such activities as its written pledge provides, the friendly and official relations between the two countries cannot but be seriously impaired.*"

III. "Listening Post" of Doubtful Value

Already, by November 24, 1937, we were finding that the value of an American Ambassador in Moscow as a "listening post" had been very much exaggerated. In a memorandum written on that date, George F. Kennan, of the Division of European Affairs in the Department of State, said:

"The Soviet policy in general: When this Government has sent ambassadors to the Soviet Union it has had a right to expect that they would be welcomed with something more substantial than formal words, and that they would be accorded by the Soviet authorities that measure of cooperation which is essential if their missions were to contribute to advancing American-Soviet rela- tions. But the experience of the two Ambassadors [William C. Bullitt and Joseph E. Davies] who have represented the United States in the Soviet Union, compels one to the conclusion that the Soviet Government has made it a policy to place every possible restriction on the activities and contacts of foreign missions in that city. The Soviet leaders appear to welcome the presence of foreign envoys in Moscow as something contributory to Soviet prestige; but they make it very evident that in their opinion these envoys—like well-trained children —should be seen and not heard.

"*In this they have little cause to fear retaliation on the part of foreign governments.* The Soviet diplomatic missions abroad constitute only one (and not always the most important) of the channels through which Russia's foreign affairs are directed. The situation in many countries—and particularly in the United States —is such that it is an easy matter for Moscow to circumvent the governments of these countries and to deal directly with private individuals, firms and organizations. It has its trade delegations, its local Communist parties, its foreign newspaper correspondents, and its various disguised agents, to help it in these efforts. Thus the Soviet leaders have been able to proceed to curb the scope of activity of the Moscow diplomatic corps, *confident that no retaliatory measures which might follow could effectively disturb their own business with the outside* world. . . .

"The presence of an American Ambassador in Moscow has apparently led to little if any change in the activities carried on in the United States by the Communist International. In 1934 (1935) this Government was compelled to make formal protest in connection with the meetings in Moscow at the VII All-World Congress of the International. *Despite this protest there is evidence that Soviet leaders are continuing to exercise authority over a certain political group in this country and are requiring members of this group to serve political interests which have nothing in common with those of the United States."*

Secretary of State Hull reveals his record of a conversation on January 13, 1938, with the Soviet Ambassador in Washington, when he read to him a memorandum which said in part:

"Ever since diplomatic relations between the United States and the Soviet Union were established the American Government has earnestly sought to make a real contribution toward maintaining them on a close and friendly basis by effecting solution of a number of matters which have been the source of irritation if not indeed of friction. That success has not attended its efforts is due, in part at least, to the attitude that has been evidenced by the Soviet authorities. . . .

"Indeed, the American Government has been constrained, in view of the conditions under which the American Embassy in Moscow has functioned ever since it was established, to consider whether the value to it of that mission is sufficient to warrant the maintenance of the Embassy on the present scale."

There are many references in the foreign-relations documents showing that American Embassy officials abroad were experiencing more and more difficulty in dealing with the Soviet Government. Thus, Loy Henderson, United States Chargé d'Affaires at Moscow, wrote to Secretary of State Hull on February 1, 1938, as follows:

"1. It should be considered as axiomatic that the ruling forces of the Soviet Union have always considered and still take the view that the presence of foreign diplomatic representatives in the Soviet Union is an evil which world conditions force them to endure;

"2. In order that the effects of this evil may be reduced to a minimum, *they consider it advantageous to follow a policy which will tend to restrict the influence, prestige, and effectiveness of the diplomatic missions in Moscow;*

"3. This policy is expressed in part by the adoption of measures, the purpose of which is to discourage the maintenance of large missions, to cause the population of the country to look with suspicion or at least with lack of respect upon these missions, to restrict the activities, freedom of movement, and number of contacts of members of these missions, and to cause members of these missions gradually to acquire a feeling that if they forfeit the good will of the Soviet authorities by fearlessly and resolutely defending the interests of the Governments which they represent they are likely to encounter increased difficulties in operating their chanceries and households with a reasonable degree of effectiveness and economy and in performing the various duties imposed upon them by their Governments, and are even likely to be attacked openly or privately as saboteurs of Soviet relations with their respective countries;

—Wide World
GEORGE F. KENNAN, U. S. Ambassador to Russia 1952

"4. One of the most effective instruments which the Soviet authorities possess for the execution of this policy is their power to decide by means of the formulation and interpretation of customs regulations the conditions under which diplomatic missions may bring articles into or take them out of the country;

"5. The Soviet customs, laws and regulations are deliberately so worded that if given a strict interpretation the life of members of diplomatic missions in the Soviet Union would be so unpleasant and the cost of the upkeep of such missions so expensive that comparatively few governments would endeavor to support diplomatic representation in that country;

"6. Since in present world conditions, the Soviet Government feels that it is necessary for it to maintain diplomatic relations with other countries, it follows the policy of interpreting and applying the customs regulations in such a manner as not to cause foreign governments to withdraw their missions from the country;

"7. The Soviet authorities apparently are of the opinion that at the present time most diplomatic missions in Moscow are maintained by governments which feel that under existing world conditions their representations in the Soviet Union must not be withdrawn even though the conditions under which such representations are compelled to work are difficult;

"8. This opinion and the rise of antiforeign feeling, particularly noticeable during the past year, undoubtedly partially explains the increasing degree of strictness with which Soviet customs regulations are enforced;

"9. This strictness will increase until it runs counter to opposition of a nature that will cause the ruling forces to find it to be the best policy to call another temporary 'breathing spell';

"10. If, therefore, the American Government and other governments maintaining diplomatic missions in Moscow permit without protest curtailments of the courtesies accorded by Soviet Customs officials to their diplomatic representations, new and more serious curtailments of such courtesies may be expected in the future;

"11. In view of the impossibility of obtaining in Moscow supplies for office and household and of the exorbitance of Soviet import and export duties, the matter of customs courtesies is much more serious in the Soviet Union than in most countries; and

"12. Since merchandise in the United States is plentiful and since exports are not subject to export duties, customs courtesies mean much more to the American Embassy in Moscow than they do to the Soviet Embassy in Washington."

DISCOURTESY TO ENVOYS—

This same situation is discussed further between Secretary Hull and the Soviet Ambassador. Here is a quotation from a memorandum by Secretary Hull written on March 26, 1938:

"After talking on another subject, the Russian Ambassador then brought up the question of the complaints in the memorandum which this Government handed to him some weeks ago relative to unsatisfactory treatment of our officials and employees and American travelers in his country. He undertook generally to deny most of these complaints, adding that he would soon present a memorandum on the subject.

"I stated that disagreeable as the small pinpricks were, there was a worse phase that our Government has in mind and that is the atmosphere created there of inconvenience and indifference and of more or less uninviting hospitality to those who go into Russia, including the constant espionage and interference with Russian employees of American citizens in the Embassy and Chancery at Moscow; that it prevents this country from improving the relations between the two countries as we are so desirous of doing, especially from the standpoint of promoting peace and mutual welfare; that regardless of the accuracy or inaccuracy of the charges presented, we are seriously handicapped in this broad way and I consider that extremely important.

"I concluded by saying that if, after we had recognized Russia, that country and this country and Great Britain and France had gone forward in the exercise of normal relations and in developing their combined moral influence for peace, the unpleasant experiences in both

the Far East and in Europe would have been reduced at least 50%, whereas the present policies of Russia in these small ways are seriously handicapping such supremely important efforts. . . ."

The most authoritative commentary on what happened before and after diplomatic relations with Soviet Russia were formally begun in November of 1933 is to be obtained from a reading of "The Memoirs of Cordell Hull" (published in 1948 by the Macmillan Company).

MR. HULL'S ANALYSIS—

Mr. Hull reviews the events leading up to the negotiations for the resumption of diplomatic relations and tells how, in advance of the step, he had called to the attention of the President that the United States should face the practical considerations concerning the conduct of the negotiations. He writes in his book:

"Consequently, I told the President we had two powerful weapons which can be used to bring about a favorable settlement of some, if not all, of our outstanding problems with the Soviet Government.

"I am convinced, from the experience of other countries, that, unless we utilize every available means of exerting pressure on the Soviet Government in order to obtain a settlement of outstanding problems, there is little likelihood that such problems can be satisfactorily solved. It is evident that if loans of any considerable amount should be extended to the Soviet Government, except as a part of an agreement involving a satisfactory settlement of such problems, one of our most effective weapons would be taken from our hands—possibly the most effective—since the Soviets, it is believed, prefer at the moment credits to recognition. I concluded by recommending that no loans be extended 'except as part and parcel of a final settlement of our relations with Russia.'

"*Thus our approach to the question was different from that of other nations then maintaining diplomatic relations with Russia. Those nations recognized Russia first and then began to discuss the questions in dispute between them. The results were generally disappointing. Having obtained part of what she wanted, Russia became less disposed to make concessions to obtain the remainder.*

"In some respects we stood to gain more than Russia by a restoration of diplomatic relations. Without relations, the Russians were probably much better informed about conditions in America than we were about the situation in Russia. The Soviets were in close touch with what was going on here through their Amtorg, or trading office, in New York, an Information Bureau in Washington, and the American Communist Party."

Mr. Hull describes the negotiations in the agreements that were formally signed and then writes:

"*But our efforts toward closer relations were again to be negated. The Communist International, with headquarters in Moscow, continued to support Communist propaganda and activities in the United States. We made verbal complaints to Moscow, without result.* Finally Russia permitted the holding of an All-World Congress of the Communist International in Moscow from July 25 to August 20, 1935. American Communists attended and took part in discussions and plans for the development of the Communist Party in the United States. Here was a flagrant violation of the pledge of noninterference given us on November 16, 1933, and we could not let it pass without protest. By agreement with the President, I sent through Ambassador Bullitt a strong note to the Soviet Government:

" *'The Government of the United States would be lacking in candor if it failed to state frankly that it anticipates the most serious consequences if the Government of the Union of Soviet Socialist Republics is unwilling, or unable, to take appropriate measures to prevent further acts in disregard of the solemn pledge given by it to the Government of the United States.'*

"But the Soviets replied with the astounding assertion that 'it is certainly not new to the Government of the United States that the Government of the Union of Soviet Socialist Republics cannot take upon itself and has not taken upon itself obligations of any kind with regard to the Communist International.' They refused to accept the protest. In other words, the Communist International, although intimately connected with the Soviet Government, could do what it wanted in American internal affairs without interference from that Government.

"In publishing both notes, I issued a statement in which I said: 'In view of the plain language of the pledge, it is not possible for the Soviet Government to disclaim its obligation to prevent activities on its territory directed toward overthrowing the political or social order in the United States. And that Government does not and cannot disclaim responsibility on the ground of inability to carry out the pledge, for its authority within its territorial limits is supreme and its power to control the acts and utterances of organizations and individuals within those limits is absolute . . . If the Soviet Government pursues a policy of permitting activities on its territory involving interference in the internal affairs of the United States, instead of "preventing" such activities, as its written pledge provides, the friendly and official relations between the two countries cannot but be seriously impaired.'

"*We were now back almost to where we had started. We had official relations with Moscow, but they rested on no bedrock of friendship and cooperation. Try as I might, I could not establish the sound relationship I deemed so necessary not only for the two countries but also as a counter-weight for peace in the scales tipping more sharply toward war.*"

IV. A Road to Negotiation

The foregoing record demonstrates conclusively that we can utilize the severence and possible resumption of diplomatic relations as an instrument of policy and that it can be, moreover, the basis for extensive negotiations.

By severing diplomatic relations with all the countries behind the Iron Curtain, the United States will in reality be adopting a policy that could prevent war and lead to a state of peace in the world.

Severance of diplomatic relations with the government at Moscow actually means opening up the road to negotiation for peace. It means in effect negotiation with the only sovereign that can make peace, namely, the people of Soviet Russia.

Such a policy should not be put into effect in a mood of pique—as if it were related to a single act that had produced irritation in our midst. It should stem from the moral force that has been the root of American idealism throughout our history.

Many persons who have conscientiously opposed this course when it has been suggested do not take into consideration the fact that severance of diplomatic relations, like its predecessor step—the opening of diplomatic relations—is a fundamental concept which can have a constructive aim. They fail to realize that it can be a constructive, rather than a destructive move and that it can conceivably awaken the world to the ways by which we can avert the outbreak of war. It can accomplish more than threats or counter-threats to use military force alone.

While it is true that severance of diplomatic relations has sometimes immediately preceded the outbreak of war, this has not at all been true in those instances where the diplomatic break has been based upon differences in fundamental policy, as contrasted with instances where some overt act led to the break itself.

History shows more instances in which a diplomatic break is an intermediate step toward peaceful intercourse rather than a final step toward war.

Within the last two years, Soviet Russia severed diplomatic relations with both Israel and then Australia—episodes in the evolution of her international policies. It didn't lead to war in either case.

It is contended that there are advantages in maintaining a "listening post" behind the Iron Curtain and that this factor is of such importance as to outweigh all moral considerations. While such an argument has some merit it suggests an excuse for inaction rather than a basic reason. For too often the philosophy of moral cowardice, which consults its fears rather than its conscience, winds up with the self-same crisis that a policy of timidity and forbearance sought to avoid.

If every time we contemplate some step in the evolution of our moral policies we are urged not to offend the other side, to repress our indignation, and so to conduct ourselves as not to antagonize tyrants who are every day oppressing millions and millions of people, then indeed it may be that Western civilization has started on the road to decay and disintegration. There is no obligation resting upon us to consult our enemies about what to do about our enemies. We must not be frightened by our own self-created bogeys.

No better demonstration of the power of moral force in world policies could be given than that which occurred during the Administration of President William Howard Taft, when the government of the Czar refused to honor the passports of American citizens if they happened to be Jews. To the credit of the Taft Administration be it said that the United States notified the Russian Government that an American passport applied equally to all citizens and that there could be no discrimination between them, if the treaty which had been signed by the Russian Government were to be honored.

The Russian Government refused to change its policy, and the United States denounced the treaty as no longer in effect.

Nobody suggested at the time that by offending the Russian Government we would create a situation of international tension which could lead to war. Nobody suggested that the United States yield to expediency and recognize a "practical" situation, because the anti-Semitic policy was an internal problem in Russia at the time.

As to the argument that it is valuable to have American diplomats behind the Iron Curtain to "listen," the record there proves this is an advantage of dubious value.

Very little information that comes through official quarters is any different from that which is broadcast by the Moscow radio or the radio stations of its satellites. Most of the information that has been obtained by the United States Government concerning conditions in Russia has come from sources other than the Embassy. Naturally the most valuable facts about internal conditions come from the hundreds of thousands of persons who travel across the borders during the course of the year in business, professional and cultural pursuits of various kinds. It is obvious that Americans living in a restricted area in Moscow are not necessarily the best sources of information about Russia. The nationals of various countries who travel back and forth are better qualified to keep us informed, particularly those who have contacts with former residents of the Soviet Union, namely nationals of Soviet Russia now in exile.

Severance of diplomatic relations would impress the Soviet people, but much would depend upon exactly how the policy was executed. If it appeared as a mere manifestation of anger it would lose its moral force.

If our argument were focused, however, on the pledges that have been broken and on the agreements that were entered into by the Soviet Government and dishonored, it would profoundly impress the people of Soviet Russia.

With the opportunities we now have for disseminating our point of view throughout the globe, it would be practicable for our own government to make a forceful presentation of all the reasons for the severance. The very debate would draw attention to the moral issues which have so long been neglected.

The severance of diplomatic relations, therefore, would be not a negative but an affirmative act. It would mean that the American people had opened their hearts and minds to the peoples of Soviet Russia and dealt with them directly in an effort to find some means of bringing about peaceful relations between the peoples. It would give hope where there is now despair. The Red Army in particular, which must make the major sacrifice in the event of war, would be especially interested to learn why America had found it impractical to deal with the present rulers in the Kremlin. For the Moscow government has never been portrayed inside Russia as the big obstacle to world peace.

Obviously this obstacle, namely a government in Moscow *which dishonors pledges,* is something which, if emphasized to the Russian people would in due time make them realize they were being represented by a government that can suddenly plunge them into war. It is a government which does not give the people an opportunity to express their wishes—a government which has become a menace to them and to mankind.

It will be said that, with the censorship of the press inside Russia, the documents sent forth by the United States would not be printed, but as news about them came over the radio this in itself would direct attention to the restrictions upon the relations between the two countries growing out of the censorship and the supression of the free flow of opinion. Radio and word-of-mouth would give it full publicity in the end.

The severance of diplomatic relations would permit a minute review of all the experiences, incidents, episodes and controversies between the United States and the Soviet Union beginning in 1933.

The mere narration of these events would be enlightening to the public opinion of the world.

It would reveal America as acting in self-defense against the encroachment of Communist agents and saboteurs.

It would constitute the greatest blow that could be struck by means of moral force, thus demonstrating to the world that the decent opinion of mankind can be more important as a means of bringing peace than the threats to use military force alone.

For when we sever diplomatic relations because of the breaking of pledges, dishonoring of agreements and the disregard of international obligations, we base our action on the highest standards of human conduct.

Our spokesmen, on the one hand, declare frequently that we do not want war. We cannot, on the other, fail to use the weapons of moral force which reach into the hearts and minds of people to prevent war.

It takes courage to exercise moral force. Even the counsel of those who propose the exercise of moral force is rejected as "leading to war." Yet the only road really open to those who shrink from the use of moral force is more and more appeasement, and finally war, because the overt acts of an arrogant enemy inevitably produce war.

V. Would the Allies Join Us?

The question will be raised as to the practicality of such a step in the event that our allies do not take similar action.

American leadership cannot be forfeited, nor can our expression of our free opinions be restrained merely because temporarily there is no agreement with us on the part of other countries.

Precisely because other governments may not concur at once, our opportunity for debate would be widened. It would lend emphasis to the discussion. On the so-called "practical" side—to those who believe that it is important to have a "listening post behind the Iron Curtain"—it should be mentioned that the American Government would have ready access to any of the diplomatic reports of any of the other governments during the interval while we who have severed diplomatic relations wait for the others to do so.

But this very interval would be of far-reaching importance. We would be urging upon our own allies that they take a course of action similar to ours. This debate would have a profound effect inside the Soviet Union. For the discussion itself would afford an opportunity anew to draw attention to the spy rings and infiltration campaigns which actually have been carried on by Soviet agents in the United States, Canada, Australia, Guatemala, Britain, France, Italy, Japan, and almost every one of the free countries.

It would not be necessary for the debate to be limited in length. It might go on for several months, with the United States pressing powerfully on the morale-force side, and with the allies one by one coming to our side as they gradually recognize the futility of further negotiations with the Kremlin government itself, or else as they perceive a change in government control there and finally an attitude which could conceivably bring about a new and better understanding between Soviet Russia and the rest of the world.

The Soviet Government itself is outwardly indifferent nowadays to the problem of maintenance or discontinuance of diplomatic relations with non-Communist countries. It believes evidently that the Western world would maintain them no matter what happened. Our failure to exercise more leverage in this situation by raising the question of whether we care to continue diplomatic relations has recently brought repeated instances of disrespect for our representatives in Moscow.

Today we seem to be unconcerned about exercising any leverage at all against the Soviet Government. We appear to be passively acquiescing in every act of the Soviet Union. We find ourselves in a strait jacket because we, of course, will not precipitate a war, and the phrase "likely to precipitate a war" is directed inside America against any policy except abject acquiescence.

Those who argue against precipitating war cannot have it both ways. They cannot, on the one hand, urge that our armed forces be immobilized, and on the other hand insist that we shall not take any steps to advance our cause in the court of world opinion.

WIELDING MORAL FORCE—

Our only opportunity today in the court of world opinion is to mobilize moral force. And the biggest instrument of moral force is in our hands, namely, the severance of diplomatic relations. It is logical, legal and clear cut and can be carried on to assure in the end the peace of the world.

Precisely as we laid down the basis for recognition by written conditions, so we can lay down the basis for the withdrawal of that recognition or the severance of diplomatic relations, and also the basis for resumption when the original conditions of 1933 have been fully met by the Soviet Union.

When there is an opportunity for the resumption of diplomatic relations we would be in the position of discussing a new state of affairs in which the Soviets would be making concessions to the rest of the world. We would not remain in the fixed position in which we are today taking affront after affront without really doing anything to impress our enemies that we might make a countermove that could be effective.

We shall not cease to express our own government's views merely because of the discontinuance of one form of technical communication between the United States Government and the Soviet Government. With radio and newspapers and the reports of those who go back and forth across the border there are many ways to discuss our relations with Russia and to bring home to the people there our views besides the method of formal diplomatic notes, which have really grown less and less effective anyway in recent years.

BASIS FOR NEW POLICY—

The true meaning of the severance of diplomatic relations, moreover, would not be lost upon the world as a whole. It would have a significance far more than the actual change which involves the withdrawal of a few diplomats from Moscow. For it could form the basis for a new policy in negotiating with the Russian peoples— a new set-up as between the United States and Soviet Russia.

America must take the leadership in such a moral cause. Those who say it is theoretically right to discontinue relations with the Soviet Government but not expedient are unintentionally condoning evil and destroying the hopes of the oppressed peoples.

The Soviet Government today has only contempt for vacillation in an adversary. That's because again and again we have been pushed back and insulted without showing the slightest bit of spirit in protest.

The long history of the periods prior to the outbreak of war shows that, when a nation fails unequivocally to express its viewpoint and to maintain its honor and insist upon the fulfillment of solemn pledges, it gives the impression of craven weakness, and ultimately it is overrun by an enemy, which miscalculates and thinks that it can win an easy victory.

The way to prevent World War III is to assert our moral position and to indicate clearly and persistently to the peoples of Soviet Russia that it is their government which is pushing us slowly but surely into a larger conflict.

As a warning against such a large conflict the severance of diplomatic relations can have a sobering effect. It can focus attention on the real issues between our governments and the dangerous steps that have been taken by the Kremlin government to infiltrate our own territory in an attempt to set up agencies to overthrow our government. Our Department of Justice, our Federal Courts, our Congressional committees for the last ten years have recorded in official testimony the acts of Soviet agents on our territory.

The question naturally will be asked as a corollary: *What effect would the severance of diplomatic relations have upon our relations with the United Nations?*

Strictly speaking, the question of the maintenance or severance of diplomatic relations with a particular government is not related in the legal or diplomatic sense to the membership which a particular nation may have in an international organization set up for specific purposes. Thus many governments now in the U.N. recognize Red China although it has not been admitted to the U.N. Conversely, there are governments recognized by the United States and diplomatic relations are maintained with those governments, but they are not members of the United Nations, though of course eligible for such membership.

It cannot be denied, however—and in fact it should be emphasized—that there is a moral relationship between the position of the United States with respect to the severance of relations with the Soviet Union and continued membership of the Soviet Union in the United Nations.

For example, all of the arguments we have made for the non-recognition of the Government of Red China and for its non-admission into the United Nations are on all fours with those which can logically be made for our severance of diplomatic relations with the Soviet Union and for its expulsion from the United Nations.

It is not logical, on the one hand, to say that we will not admit Red China to the United Nations because of its aggressive policies and at the same time permit the Soviet Union to remain in the United Nations while it continues its aggressive policies toward other members of the United Nations.

It has been frankly acknowledged by the representatives of the Soviet Union in a formal meeting of the United Nations Assembly that the Moscow government sent arms and ammunition to the Chinese and North Korean governments, and thus aided and abetted in that aggression, even though the United Nations by formal resolution had called upon all its members to refrain from sending arms to assist the aggressors.

In this connection, a few weeks ago Ambassador Henry Cabot Lodge, in a CBS radio-television discussion with some newspaper correspondents, was asked the question concerning the membership of the Soviet Union in the United Nations. The colloquy ran in part as follows:

"**Q:** Mr. Ambassador, could we get back to that word 'peace-loving' for a moment? Now, do we understand that a country, to be a U.N. member, must be peace-loving—by implication be part of a club of very peaceful, law-abiding nations? It seems, for example, to begin with, Russia wasn't one in 1945, and Russia was one of the original signers of the U.N. Charter—

"**Mr. Lodge:** Well, I think that in 1945 and 1946, at San Francisco, the United States assumed that Russia was a peace-loving nation, and the whole United Nations was based on the assumption that the alliance between the United States and the Soviet Union would continue, which, of course, was a very false—tragically false—assumption. Certainly, if we had thought at that time that the Soviet Union believed in war as an instrument of national policy, we would not have joined the United Nations with her."

From the foregoing it is clear that the Soviet Union has no moral right to continued membership in the United Nations. The League of Nations did expel the Soviet Union from that organization. The United Nations ought to have the moral courage at least to suspend the membership of the Kremlin tyrants. The seat can be declared vacant by the action of the Assembly.

It is this moral issue which is raised not only in the continued membership of an aggressor nation in the United Nations, but also in the refusal of all forward-looking nations to countenance the admission of Red China into the United Nations for the same reasons.

So by a single stroke in severing diplomatic relations we would be reopening the whole question of whether the present government of the Soviet Union should remain in the United Nations. This probably would not be decided immediately. But the moral effect of a thorough discussion would be felt around the globe. Step by step the moral forces of mankind would concentrate on evils which are now upsetting the peace of the world.

VI. An Act of Self-Defense

So, to summarize, the severance of diplomatic relations is an act of self-defense. It is a step taken to prevent the encroachment by the agents of foreign governments upon our territory in their attempt to infiltrate our institutions. Every democratic government has a right to resist such measures, by banning the use of its own territory for the conduct of operations hostile to itself.

What we say, in effect, is this: "We are not interfering with your internal affairs, but we are resenting the use of your power externally to the injury of the United States."

Sooner or later the Western world must recognize that the policies of Soviet Russia are actually hostile to them, as is proved by the many processes of subversion and internal infiltration that have characterized the so-called "cold war."

By severing diplomatic relations we also take the necessary steps toward the shutting off of all trade relationships with the United States. We can stop the flow of money to the many Soviet consulates and agencies in various countries, which are the centers of espionage. Unquestionably the Latin-American governments would eventually follow our lead, and a very important opportunity that the Soviets now have to upset Latin-American governments would be eliminated. That would be consistent with our Monroe Doctrine and the recent pronouncements of the Organization of American States.

It is obvious that the subversive movements throughout the world, conducted by the Soviet Union, could not be financed except with Russian rubles cabled to its agents in embassies everywhere, who bribe officials, newspapers, and other media of communication, especially in Latin-American countries, to help them do their work of subversion.

We know that on the continent of Africa, and in various parts of Asia, the Communist agents are busily engaged in moves to upset existing regimes, and to capitalize on existing controversies. But the money for such exploits would not be forthcoming if diplomatic relations and trade relations were cut off.

What we are advocating here is a policy of non-intercourse with the Soviet regime, which when fully explained to the people of the Soviet empire must inevitably result in some internal change. This is the hope of the world, and we must contribute toward that end by shaping our policies in self-defense against those who have made war upon us.

For the severance of diplomatic relations is merely a logical sequel to the acts of offense which have been committed by the Soviet regime upon the territories of free peoples. To condone these evils is to compound them and to deprive free peoples of their only means of protection against an enemy in the modern world which disregards all rules of sovereignty, all rules of international law, all obligations and agreements solemnly entered into and signed in formal agreements, and all assurances and guarantees given to respect the rights of others.

By interrupting diplomatic relations with the Soviet Union we would be telling the entire world that the United States of America, which has always stood in the past on moral principle, is continuing vigorously to pursue the course of morality, and that it will not resume diplomatic relations with any government which has violated its pledges to the United States Government, and which gives no practical evidence of any change in its attitude.

NO EVIDENCE OF GOOD FAITH—

We have called in the last few years for "deeds and not just words" from Soviet Russia. President Eisenhower has spoken publicly of the importance of concrete evidence on the part of the Soviet Union that it will act in good faith, but no such evidence has come forth. Under those circumstances we have no choice but to develop a policy of non-intercourse, with the definite assurance given by us that this policy will be gradually modified and relations with a new government established in Soviet Russia as soon as the Russian people express their will freely and put into office a government that will respect international obligations.

There are, of course, only two ways by which the present government in the Kremlin can be altered—that is either by external military action or internal force.

External force is out of the question because we don't wish to give the Communists an opportunity to consoli-

date their position inside the country and light the fires of patriotism and nationalism.

Internal force is the logical instrument. Revolution or peaceful change is the only means by which a despotic government can be removed without bringing on an external war.

Again and again in recent history we find that revolutions are short-lived or that the impact of pressure from the people will without bloodshed cause the resignation of unpopular rulers.

When a great nation like the United States lays the case before the world and tells the people of Soviet Russia what its government has done to impair the peace of the world, the people there must inevitably learn the truth about the danger that they face. For the real danger is that the Kremlin will involve them in a war which will require great sacrifices from the very people who only recently suffered so heavily on the battlefield.

KREMLIN CREATES WAR FEAR—

The fear of war grips everybody in the world, and the people of Soviet Russia are no exception. It is a hazard that the present rulers in the Kremlin have created which is dangerous to the future of all peoples. That is why we must never enhance the prestige of the present rulers of the Kremlin. We must not engage in "high level" conferences which can be played up in the Soviet press as examples of how the Western nations are bowing to the "great rulers" in the Politburo. We must not treat the leaders in the Kremlin as if they were our equals in the world and respectable representatives of a great nation. On the contrary, we must do as Secretary of State Charles Evans Hughes advised in 1923 when he said:

"Nothing should be done to place the seal of approval on the tyrannical measures that have been adopted in Russia, or to take any action which might retard the gradual reassertion of the Russian people of their right to life in freedom."

Only by a severance of diplomatic relations can we give convincing evidence to the people behind the Iron Curtain of the dangerous course which the evil men in power in Moscow have chosen to pursue.

When diplomatic relations have been severed and the debate begins throughout the world, the moral force of all the oppressed people will be strengthened and stimulated so that they will in their own way bring into being in Moscow a free government which will have the respect of the rest of mankind. Such a free government will have earned not only recognition, but a rightful place in the family of nations, and, of course, in the United Nations itself.

AMERICANS "FOR SALE"

DECEMBER 24, 1954

Time was when the American flag and the American uniform stood for the honor of the United States.

Time was when the rights of American citizens, if transgressed anywhere on the face of the globe, were championed by a government ready to back them up with the full power of the American people.

Time was when the rights of American citizens were recognized all over the world as inviolate—even in the early days when our infant republic courageously warned the blackmailing pirates of North Africa: "Millions for defense—but not one cent for tribute."

Time was when we landed our Marines in China along with the troops of other nations to rescue the personnel of our legation held captive by revolutionists in Peking. And we got them back, too.

Time was when the torpedoing of an unarmed merchant vessel flying a foreign flag and carrying American citizens brought forth a demand from the United States Government that such piracy cease lest America apply her military strength to protect the lives of men, women and children travelling on the high seas. We entered World War I to uphold that principle.

But today it is different.

A government in America—the land of the brave and the home of the free—actually has paid tribute and, indeed, bought freedom for Vogeler and Oatis and two American fliers who lost their course and made an emergency landing in Czechoslovakia (see page 49 for the record of the ransoms). And this very week we stand ready to bargain and barter for the release of 11 American airmen held prisoner as "spies" in Red China.

If the freedom of the 11 airmen is bought today, what does it mean tomorrow in further demands? How many more Americans have the Red Chinese in their stockpile of captives ready to be brought out for the next deal?

And does anybody who knows the Asian people believe for one moment that American prestige will be enhanced by such a barter transaction?

For throughout Asia it will be regarded as weakness on the part of the United States and her allies. It will encourage further aggression and finally war will be forced upon us as the only choice. Then many thousands of American lives will be lost, just as happened in World War II after the Munich appeasement had stimulated the arrogant aggressor to take a chance that the attitude by the allies would remain craven.

Today we have given up our own position as the protector of American rights and passed the buck to the United Nations.

More than 140,000 American boys shed their blood in order to "repel aggression" and the Korean war ended with an armistice which specifically stipulated that we were to return Communist prisoners of war and they were to return our boys. Plainly, the armistice now has been broken and the Communists have shown their contempt for the agreement.

The United Nations has just adopted a resolution "condemning" the action of the Red Chinese. The U. N. would probably never issue an invitation to a Red China representative to come to New York to address the Assembly or sit down with the representatives of other countries and negotiate. But, curiously enough, the Secretary-General of the U. N. has publicly offered to go to Peiping to plead with the head of the Communist Government for mercy. Hat in hand, suppliant, and ready to pay a ransom to the blackmailers, the envoy of the U. N. announced last week his willingness to go 8,000 miles to make the best deal he can get. Red China promptly took advantage of the humiliating proposal and accepted the offer.

This is the "new look" in American foreign policy.

This is the "collective security" which the U. N. is supposed to give us when we yield our sovereignty—presumably in the interest of "world peace."

This is the outcome of the Korean adventure for which American boys were drafted. They went to the Far East with the inspiring slogans of a noble cause. Their mission was heralded as an action that could prevent World War III.

Apologies now are in order to the dead in Korea who made the supreme sacrifice rather than surrender the honor of their country.

For the realistic truth is that an armistice has been broken and we do not choose to enforce its terms. The stark fact is that the Red China Government has imprisoned boys wearing the American uniform, and the Government of the United States has offered to buy them back. At this writing the price hasn't been finally fixed for the ransom of our fliers. But something is to be given in exchange—either the release of "frozen assets" or Chinese "students" in America. Some concession to the bandit government of Red China is in the offing as indicated by official sources in Washington.

This marks the beginning of the decay of American prestige abroad and the decline of American honor at home. What will we sell next—our souls?

FOR 1955—WHICH MOOD?

DECEMBER 31, 1954

THE MOOD OF 1954 has been characterized by a manifest reluctance to come to grips with reality and face the facts of national and international life today.

Will it be the mood of 1955?

A crass materialism has emerged to influence the mood of the age.

Europe is thriving in a new-found prosperity stimulated by American dollars. "Neutralism" and abandonment of principle are commonplace.

In this country—where high standards of living, wages unprecedented in weekly amounts, creature comforts, gadgets and the luxuries of an "abundant life" are not only fostered as a social objective but underwritten as the paramount obligation of political government—there is less and less emphasis on morals and more and more subservience to the gods of expediency.

Indeed, the ruling philosophy of the modern "intellectual" is that "in the public interest" Peter must be robbed to pay Paul and that, no matter what the words of the Constitution may say, the end justifies the means.

This insidious germ permeates the bloodstream of government.

Our judges for the most part have been chosen on the basis of their political predilections in the expectation that they will decide social questions a certain way—not in accordance with constitutional precedent but in accord with "public sentiment."

Our majorities in Congress are swayed by the passions and hysteria of a mobocracy.

The crusade for "conformity" of thought has begun to infiltrate our church organizations, our press and our educational institutions. Majority opinion is hailed as "truth." Intolerance of any minority dissent is the new "liberalism."

It really is a kind of totalitarianism born of an irresponsible mood. Freedom of speech appears to be defined as freedom only for opinions that are palatable.

The trend, moreover, is toward executive rule. The people show signs of reverting to monarchical habits. If a President speaks, the representatives of the sovereign States must not, it seems, be permitted to dissent. If they do, it is under penalty of public scorn.

These are not yet all-controlling influences. There are many parts of our country where old-fashioned Americanism still prevails and many groups who champion that faith. But there are evident nevertheless powerful manifestations of the mood of the times, which worships the doctrine of an executive autocracy.

Today the "intellectual" approach is that the Congress should function only within a limited sphere and that it must not even inquire into the operations of the departments and agencies if the Executive or his spokesmen object. True, the Supreme Court of the United States in the past has upheld the right of the people's legislature to inquire into the behavior of the executive departments and has never really placed an effective limitation on that right. But now a drive is on to insure the submissiveness of the legislative body, and, curiously enough, the majority in Congress are apparently willing to bow to it and become "rubber stamps." It is in line with the new "conformity"—an unwillingness to accept the responsibilities of American constitutionalism.

The principles of the Constitution itself have been disregarded so often that violations are condoned as "realistic." Caprice in government was dramatized on January 3, 1936, when President Roosevelt boasted to a joint session of Congress that his Administration had "built up new instruments of public power" which in the hands of a "people's government" were "wholesome and proper" but in the hands of "political puppets" would provide "shackles for the liberties of the people."

Mr. Roosevelt publicly argued also that the method of amending the Constitution in the way prescribed in the document itself was too cumbersome and that it was easier to "pack" the Supreme Court, which could rewrite the Constitution at will. The end seemed to him to justify the means.

That's the philosophy of "left wingism" today, too. Its fundamental doctrine—that anything goes if it has a "social welfare" label—is supported by many of the so-called "liberals." Unfortunately, much of the same doctrine also is beginning to be accepted by some of the conscientious but misguided advisers of the President as being the will of the people. It is a course euphemistically described as "progressive moderate."

The year 1954 recorded a tragic page in American history. The mood of 1955 will not bring back the morality and respect for constitutional principle which has guided us through many a crisis in the past unless the conscience of America is awakened from its "left wing" spree. It must be awakened—if the United States is to exhibit the courage necessary to withstand the internal and external foes who would destroy our American system of government by making a political shambles of the Constitution.

1955

POOR FRANCE!

JANUARY 7, 1955

THIS IS NOT THE TIME to upbraid France for her recent vacillation, but to give her the understanding sympathy she needs in a period of great stress.

For the France which fluctuates between dread of a resurgent Germany and fear of a ruthless Russia is not unconcerned about retaining the friendship of the United States. The liberation from Nazi oppression in 1944 by American troops has not been forgotten.

But France in ten years has not found it possible to recover her military strength. Nor has she been able to achieve that maturity of spirit which in a crisis gives a nation firmness of purpose and resoluteness of heart.

Emerging from four years of occupation under the stern heel of the Nazi armies, France has struggled to rebuild her government, only to experience 20 successive changes of Premier in a decade. She finds herself, on the one hand, with 100 Deputies in Parliament led by Communists who performed daring feats of sabotage in the underground against the Nazis. And she has hardly had time, on the other hand, to raise a generation of French statesmen capable of coping effectively with Communist propaganda or of moulding the kind of international policies which once made France a great power in world diplomacy.

France is more to be pitied than scorned.

We in America who have not witnessed the ravages of war at first hand, and who have not suffered the internal betrayals and the defeats such as left France helpless in 1940, cannot today perceive the plight of that country whose frustrated Parliament last week brought the free world to an abyss of deepest anxiety.

To an American accustomed to a two-party system, the jarring friction of 13 blocs sparring for power is something inexplicable. It is easy for some of us to complain that America has poured her billions of dollars into France only to find now that she is an unreliable or at least an uncertain ally. But this is an over-simplification.

For, while France is not starving, and indeed with our help has made substantial recovery in the last two years, she is still far from enjoying a balanced economy. Her electorate is still plagued by poverty and low wages. Domestic needs have been involuntarily neglected. The constant pressure from the Western alliance to develop France as a strong military force has coincided with the steady drain of casualties among trained officers in the long-drawn-out war in Indo-China.

France experienced a humiliating defeat in Southeast Asia. Now she is beset by the gnawing pains of internal dissension in her African possessions. Her empire is dissolving before her eyes, as her military requirements grow more and more expensive. Seldom in world history has a postwar nation been confronted with such a series of poignant weaknesses. Yet we in America expect France to overcome them all overnight.

We shall not stampede the French leaders into a wholehearted approval of something which they fear and distrust. A shift of 14 votes in the majority by which the Assembly on December 30 ratified the Western European agreements could alter the situation again. It is the continued existence of a public opinion that is uninformed, misled and confused which is responsible for the cleavage.

What is needed inside France is further elucidation of the essential reasons for the formation of the Western alliance itself. It is doubtful if the influence of certain powerful French newspapers—some of them directed by Communist propaganda—has been offset by editorials from other newspapers which, however sympathetic with the aims of the Western alliance, have failed to emphasize fundamental issues.

Certain facts have not been driven home in France. Thus, there is no basis for fearing a rearmed Germany as long as the United States and Britain stand ready to prevent any misuse of armament which could conceivably injure the French. Twice before America came across the seas to the rescue, but this time it actually maintains five divisions of troops on the Continent. This is the best assurance that could possibly be given that the alliance will not be permitted to become the tool of any European country.

The great military power of the U. S. Air Force and the U. S. Navy and the presence of the U. S. Army divisions on French soil, as well as the atomic superiority held by the United States, are in themselves safeguards against any hostility toward the French people by another misguided leadership in Germany.

It is incomprehensible why anybody who knows the facts of military power today should fear German rearmament. But the people of France do not know those facts. A campaign of education—long overdue—should be instituted so that the French people will come to feel that America and her allies will protect them.

We must not lose faith in France as she goes through the pains of re-birth. This is the time to stand fast at her side with an understanding friendship.

"A BRIDGE OF PEACE"

JANUARY 14, 1955

As A CHALLENGE to "peaceful coexistence," Pope Pius XII offers the world "a bridge of peace" based upon the reaffirmation of Christian principles.

In perhaps the greatest of the many remarkable pronouncements that have come from the present Pontiff since 1939, the peoples on both sides of the Iron Curtain are told that they—rather than the politicians of government—hold the key to peace.

The Pope's Christmas address, delayed because of illness, is hard to grasp on first reading because it is necessarily couched in implicit phrases. But the responsible officials of government and the leaders of public opinion throughout the world will find it worthy of a second reading. For it contains a positive philosophy and carries on where the-much-controverted phrase, "peaceful coexistence" leaves off.

"Cold peace," like "cold war," says the Pope, is "the mere coexistence of various peoples based on fear of each other and on mutual disillusionment." He adds that "cold peace is only a provisional calm, whose duration is conditional upon the changeable sensation of fear and upon the varying calculation of present strength," and has nothing about it which presupposes "a series of relationships converging toward a common purpose that is right and just."

His Holiness points out that "by excluding all bonds of a spiritual nature between peoples so fragmentarily coexisting, cold peace falls far short" of the precepts of Christianity itself.

The Pope describes the state of fear which exists, as one side watches the other develop new military and economic weapons. "Current political practice, while dreading war as the greatest of catastrophes, at the same time puts all its trust in war"—this is the contradiction which the Pope clearly denounces. He says leaders should be asking themselves "if deliverance from war and the ensuring of peace ought not to be sought on higher and more humane levels than on those dominated exclusively by terror."

What refreshing words these are in an era which has begun to despair that there is any other solution except an atomic stalemate!

Nor does the Pope think peace can be obtained by economic measures alone. He doesn't mention the billions of dollars being poured around the world nowadays to win allies, nor the argument over trade between the East and the West. He does, however, point out the fallacy of relying wholly on that approach. A free exchange of goods, the Pope argues, cannot bring about a "liberation of human life," if it is unaccompanied by recognition of moral values.

When it comes to moral values, the criticisms voiced by His Holiness do not spare the business organizations or the labor unions or the traders in goods who put their special interests above the good of all—nor those who advocate public ownership as an alternative to the abuses by individuals in business. He thinks the economic systems on our side of the Iron Curtain, while not by any means as culpable as those of the Communist dictatorships, will nevertheless make progress only if based on the requirements of a moral order.

"Nationalistic politics" comes in for condemnation, as contrasted with the legitimate aspirations of a national life. Emphasis is placed by the Pope on the need for unity among allies.

It is to be expected that the big Catholic political parties in Germany, France and Italy, which wield much power in their respective parliaments, will not fail to read the Pope's words.

Expressing the hope that "a bridge of peace may yet be built between opposing shores," His Holiness draws attention to the fact that "in both camps there are millions in whom the imprint of Christ is preserved in a more or less active degree." Recognizing that "in one of the two camps, the voice of those who stand resolutely for truth, for love and for the spirit, is forcibly suffocated by the public authorities, while, in the other, people suffer from excessive timidity in proclaiming aloud their worthy desires," it is the duty of "a policy of unification to encourage the former and to make heard the sentiments of the latter."

The Pontiff adds that "particularly in that camp where it is not a crime to oppose error, statesmen should have greater confidence in themselves" and they should "give proof to others of a more firm courage in foiling the maneuvers of the obscure forces which are still trying to establish power hegemonies."

In the address, many things are pointedly discussed, including the weakness of modern intellectuals in surrendering to the fallacy that all that lies between us and the Iron Curtain dictators is a difference in ideology or social approach.

The Pope's appeal for "a bridge of peace" should be heard around the world. For the only fear it concedes as righteous is the "salutary fear of God—Guarantor and Vindicator of the moral law."

THE WAR GOES ON

JANUARY 21, 1955

WISHFUL THINKERS keep talking about the state of "peace" in the world, but there is no peace.

First we are told exultantly by Government speech-makers on the stump that, for the first time in many years, there is no "war" in progress.

Then a few weeks later, when in one raid as many as a hundred bombing planes attack the islands off the coast of China—near Formosa, which we stand committed to defend—the words are altered, and it is euphemistically declared that at least there is today no "active theatre of war."

Any moment, however, according to Peiping dispatches, the Red Chinese may launch an invasion of the Nationalist stronghold on Formosa, and we shall be plunged into armed conflict.

In Indo-China every day the news dispatches tell of how the Communists are completing their conquest as they entrench themselves in an area which they promised to free from "colonialism."

Southeast Asia as a whole is nervous about Communist aggression.

Korea is seething with apprehension and unrest.

Japan is worried about how to rearm.

The sequence of events is disturbing. The Red Chinese ignore all talk about "peaceful coexistence" and announce that they have sentenced as spies eleven American airmen captured in uniform during the Korean war.

Senator Knowland, Republican leader, says a naval blockade should be applied if the flyers are not released. He is much criticized by peace-at-any-price elements who accuse him of wanting a "preventive war."

Admiral Radford, Chairman of the Joint Chiefs of Staff, comes back to Washington from a trip to Asia and says to the press that he thinks a naval blockade could be very effective.

The Assistant Secretary of State for Far Eastern Affairs, Walter S. Robertson, makes a speech declaring that Red China has a gangster government and should not be recognized or admitted to the United Nations. He cautions that expansion of trade with Red China would be a grave error.

The Secretary General of the United Nations, after a visit to Peiping, reveals in New York that he hasn't been able to win the release of the Americans held by Red China. But he states that this is only the "first stage" of his contacts and that patience is needed. Memories of Panmunjom!

What a sorry picture the Western nations present to the world! Patience is a necessary virtue, but patience can easily be misconstrued as weakness unless there is some manifestation of an intended firmness.

Congress is back in Washington and its members, irrespective of party, are restive about the situation in Asia. Senator Price Daniel of Texas, one of the ablest of the Democratic Senators, says a deadline should be set for the release of the airmen and every means available used thereafter to get them back.

Senator H. Alexander Smith, Republican of New Jersey, says he favors asking our allies to join with us in a blockade if the flyers aren't freed.

On an entirely different front, news dispatches are coming in regularly telling of spy activities within the governments of the free nations.

Also inside the most secret installation in Washington, where code analysis is carried on, Joseph S. Petersen, Jr., government employe and scientist, has been caught stealing confidential code documents and furnishing information from them to an official of a foreign embassy. For more than four years—from 1948 to 1952—Petersen has been pilfering secret documents. They were so important that much of the court proceedings were held in private by the judge. Petersen was caught partially because of a security recheck on all employes ordered by the Eisenhower Administration. He confessed his crime and was sentenced to seven years in jail.

There's a war on. But there are many persons inside and outside Washington who feel complacent about it. Some in Congress would prefer to spend their time attacking the Eisenhower Administration for the way it handles "security risks." These members of Congress are apparently interested in throwing up barriers of a legalistic nature to make it more difficult for our Government to protect itself in ferreting out the "security risks."

What catastrophe must happen before the vast body of Americans and their representatives in Congress become convinced that the enemy is infiltrating our country and our institutions and that a war is going on all over the world to undermine free governments and threaten our safety?

Wishful thinking will not bring us a state of peace. Only manifestations of courage on our part will make the enemy abandon its aggressive behavior. When will we begin to recognize that we are in a state of war? It's not the kind of war we have fought before, but a war waged by Communist imperialism inside every free country in the world.

AFTER TWO YEARS

JANUARY 28, 1955

HOW DOES ONE APPRAISE an Administration at the half-way mark? How is progress to be measured? Is it by watching the changes in the Gallup poll on the "popularity" of a President? Is it by comparing the vote cast for the two parties, respectively, in the congressional elections at midterm?

These questions suggest that we are in the habit of thinking of an Administration in terms of a man rather than of an institution. Most of the politicians, for example, are agreed that, if Dwight Eisenhower had been running in November 1954, the result would have been somewhat different. The latest poll, moreover, shows a sharp upward swing in Mr. Eisenhower's popularity.

But the Administration is more than just one man. It is a large group of officials whose responsibilities in the aggregate can be so exercised as to affect, favorably or unfavorably, the lives and property of the citizens not only of this country but of many other countries.

The newspapers necessarily give a sketchy account of what an Administration does from day to day. The sensational things get the headlines because they are news of maximum interest on subjects that are readily understood. But the unspectacular may prove in the end to yield even more sensational achievements.

Thus, the outstanding job done by the Treasury Department in putting the Government's finances in order has provided a favorable climate and incentives for business expansion which could benefit eventually every man, woman and child in the country.

Likewise, the thorough and painstaking reorganization of the Internal Revenue Service, with a program that seeks fairness for the taxpayer and the Government, is in its early stages but in the course of time can mean much larger receipts of tax money.

The Department of State, with its far-flung tasks, is unlike the other departments because it is dependent to a large extent on circumstances beyond its own control—the attitudes and actions of other governments. But here, too, some progress has been made in undoing past mistakes.

Other departments, like the Post Office and Agriculture, have made significant improvements in operation. In the long run, these will have a profound effect on many aspects of our economic life.

As one surveys the earnest efforts being made at the Department of Justice to tackle the anti-monopoly problem and a host of related issues, or the work of the Department of the Interior, with its complex obligations in the field of natural resources, one is inclined to say that important beginnings have been made toward constructive solutions of vital problems.

A start has been made by the Department of Defense toward reorganization, but the new policies have not yet been tested in an emergency.

Perhaps the most interesting experiment is in the Department of Health, Education and Welfare, where a number of sociological programs are in process of being explored. But the theme here is practicality, just as it is through the whole Eisenhower Administration.

It was Emerson who, in his "Essay on Politics," wrote a century ago: "Of the two great parties which at this hour almost share the nation between them, I should say that one has the best cause, and the other contains the best men."

This is but another way of saying that one party has a lot of good ideas, but the other party has the men who know how to make them effective and practical.

On the whole, the Eisenhower Administration has brought to Washington a great "team." But it is an unpolitical group, with a tendency to compartmentalize its talents.

It is in the over-all policy-making process that there are glaring weaknesses. The principal weakness, strangely enough, is at the White House, where the President, with the characteristic habit of a military man, is inclined to delegate important tasks to staff personnel to work out. The system is faulty, because most of those on the staff have never come up through the ranks of government service to be colonels and generals, with a sense of accountability. Yet these inexperienced staff members write memoranda and set forth conclusions that become presidential decisions.

The Presidency today is, of course, too big for any one man. We shall not overcome the defects in our present system until the Cabinet of ten or more persons gives all of its time to the Chief Executive. This should be his "staff." Each of the major departments could be managed by a deputy, but the Cabinet members themselves should have offices alongside the President and meet with him at least once a day.

After two years, it can be said that the Eisenhower Administration has made a good start. But it has a long way to go and will be successful—if it stays in office long enough. Yet tenure depends on the whim of the people at election time and on the time-tested necessities of party organization. Meanwhile, an experienced body of Democratic Party strategists has begun the battle of 1956.

A WARNING THAT MEANS PEACE

FEBRUARY 4, 1955

THE CONGRESS OF THE UNITED STATES was given last week the opportunity to tell the whole world that the American people will fight, if they must, to defend their frontiers. In this air age, these frontiers now extend to bases far overseas.

The leadership of President Eisenhower in the crisis has been in accord with the finest tradition of America. What he has done is to ask Congress to share with him the responsibility for notifying the Communist world that there are limits beyond which we will not permit hostile forces to penetrate.

Just as the late President Roosevelt once defined those limits in Europe when he said "our frontiers are on the Rhine," so today, with jet planes flying more than 600 miles an hour, another President of the United States has said, in effect, that our frontiers in the Western Pacific are close to the mainland of China.

The response of both houses of Congress, irrespective of party, has been magnificent. It's true there are those, here and abroad, who have not been able to see the forest for the trees. They still quibble about whether we should defend this or that island a few miles off the coast of China, or limit the President's authority to the shores of Formosa itself, which is 120 miles from the mainland—just a few minutes by plane. Have they forgotten that our surrender at Bataan was forced because Japanese planes were based on Formosa?

It is unrealistic to say that authority should be granted to the President to protect Formosa itself, but that bases close to the mainland of China must not be attacked if enemy planes emerge from there to bomb our aircraft carriers as they cruise in waters near Formosa. Nor is the situation met by the argument that the President already has the inherent power to issue any orders he pleases if our vessels are attacked. Shall we, in a republic, ignore the people's legislature and rely on one-man decisions, in disregard of the Constitution? Surely any plan to use the armed forces in an area vital to its interests would not be withheld from submission to the House of Commons by a British Prime Minister or to the National Assembly by a French Premier.

Nor can a decision like this be left to a strategy improvised on the spur of the moment. It must be proclaimed in advance and in terms that are explicit, so that the Communists will not have any basis for doubt as to what America will do if her ships or planes are attacked while defending Formosa.

It is regrettable to note that some Senators expressed a desire to restrict the President's authority because of fear of a larger war. This is the same old enervating philosophy of defeatism which has encouraged the enemy to think we are committed indefinitely to a supine pacifism.

The *London Daily Mail* last week boldly declared that had a warning, such as the joint resolution by Congress now gives, been expressed by leaders of the democracies prior to 1914 and 1939, two world wars might have been averted.

We must not make again the mistake we made in Korea. More than 40,000 boys were killed and 110,000 were wounded there when, at the behest of our timid allies, we told General MacArthur he could not pursue enemy planes to their bases in Manchuria.

It is to the everlasting credit of the grand old man from Georgia, Senator Walter George, Democrat, Chairman of the Senate Foreign Relations Committee, that he told his Democratic colleagues this is no partisan issue and that the defense of the United States requires the President to have unrestricted authority to use our armed forces to defend the "vital interests of the United States," as the President himself phrased it.

But what are those "vital interests"? We have American troops stationed in Korea. A Red Chinese Army of 1,000,000 men is poised in the North, ready to swoop down at any time they are reinforced. Adequate armies of the U. N. now stand guard.

But opposite Formosa on the mainland is another Red Chinese Army of at least 3,000,000 men. They are pinned down there by the presence of 600,000 troops of the Nationalist Government on Formosa and by the U. S. Navy and Air Force based on Formosa.

Not many miles away are the Philippines. If Formosa is conquered, the Philippines can be conquered through the air, or the Red Chinese armies can be released for transfer to Korea, where a military victory would affect adversely the psychology of the Japanese and give Communist infiltration its biggest boost. All Asia would then be lost, including the Southeast, where rich resources are a big prize for the potential armament of our Communist enemies.

America's decision to defend the Western Pacific brings a timely warning. The Joint Resolution does not mean war. It will avert such a catastrophe and pave the way to peace. It is the most fateful step taken since the close of World War II to reaffirm American purpose. It manifests again an unflinching courage and an imperishable faith in the strength—physical and moral —that only free men can mobilize.

YES, WE CAN ABOLISH WAR!

FEBRUARY 11, 1955

GENERAL MACARTHUR says war must be abolished. Here is a great soldier speaking, a veteran of three wars, a hero who won the adulation of his people for military achievement but who, ironically enough, became the main target of the European press as a "warmonger" because Communist propaganda falsely portrayed him as wanting to send American troops to the Chinese mainland.

What paradox is this which brings from the lips of a military man of such wide experience the most stirring plea for the abolition of war that has been heard in our times?

What fantastic suggestion, what dream of impracticality is this, ask the skeptics, as they fling at him the facts of practicality in an age of aggression.

But the idea is not to be rejected so readily. It is neither fantastic nor impractical. It is real and it is practical. It is the livest issue of our day—if we will but examine it as carefully as we do the power of a new bomb of destruction.

For here is a concept that challenges the imagination of man. It is intangible now, yet it is something the human mind can make tangible whenever there is a determined effort to do so.

Let us examine the words of General MacArthur as he spoke at Los Angeles on January 26 last on the occasion of his 75th birthday:

"It is a sad truth that human character has never reached the theological development which would permit the application of pure idealism. In the last two thousand years its rate of change has been deplorably slow compared to that of the arts and the sciences. But now the tremendous and present evolution of nuclear and other potentials of destruction has suddenly taken the problem away from its primary consideration as a moral and spiritual question and brought it abreast of scientific realism. It is no longer an ethical equation to be pondered solely by learned philosophers and ecclesiastics but a hard-core one for the decision of the masses whose survival is the issue."

That phrase—"the decision of the masses"—epitomizes the whole problem and points to its solution.

But how? Where is the blueprint? Where is the mechanism that can accomplish this worthy object? Have not men always preached the doctrines of peace? And have not wars come anyhow?

True enough, we have asked but we have never answered the real question. For we have always sought the solution through governments—when it is the governments themselves which have assumed the power to impose slavery and by their discipline to create armies.

Governments, of course, can be the honest servants and spokesmen of free peoples, but too often they are the masters of enslaved peoples. The problem is to find a way to divest rulers of their despotic power.

We shall not make peace by attending conferences or writing treaties with cliques of evil men. We cannot win them by exhortation. We can unhorse them only by reaching to the sources of their power. Anything which enhances the prestige of bad rulers helps to deceive and discourage the peoples who have been enslaved.

Our moral power should be strong enough to refrain from all contacts with evil men. The maintenance of our armament is essential only to protect us against the caprice of these evil rulers. This we must make clear to other peoples—that it is their government which threatens the peace of mankind.

Does anybody doubt that if such a message could reach the people of Soviet Russia and the people of Red China that they would react against war any differently than we do? Of course not. All human beings are instinctively in favor of survival.

Then what are we waiting for? Only for the mechanism to implement the formula whereby peoples talk to peoples, and governments begin to do what peoples want them to do. The 200 million people in Soviet Russia and the 600 million in China can at any moment remove any clique or group which is usurping authority. Armies would crumble, because soldiers, too, wish to survive.

Inventive geniuses must bring forth an electronic device to make it possible for the words of a President or the words of our spiritual leaders everywhere on this side of the Iron Curtain actually to be heard by all the oppressed peoples.

We now can amplify the human voice so that it can be heard across huge public squares in our big cities. We must look forward to the day when science will transmit words spoken in the native tongue of enslaved peoples and, again and again, convey to them the biggest truth of today—that war can and must be abolished.

The voice of humanity, speaking the language of reason, inevitably will be heard in every home in every country. When that happens, tyrants will vanish, because the concerted will of millions of people will take from such rulers the power to make war. Therein lies the salvation of the world.

200,000,000 SLAVES

FEBRUARY 18, 1955

ONE RULER WAS DEPOSED—and another took his place. Thirteen hundred hand-picked "delegates" approved. There was no dissent. It was a fantastic routine.

The people of Soviet Russia, of course—200,000,000 of them—had no voice in the selection. They were given no intimation that the change was even coming.

What thoughts go through the minds of enslaved millions when they learn that an invisible force chooses their rulers for them!

The age-old principle of free men is that governments derive their just powers to govern from the consent of the governed. But in Soviet Russia the individual lives in a reign of terror as the state—personified by a small clique of ambitious men—attempts to impose its totalitarian will on every family in the land.

There's a strange acquiescence—a bewildered compliance for the moment. But underneath there is unrest and a groping for the way out.

The plight of an enslaved people is not unfamiliar. It has been witnessed again and again in history—and always in the evolution toward a climax the same unmistakable signs are to be noted.

For Soviet Russia today is on the road to a major revolution. A nation of 200,000,000 people will not remain indefinitely in slavery.

The concentration camps contain 13,000,000 persons with relatives who day and night are scheming to find a way to liberate their kinsmen. The relatives of millions who have been killed are seeking constantly an opportunity for vengeance.

The Red Army temporarily conforms to the existing pattern of government discipline. But experience shows that, when the revolution comes, the army is the first to break ranks and overthrow the tyrants.

The Communist clique which has been governing Soviet Russia is well aware of the restlessness of the people. There's not enough food. There's not enough clothing. There's no security for anyone.

There's much propaganda talk by the Communist leadership about solving the agricultural problem—for it is well known that a food crisis persists. There's talk of mechanization so that farm machinery can be manufactured to till their vast acreages. But, as the talk goes on, the average man knows he is being condemned to perennial poverty unless some way can be found to achieve individual freedom.

Inside the Soviet Union are more than a score of major nationalities. There are only about 80,000,000 Russians. The other nationalities—around 120,000,000 persons—have little feeling of patriotism about anything Russian. The so-called "Union of Soviet Socialist Republics" is a paper description of a loose federation held together only by the iron hand of the dictatorship group.

But, as has happened so many times in human history, there's no enduring strength in a dictatorship. "Uneasy lies the head that wears the crown," irrespective of the form of despotism or the period in history.

We on the side of the free world now have an unexampled opportunity.

This is the time for us to offer the hand of friendship to the peoples of the Soviet Union and to the peoples of the satellite states.

This is the time to offer food and economic help.

We need make only one condition—that free governments must arise so as to remove the fear of war from the whole world.

For it is this fear alone which compels us to spend on armament billions that could be employed for the constructive purposes of peaceful living.

The world is not safe for democracy today because autocracy, with its myriad of agents, infiltrates our institutions and threatens us with war in numerous areas.

There can be no peace when the citizenry anywhere has no voice in the operation of its own government.

Peoples themselves never want war. Hence, we must make it clear to the enslaved in Europe and Asia that we are ready to help them, for we know they have the power to liberate themselves without bloodshed if they will but exert it in unison.

No group or clique can stand up long against the determination of 200,000,000 people in Soviet Russia to recover their liberties. Their concerted action is what the dictators really fear.

The dismissal of Malenkov reveals conspicuously the weakness of the dictatorship.

The next step is revolution.

We must, therefore, in our policies do nothing to discourage the oppressed peoples. In fact, if our statesmen only had the courage to do so, now is the time to withhold recognition from the Bulganin regime in Moscow and to exert the greatest moral force the world has ever known—the force that exalts the principle of the consent of the governed. For the only way to assure freedom from fear throughout the world is to insist on the establishment of free governments. This is the prerequisite to the abolition of war.

WHY RUSSIA SHOULD BE EXPELLED FROM THE U.N.

FEBRUARY 25, 1955

MUCH OF THE TROUBLE in which the free governments of the world find themselves today is due to a failure to steer by the compass of moral principle.

Governments that appease the aggressor go from the frying pan into the fire as they build up complications for themselves by their successive retreats.

The indictment was summed up succinctly last week by Secretary of State Dulles when he said:

"The United Nations Charter of 1945 binds sixty nations to refrain in their international relations from the threat or use of force. But there has been armed aggression in Korea which was promoted by Soviet Russia, and later Communist China was found guilty of armed aggression there."

The world for some time has known about the repeated violations of the U. N. Charter by the Soviet Union. The principal evidence was furnished by its own representative, who publicly boasted to the U. N. in March 1953 that the Soviet Union had supplied armaments to the Red China government throughout the Korean war. In that war more than 33,500 American boys were killed and 103,000 wounded.

The Soviet Union, moreover, gave military assistance to Red China notwithstanding the fact that in February 1951 the Peiping government was formally declared by resolution of the U. N. to be an "aggressor." The Moscow government ignored the U. N. warning that all members should refrain from rendering assistance to the aggressor.

The act of aggression is even more flagrant because it has been directed against the armed forces of the United Nations itself.

The United Nations is still in a state of war with both the Communist Chinese and the Communist government of North Korea. An armistice has been signed, but no treaty of peace has been consummated. Nevertheless military aid to the aggressors from Soviet Russia continues. Russian-built MIGs are commonplace in the skies of Korea.

This is in the face of the plain language of Article 2 of the Charter, which provides:

"All members shall give the United Nations every assistance in any action it takes in accordance with the present Charter, and shall refrain from giving assistance to any state against which the United Nations is taking preventive or enforcement action."

The United Nations Charter specifies exactly how offenses of a traitorous member shall be dealt with by the other members. Article 6 reads as follows:

"A member of the United Nations which has persistently violated the Principles contained in the present Charter may be expelled from the Organization by the General Assembly upon the recommendation of the Security Council."

It will be argued, of course, that the Security Council would not so recommend because the Soviet Union could block such a step by exercising her veto in the Council. The fact is, however, that the Soviet Union, being a party to the dispute, would have no right to vote at all. Article 27 of the Charter covers that point by declaring that decisions of the Security Council shall be made by an affirmative vote of seven members, including the concurring votes of the permanent members, provided, however, that "a party to a dispute shall abstain from voting."

It has been contended that the Soviet Union had obligations under a treaty with China to come to the assistance of that country on the basis of an offensive and defensive alliance. But Article 103 says:

"In the event of a conflict between the obligations of the members of the United Nations under the present Charter and their obligations under any other international agreement, their obligations under the present Charter shall prevail."

The Charter declares that membership in the United Nations shall be open to "peace-loving states" willing to accept the obligations of membership. The Soviet Union, however, has disregarded its obligations to the U. N.

By aiding Red China and North Korea, which are at war with the United Nations, the Soviet Government has forfeited its seat in the U. N. That seat should be declared vacant by a formal resolution. It would constitute notification to the people of Soviet Russia that their government had demonstrated its incapacity to fulfill international obligations, and had become a menace to peace-loving nations. The kind of government a nation chooses is its own affair, but only up to the point where such a government does not become a threat to world peace.

Some day, when a free government arises in Russia, the seat in the U. N. declared vacant could be awarded to such a new government. But today the Moscow regime must be expelled if the United Nations is to retain the respect of the world as an organization obedient to law—the words of its own Charter.

JOB CREATION OR
JOB DESTRUCTION?

MARCH 4, 1955

WHEN A POLITICAL PARTY proclaims a program of taxation based upon vote-catching, rather than sound economic principles, a serious question is raised as to its capacity to govern the nation in a responsible manner if entrusted with power.

The Democratic Party in Congress came forth last week with a proposal to give every taxpayer a $20 cut in taxes. This would cost the U. S. Treasury more than $2,000,000,000 annually in tax receipts, but it could do far more damage eventually—it could start a cycle of inflation, and, as prices skyrocketed, a breakdown of confidence in the value of the dollar would ensue.

If this is a sample of what the Democratic Party has in mind in the event of victory at the polls in 1956, there will arise at once a widespread fear for the future solvency of the American Government.

It was Thomas Jefferson, founder of the Democratic Party, who enunciated the principle: "Equal rights for all, special privileges for none." The plan to give a $20 tax cut is really a proposal to grant to certain income classes a higher percentage of tax reduction than to other groups. It is a special privilege to be bestowed upon a particular group, irrespective of the economic consequences to the nation as a whole.

The argument made by proponents of the measure is that prosperity can best be stimulated by furnishing money subsidies to certain consumers.

This was also the philosophy behind the Work Projects Administration during the depression days of the 1930's. But that policy was a failure. Unemployment remained at an unprecedented height for peacetime, and war alone came to the rescue of the national economy. It was not until 1940, when heavy-goods industries were finally given the opportunity to expand, that the unemployment figure began to drop perceptibly.

It is contended, of course, that the money saved by tax cuts will add to purchasing power. The resultant deficit in the budget, however, would have to be met by higher taxes on other income groups or by raising business taxes which are already too high.

To increase the quantity of purchasing power is futile if prices are forced upward due to lack of confidence in the purchasing power of the dollar itself. An inequitable tax scheme means a commitment to a prolonged unbalance of the whole national economy. This can only bring inflation, with its devastating effect on persons who live on pensions and fixed incomes.

What really makes America tick is a balanced economy. This means that funds must be made constantly available for investment in the expansion of business and in the replacement of worn-out equipment. Today's climate for investment, brought about by the Eisenhower Administration, is the healthiest in 30 years.

Unless saving by the individual is encouraged and the fruit of his labors invested as seed money in business, there is no chance for a system of risk capital to survive. Only the government could then provide the necessary capital. And that's the beginning of the end of individual freedom. For little by little, as State Capitalism takes hold and more and more people find themselves on the government payroll, the incentive for management to create new enterprises vanishes. Governmental restrictions on human liberty then become necessary to maintain discipline.

Why do the patriotic leaders of a great American party permit themselves to become victims of the socialistic doctrine of job destruction?

For when taxation is inequitable and men of thrift and talent are discouraged because they are taxed virtually to the point of confiscation, business enterprise falters and unemployment is the inevitable result.

Certainly, to impose taxes only on a basis of subsidy to the maximum number—without regard for the eventual good of all—is one way to liquidate the managerial class in America and to bring economic chaos, as has been the case in Russia.

Tax rates should never be determined on the basis of money grants direct to the largest number of voters. Taxes should be imposed on the basis of incentive—by means of rates that will indirectly exert the maximum influence toward job creation. That's sound economics —it's the way to deserve the vote of all groups.

The Democratic Party of today is torn between the true Democrats who wish to conserve the American economic system, and the radicals who will, if allowed to become the majority, destroy the system which has given us the strongest industrial power and the highest standard of living any country has ever known.

Will the Democratic Party return to the dynamic conservatism of Woodrow Wilson, who in the fiscal policies of his Administration maintained the principles of Thomas Jefferson? Or will the Democratic Party surrender to the insidious forces of State Capitalism which seek to break down our whole economic system?

What kind of a Democratic Party are the American people to be asked to vote for in 1956?

ARMED COEXISTENCE

MARCH 11, 1955

THE PEACE OF THE WORLD seems assured for at least three or four years.

That's the inference which we can logically draw from declarations made last week by Prime Minister Churchill and President Eisenhower.

Both statesmen confirm that the free world has the lead now in atomic weapons and may maintain it for a few years.

But Mr. Eisenhower adds that military superiority isn't related altogether to the quantity of atomic weapons made. After a certain point in numbers is reached, he thinks there is no advantage in making more. This means that, due to the progress of atomic science, destructiveness has already reached the peak of its power. If you can instantly pulverize a city with one bomb, there isn't much use in dropping ten more on the ruins.

For many months now the United States Government has exuded an unmistakable confidence. It has been apparent in the statements of our military men, and it has been specifically related to the calculated risk taken by the President in holding the armament budget down to a reasonable size.

On what is this confidence based? It is unquestionably an attitude derived from the inside knowledge which only the highest officials of the British and American governments possess—namely, that the Western powers have a decided advantage not merely in weapons but in their use from tactical locations.

The Soviet Union, for example, needs to fly her bombing planes across the top of the world or across the oceans to reach us for an attack, whereas we have bases within a few hours of the heart of Soviet Russia. Once the atomic weapons are strategically distributed along a defense line, a big war of aggression by the Soviet Union becomes improbable.

For what an aggressor faces is suicide. We, to be sure, would suffer grievously from attack, but our nation would not be destroyed. That's because our capacity to retaliate instantaneously is greater than that of the enemy, and our means of doing so is bound to be more effective because of the luck of geography.

We know in our hearts that our side will never start an aggressive war. We are, theoretically at least, opposed to a preventive war. What the situation might be if an aggressor mobilized and put his atomic force in a position really to threaten a surprise attack of large proportions is something else. We might then demand demobilization under penalty of attack. It's

in the realm of conjecture what the state of mind of the nation would be if apprised of the possibility that several of our cities might be destroyed while our forces waited for authority to retaliate.

With the development, moreover, of the guided missile which will fire atomic shells from bases in the United States or Europe, the whole nature of war itself changes. It becomes an instantaneous affair that can at any moment be unleashed without warning.

The United States today is ahead on the techniques of guided missiles. In a few years, however, Soviet Russia may have them, too.

The stalemate is already here. Both sides are aware that neither can "win." Hence both will feel that there is nothing to be gained by striking a first blow. The world is, therefore, drifting into a state of armed coexistence.

Wars in the past have been fought when national honor has been at stake or in case of invasion. There has always been time, however, to deploy defensive forces. No such interval is likely to be available now. The defensive machinery must be set—and the guided missile affords just that kind of instant defense.

We have been paying high taxes for several years now to build a deterrent force so powerful that no aggressor would dare to risk an attack.

What we are witnessing is the fruition of a policy begun under the Truman Administration. It has been a policy of deterring aggression by building up atomic armament. Mr. Eisenhower has added one decisive factor—he has convinced a potential enemy that we really will use atomic weapons. "Massive retaliation" is, to be sure, the phrase of the century.

This state of armed coexistence is by no means peaceful. It means years of uneasiness and an unbroken tension. But time gives an opportunity for the natural forces of the age to work unremittingly toward a better existence.

Moral force can, in the meantime, permeate the world. It can and must be gradually mobilized to emancipate the peoples behind the Iron Curtain.

When these peoples recover their liberties and free governments arise, resting on the consent of the governed, armament burdens everywhere will be lifted. Then will armed coexistence be superseded by peaceful coexistence. Then will the nations of the world be able to harness the great energy producers of our times and convert the new lethal weapons into the plowshares of an enduring peace.

BETTING ON AMERICA

MARCH 18, 1955

THE AMERICAN PEOPLE are constantly betting on their own future.

They bet on the foresight of skillful management in American business.

They bet on the inventive genius that saves labor and spreads human energy over more new tools.

They bet on the profits to be derived from intelligent planning and from the written and spoken salesmanship that brings sellers and buyers together.

They bet on the keen judgment which accurately estimates demand and avoids wasteful production.

They bet on the honor and integrity of men who, when they borrow other people's money, make every provision out of earnings to pay it back.

They bet on the companies that seem to promise the maximum return on the money invested.

They bet on the free-enterprise system which holds that, except for national emergencies, the citizenry shall employ its own capital and the government shall not become a competitor.

They place their bets daily in the market place where their hopes and aspirations are recorded along with their disappointments.

In recent months the stocks of various companies have steadily moved upward in price. For a long time many of these have been quoted below their actual book values. The fact that confidence does exist now seems to be something of a surprise to those observers who are unaccustomed to a stable economy.

A procession of witnesses—many of them New Dealers—has appeared before the Senate Banking Committee to answer questions in a so-called "friendly study" of the stock market. But the bearish note is uppermost. The aim appears to be to convert into an indictment of alleged sinfulness the effort by the American people to participate in the profits that accrue out of the growth of their own country.

The theory that Congress is the guardian of the public purse is acceptable. But this bestows no right to impair the freedom of an individual to win or lose as he invests his money in the securities of American enterprises. He can borrow most of the money needed to buy a house, but it now is suggested that he pay all cash to buy a piece of industrial property—a share in the appreciating values of America's businesses.

It is true that speculative excesses sometimes occur in the markets. We have had our land booms and our wild speculations in commodities. But there is far greater danger in impeding natural growth and restraining legitimate expansion by undue governmental interference with the credit mechanism than in letting the foolish speculate beyond the bounds of reason.

Had there been a genuine desire to study so complex an institution as the stock market, no kleig lights would have been necessary. It could have been undertaken by a legislative and executive commission with a staff of technicians who could have quietly made their studies in the offices of the brokers and traders in New York and in the industrial centers.

The testimony of individuals—cloistered in academic halls and possessing little first-hand knowledge of the actual workings of industry or of the things that make America tick—has now frightened the populace into thinking something is wrong with the economy. The stock market has been given a case of jitters by intimations of coming restrictions voiced by members of the Senate Committee themselves.

What is being overlooked by the critics among the Democrats is that we've been passing through twenty years of inflation—a period of loss of confidence in the dollar. Happily, under the Eisenhower Administration confidence has been returning.

For twenty years socialistic doctrines have been embraced by the Democratic Party so that American enterprise has faced the threat of gradual confiscation by government. Today the number of Democrats in Congress who openly favor government ownership of electric power is the largest in a generation. What other segments of our industrial structure will come next on the list of the destructionists?

Are the American people being given a preview of what they may expect in 1956 if the radical Democrats prevail at the polls? There are conservative Democrats who are fighting valiantly such a dangerous trend in the party of Thomas Jefferson.

There is, of course, one sure way for many Americans to lose their bet on the future of the nation's economy. It is to vote in the confiscationists.

As long as the American people can bet on the dynamic conservatives—led today by President Eisenhower and Democrats like Senator Byrd of Virginia and Senator George of Georgia—they can win.

For an expanding, dynamic America—an America in which technology makes perennial progress—is bound to return dollar for dollar more gain than any other investment anywhere else in the whole world.

Betting on America is hazardous only when selfish politicians make it so.

THE SIN OF YALTA

APRIL 1, 1955

THE SIN OF YALTA was not contained in the offhand comments by heads of governments as revealed in the Yalta papers.

The sin was imbedded in the secret decisions to carve up and award territories before World War II itself was ended.

The sin was in the flagrant denial of a great principle—the right of peoples everywhere to establish governments of their own choosing.

This betrayal of human rights has since been perpetuated at other international conferences—at Panmunjom and at Geneva—where the people of North Korea and the people of Northern Indo-China, respectively, were condemned to slavery. It is the same tyranny that was imposed in 1945 upon the peoples of the so-called satellite states of Eastern Europe.

Are we about to repeat the vice of Yalta and engage again in more of these four-power conferences where the President of the United States makes agreements committing the American people to courses of action on which they have no opportunity to vote through their elected representatives in Congress?

It was the violation at Yalta of the spirit and the letter of the Constitution of the United States which left a blot on American history.

Although the official records of the Yalta conference were withheld from the American people under one pretext or another for ten years, it is amazing that there are misguided Democrats in Congress today who are assailing their own government for bringing about at last the release of the Yalta papers.

Naturally, European statesmen favor suppression. They have been steeped for centuries in the artifices of secret diplomacy. They believe in expedient deals made in the privacy of such conferences as have been held at Teheran, Yalta and Potsdam.

America has three times in history been caught in the same dilemma—the sacrifice of many thousands of American lives for professed ideals only to see such ideals abandoned at the conference table.

The famous Fourteen Points constituting the war aims of the Allies in World War I—including the right of self-determination of peoples and the demand for "open covenants openly arrived at"—were torn up at Versailles in 1919.

The famous Atlantic Charter—pledging, as one of the war aims of World War II, the right of all peoples freely to choose their own government—was torn up at Yalta in 1945.

The famous resolution of the United Nations in 1951 declaring Red China an aggressor in Korea was torn up at Geneva in 1954. The same aggressor was awarded possession of a vast area in Indo-China while millions of innocent people were delivered into bondage.

The Constitution vests in the President of the United States the right to conduct relations with other governments. But it vests also in the Congress—as a co-ordinate branch of the Government—the right to declare war and to "advise and consent" in the making of treaties of peace.

There were no representatives of the Congress of the United States present at the Yalta conference.

There were no members of the press admitted to the Yalta meetings to tell the people of the world in detail what their representatives were doing.

It is not difficult to understand why some European newspapers are shocked by the persistent pressure in America to compel the publication of the long-suppressed documents of the Yalta conference. The American attitude toward full publicity of the public business is rooted in the concept that the people do not delegate to a single ruler the right to make commitments in their behalf.

The European idea, on the other hand, seems to be that the head of a state is a sort of absolute monarch, and even now the talk there is of a "big four" conference "at the summit."

The American people do not recognize that anybody with sovereign power sits in for them "at the summit," or anywhere else.

Ambassadors and ministers of the United States are stationed in all the capitals of the world. This is an informal and confidential means of communication. Any proposals that can lead to a better understanding in the world among nations can be made to or by such diplomatic representatives and can be referred to the President and the Congress for approval or disapproval.

There is no right on the part of the President to sit down with any foreign ruler and make a binding agreement unless Congress has delegated such particular power to him, or unless there is an opportunity for the Senate to advise for or against ratification.

The sin of Yalta was its secrecy and its disregard for moral and constitutional principles. A few individuals usurped the power that belongs only to free peoples. Nobody should be permitted to barter away the ideals of the American people on the altars of expediency.

THE RIGHT TO SURVIVE

APRIL 15, 1955

MUCH HAS BEEN SAID in recent months about the right of the individual under the Fifth Amendment of the Constitution to decline, for reasons of his own, to testify in formal proceedings.

Very little has been said about the right of the state to protect itself against infiltration by enemy agents seeking to undermine our own government.

Does the Constitution really grant rights to the individual that are superior to those reserved to the people as a whole? Must a traitor in our midst go scot-free because someone who knows of his whereabouts, or about his plotting, refuses to testify on the ground that on the witness stand he might say something damaging to himself and hence be prosecuted?

Congress wisely met that dilemma by passing a law in 1954 which specifically grants immunity from prosecution to any citizen who is willing to tell all he knows about a suspected crime.

Already a test case has arisen, in which the individual, notwithstanding an offer of immunity, has invoked the Fifth Amendment and refused to give to our government the information he possesses about Communist infiltration. Last week that case was decided unanimously by the U. S. Circuit Court of Appeals in New York, and the defendant was ordered to tell what he knows. Unless the Supreme Court now reverses this order, the judgment will stand.

For a long time there has been a controversy about the scope of the Fifth Amendment. It has been rightly argued that under its protection nobody should be required to give testimony that might incriminate him alone. But it has been difficult to understand why anyone should be protected who declines to divulge what he knows about other persons.

If a child is killed by a taxicab, does the driver of another taxicab who saw the accident have the right to say he will not testify because it might give him undue publicity or injure him in the chances of retaining employment from the same taxicab company, especially if it is to be sued for damages on the basis of his prospective testimony? Not at all. He can be summoned to court and required to testify as to what he saw. He cannot evade a subpoena.

But, under the peculiar reasoning which has been publicized by some of the "left wing" lawyers, a man who knows about a plot to assassinate a high official or to destroy our government, can remain silent and claim immunity under our Constitution. This would mean that the right of an individual supersedes the right of the state to provide for its own survival.

If perchance the Supreme Court should accept this distorted reasoning, the American people would promptly approve a constitutional amendment to make clear that the state has a right of survival which transcends the refusal of an individual to give up the knowledge he has of someone else's guilt.

Congress gave careful consideration to the immunity law before passing it. There was not the slightest intention to compel anyone to testify against himself. There was every intention to remove the last excuse that Communist sympathizers have for evading an obligation to their own government. They claim its protection for their own convenience, but are unwilling to recognize their duty to assist in the protection of all the people against a common enemy. Judge Samuel H. Hofstadter, of the Supreme Court of New York State, wrote recently an article on immunity laws in which he said in part:

"To meet the problem presented by the criminally implicated witness, the practice of granting pardons in advance of the testimony was adopted as early as 1742 in England. The first immunity law was adopted by Congress almost 100 years ago in January, 1857. Since then, immunity has been made available to witnesses testifying to violations of almost every regulatory federal statute and there are immunity statutes in probably every State of the Union."

We sometimes hear it argued that it is better that ten guilty individuals should be permitted to escape rather than that one individual who is innocent shall carry a stigma of accusation. If so, shall grand juries be deprived hereafter of the power to hand down indictments just because the publicity of a trial may be harmful to a defendant who is later acquitted?

Should a man who steals atomic secrets be allowed to furnish them to another government—which can use them to destroy us—rather than let the authorities risk drawing in some allegedly innocent person?

It is debatable what the word "innocent" means. Individuals who have made bad mistakes in judgment by joining organizations later classed as Communist fronts are not disloyal, and they can be forgiven their error. But because of possible inconvenience and the publicity they may suffer—due to their own indiscretions—are they entitled to more consideration than should be given to the safety of all the people?

Clearly the right to survive, especially in a nuclear age, is the paramount right.

MAN'S MIRACLE?

APRIL 22, 1955

AGAIN SCIENCE has come forward to save man from a dread disease.

Generations have suffered from it amid hopes that some day a miracle would be achieved.

The miracle has come. All honor to the scientists, Dr. Jonas Salk and the others, who have brought to mankind the relief so long and desperately sought as countless children have succumbed yearly to the ravages of poliomyelitis.

It is an historic coincidence that announcement of the discovery came on the tenth anniversary of the death of the late President Franklin D. Roosevelt. His valiant fight against polio, which struck him at the age of thirty-nine, helped to dramatize in later years the public drives that won so much financial support from the people of America for the National Foundation for Infantile Paralysis.

What great hope one man's struggle instilled in the minds of other victims! To what heights could they aspire—since, indeed, one whose physical movements were restricted by the paralysis of his legs could nevertheless campaign actively and become President of the United States! It was an example that conveyed a message of encouragement to millions of persons with a frustrated outlook on what the future held for them.

Today the parents of children who might otherwise be potential victims of polio can rejoice that a vaccine has been found which in nearly all cases will prove effective. While research is yet to be completed, especially as to certain strains of the disease found abroad, the door has at least been opened. Science has conquered another enemy of man—adding to victories attained heretofore over typhoid and yellow fever and tuberculosis.

It is naturally hoped that the intense study concentrated in recent years by medical experts everywhere on another disease—cancer—may in the not-far-distant future also bring a preventive. In the laboratories day and night technicians are striving for that momentous result. The prayers of mankind are directed toward what may be the next great discovery of our times in the field of medicine.

We are inclined to credit man with all such achievements. Do we forget perhaps that behind man is the guidance of the Master?

The mysteries of man's successes and defeats are not unfolded to our finite minds. For, even as man makes great discoveries in science and by his inventions changes the life of the world, nature often exhibits a power greater than any that man himself can generate.

The force of a tornado or of a hurricane can be stronger than that of a hydrogen bomb.

No invention as yet has conquered the most violent storms to assure the safety of all vessels at sea.

The sun is still a puzzling antagonist, as well as a great benefactor.

When we seek mastery over the elements, however, it is not in defiance but in self-protection against the dangers they may suddenly bring.

But, even as we manage to conquer a terrible disease, we are concerned because there are in the world today governments which threaten to use germs as an instrument of war. Our own experimentation in this field is carried on solely to teach us how to deal with such a scourge if an unmoral government some day decides to use germ warfare. The mere existence of such lethal weapons, however, is in itself a sad commentary on the deterioration of the human spirit in Moscow and Peiping, where such plots are hatched.

Of what avail is it to conquer the germs of disease that spread themselves naturally if we are to encounter the germs of man-made plagues, too?

We are reminded, moreover, that the worst epidemic of all—war itself—knows as yet no vaccine.

We have not yet found the way by which governments can be inoculated against the making of arbitrary decisions to kill innocent men, women and children. We have in our lifetime seen it happen twice. This seemed impossible, but it happened.

Can it be said that the satanic instinct in man is still battling for supremacy against the Divine Spirit?

When we learn of the amazing discovery of a vaccine to ward off polio, we are encouraged to believe that it is not the hand of man but of a Divine Providence which guides us toward new accomplishments in the field of human welfare.

Perhaps our generations have been remiss as we have glorified the achievements of man in a world of materialism. Perhaps our shortcoming has been an inability to perceive through the years of suffering that another way is open to us. Perhaps this new respite—prolongation of life through such medical discoveries—points a moral in human history. Perhaps it tells us that God may be merciful if men will only act toward one another in a manner which will deserve His blessings.

COMMUNICATION

APRIL 29, 1955

"COMMUNICATION" is perhaps the most important word in the vocabulary of our times.

Communication is not merely the transmission of written or spoken messages through the printed word or the radio.

Communication in its finest sense is the achievement of understanding between peoples, irrespective of the mistakes and blunders made by men in government who sometimes misconstrue the limits of their temporary power.

Communication sometimes belies its name by actually setting up barriers to understanding. It can be mischievous, as when propaganda seeks to mislead public opinion.

Communication must begin with the common man—with his normal and natural desire for survival. He fears no enemy if no enemy threatens him. He would prefer to live without fighting his fellow man. He wants only an opportunity for himself and his family to remain unmolested. How can he communicate his ideas and desires to everybody else?

Whether it be among the millions of people in Soviet Russia or in the satellite states or in the countries on our side of the Iron Curtain, there is everywhere an instinct for peace and a desire for friendship. When troops in allied armies were able to get together in the last war, there was a noticeable tendency among them to fraternize, irrespective of the ideologies of the governments at home.

If peoples could communicate with peoples, there would be no war clouds. If peoples could achieve the same mutual trust in the international community that they often attain in a national community, armament could be reduced to the point where only the force adequate for domestic police purposes would be necessary.

Communication, therefore, presents the biggest challenge to the world today. What can be done to advance it on the positive side, and what can be done especially to remove the negative characteristics that emerge in our present communication system?

The press and the radio, it must be confessed, are at times destructive. Though for the most part constructive, there are many instances in which the speed with which the press functions leads to sketchy reporting and fragmentary dispatches being transmitted from country to country.

Sometimes, for example, before an hour has elapsed the words of a presidential press conference, paraphrased and condensed, are transmitted to other capitals of the world. Comment is immediately sought by newsmen abroad from foreign governments. Further study of a complete text would have resulted in many cases in an entirely different kind of public comment—if, indeed, any were needed.

The same thing often happens in our country. Within minutes, an offhand comment by a member of Congress or by officials in the executive branch of the Government is relayed back and forth on the news tickers, and this frequently results in impromptu remarks that are immediately broadcast. Speed is here the creator of discord. Before there is time to think things through, emotions are aroused and friction is generated.

On the international side, we in America do not get enough information about the attitudes of other peoples, and it is evident that Europeans get a distorted picture of our own national mood and purpose.

The idea, for instance, that America or any part of it wants to go to war for war's sake is so preposterous that one wonders how anyone could transmit to Europe such a report on America's intentions. Then one discovers that, in their anxiety to get political advantage, some Senators in our own Congress have been publicly accusing American officials or other members of Congress of seeking war. This is one of the grave aspects of present-day communication.

The words of a Constitution that guarantee freedom of speech are essential, but they do not teach us self-restraint.

We must come to recognize that communication is a basic force which cannot be used constructively unless it is inspired by a God-given honesty, fairness and tolerance.

When communication in man-made controversies is faulty, it is because communication between God and man is impaired. Only when in the human heart there is a consciousness of the presence of God—sometimes called Conscience—will communication between individuals become effective in the interest of peace.

Only when all precepts of national or international policy, political or economic, pass the test of a spiritual conscience, can we begin to master in our times the real art of communication between peoples.

For when peoples can communicate their innermost feelings freely to other peoples—as honesty in communication is achieved—major conflicts will vanish from the earth and we shall enjoy an enduring peace.

"FOUR-POWER" FANTASY

MAY 6, 1955

THE SPECTACLE presented by the governments at Paris, London and Washington in seeking a conference with the Government of Soviet Russia is that of a hungry suppliant begging for almost any crumbs from the table of the absolute monarch.

This is said not so much in criticism of the sincere men who are trying to formulate the policies of Great Britain, France and the United States as it is of the many leaders of public opinion in all three countries who have fallen victim to some unfortunate illusions.

For there is no denying the fact that the threats of a political opposition—selfishly seeking in each country to ascend to power by almost any means—are influential in compelling the incumbent administrations of the three allied nations to negotiate for peace with the enemies of our civilization.

The governments themselves lack the courage to lead and instead meekly follow the will-of-the-wisps of popular fancy. The line goes something like this: "We cannot refuse to sit down and talk. If nothing comes of it, at least the air will be cleared and we shall know where we are."

We have heard this form of self-deception expressed again and again just before each successive failure of the scores of conferences we have held in the past with representatives of the Soviet Union.

When will the statesmen of today begin to heed the lessons of yesterday?

For it is written in the blood-covered pages of history that in the periods preceding the outbreak of World War I and of World War II, respectively, vacillation and cringing fear on our side encouraged the aggressor and brought on the very conflict in arms that nobody wanted.

A third world war would be horrible, and it is the obligation of free peoples to assert constantly their abhorrence of mass killing. But we must do more. We cannot assume the transformation of evil men into saints.

The simple fact is that gangsters are in control of the governments at Moscow and Peiping, and they have intensified the "cold war" throughout North Africa and in the Middle East and in Southeast Asia. They have torn to pieces the armistice agreement they signed in Korea. They have stirred up rebellion in the South of Indo-China. They are actively fomenting trouble on every continent.

Meanwhile, speeches by some of the leaders of the Democratic Party in America, by Socialist Labor Party leaders in Great Britain and by opposition parties in France tell the Communist strategists that the free world is yielding to their propaganda and is being misled into the belief that a four-power conference is a magic device which will bring peace to the world.

What a terrible example of the craven spirit that has so often preceded the decline and downfall of empires in the past! What a frivolous indifference to the proved crimes of present-day aggressors!

If, to be sure, a four-power conference was to be a real negotiation such as diplomacy has many a time tried with useful results, it would not be conducted amid the fanfare of publicity which surrounds such occasions today. Ambassadors would canvass beforehand the possibilities and indeed lay the basis for mutual agreements. But the Soviets want to show their contempt for the West in public conferences to be reported by the press of the world. What better proof do we need of the insincerity of the Communist rulers?

Why do we shut our eyes to the facts of today? Is it because we prefer not to look at the truth and because we believe the aggressor has really changed? Does the recent resumption of the Berlin blockade and the imprisonment of our fliers in defiance of a written pledge for their release indicate that the leopard has changed his spots?

The big question involved in deciding whether or not to hold a four-power conference is this: Shall we enhance in their own lands the prestige of the temporary rulers of the Soviet Union and China by sitting down with them, and, by so doing, shall we encourage these same rulers to believe that, despite our military strength, we are willing to accept almost any concessions to avoid a war?

The people of Soviet Russia and of China want freedom just as we do. We must not tighten the hold of their oppressors on them. We must open the way for their liberation by refusing to deal with gangster governments. For those governments constantly threaten the peace of the world, and there can be no safety for anybody as long as they remain in power.

There is but one way to force the disintegration of the Communist empire. It is by forgetting four-power conferences and imposing a complete quarantine on the Communist regimes. This means extermination of their agents and conspirators from all free countries.

These enemies must be driven from within our gates. It makes no sense to endeavor to negotiate with the master minds of world conspiracy.

"ONE WORLD"?

MAY 13, 1955

THERE ARE TWO fundamentally different concepts involved in the frequent use of the term "one world." It is especially important to examine them as we prepare for the coming debate over possible revisions of the Charter of the United Nations.

Everybody wants one world of peace.

Everybody wants one world of free interchange of ideas and persons.

Everybody wants unity instead of disunity, and organization instead of disorganization.

But when it comes to imposing some form of discipline to attain these objectives, we encounter basic differences of opinion and varying viewpoints.

For the mere mention of discipline implies a restriction of freedom to act as one nation thinks best. The word "right," for example, means one thing under the Napoleonic Code, which still prevails in Latin-minded countries, and quite another in countries of Anglo-Saxon background, where the English common law is accepted as gospel.

A passion for uniformity manifests itself nevertheless now and then in all countries among small groups who instinctively believe it will open the road to peace. They err primarily because they do not recognize the simple fact of a lack of uniformity which God Himself has created. Thus, there are differences not merely of color and of language but of cultures and of traditions as sacrosanct to other peoples as ours are to us.

The problem is not how to amalgamate the world under one system of government or one culture or one religion or one code of legal ethics and rights. It is how to coordinate the external action of the peoples of the world while they retain their basic loyalties to historic concepts of national sovereignty.

There can be no valid objection, of course, to the process by which nations operating under their own constitutions give up certain claims to freedom of action outside their own domain, nor to treaties signed by several governments in which they undertake mutual obligations of common defense. For essentially the principle here is one of temporary federation or alliance to fulfill special objectives. This is not super-sovereignty.

What is to be questioned is the proposition that all countries should bind themselves together in a common citizenship and that they can then govern themselves better than as separate sovereignties. It seems not only impractical but unrealistic to think in terms of an international organization—with a legislative, executive and judicial setup—which in fact means a superstate to govern us all.

The trend in the world should be not toward more mergers of states but toward more decentralization. Who will deny that, if the vast Soviet Empire with the many nationalities residing there could be split up into seven or eight really independent republics, it would be better for those same peoples? And who will doubt that this very dissolution of the Soviet merger would be better for the peace of the world?

To set up a "one world" state is to invite rule by an oligarchy or by the dictatorship of a group with special interests to serve.

The United Nations Charter can provide for a significant experiment in the federation of governments without the discipline that a superstate would require. It is true that the United Nations has failed thus far to enforce peace, but this in itself proves that a superstate could not today win the approval of independent peoples. To make agreements, on the other hand, that set forth the measures of collective security to be authorized in emergencies by the nations which are members of the North Atlantic Treaty Organization or of the Organization of American States is a proper exercise of the right of individual nations to federate temporarily in the common interest.

But it will be noted that such treaties or agreements do not involve any structural change in the constitution of each member country. They are simply voyages in the uncertain seas of foreign affairs.

We can have a world of peace, not by the use of coercive measures that put further restrictions on the sovereignty of any country, particularly in its domestic concerns, but by developing the only kind of "one world" philosophy that has ever achieved anything heretofore. It is by the appeal to the dignity of man himself—to his intellect and his sense of morality —indeed to the God-given force that is called Conscience. Tolerance and unselfishness—like morality and generosity—cannot be successfully legislated.

Man cannot make progress toward self-restraint by discipline from without. It must come from within. Hence, to impose any rigid forms of international government would actually impede the process of voluntary change going on among peoples in different stages of evolution. By reason of newly stimulated passions and frictions, it could postpone rather than hasten the day when humanity might be living in "one world" of enduring peace.

WITHOUT PRINCIPLE

MAY 20, 1955

AT PARIS

THE CYNICAL QUIP heard here among diplomats is that the West desires peace at any price while the Communists want peace at no price at all.

This is not the only paradox, however. Those in government, here and abroad, who know the inside story of all the futile efforts thus far to obtain from Moscow, through the customary diplomatic channels, some evidence of a sincere desire to negotiate peace must have a troubled conscience as they accept the enemy's propaganda trick—a spectacular meeting with Bulganin—and arouse false hopes everywhere about the prospects for peace.

Why do not men in high places give us the facts, unpleasant though they may be? Why do they unwittingly bolster the prestige of the gangsters in the Kremlin? Do they not realize that the strongest card that can be played today is to tell the masses in Soviet Russia and Red China that the fear they have of a big war is due entirely to the unmoral behavior of their rulers?

The truth is that we are making the mistake of abandoning principle for expediency. It is an error that has caused many an empire—and, indeed, many a republic—since ancient days to be overthrown by the Trojan horse tactics of an unscrupulous enemy.

An age-old mistake that has brought tragedy in democracies has been made by those who obey the impulse to tell the people only what they want to hear and to promise them anything so as to win an election. Today a selfish materialism quenches the spirit that once cried out: "What is a man profited, if he shall gain the whole world, and lose his own soul?"

Temporary equilibrium, of course, has been attained for brief periods in world history by compromising with principle. But such compromises have actually brought on major wars. Have the politicians already forgotten what happened in the '30s? Wasn't Prime Minister Chamberlain telling the people of Britain as he returned in 1938 from his two-power conference "at the summit" with Adolf Hitler that we were about to see "peace in our time"?

Wasn't this fallacy widely accepted by many of us, even as we saw the Nazi war machine growing stronger by the hour?

Millions of men, women and children are dead because of the deception that was Munich.

Forty thousand American boys are dead because of the widely spread deception that all nations were interested with us in collective security and that "to repel aggression" in Korea was to prevent aggression in Indo-China.

Our successive retreats of the last few years have not relaxed tension but have actually increased the strain.

A third world war must be avoided if it is humanly possible to do so, because the destruction of cities by atomic weapons is too horrible to contemplate. But it is precisely because a policy of weakness and craven surrender of basic principles invites attack that those who are crying for peace at any price can turn out to be the very ones who bring on a terrible war.

No such epidemic of jitters seems to have afflicted the Moscow gangsters. They now are forming new alliances of military force in Eastern Europe even as they issue transparently false propaganda about a proposed reduction of armaments. Yet spokesmen for some of the Western Powers call anything the Soviets offer "an advance" or a "sign of change," but unfortunately the Communists of the Far East still hold our airmen and still violate their solemn promises made in the armistice agreement at Panmunjom.

Whence comes this strange delusion that by a Four Power conference good faith can be established where there has been none before? And when will we learn to take our stand on principle and adhere steadfastly to it no matter what the sacrifice? For there is only one way to deter any enemy government from aggression, and that is to persuade the people behind it that their rulers are endangering their lives—and, if this fails, then to make sure our force is adequate to defend ourselves against any attack that may come.

But in Europe, where the shell-shocked populace nervously engages in wishful thinking, political parties quiver with fear of defeat at the polls unless they preach pacifism. Hence the Communists are encouraged to believe they can detach Germany from the West in the next few years, just as they now are neutralizing Austria, and thus eventually cause the collapse of the North Atlantic Treaty Organization on which the whole defense of Western Europe is based.

Governments that wish to preserve freedom must steer by the compass of basic principle. They cannot surrender to the whims of expediency now without risking the surrender of their liberties later on. But today Patrick Henry would be howled down in Europe where, if the political currents are an accurate reflection of the people's thinking, the slogan of the times would be: "Give me bondage rather than death! O, slavery, where is thy sting?"

THE GERMAN DILEMMA

MAY 27, 1955

AT BONN, GERMANY

GERMANY, DEFEATED TEN YEARS AGO and accepted now as a full-fledged ally in the common defense against a new enemy, presents a dilemma unparalleled in all history.

For the German people, bitterly opposed as they are today to militarism, did not wish to build another national army, but their new allies insisted upon it.

Germany did not desire to add to the burdens of economic reconstruction by using for rearming tax money that should be spent to remove the rubble of her bombed-out cities.

But the German people, by their repeated votes of confidence in the policies of Chancellor Adenauer, recognize that their destiny lies with the Western democracies and that the defense program of the North Atlantic Treaty Organization is essential as a deterrent force in the world.

So Germany reluctantly will rearm as a vigilant eye is fixed on any militaristic tendencies inside Germany such as brought tragedy before, and a watchful eye is focused on East Germany, whose return to the motherland is an aspiration that no political party can afford to ignore.

At what price, however, shall reunification be obtained? Shall it leave a reunited Germany, without an army, at the mercy of a militarized Russia whose promises of respect for a neutralized Republic must be regarded with misgivings?

Shall Germany accept "neutralization" and rely on the West to come to her rescue if Russia some day decides on an aggressive policy and again tears up treaties as she has done in the past?

Obviously there is no place for American divisions to be strategically placed in Europe if they must be removed from Germany in order to acquiesce in the neutralization program proposed by the Russians.

What, to be sure, are the German political leaders saying? Some of them declare that there must be a friendly attitude toward Moscow on the diplomatic side and that the Big Four conference must not make the mistake of laying down conditions in advance which will hurt a possible agreement. Others are suggesting that a broad plan of European security to include the Russians and to reorganize the whole concept of the North Atlantic Treaty Organization is necessary. This is the line taken by the opposition party—the Socialists—not because at heart they think it will work but because it furnishes a good political platform for the present.

Then there is the viewpoint of the Adenauer Administration, which has a two-thirds majority in the national parliament and which, judging by elections held since the signing of the Austrian treaty by Russia, is strongly supported by the voters of Germany.

The Adenauer Cabinet feels that the neutralization of Austria presents no parallel opportunity for Germany and that this country must line up with the West. Hence the problem is viewed not as something for Germany alone to decide but for the Western nations to consider in close cooperation with Germany and in full recognition of the internal political issue raised by Russia's new tactics in the "cold war."

The German people are sick of war, sick of militarism, and sick of the excessive nationalism that brought them disaster. They talk freely in the press about European unity on the political as well as the economic front, and they regard the French people and the British people as holding the fate of Germany in their hands as much as do the Americans. The thoughts of their leaders turn often toward a federated Europe and a free Europe. They have no illusions about any European security plan that depends on the whim of the dictators in Moscow.

Everyone in the Cabinet and in the parliamentary leadership with whom this writer talked agrees that the most critical time in the "cold war" lies ahead, that it will require courageous statesmanship in the West to avoid being entrapped in Soviet schemes.

There is, of course, a temptation to depart from principle and rely on expediency and to substitute wishful thinking for realistic analysis. Underneath is the strongest urge toward peace and away from war that any nation could experience.

To survey the destruction of homes and buildings and to see the many armless and legless veterans and the women and children in wheelchairs—victims of the bombings—is to understand what an anti-war sentiment exists here even as the call to build a national army has come once more. This call comes, however, from the victors in the war who have been aroused by the faithlessness of one of their former allies.

It is a time of paradox and contradiction, and the way out is not yet visible. For physical force is seen as the only deterrent because moral force has not yet been mobilized to persuade the peoples of Soviet Russia and Red China to restrain their errant governments as they still seek the conquest of Europe and Asia.

THE RISING TIDE OF CONSERVATISM

JUNE 3, 1955

AT LONDON

THE AMERICAN PEOPLE can well rejoice over the outcome of the British election. For it shows that the people in a democracy can tell the difference between baseless cries about misrule and the solid facts of an administration's achievements for the public welfare.

Carping criticism, vague charges of mismanagement of governmental affairs, predictions of economic doom and all the demagoguery which charges that Conservatives have no heart and that only the Socialists are truly sensitive to the needs of the people were brushed aside in an overwhelming victory for conservatism.

But the word "conservatism" must not be distorted into the meaning which the Socialists in Britain and the radical Democrats in America like to give it. For here the Conservatives, like the Eisenhower Administration officials, do not insist on a stagnant economy or governmental indifference when economic emergencies arise, as their opponents so often charge.

The true Conservative favors a flexibility of approach which recognizes social change in the nation and the importance of anticipating its requirements. There is, however, an inflexible adherence by the Conservative to the principle that governments cannot supply the brains and the initiative or the enterprise so essential to job creation or the incentives to successful management of industry.

The keen analysis of Wilfrid Sendall, political correspondent of the *London Daily Telegraph,* written on the day after the election is pertinent:

"After visiting a number of industrial constituencies in the Midlands, I had no doubt of one thing. The manifest prosperity of the highly skilled workers in this area is bringing with it a new outlook. Whereas in 1945 these workers sought security, now they are looking for opportunity. This should make them more receptive to the philosophy of modern conservatism."

But, it may be asked, what was it that basically influenced the British electorate? The behavior of the British voters is not unlike that which we observe in America. The issues here could be condensed into three words, "peace and prosperity." How often have those two issues determined an American election! They were dominant in 1916 when the Democrats won, and they were dominant in 1948 when Truman won. Apathy of the voters in the latter contest was often ascribed to overconfidence by the Dewey forces. The true reason probably was a tendency to regard the economic situation then existent as satisfactory.

In Britain they have been talking about the "apathy" and the "dull campaign." But failure to vote is not unusual when the electorate is in a state of relative contentment. The turnout at the polls was smaller than usual here this year but it affected both parties, as is always the case. In such circumstances the party in power often benefits from its more intensive organization work.

There is a question, too, as to what is meant by "dullness." Aneurin Bevan, left-wing leader inside the Socialist Labor Party, charged that "Wall Street wants a millionaire government here." He expressed himself bitterly against German rearmament and favored the Communist proposal of a neutral belt in Europe. He approved also of the Communist suggestion that the hydrogen bomb be banned, and concurred in their demand that American bases in Europe be prohibited.

Attlee, who is referred to as the right-wing leader in the Socialist Labor Party, was the champion of a moderate socialism, but he felt it necessary to express sympathy with some of Bevan's ideas on foreign policy. This didn't help him much, as Bevan accused Attlee of a "me too" conservatism. All this foreshadows an intensification of the battle for control inside the Socialist Labor Party, from which contest the Conservatives naturally should benefit.

The impressive point about the election is that the facts about economic opportunity and actual prosperity proved more effective than impassioned appeals to class prejudice through phony schemes of reduced taxation.

The election result shows that the cautious speeches by Eden and Macmillan, warning against not expecting too much from the Four Power conference, were not misunderstood by the electorate.

Sincere efforts to bring peace, while applauded by the people, do not erase the fact that peace is not solely within the control of the Western Allies. It depends more than ever on the continued solidarity of the Allies, the continued build-up of our armed forces as a deterrent to aggression, and a continued alertness to the insidious infiltration of free governments and institutions by Communist imperialism.

The British election means that America and Britain stand together now as before in a common desire to achieve "peace and prosperity" for all the world—not only for the democracies which are at present free and independent but for the many countries whose peoples are still enslaved.

THE STRATEGIC DIVERSION

JUNE 10, 1955

THE TALK IN EUROPE as well as in America is of peace—peace "at the summit," or peace at any level, but peace and a riddance from even the thought of war.

Wishfully the world fixes its eyes on words and ignores the acts of evil men.

Wishfully the world clings to the notion that governments arbitrarily conceived in the image of tyranny and governments established by the will of the people in free elections are entitled to equal status in international conferences.

Though Reality casts its heavy shadows and writes its tragedies across the map of the world, Unreality lulls free men into the fanciful belief that an era of security is about to relieve them of their anxieties.

But all around us is war—military preparation, military maneuver, and military conquest in the guise of so-called armistice and cease-fire agreements.

What do we see throughout the world today as a direct consequence either of Communist-inspired rebellions in the colonial areas of Africa or organized wars in Asia?

Terrorism reigns in Algeria and in French Morocco, where there are air bases important to the Western defense. Both Egypt and Libya are being used by the Communists as a source of supply for the Communist terrorists in neighboring areas held by the French.

France has notified the North Atlantic Treaty Organization that it will be necessary to withdraw a whole division of French troops from the defense of Western Europe to take care of the riots breaking out in the French Cameroons in Africa.

Turning to Asia, we see Communist activity in Afghanistan, Burma, Thailand, Laos and Cambodia.

Indo-China is still seething with Communist plotters, and it is an open secret that at the Geneva conference the way was cleared for the process of disintegration now going on which will permit the Communists to dominate all of Indo-China.

The so-called Republic of Indonesia, which was prematurely granted independence in 1949, is an armed camp today. There is no freedom—only tyranny. No elections have ever been held. Communist colonialism has been substituted for European colonialism.

Riots occur in Singapore, which is British territory, and Malaya—a British colony—is perennially threatened by revolt.

The Communist front line extends half way round the globe to Korea. It takes only a small number of malcontents to keep large military forces bogged down in scattered areas. To disperse the forces of your potential enemy is a favorite strategy.

We euphemistically call all this a "cold war." Yet bloodshed is frequent, and the danger is everywhere present in the undeveloped areas, where peoples not yet ready for independence are stimulated to revolution by the Communists.

We allow ourselves, moreover, to rationalize the problem as merely a matter of economic aid, or we speak vaguely of fighting Communism with "ideas" or of feeding the hungry and removing the conditions which bring on the poverty. What a surrender to illusion, and what a success the Communists are making of their strategy as they cause us to look everywhere but at the source of the trouble—Communist imperialism directed from Moscow and Peiping!

For what we are witnessing in the world today is a strategic diversion. Attention is being diverted from the main battlefields of the "cold war" to imaginary shrines where the honest demands for peace that arise from free peoples everywhere are frustrated by the dishonesty and crafty intrigues of dictators. They employ the word "peace" only as a ruse to gain their ends.

Wishful thinking does not banish tension. Billions of dollars are still being spent for armament because the Communists cannot be trusted to keep agreements.

A new phase of the diversionary strategy has just been unfolded. It is called "neutralization." First, it detaches Austria from the West. Then it seeks to isolate or immobilize Yugoslavia and Germany and projects a "neutral belt" across Eastern Europe from Scandinavia to the Mediterranean. All these moves are calculated to force the withdrawal of American troops back to the United States and to bring about the eventual collapse of NATO.

Peace must be our objective, and war must never be waged except in defense against attack. But let us not be diverted from the main issue. No pledge of good faith on disarmament or anything else given by autocracy and dictatorship is worth the paper on which it is written.

Our principal strategy, therefore, must be to concentrate on the peoples who temporarily tolerate the dictatorships. We cannot accept the word of dictatorship governments which menace the peace of the world. The sooner we resolutely tell this to the enslaved peoples, the quicker will they establish free governments. Let us not be deceived by the diversion which is Communist strategy today.

A GUARANTEED ANNUAL PROFIT?

JUNE 17, 1955

LABOR-UNION STRATEGISTS have finally forced the big auto companies to recognize the principle that they are obligated to pay wages to their employes when they are idle.

There is much to be said in sympathy for the worker who, through no fault of his own, is compelled to accept hardship as he waits for the production schedules of his employer to be readjusted each year. Hitherto employers in all industries, as a group, have contributed to unemployment insurance funds. This has been a form of humanitarian relief—not a direct charge against any one business.

But the union contract with the Ford Motor Company provides that an individual business must supplement existing unemployment insurance funds by direct grants. The plan is hedged about, to be sure, by certain safeguards and qualifications, but the principle of a direct subsidy for work not done is clearly established for the future.

The implications of this radical change are far-reaching. Not only does it start an upward spiral of prices, increasing the transportation costs of the people, but it tends to reduce the number of competitors in business.

What shall we do, also, about the plight of those companies which are not in a class with Ford, Chrysler and General Motors—the smaller companies which are having a hard time anyway competing with the larger enterprises in their field? Shall we see the "big three" swallowing up the marginal companies?

We are told the antitrust laws would be invoked to prevent such a monopoly. But this does not solve the financial problems of the smaller companies. How can they possibly meet the added expenses being forced upon big business by big unionism? There has always been a tendency on the part of labor-union leaders to aim for uniformity of pay scales throughout an industry. Today more small businesses have been forced into mergers with the larger companies as a result of union pressure for higher and higher wages than because of any other single economic reason.

If it is the obligation of each of the more successful companies to finance unemployment insurance out of their current earnings, how soon will it become the obligation of the Government—that is, the taxpayers—to subsidize the marginal companies which otherwise might have to go out of business? It can be argued with equal logic that, if it is the responsibility of the employer today to pay out of his own pocket a large percentage of the regular wages to his men when they are not working—and, hence, when they are not producing goods—then it is the duty of the Government to see to it that all the other workers get a comparable subsidy, too, when unemployment comes.

This is in line with the concept of a welfare state which is being espoused under the leadership of our socialistic brethren who are so dominant in the councils of the Democratic Party.

It seems to be old-fashioned nowadays to argue that men should not be paid for work not done. It is held to be out of step with the times to argue that business shall remain entirely on a private-enterprise basis. Yet how can we expect businesses to survive under private management when the socialistic trend is so definitely spelled out by recent developments—extortion of large sums of money for work not done? The penalty for refusal is a greater loss of earnings through work stoppages ordered by union leaders. "Negotiation" is just a euphemism for modern blackmail.

How long is the American economy going to be dominated by a labor-union monopoly which insists on setting wage levels in an industry on the basis of what the larger and more successful units can pay?

There seems only one answer in the offing—participation by the Government in a formula designed to guarantee workers against unemployment. Where it cannot be done through earnings in the case of companies operating in the red, some kind of subsidy will be urged. Will it be paid into a government fund by the larger companies, as they are ordered to help guarantee an annual profit for their competitors? Or will it come from the taxpayers as a whole?

Plainly we are facing some fundamental decisions of policy that can change the whole nature of our private-enterprise system.

The guaranteed annual wage for work not done has a logical corollary—a guaranteed profit to every company which fails to make the grade, giving it money not earned. For the recent agreements in the auto industry proclaim a new doctrine—somebody now must guarantee every worker not only a job but a steady flow of money for services never rendered.

How long can that fallacy be sustained in American private enterprise? And how long before State Socialism picks up the pieces?

ANNIVERSARY OF A HOPE

JUNE 24, 1955

IN THE TEN YEARS that have elapsed since the United Nations Organization was founded at San Francisco, the world has witnessed the rise and fall of a great hope.

With a tendency toward over-simplification of an historic problem, public opinion in 1945 delegated to the United Nations the task of preventing war and assumed that the words of a written charter would be self-enforcing.

We have witnessed in ten years many instances in which the influence of the United Nations has been brought to bear on international disputes. Sometimes the very existence of the machinery of negotiation and mediation has served to give time for cooling the passions of war. Sometimes the United Nations has exercised a direct and effective intervention—but mostly in the quarrels between smaller states.

The major experience, of course, has been in Korea. Led by the United States, the forces of 12 nations, acting in the name of the United Nations, pushed back the North Korean Army which had been furnished sinews of war by the Soviet Government. Then came intervention by the armies of Red China. The casualties were counted in the hundreds of thousands. Soviet Russia, a member of the United Nations Security Council, openly boasted of her part in supplying munitions and airplanes to carry on the conflict.

Here was an act of faithlessness which killed the United Nations as an instrument for the enforcement of peace thereafter by military measures.

The United Nations ceased to exist as a military alliance when it accepted an armistice in Korea in 1953 without having punished the aggressor and without having expelled from its ranks a traitorous member—Soviet Russia.

The United Nations, however, has continued to be and will continue as an instrument of peace in a different capacity. Instead of mobilizing military manpower, the United Nations must inevitably mobilize the moral force of mankind.

For in truth what we have discovered is that the United Nations Charter is not in itself a means of preventing war or of making peace. Rather it is the morality of the members themselves, or the lack of it, which can make or unmake the peace of the world.

As long as the United Nations can maintain a forum for debate—a means of compelling public discussion of any question which threatens the peace of the world —it will remain a useful and practical organization.

There can, of course, be no federation of governments with an organized discipline over sovereign states until international morality has reached a higher level than may be observed today.

International immorality nowadays is far more evident than international morality. Statesmen find ways to avoid passing judgment on the misbehavior of aggressor governments. There is a tendency to refrain from imposing a sentence of guilt on governments that have betrayed their pledges and have disregarded the provisions of the United Nations Charter.

The art of diplomacy today seems to be constantly one of saving face for somebody. The Red Chinese government, for example, has committed all the crimes in the law books of nations. But, bowing to the temptations of expediency, many otherwise moral governments blind themselves to the real issue and argue for admission of the Red Chinese aggressors into the United Nations.

Granted that the war in Korea resulted in no victory for either side and that the aggression was halted at the place where it began, the United Nations fails to reflect the moral indignation that should be implicit in its Charter when its members openly advocate a step that means rewarding the same aggressor with a seat in the Security Council.

May the statesmen who are gathered this week in San Francisco take counsel of their consciences and come to understand that obedience to the code of international morality requires no written mandate.

For imbedded in the minds of people everywhere is the simple truth that there can be no compromise with evil men or evil things.

Peoples must always be able to use any force they can muster to drive tyrants from power and recover their liberties. Free governments, responsive to the will of the people, constitute the only real guarantee of peace. Charters may be revised and their provisions made crystal clear, but they become futile when autocracy is given equal status alongside freedom's representatives.

The United Nations gave hope to the world in 1945 as it welcomed all "peace-loving" nations to membership. After ten years, during which we have failed to cast out the aggressors, we are celebrating again the anniversary of a hope.

It's a hope that moral force—the united opinion of mankind—someday can reach into all countries and make the words "peace-loving," now written in the Charter, mean exactly what they say.

THE TOUGH MR. MOLOTOV

JULY 1, 1955

AT SAN FRANCISCO

MANY WHO READ the speech delivered before the United Nations assembly here last week by Soviet Foreign Minister Molotov will certainly wonder if their eyes deceive them.

For here is the name-calling, arch denouncer of our times using sweet, honeyed words to proclaim that the Communist regimes have been "peace-loving" all these years and that a monster has been reared by the West which threatens an attack on the Soviet Union.

Those military bases in Europe, for example, and the North Atlantic Treaty Organization, as Molotov tells it, are all part of a plan of "aggression." Hence he wants the bases dismantled, American and Allied troops withdrawn from Germany, armaments reduced. Then "peaceful co-existence" will be ushered in with Soviet blessings.

Molotov's speech shows that he is the same master of pretense and artifice that he has been for 25 years—the same bold and brazen spokesman of a criminal gang. He evidently thinks the rest of the world will swallow his misuse of the words "peace" and "aggression" and will not see through his crafty strategy which aims at disarming the Western Allies.

Molotov says he wants peace, of course. Some American and Western weaklings may want peace at any price, but the Soviet spokesman wants peace at no price at all to Russia.

This is not the basis for a sincere negotiation "at the summit." There isn't in the Molotov address the slightest evidence that the Soviet Union is repentant or ready to acknowledge any errors. Rather the Moscow Foreign Minister glories in what he calls the "peace-loving" record of both Red China and Red Russia.

The mothers and fathers and relatives of the tens of thousands of young men killed in Korea will wonder at the effrontery of Molotov, who prates about the rights of Red China to a seat in the United Nations as a prerequisite to peace. He ignores the fact that the United Nations itself declared the Peiping government an "aggressor." He conveniently forgets that only the aggressive behavior of the Soviet Government in blockading Berlin, in sending munitions to North Korea, in helping the Communist-led armies in Indo-China and in stirring up terrorism in North Africa and in Malaya is responsible for the tension that exists today.

Molotov's cure for tension is surrender by the West. His proposals for disarmament are cleverly couched in innocent phrases which take it for granted that people in the Western countries do not read things carefully.

The loopholes in the Russian disarmament plan are well known. While atomic weapons are to be barred, the U. N. Security Council would be authorized to make exceptions—subject, of course, to the veto. One can already visualize the Soviets voting to let the weapons be used when it is to their interest and vetoing any use when it is to their own military advantage to do so.

All through the Molotov speech runs an assumed unawareness that any action whatsoever has been taken in the last ten years by Soviet Russia and her Communist stooges to disturb the peace of the world. Only the West, he claims, has been playing the evil role.

How can there be a successful negotiation when men like Molotov are in power in Moscow and speak to the world in behalf of the Soviet Government? How can the United States, Great Britain and France accept the pledges of men who distort the words and records of history to their own advantage, with a complete disregard for facts and morality?

The Soviet line shows not the slightest sign of even the spirit of a change. Instead, the line has actually hardened and the West has been arrogantly defied.

Mr. Molotov is a tough customer. He has just given the world a preview of what to expect at Geneva. He demands everything and gives nothing. There can be no safety for any free country as long as the gangsters rule in Moscow and Peiping. But it may take a few painful experiences like the Molotov speech at the United Nations assembly to convince all of the Western leaders of that simple truth.

The delegates at San Francisco received the Molotov speech with mixed impressions. Some who saw through its fakery thought he was on the defensive and was putting up a bold front, knowing that the deterrent power of the West has immeasurably increased now that West Germany has been admitted to NATO. Others saw the same inflexibility which has always characterized Soviet diplomacy.

Our Secretary of State, John Foster Dulles, with a dignity and restraint worthy of the American tradition, cut through all the bunkum of the Molotov address and, with a bit of realistic satire, told the United Nations assembly that the way for the Soviets to get peace is quite simple—obey the Charter of the U. N., refrain from the use or threat of force, and stop subversion and infiltration into other countries. It was sensible advice.

LUCKY AMERICA!

JULY 8, 1955

TWO THOUSAND MILES of travel by train around Europe and then a trip across the United States by train, all within the last two and a half months, affords the chance for a study in contrasts.

Since America was colonized originally by Europeans, it is not a question of comparing cultures or intellectual capacities. Our forebears merely found in the United States a land of opportunity, and they had the ingenuity to utilize its resources and bring forth the richest and most powerful country in the world.

These are, primarily, personal reflections about America itself—a few notes on its present mood and a look into its heart—if only for the purpose of demonstrating how erroneous is the concept of those statesmen, members of parliaments, party leaders, newspaper editors and commentators in various countries of Europe who have come to look upon the United States as a nation of impulsive, hot-headed, trigger-happy people anxious to fight another world war.

When you travel across America, as I have, through city after city in State after State larger in area than whole countries in Western Europe and realize that we have millions of miles of good roads, millions of motor cars, millions of homes with electricity, telephones and modern plumbing, comfortable trains, good hotels and motels, mammoth industries and countless retail stores with everything in them that man could desire—then you begin to wonder why on earth the United States should be accused of wanting to start a world war. You wonder why Americans should ever be willing to go 3,000 miles across the Atlantic or 5,000 miles across the Pacific to fight.

For the comparison is so favorable to America and so unfavorable to the congested life and lower standard of living in Europe, when put alongside ours, that anyone who thinks the people of the United States are war-minded and want to disturb all this should have his head examined.

Why the "Warmonger" Nonsense?

One can understand the Soviets' purpose in continuously issuing propaganda calling Americans warmongers. It is one way the dictatorship in Moscow can scare the Russian people and make them sacrifice butter for guns. But why so many persons high up in the official and business life of the principal European countries allied with us should sincerely believe that kind of nonsense is something I was unable to understand. Indeed, I argued the matter with many of them

repeatedly at private dinners, conferences and meetings at which I had an opportunity to meet truly representative men of affairs abroad.

Could it be that some "left wing" correspondents in New York and Washington, writing for European newspapers, have been skillfully distorting the American viewpoint for the last few years? Could it be the result of partisan politics in Europe itself and of the debate in parliaments so often aimed at discrediting an incumbent administration with the usual appeal to nationalism and the customary twist that the home government is "bowing to" or "accepting the dictation of" a foreign power?

The Cure—See America

Whatever it is, I can prescribe a cure—a trip across the United States by train, with plenty of stops. If in a hurry and pressed for time, the airplane is fine. But if you want to see and appreciate America, go by train —or, better yet, by automobile. For you can't feel the throb of this great country while skimming through the clouds at 350 miles an hour.

It is not the scenery alone—the fertile lands, the picturesque rivers and mountains of transcontinental America—that you will observe in a close-up view. You will meet a peace-loving, happy people. You will see them at play—fishing in the streams and lakes, golfing and playing tennis and baseball on municipal recreation grounds, or watching the contests of sport. And you will see them—eager, earnest, alert and indefatigable—at work in the factories and the fields.

Wages and accumulated savings are high. Profits and accumulated reserves for further expansion are high. If the American people look healthier than Europeans, possibly it's because we are better fed. I compliment the fine cooking of Europe. It is incomparable as an art. But, fortunately, God gave us a wonderful climate and millions of acres in which to grow corn to feed animals. The corn-fed steaks and chops of our Middle West contribute to our vitality. I believe also there is no diet anywhere in the world to compare with our cereals, our abundance and variety of fresh fruits and vegetables, our canned and frozen foods— available at relatively low prices—and the good milk that we have everywhere from coast to coast.

The physical look of European communities is different, of course, from American cities and towns. They have some skyscrapers in Europe but modern elevators in only a few of their buildings. Here in an American city it is an exception to find a building with a poor elevator. On the continent of Europe, you can go up on the "lift" but you usually have to walk down.

In European cities, they don't paint their buildings or their houses as often as we do—hence they have an untidy appearance, which even the alibi of "antique finish" fails to dispel. In Paris they say this is due to rent control. Why, it is contended, should a landlord improve a building if he can't increase the rent to pay for it?

I didn't see a new taxicab in London or Paris. Most of them are ten years old or older. The finest railroad trains, night or day, have only one toilet at each end of the car—for as many as 20 passengers. The modern bedroom car with its roomettes, so widely used now in America, is unknown abroad.

Europe with its myriads of bicycles resembles America in the 1890's. Motorcycles are increasing in number, but tractors are still rare in the rural areas. Farming is still in the horse-and-plow stage in most of Europe.

Telephones are not numerous, though increasing. Long-distance telephoning in Europe is a headache. I wondered the other day in San Francisco, as the operator dialed Washington direct for me from a pay-station telephone and I talked to my office a few seconds later, whether a European business man wouldn't faint at the shock of such prompt service.

It would be wrong to take any of this comment as disparagement. As one who favored the Marshall Plan and who still favors economic aid of substantial proportions to Europe, both from the military and humanitarian standpoints, I have no doubt that Americans can be persuaded to continue to give generously of their tax money to help build a peaceful world. But perhaps now and then an American should be permitted a rhapsody of satisfaction over the peaceful, albeit at times luxurious, position which the average citizen here in the United States enjoys in comparison with the less fortunate citizens of the rest of the world.

No Urge to "World Leadership"

Plainly, America is an independent, self-sustaining community, replete with the necessities of life, and its people unconcerned about territorial aggrandizement or colonies or even the doubtful privilege of exercising "world leadership." The fact is most of us would rather pass that compliment on to one of our older allies and be divested of the burden.

To illustrate our naïvete in world affairs, I might remind Europeans that the average American would have to stop a moment to be sure how to spell Chiang Kai-shek and, before June 1950, would probably have guessed wrong as to where Korea is on the map of Asia. I doubt if today the average American could readily locate Formosa. But he does know there is a Communist menace in the world and that 40,000 American boys were killed in Korea and 110,000 wounded because our leader—the then President of the United States—urged us to fight for the ideal of collective security and said it was important to draw a line somewhere and resist Communist aggression or it would engulf us all. That is why Americans today regard Formosa as a symbol of resistance to evil.

Bewildered By Allies' Stand

It should be no surprise to our European friends, therefore, to find Americans still idealistic, though often bewildered by the newspaper dispatches repeatedly telling us that leaders of Britain, leaders of France, leaders of Yugoslavia, leaders of India all say we should admit the Government of Red China, a proved aggressor, into the United Nations and let bygones be bygones.

Many people in America cannot accept, for example, such unpersuasive arguments in support of continued diplomatic relations with Red China as Harold Macmillan, Foreign Secretary of Great Britain, made at San Francisco last month. He said diplomatic recognition was just a historical doctrine of accepting a government that militarily controlled its country. He forgot that back in the 1940's General Petain, Hitler's collaborationist, controlled all of France while patriotic General DeGaulle was sitting in London as the head of the exiled government of France but recognized by Great Britain. DeGaulle didn't even control any offshore islands, either. Nobody in America would have ventured then to suggest that the so-called rule of diplomatic recognition should be observed and Petain should be recognized.

It will be said in rebuttal to this that a war was on in the 1940's. Well, there's a "cold war" on today, and it is costing the American people plenty to fight it. That's why many of us don't like to see official spokesmen for our allies giving encouragement to Red China. A principle of morals is still valid, whether the war is hot or cold.

The upshot of all this could be fatal for Europe. Once convince the American people that expediency rules the roost in Europe—that international morality and idealism are to be disregarded except when the mobilization of American manpower is sought to help fight wars distant from our shores—and the attitude of Americans toward defending Europe in a future war may be far different than was manifested by our armies in only a few of their buildings. Here in an American city it is an exception to find a building with a poor elevator. On the continent of Europe, you can go up on the "lift" but you usually have to walk down.

In European cities, they don't paint their buildings or their houses as often as we do—hence they have an untidy appearance, which even the alibi of "antique finish" fails to dispel. In Paris they say this is due to rent control. Why, it is contended, should a landlord improve a building if he can't increase the rent to pay for it?

I didn't see a new taxicab in London or Paris. Most of them are ten years old or older. The finest railroad trains, night or day, have only one toilet at each end of the car—for as many as 20 passengers. The modern bedroom car with its roomettes, so widely used now in America, is unknown abroad.

Europe with its myriads of bicycles resembles America in the 1890's. Motorcycles are increasing in number, but tractors are still rare in the rural areas. Farming is still in the horse-and-plow stage in most of Europe.

Telephones are not numerous, though increasing. Long-distance telephoning in Europe is a headache. I wondered the other day in San Francisco, as the operator dialed Washington direct for me from a pay-station telephone and I talked to my office a few seconds later, whether a European business man wouldn't faint at the shock of such prompt service.

It would be wrong to take any of this comment as disparagement. As one who favored the Marshall Plan and who still favors economic aid of substantial proportions to Europe, both from the military and humanitarian standpoints, I have no doubt that Americans can be persuaded to continue to give generously of their tax money to help build a peaceful world. But perhaps now and then an American should be permitted a rhapsody of satisfaction over the peaceful, albeit at times luxurious, position which the average citizen here in the United States enjoys in comparison with the less fortunate citizens of the rest of the world.

No Urge to "World Leadership"

Plainly, America is an independent, self-sustaining community, replete with the necessities of life, and its people unconcerned about territorial aggrandizement or colonies or even the doubtful privilege of exercising "world leadership." The fact is most of us would rather pass that compliment on to one of our older allies and be divested of the burden.

To illustrate our naïvete in world affairs, I might remind Europeans that the average American would have to stop a moment to be sure how to spell Chiang Kai-shek and, before June 1950, would probably have guessed wrong as to where Korea is on the map of Asia. I doubt if today the average American could readily locate Formosa. But he does know there is a Communist menace in the world and that 40,000 American boys were killed in Korea and 110,000 wounded because our leader—the then President of the United States—urged us to fight for the ideal of collective security and said it was important to draw a line somewhere and resist Communist aggression or it would engulf us all. That is why Americans today regard Formosa as a symbol of resistance to evil.

Bewildered By Allies' Stand

It should be no surprise to our European friends, therefore, to find Americans still idealistic, though often bewildered by the newspaper dispatches repeatedly telling us that leaders of Britain, leaders of France, leaders of Yugoslavia, leaders of India all say we should admit the Government of Red China, a proved aggressor, into the United Nations and let bygones be bygones.

Many people in America cannot accept, for example, such unpersuasive arguments in support of continued diplomatic relations with Red China as Harold Macmillan, Foreign Secretary of Great Britain, made at San Francisco last month. He said diplomatic recognition was just a historical doctrine of accepting a government that militarily controlled its country. He forgot that back in the 1940's General Petain, Hitler's collaborationist, controlled all of France while patriotic General DeGaulle was sitting in London as the head of the exiled government of France but recognized by Great Britain. DeGaulle didn't even control any offshore islands, either. Nobody in America would have ventured then to suggest that the so-called rule of diplomatic recognition should be observed and Petain should be recognized.

It will be said in rebuttal to this that a war was on in the 1940's. Well, there's a "cold war" on today, and it is costing the American people plenty to fight it. That's why many of us don't like to see official spokesmen for our allies giving encouragement to Red China. A principle of morals is still valid, whether the war is hot or cold.

The upshot of all this could be fatal for Europe. Once convince the American people that expediency rules the roost in Europe—that international morality and idealism are to be disregarded except when the mobilization of American manpower is sought to help fight wars distant from our shores—and the attitude of Americans toward defending Europe in a future war may be far different than was manifested by our armies

"MUTUAL TRUST"

JULY 15, 1955

ONE SOMETIMES WONDERS why, in all the welter of comment by the statesmen of the world about peace, it takes so long to get down to brass tacks. President Eisenhower seems to have isolated at last the germ of the world's anxiety—its main reason for fearing another war. He said last week at his press conference:

"In the long run, the kind of peace which we are seeking, the kind of peace that will really allow people to be really tranquil and confident in their daily pursuits, will be achieved only when nations have achieved that mutual trust of which you speak."

There has not been for years, and there is not now, any trust in dictatorships—governments which rule by force and without the consent of the governed.

The world cannot disarm, free nations cannot live without fear, so long as the mechanism to threaten world peace exists in the form of an arbitrary government which at any given moment can order an attack on a peaceful neighbor.

The remedy for the world's ills, therefore—the way to begin to build up mutual trust—is to proclaim to all peoples that no diplomatic recognition will be accorded to any government which denies its citizens the right to free and uncoerced elections.

The principle is not novel. It was affirmed in a prophetic pronouncement in 1944 by the Catholic Bishops of America, who, in analyzing the Dumbarton Oaks proposals for a United Nations organization, said:

"The international organization must never violate the rightful sovereignty of nations. Sovereignty is a right which comes from the juridical personality of a nation and which the international organization must safeguard and defend.

"However, national sovereignty may not be interpreted as absolving a nation from its obligations in the international community. Moreover, even within the state, national sovereignty is limited by the innate rights of men and families. Since civil authority does not confer these God-given rights, it may not violate them.

"The ideology of a nation in its internal life is a concern of the international community. To reject this principle is tantamount to maintaining that the violation of the innate rights of men in a country by its own government has no relation to world peace.

"Just at this moment, in the interest of world peace, our nation is exerting itself to root out some ideologies which violate human rights in the countries we are liberating.

"We hold that if there is to be a genuine and lasting world peace, the international organization should demand as a condition of membership that every nation guarantee in law and respect in fact the innate rights of men, families, and minority groups in their civil and religious life. Surely our generation should know that tyranny in any nation menaces world peace.

"A nation which refuses to accord to its own people the full enjoyment of innate human rights cannot be relied upon to cooperate in the international community for the maintenance of a peace which is based on the recognition of national freedom.

"Such a nation will pursue its own selfish international policies, while paying lip service to international cooperation."

The occasion for the making of the above statement was, of course, the war against the Nazi dictatorship. Had the free nations of the world united between 1933 and 1939 to warn the Hitler regime that it could not get raw materials or carry on trade with the free world until the people of Germany were permitted to have an unrestricted voice in their own affairs, the second world war might never have been fought.

There would be no fear of a third world war today if Soviet Russia were a republic with the customary freedoms that are enjoyed in a democracy.

There would be no Iron Curtain if the press could report to the outside world freely and without censorship what is going on inside Russia, and if the newspapers there were free to print any comment they pleased.

There would be no threat of war if the people of the Soviet Union were permitted to have parties of opposition and if a system of free elections were established so that the people could decide what armaments they needed for defense and whether they would be willing to submit always to a system of good-faith inspection.

There's not much use talking about making peace by international conferences or by paper plans for reduction of armaments when there is no "mutual trust." This can come only when all the nations of the world boldly proclaim the realism of our nuclear age—that the establishment of a free government in each country that has the capacity to menace world peace is a prerequisite to the survival of all other free governments.

There can be no disarmament or acceptable treaties or agreements until the Soviet people are free and the peoples of the satellite countries are also free. It's the only formula that will assure an enduring peace.

THE NEW TRUCE

JULY 22, 1955

THEY'RE MAKING A NEW TRUCE in Geneva this week.

It doesn't mean peace—and it doesn't mean war.

Each side will continue to build up its military forces, particularly air power.

Open hostilities will be avoided in Europe—just as now in Korea and Indo-China.

But this is a far cry from peaceful co-existence. It is co-existence, to be sure, but it can hardly be called peaceful. For the imminent danger of war will not have been removed.

It can't be removed as long as dictatorship governments in Moscow and Peiping have the capacity to disregard the wishes of the people and at any moment launch an aggression.

From 1945 to date, the aggressors of the Communist world have carried on their warfare, sometimes through puppet governments and puppet armies, sometimes with subversive elements inside some of the western countries reaching into Cabinets, parliaments, the press, the church and political parties.

This subversive activity is not to cease. International Communism has not yet been repudiated, or abandoned by Moscow, and will not be, because it is an instrument of aggression in the Western world as important to the Kremlin as are the Red military forces which dominate the satellite countries.

The Soviet-Chinese alliance is not as strong as the Western alliance. But it is fallacious to assume that the Communists are negotiating in a spirit of defeatism. It is more accurate to say they recognize their own weaknesses and seek a means of neutralizing those weaknesses by persuading the Western allies to stand still while the Communist regimes catch up in military and economic strength.

The Soviets intend to change their diplomacy mainly to ease the pressure which the West has been putting on them.

Undoubtedly, both Soviet Russia and Red China need raw materials and machinery. If, by assuming a peaceful mood and adopting conciliatory instead of blustering tactics, the East can persuade the West to modify the list of strategic goods prohibited for export to the Communist countries, it will be as big a gain as Communist imperialism could achieve.

So far as "disarmament" is concerned, the Russians are really proposing that restrictions on the use of nuclear weapons be adopted but that military forces be allowed to remain at virtually their existing strength. The Communists are thinking in terms of a military stalemate such as exists in Asia. They want to see Europe stabilized militarily for the time being. But this doesn't mean that the Russians are eager to reduce their own armies or that they will let up in their attempt to break down the North Atlantic Treaty Organization.

If by negotiation the Communists could bring it about that American troops are kept out of Germany and forced to return to the United States, this would be a great triumph for them. But the Moscow strategists are realistic enough to know they can't accomplish any such goal. So they will try to effect at least a military status quo in Europe. They really want a slow-down while they catch up.

All this may on the surface be regarded as a "relaxation of tension." There was, to be sure, a "relaxation of tension" when the Panmunjom armistice was signed. Most everybody in the West thought this was a warning to the aggressors. But the stepped up war in Indo-China came next and, after the Communists gained more territory, they agreed to a truce.

Now there is to be a new truce—primarily for Europe. But the situation in Asia will not be allowed by the Communists to stand still. Malaya, Singapore and Laos are in process of being won over to Communist influence. The next big objective is Formosa. The Communists will not be content till they have demobilized the 450,000 Nationalist Chinese troops which guard Southeast Asia for the Western alliance. Nor will they be satisfied thereafter, until they have demobilzed Syngman Rhee's 700,000-man army in Korea. Then infiltration of the Philippines becomes easy.

The whole business is a military game. That's why it's wrong to speak of the Geneva meeting as a conference to achieve peace. It's a truce conference that the President of the United States has gone 3,000 miles to attend. It merely postpones the clash that will become inevitable in future years unless free governments can be brought into being in Moscow and Peiping and in the satellite states.

In the sense that hostilities are averted or avoided, it may represent a breathing spell during which the germs of revolution inside the Communist countries can ferment to our advantage, despite the opportunity it also can give coincidentally to the dictators to build up their strength on the military and economic fronts. We will win in the long run because we are militarily strong and our cause is morally just.

HOW—

JULY 29, 1955

ASSUMING THE SINCERITY of a Soviet desire for peace and not for just a breathing spell, how can such a goal be achieved?

The statesmen "at the summit" have struggled with that dilemma. They have tried conciliatory words. They have tried fraternization. They have tried earnest argument. The net result thus far has been little change on substantive matters from the fixed positions that have prevailed now for several years.

Why? The simple answer is that, while the desire for peace may be strong on both sides, the instinct for self-preservation—a defense against possible attack—is still stronger.

Try as President Eisenhower might to persuade his former comrade in arms, Marshal Zhukov, to see that the North Atlantic Treaty Organization could protect Soviet Russia against a rebirth of German militarism, the Russian Defense Minister can hardly accept such a thesis if he is convinced that behind NATO is a military alliance aimed at Soviet Russia alone.

Conversely, when Marshal Bulganin proposes a 50-year collective-security treaty for Europe which is based primarily on the abrogation of the North Atlantic Treaty and the Paris Accords, the President and his Western colleagues naturally brush it aside as devious.

What we are witnessing is a demonstration of the impossibility of negotiating any important agreements when there is basic distrust.

How, then, can distrust be removed and trustfulness substituted? The Big Four meeting would have made more progress had it engaged in an analysis of what brought about the present differences of viewpoint rather than a discussion of proposals which, however meritorious in themselves, cannot be accepted on a background of bad faith.

Doctors tell us that, before they can prescribe a cure, there must be a diagnosis. Can the statesmen bring out the facts and outline accurately the points of digression since 1945 so that both sides may see clearly why there is an impasse?

They can, of course, yet they have preferred to assume that by wishful thinking the past can be made to seem non-existent.

But the past is there—before our eyes. So is the present. The satellites in Eastern Europe are there—oppressed and tyrannized—notwithstanding the pledges of the Atlantic Charter.

The situations in other vital areas are there—from North Korea to Indo-China and from one end of North Africa to the other, where Communist subversion has stimulated uprisings and aroused national passions.

The situations inside Latin America and, indeed, inside the United States are there, too—plain to see as the Alger Hisses and the Klaus Fuchses and the whole Soviet espionage system have infiltrated our institutions.

These pages of history must be re-examined and the facts hammered home. We must acquaint the people of Soviet Russia with the whole background of Communist faithlessness which has brought us to the point where today we hesitate to accept the word of the Moscow regime.

How can we make worthwhile agreements with a group of evil men who run a police state and keep millions of persons in Siberian prison camps? A dictatorship can arbitrarily start a war of aggression without giving the people a voice in such a momentous decision. We can photograph each other's military installations to satisfy a world craving for steps toward preventing war, but nobody can photograph the minds of evil men who can conceal from the camera their satanic purposes. How can we negotiate effectively with rulers who permit no political opposition, no free elections, no guarantees of individual rights?

The answer is that we cannot achieve peace with such a government, and the sooner we acknowledge that fact the clearer will be the air.

We should, moreover, use every device of publicity and communication to analyze the causes of the tension of today between East and West and carry the case to the court of public opinion throughout the world—and this includes Soviet Russia.

Why not ask the Soviet regime to permit inside all countries a free discussion of the causes of mutual distrust? Why not urge Moscow to stop "jamming" the Voice of America and our radio broadcasts? It's a simple way to bring out the truth. And if the Soviet rulers aren't afraid of argument—if they think they can answer it all persuasively—why should they not welcome the chance for the moral forces of the world to pass judgment on the debate?

War is not a solution. Compromise with principle is not a solution. But the building of a bridge of trust with the Russian people is a solution. Governments come and go—but relations with peoples can be placed on a basis of enduring and understanding friendship.

THEY STOOP TO CONQUER

AUGUST 5, 1955

WHATEVER ELSE HAPPENED at the Geneva conference, solemn support was given to the fateful premise that a world war should not be invoked by either the East or the West to attain their respective aims.

War certainly is not necessary for us if we are not going to be attacked. This, we have repeatedly said, is the only reason we would fight.

War certainly is not necessary for the Soviet Union if her rulers can get what they want from the West without dropping a single atomic bomb.

To be realistic, however, we should not forget that we are still engaged in an effort to bring World War II to an end. For, while the Western Allies demobilized their armies and in due time ended their occupation of West Germany, the Soviet armies have never been demobilized. They still occupy not only East Germany but Poland, Czechoslovakia, Rumania, Bulgaria, Hungary, Latvia, Estonia and Lithuania.

When we talk of peace in Europe, we mean finding a way to persuade the Soviets to end World War II and withdraw their armies to Russia, or to let them hold indefinitely what they have seized.

When we talk of peace for Asia, we mean either acquiescing in or overcoming the effects of the military occupation of the Far East by the Communists. Since 1945 they have taken China and moved their forces into North Korea and also into Southeast Asia, where they have gobbled up a large part of the territory of Indo-China. They have, moreover, extended their political leverage to Indonesia, Burma, India and other nations which call themselves neutral but actually do the bidding of Moscow out of sheer terror.

In recent weeks the Kremlin has suddenly changed its propaganda and diplomacy throughout the world—from invective to conciliation, from defiance to meekness, and from open hostility to manifest friendliness. It started by wooing Marshal Tito. It centers now on capturing the mind of President Eisenhower.

The West has been thrilled with all this. Every spokesman has uttered his sense of relief and gratitude over the outbreak of brotherly love at Geneva.

But why? Has a "better climate" for peace really been established just because Moscow ceases to snarl and now cajoles? Has any single objective in Europe or Asia been abandoned by the Soviet Government?

We of the West have had our hopes raised high before. So frightened have the Western governments become over a nuclear war that they now have apparently adopted the attitude that maybe, if the enemy will be

merciful, an effort should be made to meet him more than halfway. But we are supposed to give away our honor—the Communists are expected only to give back some of the persons and property which they never were lawfully entitled to retain.

Now our ambassador is about to sit down at Geneva with the ambassador of the unmoral government at Peiping which still refuses to accept the authority of the United Nations in unifying Korea, yet insists upon a seat in the Security Council of the U. N. The Red regime does not even acknowledge that its own troops ever intervened in Korea to repel the forces of the U. N.

There certainly is no harm in talking with the Red Chinese. We talked with them at Panmunjom, too. It's what we say to them that matters. Is it possible that, if the Red Chinese agree to return the prisoners of war they hold in violation of the pledges in the Korean armistice agreement, we will promise to lift trade embargoes so as to get from them that which, under any code of honor or justice, we are entitled to receive without offering a single concession as a ransom?

Our allies evidently are ready to go further and turn Formosa over to Red China. But do they realize that to throw away the strategic value of 500,000 Nationalist troops on Formosa is to break down also the morale of the Korean Army of 650,000 and to stimulate Communist activity in Japan and the Philippines?

Naturally many people in the United States are puzzled. They are unable to understand why we should have been required to sacrifice more than 33,000 American lives in Korea, in addition to 103,500 wounded, to defend the principle of collective security, only to see it abandoned now in a collective appeasement.

Are we to give up our powerful leverage on the economic and moral side which, if steadfastly adhered to, can liberate Eastern Europe and the peoples of Soviet Russia?

The Kremlin strategists are playing their game skillfully. If the Soviets can persuade the West to accept as permanent the control of Eastern Europe by Moscow and the domination of Asia by Peiping, and if the Communists can get trade in strategic goods opened up, too, they will have won without war the greatest triumph of all history at the least cost.

The Soviets, of course, can flatter our leaders and can pour forth soothing phrases while withholding acts of performance. For the stakes of ten years of military occupation and political infiltration are high. Moscow's rulers, indeed, can afford to "stoop to conquer."

RUSSIA'S "BIG DECISION"

AUGUST 19, 1955

(The following conversation is imaginary, but the assumptions as to Soviet policy are based on circumstantial evidence available since the death of Stalin.)

AT THE KREMLIN

BULGANIN: We have made many mistakes since 1945.

KHRUSHCHEV: Mostly we have stirred up the United States to build vast armaments.

ZHUKOV: It would be a mistake to fight the United States—a war would be suicide.

BULGANIN: Let's all agree to that. In fact, it should be a cardinal point in our policy not to have any war with America.

ZHUKOV: Will they believe us if we say so?

KHRUSHCHEV: The funny part of it is that we are really sincere on this.

ZHUKOV: I know it. I'll try to convince Eisenhower that it's true.

BULGANIN: We can at least show the world that we do not intend to fight America and that we want peaceful coexistence.

KHRUSHCHEV: The fundamental goal is the success of International Communism. We can control Europe and Asia if the United States is not in our way.

BULGANIN: Our real aim must be to bring about the withdrawal of the armies of the United States from Europe and Asia and the abandonment of their overseas bases. We can accomplish this without fighting—by negotiation and by talking "peace."

ZHUKOV: Exactly how do we go about it?

KHRUSHCHEV: By urging that international conferences be held frequently "at the summit" or at lower levels, by arranging personal missions of the high officials of our countries, by exchanging visits of students and farm groups and newspaper men, by emphasizing that we are a committee government and not a dictatorship, by removing the censorship on news dispatches of foreign correspondents—in fact, by every means that will show our friendliness. This will produce the right kind of "climate" and it will "relax tension."

ZHUKOV: What do you think will be the result?

KHRUSHCHEV: We will surely bring about a reduction of the arms budgets of all the Western countries. Their peoples will never go on spending such big sums every year for armaments if there is to be peace. And we can assure them there will be no war.

BULGANIN: If we only had thought of all this in the five years between 1945 and 1950—and if Stalin hadn't encouraged the mess in Korea five years ago—the Americans would never have built up their big Air Force or spent so much money on the development of nuclear weapons.

KHRUSHCHEV: We must not make the mistake of threatening countries in Europe, either. That only stirs up the Americans. We must play ball with Tito and offer to withdraw our troops from all the satellite countries. We'll get some concessions from the West when we do that. We should make sure that Chou En-lai says repeatedly that China doesn't want war with the United States. Let's play it peacefully all along the line. That's good Party doctrine. Lenin always said that we must adapt our strategy to circumstances and change tactics. We can depend on our good spy system. We can really achieve more by infiltration everywhere than we could get by war. In war, everybody loses—

ZHUKOV: Amen!

KHRUSHCHEV: —and if we can convince the American people that we don't intend ever to fight them, NATO will fall apart—it already is showing weakness—and we will be able to dominate Germany even if it is reunified. That should be our goal.

It's costly—this peace offensive. But our billions of rubles spent annually for propaganda have paid off. Look at the trouble we've been able to stir up in North Africa. French divisions wanted by NATO are being moved away from Europe to Africa. Look at the way we have been able to exploit the tension in the Near East. Look what we've been doing in Malaya and Singapore without involving our own troops. Look how we have scared Nehru into neutralism, and Burma, too. We've got Indonesia in the bag, and Indo-China, too.

ZHUKOV: Will Peiping stay with us?

BULGANIN: Sooner or later we will get Japan by infiltration. That will bind the Chinese to us in self-protection. If we are a bit patient, we'll also bring Chou En-lai into the United Nations. Things are going our way on that now. The Americans are softening up, and the British and French are with us.

KHRUSHCHEV: "Peaceful coexistence" is wonderful—we will slowly but surely, and in the nicest manner, guide the Americans out of Europe and Asia back to their own continent where they belong.

ZHUKOV: You think the Americans will accept all this?

KHRUSHCHEV: Sure, I do.

BULGANIN: Then what are we waiting for?

ALL TOGETHER: Horosho, poidyom! (Translated freely, "OK, let's go.")

A CODE ALSO FOR
PRISONERS OF DEFEATISM

AUGUST 26, 1955

"THE FIGHT CONTINUES After the Battle."

This is the inspirational title given by the Advisory Committee on Prisoners of War to its report issued last week under the authority of the Secretary of Defense. It tells those who may become prisoners of war in the future that a course of courageous conduct is expected of them—that they must consider themselves still in the fight even though captives.

But has the "fight" in behalf of those who recently were prisoners of war continued "after the battle"?

We must ask ourselves whether those in positions of responsibility in our country and among our allies have kept faith with the heroic soldiers who were tortured in Korean prison camps.

We must ask ourselves whether the battle for principles has been continued in the United Nations and also in those international conferences held with the Communists in recent years—or whether many of us have become prisoners of our own defeatism.

The Advisory Committee consisted of men eminent in American life. Their proposed code is in accord with American tradition. Their report, however, makes this important point:

"Our case was simple and just, but our objectives in the Korean War were frequently confused in the public mind . . .

"The causes of the war, United Nations' objectives and the need for American intervention were not clearly delineated in the public mind. This lack of understanding prevailed among citizens and American fighting men. The Communists attempted to exploit to the fullest this condition in both international propaganda and in dealing with our prisoners of war."

But who was responsible for confusing or for failing to delineate United Nations' objectives?

When General MacArthur asked that his planes be allowed to engage in "hot pursuit" if attacked by enemy planes—one of the oldest military doctrines in history—the other nations allied with us refused to agree. This was welcome news to the Soviets.

When, in the midst of battle operations, General MacArthur crossed the 38th Parallel, after having previously notified the United Nations that he was pursuing the enemy, there was acquiescence for a few weeks only. Our allies got cold feet and began to cast doubt on the move. Gradually Allied criticism of General MacArthur mounted, and President Truman summarily fired the brilliant leader of our fighting troops. Small

wonder they were bewildered and confused. This was welcome news to the Soviet propagandists.

When the United Nations declared Red China an aggressor, it was well known inside the U. N. that Soviet Russia was furnishing arms and ammunition and fliers for the Communist armies in North Korea. But the United Nations failed to declare the Soviet Government an aggressor and to expel that government from the international organization. For the Soviet Union was no longer a "peace loving" government—the basic qualification for membership in the U. N.

The new code for future soldiers asks this pledge:

"I will never surrender of my own free will . . . If I become a prisoner of war, I will keep faith with my fellow prisoners."

A new code is also needed for members of the United Nations, with this pledge:

"As long as our government continues as a member of the United Nations, we will keep faith with our fellow members. We will not surrender our ideals. We will not supply arms to enemies of the U. N. We will not reward aggressors."

Commenting on the Defense Advisory Committee's report, the *New York Times* editorially last week said:

"In the report there is no more significant statement than the revelation that more than one third of the Americans taken prisoner by the Communists in Korea died in captivity. There is no comparably outrageous record in modern times. Moreover, it is only too obvious that the record in regard to other United Nations prisoners, and especially the Koreans, is even worse."

Where is the moral courage among those leaders of the free world—in government, in the church, in the press and in the university faculties—who today are indicating that admission of Red China to the U. N. would be "logical" or "in the interest of peace," when not a word of repentance has come from these war criminals for their acts of atrocity?

Where is the moral courage among our defeatists who are so eager to expand trade with the gangster regimes and to let bygones be bygones?

The Defense Advisory Committee forgot to state one important truth: It will be difficult to inspire the soldiers of future wars with moral courage as long as the record shows a flagrant disregard of the ideals for which 30,000 of our brave young men died in Korea.

COURAGEOUS WORDS!

SEPTEMBER 2, 1955

COURAGEOUS WORDS HAVE COME from the President of the United States to dispel the fog left after the Geneva Conference by the ambiguity of Soviet utterances. For the speeches of Moscow's officials have implied that "peaceful co-existence" means an indefinite prolongation of the slavery imposed behind the Iron Curtain—an acceptance of things as they are.

Mr. Eisenhower's address last week before the American Bar Association meeting reminds the Soviet Union's rulers that, while the leaders of our country can be polite, friendly and congenial in international conferences, this doesn't mean that the United States is ready to abandon its ideals or to compromise its principles. For, as the President sees it, appeasement does not mean peace—it assures war.

Mr. Eisenhower has given dramatic encouragement to the oppressed peoples in Soviet Russia as well as in the satellite states.

For many weeks these peoples—their views reflected by refugees who once occupied posts of importance in their governments—have been increasingly apprehensive lest Great Britain, France and the United States accept the "status quo." This would mean a ratification of the Soviet grab of territory and its continued domination of hundreds of millions of people. Certainly America does not intend to abandon their cause, even though not intending any more than before to initiate in their behalf a war of liberation.

America represents the moral force of the world. Her spokesmen would be faithless to a great tradition if they failed to reaffirm a deep interest in the future of oppressed peoples everywhere. The President said:

"There can be no true peace which involves acceptance of a status quo in which we find injustice to many nations, repressions of human beings on a gigantic scale, and with constructive effort paralyzed in many areas by fear.

"The spirit of Geneva, if it is to provide a healthy atmosphere for the pursuit of peace, if it is to be genuine and not spurious, must inspire all to a correction of injustices, an observance of human rights and an end to subversion organized on a world-wide scale . . .

"Geneva spells for America, not stagnation, then, but opportunity—opportunity for our own people and for people everywhere to realize their just aspirations.

"Eagerness to avoid war—if we think no deeper than this single desire—can produce outright or implicit agreement that injustices and wrongs of the present shall be perpetuated in the future. We must not participate in any such false agreement. Thereby, we would outrage our own conscience. In the eyes of those who suffer injustice, we would become partners with their oppressors. In the judgment of history, we would have sold out the freedom of men for the pottage of a false peace. Moreover, we would assure future conflict!

"The division of Germany cannot be supported by any argument based on boundaries or language or racial origin.

"The domination of captive countries cannot longer be justified by any claim that this is needed for purposes of security.

"An international political machine, operating within the borders of sovereign nations for their political and ideological subversion, cannot be explained away as a cultural movement."

Here is a plain-spoken definition of American aims and goals—our outline of a basis for world peace, as it was expressed frequently before the Geneva Conference. But being proclaimed again now after Geneva, it carries a special significance. The President does not advocate violence but recognizes that peoples living in tyranny will inevitably invoke force if they are driven to it. He makes that point as he says:

"We must not think of peace as a static condition in world affairs. That is not true peace, nor in fact can any kind of a peace be preserved that way. Change is a law of life, and unless there is peaceful change, there is bound to be violent change."

The President takes his position unflinchingly for the support of American principles long ago written into our record in world affairs. He speaks for the whole nation, as he issues to the Soviet Union this piece of timely advice:

"Peace and security for all can be established—for the fearful, for the oppressed, for the weak, for the strong. But this can be done only if we stand uncompromisingly for principle, for great issues . . . with the zeal of the crusader."

When principle is forsaken, war comes. When men sell their souls in craven submission at international conferences, war comes. When statesmen stand steadfastly together for the right—eschewing surrender and appeasement—their faith and their moral strength can warn an enemy against the fatal miscalculations that bring on war. For a sincere spirit of conciliation must not be mistaken again—as it was at Munich in 1938—for a willingness to pay any price for peace.

THE "COLD WAR" MARCHES ON

SEPTEMBER 16, 1955

DURING A "HOT WAR" official communiqués are issued regularly, telling of the movements of the major forces from week to week.

It is equally important that the world be apprised of what is happening at the front and behind the lines in the "cold war" of today. Here is an informal communiqué on the latest action in the "cold war":

GREECE: A staunch ally of the West has been swept by waves of bitterness over the issue of self-determination for the island of Cyprus now held by Great Britain. Turkey opposes any change. The question has long been slumbering but it has been given new impetus by agents of the Communists, who play one side in Turkey and the opposite in Greece.

TURKEY: A new front has been opened up by the Communists. Taking advantage of the ill-feeling over the Cyprus issue, unknown persons dynamited a Turkish consulate in Greece. Riots in retaliation were instigated in Turkey. Finally martial law had to be proclaimed there last week. The Turkish-Greek co-operation so essential to a Balkan military alliance desired by the West has been imperiled. The Turkish Government officially blames the Communists for inspiring the trouble.

ISRAEL: The fighting with the Egyptians on the Gaza strip was intensified last week. It brought the United Nations into the picture. The Israel Government has shown signs of lining up with the West.

THE ARAB WORLD: Sympathies of the Arab countries are with Egypt in her friction with Israel, and there is no longer any secret about Russia's offer to give or sell arms to the Arab countries. Thus the Kremlin is exploiting the Israel-Egypt conflict to the utmost.

ALGERIA: Strong steps have been taken by the French to quell rebellion. Nationalism is the issue, but the poorly equipped nationalist movement has had help from the Communist underground.

MOROCCO: The Communists have definitely added momentum to the nationalist movement. It takes only a few agents and a handful of well trained terrorists to inflame the populace by instigating riots and provoking violence. American air bases in Morocco, vital in case of war, are endangered.

The net result to date has been the sending to Africa of two divisions of French troops needed by NATO in Europe. Here is a military objective that the "cold war" seems able to accomplish more easily than might be the case in a "hot war."

INDIA: Nehru is prodded on all sides to do something about annexing Goa, a Portuguese province. The Indian Premier at first acquiesced in the "non-violence" marches into Goa but soon found the situation was out of hand as the Communists stormed Portuguese consulates and excited the populace so that violence broke out in many parts of India. The Communists now are criticizing Nehru in Parliament for squelching the disturbances. The battle still goes on.

GERMANY: Just before Chancellor Adenauer left last week on his trip to Moscow to negotiate a resumption of diplomatic relations between the Soviets and West Germany's Government, it was discovered that Communist agents had infiltrated the West German Foreign Office. Communists have been active in West Germany in stirring up dissension as between the political parties and in playing upon nationalistic feelings. The German situation is at the moment the focus of Communist efforts. They hope to bring about through the Adenauer visit a bitter debate inside West Germany. The objective is to detach all Germany from the West and to prevent rearmament by offering the Germans unity in exchange for neutrality.

RED CHINA: The island of Quemoy has been shelled frequently in the last few days despite the talk that a "cease fire" has been silently adopted. The Peiping Government has released a few more Americans, and —as a ransom price—expects the present negotiations at Geneva to lead to a meeting of Red China's Foreign Minister and Secretary of State Dulles. This is an important propaganda objective of the Communists, needed to convince the people of Asia that the appeasers in America who advocate admission of Red China into the U. N. are beginning to get their way.

THE UNITED STATES: The drive to break down the security system is making progress. It is being stimulated by certain members of Congress who have exaggerated the importance of a few bungles in the handling of security cases.

But the most important development is the sudden decision of the Department of Defense to recommend to Congress a cut in armaments. Evidently it is thought that "peaceful coexistence" doesn't require as big an arms budget for America as before. The issue will split both political parties.

A "cold war" can turn into a "hot war" at any moment. Yet without a single piece of evidence that the "cold war" has abated or that any of Russia's or Red China's goals have been abandoned, the West is beginning to take at face value the Communist professions of peaceful intent. That's the biggest advance the Communists have made in many years in the "cold war."

BOOM OR STABILITY?

SEPTEMBER 23, 1955

WHENEVER THERE IS a period of stability, a tendency arises to ask apprehensively how long the "boom" will last—as if normal conditions, when achieved, are really too good to be true.

Today the business of the nation is "booming." Many factors have contributed to it—not the least of which is a genuine confidence that the forces of confiscation, the forces of over-regulation and the forces of government ownership have been held in check.

Confidence is essential to business planning. It can be frustrated by threats of interference with the natural progress of the economy.

Regulation is necessary, of course, when excesses occur. The Government, irrespective of party, has found that public opinion demands correction whenever economic power is abused by collective groups of individuals or corporations.

While political intervention in the economic life of the country to correct misuse of power is accepted generally as in the public interest, political interference with economic laws can be disastrous, especially when it is generated by pressure groups for selfish purposes.

Today interference with business expansion is at a minimum. While the Government rightly enforces anti-trust laws and applies its police power to unfair trade practices, there is a climate of reassurance because the Eisenhower Administration has repeatedly acted in ways that beget confidence. Prominent in this is the prudent management of fiscal affairs.

What America is experiencing today is an Eisenhower "boom." It demonstrates that America need not be engaged in a war to maintain prosperity.

But the stakes in a continuance of prosperity are higher than they have ever been.

A labor-union monopoly, for instance, can force the cost of production above the point where the consumers will buy.

A business monopoly can raise the price level to a prohibitive point and risk a curtailment of demand.

A government monopoly on credit can tighten the borrowing mechanism and, by unwise policies, throw the whole economic system out of gear.

It often is asserted that we have or should have a "managed economy." While some segments are regulated, the biggest single factor in business expansion—the growth of population—happily is unregulated.

As population in America increases, with a demand for more of everything, so does it increase everywhere else in the world, too. The demand for American products continues to grow. Yet the high cost of transportation and the chaotic condition of currency exchange makes it impossible to move our agricultural surpluses, for example, into areas where they can be absorbed. Hence, our own farm income is declining.

With all the lofty talk about international cooperation to utilize atomic energy, it is a sad commentary on our present situation that governments around the globe seem to lack the ingenuity to invent methods and systems to promote bilateral or triangular or even quadrangular trade in surpluses. Today the protective principle is as strongly entrenched in Europe as it is in America—each economy feels that it must protect its own minorities. Granted that this is essential, it remains possible nevertheless for an enlarged trade to be channeled into areas where it is needed. International trade deals on a worldwide scale have never been attempted except in wartime.

Our "boom" today is related primarily to international factors, particularly armament expenditures. These constitute an underpinning everywhere, but they must inevitably be supplanted in large part some day by more productive enterprises.

While this is logical, however, it must not be done suddenly or sharply. The dangers of deflation are as prevalent at present as the dangers of inflation.

The current "boom" has a sound basis. It could conceivably last over a period of many years. But the biggest single factor that can upset it is unwise action by Congress and the Executive in national and international policies. That's why the 1956 election will be the most important since 1920, when we first moved into an enlarged economy in peacetime.

It will be an election important to the maintenance of economic stability.

How encouraging, therefore, it would be if both political parties were to pledge themselves to adhere firmly to the principle which Jefferson proclaimed—that the best government is the government that governs the least. This means an opportunity for maximum reward for the individual, the entrepreneur, the investor and he who labors in farm or factory.

The American economic system is functioning very effectively today because it enjoys freedom from governmental harassment, freedom from government competition and freedom from governmental policies that the State Socialists—the twin brothers of the Communists—would foist on free America if they could get control once more of the governing power in America.

TWO GERMANYS—
THE WAY TO BREED WAR

SEPTEMBER 30, 1955

THE HISTORY OF THE WORLD is replete with instances in which a dismembered nation has nurtured its resentments and, under the perennial impulse of nationalism, has finally sought its revenge in war.

Alsace-Lorraine is the classic example. The people of France never forgot how their German conquerors took away their territory and exiled their countrymen. It was for generations one of the basic causes of ill-feeling between Germany and France. It led to the outbreak of World War I.

The continuance of two Germanys for decades to come is the apparent objective today of the Communists who rule Soviet Russia. Chancellor Adenauer in his recent mission to Moscow found that he was dealing with a ruthless enemy who scorns unification on any terms except the establishment of a Communist-dominated state. He had to agree to formal diplomatic relations in order to win freedom for the 10,000 hostages held by the Communists though, under the rules of civilized nations, prisoners must be returned after hostilities cease and peace has been restored.

For ten years the guns on the Western front have been silent. Other countries allied with Soviet Russia long ago returned the prisoners they had taken in the war. But the Communists, using the technique of blackmail—being practiced also today by Red China with respect to American citizens held captive—demanded a ransom. So Moscow got what it all along has wanted —two Germanys, each with a separate government.

The question now is whether Moscow's war lords will not themselves someday pay for their miscalculation a tragic price—a world war in which the Soviet cities will be destroyed and incalculable damage will be inflicted on the people of Germany and her allies.

For, despite all its professions of peaceful intent, the behavior of the Communist regime in Moscow in the matter of the two Germanys is clearly a sign that the Kremlin is willing to risk another world war to achieve its objectives.

To keep two Germanys in the status of separate governmental entities is not the way to heal the wounds of World War II or to bring a peaceful spirit in Europe. It is the way to breed bitterness and revenge. It means the beginning of a long struggle by the German people against Communist domination.

Actually the Soviet Government is violating the so-called "spirit of Geneva" by insisting that the East German Government is a real government and that it must be placed on an equal footing with the West German Government. Free elections have been held in West Germany, where political freedom prevails, but in East Germany there is despotism and tyranny—a government which is the enslaved puppet of Moscow.

Nationalism is a natural emotion. It is derived from patriotism and love of freedom and independence. The people of Germany will never give up their crusade for freedom and independence. They will in due time determine to risk their lives to achieve it. For Communist colonialism cannot be tolerated.

Secretary of State John Foster Dulles said last week to the United Nations General Assembly:

"The German people have now been forcibly divided for over ten years. The perpetuation of this division is a crime against nature.

"Three-quarters of the Germans are in the Federal Republic, and they are fortunate in having a great leader, Chancellor Adenauer. He stands for a united Germany that will be peaceful and that will find its mission in friendly cooperation with its neighbors. He is determined that Germany's legitimate needs for security and sovereign equality shall be met without a revival of German militarism.

"It would, however, be a tragic mistake to assume that because most of the Germans now have chosen that enlightened viewpoint, the injustice of dividing Germany can therefore be perpetuated without grave risk."

The Soviet schemers, of course, will seek by "peaceful means," as they did in Poland, to bamboozle the allies into accepting a formula for a "coalition" government. It's the same old stratagem that was successfully interjected in China to help break down the Nationalist Government there. It would mean only one, thing—another Communist-controlled state in Europe as the fruit of a flagrant aggression.

The continuance of the two Germanys will inevitably lead to incidents and outbreaks of violence that can provoke a war in which the rest of the world would certainly be involved.

America and her allies must be alert to build enough armament to deter the enemy from annexing Germany to the satellite system. For it is beginning to be painfully clear that military and moral strength—together with an announced willingness to exert it for human freedom if aggression of any kind occurs—is the only means of keeping all of us from being plunged into another world war.

ISSUES WIN CAMPAIGNS—
NOT PERSONALITIES

OCTOBER 14, 1955

THE FACTS OF POLITICAL HISTORY in America point significantly to the overriding influence of issues as contrasted with the public impression of the personalities on the rival tickets.

Millions of voters in our electorate do not really get to know either of the presidential nominees as a personality, but usually base their votes on the issues symbolized by the candidates. Surveys show that, while many voters may like or admire a man who is running for office, they do not necessarily vote for him.

In campaign after campaign for the last 60 years evidence is at hand that the more popular candidate, the abler of the two, often has lost the race because of the weakness of his party on paramount issues. Likewise, there are instances which demonstrate that even a candidate for the Presidency with no record of national popularity whatsoever can win if the issues favor his party.

These basic factors in the behavior of the American electorate may well be re-examined now in the light of current comments with respect to the coming presidential election in 1956. Three mistaken assumptions, for instance, have been widely publicized in recent months. They are:

First, that Eisenhower won the 1952 election solely because of his personal popularity.

Second, that the Republican Party was revealed in 1952 to be weaker than Eisenhower because the total vote for the Republican congressional ticket ran behind the total vote cast for the Republican nominee for the Presidency.

Third, that, because of the loss of control of the House of Representatives in the 1954 election by the Republicans and their failure to get better than a tie in the Senate, it is inevitable that the Democrats will win in 1956.

As a basis for prophecy, each one of the three assumptions is refuted by the facts of political experience revealed in the presidential and congressional campaigns since 1896.

Hence, an analysis of these campaigns with respect to the predominant issues and the popularity and unpopularity of the candidates now becomes pertinent.

There is one common denominator running through every one of these 15 presidential campaigns. It is that economic contentment can keep a party in office and economic discontent can force a change.

But there is one important qualification. If an emotional issue of protest sweeps the electorate, then economic contentment as an issue is not controlling, and the "out's" emerge victorious. Likewise, an emotional issue can be strong enough with the voters to overcome the political effects of economic discontent and thus keep an existing Administration in power.

No better example of a popular candidate who lost can be cited than the three defeats suffered by William Jennings Bryan. He was the strongest figure in the Democratic Party and a brilliant orator. He campaigned from one end of the country to the other and drew larger crowds than any man in the political history of America. There was, of course, no radio or television then, but his picture was placarded everywhere and his popular personality received more publicity in each campaign than did the other candidate. He was dynamic, while McKinley, who ran against Bryan in both 1896 and 1900, was colorless. The Republican nominee, moreover, conducted what became known then as a "front porch" campaign at his home in Canton, Ohio. He made only a few speeches and didn't travel around the country at all.

The electorate, however, still remembered in 1896 the panic and economic depression of 1893, when a Democratic President, Grover Cleveland, was in office. The Bryan campaign that year was based on an economic issue—the panacea of free coinage of silver, on a ratio of 16 dollars of silver to one of gold. The Republican slogan, on the other hand, was "sound money" and adherence to the existing gold standard.

There was for a time a theory that Bryan would win because farm prices were lagging, but they turned up before the campaign was over. McKinley won with 271 electoral votes to Bryan's 149.

In the campaign of 1900, the Republicans again stood on their economic contentment doctrine. The nation had prospered as a result of the Spanish-American war of 1898. The people were emotionally thrilled over the military victories in the Philippines and in Cuba. Bryan was the "isolationist" of that era. He cried out against American "imperialism" and wanted the United States to get out of the Philippines. But he couldn't make a dent with that emotional issue. The steady increase in employment and the excellent economic conditions made the voters feel that they had better not turn back to the Democrats. McKinley polled 292 electoral votes and Bryan 155. Thus, economic issues were decisive in both 1896 and 1900.

But it was the campaign of 1904 which illustrated the strength of economic contentment as against emotional issues that are not quite potent enough to upset the Administration in power.

Thus, Theodore Roosevelt was popular as an individual, but he incurred the opposition of his party leaders by what was considered radicalism in those days—an attack on the corporations and their trusts. He had the support of only one newspaper in New York City. He was bitterly condemned by the conservative Republicans because, they said, he didn't follow as he had promised the policies of McKinley.

Vice President Theodore Roosevelt, when he took office in 1901, was approximately the same age as Vice President Nixon is today. Roosevelt was accepted as a liberal with conservative ties. He turned down some campaign funds by the big companies but didn't hesitate to seek the support of E. H. Harriman, railroad king, inviting him to the White House in a letter saying, "you and I are practical men," and promising to consult him about legislation.

An examination of the speeches in the 1904 campaign shows the continued reliance of the Republicans on the protective tariff as the builder of prosperity in those days. Also, Judge Alton B. Parker, the Democratic nominee, tried to be a "silver Democrat" West of the Mississippi, and a "gold Democrat" in the East, where free coinage of silver was associated with the idea of an adulterated currency and inflation. Theodore Roosevelt won by 336 electoral votes to Parker's 140. The economic issues were decisive.

In 1908, the nation was riding a wave of unprecedented prosperity. Although William Howard Taft, the Republican nominee, was a colorless and relatively unknown candidate, having spent most of his career in the dignified precincts of the federal bench, the Republicans again successfully centered their campaign on economic issues and argued that the radical Bryan was unsound on economic policy. Bryan toured the country and was easily the more popular of the two candidates, but the economic-contentment issue ruled the day, and Taft won with 321 electoral votes to Bryan's 162.

Here was an example, too, of a recovery from economic recession, for the downturn of business after the panic of 1907 was widely felt. It was on the upswing that the Republicans were able to win their victory and stay in power.

In 1910, a political surprise occurred. The Democrats won the House of Representatives for the first time in 18 years, and it was widely believed that this meant the Democrats in 1912 would poll more votes for the

Presidency than the Republicans. For the economic-discontent issue was strong.

The high cost of living was blamed on the high tariff, and there were insurgent Republicans in Congress from the Midwestern States who accepted the Democratic Party's thesis. This resulted in a deep cleavage between two sections of the Republican Party.

Although Theodore Roosevelt had declared himself in 1904 against a third term, he felt that he was eligible to run in 1912 because he had been out of office for four years. A three-cornered race between Taft, Roosevelt and Woodrow Wilson ensued. The combined popular vote of the two Republican candidates, however, was larger than that polled by Wilson. Yet in the Electoral College, Wilson got 435 votes to 96 for his combined opposition.

Adverse conditions on the economic front, accentuated by the interruption of export trade after the outbreak of the European war, began to hurt the Democrats in the congressional election of 1914, particularly in the Eastern States.

In the presidential campaign of 1916, economic issues plus an emotional issue won a close contest for the Democrats. The Republican Party harmonized under the candidacy of Charles Evans Hughes, who had been a progressive Governor in New York State and who had resigned from the Supreme Court of the United States to enter the campaign. He had been drafted by the national convention without consulting his wishes.

But, while many Eastern States which were carried by Hughes showed the effects of negative voting based on economic discontent and unemployment, the Western States lined up affirmatively for the re-election of President Wilson. The slogan of the Democrats in that campaign was "peace and prosperity."

The prosperity was limited largely to the West, where wheat was selling at a phenomenally high price due to war demand. But with the aid of rural Ohio and New Hampshire—the only Northern States east of the Mississippi carried by Wilson—and, of course, with the Solid South and the West, the Democratic nominee won. It was nevertheless one of the narrowest margins in the Electoral College in our history. Wilson got 277 votes—only 11 more than the 266 necessary to win.

The emotional issue in that campaign was "peace." The American people—particularly large segments of the population which were of German or Irish ancestry—didn't want America to enter World War I. The slogan, "he kept us out of war," was powerful on the emotional side and Wilson benefited. Six months after the election, however, we were forced into the war anyhow.

The 1920 campaign saw the same elements in reverse. The very groups which had wanted to keep out of war now showed a deep resentment because of America's participation. Large groups of voters deserted the Democratic Party. But there were reasons of an economic nature, too. Wartime controls had been abruptly lifted, and prices had skyrocketed. Sugar went from the controlled price of 5 cents to 20 cents a pound. Irritations over government controls and over the Administration's handling of the railways and the telegraphs and telephones were widespread. It was a negative vote that the people cast in 1920.

James M. Cox, the Democratic nominee that year, had three times won the Governorship of Ohio, a Republican State, and was a popular figure. He made a remarkable campaign, speaking from coast to coast. His speeches were masterpieces. He defended the Wilson policies and supported American entry into the League of Nations, which at that time had become a strong emotional issue. The League was being assailed as likely to provoke more wars rather than maintain peace.

The Republicans had captured both houses of Congress in 1918 on the same anti-European sentiment, but its potency as an issue did not become apparent until the votes were counted in the 1920 presidential election.

Senator Warren Harding, the Republican candidate in 1920, was relatively unknown outside Ohio. He had served colorlessly in the Senate and was the handpicked nominee of the big conservative interests in the Republican Party. During the campaign he didn't leave the front porch of his home in Marion, Ohio, imitating the McKinley strategy.

So the popular candidate in 1920 lost and the unknown candidate won because the people were voting in a negative mood—against the Wilson Administration on both emotional and economic issues. Harding got 404 and Cox 127 electoral votes, the second biggest landslide in political history up to that time.

The campaign of 1924 was no exception to the rule of economic influence. The Teapot Dome scandals had hurt the Republicans politically, but Calvin Coolidge wasn't associated with them in the public mind because he had vigorously prosecuted the offenders.

So far as intellect and speech-making were concerned, John W. Davis, who had served brilliantly in Congress, made a great campaign and was easily the better qualified man for the Presidency. He toured the country, while Calvin Coolidge made few speeches and didn't venture out on long campaign trips.

The farm depression was being widely felt and was responsible for a big protest vote in the West.

The elder Robert M. La Follette, Senator from Wisconsin, running on a third-party ticket and seeking Democratic votes as well as progressive Republican votes, managed to take away more Democrats than Republicans in the West and drove many independent Democrats in the East into the Republican column.

There were 13 States, mostly in the West, where the combined La Follette and Davis votes exceeded that of Coolidge, but the latter won their 86 electoral votes.

The Coolidge victory, nevertheless, was due basically to economic issues, as many Democratic voters, fearing that conditions would become more disturbed by La Follette, voted for Coolidge, who polled 382 electoral votes as against 149 for his combined opposition.

By 1928 the nation's prosperity was again at a high point. Herbert Hoover had served as Secretary of Commerce but he wasn't a political campaigner in the traditional sense and had never run for office before. Al Smith, the Democratic nominee, had been elected Governor of New York three times. He made a nationwide tour of the country, drawing big crowds.

It is often said that an emotional issue—religious prejudice—decided that election. Undoubtedly some of the Southern States, where prejudice was stirred up against a Catholic as the party nominee, voted Republican for that reason. But in the North, the fact that New York State—which Smith had carried three times for Governor—failed him, too, was a clear indication that he would have been defeated anyhow for the Presidency.

For economic conditions in 1928 were good and, while Hoover wasn't as popular a candidate as Smith, the voters saw no persuasive reason to turn the Republicans out of power. Hoover was accepted as a man who would carry out the basic economic program of the preceding Administration. He got 444 electoral votes to Smith's 87.

Four years later—in 1932—the same man ran for re-election on the Republican ticket. He had had four years to acquaint the people with his progressive approach as contrasted with the conservatism of his predecessors. A worldwide depression, starting in 1929, had, however, brought America the biggest total of unemployed the nation had ever known.

While Governor Franklin D. Roosevelt was well known in New York State, he was in 1932 relatively unknown outside that State. His campaign speeches were of a conservative nature. He repudiated his own support of the League of Nations, for which, as a vice-presidential candidate, he had stumped the country in 1920. He would have been elected in 1932 even if he had stayed at Albany and made those same speeches. "Popularity" as such had little to do with the result. It was a negative vote against Hoover. Economic issues were dominant. Roosevelt won 472 electoral votes to Hoover's 59.

The election campaign of 1936 came at a time when the nation was in the midst of economic recovery, and the Republicans—of whom there had long been a majority in the country—continued to vote for the

Democratic nominee and against the return of the Republicans to power. Economic issues were again controlling, as Roosevelt won 523-to-8 against Alfred M. Landon.

In 1940, even though there was economic discontent, the people voted to continue the Democratic Administration in power because they felt the emotions of war and feared to make any change in the middle of such a crisis. Wendell Willkie was a colorful figure but he polled only 82 electoral votes in 1940, and Roosevelt won with 449. The emotional issue carried the election.

In 1944, the able Governor of New York, Thomas E. Dewey, accumulated only 99 electoral votes, while Roosevelt piled up 432, as the nation again voted not to change its Commander in Chief in the middle of a war.

The election of 1948 conformed to previous economic patterns. The country was fairly prosperous. The Republicans had come into power in Congress in 1946 because of economic discontent due to meat controls and other wartime irritations. But their program in those two years created fear rather than reassurance for the farmers of the West, who supported Truman. Economic issues were primarily responsible for the 1948 Democratic victory in the Electoral College—303 for Truman as against 189 for Dewey and 39 for Thurmond, who ran on the States' Rights ticket.

In 1952, the cry of corruption and the taint of Communist influence, together with the bungling in the Korean war, were the basic issues of an emotional nature which brought out the negative vote against the Truman Administration. They far transcended economic contentment as an advantage to the party in power. A less popular candidate than Eisenhower might, indeed, have won on the Republican ticket.

Integrity of administration is always an emotional issue in federal, State or local elections that can cut across any other issue and subordinate it if the facts are persuasive.

Turning to congressional elections, it is interesting to note that Truman in 1948 ran behind his congressional ticket. Theoretically, then, he was supposed to be weaker than his party, but the Democrats also lost ground in Congress in the 1950 elections.

Congressional elections rarely have a national flavor —they are largely local. Their outcome as a whole depends on issues vital to the sections or States in question. Economic factors, such as spotty unemployment, do play an influential part. This was emphasized particularly in the 1954 congressional elections when loss of a few seats due to the economic recession changed the party control.

For thirty years, with the exception of the 1948 election, every President who has won and every candidate who has lost has run ahead of his congressional ticket. Nobody used to suggest that this meant that the party had grown weaker than its leadership.

The disparity between the vote for President and the vote for Congress was smaller in the old days when all voting was on a single ballot. But since the introduction of separate ballots in most States, large numbers of voters do not take the trouble to vote for anyone but the President and Vice President.

From 1896 through 1948, the 14 winning candidates averaged 7.5 percentage points in total vote above their respective congressional tickets. Theodore Roosevelt polled about 14.9 percentage points above the Republican ticket in 1904, but Charles Evans Hughes got the same high margin over the Republican congressional slate in 1916 and still lost.

Franklin D. Roosevelt hit a mark of around 12 percentage points above his party in all four of his elections. Yet few persons suggested then that the Democratic Party would go out of business if someone else was chosen as its next candidate.

So it may be concluded that the results in congressional elections do not necessarily forecast the outcome of the next presidential election and that a political party cannot be ruled out today as unable to win an election just because it doesn't have a popular personality to lead it.

Parties are strong or weak at present depending primarily on whether the country is in a state of economic contentment or discontent, and on how the peace-or-war issues are met by the Administration in power.

Issues, rather than the popularity of a nominee, are the decisive influences in American politics.

THE HEART THAT FALTERED

OCTOBER 21, 1955

THROUGHOUT THE WORLD a few weeks ago the people came to know that the heart of a great man had faltered.

It was the heart of a man who in his time had won universal confidence. For he had symbolized a great hope. It was that he could bring his great personal influence to bear in ushering in an era of peace, where only suspicion and misunderstanding had prevailed before.

The whole world waited anxiously for news that his services might not be denied to the people of many countries who were depending on him, if not to work miracles, at least to push war farther and farther away.

The world struggle now, however, has been resumed with renewed vigor. There is missing the great voice of restraint which called so eloquently and so naturally for a new spirit among men. For the influence at the helm of one man—based on the power he was expected to wield in public office perhaps for five years—has suddenly diminished. As the sad tidings were carried to the far corners of the earth, it became known everywhere that the leader is to retire in just a few months. His words from a hospital bed do not carry the same weight as if he were for a prolonged period to remain the active spokesman of the free nations of mankind.

The normal channels of expression, to be sure, have not been interrupted. But there is something lacking. It is the inspiration of a man whose simplicity of appeal—almost, it might be said, his naivete in the realm of diplomacy—stirred the hopes of peoples on both sides of the Iron Curtain.

What splendid faith in the efficacy of moral force this American soldier has! It is a faith that good will can conquer all. It is a faith that constant reiteration of a sincere purpose must inevitably leave its imprint on those to whom the appeals for peace are addressed.

Human love is the great remedy which heals misunderstandings between individuals. Good will and expressions of a deep desire to find a way to live at peace with other countries are also the means of diffusing the spirit of brotherhood among nations. It is this spirit that must motivate peoples and their governments if they are to avoid the organized murders which are the essence of war.

From time immemorial, men have prayed for peace and spoken to each other in terms of peaceful intent. But the many wars in history have proved how often distrust is the forerunner of inevitable conflict.

In a dramatic effort to remove distrust, the American President had proclaimed an old faith with an earnestness that even the stern personalities of the other side were inclined to concede was genuine, as they became convinced it was direct from a great heart.

For here was a man whose life had been spent in preparation for war or in the highest command post of war. He had traveled thousands of miles to say face to face to men regarded as our enemies that the American people have no hate in their hearts for any nation and plan no war of attack on anybody. Others had expressed it but somehow, when he said it in person, it carried conviction.

The echoes of that appeal now have died down. The maneuvers of the "cold war" are intensified by the opportunists. They refuse to give up a chance to make gains in the Middle East and North Africa, even at the expense of a broken harmony that was once called "the Geneva spirit."

It was idle, of course, to expect that a single conference or a single appeal would transform men of evil into men of virtue. But behind the rulers of any totalitarian regime are the peoples to whom the words of the American President did penetrate. This particularly personal form of communication is temporarily halted—no longer is there heard the tones and words of a powerful voice. As a single heart lost its strength, so has America's appeal seemed to lose its strength.

And what of the voices heard contemporaneously inside our own land? The voices have been mostly those of ambition and of the party cliques, busily seeking advantage in the headlines.

How unfortunate that the spirit of a great heart was not able also to imbue the partisans in his own country with the good will that could subordinate the political bickering which, they must know full well, weakens our voice in the councils of the world.

The faltering of a single heart does not mean that the heart of a great nation must also falter. For the cause that America upholds is greater than any man. May even the partisans be forgiven their sins—for they know not what they do.

It is a time for the heart of America to be revealed. It is a time to speak with one accord to the other peoples of the world and to tell them that the American people—no matter who is chosen as a successor in the Presidency—expect to continue to seek peace in the self-same spirit of human love so simply expressed by Dwight Eisenhower.

RESPONSIBLE GOVERNMENT — WHEN?

NOVEMBER 4, 1955

RESPONSIBLE GOVERNMENT prevails when an Administration chosen by the people is continuously and uninterruptedly responsible to the people.

Irresponsible government prevails when a political party or leadership chosen by the people cannot instantly be held responsible to the people.

Today in the United States one political party controls the legislative branch while another political party controls the executive establishment. If the Vice President should succeed to the Presidency, and then anything should suddenly happen to remove him from office, then, under the present law of succession, the Speaker of the House, who comes from a political party that was not chosen by the people in the 1952 election to control the executive branch of the Government, would take the oath of office as President of the United States.

This is not responsible government.

When a Vice President comes into the White House, under our present system, there is no chance for the people immediately to express themselves—to approve or disapprove the new President's policies.

This is not responsible government.

Today if the President should become so ill as to make it doubtful whether or not he can discharge "the duties and powers" of his office, the exact meaning of "inability," as the word is used in the Constitution, is not defined either by act of Congress or by decisions of the Judiciary. There is no way at present to determine just when the duties and powers of the Presidency "devolve" upon the Vice President.

This is not responsible government.

Today the President, who is charged by the Constitution with the duty of conducting the foreign relations of the United States, may, due to illness, be unable to discharge the duties of his office, and hence his Secretary of State may or may not be regarded by other governments as the real spokesman of the United States. This could create worldwide uncertainty in a crisis.

This is not responsible government.

Irrespective of any question of physical inability, if a President adopts a course that the people do not favor, they should be able to replace him at once with a President who truly speaks for them. There would be no need of Bricker amendments or other constitutional safeguards with respect to the making of treaties or executive agreements if the President and his Cabinet were responsible for their tenure to both Houses of Congress and if the Congress, in turn, were directly responsible to the people at all times.

The Canadian people have such a system. It has served them well. It is known as the parliamentary system. It is in vogue in Great Britain, Australia, South Africa and New Zealand. France has a weaker form which has rightly been criticized as unstable.

As for stability under the parliamentary system, the classic example is that of the late Mackenzie King. He served as Prime Minister of Canada for a total of 22 years and 5 months during a span of about 27 years. He was on one occasion out of power for a few months and was in the minority for another five-year interval. The Canadian people, however, could have removed Mr. King from office at any time because they possessed an instant check.

This is responsible government.

In the United States, a system prevails in which even the presidential candidate who receives the largest popular vote does not necessarily win the Presidency. By indirect voting through the Electoral College, a few big cities can swing the electoral majority.

The powers of the President of the United States are greater today than any one man should possess in a fixed term. For four years he cannot be checked if he wishes to be arbitrary in matters of foreign policy or anything else. Likewise, if a Congress desires to thwart a President who is of the opposite party, it can injure the national interest by so doing. There now is no remedy until a part of the Congress is up for election once every two years.

It is out of the ranks of Congress that a President should be chosen. The majority party—which would elect its own leader—should be held responsible directly to the people, as in Canada. Any serious split in the majority party that occurs can be remedied at once by appealing to the people in an election to decide which faction or party is right.

Party responsibility means responsible leadership—and this means responsible government.

America needs a streamlined government to meet the crises of an atomic age.

A joint executive and legislative responsibility to the people would end the system of divided government that prevails in this country today. If the people were granted the right of an instant check on the Executive and on the Congress simultaneously, it would truly give the people the highest expression of freedom in our Republic. We would achieve at last a government that rested always on the consent of the governed.

A NEEDED WARNING

NOVEMBER 11, 1955

THE SOVIET GOVERNMENT is pursuing a course that can lead to the outbreak of a third world war.

The Kremlin is playing with fire in the Middle East and in North Africa.

The Moscow Government is refusing to withdraw its armies from East Germany and is openly blocking the reunification of Germany, even though World War II ended more than ten years ago.

This tends to breed a spirit of national revenge on the part of all Germans.

The Soviet game is now fully revealed. It is to hold on to the vast territory occupied by the Red armies in Eastern Europe and, at the same time, to provoke warfare in the Middle East and in North Africa.

The United States, Great Britain, and France are engaged at the moment defensively on the diplomatic front, but it must be conceded that the West's position is not as clear as it was before the "summit" conference at Geneva. At that conference the Western powers announced a desire to negotiate a settlement. The Russians, however, have mistaken this for a willingness on the part of the West to surrender on vital issues.

Before the Geneva Conference, the United States, at least, was emphasizing military power and was talking in terms of collective security pacts designed to defend the Western world against any and all attacks from the Communist regimes.

But, immediately after the Geneva Conference adjourned, many people in the Western countries jumped to the conclusion that peace was at hand. A de-emphasis on military strength began in Britain and America.

The Soviets have taken advantage of this deterioration in the Western position to press their infiltration in the Middle East and in North Africa. Outwardly Communist diplomacy appears stronger and more obdurate than it was before Geneva. The Russians seem to have concluded that the West will not fight for its principles no matter what happens.

This was the fatal miscalculation that Hitler made. It's the same mistake every aggressor makes. If, of course, an aggressor thinks he can get what he wants without a fight, he will attempt to extend his authority everywhere that he can.

But there comes a time to call a halt—to draw a line.

For the Russian aggressor has now boldly stepped out of his sovereign boundaries and is selling arms to Egypt, which country guards the entrance and exit of the Suez Canal, an important gateway for commerce and vessels of war.

The moment the Soviet Government ordered its puppet government in Czechoslovakia to sell arms to Egypt, the Moscow rulers committed an unfriendly act against the West. This alarmed the government of Israel and stimulated last week a resumption of fighting with Egypt. Too often little wars lead to big wars.

The situation will not be cured by politely-worded generalities begging Russia to keep peace in the world. Something much more explicit has to be said. The Soviet Government has to be warned that aggression in the Middle East will not be tolerated, and will be resisted by force.

The Middle East situation is not far different from that which the United States faced recently in the Far East. A line was drawn there against the Communist advance. A resolution was adopted by Congress authorizing the President to resist attacks on Formosa and related areas. There has been some skirmishing since but no major war.

Similar firmness must be shown in the Middle East and also with respect to the problems presented by the refusal of Russia to end her occupation of Germany.

The basic principle involved is that East Germany must be rid of coercion by Soviet troops so that the people there may hold elections which are truly free. The troops of the Western powers can be withdrawn simultaneously with those of the Soviets. Then the German people can choose their government in their own way. It is absurd for Russia to be talking about her need for security guarantees against Germany—a weak and virtually unarmed country possessing no nuclear weapons or factories to make them.

Russia is herself promoting the insecurity and instability of Eastern Europe.

It is the continued maintenance of armed forces in East Germany by the Soviet which is a threat to world peace.

It is the continued oppression and enslavement of the peoples of the satellite states which is sowing the seeds of a big war.

War is horrible to contemplate but the horrors of war have never prevented men from fighting where their very liberties are at stake—against slavery and for human freedom.

Realism commands the West to say frankly to the Russians that they are playing with fire, that they are engaging in acts of aggression which if not abandoned will inevitably lead to a world war.

A YEAR IS A LONG TIME

NOVEMBER 18, 1955

IT'S JUST ABOUT A YEAR before the 1956 election, and many things can happen to affect the selection of a nominee by the Republican Party before the next Convention is held nine months hence.

For one thing, it is possible to wake up some morning in the next nine months and find that a revolution has broken out in the Soviet Union and that a free government has come into power.

It is possible, also, that the satellite states, including East Germany, may be the scene of such disturbances as to cause the Kremlin to change its policies and agree to free elections and the establishment of independent states in Eastern Europe.

Neither of these two contingencies seems likely to occur in the next nine months, but if they did, war would be less likely and tension would be considerably reduced, in which case President Eisenhower might feel that he should be released from any obligation to serve further in the White House.

But, the signs point the other way—toward more, rather than less, tension.

This means that it is more than ever necessary for Dwight Eisenhower to remain as President of the United States. This writer opposed on domestic issues the various elections of Franklin D. Roosevelt, but never because of the third or fourth term issue, taking the position at the time that so long as a President's candidacy is submitted to the people at frequent intervals—and a four-year interval is too long—there should be no objection to the retention of an able public servant in time of crisis. Actually it was the world crisis in 1940 and 1944 which elected Mr. Roosevelt for a third and a fourth term respectively, in disregard of precedent.

Dwight Eisenhower stands today in a unique position of world leadership. He has the respect and confidence not only of his own countrymen but of peoples everywhere. He made a great advance at the Geneva Conference last summer. He spoke for the free world. It was a sincere gesture of conciliation and a demonstration of how the spirit of human brotherhood can be expressed in concrete terms.

It is no disparagement of Mr. Eisenhower's use of moral force at Geneva in July to find an intransigeant Russia still refusing in November to give up her dreams of world conquest, and still scheming to obtain by conference and "compromises" what she cannot win by military force or threats of war.

More than ever skillful leadership is necessary to deal patiently with these set-backs. America, and indeed the Western world, needs at the helm a man who has the background of experience that Mr. Eisenhower has acquired not only in his military career but through the last three years of intimate contact with the diplomatic complexities of the "cold war."

Mr. Eisenhower's whole being is dedicated to world peace. He is the kind of man who has been trained to risk his life for his country in military service. He is the kind of man who would gladly risk his life in the cause of world peace.

Mr. Eisenhower's decision on whether or not to run will be based neither on party considerations nor on personal convenience. It will be based on high principle. He will ask himself again and again if it is really true that he can help the world to achieve peace in our times. He will modestly assume that no man is indispensable. In theory this is right. But there is no convincing argument against accepting a call to serve one's own government if it be the wish of an overwhelming number of the people.

What greater duty is there than to respond to the call of one's countrymen in a crisis which, if mishandled by someone else, could lead us into the most frightful war of all history!

Personal wishes and personal convenience have at times motivated public men to decline public office, but it is also true that the exigencies of a situation which go beyond the personal have often compelled men to become candidates when issues of transcendent importance were at stake.

President Eisenhower may therefore be confronted in August 1956 with a unanimous draft by the Convention, even though in January 1956 he may have announced his disinclination to become a candidate.

The American people today do not want Mr. Eisenhower at present to close the door against further service in the White House. They want him to wait as long as possible—until the eve of the convention if necessary—before making up his mind whether or not to heed the call that is coming to him not only from this country but from all over the world. The people everywhere want him to remain their leader, their champion and their exponent of a spirit of human friendship—their crusader for world peace.

For we are witnessing an anomaly. The man who led to victory the biggest military force in history has turned out to be the very man to lead the biggest moral force of all times to an even greater victory—the achievement of a righteous peace.

WAS GENEVA REALLY A FAILURE?

NOVEMBER 25, 1955

SOMETIMES A "FAILURE" is merely a milestone on the road to success.

The two Geneva conferences raised high hopes which have not yet been realized. But any impartial survey of what the state of the world is today, as compared to what it was before the all-important sessions in Switzerland, must include what has been gained psychologically on the long, long journey toward peace.

The Geneva conferences are being headlined now as a "failure," yet it is significant that neither side reveals a desire to achieve agreement by any except peaceful means.

There have been periods in world history when the breakdown of a crucial negotiation turned the minds of people toward war. No such trend is visible today.

Instead, a conviction remains that somehow the objectives of the Western allies will be attained without war. For the Soviet Union must be aware that, in any war, she would lose—primarily because the oppressed peoples would seize the opportunity to break away from their rulers, as they did in the middle of World War I.

It must also be recognized that the factor of military force—the potential of the West—has not been reduced in importance merely because there have been discussions of peace. Similarly, the internal position of the Soviet Union on the military side is still that of a loosely federated alliance of states which wait only for the outbreak of a general war to pull away from the Kremlin.

What, then, to do after Geneva?

First of all, we may rejoice over the realistic truth that the Communists have failed to dissolve the Western alliance and have failed to bluff the governments of Great Britain, the United States and France into submission.

Geneva, therefore, was a "failure" only for the Soviets. They did not succeed in their objective of obtaining the surrender of the West, whose statesmen rejected "peace at any price."

Geneva was a "failure" for the Kremlin because Molotov involuntarily confessed the Communist strategy—to refuse to unite the two Germanys and to seek to maintain indefinitely things as they are in Eastern Europe.

This news is of transcendent importance to Eastern Europe. It will light up the smoldering fires of unrest among the oppressed peoples there. They know now that nothing is to be gained by appeals to Moscow. Their only chance lies in accepting the thesis of the West—that liberation of the captive nations can and will come when the moral force of the world is mobilized to its fullest strength.

The three foreign ministers on our side—Messrs. Dulles, Macmillan and Pinay—acted with dramatic unity. They literally put Molotov on the spot again and again. This has been and will be of incalculable value on the propaganda front. Therein is the true meaning of Geneva—the real victory for our cause.

Secretary Dulles gave the Soviet Foreign Minister repeatedly a chance to offer something substantial toward a peace agreement. Mr. Dulles even deliberately created an atmosphere of "optimism" for a few days to offset the feeling prevailing in the press that nothing could be accomplished. It was a maneuver to emphasize the sincerity of the West and to continue the appearance at least of a conciliatory spirit.

There is every need now to state and re-state the Western aims. It is more than ever necessary to underline them.

For the peoples of Eastern Germany, Poland, Czechoslovakia, Latvia, Estonia, Lithuania, Bulgaria, Rumania, Hungary and Albania have just been told by the Geneva proceedings in no uncertain terms that their hope for independence and the restoration of individual freedom lies not with the East, but with the West. This same craving for liberty must inevitably permeate also the enslaved peoples of Soviet Russia.

The workings of moral force are not always perceptible to the naked eye. But moral force is on the march now. Geneva gave momentum to the indestructible spirit of freedom.

Before Geneva, the Western governments were accused of being unwilling even to talk—of refusing to sit down face to face with the Russian leaders in order earnestly to discuss a possible agreement. The air now has been cleared. We have conferred. We have smiled. We have cajoled. But we have met an implacable antagonist.

The issues are clear to everybody as a result of the Geneva talks, and the West has emerged with honor.

The struggle for emancipation from slavery has only begun. The truth—the spread of it everywhere—can and will make men free.

Hundreds of millions of men and women on both sides of the Iron Curtain now know that they must not compromise with evil. They need only to unite in expressing their collective will in order to win a bloodless victory for human freedom.

WHO SPEAKS FOR THE DEMOCRATS?

DECEMBER 2, 1955

MR. STEVENSON, DEMOCRAT, calls for "moderation" and says it is "the spirit of the times."

Mr. Harriman, Democrat, says that there is no such word as "moderation" in the Democratic Party's vocabulary.

Mr. Truman, Democrat, says that Mr. Stevenson's speech at the meeting of the Democratic National Committee in Chicago recently was "the best New Deal speech I ever heard him make." It was in this same address that Mr. Stevenson used the word "moderation."

Mr. Harriman, Democrat, says the Eisenhower foreign policy is "classic in the history of bungling."

Senator Walter George of Georgia, Democrat, Chairman of the Senate Foreign Relations Committee, says that the American delegation did a good job at the Geneva conference.

Senator Lyndon Johnson of Texas, Democratic leader, praises Senator George as largely responsible for Mr. Eisenhower's decision to go to Geneva to talk with the Russian rulers.

Senator Estes Kefauver of Tennessee, Democrat, says that the Administration's objectives in foreign policy are all right, but that Democrats differ from the Republicans in the "methods" to be used in achieving those objectives.

Dean Acheson, Democrat, who used to be criticized by the Republicans when he was Secretary of State and is, therefore, entitled to strike back in the political arena, says that the Eisenhower Administration has had a bad foreign policy. He ridicules the use by Mr. Dulles of the phrase, "massive retaliation," but leaves everybody wondering if the Acheson alternative, in case of an atomic attack by Soviet planes on the people of the United States, would be "massive acquiescence."

Who speaks for the Democrats?

Obviously a frank discussion of foreign policy is always desirable and necessary. Our friends in Europe are, of course, used to the devious tactics of politicians. We now are told nevertheless that "American prestige abroad"—which seems to die every time a returning traveler speaks his partisan mind—has been "damaged" by the Stevenson-Harriman criticisms.

The truth is our foreign policy ought to be widely discussed both here and abroad. For the issue of war or peace is paramount.

So it is important to know what the Democrats propose. Did they, for instance, want Mr. Eisenhower to take Messrs. Bulganin and Khrushchev and Molotov by the nape of the neck at Geneva and give them an ultimatum to behave "or else"?

Do the Democrats now propose that American military forces be used to compel agreement by the Kremlin? If not, then why do they accuse the Eisenhower Administration of being responsible for the "failure" at Geneva? Wouldn't it be patriotic, to say the least, if the Democratic spokesmen assumed that the United States Government and its President and Secretary of State are not responsible for the intransigeance of a Molotov or the intrigue of the Kremlin Communists?

If the Democratic Party spokesmen of today begin to needle the Eisenhower Administration with the argument that it should be deliberately threatening use of military power to coerce Soviet Russia into compliance, then the impression will grow that the Democrats—in the event they win the next election—would drag the American people into a nuclear war, notwithstanding their present professions of a peaceful purpose, which also preceded the outbreaks of other wars.

The Democrats not only should be emphasizing peaceful methods but should be telling the country what they would have done differently—what proposals they would have made at the Geneva conferences, and just what frowns instead of smiles they would have used to bring the Kremlin negotiators to their knees.

As for domestic issues, does Mr. Harriman believe that "extremism" instead of "moderation" is the right word for the Democratic Party's vocabulary? Would he destroy the free-enterprise system and give state socialism further impetus? What measures would he ask Congress to repeal? And how would Mr. Stevenson champion "moderation" when, behind a Democratic President, would be the radical organizations and the labor-union bosses who put up most of the campaign funds and do most of the campaigning? Wouldn't the laws demanded by the bosses foment labor strife, and wouldn't they unsettle confidence in business expansion and bring on panic?

Is this what the extremists want—to erect on the shambles of a shattered economy an Administration dedicated to more of the New Deal's state socialism?

It's time for the Democratic spokesmen—if they can ever repair their badly split party—to clarify their position and tell the American people what the Democratic Party stands for and what really may be expected if it is entrusted with power by the people in 1956.

WHY NOT GOVERNOR LAUSCHE?

DECEMBER 9, 1955

WHEN THE UNITED PRESS last week polled 25 Democratic Governors and 44 Democratic State Chairmen and asked how they would rank Governor Frank J. Lausche of Ohio as the Democratic nominee for President, only two individuals made Lausche their first choice. Most of the others regarded him as a remote possibility.

Yet, logically, considering the normal requirements of national politics, Governor Lausche should be the first choice for the Democratic presidential nomination in 1956. For he is the best vote-getter the Democrats have today. He has proven his prowess at the polls in five elections, winning the Governorship by overwhelming majorities in a usually Republican State.

Governor Lausche, with a 221,000 majority, in 1948 carried Truman on his coattails, and the latter got a 7,000 majority in Ohio, thereby winning the State's bloc of 25 electoral votes over Dewey in that close election.

In 1950, while the late Senator Taft carried Ohio by 431,000, Lausche won the Governorship by 152,000.

Obviously, many Republicans have voted for Lausche for Governor time after time—as, for instance, in 1952 when he carried Ohio against Charles P. Taft, a brother of the late Senator, by a majority of more than 425,000 on the same occasion that Eisenhower carried the State by 500,000. Incidentally, in that election the victorious Lausche ran about 415,000 votes ahead of Adlai Stevenson, the Democratic presidential nominee.

Born of immigrant parents in Cleveland, Ohio, just 60 years ago, Frank Lausche was one of ten children. Much of the responsibility of aiding his mother fell upon his shoulders at the age of 12, when his father, a steelworker from Yugoslavia, and his eldest brother died. Young Lausche was employed for a time as a lamplighter and at other odd jobs. He became a court interpreter. He served in the Army. He played professional baseball. He attended law school at night and at 25 passed the State bar exams second from the top among 160 candidates.

As a judge, mayor of Cleveland and Governor, Frank Lausche has fought organized gambling and always has believed in keeping the government close to the people. He is a courageous and progressive champion of the public interest. He is independent-minded and wears no man's collar.

Governor Lausche has stated publicly that he will not enter the presidential contest. Many observers have wondered if he is reluctant to see the "religious issue" raised again in a presidential campaign. For Lausche is a Catholic. His wife is a Methodist.

Article Six of the Constitution says: "No religious test shall ever be required as a qualification to any office or public trust under the United States."

Is there nevertheless a "religious issue" in American politics? Was it really the cause of the defeat in 1928 of Governor Alfred E. Smith of New York in his bid for the Presidency? Certain States in the South did go Republican in that election for the first time in history, and many politicians assumed it was because of anti-Catholic sentiment.

But today two leaders in Southern States—Senator Russell of Georgia and Governor Shivers of Texas—have both warmly endorsed Lausche for the presidential nomination on the Democratic ticket. Governor Kennon of Louisiana told the United Press last week that Lausche "would make a good Democratic candidate."

The "religious issue" was thoroughly discussed by Governor Smith in an open letter to the *Atlantic Monthly* in May 1927. The full text of his letter—which was prepared after consultation with leading authorities in the Catholic Church on the relationship of church and state—is printed on the four pages preceding this article. It is a historic document and should be studied by all those who wish to know the Catholic answer to an objection sometimes raised.

The American people as a whole really didn't vote against Smith in 1928 on account of the religious issue but voted in favor of Herbert Hoover because of the economic prosperity then prevailing under the Republican Administration of President Coolidge. Smith didn't even carry his own State in the presidential election, and the popular young Franklin D. Roosevelt squeezed in as Governor of New York by the narrow margin of only 25,000 votes, as contrasted with a majority of 247,000 for Smith two years before. That's a clear indication that other issues were controlling in the 1928 election. It was not a good year for the Democrats.

The name of Governor Lausche should be given earnest consideration for 1956. The Democratic Party must not allow itself to be affected by the alleged potency of an outworn "religious issue."

Governor Lausche would poll more Republican votes than any man mentioned thus far for the Democratic nomination, and, if Eisenhower doesn't run, the Ohio Governor would have a better chance than any other Democratic candidate to win the election.

STUMBLING INTO WAR

DECEMBER 16, 1955

NO PEOPLE ever really want war—and no ruling group commits acts that could lead to war unless sure the other side will not resist.

Big wars come primarily because of miscalculation. Hitler thought Britain wouldn't fight to uphold a guarantee given Poland. He boldly took step after step, convinced that the Western allies would not mobilize effectively and that the United States would at least remain neutral.

The stage is being set today for another miscalculation.

The rulers of the Soviet Union assume that the North Atlantic Treaty Organization is crumbling and that it will be inoperative once Germany is unified on Soviet terms. The Communists are behaving as if they think they now can commit acts of aggression with impunity. A private memorandum from our London correspondent last week says:

"A top British diplomat explains the current Russian toughness this way: The Russians found out for sure at the Geneva 'summit' conference that the United States would never use the bomb unless the West were actually—that is, physically—attacked by the Communists.

"Before President Eisenhower convinced them of this once and for all at Geneva, they were not absolutely sure but, since they now know the bomb will not be used except under these circumstances, they can afford to be more venturesome. Hence, the current antics in the Middle East, India and Burma.

"The same diplomat also says that the tendency to relax in the West and elsewhere was another reason for scrapping the 'Geneva spirit' at the second Geneva conference."

It seems incredible to find the Russian rulers believing the United States will not react to Soviet aggression except in case of an actual attack on its own territory or the territory of its allies. They should remember that in Korea the Western allies did repel aggression by armed force, although no territory of any U. N. member had been attacked.

Is it possible that the Kremlin is misconstruing the pacific policies of the Western powers as a peace-at-any-price attitude? It will be recalled that the Western statesmen have been for several months insisting in their public addresses that force will not be used to reunify Korea or to unify Germany or to settle the issue in the Formosa Straits.

Is it also possible that Western acquiescence in the continuance of two Chinas, two Koreas, two Indo-Chinas and two Germanies, with an explicit statement that force will not be used to alter the status of any of these divided countries, has convinced the Communists in Moscow and Peiping that no steps of a military nature will be taken anywhere else in defense against aggression by infiltration?

If the Communists are sure the Western powers have given up the idea of using force except to repel a direct attack, then penetration of the other defense areas of the West can be continued without fear of reprisal on the basis of gradually probing the sensitiveness of the allies on the likelihood of military retaliation.

The Communists today are adopting the Hitler line in assuming the West has been terrorized into pacifism. So the Communists are helping Egypt with arms that might start a war with Israel. They are fomenting trouble in Cyprus. They are exploiting the friction in North Africa. They are trying to alienate India from the West altogether.

Infiltration, it must be recognized, can achieve the same military objectives as actual physical aggression.

Small wonder that Secretary of State Dulles, in an address last week, found it necessary to issue to the Soviet Union the following words of warning:

"We have developed, with our allies, a collective system of great power which can be flexibly used on whatever scale may be requisite to make aggression costly. Our capacity to retaliate must be, and is, massive in order to deter all forms of aggression. But if we have to use that capacity, such use would be selective and adapted to the occasion."

This can mean only one thing—that, if someday we find it necessary, we shall go to the source of the aggression, and we will hold the Kremlin itself responsible for an attack against any part of the areas around which we have drawn a line for our defense.

The course of the Soviet rulers suggests that they are recklessly moving on to foment more and more trouble in the world. They may think this will be regarded as merely a resumption of the "cold war." But they could involuntarily foment a "hot war." This might ensue as circumstances arise that cause both sides to stumble into a war. The peoples of both sides, of course, would not want such a war but, once it is started, they must finish it.

This is the tragic course that has preceded many wars in history.

The Kremlin is playing with fire.

SOMEDAY—A REAL CHRISTMAS

DECEMBER 23, 1955

SOMEDAY THE SPIRIT OF CHRISTMAS will mean more in national and international affairs than it does today.

Someday there will be peace on earth.

Someday there will be good will toward men.

When?

Can it be while men hate each other, deceive one another, envy one another, rob one another?

Can it be while men malign one another and distort truth just to win an election to public office?

Can it be while men, without basis, question each other's integrity instead of debating issues and ideas?

Can it be while those who boast of freedom and democracy practice bigotry in their own communities and deny their fellow men the rights that "freedom" must guarantee to everyone?

Can it be while men conspire to enslave their fellow men—to imprison them in isolated camps far from their homes and families?

Can it be while tyrants deny liberty to the individual and wield the scepters of despotism over millions of helpless persons?

Can it be while we prate of morals and idealism and then sell our souls amid the hypocrisies of the hour?

Can it be while men surrender principle and morality and excuse their conduct as necessary to meet "political expediency" in international relations?

Can it be while men who profess to be righteous sit down to bargain with evil regimes and to negotiate a "live and let live" philosophy that openly condones sin and cravenly runs away from the sacrifices so necessary to win a triumph for a cause that is just?

The world each year is reminded of Christmas in an outburst of generosity toward kin folk and friends. But the gifts mostly are of material things. The voice of the spiritual is rarely heard above the din of the crowd. We recite the rituals, but do we fulfill the words which speak the true creed?

This is an age of decaying morals and of crass materialism. The prophets of old have been silenced. The new prophets urge the advantages of compromise with evil —they terrorize the people with a strange fear of death. They regard sacrifice as obsolete. Jesus, they argue in effect, would better have appeased the enemy.

The motivation to resist tyrannical masters at the risk of death has always been heroic, but nowadays we are asked to buy security at any price—even at the price of ideals and moral principle.

The Great Martyr of all times had no fear of mortal death. His was to the last a voice of patience and restraint, of charity and forgiveness. There was no flinching in the test.

The lesson in the life of Jesus, well known to all of us but little heeded, is one of martyrdom for a great principle. This principle offers a firm foundation for all human relationships. It is a principle of unselfish concern for and, indeed, love of one's fellow man.

Nations will never manifest it in their relations with other nations until individuals learn its true meaning and give it effect in their daily lives.

For the principle of love is not merely affection for each other. It connotes tolerance, helpfulness, willingness to share each other's resources, and, above all, rendering unto others the respect and the consideration that equals deserve from one another.

We speak of peace as an objective. But we seldom examine the ingredients of peace that comprise the moral force of mankind.

For until the spirit that permeated the life and teachings of Jesus nearly two thousand years ago becomes the code of mankind, there will be continuous friction and misunderstanding and perhaps even war.

Peoples do not willingly fight one another. Rulers bring on war by misleading oppressed peoples, hiding the truth from them and falsely accusing other nations of threatening attack. It is the oldest crime in all history. We are conscious of its vicious impact today. Only truth can overcome it, by reaching into the hearts of men everywhere.

Someday there will be a real Christmas.

Someday the peoples of the world will rise to do homage to the principles that will assure a peaceful existence.

But the real Christmas will never come through the electric display of slogans or the myriads of tinseled trees exhibited along our thoroughfares.

The real Christmas will come when men have discovered within themselves the power that overnight can render impotent any commands issued by the despots.

The real Christmas will come when, among nations like our own and our allies, there is an impulse to follow the courageous will of a liberated Conscience.

To achieve this emancipation from the shackles of modern ideologies, we must grow a Christmas tree that doesn't wither the day after Christmas—a tree that is nourished within our own hearts and spreads its branches from man to man as it unites us all in a world of eternal love.

THE YEAR THAT COULD BE NEW

DECEMBER 30, 1955

THE PERSPECTIVE of our times is not just a year. The months roll by quickly—and sometimes a lifetime is concentrated in a moment of history.

For these are really not unusual times. They are the normal cycles of human behavior, marked hitherto by the ambitions of kings and princes and now by the aggression of tyrants new in name only.

There are, to be sure, more people on earth than in ancient times—but there are more powerful rulers now to hold them captive and shape their destiny.

Enslaved populations are numbered in tens of millions today, but the tortures of enslavement are age-old.

Freedom still lives alongside slavery—just as complacently preoccupied as in the past with its own pleasures, its own materialism.

"Am I my brother's keeper?" cried Cain centuries ago, but the echo of that voice is still heard around the world. Peoples continue to worship the false gods of a misguided expediency. They still are deceived by Trojan horses.

These times are frequently called "uncertain"—as if they ever were otherwise. There's nothing new in the terrors of war. Man is constantly devising new ways of defending himself against an unknown enemy. What is new is a widespread acceptance of the fact that war, with its aftermath, can mean only a fruitless conquest. Tyrants, however, count confidently instead on a bloodless conquest without war—by bluff and threat and infiltration.

What is yet to be learned by these despots is the simple truth that power does not finally rest with the few. The strength of a united people is slow to mobilize against dictatorships, but eventually it does mobilize.

We who live in freedom have become accustomed to lives of detachment. We imagine that the passion of revolt which stirs in oppressed hearts overseas is separate from our destiny. In relative safety, we try to convince ourselves that we can co-exist with evil and that it will never touch us.

Whence comes this curious aloofness which dominates our thinking? We find the flaming "liberal" of bygone days silent now in the face of human anguish and advocating instead the surrender of ideals as he joins the reactionary in clamoring for the maintenance of the *status quo*.

The brutal discipline enforced by dictatorships on a captive populace awakens relatively little indignation among us. Too many tongues that prate so often about the alleged abuse of "civil liberties" here in America are mute today in the face of the biggest denial of individual liberty the world has ever known—the cruel colonialism that has taken away all freedom from the people of Russia, China, Poland, Czechoslovakia, Rumania, Bulgaria, Hungary, Latvia, Lithuania, Estonia, North Korea and Northern Vietnam.

The modern aggressor doesn't invade with armies alone, but penetrates with fifth columns from within. America today is asked by various "liberal" groups to ignore the menace. A Senator naively asks, "Where is the danger?" and convokes a committee to spend thousands of dollars of taxpayers' money to protect the "civil liberties" of security risks caught in the web of associations with questionable organizations or persons. A former university president is granted 14 million dollars of philanthropic funds and devotes his entire project to a defense of the same "civil liberties."

The Communist conspiracy, it is argued repeatedly, is just a political philosophy. Nevertheless, with practical techniques, it infiltrates institutions. It adulterates our patriotism. Warnings against this trend are called "hysteria." We are even advised to advocate amnesty for those now in jail who have sought to betray us.

Well-meaning citizens—educators, churchmen, editors—cry out for a policy of leniency toward these "dissenters," though the latter are linked with an enemy government armed with weapons that can mean our destruction.

For this is the fad of the "intellectuals," who regard as heroic constitutionalism the refusal of a citizen to inform his government about traitors and their associates in our midst.

The New Year could be new. It could usher in an era of truth and honesty and good faith—of devotion to country and fidelity to principle. It could mean a rededication to Judeo-Christian ethics.

The New Year could be new—if we would only begin to see clearly that there is no substitute for simple honesty in policies, national and international, and that there is no duty or loyalty higher than the faithful fulfillment of our obligations as citizens of this Republic.

The New Year could be new if it inculcated in all of us a pride in the true spirit of America—the spirit that never compromises with evil but upholds justice, the spirit that is not afraid of sacrifice when the call to service comes, and the spirit that does not lose faith in the power of a Divine Providence "in strange ways His wonders to perform."

1956

THE MAN OF THE ERA

JANUARY 6, 1956

THROUGH THE ANNALS OF TIME we have always revered the soldier. In the face of an unknown destiny, he has dedicated his life to the service of his fellow man. On his return from war, his crusade won, we have hailed him with exultant cheers—and then his lifework has usually ended.

In this era the tale is different.

We applaud the achievements of a great soldier, but we ask him to stay on in another kind of active duty—to serve us in the battle to maintain peace.

In 1942, the great soldier of our times landed his armies on the shores of North Africa.

In 1944, the same leader, commanding the huge forces of many allied nations, invaded the coast of France in a military feat of great skill and unprecedented magnitude. It meant victory in 1945 and the end of World War II.

We recall the beaming faces in a crowded metropolis, ticker tape flung like ribbons across the streets of New York City, as the military hero was welcomed home by a grateful country.

But leadership of armies was not to be his only form of service. In 1952, the same soldier was summoned to higher duty—to be Commander-in-Chief of all the military forces of the most powerful nation in the world, and at the same time to assume the responsibilities of the Chief Executive of the entire Government.

Here was a rare opportunity to test the soldier—to learn whether among his talents was an ability to steer the ship of state through the shoals of factional strife at home and through the storms of diplomacy abroad into the quiet waters of national and international serenity.

The conscience that commanded tens of thousands of young men to go to their death in battle twinged at the thought of the many more tens of thousands who might have to go to future wars, and of the millions of innocent men, women and children who might be the victims of an atomic disaster.

To the tremendous task of peace, the soldier devoted himself. Thrusting aside protocol and precedents, he offered to go anywhere in the world at any time to make every effort to advance the cause of peace.

The Geneva conference of 1955 "at the summit," widely characterized as a failure, was not a failure for the great soldier. He went with peace in his heart and came away still believing that man can find some other way to resolve international disputes than by organized murder.

Then the hand of God intervened. Was it a mystic warning to us all in the midst of our indulgence in the excesses of materialism? Did we really deserve peace?

The heart of the soldier faltered. The whole world stood aghast—worried that he might be taken from us. The prayers of hundreds of millions of people fervently petitioned the Almighty to preserve this man—his energizing force for peace.

The power of God can humble the greatest of soldiers or statesmen and take them from us at the moment of their greatest glory.

There come to mind the lines of Walt Whitman eulogizing the stricken Lincoln:

"O Captain! my Captain! our fearful trip is done,
The ship has weather'd every rack, the prize we
   sought is won."

But today the "fearful trip" is not yet done. The ship has not weathered every rack, and the prize is not won. The world is still half-slave and half-free.

These are the days when the mysteries of Divine Guidance are no more revealed to us than before but His omnipresent influence can, if we accept it, rule mankind. It can shape human behavior. It can apply a restraining hand to an evil purpose. It can help us win in the long run a victory for honesty, for freedom and for justice. The destiny of the whole world is in the hands of those statesmen who can interpret faithfully the commands of the Almighty.

We happily are witnessing now the gradual recovery of the soldier-statesman from an illness which might have been fatal had the Lord willed it so.

Maybe this means that the crusade of the soldier-statesman is to go on and that the years of his own usefulness as the servant of his people are to continue until his mission is fulfilled.

There is ahead for Dwight Eisenhower the greatest of all calls to duty—service to the world.

For Dwight Eisenhower is the man of the era. He is the Captain who can steer the ship of state safely through dangerous seas amid the hazards of mutual suspicion and the frequent provocations to war.

On the horizon already are the dim outlines of the shore. There the true victory can be won, sooner than most of us imagine. There, rooted in the unorganized and unasserted will of the men and women of all nations, is the means by which to assure peace.

To that shore, God willing, the Captain, our Captain, must sail on until this divided world is united in freedom—until the "fearful trip is done."

A CALL TO LIBERALISM

JANUARY 13, 1956

LIBERALISM has been undergoing a steady erosion. The so-called "liberalism" of today is a philosophy of coercionism in conflict with the spirit and letter of the Constitution. It is not true liberalism.

Time was when liberalism meant freedom from excessive government—freedom from encroachment upon the rights of the people.

Time was when the Tenth Amendment to the Constitution was as sacred as any other provision of the Bill of Rights about which we hear so much from today's "liberals." This Amendment says:

"The powers not delegated to the United States by the Constitution, nor prohibited by it to the States, are reserved to the States respectively, or to the people."

Control of education, of course, was one of the powers reserved to the States and to the people. No power of the federal judiciary has until recently been exercised to set forth standards of education or to examine and rule upon the psychological influences that may or may not prevail in the classroom.

Today the Supreme Court has proclaimed that the federal judiciary has the right to determine who shall or shall not attend public schools. This disregards the wishes of the States as expressed in their laws and respective constitutions. It is a short step now to the selection of teachers and to the designation of a curriculum by federal authority.

Today's "liberal" acquiesces in this usurpation of federal power.

Control of employment has hitherto been a right reserved to the people—the right of the individual to work or to refrain from working, and the right of the employer to hire or to refrain from hiring. Neither the States nor the Federal Government were ever given the right to interfere with the freedom of individuals to contract for goods or services.

The Federal Government, under the Wagner Act and the Taft-Hartley Act, has undertaken to supervise the operations of labor unions and management where the employer-employe relationship is involved. No such power was ever delegated to Government, Federal or State, by the Constitution. It is plain usurpation.

Today the "liberal" enthusiastically champions these enlargements of governmental authority over the people.

Discrimination in economic opportunity because of race or creed or color is a shameful thing anywhere—but nothing in the Constitution grants the Federal Government or the States the power to punish employers or union officials who practice such discrimination. If the people want to abolish discrimination—economic or social—and desire to legislate morals, why not let the people adopt a constitutional provision to accomplish such a purpose? The 18th Amendment legislated on morals, but at least it was written into and taken out of the Constitution by the methods specified in the Constitution itself.

Today, without the slightest shred of constitutional power, a presidential commission coerces employers by threatening to deprive them of their right to contract with the Federal Government unless they obey its decrees on who shall or shall not be employed. This is a usurpation of power.

Granted that these objectives are desirable, shall they be achieved by usurpation? Do we really believe any more in that clause of the Constitution which prescribes the proper way to amend the Constitution, or do we believe that nine Justices may re-write the Constitution as they please?

It was Thomas Jefferson, the greatest of the true liberals of America, who first inveighed against the power of the judiciary to emasculate the Constitution. He complained that the judges could make the Constitution "a mere thing of wax" which they "may twist and shape into any form they please."

It was Thomas Jefferson who first protested against the centralized state.

Today's "liberal" believes in the mastery of the state. He wants the Government to own public-power enterprises and believes that the Federal Government is authorized to own or control every line of business.

True liberalism must be revived in America. It means a Government of laws under a written Constitution—not a Government by the caprice of men who temporarily hold public office.

True liberalism is today being ignored by so-called "liberals" who by their tactics are involuntarily enlarging the forces of reaction and stimulating extremist groups of the "right" which are as unprincipled as those of the "left."

There is only one course for the true liberal—to oppose the ideology of those who, in the name of emergency, expediency, convenience or profit, would forsake both the letter and the spirit of the Constitution.

For it is the written Constitution—the whole of it and, not just a few selected provisions—which we as citizens take an oath of allegiance "to preserve, protect, and defend."

BUILD UP ALLIES OR ENEMIES?

JANUARY 20, 1956

SHALL THE UNITED STATES engage in a competition of spending in foreign lands?

Shall our taxpayers write a blank check and leave it to the Department of State to decide where and how much money will be allocated to foreign countries?

Shall the Department of State tell the American people, and particularly the Congress, the facts about each country involved so that the people of the United States may form their own judgment as to the wisdom of the policies proposed?

These questions go to the heart of the issue of granting economic and military aid to other countries in the crusade to avert a third world war.

Speaking last week in behalf of the President, Secretary of State Dulles puts the case this way:

"The present period in history may one day be recognized as a major turning point in the struggle between Communism and freedom. It appears to be clearly a shift in the cold war, in which economic and social problems have moved to the forefront."

Mr. Dulles tells of the way the Soviet Union has been "jumping military as well as political barriers" as in India, Egypt and Burma. He then says:

"We believe that the United States must counter these Soviet efforts. We can succeed, not by outbidding Communism in sheer amounts of economic aid, but by making newly independent and newly articulate peoples feel that they can best satisfy their wants by becoming and remaining part of the community of free nations."

This is all right as far as it goes. Perhaps a warning can be read into it that the United States will be interested in helping only those countries which "become" members of or "remain" members of the free world. But there is need for further definition and for an explicit statement.

We cannot recognize such a thing as "neutralism" or "neutrality" in our foreign-aid program. The phrase "foreign aid" means "aid for the defense of the United States." Unless appropriations can clearly be allocated for such a specific purpose—for the defense of America—the money of American taxpayers should not in all honesty be used merely for a philanthropic enterprise or adventures in "competitive coexistence."

As between right and wrong, there can be no neutrality. Nehru of India, for example, condones the murder and torture of American boys in Korea. Nehru, moreover, defends the right of the Soviet Union to commit acts of treason against the United Nations. For it has been formally conceded by the Soviet Union that it furnished arms and ammunition to the North Korean and Chinese Communists to repel the armies of the United Nations.

The obligations of the Charter of the United Nations require fidelity to the principles of peace as opposed to aggression.

Yet Nehru is on the side of the aggressors and wants to reward the Red China Government with a seat in the Security Council of the United Nations.

Why, therefore, should a single dime be spent to help India unless her government abandons the tricky "neutralism" of Krishna Menon, who manages to persuade the naïve Nehru to do his bidding?

It's time to face up to the international blackmail to which we are also being subjected in the Middle East. The United States cannot police local wars and disputes. That's the task of the United Nations. But the decision of the Soviet Union to sell arms to Egypt and Egypt's readiness to accept such arms indicates that Prime Minister Nasser is trying to play one side off against the other. That kind of "neutralism" should not be supported with American dollars.

Prime Minister Nasser is represented as saying he really wants to be with the West but wishes to avoid signing any treaties or making any public commitments to the West. Why?

Vague assurances are not enough. Acts must definitely demonstrate that the nations which profess to be friends are actually on our side and not ashamed of it —and certainly not at the same time playing games with the enemy.

It's time to be realistic. We cannot "outbid" Communism. For the Soviet is making fake "bids." We are in the habit of keeping our pledges whereas the Communists make "offers" but rarely fulfill them.

The policy of the United States should be applied at all times to protect the people of the United States. If American funds can be effectively used abroad for that purpose, let Congress appropriate on a selective basis. Nations which insist on being "neutral" in the struggle between slavery and freedom and between morality and immorality can do as they like—just as we can do what we like with our own money. For this is a war—whether we call it "cold" or "hot." Our objective is to help build up our allies, not to build up our enemies.

Our motto should be: "Billions for allies, but not one cent for 'neutrals'."

FIRMNESS—NOT DEFEATISM

JANUARY 27, 1956

THE AMERICAN PEOPLE can breathe easier as a result of the pronouncements on foreign policy recently made by the Secretary of State, John Foster Dulles, and because of the outspoken support given him publicly last week by President Eisenhower.

Mr. Dulles has been speaking frankly to the world lest some aggressor miscalculate and start a war on the theory that the United States would not resist.

Irrespective of the exact wording of the *Life* magazine article which stirred up a controversy, the fact is that the governments in Peiping and Moscow have, in effect, now been told that the United States has not succumbed to the "strategy of terror" which the Communists have used through their propaganda in an effort to anesthetize public opinion here and abroad.

For many months now, the Communists have been playing a sinister game. They have endeavored to frighten the peoples of the West by emphasizing the horrors of the hydrogen bomb. But while the President tried to get an agreement to ban the use of nuclear weapons and entered wholeheartedly into a conference "at the summit" at Geneva last summer to bring about a truce in the world, the Communist governments upset those hopes shortly after the conference was held.

Marshal Bulganin said on December 31 last that he does not rule out the possibility of a nuclear war. Here was a veiled threat which had to be met, and the magazine article—reflecting in the main the views of Mr. Dulles—was an opportune reminder that the American determination to use nuclear weapons, if necessary, has not changed.

What must be avoided today is the creation of the same atmosphere as enveloped Europe just before World War I and again before World War II. In each case, a government that was planning aggression miscalculated. The belief prevailed in both instances that the United States would not enter a European war or that, if American intervention came, it would be too late to prevent a victory for the aggressor.

Adlai Stevenson in 1952 said that "the men in the Kremlin thought they would be unopposed" in Korea. Unfortunately, Secretary Acheson in January 1950 gave that impression, and America had to engage six months later in a bloody war to "repel aggression." A warning in advance might have avoided that war.

Mr. Dulles has sought in season and out to let the aggressor know in advance what is going to happen if there should be an attack in Europe or elsewhere threatening the security of the United States or its allies.

Fortunately, our allies agree with the course outlined by Mr. Dulles—namely, "massive retaliation," in case of attack, which, of course, means the use of nuclear weapons on a selective basis to achieve the most effective results in a military sense.

Our allies are glad the United States is standing for firmness and not defeatism. Prime Minister Eden of Great Britain made a public speech supporting this very point last week after some British newspapers had misinterpreted the *Life* article as meaning something inconsistent with British policy. Mr. Eden said:

"If there is less fear of world conflict today, this is due to the deterrent of nuclear weapons. Remove the deterrent, or take risks in pretending that it is not there, and the world outlook would be terrifying indeed.

"The justification of both the atomic and hydrogen bombs is that they are deterrents, so awful that no country will risk their use against itself. It is therefore true that the danger of world war should decrease unless an aggressive-minded nation gets into its head that the bomb will not be used against it, whatever it does."

It cannot be proclaimed too often that the United States and its allies mean business and are not bluffing. It is to be hoped, moreover, that Soviet Russia will not make the mistake of assuming that the petty partisans in Congress are speaking for the American people when these unwise politicians attack the Administration on a political front.

The aggressor could select 1956, our election year, as the occasion for taking risks.

It is reassuring that Senator George, Democrat, Chairman of the Foreign Relations Committee, has not shared the critical attitude of some of his colleagues.

There is no international harm in a divided political party but we must not present the spectacle of a divided Government. The world should have no doubt that we have a firm leadership in these critical times.

This is the time of all times for politicians to abandon partisan techniques and stand up for America.

The courage of the Secretary of State, Mr. Dulles, should not be derided but applauded.

The wisdom of issuing warnings to an aggressor is unmistakably clear. The episode in which Secretary Dulles recently figured has turned out to be a timely warning. It becomes a constructive contribution to world peace.

For the policy of the United States is, and should continue to be, one of firmness—not defeatism.

INSIDE THE REPUBLICAN PARTY

FEBRUARY 3, 1956

LATELY THERE HAVE BEEN rumblings about disaffection inside the Republican Party among conservative and anti-radical groups. The dissenters argue that the Eisenhower Administration has accepted too much of the New Deal doctrine, has blocked the adoption of the Bricker Amendment, or has not been vigorous enough on the issue of subversion and anti-Communism in this country.

Differences of opinion on particular issues also confront the Democratic Party.

An interesting example of how a leading Republican conservative handles the dilemma was given by Senator John W. Bricker of Ohio at one of the "Salute to Eisenhower" dinners on January 20. He said:

"Just three short years ago we were embroiled in a bloody, stalemated war in Korea. Today, the ship of state sails on calm, though still treacherous, waters of peace. In just three short years, a Republican Administration unraveled a tightly regimented economy. Today, we have a dynamic, free, and competitive economy—an economy which is providing us with the greatest material blessings in the history of man. We live in an era of uneasy peace and unparalleled prosperity.

"Only extreme partisans and demagogues will maintain that this peace and prosperity is not due, at least in part, to the leadership of the man who occupies the most powerful elective office on earth . . .

"In choosing not to emphasize President Eisenhower's legislative program on this occasion, I do not mean to impugn its general excellence. The fact is, however, that the legislative program outlined in the State of the Union Message is the work of an army of Presidential aides. We should not expect our President to be fully conversant with all the details of his legislative recommendations. That knowledge could be acquired only by a criminal sacrifice of Presidential time—the time which he devotes to life and death issues of foreign and national defense policy. President Eisenhower rightly refuses to regard the Congress as a mere rubber stamp. Accordingly, he should not be blamed for Congress' shortcomings nor given paramount credit for Congress' achievements . . .

"As an example of the President's courageous leadership, I cite the foreign policy of this Republican Administration. A President of less courage might have declared South Korea, Formosa, and South Viet Nam beyond the defense perimeter of the United States. History proves, however, that firmness and courage in foreign policy are more likely to maintain peace than attitudes of vacillation or appeasement. President Eisenhower has had the courage to take risks. Partisan critics profess to be horrified by the fact that America has been pushed several times in recent years to the brink of war. They are, however, notoriously silent about alternative methods to stem Communist aggression. We do know this. During the administrations of each of the last three Democratic Presidents, America stood on the brink of war and each time plunged over the precipice. President Eisenhower has not permitted that to happen.

"As an example of patriotic leadership, consider the President's forceful actions against subversive influences. If there is a softness toward Communism in the top echelons of government, no combination of Congressional investigating committees can uproot it from the Executive branch. President Eisenhower has not airily disregarded pertinent FBI reports. He has not promoted any Harry Dexter Whites. He has not decried undeniable evidence of Communists in government as 'red herring.'

"President Eisenhower's leadership has inspired not only America but the entire non-Communist world. Our network of mutual security alliances was never stronger. The President, almost single-handedly, showed the world how the atom could be consecrated to man's life instead of being the instrument of his destruction. Yes, even the Communist dictators have been inspired by the President. They have been inspired by the healthy fear that any overt act of aggression is apt to bring swift and deadly retaliation.

"In the area of economic policy the conservative quality of the President's leadership has produced enormous benefits. One example of this conservatism was the President's reluctance to accept standby price and wage control authority which some members of Congress were anxious to give him. No President in recent times has spurned a proposed grant of power. . . .

"President Eisenhower's leadership has been conciliatory in tone. No longer do we have a President who, for political gain, pits class against class, workers against management, and rich against poor. One result of this conciliatory leadership has been the generally harmonious relationship between the White House and Capitol Hill. Another result of this conciliatory approach has been the President's success in advancing equality of opportunity for all Americans without stepping beyond the limits of his constitutional authority . . .

"We salute him tonight and hope to salute him on five more anniversaries of his Inaugural."

RUSSIAN "ROULETTE"

FEBRUARY 10, 1956

THE RUSSIANS offer us a pistol with which to commit suicide. They assure us none of the cartridges is loaded—that the weapon contains only "blanks" to be used in celebrating "peaceful coexistence."

But we are not to know about any extra bullet. The bomb is to be concealed behind the Iron Curtain and unloosed against us in a nuclear war after we have destroyed all our atomic weapons and demobilized our armies.

What a "roulette" game to try on the most powerful nation in the world! Or do the men in the Kremlin think we are all gullible? Have they been listening to Messrs. Burgess and Maclean, the British diplomats who turned traitor and who know how to phrase conciliatory notes based on Anglo-Saxon psychology?

The two Bulganin notes of last week add up to these aims:

1. The West must destroy all atomic weapons and stop making any more. The Soviet Union, which refuses to permit any kind of inspection within its borders, will keep on with their clandestine manufacture of nuclear weapons.

2. The size of the Western armies must be reduced and all overseas bases abandoned. But the Communists would retain bases and armies of occupation in satellite countries ranging from the Baltic to the Pacific.

3. The Soviet Union must be given *carte blanche* to infiltrate other countries—neutrals and opponents alike. Russia's "sovereignty" over Poland and the other satellites would remain untouched.

The Bulganin notes reflect an illusion that the Western nations are easily deceived and that they want peace so badly that they will pay any price to get it— even the surrender of their armaments.

When President Eisenhower in his reply says that "deeds—not words" are desired now, Bulganin with feigned innocence answers:

"The conclusion of a treaty of friendship and co-operation between the U.S.S.R. and the U.S.A. would be one of the most important concrete acts in this respect, inasmuch as our two countries, once they had the very important obligations provided for in the draft treaty, would strengthen confidence and would bring tranquillity to the entire international situation.

"This would mean that our countries do not confine themselves to verbal assurances of their desire to be friends but put into actual practice the obligations which they have assumed."

When has the Communist Government in Moscow ever honored a treaty? When has it respected any written assurances, or recognized any obligations that seemed to it convenient to evade?

The record is full of broken pledges and broken treaties. It begins with the shattering of the solemn agreements entered into by the United States with the Kremlin when we recognized the Government of the Soviet Union in 1933. Sir Anthony Eden has just reminded us of a 20-year non-aggression treaty with Great Britain which Moscow tore up last year.

"Deeds" in the minds of the Soviet rulers apparently mean writing new treaties—more scraps of paper.

The second Bulganin message, received last week, speaks proudly of the reduction of the Soviet Army by 640,000 men last year. It doesn't tell how many millions merely doffed their uniforms one day to continue the next day under Army discipline in civilian labor.

The same message contends that the Russian budget on armament has been reduced. The true figures of expenditures in Soviet Russia are always concealed.

Bulganin also said a Soviet base in Finland was given up. But will the stranglehold which the Kremlin has on the Government of Finland ever be released? Its naval base can be reoccupied overnight.

The Soviet Premier points with pleasure to the fact that his Government recently signed a treaty with Austria, but why were there ten years of delay? Why does he say now that Austria has "an obligation to pursue a policy of permanent neutrality"? All the world was told, when the treaty was signed, that Austria was free to determine for herself whether and under what circumstances she will stay neutral.

Bulganin's game is clear to see. He wants America—the strongest military power in the West— to give up her arms and her bases and accept at face value the Russian promises to maintain peace. It's like the gangster who says to the city authorities: "Abolish the police force. I am going to keep on operating only within my section of the city, and you can exist peacefully in the other section."

To argue with Bulganin by means of note-writing may make interesting copy for the newspapers, but dictatorships in Berlin did the same thing prior to both World War I and World War II and managed to delay the military preparations of the democracies until the aggressors were ready to strike.

Let us pray the West will never again be the victim of such transparent deception.

IKE'S QUANDARY—AN ANSWER

FEBRUARY 17, 1956

(Paragraphs attributed here to President Eisenhower are paraphrases or condensations of statements made by him at recent press conferences. The other paragraphs are the comments of the Editor.)

MR. EISENHOWER: The question that confronts me with respect to renomination for the Presidency is not necessarily one to be decided on the basis of self-interest. It involves duty primarily to the country. Suppose that in a second term I should become ill and incapable of determining myself whether I can carry on—should the nation take that risk?

LOGIC: The nation takes that risk with any President in a first term as well as in a second term. Congress is empowered by the Constitution to enact laws providing a method of determining how and when the Vice President shall take office in case of a President's "inability." The House Judiciary Committee is engaged right now in a study of possible laws that may be enacted on this very point.

MR. EISENHOWER: The strains of the office are numerous. It is not simply a matter of organizing the job to lighten certain burdens. It isn't the quantity of the work involved. Strain can come from any single problem. I sometimes feel tired now—maybe it's just advancing age and not my heart.

LOGIC: This is the hazard which all Presidents have always faced. Nobody can say with assurance whether a man who has had a heart attack will live five months or five years or more years. The responsibilities of a President to his country cannot be measured by life insurance statistics or calculated averages. There are risks to health at every age. Theoretically, a President who does not feel physically up to his job can consider resignation during either a first or a second term.

MR. EISENHOWER: The doctors may tell me that they think favorably of my physical condition, but I alone must decide whether I should undertake a second term.

LOGIC: In public life, the individual does not always make the decision. The Government often summons young men to battle in time of emergency. It does not give them a choice. These are critical times. The word "war" is often in the headlines. The present era of tension is called a "cold war" and the public is beset with fear of a "hot war."

MR. EISENHOWER: But no man is indispensable. Certainly the people can find another leader who will satisfactorily perform the duties of the Presidency.

LOGIC: As long as a man of proved ability is available and in the opinion of his doctors, is physically able to carry on the tasks of the Presidency, the people will not be satisfied to dispense with his services.

In every presidential election, two men are selected—theoretically of equal ability. When one dies or is physically unable to serve or resigns, the other takes his place. That's our constitutional system.

MR. EISENHOWER: But suppose I feel able, suppose I feel now that I can carry on—but, because of advanced age, my health deteriorates in the second term. Remember I would be seventy years old near the end of a second term. No President in our history has ever reached that age while in office.

LOGIC: Nor has any President before Franklin Roosevelt ever been elected four times. He died in 1945 in the midst of a world war and was succeeded by a Vice President under whom the war was successfully waged and won.

Calendar age is no criterion. Clemenceau, Churchill, Adenauer and other statesmen did not feel that seventy was a maximum age for service. There are many men in public life—performing effectively—in governorships as well as in the Congress, who are far past seventy. Age limits cannot be generalized. It requires an answer for each individual case.

MR. EISENHOWER: I shall not be unduly concerned with self when I make my decision. I will do what is best for the country. I would like to be able to serve but, even if the doctors say I can do so, I alone must decide whether I will be jeopardizing the people's interest if I accept service for a second term.

LOGIC: No President should make that decision. He should lay the facts before his party, which can weigh them at its national convention. Then, if he is nominated, the electorate can also weigh the facts and decide whether to elect the presidential and vice-presidential nominees of one party or the other.

Whether Dwight Eisenhower shall continue in the Presidency for as long as he is able in a second term is a decision in which all the people in the American Republic have a right to participate.

Public service is impersonal at a time of international crisis—particularly in this dangerous age of atomic weapons. The nation is entitled to draft for service any man it may think can best serve the public interest—for one year, for two years, for three years or for four years, indeed as long as such leadership is available.

The people must rely on a Vice President to succeed a President if the Fates so require—and, as history has proved, a Vice President like Theodore Roosevelt can also become a man of destiny.

THE HONESTY OF CONGRESS

FEBRUARY 24, 1956

MEMBERS OF CONGRESS, by and large, are men of honesty and integrity—but many of them are their own worst enemies.

Day by day they play a game called "politics," which constantly impugns the honesty, integrity and motives of their political opponents.

To breed suspicion of corruption and, through committee hearings and speeches, to issue veiled innuendoes about the other fellow's alleged crookedness, together with an accusatory emphasis on "big business" or "big unionism," implying that these groups and others are the constant recipients of special privileges at the hands of Government—this is the modern concept of political strategy.

Why are such tactics condoned? Somehow men who in their personal contacts of everyday life would never think of accusing their fellowmen of wrongdoing without convincing proof, are ready, for the sake of political advantage, to cry "scoundrel" and "rascal." They would make the electorate believe their opponents are deliberately betraying the people's confidence and hence ought not to be continued in office.

There seems to be no such thing as morals in politics. It's a rough-and-tumble game, dependent for the most part on the assumption that the electorate—to use a phrase of the late Harry Hopkins of New Deal days—is "too damn dumb to understand."

But is the electorate so shallow-minded, so uninformed, so susceptible to emotional prejudice as to accept smears and unfounded accusations as a substitute for reasoned debate and thoughtful argument?

The Congress and other divisions of the Government are often held in disrepute by stump speakers who seem to think that in political warfare no holds are barred.

Lately, the American people have been given the idea that temptations beset the members of Congress on every side and that lobbyists and campaign contributors lurk in hidden places, ready to transmit their bribes to influence this or that vote.

Instances are indeed rare where violations of the law have occurred. Existing laws forbid corrupt practices and are generally obeyed, but of much more concern are the violations of the fundamental code of ethics—activities not prohibited by law—which grow out of the present system of campaign contributions.

For, when Senator Case, Republican, of South Dakota revealed recently that a Nebraska lawyer had attempted to offer his campaign fund a contribution, he was quick to say it wasn't a bribe. But the would-be donor represents a producer of natural gas, and a bill concerning the federal regulation of that commodity was then pending in Congress. Was this an attempt to influence the Senator's vote? The contributor says "no strings were attached."

Yet, are not many campaign contributions given usually in appreciation of services rendered, or in anticipation of services to be rendered?

The reports filed with the Clerk of the House of Representatives show, for instance, that in the 1954 campaign the political committees of the labor unions spent a total of about $2,000,000 and that sums ranging from $5,000 to $35,000 were spent specifically to aid certain Senators who were elected and to defeat other candidates who were successful.

Also, the same records show many corporation executives as having contributed out of their personal incomes a large total to campaign funds earmarked for certain Senators and members of the House.

If some committee of Congress or national commission now were to examine, for example, every single campaign contribution made in connection with the congressional election of 1954—and study every vote on every roll call of both Houses of Congress since then on specific pieces of legislation in which the contributors had a direct or indirect interest—would the dreaded phrase, "conflict of interest," emerge to plague some members of Congress as it has some officials in the executive branch of our Government?

Do the consciences of these individual members trouble them as they introduce or press for passage measures desired by the very organizations or groups which have given so much money to their own campaign funds?

These are practical questions which sooner or later must be faced realistically if our legislative body is to be free from all taint.

There should be a ban on all campaign contributions in excess of $50 from any individual or organization.

Donations to the party treasuries are legitimate, but large sums earmarked for particular candidates and contributed or collected by any private organization or by any citizen interested in the passage or repeal of federal laws, including Government purchases or special favors of any kind, carry with them an implied obligation and should be prohibited.

The legislative institution, like Caesar's wife, must be above suspicion.

NOW FOR UNITY

MARCH 9, 1956

THE TIME TO CLOSE RANKS is at hand.

The world has been assured that President Eisenhower will continue to exercise the leadership which the free nations of the world have entrusted to him.

America's internal politics, therefore, must not be allowed to retard the forward march of freedom.

There should be in our Congress a willingness to put aside partisanship in the national interest. The Democratic Party promised the American people in the 1954 congressional campaign that it would give the Administration wholehearted support in foreign policy. Unhappily, the captious criticism and the reckless, irresponsible speeches in the Senate in the last few days have brought dismay. They have stirred up in the minds of the Soviets the feeling that our councils are divided and that our purposes can be thwarted in this, an election year.

The Secretary of State delivered on Sunday, February 26 a well-reasoned address. It was carefully prepared many days before his testimony to the Senate Foreign Relations Committee. It was a comprehensive statement of our policy as a whole, but the politically-minded centered their fire on the extemporaneous answers given on February 24 to partisan questioning at the hearing of the Senate Committee.

Surely there are great questions on domestic affairs to be debated between the parties that will afford an opportunity to get votes without sabotaging America's world policies and striking down the prestige of the head of the Department of State. For he has just started on a tour, scheduled some time ago, on which he will visit 10 Asian countries. It is important to achieve a better understanding with the peoples of Asia.

The Senators should have offered their good wishes to the Secretary of State and given a demonstration of unity, so as to enable him to leave with the knowledge that behind him in this country leaders of both parties are united for America. This would have impressed the Asian leaders. In effect, they now are being told by press dispatches that Mr. Dulles may not have the confidence of his own legislature. Asians and Europeans think in terms of a parliamentary body and not of our Congress as a coordinate branch. When a foreign spokesman does not appear to have the support of his legislature, his words fall on deaf ears.

The weakness of democracies is their tendency to let partisan politics override considerations of unity.

What difference does it make whether the Secretary speculates rightly or wrongly before a Senate committee as to the psychological motivations behind the change in Soviet tactics from violence to economic competition? What he says has to be weighed in the light of how the Soviets themselves maneuver from day to day in the "cold war." A public hearing is hardly the place to divulge all the background of delicate matters of state.

Some of the Democratic Senators nevertheless keep on demanding that they be given "all the facts." Wasn't it only a year or so ago that we heard so much talk about a certain United States Senator who was alleged to be "encroaching on the executive branch"? Why do the Democrats in the Senate feel that they must formulate foreign policy or be given in public hearings every detail of our strategy in the "cold war"?

The most vital fact to bear in mind is that American policy is vigilant and that, no matter what the Soviets are planning, the United States and its allies are on the alert to meet whatever challenges may come.

There is allied unity today, even though differences do exist among our friends. These differences, however, are not exploited—they are submerged.

President Eisenhower at the helm will steer the Ship of State safely away from the shoals of war, if it can be done at all. His energies have been and will be concentrated on maintaining peace.

The American people are behind him. The Secretary of State speaks for the President, and the words of Mr. Dulles should be respected as such abroad.

The average American is not a partisan. He wants his Government to succeed in world affairs.

If the politicians only would realize it, their chances for individual re-election, regardless of party, are improved when they are non-partisan on foreign policies.

For non-partisanship means fairness, decent criticism, constructive advice, and an abandonment of the sniping which was so palpable last week in the proceedings of Congress.

Peace in an atomic age is hard enough to preserve without being confronted by misguided attempts to weaken the moral strength of one's own Government. For the voice of the spokesman of the United States throughout the world must be the voice not of a political party, but the voice of an unpartisan people.

It's a time to close ranks—to unite for America.

APPEASEMENT NEVER PAYS

MARCH 16, 1956

THE APPEASERS now are surveying the wreckage they have wrought in the Middle East.

The appeasers, moreover, are advocating that billions of our dollars be spent to appease India.

The appeasers are advocating, too, that we throw away 1,000,000 men—the armies of Nationalist China and the South Korean Republic, which are the main bulwark of our defense in the Far East. For a moral breakdown in Formosa and Korea would, of course, be the result if, as advocated by the appeasers, we give Red China a seat in the Security Council of the United Nations.

Appeasement leads to war. Vacillation before World War I and before World War II helped to involve us all in those two terrible conflicts. No better authority on what appeasement has meant in bringing on war could be cited than Winston Churchill. In his book, "The Gathering Storm," published in 1948, he gives a penetrating review of some of the events of 1938 and 1939 which led to the fighting of World War II under the most disadvantageous conditions. Sir Winston writes vividly of what was happening prior to 1939:

"In this sad tale of wrong judgments formed by well-meaning and capable people, we now reach our climax. That we should all have come to this pass makes those responsible, however honourable their motives, blameworthy before history.

"Look back and see what we had successively accepted or thrown away: a Germany disarmed by solemn treaty; a Germany rearmed in violation of a solemn treaty; air superiority or even air parity cast away; the Rhineland forcibly occupied and the Siegfried Line built or building; the Berlin-Rome Axis established; Austria devoured and digested by the Reich; Czechoslovakia deserted and ruined by the Munich Pact; its fortress line in German hands; its mighty arsenal of Skoda henceforward making munitions for the German armies; President Roosevelt's effort to stabilise or bring to a head the European situation by the intervention of the United States waved aside with one hand, and Soviet Russia's undoubted willingness to join the Western Powers and go all lengths to save Czechoslovakia ignored on the other; the services of thirty-five Czech divisions against the still unripened German Army cast away, when Great Britain could herself supply only two to strengthen the front in France—all gone with the wind.

"And now, when every one of these aids and advantages has been squandered and thrown away, Great Britain advances, leading France by the hand, to guarantee the integrity of Poland—of that very Poland which with hyena appetite had only six months before joined in the pillage and destruction of the Czechoslovak State.

"There was sense in fighting for Czechoslovakia in 1938 when the German Army could scarcely put half a dozen trained divisions on the Western Front, when the French with nearly sixty or seventy divisions could most certainly have rolled forward across the Rhine or into the Ruhr.

"But this had been judged unreasonable, rash, below the level of modern intellectual thought and morality. Yet now at last the two Western Democracies declared themselves ready to stake their lives upon the territorial integrity of Poland.

"History, which we are told is mainly the record of the crimes, follies, and miseries of mankind, may be scoured and ransacked to find a parallel to this sudden and complete reversal of five or six years' policy of easy-going placatory appeasement, and its transformation almost overnight into a readiness to accept an obviously imminent war on far worse conditions and on the greatest scale.

"Moreover, how could we protect Poland and make good our guarantee? Only by declaring war upon Germany and attacking a stronger Western Wall and a more powerful German Army than those from which we had recoiled in September, 1938.

"Here is a line of milestones to disaster. Here is a catalogue of surrenders, at first when all was easy and later when things were harder, to the ever-growing German power. But now at last was the end of British and French submission. Here was decision at last, taken at the worst possible moment and on the least satisfactory ground, which must surely lead to the slaughter of tens of millions of people. Here was the righteous cause deliberately and with a refinement of inverted artistry committed to mortal battle after its assets and advantages had been so improvidently squandered.

"Still, if you will not fight for the right when you can easily win without bloodshed; if you will not fight when your victory will be sure and not too costly; you may come to the moment when you will have to fight with all the odds against you and only a precarious chance of survival.

"There may even be a worse case. You may have to fight when there is no hope of victory, because it is better to perish than live as slaves."

IT'S A WAR

MARCH 23, 1956

WHEN THE COMMUNISTS stir up terrorism in Algeria and cause French divisions to be diverted to North Africa from their primary function in the defense of Western Europe, it's a military maneuver. It's the strategy of war.

When the Communists stir up the people of Cyprus to rebellion so as to wrest from the British their most important military base in the Mediterranean, it's the strategy of war.

When the Communists weaken the ties between Jordan and Britain and help to bring the Arab nations together in an anti-Western combination of states, it's a military maneuver. It's the strategy of war.

When the Communists spread their terrorism through North Africa, using Egypt as a base of operations, and when Egypt herself, succumbing to Soviet influence, enters into an agreement to buy arms from one of the satellites of the Soviet Union, it is the strategy of war.

When the Communists deliberately undermine the French Republic as well as the Italian Republic, gaining a foothold in the Parliaments of both—unmolested by any effective restriction upon subversive activities —the objective is to weaken and detach two important allies from the West. It's the strategy of war.

The Communists are infiltrating on every front in Europe, North Africa, the Middle East and Asia.

Are we in the United States immune? The Communists are striving to break down our security system, to exploit racial disputes, and yet to obtain from us technical information and as much goods as will help them build up their military armament. It's the strategy of war.

The Communists are helped inside the United States by unwitting persons, influential in the formation of public opinion. Many of the so-called "liberals," obsessed with an academic argument about the "right of dissent," are singularly indifferent to the safety of the Government itself. As Judge Learned Hand once pointed out, there is no "right of revolution" against the state.

The war in which we now are engaged is a different kind of war from any the United States has ever faced. It resembles the "fifth column" war of 1938 and 1939 that paved the way for the fall of France in 1940. Only this time the operation is masterminded by ruthless Communists instead of skillful Nazis.

Since we are at war, why do we not resist at least by financial and economic means? Why do we sit by while our allies send strategic goods to the enemy and while the Soviets transmit their gold rubles to hidden espionage centers behind our own lines in North Africa, in Asia and in Europe?

The usual argument made is that our allies must trade to make a living. But we are spending billions for military equipment to aid these same allies. Why should we not indemnify our allied friends for their losses in trade, if necessary, but still keep machinery and other strategic articles from being shipped to our enemies?

We hear "colonialism" denounced by unthinking spokesmen in America of various causes and groups who parrot the Communist line on the same subject.

Eighteen United States Senators called last week for the liberation of Cyprus from British rule, but the same Senators are not so solicitous about those who once had their independence and now have been deprived of it by the Communists—the people of Poland, Czechoslovakia, Hungary, East Germany, Bulgaria, Rumania, Latvia, Lithuania and Estonia.

China, too, has lost her freedom—enslaved by Moscow-trained tyrants. In the face of this, there are Americans who advocate policies that would virtually disband the army of 1,000,000 men now on our side in the Far East. For if Red China's gangsters are seated in the United Nations, we shall demoralize the armies of Nationalist China and of the Korean Republic. That's a military maneuver of the highest importance to Soviet strategy.

We are being lulled into inaction on the Communist front by appeals for economic aid to questionable neutrals. Billions of dollars will not instill morality or courage in the minds of those who cringe already before the Communist threat.

When will we wake up? When will we recognize that war now is enveloping us on every side? When will we fight back?

When will we mobilize our moral as well as our material strength and accept the challenge the Communists have thrust upon us? Or must we wait until our allies have been debilitated one by one and then try to battle Communism by ourselves?

It's a war—now, in 1956—as it has been for more than 10 years. It is not less dangerous because it is euphemistically called a "cold war." It is a war of infiltration and encirclement—a precursor to military conquest.

It's time to recognize the realistic facts as they are and to act in self-defense. It's a war.

WHAT ISSUES?

MARCH 30, 1956

CAMPAIGNING BY BOTH PARTIES has been in progress for several months now in anticipation of the 1956 election, but there still is no clear definition of the issues.

The Democratic Party is now in control of both houses of Congress but has not identified itself with any affirmative program visible as yet to the naked eye.

The Republican Party was in control of Congress for two years and has had its nominee in the White House for more than three years but, in terms of particular achievements, the electorate still has only a vague impression of what has been accomplished.

The Republican slogan—"Peace and Prosperity"—does outline the broad theme on which the Republicans expect to stand before the people, though it is debatable whether the "peace" we have today is based entirely on what our own Government has done or is due to the clumsy forbearance of our enemies.

"Prosperity," as a political premise, is easier to define. Normally a political party takes credit for good times and is blamed by opponents if times are bad.

The present healthy state of business in America is not an accident in politics. The Republicans can demonstrate that in a favorable climate of public policy businessmen grow confident about the future and deliberately expand their enterprises. Employment goes on to unprecedented heights.

But "prosperity" this year is not uniform. The Democrats are able to point to the drop in farm income and claim that the Republicans are at fault. The voter does not interest himself in the fine points but considers the result—the impact on him.

Between now and November some improvement in the farm situation may be expected which would tend to cut down the disaffection among farm voters. But such is the nature of the American electoral system that an adverse economic situation in a few key States can make a vast difference in the national result.

The theory that all the voters listen to campaign speeches and weigh the merits of the arguments between the candidates may seem logical as an academic position, but actually what influences 50,000,000 or more voters is something far more elemental—the impact of the economic situation on the individual. Personalities count much less than is popularly supposed, and the fluctuation of the human heart-beat is scarcely effective as a campaign issue. The voters of America for the last 50 years have been gradually turning away from steadfast allegiance to one party or the other and have switched as economic or emotional issues have swayed them.

This might be considered an advance over the times when the voter cast a ballot for the party of his grandfather, irrespective of the merits of the issues, but it is still doubtful whether a democracy can achieve its ideals as long as the "pocketbook" interest of the moment primarily governs a voter's impulse.

Perhaps the most penetrating issue on the emotional side this year will be that of "peace." On this the two parties are really not very much different. But the Democrats will have to argue that the Republicans don't know how to keep the peace as well as the Democrats would, or else that the Republicans may go over the brink into war though professing to strive for peace.

It is an argument easily twisted either way. The Republicans can ask if the Democrats want war or, if they favor peace, what they would do that isn't being done to attain it. Would the Democrats favor getting tough with the Russians or talking gently? Would the Democrats threaten more nuclear force, more air power, more armament?

Already the Democrats argue that the Administration has not kept up our defenses, to which the Republicans answer that they prefer to rely on the judgment of the military here in the White House.

It is difficult for the average voter to follow the jargon of the debate on defense. It is hard for the average citizen to understand why a budget has to be kept unbalanced so as to spend more and more for armament when the headlines reflect news of disarmament plans and international conferences in which such an objective is being constantly pursued.

The 1956 campaign thus far finds the public confused on the issues. As for the conduct of the campaign, the theatrics of the stump still are regarded as potent. President Truman thinks the electorate is best reached by a "give 'em hell" technique.

One wonders when the candidates will begin with statesmanlike intelligence to analyze the basic differences between the two major parties and restore allegiance to party and to the fundamental principles of party government in America.

The force of party can be an effective instrument of the popular will. Solidarity of party is virtually unknown in most of the democracies in the world today. Blocs and factions rule the hour as principle is shunted aside in an age of materialism.

THE POWER OF PEOPLES

APRIL 6, 1956

TOO OFTEN our minds are focused on the power of governments—and not on the power of peoples.

Too often we accept as respectable spokesmen of an oppressed people the tyrannical masters who temporarily hold the reins of government.

Too often we are tempted to accept the doctrine that "peaceful co-existence" with gangster governments is a prerequisite to our own survival.

We show a receptiveness to the enemy's maneuvers of "good will" toward Western countries but fail to perceive that at the same time we are really the victims of a strategy of terror.

Fear of an internecine conflict that will "destroy the world" has been widely generated. We are urged to disarm and to trust rulers who have again and again violated their written word.

The object of the "strategy of terror" is to anesthetize us into inaction—a form of surrender, because we are led to believe that an enemy government will attack us unless we accept its demands.

Our enemy today is the Communist government in Moscow—not the people of Soviet Russia. There are some naïve persons, even in high positions among our allies, who refuse to make that distinction. They still think that Communism is just an academic philosophy and that the Communist Party is merely a political party and not the instrument of an unmoral government which controls the machinations of agents in every country in the West. The Communist Party is allowed, for example, to sit in the French Parliament, where it holds the balance of power, while its agents plot against the French authority in North Africa.

If we in the West could see clearly our duty—to isolate the Communist imperialists and give them no quarter—the people of the Soviet Union would be encouraged to take matters into their own hands.

Fortunately, President Eisenhower has again and again given proof of the pacific intentions of the American people and thus has deprived the Moscow Government of its biggest opportunity to solidify the Russian people as against the supposed threat of attack.

It is true a gangster government can, in its desperation, try to start a war, and we must be prepared for all eventualities, but at heart Moscow's rulers are probably more afraid of the very people they might drag into war than they are of the West. Even in the midst of World War I, it will be recalled, the people of Russia revolted and turned against their despotic rulers.

The only way to assure peace is to build understanding with the tens of millions of people in Soviet Russia. It is not, of course, an easy task, but we are making progress. We must continue to tell the people behind the Iron Curtain that they have nothing to fear from us and that the only real "enemy" we have is a small group of murderers and conspirators who hold office in Moscow and Peiping.

There are signs that the Soviet peoples are being aroused to the possibilities of regaining possession of their own government.

The recent attempt to make Stalin the scapegoat for the crimes of the Soviet regime reveals internal weakness. Virtually all of the present rulers were associated with Stalin, and their hands are dripping with the same blood. The people in Soviet Russia know it, and at the right moment will strike.

The urge to freedom and independence is just as strong inside Russia as anywhere else in the world. The Soviet Union is composed of many nationalities. Russian colonialism has deprived them of their freedom and frustrated their national aspirations.

Let us hear less prating about Western "colonialism" in Africa or in the Middle East or in Asia—at least, until the present war against a common enemy is over. The fight must first be won against Russian colonialism. For there is little use of holding out hopes for the independence of any new republic anywhere while the Communists keep in bondage countries that once enjoyed their independence.

The world is not safe for any democracy today. It cannot be as long as Communist imperialism remains in Moscow and Peiping.

The power of peoples, however, is supreme and can change the face of the world. This power is often dormant, invisible, intangible, but its potentiality is immense—it can be mobilized overnight.

The 200,000,000 people in Soviet Russia, acting in unison, can at any moment brush aside the tyrants in the Kremlin.

Passive resistance has begun already in a dozen different ways behind the Iron Curtain. The fires of revolt have been kindled. The day is not far distant when the Soviet peoples and the peoples of the satellite states will be emancipated.

May we, by our firmness and our unremitting expressions of friendship and encouragement to all nations which are now enslaved, hasten the day when the power of the people shall bring freedom to Soviet Russia—and thereby give peace and security to all the world!

"DISARMAMENT"—AN ILLUSION

APRIL 13, 1956

No SOVEREIGN NATION, large or small, which has potential enemies intends to disarm.

Our own armament, we insist, is for defense.

The Communist government in Moscow says the same thing—no intention of attacking anybody, and the only purpose of existing armament is "defense."

Then why all the international conferences on "disarmament"?

Who is fooling whom?

The answer is that nowadays it is considered wise to give continuously the impression of peaceful purpose. Any nation which does not talk loudly today about "disarmament" feels it will be accused of "war mongering." Hence, "disarmament" talk is a defensive maneuver in a propaganda war.

Even the word, "disarmament," is a misnomer. No nation intends really to throw away all of its armament and actually "disarm."

The most that could be hoped for is an international agreement to limit the amount of armament—to reduce it in certain categories.

The peoples of the world believe in self-defense as their primary obligation. They will never throw away their arms as long as there is no means of being sure of the good faith of a potential adversary who has repeatedly violated his pledges.

Talk of "disarmament" is empty as long as distrust prevails among nations.

There can be no mutual trust if a dictatorship government is in the saddle anywhere to threaten war.

Peoples can achieve mutual trust only when they set up governments that actually reflect the public desire to avoid war.

Conferences on "disarmament" will be in vain unless preceded by conferences that can really develop mutual trust or make progress toward removal of the causes of distrust.

An example of the illusory reasoning of a public official was given in this magazine last week in the interview with Premier Mollet of France. His words caused repercussions throughout Europe, because the French Premier declared that Britain and America were wrong in insisting on reunification of Germany before there was disarmament. What M. Mollet was proposing, in fact, was that the discussion of "disarmament" be given priority over the question of uniting the German people—exactly what Moscow has been seeking.

Could anything be calculated to produce more distrust where so much distrust already exists than for the head of the French Government to propose that a debate which might last for a decade must be held before putting into effect or even discussing any formula for uniting the German people in a single state?

The Middle East offers a significant example of how little progress has been made on the theory of disarmament by the major nations. Soviet Russia a few months ago authorized its satellite, Czechoslovakia, to sell arms to Egypt. Now Israel wants arms, and some governments—like France—will sell them to her, though America for the present will not. A threat of war is in the air.

Sending the Secretary General of the United Nations to the Middle East to find a formula for peace makes sense, but the readiness of the larger powers to allow arms to be exported to the rival sides follows precedent also.

Thus, while we talk "disarmament," we condone larger armaments not only for the rival nations of the Middle East but for ourselves.

It has been suggested that "inspection" can be used to allay distrust and prevent war. But can it? How much can be observed from the skies by airplanes? Today all that is needed is one bombing plane and one hydrogen bomb, and the damage that could be inflicted is immense. Is it not easy to hide a dozen planes and a dozen H-bombs?

The answer to the problem of peace is not in locking up material things like weapons. It lies in the mind that orders the weapon used—not the weapon itself.

There can be no peace until peoples everywhere are in control of their own governments. It is Communist imperialism and Communist dictatorship which has given us our biggest threat to peace, not only in the Middle East but everywhere else. Only a revolution in Soviet Russia by the peoples there can save the day, and it can come when they finally realize the great danger to them and to the whole world which dictatorship has brought.

The way to peace is through the liberation of peoples. We must assist the oppressed and the enslaved.

Democratic assemblies where free speech and a free interchange of information with other peoples prevails do not make war. Only when the world is safe for democracy can there be a reduction of armament.

We have the cart before the horse—freedom must prevail everywhere before there can be confidence and faith in international agreements on the limitation of armament.

WITH WHOSE MONEY?

APRIL 20, 1956

EVERY NOW AND THEN a curious sort of propaganda line criticizing American foreign policy comes back from abroad in the form of anonymous interviews, impressions, suggestions and findings derived in good faith from persons who profess to be thinking only of the good of the United States—some of them our own officials stationed in foreign countries.

The substance of it all is a complaint that America isn't spending enough abroad in economic aid. It is apparent that the persons who feed such views to American newspapermen are absorbing the ideas of foreign officials who realize that the "gravy train" is running down and needs to be greased up again.

The propaganda is too palpable to be deceiving. It starts out usually with the criticism that America is putting too much emphasis on "military alliances," that America is attaching strings to its grants of aid, and that America is trying somehow to destroy or impair the hard-won independence of the newly-created states—now known as "uncommitted" and "neutralist."

On top of this, is the curious allegation that Americans are talking too much about war and too little about peace, and that our foreign policies are "too rigid" or "too inflexible."

Boiled down to hard realism, it means that Uncle Sam's pocketbook has become too inelastic and rigid. They are beginning abroad to suspect that there will be difficulty this time in getting billions out of the U. S.

This is the right moment, incidentally, to talk about the American people's money. The American taxpayer this very week is making his quarterly payment of income taxes and finds he is giving up a huge proportion of his earnings. The taxpayer in the past has been told it's necessary to furnish aid so as to resist Communism and strengthen our overseas defenses.

But now the new propaganda line from Europe and Asia says that America puts too much stress on resisting Communism and that this isn't a menace after all. Even the Socialist Premier of France minimizes it.

Our official spokesmen have for a long time now been talking about peace and the renunciation of force, and decrying bad colonialism, but evidently the Asians haven't heard us talking. Their ears are stopped up with glowing tales of Communist virtue.

It's strange in all these surveys, too, how little mention there is of Communist colonialism and Communist-imposed slavery in the satellite countries, which once enjoyed their independence. Yet Soviet policies in Asia are praised as exemplary.

The unnamed spokesmen in Asia hint that we should scrap our Southeast Asia treaties, discard the 1,000,000 troops on our side in Formosa and in South Korea, and recognize Red China. What a military coup for the Communists that would be!

We are reminded in these new surveys that Asians have lived in poverty for a long time and have been exploited by Europeans. We are warned that, while Asian peoples like help, they are very "proud" and don't want any conditions attached to gifts.

Somehow, it is asserted, Russia does the thing better —she gives no gifts, she just participates in "trade arrangements." But she does manage to exchange her rubles for concrete things. The first "condition" that Russia makes usually is that she get something worth-while in return. But, ah, America, she must not think of such things—America must give away her money quietly, anonymously, and ask no questions. As for Mr. Dulles, he is referred to in the surveys as a bad Secretary of State—probably because he's a good American.

It is easy to read between the lines of what these supposedly informed observers say—there's nothing wrong with the American policies abroad which a few billions of financial aid wouldn't cure. If only there were more Marshall plans, more economic agencies, more give-aways, everything would be rosy!

There is one question we might venture in all candor to ask: How do these so-called observers who have the temerity to give such pointed advice to America, expect to carry on new and enlarged programs of economic penetration? With whose money? Certainly not with the American taxpayers' money.

If underdeveloped countries are so blinded by "pride" that they don't know the difference between Communist tyranny and American generosity, it's time to stop injuring their "pride" any longer with gifts of American dollars.

If the Communist menace is, after all, a myth, then let the countries which feel that way protect themselves as best they can.

America should continue, of course, to help faithful and appreciative allies in Europe and Asia. There is, however, no obligation which requires the taxpayers of the United States to become paternalistic guardians of the "neutralist" world. If there is no military reason for American aid to certain countries who now scorn it, then America's billions might better be expended within this country for more schools, for aid to farmers, for relief of the taxpayers' burdens.

EYES ON THE DOLLAR

APRIL 27, 1956

FROM TIME IMMEMORIAL the key to the economic future of any nation has been the stability of its monetary unit.

Adam Smith, in his famous work, "The Wealth of Nations," published in 1776, emphasized the tendency of governments to repudiate their war debts. He said that almost all states, "ancient as well as modern," cheated the people by devaluing the currency.

Two world wars in the last half-century have debased the currencies of Europe and Asia. Likewise, in that period the purchasing power of the American dollar has been cut by two thirds.

We in America are at the crossroads now. We have a choice between further devaluation of the dollar and an upward rise in its purchasing power.

In the one direction lies more inflation—higher and higher prices, strikes for higher wages to meet rising costs of living, and hardship to persons with fixed incomes.

In the other direction lies stability and a greater opportunity for everybody to share in the benefits to be derived from the strong fiscal position of America.

A crucial decision will have to be made in the next few weeks on the course the dollar must take.

For, happily, the United States Treasury by June 30 next will show a budget surplus and a cash surplus—the first time in several years that this will have happened.

If, as now indicated, there's a budget surplus of about 2 billion dollars—which is nearly ten times as big as was forecast last January in the President's message to Congress—the political clamor for tax reduction will be heard from one end of the country to the other.

Politicians will be seeking to give away that surplus to those in the low-income brackets on the mistaken theory that this will be of real benefit to them. Yet this would be the very group hurt by inflation.

What would be of more benefit to more people would be to reduce the national debt by 2 billions.

As a result largely of World War II, the public debt went from around 40 billions in 1939 to 276 billions today. Measured against the wealth and income of the country, this is not in itself precarious but it is too big a sum to go untouched year after year. A government that doesn't pay off any of its debt begins to look as untrustworthy as an individual who avoids payment of his current obligations. This would be a serious detriment to the financing of a third war if it should be thrust upon us.

If a people show no desire to reduce their debt, and if they keep on curtailing their own taxes while they let the debt remain high, this must inevitably be interpreted in the monetary markets of the world as a sign of weakness—as a symbol of repudiation.

Economic advisers to both the Democratic and Republican Administrations in the past have argued that taxes should never be reduced when the nation is prosperous and that tax relief should be reserved for those occasions when it is necessary to give a stimulus to the economy, as in time of depression.

Certainly in the present boom period there is no need for further incentives to spend or borrow. The Federal Reserve Board in the last few weeks has been taking steps to restrict borrowing by business. It has done this in order to keep the boom from becoming a runaway affair and to reverse the trend toward price inflation which has been under way since last June. A tax cut would be the last straw. It could point the way to a speculative era such as that which preceded the 1929 crash.

So the best thing to do with the 2-billion-dollar surplus is to cut that amount off the public debt. This isn't much of a reduction, but it will be regarded everywhere as of transcendent importance. For it will mean that America at last has made a start toward debt reduction. The principle is worth far more than the sum involved in any tax-reduction plan.

If the dollar—which now is at about 52 cents in purchasing power compared to 1939—is to rise gradually, it will be because of the sound monetary policies pursued by the Treasury.

A tax-reduction move would be inflationary. It could send prices up so high as to cause a buyer's strike. It could devalue the dollar. Certainly it could break down the best-laid plans of industry to spend money on plant expansion. If the prices that have been figured, for instance, on construction were swept away in another upward spiral, many such commitments for spending in private enterprises would have to be revised, if not cancelled.

It is dangerous to tinker with the dollar. The whole world would be benefited if the dollar were strengthened instead of weakened. Other nations can buy more and more goods and crops from us if our price level is stable.

Throughout the world all eyes will soon be turned on the American dollar. It must remain strong. This can be assured only by a policy of sound money.

TREASON AGAINST THE U.S. AND TREASON AGAINST THE U.N.

MAY 4, 1956

FREE PEOPLES must be uncompromising in their opposition to Communism in all its forms—Communist despotism which enslaves the individual, Communist imperialism which carries on wars across the world. Communist colonialism which keeps in bondage states once independent and free, and the Communist conspiracy in our midst, engineered, directed, and financed by our enemy, the government in Moscow.

But primarily for Americans of all parties and faiths, it is Communist treason inside the United States and Communist treason inside the United Nations which today need exposition.

All Americans ought to be against treason. But there are some who do not understand the word "treason." They do not seem to realize why treason was singled out in the Constitution for special mention as the worst crime that can be committed against the United States. They fail also to perceive that the paragraph in our Constitution denouncing treason supersedes any claim to individual license. For if traitors succeed in overthrowing our Government, then the Bill of Rights becomes worthless.

Section 3 of Article III of the Constitution says:

"Treason against the United States shall consist only in levying war against them, or in adhering to their enemies, giving them aid and comfort. No persons shall be convicted of treason unless on the testimony of two witnesses to the same overt act, or on confession in open court.

"2. The Congress shall have power to declare the punishment of treason. . . ."

It will be noted that there are two clauses in the definition of treason itself—that which condemns treason as "levying war" and, separated by a comma, there is an alternative clause which defines treason as "adhering" to our "enemies" and "giving them aid and comfort."

Is there any doubt what is meant by "adhering" to our enemies?

And do we wait until treason has consummated its conspiracy and then try to punish traitors, or does the Congress have the right by law to adopt measures which will *prevent* the successful execution of plots of treason? Our courts have given us a clear answer.

It was Judge Learned Hand of the U. S. Court of Appeals who, on August 1, 1950, rendered a famous opinion that tells us why constitutional measures can be taken to avert treason. His decision was upheld by the Supreme Court. He wrote:

"The American Communist Party, of which the defendants are the controlling spirits, is a highly articulated, well contrived, far spread organization, numbering thousands of adherents, rigidly and ruthlessly disciplined, many of whom are infused with a passionate Utopian faith that is to redeem mankind. It has its Founder, its apostles, its sacred texts—perhaps even its martyrs. It seeks converts far and wide by an extensive system of schooling, demanding of all an inflexible doctrinal orthodoxy. The violent capture of all existing governments is one article of the creed of that faith, which abjures the possibility of success by lawful means. . . .

"The advocacy of violence may, or may not, fail; but in neither case can there be any 'right' to use it. Revolutions are often 'right,' but a 'right of revolution' is a contradiction in terms, for a society which acknowledged it, could not stop at tolerating conspiracies to overthrow it, but must include their execution.

"The question before us, and the only one, is how long a government, having discovered such a conspiracy, must wait. When does the conspiracy become a 'present danger'? The jury has found that the conspirators will strike as soon as success seems possible, and obviously, no one in his senses would strike sooner. Meanwhile they claim the constitutional privilege of going on indoctrinating their pupils, preparing increasing numbers to pledge themselves to the crusade, and awaiting the moment when we may be so far extended by foreign engagements, so far divided in counsel, or so far in industrial or financial straits, that the chance seems worth trying. That position presupposes that the Amendment (in the Constitution) assures them freedom for all preparatory steps and in the end the choice of initiative, dependent upon that moment when they believe us, who must await the blow, to be worst prepared to receive it. . . .

"True, we must not forget our own faith; we must be sensitive to the dangers that lurk in any choice; but choose we must, and we shall be silly dupes if we forget that again and again in the past thirty years, just such preparations in other countries have aided to supplant existing governments, when the time was ripe. . . ."

This contingency is precisely what the Congress of the United States has had in mind in enacting during the last fifteen years various laws on espionage and subversive activities.

But what has been the reaction to such legislation? Who have opposed it?

Many loyal but misguided Americans who have been duped by the Communist conspiracy have opposed such legislation. They always vaguely say, of course, that they favor some sort of protection against disloyalty, but their general opposition to the principle involved is unmistakable.

It is our duty to make clear to those who have been deceived by Communist tactics that they unwittingly give aid and comfort to the enemy when they endeavor plainly to frustrate their own Government in its efforts to protect itself against Communist treason.

What is the nature of the treason in our midst? Here is a vivid description of treason in our times—treason within the last several years, treason as defined by the man who was Commander-in-Chief of our allied forces during World War II and later was called back to duty when the Communist menace became so clear to the nations of the world that they formed the North Atlantic Treaty Organization as a measure of defense against Communist aggression.

It was Dwight Eisenhower who, in October 1952, said to an audience in Wisconsin:

"I have come to Milwaukee tonight to talk with you about Communism and freedom. . . .

"The one—freedom—knows man as a creature of God, blessed with a free and individual destiny, governed by eternal moral and natural laws. The second—Communism—claims man to be an animal creature of the state, curses him for his stubborn instinct for independence, governs with a tyranny that makes its subjects wither away.

"These two ideas are as opposed as danger is to safety, as sickness is to health, as weakness to strength, as darkness to light.

"Great truths can, at times, be startlingly simple. This one is of that kind. It is so simple a truth that it seems almost too obvious, almost stale.

"But let not our memories be too short. Only a few years have passed since many moved among us who argued cunningly against this plain truth. Their speech was persuasive, and their vocabulary clever. Remember? It went like this: 'After all, while we stand for political democracy, they stand for economic democracy. Fundamentally, these are but two slightly different roads to the same goal. We both believe in freedom.'

"We all must remember that sophisticated lie. We will never forget it. For it partly poisoned two whole decades of our national life. It insinuated itself into our schools, our public forums, some of our news channels, some of our labor unions, and—most terrifyingly—into our Government itself.

"What did this penetration into Government mean? It meant contamination in some degree of virtually every department, every agency, every bureau, every section of our Government. It meant a Government by men whose very brains were confused by the opiate of this deceit. These men were advisers in a foreign policy that—on one side of the world—weakly bowed before the triumph in China of Communists hailed as 'agrarian reformers.' On the other side of the world this policy condoned the surrender of whole nations to an implacable enemy whose appetite for conquest sharpened with every victory. This penetration meant a domestic policy whose tone was set by men who sneered and scoffed at warnings of the enemy infiltrating our most secret counsels.

"It meant—in its most ugly triumph—treason itself. . . .

". . . We have been for years the gullible victims of Communist espionage experts. These experts in *treason* have plundered us of secrets involving our highest diplomatic decisions, our atomic research. Tragically, we do not know how much more our security may have been jeopardized. . . .

"I speak not as a partisan or as a candidate but simply as an American citizen—moved to honest anger by this persistent, gnawing threat of *Communist treason* in our national life. I know that millions of both parties today are moved to anger and to action. . . .

"Armed with a clear and uncompromising respect for freedom, how then shall we defend it?

"To begin with: All of us—citizens, jurists, officials—must remember that the Bill of Rights contains no grant of privilege for a group of people to join together to destroy the Bill of Rights. A group—like the Communist conspiracy—dedicated to the ultimate destruction of all civil liberties cannot be allowed to claim civil liberties as its privileged sanctuary from which to carry on *subversion* of the Government. . . .

"To work for the United States Government is a privilege, not a right. And it is the prerogative of the Government to set the strictest test upon the loyalty and the patriotism of those entrusted with our nation's safety.

"Every official of Government must bear clear responsibility for the loyalty and fitness of his own immediate subordinates. And every official of the Federal Government—on every level—must ever be ready to answer any question from appropriate sources touching upon his loyalty and devotion to the United States of America."

Now, does anybody think that, since that speech was made in 1952, the Communists have abandoned their efforts to penetrate America? Does anyone think the goals of Communist infiltration are being sought with less vigor than before? The passage of the

Communist Control Act by Congress just 19 months ago indicates that the menace is a continuing one.

Perhaps the most up-to-date information that we have on the activities of the Communist Party and its stooges in the United States was given before a subcommittee of the House Appropriations Committee on February 1, 1956, by the Director of the FBI, J. Edgar Hoover. In this testimony Mr. Hoover says in part:

"The membership of the Communist Party at the present time is estimated to be 20,289. These are the so-called hard-core Communists of the country.

"There is no question from the investigations we have conducted that the party takes its orders and directions from Moscow. . . .

"The number of persons engaged in front activity has been estimated by Communist leaders themselves to outnumber the actual Communist Party membership by a ratio of 10 to 1, or better. . . .

"There is no question but that the Communist Party in this country is a fifth-column potential. The hard-core membership of the open party is aided by a reservoir of concealed members, the underground, which is engaged in such activities as colonization of strategic defense industries—supposedly being done on a secret basis. We have been able to keep abreast of those efforts and are aware of their activities in that field.

"They have utilized the Communist-front groups and the so-called psuedo-liberals, as I am inclined to call them: individuals who are not members of the Communist Party and who quite vociferously deny any sympathy with Communism but who, through being duped by Communist contacts, espouse causes sponsored by the Communists.

"They oppose security programs and sponsor liberalizing security measures; they oppose urgently needed internal security measures; and they advance the theory that the menace of Communism is a mere myth or hysteria.

"They contend that the Communist Party is a political party just like the Republican and Democratic parties and not a conspiracy designed to overthrow the United States Government by force and violence. It has been held by courts that the Communist Party is dedicated to the overthrow of the United States by force and violence."

Treason is not a matter of harboring abstract beliefs and keeping them secreted in one's mind. The so-called "liberals" have raised a smokescreen on that issue. They are trying to make the American people believe that many of us are seeking "thought control" or that we wish to interfere with the expression of unpopular beliefs. The so-called "liberals" ignore the fact that the late Justice Oliver Wendell Holmes of the Supreme Court of the United States told us that the right of free speech does not include the right to shout "Fire!" in a crowded theatre.

For there is no right to preach treason. There is no right to teach or advocate treason. Congress has specifically prohibited it. There is no right to hold a government job and at the same time participate in any movement which constitutes an adherence to the cause of our enemies. Acts—not beliefs alone—are the criteria.

The essential point is that our Government is not obligated to take any risk of being subjected to acts of treason. Hence, the security regulations in our governmental departments are concerned with the prevention of criminal acts—acts that have been manifested all over the world by Communist imperialism, which uses infiltration as one of its principal weapons.

Congress has repeatedly used the phrase "Communist conspiracy" in the preamble to the many laws designed to protect the national security. The Communist Control Act of 1954 declares "that the Communist Party of the United States, although purportedly a political party, is in fact an instrumentality of a conspiracy to overthrow the Government of the United States" and that "its role as the agency of a hostile foreign power renders its existence a clear, present and continuing danger to the security of the United States."

For we are dealing with a plot organized, instigated, planned, directed, engineered by a foreign government which is our enemy.

Why is the word "enemy" used here? Recently an industrialist in this country made a speech in which he naively said we should not use the word "enemy" in describing the Communist regime—it might offend them. Yet it will be noted that in the 1954 law Congress uses the phrase "a hostile foreign power" in referring to the Soviet Union.

Let us be realistic. We have already met the armies of the Communist imperialists on the battlefield. We lost more than 33,000 boys in Korea. Their mothers and fathers grieve for them today. They were the victims of the shells, or the bullets, or the bayonets of the Communists of Soviet Russia.

As a matter of fact, we still are in a state of war with Communist China. Our armies in Korea, with ammunition in their guns, are stationed on an armistice line. Our troops are alert twenty-four hours a day as they face the possibility of sudden attack by the Chinese Communists. While we have a cease-fire agreement, we do not have a peace treaty.

Although for a little while the Communist Government in Peiping disavowed responsibility and called the Chinese armies in Korea "volunteers," this camouflage was later abandoned. We know now that the Communist regime in China made war upon the tens of thousands of American boys who had been drafted for military service.

And where did the bulk of the munitions come from to kill 33,000 of our boys and wound 103,000 of them in Korea?

The bullets, the munitions, the weapons came from Soviet Russia. The late Andrei Vishinsky, in a speech before the Political and Security Committee of the United Nations General Assembly in March, 1953, confessed, admitted, conceded that the munitions of war had been supplied to the Red Chinese armies in North Korea by the Soviet Government.

To the discredit of the United Nations, it must be recalled that on hearing this statement, it took no punitive action in the Assembly.

The United Nations has had plenty of opportunity ever since to denounce the Soviet Government for its complicity in this crime of the century. For this was treason. But the United Nations has not done so.

Those of us who espoused the cause of the League of Nations in the '20's, and those of us who were enthusiastic about the United Nations when it was founded in 1945, and those of us who still believe that the United Nations can be the greatest moral force for peace in the world that has ever been mobilized, are disappointed that the United Nations failed us at a crucial moment. It evidently did not possess the courage necessary to deal with reality and truth.

Largely because the United Nations failed to denounce Soviet Russia and expel its gangster government from membership for "levying war" against other member nations—its acts of treason against the United Nations—we are today being misled into believing that "peaceful coexistence" with such criminals is a practical possibility.

Why are we now involved in many international commitments around the globe to furnish military and economic aid? Only because the United Nations as an instrument of collective security has failed us. We have found it necessary to organize regional pacts and make regional commitments to assure our safety as against a common enemy.

For the enemies of peace today in the world are the Communist Government in Moscow and the Communist Government in Peiping.

Why do we not have a peace treaty in Korea today? This writer was in Geneva in May, 1954, when the Four-Power Conference was held. Chou En-lai, Foreign Secretary of the Red China Government, in a formal address to the conference, denounced the United Nations when the United States proposed that a peace treaty which would unite Korea be drawn up under the auspices of the United Nations. Chou En-lai said a commission of "neutrals"—his kind of neutrals—should be appointed to negotiate but the commission must not have any connection whatsoever with the U. N. The position of Red China has not been modified since.

Yet we hear some well-meaning citizens in our ranks talking today about admitting Red China to a seat in the Security Council of the United Nations.

Of what avail will the United Nations be if it condones treason, if it takes its enemies to its bosom without the slightest sign of their repentance, if it allows conspirators to enter its councils and sit as equals alongside of free nations?

We who are against Communist imperialism today declare that it has not divested itself of its cloak of treason in the society of nations.

We who are against Communist imperialism today declare that it has not abandoned despotic colonialism. For Communist colonialism still imposes slavery upon the peoples of Soviet Russia and upon the peoples of the satellite countries.

A true liberal is against tyranny everywhere. A true liberal is against enslavement. A true liberal is against imperialism and against every form of colonialism that means enslavement of the people.

There are among us those who misuse the word "liberal." Many who call themselves "liberal" are not liberals at all. They are men who have been deceived into believing that "liberalism" must condone neutrality as between the aggressor and his victims in the world and must protect the right of conspirators in our midst to advocate and to practice treason.

We who believe in freedom for all peoples, we who believe in the right of self-determination for all peoples, we who believe in the right of every individual to think as he pleases, would limit individual rights only by the superior right of all the people in a nation to be protected against conspirators—those who would by force or violence overthrow a free government or aid an enemy to conquer us.

Lately we have been hearing much from the "liberals" about the Bill of Rights and "due process." A whole cult has grown up in America which preaches that individual rights are unlimited, and that the general phrases of the Constitution can be conveniently interpreted to protect traitors in our midst.

Britain, after having a tragic experience with Burgess

and Maclean, now is having the same internal debate on treason.

We should take note of a speech made in the House of Commons on March 21 last by the Secretary of State for the Home Department of Great Britain, Major Lloyd-George—son of the former Prime Minister. He spoke in part as follows:

"I should like to make three points in reply to those who may still feel that such measures are unnecessary. First, however distasteful were the measures which successive Governments over the last few years have had to take, we cannot sit back and do nothing while our security is imperilled by a menace, the existence of which is accepted on all sides.

"Secondly, while some of our counter-measures, it is true, are alien to our liberal traditions, so is the menace which they set out to circumvent. That is a point that we must never forget. As my right hon. Friend the Chancellor of the Exchequer said in the November debate, Communism has set progress back three centuries. We are now, thanks to Communist activities, back in the age when a man who holds this new creed thinks it loyal to be disloyal and has no scruple about betraying his own country. We are, therefore, driven into adopting steps which we take only because of protecting the liberal traditions that we in this country hold dear.

"Thirdly, while I do not for a moment under-rate the hardship of those who, because they are adjudged to be the dupes of the Communist creed, are moved to other work or, if it is impossible to find non-secret work for them, lose their appointments in the Civil Service, I should like to make one comment on that. Hard as their lot is, we can all make a shrewd guess as to what their lot would have been had they been employed in the Civil Service of a Communist Power, and it had been discovered that they belonged to or sympathized with a movement holding views about Communism analogous to those which Communists hold about democratic government."

Burgess and Maclean were intimately familiar with the diplomatic policies of the United States Government. They had access to the inner councils of our Government by reason of the messages sent to our allies. There is every reason to believe that Burgess and Maclean in the fateful month of November, 1950, were able to tell the Communists what was being discussed among the allied governments, particularly Great Britain, concerning the decision not to use our maximum military power in Korea.

It was important for the Communists to know whether we would apply maximum military power. They learned, undoubtedly through Burgess and Maclean, that our allies would not go along with us on that decision. Hence, the Chinese armies poured into North Korea, confident that their supply lines in the rear would not be bombed.

There is no chapter in all our history more revealing of the weakness of free nations than what occurred five months after our intervention in Korea in 1950 —when the word went forth to our military commanders that they must not use all their weapons to defend themselves and that they must acquiesce in the murder of our boys rather than allow our own airplanes to bomb the supply lines which were bringing weapons of death to kill our troops.

We heard in 1950 and we have heard ever since the cry that the use of maximum power would have involved us in a third world war. None of us wanted a third world war in 1950 and we don't want one now, but the chances of becoming involved in a third world war have been immeasurably increased by our failure to win a clear-cut victory in Korea. The failure there led to defeat in Southeast Asia and the open defiance of us today by Soviet Russia in the Middle East.

Do we have to re-read the pages of history to learn about the "fifth columns" which stimulated the processes of appeasement? We know that appeasement has led nations into war, that the real warmongers of today are the appeasers, that their lack of courage, their willingness to accept the blandishments of the enemy— anything to get peace, peace at any price—is increasing the danger to our country today and could conceivably drag us into a third world war.

It is, of course, in the nature of democracies to be restrained, to hesitate, to procrastinate, to do everything possible to prevent the outbreak of war. When we actually enter a war, however, there is no justification for any "softness" or cowardly hesitation.

President Wilson, the 100th anniversary of whose birth is being celebrated this year, tried by every possible means to prevent war, but when it was thrust upon us in 1917, he called again and again for "force, force to the utmost, force without stint or limit." The phrase, "force without stint," electrified the American people, for Mr. Wilson knew that, once we had decided to defend ourselves, there were no limitations we could impose upon our fighting men if we intended to act in good faith toward them.

When war does come—be it a little war or a big war—we must keep faith with those whom we are drafting for military service.

We must tell the mothers and fathers of today that, when their sons get up to the battlefront, they're not going to be asked to take the bullets of the enemy and the bombs from their airplanes without hitting back at the enemy's supply lines—just because some politicians back home speculate about a possible "enlargement" of the war.

We are today the victims of a strategy of terror. Again and again, public men talk loosely about the possibility that the whole human race will be destroyed by atomic bombs. Weapons of destruction have been invented which can wreak havoc on many places in the world, but the mere existence of terrible weapons that could be used against them has never prevented nations from defending themselves when attacked. The impression we are conveying today is that we will be afraid to defend ourselves if we are attacked by an unscrupulous enemy who uses nuclear weapons.

There comes a time when the risk must be calculated and when the risk must be taken. The big question is whether today, by means of the strategy of terror, we are being pressured into avoiding the risks that we should take to prevent World War III.

It must not be implied that this nation should at any time initiate a war but, when attacked, we must recognize a state of war thrust upon us and defend ourselves.

It is pertinent to refer here to a passage from "The Gathering Storm," a book by Sir Winston Churchill, which states more clearly than anything written by any modern statesman the case against appeasement. Sir Winston was describing the events leading up to the outbreak of World War II in 1939. He wrote:

"In this sad tale of wrong judgments formed by well-meaning and capable people we now reach our climax. That we should all have come to this pass makes those responsible, however honourable their motives, blameworthy before history. . . .

"There was sense in fighting for Czechoslovakia in 1938 when the German Army could scarcely put half a dozen trained divisions on the Western Front, when the French with nearly sixty or seventy divisions could most certainly have rolled forward across the Rhine or into the Ruhr.

"But this had been judged unreasonable, rash, below the level of modern intellectual thought and morality. Yet now at last the two Western Democracies declared themselves ready to stake their lives upon the territorial integrity of Poland.

"History, which we are told is mainly the record of crimes, follies, and miseries of mankind, may be scoured and ransacked to find a parallel to this sudden and complete reversal of five or six years' policy of easy-going placatory appeasement, and its transformation almost overnight into a readiness to accept an obviously imminent war on far worse conditions and on the greatest scale. . . .

"Here is a line of milestones to disaster. Here is a catalogue of surrenders, at first when all was easy and later when things were harder, to the ever-growing German power. But now at last was the end of British and French submission. Here was decision at last, taken at the worst possible moment and on the least satisfactory ground, which must surely lead to the slaughter of tens of millions of people. Here was the righteous cause deliberately and with a refinement of inverted artistry committed to mortal battle after its assets and advantages had been so improvidently squandered.

"Still, if you will not fight for the right when you can easily win without bloodshed; if you will not fight when your victory will be sure and not too costly; you may come to the moment when you will have to fight with all the odds against you and only a precarious chance of survival.

"There may even be a worse case. You may have to fight when there is no hope of victory, because it is better to perish than live as slaves."

The appeasers of yesterday brought on World War II. Let not the appeasers of today force us into World War III. We must oppose Communism in all its ugly forms—Communist aggression in so-called "little wars" around the globe, Communist colonialism which enslaves nations once independent, Communist infiltration of the free governments of the world, Communist subversion of the institutions of democracies.

Communism has encouraged treason in our midst and, by its own treason in the United Nations, has broken down the very instrument of collective security which the world set up in 1945 to enforce peace.

For Communism today is the generator of war.

THE GREAT UNCERTAINTY

MAY 11, 1956

WHAT AN ERA of confused thinking we live in today!

General Curtis E. LeMay, head of the Strategic Air Command of the U.S. Air Force, tells the Senate Armed Services Committee that we have 47 of the big intercontinental bombers and Soviet Russia has about 100 of the same type.

The Senate committee hearings give the impression we are involved in an armament race of the gravest kind—that we are relatively safe now but might not be in a war four years hence.

General LeMay says flatly that we would win if the war broke out tomorrow but that we would suffer considerable damage in America, and that five years ago we would have won with very little damage.

This means that at the time when so many weak-kneed officials in the Truman Administration were convinced that, if we used maximum air power in Korea, Soviet Russia would intervene and a third World War would result, they didn't know what they were talking about.

Evidently if we had applied maximum air power in Korea and bombed the enemy bases in Manchuria—as General MacArthur urged—we would have won a great victory in the Korean war. This would have had a deterrent effect on the Soviet policy of military aid in the war in Indo-China. It would have made less likely any such mischief by the Kremlin in the Middle East as we recently have witnessed.

But even as the Senate Armed Services Committee began talking about the need for more intercontinental bombers, the discussions at London about "disarmament" were pronounced hopeless by American officials there due to discouraging tactics by the Soviet.

Just about the time news of this turn of events was widely printed, along came the dispatches from Paris saying Great Britain, France, the United States and the West German Government had agreed to present to the Soviets a proposal that "disarmament" be considered in gradual steps in relation to the unification of Germany and possibly of Korea.

What illusions we create from day to day!

Back and forth go the protestations of peaceful intent. Everybody is led to believe that a "negotiation" of some constructive nature is actually in process, when it isn't.

Meanwhile, the battle for Asia goes on. Many misguided Americans are falling for the propaganda that the way to "win men's minds" in Asia is to give away more and more of the American taxpayers' money. The argument is made that the United States should, in some devious way, grant funds to "uncommitted nations" without any conditions. The earnings of American citizens, it is urged, should be siphoned through the United Nations or some other "multi-group" agencies. The idea seems to be to hide from the American taxpayer where his money is going and what purpose it is to serve. Fortunately, the Eisenhower Administration doesn't favor that plan.

The favorite cliché is that "no strings" must be attached. Yet the Asian spokesmen and some of their American champions would put "strings" on American appropriations by stipulating conditions under which such funds shall be used in foreign-aid programs.

The whole propaganda from abroad, moreover, emphasizes material factors. There is, for example, a good deal of indignation expressed abroad about the supposed zeal of the United States in maintaining "military alliances"—as if a strong defense against the Communist menace is no longer necessary. The Communists would like to have everybody think so.

Yet the Communists are not de-emphasizing their preparations for war. Also, while the arms race goes on, the American people are asked to forego nuclear tests or other research into new missiles and weapons because these might be misconstrued abroad as "militaristic." None of this seems to bother the Communists, who keep on with their tests and build up bigger and longer-range air forces.

Concurrently, the Communists by infiltration weaken the Western hold on smaller countries. Egypt is a victim of this strategy. The whole Middle Eastern situation is complicated by Soviet maneuvers which are plainly hostile to the West.

The wonder is that so many people in the world, including some trustful Americans, do not see through the tricks of the enemy. Why do we continue to "negotiate" with governments whose main personalities, by their shameful record of broken faith with other nations and by their tyrannical enslavement of the peoples behind the Iron Curtain, are arrogantly abrogating every principle of morality known to man?

There is only one course to follow—to steer by the compass of principle and morality. Our enemies lack both. We cannot trust them. We must, therefore, continue to arm. We must build the strongest possible force as a deterrent. For the reckless men in the Kremlin can at any moment upset the peace of the world.

A CHALLENGING PLAN

MAY 18, 1956

At LAST there has come a plan which gives promise of eventually bringing peace to the world.

It's a plan really to bind together free peoples.

It's a plan that isolates the germ of failure in the past—disunity among our own allies—and offers a constructive program to achieve unity.

It's a plan that does not depend wholly on the deterrent influence of military force but endeavors to mobilize, in addition, the moral force of nations with a common purpose.

It's a plan that does not supplant but really parallels the United Nations.

This plan, revealed last week by Secretary of State John Foster Dulles—and printed in full text in this magazine on pages 98 to 102—is a sensational development in world affairs.

The plan is an embodiment of American ideals as expressed by spokesmen in the past for Democratic as well as Republican Administrations. European statesmen for some time have nurtured the very concept which now has been crystallized by the Secretary of State.

Just as the Marshall Plan came at an opportune moment to recognize realistically that the economic situation in Europe should not be allowed to disintegrate, so the Dulles Plan seeks to stop the disintegration of political unity on our side in Europe.

We often take unity for granted. Yet it is the absence of unity on our side that gives the Soviet Government its main opportunity for mischief.

Briefly, the plan would rebuild the North Atlantic Treaty Organization by making it much more than a military alliance. The idea has been vaguely referred to heretofore as "broadening NATO." Actually, it means transforming NATO into an active instrumentality for the discussion and possible solution of any and all problems that affect world peace.

How would the Dulles Plan work? Details are not spelled out as yet. Only the broad principles have been outlined. It is, however, a simple approach. It recognizes that smaller councils are better for some things than the U. N., which is today mainly a vehicle for propaganda distribution and for log-rolling between factions of members.

Diplomacy can function best by consultation among a few, rather than in a public hall where klieg lights and cameras focus on men displaying their vanities and national prides.

The idea now is to make the NATO Council of 15 nations a living organism of diplomacy. This means that mediation and conciliation can be quietly employed to work out solutions for the complicated problems of Europe as well as of the Middle East and Asia where European powers have historic involvements.

It means also that such explosive issues as Cyprus and Algeria—which, legally speaking, are internal matters—can be dealt with tactfully and yet with due regard for the sensitivity of sovereign rights.

For it is obvious that, if the vast oil resources of the Middle East are cut off from Europe, and Turkey and Greece become hostile to each other, NATO as a military organization can overnight lose a strategic battle.

The urgency is there to come to grips with the perplexing problems of both the Middle East and Asia. But fundamentally there is even greater need to solidify Europe and begin at last to lay the foundations of a genuine peace. NATO has skirted the edges of these problems before but has not acted on them directly. As the Secretary of State says, there have been "discussions" but not "decisions." He cautions that the unity of the Atlantic community can be promoted "not by supergovernment but by common counsel."

Mr. Dulles points significantly to the unashamed way the Soviets have ignored their pledge to seek the reunification of Germany and asks: "Has the Atlantic community as a whole sufficiently focused world opinion upon the moral aspects of this problem?"

World opinion, of course, is the key to it all. It is the generator of moral force, which, if we but realized it, can at times transcend in effectiveness the military might we have necessarily assembled.

For, given the moral assignment of leadership in mediation and constructive assistance in the political as well as economic fields, a new NATO can come into being. It can affiliate intimately with the Organization of American States and with the Western European Union as well as the Council of Europe. It can cooperate with the regional organizations of an economic nature that have been set up in Asia as well as with those already striving for economic unity in Europe.

By coordinating the energies of the free governments which are ready to make great sacrifices for ultimate peace, this bold and brilliant plan initiated by Secretary Dulles can take root. It could give the world at last what it has long been praying for—a constructive program which, by its challenge, must attract the attention of peoples on both sides of the Iron Curtain. For peoples, not governments, really hold the key to peace.

THE ILLUSION OF PERMANENCE

MAY 25, 1956

WE ARE CONSTANTLY SEEKING "permanent" solutions to present-day ills.

If only this or that piece of legislation is passed, all will be well—prosperity will be permanent, and the wrongs that are corrected will be permanently removed, and forever after everything will be all right.

As we seek world peace, we talk perennially of "permanent" peace. But we rarely obtain even the degree of stability in the world which marks off in history a long era or epoch. Conditions change, we say, and new forces emerge to dispel our dreams of permanency.

But the fundamental error is in our approach. We reach out for what we blueprint as a permanent solution and we fail to achieve even temporary stability.

This weakness is often mistakenly interpreted as a kind of inflexibility in government policy. The exponents of "compromise" eagerly offer expediency and an abandonment of principle and morals as the easy way to overcome our failure to alter an enemy's behavior. Too often, however, this is the main cause of our undoing. Unwillingness to face facts and to checkmate promptly the rising power of a hostile force has brought us into two world wars.

But while appeasement never pays, it is unfortunately true that the world never seems to learn the lessons of appeasement. The temptation is to repeat mistakes. The fetish of "adjustment" or "coexistence" has served only to pile new problems on top of old ones and to delay or frustrate solutions.

Human error in the field of government is necessarily large, especially in a democracy where continuity is hampered by frequent changes in administration. But dictatorship, with its violent modifications of the economic and social order, is worse. Hitler was to remake the world. Stalin was to build up a new strength for the proletariat. But in our lifetime we have seen both repudiated even as other ideological doctrines still flounder in the realm of unvalidated theory.

Thus, in recent months it became necessary in the biggest of the dictatorship areas to concede that Stalin's philosophy had been wrong. It was an admission of guilt. It was a blow at permanence—a palpable effort to seek refuge in the doctrine of readjustment, if not retreat.

These fluctuations in the policy of the state are, of course, natural. They are the trial and error of human experiments in the power to govern. It is the striving of man to find a way to discipline or to organize into a collective society huge populations that has produced the ferments of discontent and the organized pressures of political combat.

Likewise, it is the struggle for some permanence in the international field that has brought us a galaxy of proposals, all the way from treaties that bind nations together in alliances or regional agreements, to wider federations and schemes for world government.

Here we meet the extremists—those who, with a passion for uniformity, would put all the peoples of the earth under a single sovereignty, and those who would discourage all schemes for collective security and go back to an era of irresponsible nationalism.

Why is it that we seek the hardest way instead of the simplest? It is necessary to recognize that certain problems are insoluble now. We make progress from the moment we reach that decision. For then we can devise ways and means of living with insolubility. With that achieved, we can strive for the ultimate—but in its proper perspective.

Security, it must be emphasized, is not, however, such an "insoluble" question. The law of self-preservation bids us pool our own strength and that of other nations in a common plan for defense against a common enemy. This, to be sure, is not a permanent solution. It is a temporary answer to the threats of world disturbance that we face. The North Atlantic Treaty is temporary. The United Nations is temporary. All our alliances are temporary. Peace itself is temporary.

Man, nevertheless, cannot give up hoping for a permanent solution for the problems that beset him. He must not, at the same time, in reaching for the impossible, forfeit the possible.

Basically, there is only one permanence we can all accept. It is the permanence of a God-governed world. For the power of God is alone permanent. Obedience to His laws is the only road to lasting solutions of man's problems.

This concept was affirmed by the group of prominent clergymen who, in their report to the Second Assembly of the World Council of Churches, wrote:

"Because God has not abandoned this world, because He rules and overrules its tangled history, and because we have been given a share in the power of His Spirit, we can with confidence hope and expect that what is built upon the foundations which He has laid will stand."

ERODING THE 48 STATES

JUNE 1, 1956

THE PRESENT JUSTICES of the Supreme Court of the United States by their unanimous decision last week moved a step nearer to complete erosion of the rights of State sovereignties in America.

The Court revealed a brazen indifference to the Bill of Rights—and particularly to the Tenth Amendment of the Constitution—by declaring for the second time this year that whenever the Federal Government pre-empts any field of law-making, the State Governments must stay out.

This is creeping usurpation. It is a denial of the rights which have long protected the States against the tyranny of intolerant majorities in Congress.

Specifically, the Supreme Court last week wiped out —so far as railroad employment is concerned—this provision of the Constitution of the State of Nebraska:

"No person shall be denied employment because of membership in or affiliation with, or resignation or expulsion from a labor organization or because of refusal to join or affiliate with a labor organization; nor shall any individual or corporation or association of any kind enter into any contract, written or oral, to exclude persons from employment because of membership in or non-membership in a labor organization."

Seventeen States have similar laws or constitutional provisions guaranteeing the "right to work." But the Supreme Court of the United States now proclaims that when Congress passes a prohibitory or permissive law in a particular field—such as the conditions of private employment on the railroads or air lines—the provisions of State Constitutions on the subject are automatically repealed.

The Federal law in question, passed by Congress in 1951, says that notwithstanding the law of any State, a railroad or air line may make an agreement with a labor organization requiring all employees within 60 days to become members of that labor organization.

Compulsion occurs through enforced payments of dues which the employer deducts from the pay envelope. Unless the worker is willing to pay tribute, he loses his job. He cannot get further employment on the railroads or air lines unless he is willing to sacrifice his principles and involuntarily join an organization—political and economic—to whose tenets he may have conscientiously refused to conform.

Justice Douglas, who wrote the latest opinion for the Court, makes no secret of his enthusiasm for trade unionism which he claims has strengthened "the right to work." He insists, however, that this is now a "policy" of Congress. He adds that "Congress, acting within its constitutional powers, has the final say on policy issues." He argues that if Congress "acts unwisely, the electorate can make a change."

But how can the electorate change the Justices of the Supreme Court? Must we revive the platform of the Progressive Party of 1912, which, led by Theodore Roosevelt, advocated the "recall of judicial decisions" by vote of the electorate?

The principle of compulsory unionism can, of course, be extended by Congress to all fields of employment. A worker's earnings, moreover, can now be taxed by two private economic groups—the employer and the union operating together.

It has been generally assumed as a result of a decision of the Supreme Court in 1935, that any private system of government is unconstitutional. For in that year the Court unanimously declared that Congress could not delegate to private economic groups the right to make NRA Code agreements of their own between employers and unions and thereby set up their own system of private government.

Yet Justice Douglas boldly writes today in behalf of a unanimous Court:

"If private rights are being invaded, it is by force of an agreement made pursuant to Federal law which expressly declares that state law is superseded. In other words, the Federal statute is the source of the power and authority by which any private rights are lost or sacrificed.

"The enactment of the Federal statute authorizing union shop agreements is the governmental action on which the Constitution operates, though it takes a private agreement to invoke the Federal sanction."

So now the Supreme Court sanctions a private system of government after all—a system of confiscation of the workers' earnings, moreover, by which his money—his property—is taken from him under duress.

The Tenth Amendment of the Constitution states that "The powers not delegated to the United States by the Constitution, nor prohibited by it to the States, are reserved to the States respectively, or to the people."

The Supreme Court of the United States has deliberately ignored that stipulation. In case after case in recent months, the Court has deprived the States of their basic and original rights. To paraphrase the late Justice Cardozo—this is "usurpation run riot."

THE TIDES OF HISTORY

JUNE 8, 1956

THE SPIRIT OF NATIONALISM—freedom from foreign rule—is accepted today as democratic doctrine.

The aspirations of peoples to achieve self-government are given wide support irrespective of their readiness for responsibilities and often in flagrant disregard of the rights of minorities.

The slogan of the hour is "anti-colonialism."

But somehow the hue and cry is being directed primarily toward governments in the free world.

What of the hopes and desires, however, of the millions of people who are under the yoke of the Moscow and Peking governments?

What of the peoples of Latvia and Lithuania and Estonia who had their independence taken from them almost at the beginning of World War II and whose liberties have never been restored?

What of the land of the heroic Masaryk—the highly literate and democratic nation of Czechoslovakia—which today is occupied by Soviet troops and ruled by a government of foreign commissars? What of the suffering people of East Germany who, ten years after the end of the war, are still prisoners?

What of Hungary and Bulgaria, of Rumania and of Poland? Each of these nations won their freedom from colonialism at the end of World War I when President Wilson's historic plea of "self-determination" echoed around the world. Today they are captives under the ruthless colonialism of Soviet Russia.

But do we hear any loud voices of dissent?

Mostly we hear from various newspapers of influence in Britain and France, as well as from what are often described as "liberal" newspapers in the United States, the repeated advice that we must accept all this as a necessary part of "peaceful co-existence."

George Kennan, chief adviser to Messrs. Truman and Acheson on Soviet affairs and now reported to be Adlai Stevenson's principal mentor on foreign policy, declares in his speeches that there is a "finality" about the present situation in Eastern Europe. He apparently favors our acceptance of the *status quo*—even though it means the surrender of all our ideals.

Perhaps the most significant demonstration of the defeatism which has afflicted the "liberals" is their attitude toward the word "liberation" itself. When John Foster Dulles used the word, he was promptly assailed as a "warmonger" by spokesmen for the Democrats. Although he denied that he was advocating a war of liberation in behalf of the satellite peoples and said he favored their "peaceful liberation," criticism of him on this point by the "liberals" has never abated.

There is, on the part of these same critics, a noticeable tendency to urge the soft-pedaling of any policies which encourage the peoples of the satellite states to revolt.

Why do so many of our American "liberals"—Walter Reuther, for instance, who has been making a lot of speeches lately criticizing Western "colonialism"—overlook the importance of sustaining the morale of the peoples of the satellite states? Why forget the peoples of the Ukraine and the many other colonies in the Soviet Union where national aspirations have never died? They are even more deserving of attention than the revolutionaries in Algeria, in Tunisia, in Morocco, in Cyprus, in Goa, and in Indo-China.

Why are Sukarno of Indonesia and Nehru of India so vocal about freedom for the half-civilized tribes of Asia and Africa and yet so silent about the peoples of Eastern Europe who only a few years ago enjoyed independence and freedom? Why do many Asian and European and American spokesmen wax so eloquent about the evils of "colonialism" and say nothing at all about the deep craving of the people of South Korea to be united with their brethren in North Korea now held in bondage by the cruel colonialists of Peking?

The fact is that Soviet colonialism today holds captive hundreds of millions of people.

We will not be true to the principles of the Declaration of Independence if we allow ourselves to remain indifferent to the plight of the people behind the Iron Curtain. We need not, of course, go to war to help them win freedom, but we can refrain from giving moral support to their oppressors.

We must, for this reason, stop building up the respectability of gangster governments in the eyes of the world. For, by fraternizing with their envoys and missions, we enhance the Soviet Government's prestige and discourage the people behind the Iron Curtain who look to us for moral support.

To accept "peaceful co-existence"—the slogan of Soviet imperialists—is to betray our heritage.

If we believe in the emancipation of the enslaved, we must frequently, unequivocally and outspokenly take our stand beside the peoples who are oppressed by Soviet tyranny.

For, if the tides of history mean anything, they mean that the peoples now imprisoned by the Soviet Government will, if encouraged by the free world, strive unceasingly to win their freedom from Soviet colonialism.

THE ROAD TO WAR

JUNE 15, 1956

IT'S THE 1930's all over again.

Then, the League of Nations faltered by failing to enforce an economic embargo on Mussolini in his war of aggression against Ethiopia.

Today, the United Nations has failed to enforce an embargo on shipments of war materials to Red China, though the government at Peking was formally declared by the U. N. in 1951 to be an aggressor in Korea.

When Mussolini saw the League of Nations unable to enforce its own embargo in 1935 and 1936, he was encouraged in his aggression—and so was Hitler. As a consequence, in 1939 the world was at war.

Today we are witnessing a strange parallel. Great Britain, a member of the U. N., has broken ranks by consenting to the shipment of rubber from Malaya to Red China. Promptly the Indonesian Government, also a member of the U. N., announced last week that what Britain had done meant that the U. N. embargo was no longer in effect and hence she, too, now will ship rubber to Red China. Indonesia is the largest producer of natural rubber in the world.

In the 1930's Italy could not have waged war without oil and war materials from the Middle East and this hemisphere. The ministries of Great Britain and France floundered. They passed the buck to the United States by trying to give the impression that, because this country was not a member of the League of Nations, no embargo could be effective. But the late President Roosevelt advised them that he was willing to act separately to enforce the embargo in accordance with a then-existing law passed by Congress.

The truth is that London and Paris weakened at the critical moment in the face of economic and political pressures from within. This enabled Mussolini to win his war in Ethiopia. Taking advantage of the breakdown of allied unity, Hitler began building up his war machine and his stockpile of strategic materials with shipments from the West that were permitted up to the very eve of the outbreak of World War II.

But rubber in unlimited quantities is now to be shipped to Red China and, if the embargo imposed by the U. N. is to be wilfully disregarded by its own members, all strategic materials soon will be exported to the enemy. For Red China is still an unrepentant enemy. No peace treaty has ever been signed in Korea, and the terms of the armistice agreement there are being violated every day.

History tells us that, as the moral force of the League of Nations went to pieces in the 1930's, the statesmen of the West resorted to the direct approach in diplomacy. They fraternized with the aggressors and exchanged many trade missions and visits of high officials. The cry in Britain and France was, "You can do business with Hitler." And in September 1938, at Munich, Chamberlain and Daladier proclaimed that "peace in our times" had come at last.

But the dictators also turned then to the direct approach and won Stalin's help, first with a "neutrality" pact and then later with an agreement giving the Nazi armies a free hand in Western Europe without immediate fear of a second front.

Today, Khrushchev has won Tito of Yugoslavia and Nasser of Egypt and Nehru of India to the cause of "neutrality." This means a free hand for Soviet Russia in the Middle East and in Southeast Asia. What a feat of military strategy!

We may ask ourselves whether the dictators in Moscow and Peking now may take the risk of encouraging some of those so-called "smaller wars" which can bring on a world war. Hitler, too, was confident that Britain and France would not fight to save Poland in a small war. Must we again expend human lives to disprove a fatal miscalculation by dictators?

This is a dangerous time in world affairs. The Communists see a divided alliance in the West, a collapsing U. N., a faltering NATO, and now a faltering SEATO as the faith of our allies in the Western Pacific is shaken by the unfortunately-phrased remarks of the White House press conference last week which had the disastrous effect of encouraging the "neutralists" in Europe as well as in Asia.

Will the dictators in Moscow see the coming months as a time to solidify their internal situation by seeking new conquests in the international field?

It is a dark prospect for the world. Overnight the chances of involvement in a world war have been increased. For as the disarmament intrigue progresses, it is possible that both sides will agree never to use nuclear weapons. Then conventional war could be thrust upon us as Soviet Russia's master stroke.

Whatever kind of war is threatened, the American people, through wise statesmanship, can and must be protected against its outbreak. Responsibility for carrying out that objective rests as much upon London and Paris as it does upon Washington.

War materials must not be shipped to the aggressors. We have kept the faith. But last week's news of the breakdown of the U. N. embargo was, indeed, ominous.

A CONFUSED COURT

JUNE 22, 1956

SITTING AS THE HIGHEST COURT of law—supposedly aloof from the polemics of partisan politics and ideological friction—the Supreme Court of the United States has long been held in reverence by the American people.

But today the Supreme Court, its decisions characterized by palpable inconsistencies and extremist philosophies, presents a picture of confusion that is causing dismay among the lawyers of the nation. Many of the Court's opinions and dissents sound like speeches on the political stump or like the impassioned arguments of "cause" groups in their mass meetings.

Three Justices—Reed, Clark and Minton—have for the most part refused to join the majority of the Court in their attempt to write new legislation. Occasionally, two other Justices—Harlan and Burton—have supported the dissenters to make a majority, but sometimes, by their concurrence, they have given majority sanction to the extremist position of Justices Black, Frankfurter, Douglas and Warren.

Here are some rulings of our highest tribunal in recent weeks:

1. By a 6-to-3 vote, the Court declared that a worker in California could be fired for being a Communist when the union-and-employer contract includes a provision for dismissal for "just cause." But Justices Black, Douglas and Warren held that being a Communist is a matter of "political belief" and that the Communist Party is just another political party like the Republican and Democratic parties. Congress wrote in 1954 a declaration that the Communist Party here is "the agency of a hostile foreign power."

2. The President was authorized by Congress in 1950 to determine at his discretion which agencies of the Government are "sensitive," and, by Executive Order, in 1953 all of them were designated as related to the national security. Six Justices—Frankfurter, Black, Douglas, Warren, Burton and Harlan—"repealed" this statute and said the loyalty-security program cannot, under existing law, be applied to "nonsensitive" agencies. A traitor in the Government is presumably outside the jurisdiction of the loyalty-security program if he doesn't work in a "sensitive" agency. Justices Reed, Minton and Clark vigorously dissented from the decision and said the majority "has stricken down the most effective weapon against subversive activity available to the Government."

3. By a 6-to-3 vote, Justices Frankfurter, Black, Douglas, Warren, Clark and Harlan ruled that a State

may not punish treason because Congress intended that the Federal Government act exclusively in this field. The majority of the Court disregarded the expressed intent of the authors of the law as written in the Federal Criminal Code itself. Justices Reed, Minton and Burton, in their dissent, said the majority ruling "cannot be reconciled with a clear authorization" by Congress permitting State legislation on the subject.

4. By a 5-to-4 vote, the Court's majority—Justices Black, Douglas, Frankfurter, Warren and Clark—ruled unconstitutional the summary dismissal of a school teacher by New York State authorities for refusing to tell whether or not he was a Communist. The dissenting Justices—Reed, Minton, Burton and Harlan—said this "unduly circumscribes the power of the State to insure the qualifications of its teachers."

5. By a 7-to-2 vote, the Court's majority—Justices Frankfurter, Reed, Minton, Clark, Burton, Warren and Harlan—upheld a 1954 law of Congress which grants immunity to a witness who might otherwise incriminate himself if he told his Government the truth about Communist activities as he knew them. Justices Black and Douglas dissented and said no immunity law could require a man to help his own Government if he chose not to do so.

6. By a 5-to-4 vote, the Court's majority—Justices Black, Douglas, Frankfurter, Warren and Clark—ruled that the laws of the State of Illinois didn't provide proper procedures because a convicted burglar was required to furnish for his appeal a copy of the court record and didn't have the money to pay for it. Justices Reed, Minton, Burton and Harlan dissented and thought the State of Illinois should be allowed to deal with that kind of local problem.

Need any more examples be given?

The Supreme Court cannot be reversed except by constitutional amendments or by new laws that meet the objections of a capricious and arbitrary court. Woodrow Wilson wrote in 1907:

"Every government is a government of men, not of laws, and of course the courts of the United States are no wiser or better than the judges who constitute them. A series of bad appointments might easily make them inferior to every other branch of the government in their comprehension of constitutional principles, their perception of constitutional values. But that would be because the government had fallen into wrong hands, and would not invalidate the principle upon which our courts are constituted and empowered."

IF—

IF SOVIET RUSSIA drops H-bombs on the territory of the United States, we will retaliate instantly with superbombs.

If Soviet Russia, however, starts a war in Europe or Asia and does not use atomic weapons, we will not use them either. There is no agreement to this effect now. There may never be. But it is clear that public opinion within the Western nations will not sanction the actual use of atomic bombs unless and until the other side employs them. We already have shown that we preferred to lose the war in Korea rather than use atomic weapons.

If Soviet Russia attacks any country which is a member of the North Atlantic Treaty Organization and does not use atomic weapons, the United States stands committed to resist such an attack but not necessarily with atomic weapons. The decision whether to use nuclear weapons must be made by the civilian governments of our allies because they control our overseas bases. It will not be made by the military commanders. This is the assurance that has been given publicly by the British and French parliaments.

If only conventional weapons are used to resist an attack by the Soviet Union on Western European countries and no atomic bombs are employed, Soviet Russia will dominate the conflict because it has a land army of more than 10,000,000 men even after the reduction of 1,200,000 recently proposed.

If a conventional war is fought in Europe, the Soviet Union would be an easy victor because the land armies of NATO are small and there is already a movement in Western countries to cut down the term of conscription, to curtail navies and armies and to depend on nuclear weapons even though it has become doubtful whether they would be used.

If the Soviet Union threatens to use nuclear weapons on the Western countries in the event that they say they will allow their bases to be used by American bombing airplanes carrying conventional bombs, it is likely that "neutralist" sentiment will increase in those countries and hamper the defense of those allied countries by the military forces of the United States.

If the next war, therefore, is not to be fought with nuclear weapons—and every day it seems more certain that Soviet Russia will not use them and we most surely would not initiate their use—then, it may be asked, of what avail is the "new look" in armament and the tendency of Congress to appropriate more and more money for weapons that will not be used?

If the United States doesn't keep up with Soviet Russia in building more and more planes and more and more superbombs, the chances of deterring a big war and preventing the use of nuclear weapons are lessened. So the United States must continue to appropriate large sums for both conventional and unconventional weapons. This means an increased burden for the taxpayers of this country and of our allies.

If there is an indefinite continuance of the armament race on the scale outlined, the economic load will become unbearable and the Western system of democracies will be gravely impaired or broken down altogether.

If there is to be any security in the world, it is not the atomic weapons which must be abolished but the dictatorships which at any moment can suddenly order the use of those weapons.

If the world is to be made safe for the democracies to live in, then autocratic governments must be put out of business. Only governments that are based on the consent of the governed should be permitted to take their place. The issue for each of our countries is not some scheme for world government or world tyranny but survival of independent nations.

If we are to prevent wars, there must be free governments everywhere.

If we want to assure the establishment of free governments, we must reach peoples.

It is not really a matter of money to furnish economic aid to so-called "uncommitted" or "neutralist" countries. These should not be the primary source of our concern. We should concentrate on ways and means of laying before the peoples of Soviet Russia and the satellite states all the facts about the international menace of dictatorship.

We have the example of freedom on our side. The dictatorship in the Kremlin is already making confused alibis and explanations. Now is the time to insist on laying the case directly before the other peoples of the world. We ought to have the ingenuity to do this huge job of persuasion. Means are not lacking. The President's voice is a powerful one.

Once the implications of the non-use of nuclear weapons are fully understood, the American people will be better able to see the grave danger that lies ahead for all democracies. We must win the peoples of Soviet Russia and their many oppressed nationalities to the banner of freedom. They alone can save us. It's our only chance.

CONFORMITY BY COERCION?

JULY 6, 1956

IT IS NECESSARY to come to grips with the issue of enforced integration in the nation's schools. It is a legal issue, a moral issue, a sociological issue, and a political issue.

Yet all these diverse approaches only accentuate the real question—conformity or non-conformity in organized society. It is an issue that for generations has confronted mankind.

The perennial conflict fundamentally is between theoretical equality and actual equality.

Government usually is concerned with theoretical equality. But too often, in the passion for uniformity, obstacles arise to the practical application of the law. Sooner or later revision is found necessary. An adjustment to realistic conditions becomes inevitable.

Obedience to law is a precept with which few will disagree, but disrespect for a law written by agents of the people in contradiction of the real will of the people leads to disobedience, disregard or repeal.

Conformity itself is a dangerous dogma when dependent solely on coercion. It is a device by which freedom often has been destroyed and totalitarianism substituted. Conformity of thought imposed by law is the tool of despots.

Conformity means that everybody must think alike, act alike, and obey the edicts of a central authority.

Our Constitution was built upon the fundamental principle that government derives its just powers from "the consent of the governed."

Realizing that our republic was founded by groups with conflicting interests, often widely separated by big distances, our forefathers conceived the idea of separate States. Each State was to be sovereign—endowed with the right to govern itself within its own area. Only in the case of infringement upon other States was the national authority to be invoked.

The founding fathers, to be sure, realized that they could not apply a rule of conformity over the people of a vast territory. So they delegated to the several States the right to deal with their own sociological problems. This is why education, for example, has always been a local problem. It is also one of the reasons why the maintenance of law and order has been primarily a State and city responsibility.

Conformity cannot be successfully compelled where the customs and morals of the people are in conflict with statutory law. It has often been truly said that "government cannot legislate morals."

Perhaps the best demonstration of this in recent years was the experience of the nation with the 18th Amendment. For decades there had been attempts to solve the prohibition problem. Many States had passed "dry" laws. Congress tried to regulate the liquor traffic across State lines. The federal courts, while upholding the interstate aspects, were careful to refrain from imposing upon each individual State an obligation to conform to a moral code which specified that people must not drink intoxicating liquors.

When the 18th Amendment, however, was ratified in 1920 as a part of the Constitution, the entire nation was asked to conform to a formula which forbade the manufacture and sale of intoxicating beverages anywhere in the United States. This meant that the will of a State was superseded entirely by national law.

What was the result? The effort to produce conformity failed. This was because the evils which came in the wake of the 18th Amendment proved to be far greater than the evils which the Amendment sought to correct. Disobedience of law became widespread.

Bootlegging, which began to thrive immediately after the Amendment was adopted, brought in its wake vice and crime and organized gangs. Some of these gangs which had their origin at that time have not been entirely eradicated from our communities to this day.

It will be recalled that, while the 18th Amendment was a part of the Constitution for nearly 14 years, it took less than ten months during the year 1933 to get it repealed by the States after Congress submitted it to them.

This did not happen because public thinking on the use of intoxicating beverages had actually undergone any substantial change. Many people continued to think that the sale of intoxicating beverages was harmful to the community and that the manufacture of such products should be prohibited. Several States still have prohibition laws, varying according to local conditions. But the nation voted for repeal because of a general condition—the American people found that, despite vigorous efforts to enforce the law, the illicit manufacture and distribution of liquor had intensified.

Historical experience should have taught us that there is a distinct difference between the theory of equal rights and the conditions sometimes provoked by the application of laws which go counter to public sentiment in a community.

But, while we profess to believe in the right of a community to govern itself, do we always apply the doctrine in practice? We have tried in America to give city and State communities the right to govern themselves. Yet we interpose a federal authority sometimes and virtually disregard local self-government. Thus we impair a great principle—the right of self-government.

We have, for example, said, in effect, that, because the people in the Northern, Eastern and Western parts of the United States constitute a numerical majority, their will must prevail over the people in Southern communities.

What we are attempting to do today in America is to compel the minority in the South to conform to the supposed will of the majority in the North. Do we aim thereby to wipe out State autonomy altogether?

There are basic rules to which both minorities and majorities will give their support. Thus, individual rights of association—the practice of religion, the right to educate children in accordance with local custom or tradition, and the right of the minority, even though living in the same community with the majority, to pursue its own racial or religious customs—have all been recognized as just principles in organized society.

The theory of equal rights means that there can be no denial of any public rights to citizens. Thus, the right to vote is a public right. The right to hold office is a public right. The right to own property is a public right. The right to obtain an education in a city or county school is a public right.

There are, to be sure, certain public utilities, such as conveyances, and certain public facilities where rules of limitation should not be imposed by the majority which would put the minority at a physical disadvantage.

But this is a far cry from requiring that each community must compel conformity in the educational process.

If education were entirely an impersonal affair and there were no social life at all in the schools, we would be dealing with a different problem.

But majority as well as minority groups have an equal right to freedom of association or non-association. Voluntarism is the key.

If one individual, for example, does the same work as another, he is entitled to equal pay irrespective of race or creed or color. In some occupations where majorities object to working alongside of minorities, a problem of adjustment presents itself which in many instances can be solved by patience and some physical rearrangement of locker rooms and personal facilities so as to remove barriers to employment.

But attempts to impose conformity by coercion, whether in the legal or economic or social sphere, usually produce conditions not unlike those which followed the attempt to enforce the 18th Amendment.

We already hear zealous extremists advocating that troops be sent "to enforce the Constitution" and compel the South to integrate its public schools.

It is not a problem that will ever be settled by bayonets. Nor will it be settled by exhorting people to forget prejudices bred in them.

II—An Era of Friction

We have recently seen evidences of anger and violence in the North and South. We have also witnessed the use of retaliatory measures in communities in the South where the most amicable relations previously had prevailed between the races in the South. Voluntarism had made progress. Talk of coercion now retards progress.

It is an illusion to suppose that, under the threat of "law enforcement," these difficulties are going to lessen with the passage of time. For social customs and social life do not function by any rule of conformity. They are bound to continue in the diversity that human nature has provided.

There will inevitably be passive resistance to laws of enforced integration. The public-school systems of the South may even disintegrate so that education in that region may lag behind the rest of the country. It would be a tragic price to pay. But men of determination have been known to pay almost any price for what they consider to be the preservation of their inalienable rights. Prejudice cannot be legislated out of existence by law.

A compromise formula—segregation through equal but separate facilities of education—was first sanctioned in a Northern State. It was upheld by the Supreme Court of the State of Massachusetts in 1849.

For 30 years after the War Between the States, the Supreme Court of the United States wrestled with legal issues growing out of racial conflict, and in 1896 ruled that systems of "equal facilities, even though separate" were constitutional. This permitted minorities to live alongside majorities in harmony.

Now, however, 60 years later, the Supreme Court of the United States, having reversed itself, is attempting to impose conformity. It should be noted that the Court, in its decision in 1954, did not say the separate educational facilities previously provided had been unequal —indeed, they have at times been even superior for the Negro. The Court took the position that, although the facilities were equal, they could not be permitted to be separate. Reliance was placed on sociological reasons— not legal precedents. The basic argument accepted was that a psychological impact of an adverse nature had occurred—that Negro children felt themselves inferior wherever segregation was legalized. It was the act of "discrimination" itself which the Court held to be illegal.

Now, as a consequence, however, a counter-conflict on the sociological front has arisen. White parents in the South are arguing that the impact of integration will prove harmful to their children. Will the Court now give equal weight to this plea, or tell the white parents to send their children to private schools, which so many citizens cannot afford?

III—Social Relationships

So we are back again in the realm of the sociological —how can we get majorities and minorities to live harmoniously in the same community?

But it will be asked whether the right to attend a public school does not include the right to attend any public school. The right of assignment of pupils is a local—not a national—function. Even today, the most ardent exponent of equal rights would not deny that it is within the power of the State to set up schools in which there is segregation by reason of sex—all girls in one school and all boys in another school, irrespective of color.

If, for sociological reasons, it is deemed desirable to separate the sexes in the schools, there would be no constitutional barrier against this even though one State chooses to adopt the plan and another State does not. For we usually recognize as absolute the right of each State community to regulate its social life, provided there is no denial to anyone of the right to public education itself. The States can, moreover, if they wish, subsidize private schools—provided they do not discriminate as between individuals in allocating funds.

The question before the country today is whether communities are free to adjust their school systems to meet their own local conditions and local sentiment. Those States which desire to integrate their schools ought to have the sovereign right to do so, and those which desire to operate mixed schools in some counties and separate their schools in other counties, either by color or by sex or by intelligence tests, should have the same sovereign right.

It is argued, on the other hand, that, since the public schools are tax-supported and because tax receipts come from all citizens, all public schools must be opened to all citizens. But the same point—equality of participation—could be made with respect to admission to church organizations, private clubs and private schools. They, too, are supported by all taxpayers because an exemption from State and federal income taxes is given them as "non-profit-making" institutions.

Theoretically, wherever the Government confers its favors, there rests authority to regulate—to withdraw those favors unless the regulation which imposes conformity is accepted. Today the President's Commission on Interracial Discrimination has adopted this principle as the genesis of its power. The Executive Order under which the Commission functions provides that whosoever benefits from any government contract must conform to its requirements against discrimination in employment if based on "race, creed, color or national origin."

The central issue in the school question, however, is one of social relationships. Rooted in the minds of many people in the South is a fear that personal associations begun in the elementary schools will lead to a state of mind among youth that will bring more intermarriage of races.

If intermarriage became widespread, it seems certain that communities would insist upon some other way of preventing them—either by ostracism or by curtailing economic opportunities in the community to those who deviate from custom.

If there were only a few intermarriages in a given State, they probably would not attract much attention. But once they became numerous, the local communities would frown upon them. Public sentiment sometimes is stronger than law in bringing about a reform or change which the law itself could never impose.

What are the limits of conformity? Conformity in theory is justified, especially when the entire national interest is involved—in times of national peril. Thus, in theory, we are not supposed to recognize any distinctions when it comes to military service. But actually we do discriminate here, too. Even the conscientious objector is allowed to refrain from participation in active combat. Able-bodied women are not compelled to fight in the front lines though women have equal rights of citizenship. "Equality" has its exceptions.

At most it must be said that the problem is not going to be solved if there is a failure to analyze studiously the viewpoints of the opposing groups. It is a situation that ultimately will have to bow to the enlightened principle that majorities and minorities each have a right to regulate their own lives and their own customs.

Thus, treaties signed at the end of World War I established an obligation upon some of the new governments in Central Europe to allocate public funds for educational, religious and charitable purposes to "racial, religious, or linguistic minorities" within their borders. The League of Nations was given the task of guaranteeing the observance of these minority rights.

The more we examine the formulas that have been developed throughout the world to permit minorities to get along with majorities, the more we will find that adjustments precisely of this nature have been conducive to conditions of harmonious living.

IV—Is The 14th Amendment Valid?

We hear the argument, "But it's the law of the land." There is a grave question whether the 14th Amendment, under which integration is ordered, was ever legally submitted to the States and legally ratified. The specific point has never been passed upon by the Supreme Court, though the public has taken it for granted for years that the 14th Amendment is an integral part of the Constitution.

What are the facts? It is necessary as an initial step for any amendment to the Constitution to be passed by a two-thirds vote of both houses of Congress. Yet, in June 1866, when the 14th Amendment was voted upon in Congress, each House had excluded all persons appearing with credentials in the first instance as Senators or Representatives from the ten Southern States of Virginia, North Carolina, South Carolina, Georgia, Florida, Alabama, Mississippi, Louisiana, Arkansas and Texas. If these Southern States had been permitted to vote in Congress, the Amendment would not have passed.

Then, when the Amendment was submitted to the legislatures of the several States, it needed to be ratified by 28 States, which was three-fourths of the 37 States then in the Union. Ten States, therefore, were able to block ratification.

But the 14th Amendment was never ratified by California, and was rejected at the time by Kentucky, Delaware and Maryland. It was rejected during the latter part of 1866 and the early part of 1867 also by the legislatures of the ten Southern States. For the 14th Amendment had in it many objectionable clauses. Apart from its provision requiring States to guarantee "equal protection of the laws," the Amendment sought to punish former Confederate soldiers by forbidding them to hold office even in their own States unless Congress by a two-thirds vote removed the disability.

It was argued, moreover, in those days that the State governments in the South were not legal governments but were merely "rebel States." Yet these States at the time had already received presidential recognition, and when the same Southern legislatures in 1865 had ratified the 13th Amendment—which abolished slavery—their action was accepted as legal by the Secretary of State. For the South had, by its vote, made possible the three-fourths vote of the States necessary for the adoption of the 13th Amendment.

Furthermore, in the Reconstruction Act of 1867 Congress arrogantly proclaimed that self-rule would be restored to the States and they would be permitted representation in Congress once more only when they adopted the 14th Amendment. It was so stipulated in the law which had been passed over the veto of President Andrew Johnson. He emphasized its injustices and unconstitutional aspects, and denounced it as "a bill of attainder against nine million people."

Here is what Senator Doolittle of Wisconsin, a conservative Republican of the North, said about the proposal on the floor of the Senate:

"My friend has said what has been said all around me, what is said every day: the people of the South have rejected the constitutional amendment, and therefore we will march upon them and force them to adopt it at the point of the bayonet, and establish military power over them until they do adopt it."

This was a flagrant case of conformity by coercion.

The Act of Congress was a direct violation of the letter of the Constitution. For Congress has no power to coerce the States when they pass upon the question of whether or not they will ratify or reject proposed constitutional amendments.

"Puppet" governments established in the Southern States did finally "ratify" the 14th Amendment in 1868 but only under duress—with registration of voters being supervised by military commanders from the North and with millions of white voters deliberately disenfranchised by the Reconstruction Act because they had fought in the war against the Union. Ohio and New Jersey attempted unsuccessfully that same year to withdraw their acts of ratification before the Secretary of State formally proclaimed the Amendment as adopted. Doubt was expressed at the time by the President as to the validity of the alleged ratification.

Can it be said that all this action was in accord with the spirit of American fair play? Will this record stand up as constitutional—as the "consent of the governed"? Would we say today that the people in any place under military occupation are able freely to exercise their sovereign rights? The Reconstruction Act for many years deprived the Southern States of their powers of governmental autonomy. They recovered these powers only after a long and tragic era of military compulsion.

Should not the Supreme Court today re-examine the validity of the 14th Amendment? If an important decision of 1896 can be reopened and reversed by the Supreme Court in 1954, is it not logical to resurvey the doubtful procedure whereby the 14th Amendment itself was forced into the Constitution? The present Court has shown itself quite solicitous lately that persons in our midst charged with disloyalty be given the protection of "due process." Cases involving Communists have, on the slightest pretext of technicality, been ordered for retrial. Can't we give the same consideration to the States which have demonstrated their loyalty to the Union?

If it were presented anew today, there would not be a two-thirds vote of both houses of Congress to approve the 14th Amendment unless a specific reservation were made on the points now at issue.

The reason is clear. More than a third of the membership of both houses at present feel that the 14th Amendment was itself amended by the Supreme Court in 1954 and that, as long as this new legislative action by the Court stands as the official interpretation, it makes the original language of the 14th Amendment inadequate.

V—The Philosophical Approach

What do the philosophers of history say about conformity?

George Santayana in "Dominations and Powers" (1951)—a work sometimes referred to as comparable to Plato's "Republic" or to the "Ethics" of Aristotle—makes this pertinent comment:

"This ideal of a perfect ultimate democracy rests on two assumptions: that human nature in all men is essentially similar, and that consequently mankind could not fully develop its vital liberty without coming to a unanimous vision of the world and a cooperative exercise of the same virtues. I think this is a biological error, and that what is identical in all life is only its germ, from which all plants and animals have developed centrifugally, as circumstances have allowed them to develop. . . .

"The uniformity in American principles, as proclaimed publicly and as genuinely felt by most people, is no index to a natural unity in the vital forces at work among them. The proof appears if we consider a notorious fact: the Constitution of the United States, since the Civil War, establishes the equality of all citizens, irrespective 'of race, colour, or previous condition of servitude.' And this is not merely a constitutional sham, like so many of the provisions in paper constitutions in other countries. It expresses an earnest conviction, dearly defended, by a great part of the people.

"Nevertheless whenever a difference of race, colour, religion, or breeding is not so overcome in the rush of common work or duty as to pass unnoticed or even unknown, if an attempt is made to ignore it in comradeship, society, marriage, or place of residence, the real difference in the soul is instantly recognized, and an irresistible impulse causes the groups to segregate.

"This is set down by democratic doctrinaires to prejudice or snobbery. They do not perceive that contrast of character and taste can be ignored when people are engaged in some *instrumental* action, to which their moral diversity is irrelevant; but that as soon as the labour is over, and the *liberal life* of play, art, affection, and worship begins, both sides equally require moral comprehension and are equally chilled, bored, and rendered sterile when comprehension is absent.

"That a white man *ought* to hobnob with a Negro because otherwise he would not be Christian or unselfish involves a flagrant assumption of superiority. The Negro, if he is not a fool, loves his own inspiration, and expands in the society of his own people. Vital liberty differentiates. Only vacant freedom leaves all in the same anonymous crowd."

G. K. Chesterton, in his famous work "Orthodoxy," wrote in 1908:

"In modern ideal conceptions of society there are some desires that are possibly not attainable: but there are some desires that are not desirable. That all men should live in equally beautiful houses is a dream that may or may not be attained. But that all men should live in the same beautiful house is not a dream at all; it is a nightmare."

Alexis de Tocqueville, of France, a renowned philosopher who visited America in the 1830's and compared it with the systems of government in vogue from ancient days, expressed himself vehemently on the subject of tyrannical majorities—the effort by law to impose upon the minority certain customs and rules that did not have universal sanction.

Yet de Tocqueville was hopeful about America's future, little realizing the grave conflicts that were to come in later years because of the abuse of the very principles about which he wrote in 1835:

"But in the United States, the majority, which so frequently displays the tastes and the propensities of a despot, is still destitute of the most perfect instrument of tyranny.

"In the American republics the central government has never as yet busied itself except with a small number of objects, sufficiently prominent to attract its attention. The secondary affairs of society have never been regulated by its authority; and nothing has hitherto betrayed its desire of even interfering in them.

"The majority has become more and more absolute, but has not increased the prerogatives of the central government; those great prerogatives have been confined to a certain sphere; and although the despotism of the majority may be galling upon one point, it cannot be said to extend to all. However the predominant party in the nation may be carried away by its passions, however ardent it may be in the pursuit of its projects, it cannot oblige all the citizens to comply with its desires in the same manner and at the same time throughout the country.

"When the central government which represents that majority has issued a decree, it must entrust the execution of its will to agents over whom it frequently has no control and whom it cannot perpetually direct.

"If an oppressive law were passed, liberty would still be protected by the mode of executing that law; the majority cannot descend to the details and what may be called the puerilities of administrative tyranny. It does not even imagine that it can do so, for it has not a full consciousness of its authority."

Perhaps it is in recognition of these very difficulties that Robert Morrison MacIver, whose name means as much to modern sociology as does that of John Dewey to philosophy, gives some pointed advice in his book, "The More Perfect Union," excerpts from which appear on pages 106-133 of this issue. He offers a "program for the control of inter-group discrimination." It is definitely sympathetic to integration. Yet he gives this word of caution:

"Discrimination and its evils are likely to be exacerbated by any changes that increase tensions or promote crises in a society, no matter what their source, whether economic, political, ideological, or any other. On the other hand discrimination is likely to be diminished by any changes that make for the general well-being of a society or that provide more constructive outlets for the aggressive tendencies of its groups."

VI—Lincoln On "Social Equality"

It is sometimes asserted, though mistakenly, that, once the Supreme Court has ruled upon a subject, there is no appeal—not even to public opinion. Lincoln didn't think so. He denounced the Supreme Court for its decision in the Dred Scott case. He was outspoken against "social equality."

When Lincoln argued against slavery he pointed to the impairment of personal freedom within the community—the individual had been deprived of his liberty—the right to make his own life. But Lincoln said this did not mean enforced association between the races. Debating in Illinois with Stephen Douglas, in September 1858, Lincoln said:

"I will say then that I am not nor ever have been in favor of bringing about in any way the social and political equality of the white and black races—that I am not, nor ever have been, in favor of making voters or jurors of negroes, nor of qualifying them to hold office, nor to intermarry with white people; and I will say in addition to this that there is a physical difference between the white and black races which, I believe, will forever forbid the two races living together on terms of social and political equality. And inasmuch as they cannot so live, while they do remain together there must be the position of superior and inferior, and I as much as any other man am in favor of having the superior position assigned to the white race."

But it is insisted: "The Supreme Court has spoken." De Tocqueville's eloquent answer may be applied to the issue today. He wrote:

"When I refuse to obey an unjust law, I do not contest the right of the majority to command, but I simply appeal from the sovereignty of the people to the sovereignty of mankind. Some have not feared to assert that a people can never outstep the boundaries of justice and reason in those affairs which are peculiarly its own; and that consequently full power may be given to the majority by which it is represented. But this is the language of a slave.

"A majority taken collectively is only an individual, whose opinions, and frequently whose interests, are opposed to those of another individual, who is styled a minority. If it be admitted that a man possessing absolute power may misuse that power by wronging his adversaries, why should not a majority be liable to the same reproach? Men do not change their characters by uniting with one another; nor does their patience in the presence of obstacles increase with their strength. . . .

"When an individual or a party is wronged in the United States, to whom can he apply for redress? If to public opinion, public opinion constitutes the majority; if to the legislature, it represents the majority and implicitly obeys it; if to the executive power, it is appointed by the majority and serves as a passive tool in its hands. The public force consists of the majority under arms; the jury is the majority invested with the right of hearing judicial cases; and in certain States even the judges are elected by the majority. However iniquitous or absurd the measure of which you complain, you must submit to it as well as you can."

VII—Jefferson On Judicial Tyranny

Thomas Jefferson warned against the tyranny of judges. He wrote in 1804:

"But the opinion which gives to the judges the right to decide what laws are constitutional, and what not, not only for themselves in their own sphere of action, but for the Legislature and executive also, in their spheres, would make the judiciary a despotic branch."

Then, long after Jefferson left the Presidency, he wrote in 1820 and 1821:

"It is a misnomer to call a government republican, in which a branch of the supreme power is independent of the nation . . .

"A judiciary independent of a king or executive alone, is a good thing; but independence of the will of the nation is a solecism, at least in a republican government . . .

"To consider the judges as the ultimate arbiters of all constitutional questions (is) a very dangerous doctrine indeed, and one which would place us under the despotism of an oligarchy . . . The Constitution has erected no such single tribunal . . .

"The great object of my fear is the Federal Judiciary. That body, like gravity, ever acting, with noiseless foot, and unalarming advance . . . is engulfing insidiously the special governments into the jaws of that which feeds them."

How much this is like the doctrines of Thomas Hobbes! In his famous work "Leviathan," he wrote in 1651:

"Princes succeed one another; and one judge passeth, another cometh; nay, heaven and earth shall pass; but not one tittle of the law of Nature shall pass, for it is the eternal law of God. Therefore all the sentences of precedent judges that have ever been cannot altogether make a law contrary to natural equity."

A modern writer—Walter Lippmann—in his book "The Public Philosophy" (1955), says:

"There is a hiatus between the highest wisdom and the actual perplexities with which men must deal. An encyclopedia of all that the prophets and the philosophers have taught will not tell a man clearly and definitely how to make laws, how to govern a state, how to educate his children—how, in fact, to decide the problems that the priest encounters in the confessional, the doctor with his patients, the lawyer with his clients, the judge with the litigants, the man of affairs in his business."

VIII—Facing The Real Issue

Many people today are urging caution with respect to the integration problem—an approach that has come to be known as "gradualism." Its fallacy lies in the belief that what cannot be resolved now will be resolved by postponement. It assumes that equality is a natural right in the community and that all forms of discrimination can be abolished by the passage of time.

The fetish of conformity, however, has demoralized the life of many nations in the world through the centuries. Where minorities have been suppressed and the right to pursue their own lives and customs has been impaired, there has been discontent and, at times, eruptions of violence.

We see today in the island of Cyprus a bloody war because nobody has yet devised a plan whereby the Turkish minority can live alongside the Greek majority. We see the same tragedy in Algeria—as between the French minority and the native majority.

Self-determination does not mean the delegation of power to a tyrannical majority. It means adjustment of minorities alongside of majorities. In no other way can there be a maintenance of equity for all concerned.

Can we not in America find a way whereby majorities and minorities may get along with one another in peace? The Constitution of the United States provided for separate but not equal States. There was no provision that each State must be equal to the other in voting for President or in choosing members of the House of Representatives. Equality of representation was provided only in the Senate.

Theoretically, all men are created equal. It is a doctrine that could mean that all wealth in the community must be divided equally between all citizens. The Communists believe in such a doctrine. There have been men in America who have argued for the "redistribution of wealth." Do any of us honestly believe that harmonious society can ever be achieved by a law that requires all incomes to be equal, or that the possession of property should be equalized between all citizens?

Equality is a theoretical goal. Its application will depend always on the mores of the community. Even in our day some of the loudest voices declaiming against discrimination are men who in their business and social relationships are practicing discriminations of various kinds. It is common knowledge that membership in some of the principal clubs and organizations in many of our large cities and in the fraternities in almost all of our colleges is barred to persons of certain races or religions, as the case may be. It is common knowledge also that employers in the North, for the most part, give preference to applicants of certain ethnic origins or races as against others. There is, therefore, continuously applied a doctrine of discrimination which negates the theory of equality.

One need not agree at all with the reasons given for such discriminations—indeed, one may be offended by their practice. But if we are to rely on theory, there is as much right to discrimination as there is to non-discrimination. It is really the misguided attempt to override these separate and distinct rights of the individual by public law that causes the conflict of today.

Conformity by coercion is not liberalism. The answer is to be found in voluntarism—freedom's greatest vehicle of progress. It offers us the only solution to the vexatious problems of sociology in our republic.

CONGRESSIONAL "RACKETEERING"

JULY 13, 1956

THE HOUSE OF REPRESENTATIVES last week, by a vote of 225 to 192, recorded its view that, unless the Southern States abandon their convictions and surrender their principles, they should be punished by the withholding of federal funds for the erection of new schools and for other educational purposes in those States.

Fortunately, this amendment to a general bill which was to provide federal aid to education was nullified later when the entire measure was rejected. But the vote on the issue stands out as a disgraceful piece of attempted coercion.

For this was an effort to enforce conformity of thought in America.

The whole bill, of course, threatened an invasion of the historic right of the States to control their own educational systems. It never was intended that billions of dollars of taxpayers' money should be used to transfer control of our 48 separate educational operations from the States to a centralized bureaucracy in Washington.

Last week, moreover, the voting happened to be on a stipulation that certain Southern States must give up their lawful right to appeal from adverse court orders in any proper steps they may seek to take to postpone integration, even temporarily.

Next time the voting could be on a provision in an appropriation bill declaring that no funds be granted for any school unless there is conformity to a national curriculum of studies.

Once the principle of usurpation is accepted under the guise of financial paternalism directed by the national government, arguments about unconstitutionality will be of little avail. Even without a vote in Congress on any specific amendment, administrative action could be taken by an executive department to deny funds for schools in Southern States.

Fears of just such a contingency are well founded. Thus, there is no warrant of law today for the action of the President's interracial commission which asserts the right to withhold Government contracts from companies that do not comply with an Executive Order forbidding employers to discriminate in employment on the basis of race or creed or color or national origin. Companies which refuse to do the bidding of the Federal Government are threatened with loss of contracts. The present Executive Order could even now be readily broadened to deny to Southern schools aid of any kind, such as the payment of veterans' tuition under measures like the "GI Bill of Rights."

States, therefore, which decline to accept the discipline of an executive agency in Washington in the conduct of their schools could, under any bill in the future providing aid in general to education, find themselves unable to construct the necessary buildings in their localities or to keep up with the growing needs of an increased school population.

The Eisenhower Administration, to be sure, has publicly frowned upon the imposition of any conditions in connection with the grant of federal funds to aid the public schools of the States. The roll call nevertheless showed 148 Republicans and 77 Democrats from the North voting for the coercive amendment sponsored by Representative Powell, Democrat, of New York City.

This punitive proposal was a mockery of America's boasted freedom of conscience and freedom of thought.

It will be recalled that the Supreme Court of the United States itself, in its 1954 decision, placed no time limit on the specific orders that it expected the lower courts to issue in bringing about a gradual adjustment to the integration mandate. But if the amendment voted on last week by the House had become law, it would have foreclosed the opportunity to some Southern States to get federal funds during the interval that lower court orders on specific points were being argued or appealed to higher courts, as permitted under lawful procedures. The States were to be told, in effect:

"Give up your constitutional right of appeal or you get no money. Accept now without argument whatever orders are to be issued by the lower courts hereafter, or you will pay the penalty of having millions of dollars for schools withheld from your State in the meantime. Even if you do comply, a bureaucrat in Washington will have to be satisfied as to the exact nature of your compliance before your State gets any money."

What a tragic example of organized punishment and organized bribery—and this in free America, where the States are supposed to be sovereign and where even a Communist is given his full right of appeal from the lowest to the highest courts!

What new crimes will be committed in the name of "liberalism" and "equal rights under the law"?

What new extortions and demands will be made upon the minority by an intolerant majority which seeks to use the devices of legislative "racketeering" to establish conformity of thought in the House of Representatives today?

ILLUSIONS OF 1922 AND 1956

JULY 20, 1956

BACK IN 1922, they were saying there wouldn't be another war—it would be too terrible, there would be mutual destruction. It was believed then that at last the deterrent force had been found—poison gas. Yet a world war broke out in 1939, and poison gas wasn't used on either side.

Today we read that, because nuclear war would destroy mankind, this will prevent either side from beginning a war. We know that the mere possession of nuclear weapons did not prevent the Korean war from happening. Nor did it avert the long war in Indo-China.

It is interesting, therefore, to read exactly what Brigadier General Amos A. Fries, then Chief of the Chemical Warfare Service of the U. S. Army, wrote in the *Current History Magazine,* as condensed and published in *The Reader's Digest* in its issue of February 1922:

"War is today at the beginning of a complete change in armament. Greater progress has been made since the close of the war in perfecting and developing poison gas bombs than any nation foresaw three years ago. Poison gas, in this very brief period of time, has become the biggest potential military and naval problem of the world.

"1. Recent bombing tests off the Atlantic coast demonstrated that our coasts are almost impregnable against a foreign enemy who has to cross the ocean. If bombs containing poison gases can be dropped from airplanes upon or around enemy warships, if submarines can lay mines containing gases, and if gases in solid form, which will burn on water as well as on land, can be utilized to protect our coasts, chemical warfare is bound to have a great influence upon our methods of defense.

"The most expensive forms of armament are those most readily visible. Thus battleships, huge guns on railroad mounts, permanent fortifications, submarines, airplanes and numbers of soldiers themselves, are items that cannot be maintained or developed secretly in peace. All are subject to easy inspection, which will at once reveal whether or not a nation is keeping its agreement. But limitation of armament is not disarmament, nor is it necessarily abolition of war. Preparation for war can be neither successfully supervised nor repressed. . . .

"2. With the realization of this power of defense has come also the realization that great military power in the future will be measured far less by numbers of soldiers than in the past. The nation which has a coal supply sufficient to furnish power and coal tar products can make all the high explosives and war gases needed.

With the development of an air service she can, with comparatively small numbers of men, defend her shores against any enemy.

"We must expect that new gases, new methods of turning them loose, and new tactical uses will be developed. Gas is the only substance used in war which can be counted upon to do its work as efficiently at night as in the daytime. Chemical warfare has come to stay, and just in proportion as the United States gives chemical warfare its proper place in the military establishment, just in that proportion will the United States be ready to meet any or all comers in the future, for the United States has incomparable resources in crude materials that are necessary in the manufacture of gases.

"3. So long as wars were carried on solely by men trained in peace for that purpose—in other words, by a standing army—definite rules of warfare could be enforced. In other words, so long as the numbers of each nation not engaged in a war were much larger than the forces engaged, there was a sufficient force to make armies live up more or less well to fixed rules of carrying on warfare. When, however, whole nations became involved in war, and the fate of the entire nation hung in the balance, it became evident to thoughtful men that no set rules of warfare could be guaranteed. In other words, a nation fighting for its life will use any means that offer a chance to win.

"This must be accepted as fundamental and axiomatic, and all plans for future defense should be based thereon. Thus, no method of warfare that promises results can be abolished by agreement, unless all warfare can be so abolished. The last year, however, has been remarkable for the growth of feeling that the burden of preparation for war is too great, and with the growth of that opinion has come the feeling that the expensive forms of armament might safely be reduced by agreement. . . .

"Every development of science that makes warfare more universal and more scientific makes for permanent peace by making war intolerable, and I, for one, believe that all nations should be given to understand that if we are forced into a war we shall use every known chemical method of warfare against hostile forces wherever they are located. That would be our permanent guarantee against attack."

Will history repeat itself?

We are again being told that there will be no world war because neither side will venture to use H-bombs. But if war breaks out and no superbombs are used, who will win that war?

THE HONEYMOON IS OVER

JULY 27, 1956

No ACTION IN RECENT MONTHS has symbolized so effectively the dubious mood of Congress and of the American people toward giving away taxpayers' money to so-called "uncommitted" or "neutralist" nations, as the announcement last week by Secretary Dulles that the United States Government has withdrawn its offer to help Egypt build the Aswan Dam.

This project would have taken some 12 to 15 years to construct and would have cost about $1,300,000,000. The bulk of the money was to come from the United States. Unquestionably, this plan for irrigating a vast area and enabling the people to produce agricultural products on a large scale meant much to the future development of Egypt and its neighbors along the Nile.

But Premier Nasser fumbled the ball. By threatening a deal with the Soviets, he tried to play America off against the Communists. This is euphemistically described nowadays as "competitive coexistence."

Britain stood firm with the United States. Both governments saw through the maneuvers whereby Nasser was creating in the Middle East a hostile sentiment toward the West among the Arab States and decided that the project had better be abandoned.

The official reasons given by the United States and Britain are that Egypt herself could not furnish the necessary economic cooperation and that the other countries adjacent to Egypt have not worked out the necessary agreements on water rights. But the plain meaning of the cancellation is that Uncle Sam is tired of being played for a sucker in the world and has decided to let Moscow try to make good on her promises of economic aid to "uncommitted" countries.

Certainly the millions of people of Soviet Russia who haven't bread or clothing would look askance at a "giveaway" to Egypt—a country with which Moscow at best can have only tenuous ties. Also, the people in the enslaved states in Eastern Europe would be indignant at the spectacle of such a huge outpouring of Soviet funds by Moscow to a country strategically as far away as is Egypt.

So the policymakers of the United States Government wisely decided to call the Soviet's bluff. Naturally, the Egyptian Government, which has been playing "footsie" with the Moscow rulers, is surprised. But there are other surprises due—the Western nations may come to feel that other "neutral" leaders who have been snuggling up to the Soviet Union are perhaps not as good partners, after all, as they profess to be.

The news about the Aswan Dam came at the same time that Messrs. Nasser, Tito and Nehru were engaged in a conference deliberately planned to embarrass the West and to build up their own positions for trading purposes. Back of it all were the Communist strategists.

Unfortunately, in America and in Western Europe there are persons loyal to our side who believe it is wise to give taxpayers' money away to foreign governments without any strings. This has been dramatized as the way "to win men's minds." Along with it has come the familiar denunciation of "military alliances" which, to be sure, has coincidentally been emphasized in the Communist party line for a long time.

Yet for what other purpose but military defense do the American taxpayers make sacrifices? To build up Communist influence in India and in the Middle East? To let whimsical "neutralists" decide whether Moscow's tremendous preparations in armament are "peaceful" in intent? After all, it is the American family and the American city which will suffer if Soviet H-bombs are dropped. The "neutralist" leaders are not responsible for the safety and security of the American people. Only the American Government has that responsibility —and Congress, as the coordinate branch, has the duty of appropriating the money.

The recent antipathy in Congress, moreover, toward the grant of any further funds to Yugoslavia has been pronounced. The State Department has been hoping Tito would see the light and has asked that the door be kept open for him. But Congress recently has shown skepticism about such a policy. The days of giving away money with no questions asked are passing. The honeymoon is over.

Mr. Nasser, of course, has injured the chances for American aid to Egypt under his regime. The people of Egypt now must decide whether his leadership will force them more and more into the clutches of the Soviet Union or whether they should elect other leaders —if an uncoerced ballot is available—and join up with the West. That's where Egypt really belongs.

Countries that hesitate to make up their minds on a simple issue—whether the gangsters in Moscow are better partners than the leaders of the free governments of the West—perhaps need a period for meditation. And that's what they undoubtedly will have now. It's to be hoped they will soon perceive the difference between immorality and morality—between slavery and freedom, between insecurity and security, and between economic chaos and economic opportunity.

THE "GIVEAWAY" CONGRESS

AUGUST 3, 1956

THE FREEST IN SPENDING, the most extravagant in giving away the taxpayers' money, the biggest in "log-rolling" deals—the system whereby members reciprocate in aiding each other's projects—this is the strange record of the 84th Congress.

More than 60 billion dollars were appropriated at this session, and much of it as a plain subsidy to big voting groups. On the list is everything from expansion of federal payments for milk to be given free to children in public schools and summer camps—irrespective of their parents' ability to pay for it—to big projects benefiting particular localities and privileged groups in the electorate. It is perhaps the biggest variety of items in legislative history.

Even in the 34.6 billion dollars for armament, the "log rolling" for military expenditures by representatives from certain States and localities was palpable. Thus, 900 million dollars more than the Executive asked for was given him to spend. The Air Force, on which this bounty was bestowed, must now try to figure out how to spend it. What a travesty on government that Congress provides surplus funds before there is even a request from the Executive or a planned project for its use by the military department most concerned!

Beginning with the "soil bank" for the farmers, which cost 1.2 billions and which was designed primarily to head off a bigger "giveaway" by the opposite political party, the Republican Administration laid down the principle that the Federal Government and the local governments should share in the development of natural resources. This now has been interpreted by Republicans and Democrats to justify the largest series of projects of benefit to their particular areas that has been ushered in since the days when "pork barrel" legislation was the order of the day.

To meet the inflationary trend of the times, there were increases of pay voted for legislators, judges and executive officials. Increases in pensions were authorized, as well as new grants under the Social Security system, and, with all of this, the beginnings of a program which may open the door to medical insurance.

Though the nation is in a period of unprecedented prosperity, Congress authorized the largest amounts of "welfare" money ever voted.

Many of the schemes, moreover, call for relatively small payments at first—just a few millions a year now—but they build permanently into the governmental scheme of things a new series of expenditures which will pile up new appropriations for future Congresses to provide annually.

Broadly speaking, this was a non-radical Congress, in the sense that a coalition of conservatives in both parties managed to prevent the government-ownership advocates from getting the upper hand. The latter were balked in their efforts to get public-power projects enacted that could start the downfall of private electric power companies. There was a failure to break down the Taft-Hartley Act. This is because the Southern Democrats were able to block action on amendments. Fear that more unionization in the South would upset their own political power was the main reason. There was a noticeable opposition, too, from conservatives in both parties to various socialistic features of public housing.

If it hadn't been for the segregation issue, a construction fund for public schools amounting to a total of 1.6 billion dollars would have been voted. As it was, more than 368 million dollars was appropriated for school aid in areas where military installations have caused unusual increases in school populations.

Only in foreign aid was there a tendency to economize drastically. The Administration's original program was cut down by more than a billion dollars.

In the face of all this spending, almost nothing was heard about reduction of income taxes. The Treasury's surplus of 1.8 billion dollars was not enough, of course, on which to base a program of tax reduction. But who can say that restraint on spending would not have provided the American people with a bigger surplus which could have been used either to reduce taxes or to cut down the public debt? This debt now stands at 273 billion dollars.

Where is all the money coming from to meet the new obligations just piled on the taxpayers by Congress? It may turn out that the 84th Congress made a new record of some kind in preventing any income-tax cuts for many years to come. The spending drive now is so strong that, if the American people do not check it, they will find the 85th Congress outdoing its predecessors in giving away public funds.

What is needed now are nonpartisan groups of taxpayers in every congressional district to organize a lawful revolt and to encourage those candidates to run for office who will check the spending streak. For the 84th Congress was the "giveaway" Congress of the century.

WHOSE DEMOCRATIC PARTY?

AUGUST 10, 1956

THERE WAS A TIME when the Democratic Party was the great defender of the rights of the States and of the rights of the people as against a centralized government.

There was a time when the principles of Thomas Jefferson and of Andrew Jackson and of Woodrow Wilson were the guiding concepts of the Democratic Party's national platform.

There was a time when individual liberty was protected against any encroachment by federal or State governments.

There was a time when the Democratic Party proudly boasted that it was the party of individual freedom and the foe of governmental despotism.

But the Democratic Party under the New Deal and the Fair Deal deserted its ideals of the past and went over to the concept of federal absolutism sponsored by Madison and Hamilton—the fundamental doctrine of the Republican Party throughout its history.

The only legitimate descendant of the Democratic Party of Jefferson, Jackson and Wilson today is the Democratic Party in the Southern States.

All lingering doubts as to the continuance of these fundamental differences in party concepts were removed by the avowed support given lately to the usurping Supreme Court by Democratic Party leaders of the North. When the highest court ruled that States now have lost their powers to legislate on many questions long reserved to the States, the Constitution was flagrantly violated. Many Democrats at the last session of Congress protested against this usurpation, but a Northern majority ignored them.

The South, which has long been the citadel of brave devotion to principle, now stands at the crossroads. It has perennially supported the Democratic Party's nomination for the Presidency and Vice Presidency, even though in recent years the selection of candidates has been vested largely in the party bosses of the big cities of the North and in the labor bosses.

Under our Electoral College system, each State may choose its own electors. The people may, in the first instance, write in the names of new electors if they choose to ignore the "organization" electors. We witnessed in the last election for United States Senator in South Carolina the effectiveness of a "write-in" campaign as against a regular party nominee.

The South cannot stand by and let a Northern faction write a platform which negates every principle the Democratic Party has stood for in decades past.

The South is in the midst of a life-and-death struggle —to preserve the right to control its own systems of education.

This is more important than the political ambitions of individual Democrats anywhere who feel they must play ball with the Northern organizations of so-called Democrats and accept the "compromise" planks on civil rights that are good only for the duration of the campaign.

The South can challenge the right of these so-called Democrats of the Northern States to use the party name. It can challenge this morally and legally.

There is no need for a third party. There is every need for a strong, independent stand within the Democratic Party, even if it means abstention from voting for the candidates of the Chicago convention when the Electoral College meets. This is an important veto power—long neglected but thoroughly constitutional.

The South must make its protest felt. Too long have the Northern Democrats taken the South for granted. Indeed, this is one reason why the leadership of the Party in the last 25 years has been free to woo the votes of former Republicans in the big city areas by telling them that the alleged rights of a federal bureaucracy supersede the basic rights of the States.

As long as the Democratic bosses in the North can feel sure that the Southern electoral vote will be theirs anyhow, the process of letting the Federal Government usurp State powers will go on.

The National Convention of the Democratic Party in Chicago next week gives the South its chance. Will the South make a stand on principle or surrender to the jargon of expediency which the professional politicians constantly preach?

This is the hour for decision. When will the Democratic Party rise again to defend the freedom of the individual as against unconstitutional acts committed in the name of the Federal Government? Will the Chicago convention denounce the several decisions of the Supreme Court which have ignored the words of the Tenth Article of the Bill of Rights? For that Article plainly says that all rights not specifically delegated to the Federal Government are reserved to the people.

Who delegated the control of education to the Federal Government?

Whose Democratic Party will speak in the platform to be adopted in Chicago next week—the Party of the usurpers or the Party of individual freedom and States' rights?

"THE PROMISES MEN LIVE BY"

AUGUST 17, 1956

WHAT WOULD HAPPEN in the world if, when business contracts were suddenly torn to pieces, no means of redress were available to the aggrieved party? It would mean economic anarchy.

When governments dishonor their contracts and abrogate treaties, it often leads to war.

Back in 1914, the Kaiser's government in Germany made a "scrap of paper" of the treaty which it had signed many years before guaranteeing the territorial integrity and independence of Belgium. It was the beginning of World War I.

Back in 1936, Hitler marched into the Rhineland in deliberate violation of the terms of the Versailles Treaty. Unchecked, he broke agreement after agreement. This led to the outbreak of World War II.

The world today is confronted with another dictator —Nasser of Egypt. He doesn't control a big enough army himself to start a world war, but he can set in motion the alliances which can spark a conflagration in the Middle East and bring on World War III.

For Nasser has made a "scrap of paper" of the treaty of 1888 by which nine nations became guarantors of international operation of the Suez Canal.

It is not a question of mere "nationalization" of property. The Canal itself is within Egyptian territory, and there is every right—at the proper time and in a legal manner—for Egypt to acquire complete ownership of the Canal.

But there is, in the meantime, no right of confiscation. A contract—a treaty—is in effect. It has twelve more years to run. If Nasser considered the terms onerous, he could have sought a reopening and a negotiation. Reasonable parties usually modify by mutual consent any inequitable provisions in contracts. Nasser, however, seized the Canal. It was, as Prime Minister Eden said to Parliament last week, "an act of plunder."

To condone such an act, to acquiesce in it, is to encourage more plunder and even aggression.

The damage done by Nasser to Egypt's future goes far beyond the impairment of the Canal property. He has ruined Egypt's entire credit standing in the world—public and private. No sensible government now will lend any Egyptian Government money if Nasser is at the head of it. Even Russia will be wary. No private investors will extend credit. Egypt's economic growth is stagnated. The Canal itself needs millions for improvement. Pipelines and other waterways now will be built to avoid using the Suez Canal.

So "nationalism" can become a form of national suicide. It can affect adversely the lives of millions of men and women who, though themselves innocent of wrong, must resort perhaps to bloodshed to get rid of their dictatorship government.

The British Prime Minister told the world last week:

"He (Nasser) has shown he is not a man who can be trusted to keep an agreement. And now he has torn up all his country's promises toward the Suez Canal Company and he has even gone back on his own statement . . .

"We all know it is how Fascist governments behave and we all remember only too well what the cost can be in giving in to Fascism . . .

"Just now Colonel Nasser is soft-pedaling. His threats are being modified, but how can we be sure that the next time he has a quarrel with any country he won't interfere with that nation's shipping or that the next time he is short of money he won't raise the dues on the ships that pass through the Canal? . . .

"If Colonel Nasser's action were to succeed, each one of us would be at the mercy of one man for the supplies upon which we live. We could never accept that. With dictators you always have to pay a higher price later on—for their appetite grows with feeding."

What plain-spoken words—and so much needed in these times!

For we have just seen Sukarno of Indonesia repudiating the debt held by Dutch investors.

We have seen in recent years attempts at organized plunder of foreign property in Iran. The people, fortunately, set up a decent government and then imprisoned Mossadegh for treason.

We have witnessed in the Nasser tragedy something even more disturbing than the mere outburst of nationalistic passion. It is a kind of blackmail which governments in other parts of the world, inspired by revolutionary parties and Moscow intrigue, may also be foolish enough to try out.

All this teaches us that perhaps we have been stampeded into unwarranted and superficial attacks on "colonialism" before the colonial countries really showed themselves capable of self-government.

We see clearly now how the immorality of "neutralism" in these newly independent countries is stimulated by the immorality of "nationalism."

When peoples with a conscience choose governments with a conscience, then the promises men live by will be kept—and then only will conditions prevail that are conducive to peace in the world.

WRONG CAMPAIGN, AT WRONG TIME AND PLACE

AUGUST 24, 1956

THIS IS NO TIME for a presidential and congressional campaign.

This is no time for the United States—the leader of the free world—to be paralyzed with disunity. A crisis that might mean war is on this very week in the whole Middle East.

This is no time for a change in Government, either. Yet if the incumbent party is defeated in an election, the Constitution compels the nation and the world to wait for nearly three months while a discredited Administration remains helpless to conduct the policies of the United States. Much can happen in three months.

Our forefathers contemplated that the Constitution would be changed over the years to meet changing conditions. Must we wait for a catastrophe to befall us before we remove the handicaps of our rigid system?

It is a mockery of free government to require an intelligent electorate to make a choice every four years between two candidates selected by a convention system that presents a grotesque spectacle of irresponsibility and has no sanction in law.

Who can persuasively assert that the two men best qualified to be President of the United States are chosen as nominees at our national party conventions?

Who will say that there are not in the Senate or the House at least a dozen men better qualified—by training in legislative affairs and by long familiarity with all the complexities of Government—to lead the nation?

We all know these truths to be self-evident. Yet we accept the Convention system and risk a hazardous interregnum from November through January.

What a time for a foe to conspire to attack us!

What a time for an enemy alliance to contrive to weaken our influence in world affairs and perhaps to light the fire that can envelop us in a world war!

One needs only to read the text of the foreign policy plank of the Democratic National Platform proclaimed last week—and it's the same type of platform adopted in past conventions by the party out of power—to discover that the principal objective, as always, is to discredit the incumbent Administration.

If a viciously partisan indictment of the foreign policy of the United States—such as was expressed in the Democratic Platform and advertised to the world last week—is believed by the American people and the Democratic nominee is elected next November, a repudiated Government must stagnate for nearly three months, unable to carry on effectively.

Must the mothers and fathers of American boys suffer the casualties of a war that can come because of this dangerous interval between Administrations?

Must the nation's economic system suffer the shock and the damage of such a hiatus in Government?

Such a crisis arose in our economic life between November 1932 and March 4, 1933—the interval between the time Herbert Hoover was defeated and Franklin Roosevelt was inaugurated. All the banks had to be closed. A frightful increase in unemployment resulted. Full employment was not restored until World War II broke out in 1939.

Cooperation between the two Administrations was regarded in 1932-1933 as politically impossible, and as a consequence the nation suffered grievously.

Must the ambitions of selfish politicians and the rivalry of parties today destroy the chance of American unity at a critical time in national and international affairs?

The parliamentary system in Canada and in other English-speaking commonwealths is a big improvement over our own system. It can be modified to meet American customs.

We hear much nowadays about picking the right man for Vice President. Adlai Stevenson made quite a point of it last week when he himself was nominated for the Presidency. Only the parliamentary system, however, provides a method whereby the best qualified leader—the man who has won his spurs in the legislative and executive operations of Government—can succeed at once when the top man can no longer serve. If the new leader does not prove satisfactory to the nation, he can be removed promptly. If deemed necessary, an election can be held at once to replace him.

Basically, this system provides a union of the executive and legislative powers in a majority party responsible to the people at all times—not just every four years—and subject to an election only when the nation really feels it can afford the luxury of a bitter conflict between the major parties.

Certainly for several months now we have been waging the wrong campaign—at the wrong time in world affairs and in the wrong place—within the very country on whose military might and in whose leadership all the other free nations place their reliance and dependence to avert the holocaust of an atomic war.

When will America wake up to the dangers of the Party Convention system?

HOW DO 100,000,000 PEOPLE REACT?

AUGUST 31, 1956

THERE ARE ABOUT 100,000,000 men and women eligible to vote, and if 63 per cent should go to the polls in the presidential election this year it would be the highest rate of participation ever recorded.

As the national campaign progresses, we shall be examining the strategy of the managers—their concepts of what impresses the voters. It is not always realized by those managers that human nature doesn't change from campaign to campaign.

The voters probably will react this year in much the same way as they have reacted in previous years. Television has introduced a means of communication to larger audiences, and much of the campaigning will be done on the screen. When the radio first came into use, it was insisted that this would increase the effectiveness of campaigning. But has it?

The truth is the mechanical means of transmitting facts doesn't improve the argument for one side or the other, nor furnish persuasive issues when there are none.

The facts don't change just because more people can be reached with the facts. Scientific polls show that, no matter how large the audience, the result derived from a substantial sample remains approximately the same. It is often said that the radio and television and the increased space given to political campaigns by the press can bring more voters to the polls. But all the get-out-the-vote appeals in the past do not seem to have moved up much higher the percentage of participation.

Until 1952, the highest percentage of the eligible voters to participate in any election was in 1940, when 59.1 per cent of the electorate voted. Willkie was running against Roosevelt that year and both personalities were colorful and interesting. History, however, has proved again and again that the issues and not the men bring out the vote and decide elections. The people vote out the party in power when there is something deep-seated for them to protest about, and they continue a party in office when they feel it is not "time for a change."

The people usually do not want a change in the midst of emergencies. Thus, during World War II they didn't want to "swap horses in midstream." They did want a change in 1952, and 55.4 per cent of those who voted expressed mostly their protest against the Korean War, against Communist infiltration and against corruption in government—all of them emotional issues at a time when the country on the whole was prosperous.

The basic formula which this writer has found uniformly applicable in the last ten presidential campaigns involves two main doctrines. One is that economic contentment or discontent is a controlling issue. The other is that emotional issues can deprive the incumbent party of the benefits of the economic contentment issue and shift the vote to the opposite party.

Looking back at presidential campaigns of the past it is interesting to note that again and again the better man did not win, but the better issues did.

Too much emphasis is usually placed on men—on the candidates themselves—when the truth is the voters are interested primarily in the issues. Candidates are supported by the voters to the extent that they expound effectively the pocketbook or emotional issues. The stay-at-home vote is also affected in a negative way by the way the issues are explained or not explained. Often many millions of voters do not care to vote because they feel it doesn't make any difference who is elected.

A wide variety of small groups in an electorate are influenced by prejudices of different kinds. Many voters are impressed with the looks of a candidate, how he talks, and what they read or hear about his personality. But these fragmentary blocs tend to offset one another. When the voting group is as large as 60 million persons, past experience indicates that major issues sway the maximum number.

The biggest issue of all sometimes is an emotional one, such as the issue of peace and war. It affects the drafting of youth, and the killing of American boys in faraway wars. Korea was a handicap to the Democrats in 1952, just as the peace issue is an asset to the Republicans in 1956.

Economic contentment and discontent this time will affect the result in different ways in different States. If the farm depression is still serious, it will reduce the customary Republican majority and perhaps even turn some farm States to the opposite column. But, on the other hand, in the other States, the prosperity issue may conceivably increase the Republican majorities.

President Eisenhower is politically popular today because he symbolizes the issues. But if the economic contentment and peace issues were tried out with any other Republican nominee, they would probably bring almost as big a vote. For while candidates are theoretically "popular" as personalities, the voting record of 100 years shows that it is the issues—not the personalities of the candidates—which win presidential elections.

THE PEOPLE WANT TO KNOW

SEPTEMBER 7, 1956

THE PEOPLE HAVE A RIGHT to know what the policies of each candidate for the Presidency will be if he is elected in November.

The record of President Eisenhower during the last three and a half years is an open book, and his course of action in public office may be expected to continue along the same lines if he is given a second term.

But we were told by former President Truman that the Democrats nominated at their Chicago Convention a man who does not have "the experience and the ability to act as President immediately upon assuming that office without risking a period of costly and dangerous trial and error."

Mr. Truman said Governor Harriman has these qualifications and implied that Mr. Stevenson does not. A few days later, however, Adlai Stevenson was nominated and a national platform was unanimously adopted by the Convention which contains a series of pledges that the nominee is morally bound to fulfill if elected.

The people, therefore, have a right to know the extent to which Mr. Stevenson agrees or disagrees with his party platform and in what areas of public policy he will "go it alone." Here are some points on which the people will want further information:

1. The Democratic platform says: "The current crisis over Suez is a consequence of inept and vacillating Republican policy."

Does Mr. Stevenson think Nasser was right in seizing the Suez Canal and that America put him up to it?

Does the Democratic nominee favor the lending of more than a billion dollars—most of it from American taxpayers' funds—to build the Aswan Dam in Egypt? Or does he think that the Department of State was right in declining to support that plan?

What Republican policies have, as the platform alleges, produced "the risk of atomic war" for the United States?

2. The Democratic platform favors a "multilateral approach" and advocates that the funds for foreign aid be "pooled" to help other nations in their economic development.

Does this mean Mr. Stevenson favors the giveaway of American money without a voice in what happens to it abroad? Does he favor, for example, building up facilities for the growing of Egyptian cotton so it may undersell the cotton of our own Southern States?

3. The Democratic platform says that since 1953 the Republican Administration has been "standing silent when the peoples rise in East Germany and Poland, and thereby weakening the positive Democratic policy of halting Communist expansion."

Does this mean that Mr. Stevenson would embark on a war to "liberate" the satellite countries?

4. The Democratic platform pledges that it will "reduce interest rates" on the public debt.

How? By taking over the Federal Reserve System and dominating the whole credit mechanism from the Office of the Secretary of the Treasury? Businessmen will want to know about this as soon as possible, for this could threaten the financial stability of the nation.

5. The Democratic platform promises the "repeal of the Taft-Hartley Act."

How does Mr. Stevenson intend to deal with the Democratic Senators and Representatives in Congress from the Southern States who have blocked even the mildest form of amendments to the Taft-Hartley law? Will he browbeat them into compliance? Without their votes, of course, the Act cannot be repealed.

6. The Democratic platform says the Taft-Hartley Act must be repealed "because its restrictive provisions deny the principle that national legislation based on the commerce clause of the Constitution normally override conflicting State laws." This is an obvious reference to the "right to work" laws of the several States, most of them Democratic States. How does Mr. Stevenson expect to get any of the voters who believe in States' Rights, whether in the North or in the South, to accept this so-called principle?

7. The Democratic platform advocates a program of government ownership and promises to "preserve and strengthen the public-power competitive yardstick in power development" and in "other future projects, including atomic power plants."

What "other projects"? Does Mr. Stevenson favor the sabotage of the electric light and power industry in America and the consequent loss to private investors who have put billions of dollars of their savings into the plants of that industry?

These are only a few of the many problems raised by the Democratic national platform whose declarations Mr. Stevenson accepted at Chicago.

When the Democratic Party nominee asks the voters for their support, they have a right to be told what deviations from the present policies of the Government he has in mind and what new policies may be expected from him in that period of "costly and dangerous trial and error" which, we have been warned, will follow if Adlai Stevenson is elected.

"EVERYBODY FOR HIMSELF AND—"

SEPTEMBER 14, 1956

PRIMARILY OUR NATIONAL ECONOMY runs itself. Sometimes, of course, it runs itself into the ground. When self-control is abandoned, economic anarchy is the sequel.

Today the only broad restraint that government imposes is on the supply of credit.

This is supposed to be the way to prevent or stop inflation. But credit brakes are only temporary. The cycles of rising prices are always resumed in due time as the nation moves on toward another danger line. For the impulse to get the maximum advantage, irrespective of the effect on anybody else, is not dormant.

Organized selfishness is the basic evil.

Big corporations used to be the main offenders. Now big unions exercise an even more powerful influence on the economy.

Decades ago Congress recognized that price-fixing by concerted action of corporations was against the public interest, and the Sherman Antitrust Law was passed to make such practices unlawful. When this didn't prove effective enough, amendments were adopted designed to prevent the further growth of monopoly.

But monopoly has been bred faster than it has been restrained.

Thus, for example, the excess-profits-tax laws—passed by Democratic Administrations—have done more to put small business out of the running in competition with big competitors than all the lawsuits ever brought under the antitrust laws.

The secret of effective competition, to be sure, is the ability of a company to obtain equity capital or to retain enough earnings after taxes to justify long-term loans for expansion purposes.

The big corporations have been permitted during wartime to amass huge amounts of capital because they pay less taxes proportionately than the smaller businesses. In the tax laws passed during World War I and World War II, and also during the Korean war, the base on which excess profits were computed for corporations always favored the big fellows. The smaller companies, which might have gotten a start toward becoming real competitors, were severely penalized.

So when the Democrats talk now about their concern for "small business," they are forgetting their own guilt —their own responsibility for the tax laws that fostered the growth of bigger and bigger businesses against which smaller units now find it difficult to compete.

When abuses develop and credit controls have to be exercised, the big companies—because of their huge surpluses—do not suffer. Their plant capacity is usually adequate for a high rate of production, and expansion plans can be deferred without harm.

The smaller companies, on the other hand, must, in a tight-money period, postpone their expansion—their opportunity to become strong competitors.

The present movement to make money tight is sponsored by a conscientious Federal Reserve Board which sees the national economy getting out of hand. It fears that the consequences may well be worse if the boom is not checked now.

But what produced the inflation? What are the economic and political factors that have brought us an unbalanced economy? Who tightens these up?

One of the main factors is obvious, but nobody in Congress lifts a finger to check the trend. It is the unrestrained selfishness of labor unions which is now upsetting the economy. There is no limit to union demands —no limit because the unions know that the employers cannot stand costly strikes and hence must yield to economic coercion.

Organized business has been properly restrained from price-fixing. But organized unionism evidently is not prevented from forcing prices upward by means of wage-fixing in whole industries at a time.

The recent settlement of the strike in the steel industry is a case in point. The unions had demanded higher pay—not because of any problem of living costs or because the wages were deemed low, but simply because the steel companies were regarded by the union leaders as able to absorb the increased wages out of current profits or else to pass on a considerable part of the increased costs in increased prices to the consumer. Naturally, the price of steel was immediately raised. It set a pattern for other industries.

The wage-and-price spiral is moving upward every year. This is a recklessness which can break down the national economy. If everybody seeks the most without regard for the effect on anybody else's interest, we will be headed for depression and disaster.

What forces of public opinion can be mobilized against the everybody-for-himself doctrine that can lead us to a socialistic government? For once the breakdown of the private enterprise system occurs, so much distress will be generated that the voters, in desperation, will accept almost any solution.

Credit is being restrained, but when will organized greed be restrained? That's the question of the hour— and of the age.

THE ELECTION THAT ISN'T WON

SEPTEMBER 21, 1956

THERE MAY BE more persons in the United States today who "like Ike" and want to see him reelected than there are who want a change in government. But if millions of those who favor the continuance of the President in office do not go to the polls, and the opposition does get out its vote, the country can witness the political surprise of the century.

This is but another way of saying that nothing counts in an election like the votes themselves.

As of today there is a noticeable lethargy in the nation. Some call it "complacency." But it is due really to an erroneous assumption—that elections are won by the more popular candidate no matter what the issues or the work of intensively operating organizations.

There are in America today four national organizations engaged in political campaigning.

The Republicans have their regular party organization and the Citizens for Eisenhower clubs.

The Democrats have their regular party organization and the AFL-CIO Political Action Committees.

It so happens that the Republican political organizations are relatively weak because they do not control the mayor's office in the big cities which dominate so many States with large electoral votes.

The Democrats, on the other hand, have the advantage of such organizations in the big cities.

Also the Democrats have in the AFL-CIO operation something far more concentrated than the scattered and improvised groups of "Citizens for Eisenhower."

In fact, the practical politicians are only now beginning to recognize that, important as the customary effort by political workers happens to be, the man-to-man pressure inside the factory is even more penetrating and influential in lining up Democratic votes. This was proved last week by the election figures of the pivotal cities in Maine. It was also plainly apparent in 1954 in the States where the Democrats elected Senators because of CIO help in major cities.

The labor-union leaders cannot, of course, dictate to the workers how they shall vote in a secret ballot, but they can persuade. And what they say in their intimate talks to the workers each day during the lunch hour doesn't get into the newspapers. The whole solicitation is done quietly by the labor-union canvassers.

The workers and their families can, of course, be interviewed at their homes through local organizations, but it takes more time.

The main difficulty with the Republican campaign is that it has depended too much on a single personality or rather on the President's popularity. The Republicans won in 1952 not because of Ike's personal prestige but because the country was resentful of the Truman Administration.

Today there are, as always in a four-year period, things that the voters don't like. Discontent of all kinds can be mobilized by an opposition party. This has to be countered by affirmative work in behalf of the achievements and future pledges of the party in power.

The real issue before the country is one that must give all citizens much concern: Should there be a change of government at this critical time in world affairs?

Shall the Communists be encouraged to believe that the policies of the present Administration—which, to say the least, have been characterized by patience and restraint—are to be repudiated and that the nation wants to take up arms to "win the cold war" and check Communist infiltration?

Or does the country want deliberate appeasement, which history tells us usually leads to war?

Precisely just what do the voters want who are seriously thinking of changing horses in midstream? Are they indifferent to the dangers in the international situation? Do they realize the risks in the period of transition that could begin in November?

Turning to domestic issues, do the voters want an era of chaos in the business world? Most businessmen today feel that the present Administration has been fair and impartial as between management and labor and that this encourages business growth. Do the voters want to destroy this basic confidence and cause a sudden let-up in business expansion, with consequent unemployment? Do the voters really want to reverse engines and unwittingly start business going downhill? Why risk a change when things are going all right?

The burden of proof is on those who are urging a change. Do the voters really want it?

Talking face to face with the voters, these are the issues to be debated in the home, in the factory, and on the farm.

The fight to get out the vote is only beginning. Judging by the results in Maine, where more Republicans stayed at home than voted, the present Administration can be defeated and a radical regime installed in power. The nation would then face what Mr. Truman has accurately predicted would be "a period of costly and dangerous trial and error."

This election is not yet won for either side.

WHICH PARTY FOR LABOR?

SEPTEMBER 28, 1956

WE HEAR IT SAID on the stump that the Republicans are the "rich man's party" and the Democrats are the "poor man's party."

We hear it said that the Republicans are the party of "big business" and that the Democrats are the party of "the little man" or of "small business."

We hear it said that the Republicans are against labor, and that the Democrats are for labor.

But the real question is whether the confidence that businessmen have today in the future—which can mean the creation of more and more jobs—will remain or whether it will be shaken, thus resulting in stagnation and unemployment.

Will Adlai Stevenson, for example, feel obligated to do what labor demands if he is elected through the intensive organization work of labor unions plus their expenditures in his behalf of millions of dollars, especially in the big cities?

There is a truce today between management and labor—a balancing of the scales that has rarely been attained. Will the labor-union strategists demand as their pay-off that this balance be destroyed? Will it not usher in an era of labor-management strife with strikes more costly than we have ever witnessed in America?

Mr. Stevenson is for the "repeal" of the Taft-Hartley Act. This would mean a return to the one-sided philosophy written into the Wagner Act.

Nothing could be more calculated to upset the stability of American industry and stop expansion—and hence halt the increases in employment—than such a threat of war on business.

The Eisenhower Administration did try to correct certain defects in the Taft-Hartley Act but was prevented from doing so by a coalition of Democrats in Congress, some of whom thought the amendments went too far and some that they didn't go far enough. But the fact remains that behind the effort to repeal the law is a deliberate plan to bring about an attitude in Congress and in the Executive branch of the Government prejudiced in behalf of labor and against business.

Already this is apparent in the debate that has been going on concerning the decisions of the National Labor Relations Board. Judging by some of the speeches by Mr. Stevenson and his Democratic supporters in Congress in the North who are beholden to labor unions for their financing of past campaigns, a Democratic Administration, if entrusted with power, would proceed to do the very thing it accuses its opponents of doing— "packing" the Labor Relations Board.

The demands of the labor-union politicians, however, go deeper than mere control of the National Labor Relations Board. There is evident an avowed hostility to business and a mistaken passion for the shackling of American enterprise.

Simply stated, labor and management should have the same goals—the development of more and more businesses with more and more profits and hence more and more employment opportunities. For to encourage this trend means higher and higher wages and more and more benefits for the workers and their families.

Union labor, on the other hand, by the utterances of its leaders, often gives the impression that it wants to break down the profit system and substitute state socialism. There are some leaders who are bitterly opposed to such a course and say so openly. But there are too many who hammer away for more and more restrictions on business and for higher taxes on corporation earnings, without the slightest regard for the damage this would do to the most delicate machinery of our whole national economy—job creation.

If business men become frustrated, if they begin to lose confidence in the opportunity of their companies to earn a fair return for investors and to accumulate a surplus out of which to pay the cost of new plants and equipment for future expansion, America will face a severe depression and unemployment.

The record of the Roosevelt Administration in this respect is significant. From 1933 to 1940 it could not get below a 7,700,000 figure on unemployment. Only the outbreak of total war saved the day. That's what the Republicans mean when they say that the country has never had full employment under the Democrats except in time of war.

If the Democrats want to risk another depression, they can do so by upsetting the confidence of businessmen so that they will be compelled involuntarily to postpone or cancel their present plans for capital-goods expansion at a time of its greatest growth.

It was the failure to understand the importance of job creation and the capital-goods side of our economy which prevented the Democrats from restoring prosperity in the '30s. They insisted instead—as their advisers do now—on an approach which means subsidizing purchasing power through WPA's and boondoggling.

The country faces a choice between instability, with severe unemployment, and continued prosperity, with the highest scale of living ever achieved in any country in the world. Which party for labor?

WHAT IS "THE LAW OF THE LAND"?

OCTOBER 5, 1956

FAR AND WIDE we hear the cry: "It's the law of the land—it must be obeyed—the Supreme Court has decided—it is final."

But what really has been decided on "desegregation"? What is "the law of the land" that all citizens are supposed to obey?

The quandary arises when we endeavor to determine whether voluntary or enforced integration in the schools is "the law of the land."

Of particular interest in this regard is the transcript of a recorded interview with Dr. Omer Carmichael, Superintendent of Schools in Louisville, Kentucky, which begins on page 46 of this magazine. Dr. Carmichael says that white children are attending certain schools in Louisville which have no Negro children in them, and Negro children are attending certain schools which have no white children in them, but that both whites and Negroes are attending other schools which are mixed. Under this system parents are allowed to exercise "freedom of choice," and requests for "transfer" are granted insofar as is practicable within the available school facilities.

This is "permissive" segregation. It is also being called "voluntary" integration. In any event, authority is being exercised by a subdivision of a State government—the school board—to assign pupils on a basis conforming to local conditions and local sentiment on the race question.

It is a noble experiment. But is it really constitutional? If it is, then the Supreme Court of the United States must say so and, if it someday does, it will, in effect, be reversing a vital point in its decision of May 17, 1954.

The Louisville plan happens to be buttressed for the time being by a significant ruling rendered on July 15, 1955, by a federal court in South Carolina composed of two members of the U. S. Circuit Court of Appeals and one U. S. District Court judge. This ruling, which has not been passed upon by the highest court one way or the other, says in part:

"It (the Supreme Court) has not decided that the federal courts are to take over or regulate the public schools of the States.

"It has not decided that the States must mix persons of different races in the schools or must require them to attend schools or must deprive them of the right of choosing the schools they attend.

"What it has decided, and all that it has decided, is that a State may not deny to any person on account of race the right to attend any school that it maintains.

This, under the decision of the Supreme Court, the State may not do directly or indirectly; but if the schools which it maintains are open to children of all races, no violation of the Constitution is involved even though the children of different races voluntarily attend different schools, as they attend different churches.

"Nothing in the Constitution or in the decision of the Supreme Court takes away from the people freedom to choose the schools they attend. The Constitution, in other words, does not require integration. It merely forbids discrimination. It does not forbid such segregation as occurs as the result of voluntary action. It merely forbids the use of governmental power to enforce segregation."

But, after we have read the above, we must compare it with what the Supreme Court of the United States said in its famous decision of May 17, 1954. The Court confessed its inability to find anywhere in the Congressional debate on the Fourteenth Amendment anything conclusive to support the theory that desegregation in the schools was the intent of the sponsors of the Amendment.

Then, without any basis in precedent or in constitutional history, the Court arbitrarily decided that the time had come to adopt a psychological rather than a legal yardstick for measuring the effect of segregation on school children. The Court said:

"Does segregation of children in public schools solely on the basis of race, even though the physical facilities and other 'tangible' factors may be equal, deprive the children of the minority group of equal educational opportunities? We believe that it does. . . .

"To separate them from others of similar age and qualifications solely because of their race generates a feeling of inferiority as to their status in the community that may affect their hearts and minds in a way unlikely ever to be undone. . . .

"Whatever may have been the extent of psychological knowledge at the time of *Plessy* v. *Ferguson*, this finding is amply supported by modern authority. Any language in *Plessy* v. *Ferguson* contrary to this finding is rejected."

In the *Plessy* v. *Ferguson* case—decided in 1896 by the Supreme Court—the doctrine of "separate but equal" facilities had been upheld. It remained "the law of the land" for 58 years thereafter.

How has the new "law of the land" been determined? By Congress? By "judge made" rules? In spite of the fact that no testimony whatsoever from experts was taken in the trial court, the Supreme Court set itself up as the final authority on "psychological" matters and handed down a mandate based upon its own examination of these same "psychological" factors.

The opinion of the nine Justices declared frankly that they relied on out-of-court assertions contained in the writings of a few sociologists. These were primarily critics of segregation. It is axiomatic that "expert" opinion cannot be considered in court unless the testimony is subject to refutation in cross-examination.

But what will the Supreme Court say now about the actual experience in the Louisville schools? There, by reason of freedom of choice and parents' preference, certain children are permitted to attend all-white schools, and certain parents have selected all-Negro schools. So far as legal authority is concerned, the parent of a child cannot insist upon his choice, and the school superintendent may put Negro children and white children in any school he pleases. This may, in a broad sense, satisfy the legalities. But—on the "psychological" front—does it not disprove the Supreme Court's "finding"?

Thus, for example, if the Court is right, will not the children who are in all-Negro schools have a "feeling of inferiority" to whites because they have been persuaded by one means or another not to go to the same school with whites? How is it proposed to remove such "psychological" barriers? Isn't it "the law of the land" that these barriers must be removed?

Likewise, what will be said as to the effect hereafter on the white children who are compelled to attend school with Negro children, especially when the cultural training of the white children and the whole philosophy of Southern families has been psychologically set against mingling of the races on a social or quasi-social basis?

Can it be persuasively argued that Negro children are adversely affected by enforced segregation but not by voluntary segregation? Can it be logically contended that some white children are not unfavorably affected in their educational opportunities when integration is ordered by the school authorities? The testimony before a House subcommittee last week on the experiences in the integrated schools of the District of Columbia revealed some startling facts on these points.

Surely the Supreme Court cannot now refuse to consider evidence on "achievement" tests and other related factors which it failed to request in the first instance as the Court constituted itself virtually a commission on psychology, without regard to testimony or cross-examination of witnesses on both sides. Was this really "due process"?

There is a further dilemma. Former Governor James F. Byrnes of South Carolina, who was also an Associate Justice of the Supreme Court of the United States, pointed out last week in a speech before the Vermont Bar Association that the Supreme Court really does not have any power to "enforce" integration. He contends that the Fourteenth Amendment itself specifically gives to Congress alone the power to enforce its clauses. But Congress has not legislated.

Is it "the law of the land," therefore, for the judiciary itself to issue orders to enforce "desegregation" when this power can only be exercised by Congress, as provided in the Constitution?

The text of Mr. Byrnes' speech, printed on pages 100-104 of this issue, is illuminating. He indicates that more problems have been raised than have been settled by the Supreme Court decision. Already free speech in the South has been repressed by federal court order on the ground that speeches against desegregation may tend to incite violence. The question of jury trial for those held in contempt is stressed by former Justice Byrnes, who significantly asks:

"If the speech of a citizen urging students not to attend an integrated school is held violative of a court order enjoining interference and is punished by imprisonment without a jury trial, then what about a speech by a labor leader urging employes not to work when interference is similarly enjoined?"

Guns and bayonets have been used in recent weeks to "enforce" the anti-segregation decree of the Supreme Court of the United States—to escort children to school. Is this "the law of the land"?

Will those workers who are willing to enter a plant during a strike now be escorted into the factory by troops? Is this "the law of the land"?

To say the least, "the law of the land" on the school question is far from clear today. Proposals to achieve "equality" among unequals amid the vicissitudes of the classroom are not susceptible of enforcement by law. To engage in such empiric adventures is hardly the function of the Supreme Court of the United States as prescribed in the Constitution itself. Plainly this is a departure from our accustomed reliance on constitutional law and historic procedure.

Voluntarism, instead of coercion, is certainly a desirable means whereby the States can handle their school problems. But is voluntarism sanctioned by the Supreme Court of the United States?

We must, therefore, still ask: Just what is "the law of the land" on "desegregation"?

WHICH COMMANDER-IN-CHIEF?

OCTOBER 12, 1956

WHEN THE AMERICAN PEOPLE go to the polls in a few weeks, they will choose the man who—beginning on January 20th next—is to be Commander-in-Chief of all the armed forces of the United States.

This means command of the largest Navy and the largest Air Force in the world today and of the largest Army the United States has ever maintained except in time of actual war.

This means that the power of decision—where and when to deploy these forces, how to maintain them in the best possible positions so as to deter a war from breaking out or to fight a war if it does break out—is in the hands of the President of the United States who is elected next month.

This means also that the delicate questions of diplomacy and of military policy, which are so closely interwoven nowadays, must be determined by the man who, under the Constitution, not only commands the armed services but is charged with the responsibility for conducting all our relationships with foreign governments. A President may have many counsellors and subordinates, but the power of decision is his, and his alone. The quality of his judgment and the expertness of his background can mean the difference between victory and defeat—survival and disaster—in a nuclear age.

What a fortunate thing for America that during the last three and a half years the Commander-in-Chief has been the same man who led the biggest military force in history to win the greatest military victory of all times for the United States and its allies!

Military men have often been pictured as eager for war. But President Eisenhower has shown himself to be even more eager for peace. He brushed aside cries of possible "appeasement" and forthrightly ventured to the Geneva Conference in 1955 to meet personally the leaders of the Communist regime. He had no illusions as to their insincerities, but he wanted to make clear to all nations that he meant what he had been saying all along—that he would go anywhere in the world to advance the cause of peace.

The fact, moreover, that there has been a period of non-war doesn't mean that war has been removed as a possible contingency in our lives. The Congress—including the leaders of both parties—have not abated one bit a determination to maintain the armed forces necessary to deter a war. We are spending around 40 billion dollars a year on our armaments.

The President commands at this moment large American forces in Europe and the Far East.

These are times when one man's decision can mean the difference between war and peace.

Congress, for example, vests in one man alone—the President—the power to order the super-bomb to be dropped, or not to be dropped.

The United States, moreover, is today signatory to the North Atlantic Treaty because the Senate, in an action unprecedented in our history, ratified an agreement which provides that an attack in Europe and North America on any of the countries of the North Atlantic Treaty Organization—now numbering 15—is an attack on this country.

For three and a half years as President, and prior to that for several years as military commander, Dwight Eisenhower has become familiar with every angle of the perplexing situations that exist in Europe, where war can break out at any time. He has also had first-hand experience with the problems of Korea and the Far East. He obtained from Congress last year, by virtually unanimous vote, the authority to act at once in the Formosa Straits if there should be any attack on United States interests there. War is a continuous threat in and around Formosa.

When the American people vote next month, will they turn out the present Commander-in-Chief and select a novice to take his place?

Obviously one of the two presidential nominees does have the needed experience, and the other plainly does not. Shall other factors then—group grievances and the promises of materialistic gains for farmers or labor-union politicians—be given more consideration by the voters than they give to the military ability and judgment of a Commander-in-Chief who happens also to have an accumulated knowledge of every phase of world diplomacy?

Shall this leader, recognized as such by the free world, be turned out of office?

Of what avail are the material gains of the day for any group of voters if the lives of any of our sons are to be lost in a war that could be avoided?

Is this the time to change the Commander-in-Chief?

Is this the time to take the risks of transition and of "a period of costly and dangerous trial and error," such as Mr. Truman prophesied would ensue in the event of the election of Mr. Stevenson?

Is this the time to change horses in midstream—to swap the nation's most experienced man in military affairs for an inexperienced Commander-in-Chief of the Army, the Navy, and the Air Force?

WHICH ROAD?

OCTOBER 19, 1956

THE AMERICAN PEOPLE stand at the crossroads. Which way shall they go?

One road leads them to instability—to the hardships of a worrisome era in business. Continuing on the other road means expanded business, stability and security.

For the American economic system is a sensitive thing. It derives momentum from the psychological confidence that enterprising individuals feel in the future—in their opportunities to produce and sell goods in a market unhampered by the hand of the state.

Such confidence begets a feeling that long-range plans can be made, that more workers can be hired, that more money can be borrowed or capital invested, with an assurance that sufficient earnings will be accumulated to take care of all obligations and yield a surplus.

Confidence in business planning is essential to the taking of risks with invested funds. It means that, as new plant and equipment are bought and production is increased, more employment opportunities are created for our growing population. Also, as labor increases its productivity, the worker earns higher and higher wages.

This is the American business system—the envy of the whole world.

For here in America business men are free, labor unions are free, and the Government intervenes to regulate only where there are abuses or, at times, to lend when private capital naturally cannot be expected to take the risks of a great need, usually in wartime.

The American people today, however, are being told that "big business" rules in Washington and dominates every decision of Government to the detriment of the working man. It's the campaign theme of the Democrats. The inference is plain—large businesses must be shackled and, little by little, must be broken up so that in the long run we shall have a communal system. Over the years this can mean the socialization of our business enterprises. This is the road to nationalization which has all but ruined many a European country.

Can it be that, if the Democratic nominee becomes President, he will feel he has a mandate to break up large-sized business? Where will he start? Will he demolish General Motors on the theory that this company—owned by more than 612,000 citizens—is not good for the country? Will he dissolve the Ford enterprise, with its 320,000 investors? Will he say to Chrysler, with its 90,000 individual owners, that it must abandon the making of cars in different price fields and undergo political surgery?

What is to happen, moreover, to the hundreds of thousands of workers in the automobile industry and in the industries which supply raw materials and parts and accessories? Must these workers be made the guinea pigs of an unemployment cycle in which the state seeks to harass and disintegrate "big business"?

Also will the telephone systems, the railroads, the steel companies, the oil companies, and the big food chains feel the heavy hand of a giant Government which in the guise of regulation seeks to take them over one by one or to break them up into many artificial units? Will these enterprises that now employ millions of workers be subjected to government by the politicians and for the politicians?

What plans has the Democratic nominee, moreover, for the big unions of the country?

What has made possible the negotiation of the big contracts by the labor unions? Has it not been that the large companies—"big business"—have been successful and hence prosperous enough to take the lead in meeting the wage demands of the unions? Does anyone seriously believe that labor unions can benefit from the recessions and unemployment that would follow the disruption of the modern business system?

Which road, then, shall the voter choose?

Shall it be the road that leads to the frustration and stoppage of American business expansion—to economic chaos—a road that winds back to more and more Government "pump priming" and great uncertainty for everybody?

Or shall the voter take the road of confidence? This means encouragement for business and labor, owner and investor, in an era of better understanding between management and worker. It means better earnings for those who invest their savings. It means surpluses for the Government, too, and it can make possible a steady reduction of tax rates.

Shall the United States continue on the road that we have been traveling under the leadership of President Eisenhower since 1953?

It's a road that leads away from class vengeance and class bitterness toward the goals of a better America:

A nation indivisible by class strife.

A nation impregnable against attack by any foe, internal or external.

A nation enjoying, under the free-enterprise system, an unprecedented prosperity for all.

THIS IS NO TIME FOR A CHANGE!

NOVEMBER 2, 1956

THE WORLD IS ASTIR with the cries of oppressed peoples calling for freedom from tyranny.

The fires of revolt are beginning to sweep Eastern Europe. The Middle East is aflame.

It is a time of great danger—when reckless men in the Kremlin can at any hour, by impulsive action, force the start of a big war.

Desperate rulers in Moscow, seeking to escape from internal pressures, may decide that an international conflict is the only way out for them. For, in the face of external war, domestic issues become subordinate and peoples are quickly rallied to unity by appeals to patriotism.

This is a time of crisis in the world.

It is not a time in which to change leaders, but a time to retain the men of experience at the head of our own Government.

It is not a time to inaugurate an era of bewilderment and confusion among our allies and compel them to wait months and months for new policies to be shaped by an inexperienced Administration.

For the power vested in our Chief Executive is extraordinary. It is the President's responsibility to conduct war if it comes, but also to maintain peace.

The peoples of all the world want peace. They want security against sudden attack. They want freedom from fear. But as long as irresponsible leaders are exploiting the hundreds of millions of persons behind the Iron Curtain, the American people and the people of allied countries cannot feel safe.

This is no time for adventurers—those who would gamble with our safety by grasping at theory and ignoring reality.

Our Government has sought again and again by continuous negotiation to test the sincerity of the Communist regime in Moscow, and has found no sincerity there. The record of broken treaties and shattered pledges is an open book for the world to read. To give the Kremlin another chance to violate a treaty—and at our expense—would be folly.

This is not the time to abandon tests of H-bombs—our most powerful deterrent—as Adlai Stevenson has proposed to do. We can agree to this only when free governments arise to honor agreements that will end not merely tests but the use of nuclear weapons.

Until free peoples are in control of their own governments everywhere, there can be no mutual trust. For peoples do not make wars. Only unscrupulous leaders plunge peoples into wars.

Meanwhile, the conditions of an armed truce will prevail. But in an armed truce you never throw away your weapons on the hopeful assumption that a ruthless enemy will not attack. Indeed attack is likely when a nation shows weakness or irresoluteness.

President Eisenhower, by his masterful statement last week on the issue of H-bomb tests, has persuasively refuted every argument made by Messrs. Stevenson and Kefauver. The present propaganda of the Soviet Union designed to stop development of nuclear weapons in America and to ally some of our gullible scientists here and there behind the Communist drive has not fooled anybody in the Government in Washington. But there are signs that it might fool Mr. Stevenson, who already has won the plaudits of Bulganin.

Our nation cannot take chances on a change in Administration now because of the perils involved in upsetting our foreign and domestic programs at this time. The two are interwoven.

We are witnessing the success of the President's policy in maintaining adequate armament to deter the aggressor from attacking us in a big war, while at the same time exercising forbearance and restraint.

President Eisenhower, at Geneva in 1954, took away from the Soviet propagandists their most telling argument. He spoke dramatically for an America peaceful in intent—ready to convert its atomic swords into atomic plowshares. This may have been the turning point in the "cold war" itself. For the attention of the peoples in East Germany, in Poland and in Hungary, and to some extent inside Soviet Russia itself has been turned inward ever since—toward domestic reform and the building up of pressure against tyrannical governments.

This is no time to weaken our moral leverage for the peaceful liberation of oppressed peoples.

This is no time to rock the boat in America—to unsettle the very diplomacy that has kept American boys out of war.

This is no time to risk the "period of costly and dangerous trial and error" that Mr. Truman rightly predicted, at the Democratic Convention last August, would follow if an inexperienced man like Adlai Stevenson were elected President in November.

This is no time to turn out General Eisenhower as Commander-in-Chief of the Army, the Navy and the Air Force, and to put the inexperienced Adlai Stevenson in command of our destiny.

This is no time to swap horses in midstream.

THE USE OF FORCE

NOVEMBER 9, 1956

THE WORLD IS CONFRONTED once more with the dramatic assertion by spokesmen for peace-loving governments that, in dealing with a dictatorship, there is no substitute for the use of military force.

The world is confronted again with the simple truth that wars come when there is no satisfactory method of resolving the international disputes which arise out of questions of law.

For there is today no court to which nations are required to submit their disputes if one or the other of the parties is unwilling to do so. There is no court which, on its own initiative, can examine the legal issues and tell the world who is right or who is wrong.

Diplomacy cannot succeed in a vacuum. It is very difficult to avoid war when irresponsible dictators, by their disregard of law, provoke the punitive use of military force against them.

Pacifism gives us no answer. Appeasement and disregard of the aggressions of a Hitler or a Mussolini or a Nasser mean the use of military force in the end.

Moral force cannot function without adequate means of mobilizing world opinion.

The dispute over the illegal seizure of the Suez Canal could have been settled by a competent tribunal set up for that purpose by the nations of the world. Such a settlement of legal questions was blocked by the partisanship of the governments in Moscow, in New Delhi and in the Arab capitals which, siding with Nasser, saw only the narrow issue of "nationalization," while ignoring his action in tearing a treaty into scraps of paper.

However we may differ about the wisdom of the military steps just taken by Britain and France to protect their legal interests in the Suez Canal area, we must speak out even more vehemently in criticism of those who sent arms to Nasser and spurred him on as he scorned all international conferences and rejected the many reasonable measures proposed to him for a fair and equitable settlement of the problem.

The use of force becomes inevitable in certain contingencies. We found it the only way in 1917 when our rights on the high seas were transgressed. We also found it the only way in 1941 when we were attacked at Pearl Harbor. We, too, shall use force if attacked in the future—even as Britain and France and Israel have acted to repel the aggression by Nasser.

We do not disapprove of the use of force today by the patriots of Hungary as they strive to throw off the yoke of a foreign army which, without legal or moral right, has occupied that country ever since 1945. President Eisenhower last week rightly extolled "this brave people" who "offered their very lives for independence from foreign masters."

Can we say then that Israel must not use force to defend her very life? Is there any difference between the case we make for Hungary's patriots and the case we make for a republic that is surrounded on all sides by enemies which raid her territory constantly, blockade her ports, and refuse to let her ships go through the Suez Canal in defiance of the treaty itself?

We cannot merely pronounce a pious judgment against the use of military force. We must instead seek conscientiously to remove the conditions that give rise to the impulsive decisions to use such force.

There is much wisdom in the President's statement last week that "there can be no peace without law." He is right, too, when he says that "the passionate longing for peace—on the part of all peoples of the earth—compels us to speed our search for new and more effective instruments of justice."

Mr. Eisenhower pointedly declares that "the processes of the United Nations need further to be developed and strengthened" and that this must be done by "increasing its ability to secure justice under international law."

Unfortunately, the United Nations in recent years has become a political body where "log rolling" and the "expediency" of opportunism rules the day. Partisanship has superseded objectivity. The Soviet Government, for example, by openly helping the aggressor in Korea, violated the United Nations Charter but still remains a member of the U. N. Also, the Red China regime, which was formally denounced by the U. N. as an aggressor, is actually being sponsored today for membership in the U. N. by many of the so-called "peace-loving" nations. Yet Red China has never atoned for or repented her crime.

While the United Nations last week, by resolution of the General Assembly, asked for a cease-fire and withdrawal of British, French and Israeli troops from Egypt, it made the mistake of asking for the reopening of the Suez Canal itself without providing a means of dealing with the illegality which was the original cause of the whole tragedy.

International rights are readily defined. The historic principles of rectitude in international behavior are well known.

The time has come to establish the rule of law.

TRIUMPH AND TRAGEDY

NOVEMBER 16, 1956

A GREAT LEADER in the free world was re-elected President of the United States last week by the American people. They gave him a vote of confidence unmistakable and unqualified.

The tribute to President Eisenhower was well deserved. For he rose above partisanship as he offered a record of solemn devotion to duty and a conscientious pledge to help America avoid involvement in war.

In contrast, the campaign made by Adlai Stevenson was indefensible. It was, to a large extent, an attempt to scare the American electorate—by palpable exaggerations of the alleged ill-effects of the "fallout" from H-bomb tests and by speeches implying that the President was somehow responsible for the misbehavior of the Soviet rulers and even for the policies of the British and French governments in resorting to force in meeting Nasser's aggression in the Middle East.

Most regrettable were Mr. Stevenson's constant innuendoes uttered during the campaign in which he intimated that the President would not live out his second term. The Democratic nominee, discussing a possible Republican victory, went so far as to predict that, according to "scientific evidence," Vice President Nixon "probably would be President of this country within the next four years."

The effort to make Vice President Nixon personally an issue, by an attempt to impugn his integrity, was futile. Mr. Stevenson should have realized that, since Dwight Eisenhower works intimately with the Vice President and has given him his complete trust and confidence, this was sufficient to dispose of that spurious issue. Mr. Stevenson used up time and energy that might better have been devoted to a thorough debate on domestic questions of an economic nature.

Foreign policy, of course, should never have been made an issue in the campaign. Long before the Middle East crisis developed, however, the President was conceded by political leaders, by poll-takers, and by editors in all parts of the country to be running ahead of his opponent by a substantial margin. But the trouble in Egypt did focus attention sharply on what a change in government could mean at this time—especially with a Democratic candidate who talked of ending the draft and the H-bomb tests, too.

In describing the election as a victory for President Eisenhower and his record, it must be said also that it was a victory for decent campaigning.

While there is satisfaction, however, in the nationwide approval of the conduct of the executive branch of the Government by the Eisenhower Administration, it is a tragedy that the electorate failed to give to the President a working majority in Congress.

If party responsibility in America is repeatedly ignored, we are in for some perilous times in government. The past two years in Congress have furnished example after example of obstruction by the Democrats which has deprived the country of needed legislation.

Nor did political campaigning end last week. It will go on now in both houses of Congress as the Democrats, conforming to the customs of an "opposition" party yet exercising the majority control, will seek to avoid enactment of the Executive's recommendations except in those few cases where the public understands the issues and makes its opinion felt.

Why, it may be asked, did not the voters last week elect a Republican majority in both houses? One reason is that in "one-party" districts in the South and Border States there were 66 House seats uncontested by the Republicans. Six Democrats were elected to the Senate without contests.

With respect to the seats in the House for which there were contests, the Republicans won 200 and the Democrats 169. In the Senate—leaving aside the six uncontested seats in the South—the Republicans won 17 and the Democrats won 12.

To get a working majority of 25 in the House of Representatives, the Republicans must win at least two-thirds of the seats in the North to overcome their handicap in the South. They can only achieve such a majority when economic conditions are uniformly favorable, which they were not this time because of the farm depression in the Western States. Indeed Mr. Eisenhower himself did not get a majority in certain Congressional districts in the West which previously had been Republican, and naturally the Congressional candidates lost, too. It cannot be said, therefore, that the Republican Party is inherently "weaker" than the Democratic Party. When economic factors are decisive, the intrinsic strength of a political party is not at stake.

The country faces a coalition government in Congress. But, while many of the Southerners think ideologically like the Northern Republicans, there are vital issues on which party lines are sharply drawn.

The American people have not yet been educated to understand—as is the case under the parliamentary system—the importance of making a single party responsible for both the executive and the legislative branches of the Government.

THE NEW BALANCE OF POWER

NOVEMBER 23, 1956

FOR MANY DECADES in modern history, the military power of one set of allies has offset the strength of the rival group of nations. An equilibrium has been involuntarily maintained for certain periods of time. This uneasy peace has been called the "balance of power."

When one or the other of the two groups of nations, however, tipped the scales of military force and endeavored to widen its sphere of influence or to conquer the other side, war usually ensued.

Recently the Soviet Union has built up its own system of alliances in Europe and has been reaching out for more allies in the Middle East and Asia to balance the Western alliance, with its control of the seas and many air bases.

It was Woodrow Wilson who, in a speech at London in 1918, a month after the ending of World War I, called for the end of the system of alliances and an abandonment of the balance-of-power doctrine. He urged instead collective security under the League of Nations—to guarantee the political independence and territorial integrity of every member country.

But the League failed because it had no enforcement machinery of its own. This omission was corrected by the United Nations Charter in 1945, which provided for an international police force.

The U. N., however, sent an international army into Korea to repel aggression there only to discover that Soviet Russia was disobeying the resolution which had called on all members to refrain from aiding the aggressor in Korea. The Moscow regime was not punished, and no machinery for punishing Communist China for her aggression has yet been adopted by the United Nations. Indeed, India and a bloc of other nations offered only last week a proposal in the U. N. to admit Red China to the Security Council—a brazen indifference to her aggression. It was defeated by a vote of 47 to 24.

It has become apparent, therefore, that, unless the major powers are agreed, no international army can be sent to any troubled area to punish the aggressor.

By a curious turn of events, the United Nations has been able in the last few days to try, for a different reason, the device of an international army. This time it is designed to take over the positions previously held by the combatant armies. Neither Soviet Russia nor the United States are—by resolution of the U. N. General Assembly—permitted to participate in the actual military force. Yet it is basically the formal support given the proposal itself by these two major powers which makes the action possible at all.

We are witnessing really a unanimous agreement by the strong nations—including Great Britain, France, Russia and the United States—to enforce the resolutions of the United Nations in seeking to stop a local war.

What the United States, under the policy of President Eisenhower and Secretary Dulles, has just done is to give support to a new balance of power in the world.

Whether for any long period of time this can spare the world the horrors of a big war may be debatable, but there can be no doubt of the President's broad objective. It is to apply the principle expressed in diplomacy as a "modus vivendi"—a way to get along or to live with existing problems without a war.

Unfortunately, abstention from the use of military force sometimes leads to war anyhow, because appeasement of an aggressor only whets his appetite for more aggression. Nor does human passion for liberty and freedom stagnate. It refuses to be anesthetized by any form of diplomatic opiate. The people of Hungary, for instance, will go on pressing for liberty and indirectly threatening the new balance of power, just as the peoples of the Middle East will insist on fulfillment of their goals of nationalism and individual security.

The Egyptian people cannot long endure Nasser's dictatorship. Nor can the people of the Arab world or Israel assure themselves of safety if Soviet Russia continues to carry on her intrigue and stir up rival nations in the Middle East to fight each other.

The entire world will hope and pray that the new balance of power will gain what is most necessary —time. The chances of bringing to bear the pressures of moral force are not lessened but increased by a period of "cold" peace. Inside Soviet Russia, the fires of revolution are smoldering. A world war would afford an opportunity for the Kremlin to tighten the shackles of enslavement. If, on the other hand, the two major powers—the United States and Soviet Russia—do not go to war, the struggle for freedom can progress everywhere inside the smaller countries, as indeed the peoples of Hungary and Poland have just confirmed.

The new balance of power may be temporary, but it may prove a useful counterstroke in the battle for human liberty. When all peoples are free, and military action can be controlled by governments established only by the consent of the governed, there will be less need for a balance of power—and then the ideals of a system of collective security will truly have been achieved.

THE ROOT OF THE TROUBLE

DECEMBER 7, 1956

WORLD PEACE can be achieved in two ways—either by the restraint that free nations impose upon themselves, or by the restraint which an international authority imposes upon any dictatorship government that threatens to bring on a war.

The free nations have been building a system of defensive alliances as a deterrent to war.

The Soviet dictators on their part have been setting up a rival system of military alliances and a diabolical mechanism of political infiltration, gradually drawing into their orbit the so-called "neutralist" nations.

The two systems cannot continue long before bringing on the very conflict that the world has dreaded.

The time has come to go back to the original concept—a world alliance.

The United Nations originally endeavored to make of itself a body that would "enforce" peace. All the necessary words were included in the long and comprehensive provisions of the Charter.

One big obstacle, however, has always remained—what to do if one of the major powers openly provoked disunity and clandestinely fomented small wars.

A test came in Korea in 1950. The free world sent its brave soldiers to repel aggression. The Soviet alliance, however, defied the United Nations, aided the aggressor and scoffed at its resolutions.

"Peaceful coexistence" between the two rival sets of powers now has proved a sham. "Armed coexistence" has taken its place. In recent months the Soviet rulers have been sending vast quantities of arms to Nasser in Egypt. It was they who encouraged him to seize the Suez Canal. It was they who initiated the Middle East crisis, and it is they who now are aggravating that crisis by dispatching a substantial amount of arms to Syria, to incite more fighting in that troubled area.

We have seen the Soviet Union, moreover, forcing puppet governments upon the nations of Eastern Europe. We have seen the Soviet Union denying even to the United Nations' representatives access to the territory of suffering Hungary.

Why do we hesitate any longer to face the root of the trouble—the regime in Moscow?

Misuse of the veto by the Soviet Union from the start of the U. N. has led to the whole series of defensive alliances and counter alliances. There is no use avoiding the basic issue any longer.

As a first step, we must put our whole moral and military strength behind the United Nations. It is the only organization available to us today through which world opinion and world military power can be mobilized on the side of justice and freedom. The U. N. must be transformed into a world alliance of free governments.

Dictatorships must go. They are a menace to world peace. Only free governments must be permitted to be members of the world alliance. Sovereignty would, of course, remain in each country. Participation in the world alliance should be wholly voluntary. It is a league of defense—not a world government—that must emerge from the new United Nations.

The Moscow Government is not a free government. It does not represent the will of the peoples who comprise the many nationalities in the Soviet Union today.

There must be instituted at once a systematic exposure of the facts of the Soviet plot which is threatening to disturb world peace. The investigative processes of the United Nations should be invoked, and the membership of the present Soviet Government suspended while this extraordinary trial is held.

We should proclaim at once the principles for which we and the other nations of the free world shall fight—if we must—to assure all peoples security from attack by the irresponsible men in the Kremlin:

First, that the political independence and territorial integrity of each free nation will be guaranteed and any violation by an external power will be resisted.

Second, that no nation may maintain troops on the soil of another country unless requested by a government that has been established in such a country by free elections, and then only through the authority of the world alliance. Every government that denies free elections must be regarded as suspect—as outside the world alliance.

Third, when nations seeking autonomy are capable of self-government and ready for it in an economic sense, too, they will be guaranteed their political independence. Free elections in troubled areas should always be observed by the world alliance, so as to make sure there is no outside interference.

Fourth, whenever legal questions arise such as Nasser's unlawful seizure of the Suez Canal in violation of a treaty the U. N. should request from the world court of justice a formal opinion as to which party is right.

The peaceful nations of the world have the moral and military power to bring about international discipline. If they falter now and do not pool all their resources, a general war will ensue within the next few years. There is still time to prevent World War III.

AMERICA TO THE RESCUE

DECEMBER 14, 1956

EUROPE is in a serious economic plight again. The recent closing of the Suez Canal has interrupted oil shipments and forced a curtailment of automobile production. It has brought a general breakdown of trade with the Middle East. It has put in a critical position not only England and France but other countries nearby.

Most of us have been assuming that Europe's economy has fully recovered from the last war. It needed only the Suez episode to show the weakness of the whole business structure of Europe.

For there is today virtually a run on the pound and on the franc. Currencies in other countries are bound to be affected.

Nothing is more important to a world economy than stability of monetary units.

America cannot afford to see Britain and France so weakened that neither country can finance a defense budget adequate for its own needs. Otherwise, the drain on American manpower would be very great. An increase in our own draft calls could become necessary if our allies in Western Europe found it impossible to support their armed forces at present size.

It is natural to blame the British and French governments for their impulsive intervention in the Egypt-Israel war. But even before this step there was a growing hazard of a big war in the Middle East due to Soviet penetration and the sending of arms to Arab states during the last two years. This was bound sooner or later to produce a crisis even more dangerous than what we have witnessed in the last forty days.

Vice President Nixon in a speech last week wisely commented on the Suez crisis as follows:

"Now is the time for all of us to recognize that recriminations and fault-finding will serve no purpose whatever. The cause of freedom could suffer no greater disaster than to allow this or any other incident to drive a wedge between us and our allies."

What can America do now to help? First of all, there must be a strengthened North Atlantic Treaty Organization as a backstop to the United Nations. But to build strong political ties will be impossible unless the economic foundations in the free countries of the world are also strong.

When all the facts have been gathered and the European countries have decided among themselves what is needed, the United States can consider how far it can go in meeting the needs of its allies. Congress, of course, will have to appropriate any funds required. It may take 2 or 3 billion dollars. This could prevent any tax reduction for the American people next year.

Basically, however, a way must be found to protect Europe against further interruptions in the flow of oil. Whether this means new pipelines to the Mediterranean to diminish dependence on the Suez Canal or whether it means the building of more tankers so as to permit a larger flow of oil from the Western Hemisphere to meet the needs of Europe are questions that will not be answered overnight.

But before many days have passed certain relief measures through the International Monetary Fund and the Export-Import Bank may be expected, and later on some comprehensive plan developed to give the European economy the bulwark it needs in these days of fluctuating currencies.

Broadly speaking, Americans do not realize what World War I and World War II did to Britain, France, Germany and Italy, as well as to Belgium, Holland and Norway. A whole generation, comprising many millions of able human beings, was wiped out in each of the two world wars. Credit arrangements of long standing and systems of distribution of commodities were twice broken up. When one considers that it took the South nearly a half-century to get on its feet after our own War Between the States, it can be imagined what Britain, France, Italy and Germany have been up against in the eleven years since the last war.

The Marshall Plan, begun in 1947, was a timely program of aid to Europe. But it has not achieved the permanent improvement that had been hoped for by its sponsors. America must help Europe now to make sure that another economic collapse of the European economy does not have dangerous repercussions on the economy of the United States.

It will be recalled that in 1931, when the British and French asked the United States for suspension of payments to this country on war debts, all Europe was in a weakened condition and Germany was on the verge of collapse. The vast unemployment there in 1933 produced the conditions that gave Hitler his chance.

It is to our interest to spend dollars now so as to avoid the spending of human lives later.

America can afford to help Europe not only as a matter of self-interest, but to prevent the chaos that could make it easier for Communist dictators to control the political parties of free governments.

America must come to the rescue, with material as well as moral support, in Europe's hour of need.

JUDGE-MADE CHAOS

DECEMBER 21, 1956

THE AMERICAN PEOPLE must stand aghast at the edict by a federal judge that anyone who speaks his mind in urging non-attendance at a mixed school in Clinton, Tenn., may be guilty of contempt of court.

This means that, without a trial by jury, citizens in supposedly free America can be put in jail for their utterances. Free speech is thereby squelched and thought control imposed.

This is a sweeping and arbitrary extension of judicial power.

It is not sanctioned by any act of Congress.

It is not authorized anywhere in the Constitution.

The "supreme law of the land" today—and it has not been reversed by the Supreme Court of the United States—was laid down by two judges of the U. S. Circuit Court of Appeals and a District Court Judge in July, 1955. The three-judge opinion of the court said in part:

"The Constitution does not require integration. It merely forbids discrimination."

The school board in Clinton, Tenn., complied fully with the Supreme Court's order—it opened its doors to everyone, irrespective of race. Beyond that it did not need to go. A federal judge there, however, evidently feels that his injunction, ordering nobody to "interfere" with "integration," covers also the acts and speeches of citizens and the distribution of printed matter anywhere in the community outside the school.

On Monday of last week an extraordinary thing happened in Clinton. Eugene Joyce, the County Attorney of Anderson County, at the request of the school board, made a speech in which he read this federal injunction to the assembled high-school students. The full text of his remarks, as stenographically recorded, appear on page 59-61 of this issue. Certain passages are startling. The County Attorney, for example, said:

"To my knowledge in all of American history it has never been necessary to read an instrument such as this, a federal injunction, before an especially called assembly of a student body."

Mr. Joyce went on to say:

"Questions have been asked of me and other law enforcement officials as to the enforceability of this injunction. I think the actions of the past few weeks or the past few days, particularly, speak in unmistakeable language that this injunction is enforceable.

"The other question so frequently asked is: Will this injunction apply to students under 21 or to acts inside the high-school building? The answer is that this injunction has no limits; it applies to everyone, every-where, be they minors, adults, inside or outside any building in this county."

Any reading of the text of the injunction confirms Mr. Joyce's view. It is in truth an injunction without limits. It covers every act and every speech or writing and every meeting of citizens in the community and county which a federal judge—without jury trial—may decide to punish as violative of the spirit or purpose of the injunction itself.

It is important to note, moreover, that the County Attorney told the students that, while the school principal would hereafter expel "any student that is guilty of misconduct," their troubles might not end there. He added:

"They (the members of the Board of Education) have also instructed the faculty to pass on to the Federal Bureau of Investigation any actions on behalf of the students that might be construed as violative of the injunction."

What a means of intimidation this federal injunction turns out to be! In free America the boys and girls in a public high school are being taught, in effect, that State government has been abolished, county government has been abolished, and that an all-powerful dictatorship by the judiciary, acting upon "evidence" obtained through investigations made by the federal secret police, will now suppress the right of any citizen even to talk about segregation or integration.

The students in Clinton thus are given a false picture of their own system of government. They are not taught that they have a right to express themselves for or against segregation or integration. They are not taught, moreover, that under the Federal Constitution any assault or misdemeanor or any form of intimidation or threat is a case for State and county prosecution unless the State of Tennessee intends to abdicate all responsibility for maintenance of law and order.

Nobody, of course, should condone violence. But under the Constitution it is the exclusive duty of the State to prosecute any criminal offenses committed within the State. This is the "supreme law of the land" as laid down again and again by the Supreme Court of the United States.

This whole chain of events, which has come to a head in Clinton, Tenn., was forecast by James F. Byrnes, formerly an Associate Justice of the Supreme Court of the United States. In a speech on September 22 last, before the Vermont Bar Association, he declared

240

that only Congress, by appropriate legislation, can enforce the Fourteenth Amendment. Mr. Byrnes added:

"But the Supreme Court that was unwilling (in 1954) to leave the amendment of the Constitution to the Congress and the States, as provided in that instrument, likewise was unwilling to leave to the Congress the enforcement of the Fourteenth Amendment. It has substituted for congressional legislation the power of the courts. That means the power of injunction. It is a dangerous power, often abused.

"Already the press reports a blanket injunction by a United States judge against the people of a community, prohibiting interference with the integration of a school.

"Assuming the report to be correct, it suggests many problems. What constitutes 'interference' may not be set forth in a court order in the precise language of a criminal statute. If left to the discretion of a judge, it will differ in various jurisdictions.

"Heretofore, a judge could imprison a citizen for contempt committed in his presence. For refusal to comply with an order directing an affirmative act, like turning over assets, a citizen could be imprisoned by a judge solely to coerce him into complying.

"But in cases of criminal contempt, or proposals to imprison as punishment for some act already done—not in the presence of the court—the citizen was entitled to a jury trial.

"Now it is evident efforts will be made to deny the citizen a jury trial. The precedents about to be established by the expansion of the injunctive power will have far-reaching effects. They may place new restrictions upon the right of free speech. Certainly they will raise serious questions for the leaders of organized labor.

"If the speech of a citizen urging students not to attend an integrated school is held violative of a court order enjoining interference and is punished by imprisonment without a jury trial, then what about a speech by a labor leader urging employees not to work when interference is similarly enjoined?

"As a result of the Supreme Court's decision, a district judge has the authority to enjoin school officials from refusing to admit a student solely because of his race or color. More than that he should not do. He should not set himself up as a glorified school administrator."

It is clear, moreover, from a reading of many decisions of the Supreme Court, that the Fourteenth Amendment can be enforced only by legislation passed by Congress.

Justice Jackson, speaking for the Court in a decision ten years ago, emphasized that the fifth section of the Fourteenth Amendment specifically vests in Congress the authority to enforce it by statute. Citing an enforcement statute on certain phases of civil rights enacted by Congress on March 1, 1875, he wrote:

"This statute was a factor so decisive in establishing the Negro-case precedents that the Court even hinted that there might be no judicial power to intervene except in matters authorized by acts of Congress. Referring to the provision empowering Congress to enforce the Fourteenth Amendment, it said that 'all of the amendments derive much of their force from this latter provision. It is not said the *judicial power* of the general Government shall extend to enforcing the prohibitions and to protecting the rights and immunities guaranteed. It is not said that branch of the Government shall be authorized to declare void any action of a State in violation of the prohibitions. It is the power of Congress which has been enlarged. *Congress* is authorized to *enforce* the prohibitions by appropriate legislation.' "

Where are the so-called "liberals" of today in this controversy? They always are alert enough to raise their voices when a Communist sympathizer is dismissed from a government post because he allegedly holds different "opinions" than his superiors. It usually is protested that the Federal Government is seeking to impose "thought control."

But not one of the civil liberties organizations has cried out in protest against the patently outrageous extension of federal authority in the Clinton injunction.

The Bill of Rights of the Constitution guarantees free speech, free assembly and the right to a jury trial.

Do not the "liberals" believe in giving the boys and girls and their parents in Tennessee these rights?

Or do we have one standard for Communist sympathizers and another standard for loyal Americans who hitherto have been taught to believe that the States are responsible for the exercise of the police power in maintaining law and order within the States?

The Constitution plainly vests authority to enforce the Fourteenth Amendment only in Congress. This is "the supreme law of the land" today.

Is the legislative power of Congress to be circumvented by the subterfuge of a federal injunction issued in an unprecedented era of judicial tyranny?

Extreme measures usually beget other extreme measures. Will the Southern members of Congress now try to amend the Department of Justice's appropriation bills at the next session and filibuster against their passage unless "riders" are adopted defining the limits of federal and State authority?

"Integration" will never be accomplished at the point of a bayonet or by giving to the judiciary an enforcement power it has never possessed.

Judge-made law can only result in judge-made chaos.

1957

1957—A YEAR OF MORE WAR?

JANUARY 4, 1957

WHO WOULD HAVE THOUGHT that in the year 1956—so soon after World War II—the Soviet Union would suddenly disregard the provisions of the United Nations Charter and upset the equilibrium of Europe by supplying arms to an aggressor in the Middle East?

Who would have thought that in the year 1956 another Hitler, in the person of Nasser of Egypt, would arise to tear up treaties and seize an international waterway vital to the commerce of the world?

Who would have thought that in the year 1956 the arms supplied by the Soviet Union would be used by Nasser to threaten the continued existence of the little Republic of Israel, causing this victim of constant raids by Egyptian troops to act in self-defense?

Who would have thought that in the year 1956 Great Britain and France, their lifeline impaired by Nasser's illegal seizure of the Suez Canal, would land troops in the vicinity of the waterway in an effort to keep Egypt from capricious interference with commerce?

Who would have thought that in the year 1956 the United Nations would send an international police force to supplant British and French troops, and then let the situation revert to its previous status, as the whim of one man arrogantly determines when and how the Canal will be cleared and he himself goes unpunished for his illegal acts, including the deliberate sabotage of the Canal itself?

Who would have thought that in the year 1956 Syria—now coming under Communist control—would deliberately sabotage the pipelines that carry oil overland from Arab countries to the Mediterranean?

This is the traditional sequence. It's the way little wars begin and usually lead to big wars.

For war over a large area, and involving millions of innocent people, is the inevitable consequence of timidity, fear and appeasement of dictators.

What we have witnessed is a series of unilateral acts—a chain of events based on the doctrine that sovereignty means the right to be irresponsible and that the "national interest" as interpreted by a single country is paramount, irrespective of the impact on the peoples of many other countries.

It has been the hope of the world that some form of international discipline might be established after the sacrifices made in the last two world wars. But the Soviet Union and Red China, by their aggression in Korea and Indo-China, tested the courage of the United Nations and found it wanting. So today we are paying the penalty for compromises, retreats and appeasements, as the Soviet Union reaches down, with her infiltration of weak governments, into Asia and Africa.

Misleading cries about "imperialism" and "colonialism" have duped many people in the free world into believing that we are witnessing only the struggles of the smaller nations for independence. What we are really seeing is how again and again the grant of complete independence to such nations leads to a loss of the military protection of the former sovereign as the newly-established governments become easy victims of Soviet penetration and control.

For, instead of the enlightened colonialism of the British and the Dutch and the French, we now have the subtle and dangerous colonialism of the Soviet Union as we see Communist infiltration in Indonesia, India, Burma, Syria, Egypt, Algiers, Libya, and Morocco.

Concurrently, the Soviet tyrants employ with brutality their military forces in Eastern Europe to keep the satellite states in subjugation. Rebellion, to be sure, has broken out and freedom's fighters are bravely resisting, but they have neither the arms nor the money to carry on active war. They can conduct guerrilla raids and harass the Communist puppet governments, but Soviet military power still hangs like a pall over all Europe, as the organized military power of the free world shows signs of weakness. What a tempting opportunity for the aggressors to take a chance!

Meanwhile, the misguided theorists on our side are already urging that we give Nasser more money to finance the Aswan Dam, and that we voluntarily withdraw our troops from Germany and thus weaken NATO's defenses. All this reflects appeasement—the belief that by concessions you win over the dictators.

When appeasement is the ruling policy, war comes dangerously near.

America has chosen to support the moves and programs of the United Nations as a means of enforcing some kind of international discipline. This is a commendable policy for the time being. But we must be prepared for the collapse of such efforts. In fact, the United Nations cannot insure peace unless it is ready to act firmly with Nasser of Egypt and compel some sort of settlement of both the Canal question and the little wars in the Middle East.

While we may indulge in wishful thinking, the fact remains that the passions which can give rise to another world war have been fully aroused, and 1957 may turn out to be a year of more war. Only by facing up to the real dangers can the catastrophe be averted.

245

THE COURAGE TO PREVENT WAR

JANUARY 11, 1957

IT MAY SEEM PARADOXICAL, but it is much easier nowadays unwittingly to encourage aggression than to check it and thus prevent a world war.

It's easy to appease—to adopt policies which make it appear that America is really afraid of becoming involved in a conflict of arms. This, however, is what invites a miscalculation by the aggressor who mistakes pacific intent for lack of courage.

Free governments are particularly at a disadvantage in making clear to a potential enemy their basic intentions. The necessity under our Constitution for the Executive to consult the national legislature affords an opportunity for partisan expression by petty-minded men, who often do not realize they are putting political partisanship and personal ambition above the national interest. The sour note of Adlai Stevenson, Democratic presidential nominee, in his statement while visiting at the Capitol last week, is a tragic illustration of this tendency. It was in sharp contrast to the statesmanlike pronouncement of Speaker Rayburn, Democrat, who called for a united stand behind the President.

There come times, therefore, when public opinion must assert itself unmistakably against allowing a vital question of foreign policy to become entangled in the political struggles of the day.

Thus, for example, there is a small group in Congress today which wants to "investigate" all the incidents and episodes which have led up to the President's decision to ask Congress for authority to use the armed forces of the United States in certain contingencies in the Middle East.

To publish the contents of messages and communications and the backgrounds of the talks between friendly governments which happen to have differences of opinion on current problems would bring out the full story, to be sure, but it would also breed acrimony and discord as between allied governments and ourselves—the very thing our enemies would welcome. Why rake over past disputes with our friends?

It requires statesmanship of the highest order to keep partisanship out of a congressional debate on foreign policy and to confine such inquiries by committees to a presentation of the facts necessary to obtain an understanding by Congress of the fundamental issues in the crisis that has arisen in the Middle East.

The United Nations machinery can be expected to deal concretely with the controversies that have arisen over control of the Suez Canal and the aggression which Nasser has perpetrated by his constant raids against Israel as well as his refusal to let the ships of Israel use the Suez Canal. He has sought to utilize Soviet arms and technical advisers in helping him form a military alliance of Arab states against the little Republic created by edict of the U. N. itself. But as against the main Communist aggressor, operating already with military weapons in North Africa and in the Near East generally, there is only one power able today to checkmate that advance. It is the power of the United States.

America, with its military and moral force, can bolster the U. N. in its efforts to settle the local disputes in the Middle East. But in the final analysis there must be some steps taken to make clear to the Soviet Union that, should the U. N. fail to check Communist aggression, American armed forces, allied with the military strength of other nations in the Middle East and in Western Europe, will challenge on the battlefield, if necessary, any military invasion of the free world.

We have drawn a line in Western Europe against the Soviets by participating in the North Atlantic Treaty.

We have drawn a line in Southeast Asia by sponsoring the Southeast Asia Treaty Organization.

We have drawn a line in the Far East by means of our bilateral treaties with the Philippines, Nationalist China and the Republic of Korea.

We have specifically drawn a line in and around Formosa to warn Red China against aggression there.

There is only one gap—the Middle East. We have the friendship and support of Greece and Turkey, of Iran and Iraq, and of Pakistan. We need to close up the openings in this exposed flank and let Moscow know we have drawn a new line of defense across which the Soviets must not go.

This is why President Eisenhower is asking for authority from Congress to use the armed forces of the United States to check Soviet aggression in the Middle East. When Congress similarly granted the President the power to use our armed forces to protect Formosa, both houses voted for it almost unanimously.

May Congress do likewise now, and thereby serve warning on the would-be aggressors that their moves will be resisted!

A courageous decision now may well avert a big war later on.

For Congress, by approving the resolution, will be proclaiming America's readiness to fight in defense of freedom, even if it involves nuclear war. That's the best way to prevent an aggressor from starting any war.

THE GREAT DANGER

JANUARY 18, 1957

GREAT AS IS THE DANGER of Soviet mischief-making in world affairs, a more immediate danger exists in our domestic affairs.

It is the danger that the national economy may break down.

For we are in the midst of a reckless and uncontrolled inflation. Prices have been steadily rising. Wage demands are continuing to be made for higher and higher "take-home pay." Meanwhile, the purchasing power of the dollar is slowly going down.

The tightening of credit by the Federal Reserve Board has restricted only one factor—the money supply. It does not go to the root of the trouble—the wage-and-price inflation spiral.

President Eisenhower is aware of the danger signals. He devoted a significant passage in his address to Congress last week to an appeal for "self-discipline." He pointed out to the powerful economic forces of our country—business management and the labor unions—that if wages continue to rise, if prices continue to go up and if there is no corresponding increase in productivity from labor, we shall be confronted with an economic crisis. This would compel the Government to intervene, and would bring back controls such as we had in wartime. The exact words of the President on this point are worth repeating here:

"The national interest must take precedence over temporary advantages which may be secured by particular groups at the expense of all the people.

"In this regard I urge leaders in business and in labor to think well on their responsibility to all the American people. . . .

"Freedom has been defined as the opportunity for self-discipline. This definition has a special application to the areas of wage and price policy in a free economy. Should we persistently fail to discipline ourselves, eventually there will be increasing pressure on government to redress the failure. By that process freedom will step by step disappear. No subject on the domestic scene should more attract the concern of the friends of American working men and women and of free business enterprise than the forces, latent and active, that threaten a steady depreciation of the value of our money." (For remaining text on this topic, see page 26.)

An uncontrolled inflation is like an uncontrolled automobile—it lands us all in the ditch.

The President spoke also of the international implications. He said: "Any program that endangers our economy could defeat us."

Soviet Russia has been patiently expecting the American system of capitalism to break down.

Our system of private enterprise is being gradually undermined by two big forces in our economy.

There is the uncontrolled force of businesses themselves, which, feeling the pressure of rising costs, raise their prices to meet the added expense.

There is the force of "big unionism" which sets wage scales on a nationwide basis, irrespective of the capacity of the smaller business located in low-cost-of-living areas to pay those same scales.

Labor-union leaders—pressed by ambitious rivals inside their own organizations—are striving each year to obtain agreements for higher and higher wage rates and benefits without regard to whether this pushes upward the price scale of several industries. The pattern of settlement in one industry usually influences other industries which buy supplies from it, and thus a chain reaction sets in for price increases. This inevitably weakens the whole economic structure.

Total profits after taxes are declining. Liquid assets are at the lowest point in recent years, as businesses dip deeply into working capital to get funds for more plant and equipment in a desperate effort to cut costs.

The biggest question of the present era is whether "big unionism" can apply self-restraint, or whether government must inevitably control both wages and prices to save the nation from an economic collapse and widespread unemployment.

The crisis presents a challenge to common sense in American business management and labor. Strikes are costly, and individual businesses feel helpless nowadays to resist union demands. But there must be a halt sometime to the steady upward climb of prices. For eventually the buyers do not buy and the employers begin to lay off employes and we are confronted with a full-fledged depression.

Is a big depression, therefore, inevitable? Can it be prevented by any measures taken now—a year or two before a crash comes? It is too late to put out a blaze when it has already enveloped a whole community.

Now is the time to take to heart the warning that the President uttered in his very important message to Congress. Can the American system discipline itself? This is really the most challenging question before the country today.

For if there is no self-discipline, government must act, and this could mean the beginning of the end of the whole private enterprise system.

HOW MUCH "BUTTER"?

JANUARY 25, 1957

WHETHER IT'S A HOT WAR or a cold war, the big question before every nation today is how to supply each year enough money for both "guns and butter."

Armament eats up an unprecedented proportion of a nation's funds nowadays. Most of the guns, moreover, become obsolete in a relatively short time and must be replaced by new guns. The whole process is unproductive, if compared with the more stable form of job creation in "peacetime" enterprises—the normal economy.

While recognizing that national security is paramount, we go on spending billions as usual for more and more of the nonmilitary objectives.

Yet the real issue is how much can the nation afford to spend for security and still maintain a normal rate of progress. For we know that the demand for social welfare programs increases as the population increases.

Boiled down, therefore, to the essential point, we must ask ourselves: How much "butter" can we afford, or, to put it another way, how much "butter" can we risk? Theoretically, the public interest demands that the needs of the people for better housing conditions and bigger incomes and a higher standard of living be fulfilled.

But theoretically also the national safety requires that every sacrifice be made to insure enough expenditure for armament to protect the nation in the event of war, whether or not it be fought with H-bombs.

The answer inevitably is a compromise. The judgment of the President and his Cabinet, the judgment of Congress, the mood of the people, and especially their readiness to understand the real issues or to accept the misleading slogans of the demagogue—all these factors are involved in the final decision as to what shall be done with a budget such as President Eisenhower submitted last week.

But do the people of America really understand or weigh seriously the whole world situation, with its many potentialities for the sudden outbreak of war? Do they understand that "foreign aid"—both economic and military—isn't just a largesse and that Uncle Sam isn't playing Santa Claus but is trying earnestly to bolster the weak countries where the aggressor, with his subversive tactics, may invade?

How much, moreover, do the American people understand what it means to them to live in freedom while so many hundreds of millions of enslaved people are suffering under the yoke of a ruthless tyranny?

The American people cannot live in isolationism. Yet it is evident that their minds are in large part isolated from the world situation. The headlines are perused occasionally with deep concern, but the whole idea of war seems to people generally something remote—especially the thought that "little wars" in the Middle East can ever affect us.

It is the danger of war that the American people have not yet been willing to face in all its implications.

There is only one way to prevent war—to be militarily strong enough to defend ourselves so that no aggressor will risk destruction by our massive retaliation.

But we cannot be strong if we overdo the pressure for armament on the theory that mere quantity brings safety. The armament problem of today is a problem in selectivity. Nobody disputes the basic need.

So must it also be with social welfare programs. Is a certain appropriation really necessary? Can it be postponed to some future time? Can we not persuade individuals and their families to do more for themselves so that the Government will have to do less? Must we indulge in luxuries when there is a war to be prevented?

This is the kind of approach we need. Programs of "austerity" which some nations have had to adopt—and have indeed borne with fine spirit—are, fortunately, not a requirement for us. All we in America have to do is to forego some luxuries—not necessities.

Congress has a solemn duty to perform. It is to join with the representatives of the executive departments in a nonpartisan, statesmanlike approach to the cutting of the budget. Senator Byrd of Virginia, Democrat, Chairman of the Senate Finance Committee, has pointed the way. Secretary of the Treasury Humphrey says frankly he would welcome budget cuts.

But everybody knows that fundamentally the obstacles are political. If one party decides to exploit and attack the refusal of the other party to appropriate money for a worthy but not essential object, such an attitude can only lead to a retreat by the party sponsoring economy, and thus bring about more and more expenditure and more and more inflation, with higher and higher prices.

By prudent policy a surplus can be accumulated in the Federal Treasury which will be big enough gradually to pay off our public debt and also to bring about a steady reduction in taxes. But it means a tightening of the belt at the Capitol and, in turn, throughout the country among the people generally.

We can have our guns and our butter, too. But the penetrating question now is: How much "butter"?

THE BUDGET THAT'S TOO HIGH

FEBRUARY 8, 1957

SEVENTY-TWO BILLIONS OF DOLLARS is a big sum of money for a federal budget. It is an amount difficult, even for members of Congress, to evaluate. They cannot possibly familiarize themselves with the wide variety of items in a budget.

Someday the American people will demand that the system of budget-making be reformed. Today's methods are obsolete and inadequate. The Government is too big to be run as it was 36 years ago when the present budget law was passed.

For the truth is Congress created a Bureau of the Budget but made it a subdivision of the office of the President. It gave no power to the Budget Director himself to change the estimates furnished by heads of departments and other governmental agencies. It made the Budget Director only a sort of information-gatherer for the President. It did not even require the Budget Director to be confirmed by the Senate.

No member of the Cabinet—not even the Secretary of the Treasury—has the official duty of reviewing the whole budget to determine what items should be included or eliminated.

The President receives estimates from each department or agency and depends on the Director of the Budget for explanatory data. But the decision in the last analysis as to how much shall be included must, by law, be made by the President himself.

Does anybody believe for a moment that any President can make a detailed examination or review of a present-day budget of the Government of the United States and do anything else?

There are, of course, items that do not change from year to year—obligations that grow out of existing laws or previous commitments. The President cannot, for instance, assume that certain laws will be repealed even though he may dislike them, yet they involve recurrent expenditures of many billions every year.

A President, to be sure, is the head of the Government and represents the national interest. He cannot be biased in favor of this or that special interest or locality. He must weigh judicially the demands of pressure groups. He must be sensitive to public opinion—for the continuance of his party in power depends on whether he has in general satisfied the wishes of the electorate.

When the budget law was passed in 1921, it was recognized that officials of the various departments might not be satisfied with the sums allotted to them in the budget and might complain to Congress. Strict regulations—which are still in force—were, therefore, issued by the President forbidding executive department employes from going to Congress to obtain higher appropriations than those set forth in the budget. This has been ingeniously circumvented by Congress itself. Officials are usually invited to testify at congressional hearings, and from them is elicited the information on which champions of particular causes base their demands for enlarged appropriations.

The voting of about a billion dollars more than the President and the armed services themselves asked for at the last session of Congress was so transparently the result of political demagoguery and collusion with overzealous advocates of larger spending within the executive departments that the incident makes one wonder whether strong laws rather than mere regulation should not hereafter govern the behavior of executive employes who connive with members of Congress to lobby for increases in the budget.

In all fairness, however, it must be said that the armament-spending group doubtless felt it was as much entitled to the taxpayers' money as the groups pressing for some of the so-called "welfare" items in the budget.

But who is to weigh all the facts and say for what the taxpayers' money shall be spent? The budget recently presented by the President was, according to his own admission, very high. He said he hoped it could be cut.

Congress has the sole duty of deciding what the final budget shall be. Under the British and Canadian system, the budget is submitted by the Prime Minister and then the Parliament must accept or reject it as it is, for both the executive and the legislative branch are controlled by the same political party. In America, where divided government prevails today, the people pay a high price for their failure to fix responsibility in a single party.

Someday Congress should set up large enough committees with proper staffs—perhaps a joint committee of both houses—to study continuously throughout each year the workings of the budget system and gather the necessary information to guide Congress.

Nobody likes the size of the new budget—neither the President nor the Congress. Certainly the taxpayers don't like it. For they see the federal budget going higher and higher, with no relief in sight from heavy taxes on the incomes of individuals and businesses.

How much longer will taxpayers tolerate such a haphazard system of budget-making as we have today?

THE HIGH COST OF FEAR

FEBRUARY 15, 1957

GOVERNMENTS EVERYWHERE in the world are under strain because of the size of their national budgets.

Yet governments everywhere must face the problem of protection against sudden attack.

Wherever one turns, fear is uppermost.

Many governments are afraid of each other. Alliances and counter-alliances are the order of the day.

Peoples under despotic rule are afraid of their own governments—that they may at any moment be plunged into a war nobody wants.

What an unprecedented era of social and economic progress all nations could enjoy in a world without fear—a world without competitive armaments, a world in which tension would vanish and everybody could concentrate on the pursuits of peace!

We recall the words of Isaiah's immortal prophecy:
"And He shall judge between the nations,
And shall decide for many peoples;
And they shall beat their swords into plowshares,
And their spears into pruning-hooks;
Nation shall not lift up sword again nation,
Neither shall they learn war any more."

This ideal, in the modern world, is called "disarmament." But it would be folly today to assume that peace can be achieved either by an international agreement to discard arms or by terrorizing peoples with talk of the awfulness of H-bombs.

Terror in and of itself will not prevent war. Mere agreement to bar the use of certain weapons of destruction will not assure peace if those who sign the agreements cannot be trusted to honor their pledges.

Fear emerges from the presence in the world of evil rulers who control hundreds of millions of people and can order them into war.

As fear begets fear, the world staggers today under armament burdens that are growing larger each year.

What is the answer to it all?

We have invented weapons of destruction, but we have not invented means by which peoples can persuade each other to live in peace.

When will we begin to recognize that the power to prevent war lies with peoples?

When will we appropriate enough dollars to build effective channels of communication with other peoples?

The task of removing fear is not one for underlings and bureaucrats with an abundance of radio stations and transmitters at their disposal, important and essential as these devices may be.

The central responsibility lies in free governments themselves. We have a powerful voice in the Presidency. We should have, but do not have, powerful voices in our national legislative body. There we have mostly captious critics so eager to win future elections that they would crucify their highest officials on the cross of bitter partisanship.

To speak as a nation in the councils of the world, we must speak with one voice of patriotism.

America's influence grows—indeed, the influence of any alliance of free nations grows—when there is unity of purpose inside the ranks.

The desire for peace must be supplemented by an active crusade for peace.

Challenging plans are needed—imaginative plans and programs. What benefits, for example, might flow to the people of Soviet Russia if their armaments were converted to "plowshares"! What progress could civilization make with the huge sums of money that would become available to improve the lot of hungry, starving countries where there is need for machinery to build a new economy!

But first steps must come first. There must be a constant preachment about the need for the removal of tyrannical rulers so that peoples may freely choose their representatives.

There is no fear of war between Canada and the United States or between this country and its neighbors to the South. There is no fear of war as between France and Great Britain. There is no fear of war between most of the peoples of the earth because, wherever there are free governments, there is no menace to peace.

We must concentrate, therefore, on the few capitals of the world where tyrants rule. The way to peace does not lie in appeasing the rulers in Moscow and Peiping. We must not enhance their prestige by treating them as equals. We must speak directly, constantly, boldly and forthrightly to the peoples of Soviet Russia and Red China. We must again and again strive to deal only with representatives of the people—chosen in really free elections.

For the doctrine of genuine freedom, when embraced by all the peoples of the world, contains the key to peace.

It is the one way to banish fear from the face of the earth—to win the crusade for universal freedom. The people everywhere in their own interest can achieve that victory—for they themselves have the power to destroy fear.

ABOVE THE LAW?

FEBRUARY 22, 1957

IS THE PRESS ABOVE THE LAW? Has the press any responsibility whatsoever to cooperate with constituted authority when a difficult and delicate issue of international policy is at stake?

The United States Government recently asked American newsmen not to go to Red China and declined to validate their passports for travel to that country. Three newsmen, permitted by the Peiping Government to go to the mainland, ignored the State Department's request, declaring that the Department has no legal authority to invalidate their passports. Assuming, however, that there is such a right of travel for newsgatherers, as distinguished from the limitation on the rights of any other businessman, is it wise or patriotic for the press to fly in the face of constituted authority, especially in a matter that involves an enemy government which still holds American citizens as hostages?

But there is in this case a plain contravention of the regulations issued by our Government.

There is today a law on the statute books known as the "Trading With The Enemy Act." It restricts commercial intercourse with Red China, particularly the carrying of any American funds into that country by American citizens.

There are American businessmen who want to ship goods to Red China and to go there to negotiate business deals. The State Department has refused to validate passports for travel there, or to approve any transactions of commerce with Red China. Is the press, however, a group by itself—immune from such laws?

While the Constitution says that Congress shall make no law "abridging the freedom of the press," the Supreme Court of the United States has again and again limited that immunity by declaring that the press must obey the regulatory laws of the land as they apply to all businesses.

The Supreme Court of the United States has said:

"The fact that the publisher handles news while others handle food does not . . . afford the publisher a peculiar constitutional sanctuary in which he can with impunity violate laws regulating his business practices."

In another case, the Supreme Court also said:

"The publisher of a newspaper has no special immunity from the application of general laws. He has no special privilege to invade the rights and liberties of others. He must answer for libel. He may be punished for contempt of court. He is subject to antitrust laws. Like others, he must pay equitable and nondiscriminatory taxes on his business."

But even if there were no question of legal right involved, what is the true responsibility of the press?

When the Weinberger baby was kidnapped, most newspapers cooperated fully with the police request to suppress temporarily any mention of the kidnaping or ransom efforts, but one newspaper in the area did not. The end result was a tragedy—the baby was left to die when the kidnaper was scared off by crowds which had gathered near the ransom spot as a result of the publicity. It was the right of the press to gather the news—but was it wise and in the public interest to print it?

On December 4, 1941—just a few days before the Japanese made their attack on Pearl Harbor—several American newspapers published secret documents from the defense files of our Government in which Admiral Stark and General Marshall were revealed as having prepared a joint strategic estimate of the action to be taken by the United States if war broke out with the Axis Powers. Hitler, in announcing on December 11 the German-Italian declaration of war on the United States, explained that his final decision had been provoked by these newspaper revelations in America. The Secretary of the Navy called the documents "the most secret" papers in possession of our Government.

It was the right of the press to gather this news. But was it wise and patriotic to print it?

Red China today is an enemy government. American troops guard the armistice line in Korea, where a state of war still exists between the Communists and the United Nations. No peace treaty has been signed, and the armistice has often been violated.

Red China's Government, of course, wants American newsmen to come to China as a vehicle for its propaganda, but will not let them travel where they please or interview anyone they choose.

For many months now the American Government has been trying patiently in negotiations at Geneva to obtain the release of American prisoners still held in violation of the Korean armistice. The State Department has declined to give passports to relatives of American prisoners in Red China. Naturally, the United States Government has the duty under international law to protect American citizens wherever they go.

The Department of State wishes to avoid further complications. Is it asking too much for the dissident members of the American press to cooperate patriotically with their own government in a delicate and difficult issue of international relations?

TAMPERING WITH THE BALLOT BOX

MARCH 1, 1957

WHEN THE HIGHEST COURT OF A STATE begins to tamper with the ballot box and sets itself up as superior to the Legislature—or even to the Constitution of the State—as has just happened in Rhode Island, such action is a plain usurpation of power by the judiciary.

Although the Supreme Court of Rhode Island handed down on January 1 last a brief memorandum of conclusions, it issued only a few days ago the text of its formal opinion. It gives for the first time a detailed argument seeking to defend this amazing deviation from justice.

The absentee ballots of 5,454 citizens of Rhode Island were discarded by order of the Court because they were cast before Election Day, while 648 absentee ballots were accepted by the Court because they were cast on Election Day.

This rejection was in disregard of the specific wording of the law of Rhode Island which says that voting by absentees "may be done on or before said Election Day."

The Court's decision changed the election result, giving Rhode Island a Democratic Governor by 63 votes, although the voters had elected a Republican.

Many States have similar laws about absentee voting. If the technical and tortuous reasoning disclosed in the decision of the Supreme Court of Rhode Island becomes a precedent for other States to follow, many shut-ins and persons who happen to be ill at election time will lose their right to vote.

The facts are clear: The people of Rhode Island in 1948 adopted an amendment to their State Constitution which specifically says that persons "who are absent from the State, or who, by reason of old age, physical disability, illness or for other physical infirmities, are unable to vote in person, being otherwise qualified to vote at the general election held bi-annually, on the Tuesday next after the first Monday in November, shall have a right to vote in all elections in the State . . ."

In that same constitutional provision was a broad grant of authority to the State Legislature declaring that "the General Assembly shall have full power to provide by law for carrying this article into effect and any ballot cast under the provisions of such law shall be received and counted with the same effect as if given by such elector in open town, ward or district meeting."

The Rhode Island Legislature in 1953 passed a law which authorized absentees to vote "before or on said Election Day." Now the Supreme Court of Rhode Island argues speciously that, while in a 1944 amendment to the State Constitution military personnel were permitted to vote at any "time" fixed by the Legislature, it was somehow significant that this wording was omitted from the constitutional amendment adopted in 1948 which opened the right of absentee voting to all citizens, including shut-ins and ill persons. Hence the Court accepted as valid only the votes of 648 absentee civilians because their ballots were notarized as having been cast on the regular Election Day.

Yet no restriction had been imposed anywhere in the Rhode Island Constitution itself on the right of the Legislature to set forth by law the details of absentee voting. Certainly, since the Legislature in 1948 was given by constitutional amendment "full power" to deal all inclusively with absentee voting, it acquired the full right to provide by law exactly when and how the ballots could be cast—that is, on or before Election Day. Had the people wished to deprive the Legislature of the power to arrange the voting at a time convenient to absentees, they would have said so.

The Court's opinion notes that the Legislature in 1942 had asked for an advisory opinion and that the Supreme Court of the State in that year had said the Legislature did not have the power to permit absentee balloting before Election Day. But the 1942 ruling was rendered before adoption of the 1948 amendment to the Rhode Island Constitution which gave the Legislature "full power" to deal with absentee voting. An advisory opinion, moreover, rendered in prior years by a court does not supersede the plain phrasing of a constitutional amendment adopted in subsequent years by a vote of the people themselves.

Plainly, a constitution is not a series of legislative enactments. It is a charter that grants broad powers to the Legislature to carry out by appropriate laws the stated purposes of the constitution.

The Rhode Island Legislature, taking into account all the difficulties that surround absentee voting, deemed it fair and practical to let absent citizens mark their ballots before Election Day. This was a proper exercise of legislative power.

To count a certain number of ballots as valid and arbitrarily to invalidate others is to take away from the Legislature "full power" to enact legislation that treats all absentee voters alike. The Court's decision is a plain discrimination between citizens. It is a denial of "the equal protection under the laws" guaranteed to the citizens of Rhode Island by the Federal Constitution itself. It is a palpable tampering with the ballot box.

TURNING THE CLOCK BACK?

MARCH 8, 1957

STRANGE VOICES are being heard nowadays in the United States Senate. They are reminiscent of the 1920's, when the United States Government rejected the principle of collective security. They remind us also of the 1930's, when a vacillating America failed to announce in clear-cut terms in advance that we would come to the aid of the victims of aggression—a circumstance that led Hitler to believe he could win a war in Europe before the American Congress could make up its mind what to do.

What we are hearing in the Senate today is not the voice of the Democratic Party of Speaker Sam Rayburn of the House of Representatives, or of the three Democratic Presidents of the last half-century.

We are hearing instead from various Democratic Senators the voices of a revived isolationism.

We are being told again that we must not "meddle in Europe or Asia."

We are being told again that the President might plunge us into war without consulting Congress.

We are being told again that there must be no "advance delegation of the power to declare war."

We are being told that, if serious trouble comes, the President can always call the Congress into session and obtain whatever authority he needs.

We are being told that alliances of a military nature are bad, and that America had better rely on her own strength and keep out of "foreign entanglements."

We are being told that American taxpayers' money must not be spent abroad when there are "so many better ways to use the money at home."

We are being told that to furnish any economic aid to Egypt means an increase in cotton production there and more competition for our Southern cotton-growers.

We are being told that American foreign policy seeks primarily to protect American oil companies with investments in the Middle East. The fact that it is vitally necessary to supply oil to sustain our allies in Europe seems to have been ignored.

We are being told that American foreign policy is drifting, rudderless, purposeless, that the Soviet threat in the Middle East does not create an urgent situation, and that the President, in pressing for the passage of the Eisenhower Doctrine resolution, is ill-advised.

But these are mere excuses and quibbles. The startling development is that so many of the Democrats, joined by two or three Republicans, are looking at things through the eyes of the old isolationists. They are trying to get rid of the whole problem of the "cold war" or the threat of a "hot war" by wishful thinking. They would issue at this time a meaningless statement of generalities as a substitute for the Eisenhower Doctrine resolution. This would tell the world that America is disunited and may not make up its mind what to do until the Soviets have already grabbed off the Middle East.

We are hearing today the kind of talk which, if accepted by American public opinion, will produce the very conditions that can lead to a third world war.

Isn't this an atomic age in which we are living?

Didn't the Senate by an overwhelming vote of both parties accept the leadership of a Democratic Administration and ratify a treaty that obligates the President,—without going again to Congress for authority—to resist an attack on any of the 15 countries now members of the North Atlantic Treaty Organization?

Didn't the Senate in 1955, with only two negative votes and with the overwhelming support of the House, authorize the President in advance to use our armed forces to protect Formosa against Red China?

What the world faces nowadays is the threat of an atomic war. It is academic whether a President is or is not already authorized to use armed forces in an emergency. It is more important that the President be authorized now to employ the deterrent power of the United States to prevent a war. The Congress must let the whole world know that the President has been fully authorized to act. It will be too late to argue these points in Congress when the bombs are falling.

What President Eisenhower and Secretary of State Dulles are trying to do is to win a "cold war" now, so that there may be no "hot war" later on. It is imperative that American intentions be made clear now.

We need allies because we need military bases overseas and the help of their manpower. We should not spend a cent for boondoggling, but we should spend billions, if necessary, for military protection through allies in Europe and Asia and anywhere else in the world.

Let us not turn the clock back.

This is 1957. The American people want peace no matter what it costs in money. They want to save the lives of their sons. They will pay even higher taxes if it means that a world war can be averted.

This is the time for unity in America, for nonpartisanship and objectivity. It is a time for the Democratic Party to be true to its traditions and support the Administration's policies that seek to avoid war.

INVISIBLE GOVERNMENT

MARCH 15, 1957

REVELATIONS OF THE INSIDIOUS INFLUENCE and far-reaching power of some of the leaders of a national labor union have recently shocked the country.

A Senate committee—headed by the able and conscientious Democratic Senator from Arkansas, John L. McClellan—which is investigating labor rackets, has thus far only scratched the surface. Senators on the committee are telling the press there are more exposures to come.

It will not be an adequate answer to say that most of the union leaders in America have nothing to do with rackets and are dedicated to the cause of labor and nothing else.

What the Senate committee has brought out into the open is the existence of an invisible system of government which elects its own mayors and its own district attorneys, and compels the choice of its own police chiefs—to say nothing of the use of large sums of workers' dues and forced contributions to elect Governors and even members of Congress to do the bidding of these self-styled leaders. It is this misuse of financial and economic power which now rightly concerns the American people.

Time was when corporations perpetrated many an abuse against their stockholders and against the innocent public. Congress stepped in and wrote laws, not to restrain the legitimate activities of corporations, but to make sure there was no opportunity for illegitimate power to be exercised.

Labor unions have grown in membership in large part because they have obtained from employers by duress the "union shop," which is, of course, a form of "closed shop." By whatever term it is described, the basic requirement is that a man must join a labor union if he wishes to keep his job, for the employer is by contract required to dismiss anyone who refuses to join a union after 30 or 60 days of employment.

What, in the name of "liberalism," is this but a form of compulsion—a denial of the "privileges and immunities" of a citizen? How can so-called "liberals" consistently argue for "civil rights" legislation, while at the same time they never protest against compulsory unionization?

At the heart of the labor-union structure today is a rule of coercion. It takes away job opportunities from those who refuse to accept the discipline of a union.

In many occupations, there is a waiting list of workers. The applicants are told they must join a union but, even when they are ready to join, it is the union which, in effect, determines the priority in hiring. Isn't this a system of private government, with control over the lives and destinies of millions of our citizens in a supposedly free America? Is it any wonder that some of the national unions with many millions of dollars in their treasuries—accumulated largely as a result of this power to monopolize job opportunities—find it possible to use such funds for improper purposes?

It is apparent from the testimony recently taken by the Senate committee that union funds and power are used locally for improper purposes—to control elections in cities and States where enforcement officers turn their eyes away from vice-ridden areas because union officials have a vested interest there. This raises the question whether there is on the statute books adequate legislation to safeguard the funds of the workers. It is the basic legislative reason behind the current investigation.

One remedy, of course, is to require full disclosure. The Securities and Exchange Commission was created by Congress to receive and examine the financial reports of corporations, and a great deal of data is filed during the year about the relations of the corporations to their stockholders and long-term creditors. Is it not desirable to require labor unions to submit to the same kind of minute supervision so that the money they collect from working men will not be wrongfully used?

We now have strict antitrust laws that prohibit corporations from engaging in monopolistic practices. Political influence by the labor unions thus far has prevented the antitrust laws from being extended by Congress to cover labor-union practices.

National labor unions nowadays fix prices in a whole industry by fixing uniform labor costs throughout that industry. By ordering a strike or a boycott, they can destroy a business man who refuses to do the bidding of a labor union, and they can favor a competitor who is willing to act in collusion with the union and pay tribute to it.

Should not the 30 States, moreover, which do not yet have provisions in their Constitutions or State laws guaranteeing the citizen the right to work—the right to join or refrain from joining a union—be encouraged to adopt such measures?

The civil rights of citizens of every race, creed and color are being abused in the numerous labor-union rackets of today.

It is time to bring about the abolition of invisible government in America.

U.N. ASSEMBLY IS
NO SUPER-GOVERNMENT

MARCH 22, 1957

AN IMPRESSION has been developing that the United Nations General Assembly, particularly in the Egypt-Israeli dispute, is acting as a super-government.

The public is beginning to believe that because the Secretary-General, Dag Hammarskjold, and his Under Secretary, Ralph Bunche, conduct conferences with President Nasser of Egypt, the U. N. officials can issue orders to both sides to keep the peace.

But the truth is the Secretary-General and his assistants have no such authority, and the U. N. General Assembly has no power of that kind, either.

Disappointing as it may be to many in our midst who have hoped for an immediate settlement by the U. N. of the Israeli-Egypt controversies after the recent withdrawal of the troops, the fact is that the United Nations Emergency Force is in Egypt and in the Gaza Strip only through the consent of the Egyptian Government.

While it is true that Egypt has no sovereignty over the Gaza Strip, actually Egypt was given, by the terms of the Arab-Palestine armistice of 1949, the military right temporarily to occupy the Strip.

The U. N. General Assembly resolutions merely call on the parties concerned to settle the disputed points, but, legally speaking, the U. N. representatives can only plead with the Egyptians to allow certain steps to be taken looking toward a settlement.

Thus, we may have a situation again in which Egypt can, with impunity, send raiding parties into Israeli territory through the Gaza Strip and block the Gulf of Aqaba and the Suez Canal to Israeli ships.

There is no power in the U. N. Assembly itself to restrain Egypt's aggressions except, of course, to exert force in the court of public opinion.

There are signs that Moscow pulls the strings in Cairo and controls the inflammatory press and radio there, and thus keeps at fever heat the emotional tensions in the area. This prevents direct negotiations between Israel and Egypt, who might otherwise find a means themselves of settling their controversies peaceably.

But if the U. N. General Assembly has no power except to "recommend" measures, where is there any authority in the U. N. to stop local wars and compel a settlement?

The answer is that the Security Council, in which the major powers each has the right of veto, is the only part of the United Nations Organization that can take military and economic measures, occupy territory and compel a settlement on the terms proposed by the Security Council.

While the Security Council, of course, did authorize in June 1950 military action to "repel aggression" in Korea, no similar step has since been ordered.

The Security Council has not decided to intervene in the Middle East, presumably because the Soviet Government is not anxious to bring peace but wants to keep the Middle East aflame.

Britain, France and Israel all were cognizant of the weaknesses of the United Nations structure when they took military action last autumn against Egypt. Moral force came into play later and persuaded the British and French first, then the Israelis subsequently, to withdraw their troops without exacting any agreement in advance from the Egyptians as to what they would do in the interest of an equitable solution of pending problems.

Granted that the military action last October was inopportune, even though the British and French and Israeli governments felt they had ample justification because of Egypt's disregard of the Suez Canal contract and because of other provocations, the simple truth today is that, if Egypt does not respect moral force, there will be left only military and economic force again to deal with any further crisis.

Next time, of course, the United States would become directly involved. For President Eisenhower and Secretary of State Dulles have publicly stated that, by withdrawing her troops, Israel could feel assured of a fair settlement of the issues and particularly could expect freedom of navigation for her ships through international waterways.

If Egypt, however, insists on a "legal" right to govern the Gaza Strip and continues to bar all Israeli ships from using the Suez Canal or the Gulf of Aqaba, the Middle East situation will not have advanced toward peace but toward more war.

Only joint action—moral or military—by the big powers can then make the disputants accept the settlements that must be devised by those major powers if there is to be peace.

For the U. N. General Assembly is not a super-government. The real power of discipline is still in the hands of the United States and its allies. This country now has proclaimed to all the world that it has a paramount interest in the Middle East and that it is ready to assume direct responsibility in that area of the world.

SOMEBODY ELSE'S MONEY

MARCH 29, 1957

A SHOCKING STORY about misuse of the funds of labor unions is being exposed by a Senate committee investigating "rackets."

When workers join a union and pay dues regularly out of their hard-earned wages, either for pensions or any other purpose, they expect their money to be put into the equivalent of a trust fund.

This money is not paid in by the workers to be used in any enterprise that union officers happen to decide is a "good investment." Certainly the lending of union funds to friends of union leaders is not a proper use of the workers' money.

Trade unions have a legitimate purpose. They are useful, especially in large industries, as a means of fostering the best interests of the workers in their relations with employers. But unions should be democratically organized and democratically operated.

Too many unions are dominated by arrogant minorities. Too many owe their large membership lists primarily to tactics of coercion or intimidation.

Workers who are forced to join a union are not likely to participate in its meetings. Those who have been bludgeoned into joining in the first instance fear strongarm methods if they venture to raise their voices against the few who run the union.

Some of the older and more experienced unions in America have provided in their respective constitutions a system of checks and balances so that power cannot be abused. The machinery is sometimes cumbersome but it is better than the dictatorship type, where one man or a small clique makes the decisions, as ratification is voted at meetings controlled by a few henchmen.

Funds amounting to hundreds of millions of dollars have been collected annually by labor unions either for pensions or for organization expenses. The collection of dues has been made automatic in many instances, so that the employer actually withholds them from the worker's pay envelope and transmits the money directly to the union treasurer. Sometimes what are called special "assessments" are levied by the unions, but often the information as to the real purpose of such assessments is vague.

When we read, therefore—as was revealed in the committee proceedings last week—that $100,000 in cash was placed at the disposal of one or two men in the Teamsters Union to be used for political purposes, and no accounting was required to any public authority of the State in which the political influence was to be ex-

erted, we begin to wonder how long the rank and file of the American workers will tolerate such abuses.

Every citizen has a right to his own political beliefs, and it is deplorable to find labor unions collecting money to support candidates that many workers do not themselves favor.

The customary alibi given is that money for political campaigns is collected separately from dues and that these are "voluntary" contributions. But many a worker has found to his sorrow that he must either contribute "voluntarily" or risk the penalties that come when a worker incurs the disfavor and hostility of the powers-that-be in a union.

Letter after letter has come to members of Congress for years complaining about the terror that exists inside labor unions. The Congress has been told again and again that compulsory unionization is a violation of the civil rights of the citizen. But no legislation has been passed to prohibit compulsory unionization. It is still necessary in free America to join a union in order to keep a job in many industries and businesses.

Revelations by the Senate committee investigating union activities are opening the eyes of the American people.

History is replete with instances of the wrongful use of "somebody else's money" invested in corporations by stockholders who could not possibly know what was being done with their savings. The scandals uncovered by congressional committees led to the passage of strict laws that require independent accountants to audit and certify to the books of corporations. Various statutes make it necessary for certain reports to be filed by corporations periodically with governmental agencies.

But, while unions should be required to make similar reports and to obey State laws such as those enacted for corporations, these evils will not be remedied by statutes alone.

What is necessary is full disclosure of all the financial data of unions, so that each member may at least have all the facts. Next it is important to insure protection for minorities inside unions—the right of free speech and the right to be protected against reprisals if they vote in dissent.

The biggest corrective, however, will come from the outraged workers themselves. They will not long be ruled by men who lack integrity.

The handling of somebody else's money is and ought to be always an inviolable trust.

"MODERN REPUBLICANS" AND "MODERN DEMOCRATS"

APRIL 5, 1957

SPONSORS OF THE PHRASE "modern Republicanism" seem to have encountered within their own party a mixed reaction. Some Republicans regard the new label as a slur upon the sound principles of conservatism. Other Republicans hail it as a means of matching whatever advantages among the voters the Democrats in the North may have been deriving from the so-called "liberalism" of today.

Likewise, the radical wing of the Democratic Party, through its newly created "Advisory Committee," has been publicizing a definition of "modern Democrat" that seems to disregard the views of the conservatives of the South, so many of whom happen to be chairmen of the powerful committees in both houses of Congress.

But isn't the writing of such definitions today really an opportunistic effort to interpret the purposes of each party as being loftier in theory than in performance? Can this be accomplished by hurling epithets of disdain at the faction in each party which, by conviction, upholds the traditional principles of government in America?

It is nothing new, of course, to see a President of the United States trying to make his party over in the image of his own Administration's policies. The amazing thing is that so few who espouse "modernism" are aware of the programs for human betterment that were enacted 50 years ago.

Basically, the struggle in the political arena has always been waged between the "haves" and the "have nots." It goes on generation after generation. Redistribution of wealth is not a "modern" doctrine. It is truly ancient. Yet a "modern Republican" or a "modern Democrat" gets his biggest applause nowadays when he champions what is known as the "welfare state." It is a doctrine whereby the individual depends primarily on the Government to take care of him.

In recent years, moreover, the "general welfare" clause of the Constitution has been deliberately distorted to support the view that the Government can spend almost any amount of money and for any purpose it chooses. Some of the "modernists" have gone so far as to argue that it also means the exercise of any power the Federal Government might choose to exercise. Yet we are supposed to have a written Constitution which enumerates the specific powers that are delegated by the people to the Congress. Usurpation is not "modern." It's the same old scheme by which a tyrannical majority rides roughshod over a helpless minority.

The currently espoused "liberalism" which would, by drastic methods of taxation, deprive the citizen of his property or confiscate his savings under the guise of a benevolent purpose, also is not "modern," although this is today euphemistically called "humanitarian" by the politicians. Anyone, of course, who opposes such programs nowadays is usually characterized as a "reactionary" or a "person without a heart."

This is because sociology is solemnly cited as "modern" authority in interpreting the Constitution. "Forced association" in schools, for example, is imposed not because there is anything in the Constitution which gives the Federal Government power to regulate school attendance in the States, but because the sociologists persuasively recommended it to the Supreme Court as essential to the development of "modern" education.

Such worship of the gods of political expediency is not "modern." It is the gospel of Machiavelli.

Hardly any of the terms we hear in today's politics is of recent origin. "Inflation," for instance, is not "modern." It is a process by which the monetary unit of a nation is slowly depreciated. The trick is as old as money itself. Adam Smith, in his work, "The Wealth of Nations," published in 1776, refers to this form of deception as having been practiced often by "ancient governments." But today we call it "modern."

It isn't "modern" to rob Peter to pay Paul or to spend far more money than you can pay back. The list of governments which have violated that rule goes back quite a distance in history.

It isn't "modern" to pooh-pooh subversion and to admit the enemy within your gates when he deceives you with a smile. The story of the Trojan horse is many centuries old.

It isn't "modern" to advocate the supremacy of a centralized government over the States. Hamilton favored it, and Jefferson opposed it.

It isn't "modern" to spend public funds for direct grants to the citizens. The grant of public lands for homesteading and rights-of-way for railroads was recognized as a necessary principle of federal aid in the early days of the development of the Republic.

Nor is there anything "modern" in the "isolationism" that emerges nowadays in the speeches of prominent Democrats of the "liberal" school of thought in Congress, paralleling the utterances of a small Republican faction. They quote George Washington's advice against engaging in foreign wars, but they ignore the fact that in 1812 we participated in our first world war, using such military and naval power as we had to fight the British, who were then in the midst of the Napoleonic Wars.

It isn't "modern" to find a President asking Congress to proclaim a United States doctrine warning the Communists to keep "hands off" in the Far East or in the Middle East. In 1821, President Monroe announced a policy for the United States that told European imperialism to keep out of the Western Hemisphere.

Nor is it "modern" for the Democratic or the Republican Party to contain an "isolationist" group which opposes internationalism. Indeed, in 1900 we saw William Jennings Bryan, Democratic candidate for the Presidency, making his campaign on the issue of "imperialism" because our naval forces fought Spanish forces in Manila Bay and acquired the Philippines. We saw also William McKinley, the Republican nominee in that same year, winning out on the premise that America had become a "world power."

Turning to domestic policy, there has always been, of course, a fundamental difference between the experimentalist who is willing to take dangerous chances in the use of governmental authority as it affects our economic problems, and the experimentalist who wants to proceed cautiously with the minimum of risk—but who does want to try out new ideas.

There is, on the other hand, the stagnant mind which wants to "leave well enough alone" or which has a preconceived conviction that all experiments will turn out to be wrong anyway.

It is not necessary to confine our definitions to the debates in politics. The same attitudes are to be found in the field of economics, or in science, or in religious circles. There are men who become "reactionaries" in their early years, and men who become "radicals" in their advanced years. Age itself is not a consistent guide.

Conservatism and radicalism are really characteristics of differing personalities and, when applied to political parties, more often than not reflect the conflict between those who fear reckless extremists and those who believe propaganda can make the public approve almost any reform for reform's sake.

What Ralph Waldo Emerson said more than a century ago in his famous essay on "Politics" still reads as if it were penned last week. He wrote in 1844:

"Of the two great parties which at this hour almost share the nation between them, I should say that one has the best cause, and the other contains the best men. . . .

"The spirit of our American radicalism is destructive and aimless; it is not loving; it has no ulterior and divine ends, but is destructive only out of hatred and selfishness.

"On the other side, the conservative party, composed of the most moderate, able and cultivated part of the population, is timid, and merely defensive of property. It vindicates no right, it aspires to no real good. . . .

"From neither party, when in power, has the world any benefit to expect in science, art, or humanity, at all commensurate with the resources of the nation."

Much progress, however, has been made in America without the aid of Government and despite the ineptitude of our political parties.

What we need today is a realistic application of a principle that has stood the test of ages. It's a principle as modern as the Sermon on the Mount and as old as the Ten Commandments. It tells us to search our own consciences and to decide whether a particular policy proposed is in itself honest. It tells us to ask ourselves: Is the benefit to the people likely to be lasting or eventually destructive of self-reliance and of our system of private initiative? Will the policy really benefit the maximum number of persons in the country, or is it a policy merely to corral the votes of the supposedly uninformed or misguided citizens on the theory that the end—the winning of political office—justifies the means?

These questions have little to do with the slogans of political parties, but they have everything to do with what is moral or unmoral.

Politics today can and must be ruled by the same basic principle that our forefathers expressed when they acknowledged in the Declaration of Independence "a decent respect to the opinions of mankind."

When we begin to apply such a principle, the terms "modern Republican" or "modern Democrat" will mean what they ought to mean—a sincere devotion to what is really in the public interest.

This means forsaking hypocrisy and putting in its place fundamental honesty.

This means abandoning demagoguery and self-seeking—and substituting instead a spirit of unselfishness.

This means reliance no longer on the distortion of constitutional clauses, but a dependence instead upon the plain words of the law of the land.

This means a revision by the politicians of the low estimate they have been placing on the intelligence of the electorate, and the courageous display instead of an abiding faith in the common sense and integrity of the American people.

IRRESPONSIBLE GOVERNMENT

APRIL 12, 1957

WE HAVE BEEN REMINDED lately that, if a President of the United States becomes seriously ill and is temporarily unable to function, the Constitution does not say whether the Vice President lawfully can act in his place and for how long.

We have also been reading recently that, when the President submitted the annual budget to Congress, the Secretary of the Treasury said it was too high, and then the House of Representatives, in turn, asked the President to indicate how the budget could be cut. This seemed to many observers to be an example of "buck-passing." But actually it was a conspicuous example of a lack of well-defined responsibility in our governmental system. The sequel—budget-cutting by the "meat ax" method, as revealed last week in the fluctuating votes of congressional committees—is a dramatic example of irresponsible government.

There would be no argument today over the problem of succession during the temporary "inability" of a President, nor would there be any dispute about who is really responsible for the budget if we had a parliamentary system such as our neighbors in Canada enjoy.

There is little difference to them in substance between the inability of a Prime Minister to function because of his own ill-health and the situation that arises when the well-being of a nation suffers because of a lack of confidence in the policies of the Prime Minister.

Both types of problems can be handled promptly under the parliamentary system by a majority vote of the legislature. If the Prime Minister—who is the Chief Executive—doesn't feel impelled to resign, he can carry the issue to the country in a general election. There the people decide whether a new majority in the parliamentary body or the party of the incumbent Executive shall form the governing Cabinet.

Under a parliamentary system, the Executive is chosen from the legislative branch because over the years he has won his spurs in debates there. He usually has attained the leadership of his party because of his knowledge and experience in public affairs. This method also gives an answer to the question of whether a man chosen as Vice President in a previous election fits the particular situation confronting the nation when a new leader has to be selected. The utmost flexibility is afforded to make a new choice.

The argument against the parliamentary system, of course, is that it leads to frequent elections and instability. In some countries this happens, but the defect can be remedied by constitutional reform—as, for ex-

ample, by limiting the chances of arbitrary action through a two-thirds rule or specific provisions allowing "a vote of confidence" to be taken only on certain major issues and at fixed intervals.

Where the parliamentary form of government prevails, budget-making is the core of party responsibility. The political party which has won a majority of the seats in the parliament must take responsibility, along with the Executive, for the voting of a budget.

In America, however, we have today one party in control of the national legislature and another party in control of the executive branch of the Government. There is no party responsibility for the budget either in whole or in part and, even when the same party which wins the majority in Congress has elected its candidate for the Presidency, factional differences produce opportunistic coalitions of voting on various items in the budget. Hence, responsibility for the appropriations finally passed cannot be fixed anywhere—either in the party controlling Congress or in the Presidency.

Nobody really represents the "national interest" today except the President. Members of Congress represent primarily their local constituencies. The importance of the President as the spokesman of his party and of the Government itself was emphasized in February 1913, by Woodrow Wilson, as President-elect. Giving his views on presidential tenure, he declared that four years was "too long a term for a President who is imposed upon and does not lead" and that four years was sometimes "too short." Obviously he had in mind the flexibility of a parliamentary system. He added:

"Sooner or later, it would seem, he (the President) must be made answerable to opinion in a somewhat more informal and intimate fashion—answerable, it may be, to the Houses whom he seeks to lead, either personally or through a Cabinet, as well as to the people for whom they speak. But that is a matter to be worked out—as it inevitably will be—in some natural American way which we cannot yet even predict."

The time has come for Congress to create a commission composed of some of its best constitutional lawyers and other prominent citizens to study ways and means of establishing a system of "responsible government" in America.

We can never forget the poignant words of Lord Macaulay in his famous letter of 1857, written after a visit to the United States, when he warned: "Your Constitution is all sail and no anchor."

PEOPLES ABOVE GOVERNMENTS

APRIL 19, 1957

TOO OFTEN in our present-day thinking we focus on governments, on rulers, on administrations temporarily in power—and fail to keep our eyes on peoples.

The peace of the world can be disturbed, of course, by capricious rulers, but it also can be maintained only by what peoples do to restrain such rulers.

We have grown accustomed, for example, to thinking about the men in the Kremlin as typifying the Soviet Union, instead of fixing our sights on the peoples of the several Soviet "republics."

We talk much of Nehru and his idiosyncrasies, but we are little disposed to learn about the problems faced by the hundreds of millions of people of India.

We become aroused over the idea of inviting Tito to sup with our President at the White House, but we overlook the importance of communicating our thoughts to the people of Yugoslavia.

There is always, to be sure, the hazard that publicized visits between our leaders and dictators in foreign countries who have ideological ties with our enemies may be misconstrued by the people abroad and enhance the prestige of such rulers, thus weakening the potential resistance to them.

But the advantages may outweigh the disadvantages. Sometimes the device opens up opportunities to channel ideas directly to the peoples in countries where strict censorship of the American viewpoint has prevailed.

The task of communicating with peoples over the heads of governments is a challenging one.

There are, on the other hand, in the United States many well-intentioned, patriotic persons who seem to feel that America can get along without worrying about what's happening abroad. They argue, for instance, against all "foreign aid" as extravagant and a waste of funds that could better be used at home.

Too often we hear the cliché that "you can't buy allies" or "you can't buy friendship with money." If, indeed, a proud people is approached with such crude tactics, there is bound to be suspicion of our motives as well as resentment.

Mindful of these pitfalls, the Secretary of State has just laid before Congress a new program of foreign aid. His statement, printed on page 158 of this issue, is very constructive. The principles enunciated by him won instant support last week from both parties in the Senate Foreign Relations Committee.

The main idea is to grant funds for strictly military defenses erected in the free world and to handle economic aid so far as possible on a public as well as private loan basis. This is business-like and sensible.

Many Americans, of course, forget that "foreign aid" gave the American republic its economic stimulus. Our railroads owe their early development to the investment of large sums of European capital. It is unpleasant, moreover, to recall how much money the Europeans lost in our enterprises when bankruptcy after bankruptcy forced a repudiation of foreign debts.

True enough, the Europeans in those days originally saw a good opportunity from a business standpoint. So today we, too, may see business opportunities, especially through the enlarged demand for our own products.

We cannot live in a vacuum, politically or economically. It must be assumed, whether we have a Democratic or a Republican Administration, that there will henceforth be an awareness of the mistakes in judgment and administrative weaknesses of the past.

But we have learned by experience, and the way is opened now for effective action by such institutions as the World Bank, the Export-Import Bank and the new lending agency proposed by Secretary Dulles which is to operate a revolving fund for foreign loans. This must inevitably encourage more investment of American private capital, too, in enterprises abroad.

Peoples who help other peoples will win a lasting reward in the hearts of individuals everywhere. The real story of such efforts finally does penetrate by word-of-mouth—that America means to help and not to destroy, to take a deep interest in the welfare of other peoples rather than to remain coldly indifferent to their plight.

We must, therefore, look beyond the errors of temporary rulers and take a long look ahead. We must by our example of national unselfishness—we covet nobody else's territory—implant in the minds of peoples everywhere this basic thought: there can be peace, there can be economic well-being, there can be beneficial interchanges of goods between the peoples of the world.

These aspirations for human betterment require broad-gauged statesmanship in the policies of government but an even broader understanding by the people of America of the great opportunities they have to form and maintain friendships with other peoples. For it is the people everywhere who decide whether there shall be war—they alone must do the fighting. And it is the people in every country who alone must decide whether they wish to enjoy the fruits of peace.

Let's keep our eyes on peoples—in their hands rests the destiny of our world.

"PENNY WISE AND POUND FOOLISH"

APRIL 26, 1957

FOR CENTURIES, back to the days when we still used the English pound instead of the dollar, the expression quoted in the headline above has been used to warn against economizing unwisely.

From one end of the country to the other in recent weeks there has arisen a proper demand that government spending be curtailed lest it get out of hand in future years. This demand is in itself a warning against the dangers of a loss of public confidence in the dollar —a possible forerunner of an inflation panic.

But the other extreme can be equally dangerous. We must not ruin the effectiveness of the dollar we are spending by slashing the budget recklessly. It has often been said that any building can be toppled over if one is permitted to select and tear out just ten per cent of the bricks anywhere in the structure.

Many citizens, eager to see their taxes reduced, are joining a chorus which, in effect, says, "Let's cut the budget, irrespective of the consequences."

Other citizens, urged on by well-intentioned associations and organizations seeking early tax reduction, denounce as wasteful certain categories of expenditure, such as "foreign aid," or blandly classify as "boondoggling" many an item with whose purpose they are unfamiliar. There are also those who, without examining all the facts, just call the whole spending program a reversion to "New Dealism."

There must soon be a turn to common sense and realism. The agitation for a reduced budget is, of course, salutary. It is one of the healthiest symptoms of public interest in a complex subject that has been manifested in a long time. But we must nevertheless proceed on the basis of facts and not just wishful thinking.

How many newspapers will give the necessary space to print the full text of the letter on this subject just written by President Eisenhower to Speaker Rayburn of the House of Representatives?

Without a knowledge of the viewpoint and the facts contained in that letter, no citizen can argue intelligently about the cuts that ought to be made in the federal budget. The readers of this magazine will find the letter on pages 91-94.

The President wants to cut the budget. But it cannot be done with a hatchet, as Congress is doing. For this will prove far more costly in the long run than the sums allegedly saved now.

Take, for instance, the unwise cut made by the House of Representatives last week in the $144,000,000 requested by the President for the use of the United States Information Agency. The amount was reduced to $106,000,000. That's a reduction of almost one third. Isn't it obvious that what the House really did was to disapprove a policy?

The projects recommended originally were the result of months of study of how America might combat Communist propaganda in different parts of the world. Men expert in the field of transmitting ideas to peoples in various countries worked out the plan but, in a few hours, a majority of the members of the House, who could not possibly be familiar with the specific conditions abroad in which America is fighting the spread of international Communism, slashed the program with a meat-axe. An information agency of the Government which seeks to prevent war by reaching the hearts and minds of other peoples was frustrated. Yet its cost represents only one third of one per cent of what we have to spend for armament.

If we do not win the "cold war," we will find ourselves in the midst of a "hot war." And who will have to fight that war, and what will it cost? Not only will our sons be drafted and the lives of many of them sacrificed, but in a nuclear war the civilian population will be decimated—and the budget will skyrocket.

The American people cannot afford meat-axe cutting of the budget. Federal spending, as the President says in his letter to the Speaker of the House, can be reduced and he points the way. But, with 45 billion dollars for armament and national protection and 17.6 billions for fixed items like veterans pensions and interest on the public debt, only 9 billions remains for all the other activities of the Government. Hence, the President says, "a multi-billion-dollar reduction as evidently envisaged by the House resolution would destroy or cripple many essential programs if concentrated in this limited area of the budget." He declares that a "substantial reduction" in 1958 expenditures "can be accomplished only at the expense of the national safety and interest."

The President is right. His letter is supported in its entirety by Secretary of the Treasury Humphrey. Certain cuts in spending authority for future years are recommended by Mr. Eisenhower, together with a sensible procedure to achieve a system of economical spending.

This is not a time to play politics. It is a time for common sense. We must not be "penny wise and pound foolish."

THE HIGH COST OF GREED

MAY 3, 1957

THE TRUTH ABOUT THE CONTROVERSY over the size of the federal budget is slowly coming to the surface.

We are discovering that in large part the budget is high because the cost of the things the government buys has gone up in the last several years.

Out of the 72 billion dollar budget of today, 41 billions are directly attributable to the higher prices which the government has to pay for the same things it bought in 1940.

The article on pages 27 through 30 of this issue—prepared from data compiled by the economic division of "U. S. News & World Report"—is a startling revelation of what inflation has done to the federal budget.

How long can we go on acceding to every pressure to move wages and prices upward and then expect the federal government to cut down its services to the people in order to have money enough to buy the same amount of goods it bought before?

We hear much about "waste and extravagance" and "social welfare" programs and there is much in the criticism that is sound. But inflationary dollars cannot be cut out and the purchasing power of the dollar restored by the carping complaint that the Eisenhower Administration "has gone New Dealish."

President Eisenhower did not order the labor unions to demand higher and higher wages and the business and industrial executives to order higher and higher prices. The responsibility for the present inflation rests with those who refused to apply government controls at the right time when war came upon us.

On this point, the words of Bernard M. Baruch, America's elder statesman, which were uttered in a speech before the City College of New York just three years ago—May 11, 1954—are remarkably prophetic. He said:

"Since 1914 we have either been going into a war or coming out of one. Twice—and this does not include the lesser ordeal of Korea—we have had to turn our economy inside out to meet the needs of war and, when the shooting was over, to turn the economy outside in to meet the needs of peace.

"In that entire period, which more than covers your own lifetime, hardly a year could be considered free of the pressures or shadow of war or post-war adjustment. Yet through this period most economic thinking assumed that we were dealing with peacetime problems."

Mr. Baruch blames those in government who yielded to popular clamor and failed to impose controls on wages and prices at the right time. He adds:

"In both of the last two war emergencies—World War II and Korea—although what needed to be done was clear—action was delayed until too late and not before prices had jumped over the moon.

"The failure to impose effective controls at the outset of World War II increased the cost of that war by perhaps 100 billion dollars. The repetition of this failure when the Korean war broke out has added at least 40 billion dollars to defense costs since then. Taken together, in other words, more than half of our national debt, which burdens us so heavily today, represents the needless tribute exacted by inflations which could have been largely prevented.

"As a result of these inflations, millions of persons with low or fixed incomes have been cruelly squeezed. The budgets of all our governmental units, colleges, hospitals and other institutions have been deranged. Here in New York the subway fare is increased but the additional revenue is swallowed almost in one gulp by higher operating costs. Teachers, firemen and others, whose incomes lagged in the inflationary race, clamor for relief and justifiably so.

"The inflation of the war and after-war years also pushed our whole price structure up onto stilts, far above levels that can be maintained under ordinarily competitive conditions. Now we face the painful process of readjusting those prices and costs, wages and rents."

Yet today, when the Federal Reserve Board tries to restrain the excesses of an inflationary boom, "tight money" is assailed and the petty politicians in Congress try to break down those restraints.

Greed and selfishness are at the root of the inflation. Mr. Baruch put it this way:

"The inflation of recent years was caused largely by the selfish struggle for special advantage among various pressure groups. Instead of accepting a common standard fair to all and which would have kept down all costs and prices, each group tried to keep its prices or wages free, even while arguing 'control the other fellow.'

"This same contest for special advantage is being repeated now in the process of readjustment. Each group seems bent upon having the burden of dislocation borne by someone else. Each wants tax relief for itself but not for others. Each argues that 'to avoid a depression' its wages or its prices or its profits must be kept up, and that it is the other fellow's income which should come down first. . . .

"We will have to pay some price of adjustment for the inflationary neglects of the past. How heavy that price may be will depend mainly on two things—on our success in subordinating to the higher national interest this battle for selfish advantage now raging among the various segments of our economy and upon our skill in adjusting to the changed conditions of supply and demand all over the world."

What, however, are we hearing today? Cries that everything will be rosy if the federal budget is cut and the taxes are reduced. With our enormous national debt, surpluses should be used not for tax reduction but for debt retirement. Mr. Baruch in his speech said:

"I have opposed all tax reductions until first, the needs of national security are met and, second, the budget is brought into balance. To reduce taxes with an unbalanced budget and so swollen a national debt is both uneconomic and immoral. It puts a premium on efforts to escape bearing a fair share of the heavy cost of the cold war."

Basically we have a conflict between the natural laws of supply and demand and the governmental powers that are exercised by political forces in our midst. Mr. Baruch has some sage advice on this as he continues:

"Even where we have known of these natural laws and how they operate we still have failed to work in harmony with them. Often we grab greedily what we can for the day, letting the morrow bring what it will. We put off doing what we know is necessary because it seems unpleasant or unpopular. Yet, particularly in these times when our whole civilization is under constant attack, neglect is one thing that never seems to go down in price."

There is, of course, constant need for readjustment when the laws of supply and demand are permitted to operate. Mr. Baruch refers to that very delicate process as follows:

"As these adjustments take place people worry whether the whole structure will collapse into another depression. There is much agitation over the government's responsibility to forestall or prevent such a depression. But hardly anyone explains how the government is to discharge such a responsibility unless it first has learned to prevent the inflationary booms which cause the busts.

"Can we just inflate, inflate and inflate and then, having run the whole gamut of economic sins, turn around and, like a penitent child, say 'We want to behave now. Do something so we won't have to pay for the mess we have made.'?"

Too many people in labor, in business, in finance, in fact in government, are unmindful of what a post-war readjustment really means and how long it takes for a nation to accommodate itself to the consequences of war. Mr. Baruch stressing the need for realism, says:

"The postwar sellers' market is gone. New competitive conditions confront us everywhere. The adjustment to these new conditions cannot be made by the government. They must be made by individuals—by each of us in our businesses, on our jobs, on our farms. We must cut costs, work harder, sell harder. If we lose one market, we must find another. If what we produce has been outstripped technologically by some new development we must find new uses for our product or shift to what is in demand.

"The sooner these adjustments are made the better. At the same time we cannot—and need not—let these adjustments go too far. Adjust? 'Yes.' Bust? 'No.'

"I have long maintained that in our complex, urbanized society a floor had to be kept under our economy at all times. But that is quite different from contending, as some do today, that there should be no downward adjustment from sky-high ceilings."

These are days when we dislike to look facts in the face. It is so easy to condemn the Administration for all ills, past, present or future. It is easier to snipe at the President—to emphasize trivialities and to avoid coming to grips with the main issues of the day.

These issues have not changed a bit since they were outlined by the President three months ago in his State of the Union message.

These are by no means normal times. The government itself by the enormous expenditure annually of at least 38 billions for armament constantly creates a demand for certain materials and services which is absolutely necessary for our national security but which is bound to have inflationary effects.

We must, therefore, exercise our respective responsibilities in business and labor with due restraint or find ourselves in a controlled economy with politically imposed regulations.

Since the war days our economic system has been relieved of the heavy hand of government management and allowed a freedom of action both in wages and prices—which is in keeping with tradition but which has often turned out to be an abuse of economic power.

Unless selfishness is curbed and an enlightened self-interest is substituted the nation as a whole will pay a terrible price for this irresponsibility. Greed has already imposed too high a cost on the national community.

GAMBLES IN THE "COLD WAR"

MAY 10, 1957

IT WOULD BE A SIMPLE MATTER to operate any business—even a governmental department dealing with foreign aid—if there were no risks involved and if one could be certain that every dollar spent was sure to achieve the objective desired.

But in a "cold war," just as in a "hot war," the commanding general must take what is known as a "calculated risk." He is bound by the adage, "nothing risked, nothing gained."

The decision of the United States Government to send to Poland approximately $125,000,000 worth of wheat and other needed products is a risk. Whether it is worth taking depends on what purpose is being sought and what are the consequences likely to follow.

In this age of superficiality and snap judgments, it is easy enough to say that, because Poland is Communist-controlled, no aid whatsoever should go there.

The charge is made, moreover, that the wheat would merely be stolen by the Soviets and used to take care of their own shortages.

Accepting this as a possible eventuality, such a development might, on the other hand, turn out to be something on which the American Government can capitalize. For this kind of situation would not long be kept a secret. If the Russian people were to discover—as they inevitably must—that they were being aided by the generosity of the American people, it could conceivably make it harder for the men in the Kremlin to whip up a war spirit against us inside Russia.

But the danger to the Moscow dictators would be even greater if American wheat, intended for the Poles, were consumed by the Russians. To deprive the Polish people of needed food would mean a stimulus to rebellion. The situation is somewhat tense already, as is described in an article on page 47 of this issue. Moscow cannot afford to lose Poland. It is contiguous to East Germany. The whole Communist situation in the satellite countries would begin to crumble if Poland should become independent like Yugoslavia.

Indeed, it is an interesting fact that Marshal Tito was able to start detaching himself from the yoke of the Kremlin only when he was assured of American economic and military aid. Lots of us in America do not like Tito and feel that he is a Communist dictator. Just as it was considered militarily desirable, however, during World War II to accept Stalin as an ally after he had been Hitler's associate, so in the desperate game in Eastern Europe today the gamble with Tito is worth taking.

Certainly the rulers in Moscow have again and again sought in the last two years to ensnare Tito and to force him into an alliance. But he has been too foxy for them. The fact that Tito manipulates American aid to his advantage may be displeasing to many of us but in a "cold war" the end does justify the means. It's important to deprive the Soviets of a chance to send their occupying armies into Yugoslavia and to prevent their using the shores of the Adriatic Sea as a base of military operations against us in the Mediterranean.

The stakes are high—world peace. To win the hearts and minds of the peoples now behind the Iron Curtain is worth any gamble involving just a few millions of dollars as compared with the many billions—and the lives of American boys—that would have to be spent in a war.

There has been much criticism abroad about the extension of American aid because of "strings" or conditions allegedly attached. Naturally, Moscow harps on that point in appealing to the pride of various countries which receive or are considering American aid. But we impose no conditions affecting the independence of a recipient country. The dependence, however, on America—when any aid is extended—is something else. Thus, the Polish peasants have been forced heretofore to make heavy contributions from their farms to the Communist Government. They cannot do so and survive. Once the American Government comes to the rescue, a machinery for the future is established which will be hard for the Poles to discontinue.

It is the Moscow regime that should be worrying about the prestige and intangible benefits that American diplomacy will derive from the export of wheat to Poland.

After all, the responsible officials of the executive branch of our Government get intelligence reports constantly from countries behind the Iron Curtain. Our officials have all the facts on which to base an estimate of probabilities. They know all the arguments pro and con and, when they decide to go ahead with aid to Poland, their action must be accepted as a "calculated risk" and should be supported.

The commanding general in the "cold war"—President Eisenhower—cannot let the initiative be taken by the enemy. He must move into every situation where there is a chance of driving a wedge between the peoples of Communist-controlled countries and their temporary masters. It costs money to do these things—but they are the necessary gambles of a "cold war."

FACTS—NOT DISTORTIONS

MAY 17, 1957

MANY PEOPLE who have been talking about the federal budget lately have been expressing views based on misinformation.

The public has been given the impression, for example, that there is something unprecedented about the budget submitted last January by the President.

What are the real facts and their true significance?

Fact No. 1: It was in the year 1953 that we had the biggest federal budget since World War II ended—not in 1957. The amount was 74.3 billion dollars for 1953. The budget prepared by President Eisenhower for the fiscal year 1958 is 71.8 billion dollars.

Fact No. 2: Secretary of the Treasury Humphrey did not disavow the President's budget and say, as was reported in the press on January 16 last, that, if it were adopted, we would have "a depression that will curl your hair." What he did say was this:

"I think this budget as now drawn has been prepared with the very greatest care, and I think that it is the best that we can possibly do right now . . . I don't think there is anything in sight at the moment that can be done better than is now proposed in this budget, but I think we ought to improve it as time goes on."

Later on, in the same press conference, Mr. Humphrey was asked whether "there is any hope anywhere in the world situation that you can do any cutting in defense spending in the next few years." Mr. Humphrey's answer was that he would "certainly deplore the day that we thought we couldn't ever reduce expenditures of this terrific amount." He then added that, if "over a long period of time" it wasn't done, he would predict "a depression that will curl your hair."

The foregoing did not imply in the slightest any criticism of the Administration or its competency in handling the budget. It was an answer to a specific question on armaments—something that has been giving concern to statesmen throughout the world as reflected recently in the comments of Prime Minister Macmillan, Premier Mollet and Chancellor Adenauer.

Fact No. 3: The Soviet Government, in effect, regulates nowadays the size of our federal budget by stirring up trouble all over the world and menacing our safety and that of our allies. Unless we are willing to appropriate money for adequate armament and yet at the same time spend what really are relatively small sums for insurance—through projects of the psychological-warfare type which can reach the hearts and minds of the peoples behind the Iron Curtain and the peoples of other countries that may become our allies—we shall not be moving toward a worldwide reduction of armament expense. We shall instead be placing ourselves at the mercy of the men in the Kremlin.

Fact No. 4: Spending has been rising in America not merely inside but outside the Federal Government. Total spending of all kinds in the United States—public and private—has gone up from 363 billion dollars in 1953 to 412.4 billion dollars in 1956. Much of this is due to the effect of inflation.

Fact No. 5: State and local governments—which spent a total of 24.9 billion dollars in 1953—actually spent 32.8 billion dollars in 1956. Certainly nobody in the Eisenhower Administration can be blamed for this.

Fact No. 6: While many people have been talking glibly about "waste" and "extravagance," the real culprit—inflation—has been largely ignored. Thus, the federal budget went from 64.6 billion dollars in the fiscal year 1955 to 71.8 billion dollars for fiscal year 1958. This is a jump of more than 7 billion dollars in only three years but the same budgets, in terms of the purchasing power of 1940 dollars, showed a rise from 30.1 billion dollars to only 30.9 billion dollars.

Fact No. 7: Comparing the actual 1953 budget with the one now proposed for 1958, we find that national security and defense expenditures have come down—due to the ending of the Korean war—from 52.6 billion dollars to 45.8 billion dollars. Foreign aid and military assistance abroad are included in this category, and there has been relatively little change in their amounts for several years. In fact, for 1958 they are less.

Fact No. 8: The nondefense expenses for 1953 amounted to 21.7 billion dollars. This total now has risen to 26 billion dollars for 1958. But the increase is due primarily to appropriations for farm aid, for veterans' benefits, higher interest rates on the public debt, health and other programs enacted by Congress during the last four years by overwhelming votes of both parties. Congress must repeal these laws if it wants these expenditures eliminated. The President has to recognize their legal existence when he makes up a budget for the ensuing year.

The American people cannot afford the irresponsible tactics of those committees of Congress which are applying a meat-ax to the budget. There are always some economies that can be made, but the sooner the budget is taken out of politics and reviewed on its merits in a bipartisan way, the happier will be the result for our country. The sounder, too, will our national economy be in this dangerous era of international friction.

LET THE COMMUNISTS TAKE OVER?

MAY 24, 1957

THERE'S A NEW REFRAIN being echoed nowadays by too many people in America. The cry is: "Stop all foreign aid."

When it is suggested that this plays into the hands of the Communists, we are met with a shrug of indifference about the fate of Europe, Asia and Africa, as if to say: "Then let the Communists take over!"

Even in these days of the intercontinental bomber, the guided missile and the hydrogen bomb, there are some Americans who favor the withdrawal of our forces from other parts of the world and letting our allies shift for themselves—although all of them combined are weaker than Soviet Russia.

Do we really want to take the big gamble and withdraw from Europe and Asia, as the Communists have repeatedly been demanding?

If so, have we appraised the consequent cost of enlarging our own defense establishment?

How many Americans with sons of draft age will want to see the draft calls each month trebled and quadrupled as we find ourselves compelled to maintain larger standing forces at home in order to meet any emergencies that might arise?

Our military chiefs are not involved in partisan politics. They have only the duty to say what is or is not an adequate defense for the United States. They have recommended that we push the frontiers of our defense to bases overseas—far from our homeland.

Examining the strategic situation throughout the world, we find first of all that in Western Europe we are committed by the North Atlantic Treaty, which was ratified by the overwhelming vote of both parties in the Senate. By the terms of that treaty, an attack on any one of the 15 member countries is automatically to be considered an attack on the United States.

Shall we surrender our strongholds in Western Europe now and let the Communists take over?

The North Atlantic Treaty Organization is primarily a military alliance. American troops are in Germany, and our military supply organizations are in France. We have the use of naval and air bases in Italy and Spain and North Africa. We have a large fleet based in the Mediterranean, with aircraft and missiles to protect the southern tier of countries in Europe and to reach out to the Middle East, if necessary.

Shall we now surrender the Middle East to the Communists? Shall we forsake Turkey and Greece and reverse the doctrines we have proclaimed since the close of World War II?

Shall we give up Southeast Asia? We have spent many years developing our close relations with the Philippines. We have naval and air bases there as well as bases in Formosa, where we now have set up guided missile stations so as to be able to resist instantly any attack from the Communist Chinese.

We have our own armed forces in South Korea, on the armistice line. To the north, the Communist Chinese maintain a large army and air force, with big airfields. Shall we surrender this whole area and give up our alliance with Japan?

Why should the United States hand over all these military advantages to the Communist empires of the Soviet Union and the Red China regimes in Europe and Asia? Is it worthwhile doing all this just to save three billion dollars and in order to divide among individual taxpayers in America something less than $40 apiece?

Would we not risk a big toll in lives later on?

If the Communists take over these large areas in Europe, Asia and Africa, where is the guarantee that they will let us alone, that they then will not penetrate South America and begin to encircle our remaining bastions on this continent?

"Let the Communists take over" is a dangerous slogan. Many people will deny they mean to go that far. But if the three billion dollars set aside in the President's budget for our military security abroad is wiped out, the net result could be the same.

The President has proposed an additional item of less than one billion dollars to bolster the economic situation in countries friendly to us which could otherwise become centers of Communist strength. There may be room for argument about exactly how large this amount should be and what cuts can be made in it. But a sum somewhere between three and four billions is absolutely essential for the whole "foreign aid" program unless we really do want the Communists to take over.

If a war ensues, there would be no budget but an astronomical increase in the national debt—no tax reduction, no relief from the draft. Billions of dollars would have to be expended for bomb shelters, as the lives of millions of Americans would be imperiled.

Shall we pay the small amount of insurance against war, or shall we take chances? We are not starving in America. Personal incomes are the highest in our history. We can stand high taxes when it is necessary—and our military men are unanimous in saying we face the gravest danger of all times.

WHO IS FORSAKING THE REPUBLICAN PLATFORM?

MAY 31, 1957

THERE HAVE BEEN sharp criticisms expressed lately that President Eisenhower "has gone back on his platform pledges of the 1956 campaign." The argument has been made by critics that the submission of a 71.8-billion-dollar budget violates these pledges and that tax reduction was pledged, instead of "more spending." The further comment has been heard widely that the President has "gone New Dealish" and that he has deserted his party.

These points must be examined in the light of what the Republican national platform did say. The full text of that document appears on pages 126-138 of this issue.

This is the platform that was adopted by a unanimous vote of the Republican National Convention in San Francisco just nine months ago.

This is the platform, moreover, on which Republicans were elected to the House and Senate. For the convention proceedings show no record of protest then, but an appeal by a united party for support at the polls.

Careful reading of the pledges discloses, first of all, that the so-called "welfare" and "international" planks of the platform are as prominent as those which extoll policies of fiscal soundness.

Thus, "further reductions in Government spending" are advocated but "without weakening the support of a superior defense program or depreciating the quality of essential services of Government to our people."

As for fiscal policy, a "continued balancing of the budget" is pledged, along with a "gradual reduction of the national debt."

With respect to tax reductions, we find the platform stating explicitly that "insofar as consistent with a balanced budget," the party pledges itself "to work toward these additional objectives." Then are listed "further tax reductions with particular consideration for low and middle-income families," the "initiation of a sound policy of tax reductions which will encourage small independent businesses to modernize and progress," and, finally, the promise of a "continual study of additional ways to correct inequities in the effect of various taxes."

There is nothing in the platform which says that at a particular time a tax reduction must be put into effect. Even the Democratic leaders—who earlier had been proclaiming their intention to pass at this session of Congress legislation reducing taxes—changed their tune last week and now say they cannot tell when a tax bill will be sponsored by them.

Also, the staff of experts of the Joint Committee on Internal Revenue Taxation in Congress just a few days ago pointed out that the carry-over spending from obligations and contracts made in previous years would bring federal spending next year above the 71.8-billion-dollar mark no matter how much the new budget is cut in "appropriations" or "authorizations."

A tax reduction which gives an enlarged purchasing power to the people at a time when, due to military contracts in process, the amount of spending is not reduced, would merely send wages and prices upward in another inflation spiral. Incidentally, the platform specifically endorses the "tight money" policy of the Federal Reserve System and warns against inflation.

To those who think "foreign aid" or "mutual security" is a brand new idea developed by Mr. Eisenhower since his re-election, the following quotation from the Republican platform seems pertinent:

"We recognize that no single nation can alone defend the liberty of all nations threatened by Communist aggression or subversion. Mutual security means effective mutual co-operation. Poverty and unrest in less-developed countries make them the target for international Communism. We must help them achieve the economic growth and stability necessary to attain and preserve their independence."

As for social welfare in America, the Republican platform says:

"We are proud of and shall continue our far-reaching and sound advances in matters of basic human needs—expansion of Social Security—broadened coverage in unemployment insurance—improved housing—and better health protection for all our people. We are determined that our Government remain warmly responsive to the urgent social and economic problems of our people."

If this sounds "New Dealish," many millions of so-called "conservatives" raised no voice of protest to it last summer at the convention or in the campaign.

It is worthwhile re-reading the social welfare and all the other planks of the Republican platform if only to note how closely the two recent television addresses by the President parallel the various pledges made in the last campaign which helped to win him his overwhelming victory at the polls. Certainly Dwight Eisenhower has not forsaken his platform even if many Republicans, impatient for Rome to be built in a day, have forgotten what the document really promised.

JUSTICE TO THE MEMORY
OF SENATOR McCARTHY

JUNE 7, 1957

TRUE LIBERALISM often requires the championship of causes that at the moment may be unpopular. For true liberalism is not intimidated by the passions of the hour. True liberalism fights for the ultimate verdict—the justice that sometimes comes only in the court of public opinion.

Liberal-minded President Wilson once said in a public speech:

"I would rather fail in a cause that I know some day will triumph than to win in a cause that I know some day will fail."

True liberalism challenges us today to rectify a wrong done to the cause of freedom of speech in America.

Such a wrong was committed on December 2, 1954, when the Senate of the United States adopted a resolution in which it cited specifically the views expressed in public forums by Joseph R. McCarthy, the junior Senator from Wisconsin, and then formally "condemned" his utterances as "conduct" tending "to obstruct the constitutional process of the Senate."

For either house of Congress to adopt a resolution "condemning" a member because his views may be distasteful, or because the individual who uttered them may himself be disliked, is to restrict, if not to deny, freedom of speech in America.

We may accept as our guide to true liberalism the historic definition of free speech bequeathed to us by Justice Oliver Wendell Holmes of the Supreme Court of the United States—the greatest of the liberal jurists. He wrote in a famous opinion that free speech is "freedom for the thought we hate."

We must ask ourselves, then, liberals and non-liberals alike: Are we tolerant enough, are we courageous enough, to endure the opinions of those in public office whom we dislike?

Now that Senator McCarthy is dead, it may be possible to examine without feelings of personal rancor the basic issues involved in the controversy which raged in the Senate in the autumn of 1954. It may be, of course, that there are still men in the Senate who cannot forget their personal animosities or their wounds of pride. But at least they can strive to reconsider impersonally the issues involved. They can examine their consciences and ask themselves in all humility whether the vote as taken should be left unchanged in the proceedings of the Congress of the United States, or whether it should now be reversed on the initiative perhaps of the very men who originally pressed it for passage.

For, if the resolution stands, it will remain as a blemish on the picture we have painted to the world of a nation dedicated to free speech. It is today a blot on the record of constitutional guarantees long extolled and respected in America.

To refresh our memories, it is necessary to read anew the full text of the resolution itself. It was in two sections.

One of the two sections said:

"Resolved, that the Senator from Wisconsin (MR. McCARTHY) in writing to the chairman of the Select Committee To Study Censure Charges, after the Select Committee had issued its report and before the report was presented to the Senate charging three members of the Select Committee with 'deliberate deception' and 'fraud' for failure to disqualify themselves;

"In stating to the press on November 4, 1954, that the special Senate session that was to begin November 8, 1954, was a 'lynch party'; in repeatedly describing this special Senate session as a 'lynch bee' in a nationwide television and radio show on November 7, 1954;

"In stating to the public press on November 13, 1954, that the chairman of the Select Committee was guilty of 'the most unusual, most cowardly thing I've heard of' and stating further: 'I expected he would be afraid to answer the questions, but didn't think he'd be stupid enough to make a public statement'; and

"In characterizing the said committee as the 'unwitting handmaiden,' 'involuntary agent' and 'attorneys-in-fact' of the Communist Party and

"In charging that the said committee in writing its report 'imitated Communist methods—that it distorted, misrepresented, and omitted in its effort to manufacture a plausible rationalization' in support of its recommendations to the Senate, which characterizations and charges were contained in a statement released to the press and inserted in the *Congressional Record* of November 10, 1954, [Senator McCarthy] acted contrary to senatorial ethics and tended to bring the Senate into dishonor and disrepute, to obstruct the constitutional processes of the Senate, and to impair its dignity; and such conduct is hereby condemned."

This is an indictment of free speech. However unpleasant may be the words and however displeasing to individual members of the Senate, the fact remains that Senator McCarthy's statements were expressions of opinion concerning the members of a committee who, Senator McCarthy was convinced, were unfairly trying to stigmatize him.

It will be noted that none of Senator McCarthy's statements was made during sessions of the Senate. The Senate, by its rules, may "call to order" anyone who speaks discourteously of another Senator on the floor of the Senate, and, of course, any member of Congress who is criticized outside the sessions of Congress may have recourse to the courts, where the laws of libel and slander can be invoked.

The Senate of the United States is, however, not vested with the power to punish its members for speeches made or even acts committed outside the Senate, except that it may expel a member for any reason whatsoever.

But the Senate did not in its action in the case of Senator McCarthy raise the question of expulsion. It adopted instead a resolution of "condemnation." The comments it considered objectionable were all made outside the Senate and on subjects highly controversial —emotional expressions of bitterness that were obviously the result of continuous provocation.

"Provocative Speeches"

Indeed, the Select Committee itself, which considered the "censure" charges, said in its report that it had eliminated one of Senator McCarthy's denunciations of a fellow Senator as a basis for "censure" and acknowledged frankly that his outburst was due to the other Senator's "provocative speeches."

What price provocation? If we examine all the statements made against Senator McCarthy in the long period of controversy prior to the time when the Senate voted its resolution, we will find that the words he is cited in the resolution as using are mild and restrained as compared with the epithets and invectives hurled against the junior Senator from Wisconsin by some of his colleagues, both on and off the floor of the Senate.

Let us examine a few of them:

1. On September 28, 1951, a United States Senator demanded in the Senate the expulsion of Senator McCarthy. In a ten-point indictment Senator McCarthy was accused of lying under oath, accepting influence money, hoaxing the Senate, practicing calculated deceit, engaging in election frauds, and making irresponsible, libelous and false statements.

2. On February 10, 1952, in a speech outside the Senate, the same United States Senator declared that Senator McCarthy "has now added blackmail" to "deceit and falsehood" in attacking those who disagreed with him.

3. On May 7, 1954, a United States Senator characterized the hearings being conducted by Senator McCarthy, chairman of a Senate investigating committee, as "unsavory" and "sordid" and declared that "the American people can see at first hand some of the methods that have been employed, such as doctored pictures and counterfeit, phony letters."

4. On June 1, 1954, a United States Senator said of Senator McCarthy: "Were the junior Senator from Wisconsin in the pay of the Communists he could not have done a better job for them." The same Senator added later:

"The real heart of the mystery concerns the personal relationships of the Army private, the staff assistant and the Senator."

Another statement:

"His (Senator McCarthy's) anti-Communism so completely parallels that of Adolf Hitler as to strike fear into the hearts of any defenseless minority."

5. On June 12, 1954, another United States Senator, in a public speech outside the Senate, said:

"What is the source of the most effective damage being done to the United States today? What network of Communist spies and saboteurs could have succeeded in turning this nation upside down and inside out, in paralyzing the Army and Congress and in sabotaging the defense effort in terms of delay and interruptions beyond any reckoning of it? No Communist could have done it. But McCarthy has accomplished it as a mere side effect of his activities."

6. On June 13, 1954, a United States Senator, in a nationwide television broadcast, declared that Senator McCarthy was seeking to be the "sole private eye, prosecutor, judge, jury and sentencer."

7. On June 27, 1954, a United States Senator made a statement similar to the one of June 1 about Senator McCarthy's position. He said: "It very closely parallels the fanaticism that Hitler had over his people."

8. On July 18, 1954, a United States Senator, in a speech in the Senate, referred to the excesses and crimes of Hitler and Fascism and then declared:

"Each of these features finds its parallel, though it must be admitted to a weaker degree, in the career of the junior Senator from Wisconsin."

Need there be given any more citations of "contumacious conduct" or of vilifying statements against Senator McCarthy in the months that an organized campaign against the junior Senator from Wisconsin was being carried on, which was finally climaxed by the Senate's decision to appoint a committee to consider the proposal of "censure."

Every one of the statements recited in the Senate resolution which "condemned" Senator McCarthy was made by him after the Senate committee on "censure" had assailed him, either at its hearings or in its report filed on September 27, 1954.

It might be argued that the long list of statements by other Senators excoriating Senator McCarthy should also have been subject to a resolution of "condemnation." If, indeed, the precedent established in the resolution voted by the Senate itself on December 2, 1954, became Senate "law," then not only was the Senate remiss in 1954, but it is remiss now in failing to pass resolutions of "condemnation" of the statements of similar import made inside and outside the Senate since 1954 by those Senators who have publicly impugned the character and integrity of their colleagues and of the President of the United States.

A "Rule" for One Senator Only?

It is difficult to see why, in view of the record of abuse directed at Senator McCarthy, it is what he alone said that was considered "contrary to senatorial ethics." Will history say that only a Senator who had the temerity to fight, though clumsily at times, the menace of Communist infiltration in America was singled out for "condemnation"? Must it not be conceded that Senator McCarthy was the center of a very bitter controversy and that he fought back as viciously as did those who fought him?

Do words themselves actually "obstruct the constitutional processes of the Senate"? If so, then why is it that a "filibuster" by an individual Senator lasting hours and hours—tactics designed deliberately to block the passage of legislation desired by a majority—is never made the basis for a resolution by the Senate such as that which was voted against Senator McCarthy? Are there any "rules" even now that can be applied equally to all Senators who may be guilty of violent outbursts, or does the "rule" apply only to a certain type of Senator with a certain type of views?

The answer must be that, no matter how intemperate the expressions of opinion, it is the intent of the Constitution to allow all manner of speeches to be recorded in Congress and to let the jury in the court of public opinion decide on the wisdom of such utterances.

It is necessary next to examine the remaining section of the resolution adopted by the Senate. It reads, in full text, as follows:

"Resolved, that the Senator from Wisconsin (MR. MCCARTHY) failed to cooperate with the Subcommittee on Privileges and Elections of the Senate Committee on Rules and Administration in clearing up matters referred to that subcommittee which concerned his conduct as a Senator and affected the honor of the Senate and, instead, repeatedly abused the subcommittee and its members who were trying to carry out assigned duties, thereby obstructing the constitutional processes of the Senate, and that this conduct of the Senator from Wisconsin (MR. MCCARTHY), is contrary to senatorial traditions and is hereby condemned."

This refers specifically to the efforts of the Senate Subcommittee on Privileges and Elections to obtain in 1951 and 1952 testimony from Senator McCarthy with respect to various unproven charges which were in circulation at the time.

But the Senate Subcommittee on Privileges and Elections said on January 2, 1953, in filing its final report on the subject, that "a number of its aspects have become moot by reason of the 1952 election." This was one way to take cognizance of the fact that Senator McCarthy had won re-election to the Senate. In this connection, the report said:

"Such facts therein as were known to the people of the States particularly affected have been passed upon by the people themselves in the election."

For it is a fact that all the important issues in the proceedings of the Senate Subcommittee on Privileges and Elections were published in the press before or during the campaign of 1952 in which Senator McCarthy was up for re-election.

Indeed, when the people of the State of Wisconsin on November 4, 1952, had an opportunity to defeat Senator McCarthy, they knew virtually everything he had said and all that had been said against him in his controversies. For this was a matter of record in the press of Wisconsin.

There were a few incidents later on—after the election. One was the refusal by Senator McCarthy of a written invitation to testify, sent him by the same Senate subcommittee on November 21, 1952. Incidentally, this was the first formal invitation to testify ever sent to Senator McCarthy by instruction of the subcommittee during its 16 months of life. He actually had testified voluntarily before this subcommittee on July 3; 1952, and could then have been asked any questions the members desired. For the charges against him had been widely published by that time.

Another point cited against Senator McCarthy was that he wrote on December 1, 1952, a denunciatory letter in which he charged that the Senate Subcommittee on Privileges and Elections had impugned his honesty and integrity without evidence to support its charge. He declared also that the subcommittee was politically motivated.

But these are plainly expressions of opinion by a United States Senator. If they were violations of senatorial conduct, the Senate had a right on January 3, 1953—the day after the subcommittee's report was submitted—to ask Senator McCarthy, as he presented his credentials of admission for a second term, to step aside while his qualifications for membership were examined, and to ascertain whether he had "obstructed constitutional processes." Indeed, Senator McCarthy reviewed the charges against him in the subcommittee's report on the day it was filed—on January 2—and publicly challenged the Senate to refuse to seat him. But the Senate ignored the subcommittee's report and admitted him the next day for a new term.

It is a fact, moreover, that the same Senate subcommittee which had been investigating Senator McCarthy never issued a subpoena requiring the presence of the Senator at its hearings. It merely issued "invitations." No Senate rule, therefore, was violated by Senator McCarthy in refusing to testify a second time. No legal processes were "obstructed."

Again and again Senators for various reasons decline "invitations" to testify. So do many citizens. It is an established custom. It implies no illegality.

The LaFollette Precedent

What, however, were the "senatorial traditions" in cases in which a Senator was under charges of misconduct? The record shows that the elder Robert M. LaFollette, senior Senator from Wisconsin, in a parallel case, declined to testify before a Senate Subcommittee on Privileges and Elections and ignored letters from the same subcommittee.

The case arose when a resolution was offered in the Senate demanding the expulsion of Senator LaFollette because he was charged with being "a teacher of disloyalty and sedition, giving aid and comfort to our enemies, and hindering the Government in the conduct of the war." The charge was first filed by the Minnesota Commission of Public Safety in September 1917, during World War I, because of speeches made by Senator LaFollette allegedly interfering with the prosecution of the war. Both houses of the Legislature of the State of Wisconsin, by overwhelming vote, requested the United States Senate to expel the Wisconsin Senator.

Senator LaFollette, however, demanded the right to cross-examine witnesses and said publicly that the committee "denies me the right to a definite statement of the offense of which I am accused and the evidence upon which the charge is supported—a right which is accorded to every man called to answer even for a mere misdemeanor."

This was precisely the position taken in 1952 by Senator McCarthy. He said that he would appear in response to a subpoena but that he would demand the right to have his attorney cross-examine witnesses and to be advised of the charges against him. The Senate Subcommittee on Privileges and Elections never issued such a subpoena. It never assured him of the right to cross-examine witnesses and to be advised specifically of the charges against him. Though this is the very code that so-called "liberals" have lately espoused in urging similar rights for those accused of Communistic activities or associations, the subcommittee did not afford Senator McCarthy "due process." Only when the "censure" committee started its proceedings were Senator McCarthy and his counsel permitted to cross-examine

witnesses. He himself was interrogated at length and submitted to cross-examination.

The record shows that, when Senator LaFollette appeared briefly before the Senate Subcommittee on Privileges and Elections on October 16, 1917, he filed a long letter and defiantly walked out without permitting any questioning or cross-examination. The committee heard Gilbert E. Roe, attorney for Senator LaFollette. He made a lengthy argument disputing the Senate's right to punish Senator LaFollette except by expulsion. A number of constitutional lawyers of eminence in the Senate at the time sat on that committee. Mr. Roe told the committee:

"Now, the power, under the constitution of the Senate, to expel is unlimited. The power, however, to punish is limited to punishment for violation of its rules and for disorderly behavior. And in this case either Senator LaFollette's speech is sufficient to put him out of the Senate or no action can be taken upon it at all."

"Do you think," asked Senator Kenyon, of Iowa, "the Senate has inherent power to censure?"

"No, sir, not at all," replied Mr. Roe. "There is no doubt about that question."

The Senate subcommittee finally decided not to recommend the censure or expulsion of Senator LaFollette.

Yet the Senate in December 1954 said, in effect, that refusal by Senator McCarthy to accept an "invitation" to testify and his denunciation of a committee for activities which the Wisconsin Senator deemed improper and politically motivated made him guilty of "obstructing the constitutional processes of the Senate" and of having acted "contrary to senatorial traditions."

Can the Senate today in all fairness disregard the precedent established in the case of Senator LaFollette, whom it has now selected as one of the five great Senators whose portraits are to be placed in the Senate's own Hall of Fame?

The vote in 1954 on the resolution to "condemn" Senator McCarthy was bitterly partisan so far as the Democrats were concerned.

While the Republicans split and voted 23 to 22 to "condemn" Senator McCarthy's refusal to testify before a Senate committee and 25 to 19 against "condemnation" of Senator McCarthy's utterances, the Democrats voted solidly in favor of both sections of the resolution of "condemnation."

Why wasn't there a single Democratic Senator, out of the 48 in the Senate at that time, willing to recognize the free speech issue as transcending party passion?

This is so out of keeping with the traditions of the party of Thomas Jefferson, and so far afield from the great traditions of the Democratic Party itself, that apparently only ephemeral considerations of partisan politics influenced the Democrats to vote as they did.

Unquestionably at the time the Republicans were embarrassed by the split in their own party. It was presumably considered "good politics" by the Democrats to compound the embarrassments of the Republicans.

But the record of the Democratic Party on the subject of intemperate language and invectives is not too clean, either.

President Truman, in a speech in Oklahoma City on September 28, 1948—as recorded and transcribed by the New York *Times*—said:

"The fact of the matter is that the Republican Party is unwittingly the ally of the Communists in this country. This is clearly shown in the election record of the Communist party."

Yet some Democrats have been saying they felt aggrieved at Senator McCarthy because he had implied that the Democratic Party was "a party of treason."

Both implications are to be deplored. Yet, after all, these are expressions of opinion, and certainly it is a sorry day for the American Republic when formal resolutions are adopted in the United States Senate "condemning" one of its members for mere words in the polemics of the political forum.

No Senator, moreover, should have been permitted to sit in judgment on this case who had himself been a party to the proceedings against Senator McCarthy— neither the members of the committee which sought to uncover alleged irregularities in his personal affairs nor those who filed "censure" charges on the floor of the Senate. Did not these Senators constitute themselves simultaneously as judge, jury and prosecutor? Should not many of these Senators have voluntarily disqualified themselves from voting? Senator McCarthy, to his credit it must be said, was present but did not vote for or against the resolution "condemning" him.

If a Senator commits an offense on the floor of the Senate, he is subject to the rules of the Senate. No resolutions of "condemnation" are adopted when Senators speak ill of each other. The presiding officer merely "calls to order," and the speakers proceed as usual.

The Constitution itself says explicitly that Senators and Representatives are immune from arrest during their attendance at the sessions of their respective houses and that "for any speech or debate in either house, they shall not be questioned in any other place."

If any Senator or member of the House is convicted of a crime in a court of law, he is properly subject to expulsion from Congress. But the least that traditional justice has required is that the courts of law be permitted to take their natural course. It is not justice to administer punishment to any man until his guilt is proved in a court. To do so is to condone a form of "lynching."

For what the Senate Subcommittee on Privileges and Elections was undertaking, prior to the election of November 1952, was an investigation of the personal income taxes and finances of the junior Senator from Wisconsin. It so happened that the Internal Revenue Bureau had begun an inquiry as a result of widely circulated charges on these very points. Senator McCarthy rightly refused to furnish political capital to his enemies by dignifying the charges.

Official Record Acquits

In October 1953—more than a year before the so-called "censure" resolution was voted on—the Attorney General of the United States wrote to the Senate Committee on Rules and Administration that the report of its Subcommittee on Privileges and Elections with respect to the personal affairs of Senator McCarthy—submitted to the Department of Justice in January 1953 —had been "carefully reviewed" by the Criminal Division of the Department "as to possible offenses within the Department's jurisdiction" and that the "report fails to show the commission of any such offenses."

At that time—in 1953—the Department of Justice said it had not yet received the report of the Internal Revenue Bureau on the income taxes of Senator McCarthy. The same Senate subcommittee had implied previously that the Senator did not report in his income certain sums, allegedly used for his personal benefit, which were raised to finance his fight against Communism. The Treasury Department under the Truman Administration had investigated the same charges, as did the succeeding Administration. Then on April 19,1955, Senator McCarthy received a check from the Internal Revenue Bureau of $1,046.75 as a refund for overpayment of taxes. The Bureau's letter of that date gave him a clean bill of health for all the tax years in dispute, from 1946 through 1952.

These have always been properly matters for the Bureau of Internal Revenue of the Treasury Department to settle or prosecute, as the case may be. It has never been the province of a Senate committee to prosecute alleged violations of the law.

This final action by the Treasury Department on April 19, 1955, came less than five months after the Senate had adopted its resolution of "condemnation." The official record, therefore, now attests that Senator McCarthy was found innocent of any crime and that there was no deficiency in his income taxes—that, in fact, he had overpaid them.

Will the Senate now do justice to a man proved innocent of the charges and innuendoes levelled against him by a "kangaroo court" of the Senate?

The writer, in an editorial on these pages on October 29, 1954, wrote with reference to the "censure" resolution then pending in the Senate:

"The proposed action is unprecedented in the entire history of the Senate.

"There have been three cases in the past in which 'censure' has been voted. Two of them involved physical behavior—fist fights on the floor of the Senate—and the third was concerned with the ineligibility of a member of a Senator's own staff to attend executive sessions of a committee over which the Senator in question presided as chairman.

"While the Constitution specifically grants to the Senate the power to punish its members for 'disorderly behavior,' there has been no 'censure' ever voted for 'disorderly' speeches or statements of individual Senators. Before the special Select Committee submitted its report proposing to 'censure' Senator McCarthy, there was never offered in the Senate such a proposal to curtail freedom of speech.

"The Senate, of course, can adopt any new rules that it pleases. But never in the past has the Senate sought by *ex post facto* action to apply retroactively any new rule or code of behavior. To do so violates the spirit as well as the letter of the Constitution. It is not dislike of a man which is the issue, but a procedure that will affect our system of government for generations to come. It is of transcendent importance to the preservation of the freedom of the Senate itself to examine the basis for the most unusual action now recommended."

Fortunately, the Senate did decide finally not to use the word "censure" in its resolution. Nor did it claim that the resolution was being passed under the power to "punish" which is mentioned in the Constitution. For no penalty was imposed.

By the use of the word "condemned," many members of the Senate undoubtedly felt they were softening the blow. They declined to apply "censure" in the legal sense in which the term "contempt" is used.

But the whole world was nevertheless informed that in the Senate of the United States, whenever the views of a minority member do not find favor with the majority, he may receive the "condemnation" of his colleagues. He is warned and may be intimidated by the prospect that, if he does not alter his views or mode of speech to conform to the majority will, he may be subject to punishment by expulsion.

Senate Can Erase Its Mistake

The Senate can undo today the grave injury it has done. It can adopt a simple resolution expunging from the record the vote of December 2, 1954, with respect to the junior Senator from Wisconsin. This would serve notice to generations to come that the Senate in a moment of passion, in a moment of political bitterness directed at a Senator who had himself been the victim of provocative statements, passed a resolution which does not belong in the record of the Senate of the United States. Millions of voters feel that the death of Senator McCarthy on May 2, 1957, was due in part to a physical condition brought on by months of agonizing tension growing out of the persecution he suffered at the hands of the Senate. These are matters of sentiment. What we are concerned with here are principles that are above personalities—principles of constitutional law and of simple justice.

It may be that more years will have to elapse before Senators now still harboring their grievances against Senator McCarthy have passed from the stage, and other Senators are elected who will in due time examine impartially the whole record and do justice. But it would be a tremendous encouragement to true liberalism in the world today and a fine example of confession of error for the Senate now to cast from its record the resolution which it passed on December 2, 1954.

Just as the elder Senator LaFollette is now elevated to the Hall of Fame of the Senate—thereby setting aside the many bitter things that were said about him and apparently forgiving him for his refusal to testify before a Senate committee—so today may the Senate restore its own dignity and repair its own prestige by showing that it has the courage to admit that it made a mistake in its resolution of December 2, 1954.

Joseph R. McCarthy, twice elected Senator from Wisconsin, is dead—but the memory of the injustice done him by the Senate of the United States lives on. When will justice be done? Must history wait? **[END]**

VIOLENCE OR REASON?

JUNE 14, 1957

WHAT SHALL WE SAY to the youth of the nation at this "commencement" season?

What sins of omission shall we, their elders, confess?

Need we remind anyone that war is the most terrible menace that faces mankind? Theoretically, everyone is against war. The men who are mobilized to fight hate it as much as do those who send them to battle. Yet, in the very build-up of armaments and by the continuance of trained armies and navies and air forces, we concede that human passion can be ungovernable—that Violence may have to prevail as a means of defense against those rulers who lose their heads and plunge us into physical conflict.

But we know that, while military power has won many a war, it has not been able to assure peace—it gives us only the armistice that we fear may be broken.

Is it not time to give Reason its chance, even as we continue our military preparation to safeguard against the possible failure of our efforts? We talk nowadays of military disarmament when the truth is we must find a way to disarm the belligerency of man himself.

The challenge, of course, comes when we seek to apply Reason. We have only lately accepted the principle that the peoples who are called upon to bear the sacrifices of war can, by concerted will, maintain peace. We must, therefore, focus on peoples—not just governments or rulers. But, in doing so, we look out on a mass of individuals and wonder how much the rule of Reason has penetrated in their own lives, in their own society and environment.

I. RESPONSIBLE INTERNATIONALISM

We turn to moral force—not as the substitute for, but as the hopeful alternative to military force. Moral force is idea power in action. Idea power is the instrument of Reason.

With our modern systems of communication, the opportunities to reach the hearts and minds of people everywhere are limitless. They are, unfortunately, restricted in totalitarian countries, but even such barriers can be overcome. With all due respect to the printed word, the most far-reaching form of communication today is by word-of-mouth. Neighbor talks to neighbor. Human reaction is the same everywhere. The radio reaches across boundary lines to transport a daily nucleus of ideas to countries where the printed word is censored and prohibited. Ideas have wings.

Idea power attains its maximum effectiveness when it actually persuades vast numbers of people—when it achieves their active acceptance of the ideas that can emancipate them from bondage.

Idea power, on the other hand, has been, and can still be, abused when manipulated by the hand of the dictator.

But, in the long run, the steady persistence of Reason overthrows such governments—and often, too, by bloodless revolution.

The strength of idea power, backed by the sincerity of Reason, is incalculable. It may be slow-moving. It may not penetrate an "iron curtain" today or tomorrow, but it will ultimately penetrate any barrier.

The greatest example of idea power in history is the Judeo-Christian concept of human ethics. It has persisted throughout many centuries of time. However it may have been disregarded or violated in the relations of nations and governments and in the everyday life of many of us as individuals, the fact remains it has survived as the ideal of human conduct. It is acknowledged as the guide and charter of our own society. Even among the so-called "backward" peoples of the earth we find an instinctive reaching-out for the help of a Supreme Being. This is the common denominator of mankind today. This is the first rung of the ladder on which governments—our own and others—can climb upward to the higher planes of an international society.

II. RESPONSIBLE NATIONALISM

But here we come face to face with the heart of the problem—the formation of national opinion as it influences the policies of a representative government. Here we find many handicaps. We ourselves do not speak with one voice to other peoples who hear too often the strident voices of friction within our legislative halls. This discord reflects the disunity of the world itself.

Can we rise above partisan passion in America and express our idealism with a singleness of purpose that the whole world will understand?

Will the free peoples of other countries exert a similar influence, so that their own governments may help to make our alliances a vehicle for the true expression of the greatest power of all—moral force?

Even as we ask these questions, we know the answers. For, despite centuries of progress in science and invention, despite, for instance, the material benefits that have been so widely distributed in our own country, we do not yet speak unitedly with the voice of Reason.

The fault is not entirely in systems of government.

We happen to believe in a written Constitution—and a rule of law. But we differ too frequently as to how the law shall be interpreted or applied. Tyrannical majorities in legislative bodies seek to impose their will on dissenting minorities. Demagoguery shouts down the voice of Reason. Legislative assemblies too often yield to the demands of materialism and selfishness and to the pursuit of individual ambition.

Internal Friction

We realize, of course, that a rule of law is paramount, and we ask ourselves again and again: What is the meaning of "law" itself? Therein we find the germ of discontent. For statutes are not rigid formulas—straitjackets for man to wear. What gives rise to internal friction is that too many peoples confuse fair rules for the conduct of human relations with the demand for laws based solely on political expediency.

President Woodrow Wilson said in 1916:

"A point in national affairs never lies along the lines of expediency. It always rests in the field of principle. . . . Justice has nothing to do with expediency. Justice has nothing to do with any temporary standard whatever."

If we examine the motif of the rule of law, we will understand what stimulates the passions of friction. For the rule of law represents a hope for justice, an aspiration to fairness in regulating the relations of man to man—and when we attempt to regulate human behavior or to "legislate morals," we run into trouble.

In an honest search for the answer, we must never be misled by political slogans calling for theoretical equality.

For we cannot overnight give the poor man the riches he has not obtained for himself.

We cannot overnight give the man of limited vision a broader vision by the fiat of law.

We cannot award equal marks on the examination papers of life where there is more capacity on the part of one man and less capacity on the part of another to pass the tests of individual achievement.

But we can open the doors of opportunity in the economic world to those who are efficient or who can be trained to efficiency.

We can by all means open the doors of human kindness and benevolence to one another in the congested thoroughfares of everyday life.

Ethics and equity, and the principles of justice, do not change with the calendar. The Ten Commandments and the Sermon on the Mount have not become obsolete because sociological conditions have changed in a Republic whose population has grown to 171,000,000. A rule of law is not necessarily just because it is the 1957 model with a convertible top.

There is, moreover, a distinct difference between obedience to the statutes and questioning the wisdom of continuing such statutes. We have changed our Constitution many times. We have repealed some provisions and added others. So, too, we have passed many laws and repealed many. Debate as to the kind of laws we shall have is a fundamental and inherent right of free expression. It is a rule of law that such debate shall neither be prohibited nor restricted. This, to be sure, is one of the most effective ways to avoid Violence. We sometimes call it "blowing off steam." It enables the citizen to apply the rule of Reason in periods of emotional stress and strain.

If we examine carefully the basis for much of the friction in our country, we find it is as often due to arbitrariness of judgment or usurpation of power in our governmental process as it is to a lack of knowledge by the people concerning the extent of the authority which they themselves have delegated to government.

Voluntarism—Not Coercion

Ingrained in our minds is the rule of law which says that the individual submits voluntarily to certain restraints in the common interest. Law makes its greatest progress under voluntarism—not coercion. Years ago we would have thought it highly unreasonable if the mayor of our city or town had issued an ordinance saying that we couldn't leave our horse and buggy at the hitching post in front of our own property. But today the congestion of traffic requires regulations that severely restrict the freedom to park our vehicles anywhere we please.

Thus we submit understandingly to rules made in the interest of an adjusted society. Self-government is the fundamental principle behind it all. And yet self-government by Constitution, written or unwritten, must always mean a government of specifically enumerated, rather than blanket, powers. The people never willingly consent to a surrender of all their sovereignty to the state—their servant.

Representative government is the key. For the test of freedom is whether government is the agent or the master of the people. Internal peace depends on whether laws and constitutions are instruments of tyranny exercised by cliques or political parties or pressure groups. Capriciousness in government is the instigator of Violence. Reason is the generator of Conciliation.

III. RESPONSIBLE INDIVIDUALISM

We come, then, to the most important source of idea power in dealing with these national and international challenges of our times. We hear many terms in contemporary debate throughout the world—socialism, communism, fascism, statism, conservatism, liberalism and all the political "isms" of a free republic. But the most important of all is responsible individualism. It can thrive only in a democracy. By its example, it can in time reach into the hearts and minds of people everywhere. It can prompt them of their own free will to throw off the shackles of totalitarianism and to embrace the rule of law.

Responsible individualism means an acceptance by the individual of certain obligations and duties. We cannot see beyond into the larger world of international action if we have not first defined for ourselves the obligations and duties of the individual—if we have not organized a free constituency from which governments shall derive their power and authority.

We hear much about what the government should do for the individual. We hear little about what the individual should do for his government—the part he can play in the formation of public opinion.

If governments are sometimes autocratic or tyrannical, it must be primarily because there is no constituency behind them with a sufficient respect for the duties and obligations of a courageous citizenship. How did it happen, for instance, that the Germans allowed Nazism to flourish? Was Christianity dormant? Was education inadequate?

We are told that the personal tragedies of economic depression in the 1930s, with its widespread unemployment and suffering, caused many people in Germany to grope for and accept any solution just to survive.

Little by little, when usurpation by government is tolerated in exchange for material benefits, the contest for freedom is lost. Despotism gets the upper hand. This is the very way that the masses in the Soviet Union today are being deceived as their rulers allot them a few crumbs with each newly announced plan for economic improvement.

What we need in the world is a spiritual influence strong enough to put in the heart and mind of the individual a sense of responsibility which will encourage him to support those leaders who dare to scorn the bribes of materialism as a substitute for human liberty. What profiteth a man that he gain the whole world if he lose his own soul? This is a warning from the Scriptures which ought not to be forgotten.

Education, through schools and colleges or through the press, television and radio, can bring knowledge to the individual. But there must be something else developed within the individual in resistance to the human failings that have caused us at times to sell ourselves for a few pieces of silver or to ignore the twitchings of an ever-present conscience.

Whatever approach we take, therefore, we come back to the individual—the task the individual must perform in his own life. But, it will be said, this has long been clear, and it is man's own indifference, or selfishness, or greed, or blindness to folly which bars the way to understanding. We see the consequences—wars between nations, wars between groups within our own country, friction in the courts, friction on the industrial front and friction in the home. We know that human friction needs a solvent. Without spiritual help, however, there can be little diminution of that friction.

One of our difficulties today is that we are always advocating "permanent" solutions of present-day problems. Many of them are unsolvable today. They may be solved when the rule of Reason is applied. Solutions sometimes come when both sides in a dispute recognize that there is no solution in sight. The moment we decide what is or is not solvable in life, we make real progress toward an ultimate solution. For, as we devise ways and means of living with insolubility, we apply the rule of Reason to solutions we never conceived of before.

Impatience is the forerunner of anger. Patience is the most essential ingredient of human love.

Human Happiness

In a famous essay written nearly 75 years ago, entitled "The Greatest Thing In The World," Henry Drummond put together from the Scriptures what he described as "the spectrum of love," in nine ingredients: "Patience, Kindness, Generosity, Humility, Courtesy, Unselfishness, Good Temper, Guilelessness, Sincerity."

These, Drummond said, make up the supreme gift— "the stature of the perfect man." It should be noted that "patience" is put foremost.

For the greatest achievement of human love is the will and readiness to understand one another. It is the whole basis of the rule of Reason. World peace depends upon it. Internal peace depends upon it. Human happiness in the home depends upon it.

But, above all, these three ideals depend upon the spiritual rebirth of man—responsible individualism. This is nothing less than the responsibility of man to God Himself.

DISARMAMENT TALK—AND THEN WAR?

JUNE 21, 1957

WILL HISTORY REPEAT ITSELF?

Three times now disarmament crusades have preceded big wars.

In 1912 Winston Churchill, then head of the British Admiralty, made a speech in the House of Commons in which he proposed to Germany a limitation on naval building. He said that "any retardation or reduction in German construction will, within certain limits, be promptly followed here . . . by large and proportioned reductions."

This plan was described as a "naval holiday." Missions of high officials travelled back and forth between Berlin and London. Negotiations were extensive. The press was filled with hopeful talk.

But two years later the German Emperor ordered the attack and World War I began.

The United States, Japan, Great Britain and France did agree in 1921 to a limitation of naval armament but Japan at the disarmament conference in London in 1934 served notice she was abandoning the agreement.

The United States failed nevertheless to heed Japan's warning and did not build up its own naval strength.

Britain and France, too, lagged behind in military preparation—to save money—while the Nazis under Hitler built a big submarine fleet, a big army and also plenty of tanks and airplanes, in disregard of the limitations imposed by the Versailles Treaty of 1919.

In the autumn of 1938 came the appeasement at Munich. Britain's Chamberlain sacrificed Czechoslovakia because England was militarily unprepared for war. It had "disarmed."

Within 12 months, Hitler struck and World War II broke out. It lasted for six years.

After the war ended, Soviet Russia continued to maintain an ever-increasing military establishment while her allies demobilized.

But from 1947 to 1950 the United States, listening to the popular cries for economy, did exactly what had been done before—it "disarmed." The budgets of our military men were drastically cut by Congress.

In June 1950, the Communist enemy took advantage of our military weakness to challenge us in Korea.

For all this, the United States, acting for the United Nations in Korea, paid a terrible penalty in lives and money. Russia later boasted publicly that she had supplied the arms to the Communist Chinese armies in Korea. But nevertheless the Soviet Union is still a member of the United Nations.

Today disarmament talk fills the air, even as Russia is building the biggest submarine fleet ever known. The Soviet conspiracy, moreover, to influence America to stop testing nuclear weapons and thereby give Russia a military advantage is well under way.

War comes always when the aggressor is assured of a military advantage and feels confident that a quick victory can be won. Khrushchev evidently doesn't fear total war by H-bombs. He said in a public speech this month that in a nuclear war only capitalism would be destroyed anyway and that Communism would survive.

Human nature—in both dictators and their victims—doesn't change very much. The news dispatches and speeches of 1912 or 1938 could be written these days with only slight changes in names and places.

We are today capitulating once more. Britain, breaking away from her agreement with the United States, has decided to sell goods that will industrialize Red China. This will build up an enemy for World War III.

Why should any free government help the Communists—Soviets and Chinese—to build factories in which to make the weapons that can defeat us?

This is the road to war. Historically speaking, the present sequence of events—paralleling Britain's trade with Hitler almost up to the opening of World War II—logically points to a big war within the next few years. For the handwriting on the wall is the same.

When will we learn not to disarm while we arm our enemies? When will we begin to direct our energies to winning the people who can get rid of the dictators?

We are constantly dealing with dictatorship governments that are potential enemies and we are forgetting that the biggest need of all is to communicate with peoples who can overthrow those governments. We spend billions for armament and deny our information agencies the few dollars they need to transmit messages from the orbit of freedom to the orbit of slavery.

The big fallacy remains. It is that free governments by negotiating disarmament "agreements" with treacherous governments still think they can thereby prevent wars.

Unless we can count on the support of the peoples behind the Iron Curtain today by persuading them to oust the dictators, we are doomed to another world war.

The world must first be made safe for democracy and unsafe for dictatorship. Then only will it be logical to consider a world-wide reduction of armaments.

TREASON'S BIGGEST VICTORY

JUNE 28, 1957

THE RIGHT OF AN INDIVIDUAL to be protected against prosecution, even if he advocates publicly the forcible overthrow of our Government, has just been upheld by the Supreme Court of the United States.

Punishment can come only if it can be proved that, as a result of this preachment, a specific step was taken to carry out a treasonable purpose.

Nor can such an advocate be convicted by any court in any of the 48 States of the Union. For treason as an "abstract doctrine" has now been legalized by the Supreme Court and given the protection of the First Amendment to the Constitution.

Not only are the courts put in a strait jacket of impotence, but the Congress of the United States has been notified that it no longer can carry on penetrating investigations designed to expose any wrongdoing, even if it seeks information for use in writing future laws that could prevent a recurrence of such wrongdoing.

In many respects, the series of decisions rendered at the present term of the Supreme Court of the United States are more devastating and more destructive of the rights of Congress to function as a co-ordinate branch of the Government than any decisions ever rendered by our highest Court in its entire history.

The rights of the individual now are ruled as superseding those of the Government itself and of all other citizens in the Republic who may be imperiled thereby.

The rights of the individual, moreover, now are held to be more sacred than the right of the people, through their Government, to be made secure against foreign enemies whose agents operate inside our borders.

Overnight a historic function of Congress has been curtailed and weakened—the right to investigate and inform itself on matters that may require legislation.

No longer can Congress compel a witness to tell what he knows, for instance, about other individuals engaged in Communist activity, even though he himself may not be a Communist or a traitor. The citizen, of course, can volunteer such information, but the witness now is to decide for himself whether a question asked by the interrogating member of a congressional committee is or is not "pertinent" to a "legislative purpose."

The Supreme Court says Congress has not hitherto explained fully, and maybe doesn't itself know, the "legislative purpose" for which it seeks information through its investigations, and hence doubts must be resolved in favor of the recalcitrant witness.

Presumably committees of Congress hereafter will not be able to compel answers to their questions unless each query appears to be specifically authorized under the wording of a resolution adopted by either the House or the Senate. Even then, the Supreme Court intimates that it can rule later that the resolution was "loosely drawn" or "too broadly drafted." As a practical matter, this sabotages the effectiveness of investigations based on the subpoena power.

It means that crooks who operate shady businesses, crooks who dominate certain labor unions, and traitors who do the bidding of foreign agents and institutions cannot be exposed by Congress. The Supreme Court says that to do so might damage the reputation of these individuals and that to preserve this is more important than the safety or the integrity of the State.

Path of Traitors Made Easier

Last week's decisions rendered by the Supreme Court of the United States are epoch-making. They are so sweeping that for a long time to come the path of the traitor in our midst will be made easier—unless the appellate jurisdiction of the Court is limited, as the Constitution says it can be, "under such regulations as the Congress shall make."

A new concept of the citizen's "duty" now is brought forward by the Supreme Court when it says, in effect, that a witness need not answer even though he knows just where the time bombs are hidden which may blow up thousands of his fellow citizens.

It seems that the First Amendment now includes a right of "association" and that the relations between citizens and traitors are protected by the Constitution.

This is legalism run riot. This is technicality glorified. This is caprice that defies realism. It ignores the very existence of Soviet infiltration, Soviet espionage and the Soviet conspiracy to render the American military establishment someday too weak to resist attack.

The Supreme Court, in its latest opinion, examines the phrasing of the resolution—first adopted by the House of Representatives in 1938 and re-adopted seven times since—which authorizes its committee to investigate "un-American" activities. The Court now finds this resolution defective. The majority of the Justices belittle the name of the committee by asking if anybody knows what "un-American" means.

Is it possible that in this day and age the Congress of the United States is being instructed that it must define "un-Americanism" to the satisfaction of every witness who may be called by an investigating committee before he can be compelled to answer questions? Didn't the House committee itself set out to learn what sort of activities hostile to American interests were being carried on?

In one instance, on the other hand, wherein the chairman of the House committee did outline in detail at a certain hearing that Congress wanted to know specifically whether labor unions were dominated by Communists, the Supreme Court now insists that even this is too vague a statement of the "legislative purpose" because it is noted that six of the nine witnesses examined apparently had no connection with labor unions.

But Justice Clark, in his dissenting opinion, inquired in substance as follows: Who is to say that the supposed non-labor witnesses were not stooges, instruments of communication or contact between the Communist traitors and the misguided, gullible members of the union? Wouldn't the Communists use "drops" or "cover-up" agents to do their work? Did the Supreme Court majority ever hear that secret agents have accomplices among persons not necessarily members of a union?

The Supreme Court seems to imply that the menace of Communist infiltration has vanished. It says witnesses now are asked by Congress to talk about "past associations" and to be "judged by current standards rather than those contemporary with the ones exposed." When was treason ever judged by any standard provided by the chronology of the calendar? At what time in a man's life does the concealment of the traitorous behavior of persons other than himself become righteous through obsolescence? When does it become permissible in retrospect to have accepted the discipline of a foreign government's agents or stooges who seek to overthrow one's own Government?

Many of our citizens who were duped by the Communist line have since denounced it in public. They have been forgiven. They have been applauded for their courage and renewed allegiance. But today it is the coward who is extolled. It is the traitor who is advised that not only will his own secrets be protected, but that he can continue to protect the agents of foreign governments and others who listen to their propaganda or become a part of their "apparatus."

The Supreme Court, in its opinion, repeatedly proclaims that a congressional committee should not have the right to explore details of the background of a witness because this might hurt his reputation or that of his friends and associates. Why should such solicitude be shown for the reputation of shady characters or for those who have in one way or another made the mistake of coming under Communist influence?

The Supreme Court seems obsessed with the idea that "public stigma" is too harsh for a man who is called to testify before a congressional committee and refuses to tell what he knows. The Court argues that

the safety of the state is too abstract an objective to justify the requirement that a witness tell all he knows about Communist infiltration. If there is to be an error, the Court feels it should be on the side of the traitors and that this is a "small price to pay." But what about the price that the loyal citizens must pay with their lives when the acts of treason eventually are consummated and the enemy is given a military advantage?

The clumsy barriers erected by the Supreme Court will kill, for all practical purposes, the searching type of inquiry which Congress has found so useful in the past in exposing corruption and crime long after the statute of limitations has run in particular cases.

Yesteryear Liberals

Woodrow Wilson, in his book on "Congressional Government," wrote: "The informing function of Congress should be preferred even to its legislative function."

Felix Frankfurter, as a professor of law at Harvard Law School, used that very quotation approvingly in a magazine article he wrote when a Senate committee was investigating the Teapot Dome scandals in the 1920's. The article appeared in *The New Republic* for May 21, 1924, and was entitled, "Hands Off The Investigations." Justice Clark cited this article in his dissenting opinion last week.

Excerpts from Mr. Frankfurter's article are as follows:

"If these aren't 'leads' properly to be pursued, then we had better frankly admit that the power of congressional investigation is a sham and not an effective instrument for ventilating issues for the information of Congress and of the public. . . .

"The real issue is whether the danger of abuses and the actual harm done are so clear and substantial that the grave risks of fettering free congressional inquiry are to be incurred by artificial and technical limitations upon inquiry. . . .

"For the same reason congressional inquiry ought not to be fettered by advance rigidities, because in the light of experience there can be no reasonable doubt that such curtailment would make effective investigation almost impossible."

Hugo Black, as United States Senator from Alabama, when he headed an investigating committee exposing the misbehavior of utility magnates, wrote an article in the February 1936 issue of *Harper's Magazine*. Justice Clark last week also cited this article. It is just as persuasive today as the day it was written.

Senator Black wrote:

"There is no power on earth that can tear away the veil behind which powerful and audacious and unscrupulous groups operate save the soverign legislative power armed with the right of subpoena and search. . . .

"This controversy has brought forth many legal arguments, filled many pages of parliamentary records, evoked multitudinous editorial protests, and sent many recalcitrants to prison. Notwithstanding this continuous opposition, the House and Senate have uniformly sustained the right of their committees to obtain such evidence since the first congressional investigation was ordered by the House in 1792. The courts have upheld them. . . .

"Witnesses have declined to answer questions from time to time. The chief reason advanced has been that the testimony related to purely private affairs. In each instance with which I am familiar, the House and Senate have steadfastly adhered to their right to compel reply, and the witness has either answered or been imprisoned."

Earl Warren, as attorney general of the State of California, issued a statement on November 28, 1941, denouncing the California Prison Board of Terms and Paroles for the release of three murderers sentenced to a 20-year term who had just been set free after serving a little more than four years. Mr. Warren wrote:

"Human life has indeed been cheapened. The murderers are free today not because they are rehabilitated criminals but because they are politically powerful Communistic radicals. Their parole is a culmination of a sinister program of subversive politics, attempted bribery, terrorism and intimidaton which has evidenced itself in so many ways during the past three years."

These three liberals of yesteryears—Messrs. Frankfurter, Black and Warren—were then living in a world of reality. But today Justices Frankfurter and Black and Chief Justice Warren live in the vacuum of an equivocal "liberalism." They are three of the six Justices who made possible the sweeping decision of last Monday destroying the future effectiveness of congressional investigations in all fields of inquiry, including Communist activities in the United States.

True enough, Chief Justice Warren holds out hope that in the future a "measure of added care" may make it possible for Congress to exercise its investigating powers. But, as Justice Clark points out in his dissent, the phrase "added care" isn't spelled out, nor is there any intimation of what these words mean today or may mean in the future. This is confusion worse confounded.

Not content to strike down the investigative powers of Congress, the Supreme Court also demolished on the same day, in another case, the investigating authority of State Legislatures throughout the nation.

Hamstringing Law Enforcement

Nor is all the damage confined to investigative powers of Congress or the States. Much worse is the blow struck at the law-enforcement work of police agencies in city and county governments as well.

Thus, the Federal Bureau of Investigation and every Police Department throughout the country must now be ready to make public in court the copies of all confidential reports made by detectives concerning all witnesses who are called to testify by the prosecution. Even state secrets covered in such reports must be divulged, or else the prosecutor will have to give up the right to use the witness. Undercover agents have to be revealed, and, of course, their future usefulness is impaired when they are identified publicly.

Who now will telephone a tip to the FBI or the Police Department of any city or county if his name is to appear in a detective's report made public in court? The informant will know that he can be subjected to reprisals from the members of the family of an accused person or his partners in a crime ring. What a blow to law enforcement!

So the net result of the recent decisions of the Supreme Court of the United States has been to do the following things:

1. To make easier the escape of criminals and traitors from prosecution or exposure, and to make harder the process of detection.

2. To cripple the investigating power of State Legislatures and city and county governments in studying corrupt operations not yet covered by any laws.

3. To hamstring the Congress and deprive it of the best way to get the information about the operations of criminals and traitors needed to write the necessary laws to fight such criminals and traitors.

4. To make it easier for foreign governments hostile to us to operate on American territory through parties and groups and "fronts" that can destroy not only the Bill of Rights but the lives and property of our citizens when the time comes to complete the conspiracy by infiltration or war.

Treason has won its biggest victory.

"GOOD BEHAVIOR" OF JUDGES— WHO DEFINES IT?

JULY 5, 1957

DOES THE CONSTITUTION of the United States really provide for the life tenure of Justices of the Supreme Court? The words "life tenure" do not appear anywhere in the Constitution.

The prevailing impression, however, is that, once appointed to the bench, a judge can be removed only by impeachment. But the Constitution says that the impeachment power can be invoked solely in the case of "treason, bribery, or other high crimes and misdemeanors."

Supposing, therefore, that no such crime or misdemeanor is committed and that in all sincerity the Supreme Court Justices render judgments which nevertheless have the effect of nullifying important provisions of the Constitution, what steps then are available to the President or to the Congress to see that the Constitution is not destroyed by decrees of the judiciary?

Where is the protection against arbitrary and capricious action by the judges? Five Justices of the Supreme Court, constituting a majority of the nine, are able to establish themselves as an oligarchy and rule the United States. How does our famous system of "checks and balances," inherent in the Constitution, deal with such a contingency?

The Constitution says:

"The judicial power of the United States shall be vested in one Supreme Court, and in such inferior courts as the Congress may from time to time ordain and establish.

"The judges, both of the Supreme and inferior courts, shall hold their offices during good behavior, and shall at stated times receive for their services a compensation, which shall not be diminished during their continuance in office."

Since Supreme Court Justices may hold office only "during good behavior" and since obviously the Court itself cannot be the judge of its own "behavior," it follows logically that the President and the Senate, acting together, have the constitutional power to determine just how "good behavior" shall be defined.

The Constitution does not use the word "confirmation" but says that "by and with the advice and consent of the Senate," the President "shall appoint ambassadors, other public ministers and consuls, judges of the Supreme Court, and all other officers of the United States, whose appointments are not herein otherwise provided for, and which shall be established by law."

Since the Senate can give "consent," it can withdraw "consent," as Alexander Hamilton once argued in *The Federalist*. There is nothing in the Constitution which says that the Senate must acquiesce in the retention of any judge who does not conform to the standards which may be set up to define the term "good behavior."

Congress could require by statute that every Justice come before the Senate periodically—perhaps every six years—for "reconfirmation." There is no hint in the Constitution that confirmation once given is an irrevocable action. Reconfirmation occurs regularly now on the reappointment of various administrative officers of the United States, and in the case of judges of the Court of Tax Appeals and members of quasi-judicial bodies such as the Interstate Commerce Commission, the Federal Trade Commission and the Federal Communications Commission. In all these instances, the term of office is definitely fixed by Congress.

Where the tenure is not fixed, however, as in the case of "ambassadors and public ministers," the process of reconfirmation becomes merely a method of re-examination looking toward the termination or extension of the period of service.

The phrase "good behavior" in the Constitution indicates a continuing jurisdiction by the President and the Senate over the tenure of the judges.

The Supreme Court, on its part, has recently proclaimed a "continuing jurisdiction" over the States and all their schools and over all citizens who may do or say anything in connection with court orders issued in segregation cases. This "continuing jurisdiction" is accomplished through injunctions issued by the judges which may not be terminated for decades to come.

There is no reason, therefore, why the Senate of the United States on its part may not maintain a "continuing jurisdiction" and a process of observation to determine whether the Supreme Court Justices are confining themselves to those judicial functions specifically granted to them by the Constitution or by Congress.

Congress can clarify the whole problem in a law—indeed, there would appear to be no need for a constitutional amendment—which would provide a suitable method of establishing whether the official conduct of such Justices still complies with the meaning of the words "good behavior." Such a law should provide that a two-thirds vote be required for an adverse judgment—withdrawal of consent by the Senate.

The President, because he is a part of the appointive power, should be given by law the authority to consent or refuse to consent to the Senate's judgment.

This would give both the executive and the legislative branches an opportunity to share in the responsibility for whatever action is taken. The American people would be able to fix responsibility, too. They could deal at the polls every two years with a mistaken Congress and every four years with a mistaken Executive.

The hearings in the Senate in each instance relative to the determination of whether "good behavior" has been achieved or disregarded should be based on the specifications set forth in such laws as Congress may pass concerning "appellate jurisdiction." For the Constitution does give Congress the right to say what cases may be appealed to the high court and to define what authority the Supreme Court shall have in particular cases. This power is derived from the Constitution, which says:

"In all cases affecting ambassadors, other public ministers and consuls, and those in which a State shall be party, the Supreme Court shall have original jurisdiction. In all the other cases before mentioned, the Supreme Court shall have appellate jurisdiction, both as to law and fact, with such exceptions, and under such regulations as the Congress shall make."

Certainly if a Justice has not lived up to the rules set forth by Congress when it defines by law the "appellate jurisdiction" of the Supreme Court, or if he refuses to appear before the Senate for reconfirmation, he would not be fulfilling the meaning of the term "good behavior" as defined by Congress, and his term could thereupon be ended. If he still disobeyed, he could be impeached and removed for violating a specific law.

It is to be noted that to Congress is given the power of "regulation" of the Supreme Court's jurisdiction.

This is the main safeguard which the American people possess as against what a member of the Supreme Court itself once described as a power "inherently oligarchic." Thomas Jefferson all his life regarded the Supreme Court as "an irresponsible body" and "independent of the nation itself."

It was never intended by the Founding Fathers that the American people should be governed by five men, sitting as a majority of the Supreme Court, who could by judicial order frustrate the FBI, release confessed rapists, and prevent law-enforcement officers in federal, State and city governments from nipping treason in the bud or stopping corruption before plots of this kind can be consummated and grave damage done to the nation.

One of the laws which Congress clearly has the power to make relates to the conduct of its own proceedings, including investigations. Congress has the right to say by statute that the Supreme Court shall not be permitted to pass on cases which involve in any way a change in the rules of the Senate or the House. This must be respected by the Supreme Court because the Constitution explicitly says:

"Each House may determine the rules of its proceedings, punish its members for disorderly behavior, and, with the concurrence of two thirds, expel a member."

The Supreme Court in a recent decision conceded that a legislative "investigation is part of lawmaking." Plainly, therefore, there is no right bestowed on the Supreme Court to tell Congress what rules it may or may not make for the conduct of its own investigations which are admittedly part of those proceedings.

But the Court nevertheless undertook to tell the Congress that whatever "rules of its proceedings" it might adopt, these are subject to further review by the Supreme Court of the United States. This is a plain violation of the Constitution.

Can it be persuasively argued that the framers of the Constitution ever intended to leave the President and the Congress helpless to carry out their constitutional functions in the face of such deliberate interference by the judiciary? Can it be said that no means of restraint at all was provided in the Constitution against such arbitrariness on the part of members of the Supreme Court who could indefinitely constitute a majority and issue decisions with all the force of law?

The obvious answer is that Congress, as the body which is representative of all the people, was given such power. It is up to Congress, therefore, to exercise it promptly by defining "good behavior" and at the same time limiting the "appellate jurisdiction" of the Supreme Court.

This, to be sure, is the system of "checks and balances" which the American people have written into their Constitution. It is time for the American people, through their elected representatives, to stop judicial usurpation and to prevent the growth of judicial despotism.

It is time to bring well-meaning but misguided justices to a realization that they cannot and must not expect to function in contempt of the Constitution itself and still remain in office.

DEPRESSION—THE ONLY CURE?

JULY 12, 1957

THE NATIONAL ECONOMY is traveling along at a reckless pace.

Labor costs rise, and then industrial prices rise.

As industrial prices rise, the cost of what the farmer buys—equipment and everything else—goes up. So the price of what the farmer sells must also go up. And the Government pays a subsidy to maintain a certain level of prices to the farmer.

As the costs of food and its distribution are increased to the consumer, the "escalator" clauses of labor-management agreements—based on a rise in the cost of living—call for proportionate increases in wages. Other rises in wages—not tied to the cost of living—are also written into labor contracts to take effect automatically on fixed dates in the future, irrespective of the economic conditions prevailing at the time.

As the wage and price spiral continues, the purchasing power of the dollar steadily goes down. More and more dollars are then needed to buy the same quantities of goods.

It's a case of the dog chasing his tail.

It's the same old story that has plagued nations from time immemorial.

Centuries ago, to meet inflation, governments began to devalue their monetary units and to engage in juggling tricks to pay off national debts.

Today the people are cheated in a different way. Millions and millions of persons with fixed incomes—pensions and insurance funds—are the victims as their dollars steadily depreciate through the persistent rise in prices acquiesced in by government.

A savings bond bought a few years ago and put aside to pay for a child's college education buys less and less as the time approaches for college entrance.

Too many people lately have vented their indignation at "federal spending"—as if this were the sole cause. It is only one of several causes.

One reason, of course, for today's inflation is past wars and defense preparations against the next war. The dangerous men in the Kremlin are the real culprits.

But there are other causes which are well within our control.

More than six decades ago federal laws were passed to prohibit corporations from forming monopolies or fixing prices. These statutes have been rigidly enforced.

Today, however, the biggest single influence in the fixing of prices—national labor unions—goes unrestrained. Agreements are made nowadays on an industry-wide basis. No law exists against industry-wide bargaining. Yet it is an obvious device to fix prices. It's a concerted action within industry after industry that directly affects the cost of goods in interstate commerce. Employers are helpless to fight wage demands. They usually capitulate rather than face the high cost of a strike.

So with government acquiescence—or negligence—an economic power unparalleled is wielded by a few union leaders who control our economic destiny.

The management of a big company today must calculate in advance how high its prices can be permitted to go without meeting sales resistance.

Sometimes management does guess wrong—or rather it has no choice. Businessmen know that a price rise can mean diminished demand and buyers' resistance. But they must move prices upward just the same and be content with a smaller volume of sales in order to make any profit or to hold losses at a minimum.

When buyers' resistance comes, recession comes, too, and then depression.

We sometimes call the incipient stages "readjustment" or "correction." But the truth is that, in our uncontrolled economy, recession or depression is emerging as the only cure. Evidently there has to be a severe decline of some kind before prices and wages can be held static while waiting for economic recovery.

What is the alternative? Nobody wants wage and price control by government. Everybody favors a "free economy."

The President has been appealing repeatedly to labor and management to exercise self-restraint. But such appeals are not effective because there are so many factors operative at the same time.

Productivity of labor, for instance, has not risen commensurate with the rise in wages. Statesmanship in labor is missing. Leadership of the big unions, for the most part, thinks only in terms of vote-getting in union campaigns. The labor leaders know the facts, but the demand constantly is for higher and higher wages, irrespective of the productivity of labor itself and irrespective of the nation's capacity to absorb the higher prices forced by the wage increases. Taxation limits profits, but nothing limits wage demands.

It is a dangerous cycle in which we are living today. Congress lacks the courage to expose excesses. Everybody seems to be waiting for the inevitable depression, with its waves of unemployment.

What a painful way to learn the lessons of economic self-discipline!

"CIVIL RIGHTS" THAT
BREED "CIVIL WRONGS"

JULY 19, 1957

WHAT IS BEING PROPOSED in Congress these days in the name of "civil rights" and what is being decreed by the Supreme Court makes a mockery of a written Constitution.

For, under our Constitution as written, there has always been reserved to the States of the Union the right to determine the qualifications of the voters. But now the Federal Government, without the slightest sanction from the same written Constitution, is trying to deprive the States of the right they have always exercised—to specify by law the qualifications for eligible voters. To take away this right is a "civil wrong."

Every State has restrictions on the voting privilege. Some require educational tests. Some specify property ownership. Others fix the time of residence within a State. All States fix the age limits. An article on pages 45-47 of this issue gives a summary of such laws.

The right of each State to pass its own laws governing qualifications for voting is not challenged anywhere in the Constitution, except that the right to vote cannot be abridged because of race, color or sex.

But it is alleged that, under cover of educational or literacy tests, there are some denials of voting rights in the South because of race or color. So the Federal Government, through a "civil rights" bill, now is proposing to become a policeman and psychology expert—to inquire into the motives of the State officials everywhere and to harass them by the investigative process of a national commission set up for the purpose.

It is a fact that more than 1,500,000 Negroes do qualify for voting in the South and that, in three Southern cities, Negroes have recently been elected to city councils. The issue, therefore, is not whether any Negroes are being permitted to vote, but whether the Federal Government shall review in each case the actions of a State election board on the suspicion that the State's requirements have not been or will not in the future be uniformly applied.

If election boards can be punished, the Federal Government can coerce the Governors and the members of the State legislatures and the mayors of our cities and the governments of our counties.

Is there any limit, then, to the federal power? Are we to have an era of "civil wrongs" perpetrated in the name of "civil rights"—a return to the tragic follies of the "Reconstruction" years of 1866 to 1880?

The "civil rights" legislation now proposed would enable the Federal Government—by force of arms, if necessary—to compel the "integration" of races in the public schools. This is a "civil wrong."

Furthermore, the proposed law would set up a system whereby suits would be filed in the name of the "United States" instead of by individual complainants. Thus automatically would trial by jury be prohibited. This is a "civil wrong."

But where is there any concern shown by the President and the majority of Congress for the "civil rights" taken away from white and Negro citizens alike throughout the United States when, against their will, they are obliged to join labor unions to keep from being dismissed by an employer acting under the duress of a labor contract? This is a "civil wrong."

Where is there any concern for the "civil rights" of the tens of millions of citizens who wish to be protected against the enemy's infiltration of our institutions but who now see the Supreme Court of the United States rewriting the First Amendment to the Constitution to permit Communists and Communist sympathizers to be immunized from congressional inquiries? This is a "civil wrong."

Where is there any concern for the "civil rights" of Congress itself when it wishes to obtain by investigation the necessary information for the law-making process but now is impeded by the fiat of a reckless Supreme Court? This is a "civil wrong."

Where is there any concern for the "civil rights" of the American people as a whole when the Supreme Court rules that it is lawful now to advocate publicly the forcible overthrow of the Government of the United States?

The establishment of a judicial oligarchy and a federal despotism is not the way to assure "civil rights." It is the way to inflict more "civil wrongs."

It is a deliberate defiance of everybody's "civil rights," particularly the rights of the people themselves and of the several States as guaranteed to them heretofore by the Tenth Amendment.

It is the way to disunity and national frustration.

It is the way to a breakdown of the spirit and letter of the Constitution itself.

It is the age-old way of coercion and tyranny that leads inevitably to violence. It is not the way of volition, the way of patient persuasion, the way of reason.

WHY NOT "FREEDOM OF ASSOCIATION" FOR EVERYBODY?

JULY 26, 1957

THE SUPREME COURT of the United States on June 17 last added to the Bill of Rights of the Constitution a new phrase—"political belief and association."

The Court said: "Nor can the First Amendment freedoms of speech, press, religion, or political belief and association be abridged."

The words "political belief and association" have never been in the Constitution, nor has there ever been a definition by the Supreme Court of what is included under "political belief and association."

We are ordered now, however, to accept as the "supreme law of the land" this edict from the Court:

"Merely to summon a witness and compel him, against his will, to disclose the nature of his past expressions and associations is a measure of governmental interference in these matters."

This means that the citizen who knows, for instance, through his "associations" that members of a so-called political party are plotting the overthrow of his own government, is under no obligation to divulge his knowledge of a prospective crime of treason.

This raises a significant question: Does such iron-clad protection for Communists and subversives extend to the "political belief and association" of loyal Americans?

Many workers, for example, conscientiously hold, as a right of "political belief and association," that they should not be compelled to join a labor-union organization—and, of course, labor unions are in politics. But employes are forced to sacrifice their beliefs as the price of a job.

Many employers hold, as a right of "political belief and association," that they should not be compelled to dismiss employes who decline to join unions. But federal law today compels the employer to dismiss such employes unless they are willing to conform to the "belief" of the majority in a plant.

May we assume now, therefore, that the right of "association"—which, in theory, is a right given to the employe and the employer alike—cannot hereafter be abridged and that this provision of the existing law now violates the First Amendment?

What shall be said, moreover, of the "compulsory process" visited on the employer by the same statute requiring him to bargain collectively with the agents of a majority of his employes? The employer today is not permitted to recognize any minority of individuals who may wish to make separate arrangements with him for compensation.

Since by mere fiat of the Supreme Court the Constitution is now so readily amended, it would appear logical to petition the Court to add just a couple more words so that the phrase will read: "political, economic and sociological belief and association."

An economic or sociological right is as precious as any political right. Indeed, the three are inseparable.

As for "sociological" belief and association, the Supreme Court can hardly forget that it specifically emphasized "sociological" considerations when it ruled in 1954 in favor of mixed schools. Sociology can be regarded now as a part of political science, anyway.

Surely citizens who band together to choose the companions for their children in public schools are entitled to all the "privileges and immunities" that members of the Communist Party now are to enjoy. Should not "freedom of association" be applicable also to education generally? Is it to be limited solely to the professors and teachers and not granted to the parents or to the students themselves?

If, for instance, some citizens wish to join with others in establishing mixed schools for their children, should not this right of "association" be respected, along with the right of a community to provide "separate but equal" facilities so that all-white "associations" and all-Negro "associations" can be preserved through processes of volition rather than compulsion?

For if "freedom of association" is now an integral part of the Constitution, this freedom should be available to the millions of citizens who never have faltered in their faith in the American system of government. It should not be confined to those who now have been given by the Supreme Court the right to advocate publicly the forcible overthrow of our Government and to conceal their "association" with a political party having secret alliances with a foreign government that is hostile to us.

Let us hope that the Supreme Court, which now has become virtually a legislative body, will, as Congress does, respect the right of petition.

May the Supreme Court of the United States listen to the pleas of the people and apply the "equal protection of the laws" to all citizens, so that not just a few thousand Communists but everybody may enjoy "freedom of association."

AN EDITORIAL
BY THOMAS JEFFERSON

AUGUST 2, 1957

(Thomas Jefferson saw our Government in operation for 37 years. He was Secretary of State, Vice President and then President for two terms. He criticized the Supreme Court in many letters made public at the time. Here are extracts from some of them. They constitute today as timely an editorial expression as when they were first penned.—DAVID LAWRENCE, Editor)

1804: But the opinion which gives to the judges the right to decide what laws are constitutional, and what not, not only for themselves in their own sphere of action, but for the Legislature and executive also, in their spheres, would make the judiciary a despotic branch.

1816: It has been thought that the people are not competent electors of judges *learned in the law*. But I do not know that this is true, and, if doubtful, we should follow principle. In this, as in many other elections, they would be guided by reputation, which would not err oftener, perhaps, than the present mode of appointment.

1820: The judiciary of the United States is the subtle corps of sappers and miners constantly working under ground to undermine the foundations of our confederated fabric. They are construing our Constitution from a co-ordination of a general and special government to a general and supreme one alone. This will lay all things at their feet. . . . We shall see if they are bold enough to take the daring stride their five lawyers have lately taken. If they do, then . . . I will say, that "against this every man should raise his voice," and more, should uplift his arm. . . .

Having found, from experience that impeachment is an impracticable thing, a mere scare-crow, they consider themselves secure for life; they sculk from responsibility to public opinion. . . . An opinion is huddled up in conclave, perhaps by a majority of one, delivered as if unanimous, and with the silent acquiescence of lazy or timid associates, by a crafty chief judge, who sophisticates the law to his mind, by the turn of his own reasoning.

1820: To consider the judges as the ultimate arbiters of all constitutional questions [is] a very dangerous doctrine indeed, and one which would place us under the despotism of an oligarchy. Our judges are as honest as other men, and not more so. They have, with others, the same passions for party, for power, and the privilege of their corps. . . . Their power [is] the more dangerous as they are in office for life. . . . The Constitution has erected no such single tribunal, knowing that to whatever hands confided, with the corruptions of time and party, its members would become despots.

1821: It has long, however, been my opinion, and I have never shrunk from its expression . . . that the germ of dissolution of our federal government is in the constitution of the federal judiciary; an irresponsible body—for impeachment is scarcely a scare-crow—working like gravity by night and by day, gaining a little to-day and little to-morrow, and advancing its noiseless step like a thief, over the field of jurisdiction, until all shall be usurped from the States, and the government of all be consolidated into one.

To this I am opposed; because, when all government, domestic and foreign, in little as in great things, shall be drawn to Washington as the center of all power, it will render powerless the checks provided of one government or another, and will become as venal and oppressive as the government from which we separated.

1821: [For the] difficult task in curbing the judiciary in their enterprises on the Constitution . . . the best [remedy] I can devise would be to give future commissions to judges for six years [the senatorial term] with a re-appointmentability by the President with the approbation of *both* houses. If this would not be independence enough, I know not what would be. . . .

The judiciary perversions of the Constitution will forever be protected under the pretext of errors of judgment, which by principle are exempt from punishment. Impeachment therefore is a bugbear which they fear not at all. But they would be under some awe of the canvas of their conduct which would be open to both houses regularly every sixth year.

It is a misnomer to call a government republican, in which a branch of the supreme power is independent of the nation.

1822: Let the future appointments of judges be for four or six years, and renewable by the President and Senate. This will bring their conduct, at regular periods, under revision and probation, and may keep them in equipose between the general and special governments.

We have erred in this point, by copying England, where certainly it is a good thing to have the judges independent of the King. But we have omitted to copy their caution also, which makes a judge removable on the address of both legislative Houses. That there should be public functionaries independent of the nation, whatever may be their demerit, is a solecism in a republic, of the first order of absurdity and inconsistency.

AN EDITORIAL
BY ABRAHAM LINCOLN

AUGUST 9, 1957

(On this page last week Thomas Jefferson's views criticizing the Supreme Court were presented. Here are the views of Abraham Lincoln, with particular reference to the right to criticize the Supreme Court, the right to urge a reversal of its decisions, and, indeed, the duty to urge such reversal.

These statements are as timely today as any editorial expression that could be made on recent decisions of the Supreme Court.—DAVID LAWRENCE, Editor)

June 26, 1857—Speech at Springfield, Ill.

But we think the Dred Scott decision is erroneous. We know the Court that made it has often overruled its own decisions, and we shall do what we can to have it to overrule this. We offer no resistance to it. . . .

If this important decision . . . had been before the Court more than once, and had there been affirmed and reaffirmed through a course of years, it then might be, perhaps would be, factious, nay, even revolutionary, not to acquiesce in it as a precedent.

But when, as is true, we find it wanting in all these claims to the public confidence, it is not resistance, it is not factious, it is not even disrespectful, to treat it as not having yet quite established a settled doctrine for the country.

July 10, 1858—Speech at Chicago, Ill.

All that I am doing is refusing to obey it [the Dred Scott decision] as a political rule. . . . Somebody has to reverse that decision, since it is made; and we mean to reverse it, and we mean to do it peaceably. . . .

The sacredness that Judge Douglas throws around this decision is a degree of sacredness that has never been before thrown around any other decision. I have never heard of such a thing. Why, decisions apparently contrary to that decision, or that good lawyers thought were contrary to that decision, have been made by that very Court before. It is the first of its kind; it is an astonisher in legal history. It is a new wonder of the world. It is based upon falsehood in the main as to the facts—allegations of facts upon which it stands are not facts at all in many instances—and no decision made on any question—the first instance of a decision made under so many unfavorable circumstances—thus placed, has ever been held by the profession as law, and it has always needed confirmation before the lawyers regarded it as settled law.

July 17, 1858—Speech at Springfield, Ill.

I think that in respect for judicial authority, my humble history would not suffer in comparison with that of Judge Douglas. He would have the citizen conform his vote to that decision; the member of Congress, his; the President, his use of the veto power. He would make it a rule of political action for the people and all the departments of the government. I would not. By resisting it as a political rule, I disturb no right of property, create no disorder, excite no mobs.

Oct. 13, 1858—Speech at Quincy, Ill.

But we nevertheless do oppose that [Dred Scott] decision as a political rule which shall be binding on the voter to vote for nobody who thinks it wrong, which shall be binding on the members of Congress or the President to favor no measure that does not actually concur with the principles of that decision. We do not propose to be bound by it as a political rule in that way, because we think it lays the foundation not merely of enlarging and spreading out what we consider an evil, but it lays the foundation for spreading that evil into the States themselves. We propose so resisting it as to have it reversed if we can, and a new judicial rule established upon this subject.

Sept. 17, 1859—Speech at Cincinnati, Ohio

The people of these United States are the rightful masters of both congresses and courts, not to overthrow the Constitution, but to overthrow the men who pervert the Constitution.

March 4, 1861—First Inaugural Address

I do not forget the position, assumed by some, that constitutional questions are to be decided by the Supreme Court; nor do I deny that such decisions must be binding, in any case, upon the parties to a suit, as to the object of that suit, while they are also entitled to very high respect and consideration in all parallel cases by all other departments of the government. And while it is obviously possible that such decisions may be erroneous in any given case, still the evil effect following it, being limited to that particular case, with the chance that it may be overruled and never become a precedent for other cases, can better be borne than could the evils of a different practice.

At the same time, the candid citizen must confess that if the policy of the government, upon vital questions affecting the whole people, is to be irrevocably fixed by decisions of the Supreme Court, the instant they are made, in ordinary litigation between parties in personal actions, the people will have ceased to be their own rulers, having to that extent practically resigned their government into the hands of that eminent tribunal.

AN EDITORIAL
BY FRANKLIN D. ROOSEVELT

AUGUST 16, 1957

(In successive issues in the last two weeks, there have been presented on this page extracts from speeches and letters by two Presidents of the United States—Thomas Jefferson and Abraham Lincoln—in criticism of the Supreme Court. Here's the last of the series. Coming from the pen of a more recent President—Franklin D. Roosevelt—this week's selection constitutes an "editorial" that could be written today, not only in support of the right of criticism of the judiciary but to prove that public opinion, when sufficiently aroused throughout the country, does have its effect on the decisions of the Court itself.

Mr. Roosevelt proudly asserted in 1941 that the so-called "Court-packing" fight in 1937 was a decisive victory for him and his viewpoint on how the Court should decide questions of social and economic importance.

It so happens that two of Mr. Roosevelt's appointees—Justices Black and Douglas—are today generally considered by many lawyers to be "dominating" the Chief Justice and other members of the present Court.—DAVID LAWRENCE, *Editor)*

Radio speech, March 9, 1937:

But since the rise of the modern movement for social and economic progress through legislation, the Court has more and more often and more and more boldly asserted a power to veto laws passed by the Congress and State Legislatures in complete disregard of this original limitation.

In the last four years the sound rule of giving statutes the benefit of all reasonable doubt has been cast aside. The Court has been acting not as a judicial body, but as a policy-making body. . . .

The Court in addition to the proper use of its judicial functions has improperly set itself up as a third House of the Congress—a super-legislature, as one of the Justices has called it—reading into the Constitution words and implications which are not there, and which were never intended to be there.

Introduction, dated June 3, 1941, written by Franklin D. Roosevelt as a preface to the 1937 volume of his public papers and addresses:

. . . I regard the effort initiated by the message on the Federal Judiciary of February 5, 1937, and the immediate results of it, as among the most important domestic achievements of my first two terms in office. . . .

The problem was a simple one to state; but an almost impossible one to solve. Was the majority of the Court to remain what Mr. Justice Brandeis had characterized as a "super-legislature," passing upon the wisdom of legislation on the basis of their own personal political and economic philosophy? Was the electorate to be powerless to insist upon solution of its national problems through its Congress, without having to risk judgments of unconstitutionality based not on constitutional limitations but on personal predilections of five Justices not elected by it? Or was this nation to retain its full powers to serve its own citizens, and to use those powers in a steady drive to meet the modern needs of humanity? . . .

By the time the Court term was over in June of 1937, it was very clear that the entire approach of the Court to the many problems confronting us had completely changed. The views of the liberal minority of 1935 and 1936 were being gradually adopted by the one or two Justices on the other side necessary to make them the views of the majority.

The blunt fact, therefore, is that by this time the Supreme Court fight had actually been won, so far as its immediate objectives were concerned.

The legislative fight was not discontinued immediately, however, because it was not certain whether this victory was permanent or temporary. Furthermore, even with a liberal Court, the basic principle of insuring a steady flow of new vigor and new intellectual approach into the personnel of the Court would still be a sound one. For only with that continuing process could we ever be sure that the Court would continually be kept personally abreast of changing social conditions by the addition of new men, brought up and moulded in such conditions.

The result of the Supreme Court fight in the political halls of the Congress is now well known. Owing to many factors, the most important of which was this reversal of the Court's attitude itself, the portion of the bill dealing with the Supreme Court itself was defeated—although many other provisions of the bill were adopted in 1937 and later.

It was not until after the end of the judicial term in June, 1937, that a single vacancy on the Court actually occurred. The about-face in the decisions of the Court had come from the very same personnel that had been on the Court since my first inauguration. The victory, therefore, cannot be attributed to the new Justices. It was rather a realization by one or two members of the Court that the Court had exceeded its powers, that it had strayed away from the Constitution itself, and that the liberal minority of the Court had been correct in its conclusions.

PRIDE OF COLOR

AUGUST 23, 1957

IN THE EMOTIONAL DISCUSSIONS of the hour, we hear frequently the words "inferiority" and "inequality" as population groups are invidiously compared.

We hear too infrequently of the pride of color or the pride of race which, though not often expressed openly, is felt deeply by man throughout the world.

Preachments of "equality" are not truly satisfying. Does any population group inside or outside this country really feel itself merely the "equal" of another? Does one group actually concede to any other group a status of "superiority"?

This writer recalls two incidents in point which occurred when he and about 50 other correspondents travelled across the Atlantic in December 1918 to report on the Paris Peace Conference.

One night aboard ship, Robert R. Moton, head of Tuskegee Institute and the successor to Booker T. Washington, was invited to speak to us on any topic he wished. He spoke on pride of color.

"As I look at you folks," he said good-humoredly, "you seem so pale of face. That's what the red man noted, too, when he first saw you. For really you have no color. We Negroes, on the other hand, have a full color, and there are many things we can do which you can't do."

Bob Moton thereupon sang some Negro spirituals, which brought down the house. He had pride—and, with it, an unforgettable dignity.

A few weeks later I was walking with a Japanese newspaperman near the French Foreign Office, where the sessions of the Peace Conference were being held. We were discussing a proposed resolution declaring all races are "equal." The Japanese delegation particularly was anxious to have that doctrine proclaimed so as to overcome the then-existing bans on immigration to the United States from the Far East.

"Do you really believe a Japanese is the equal of an American?" I asked my Japanese friend, and urged him to give me a candid answer.

There was a moment of hesitation, and then he replied proudly: "Of course not. I hope I will be pardoned if I say a Japanese is superior. I mean no reflection on Americans."

"Well," I remarked, "since the average American usually thinks of himself as superior to the citizens of any other country in the world, and the average Japanese thinks he is superior to any other race of people, a declaration of mere 'equality' seems somewhat irrelevant, doesn't it?"

On this we agreed, and maybe, if we ourselves had been writing the resolution, we would have favored giving each nation the doubtful but at least the realistic right of feeling superior to the other.

I've thought many times of these two episodes, and of how sometimes we pay lip service to a declaration of "equality" that sounds fine but is hypocritical on its face.

Conflicts between the races have today created almost unsolvable problems in Algeria, Cyprus, the Middle East, South Africa and in our own country.

The sociologists still argue inconclusively about the relative status of some races as "inferior" to others. But it cannot be denied that talented individuals of every race and color have won recognition for their exceptional achievements.

Perhaps one reason for our regrettable tendency at times to demote various groups is that we as a nation know little about the cultures of other peoples—as, for example, the intellectual attainments of the Arab world, the philosophy of the Moslems, or the literature and arts of the Orient. Too many of us know the peoples of Africa and Asia only as "black" or "brown" or "yellow" or perhaps all-inclusively as "non-white."

America's responsibilities of leadership in the world have increased faster than our own educational training can meet them. We must not only teach in our colleges the languages of all other peoples, but we must come to know their basic cultures.

For as we survey the cultural accomplishments of the Latins or the Slavs or the Greeks or the Arabs or the Hindus or the Chinese or the Japanese or the Koreans, and especially of those peoples whose color varies from our own—their many contributions to the arts, to medicine and to science—we must recognize the simple fact that God created them all. What His purpose was in giving distinguishing colors to different nations we do not know, but shall it be said that on the people of only one color was bestowed a badge of favor?

Might it not be better said that color can be a badge of distinction which challenges every individual within every group to aspire to great achievements in which all mankind may share?

The right of the individual to choose his companions or associates is basic in our theory of individual freedom and natural law. But the right of every man, irrespective of race or creed or color, to serve the cause of mankind as a whole is never questioned by sensible men anywhere in the world.

WHAT 'DOCTRINE' NOW?

AUGUST 30, 1957

SOVIET RUSSIA has suddenly disturbed the peace of the Middle East and created new tensions in the world by virtually taking over Syria.

President Eisenhower described it this way to his press conference last week:

"The pattern that is seemingly emerging is an old one for the Soviets—to insert or offer economic and military aid and, through doing so, to penetrate the receiving country with their agents, for these to get into power, to find stooges that will do their will, and, finally, to take over this country. . . .

"It is not one of those instances that at present justify any kind of action at all under the Mid-East Doctrine."

The reference is to what has been popularly called the "Eisenhower Doctrine." This provides for military intervention only upon the request or invitation of the existing government. In this case, of course, the Soviets control the present government in Syria.

What, then, to do when Communist infiltration amounts to conquest and when the country affected is either helpless to resist or pro-Communist elements are in control of the governmental machinery?

The problem is not novel, and Mr. Eisenhower rightly says "there are very definite limitations on what you can do in the internal affairs of any other country."

The world, however, has progressed from the old formalism of diplomacy, which stood aloof at the borders of a country and saw the immunized territory then used as a base for aggression against other countries.

Nazism, too, was an "internal" affair, but it became a threat externally to the peace of the world.

Today what the Soviets are doing in Syria and elsewhere is analogous to what the Nazis did. Country after country is being taken over as a prelude to a major aggression and an attempt at conquest of the whole Middle East—the world's biggest source of supply of oil, which is, of course, the most strategic commodity of war and peace.

How long can the Western powers stand by and see Syria and Egypt operating together to entrench Communist authority in the Middle East? Will Turkey, Iraq and Iran allow this warning of danger to go unheeded?

Under the Eisenhower Doctrine, these three countries can invite the aid of the military forces of the United States and of other members of the free world.

But the initiative must come from those Arab nations which wish to preserve a free government. The Eisenhower Doctrine can be broadened to include the aid of other countries willing to set up a wall of defense against the Soviet aggressor.

The Syrian people can be helped only if they manifest in some way a desire to be helped. There are elements within Syria—just as there were within Hungary—sympathetic with the West.

Measures can be taken to assist the Syrian people. Their Arab neighbors can provide such assistance, and the West will supply the necessary sinews.

The essential point, however, is that a nation taken over by international Communism must not be permitted to drift and become a captive within the Soviet orbit. For if the process is not checked, the whole Middle East can be gobbled up even as other nations wishfully pretend this is but an "internal" matter.

There come crucial moments in history when a decisive step must be taken. The hour for it is at hand. The United States must enlist the diplomatic cooperatin of all the countries interested in resisting Soviet aggression in the Middle East. It is not the concern of any one nation but of the whole free world.

For a union of free governments must protect the Middle East against Communist subversion and infiltration. Firm action in this region will provide a salutary lesson to the Soviets. It will bring encouragement to the peoples of the "satellite" countries of Eastern Europe. It is important to forget the bickerings of yesterday among our allies and to concentrate on the dangers of today and tomorrow.

It took resoluteness and courage for the United States to organize the free nations to repel aggression in Korea. The machinery of the United Nations is still available for an allied operation.

Obviously the U. N. Security Council can veto proposals for action but, under Article 51, the free nations can take whatever military and economic steps they desire in order to rid Syria of the aggressor.

There must not be any hesitancy to affirm before the world the right of all peaceful nations to take cooperative measures to halt aggression. For what has happened in Syria is just as much a violation of the sovereignty of that country as the march of Communist troops into the territory of the Republic of Korea.

There is only one "doctrine" to invoke now in the Middle East, and that's the doctrine of organized resistance to aggression. To condone Soviet infiltration now is to run the risk later of a third world war under the most unfavorable conditions—with the Middle East under enemy control.

WHICH "CONSTITUTION"?

SEPTEMBER 13, 1957

PRESIDENT EISENHOWER, in telegraphing to the Governor of Arkansas last week, said:

"When I became President, I took an oath to support and defend the Constitution of the United States. The only assurance I can give you is that the Federal Constitution will be upheld by me by every legal means at my command."

But which Constitution?

Is the so-called Fourteenth Amendment, under which "integration" is being forced today upon an unwilling population in the South, really a valid part of the Constitution?

The Southern States, after the war was over, ratified the Thirteenth Amendment abolishing slavery and this was accepted as legal by the Federal Government. Yet when the same legislatures in the South subsequently assembled lawfully and rejected in due form a proposed Fourteenth Amendment, all Southern members of Congress were deprived of their seats in the Senate and the House. Federal troops were ordered to take charge of these State legislatures. Puppet legislatures finally did "ratify" under duress.

The Supreme Court in the last 89 years has never ventured in a single instance to decide the issue of whether this "ratification" was actually lawful.

Why, therefore, are some of us so explicit and eloquent nowadays in sanctifying the phrase—the "supreme law of the land"—as requiring compliance with the vague and undefined edicts of a Supreme Court that has plainly disregarded the illegality of the so-called Fourteenth Amendment?

Where in the Constitution are the federal courts given the right to control or regulate the schools of the nation and to dictate to them whom they shall admit as students and whom they shall refuse to admit?

Where in the Constitution is there any delegation of power to the Federal Government to put in jail parents who wish to persuade other parents to refrain from sending their children to mixed schools? Yet federal injunctions today seek to coerce these citizens and deprive them of their right to speak freely as guaranteed under the First Amendment of the Constitution.

The President's telegram to the Governor of Arkansas will become a historic document. It may have unfortunate consequences in the future relations between the States and the Federal Government. It appears to be an ill-advised statement prepared for Mr. Eisenhower by overzealous lawyers in the Department of Justice. The telegram said in part:

"You and other State officials—as well as the National Guard, which is, of course, uniformed, armed and partially sustained by the Federal Government—will, I am sure, give full cooperation to the United States District Court."

Where in the Constitution is any power given to the President or to anyone in the Federal Government to say to the Governor of a sovereign State that he must not use the National Guard—State troops—to maintain order? And since when does the fact that the National Guard receives funds or uniforms or guns from the Federal Government deprive the Governors of our States of their right to use these troops for State purposes without first obtaining the permission of the Federal Government?

Does this mean, too, that the allocation of federal funds to schools, which has been urgently advocated in recent months by the President, will give the Federal Government some new and hitherto unbestowed grant of power to pass judgment on the efficiency of a State Governor or to question his motives when he attempts to do his duty, as he sees it, under the Constitution of his own State as well as the Constitution of the United States?

Since when, to be sure, is it the duty of the National Guard to execute federal injunctions? Since when has the National Guard become an instrument of the federal judiciary? Since when has an injunction or order issued by a lower court become a final decree that must be obeyed under threats of reprisals by the Chief Executive even before the court order has been properly reviewed on appeal to the higher courts?

Are the Governors and State legislatures now mere puppets, and have our several States suddenly become "satellites" which can function only with the consent of a federal dictatorship?

There is only one Federal Constitution in America. It is in the Articles and lawfully-adopted Amendments to the document itself. All misguided attempts to amend this Constitution by the fiat of nine judges must be deplored as a usurpation of power and a defiance of the Constitution itself.

For to the people alone—uncoerced by military force—is given the power to change the Constitution. The method is specifically prescribed in the Constitution itself.

This is the way to preserve our dual system of government. It is the only way by which the nation can maintain internal peace and national unity.

"THOU SHALT NOT FEEL INFERIOR!"

SEPTEMBER 20, 1957

"TODAY, education is perhaps the most important function of State and local governments."

These are the words of the Supreme Court of the United States in its decision of May 17, 1954, by which desegregation of the races in the public schools of the United States was ordered.

The Court's opinion specifically excluded any mention of the Federal Government as a participant in the American system of education. For nowhere in the Constitution is education placed within the jurisdiction of the Federal Government.

The Supreme Court based its ruling entirely on the so-called "Fourteenth Amendment," which says that no State shall "deny to any person within its jurisdiction the equal protection of the laws."

But which governmental body is to say what the phrase, "the equal protection of the laws," really means and whether separate schools are sufficient? The key is to be found in the provision in the "Fourteenth Amendment" itself which reads as follows:

"The Congress shall have power to enforce, by appropriate legislation, the provisions of this Article."

Congress, however, has never passed a single law forbidding segregation or requiring integration in the schools.

The Supreme Court nevertheless in its 1954 decision declared that, even if equal facilities—equally good buildings, equally good teachers, equally good textbooks, equally good courses of study—were provided in the public schools attended solely by Negroes, there was an intangible factor which had not been equalized.

This intangible factor, the Court said, was so important that, unless the alleged barrier was removed, a child would actually be deprived of "equal educational opportunities."

The intangible factor named was "inferiority." The Supreme Court opinion said on this point:

"To separate them [the Negro children] from others of similar age and qualifications solely because of their race generates a feeling of inferiority as to their status in the community that may affect their hearts and minds in a way unlikely ever to be undone."

This, of course, disregarded all precedents of law and all interpretations of the Constitution on the subject which had been recorded in the history of the United States since the Republic was founded.

Never before had the nine Justices of the Supreme Court set themselves up as nine psychologists or sociologists to determine the mental reaction of students to their environment.

The Court omitted any mention, on the other hand, of the mental reaction of white students to situations thus created that were in violation of the views taught them by their parents or of their traditions, customs and attitudes of life. The tribunal brushed aside also the inalienable rights of parents to freedom of association for their children.

Most disconcerting, moreover, was the pointed reflection on the Negro himself which the Supreme Court opinion unwittingly recorded. For is it really true that an educated Negro feels himself "inferior" to a white person? Is it really true that, just because an intelligent Negro was continuously separated from whites in other public school buildings, he was not able to obtain a good education and is today not equipped to carry on his profession in the fields of law or medicine or in the press or in politics or in the teaching world?

Will any educated Negro, proud of his color, concede today that, because he once attended a separate school with members of his own race, he became "inferior" and that this affected "his heart and mind in a way unlikely ever to be undone"?

Are the Negroes of our land really willing to admit that, even under competent teachers, they cannot possibly acquire an education in history, mathematics, science, geography, English literature and languages unless white students are at their side in the classroom?

Are we being told that there is no pride of race which will say: "Give us the same education and we will prove we are not inferior"?

What, it might now be asked, will the Court do about the psychological effect on the individual Negro in an "integrated" school when the day-after-day contacts on the playgrounds emphasize the separation on the social side which, at least in the South, will exist for many years to come?

Will the federal courts be expected to issue injunctions, with the threat of jail sentences, to all those persons who supposedly induce a feeling of "inferiority" in others? Or does the solution lie in the issuance by the Supreme Court of a new commandment which, in effect, shall say: "Thou Shalt Not Feel Inferior"?

Presumably, once this doctrine is proclaimed as "the law of the land," all friction will cease and we shall have internal peace once more in America. What a challenge to the Supreme Court of Sociology!

THERE IS NO
"FOURTEENTH AMENDMENT"!

SEPTEMBER 27, 1957

A MISTAKEN BELIEF—that there is a valid article in the Constitution known as the "Fourteenth Amendment"—is responsible for the Supreme Court decision of 1954 and the ensuing controversy over desegregation in the public schools of America.

No such amendment was ever legally ratified by three fourths of the States of the Union as required by the Constitution itself.

The so-called "Fourteenth Amendment" was dubiously proclaimed by the Secretary of State on July 20, 1868. The President shared that doubt.

There were 37 States in the Union at the time, so ratification by at least 28 was necessary to make the amendment an integral part of the Constitution. Actually, only 21 States legally ratified it. So it failed of ratification.

The undisputed record, attested by official journals and the unanimous writings of historians, establishes these events as occurring in 1867 and 1868:

1. Outside the South, six States—New Jersey, Ohio, Kentucky, California, Delaware and Maryland—failed to ratify the proposed amendment.

2. In the South, ten States—Texas, Arkansas, Virginia, North Carolina, South Carolina, Georgia, Alabama, Florida, Mississippi and Louisiana—by formal action of their legislatures, rejected it under the normal processes of civil law.

3. A total of 16 legislatures out of 37 failed legally to ratify the "Fourteenth Amendment."

4. Congress—which had deprived the Southern States of their seats in the Senate—did not lawfully pass the resolution of submission in the first instance.

5. The Southern States which had rejected the amendment were coerced by a federal statute passed in 1867 that took away the right to vote or hold office from all citizens who had served in the Confederate Army. Military governors were appointed and instructed to prepare the roll of voters. All this happened in spite of the presidential proclamation of amnesty previously issued by the President. New legislatures were thereupon chosen and forced to "ratify" under penalty of continued exile from the Union. In Louisiana, a General sent down from the North presided over the State legislature.

6. Abraham Lincoln had declared many times that the Union was "inseparable" and "indivisible." After his death, and when the war was over, the ratification by the Southern States of the Thirteenth Amendment, abolishing slavery, had been accepted as legal. But Congress in the 1867 law imposed the specific conditions under which the Southern States would be "entitled to representation in Congress."

7. Congress, in passing the 1867 law that declared the Southern States could not have their seats in either the Senate or House in the next session unless they ratified the "Fourteenth Amendment," took an unprecedented step. No such right—to compel a State by an act of Congress to ratify a constitutional amendment—is to be found anywhere in the Constitution. Nor has this procedure ever been sanctioned by the Supreme Court of the United States.

8. President Andrew Johnson publicly denounced this law as unconstitutional. But it was passed over his veto.

9. Secretary of State Seward was on the spot in July 1868 when the various "ratifications" of a spurious nature were placed before him. The legislatures of Ohio and New Jersey had notified him that they rescinded their earlier action of ratification. He said in his official proclamation that he was not authorized as Secretary of State "to determine and decide doubtful questions as to the authenticity of the organization of State legislatures or as to the power of any State legislature to recall a previous act or resolution of ratification." He added that the amendment was valid "if the resolutions of the legislatures of Ohio and New Jersey, ratifying the aforesaid amendment, are to be deemed as remaining of full force and effect, notwithstanding the subsequent resolutions of the legislatures of these States." This was a very big "if." It will be noted that the real issue, therefore, is not only whether the forced "ratification" by the ten Southern States was lawful, but whether the withdrawal by the legislatures of Ohio and New Jersey—two Northern States—was legal. The right of a State, by action of its legislature, to change its mind at any time before the final proclamation of ratification is issued by the Secretary of State has been confirmed in connection with other constitutional amendments.

10. The Oregon Legislature in October 1868—three months after the Secretary's proclamation was issued—passed a rescinding resolution, which argued that the "Fourteenth Amendment" had not been ratified by three fourths of the States and that the "ratifications"

in the Southern States were "usurpations, unconstitutional, revolutionary and void" and that, "until such ratification is completed, any State has a right to withdraw its assent to any proposed amendment."

What do the historians say about all this?

W. E. Woodward, in his famous work, "A New American History," published in 1936, says:

"To get a clear idea of the succession of events let us review [President Andrew] Johnson's actions in respect to the ex-Confederate States.

"In May, 1865, he issued a Proclamation of Amnesty to former rebels. Then he established provisional governments in all the Southern States. They were instructed to call Constitutional Conventions. They did. New State governments were elected. White men only had the suffrage [the Fifteenth Amendment establishing equal voting rights had not yet been passed]. Senators and Representatives were chosen, but when they appeared at the opening of Congress they were refused admission. The State governments, however, continued to function during 1866.

"Now we are in 1867. In the early days of that year [Thaddeus] Stevens brought in, as chairman of the House Reconstruction Committee, a bill that proposed to sweep all the Southern State governments into the wastebasket. The South was to be put under military rule.

"The bill passed. It was vetoed by Johnson and passed again over his veto. In the Senate it was amended in such fashion that any State could escape from military rule and be restored to its full rights by ratifying the Fourteenth Amendment and admitting black as well as white men to the polls."

In challenging its constitutionality, President Andrew Johnson said in his veto message:

"I submit to Congress whether this measure is not in its whole character, scope and object without precedent and without authority, in palpable conflict with the plainest provisions of the Constitution, and utterly destructive of those great principles of liberty and humanity for which our ancestors on both sides of the Atlantic have shed so much blood and expended so much treasure."

Many historians have applauded Johnson's words. Samuel Eliot Morison and Henry Steele Commager, known today as "liberals," wrote in their book, "The Growth of the American Republic":

"Johnson returned the bill with a scorching message arguing the unconstitutionality of the whole thing, and most impartial students have agreed with his reasoning."

James Truslow Adams, another noted historian, writes in his "History of the United States":

"The Supreme Court had decided three months earlier, in the Milligan case, . . . that military courts were unconstitutional except under such war conditions as might make the operation of civil courts impossible, but the President pointed out in vain that practically the whole of the new legislation was unconstitutional. . . . There was even talk in Congress of impeaching the Supreme Court for its decisions! The legislature had run amok and was threatening both the Executive and the Judiciary."

Actually, President Johnson was impeached, but the move failed by one vote in the Senate.

The Supreme Court, in case after case, refused to pass on the illegal activities involved in "ratification." It said simply that they were acts of the "political departments of the Government." This, of course, was a convenient device of avoidance. The Court has adhered to that position ever since Reconstruction Days.

Andrew C. McLaughlin, whose "Constitutional History of the United States" is a standard work, writes:

"Can a State which is not a State and not recognized as such by Congress, perform the supreme duty of ratifying an amendment to the fundamental law? Or does a State—by congressional thinking—cease to be a State for some purposes but not for others?"

This is the tragic history of the so-called "Fourteenth Amendment"—a record that is a disgrace to free government and a "government of law."

Isn't the use of military force to override local government what we deplored in Hungary?

It is never too late to correct injustice. The people of America should have an opportunity to pass on an amendment to the Constitution that sets forth the right of the Federal Government to control education and regulate attendance at public schools either with federal power alone or concurrently with the States.

That's the honest way, the just way to deal with the problem of segregation or integration in the schools. Until such an amendment is adopted, the "Fourteenth Amendment" should be considered as null and void.

There is only one supreme tribunal—it is the people themselves. Their sovereign will is expressed through the procedures set forth in the Constitution itself.

ILLEGALITY BREEDS ILLEGALITY

OCTOBER 4, 1957

THE STATE OF ARKANSAS last week had its constitutional rights taken away at the point of federal bayonets.

In disregard of every precedent of law and of the provisions of the Constitution of the United States—which places on the States the primary responsibility to preserve order and prevent violence within their borders—a federal army of occupation, under the direction of the President, moved into Arkansas.

Never in the peacetime history of the United States, since Reconstruction days, has any President—without the cooperation of the Governor of a State—sent federal troops into a State "to prevent violence."

In every instance of disorders since George Washington's day there has been federal cooperation with the State authorities.

But last week President Eisenhower did not permit the Governor of Arkansas to furnish State militia or U.S. Deputy Marshals. Instead he "federalized" the National Guard and deprived the Governor of his largest police force. The President did all this so hastily that the people of Arkansas were not given even 24 hours to comply with his proclamation demanding order. Before the citizens of Little Rock had a chance to read the morning and afternoon newspapers on Tuesday, Sept. 24, or to digest what was said in the proclamation, federal troops were ordered to Arkansas on the specious ground that the proclamation issued the night before "had not been obeyed."

The truth is that the proclamation was made public at 4:45 p. m. (Little Rock time) on Monday, Sept. 23. During Tuesday forenoon all the press dispatches reported there was quiet in the vicinity of the high school at Little Rock. Yet at 10:22 a. m. (Little Rock time) on Tuesday the executive order was issued declaring that the command in the proclamation "has not been obeyed" and that a "wilful obstruction" of a court order "still exists." Who was obstructing it? Certainly not the Governor and the National Guard, who had obeyed the court order.

The Mayor of Little Rock on Monday afternoon, in order to prevent violence by the people, had suggested that the Negro students be withdrawn temporarily from the school so as to forestall disorder within the school. This was exactly what the Governor previously had felt was the only thing to do for the time being.

Apparently the President, however, was not so much concerned with quelling disorder as he was with enforcing "integration."

But there Mr. Eisenhower erred. He has no right to use federal troops to enforce federal court orders unless the civil process has actually broken down. He did not wait to see if it had. President Cleveland, in using military force at Chicago to break a railway strike in 1894, had demanded clear proof of the failure of judicial process before he acted. In that instance, the State of Illinois furnished almost all the troops and 5,000 deputy marshals.

The statute which President Eisenhower cited in his proclamation was passed in 1871—during Reconstruction days. It provides that the President "shall take such measures as he considers necessary to suppress in a State, any insurrection, domestic violence, unlawful combination or conspiracy" but only if "the constituted authorities are unable, fail, or refuse to protect" the rights of the people or if "the execution of the laws of the United States" has been obstructed.

The Arkansas Governor complied with the court's order on Friday, Sept. 20—three days before the federal proclamation was issued. Any alleged "obstruction" by the State itself was removed that same day when the original orders issued to the National Guard by the Governor were withdrawn.

Why wasn't the Governor of Arkansas formally requested by the President to aid in the appointment of deputy marshals to enforce the "judicial process"?

Why was the Arkansas Governor prevented from exercising his judgment as to how to maintain order in his use of the National Guard?

Are not the President and the federal judge both responsible for interfering with the constitutional processes of the State—first, by enjoining the Governor from the exercise of his executive judgment with respect to the National Guard, and secondly, in failing to call upon the Governor to help provide the necessary deputy marshals to enforce "judicial process"?

Here is illegality—military rule—tearing to shreds the specific provision in the Federal Constitution that the Federal Government "shall guarantee to every State in this Union a republican form of government."

Here is a President of the United States ignoring the statutes which place upon him the responsibility of taking measures in cooperation with the Governor of a State in maintaining order.

What Mr. Eisenhower's legal advisers also disregarded last week was the law passed by Congress in

1878 specifically limiting the use of the Army in quelling disorders. It says:

"It shall not be lawful to employ any part of the Army of the United States, as a *posse comitatus,* or otherwise, for the purpose of executing the laws, except in such cases and under such circumstances as such employment of said force may be expressly authorized by the Constitution or by act of Congress."

The law which "expressly authorized" use of the federal troops in "civil rights" cases was repealed last summer by Congress.

There is nothing in the Constitution that makes the President a dictator—nothing that says the President can use military power whenever he pleases. He has no such unlimited authority outside the United States, and he certainly has no such unlimited authority inside the United States. Obviously he can use federal troops to protect property of the Federal Government, but the schools in Arkansas are not federal property.

When the President, moreover, instructs the General in command of federal troops in Arkansas to enter the classrooms of a public school—operating with State funds and under State laws—and the General tells the pupils that there is a "law" which compels the "integration" of students and that the pupils must not take any step which might lead to disorder, this is, in effect, saying federal troops can be used whenever and for whatever purpose the Executive demands. For there is no such law.

Thus we see the same military commander, on instructions of the President, asserting the right to exert discipline inside the public schools without any authorization of Congress and without regard to any constitutional power of the States.

What is the proper procedure? What is the alternative if a State does not preserve order? The Constitution expressly says that the Federal Government must come to the aid of a State if the legislature of a State requests it or when the Governor makes such a request, in the event the legislature is not in session.

But supposing a Governor does not want to request federal military aid, then what? Many critics have said that "there is no alternative" except to send federal troops to that State when a federal law is involved. This is a mistaken conception of the way our judicial system operates. Whenever a federal court issues an order and the U. S. Marshal cannot enforce it alone, he is authorized to deputize as many citizens as he needs.

Certainly the U. S. Marshal at Little Rock could have endeavored to obtain in Arkansas a thousand deputies or more if necessary to carry out his orders. He could

have ordered the arrest of anyone who interfered with the serving of his orders.

Was the assembly of a lot of citizens in the streets in Little Rock last Monday night really a disobedience of the command of the proclamation? Who in the Department of Justice, or elsewhere, determined the "intent" of these citizens over the weekend?

Didn't the Supreme Court in a decision last spring say that a citizen now can preach publicly even the overthrow of the Government of the United States by force but, until there is an overt act directly growing out of the utterance, it is merely "free speech" and "free assembly," guaranteed by the First Amendment.

We have in the Arkansas tragedy an example of civil law disregarded by President Eisenhower. It was an analogous procedure which led the Supreme Court in *Ex Parte Milligan* to criticize President Lincoln so severely after the war for having suspended certain civil rights during the war. "Emergencies do not create power"—the Supreme Court has said again and again.

The far-reaching significance of President Eisenhower's tragic error may not be fully realized for a long time to come. It is a cruel and unconstitutional precedent that has been established.

Even if we assume the validity of the Fourteenth Amendment, this same amendment plainly declares that only Congress—not the Supreme Court of the United States and not Federal troops—"shall have power to enforce, by appropriate legislation, the provisions of this Article."

Congress has passed no law forbidding segregation in the schools. The Supreme Court for nearly 60 years approved "separate but equal" facilities as being constitutional under the Fourteenth Amendment. Now, without consulting the people, the so-called "law of the land" is arbitrarily changed by nine men—a judicial oligarchy—who argue mainly in terms of sociology and not of law.

The American people are being told today that, so long as the objective is good, it doesn't make much difference what methods are used by their government to attain the objective—that the end justifies the means. This philosophy of "might makes right" could mean the end of free government in America.

The illegalities of Reconstruction days are with us again. Arbitrary actions, military force, capricious and arbitrary decrees of the judiciary, mob violence, threats to pupils in the schoolroom itself uttered in speeches by uniformed commanders—this is not government of the people and by the people and for the people. It is illegality run riot.

THE VOICE OF REASON

OCTOBER 11, 1957

MUST WE CONCEDE that in free America only military force can achieve obedience to what is often termed "the law of the land"?

We have been preaching to the world for several years now that "renunciation of the use of force" is the best means of preserving international peace.

Isn't that true also of internal peace?

Looking back at the events in Arkansas, can it be said that we exercised the same forbearance and restraint as we call on other countries to apply when passions run high and local riots break out?

The President, in his "Notes on Legal Principles," said last week that the "formulation of plans effecting desegregation" is a "function left to the community where maximum understanding of local problems exists," and that, in the 1954 decision, this was "clearly recognized by the United States Supreme Court."

Wouldn't it have been better for the federal judge at Little Rock to have granted the delay formally requested by the school authorities there till tempers cooled?

Wouldn't it have been better for the President to have directed the Department of Justice to assist the federal marshal in carrying out the orders of the federal court through the deputizing of enough citizens, as assistants to the marshals, to arrest any persons interfering with the court's injunction?

Wouldn't it have been better for the President—in issuing his proclamation on Monday, September 23, which called on the people of Little Rock to preserve order—to have given the people at least several days in which to listen to the voice of Reason?

Are we admitting that our "civil process" and appeals to the citizenry would have been of no avail?

Must we proclaim that we in free America will not respect the normal processes of the judiciary except at the bayonet points of federal troops?

We have only ourselves to blame for the taking of what is an ordinary condition of riot in a small town and magnifying it into a dramatic exhibition before the whole world, as the President of the United States did when he sent in federal troops to squelch a local disturbance.

Why did we have to assume that we could not settle our difficulties locally through the State police and federal court processes and that only federal troops could secure compliance with a court order when there were other means available?

This is the real tragedy of Little Rock.

The President himself outlined the alternative means at a press conference at the White House on September 11, 1956, when he was discussing the case of Texas militiamen who had prevented the entry of Negroes into a public school. He said:

"Well, the federal judge, of course, is a federal officer in the judiciary branch. Now, I assume that if that marshal is not able to carry it out by himself, he has got the right to deputize any number of deputy marshals to help him carry it out. I really don't know what the next step is.

"I do know this: In a place of general disorder, the Federal Government is not allowed to go into any State unless called upon by the Governor, who must show that the Governor is unable with the means at his disposal to preserve order. I believe it is called a 'Posse Comitatus Act' of 1882—and I am now going back to my staff school of 1925—and that is the thing that keeps the Federal Government from just going around where he pleases to carry out police duties."

On August 10, 1956, Congress approved the recodification of the "Posse Comitatus Act" originally passed in 1878. This specifically forbids the use of federal troops "to execute the laws" unless "expressly authorized by the Constitution or act of Congress."

This was "the law of the land" only a year ago. Why isn't it respected as "the law of the land" today?

What is to be done now? There must be an abandonment of the quibbling, pettifogging attitudes which caused the collapse last week of the negotiations for the withdrawal of federal troops from Arkansas.

It is not too late to return to the normal processes of law enforcement in America and to rely on the good sense of a community whose feelings have understandably been aggravated by an unlawful use of federal troops.

Withdrawal of these troops, it became clear to everybody last week, is the first step toward peace at Little Rock.

All parties who wish to challenge any phase of the law can do so at any time by proper proceedings in the court.

Decisions of the Supreme Court of the United States, it must be emphasized, have never been and are not now "the law of the land" but the law of the case.

Only the Constitution and acts of Congress are "the law of the land."

What we need is a return to common sense—to heed the lessons of history and listen to the voice of Reason.

COMING DOWN TO EARTH

OCTOBER 18, 1957

MANY PEOPLE IN AMERICA—particularly the politicians—went "up in the air" last week.

Just because the Russians managed to spin a ball in outer space, a sort of hysterical terror seized too many persons in this country. If the Russians can do this, it was lamented, what couldn't they do to us with an intercontinental missile?

It's necessary to come down to earth—to put what has happened into the perspective of military facts. We must go from the speculative or conjectural to the realistic and the actual.

If the Russians really can fire an intercontinental missile into space, they—as well as we—have much to do yet in perfecting its aim. It could circle the earth and come back to kill Russia's own people.

There is no reason, therefore, to begin to yield in craven submission to the totalitarian enemy, which is already demanding a "change" in our foreign policy. There is every reason instead to continue our steady production of counter-weapons.

For not all missiles can get through to their targets. Interception devices are being developed. Also if the free world is attacked, there will instantly be a massive retaliation—scores of hydrogen bombs will be dropped on selected targets.

So the situation has not been changed a bit because a harmless device has been spinning around the world in outer space. The big stalemate remains.

We can destroy a big part of Russia and the Communists can destroy a big part of this country.

Death-dealing weapons already have reached a sufficiently high point of effectiveness.

No military advantage has been added or subtracted by the launching of the earth satellite.

Whether Russian scientists are better than ours or whether they have had more money to spend—some estimates are that 14 billion dollars have been spent by Moscow on the experiments thus far—the fact remains that there is no military value in the earth satellites as such. The hydrogen bomb, carried by fast-moving jet planes from bases within a few minutes' flight from the Soviet Union, can produce as many if not more casualties than several intercontinental missiles.

Under such circumstances, is not the true significance of last week's events that peoples now become more important than tyrants and dictatorships? Will any people submit long to the rule of a small group of men who can plunge them into a destructive war overnight?

Much has been said about the "propaganda victory" of the Kremlin. Victory over what? Will the peoples of the world suddenly forget the cruelty and tyranny of the Soviet leaders and hereafter consider them saints because of their success in launching the iron ball?

Will the world now forgive all that the Communist criminals have been doing and embrace them as trustworthy friends? Are the peoples of the West and of the "neutral" areas really so fickle and so easily misled?

America's position in the world rests upon this great and simple truth—we covet nobody's territory and we do not wish ever to interfere in the right of any people to be free or to choose whatever form of government they desire.

We are not concerned militarily with internal policies in any country. We are concerned with external policies—the possibility that a dictatorship might sweep helpless countries and enslave their peoples and engulf us in a war.

From the standpoint of idealism, we are concerned, of course, with the evil that dictators do to the people they temporarily command. We are anxious to offer moral support to the oppressed. But we have never said we would use military force to emancipate any nation from bondage. This must come from within.

Nor is the prospect of revolution in Soviet Russia lessened by recent events. Actually, this may have been advanced. For how long can a people, held in slavery, tolerate a regime that spends billions of rubles for stunts and not enough rubles to improve the standard of living of its people?

The Russian people will find that the enhancement of the prestige of their tyrannical rulers, with misguided applause coming from other countries, will not win them freedom.

The futility of war as a means of settling international disputes has been evident to mankind for centuries. The development of lethal weapons in the last decade has made war seem more and more impracticable as a method of assuring any nation or group of nations a permanent position of advantage in the world.

The building up of deterrent strength, of course, has become even more important than ever before.

Peace will not be accomplished through a resort to pacifism and disarmament. It will come only through the rise of free peoples against dictatorships. For only when the power everywhere is in the hands of free peoples will the world be safe for democracy.

It's time for everybody, including the politicians in America, to come down to earth.

A TIME FOR COURAGE

OCTOBER 25, 1957

THERE COMES A TIME in the life of a nation when resoluteness becomes essential to survival and when cowardice can bring destruction.

It is a time when weakness and vacillation can encourage an enemy to misconstrue our purposes and miscalculate our strength.

It is a time when America must not leave any doubt anywhere that we intend—if we are pressed by our enemies—to use every force we can command to fulfill American obligations in the world.

The recent behavior of the Soviet rulers is ominous. They launch a "satellite" to impress the world with their scientific progress, but the same week they connive with Egypt and Syria to threaten a new war in the Middle East which inevitably would engulf the rest of the world.

The Moscow dictatorship presumably doesn't want a world war any more than the Nazi dictatorship did in 1939. But just as Hitler miscalculated and wouldn't believe that the forces of the United States could arrive overseas in time to save Britain and France, so today Khrushchev evidently thinks the American people are scared to death because of the gyrations of his metal ball around the earth and that the threat of his missiles, as yet unperfected, can bluff the American Government into submission to Moscow's dictation.

Our Secretary of State, John Foster Dulles, has met the Russian threat with a frank declaration that, if Turkey is attacked, the United States and her allies will defend that country.

This is a grave warning which Moscow should not misunderstand. Just before the Korean war broke out in 1950, we were foolish enough to tell the world that Korea was outside the "defense perimeter" of the United States. It was this, among other things, that prompted the Soviets and the Red Chinese to feel safe in launching a local war. It cost them and it cost us heavily.

Today the United States serves notice in advance. This is the wise thing to do because the Moscow rulers must not for a moment be left to guess America's intentions. They could guess wrong.

There are Americans, of course, who want to surrender. They will not admit it, but their words keep saying so and Moscow keeps reading them. After all, the familiar argument goes, aren't the Soviets in control of the states of Eastern Europe? Is it worthwhile to worry about the reunification of Germany? Isn't it better to accept the "status quo" and forget all about "liberating" the captive countries of Eastern Europe? And aren't the Red Chinese in complete control of the mainland of China, and isn't it better to recognize that fact and let bygones be bygones as the gangsters are welcomed into the United Nations without a single act or word of repentance for their aggression in Korea?

This is the chant of defeatism. It is not our boasted adherence to principle. It is the same old surrender to expediency on the mistaken theory that, if you yield to the enemy, he will be kind to you thereafter.

Human experience shows that tyrants are never satiated and that each surrender means further demands and a higher price in their blackmail. The historic writings of Winston Churchill remind us of the repeated appeasements of the Nazis, in step after step, as Hitler's military strength was concurrently being enlarged. Then the fateful moment of decision came when the dictator thought it was opportune to strike. The world knows now the tragic necessity that forced us all into a conflict that swept the globe. It left behind the wreckage of millions of human lives—civilians as well as soldiers. It left a devastation of trade and commercial relationships. It left a huge public debt which this generation is struggling with in an era of depreciated currencies and economic distress throughout the free world.

The time to prevent a war is in the incipient stages when tyrants, intoxicated with their own power, begin to feel their strength.

We have unwittingly helped to enhance the prestige of the Moscow tyrants. We are being told that we must "congratulate" the Soviet scientists and forget they are Communist puppets—as if this were a game of courtesy and chivalry. It is, in fact, a game of Russian roulette in which we are asked to put a pistol to our heads and take chances.

The free world is bound together by alliances and pledges of mutual aid. Our allies are looking to us for courageous leadership. We must not fail them.

If Khrushchev and his coterie of gangsters who have enslaved hundreds of millions of people really believe their scientific advances in recent months entitle them to bluff the rest of us into surrender and submission and that the Middle East is to be the testing ground, the time has come to meet that test.

May the President summon not the petty partisans but the patriotic leaders of both parties to form an American council of defense in this critical hour.

It is not a time for faltering or bickering or mutual recrimination on the political front. It is a time for statesmanship. It is a time for courage.

AN "UNWRITTEN CONSTITUTION"?

NOVEMBER 8, 1957

HAS THE TIME COME for the American people in self-protection to adopt the system of government known generally as an "unwritten Constitution," whereby the national legislature makes the supreme law of the land?

No such question would be presented now for consideration if there had not been forced upon us recently a situation in which nine men, appointed for life, have been rewriting our Constitution at will. These nine men today rule the nation—they are the Constitution.

It was never intended by the Founding Fathers that there should be a judicial oligarchy in America. Jefferson vehemently opposed it from the beginning. Abraham Lincoln inveighed against it.

The Supreme Court was established solely to interpret the Constitution and the laws made under it—not to legislate.

Today, nevertheless, the Supreme Court legislates.

It adds to the Constitution words that have never been in that document.

It makes laws for the States, though the Constitution itself forbids the Supreme Court to make any such laws.

It orders the citizens to obey court decrees which are publicly referred to by the President himself as "laws," though they have not been voted by the Congress.

There is as yet no immediate check upon the excesses of the Supreme Court of the United States.

We have the disadvantages of the formula of an "unwritten Constitution" but none of the advantages of a democratic method of operating it, such as are enjoyed, for example, by the people of Great Britain.

If we in America turn to an "unwritten Constitution," full power to make the supreme law must be exercised only by the people's legislature.

Would it not be better—if we must have opportunistic government—for Congress and the State legislatures to agree on how to handle important questions of public policy, such as whether the States or the Federal Government shall control public schools, whether Communists shall be allowed to preach the overthrow of the Government by force, whether Communists shall be permitted to hold government jobs or professorial posts in our colleges, rather than to leave all these and kindred questions to be legislated upon by nine men who are responsible to nobody in the Government?

Federal and State relations are in a chaotic condition today, though there is no valid reason for it. The Tenth Amendment says clearly that the powers not delegated to the Federal Government in the Constitution itself nor prohibited to the States by the Constitution "are reserved to the States respectively, or to the people."

If the American people should wish to adopt an "unwritten Constitution," it would not necessarily mean the scrapping of our Federal Constitution, for there is really nothing wrong with the document itself. The Supreme Court and the State courts could still retain their interpretive functions, but we do need a check against usurpation of power by the judiciary. We must plug a loophole.

A simple change would assure the rule of the people. An amendment to the present Constitution could provide that all decisions of the Supreme Court shall be subject to review at will by a two-thirds majority of Congress and that no decision shall be valid if rejected by the Congress.

The people at an election every two years could check an errant Congress. By requiring a vote of two thirds of both houses in order to reverse decisions of the Supreme Court, the excesses of an impassioned majority of lesser numbers would be avoided.

This principle, to be sure, is not novel. The idea of periodic review by Congress was inherent in Jefferson's suggestion that the Supreme Court Justices be appointed for four or six year terms and confirmed by both Houses of Congress. Former President Theodore Roosevelt, in his campaign as a Progressive Republican in 1912, favored the "recall of judicial decisions" in the States. One platform plank read as follows:

"The Progressive Party demands such restriction of the power of the courts as shall leave to the people the ultimate authority to determine fundamental questions of social welfare and public policy."

It would be a matter of universal regret if it became necessary in the United States to forsake the system of a written Constitution. The pressures of the extremists of our day, however, are compelling us to examine remedial measures—how we can best assure protection for the rights of the people.

The basic question is: Who shall make "the law of the land"?

As between a judicial oligarchy of nine men appointed for life and a two-thirds vote of both houses of Congress, there are millions of Americans who would prefer to put their trust in the people's own legislature.

THE ONLY ANSWER?

NOVEMBER 15, 1957

PRESIDENT EISENHOWER was at his best in his speech to the nation last week—unpolitical, forthright and frank. He outlined without bluster America's military strength. He gave us the first authoritative word of the great strides the United States has made in the scientific development of new weapons, especially missiles. He emphasized that we have sent a missile into outer space and have solved the problem of re-entry through the earth's atmosphere and return to a specific target—something it has not been clear whether the Russians have achieved.

If the speech had been one of exultant self-satisfaction—assuming that America had launched the first "satellite"—it would have been promptly interpreted by the Communist countries as a military threat and as a harbinger of war. Instead, circumstances have made the President's posture before the world one of defense rather than offense. Yet his message gives reassurance to the American people that they possess a strong means of repelling sudden attack, and it tells the people of the world that America's power will never be used for aggression but only to deter or resist an enemy.

In measured phrases, the President describes America's military position as follows:

"It is my conviction, supported by trusted scientific and military advisers, that, although the Soviets are quite likely ahead in some missile and special areas, and are obviously ahead of us in satellite development, as of today the over-all military strength of the free world is distinctly greater than that of the Communist countries. We must see to it that whatever advantages they have are temporary only."

Thus the armament race in the world goes on. Who and what can stop it?

The President rightly says:

"What the world needs today, even more than a giant leap into outer space, is a giant step toward peace."

Unhappily, the self-sufficient rulers in Moscow do not agree with this. They talk peace but they do not mean it. They have just withdrawn from all discussions in the United Nations on the subject of disarmament. They have recently been instigating trouble in the Middle East. They have been provoking mischief internally in every country in the world, including our own. They rely on the naive in our midst and in allied countries who still talk of holding "round tables" with Soviet scientists or more "summit" conferences with their leaders—as if mere conversation ever budges the intransigent men in the Kremlin.

Appeasement is fruitless. The road to "Munich" leads only to war.

The road to peace does not begin in the Kremlin but in the cities and towns of the Soviet empire. It's the people of Soviet Russia who must be reached and persuaded if the world is ever to halt its armament race.

The President puts it realistically as follows:

"But, in the main, the Soviets continue to concentrate on the development of warmaking weapons and supporting industries. This, as well as their political attitude in all international affairs, serves to warn us that Soviet expansionist aims have not changed.

"The world has not forgotten the Soviet military invasions of such countries as Finland and Poland, their support of the war in Korea, or their use of force in their ruthless suppression of Hungarian freedom.

"Eternal vigilance and increased free world military power, backed by our combined economic and spiritual strength, provide the only answer to this threat until the Soviet leaders themselves cease to consume their resources in warlike and expansionist purposes and turn them to the well-being of their own peoples."

But is it the only answer?

We mobilize the best brains in the scientific world, yet what "missiles of information" have we invented to reach the people of Soviet Russia, who alone have the answer to the question of whether there will be war?

Internal upheavals are inevitable. They do not happen overnight. It takes a long, long time to organize revolt. In the annals of history, however, years are but minutes. The inexorable laws of mankind do operate eventually to secure emancipation from slavery.

The people of Soviet Russia do not want war any more than we do. They are paying a heavier cost than we in the armament race. They are being deprived of adequate food and clothing. The hundreds of millions of people in Red China and in the states controlled by the Kremlin are suffering great privation. Surely here are the ingredients of the "missiles of information" which we should be able, by scientific invention, to transmit to every citizen behind the Iron Curtain.

We must learn how to launch "satellites" that encourage, that inspire, that stimulate the people of Soviet Russia to join with us in assuring peace.

For the only answer to the threat of another world war lies with the people of Soviet Russia. By concerted action, they can overthrow the tyrants in the Kremlin. They can lift the burden of armament from peoples everywhere. This is the only answer.

THE NEED FOR CABINET GOVERNMENT

NOVEMBER 22, 1957

THE PRESIDENCY is a superhuman task. This has been said again and again, but it may take a catastrophe to awaken the American people to the need for a constructive remedy. How long can we afford to consider the Presidency as a one-man job?

Certainly the same individual who, under our Constitution, must serve as Commander-in-chief of the armed forces and also as the executive head of the civil establishment and as the vigilant guardian and constant spokesman of the national interest, cannot be expected to do all this by himself.

For years the theory has prevailed that we have a Cabinet system. Actually, we have administrators of big departments of government.

The enlargement of the President's staff in recent years has failed to solve the real problem, which is not merely administrative efficiency but policy-making. The subject is neither political nor partisan. The same criticisms have been made here with respect to Democratic as well as Republican Administrations. Thus, on April 30, 1934, on this page, a different function for the Cabinet was urged, as follows:

"The country expects to see in the Cabinet men who are able to advise the President. But it is a paradox of the present arrangement, both under this and preceding Administrations, that the Cabinet officers really have no time to do any substantial amount of advising. Their opinions are asked and given on specific matters that arise in the routine of governmental operations. But the study and analysis of current policies by committees of the Cabinet devoting themselves wholly to such tasks has been virtually impossible.

"Cabinet officers work late into the night—but usually on detail that could just as well be handled by managers of the government departments. The difficulty lies in the fact that seldom is a distinction made between the formulation of departmental policy—which ought to be done by the Cabinet officers—and execution of the same policy in the hundred and one different cases of administrative detail which arise from day to day. This ought to be delegated entirely to the manager of a department who, after all, should be responsible for administrative efficiency."

The idea was advanced at the same time that in a presidential building the Cabinet officers would have their regular offices at the elbow of the President and would be consulted there by the managers of their own respective departments and by the heads of independent commissions. The principal duty of Cabinet officers would be to advise the President. For the Government of the United States is the only big business in the world that does not have a conference of the executive committee of the board of directors two or three times a week.

Again on November 14, 1952, when a Republican Administration was coming into power, the same question was raised on this page, with the following comment:

"Government has grown beyond any one man. The Presidency today cannot be just an administrative office like that of the general manager in private business. It is a policy-making job."

On the same occasion the suggestion was made that a five-man council be created in the Department of State, with the Secretary of State as chairman and with all the members nominated and confirmed by the Senate. It was also recommended that similar councils be established for other departments of the Government.

Too many matters of the highest importance are decided nowadays by the President in consultation with a single Cabinet officer.

The meetings of the present Cabinet—held once a week—include not only the heads of the ten departments of the Government but also the heads of other governmental agencies and commissions. It is a large group. Few of the participants are familiar with the problems of departments other than their own. These sessions should, of course, be continued but they cannot possibly accomplish the purpose that could be served by an intimate council of five to ten members.

A Presidential Council is essential to the making of public policies. The group could be enlarged on occasion, when specific subjects arise requiring the advice of persons particularly familiar with given problems.

The first step is to separate the Cabinet officers from the administrative work of their departments and to give them policy-making functions. An executive manager should be appointed for each department.

The next step is to form committees of the Cabinet with which the heads of other agencies of the Government would consult. This would permit the Cabinet officers to give all their time to policy-making.

The third step is to form within the Cabinet a Presidential Council which could meet daily to discuss questions pressing for decision by the President.

These reforms in a Department of the Presidency are long overdue.

THE UNNECESSARY "RECESSION"

NOVEMBER 29, 1957

THE NATIONAL ECONOMY is in the midst of a "recession" or, to use a somewhat more palatable synonym, a "rolling readjustment."

"Fundamentally," as the saying goes, "things are sound." This is but another way of asserting that there is nothing in the situation that a little self-restraint cannot cure. For abuses of economic power, rather than any cracks in the foundation of our free-enterprise system, are causing the present maladjustment.

We hear much about "tight money" as a negative influence recently on business growth and as threatening the continuance of high employment. Or else we read articles on "government spending" and large budgets as the cause of our troubles. Usually it is not a single element but a lot of different elements combined which bring on the crisis.

As we survey the irresponsibility of economic forces, the pursuit of greed and the tendency to assume that we can go on and on feeding an inflation inherited from the war years, the wonder is that we don't have more recessions and perhaps a deep depression.

For we seem to drift along in a state of indifference to economic shoals. Then, when things really get bad, we expect the Administration in power to use all the Government's functions and all the resources at its command to rescue the stranded ships of trade.

Fortunately, due to the great improvement in our methods of gathering statistics, we can do some introspection every month by examining the curves in the ups and downs of business charts. This prompts the experts to call for corrective measures soon after a dangerous trend has already appeared.

Too much reliance, however, is placed on governmental devices to help us out. It is so easy to blame all our afflictions on "tight money" and on the high interest rates imposed by the Federal Reserve Board—as if monetary controls could cure everything. Actually, the control of interest rates is a way to stop certain excesses rather than a means of preventing their recurrence.

When, a week or so ago, the Federal Reserve Board began to reduce interest rates, it reversed a policy of two and a half years, during which money rates have been moving steadily upwards. This is a constructive move which notifies the business community it is approaching bottom or that a new plateau has been reached in the incessant struggle with inflation.

Yet of what avail is a relaxation of the curb on interest rates when no restraints have been placed on any other factors in the business mechanism?

What evidence, for instance, is there that the labor-union leaders responsible for the recent wave of inflation have been taught any lesson and that they, too, are ready to reverse themselves? And what can they do inside their own organizations when they have been elected to office on the pledge that they will obtain wage increases every year, come hell or high water?

Management, often without a fight, has acquiesced in and accepted "built in" escalator clauses. These are predetermined wage increases affecting future years. They are embedded in labor-union contracts. In 1958— when the nation's consumers may be buying less goods due to high prices—many employers will not be able to reduce the prices of their products without going into the red. There is now no such flexibility in the price structure as we had before the labor-union monopolies began virtually to fix prices by taking command of the cost side of business.

The Sherman antitrust law was enacted by Congress in 1890 to break up price-fixing by the sellers of goods. The public was being gouged by the concerted action of the producers who had stifled competition.

When the Supreme Court, however, ruled that "restraint of trade" as used in the antitrust laws could not be applied to labor-union activities, the doors were opened to periodic recessions and depressions, with grave consequences to the workers themselves.

Today, with industry-wide bargaining, the American people see the big monopoly of national labor unions forcing the costs so high that sellers have no other choice—they must keep on raising their prices.

Inflationary forces—not just extravagances— have sent upwards the cost of federal, State and city governments in America. Higher taxes have been the inevitable result.

When will the monopoly of organized labor be tackled by Congress? "Rackets" such as we have read about recently are deplorable, but the real problem is not with the few union officers who misuse money in labor-union treasuries. The biggest danger comes from the legalized monopoly exercised by the national labor unions themselves.

Statesmanship and self-restraint by labor-union leaders could theoretically, without more laws, cure the excesses. But human nature being what it is, there must be additional legislation.

As has been said many times, there is enough in America for everybody's need—but there's not enough for everybody's greed.

"AMERICAN PRESTIGE" ABROAD

DECEMBER 6, 1957

Is "AMERICAN PRESTIGE" ABROAD really a one-man affair? Does it go up and down like the stock market? Or is it something more enduring?

These questions become pertinent now because only a few weeks ago America was being criticized abroad for failing to exercise "leadership" in "sputniks." The criticism was diminished somewhat when it was announced last month that the President would attend the NATO conference in Paris. In contradiction, however, last week—as the first news of the President's illness was published—various London newspapers editorially called on Mr. Eisenhower to "resign" at once.

The American press has never undertaken to select a Prime Minister for Britain. Nor did such a demand upon the leader of their own Government ever come from the British newspapers when they suppressed the facts about the "complete paralysis" suffered for a time in 1953 by Prime Minister Churchill. It was not until 1955 that the truth was revealed by the Prime Minister himself just before his withdrawal from public life.

"American prestige" abroad seems to have many lives. It appears to have been "killed" when Congress was investigating Communists in our midst—if the foreign press is to be believed. Then our "prestige" was subsequently revived when a Wisconsin Senator was "censured." It was "killed" again when we sided against Britain and France in the Suez dispute.

What is this intangible called "prestige"? What is the real clue to it all? Is it money? Is it a fear that Mr. Eisenhower will not be sufficiently effective in leading his party, which has not been as generous with "foreign aid" funds as were Mr. Truman and the Democrats? The British press enthusiastically favored the election of Mr. Stevenson in 1956.

Is "American prestige" to be judged by materialistic yardsticks? Is it to be appraised solely in terms of whether our governmental leaders are lukewarm or enthusiastic at the moment about pouring out more of America's billions, particularly in the "undeveloped areas" or in the "uncommitted countries"? The cliches in the European press—often echoed here—call for "bold and imaginative ideas." But what is usually meant is more and more dollars for "foreign aid."

Let there be no mistake. Financial co-operation between this country and the rest of the free world is essential, but money is not the only American asset.

Actually, the United States has won her position of leadership through good fortune and inherent ability. The peoples of every nation have been encouraged to settle here on a continent rich in natural resources and blessed with an abundance of food acreage. But there are other parts of the world also blessed with valuable resources and food potential. The people who came to America, however, had the ingenuity and the courage and the persistence to develop and make maximum use of those resources. No other nation has as yet achieved anything like it. Our "prestige" in that sense may be envied but it has not been duplicated.

The fiction that to retain "prestige" abroad America must lead in everything, including "sputniks," is widely accepted nowadays. It is forgotten that American medical men, inventors and scientists in past decades have had to learn a lot from men of achievement in other countries and have always been willing to take lessons from trained minds in Europe and Asia.

The "sputnik" race isn't over yet. As for intercontinental missiles, it is one thing to develop them and another thing to produce them in the quantity that an American production line can turn them out.

The prestige of the United States is by no means a one-man affair. It is what the American people collectively make it. And just now America's prestige should be at its highest point in our history because America has not only developed material advantages but, in a spirit of idealism and unselfishness unequalled in our times, has been willing to share them with other nations.

Every American taxpayer contributes annually a substantial part of his income to help maintain the economic and military strength of other countries thousands of miles away from our shores. What other nation has ever done this and for so long a period of time?

Only six or seven years ago, moreover, 1,200,000 American troops—not just a "token" force—were sent 5,500 miles across the Pacific. They did not go there to annex a single foot of territory, or to gain commercial advantage for the United States, or to pursue goals of "imperialism" or "colonialism." They went to Korea to fight for an ideal known as "collective security."

The sacrifices made by our manhood in the Korean war, in World War II and in World War I constitute an unequalled record of altruism. It is to peoples everywhere unparalleled evidence of the immutable prestige of the United States in the world.

It is a prestige maintained by our unremitting pledge to defend the free world if any member country is attacked. It is a prestige held aloft by our continuing devotion to the cause of universal peace.

DEFENSE AGAINST WHAT?

DECEMBER 13, 1957

WE USE NOWADAYS in our official vocabulary such terms as "deterrent" power, "massive retaliation" and "defense against sudden attack."

But what is really meant when we say we will defend ourselves only if we are actually attacked?

Must America wait till after our big cities have been demolished and after the British and the French parliaments have finished debating whether our military forces stationed on their territory are to be allowed to launch bombs or missiles?

Are we in America to see New York and Detroit and Chicago and Washington destroyed simultaneously and our principal air bases and many of our planes rendered useless before we authorize "massive retaliation" with what military power we have left? Interception, it is conceded, will not prevent a large percentage of enemy bombs and missiles from reaching their targets, nor will we be immune from attack by missiles fired from enemy submarines roving up and down our coasts.

We in the free world have not yet faced up to these particular contingencies.

The problem is not changed very much just because Soviet Russia sends a "sputnik" into outer space and we later duplicate the feat. Missiles have been in process of development for some time, and so have experiments with anti-missile missiles.

The fact is that the power of sudden attack—instantaneous destruction of many of our cities and of our defense arsenals from which retaliation would be ordered —is vested in an unscrupulous enemy government.

We content ourselves by saying that America will never fight unless attacked and that, by accumulating enough military strength, we will make it unwise for an enemy to invite the blows of destruction that we can inflict on his territory.

Time is of the essence when nations are ready to fight. In 1941 we had a better fleet than Japan had, but the Tokyo planners decided on sudden attack and crippled our Navy for many months. The strategy of a "Pearl Harbor" appeals to the military mind—it has long been known in the glossary of military techniques as the "surprise attack."

Today our main reliance against surprise attack is "massive retaliation." Even this concept has been ridiculed by some in our midst who think of it as an improbable sequence and argue that it is better to develop strong forces of the conventional type so as to be able primarily to fight small wars.

The unpleasant truth is that no nation is secure unless it is able to fight both small wars and big wars. For a little war might grow overnight into a big war.

We in America and our allies abroad are faced with the danger of being destroyed because we are unwilling to strike the first blow. For us to strike the first blow is called "preventive war," and the idea is promptly waved aside as unthinkable. But where is the guarantee against surprise attack?

There is a middle course between the two extremes. Soviet Russia must not be led to believe that we will take the first blow. Our forces must be ready overseas and in this country to strike not only when—through our devices of detection—Soviet planes or missiles are known to have left the ground but when the mobilization for attack against us begins.

With the new inventions that permit aerial inspection high above the earth's surface, it is possible to know what an enemy is doing by way of assembling his weapons of war for attack.

We should agree to permit actual inspection of what we ourselves are doing inside the free world, but only if some trustworthy form of international action has been taken to prevent war. This is why we tried to get a "disarmament" agreement.

An unfortunate impression prevails that the free world today is at the mercy of Soviet missiles. This isn't so. The big bombers we have stationed in this country and abroad can inflict terrible blows on the enemy, and it can be done with our Air Force bombers and the Navy planes that carry hydrogen bombs from aircraft carriers, provided they are ordered to operate at the instant of a coming attack. The enemy should not be permitted to count on the devastating effect of its own first blow to compel our surrender.

Under all the circumstances, it is desirable to reappraise the real meaning of the "first blow" and to demand an ironclad agreement limiting or abandoning the use of atomic bombs and missiles. Unless such an international agreement is achieved, the free world will be compelled to be ready not merely to intercept the first blow but to deliver our own first blow the moment it is clear that the enemy mobilization has reached the danger point for us.

Defense against attack must mean defense by means of a calculated offense. The very knowledge that such a policy of defense has been decided upon can deter an enemy. It is important that America and her allies agree at the forthcoming NATO conference to examine the critical problem involved in that "first blow."

ONLY 19 MONTHS AGO

DECEMBER 20, 1957

Sometimes we feel the world moves fast, and we tend to think in terms of days instead of years. But it takes time for ideas to sink in—for action to follow planning.

This week at Paris we hope to see the fruition of a great ideal—the strengthened union of free peoples as represented at the NATO conference. For it was only 19 months ago that the foundations were laid, as described in the following editorial on this page, entitled "A Challenging Plan":

AT LAST there has come a plan which gives promise of eventually bringing peace to the world.

It's a plan really to bind together free peoples.

It's a plan that isolates the germ of failure in the past—disunity among our own allies—and offers a constructive program to achieve unity.

It's a plan that does not depend wholly on the deterrent influence of military force but endeavors to mobilize, in addition, the moral force of nations with a common purpose.

It's a plan that does not supplant but really parallels the United Nations.

This plan, revealed last week by Secretary of State Dulles, is a sensational development in world affairs.

The plan is an embodiment of American ideals as expressed by spokesmen in the past for Democratic as well as Republican Administrations. European statesmen for some time have nurtured the very concept which now has been crystallized by the Secretary of State.

We often take unity for granted. Yet it is the absence of unity on our side that gives the Soviet Government its main opportunity for mischief.

Briefly, the plan would rebuild the North Atlantic Treaty Organization by making it much more than a military alliance. The idea has been vaguely referred to heretofore as "broadening NATO." Actually, it means transforming NATO into an active instrumentality for the discussion and possible solution of any and all problems that affect world peace.

How would the Dulles Plan work? Details are not spelled out as yet. Only the broad principles have been outlined. It is, however, a simple approach. It recognizes that smaller councils are better for some things than the U. N., which is today mainly a vehicle for propaganda distribution and for log-rolling between factions of members.

The idea now is to make the NATO Council of 15

nations a living organism of diplomacy. This means that mediation and conciliation can be quietly employed to work out solutions for the complicated problems of Europe as well as of the Middle East and Asia, where European powers have historic involvements.

It means also that such explosive issues as Cyprus and Algeria—which, legally speaking, are internal matters—can be dealt with tactfully and yet with due regard for the sensitivity of sovereign rights.

For it is obvious that, if the vast oil resources of the Middle East are cut off from Europe, and Turkey and Greece become hostile to each other, NATO as a military organization can overnight lose a strategic battle.

The urgency is there to come to grips with the perplexing problems of both the Middle East and Asia. But fundamentally there is even greater need to solidify Europe and begin at last to lay the foundations of a genuine peace. NATO has skirted the edges of these problems before but has not acted on them directly. As the Secretary of State says, there have been "discussions" but not "decisions." He cautions that the unity of the Atlantic community can be promoted "not by supergovernment but by common counsel."

Mr. Dulles points significantly to the unashamed way the Soviets have ignored their pledge to seek the reunification of Germany and asks: "Has the Atlantic community as a whole sufficiently focused world opinion upon the moral aspects of this problem?"

World opinion, of course, is the key to it all. It is the generator of moral force, which, if we but realized it, can at times transcend in effectiveness the military might we have necessarily assembled.

For, given the moral assignment of leadership in mediation and constructive assistance in the political as well as economic fields, a new NATO can come into being. It can affiliate intimately with the Organization of American States and with the Western European Union as well as the Council of Europe. It can cooperate with the regional organizations of an economic nature that have been set up in Asia as well as with those already striving for economic unity in Europe.

By coordinating the energies of the free governments which are ready to make great sacrifices for ultimate peace, this bold and brilliant plan initiated by Secretary Dulles can take root. It could give the world at last what it has long been praying for—a constructive program which, by its challenge, must attract the attention of peoples on both sides of the Iron Curtain. For peoples, not governments, really hold the key to peace.

THEY DON'T BELIEVE IN GOD

DECEMBER 27, 1957

THERE WAS A VACANT CHAIR at the meeting in Paris last week.

The chair should have been occupied by the head of a free government that could have represented the many nationalities living in a vast area from the Baltic to the Pacific.

The reason why such a government does not exist today is because a few willful men hold the reins of power in Soviet Russia. They govern with a despotism that denies liberty to tens of millions of people.

Fifteen governments—freely chosen by the people in each country—sent their chief executives or prime ministers to the Paris meeting to take steps to defend their territory against the threat of attack persistently raised by the irresponsible group in the Kremlin.

If a free government existed in Moscow, the Paris conference could have been devoted to the fulfillment of the ideals of progress and human betterment in a peacetime world.

But the "enemy" government—master, for the time being, of friendly peoples who really wish to live in peace with the rest of the world—continues its strategic game of menace and intimidation.

The whole world is kept in a state of incessant fear because the rulers in Moscow have no morals—no sense of right and wrong.

For the fact is that the leaders of the Communist regime do not believe in God. One of their main tenets is an antagonism toward all churches and all religions.

Those who do not believe in God make their own rules. They avow that the end justifies the means.

Those of us who do believe in God avow a faith in the rightness of moral teachings as derived from the Bible itself. Man thereby feels an obligation toward man—as brother to brother. There is no desire to kill, no desire to destroy savings and the fruits of toil, no desire to threaten the unity of millions of homes throughout the world. There is only a desire to live and let live.

The Moscow rulers, of course, argue that this is exactly what their proposals of "peaceful co-existence" mean. Unhappily such professions are not persuasive because they are built upon an atheistic doctrine which is quite ready to promise anything and then treacherously to violate the most solemn of promises.

There is expressed by some gullible persons in the free world today the wishful thought that the Soviets seek an "armistice" with the West and that the time has come to "negotiate a deal." From many well-meaning persons in our midst here and abroad comes the renewed suggestion that there be another "summit conference" like the one in Geneva in 1955. It is being said again with the same naïveté as before that the conference plan is worth trying because, even if the effort fails, we shall know where we stand.

But by this time don't we know where we stand? Don't we know that such conferences are merely vehicles for more propaganda and flagrant defiance of the ideals of free men?

Our Secretary of State, John Foster Dulles, in a recent article in *Life* magazine, aptly expressed the meaning of such proposals when he wrote:

"We have an armistice agreement with the Communists in Korea. But it is worthy of note that the Communist side violates every provision of that agreement *except the one provision that we enforce;* namely, that they shall not advance militarily beyond the armistice line."

We of the West have drawn such a line in Europe, too, and, as a result of the sensible agreement made in Paris last week by the NATO Council, we are preparing to establish bases in Europe for our missiles and stockpiles of atomic weapons. We do this because we think it is the only way to prevent war.

If we were dealing with men of conscience, all of Europe could be disarmed. There would be no need of missile bases or stockpiles of nuclear weapons.

But we are dealing with men who boast of their contempt for religion—they do not believe in God.

In the Western world, theism is the basis of every constitutional right, every principle of free government. We are confronted in Moscow not with theoretical or philosophical atheists, but with practicing atheists.

For atheism is unmorality. It has no regard for human life. It worships instead at the shrine of a materialistic and godless ideology.

This is not just a question of tolerating a belief contrary to our own. It involves realistically a stern threat to survival itself.

The world is not going to be safe for any of us as long as atheistic Communism is enthroned in Eastern Europe. There is nothing else to do but to shore up our defenses. At the same time we can fervently speak what is in our hearts to the peoples behind the Iron Curtain and pray with them for deliverance. For in the millions of them who still believe in God rests the hope of mankind. They must inevitably find a way to set up a government of freedom. Their faith and our faith together can alone save the world from another war.

1958

THE FUTURE THAT NOBODY KNOWS?

JANUARY 3, 1958

THIS IS THE SEASON OF PROPHECY when we ask ourselves: What will the new year bring?

The past is recollection. The present is actual experience. But of the future we say: Who really knows?

Certain truths, however, can guide us. For human nature does react always with characteristic self-interest, whether as individuals, striving to obtain material rewards, or as nations, endeavoring to unite in the face of a common peril.

We know all too well the ingredients of man-made friction in both the world at large and in the narrower confines of our home communities. We know the factors that bring discord. We are also aware of an instinctive duty to find ways of accommodation—an heroic means of adjustment which shall remove the influences that keep us in conflict with one another.

We are, therefore, not lacking in knowledge of things to do to make a better world. What we lack is the will-power to do them.

For war is not a phenomenon merely of nations. War is also the battle of men against men, in every walk of life. Eventually, the strident voices of individuals make up the babel of a distraught world.

Whatever the vicissitudes of the times, the human struggle continues with more periods of fear than of repose. The contest for supremacy over other peoples is unceasing. The age-old passion for superiority does not subside—mere equality does not seem to satisfy.

The common fallacy is that there is something new in the offing—a magic remedy for all this. The perennial friction of class, of race, of creed, of political or economic factionalism is regarded as just a malady of the times. We assume that what has happened before is obsolete, and hence not worth re-examining. Too often we disregard the lessons of the past as meaningless, because, as we rationalize it, they supposedly apply to a different set of circumstances than we observe today. Yet history repeats itself.

We look admiringly at our new inventions. But some of the "improvements" of our day are illusory. We have developed many mechanical devices to get more enjoyment out of life but we have never invented a better formula for human behavior than the Sermon on the Mount.

We are perfecting now the most effective means of "organized murder"—as Lloyd George once called war—that the world has ever known. But the weapons of organized peace are still in the laboratory stage.

The foundations, however, of understanding between men were long ago established. Man has accumulated enough knowledge of the necessary principles of law and order to build a free society. Our moral philosophy is now, as always, a combination of faith and conviction based on everyday experience in the busy thoroughfares of life. We know full well what really constitutes fundamental truth, no matter how much we discount it in our everyday living.

For whether we pay homage to the doctrines of Mohammed or Confucius or Moses, or whether we worship at the shrines of the Christian world, we know that there is a Force stronger than ourselves which moves among us everywhere, everyday. Acknowledgment of the existence of a Supreme Being is the starting point of human progress.

What we have not yet been ready to utilize effectively, however, is the knowledge that God's infinite power does invest the earth in countless places, and does govern the behavior of men, even as they seemingly submit to leaders who oppress and enslave.

The transgressions of men—or their passive acquiescence in sinful deeds—are not the result of any dearth of knowledge of what is right, or what is required of us. These errors come because many of us deviate from basic principles, though in our hearts we know that these principles are inflexible and cannot be bent to suit the expediencies or whims of the hour. Evil survives in the world primarily because good men fear to make the sacrifices that must be made to win and retain freedom.

We do not know the future? Of course we do. The real question is whether we are willing to meet its tests—whether we will let greed and selfishness reign where we know there must be generosity and unselfishness, whether we will be craven and cowardly where we know we must be brave and resolute, and whether we will extend the hand of friendship and with love open our hearts to other human beings, or whether we will shirk the obligations which inner conscience and the pages of history tell us to fulfill.

For we do know the future—because we do know the past!

Human knowledge does not perish. It lives on under the inspiration of Divine Providence, whose reminders of what truth really is come to us every moment of our lives. With faith in His Wisdom we can face the challenges of the future, courageous and unafraid.

"COMPULSORY" DISARMAMENT?

JANUARY 10, 1958

IS THE TIME near at hand when the peoples of the world will have to insist upon the making of an ironclad agreement to ban nuclear weapons?

Today the question of whether "disarmament" shall or shall not be negotiated is tossed back and forth between the East and the West, and meanwhile the public is unaware of the serious implications of these delays.

The simple fact is that peoples generally do not yet know the dangers growing out of the intensified rivalry in missiles and nuclear weapons. Recently, in this magazine, articles were printed raising the question of whether America really must take the "first blow." To many persons this was a surprising question because it had been assumed right along that, no matter what Soviet Russia did, the United States would wait for the "first blow" and then try to retaliate.

The main problem is that the new Soviet weapons could conceivably render America helpless someday and that, when our big cities and our principal air and missile bases were simultaneously destroyed by the "first blow," there wouldn't be much of anything left with which to retaliate.

Americans have been slow to realize the peril that may confront them. For the last three years, however, strategy experts of the Soviet Union have been writing in military journals about the "first blow."

Perhaps the most up-to-date analysis of the discussions carried on by the Soviet military men is given by Herbert S. Dinerstein in the January issue of the magazine *Foreign Affairs,* published quarterly by the Foreign Policy Association of New York. Mr. Dinerstein, who is on the staff of a non-profit organization which conducts research for the U. S. Air Force, writes:

"The very magnitude of the investment in the present military posture makes it doubtful that the Soviets will turn back to what Malenkov advocated—primary reliance on deterrence.

"Yet the strategy imposed by present conditions cannot be completely satisfactory to the Soviet leaders. The strategy of fighting a preemptive war—getting in the first blow against an opponent poised to strike—as advocated by General Rotmistrov and officially adopted in 1955, is essentially a strategy of the second-best. For under these conditions, it is the opponent who chooses war; the Soviet Union simply makes the best of it in seeking by earlier action to blunt the opponent's first blow. As long as the Soviet Union has no hope, in its first strike, of hitting the opponent's striking forces ef-fectively enough to preclude retaliation, the initiation of war is an act of extreme desperation. If the Soviet Union could create a weapons system permitting the elimination of our striking force without fear of effective retaliation, the Soviet leaders could attack if and when they pleased.

"If the Soviet Union should continue to gain technologically while the NATO alliance made little progress, the Soviet Union would be able to make war without fear of the consequences. It will be difficult to attain the ability to eliminate the opponent's nuclear striking forces in a single blow. But that is the goal which the Soviet leaders must strain to reach. If they should acquire such preponderant military strength, they would have policy alternatives even more attractive than the initiation of nuclear war. By flaunting presumably invincible strength, the Soviet Union could compel piecemeal capitulation of the democracies. This prospect must indeed seem glittering to the Soviet leaders."

Do the American people, therefore, wait for the Soviets to perfect weapons which can achieve a simultaneous destruction of our principal cities and bases? The problem was posed with prophetic insight by the late Senator Brien McMahon, chairman of the Joint Committee of Congress on Atomic Energy. Chatting informally with this writer in 1950 about the dangers of new atomic weapons, the Senator said:

"Suppose you lived in an isolated area and the man living nearest you had threatened to kill you. Suppose he told you he was working on a new gun which he expected to finish in a few weeks and with which he could kill you from afar without anyone knowing who did it. Would you wait until he finished developing that weapon before doing anything about it?"

What then do we do in the year 1958 about the prospect of a "surprise attack" or the "first blow"? Do we wait until we are fatally hit two or three years hence, or do we let the people of the Soviet Union know that a disarmament agreement has become imperative for all concerned? Otherwise, believing that it is truly acting in self-defense, either side may feel compelled to inflict the "first blow" as the real deterrent.

This is why the subject of disarmament negotiations is no longer academic. This is why it is absolutely essential that the production of atomic weapons shall be subject to constant control. This is why any government that refuses to permit continuous inspection may be precipitating a nuclear war.

PEOPLE TO PEOPLE

JANUARY 17, 1958

THE PRESIDENT OF THE UNITED STATES began last week an epochal conversation at the "summit." He spoke on behalf of the people of America and addressed directly the people of the Soviet Union. This is the start of a process of communication that can build the foundation of world peace. Mr. Eisenhower said:

"My call for action is not primarily addressed to the Congress and people of the United States. Rather, it is a message from the people of the United States to all other peoples, especially those of the Soviet Union. This is the spirit of what we Americans would like to say:

" 'In the last analysis, there is only one solution to the grim problems that lie ahead. The world must stop the present plunge toward more and more destructive weapons of war, and turn the corner that will start our steps firmly on the path toward lasting peace.

" 'Our greatest hope for success lies in a universal fact: The people of the world, as people, have always wanted peace and want peace now.

" 'The problem, then, is to find a way of translating this universal desire into action. This will require more than words of peace. It requires works of peace'."

Here is an appeal above the heads of government to the people of the Soviet Union, voiced by a Chief Executive elected by the votes of a free people in America.

Here is the expression of an idealism that in our Republic has given liberty to all men and slave-labor camps to none.

Here is an open bid to the people of the Soviet Union to consider the American example and to participate in the greatest enterprise of our times—the making of a lasting peace.

It was President Woodrow Wilson who in 1917 told the Congress that the United States had "no quarrel with the German people" but only with the Imperial German Government. Eventually the people deposed their Emperor and made peace, only to be robbed of it later by another autocratic ruler and dictatorship. We are today friends again with the people of a new German Republic which stands as a beacon of hope for all enslaved peoples.

President Eisenhower last week emphasized before the world the threat that has come from the Soviet dictatorship. He said:

"The threat to our safety, and to the hope of a peaceful world, is simply stated. It is Communist imperialism."

There is no quarrel with the people of the Soviet Union. Mr. Eisenhower went on to say:

"This threat is not something imagined by critics of the Soviets. Soviet spokesmen, from the beginning, have publicly and frequently declared their aim to expand their power, one way or another, throughout the world.

"The threat has become increasingly serious as this expansionist aim has been reinforced by an advancing industrial, military and scientific establishment.

"But what makes the Soviet threat unique in history is its all-inclusiveness. Every human activity is pressed into service as a weapon of expansion. Trade, economic development, military power, arts, science, education, the whole world of ideas—all are harnessed to this same chariot of expansion.

"The Soviets are, in short, waging total 'cold war.'

"The only answer to a regime that wages total cold war is to wage total peace.

"This means bringing to bear every asset of our personal and national lives upon the task of building the conditions in which security and peace can grow."

Opportunities to apply this approach in specific ways will develop as we encourage the Soviet people to join us in "building the conditions in which security and peace can grow."

For peace can come only when the regime in Moscow is driven from power by the concerted will of a people determined to choose their own rulers and to win for themselves the liberties free nations enjoy.

Disarmament conferences will no doubt someday be resumed, as a formality, with representatives of the Communist Government if only to offset the propaganda that America does not want disarmament. But such conferences will prove of little avail until the people of the Soviet Union are free. As the President pointed out, any agreement must provide "reliable means to ensure compliance by all."

There can be no reliance, however, on dictatorships.

There can be reliance only on governments chosen by free peoples.

President Eisenhower's appeal is one of the most constructive peace efforts of current history. His address was perhaps the greatest state paper of our times. It was a message of resoluteness, of confidence, of determination. It was a message that can help to bring mankind out of the "age of terror" and into an age of mutual respect and enduring friendship.

The key to it all is the direct appeal from people to people. For theirs alone is the sovereign power—the true power to be invoked at a "summit conference."

WHOSE "SPUTNIK"?

JANUARY 24, 1958

MAN TALKS OFTEN NOWADAYS of the universal destruction that hangs over him.

Hydrogen bombs are conceived of which have such force as could instantly destroy whole nations.

In the vocabulary of our times, "international suicide" is the phrase used by governmental spokesmen to describe the menace that threatens our lives and our civilization.

Man's biggest venture into outer space—a mechanism that circles the earth in 96 minutes—has increased the fear of a devastating war.

Peoples everywhere are terrorized now by the possibility that missiles of destruction can be hurled at them from globe-girdling devices of incredible power.

What is the meaning of this revelation? Is it just a manifestation of Man's advance in the realm of science?

Dean Bernhard W. Anderson of the Theological School of Drew University, in his recent book "Understanding the Old Testament," writes:

"Is the historian's view too narrow if he fails to see God at work in political events? Is history not just the narration of human deeds, but of the acts of God as well?"

Despite advances in the arts and sciences, each generation in primeval history, impelled by rebellious influences, sought to assert their will and "to take things into their own hands in their desire for greatness and power." The story is told of how God repeatedly imposed His punishments and how, when He could not find even ten righteous men in the evil cities of Sodom and Gomorrah, He caused to rain upon them "brimstone and fire," wiping out the cities and all the inhabitants and their crops.

Whether symbolic legend or historical fact, the interpretation is ominous—Man failed to accept the blessings of life as neighbor fought with neighbor.

Is history so much different today?

Man is at war almost all the time in some part of the world. Friction is perennial, and the battle for power over other men goes on continually. Slavery is no longer a matter of local tyranny. Hundreds of millions of human beings are held in bondage within vast areas of the earth's surface. Until recently armed conflicts were local or regional. They have lately become intercontinental and now may even become truly global in the extent of their devastation.

Is there a hidden meaning therefore—a fateful warning—in the "Sputniks" of today?

One nation may possess for the moment a military superiority over the other but from the skies there may come at any time an age-old "Sputnik"—"fire and brimstone"—to inflict greater destruction on the nation that initiates wars. For Man cannot harness the meteors of nature itself, nor can he foresee when they may again become the "Sputniks" of a Divine wrath.

We read in Second Chronicles this message:

"And the Lord appeared to Solomon by night, and said unto him, I have heard thy prayer, and have chosen this place to myself for an house of sacrifice.

"If I shut up heaven that there be no rain, or if I command the locust to devour the land, or if I send pestilence among my people;

"If my people, which are called by my name, shall humble themselves, and pray, and seek my face, and turn from their wicked ways; then will I hear—from heaven—and will forgive their sin, and will heal their land."

Man is urged to heed the portent of his own revolt against Higher Authority. But somehow, as we peruse Biblical history, we find that Man often does not see the light until it is almost too late.

Jesus, in words of prophecy that have come down to us in the New Testament, expressed it this way:

"And ye shall hear of wars and rumours of wars: see that ye be not troubled. . . . be not terrified. . . . Nation shall rise against nation, and kingdom against kingdom; and great earthquakes shall be in divers places, and famines, and pestilences; and fearful sights and great signs shall there be from heaven. . . .

"And when these things begin to come to pass, then look up, and lift up your heads; for your redemption draweth nigh."

Man has always derived inspiration from the teachings of the Scriptures and from the sacred books of the many religions of the world. Maybe these apocalypses will reveal to Man the true meaning of the "Sputniks." For, while missiles, rockets and satellites are man-made, are they not subject to Higher Law?

The deadliest weapon of today is not mere metal and liquid. It is the human hand that triggers the "Sputniks" of war. It is Man himself who must answer for the destruction that may be wrought by his own contrivances. Man can find the way to his own redemption—to "works of peace"—only through moral force.

For moral force—human love and sacrifice, and a willingness to share unselfishly with others less fortunate the material things of life—can alone bring all God-fearing peoples together in a common destiny.

"PEOPLE TO PEOPLE"

JANUARY 31, 1958

(Forty years ago, just after the people of Russia had revolted against the despotism of the Czar, they chose a Constituent Assembly—the only freely-elected parliament in their history. It was crushed by the Communists after just one day's session, January 18-19, 1918.

To remind the world of this grim event, "Radio Liberation," an organization of private citizens from the free countries of the world, last week broadcast over powerful transmitters, in Russian and 17 other Soviet languages, some pointed messages. These were not only from leaders of both political parties in the Congress of the United States but from authors, playwrights and editors, and were supplemented by statements from prominent members of the parliaments of the free nations of Europe.

This is an excellent example of the way communication can be established between the peoples on both sides of the Iron Curtain.

Extracts from some of the messages sent by American leaders of opinion are given here.—David Lawrence, Editor.)

Senator Lyndon Johnson, Majority Leader of the Senate: "The dissolution of the all-Russian Constituent Assembly was a crushing blow which ended the hopes of the Russian people for democratic government. But the dream of freedom is one that can never be completely crushed. And men of good will everywhere join in the hope that Russia will some day be free."

Senator William F. Knowland, Minority Leader of the Senate: "In the only free election the people of Russia have enjoyed, we remember that the Communist Party received an overwhelming defeat. All of the people of the free world look hopefully to the future— that the people of Russia will again have the opportunity to select freely their own government and official representatives."

Senator Paul H. Douglas, Democrat, of Illinois: "Russia needs a democratic government today to replace the present brutal dictatorship and when this happens there will again be a Russian parliament."

Senator John F. Kennedy, Democrat, of Massachusetts: "Undoubtedly the passage of forty years has not dimmed the eternal yearning of the people of the Soviet Union for a truly representative Constituent Assembly."

Senator Joseph Clark, Democrat, of Pennsylvania: "The Constituent Assembly was an expression of the will of the majority for an open society, with representative political institutions. Its dispersal by force of arms was the first in the chain of violent tragedies leading to the subjugation of many proud nations."

Senator Clifford P. Case, Republican, of New Jersey: "We in the United States know that, like us, the peoples of the Soviet Union want the opportunity to develop and utilize their talents and resources in freedom and in peace. We have no doubt that if a truly free election could be held in the Soviet Union the Soviet peoples would again choose the way of democracy."

Senator Leverett Saltonstall, Republican, of Massachusetts: "I join my fellow Americans in extending to the Russian people our fervent wish which we hold for all peoples of the earth that you may be permitted and that the peoples of all other nations be permitted to establish, as we have, a government of your own choosing."

Senator Irving M. Ives, Republican, of New York: "Let this tragic anniversary remind you that democracy once lived in Russia. May it live again so that the lives of the Soviet peoples will be happier and the dangers to world peace inherent in overly concentrated power can be eliminated."

Senator Hubert H. Humphrey, Democrat, of Minnesota: "On this tragic anniversary the American people could wish for nothing better for people in the Soviet Union than the re-establishment of genuine representative institutions."

Representative Emanuel Celler, Democrat, of New York: "Only representative government can claim to be free. Tyranny began when the free parliament ended."

Mrs. Roosevelt: "This is Mrs. Franklin Delano Roosevelt speaking over Radio Liberation to the peoples of the Soviet Union. Just a few short months ago I visited your country and traveled thousands of miles in many directions. I had the opportunity of meeting and talking with individuals in all walks of life— students, doctors, farmers and government officials. There I confirmed at first hand what I have always known—that the people of your country want above all else peace, a lasting peace which will permit you to continue the remarkable work of rebuilding your nation after the devastating war in which our peoples fought together as allies.

"In Russia, too, I saw that your people have reached a level of education and scientific achievement as high, and in some respects higher, than anywhere in the world. And I wondered why such a talented people still lack their own freely elected government—a government responsible to their will."

TALKING BACK TO RUSSIA

FEBRUARY 7, 1958

(EDITOR'S NOTE: *Last week on this page extracts were presented from a number of statements written by many prominent men in the free world and broadcast in several languages to the people behind the Iron Curtain by the American Committee for Liberation. This organization of private citizens has been crusading for "freedom for the peoples of the USSR."*

Twelve United States Senators and five Representatives of both parties gave statements urging freedom for the people of Soviet Russia.

The broadcasts were made in connection with the 40th Anniversary of the Communist suppression of the First Constituent Assembly—the only free parliament elected by universal suffrage in Russian history.

The Soviet Government's principal newspaper, Izvestia, *promptly denounced the American speakers as having "a gay time at a funeral banquet for the Assembly." But "Radio Liberation," using powerful transmitters in West Germany and the Far East, now has broadcast several rebuttals, two of which are printed below.*—David Lawrence, Editor.)

Senator William Knowland, spokesman for the Eisenhower Administration in the Senate: "I have enough confidence in the common sense of the people of the Soviet Union to believe that their reaction to the Communist Government dictated *Izvestia* article of January 23rd will be: 'A confession of guilty as charged—guilty of destroying free government in Russia.'

"Today, I should like to make it clear that we paid tribute to the freely elected Constituent Assembly of 1918 not because we want to turn back the clock, to revive the past. On the contrary, it is my conviction, and I believe it is shared by the overwhelming majority of people in the democratic world, that a freely elected parliament represents the *future* of the Soviet peoples rather than the *past.* Unlike *Izvestia,* we have confidence that the Soviet people are mature enough and wise enough to govern themselves freely, through freely elected representatives, and to vote out of office leaders who do not carry out their will.

"*Izvestia* claims that the Soviet public is satisfied with the present political order; if this is true, there is a simple way to prove it: hold free elections under conditions which would guarantee Soviet citizens freedom of choice at the polls between persons and groups of different viewpoints.

"The democratic world has enough confidence in the good judgment of the Soviet public to abide by the results of such an election.

"Finally, I am confident that I speak for the overwhelming majority in the United States when I say that our Government would welcome talks at the summit with the spokesmen of a freely elected parliament truly representing the peoples of the Soviet Union.

"We are confident that such an elected leadership would work for genuine peace, disarmament and the removal of the barriers that divide the western world from the people of the Soviet Union. I am sure the people of both our countries desire peace with honor based on freedom."

Norman Thomas, many times candidate for the Presidency on the national Socialist ticket: "Over this radio I spoke to you briefly on the 40th Anniversary of the day when Lenin and Trotsky forcibly dissolved the Constituent Assembly which originally they had favored. Frankly I had doubted how many of you would ever hear what I, along with other Americans, said on that occasion. Imagine then my pleasure to learn from *Izvestia*'s long diatribe against us that our remarks must have received your attention.

"To be sure, *Izvestia* says that 'Norman Thomas hysterically questioned his hypothetical Soviet listeners.' Obviously, it would not have troubled to reply if all my listeners were hypothetical. And I am quite sure that those listeners, whatever their silent answers to my questions, would agree that neither the questions nor the manner of my asking them was hysterical. . . .

"On questions of American policy our speakers represented on January 19 different views. Many of them would challenge my socialism, but none my right to speak to you in a friendly fashion as an American and a Socialist. . . .

"My position and my party's on this and other matters critical of our Government was well known. Nevertheless the Federal Government has never kept me from speaking to you or my own countrymen, or denied me radio facilities to speak to you about peace and freedom.

"I should not impose this personal statement on you except that it justifies my raising a question not only for you but for the editors of *Izvestia* to consider: Is there any writer, speaker, labor leader or political figure in your own great country who has been on occasion as openly critical of your Government as I of mine, who has been allowed to speak and write in freedom in Russia, or been offered the facilities of Radio Moscow to speak to Russians in the name of peace and freedom for us all?"

ENFORCE THE "LAW"!

FEBRUARY 14, 1958

WHEN THE DEPARTMENT OF JUSTICE started in the 1930s to enforce vigorously the Prohibition laws enacted under the 18th Amendment, the American people soon demanded repeal. In less than ten months after the 21st Amendment was submitted to the States by Congress, it was duly adopted and, thereafter, control of liquor sales was vested in the States.

Today, after nearly four years, the edict of the Supreme Court of the United States ordering segregation banned in the public schools has not been enforced throughout the country—even in the North—so as to accomplish the purposes set forth by the Court.

For on May 17, 1954, "the supreme law of the land" was proclaimed as follows:

"We come then to the question presented: Does segregation of children in public schools solely on the basis of race, even though the physical facilities and other 'tangible' factors may be equal, deprive the children of the minority group of equal educational opportunities? We believe that it does."

The Court went on to stress the importance of "intangible considerations," such as "ability to engage in discussions and exchange views with other students," and then added:

"To separate them from others of similar age and qualifications solely because of their race generates a feeling of inferiority as to their status in the community that may affect their hearts and minds in a way unlikely ever to be undone."

Relying on that declaration, the Chicago branch of the National Association for the Advancement of Colored People complained recently that in that city only 9 per cent of the elementary schools are mixed racially, that 70 per cent are predominantly white, that 21 per cent are predominantly Negro, and that, as a consequence, "90 per cent of Chicago public-elementary-school pupils attended de facto segregated schools."

In New York City the situation is best described in an article in the New York *Times* by its education editor, Benjamin Fine, who writes:

"The majority of children attend schools of their own ethnic group. Although integration is now one of the 'cardinal principles' of the School Board, three out of four pupils go to a school that is in effect segregated. These are either schools where Negroes are in the vast majority, or where the white children are concentrated. Most of this is caused by residential patterns.

"Despite consistent urging by the Urban League, the National Association for the Advancement of Colored People and other groups, little change has taken place in district lines for elementary schools. A central zoning unit, authorized by the Board of Education several months ago, is still little more than a paper agency. . . . The unit has received $100,000 to study zoning lines and change them where necessary to help integration."

The *Times* writer goes on to say that "it is doubtful that complete integration—if by that term is meant the elimination of segregated schools—can ever be accomplished in the city" because the school administration is insistent "that the principle of neighborhood schools remain intact."

But what of the rights of the Negroes under "the supreme law of the land" to enjoy "equal educational opportunities," regardless of residence?

New York City's School Superintendent in a recent report said that 1,500 children are being taken short distances by bus from one school to another, to relieve overcrowded conditions and incidentally to help integration.

What about the Negro pupils, however, whose parents are willing to pay bus fares over a long distance to a white school and secure the advantages to which the Supreme Court says the Negro children are entitled? How long can the subterfuge of "residence requirement" be maintained in the face of the declaration by the Supreme Court that no Negro student can get the proper education unless permitted to attend a white school and mingle with white children?

Negro leaders in New York City argue that any New York school in which more than 40 per cent of the pupils are Negroes is not properly "integrated" and that to achieve a "racial balance" each school should contain about 15 per cent Negroes, since about 15 per cent of New York's 1,300,000 public school pupils are Negroes.

It follows that every public school in the United States—in order to carry out the doctrine enunciated by the Supreme Court—must have in it a uniform proportion of Negro students based upon the population ratio of that city or area.

The Supreme Court has ruled that "separate educational facilities are inherently unequal."

When will "the supreme law of the land" be enforced?

The quickest way to get "repeal" of the Supreme Court decision is to enforce the so-called "law." The people will act when they fully understand that the States are being deprived by federal authority of their right to control and regulate their own schools.

JOB CREATION

FEBRUARY 21, 1958

WE HEAR MUCH about the need for increasing the "purchasing power" of the low-income groups as a means of stimulating business and of diminishing unemployment. This looks like good politics, but it is bad economics.

We hear, too, that taxes should be reduced so that everybody would have about two or three dollars a week more. This looks like good politics, but it is bad economics.

We hear also that, with the tax revenues expected to be two or three billions less than estimated anyway, Congress should deliberately authorize five or six billions more to be spent for projects of various kinds even though the Treasury thereby goes into the red seven or eight billion dollars next year. This looks like good politics, but it could be disastrous economics.

The big question is whether or not we want an inflationary "shot in the arm" and the start of a cycle that could send prices skyrocketing and shatter all confidence in the purchasing power of the dollar.

It is more important for us today to plan a sound long-range program that insures stability.

Our experience in the 1930s should be a lesson to us. First we had the "Hoover depression," which was aggravated by the breakdown of our export trade due to the collapse of European economies. This came as a consequence of their World War I debt burdens, which we refused to relieve. But when, in the summer of 1932, Europe was beginning to recover and the League of Nations economic bureaus in Geneva were giving us encouraging news from all over the world, the United States just then had to have a presidential election. The uncertainty about the future stopped the wheels of business, and the fatal four months from November 1932 to March 1933 created a panic in the minds of the business and financial men of the nation.

There were rumors about the condition of the banks and of a possible revaluation of gold. This writer, in the week after the election, advocated that the President and Vice President should resign in favor of the President-elect, Franklin D. Roosevelt. This could have been done by giving him an appointment as Secretary of State as provided by the law of succession in those days.

Had there been a quick transfer of power, much damage to the economy could have been averted. As it was, Mr. Roosevelt refused absolutely to cooperate with the outgoing Administration and the result was a "bank holiday" which was so severe that it brought on the "Roosevelt depression." This lasted far longer than the "Hoover depression" and gave America a bigger total of unemployed than ever before. It was not until 1940 that this country saw the beginning of full employment.

One reason for the delay in recovery was the fallacious doctrine of the New Deal that, by "leaf raking" projects and cuts in taxes for the low-income groups, with higher taxes for the middle and upper groups and extra burdens on corporations, the economic situation would be improved. For the fact is that, while we had 12.8 million unemployed in 1933, we still had 9.5 million unemployed six years later. It was only when the heavy-goods industries were revived by the armament programs undertaken after World War II broke out that economic recovery really started.

These mistakes could be repeated. There are socialistic Democrats who today are talking about "anti-recession" measures that involve the same fundamental errors which characterized the policies of the 1930s.

The talk now, for instance, is for a cut in the taxes of the low-income groups. If any reductions in tax rates are to be made, the taxes on corporations should be reduced from 52 per cent to 35 per cent. This would create such a high level of economic activity that the receipts of the Treasury would ultimately be increased beyond present-day revenues. It would promote efficiency and enable companies to accumulate surplus funds which they could put into the building of new plants and the modernizing of old equipment.

Our plant capacity is large but not adequate for future demand. It has been financed recently on short-term bank credit. This has rightly been halted by the Federal Reserve Board. Such projects should utilize the long-term funds that come from individual and corporate savings.

Many of our office buildings throughout America have grown obsolete. Many of our homes need improvements. There will be more employment and better wages when the heavy-goods industries are again going at full speed.

Job creation should not be treated as just an emergency measure. It is surprising that, with all the commissions and boards available to us on everything else, there is no outstanding study being made of the sources of job creation and of the retarding effect that high corporate taxes have on the pace of employment.

Job creation on a national scale is America's most important task. It is far more important than any local emergency measures. We need a national perspective on job creation to assure American prosperity.

HOW TO GET OUT
OF THE RECESSION

FEBRUARY 28, 1958

THE MAIN REASONS why there is an economic recession in America today are clear enough, but we are reluctant to take the steps to cure what's wrong.

We place reliance, unfortunately, on the erroneous concept that, if the economic situation gets very bad, the Government somehow, by one magic device or another, can "prime the pump" or, by reducing taxes, can create "purchasing power," and then supposedly recovery will promptly ensue.

The people themselves, however, must bear much of the blame for the present recession. For it is largely the indifference of the electorate to the growth of group power, group monopoly and organized greed which is responsible for our present plight.

Self-restraint is the most difficult form of discipline to administer in a free economy. But the need for it was never greater than it is today.

Thus we now are faced with the effects of an inflation spree. Labor unions have utilized their stranglehold on business in recent years to extort higher and higher wages under penalty of strikes that would be so costly as to make it impractical for employers to resist the unions' demands. The only alternative for the companies was to raise prices.

Gradually the purchasing power of the dollar has been depreciated. The laborer gets higher wages numerically, but his dollar buys half of what it did before. As for the vast number of persons with fixed incomes—those living on pensions or retirement pay—they are suffering hardships. They have been cheated. They worked many years to save money to care for themselves and their families in later life, only to find now that someone has robbed them of their earnings.

Time was when labor unions recognized that every dollar given in wages must represent a given schedule of work performed. This has been called the "productivity of labor." Hours may be shortened and wages may be increased but sound economics requires that there be a corresponding increase in the productivity of labor. This can come from the use of improved machinery or from more efficient methods. Technological progress is essential if wages are to be raised. More pay for less work spells bankruptcy.

But today the theory is advanced that union labor has a right to a share in the profits of industry even before adequate sums are set aside to modernize plant and equipment or to accumulate the surpluses needed to finance deficits when depression comes.

Naturally the volume of business grows as the nation expands, and profits are larger numerically. But the rate of return on the investment has not grown perceptibly in many industries. Due to the monopoly exercised by national unions, the bigger businesses, with their large surpluses available to buy better machinery, can produce at a lower cost and can actually afford to pay the higher wages which many of their competitors cannot pay. Labor-union strategy nevertheless forces the marginal competitors to pay the same high wage scale or go out of business altogether. This kind of squeeze is largely responsible for the recent wave of mergers. It's the principal reason why big business gets bigger and small business suffers.

Prices as well as wages must be stabilized if we are to get out of the recession. They cannot be stabilized unless labor unions are willing to sign two- or three-year contracts without wage increases so that their workers may be given a chance to increase productivity.

Government cannot help us out of the recession by artificial measures, such as the reduction of taxes in the low-income groups. Two or three more dollars a week in the pay envelope for everyone does not create the general prosperity that makes possible purchases of more automobiles. Nor can this bring the resumption of employment in the hard-hit industries which manufacture durable goods.

Government does have a very important part to play. It can fearlessly reveal the truth about our economy—the factors that have brought on the recession. The people must not be frightened by the political claptrap of those who want to exploit adversity. The people must let all organized groups, such as business and labor, know that this is a time for partnership and for intelligent cooperation. It is not a time for strikes or threats of strikes. It is not a time for raising prices. It is not a time for huge deficits in the Treasury.

The way out of the current recession is to persuade the organized groups in our economic system to give us an assurance of stability in wages and prices. Only an enlightened public opinion can achieve that result.

We can come out of the recession before another year has passed, but we cannot do so if everybody demands all he can get. We must proclaim again and again the maxim of that eminent exponent of Christian philosophy, the Reverend Samuel M. Shoemaker: "There is enough in the world for everybody's need, but not enough for everybody's greed."

FAMOUS JUDGE REBUKES
SUPREME COURT

MARCH 7, 1958

JUDGE LEARNED HAND, now retired, is one of the most eminent men ever to sit on the federal bench. For many years he presided over the Second Circuit Court of Appeals in New York, and his opinions were usually accepted by the Supreme Court of the United States. Indeed his opinions came to be regarded by the legal profession as among the most persuasive expositions of "the law of the land."

Recently Judge Hand delivered a series of three lectures before the students at Harvard Law School. He dealt with the widely debated concept that the Supreme Court may "legislate" at will.

These lectures have just been published by the Harvard University Press. While they are written in dispassionate and restrained phrases, the lesson contained therein is unmistakable. It is one of sharp rebuke of the Supreme Court for a tendency to set itself up as a "third legislative chamber."

Judge Hand issues a warning as to what the American citizen faces whenever the Supreme Court not only restricts the right of legislative bodies to legislate but itself assumes a legislative function.

Judge Hand does not confine his criticism merely to the present-day Supreme Court. He points out that an 1894 opinion of the Court foreshadowed current trends. He quotes the Court's declaration at that time that a State Legislature's "determination as to what is a proper exercise of its police powers is not final or conclusive, but is subject to the supervision of the courts."

Judge Hand observes that "such a definition leaves no alternative to regarding the court as a third legislative chamber." He then notes the subsequent disavowals of such a doctrine by the Supreme Court and cites a 1952 opinion which says:

"Our recent decisions make plain that we do not sit as a superlegislature to weigh the wisdom of legislation, nor to decide whether the policy which it expresses offends the public welfare."

Judge Hand remarks: "One would suppose that these decisions and the opinions that accompanied them would have put an end—at least when economic interests only were at stake—to any judicial review of a statute because the choice made [by Congress or the State Legislatures] between the values and sacrifices in conflict did not commend itself to the Court's notions of justice."

Judge Hand finds, however, that the Supreme Court recently has not only proceeded to impose its own view of what is wise or unwise legislation, irrespective of constitutional powers, but seems to have applied hostile rules where "property" was involved and softer rules where "liberty" was at issue. He says:

"I cannot help thinking that it would have seemed a strange anomaly to those who penned the words in the Fifth [Amendment] to learn that they constituted severer restrictions as to Liberty than Property, especially now that Liberty not only includes freedom from personal restraint, but enough economic security to allow its possessor the enjoyment of a satisfactory life.

"I can see no more persuasive reason for supposing that a legislature is a priori less qualified to choose between 'personal' than between economic values; and there have been strong protests, to me unanswerable, that there is no constitutional basis for asserting a larger measure of judicial supervision over the first than over the second."

Judge Hand puts his finger on the cases that today transcend all others as examples of usurpation of power by the Supreme Court. He says:

"The question arose in acute form in 'The Segregation Cases.' In these decisions did the Court mean to 'overrule' the 'legislative judgment' of States by its own reappraisal of the relative values at stake? Or did it hold that it was alone enough to invalidate the statutes that they had denied racial equality because the [Fourteenth] Amendment inexorably exempts that interest from legislative appraisal?

"It seems to me that we must assume that it did mean to reverse the 'legislative judgment' by its own appraisal. It acknowledged that there was no reliable inference to be drawn from the congressional debates in 1868 and it put its decision upon the 'feeling of inferiority' that 'segregation' was likely to instill in the minds of those who were educated as a group separated by their race alone.

"There is indeed nothing in the discussion [by the Supreme Court] that positively forbids the conclusion that the Court meant that racial equality was a value that must prevail against any conflicting interest, but it was not necessary to go to such an extreme. *Plessy v. Ferguson* [the 1896 case approving 'separate but equal' facilities] was not overruled in form anyway; it was distinguished [differentiated] because of the increased importance of education in the 56 years that had elapsed since it was decided.

"I do not see how this distinction can be reconciled with the notion that racial equality is a paramount value that State Legislatures are not to appraise and whose invasion is fatal to the validity of any statute.

"Whether the result would have been the same if the interests involved had been economic, of course, I cannot say, but there can be no doubt that at least as to 'Personal Rights' the old doctrine seems to have been reasserted.

"It is curious that no mention was made of Section Three [of the Fourteenth Amendment], which offered an escape from intervening, for it empowers Congress to 'enforce' all the preceding sections by 'appropriate legislation.'

"The Court must have regarded this as only a cumulative corrective, not being disposed to divest itself of that power of review that it has so often exercised and as often disclaimed.

"I must therefore conclude this part of what I have to say by acknowledging that I do not know what the doctrine is as to the scope of these clauses; I cannot frame any definition that will explain when the Court will assume the role of a third legislative chamber and when it will limit its authority to keeping Congress and the States within their accredited authority."

Judge Hand says he "has never been able to understand" on what basis other than as a "*coup de main*" the Supreme Court adopted the view that it may actually legislate. By "*coup de main*," he means, of course, arbitrary usurpation of power.

Should we establish a "third legislative chamber"? This is the penetrating question asked by Judge Hand, but he adds quickly: "If we do need a third chamber it should appear for what it is, and not as the interpreter of inscrutable principles."

But Judge Hand doubts the wisdom of letting a judge "serve as a communal mentor" and deems inexpedient any such wider form of review based on the "moral radiation" of court decisions. He gives these reasons for his view:

"In the first place it is apparent, I submit, that in so far as it is made part of the duties of judges to take sides in political controversies, their known or expected convictions or predilections will, and indeed should, be at least one determinant in their appointment and an important one.

"There has been plenty of past experience that confirms this; indeed, we have become so used to it that we accept it as a matter of course.

"No doubt it is inevitable, however circumscribed his duty may be, that the personal proclivities of an interpreter will to some extent interject themselves into the meaning he imputes to a text, but in very much the greater part of a judge's duties he is charged with freeing himself as far as he can from all personal preferences, and that becomes difficult in proportion as these are strong.

"The degree to which he will secure compliance with his commands depends in large measure upon how far the community believes him to be the mouthpiece of a public will, conceived as a resultant of many conflicting strains that have come, at least provisionally, to a consensus.

"This sanction disappears in so far as it is supposed permissible for him covertly to smuggle into his decisions his personal notions of what is desirable, however disinterested personally those may be.

"Compliance will then much more depend upon a resort to force, not a desirable expedient when it can be avoided."

Those last words could apply to the use of troops at Little Rock, which certainly was "not a desirable expedient" and could have been avoided.

There seems no doubt that Judge Hand would like to see the Supreme Court adhere to its basic function of interpreting legislation without adding laws not written by the people's legislatures. He evidently deplores the tendency to vest political power in the Supreme Court of the United States whose Justices are appointed for life. He concludes:

"For myself it would be most irksome to be ruled by a bevy of Platonic Guardians, even if I knew how to choose them, while I assuredly do not. If they were in charge, I should miss the stimulus of living in a society where I have, at least theoretically, some part in the direction of public affairs.

"Of course I know how illusory would be the belief that my vote determined anything; but nevertheless when I go to the polls I have a satisfaction in the sense that we are all engaged in a common venture."

Judge Hand has rendered a great service to contemporary understanding of the true limits of the Supreme Court's powers. For there are limits, and the Congress, acting for the people, can and should impose such limits lest we fall victim to absolutism in our own institutions.

INCENTIVES TO PROSPERITY

MARCH 14, 1958

IT'S AN ILL WIND that blows no good—and the belated discovery in recent months that talented people should be stimulated by scholarships and other inducements to excel in the field of science applies as well to other fields of human endeavor.

The nation that seeks to standardize all individuals will find itself plagued by mediocrity.

The nation that carries the abstract principle of equality to the point where success is penalized retards its own progress.

The nation that restricts the gifted and the enterprising and virtually confiscates their earnings will not thereby accomplish the maximum good for the maximum number. In fact, the very opposite will be the result.

We can attain real prosperity by recognizing the importance of incentives to prosperity.

The biggest single incentive that could be applied in America today is in the field of taxation. The current "recession" and the economic convulsions of our times are directly related to the punitive rates in our tax system.

Low tax rates that are productive would bring in more revenue to the Treasury than it has ever received before. For when earnings are stimulated, the Government receives a larger and larger total—a share not only of the bigger profits earned by corporations but a share of the increased payrolls derived from full employment.

Tax revision cannot be achieved all at once, but a start can be made with a five-year program which brings the individual tax rates within a range of 15 per cent at the low point and 42 per cent at the top and puts a ceiling on corporate taxes at 42 per cent of net income. This is, in brief, the proposal made in the bill introduced by Representative Sadlak, Republican, of Connecticut, and Representative Herlong, Democrat, of Florida.

The theory that individuals with large incomes spend it all on themselves is fallacious. There's a limit to the luxury that any individual can enjoy. Probably more than 90 per cent of a rich man's income above ordinary living expenses and charitable contributions is usually invested in productive enterprises, thus helping to build new businesses and create employment opportunities.

There is no sensible reason for stifling the initiative of the most successful individuals in our midst. Even the Moscow regime has discovered that, when every-body works for the Government, there is lassitude and that money incentives become necessary to stimulate ambition and increase efficiency.

The worst mistake we make in our tax system is in the field of corporate rates. Here we expect the enterpriser who takes the risks of everyday business to be enthusiastic about his position as a minority partner. There isn't much incentive felt in being a 48-per-cent partner, while the Government takes the major share —52 per cent—of all net income.

Apart from the psychological discouragements of such a disproportionate partnership between the Government and businessmen, this system fails to build the necessary surpluses for modernization and expansion of plant.

America would have an era of unprecedented prosperity if the tax structure were revised so that, by a reduction of 2 percentage points a year, for instance, companies could see in the next five years a chance to plan ahead with an assurance of a fair return on the money and energy invested by them. It would be the quickest way to restore confidence among businessmen and bring an early end to the current "recession."

Until we become realistic about the handicaps in our tax structure, we shall not absorb the more than 900,000 new workers who are added to the total labor force every year. Thus, in January 1958, there were actually only 340,000 less persons employed than in January 1957, but we have not made it possible for business and industry to absorb the new workers. Our population is growing, and we must find a way to enable business to create more and more jobs.

A simplified tax structure based on such incentives would solve our current problems and avoid "recessions" in the future. It would bring balanced budgets and large surpluses long before the five-year period elapsed. It would pave the way for even lower tax rates in subsequent years.

Reform of the tax structure is necessary to cure us of our chronic "recessions"—but this will not come until an informed public opinion persuades the politicians that the best politics is sound economics.

It is the duty of our leaders, both political and economic, to take a long-range view and begin to lay the basis for a sound prosperity.

We must face up now to the need for a fundamental program that will enable America to stabilize prices, to arrest inflation and to create more and more job opportunities in an expanding economy.

THE NATIONAL MOOD

MARCH 21, 1958

THE EMOTIONS THAT SWEEP A NATION when people begin saying that "times are not good" betray a tendency in human affairs to consider material values as all-important.

We begin to fear that life will not be as easy, as comfortable, as carefree as it was before. Unemployment figures come as a shock even though only a small percentage of the total labor force in the nation is idled. Usually there has been little preparation for such misfortune. Too many of us assume blandly that good times are never interrupted.

Conditions today, to be sure, are somewhat different from what they were in the 1930's, because America has built into its economic mechanism an instantly-operating system of unemployment insurance. These money benefits are paid by government for a half year or so, and the period will be extended if the present economic recession is prolonged. This does help many a family to weather the storm. There are no "breadlines."

Even unemployment benefits, however, do not bring self-assurance or confidence about the future. The individual who is not a victim of unemployment is worried, too. Fear begets fear.

The politicians naturally suggest solutions as they come forth with their own brand of altruism. They insist that it is the duty of the Government to restore employment by expending more funds for a variety of purposes. They propose that almost normal wages be paid out to the unemployed. They appeal to our material instincts by demanding that Congress grant all kinds of tax cuts, including even tax forgiveness for everybody for months at a time.

There can be no doubt that the basic principle of help by the Government to the unemployed is sentimentally logical, but in its application there is sometimes a danger that unsound plans will do harm to a vast number of employed people. For if what are termed "inflationary" policies are pursued, the purchasing power of the dollar could be diminished and a loss of confidence in the monetary unit could ensue. Then the distress would extend to many millions of persons who do have jobs but whose pay envelopes would be reduced in value.

The function of government in an emergency must always be to achieve the maximum good for the maximum number, and this could mean temporary hardships for some while the Ship of State steers away from the shoals of unwise experimentalism and the various unsound "remedies" usually proposed.

The need was never greater than today for confidence and common sense in the formulation of anti-recession measures. Unhappily, we do not have a united Government. One party controls the Congress and the other controls the executive branch of our Government. The leaders of each side profess non-partisanship, but many of the speeches and statements do not reflect such righteousness. On the contrary, some of the members of Congress continue to preach "gloom and doom" and thus intensify the doubts and fears of the populace. All this is supposed to come under the heading of "good politics," but it is really injurious to the public interest.

Selfishness, whether it be political or economic, cannot help us to pass safely through the present readjustment in our economic life. Everybody who is familiar with economic trends knows that pressures of an inflationary nature forced prices up, that greed among our economic groups gave us a bloated condition and that it became imperative to apply restraints. The "boom" really had to be slowed down so that it would not bring a run on the dollar such as we have witnessed in other countries in recent decades.

It is a time for the utmost caution in public policy. Politicians must not rock the boat by demanding the impossible from government. The future growth of America is assured. The recovery movement is already underway. Whether it takes weeks or months to bring back normal employment, there can be confidence in the inevitability of such a development. Nations everywhere expect this from the richest country in the world. We indeed have the resources to bring about a prosperous economy, provided we do not let organized greed or political chicanery defeat us.

It is a time to think in terms of the entire community and of the basic principles of economic law that eventually can restore our business equilibrium.

It is a time, too, to think of spiritual values rather than material desires. The blessings we do enjoy cannot be minimized. We are not at war. Our lives are not endangered. Our homes are in large part paid for and our children are enjoying a healthy era, devoid of the ravaging epidemics that we have known in the past. There is a superabundance of food.

It is a time to remind ourselves that "money isn't everything." It is a time, moreover, to turn to the other side of the coin and take to heart the words of faith our forefathers inscribed for us: "In God We Trust."

OUR OWN DICTATORSHIPS

MARCH 28, 1958

THE AMERICAN PEOPLE have been shocked by the disclosures in testimony before the Senate committee that has for the last 12 months been investigating rackets in the field of employer-employe relations. Not only have labor-union funds, estimated at $10,000,000, been "stolen, embezzled or misused" —as the formal report issued this week by the Senate committee phrases it—but there have been many acts of violence and a flagrant disregard of human rights.

The truth is that a private system of government, beholden to nobody but its own autocratic rulers, has sprung up in the United States.

The "clean" unions protest vehemently that they have been scrupulously mindful of their trusteeship and that only a few miscreants in some of the large unions are involved. It is always true about crime, however, that only a few citizens transgress, but the law is intended to punish them and deter others.

Lawlessness must not be permitted any longer to surround the labor-union movement. Many of the unions, though handling their funds properly, seem nevertheless to condone violence on the picket front. It is a sad commentary on trade unionism to find compulsion and intimidation apparently considered necessary to maintain membership or to win strikes.

What has become of our boasted virtue—the power of persuasion by the processes of reason?

Why the indifference heretofore to the rackets? To what extent is Congress dominated by labor-union influences?

The records show that 175 members of Congress owe their election, in part at least, to labor-union contributions or to the campaign efforts of unions.

Representative Ralph W. Gwinn of New York, Republican, in a speech inserted a few days ago in the *Congressional Record* says that a total of $725,000 was spent by a single union to elect a United States Senator, and points to the many members of Congress elected with the aid of labor-union money.

Why do we hear so little about the "conflict of interest" which arises when a member of Congress who has benefited by campaign funds from labor unions seeks to protect their legislative interests?

The American people must insist upon complete exposure of such influences so that persons may be elected who are not obligated to any special interest.

All honor to courageous men like Senator John McClellan of Arkansas, Democrat, and to those of his colleagues on the committee who have helped to reveal to the American people the facts about the labor-union rackets.

Even the American Civil Liberties Union now finds it necessary to urge the AFL-CIO to adopt "a labor-union 'bill of rights' aimed at safeguarding the civil liberties of workers within unions," though nothing is said about safeguarding the civil liberties of workers outside unions. In a statement issued last week, this civil liberties group says:

"Congress has accepted as a legitimate extension of collective bargaining a provision in a contract between a labor union and an employer that all of his employes must join the union if the majority of them so decide. An organization with far-reaching control over the power of its members to earn a living must guarantee to them in internal democracy the equivalent of what the Constitution requires our Government to guarantee to its citizens—free speech and fair procedures and nondiscrimination."

Then why acquiesce in the discrimination against a citizen who doesn't wish to belong to a union? Why is membership in a labor union today made compulsory in many industries as the price of a job in free America?

Many employers have been forced by economic pressure into conspiracies to deprive American citizens of their constitutional right to a job.

For isn't the right to work really guaranteed by the Constitution of the United States, which says that no person shall be "deprived of life, liberty, or property, without due process of law"?

Disclosures by the Senate committee, moreover, of what has been happening on the picket lines present a tragic and disgraceful picture in a country that prides itself on its freedom and democracy. Mayors, sheriffs and police chiefs obligated to labor unions for political help are revealed in various cases as refusing to protect the citizen who wants to cross the picket line. These breakdowns of law and order are the product of labor-union dictatorships.

We must not in America condone any form of totalitarianism.

The American people at the polls, by voting for candidates for Congress pledged to protect constitutional rights—inside and outside labor unions—can once more assure freedom of opportunity to the American workingman.

ONE GLASS OF VODKA AND—

APRIL 4, 1958

THE PEOPLE OF THE SOVIET UNION were suddenly told last Thursday by press and radio that they have a new "Premier."

The people of the Soviet Union did not choose him. He chose himself.

A nation of 200,000,000 persons was not informed why Bulganin resigned the office of "Premier" nor why Khrushchev alone was considered eligible to succeed him. No views on public policy were expressed. No opportunity was given to weigh the qualifications of anybody else. It was as brazen a defiance of the people as the act of any medieval despot.

Yet all this is happening in the modern world in a country which is hailed as rivaling the free nations in the fields of science and education.

All this, moreover, is falsely labeled as "democracy." That's the word the Moscow radio stations use night after night in their worldwide broadcasts describing the alleged virtues of the Communist system.

But it really is a travesty on freedom. When a people have no voice at all in selecting their own rulers, despotism is enthroned. The word "Premier" is a sham. There is in the Soviet empire today only a fake imitation of true parliamentary government.

The new developments make a mockery of the claim reiterated for two years now by Khrushchev himself that the Soviet Union is governed at the top by a "committee" system. For he is today in as complete control of the government as was Stalin.

The new "Premier," of course, used the "committee" device temporarily so as to strengthen his own hand until the time was ripe for the final step of transition to a one-man dictatorship.

Whom does Khrushchev represent now? If he is accepted in official embrace by the heads of the Western governments at the proposed "summit" conference, what evidence is there that he speaks for the people of the Soviet Union?

It must indeed be questioned whether any agreement or commitment or pledge or promise given by a one-man government can ever be trusted.

When a dictator has defrauded his own people, he will not hesitate to let the end justify the means in his dealings with other governments and other peoples. There are some leaders in the West who think it possible to "do business with" a dictator. The same kind of rationalization was heard in the 1930s as, in step after step, the democracies appeased Hitler.

Again pressure for appeasement is growing. Once more, on the other hand, there is grave doubt in many quarters as to whether a ruthless dictator will keep the peace. One glass of vodka too many could mean a one-man decision to plunge the world into a nuclear war. For it is so easy for him to order the trigger pulled somewhere in the wilds of Siberia or even Red China where the origin of the missile could not be readily determined by us.

Possessing nuclear weapons with a terrible power of destruction, the Kremlin dictator will try to terrorize the world into submission. He will seek to disarm the West by offering to give up nuclear tests without waiting for an international agreement. But who could rely on his word? The world will not soon forget that Khrushchev on one occasion threatened to "bury" us if we do not surrender to his demands. Weak-kneed politicians in some of the Western countries are unwittingly giving him aid and comfort. For they are naive in their belief that it is possible to "negotiate" with a gangster regime.

Would that the statesmen in the democracies had behind them a united public opinion so that they could boldly refuse to recognize the Khrushchev regime as a government that truly represents the people of the Soviet Union! It would be an example of the timely use of moral force. It would thrill the world and restore idealism to its rightful place by overriding the materialism of the hour. Only when there is evidence of an expression of the free will of the people should recognition ever be extended.

For as long as there is a dangerous dictatorship in Moscow, there can be no assurance of world peace.

Already many nations have become victims of the Kremlin's imperialism. A new colonialism—engineered by Kremlin propaganda, with financial and military aid surreptitiously given—is sweeping North Africa, the Middle East, Indonesia and a vast domain in Asia.

The march of dictatorship can be arrested when peoples everywhere, including the Soviet peoples, become convinced that the danger of war has been increased by the emergence of a heavy-drinking, unstable man as the dictator of the Soviet empire.

History has repeatedly demonstrated that dictatorships are overthrown when the people, by concerted will, decide that they must take into their own hands the power a few men have usurped. Peoples move slowly toward revolution, but inevitably they do exercise their sovereign power of self-government.

WHY SUSPEND ONLY BOMB "TESTS"?

APRIL 11, 1958

THE SOVIET UNION'S PROPOSAL temporarily to suspend, of its own accord, the testing of H-bombs has been hailed by some newspapers here and abroad, and by some partisan politicians in Congress, as a great "propaganda victory" for the Communists.

To the gullible and the craven, to the weak-kneed and the "practical"—who used to advocate doing business with Hitler and who now want to do business with Khrushchev—the Moscow proposal is a "stroke of genius."

But to the President of the United States, who has faith in the truth, the Communist stratagem is a "gimmick" and a diversionary tactic. To all straight-thinking people throughout the world, the Soviet proposal is a transparently phony scheme.

For the Communists have just completed their own series of tests, and they know that the United States is about to begin a new series of tests. Prime Minister Macmillan told the House of Commons last week that Great Britain now has "specific evidence" that not all nuclear tests can be detected by other governments. The Soviet Union, indeed, rejected the resolution overwhelmingly adopted last November by the United Nations General Assembly calling for a supervised ban on nuclear tests and the ending of the production of nuclear weapons, with controls. Khrushchev now says he favors "international control" of tests but avoids endorsement of the U. N. plan. What he really wants is his own kind of supervision.

Why, incidentally, was the offer made by the Soviet Union to ban only the tests of H-bombs? Why didn't Moscow announce a decision to accept proposals already made by Western governments to abandon completely the manufacture and use of nuclear weapons under an inspection system that would insure compliance? If testing is a crime against humanity, then the use of nuclear bombs hereafter would be an even worse tragedy for mankind.

Throughout the 8,000-word speech of Soviet Foreign Minister Gromyko, there is only one sentence about a possible abolition of the use of atomic bombs, and this is couched in the vaguest terms as an aim or hope. Yet every word uttered against nuclear tests could be applied even more effectively against the production and use of any nuclear weapons.

The argument of the naive in our midst is that the suspension of the tests will be a "good beginning." After this—it is wishfully argued—may come other agreements. It is a familiar refrain. It has been heard every year since 1945. Yet after we engage in talks and conferences, we find out what we knew before— that the Communists break their pledges and will not accept anything but the unconditional surrender of the Western world. Once we agree to stop testing, and the agreement is subsequently broken by the Soviets, then—as the cliche goes—"we will at least know where we stand." To put it more realistically, Khrushchev will be in a position to terrorize the Western nations and tell them where they will be "buried."

Every one of the Soviet proposals, including the recent demand that American bases be abandoned and our troops be withdrawn from Western Europe, has a single military objective—to win domination for the Communists without firing a shot.

There are groups—here and abroad—who are tired of the fight for ideals. They want to appease the Communists—by accepting the present enslavement of the captive countries as irretrievable.

Why do not some of these same unwitting apologists for the cause of the Communists demand the suspension of a few other things besides the testing of H-bombs? Have they no interest in the fate of the Hungarian people and the peoples of the other captive countries who are being tortured every day, not by Soviet "tests" but by Soviet acts of brutality?

Under certain conditions, we would agree to suspend the use of nuclear weapons altogether, and we have indicated this position frequently in the past. But the Soviet Union first must establish the sound conditions that would warrant the taking of such steps by the free nations of the world today.

The Kremlin could, for example, liberate the peoples of Eastern Europe. It could give East Germany back to the German people. It could permit free elections in all the countries now held in bondage by the Moscow regime. It could by "unilateral" action lift the yoke of tyranny that has deprived hundreds of millions of people of their liberty and freedom.

Acts like these would truly be victories for mankind. But they will not come as a result of any decision by the conscienceless men in the Kremlin today. They will come only when the aroused peoples of Eastern Europe and Asia take concerted action and overthrow the dictatorships.

This is the truth that needs to be broadcast unceasingly. For there can be no compromise with evil. We must say again and again to all peoples everywhere that "the truth shall make you free."

WAGE AND PRICE CEILINGS

APRIL 25, 1958

THE PRINCIPLE that the Government should intervene in the economic life of the country to help the nation recover from a recession in business has been accepted in recent years by both political parties.

To cut down unemployment has become a responsibility of Government. What the people cannot do for themselves, the Government must do in order to achieve the maximum good for the maximum number.

Today, due to the irresponsible behavior of organized groups, the total number of persons seeking jobs is an abnormally large percentage of the labor force of the nation. We are in the midst of a recession that has been foisted upon the country by Big Unionism.

Government regulates competition in industry through the antitrust laws, and price-fixing by competitors is forbidden. Yet wage rates, the largest single factor in price rises, are virtually fixed nowadays for all competitors in a given industry through collective bargaining—in reality, collective bludgeoning—carried on by Big Unionism.

Thus, while Big Business is regulated by Government and its profits are heavily taxed, Big Unionism can at will push prices to higher and higher levels. No law operates against such monopolistic practices.

Under these circumstances, there is only one thing to do—to demand that the excesses of the labor-union monopoly be regulated by Government so that the adverse effects on the economic situation in the country may at least be limited.

The time, therefore, has come for the Government to impose ceilings on both wages and prices. The automobile industry, for instance, is said to have priced itself out of the market. But the auto industry has had a gun at its head for many years now and has been compelled to knuckle under to Big Unionism or pay a penalty in strikes of prohibitive expense.

Why, it may be asked, are the leaders of Big Unionism today clamoring so loudly for tax cuts? Merely to increase purchasing power? Or to establish a foundation for more increases in wages?

Congress would stultify itself if it passed the various tax-cut measures being currently proposed only to find that, the moment car sales showed an increase, the auto unions would demand higher and higher wages. This would merely pave the way for a recurrence of the buyers' strike. It could bring even more unemployment as soon as the effects of the first shot in the arm—through tax reduction—had worn off.

There is only one way to keep the American economy from again running into the ditch. It must be regulated on the wage and price front.

But, it will be argued, this isn't "wartime," when such controls are grudgingly accepted. But aren't we spending 40 billion dollars a year on armament? Aren't we feverishly building missiles and "sputniks" and nuclear weapons? Isn't the international situation, with its tensions, a threat to our lives and property? Aren't newspapers throughout the world expressing every day their fears that a slump in America will hurt other countries in the free world in their battle against Communism? Aren't we fighting an economic war around the globe against Communist imperialism? Aren't many of us for that reason urging a mutual-aid program to help the weaker nations on our side?

Certainly the circumstances that face us in the world today are not normal. A strong American economy is absolutely essential if we are to prevent a nuclear war. This is wartime in the sense that we are already engaged in a worldwide "cold war," and it behooves us to mobilize our economic forces so the enemy will not be tempted to miscalculate about our weaknesses and plunge us into a "hot war."

We must take emergency measures now. We should not and need not give up the principle of free enterprise. We must not resort to "nationalization" of industry, as so many of the socialists abroad have urged. But we must put an upper limit on wages and prices lest we see the irresponsible elements in our midst forcing a runaway inflation that can reduce immeasurably the purchasing power of the dollar.

The governmental mechanism for wage and price limitation can be very effective if Congress gives to an independent board or commission the power to fix ceilings on wages and prices.

Isn't the best politics, after all, that which will permit America to emerge from the current recession with machinery sufficiently strong to prevent a runaway inflation?

Only when there is a limitation on wages and prices can a tax reduction really be effective in spurring the general economy. For expenses could be reduced considerably and the budget could show a surplus, even with a tax cut, if the prices of the goods bought by the Government were to be stabilized at least for the next two years.

The fixing of ceilings on wages and prices during this era of economic anarchy has long been overdue.

THE IMPERATIVES OF THE HOUR

MAY 2, 1958

THE TASKS BEFORE US today are these:
We must organize our armed forces efficiently in this nuclear age so as to be prepared to thwart an attack by the enemy.

We must build enough military power to deter any government from deciding to launch such an attack.

We must keep on testing nuclear weapons so as to be able to eliminate "fall-out" almost completely and, if war comes, to limit our blows to military targets— a return to "civilized" warfare.

We must assist our present and potential allies so that they will grow in economic and military strength and thus help to protect our own country.

We must continue to press for a disarmament agreement—safeguarded by a system of mutual inspection that guarantees absolutely against any violation.

We must abandon partisanship in our debates on foreign policy so that unity at home will mean effective leadership abroad.

We must pull ourselves out of the economic recession that has stopped our progress at home and now threatens to disturb the economic equilibrium of the rest of the world, too.

We must care for the unemployed while economic readjustments are under way.

We must use governmental funds in such a way that the economy will be stimulated and yet dangerous inflation will be avoided.

We must prevent the cost of living from increasing.

We must keep prices generally from rising.

We must persuade labor-union leaders to co-operate with management in holding down wage increases during this period of recession.

These are among the imperatives of the hour. To recite a few of them is to emphasize the paradoxes they present.

We are groping indeed, inside and outside our country, for solutions that depend really on the self-restraint of man. We do not always perceive how essential is sacrifice, or how unselfishness can become the highest form of enlightened self-interest.

The tendency of man is to be self-centered. So is it also with governments.

Much of the energy of the politician is consumed in seeking specious rewards—the applause of those who clamor for special privilege at the expense of the national interest. Organized greed is the sponsor of organized politics.

Much of the energy of the individual is absorbed in seeking material things. We give lip service to spiritual values, but too often expediency brushes aside honesty and fair dealing.

Invisible government by private groups, moreover, flourishes today. Scandalous conduct, for instance, by labor-union officers in some of the major unions has continued for years under the very eyes of our local governments, only to have wrongdoing exposed finally by an investigating committee of the Congress. But why has the local police authority failed to preserve in every community the moral codes of law? What corruption has resulted from the misuse of political campaign funds to win immunity from prosecution?

Truth is the rarest, if not the most unpalatable, food of our times. Only when we begin to suffer do we sometimes recognize realism.

Is it possible that these recurring periods of adversity which we experience may have a mystic meaning? Are we being reminded perhaps how helpless man really is when forces stronger than any individual are let loose in the community?

Are we being warned, too, in the world at large that man-made weapons of destruction absolutely demand man-made modes of control? Is this the true challenge of the H-bomb?

The answer does not lie merely in abolishing deadly weapons. It is to be found in abolishing the hates, the covetousness and the insatiable greeds of factions and groups within nations, and in overthrowing the tyrants who make themselves masters of peoples. It is not the trigger itself, but the mind that orders the trigger to be pulled, which can wreak havoc.

In the will of man—the concerted will of peoples —is the key to a better world.

Man must perennially make sacrifices for freedom. People in bondage will not always accept the crumbs that are flung at them in place of the bread of life itself—liberty.

Where shall we look for inspiration in these troublous times? When shall we rediscover the true meaning of human sacrifice?

May the words of the "Recessional" by Rudyard Kipling come back to remind us:

"The tumult and the shouting dies;
"The Captains and the Kings depart;
"Still stands Thine ancient sacrifice,
"An humble and a contrite heart.
"Lord God of Hosts, be with us yet,
"Lest we forget—lest we forget!"

PROSPERITY UNLIMITED

MAY 9, 1958

SEVERAL YEARS AGO this writer was standing on a street corner in a Midwestern city, chatting with Charles F. Kettering—the genius in engineering and invention who has played such a vital role in developing many of the products of General Motors. The conversation went like this:

"See all those office buildings," said Mr. Kettering as he gestured with a wave of his hand toward a group of business edifices which from the outside at least looked all right. "They all ought to be torn down. Not one has air conditioning, good elevators. None of them makes efficient use of the space for offices. Nor have they a lot of other things that would make for better living for the thousands of persons who have to spend at least eight hours of their waking day in them."

"Why aren't they torn down?" the writer asked.

"The bookkeepers in Government," he replied.

"What do they have to do with it?"

The answer that Charles Kettering gave then applies even more today in the midst of economic recession than it did when he first explained the effects of our obsolete policy on "depreciation."

For, as Mr. Kettering pointed out, the "bookkeepers," according to the Internal Revenue Code, allow only a two per cent deduction on income taxes per year for "depreciation." This means 50 years must elapse before the capital to replace the building can be accumulated. Meanwhile, costs of construction have risen immeasurably. Farm buildings, for instance, cannot be replaced by this means in less than 25 years. Some farm equipment, like tractors, cannot be given "depreciation" allowances in a period of less than 10 years. This very problem of "depreciation," if tackled promptly and effectively by Congress, could soon lift us out of our economic plight.

For we are hearing much talk today about "capital formation" as the weakness that helped to precipitate the present recession.

We are hearing also that the heavy-goods industries —where most of the unemployment has occurred—are stymied because America today has more than enough plant capacity to meet the current demand for goods.

We are being told that in another year or two—as demand catches up with current supply and as an increase in population comes along—the makers of machinery and machine tools and equipment may be busy again.

What a haphazard way of running an economy!

What we need in America is a better understanding of "capital formation." We call our system "people's capitalism," but we put roadblocks in the way when people seek to accumulate capital for investment purposes.

It is right, of course, to tax individual incomes and corporate profits as such. But it isn't sensible to put a penalty on the formation of capital.

To a small degree, we now recognize the principle when an individual sells his home at a profit. The law permits him to reinvest in a new house the sum he obtained on the sale of his old house. He is not required to pay what is ordinarily known as a "capital gains" tax. This, at least, is a step in the direction of a sound policy on investments. If it were applied also to businesses or individuals who own more than one house, it would generate an unending era of construction and reconstruction in America. New up-to-date homes could then replace the old ones at least every ten years.

The federal income tax laws, moreover, should encourage corporations—through tax incentives—to set aside in a surplus account a certain percentage of profits each year to be used for reinvestment purposes.

The Government should also permit individuals and corporations to fix their own schedule of "depreciation" over a given period. This principle, incidentally, is what the Secretary of Commerce, Sinclair Weeks, urged in a speech before the U. S. Chamber of Commerce meeting last week in Washington.

If businessmen could promptly replace worn-out equipment, if they could substitute new and up-to-date plants for old, high-cost plants, if new farm buildings and new equipment could be substituted for the obsolete by means of tax deductions spread over shorter periods of "depreciation," America would have an unlimited opportunity for constant growth.

For America would be rebuilding itself right along. The incentive to new and up-to-date equipment and office buildings, shops and stores would be continuous.

The way to an unprecedented expansion in America is thus open to us. Profits can be progressively increased, and the gain in tax revenues in the long run can more than offset any temporary drop. The chain reaction on industry after industry could swell tax receipts.

It is the way to satisfy a pent-up demand for goods and materials.

It's the road to unlimited prosperity.

329

STOP THE DICTATORSHIP!

MAY 16, 1958

SOMETIMES WE DON'T SEE the forest for the trees. Our eyes are focused, for instance, on widely publicized demands that the testing of nuclear weapons be stopped—as if, by doing this, the world would be saved from a horrible catastrophe.

But the real danger is overlooked—it is the mind of the dictator that can trigger the bomb, disregarding at will any previous pledges given to stop nuclear tests.

The world faces the frightful prospect of a nuclear war that can come at any moment because one man in Moscow can order the fateful blow.

It isn't the "testing" of bombs, but dictatorship in Moscow, that must be stopped.

So long as this dictatorship continues, there can be no safety for the free world.

As President Woodrow Wilson put it 41 years ago in his address to Congress, "the world must be made safe for democracy."

That message of 1917 is as clearly applicable to the world situation today as it was when we were compelled to enter World War I. Mr. Wilson said:

"Neutrality is no longer feasible or desirable where the peace of the world is involved and the freedom of its peoples—and the menace to that peace and freedom lies in the existence of autocratic governments backed by organized force which is controlled wholly by their will, not by the will of their people. . . .

"A steadfast concert for peace can never be maintained except by a partnership of democratic nations. No autocratic government could be trusted to keep faith within it or observe its covenants. It must be a league of honor, a partnership of opinion. Intrigue would eat its vitals away; the plottings of inner circles who could plan what they would and render account to no one would be a corruption seated at its very heart. Only free peoples can hold their purpose and their honor steady to a common end and prefer the interests of mankind to any narrow interest of their own."

The quarrel then was not with the German people, and it is not now a quarrel with the people of the Soviet Union.

For at the head of the Soviet Government is a dictatorship of one man. It is his power, his authority, his capricious mind that can send millions to death.

All pretense that "collective leadership" has been in command in Moscow now can be swept aside. One man controls the destiny of hundreds of millions of people behind the Iron Curtain.

It may be reasoned that war would not be expedient, that it would mean suicide. No dictator is concerned with such counsel. He starts a war because he thinks his adversary either cannot or will not fight.

Today the resolution of the free world is being weakened by internal friction.

It is a time when miscalculation can occur.

In France, the Communists hold the balance of power in the parliament.

In Italy, the Communist Party is in a key position in the formation of parliamentary majorities.

In Britain, the Communist viewpoint on banning missile bases in Europe is shared by an important segment of the Labor Party, which may soon take over the governing power. Thus NATO is of doubtful strength.

In Latin America, the Communists have made inroads.

In Asia, the Communists control Indonesia with its valuable resources, and, of course, Red China occupies a pivotal position in a military way in the entire area.

A big army in Korea and on Formosa is the frontline defense of the free world. But the agitation to throw away this military advantage by appeasing the Red Chinese and weakening Korea, Japan, Formosa and the Philippines is continued by some misguided Americans whose words get wide attention.

Scarcely a day goes by, moreover, that prominent scientists do not berate our Government for trying to perfect nuclear weapons of defense. The same viewpoint was evident from 1947 to 1950, when a few American scientists strayed beyond their field and succeeded for a while in preventing us from developing the H-bomb.

Scientists must be respected when they give judgments on technical questions, but their judgments on what national or international policy should be are entitled to no more weight than those of other citizens, who have not won Nobel prizes. Yet many newspapers give display to a persistent propaganda by certain scientists that could, if successful, result in weakening the military position of the United States.

Our enemy is the dictatorship in Moscow. If the publicity power generated to stop nuclear tests could be devoted to an agitation aimed at ending the dictatorship of Khrushchev, the people behind the Iron Curtain would soon learn that they have the moral support of the people of the United States in taking any steps necessary to remove the tyrants in the Kremlin.

What is needed is a worldwide concentration on a single objective—the stopping of dictatorship in Moscow. The emergence of a free government there would assure the peace of the world.

INTERNATIONAL ANARCHY?

MAY 23, 1958

WE ARE WITNESSING TODAY in the world a breakdown of national disciplines and a disregard for the simple amenities of international intercourse.

The Vice President of the United States and the flag of this country were subjected to indignities last week as mobs tore to shreds the rules of courtesy and protection to which visiting citizens from other countries have always been entitled.

These were not the acts of the freedom-loving peoples. These were the acts plotted by malcontents which the governments of Venezuela and Peru were unable or unwilling to prevent because they themselves are not stable or do not yet exercise effective control.

The weakness of every free government today is that it can easily become the victim of foreign infiltration and subversion. Plenty of money sent by the Moscow Government to the trained agents of its espionage apparatus can readily embarrass any of the free governments of the world.

For the truth is we have not yet learned how to fight this modern type of invasion.

In the United States, for example, we have become confused by the issue. A so-called "liberal" element—naive, gullible, and emotionally preoccupied with abstract theory instead of the condition that confronts us—would wait until an insurrection is underway before trying to squelch the uprising.

Even so august a body as the Supreme Court of the United States says it is all right to preach treason—and declares it is only when agitators actually succeed in persuading the audience to commit acts of violence that punishment may be inflicted.

Thus today the simple tenets of self-defense against subversion are brushed aside as "unconstitutional" or as "illiberal."

Yet, from the days of the Trojan Horse, we have known that governments which do not fight deceptive invasion will inevitably be crushed.

We can hardly blame the weaker Latin American governments when we permit Soviet infiltration here in the United States. Efforts nowadays to alert and warn the American people are contemptuously brushed aside as "hysteria" or "witch hunting."

Present-day attitudes are both pussyfoot and pacifist. In some quarters of our national capital last week indignation was expressed at the behavior of the mobs in South America, but no small amount of criticism was immediately directed at our own Government for letting the Vice President go to Latin America at all. Shouldn't we have known, it was asked, that these things might occur?

But, on the other hand, should we have offended the governments which had invited our Vice President to tour their countries and pay goodwill visits to their peoples? Should we have proclaimed that the great Government of the United States was afraid? Should we, in ignominious isolation, have announced our withdrawal from contact with our neighbors? Why should we ever yield to such a counsel of cowardice? To ask these questions is to answer them.

Plainly, the Soviet Government is responsible for the troubles in many parts of the world. Through its stooges inside political parties, as in France and Italy, and through active and well-financed underground organizations, the Moscow Government carries on a war of subversion—even forcing into being countermovements. When will the Western nations all decide to deny these privileges to the agents of such a hostile government?

Unless we are ready to meet on all fronts the challenge of an unscrupulous enemy in this "cold war" we shall find ourselves plunged into a "hot war" by provocative incidents. Appeasement is the certain road to an enemy's miscalculation and to all-out war.

The time has come to call on the Soviet Government to stop its infiltration of the Western Hemisphere lest it be necessary to sever diplomatic relations. The Monroe Doctrine must be respected.

The time has come to announce also our unwillingness to attend any "summit" conference with the head of a government which is making war on us.

The time has come, moreover, to consider expulsion of the Soviet Government from the United Nations for violating the spirit as well as the letter of the Charter, which explicitly demands respect for the sovereign rights of all member nations.

We have moral force on our side, but sometimes it takes as much courage to exert it as to apply physical force. For there has been in the free world a deterioration of firm purpose and a creeping paralysis of fear—mostly brought about by the machinations of the Communist Government and its policies of intimidation. Unless we meet the threat boldly, we will find the whole world drifting into a dangerous era of international anarchy.

It is time for us to take the leadership in a determined movement to restore discipline and order in the world and to put a stop to the infiltration of free governments by the conspirators in the Kremlin.

THE BIG PARADOX

MAY 30, 1958

WE ARE SPENDING billions every year for armament. The objective is to deter a potential enemy. Yet disorder spreads around the world.

Why?

Because no concerted force preserves order.

This requires either an alliance of a few powers as in the past or a new concert of several nations strong enough in the aggregate to win respect.

Theoretically this is what the League of Nations was supposed to do and what the United Nations Charter specifically sets forth as the collective responsibility of its members.

But there is no peace.

There is instead a growing anarchy.

The means to enforce peace exists, but there is no mobilization for peace.

There is instead hesitation and frustration.

We all desire peace, but where is the readiness to make sacrifices for peace? It's the big paradox of our age.

Are we at heart afraid of our own power in the world? And by "we" is meant the free nations of all continents—the democratic peoples everywhere. Do we know yet the price we must pay for the opportunity to enjoy the blessings of liberty and freedom?

To regard the world situation of today as just a phenomenon of national uprisings here and there is to blind ourselves to reality. The passion for independence burns ever in the minds of people whose local government is subordinate to a foreign government. But there must emerge some method of achieving political autonomy by a sensible process of evolution rather than by revolution. Economic progress is never achieved by political disintegration. Poverty and suffering are the inevitable consequences.

Revolution is justified when an autocratic government takes away human rights. But it becomes futile when aided and abetted by a rival foreign power that seeks to substitute its own authority for that of the incumbent rulers.

The plain purpose of the Communist imperialists in Moscow is to dominate the countries to which they furnish money and arms. The object is to build a Communist bloc strong enough to conquer the free world without the necessity of resorting to a big war.

In every one of the trouble spots—the Middle East and North Africa as well as Southeast Asia and Latin America—the meddling by the Communists has been effective because the free world has mistakenly assumed that the factional movements in these smaller countries were solely nationalistic. While conceding the presence of the Communists as a collateral influence, the tendency has been to pooh-pooh the menace of Moscow.

But the time is approaching when the very multiplication of disorders throughout the world can threaten the peace of the nations not now involved directly in the struggle. Does anyone believe that if, for example, a new empire is built by Nasser in the Middle East, it will not be a pawn in the hands of the Kremlin? Surely the strategists in Moscow do not lightly toss their rubles in the direction of Egypt or Indonesia without counting on the military advantages they are to collect in return.

We must realistically face the fact that the Communist type of "cold war" can be the forerunner of a "hot war" and that perhaps the biggest factor favoring the continued infiltration of the smaller countries by the Kremlin is the belief that the West will not fight.

This, tragically enough, is the reason why world wars do occur. The Kaiser in 1914 was sure his armies could win. Hitler in 1939 was convinced that, by a "blitz," he could achieve victory.

Is it any different today?

The Kremlin thinks that a surprise attack with nuclear weapons could succeed in demolishing the Western strongholds and force a surrender—or alternatively that, because the West fears any war, it is ready to make peace at any price.

Where is the evidence that the West will fight? Where is the manifest readiness to put down the smaller wars? Doesn't its absence indicate our unreadiness also to fight a big one?

Isn't it time to bring about collective action to resist aggression in the Middle East and anywhere else that it rears its head, whether instigated or aided indirectly by the men in the Kremlin?

Sooner or later the West must adopt an attitude of resoluteness which must not be weakened by the petty politicians in any country. Above all else comes the duty of self-preservation.

"United we stand, divided we fall"—it's the only answer to the paradox of our times.

Unless every one of the nations of the free world is ready to put aside its internal quarrels and present a united front of armed forces, ready to fight if need be, there is grave danger that we shall drift into a third world war.

SO THERE IS A "RIGHT TO WORK"!

JUNE 6, 1958

UNIONS, WITH THEIR MONOPOLY POWER, have mistakenly come to be regarded even by some of their own members as having some of the absolute powers of government. The threat of expulsion hovers constantly over the non-conformist in union meetings. Under a federal statute, moreover, a worker today can be required to join a union in order to retain his job. Workers who have conscientious objections to union membership can lose their jobs when a plant is unionized. Efforts to correct this by state laws that would prohibit compulsory membership and would protect the "right to work" have been met with hostility by labor union leaders.

So it is refreshing to read the opinion handed down last week by the Supreme Court of the United States which upholds the principle that nobody can lawfully interfere with an individual's right to work.

The issue arose in a picketing case in 1951. Paul Russell, not himself a union member, sought to continue working at an Alabama factory during a strike. Justice Burton, speaking for the Court's majority, writes:

"Such pickets, on July 18, by force of numbers, threats of bodily harm to Russell and of damage to his property, prevented him from reaching the plant gates. At least one striker took hold of Russell's automobile. Some of the pickets stood or walked in front of his automobile in such a manner as to block the street and make it impossible for him, and others similarly situated, to enter the plant."

This kind of "picketing" has happened hundreds of times in recent years in America without effective intervention by federal or State authorities. Hence the intimidation has been successful. In such cases, the proud boast of trade unionism that it rests on volition rather than coercion becomes an empty claim.

It is, therefore, commendable that six Justices of the Supreme Court—Burton, Whittaker, Brennan, Clark, Harlan and Frankfurter—all voted to uphold the right of a State court to impose damages. Russell was permitted not only to recover back pay but to collect punitive damages for the emotional harm done to him by the incident.

The dissenting members of the Court—Chief Justice Warren and Justice Douglas—argued that only federal law applied. This meant that only back pay would be obtainable and no redress would be possible for bodily harm or damage to one's automobile. In fact, the minority of the Court takes the political view that it would be bothersome to labor unions if they were subjected to such suits in State courts. No similar solicitude seems to have been exhibited for the rights of the individual worker. Chief Justice Warren says:

"There is a very real prospect of staggering punitive damages accumulated through successive actions by parties injured by members who have succumbed to the emotion that frequently accompanies concerted activities during labor unrest."

How easy it is glibly to rationalize violence as just emotionalism!

Here is an example, too, of indifference to human suffering which will come as a surprise to those who have believed the so-called "liberals" on the high court are more concerned with humanitarianism than with absolute legalisms.

Fortunately, the majority of the Court did not hesitate to reaffirm the principle of State protection against physical interference with the right to work.

"The issue before us," says Justice Burton's majority opinion, "is whether a State court, in 1952, had jurisdiction to entertain an action by an employe, who worked in an industry affecting interstate commerce, against a union and its agent, for malicious interference with such employe's lawful occupation. . . . we uphold the jurisdiction of the State courts in this case."

A lawful occupation, the Supreme Court says, in effect, must not be interfered with, and the warning is clear that, if the local police do not furnish protection to the citizen, he may sue the union whose pickets have forcibly prevented him from working at his job.

The Supreme Court majority last week also held that a worker unjustly expelled from a union could sue it for damages in State courts. The point was emphasized that expulsion of a member for ill-founded reasons is a breach of contract by the union.

The right to work, whether exercised by a member or nonmember of a union, is an inherent right of the individual. It is protected by the Federal Constitution, which says that nobody shall be "deprived of life, liberty, or property, without due process of law."

It is time for the so-called "liberals" and the labor-union leaders of the country to accept these basic principles of constitutionalism. A trade-union movement that is dependent for its progress on measures of coercion cannot survive. Only when the organizing methods are voluntary can the concerted activities of private individuals ever win lasting respect.

TOO MANY "GENERALS"

JUNE 13, 1958

IT'S NOT OUR FORM of government, but the weakness of our operating formula which is handicapping us in the cold war.

Some critics are inclined to oversimplify the problem with vague demands for "bold, imaginative leadership."

But leadership depends on persuasion and volition. It can never be absolute as in a dictatorship.

It isn't really leadership we lack today, but unity.

A house divided cannot be as strong as a house united.

Political dissension among us has become the positive danger.

We used to say that "partisanship ends at the water's edge." Unfortunately it intensifies now, as partisanship splits us apart on the "cold war" front, especially on many phases of economic and international action. This can make the difference some day between victory or defeat in the battle for survival.

Nuclear bombs may never be used, but an insidious weapon more deadly is being employed against us now throughout the free world. The Communist infiltration is beginning to eat away at the vitals of free government on every side. Too many in our midst are pooh-poohing the Communist menace and are carelessly treating it as just a rival political doctrine.

But every day we are forced to fight against the Communist legions on the battlefront of economic and financial war. We are up against the well-financed internal organizations that have gained a foothold in the political parties of every one of the parliaments of Western Europe and are now reaching out to do the same thing in Latin America.

We in America cannot win the "cold war" by enjoying the luxury of partisan bickering. On one day the Democratic leader of the Senate, for instance, inveighs against our aid to dictatorships in the past. But only a few days before, the Democratic chairman of the Senate Foreign Relations Committee was urging us to take back to our bosoms the dictator who rules the Egypt-Syria merger. One day the Administration favors proposals to give the Executive discretion in sending economic aid under certain circumstances to strategically-placed countries—captives of the Communists—only to back away later because of divisions in Congress.

Then there are the frequent speeches by individual members of the Foreign Relations Committee sniping away at our foreign policies. All of these utterances are, perhaps, well-intentioned, and presumably designed to produce a constructive result. But we cannot make progress if we have too many "generals" taking command and attempting to speak to the world with a voice of authority in behalf of the United States.

Europeans think of our Government as a single entity. They do not understand how one political party can control the legislature and another party can control the executive. Nor do the American people themselves realize as yet the perils of such a division.

It is imperative, therefore, that there be unity in our foreign operations.

If there is a temptation in Congress to utter criticism, let account be taken beforehand of the use that will be made of it by our enemies. It isn't fair for any political party or its factions constantly to drag foreign policy into open debate during the "cold war."

What we need in America is a new formula of operation to meet the exigencies of these days of crisis.

We need to unify our forces—not merely in the Pentagon but throughout the Government.

The day by day complexities of the "cold war" are difficult enough as the executive departments combat the moves of the common enemy. But in Britain, as well as in the United States, cooperation between the political parties is not what it should be. Often lip service is paid to the principle, but in actual operation the concept becomes meaningless.

What we should set up in our Government is an Operating Council that can consult with similar councils in the allied governments. The Council, so far as our own Government is concerned, can be informal and need not be formalized by statute. The National Security Council omits congressional participation.

It is essential that the responsibility for cooperation between our political parties be fixed in relation to world policy. This can be done by inviting to the Operating Council the leaders of both parties in the House and Senate who could sit regularly with the Secretary of State and the heads of all the international economic and financial agencies of the Government. They all play a part in the "cold war."

If we can forego partisan zeal and selfish ambitions, we in America can establish an operating unity in government that will be a splendid example to all the world. There are too many "generals" today. We need a unified command in the "cold war" embracing all branches of our Government and of the other free governments. It is the acute need of the hour.

A START TOWARD UNITY

JUNE 20, 1958

PROGRESS WAS MADE last week toward a solution of the practical problems of financial and economic co-operation that confront the Western allies.

Critics have said that we have been emphasizing military rather than economic requirements. This implies that the armament needs of the West have been overestimated, which is not the case. Where we have failed is in not giving equal weight to the economic factors that must be dealt with if we are to be strong militarily.

We cannot brush aside the needs of the Western nations and assume that the United States may safely ignore the dangerous developments on the political and economic fronts as they affect the solidarity of our allies. To do so would expose us to the inroads of the enemy not only in Europe but in Africa and in Asia as well as in Latin America.

We must recognize the practicalities of a situation resulting from two world wars and the local but costly wars in Indo-China, Korea, the Middle East and North Africa. Empires involving a long-standing network of financial and trade relationships have been shattered.

We are in a period that demands co-operation with all our allies so that the free world may be restored to economic health. We ourselves are in the midst of a serious recession. We shall come out of it in a few months, but a new economic threat in the world could involve us in another recession of grave proportions.

What the visit of Prime Minister Macmillan of Great Britain to Washington last week pointed up clearly was the need for a new approach to economic policy on the international side. The object, he said, should be "to help the economies of the free world to achieve stability with steady expansion."

Too much of our thinking is provincial. We cherish the illusion that, if we can adjust our own national economy, all will be well elsewhere. But we forget that many of the free countries of the world are weak economically. Nor will they be helped by mere hand-outs and subsidies from us.

The real solution lies in moving toward the normal balances of trade that must prevail if a sound basis for growth is to be established. This is but another way of saying that private capital as well as public funds must be utilized to bring about a better exchange of goods.

For decades we have struggled with the perplexing question of tariffs. Often it is not just a high tariff rate that will prevent injury to a domestic industry. The United States must have available a flexible system of import quotas that can be adjusted to changing circumstances. This is the method in use by some of our allies.

The problem cannot be simplified with the negative statement that a governmental means of restricting trade shall be used only occasionally. The reciprocal trade bill passed last week by an overwhelming vote of the House of Representatives would extend for five years the executive authority to make remedial changes in tariff rules so as to encourage world trade without doing serious damage to any American industry. Once this legislation has been enacted, however, it becomes necessary to take a wider look at the problems of world trade.

We are supposedly at peace but we are actively engaged in a "cold war." The Soviet Union and Communist China want to trade with us but only to get dollars which they then would be able to use for infiltrating the underdeveloped countries where Communist imperialism wishes to extend its domination.

Surely we can play the game of currencies and foreign exchange as effectively in the interest of the free world as the Communists can in their areas. What is needed now is a re-examination of all the funds available to the international agencies of our government and other governments on our side to see how far such money will go toward stimulating private capital to embark on new projects.

Our recession would come to an earlier end and we would be putting our economy on a sounder basis for the future if we could find a way to provide outlets for industrial machinery and other American products desired by the people of many countries.

We must avoid any entanglement with the Communist powers and maintain a cautious aloofness toward their trade projects. Our European allies want to increase trade with the Communists largely because it is felt other markets are not available. A careful study of world markets, on the other hand, will reveal that the non-Communist world needs as much as can be produced by all the larger countries of the West. What is essential is a mechanism of exchange, and this means a financial stimulus from private as well as public funds.

Economic statesmanship is as important as political statesmanship or military leadership. We are on the threshold of such a turn in world affairs. The British Prime Minister's visit was helpful in arousing us to the acute need for economic statesmanship.

A start has been made toward unity.

THE LEOPARD UNCHANGED

JUNE 27, 1958

THE MEN IN THE KREMLIN have once more shown their perfidy.

The solemn promise that no harm would come to former Premier Imre Nagy of Hungary if he left the Yugoslav Embassy in Budapest, in which he had taken refuge in 1956, has been violated.

It is another example of wanton disregard of the pledged word.

President Eisenhower rightly says the episode is "a serious obstacle" to further consideration of a "summit" conference. For of what avail can it be to make an agreement with a government which repeatedly gives conspicuous evidence that it will not abide by its agreements?

Certainly there is no reason to believe now that a mere meeting of the heads of the four governments would be conducive to the making of a stable peace. Indeed, the idea of a "summit" conference, which the Soviet Union has urged so persistently, has been revealed as a transparent piece of propaganda. It has emerged as a stratagem without an honest purpose.

For it has been demonstrated again to the Western nations that the Soviet rulers, while professing to be peaceful, are not true to their own words. They have sought, for instance, to give the impression that the smaller countries contiguous to them—the captive nations—are really independent and may rule as they please. But this hoax is now fully exposed.

The story of the tragedy of the Hungarian revolution in 1956 was graphically told to the peoples of the free world, but nevertheless there have since arisen in our midst apologists who say that agreements with the Soviet Government still can be made—as, for example, to suspend nuclear tests. It is insisted that we should take the risk of weakening our military strength. If the Communists disregard their pledges, it is recklessly asserted, we can detect such action and resume testing. But in the meantime, of course, we lose the benefit of the time and knowledge we would have gained had we continued our tests. Even some prominent members of the Democratic Party in Congress have fallen victim to the illusion that a Soviet pledge to suspend nuclear tests can be accepted as valid.

The controversy over nuclear tests has been kept going artificially by the Communists. They have enlisted on their side a lot of misguided pacifists and wishful thinkers who believe that, since Stalin's days, there have been marked changes for the better in the attitude of the Communist Party and of the Kremlin.

But now suddenly we see Stalinism boldly exhibited in all its brutality. What will it take to convince our defeatists that the Soviet rulers really cannot be trusted and that we cannot accept assurances from any government in Moscow unless it is chosen in free elections by an emancipated people?

Must we endure the painful penalties of self-deception that are bound to follow if we yield to the argument of some of the "intellectuals" of the West who say that Communism is "here to stay" and that we "must find a way to live with it"?

Surely free men will not be so lacking in the courage of their convictions that they will accept tyranny as commonplace and despotism as inevitable!

Rather the history of free men teaches us that they prefer the risk of death to life under slavery. They have heroically exercised their right of revolution in the past. They will do so again.

Today even the "neutralist" world, as typified by India's Nehru, expresses a sense of shock over the disclosures that four leaders in the Hungarian revolution have been executed after a secret trial.

The irony of the affair is that Moscow has been portraying Hungary as an independent nation and now pretends that the revolution's leaders were punished by the local government in Budapest. The world, however, is convinced that Moscow ordered the executions and that, in the captive countries, Moscow's word is law. Both houses of our Congress unanimously adopted last week a resolution expressing America's "deep sense of indignation" over the Soviet murder of Premier Nagy and his associates.

With characteristic arrogance, the tyrants of the Soviet Union have publicized the execution of the four Hungarian leaders as "a lesson for all those who are planning plots against the people." The threat to all the captive countries in Eastern Europe is clear.

Communist imperialism still defiantly waves its bloodstained hands before the world. There must be no letup in our resistance, through the "cold war," to the Soviet schemes. For the Communists are engaged in a desperate game of deception. They are actively trying to infiltrate and subvert the free governments of the world. The Communist movement is not just a "political belief," as some of our cloistered Supreme Court Justices naïvely have declared. The Communist conspiracy is international. It is a military menace.

The Communist leopard showed conclusively last week that it cannot change its spots.

WHY CONTINUE DIPLOMATIC RELATIONS WITH THE SOVIETS?

JULY 4, 1958

THE SOVIET GOVERNMENT last week staged a demonstration against the American Embassy in Moscow. The demonstrators cried, "Yankees, go home."

If the members of the American Embassy are not welcome in the Soviet capital, why should they remain there to be insulted by mobs instigated by the Soviet Government itself?

The maintenance of diplomatic relations among peaceful nations is designed primarily to afford a means of exchanging views on questions arising between them. But the Moscow Government does not carry on important exchanges of views through Ambassadors. The Soviets make public their notes and pour out a constant propaganda to the world.

Again and again the United States has attempted through diplomatic channels to achieve agreements with the Soviets, but repeatedly these efforts have been frustrated by the Kremlin's disregard of even the customary courtesies.

The Soviet Government, moreover, has sent to the United States an Ambassador, Mikhail Menshikov, who, upon instructions from Moscow, has deliberately misused his position here to hurl public insults at the very government to which he is formally accredited. Recently he told a nationwide television audience that he could not make up his mind whether the Government of the United States wants to start a war against his country, though he was sure the American people do not wish to do so. He also lied to the American people when he blandly declared over a television network that there is no censorship of press dispatches transmitted from the Soviet Union.

Of what benefit to America is "recognition" of a government openly hostile to us?

Can it be doubted that the Soviet Government is behind the prolonged detention of American citizens in Red China, and now has directed the imprisonment of nine American servicemen whose unarmed helicopter strayed into East Germany during a storm?

As the ransom price for these American citizens, the Moscow Government has demanded that our State Department deal with the East German regime. This is a palpable attempt to maneuver us into a diplomatic recognition of the puppet government in East Germany.

The State Department has agreed to talk with and negotiate with the East Germans as local authorities, in accordance with the existing military agreement which governs the so-called Soviet zone, but does not wish to do anything that could be construed as a formal act of diplomatic recognition. This evidently has not satisfied the Soviets, so the Americans last week were still being held in jail.

We hear much these days about the sacred right of Americans to travel anywhere in the world, but are we prepared to support that right by measures that will compel the respect of other governments for our citizens? We announced in 1911 our intention to abrogate a treaty of commercial intercourse with Czarist Russia for refusing to honor the passports of American citizens of a particular religion. Why therefore, should diplomatic relations be continued with the Soviet Government which has seized American citizens?

What better way to gain the respect of the whole world than by applying moral force? The late President Franklin D. Roosevelt advocated a "quarantine" when another lawless dictatorship was rampant in the world. We should today follow that advice. We should ostracize and isolate the Moscow Government.

The record shows that every single provision of the agreement by which we extended diplomatic recognition to the Moscow Government in 1933 has been violated by the Soviet Government.

It has been argued that we should continue to deal with the Soviet regime because "peaceful coexistence" is a practical necessity. But, unfortunately, the "coexistence" isn't peaceful. It is warlike. The Soviets recently agreed, for instance, to send technicians to an international conference at Geneva to study methods of inspection, looking toward an eventual agreement to suspend the testing of nuclear weapons. But the Moscow Government later demanded—as a condition of its participation—an agreement in advance to suspend the testing. This is an example of the trickery and deceit practiced by the Communist dictatorship.

Why continue any longer to treat a bandit government as a civilized entity?

Why accord the ruthless men in the Kremlin the prestige of membership in the family of governments?

Why not instead indicate to all the peoples behind the Iron Curtain that the United States will maintain diplomatic relations with any government regardless of its economic ideology—but only if such a government is truly chosen by its people and is not a menace to the peace of the world.

PLAYING WITH FIRE

JULY 11, 1958

THE SOVIET GOVERNMENT is playing with fire in Lebanon. It is doing so through its puppet Nasser, military chief of the Egyptian-Syrian "merger."

The free world is being tested, if not challenged, to determine whether such an aggression—against a small republic which seeks to remain free—will be tolerated.

Lebanon is friendly to the West. The fomenting of revolution within her borders, aided and abetted by Soviet Russia, is an act of hostility directed against the free nations of the world. It is a move toward conquest of the Middle East by the Communists. If unrestrained, it will lead to other aggressions.

The United Nations chose to repel aggression in Korea with armed forces. The situation in Lebanon could be parallel because the so-called "volunteers" who invaded Korea have their counterpart in the "rebel" armies which are being supplied with arms by Nasser. He, in turn, is taking orders from Moscow.

Many Americans would prefer to brush off the disturbances in the Middle East as remote and of no direct concern to us. Such indifference has often preceded big wars. We cannot wait till armed conflict is almost upon us before we try to stop a war.

The virtual stalemate in the use of nuclear weapons has led to an assumption that big wars are not likely but that local wars may occur. The danger always is, however, that a so-called "limited" war can overnight become unlimited.

America is today on the brink of military action in the Middle East. Most people aren't yet aware of the danger. The Soviets are playing with fire. They are miscalculating that the American people will not become concerned and will acquiesce in the gradual absorption of the Middle East into the Soviet orbit.

Secretary of State John Foster Dulles, at a press conference here last week, was asked to define the circumstances under which the United States would be willing to render direct military assistance to Lebanon. He replied:

"The normal way to deal with these problems is through the processes of the United Nations, and the Government of Lebanon initiated such a process when it took its case to the Security Council and obtained the resolution for observation under which the Secretary-General is now acting and under which I believe some results at least are being obtained.

"Now we have never believed that you could only act under such processes. Indeed, Article 51 was put into the Charter to meet the contingency that it might be impractical, because of the veto power or otherwise, to obtain appropriate action from the United Nations. Article 51, as you will recall, talks about collective defense if an armed attack occurs.

"Now, we do not think that the words 'armed attack' precludes treating as such an armed revolution which is fomented from abroad, aided and assisted from abroad. Indeed, you will recall perhaps, in the report on the North Atlantic Treaty, that the Senate Foreign Relations Committee indicated that that kind of a civil disturbance could be treated as an armed attack. In our Japanese Security Treaty that is expressly spelled out.

"However, we believe that the best way to deal with these things is through the processes of the United Nations. We do not think it is proper yet to conclude that those processes have failed or will fail. If and when we had to reach that conclusion then there would be a new situation which we would have to deal with in the light of the new circumstances at the time."

The Secretary also pointed out that there is no "analogy whatsoever between the situation in Lebanon, where the lawful government is calling for assistance, and the Suez case, where the armed intervention was against the will of the government concerned." He added:

"We do believe that the presence in Lebanon of foreign troops, however justifiable—and it is thoroughly justifiable from a legal and international law standpoint—is not as good a solution as for the Lebanese to find a solution themselves. It would be, as you put it, a sort of measure of last resort."

These words are a plain warning to the men in the Kremlin. Will they heed it or continue to play with fire? The Soviet policy will be influenced by the extent to which American public opinion seems to be alerted to the risky game of the Communists.

The American point of view now has been clearly stated by the Secretary of State with the approval of the President of the United States. It is that, first, the United Nations must strive to prevent war in the Middle East. If that fails, armed intervention under Article 51 of the United Nations Charter will become necessary.

There should be no doubt left anywhere that this is the policy of the West. For a miscalculation by Moscow as to the willingness of the West to defend free peoples against aggression could bring on a chain of events that would lead to World War III. The Kremlin is playing with fire.

LEGALIZING TREASON?

JULY 18, 1958

FIVE JUSTICES of the Supreme Court of the United States—Chief Justice Warren and Justices Frankfurter, Black, Brennan and Douglas—have ruled that, even if an American citizen is a member of the international Communist conspiracy, he cannot for this reason alone be barred from travel to and from hostile countries and is entitled to a passport carrying the seal of the Government of the United States.

The Court has ruled, too, that this "right to travel" cannot be interfered with even if our Government feels that the citizen may be going abroad to furnish military secrets to the Soviet Union.

The Court has not as yet ruled directly that the "right to travel" is protected by the Constitution itself but hints broadly that in the future it may bar as unconstitutional any restriction whatsoever, whether in peacetime or wartime, depending upon whether the Court itself feels that the national security is adversely affected by the issuance of the passport.

The Supreme Court thus takes over the conduct of the foreign relations of the United States.

President Eisenhower last week in a special message urged Congress to pass a law specifically affirming the right of the Executive to control the issuance of passports in a time of national emergency.

But the Court, under its recent opinion, has threatened to declare invalid any denial of a passport solely because of an applicant's connection with the Communist conspiracy.

The Court, moreover—even in the face of world conditions today—insists that membership in the international Communist movement is merely "a political belief and association."

This means that the Court is not concerned with acts of treason a citizen may commit while he is traveling abroad. The Government of the United States, knowing of his errand, would be powerless to restrain anyone making frequent trips back and forth to contact enemy agents abroad.

Four members of the Court—Justices Clark, Burton, Harlan and Whittaker—directly contradict the majority. They condemn their colleagues for ignoring a Presidential proclamation—in effect since 1950—which declared a national emergency. The minority says:

"Were this a time of peace, there might very well be no problem for us to decide, since petitioners then would not need a passport to leave the country. . . .

"In a wholly realistic sense there is no peace today, and there was no peace in 1952. At both times the state of national emergency declared by the President in 1950, wherein he stated that 'world conquest by Communist imperialism is the goal of the forces of aggression that have been loosed upon the world' and that 'the increasing menace of the forces of Communist aggression requires that the national defense of the United States be strengthened as speedily as possible,' was in full effect."

But the five Justices of the majority flatly refuse to take into account the menace of Communist imperialism or the acts of subversion and infiltration in our midst or the manifestations of hostility by the Communist rulers against the United States which daily fill the press. The majority opinion, written by Justice Douglas, says:

"We deal with beliefs, with associations, with ideological matters. We must remember that we are dealing here with citizens who have neither been accused of crimes nor found guilty. They are being denied their freedom of movement solely because of their refusal to be subjected to inquiry into their beliefs and associations. They do not seek to escape the law nor to violate it. They may or may not be Communists. But assuming they are, the only law which Congress has passed expressly curtailing the movement of Communists across our borders has not yet become effective."

It is true that a statute requiring registration of the Communist Party has not yet become fully effective because of pending litigation. But do we need a law to tell us that Americans involved in the Communist conspiracy ought to answer forthrightly all questions asked them on an application for a passport?

Actually, there are plenty of statutes requiring such information which do not happen to mention Communists. Does this mean that Communists are immune from all laws unless specifically mentioned?

Must the Government of the United States wait until a citizen engages in acts of treason abroad and then try to revoke a passport? How can the Government of the United States set up a policing machinery in foreign lands? Why shouldn't any citizen be willing to swear before his own Government that he does not belong to a Communist conspiracy?

If the Supreme Court had ruled that treason now is lawful, it could not have dealt a more devastating blow to the safety of the people of America than it did in the five-to-four decision ordering passports issued to any person of American citizenship irrespective of his loyalty to the United States.

A STEP IN TIME

JULY 25, 1958

THE ACTION IN THE MIDDLE EAST taken last week by the United States and Great Britain is a step in time.

For several years now we have been appeasing the Communist dictators. We have had "summit" talks. We have exchanged lengthy notes on disarmament and peace. We sought to repel aggression in Korea, but we hesitated to bomb the bases in Red China from which the Communist armies were supplied.

We tried by peaceful means to deal with Nasser's grab of Suez. We have passively acquiesced in Nasser's further aggression as he has taken over Syria. He now threatens to annex Iraq, Lebanon and Jordan.

Nasser today—the stooge of Moscow—is the Mussolini of yesterday. Khrushchev is the present-day Hitler.

The League of Nations was hesitant to impose embargoes and prevent various aggressions by totalitarian states in the 1930's.

Will the United Nations be equally ineffective now? Will we ultimately have to fight a big war? The lesson of the past should be re-read—appeasement never pays.

In his book, "The Gathering Storm," published in 1948, Winston Churchill writes vividly of what was happening prior to the outbreak of World War II in 1939:

"In this sad tale of wrong judgments formed by well-meaning and capable people, we now reach our climax. That we should all have come to this pass makes those responsible, however honourable their motives, blameworthy before history.

"Look back and see what we had successively accepted or thrown away: a Germany disarmed by solemn treaty; a Germany rearmed in violation of a solemn treaty; air superiority or even air parity cast away; the Rhineland forcibly occupied and the Siegfried Line built or building; the Berlin-Rome Axis established; Austria devoured and digested by the Reich; Czechoslovakia deserted and ruined by the Munich Pact; its fortress line in German hands; its mighty arsenal of Skoda henceforward making munitions for the German armies; President Roosevelt's effort to stabilise or bring to a head the European situation by the intervention of the United States waved aside with one hand, and Soviet Russia's undoubted willingness to join the Western Powers and go all lengths to save Czechoslovakia ignored on the other; the services of thirty-five Czech divisions against the still unripened German Army cast away, when Great Britain could herself supply only two to strengthen the front in France—all gone with the wind.

"And now, when every one of these aids and advantages has been squandered and thrown away, Great Britain advances, leading France by the hand, to guarantee the integrity of Poland—of that very Poland which with hyena appetite had only six months before joined in the pillage and destruction of the Czechoslovak State.

"There was sense in fighting for Czechoslovakia in 1938 when the German Army could scarcely put half a dozen trained divisions on the Western Front, when the French with nearly sixty or seventy divisions could most certainly have rolled forward across the Rhine or into the Ruhr.

"But this had been judged unreasonable, rash, below the level of modern intellectual thought and morality. Yet now at last the two Western Democracies declared themselves ready to stake their lives upon the territorial integrity of Poland.

"History, which we are told is mainly the record of the crimes, follies, and miseries of mankind, may be scoured and ransacked to find a parallel to this sudden and complete reversal of five or six years' policy of easy-going placatory appeasement, and its transformation almost overnight into a readiness to accept an obviously imminent war on far worse conditions and on the greatest scale.

"Moreover, how could we protect Poland and make good our guarantee? Only by declaring war upon Germany and attacking a stronger Western Wall and a more powerful German Army than those from which we had recoiled in September, 1938.

"Here is a line of milestones to disaster. Here is a catalogue of surrenders, at first when all was easy and later when things were harder, to the ever-growing German power. But now at last was the end of British and French submission. Here was decision at last, taken at the worst possible moment and on the least satisfactory ground, which must surely lead to the slaughter of tens of millions of people. Here was the righteous cause deliberately and with a refinement of inverted artistry committed to mortal battle after its assets and advantages had been so improvidently squandered.

"Still, if you will not fight for the right when you can easily win without bloodshed; if you will not fight when your victory will be sure and not too costly; you may come to the moment when you will have to fight with all the odds against you and only a precarious chance of survival.

"There may even be a worse case. You may have to fight when there is no hope of victory, because it is better to perish than live as slaves."

" 'WELCOME,' MURDERER!"

AUGUST 1, 1958

SOMEHOW, TO CARRY ON CONFERENCES at the United Nations with Sobolev or some other Ambassador from the Soviet Government seems tolerable to a degree as a formal mechanism of diplomacy, but to sit down and fraternize with the arch-conspirator—the man who ordered guns and tanks to shoot down and trample upon men, women and children in Hungary just a few short months ago—this is something else again.

If "summit" meetings are to be held with rulers whose hands are soaked with the blood of thousands of human beings killed in Eastern Europe, then indeed have we lost sight of fundamentals and succumbed to a passion for appeasement of the present-day Hitler.

Only two weeks ago, the United Nations, in a special report, was deploring the fact that the Soviet Union had disregarded the resolutions of the General Assembly which had demanded information about the trial and execution of the patriots in Hungary. Henry Cabot Lodge, Ambassador to the U.N., said on July 16:

"This new and revealing report shows that the United Nations has good reason to remain deeply concerned over the tragic situation in that country. The murders of Imre Nagy, General Maleter and other Hungarian patriots will never be forgotten. The perpetrators of these acts have reverted from civilized behavior to the law of the jungle. These frightful acts are obviously not the acts of free Hungarians but of puppet rulers kept in power by Soviet military forces. In the name of simple humanity, these killings must stop."

And here is what the Government of the United States said about it in a special statement issued by the Department of State on July 17:

"The U. N. report makes it abundantly clear that the Hungarian regime, which was forcibly imposed by the Soviet Government in November, 1956, and has since been supported by the presence of Soviet troops in Hungary, secretly tried and executed Imre Nagy and his associates in flagrant violation of assurances of safe conduct and of recognized conditions of immunity. . . .

"The Committee (of the U. N.) also calls attention to the fact that the Soviet and Hungarian governments have continued to persist in their refusal to comply with resolutions of the United Nations General Assembly and to cooperate in any way with the Committee. . . .

"The United States Government is convinced that the nations of the world, feeling a deep sense of shock and revulsion at the events in Hungary, will not assume an attitude of indifference permitting the Soviet and Hungarian governments to escape the full weight of the opprobrium that they must justly bear because of their actions."

The Committee reported also that it has evidence that 33 patriots have been sentenced to death and that more may shortly share their fate.

Who gives the command for these murders to be committed? Naturally, it's the man who holds the top post in the Kremlin—none other than Nikita Khrushchev.

This is the man we are asked to "welcome" at a "summit" conference.

What a strange delusion has swept the world, and particularly so many misguided persons in the parliaments of the free peoples, as they enthusiastically urge "summit" conferences! Is it that somehow, by sitting down under the glare of the kleig lights and television, with cameras clicking and thousands of newsmen looking on, some sort of "deal" can be arranged which supposedly will—as Munich falsely promised—give us "peace in our times"? What nonsense!

Have we lost our perspective? Are we to forgive and forget the murders of innocent persons in Siberia? Are we to deprive the enslaved peoples in Eastern Europe and in the Middle East of their hopes for emancipation?

What of the traditional ideals of the liberty-loving peoples of Britain, France and America? Do we believe in them still? Or do we rush with open arms to welcome the man who has blasphemed us, the man who stirred up rebellion in the Middle East and sent weapons to Nasser to help him threaten and then annex, one by one, the defenseless states adjacent to Egypt?

What principle of humanity beckons us to do aught but deal sternly with the murderer who is today the foremost enemy of peace in the world?

What principle of "diplomatic courtesy" requires us to remain silent when the man who has threatened to "bury us" comes to our shores supposedly to "negotiate" some vague agreement that will never be honored by him—if, indeed, one is ever signed?

We should, of course, assure the personal safety of Khrushchev, but we should din in his ears daily the case against murder and tyranny.

Let the kinsmen of the patriots of the captive states parade flag-draped coffins down the streets of New York City day after day during Khrushchev's visit so he may be reminded that in America, at least, we do not glorify murderers. Let the placards read: " 'Welcome,' Murderer!"

THE PEOPLE SPEAK

AUGUST 8, 1958

It was no "mob" incited by "agitators" that went to the polls last week in Arkansas.

It was no "small group of zealots" determined to "defy the supreme law of the land" that voted overwhelmingly to assure Governor Faubus a third term—unprecedented in more than half a century.

It was the electorate of Arkansas, expressing in a calm and deliberate manner its belief that the wording of the Constitution of the United States must be accepted, rather than any fortuitous ruling by the Supreme Court deviating from the Constitution.

The electorate of Arkansas reiterated by its vote a belief that the Fourteenth Amendment should be enforced not by bayonets but by a law of Congress. Such a law has never been passed even though the Amendment specifically says:

"The Congress shall have power to enforce, by appropriate legislation, the provisions of this article."

What is the "provision" that has been deemed pertinent by the Supreme Court? The Fourteenth Amendment says that "no State shall . . . deny to any person within its jurisdiction the equal protection of the laws."

For decades past "equal protection" has been construed by the Supreme Court to mean that equal facilities for education may properly be provided by the States through separate schools.

Ever since the founding of the Republic, education has been considered solely within the right of the States to administer. Nowhere in the Constitution is the word "education" mentioned, and certainly the debates in Congress when the Fourteenth Amendment was adopted do not reveal a scintilla of evidence to prove that the Amendment was intended to give Congress the power to take away from the States the right to control their own educational systems.

There is nothing in the Constitution, therefore, which prohibits the States from assigning pupils to public schools on whatever basis the State feels will give the best education to the children of its citizens.

From the very beginning of our history—confirmed indeed by a specific decision of the Massachusetts Supreme Court in 1850—the right of a State to set up separate schools for different races has been upheld. In 1896 the United States Supreme Court formally recognized the custom when it said that "separate but equal facilities" do not violate the Fourteenth Amendment.

The people of Arkansas have as deep a respect for the Constitution as the people of any other State of the Union. There would not have been cast for Governor Faubus last week the largest percentage of votes ever polled by any candidate in a Democratic primary election in Arkansas—70 per cent of the total vote—if the people had not wished to assert their right to interpret the plain words of the Constitution as they are written.

The people of Arkansas have refused to uphold the usurped right of the nine Justices in Washington to say that modern psychology or emotionalism is more important than the letter of the Constitution itself. The people of Arkansas reserve the right to control their own emotionalism, especially inside the schools.

The people of Arkansas have been abused on the radio and on television and in the Northern press as "lawless." They have been told that their action—in controlling their own educational system—is a blot on America's record before the world, especially in Soviet Russia.

But the free election last week, is, on the contrary, a dramatic example of freedom of choice. Nowhere in the Soviet empire could there be such a vote recorded in opposition to the policies of the central government.

Arkansas has not merely upheld its Governor. It has gone beyond any question of personalities. It has upheld a great principle—the doctrine of "States' rights" which Thomas Jefferson gave us.

The Tenth Amendment to the Constitution declares: "The powers not delegated to the United States by the Constitution, nor prohibited by it to the States, are reserved to the States respectively, or to the people."

The problem of mixing the races in public schools cannot be solved overnight. It is one that is rooted in the customs and habits of the people.

This writer was enrolled for 12 years in integrated public schools in the North and never has had any personal objection to integration. The people of every State, however, are entitled to their right of self-government. If it was intended by the Constitution that there be uniformity of law throughout the States, then logically the Supreme Court long ago should have declared invalid all those laws which vary from State to State in different fields of human relations.

The people of Arkansas have spoken. They have said that the Constitution itself is the only "supreme law of the land." By their virtual unanimity, they have advised the Supreme Court to halt its usurpations and to follow the Constitution itself.

LABOR'S "VICTORIES"?

AUGUST 15, 1958

JUST A FEW YEARS AGO this writer was dining in the restaurant of the House of Commons in London with Aneurin Bevan, the British Labor Party leader, and some of his associates. The conversation turned to the American system of "free competition." Mr. Bevan cynically remarked that he didn't think we really had any such thing in the United States. Nor did he believe in free competition. Instead, he favored monopolies, and said we had them in America but, unfortunately, they were controlled by private persons instead of by the Government. That's why he argued for "nationalization" of big industries.

This incident came to mind last week as the newspapers reported the alarm of certain members of Congress over the recent rise in steel prices. There were the customary suggestions on Capitol Hill that "there ought to be an investigation." But, as usual, almost everybody forgets quickly what starts the price rises and what are the motivating influences in the making of prices in America today.

The truth is that, because of industry-wide bargaining and the tremendous power wielded by national labor unions, a battle is being waged between Big Unionism and Big Business that concerns the future of our whole economy—from automobiles to kitchens. The public is the innocent bystander. The people as a whole suffer because the Congress hasn't the courage to tackle Big Unionism. That's perhaps because too many millions of dollars of campaign funds come from the unions to elect the Democratic majority and to infiltrate the so-called "liberal" groups in the Republican Party.

So monopolies grow, and feeble cries arise here and there for wage and price control. It is a logical demand, of course, but, unless the political power of Big Unionism is curbed, there is little chance that any governmental board or commission would order the fixing of equitable rates of wages and prices.

The biggest single fact about the steel industry today is conveniently overlooked by the demagogues in Congress. It is that labor costs are skyrocketing and no curb is being placed upon them.

It is pertinent today to re-read an interview in the June 7, 1957, issue of this magazine with Joseph L. Block of Chicago, President of the Inland Steel Company. He was asked: If labor keeps demanding higher wages, and prices keep on going up, where will the spiral end? He answered:

"I wish I knew. I am not as concerned about the spiral per se as about the relationship. If you had everything in proper balance—which you don't—then you could say that labor advances could go up directly in proportion to productivity without ever raising the price again. But you haven't got that.

"Your labor costs have gone up substantially more than your steel prices, with the result that steel prices are not adequate for the new costs—the costs of new equipment and replacement."

If productivity of labor doesn't keep pace with wage increases, then the companies must build new plants and seek new equipment, technologically more efficient, so as to produce steel at lower and lower costs.

But where are the billions of dollars coming from to invest in new plant and equipment? Only from investors who see adequate earnings and favorable dividends. That's the basis of the system of private enterprise.

As long, however, as there is a monopoly power to fix labor costs through industry-wide bargaining, the investor will be hesitant, and sooner or later the larger and more successful of the steel companies will gobble up their weaker high-cost competitors.

The recent price rises in steel offset only a part of the increased costs that are coming, especially in the purchase of raw materials and services. The larger companies, with their more efficient plants and their own sources of supply, are able to absorb a bigger proportion of the increased wages than their non-integrated competitors can. Yet wage rates apply uniformly.

Do not the labor leaders realize that their monopolies in all the big industries are driving us headlong into "nationalization" and a state-controlled economy? Labor will not like such a result any more than management will, but the union leaders are today overstepping the bounds of common sense, just as irresponsible officers of corporations used to do before the antitrust laws were adopted to curb excesses.

The day the Congress of the United States gave labor unions immunity from our antitrust laws, the spectre of nationalized industry was raised in America.

Will we, before it is too late, make all monopolies subject to federal laws that forbid restraints of trade and encourage competition? Will we face up to the danger or just drift into economic anarchy, when the "solutions" will inevitably be more drastic?

Union monopolies are winning their biggest victories while Congress, intimidated by labor's power, waits for an informed and aroused public opinion to make itself heard.

"BALLISTIC BLACKMAIL"

AUGUST 22, 1958

ONCE AGAIN a President of the United States has enunciated in behalf of the American people great principles for the guidance of peaceful nations.

As President Wilson did in his famous addresses in 1918, as President Roosevelt did in the Atlantic Charter in 1941, as President Truman did in authorizing our military forces to forestall Soviet aggression in Greece and later to repel Communist aggression in Korea, so did President Eisenhower, before the United Nations General Assembly, proclaim last week the historic principles now guiding us in the Near East. They have guided us from the very beginning of this Republic.

The United States has stood always as the protector of small nations—as the defender of the nations of this hemisphere against invasion by any European power and as the defender of the small nations of Europe itself in fighting against totalitarian dictatorships in World War I and World War II.

America, supported now by free governments everywhere, takes her stand again for the same principles in responding to the requests of Lebanon and Jordan for aid against aggression.

President Eisenhower recalled the crises in connection with Soviet aggression in Iran, in Greece and Turkey, in the Berlin blockade, in Korea and in the Straits of Formosa, and said:

"A common principle guided the position of the United States on all of these occasions. That principle was that aggression, direct or indirect, must be checked before it gathered sufficient momentum to destroy us all—aggressor and defender alike.

"It was this principle that was applied once again when the urgent appeals of the governments of Lebanon and Jordan were answered."

Mr. Eisenhower announced that the United States "reserves, within the spirit of this Charter, the right to answer the legitimate appeal of any nation, particularly small nations."

The President replied forcefully also to the hypocritical claim of the Soviets that the presence of American and British forces in Lebanon and Jordan constitute "aggression." He said:

"If it is made an international crime to help a small nation maintain its independence, then indeed the possibilities of conquest are unlimited."

This is a reiteration of an American principle long established. We have followed it in the Monroe Doctrine. We have followed it in stating our aims in World War I and in World War II. We have followed it in the "Truman Doctrine" in Greece, and we have followed it in the "Eisenhower Doctrine" in the Far East and in the Middle East.

There comes a time in world affairs when an internal crisis has an external impact. Small nations could be gobbled up easily if larger powers were indifferent to their plight. This would inevitably bring on a big war.

Today we are confronted by the same dilemma that has faced the world so often in the 19th Century and in the first half of this century. Totalitarianism is on the march in Eastern Europe, in the Far East, in the Middle East, in the Near East and in Africa. As a consequence, the free world, tired of war and anxious to pursue paths of peaceful development, is being compelled by contemporaneous events to build larger and larger armaments.

One government—a dictatorship in Moscow—today threatens world peace by meddling in troubled waters everywhere. Mr. Eisenhower's warning is unmistakable. He says:

"This world of individual nations is not going to be controlled by any one power or group of powers. This world is not going to be committed to any one ideology. Please believe me when I say that the dream of world domination by one power or of world conformity is an impossible dream."

This is notice that the free world can and must defend itself. It will not be terrorized. Nations "under aggressive leadership," said the President, may "seek to exploit man's horror of war by confronting the nations, particularly small nations, with an apparent choice between supine surrender, or war." He added:

"This tactic reappeared during the recent Near East crisis. Some might call it 'ballistic blackmail.'"

But the United States and its allies will not succumb to the threat. They are ready and anxious to set up a United Nations machinery to keep the peace in the Near East, to stimulate plans for economic development, but "indirect aggression" will not be tolerated.

If the Soviet Union wants to push this country and its allies to the brink of war, it will find that the free nations will make any sacrifice necessary to preserve their liberties.

The free nations will not be frightened by "ballistic blackmail."

The free nations will not choose the path of "supine surrender."

THE CONGRESS THAT FAILED

AUGUST 29, 1958

THE 85TH CONGRESS, which was entrusted with the legislative power two years ago, has failed the American people.

The Congress has failed to deal with the subversion in our midst which is directed and financed by the Communist regime in Moscow.

The Congress has failed to deal with racketeering in our midst which is carried on by irresponsible leaders of a minority of labor unions.

The Congress has failed to amend federal law so that all persons permitted by a Supreme Court decision to preach openly the forcible overthrow of our Government could be prevented from doing so. The proposed amendment would have punished the advocacy as well as the practice of treason.

The Congress has failed to pass a law, adopted by the House, which would give the States as well as the Federal Government the power to punish those who would overthrow the Government by force.

The Congress has failed to pass legislation to prevent the foreign policy of the United States from being sabotaged abroad by citizens carrying American passports.

The Congress has failed to pass laws correcting the decisions of the Supreme Court which permit confessed rapists and other criminals to go scot-free on technicalities.

The Congress has failed to checkmate the usurpation by the Supreme Court which has restricted the power of Congress to get information needed for legislative purposes.

The Congress has failed to deal with the monopoly power of labor unions which, through industry-wide bargaining, virtually fixes prices and prevents free competition in America by favoring the larger against the smaller businesses of the nation.

The Congress has failed to economize on governmental spending and has, in some instances, appropriated more money than was asked for by the executive branch of the Government. A 12-billion-dollar deficit now faces the country, and the end of such deficits is not in sight.

The Congress has failed to stop the trend toward runaway inflation which today threatens the purchasing power of the dollar and particularly the welfare of the millions of persons in the fixed-income groups in America—the retired persons living on pensions as well as those widows and orphans depending on the income from bonds and mortgages.

The Congress has failed to pass legislation defining the powers of the States and of the Federal Government to cover the "no-man's land" in labor disputes exposed by recent Supreme Court decisions.

The Congress has failed to deal with the use of money to influence legislation. Millions of dollars have been spent by labor unions, for example, to get members of Congress elected who will favor the legislation desired by labor unions and oppose that which the labor unions dislike. The charge has been openly made in speeches in Congress that a substantial number of the members owe their elections to labor-union money. Congress failed to investigate itself, though it spent lots of money investigating the executive branch in search of campaign issues.

The record of inaction of the 85th Congress is palpable. It will be glossed over, of course, by partisan speeches boasting how much legislation was actually passed at this session. There was indeed a wide variety, but much of it serves special interests. Quantity, moreover, is no substitute for quality. Action on some worthy proposals is no answer to inaction on many other proposals equally worthy.

Why did all this happen? Because there is no such thing as party responsibility in Congress any more. Theoretically, the Democrats were in control of both houses at this session, but actually there were Republicans, for example, who joined with Northern Democrats to do the bidding of the radical and socialistic organizations which have been lobbying so successfully to prevent any legislation being passed which deals with the usurpations by the Supreme Court.

Government in America has indeed reached a serious impasse as judicial tyranny is ignored by Congress. The report (see pages 62 and 63) criticizing the Supreme Court which was issued by the Chief Justices of ten States—seven in the North—points up the danger. The same facts would have been available to any of the investigating committees of Congress.

The 85th Congress has failed. It has been faithless to the trust imposed upon it by the people.

What can the voters do? They can inform themselves as to which Republicans and which Democrats participated in this debacle, and then vote against them in the primaries and in the final elections. The protest vote may be small at first, but there must be a start made eventually to remove from public office all those who have failed the people in these days of international as well as national emergency.

A DANGEROUS GAME

SEPTEMBER 12, 1958

WHILE OUTWARDLY PROFESSING a desire for a "summit conference" with Western leaders to discuss Middle East problems, Nikita Khrushchev suddenly went to Peiping last month for a conference with the head of the Red China regime. For two months before there had been daily conferences between the Soviet and Red Chinese top military commanders. What was this all about?

It turns out now that, while calling off their puppets in the Middle East, the Communists were hatching a plot to shift the scene of battle to the Far East. America and Britain had landed military forces in Lebanon and Jordan. Aggression by the Communists had thus been checked in that area. So the Moscow-Peiping alliance decided it was opportune to probe the situation in and around Formosa.

Unfortunately, too many observers here and in Europe have been viewing the Far Eastern developments as local and not as part of the world-wide game being carried on by the Soviets. Whatever the Soviets do in one region of the world is always related to what they are doing in other regions. They are constantly infiltrating the governments of free countries and taking advantage of the natural partisanship of opposition parties. The Communists have been encouraged to believe the West was weakening. So they decided to test the determination, if not the military strength, of the United States and its allies.

It is not surprising to see the Kremlin strategists moving forward and then backward whenever they find it convenient to do so. Thus, it has suited Moscow to play down the tension in the Middle East in order to gain more time to develop new intrigues inside the Arab world. For the moment, as the Secretary-General of the United Nations explores the situation with Nasser and seeks a formula for a truce, it is thought desirable by the Soviets to let things cool off. But this doesn't mean the situation has by any means been solved. It merely means that the Far East takes over now as the primary place to test the willingness of the United States to fight in defense of the free world.

On this page, November 11, 1955, the following was written:

"The Soviets have taken advantage of the deterioration in the Western position to press their infiltration in the Middle East and in North Africa. Outwardly Communist diplomacy appears stronger and more obdurate than it was before Geneva (the "summit conference" of July 1955). The Russians seem to have concluded that the West will not fight for its principles no matter what happens.

"This was the fatal miscalculation that Hitler made. It's the same mistake every aggressor makes. If of course, an aggressor thinks he can get what he wants without a fight, he will attempt to extend his authority everywhere that he can.

"But there comes a time to call a halt—to draw a line."

It was urged then that such a line be drawn in the Middle East just as it had been in the Far East in January 1955. Congress passed in March 1957 a similar resolution which authorized American military forces to be used in the Middle East to protect the free countries there against aggression.

Moscow tested our good faith last July by setting off a revolution in Iraq which threatened to engulf both Jordan and Lebanon. America, fortunately, made good on her pledge and was joined by Great Britain.

Turning now, therefore, to the Far East, the Soviets and the Red Chinese are seeking to determine if the United States is in earnest. Doubts about our position have arisen because of the gradually-increasing support for the Communists manifested in influential circles in this country and in Canada with reference to the admission of Red China to the Security Council of the United Nations.

The American policy in the Far East, however, is unequivocal. If the Soviets want it, there will be fighting in which American forces will be engaged. The United States cannot afford to let her defense line in the Far East crumble—and that line includes Korea, Japan and the Philippines, as well as Formosa, with millions of troops available to our side.

What was written here on November 11, 1955, needs to be said again:

"Realism commands the West to say frankly to the Russians that they are playing with fire, that they are engaging in acts of aggression which, if not abandoned, will inevitably lead to a world war."

Certainly Red China would not have moved against Quemoy last week without the open support and inspiration of the leaders of the Soviet Union. What we are witnessing is another example of "indirect aggression" that has become direct aggression. We cannot ignore it. For if we do, the enemy may misconstrue our weakness as consent to or acquiescence in further aggression—and thus are big wars born.

"IS IT A CONSTITUTION OR IS IT A SHAM?"

SEPTEMBER 19, 1958

(The question, "Is it a constitution or is it a sham?" was asked at the Conference of State Chief Justices in a report approved last month by a vote of 36 to 8. It severely criticized recent decisions of the Supreme Court of the United States.

When the Chief Justices of three quarters of the States of the Union declare that the present Supreme Court is overstepping its bounds, such a pronouncement is well worth the attention of the American people.

Because of the Supreme Court's ruling last week disregarding the Tenth Amendment to the Constitution, added significance attaches to the following excerpts from the conclusions reached by the 36 State Chief Justices.—David Lawrence, Editor)

We believe that in the fields with which we are concerned, and as to which we feel entitled to speak, the Supreme Court too often has tended to adopt the role of policy-maker without proper judicial restraint. We feel this is particularly the case in both of the great fields we have discussed—namely, the extent and extension of the federal power, and the supervision of State action by the Supreme Court by virtue of the Fourteenth Amendment. In the light of the immense power of the Supreme Court and its practical non-reviewability in most instances no more important obligation rests upon it, in our view, than that of careful moderation in the exercise of its policy-making role.

We are not alone in our view that the Court, in many cases arising under the Fourteenth Amendment, has assumed what seem to us primarily legislative powers. See Judge Learned Hand on the Bill of Rights. We do not believe that either the framers of the original Constitution or the possibly somewhat less gifted draftsmen of the Fourteenth Amendment ever contemplated that the Supreme Court would, or should, have the almost unlimited policy-making powers which it now exercises. It is strange, indeed, to reflect that under a constitution which provides for a system of checks and balances and of distribution of power between national and State governments one branch of one government —the Supreme Court—should attain the immense, and in many respects, dominant, power which it now wields. . . .

It has long been an American boast that we have a government of laws and not of men. We believe that any study of recent decisions of the Supreme Court will raise at least considerable doubt as to the validity of that boast. . . .

We further find that the Court does not accord finality to its own determinations of constitutional questions, or for that matter of others. We concede that a slavish adherence to *stare decisis* could at times have unfortunate consequences; but it seems strange that under a constitutional doctrine which requires all others to recognize the Supreme Court's rulings on constitutional questions as binding adjudications of the meaning and application of the Constitution, the Court itself has so frequently overturned its own decisions thereon, after the lapse of periods varying from one year to seventy-five, or even ninety-five years. . . .

The Constitution expressly sets up its own procedures for amendment, slow or cumbersome though they may be. If reasonable certainty and stability do not attach to a written constitution, is it a constitution or is it a sham?

These frequent differences and occasional overrulings of prior decisions in constitutional cases cause us grave concern as to whether individual views as to what is wise or desirable do not unconsciously override a more dispassionate consideration of what is or is not constitutionally warranted. We believe that the latter is the correct approach, and we have no doubt that every member of the Supreme Court intends to adhere to that approach, and believes that he does so. But to err is human, and even the Supreme Court is not divine.

It is our earnest hope which we respectfully express, that that great Court exercise to the full its power of judicial self-restraint by adhering firmly to its tremendous, strictly judicial powers and by eschewing, so far as possible, the exercise of essentially legislative powers when it is called upon to decide questions involving the validity of State action, whether it deems such action wise or unwise. The value of our system of federalism, and of local self-government in local matters which it embodies, should be kept firmly in mind, as we believe it was by those who framed our Constitution. . . .

Surely, it is no less incumbent upon the Supreme Court, on its part, to be equally restrained and to be as sure as is humanly possible that it is adhering to the fundamentals of the Constitution with regard to the distribution of powers and the separation of powers, and with regard to the limitations of judicial power which are implicit in such separation and distribution, and that it is not merely giving effect to what it may deem desirable.

WHAT THREE SUPREME
COURT JUSTICES HEARD—

SEPTEMBER 26, 1958

LAST MONTH a memorable episode occurred at a dinner given by the Conference of State Chief Justices in Los Angeles.

It was memorable because three members of the Supreme Court of the United States—Chief Justice Warren, Justice Clark and Justice Brennan—sat at the head table as Chief Justice John R. Dethmers of Michigan delivered an address criticizing the Supreme Court of the United States.

The fact that, under our American system of free speech, the members of the highest court in the land can be criticized to their faces is in itself a tribute to the greatness of the First Amendment.

But the occasion was far more significant than as an example of freedom of expression. It was the climax of a meeting of the Conference of State Chief Justices which had approved, by a vote of 36 to 8, a report submitted after exhaustive study of recent decisions of the Supreme Court of the United States. The report did not discuss the segregation issue but limited itself to many rulings deemed contrary to the basic interpretations of the Constitution throughout our history.

Chief Justice Dethmers of Michigan, who was chairman of the Conference of State Chief Justices, reviewed the work of the Conference during the last ten years, stressing its many successful efforts in helping to overhaul and modernize State court systems. But his main point was the growing conflict between the Federal Government and the States as to the rights granted each under the Constitution. He said:

"Of transcendent importance to the nation, overshadowing all others in the concern of the Conference, is the matter of federal-state relationships as affected by judicial decisions. Increasingly, in recent years, members of the Conference had been expressing themselves in terms sharply critical of what they viewed as a trend in this area.

"Accordingly, at the sessions of the Conference in Dallas, two years ago, the formal program was in large part devoted to the subject of the division of powers between the federal and State governments. In New York, last year, several members urged adoption of resolutions strongly condemnatory of that asserted trend. The majority, shunning hasty or precipitate action, determined on the appointment of a committee to devote the ensuing year to a study of the subject and to report to the 1958 session with recommenda-

tions for achieving sound and appropriate relationships. . . .

"Time will not permit, nor is this the occasion for detailing the treatment in the report of specific phases of the subject and the decisions of the United States Supreme Court relating thereto. . . . In general, it expresses the concern of its framers and adopting members of the Conference over the constant expansion of the powers of the national government and consequent contraction of the powers of State and local governments, which result from Supreme Court interpretations of constitutional and statutory provisions. Note is taken of what is viewed as an assumption by the Court of the legislative function and the role of policy-maker in this area of federal-state relationships.

"Maintenance of the historic division of powers between national and State governments, and retention of the highest possible degree of local self-government compatible with national security and well-being, are deemed of the utmost importance by members of the Conference, as they were by the Founding Fathers, only as they serve as effective instrumentalities for the preservation of the liberties of the people and the perpetuation of our free institutions. No other, or sectional, interest was sought to be subserved by the report.

"It is the feeling of the members of the Conference that, as judicial officers, entrusted by the people with positions of high responsibility and trust, they would be remiss in their duties, indeed, if they were to cower in a corner and neglect to speak out in temperate tone, to alert the public to trends and developments of tremendous moment to the people. Particularly is this true in view of the peculiar training, experience and contact with events that especially equip Justices of the State Appellate Courts to discern such trends and to appreciate their significance. Where can it be said that greater obligation rests than on them to call public attention to a gradual sapping of State and local powers and rights, portending peril to the rights of the people. Inasmuch as the people must make the final judgments on these matters, existence of the problems and the involvements must be proclaimed. It is intended that the report shall serve that office.

"Abraham Lincoln once said that resistance to decisions of the Supreme Court 'meant an attack on our whole system of republican government, a blow that would place all our rights and liberties at the mercy of passion, anarchy and violence.' The Conference has moved in full recognition of the utter importance of upholding public confidence in the courts and the judicial process, and the high duty of lawyers and Judges to upbuild it. Constitutional guarantees of freedoms and liberties avail but little except as the courts breathe the breath of life into them and make them effective and meaningful. This they can only do, successfully, as they are supported by the public. As American Bar President Charles S. Rhyne has said so pointedly: 'Our free institutions and system of government are no stronger than the public opinion supporting them.'

"Accordingly, you will find the Conference report, despite certain newspaper headlines to the contrary, completely temperate and restrained, couched in terms of fullest respect for the United States Supreme Court as an institution of government charged with responsibility for giving life to human liberties, and also respect for the intelligence and integrity of the members of that Court.

"At the same time, in a government by the people, views on vital national issues not only may, but must be voiced if that system is to be maintained. It will be recalled that Abraham Lincoln, also, in discussing the Dred Scott decision, said, 'We know the Court that made it has often overruled its own decisions and we shall do what we can to have it overrule this. We offer no resistance to it.'

"We do not forget that Mr. Justice David J. Brewer of the United States Supreme Court, speaking in 1898, said, 'It is a mistake to suppose that the Supreme Court is either honored or helped by being spoken of as beyond criticism.'

"The Conference report, so far from attacking the Court, expresses only its concern with certain of the decisions. It contains no applause for suggestions on the political front that the Court be stripped, by congressional action, of any of its traditional powers. The power of the Court to uphold and preserve human liberty and the rights of the people must not be crippled, curbed or destroyed. The Conference report would have none of this. It concludes, therefore, in most respectful and temperate terms, and with extreme restraint, to urge upon the Court, that, particularly in the field of determining federal and State powers and relationships, it exercise that greatest of all judicial powers, the power of judicial self-restraint, by constant recognition and giving effect to the vital difference between what, on the one hand, the Constitution prescribes or permits and that which, on the other, may, from time to time, to the majority of the Court, seem desirable or undesirable, and by adhering firmly to its tremendous, strictly judi-

cial powers and eschewing so far as possible the exercise of essentially legislative powers, contenting itself with use of the policy-making role, where at all necessary, with only the utmost care and moderation.

"Such is the general tenor of the report, offered in a spirit of good will and cooperation in the public interest. If, perchance, it should come to the attention of the esteemed members of the Court, it is our fervent wish and hope that it will be received and considered in like fashion.

"Mention has been made of the dread responsibility of members of bench and bar for enhancing the prestige of courts and the judicial process in public esteem and the consequent duty to criticize court decisions, if at all, with only the greatest restraint. That responsibility and that restraint must be deemed to apply not only to the critic but as well to the formulator of court opinions and the making of court decisions. We, lawyers and judges, share, as advocates, as critics and as final arbiters of right and law, one common responsibility to the people in that regard. If, in public appraisal, we do not make our system work, as an instrument for good and for human freedom, it must fail."

When Chief Justice Dethmers prepared his speech, he did not know, of course, who would be in his audience. It will be noted that he did not touch at all on the segregation issue and did not give endorsement to recent legislative efforts in Congress to limit the jurisdiction of the Supreme Court.

Incidentally, on this page last week, several excerpts were presented from the report to the Conference of Chief Justices, the text being furnished by the office of the Council of State Governments, which now advises regretfully that it furnished in error a copy of the preliminary draft. It happens that two sentences of those published here were eliminated before the report was submitted to the Conference by the committee. The sentences were these: "If reasonable certainty and stability do not attach to a written constitution, is it a constitution or is it a sham? . . . But to err is human, and even the Supreme Court is not divine."

Much more forceful language, however, on this point was adopted by the Conference itself when, in approving the report as a whole, it was resolved:

"That this Conference, while recognizing that the application of constitutional rules to changed conditions must be sufficiently flexible as to make such rules adaptable to altered conditions, believes that a fundamental purpose of having a written constitution is to promote the certainty and stability of the provisions of law set forth in such a constitution."

"EQUAL" IN THE SIGHT OF MAN?

OCTOBER 3, 1958

PRESIDENT EISENHOWER last week, in criticizing the closing of public schools in Virginia and Arkansas, said:

"Most of us in the United States, as part of our religious faith, believe that all men are equal in the sight of God. Indeed, our forefathers enshrined this belief in the Declaration of Independence as a self-evident truth. Just as we strive to live up to our fundamental convictions, we constantly strive to achieve this ideal of the equality of man."

The President has oversimplified the issue. There is no question about the equality of citizens before the law. They must be treated alike where "civil or political rights" are concerned. But social rights are not civil or political rights. Nor can man be made equal in the sight of man merely by proclaiming an ideal.

God created men of different colors, just as He created birds of different colors. We know the old saying that "birds of a feather flock together." And the Supreme Court of the United States has recently upheld the right of individuals to "freedom of association."

Social discrimination may be deplored in theory, but in every big city in the United States there are "exclusive clubs" and other tax-exempt organizations which select members on the basis of color and religion.

Many persons who today are vehemently advocating "integration" are members of such clubs. Lots of people, too, are sending their children to "exclusive schools" because they want them to "grow up with the right sort of children." This may not be moving toward the ideal of "social equality," but who, including the President of the United States, will come out now and call such "freedom of association" a violation of the Declaration of Independence?

For there is a difference between legal rights to a public facility and a citizen's legal privilege to operate a school as a private facility. No public school can be used for an illegal purpose—and if the "law of the land" bars the use of such a building to private citizens, then are we to deprive the parents who formerly sent their children to public schools in Virginia and Arkansas of the right to try out the private-school method in some other buildings if they choose?

The President says we have come to regard "as a fundamental right—the right to a public education," and he unwittingly gives the impression that private-school education cannot be equal to public-school education. This is a fallacy. Indeed, our private colleges and universities, including sectarian institutions, rank higher in scholarship and educational achievements than do many of our State-supported institutions.

To deplore the closing of public schools in Virginia and Arkansas and to say the consequences could be "disastrous" is to say that the people of these two States cannot possibly achieve by private schools what they have hitherto achieved through public schools.

Maybe the people of Virginia and Arkansas will not succeed in giving their children better schooling through private institutions, but at least they have the right to try. For there is no right on the part of the President or anyone else in the Federal Government to seek to control the educational processes of the several States. This is a matter which Congress again and again has said in its laws must remain "forever" in the "exclusive control" of the States. This same language was in the law recently passed by Congress admitting Alaska to the Union.

Nor is the maintenance of public schools necessarily a State's legal obligation. Each State can, within its discretion, provide public schools or decide to aid private schools. This, too, has been upheld for many years by the Supreme Court. Also, Congress has for several years been appropriating money for tuition grants to veterans under the "GI Bill." The money was awarded to the individuals directly, and they alone chose the schools or colleges they desired to attend.

In America, parents have a right to decide to what schools they shall send their children. In Soviet Russia, where "equality" in almost everything is enforced at the point of the bayonet, no choice exists.

How far does "equality" really go? Must we enlarge the Supreme Court to ten, so that there can be five men and five women Justices? Should at least five of these Justices be Negroes?

Must the initiative of the enterprising individual be stifled and the pace of his mind and physical activity be reduced to that of another man less fortunate?

Is it "equality" for one man to pay more taxes than another? Is it "equality" for one man to accumulate more property than another? Will we be hearing soon that, because all men are "equal in the sight of God," it behooves us now to redistribute private wealth so that everybody will have an equal share?

For if we are going to make a fetish of "equality" and apply it to the relations of man to man, then indeed we may soon be asking ourselves: "O Communism, where is thy sting?"

PRIVATE SCHOOLS—
BETTER EDUCATION

OCTOBER 10, 1958

IT'S AN ILL WIND that blows no good—and the current discussion among the people of several States of plans to concentrate on private rather than public schools in some localities affords an opportunity to improve the educational process in America. In this respect, the controversy over "integration" may turn out to be a salutary development.

Bona fide private schools, financed by private individuals and operated in private buildings, are clearly constitutional. Generally they have been very successful as educational institutions. Private schools, moreover, have become preeminent in producing the leaders of Great Britain, France and Germany.

The critics of the American public-school system have all along been saying that "mass education" in the public schools has been a failure and that other countries are outstripping us. Interviewed in the January 24, 1958, issue of this magazine, Professor Arthur Bestor of the University of Illinois, nationally known educator, revealed many of the weaknesses in the American public-school system. He said:

"There's another reason why such an alarming percentage of our ablest young men and women feel no desire to complete their education. Their intellectual interest and intellectual curiosity have been deadened because they have been held back to the level of the mediocre student so long that they have become completely bored. A 'soft' educational system has put their brains to sleep. . . .

"We like to think of America as a land of opportunity, and we have gladly spent billions trying to make it a land of opportunity so far as schooling is concerned. But actually we don't offer our brightest young people the kind of educational opportunity they would have if they were born in other countries. . . .

"Our standard for high-school graduation has slipped badly. Fifty years ago a high-school diploma meant something."

Asked if American students generally would be able to win a diploma in the high schools of England, he replied:

"I do not think that the ordinary graduate of an American high school could pass satisfactorily the exams which are required at the same level abroad."

Why has all this happened? Because public-school systems are controlled by governmental bureaucracies which tend to standardize education at levels that conform to the "mass education" idea. Because of the large classes, the better students are held down to a lower level of educational attainment.

Unfortunately, the American public-school system is handicapped because there is a taboo on all religious instruction. The Supreme Court has ruled that to teach religion in the public schools is a violation of the First Amendment of the Constitution.

An "ingenious" circumvention, however, has been accomplished in recent years through the "released time" method. States have passed laws which permit the public-school authorities—State agencies—to arrange with private religious schools for students to leave the public-school buildings for certain hours during the week. Those students who do not desire this kind of instruction are compelled to remain in other classes. This scheme has not been held by the Supreme Court to be an "evasion" or a discrimination between students, but someday it might be. Hence, those Americans who really want their children to get some kind of religious instruction may wish to begin thinking of enrolling them in private denominational schools. Certainly juvenile delinquency might well be decreased if there is more opportunity for religious instruction of our teenage population.

Teachers will be receiving higher pay in private schools than in public schools. There will be better retirement systems for such teachers than in public schools. A better quality of teaching will result.

There is no need, of course, to do away with public schools as such. These schools are required for the huge number of children who must be given education of some kind, even if it is inferior. But the States can readily arrange to finance the tuition of all those children whose parents want them to attend private schools. The argument that only the rich can attend private schools is fallacious. Tuition grants under the GI bills passed by Congress have been made directly by the Federal Government to private citizens, who can choose whatever school they wish. The States can likewise make tuition grants each year. The taxpayer would welcome a system whereby he could decide how and where his children shall be educated.

The days of regimented education with low standards would seem to be numbered. Private schools may at last come into their own in America.

PRINCIPLE OR EXPEDIENCY?

OCTOBER 24, 1958

WHAT SHALL the American voter do this autumn? He is usually importuned to vote against things. He is told that, if he has been unemployed or if farm income is down, it is the fault of the incumbent party. If he has a son of draft age, he is warned that the success of one party at the polls may bring on war and that the other party, if retained in office, will insure peace.

Expediency, which has become the guiding philosophy of the politician, now afflicts also many of the mentors who advise the citizenry in the press. The cry is that the Government owes the citizen a living and that the Government must provide jobs no matter how much it costs or how big the deficits in the Treasury. Runaway inflation and eventual bankruptcy are dismissed as "impossible." Governmental paternalism is deeply imbedded in the political doctrines of today, irrespective of the fiscal consequences.

To be in favor of taxing heavily anyone who has the brains to earn a substantial income is called "liberal." To insist that private enterprise and individual initiative should be the basic American platform is derisively regarded nowadays as "reactionary."

The drift plainly is towards socialism—the mastery of the state over the individual. Nobody is ready to admit that such a course has been deliberately set—not even the factions that seek control of the Democratic Party today. But the trend is inevitable if present-day "liberals" can continue to masquerade under the cloak of benefactors to the common man.

The Democratic Party in the North really favors socialism, though it never uses the term. The Democratic Party in the South holds just the opposite philosophy, and if it had not been for Democratic leaders from the South in the last session of Congress who repressed some of the spenders in their own party, America now would be facing economic disaster.

The Republicans, on the other hand, have a "modern" clique that apes the radicals in the Democratic Party. The conservative Republican in many a State feels he is being pushed out of his own party except when the campaign funds are being solicited every two years.

What shall the American voter do who believes in the right to work without being compelled to join a union or any organization in which he does not conscientiously believe? What about the right to "life, liberty and the pursuit of happiness" without the extortions of Government or the oppressive hand of union monopoly? When will we find out how much money was really spent by the labor unions to elect their candidates in the current campaign? Will a Congress which has been elected through union funds investigate itself?

The voter who wishes to be true to America's finest traditions must vote for principle as against expediency. He must support those candidates who have an understanding of the conflict in America today between freedom and totalitarianism.

The "popular" philosophy nowadays is that the end justifies the means and that, if the Constitution doesn't provide a reform, the Supreme Court may order it anyhow. Precedent is disregarded as old-fashioned.

Yet the year a principle was born has nothing to do with its validity. Human nature doesn't change the fundamental rules of conduct just because 2,000 years have elapsed since the Gospel was preached by the Disciples. The martyrs who suffered torture for Christianity's principles were not cowed by successive defeats. They were true to their consciences—they knew that right must win in the end.

Woodrow Wilson once said: "I would rather lose in a cause that some day will triumph than to triumph in a cause that I know some day will fail."

How many of us on the American political scene today actually care enough about principles to risk defeat or "unpopularity" in espousing them?

Men of character are needed who, on becoming candidates for office, will champion fundamental principles and stick to them irrespective of whether this will win the election in a particular year.

The progress of parties goes up or down in accordance as the quality of the candidates reflects the determination of the voters themselves to see certain principles of government maintained.

Americans do not want a dictatorship by any branch of the Government in the guise of a democracy, nor a liberalism that is based on coercion. Hitler in 1933 followed the letter of the German Constitution when he rose to power. We all know the story of what his subsequent usurpation brought to the world. Yet the real story—the indifference of the German people who acquiesced—seems never to have been driven home to those people in the democracies who still worship the doctrine that the end justifies the means and who believe that expediency is to be preferred to principle.

It's a time for loyalty to principle, loyalty to fundamental constitutionalism, loyalty to the American system of private enterprise as opposed to all forms of socialism. It's a time for loyalty to conscience as one enters the voting booth.

WHAT MANDATE!

NOVEMBER 7, 1958

WHAT IS THE MANDATE of the people in the congressional elections held this week?

Can anyone be sure what the Democratic gains in the House or Senate really signify? Do we have two major parties, each with a recognized obligation to advocate certain policies of government in the field of national and international affairs?

In Britain they still believe in party responsibility. Each party goes before the people with a specific platform, adhered to by all its candidates for parliament. When the incumbent party, moreover, loses the parliamentary election, a new prime minister takes office.

But in the United States we have divided government. For four years now we have had the Democratic Party in control of both houses of Congress. Knowing that we shall continue to have a Republican President in control of the executive branch of the government for another two years, millions of voters this week expressed their desire to continue control of Congress in the Democratic Party.

Unfortunately, the peoples of the rest of the world who are familiar with the ways of parliamentary government will be tempted to assume that the Democratic Party's victories in various States in the election this week of Representatives and Senators to our national legislative body means a repudiation of the policies of the President and the Secretary of State.

Having read dispatches quoting the campaign utterances of leading Democrats, the people in Europe, Asia and Africa will be told by Soviet-controlled radio broadcasts that a triumph of the Democrats means the President must stop supporting the Nationalist Chinese and must surrender our strategic position in the Far East.

The American people, despite the claims of some Democrats, did not intend by the election to be put in the position of repudiating the foreign policy of the present Administration. It would be a mistake for Moscow to proceed on any such assumption.

But, even while refuting such a possible misinterpretation of the election results as bearing on foreign policy, it is evident that the ambiguities in domestic policy are not so readily dismissed.

Do the gains of the Democrats mean that we are in for an era of public spending irrespective of deficits?

Are we now to increase taxes on corporations and on individual incomes so as to balance the budget? Are we to ignore the fact that the inflationary movement may reduce the purchasing power of the dollar?

The "pocketbook issue" has been useful in winning votes for the Democrats in areas where unemployment has occurred. But if all the unemployed do not get jobs in the next two years, will the Democratic Party in Congress be held responsible for this in the 1960 congressional and presidential elections?

The answer is that the electorate will be urged again to hold only the President responsible for economic adversity even though a partisan-minded Congress may have blocked sound measures proposed by the Administration to insure economic stability.

The truth is there is no clear mandate to be derived from the 1958 elections. There is today no party responsibility on either side of the aisle in the Senate or in the House. Each side has been betting apparently on the capacity of its orators to take advantage of the ignorance of an uninformed electorate.

But, while we know there was no general mandate given by the people as a whole, we must face realistically the fact that the new Congress is to be controlled not by the Democratic Party as such but by a clique of union bosses. The labor unions through their political auxiliaries have spent in several instances more money to elect this week the candidates of their choice—almost all of them Democrats—than have the organizations of the nominees themselves.

The mandate to be given by the labor unions to their henchmen in Congress will become clear enough next January. They must try to amend the labor-management laws so as to give more advantages to the labor unions. They must try to repeal the law permitting the States to pass "right to work" laws. They must be ready to defeat any further legislation that might effectively deal with labor racketeering.

To achieve a majority in the Congress, labor unions have spent time and money in electioneering. Businessmen have not risen to the challenge.

Now the question is whether the economic power of labor unions will be curbed. Higher and higher wages will be extorted from management under the penalty of costly strikes. Eventually, as prices must be raised to meet increased wage costs, the result could be a buyers' strike and finally a depression which certainly would bear the union label.

The 1958 election, instead of bringing an era of prosperity, may in time prove to have been the turning point in favor of those forces which really seek a breakdown in the private-enterprise system. Was this the intended mandate of the voters?

20 YEARS OF COURT "PACKING"

DECEMBER 12, 1958

FOR 20 YEARS NOW the Supreme Court of the United States has been "packed" with Justices selected from a cult that believes the Constitution can be rewritten at will by the judiciary.

The late Samuel Gompers, president of the American Federation of Labor, once proposed a constitutional amendment "to curb the power of the Supreme Court over Congress, the Constitution and the rights of the individual citizen." He wrote in 1924:

"Labor and the Progressives do not attack the Supreme Court or any court. Their proposal to check the present assumption of power arises wholly from two facts: first, that the Supreme Court, whether by usurpation or by a sound interpretation of the Constitution, has exercised supreme power over our entire governmental structure; and, second, that this Court is selected in the most undemocratic manner conceivable under our governmental system, namely, appointment by the President for life. . . .

"According to Thomas Jefferson, the danger to our Constitution lies, not in lessened power of the courts, but in their augmented powers. He said:

" 'The germ of dissolution of our Federal Government is in the judiciary—the irresponsible body working like gravity, by day and by night, gaining a little today and gaining a little tomorrow and advancing its noiseless step like a thief over the field of jurisdiction until all shall be usurped.'

"If this process of judicial usurpation outlined by Jefferson should continue, it would inevitably lead to a revolutionary explosion. For a judicial autocracy is no better than any other form of tyranny."

Mr. Gompers pointed out that the Supreme Court is not supreme over the Constitution because Congress can at any time increase the number of Justices and, by this means, a Congress and the President "can overthrow this judicial autocracy." But the labor leader said this was a "very dangerous" method and he preferred instead a constitutional amendment limiting the powers of the Court.

The late President Franklin D. Roosevelt, however, did propose in 1937 just such a plan to increase the number of Justices. He hoped to be able to appoint Justices sharing his viewpoint so as to achieve a new majority. This move failed in Congress, but Mr. Roosevelt won his victory anyway. It was a victory for the philosophy that believes in "adapting" the Constitution to the demands of the hour—ignoring the amending process.

Mr. Roosevelt gloated over his victory. Having made several appointments to the Court to fill successive vacancies, he wrote in 1941, in the introduction to the 1937 volumes of his public papers, as follows:

"By the time the Court term was over in June of 1937, it was very clear that the entire approach of the Court to the many problems confronting us had completely changed. The views of the liberal minority of 1935 and 1936 were being gradually adopted by the one or two Justices on the other side necessary to make them the views of the majority. . . .

"It was not until after the end of the judicial term in June, 1937, that a single vacancy on the Court actually occurred. The about-face in the decisions of the Court had come from the very same personnel that had been on the Court since my first inauguration. The victory, therefore, cannot be attributed to the new Justices. It was rather a realization by one or two members of the Court that the Court had exceeded its powers, that it had strayed away from the Constitution itself, and that the liberal minority of the Court had been correct in its conclusions."

But the fact is that the few decisions of this brief period which did represent a change were not as fundamental as those that came afterwards from the Court that Mr. Roosevelt did "pack."

This writer in 1936 wrote a book in defense of the Supreme Court as an institution and particularly emphasized the long line of decisions that had affirmed and reaffirmed what Abraham Lincoln once described as "settled law." The Court decisions prior to 1936 were commended as in accord with basic constitutional principles. But by 1941 it was apparent that "settled law" was being tossed aside by a new majority made up in large part of Justices appointed by Mr. Roosevelt. In an editorial here on June 13, 1941, this writer commented on the change as follows:

"The opinions handed down in the session of the Court just ended are amazing in their deviation from accepted principles of constitutional law. Words not written in the statute have been supplied by the Justices. What Congress meant to say or did not mean to say—though not revealed in the statute—are glibly interpolated through judicial legislation. Principles that have stood the test of time in their thoughtful balance of relationships between the Government and the citizen are demolished overnight. The lower courts are bewildered. The bar is stunned. The basic guide to human intercourse—that principles once settled are immutable but that details and applications of principles in specific cases alone may change—is now brushed aside. . . .

"The members of the bar who have been reading the decisions of the five 'yes men' stand aghast. For they see a Court 'packed' with men who are engaging in the very practices Mr. Roosevelt so vehemently condemned —the writing of legislation. . . . They see the Court voting almost always as a unit on New Deal issues."

There has been a lot of misrepresentation of the current criticism of the Supreme Court. It is mistakenly argued that the attack is against the Supreme Court as an institution and that this tends to undermine the prestige of the Court.

Nobody can undermine the prestige of the Supreme Court of the United States except the Justices themselves.

By their decisions they twist the Constitution out of its accustomed and natural meaning, as they assume the power to legislate or as they supply words to the law and to the Constitution which never were there in the first instance. When they do this, they provoke widespread condemnation.

An effort is being made nowadays to make it appear that the criticism of the High Court is due wholly to its decision in the desegregation cases. This simply is not true. The report which was approved last summer by a vote of 36 to 8 by the Chief Justices of the State supreme courts did not even mention the segregation issue. It did accuse the High Court of a lack of "judicial self-restraint" and cited a long list of decisions in recent years to back up the indictment.

The trouble is not wholly in the Court itself. It is in the law schools, too, where many of the new cult hold sway. Students are taught that the Supreme Court need not respect the intent of Congress nor the decisions of the past but instead can at any time ignore the "law of the land" and issue its own amendments to the Constitution.

Up to recent years it was accepted that the Supreme Court should make an initial interpretation of the Constitution and, once this was proclaimed as the "law of the land," it would not be changed unless some new legal point was raised or new legislation passed by Congress or a new amendment added to the Constitution.

America didn't depend on Supreme Court decisions to change the Constitution in order to permit a federal income tax to be levied or woman suffrage to be adopted or prohibition to be imposed and later repealed. The people had an opportunity in each instance to vote on a constitutional amendment. This is as it should be.

But today we have what Judge Learned Hand of New York—perhaps the ablest of the Federal Circuit Court judges of our times, now retired—recently described as a "third legislative chamber."

Criticism of the Supreme Court is not only legitimate but essential to a free republic. There are voices heard which would stifle criticism and require of everybody a sycophantic obeisance.

It is healthy to discuss all phases of public questions. The American people have not yet been aroused to the dangers of judicial tyranny that face them. It is time to expose the true meaning of the philosophy of the cult which is teaching our youth that we no longer need to amend the Constitution and that the Supreme Court—nine Justices appointed for life—hereafter will perform that task for us.

How easy it is to fall into the ways of totalitarianism—to let an autocracy rule the people because presumably the people are unable to rule themselves!

The fight for constitutionalism must go on. Sam Gompers won his fight by public agitation, as Congress in 1932 passed the Norris-LaGuardia Act curbing the courts' jurisdiction over labor disputes by prohibiting injunctions in a large variety of cases.

Franklin Roosevelt won his fight when he appointed only those Justices that he knew were believers in an elastic Constitution which could be altered at any time to satisfy the whims of so-called "liberalism."

Unfortunately, the Presidents who have followed him, misled by some of the same cult in the Department of Justice, have selected several Justices known to be dedicated to the belief that the Supreme Court can rewrite the Constitution at will.

Thus, we have had 20 years of Court "packing"— and the time has come for the people to checkmate that practice by limiting its effects. This can be done by a constitutional amendment prescribing a limited tenure for Justices and requiring that, among their qualifications, they be experienced, not in party politics but at the bar or on the bench. Also, it should be provided in the Constitution itself that, once an initial interpretation is made by the Supreme Court, this interpretation can be changed only by a constitutional amendment when a provision of the Constitution is in dispute—or by a valid Act of Congress when a previous federal statute has been declared unconstitutional. This is the historic doctrine—known as *stare decisis* or "settled law"—bequeathed to us by the Founding Fathers.

WHAT DID THE PEOPLE SAY?

NOVEMBER 14, 1958

WHAT DID THE AMERICAN PEOPLE SAY by their votes in the congressional election last week?

Did they say they wanted more billions spent by the Government?

Did they say they favored appropriations for "welfare" purposes, even if it means inflation and a reduction in the purchasing power of the dollar?

Did they say that Quemoy and Matsu should be surrendered to the Communists and that the Red China Government should be recognized by us?

Did they say they wanted America to cut down or enlarge its foreign aid program?

Did they say the policies of the Administration toward our allies in Europe should be changed?

Did they say our policies toward the Soviet are wrong and should be modified to appease Moscow?

Did they say that the American armament program is not big enough or should be reduced because of the enormous expense to the taxpayers?

Did they say they wanted taxes lowered, no matter how much this might enlarge the present Treasury deficit of 12 billion dollars?

What did the electorate mean when it chose 282 Democrats for the House of Representatives and gave the Democrats 64 members of the Senate—the biggest majority in a quarter of a century? What platform was approved by the people, and how much did the voters know about its unwritten planks?

Where can responsibility be placed during the next two years for the conduct of the Government of the United States?

What shall the other nations be told—shall foreign governments look for guidance to those partisan members of the Senate Foreign Relations Committee who so often rush into print to express their capricious attitudes toward Administration policy in Europe, Asia and Latin America?

Plainly, what we have witnessed in the election last week is a tragic manifestation of irresponsibility in our system of government. A few more elections such as we've just had will inevitably move us toward a debacle like that which France has just encountered and which finally compelled a drastic revision of its Constitution.

Our Constitution should be amended so that when the people vote a party into power, the President of the United States shall be chosen along with the elected majority in Congress. Whether the election should be held every two years or every four years may be de-bated, but some formula must be established whereby a single party will be responsible for the leadership of both the executive and legislative branches of the Government. This has long been the custom in parliamentary governments abroad.

If we do not make such a change, one of our fixed election days will plague us some day in the midst of a dangerous crisis in international affairs, and the people may again find themselves electing the leader of one party to the White House and the members of the opposite party to a majority control of Congress. In an atomic age, this kind of contingency is unrealistic. It should be removed at once from even the realm of possibility.

Although the headlines have told us the "Democratic Party" obtained control of both Houses of Congress, such control is meaningless today in terms of party responsibility. For in the Southern States, no candidates from any opposing party were even nominated, except in a handful of districts.

The South, nevertheless, by virtue of the seniority system in Congress retains all the important chairmanships of committees in both Houses. Did the American people by their votes last week mean to approve this system?

Did the American people by their vote approve or disapprove the viewpoint of those Southern leaders who denounced the use of federal troops at Little Rock?

For four years now, the Southerners have been condemned by their Northern brethren as undemocratic and reactionary and as defiant of the Constitution itself on the vital issue of States' Rights vs. Federal control, usually referred to as "Civil Rights."

There is very little in common, moreover, between the economic philosophy of the Democrats of the South and that of the Democrats in the other regions of the country.

In reality, there are two Democratic Parties in the United States today and no system of party discipline exists within any party.

Our forefathers thought they were establishing a system of responsible government. The Constitution can be amended to give us such a system now.

The people today have no means of assuring themselves of a majority in Congress which will support a definite program that has been submitted in advance to the electorate in a congressional election.

What did the people really say by their votes last week? Who knows?

—AND WHAT ABOUT
INTERMARRIAGE?

NOVEMBER 21, 1958

THE CATHOLIC BISHOPS of America have again, by their annual pronouncement, given the people of all faiths something worthwhile to think about.

The statement just issued—full text on page 74—is an eloquent defense of the rights of Negroes. It is a powerful brief on the theory of equality. But it doesn't mention the basic question often raised in discussing actual equality—namely, intermarriage between white and colored.

The statement of the Bishops displays a spirit of tolerance toward opposing views. It rightly counsels "prudence" in any attempts to upset the traditions rooted in centuries of experience and customs.

There can, of course, be no persuasive dissent from the proposition that, so far as the state is concerned, all men should have equal opportunity and should enjoy equal rights of citizenship. There can be no disagreement either over the simple proposition that education is essential to good citizenship and that a good education is necessary to the fulfillment of economic opportunity. "Separate but equal" educational facilities was the "law of the land" for generations. The doctrine was affirmed as late as 1950 by the same Supreme Court Justices, with one exception, who reversed it in 1954.

But in the tragic problem of enforced integration in the public schools, we are not dealing solely with education. Were it simply a matter of transmitting information from books or teachers to this or that pupil, there would not be the furor today that has been raised over the segregation issue.

The truth should be faced, no matter how unpleasant the topic may seem. For the root of the whole problem is intermarriage. The people who oppose enforced integration regard school life as social life. In the November 7 issue of this magazine, a white girl who has just spent the last four years in an integrated high school in Milwaukee told of her experiences there. She did not recommend any particular solution but related objectively what she saw. What she observed was that in the social life of the school several of the white girls gradually began "dating" colored boys clandestinely out of school. The Milwaukee *Journal,* which approves integration, commended the girl's story and said she had attempted to be "factual and fair." (See page 10.)

In the November 14 issue of this magazine, an excerpt was published from a speech by Allan Nevins, long-time professor of American history at Columbia University and twice a Pulitzer Prize winner. In his enthusiasm for integration, he comes to grips boldly with the question of intermarriage. He says:

"In broad terms we must plan, North and South, to raise the Negro race to a plane in character, cultivation and manners where it will be entirely fit to intermarry with the white race.

"As a historian, I do not for a moment believe that, in our mighty American river of many nationalities, two currents can flow side by side down the centuries without ultimately becoming one.

"At first the fusion will be imperceptible; then it will be perceptible but slow; then it will move with a rush. I could cite a dozen analogies from history to prove that such a process is inexorable, irresistible. Any sociologist could cite a dozen reasons why it is inevitable."

The statement of the Catholic Bishops gives us no explicit advice on this point. Do they favor the encouragement of intermarriage of the races as between members of the Catholic faith? If they do, then what is the reasoning behind such a view? It is on this point that persons of all religious faiths need enlightenment, and it is regrettable that the chief objection to integration in the schools in the South, especially among the womenfolk, was not discussed.

The theory of integration, the theory of equality of the races in political and civil rights, is easy to rationalize and for most of us to accept but, as has often been said, it's a condition and not a theory that faces us. We need advice, and we must pray for guidance on the important question of how the problem of intermarriage shall be met.

Many people may not know it, but the Supreme Court of the United States, which is supposed to proclaim the "law of the land," has ruled that the existing laws of several States forbidding marriages between white and colored persons are constitutional.

How then can the statement of the Catholic Bishops help to meet this sociological problem as well as the constitutional issues that trouble so many people in the South who are receptive to the ideals ably expounded by the Catholic Bishops? It is to be hoped that some religious group will soon give us the answer as to how to put these ideals into practice.

WHITHER AMERICA?

NOVEMBER 28, 1958

WHAT IS THE DESTINY of America in the world? How can we best serve mankind and at the same time keep from dissipating our energies and our resources?

These questions go to the heart of public policy today. They are not solely international. They also challenge the fundamentals of domestic policy.

For what doth it profit a nation to seek laurels abroad if it forsake its ideals at home?

We have in America today two basic philosophies at work inside our two political parties.

One philosophy is that the end justifies the means—that the attainment of a meritorious objective must be compelled even if this means disregard of a written Constitution.

The other philosophy holds true to the principles on which this Republic was founded—that we must have a "government of laws" and not yield to the concept of a "government of men." Progress in government achieved at the expense of a violated contract inspires no faith or spirit of permanence. It fluctuates with the will of the mob. The intolerance of majorities has throughout history left in its wake a casualty list of human freedoms destroyed.

Too many people in America today would indignantly disavow any thought of totalitarianism, but they are often ready to accept some of its ways. They cry out that the process of amending the Constitution is too cumbersome or "time-consuming." They do not advocate, as they could, a change in the method of amending the Constitution as already prescribed in that document itself. They prefer usurpation instead—even the seizure of a whole industry to curry favor with labor leaders or the use of federal troops to enforce a sociological doctrine. It is defended as a quicker process. So is dictatorship.

Too many people believe that the writing of laws should not be confined to Congress but that the Supreme Court of the United States must legislate. Many of the professors in our law schools and many of their deans are resentful of any criticism of the Court and say frankly that it is up to the Court to reconcile the past with the present—to take care of evolution and "adapt" the Constitution to changing conditions.

This is reminiscent of the speech which Hitler made in the 1930s when, after accepting election under the legal process of the German Constitution, he proclaimed that the courts should take into account "public sentiment" in writing their decisions.

We have today many perplexing problems to solve in America. We have severe competition now with goods made abroad, where labor is cheaper and trade unions have no such economic power to raise prices as they have here in the United States.

We fought successfully for decades against monopoly by corporations, but today we have in our midst a far worse monopoly power in the labor unions. The unions win political elections by the expenditure of many millions of dollars. They influence a sufficient percentage of voters to swing elections. Labor unions have become a sort of supergovernment.

We have also a serious problem in combating the inflationary trend that has come upon us. We have taxes that are almost confiscatory and a 12-billion-dollar deficit this year.

How can we assume, as some critics repeatedly suggest, that "bold and imaginative ideas"—which means American money for the underdeveloped nations—are all that's necessary to make American leadership supreme and thus counteract Soviet infiltration?

We must continue certainly to spend billions for armament so as to deter a potential enemy. This in itself is draining our resources and frustrating our normal progress. We cannot, however, take on the support of all the rest of the world, too.

There are some things we can do in world trade and through developmental loans, but these should be largely by private capital. The era of lavish expenditure in the form of grants and gifts is about over. It is time to take a good look at internal America and put our own house in order.

Unless we start now to readjust our domestic position, we shall have a depression in the next five years that will weaken our world position. This is not a time for starry-eyed sprees in "welfare" spending.

It is a time, moreover, to examine critically the functioning of our system of government.

It is a time for a crusade to restore the constitutional system our forefathers gave us and to use it as they prescribed. For if we give up government by law and yield to government by the caprice of individuals, we shall destroy the American Republic and find ourselves surrendering gradually to the totalitarian concepts of our chief adversaries.

The best way to advance American leadership abroad is by maintaining solvency and adhering to constitutional government at home. Then we will by example prove that the United States is succeeding and will continue to succeed as a great republic.

EVERY DAY IS THANKSGIVING DAY

DECEMBER 5, 1958

ON THE THANKSGIVING DAY just passed, did we remember to give thanks to Divine Providence for all the many blessings bestowed upon us as a nation? To name only a few:

Thanks for the avoidance of war and the continuance of peace.

Thanks for the absence of famine in our country and the abundance of food.

Thanks for the unexampled health of the nation—for the Salk vaccine, for the progress of cancer research, and for the great advances being made in the field of medicine to relieve many forms of illness.

Thanks for the steady improvement in our standard of living.

Thanks for the increase in living comforts—for those products of inventive genius and the techniques of mass distribution so necessary to an expanding population.

Thanks for the achievements in communication—the miraculous benefits of the telephone, the radio and television.

Thanks for the airplane, the railroad locomotive and the automobile and for what they have meant to the transport of goods as well as to the enjoyment of travel by the whole family.

Thanks for the public spirit of the many individuals in our midst who conduct the drives for charity and for the unselfishness which animates the people who respond to these appeals.

Thanks for the dedicated men who serve in our armed forces ready at a moment's notice to make the supreme sacrifice.

Thanks for the decent, incorruptible men and women in the labor unions who so conscientiously strive to help their fellow man.

Thanks for the courage of the legislators who have exposed the corruption and misuse of power by certain leaders and their henchmen in labor unions.

Thanks for the many humane employers who do care about the welfare of their employes.

Thanks for the fraternal spirit that stimulates free men everywhere.

Thanks for the enduring ties with our allies—closer than ever before.

Thanks for the widespread recognition of the difference between human slavery and human freedom—and for the moral support being extended constantly to the millions of people who are captives of dictatorship in various parts of the world.

Thanks for the unsung heroes in the government service—in the townships and villages, in the cities, in the counties and in the States as well as in our National Government—and for the service they render us all.

Thanks for the guardians of the law who risk their lives in fighting fire, in fighting crime, in fighting the hidden subversive that could destroy us from within.

Thanks for those judges who do dispense justice uninfluenced by the passions of party or faction or by the caprice of power.

Thanks for the men and women who teach in our schools—inspired only by devotion to the single cause of a trained youth.

Thanks for those who serve in our hospitals and institutions, caring for the sick and the handicapped.

Thanks for the devoted persons in the priesthood and in the convents and in the ministry of all churches who heed our calls in hours of anguish.

Thanks for the parents who do not neglect their growing children in order to pursue their own pleasures, but who recognize that juvenile delinquency must in large part be due to adult delinquency.

Thanks for the thrifty among us who save and by their example teach others to conserve during the days of plenty in order to meet the exigencies of days of scarcity.

Thanks for the many voices of reason that rise above the din, mistaking not the noisy clamor of the mob for the true will of a God-loving people.

Thanks for the freedoms proclaimed in the Bill of Rights.

Thanks for the opportunity to debate without fear the most controversial issues of the day.

Thanks for the men of deep conviction who do not regard the winning of an election as in itself worth the sacrifice of principle to expediency.

Thanks for the continuing benefits we receive each year from the teachings of our forefathers—particularly the written Constitution that must guide the nation as we try to solve current problems at home and abroad through the processes of reason.

Thanks for those churchmen whose voices rise above the secular bedlam as they encourage us to seek Divine guidance.

Thanks for helping us to maintain an unswerving belief in the innate morality of man and in the tenets of our Judeo-Christian philosophy.

Every day can be Thanksgiving Day.

THE "MESS" IN THE WORLD

DECEMBER 19, 1958

The thoughts here expressed are in response to a letter from the minister of the First Congregational Church in a Kansas town. He writes that, when he is called upon to address various organizations and it comes time for the question period, many people ask: "Why is the world in such a mess and what can we do to build a better world?"

THE WORLD IS IN A MESS—if by this is meant the threat of war and of large-scale destruction of human beings.

The world is in a "mess"—if we concede that human ingenuity and human reason have failed to bring acceptance of a universal morality and that we are to be entirely dependent instead on physical force and armed might for self-preservation.

What can we do to build a better world? No one person and no one government is alone responsible for the "mess"—nor just our own generation. There is no lack of knowledge of the elements that cause human friction and no lack of emphasis on the need to heal the wounds of friction. The unanswered question, written in large letters on the pages of history, is: When shall we do the things we know must be done to change the millions of individuals who are indifferent to their own God-given power?

Do we doubt that a hostile autocracy threatens the survival of free nations?

Do we doubt that a nation of millions, acting together, can at any time unseat an unscrupulous dictator who has ruled them?

Do we doubt that an army will turn away from a leader who is found disloyal to the best interests of his people?

Do we doubt the power of any people to choose their own rulers when they do decide to manifest their concerted will?

Obviously people can protest a dictatorship or acquiesce in its tyranny. What then will prompt them to reach the decision to rule themselves? Will education do it? Will information about the hardships of their fellow men do it? Will the threat of war do it?

Many people nowadays seem too much concerned with materialistic goals and not enough with the spiritual obligations of everyday living. As long as people go their separate ways believing that somehow government is a thing apart and that, by waving a magic wand, it can cause stormy waters to become still, there will be indifference to the "mess." But sometimes we mistake inaction for acquiescence. There comes a time when tyranny goes beyond the point of endurance. The instinct to freedom is ingrained in all of us, irrespective of geography.

Nations are collections of individuals. Inherently the people of the Soviet Union are like us in America—they have the same dread of war, the same love of peace and the same desire for freedom. Our concept of morality may not be the same as it is on other continents. What is the maximum good for the maximum number may be one thing in Christian countries and quite another in non-Christian areas. But fundamentally man everywhere believes in a higher influence than his own—at least, he accepts death as the terminal point of his earthly power.

We meet on common ground, therefore, as we face destruction by nuclear weapons. There are ingenious defenses, to be sure, in the offing, but nothing is certain now except that millions of human beings can be destroyed in a matter of minutes.

International peace rests on national peace. And national peace rests on individual peace.

This means peace of mind as between the conflicting demands in America of a life enriched by many blessings but tortured by many worries about what is going on overseas, even as our hearts and consciences are touched by the poverty of our fellow human beings in various parts of the world.

We have the simple duty to become better individuals—more useful individuals—so that our nation may be more effective in partnership with other nations. We have, of course, an obligation to the human family. And we can help other peoples—but they must help themselves, too. We are still our brother's keeper —but sometimes our brother needs a forthright mentor as much as he needs material things. He must learn to do certain things for himself if he is to win the co-operation of people in other countries.

There is an answer to the "mess." It will come to us through the spiritual regeneration of the individual, irrespective of race or creed or color. God moves in strange ways His wonders to perform. His challenge to us today in a nuclear era is plain enough. When will we begin to apply the doctrine of unselfishness that has been so clearly indicated to us?

As we make of ourselves better individuals, so shall we make a better world.

We have courageous leaders. We need courageous followers. Regeneration begins at home.

1959

SAVE THE DOLLAR!

JANUARY 2, 1959

THE DOLLAR is the symbol of America's strength in a world where there is uneasiness nowadays about the future of the currencies of several nations.

Furthermore, no monetary unit anywhere would be safe from decline if the dollar's value started downhill.

World trade would be demoralized, and many of our own factories that sell goods for export would be forced to lay off millions of employes.

Even more important is the dollar's purchasing power at home. If prices start soaring, wage increases cannot be expected immediately to offset the rise in living costs. There are millions of persons, moreover, including government workers, who are unable to get increased incomes quickly enough to keep pace with the rising prices.

It is gratifying, therefore, to read the announcement by President Eisenhower that he will request Congress to maintain a balanced budget in the coming fiscal year, and that he will recommend holding the line against increased expenditures—a decline in the budget spending of more than $2,200,000,000.

Lately in different parts of the world suspicion has been expressed that the dollar is weakening. In last week's issue of this magazine there was printed the full text of an address by William McChesney Martin, Jr., Chairman of the Federal Reserve Board, on the importance of maintaining a stable dollar. Discussing his trip abroad, he said:

"One distressing experience was to find among intelligent and perceptive men in those countries a growing distrust over the future of the American dollar. . . .

"To the foreigner, much more than to Americans, the dollar is the symbol of this country's strength. A decline in the value of the dollar would suggest to him a decline in the faith and credit of the United States, signaling in his mind a decline not only in American economic strength but also in moral force. Naturally I was interested in the basis of distrust.

"Two matters appeared uppermost. One was the conviction that, not necessarily at the moment but in a fairly short time and more markedly in the extending future, American goods are going to find themselves priced out of the market.

"Indeed, I was told that some countries to which we have made loans conditioned upon the purchase of American goods would, except for that restriction, already be turning elsewhere for their purchases.

"You will recall that this same sort of talk was directed at Britain for about a year before the British got into trouble and had to devalue the pound sterling. . . .

"The other thing cited to me as a reason for foreign distrust of America's ability or will to preserve the buying power of the dollar was the 12-billion-dollar deficit that has developed in the United States budget, plus possibilities that further deficits may follow. It was amazing to me how closely our budgetary developments were being followed in such remote areas as Thailand and Hong Kong, and how many people there knew our precise budget figures better than most Americans."

Mr. Martin might have added that Hong Kong is a speculative center where fluctuations in world currencies have been meticulously watched for decades.

But if the dollar is in trouble, it is not alone because of our budgetary deficits. It is because our price level is being driven upward in the most reckless wage-price spiral which the United States has ever experienced.

The American people can apply a check to the "spenders" in Congress by threatening to defeat legislators who refuse to vote for curtailed expenditures, and who insist on their pet extravagances. But, what can the people do to check the irresponsibility of labor unions?

We have, in effect, a super-government—a labor union monopoly that ignores the public interest, as it seeks selfishly to extort more and more, even from companies that are operating in the red. The strikes on the airlines and the shutting down of all the newspapers in New York City are examples of a shocking disregard of the simple laws of economics.

The President must take the lead in calling for a labor-management conference. Public opinion must assert itself. There are three parties to every labor dispute—the employers, the unions and the public. The President can speak for the public and, if restrictive legislation becomes necessary, Congress must begin to act for the public.

The dollar must be saved from a further decline in its purchasing power. Fixed incomes received by millions of citizens each week are at stake. So also is the whole American economic system. Unless private capital can be accumulated steadily under a stable price level, job creation is impaired.

We have reached the climax in the battle between the "spenders" and the "savers." It's a fight to maintain a stable dollar. It's a fight against the organized greed of pressure groups. It vitally concerns every man, woman and child in America.

DO WE REALLY GOVERN OURSELVES?

JANUARY 9, 1959

THE BOAST IS OFTEN MADE that we govern ourselves. But do we? Is the will of the majority always expressed? Who represents the "public interest," for instance, in a labor dispute?

The fact is that any organized minority can damage the public interest and go scot-free.

Crimes against individuals or wrongs done to them are punishable by law, but an organized group can damage the public to the extent of hundreds of millions of dollars, causing inconvenience and hardship to a community, but neither the Federal Government nor the State Government nor the city government customarily does anything about it.

For, when there is a strike affecting the lives and welfare of citizens throughout the country, such as the stoppage of operation of several airlines or of the publication of all the newspapers in the biggest city in America, no law or instrument of the law is utilized to protect the public interest.

This is not self-government. It is a form of anarchy. Indeed, it is a kind of supergovernment by a minority which, under the slogan of "the right to strike," now can override the public interest while the majority of the people appear helpless to apply a remedy.

In the last election campaign, six States sought to enact "right to work" laws so that individuals need not belong to a union in order to keep their jobs. But the labor unions spent millions of dollars for propaganda to distort the issue and to persuade many voters that the measure was really aimed at self-organization.

There is every reason to encourage collective bargaining by the workers. No provision of law interferes now or should ever interfere with the right of a majority in a plant to select their own leaders and their representatives to negotiate with the employer. But the minority have rights, too. No contract should be lawful which coerces the employer into firing any worker who, for conscientious reasons of his own, does not wish to join a labor organization.

Actually, it was the indifference of millions of citizens which defeated the "right to work" proposals in five States. Evidently the public interest must suffer a great deal more before a lethargic electorate will begin to see clearly the monopoly power usurped by the labor unions.

There is also an even more vital reason for the reform. The members of a union must not only be permitted the right of protest which goes with the right to resign from the organization without penalty, but they also must be given by law the opportunity to hold frequent elections so as to exercise a check upon leaders who do not effectively or honorably represent them.

In the strike which stopped the publication of all New York City's newspapers—accomplishing what, under the Constitution, no law of Congress may bring about, namely, the suppression of any newspaper—a flagrant weakness in our governmental system was exposed. This emerged also in the airline strikes. It is the failure of the public interest to attain priority over the private interest of organized minorities.

Federal mediation was applied in all these instances. But mediation without any compelling force behind it to require acceptance is not always effective.

Should we, therefore, enact laws providing for compulsory arbitration in labor disputes? This, too, has its disadvantages. The selection of arbitrators sometimes is affected by political influences. Confidence in arbitration is not as high as it used to be, mostly because it is not easy to be assured of impartial arbitrators. Panels of arbitrators, however, can be set up by a governmental process to overcome this difficulty.

We need laws, moreover, to provide for government seizure of plants when there is a hopeless deadlock in labor negotiations. The airlines are governed by the Railway Labor Act, which contains no provision for seizure and government operation. The Taft-Hartley Act, which does not cover common carriers, provides for court injunctions to prevent a strike only during an 80-day "cooling off" period.

While government seizure and operation in an emergency is not a desirable alternative to settlement by the parties themselves, it is better than allowing severe damage to be inflicted upon the public.

There are often, to be sure, what seem to be irreconcilable differences. The desire for equitable settlement is not always found on the side of the union or of the employer. The public has the superior right—to require continued service in an essential industry. This means, in extreme cases, an imposed settlement before and not after the damage has been done.

The American people are supposed to govern themselves. They do in most things, but apparently not where organized economic groups usurp the power of government itself.

How long are we to continue to acquiesce in domestic anarchy? When will the people really begin to govern themselves in the economic domain?

REACHING FOR THE MOON

JANUARY 16, 1959

As we reach for the moon, shall we lose the battle on earth? Will moon-gazing become a national pastime? The game is harmless so long as it is confined to those tired souls who long to get away from their earthly chores, but it becomes harmful indeed when we are asked to spend billions of dollars to win a stunt contest in outer space.

Laudable is the spirit of patriotism which seeks to win every race for our country. But we haven't always won the Olympics, and we have managed to adjust our lives to such ephemeral disappointments.

Military values are preeminent. Whatever is necessary to test out guidance systems for missiles must have a proper place in our defense budget. But a contest in launching satellites merely to outdo the Soviets makes little sense.

The "Sputniks" last year threw us off our course and started a wave of spending in Congress. It is to be hoped that the psychological effect of the "Luniks" will not be such as to open the floodgates to more indiscriminate expenditures for the spinning of metal balls in orbit around the sun or the moon.

Many members of Congress seem to have become intrigued with the possibilities of space travel. They look upon the competition of our scientists with those of the Soviet Union as a gripping matter deserving priority above all else.

But the fact remains that the votes which elect our Representatives and Senators are to be found among the peoples living on the firm ground of the 49 States of the Union—not in outer space.

There is great need for a down-to-earth point of view in the present Congress. All the artificial planets that whirl around the sun will not create employment here in America where there is unemployment, nor bring taxes down from their painful heights, nor stop the raids on the American dollar.

The most important task for our legislators today is to conserve the economic strength of the United States of America. We are engaged in a "cold war" of frightening proportions. The war of missiles and nuclear bombs may never take place, but the economic war throughout the world is actually in progress now on a dozen fronts and on every continent.

This is not just a matter of distributing grants of money to buy allies, but of assuring economic stability for the United States, too. The world is a trade unit. We are dependent on continuing trade arrangements that encourage the sale of our domestic production in various parts of the world and that make possible the purchase abroad of materials needed for use here in our own country.

Our biggest concern today is the constant infiltration by the Moscow regime in certain countries of the free world by means of loans and by barter exchange of commodities. We are witnessing an economic war such as the world has never known. The stakes are high. It could mean political control of vast areas for the Communists. Their strategy is to burrow in and subvert the recipients of Soviet favors.

Once our own fiscal position is improved, we can look forward to using more and more funds to check the Soviet advances on the economic front in Asia, Africa and Europe, as well as in Latin America. This is not a battle that will be settled in one year—it is a struggle that will last for many years to come.

There is already a significant counteroffensive being made by the free world with financial weapons. The expansion of the various governmental lending agencies—such as the World Bank, the International Monetary Fund, the Export-Import Bank and the new Development Loan Fund, for which Congress has been appropriating relatively small sums—will mean a multiplication of private loans. The way is being opened in several countries already to sound development where foreign credit is needed and can be repaid.

But all this can be nullified unless there is respect for integrity of contracts. It is discouraging to find a government, such as the new one in Venezuela, becoming hostile to American investors after they have for decades poured their savings into that country.

If the end result after an era of lending is the emergence of nationalistic governments which, under Communist prodding, repudiate their obligations and welsh on their commitments to foreign property-owners, private investors will be discouraged from again risking their savings.

Moral standards apply to nations—they must respect property, for it is never right to rob Peter to pay Paul.

We have many perplexing problems to solve in the economic field today. These involve down-to-earth questions of great difficulty. It is not a time for moon-gazing. We have plenty of work to do on earth.

Congress might well bear in mind that it is the people of the United States whose interests are paramount and that just now we are engaged in a battle for survival on this planet and not in the vapors of outer space.

CUBA'S TRAGIC ERA

JANUARY 23, 1959

CUBA WON HER INDEPENDENCE from Spain 60 years ago with the aid of the troops of the United States.

During the years that have since elapsed, Cuba has had some free governments and some dictatorships.

The United States for a long time exercised a kind of guardianship over the island under the so-called Platt Amendment, through which Cuba gave this country the right to intervene with arms at any time to maintain order.

The Cuban people, believing that they had achieved maturity and could govern themselves, persuaded the United States in 1934 to abandon the Platt Amendment, which had previously been a part of the Cuban constitution.

As Cuba prospered—and the financial investments of foreign companies of all kinds increased—the stakes in the possession of governmental power among the Cubans also became higher. Political groups vied with one another for control of Cuba. It is unhappily true that, by intrigue and a disregard of constitutional methods, dictators came into control of Cuba. They maintained order. They curried favor with the State Department in Washington through the influence at times of American companies anxious, for business reasons, to see an existing regime sustained.

Batista was a dictator of the kind frequently found in Latin America. He carried on friendly relations with foreign governments but he ruled internally with an iron hand. The inevitable reaction finally came in the revolution led by Fidel Castro.

The Government of the United States, faced with the problem two weeks ago of whether to extend or withhold recognition, decided to begin formal diplomatic relations with the provisional government established by the revolutionists.

Today millions of people in the United States wish that recognition had not been extended so precipitately. They feel that there should have been a period of waiting—to see how the new regime would behave.

The newspaper headlines throughout the world told last week of the wanton murder of hundreds of Cubans, many of them civilian officials of the Batista administration. Whether they were guilty, as charged, of cruelties to other Cubans hostile to them cannot be known, for they were not given any trials in courts of law.

Can any influence in behalf of the use of judicial institutions be exerted at a time of revolutionary reprisals? Is it not the function of a government like ours to exhibit such concern and to manifest plainly the solicitude of the whole civilized world?

We should not, of course, intervene with military force unless the lives of our citizens are placed in jeopardy.

But we do have opportunities to help the new government or to indicate our disfavor. It involves risks. Events that give rise to a counter-revolution could result from the assumption by the United States of a detached and neutral position. For there are in such circumstances groups always ready to take advantage of the weakness of a revolutionary regime when it is in its incipient stages of organization.

The United States in 1913, under President Wilson, proclaimed a policy of non-recognition of any government that came into power as a result of military force. Within a decade later this policy was reversed and the old rule of diplomacy, which extends recognition to the government in military control of an area, was once more adopted.

It has always seemed to this writer that a distinction should be drawn between "de facto" and "de jure" recognition. In the former case, military control by a faction or party is accepted as a fact and diplomatic relations are carried on by subordinate members of a legation or embassy. When, later on, an election has been held and the people have by constitutional means indicated their support of an established government, then "de jure" recognition—an acceptance of the lawful government—can be proclaimed by our own government and other governments of like mind.

When full recognition is extended, an ambassador or minister would be sent to the new government. It would be notice to the whole world that a demonstration has been given of the capacity of a new government to honor international obligations.

The principle of "de facto" recognition applied to Cuba could mean delay in sending an ambassador until it is plainly evident that the new government is capable of discharging international obligations. Manifestly, a government that violates the traditions of human freedom—by failing even to give a trial to those accused of crime—is not stable enough to warrant the belief that it can protect the lives and property of American citizens.

Why shouldn't all the governments of Central and South America be asked to support means of dealing with the problem of recognition in states emerging from revolution? Such a discussion now could have a salutary effect in Cuba and elsewhere in Latin America.

"FAREWELL, MURDERER!"

JANUARY 30, 1959

ANASTAS MIKOYAN was not officially invited to visit the United States. He obtained a visa for the purpose of visiting the Soviet Embassy in Washington.

But, for all practical purposes, the journey was a carefully planned maneuver by the Soviet Government adroitly designed to test out whether the American people, by their overwhelming vote against the Republican Party in the last congressional election, had in fact repudiated the leadership of President Eisenhower in world affairs. If so, then, by driving a wedge between the American people and their Government, the Soviets hoped to pursue their campaign to oust allied forces from West Berlin and gain another victory in the "cold war."

A Democratic Senator assured the Soviet Deputy Premier that there is unity in Congress on world policy.

Mikoyan was feted by some businessmen and some labor leaders. He was, on the whole, treated courteously by the people. He was given lengthy audiences by the President and the Secretary of State. The American press gave him headlines and plenty of space, as did television and radio.

But, while our government officials were scrupulously polite because they had to be, it is a matter of considerable puzzlement that the American press fell down so badly in exposing Mikoyan. Only here and there did editorials appear referring to the record which shows his hands dripping with the blood of Hungarian patriots.

Basil Brewer, publisher of the New Bedford, Mass., "Standard-Times," felt so badly about the lack of attention to the facts that he bought advertising space in several newspapers in the East to reprint his editorial entitled "This Monster, Mikoyan." The editorial said in part:

"Deputy Premier Mikoyan was sent to Budapest to take charge for Moscow, when the freedom-fighters deposed the puppet regime and set up a new government under Premier Imre Nagy.

"On Oct. 31, 1956, Mikoyan personally assured Zoltan Tildy, minister of state of the new Hungarian Government, that Soviet troops would be withdrawn from Hungary. This welcome news was announced over the Budapest radio by General Maleter, defense minister in the new Hungarian Government, and reported from free-world news correspondents on the scene.

"Even as Mikoyan gave his pledge, however, he was calling for Soviet troop reinforcements to mass outside Hungary, in preparation for the attack of Nov. 3-4.

"Having put the Hungarian leadership off guard, Mikoyan arranged a series of conferences between Soviet and Hungarian military leaders, 'to plan the withdrawal.' After several sessions, an emergency 'parley' was arranged for 10 p. m. Nov. 3, at Soviet military headquarters outside Budapest.

"Once inside the conference room, General Maleter and his aides were arrested, and, immediately, the signal was given for a massive Soviet tank and infantry attack on Budapest. While Premier Nagy, unaware of the trap, implored over the radio for General Maleter to return to his post, the Soviet forces moved in for the kill.

"A few days later, with Mikoyan still in full charge for Moscow, Nagy himself was tricked into leaving asylum in the Yugoslav embassy and taken prisoner.

"Mikoyan's vital role in this bloody chapter of history has not been as widely reported as it should have been. The Soviet Government has never mentioned it, and witnesses who would have testified to it have gone—by death in the fighting, by deportation and by execution. The voices of General Maleter and Premier Nagy were silenced by firing squad. As is his custom, Mikoyan tried to leave no trace!

"It is an insult to the American people for this arch-murderer Mikoyan to pretend to be a good-will ambassador to the United States. Only disaster can come from American businessmen and officials fawning over this Machiavellian monster."

Our State Department has confirmed the facts related above.

The Soviet Deputy Premier surely didn't convert many American businessmen. Most of them attended the social functions out of curiosity.

Why, however, was Mikoyan given the "red carpet" treatment by any private organizations or persons? Why were the few pickets and demonstrators who did appear reprimanded in our press?

Can it be that we haven't enough proof yet of the perfidy of the Communist regime? President Eisenhower did not hesitate to say in his message to Congress just after Mikoyan arrived:

"We have learned the bitter lesson that international agreements, historically considered by us as sacred, are regarded in Communist doctrine and in practice to be mere scraps of paper."

That's why we cannot trust the Soviet regime. That's why we must remain armed to the teeth.

Recalling the tragedy in Hungary, we say to our departed "guest" Mikoyan: "Farewell, Murderer!"

TOWARD PEACE

FEBRUARY 6, 1959

THE GENERAL TREND in the world is toward peace. The mere pronouncements of high purpose by various governmental spokesmen here and in Europe do not alone assure peace. Nor do the rival boasts of missile strength or of adequate defense against new weapons.

It is rather the certainty of almost total destruction in war that is accepted now as a realistic fact.

Two powers, each possessing war-making strength of unprecedented proportions, have achieved what used to be known as a "balance of power," but which today is being called a "balance of terror."

A big fear, however, is of accidental war.

There is only one way to deal with such a contingency—it is to make sure that there is rigid control by the governments possessing missiles and nuclear weapons so as to insure against accidents.

This very subject has been discussed by the major powers in international conferences. A parley on the problem of "surprise attack" has been going on intermittently as a natural sequel to what military experts pointed out in articles in this magazine a few years ago. They argued that America must not be compelled to take the "first blow." At the time it was erroneously assumed by some critics that this involved the concept of "preventive war." Actually, it concerns another doctrine, termed "pre-emptive war," and, since this has been adopted officially as the military strategy of the Soviet Union, it was necessary to examine it in the recent conference at Geneva, which was unfortunately suspended by the Soviets.

Under the "pre-emptive war" theory, a nation claims that it is not itself inflicting the "first blow" as an aggressor, but is deploying its forces outside its own boundaries to intercept or forestall an expected "first blow" from the enemy.

For many months now the air forces of the United States have been kept constantly in the air outside our boundaries on reconnaissance missions designed to help intercept an attack.

Oddly enough, in international forums more emphasis has been placed on the dangers of "fall-out" from atomic tests than on the hazards of bomber forces constantly operating near rival boundaries.

The truth is that all the new inventions in the missile category and the improvement in the destructive power of nuclear weapons have only served to accentuate the simple point that the weapons themselves are not the real problem. It's the hand that can pull the trigger which imperils mankind.

Whether America is or is not behind in missile development has been lately argued in committees of Congress and in the headlines. We are assured by the President that the basis of measurement should not be a particular category of weapons but the total strength of all our defensive weapons at a given time.

Our military chiefs are confident of the capability of the United States today to inflict such destruction from our bases in different parts of the world as to deter the enemy from starting a conflict. Despite the overtones of challenge in the discussion nowadays, the basic fact is that enough weapons are already available to inflict destruction. No new inventions are needed from that standpoint unless they help to cut down the perennial expense of preparing for what a British statesman once called "organized murder."

The debate over preparations for a missile war has its frightening aspects but, as people everywhere become informed on the certainty of terrible devastation of whole countries, the pressure for restraint grows.

The over-all progress toward peace is difficult to measure in times when the biggest emphasis is on the deadliness of weapons. Actually, there now is even greater progress, slow though it be, in bringing peoples closer together. The press and radio are persistently trying to break down barriers in communication. Despotic rulers may talk arrogantly, but at heart they fear the power of peoples. As the story of what war can do percolates more and more, the power of the populace to restrain arbitrary rulers will grow. It is already growing fast even behind the Iron Curtain. The Moscow rulers keep assuring and reassuring their people every day that they are striving for peace. They can't do otherwise and stay in office.

Though at times it is imperceptible, there is real progress toward peace. It is the product of a moral force in the world that is steadily advancing. Such growth is less spectacular than the performance of missiles, but it is nonetheless effective in keeping a major war from breaking out and in applying restraints even in the areas where a "limited war" might develop into a world war.

We may give thanks that debate throughout the world is producing some tangible results in a wider and wider understanding of the terrible menace to mankind that has arisen through the prolonged acquiescence of the Soviet people in a one-man government which has the decision power to destroy us all.

SEND MENSHIKOV HOME— RECALL OUR AMBASSADOR!

FEBRUARY 13, 1959

WE HAVE REACHED the end of the line with the present government of the Soviet Union. Diplomatic relations no longer are of any practical value.

When a government—through its Deputy Premier, through its Foreign Office and through its accredited Ambassador—lies repeatedly to another government, there can be no trust in any promise or pledge or so-called "agreement" emanating from such a regime.

Ever since September 2 last, when 17 American airmen were deliberately murdered as their unarmed transport strayed a few miles over Russia due to a navigational error, the United States has been trying to elicit the facts from the Soviet Government.

The Moscow regime, its Deputy Premier and its Ambassador in Washington have persistently disclaimed any knowledge, except that the plane crashed and that six bodies were recovered.

Yet, in an aviation journal published in the Soviet Union, about two weeks after the episode last September, there is given in detail an account of a so-called "practice" mission which parallels in large part what actually happened when the American transport was shot down. The same information and almost identical radio conversations between the attacking pilots were recorded on a tape—obtained by American authorities through its efficient intelligence system—at the exact time and place that the American plane went down.

This tape recording tells in dramatic manner how the American plane was shot down even though it was fully recognized as an unarmed transport, and hence entitled to be guided to a safe landing. But the recording of the conversation of the Soviet flyers shows also how they gloated over the murder of the American airmen. All the evidence and the written transcript of the tape recording was presented last November directly to Soviet Ambassador Menshikov in Washington.

When Soviet Deputy Premier Mikoyan came to this country in January, he was asked specifically by Vice President Nixon and Secretary Dulles about the facts uncovered in the tape recording. The State Department declared last week in a formal statement concerning the Mikoyan conference with Mr. Dulles:

"Mr. Mikoyan said that the Soviet Government had done all that it could, that all the bodies had been returned and that the Soviet Government did not know about any other personnel. . . . He denied that the plane had been shot down, asserting that it had crashed."

How can any government in the Western world—in the face of the evidence presented—any longer do business with the Soviet regime? Of what use are "new ideas" or the historic devices of diplomacy itself when dealing with a crooked government? Of what avail are "summit conferences" or tours of Soviet Russia by high officials of the West?

The time has come for the United States to take the lead in cutting off all diplomatic relations with the barbaric dynasty that rules in Moscow.

The time has come for the United States to urge all its allies to do likewise and to embargo all trade with the Soviet empire.

There is no need to go to war—ostracism is a salutary alternative. There is every reason to isolate the Soviet regime and, applying the words of the late President Franklin Roosevelt, to impose a "quarantine" on the Moscow government. Had such a course been followed by our allies in the 1930s the Hitler government would never have gotten the munitions it needed so acutely in order to build up its war machine.

America has been studiously patient. The facts about the tape recording were available to the Soviet Government as far back as last November. The United States tried for months, quietly and without publicity or the display of public emotion, to get the Soviet Government to co-operate at least in establishing the facts—the discussion of responsibility for the error of the unarmed transport could come later.

Most insulting of all, however, was the attitude of Ambassador Menshikov in his meeting with the Deputy Under Secretary of State, Robert Murphy, on November 13 last. The State Department's indictment says:

"Mr. Murphy said that it was Ambassador Menshikov's responsibility, as Soviet Ambassador to the United States, to listen to the representations that were being made to him. The Soviet Ambassador nonetheless refused to listen to the tape recording."

Why should the United States continue to deal with any Ambassador who shows such discourtesy to the government to which he is accredited? Why should we keep an American Ambassador in Moscow who is refused information about the cold-blooded murder of 17 American citizens?

Millions of Americans would answer: Send Menshikov home—recall our Ambassador!

"HUMAN VALUES"

FEBRUARY 20, 1959

PRESIDENT EISENHOWER was asked at his press conference last week whether, in view of his limited recommendation on school aid, he had decided that "it's more dangerous to unbalance the budget now than to run the risk of more inadequately educated citizens later." The interrogator suggested that Mr. Eisenhower differentiate between "difficult fiscal values and human values."

The President said, first of all, that he isn't sure there can be such a differentiation. He then added:

"The human values in America are not going to be promoted unless we are sane and sensible in our fiscal policies. . . . I know of nothing that could injure more the great population—174,000,000 people—we have got, than to allow the budgetary process to get out of control, fiscal measures going loosely, in such a way that inflation would absolutely be inevitable."

There seems no question but that every lobby is pressing Congress today for more funds. Each claims the right to assert that "human values" are above all other values.

But what really are the overriding values in the controversy over whether the budget shall continue to go unbalanced? Oddly enough, there isn't any agitation for a surplus, to be used to pay off debt. The drive seems to be to spend more than the Government takes in. Nor are there any signs yet of proposals for higher taxes so as to get the necessary revenues to balance the budget or to meet any increase in expenditures.

Are those "spenders" who really are pursuing a course that could lead to national bankruptcy thinking at all of basic "human values"? Are they aware of what has happened in past history as governments have spent money—and printed more and more paper money—for expenditures that seemingly were to benefit the community but resulted later only in hardships to the individual and indescribable tragedy to the populace as a whole?

We should re-read the story of what happened to paper money during the French Revolution in the 18th century and more recently in the 1920s in Germany, when the Weimar Republic went on the rocks. This writer happened to be in Berlin in 1923 when a taxi ride within the city was paid for by many millions of paper marks. In 1914, the exchange rate had been 4 marks to the dollar. By 1919, it was 30 marks to the dollar, and four years later, 2 billion marks to the dollar. The German monetary unit had dropped to the point where the mark wasn't worth the paper it was printed on.

And what followed this period of economic and financial chaos during which the cost of living rose to fantastic heights, property values were destroyed, and widespread unemployment brought political upheavals? On the crest of that wave of discontent, which lasted several years, Hitler came into power and was welcomed by the people as a savior. Thus are dictatorships born and "human values" destroyed.

But it will be said: "It can't happen here!" No bigger illusion could be concocted by a wishful-thinking generation. No nation is safe from financial danger if it ignores the laws of arithmetic. The people will not indefinitely retain their confidence in the monetary unit if they come to believe that the Government is wasteful and does not intend to honor its obligations.

There are disquieting symptoms already visible. Our own Government has been trying lately to convert its relatively short-term bonds into longer-term securities. The public balks. The last offering ran into difficulties, as more holders of maturing securities than had been expected demanded cash rather than accept an exchange even at a very attractive interest rate. The holders of securities showed uneasiness about the future value of the bonds they would be buying today. It is important for Congress, by a sound fiscal policy, to do at once the things that will remove such fears.

Confidence is an intangible. Nobody knows how long it will remain, and nobody can predict when a "run" on a monetary unit's value actually will begin.

There's only one safe course—to consider the "human values" of the millions upon millions of citizens whose fixed incomes and whose savings will be impaired if the Congress fails to heed the age-old laws of thrift. The legislators must soon convince the country that they do not intend to allow the public debt to be increased.

At a time when the nation's safety and perhaps its survival requires more than 42 billion dollars for armament every year, we must begin to realize that we cannot have all the "butter" we want when we need so much to pay for the "guns."

No government—any more than an individual—can long continue to spend more than it receives. To do so would destroy not merely all hope of adding the very "human values" that the "spenders" keep publicizing in their unwitting drive to bankrupt the Treasury but also the basic "human values" already imbedded in American life.

A TRIUMPH OF CHARACTER

FEBRUARY 27, 1959

THEY RIDICULED his phrases—but now they are singing his praises!

Why is there today wide acclaim for John Foster Dulles, Secretary of State, when only yesterday there was such bitter criticism? Americans have been told repeatedly by Democratic Party spokesmen for the last two or three years that the United States has "no friends in Europe," that our allies have been "alienated," that the Administration really has had "no foreign policy," and that Mr. Dulles is to blame.

Still more recently, certain members of Congress made the headlines by crying out that our policy is "inflexible," that Mr. Dulles is "too rigid," and that we should get off "dead center."

The Kremlin, of course, has long been saying through its propaganda—over the radio and to newsmen through Soviet Ambassadors everywhere—that the main obstacle to the ending of the "cold war" is John Foster Dulles. If only he could be removed as Secretary of State, the Communists have said openly, everything would be rosy.

Plainly the Soviets do not like Mr. Dulles because he will not appease, he will not surrender, and he will not barter away the basic principles of international morality for the sake of expediency.

Events have proved Mr. Dulles was right in his stoical resistance to the insidious propaganda of those who sought peace at any price. That's why there has come, at last, a true appreciation of his services, just as he faces the tragic months ahead in fighting cancer.

There have been some occasions when Mr. Dulles has incurred the displeasure of our allies, especially in his stern stand against a punitive war over Suez. But what has happened since proves he was right.

Time and again Mr. Dulles has been assailed for views which were deliberately distorted in the press of the world. Even today, some critics still say he was wrong in espousing the cause of "liberation" for the peoples of the captive states of Eastern Europe. His plea for "liberation" was twisted to mean a threat to use military force.

The critics did not—or would not—perceive that moral force has always been the principal weapon in the arsenal of John Foster Dulles.

The Secretary is, however, no pacifist. His phrase "massive retaliation" has stood the test of time—the concept has proved a powerful deterrent of war. He has always been ready, as he once acknowledged, to go to "the brink of war" to show the sincerity of American purpose and a willingness to make every sacrifice for principle. The critics derided this as "brinkmanship," but they witnessed a successful manifestation of it recently in our decision to protect Quemoy and Matsu if it appeared that any military measures taken there by the Red Chinese were to be the forerunner of an invasion of Formosa itself.

Although Congress, by joint resolution in 1955, had given the President full power to deploy our military forces in defense of Formosa, there emerged in recent months some faint-hearted men in Congress and elsewhere who exhibited "peace at any price" weaknesses. They were inclined to a deal whereby Red China would be taken into the bosom of the free nations of the world and we would let bygones be bygones. But Mr. Dulles never forgot the sacrifices made by American boys in Korea—the many who died or suffered grievous wounds to repel the attack of the Communist Chinese, aided openly, as they were, by the Soviets. He could see no reason to reward an aggressor.

In its latest threat, the Kremlin startled the world by trying to detach Berlin from West Germany. The Moscow Government thought the time had come to test out the strength and determination of the West. This was promptly countered by the conference of Secretary Dulles with the heads of the British, French and West German governments. Though suffering excruciating pain physically, Mr. Dulles, undaunted, continued to perform his great mission. He was able to bind together the members of the Western alliance. A demonstration of allied unity has in itself proved to be one of the best ways to prevent the Soviets from assuming that the West is weakening. A miscalculation on that point by Moscow could plunge us into war.

John Foster Dulles has steadfastly adhered to principle. He has tenaciously maintained the ideals of free peoples everywhere. He has refused to be bullied by the Communists abroad or disheartened by the snipings of the partisans at home. He has fought for the best interests of the United States just as bravely as if he were a soldier facing the fire of the enemy. The world has indeed witnessed in his skillful conduct of American policy a heroism which will be engraved on the pages of history.

While the years of life itself are numbered, the years of a man's fame are unnumbered. In the career of John Foster Dulles, we see a triumph of courage, a triumph of unselfish devotion to public service, and, above all, a triumph of character.

"DON'T KILL THE GOOSE—"

MARCH 9, 1959

THE GOVERNMENT OF THE UNITED STATES is a 52 per cent partner in every American business.

Partners share the losses as well as the profits.

But the Government is a silent partner in private enterprise—it has to sit by while pressures of various kinds curtail or wipe out profits. Yet profits are necessary not only to furnish tax money to the Government but to replenish worn-out tools and to pay the wages of the investors.

Nation-wide labor unions lately have become the outspoken foe of bigger profits. Every time statistics are published showing that some companies in an industry are making somewhat larger profits than in the preceding year, union leaders demand higher wages. Unless these are granted, costly strikes ensue. This has little to do with whether the worker is going to produce more. The modern labor-union doctrine holds that the worker is entitled to more wages, irrespective of efficiency or productivity.

But if this trend continues, where will the Government wind up?

Thus, in the current fiscal year, as a result of the business recession, the estimated tax receipts from the profits of corporations have gone down from 20.1 billion dollars to 17 billion dollars.

If labor unions insist that they have a right to a bigger and bigger share of the income of corporations, the Government will lose in two ways:

First, every wage expense is a deduction on which the Government suffers a 52 per cent loss of revenue.

Second, the increased revenue from individual income taxes does not make up for all the losses suffered by the Treasury from a drop in corporation profits. In the current fiscal year, for instance, individual income tax receipts, as estimated by the Treasury, have gone up by 2.2 billion dollars at the same time that the corporation taxes have declined by 3.1 billion.

The dependence of the Federal Treasury on the profits of business is not fully appreciated or realized throughout this country. President Eisenhower said on this point at his press conference last week:

"We shouldn't be so prone, I think, to talk about and decry profits in our economy.

"You must remember that the people now expect all sorts of services from the Federal Government, starting with that of national defense and go right on down to the last item that you want to find in the Department of Health, Education and Welfare.

"We tax largely profits. We don't tax industrial activity as such—we tax profits. That is what the income tax is. So if you are trying to get profits down to zero, you are going to have to find some other way of finding federal revenue, if we are going to run this Government, I assure you."

America has achieved her greatest progress under the system of private initiative. Experience proves that government operation of business projects is wasteful. Also, a big volume of tax dollars that would otherwise be collected is lost to the Treasury.

President Eisenhower has stated the issue plainly: How can there be appropriations for social welfare unless the Government takes in enough money from taxes to pay its bills? The President said last week in a speech to the United States Savings Bond Conference:

"Now, we have among us those who are calling for heavier and heavier expenditures, saying that these heavier expenditures on the part of the Federal Government would mean and, in effect, would cause, economic expansion. I cannot think of any doctrine or statement that is so false as this one. . . .

"When the Government spends more money than it is getting in the form of taxes, the Treasury must do just exactly what a family or a business would have to do, under similar circumstances: It must go out and borrow whatever is needed to finish paying the bills. When part of the borrowing it must undertake comes from commercial banks, the money supply is increased and the conditions are created for an inflationary price rise.

"Inflation weakens the economy. It brings serious hardships to those of our citizens who are living on pensions or other fixed incomes, and works against those who are unable to bargain effectively for higher wages. Most dangerous of all, inflation weakens the incentive to save. It gives rise to a fear that the dollar will continue to decline in value and that speculation will be the only way to keep ahead of the game."

What is the answer? It is to be found in one word—self-restraint. Business must restrain itself on prices. Labor must restrain itself on wages. The spenders in Congress must restrain themselves on appropriations for "social welfare."

Steady growth and a stable dollar are certain to result from such restraint.

But what must be borne in mind above all else is that profits derived from private business are necessary to support the Government. We must never "kill the goose that lays the golden egg!"

THE "FIRST BLOW"

MARCH 16, 1959

THE SECRETARY OF DEFENSE, Neil McElroy, at a hearing last week, was asked by Representative John McCormack, Democratic leader of the House, whether it is still the military policy of the United States that "under no conditions will we attack first." Mr. McCormack inquired whether this isn't an untenable position in the event of a grave emergency.

The Secretary agreed that it is "a very difficult thing militarily." Then he explained that the policy not to attack first is "currently true," and added: "Whether that will always be true, I think, could be something else."

Representative McCormack promptly said he was glad to get such an assurance of possible change. For he believes that America should say it reserves to itself the same freedom of action as the Soviets now enjoy.

Thus, at last, there has come into the open a phase of Communist tactics which is largely responsible for the cockiness of the Soviets in the "cold war."

For Moscow has known that the United States policy is to accept the "first blow" and that, indeed, Chicago or Detroit or New York or Washington—or perhaps many of our air bases—could be destroyed before any retaliatory blow would be struck.

What is truly involved is the official strategy adopted by the Soviet Union in 1955 when, through the influence of Nikita Khrushchev, the military policy of attacking a potential enemy first was formally decided upon in the councils of the Kremlin. This was not termed "preventive war" but "pre-emptive war."

The policy has been fully set forth by high military officers of the Soviet Union in its military journals. Excerpts from these articles and comments by Western military men were published in "U. S. News & World Report" on June 10, 1955, December 13, 1957, and February 7, 1958.

The "pre-emptive war" doctrine now should also be adopted by the United States in its own defense. This is perhaps the best way to prevent war from ever happening. The doctrine, as the United States could pursue it, was outlined by Captain W. D. Puleston, retired naval officer, who, in an article in this magazine on December 13, 1957, wrote:

"Our Government should also make it equally clear to the Soviets that we will not stand idly by and wait to be attacked—that we will not permit any nation to prepare and mount a surprise attack upon this country or any of its allies.

"If Russia—or any other nation—should give positive evidence that it is preparing such an attack, the United States should immediately:

"1. Alert its armed forces and deploy them for instant attack upon the threatening nation.

"2. Serve immediate notice upon the threatening nation that, unless it dismounts the attack preparations within a specified brief period of time, the United States will attack in self-defense, without waiting to be hit first.

"Then, if the Russians or their satellites should defy this warning, the United States would be in a position to get at least an even break. If the enemy should attack, we could attack simultaneously. If the enemy should persist in its preparations to attack, we could—with honor—attack first, and thus gain the initial advantage instead of conceding it."

The frank discussion of this terrifying contingency is a healthy sign. There must be a resumption at once of the international conferences, recently suspended at Geneva, dealing with the subject of "surprise attack." Although the United States has said it would accept the "first blow," it is clear now that our Government may wish to consider a change. This fact —even though no change has as yet been decided upon —at least moves the problem nearer to solution.

For at the moment the Soviets have a free hand. They can bluff us out of Berlin and out of our bases in Europe. They can threaten to destroy our big cities. They can threaten us everywhere with their new missiles. And we are supposed to wait for the "first blow," however devastating it may be, and then conduct our "massive retaliation" with "most of what you have left," as Secretary McElroy said to Mr. McCormack.

Mr. McElroy told his press conference last week that preparations for an attack by bombers or missiles in the "foreseeable future" would be so complex that they would most certainly be discovered by the free world before the blow could get under way.

But what do we do when we discover it?

In self-defense, we should announce now that we will intercept or forestall the "first blow." We have the same right to apply the doctrine of "pre-emptive" force that our adversaries do. To avow this is to hasten the day when an ironclad agreement can be made to insure against the mobilization of missiles and bombers by either side. For such a mobilization itself can be a signal for the outbreak of war, even as it has been in the past. This is the most pressing problem before the world today.

A CRIME AGAINST HUMANITY

MARCH 23, 1959

WOULD THAT SOMEHOW the facts of life could be made plain to Nikita Khrushchev!

For now the record is clear—the dictator in the Kremlin is threatening a crime against humanity.

When World War II was ended, the military forces of the major allies, including those of the Soviet Union, occupied all of Germany. Four zones of occupation were carefully defined. Over one of these—in East Germany—the Soviets were given jurisdiction.

Moscow now claims it is ready to give up formal jurisdiction over East Germany. The United States, Britain and France in recent years bestowed complete sovereignty on West Germany.

If there were a chance of East Germany becoming an independent nation with an independent government, and if this were the only question to be resolved, there would be no difficulty in arriving at a peaceful solution.

But the Soviet Government now threatens an act of aggression. It demands the consent of its wartime associates to the proposition that a portion of the territory hitherto occupied by the Western powers should be detached and a new kind of "internationalized" regime established in West Berlin, over which the Soviets would obtain a measure of control.

Even assuming that it were desirable to make Berlin an independent entity—something, incidentally, that the West German people do not want to see happen, for they wish to reunify rather than further disunite their country—by what right does one partner to the wartime alliance suddenly threaten that, notwithstanding the wishes of the other partners, a certain piece of territory will be forcibly removed from the scope of the wartime agreement just to suit one partner's evil purposes?

What we have here is a simple case of threatened aggression. Unless the Western powers agree, the Moscow Government intends to use force to get its way.

Though the existing agreement specifically grants free access to West Berlin for the military traffic of the Western Allies, the threat now by the Soviets is to remove such communication facilities from the control of the Western powers unless West Berlin is "internationalized."

Naturally, the Western governments have announced that they would resist any force compelling them to withdraw from Berlin.

The basic issue is not what kind of government shall be created in Berlin. Nor is it whether Berlin would or would not be better off as a "free city."

The real question is whether a member of the wartime alliance shall now threaten to use military force to violate an existing agreement.

If the last two world wars have not taught dictators the lesson that force does not pay and that, when peace is disturbed by aggressive acts, all humanity suffers, then the sacrifices made by millions of soldiers—including those of the Soviet Union—would seem to have been made in vain.

The principal reason for the unrest throughout the world today is that some nations do not respect law and their pledges as given in signed contracts. This means that, in self-defense, other nations are compelled to build costly armaments to protect themselves against the whim and caprice of so-called civilized powers.

If there were faith in each other and mutual trust, no crisis would arise over Berlin. The people of West and East Germany would then decide for themselves in free elections what kind of government they wished and whom they desired to elect as their rulers.

The main reason the Moscow Government is so deeply concerned about the future status of Berlin is that the Soviets mean to hold East Germany indefinitely as a puppet. It is psychologically, if not strategically, important for the Soviets to get military control of Berlin.

The same government that breaks its word to all other governments cannot now expect to be trusted. We shall, of course, go through the motions of Foreign Ministers' meetings and perhaps even "summit" conferences, but these will not restore faith or bring "peaceful coexistence."

When the Soviets fixed the May 27 deadline for agreement, this was virtually an ultimatum. Negotiation under·duress is intolerable.

Civilized people stand aghast as a dictatorship, holding sway over hundreds of millions of people, now threatens war against the peace-loving millions of the free world.

War is a crime against humanity.

To announce now a readiness to defend ourselves to the limit is to warn the men in the Kremlin that they must not commit this crime, lest they themselves and millions of their innocent countrymen be destroyed.

Would that somehow these facts of life could be communicated not merely to Nikita Khrushchev, but to all the people behind the Iron Curtain!

WASHINGTON'S WORRY

APRIL 6, 1959

THE CITY OF WASHINGTON now has a population that is 53 per cent Negro. There has been a continuing exodus of white residents in the last few years. Parents unwilling to send their children to integrated schools have been steadily moving their homes to nearby Maryland and Virginia.

That the situation worries the Washington "Post and Times-Herald" is revealed in its editorial on March 4. The "Post" has been a courageous champion of integration in a community where sentiment on the subject is sharply divided, and has consistently defended the Supreme Court. The "Post" editorial is entitled "New Form of Segregation." Here it is in full text:

"Washington's population problem comes into sharp focus with the publication of the 1958 census estimates. If these calculations are correct, the District now has 387,000 white residents and 438,000 nonwhite residents, or 47 per cent white and 53 per cent nonwhite. The breakdown by age groups indicates, moreover, that the nonwhite residents are virtually certain to increase in number and the white group to shrink. Only a small portion of those over 65 is nonwhite. The white population also predominates in the middle-aged group, but nonwhite children from 5 to 17 years of age outnumber the white children nearly two to one.

"Of course, these statistics alone give a distorted picture of the situation in the Washington area as a whole. The Census Bureau points out that in the metropolitan area, comprising the city and the Maryland and Virginia suburbs, there is little change in the total makeup of the population. It continues to be about 76 per cent white and 24 per cent nonwhite as it has been for many years.

"The present problem arises because the District proper is moving very rapidly toward becoming a largely Negro city. We do not think that this sort of imbalance is good for either the white or the colored race. Certainly it is not good for the National Capital or for the District as a civic community. The Commissioners have made a strong case for more federal aid because the District's changing population increases the outlays for schooling and various forms of community service without any corresponding increase in revenue.

"What is happening in Washington is not very different from what is happening in many other large cities. The more prosperous families tend to flock to the suburbs and the central city is filled up with people earning lower incomes. It is incidental that many of these happen to be Negroes. Nevertheless, in effect this is a new form of segregation. It should be deliberately attacked as such.

"Fortunately, there are many steps that can be taken to curb the trend toward an all-Negro District and all-white suburbs. One of the most important is a proper distribution of luxury, medium-priced and low-rental housing. At present very little low-cost housing is being built in the suburbs and no public housing is available there. Low-income families in the area are virtually forced to seek shelter in the District slums.

"This situation could be relieved in some measure by large-scale clearing of slums to make way for close-in housing for medium and high-income families. But such a course is frustrated in large measure by the absence of any public housing to which displaced slum dwellers unable to pay an economic rent can be moved. The provision of such housing in the suburbs as well as in the District must be regarded as urgent.

"Improvement of the city's mass transportation system to the suburbs is also needed to encourage a dispersal of low-income families. Some dispersal will be necessary in any event to make way in the central city for new Government buildings, freeways, commercial structures and so forth. If these major improvements go hand in hand with reclamation of the slums, they can help greatly to restore a balance of population.

"One other factor is important. The District attracts a large influx of low-income families because it has never succeeded in adequately enforcing its housing standards. So long as several families are allowed to crowd into a substandard house unfit for even one, the whole problem of lifting standards and bringing about a healthy distribution of low-income families will be gravely complicated. The time has come when these difficult problems must be faced realistically to avoid a state of affairs that would be deeply regretted by the whole country."

The Richmond, Va., "Times Dispatch" on March 7 commented editorially on the foregoing as follows:

"The time seems not far distant when the population of the Capital of the United States will be 75 per cent, even 90 per cent colored—by far the biggest percentage of Negroes in any large city in the country, North or South. Just how this will benefit either the white or the Negro race is by no means clear."

Will we soon hear suggestions that the Civil Rights Commission should, by "court order" or otherwise, persuade those white parents—especially Government employes—who move away to avoid integration that they are violating the spirit of "the law of the land"?

"PEOPLE IN GLASS HOUSES—"

APRIL 13, 1959

THE MEMBERS OF BOTH HOUSES of Congress must be persons of integrity—the public rightly expects it. Hence, the current furor over the employment of relatives by a few members of Congress is understandable. But it should not be permitted to become a blanket indictment of Congress as a whole.

Mistaken judgment—or perhaps "imprudence" is the better word—has, to be sure, brought innuendoes of a lack of integrity in individual instances. Yet it would be a sad day for America if Congress as an institution suffered as a consequence of the blunders of a few of its members.

For Congress, because of its investigative power, its power of impeachment under the Constitution, and its authority to pass punitive legislation to correct wrongdoing in other branches of the Government, as well as in the country at large, must retain the respect and the confidence of the people.

The facts concerning the misuse of the public's money have been exposed by the press. It has been found that some of our legislators have put relatives on the payroll at large salaries for part-time work. Were these employes competent? Were others given an equal chance to apply for these same jobs? Was it proper to charge the Government a rental fee for the use of a front porch in a member's home?

Questions like these are being asked by the voters in the districts or States whose representatives in Congress have been engaged in such practices. History tells us there are no more penetrating issues in American politics than those that concern the integrity of Government personnel.

It goes without saying that every public official should, like Caesar's wife, be above suspicion. Those members of Congress who have blundered in the handling of their staffs not only have done a disservice to their colleagues but have hurt the dignity and prestige of the National Legislature itself.

A member may for years have properly employed his wife as a private secretary. He may also during his public service have paid money out of his own pocket for which there was no way to be reimbursed. Each case should be judged on its own facts.

It, therefore, behooves the Democratic Party, which is in control of both houses of Congress, to deal promptly and effectively with the whole question.

It is no solution to compel every member to disclose annually the details of his regular payroll. Internal jealousies can be bred that impair efficiency. Most companies, in the interest of a necessary privacy, do not publicize the salaries paid to individual employes.

Nor is there any advantage in asking each member to make his income tax returns public each year for the benefit of his political opponents.

There have been some proposals from well-intentioned legislators who have recommended that each member of Congress should be required to publicize his financial holdings. What good would it do? More waves of suspicion would be set in motion, and the member of Congress would thereafter be prevented from expressing his honest convictions on economic issues for fear of being subjected to unwarranted criticism. For no matter what a member's holdings happen to be—even if everything were in the form of cash in the bank—there is scarcely a subject of legislation which does not affect either the purchasing power of the dollar or the value of bank savings.

There is no legislative way, of course, to create a conscience if it is missing in a member of Congress.

The "conflict of interest" doctrine, however, does need definition. Should members of Congress accept the benefits of campaign contributions from pressure groups that are active in pushing legislation to serve their own ends? Should members disqualify themselves from voting on any labor legislation if they have been elected with the help of contributions from corporation executives or labor unions?

Congress could, of course, amend its rules to require Civil Service examinations for its employes. It could provide also that no relative may be employed except with the consent of the majority of either house. This action would be taken only after consideration of all the facts by a committee set up for the purpose. A housekeeping committee should be composed of veterans in Congress who could discourage their younger colleagues from violating the proprieties. There is need, moreover, for an unambiguous code of ethics on a number of matters that relate to good government, especially the proper conduct of members of Congress toward quasi-judicial commissions or boards.

Unless some such remedial steps are taken at once, Congress will continue to be smeared, and many honorable public servants will be unjustly circumscribed in the pursuit of their investigative powers as well as in their votes on important legislation—and we shall be plagued again and again with the cynical cry that "people in glass houses shouldn't throw stones."

JOB DESTRUCTION

APRIL 20, 1959

SEVERAL THOUSAND unemployed workers assembled in an artificially contrived demonstration in Washington last week to attempt to prove that the Administration isn't doing enough to create jobs.

The prescription offered—that the Government spend more money on various projects reminiscent of the "boondoggling" of the 1930s—was quickly embraced by some Democratic leaders. Indeed, it was suggested that a commission be appointed to investigate the plight of the unemployed in various areas. There were unmistakable signs of an effort to engage in political exploitation.

Memories are short. All the "made-work" appropriations in the period of the Hoover-Roosevelt depression from 1933 to 1940 did not at any time reduce the unemployment figure below the 7,700,000 mark. It still stood at 9,480,000 in 1939. Only defense projects necessitated by World War II ended use of the opiates that had proved so illusory in the attempt to increase employment. No effective substitute had been found for the normal processes of job creation, especially in the capital-goods industries which had been particularly neglected in the so-called depression remedies.

So it is today. Those economists with a nostalgia for the old New Deal pattern still urge the appropriation of billions of dollars of public funds for a variety of special projects aimed at stimulating the creation of jobs. They talk glibly of the expanding population and the "growth" that's ahead of us. But they do not put their finger on the poison that is stunting our growth today—the job destruction that has been consistently, though unwittingly, carried on by the organized-labor monopoly.

Certainly there is need for a commission to investigate, as Senator Lyndon Johnson, Democrat-majority leader in the Senate—has proposed, but it should do more than seek headlines to emphasize for political reasons the fact that there is unemployment. What the commission should do, of course, is to investigate and expose the persistent destruction of jobs in the last several years.

It will be found that labor unions have forced prices up to the point where the products of many companies have been priced out of the market as bigger competitors, with better tools and equipment, have taken over.

It will be found that union labor has all too often abandoned at the collective-bargaining table the states-manship of only 10 years ago when the AFL sent out a guidance memorandum to its local labor unions recommending that they take into account the financial and price problems of the employer before submitting requests for wage changes.

It will be found that the number of mergers, particularly among small businesses, has been large and that failures have increased because of exorbitant demands by labor unions which in many an industry make the small business pay the same wage rates as the big business.

It will be found that, whereas in 1956 American businessmen had approved plans for capital goods expansion—the building of new plants and the purchase of new tools and equipment—many of these projects had to be laid aside in the next two years because the cost of borrowing money had substantially increased and there was an inadequate supply of capital.

It will be found that plans on the drawing board today for normal expansion of American business would create more jobs than all the billions of public money which Congress is being urged to spend outside the budget.

It will be found that, whereas 850,000 youngsters come into the labor market each year, the big labor monopoly shuts many of them out as it continues the process of job destruction through the forcing of higher and higher prices beyond the consumer's capacity to pay.

It will be found that the drive for more and more government spending for special interests has unbalanced our budget and produced around the world a loss of confidence in the American dollar.

It will be found that there are vast opportunities for American trade abroad even under existing tariffs and quotas but that the American workingman is not getting the benefit of such expansion because the American price level is inflated.

For the fact is that the labor monopoly and inflation have stunted job creation.

A commission appointed to "play politics with human misery" is indefensible. But a commission that will open the eyes of the American people to those forces and influences which have been carrying on for several years now a steady campaign of job destruction would be helpful. Such a fact-finding inquiry should, of course, be conducted by a body of broad-visioned citizens who are without political motivation and clearly without ties to the pressure groups.

THE MAN WHO HAS
KEPT US OUT OF WAR

APRIL 27, 1959

JOHN FOSTER DULLES will be known in history as the man whose bravery kept his country out of war.

For it takes no courage to appease, to retreat, to accept the promises of an unscrupulous enemy at a time when it is being urged that "concessions" and "compromises" are the way to avoid bloodshed.

It takes no courage to argue that, because the Communists are strong militarily and have already achieved a sort of "right of conquest" in Eastern Europe, we must therefore "accept the status quo."

It takes no courage to become so "flexible" as to desert moral principles in international life.

It takes no courage to yield to the temptations of domestic politics and to seek political advantage by claiming to be a crusader for "peace"—even if it's peace at any price.

But it does take courage to fight the insidious doctrines of those, inside and outside of our Congress and the parliaments of the West, who think that the easiest way to deal with your adversary is to appease him.

One reason why John Foster Dulles has been able to see through the deceptive tactics of the Communists is that he has had a long experience in diplomacy—covering perhaps the longest span of any living American.

The critics of the outgoing Secretary have been so preoccupied with one objective in the last three years—to force the resignation of Mr. Dulles—that they have discounted his consummate skill in dealing with the ever-changing wiles of the Communists.

Thus there has been no lack of conferences at high level with the Communists on almost every subject—from the question of suspending nuclear tests to the matter of "cultural" exchanges. Even the artificially stimulated campaign to secure the admission of American press correspondents to Red China resulted in Mr. Dulles making a concession only to find, as he had suspected, that the Communists were not sincere. For they immediately insisted on a diplomatic package involving, in effect, the right to send a host of espionage agents into the United States as the price of admitting American newsmen to the Chinese mainland.

The critics have made much of the "liberation" policy advocated by Secretary Dulles. He never implied that America would use force to liberate Eastern Europe, but his opponents mischievously distorted his words in trying to impute such a purpose to him. By upholding the cause of peaceful liberation as a goal, he has kept the fires of freedom burning in the hearts of the peoples of the captive states.

Among those who so often have assailed Mr. Dulles for the phrase "massive retaliation" are many of the unwitting appeasers. They shortsightedly took his words to be an empty threat. They shuddered at a policy of resoluteness. Yet this is the only way to warn a potential enemy not to miscalculate our strength or our purpose.

Today "massive retaliation" is the embodiment of the military power of the West, though there has lately been more frequent use of the phrase "deterrent power." Actually, peace rests today on the knowledge in Moscow that an atomic attack on any country now a member of the North Atlantic Treaty Organization will result in a massive blow from our bombers based both overseas and in this country.

To John Foster Dulles belongs the accolade for having effectively warned the men in the Kremlin of what America would do if they started any general attack. President Eisenhower deserves the greatest credit for his unswerving support of these policies.

The strength of our determination has been tested at Quemoy and in Lebanon and in Indo-China and lately in the West Berlin crisis. At no time has there been any doubt that Mr. Dulles would recommend military action in our defense if he thought it necessary. He was chastised in the press for using the phrase "brink of war." This has often been sarcastically referred to as "brinkmanship." Yet it is this basic readiness to fight if necessary—to let your enemy know you are willing to risk war to avoid war—which is the essence of "brinkmanship."

It is to be regretted that in the 1930s we didn't let Hitler know that Britain and France and America would join in fighting him if he started a war. He was convinced that, with the Soviet Union as an ally on his eastern flank, he could quickly finish off the Western countries. It took a tremendous sacrifice of human beings to show the Nazis the error of their way. May no such demonstration of error ever be necessary again!

If a world war is averted in the next decade, it will be because in the United States, irrespective of whether a Republican or a Democratic Administration is in power, the principles that have been applied by John Foster Dulles in shaping America's policies in world affairs have been faithfully followed by his successors.

WHERE ARE THE STATESMEN?

MAY 4, 1959

FOURTEEN MONTHS remain before the national political conventions which are to nominate two candidates for the Presidency of the United States—and do we know what the two parties really stand for? Where are the statesmen who can accurately interpret for us American ideals and purposes? Where are the planners with constructive proposals for reform that truly reflect the will of the American people?

Where are the statesmen who can give convincing evidence of the quality of their leadership?

Where, indeed, are the party spokesmen who can do more than merely condemn their opponents? When will we be given an inkling of alternative policy?

For, though there are would-be nominees in abundance, they really tell us little about the programs they would sponsor or of the corrective laws they would ask Congress to enact so that monopolies and economic blocs will not continue to hold back the progress of the people.

The challenge of tomorrow is greater than ever before. Population multiplies daily. The boundaries of cities and counties are becoming coincident as they merge into bigger and bigger metropolitan areas. States are crisscrossed by wide strips of contiguous cities. Our forefathers visualized the several States as huge areas of sovereign power. But today all the States are blended into one another under a single code of interstate-commerce law. Yet, while federalism is absolute, these same States are themselves still divided into many governmental units for purposes of more regulation and multiple taxation.

Duplication and overlapping in government are sapping our economic vitality while politicians fear to fight the organized greed of private groups. Unemployment is chronic, but we confidently assume that the public purse can create jobs or subsidize the idle.

Look around the country and see the State treasuries struggling with deficits! Some States are still solvent, but others are on the edge of disaster. When will the politicians stop telling the citizens they can indefinitely remain wards of the Government—tied always to the apronstrings of a goddess of unemployment compensation?

Our problems are complex and diverse. They are evaded by the politicians of today because the right decisions might mean more taxes for all voters and less power for the pressure groups—and it is considered fatal to advocate anything that could cost votes.

Political parties today are not instruments of progress—they are the makeshift organs of negativism! They forsake ideals in a welter of ambiguities that abound in the national platforms. The basic causes of disunity are ignored by the party leaders as they expediently plead for harmony every campaign year.

Some of us are inclined to rationalize that men and not parties are the magnets that attract voters in present-day campaigns. But if the enunciation of principles must be brushed aside as perhaps too intellectual nowadays to get a high enough rating on the surveys that measure the reaction of television audiences, what sort of guidance are we really to expect from those individuals who thrust themselves forward as our new leaders? What, indeed, is the texture of their respective candidacies? What is their capacity to administer our huge Government? What is their vision of new policies, and what are the solutions they would offer to our pressing problems?

The world is in crisis. We see clearly the age-old threat of war emanating from a one-man dictatorship abroad. We see a totalitarian government maneuvering for admission to respectable society on the ground that only a new ideology or philosophy of government has been introduced. And we also perceive all around us at home the floodwaters of economic anarchy rising to even more menacing heights as unprecedented spending, especially for armament, threatens the integrity of our monetary unit.

These are years of mounting adversity as many countries in the world seethe with internal strife and as the threat of an atomic war hangs over us all.

America is called upon for dollars to bring economic stability to the world, for manpower to meet sudden emergencies, and for weapons to insure an allied defense against a mad enemy on the rampage.

It is not a time for the timid or the reckless. Dictatorships can be curbed without war—but it is necessary to risk war to avoid war. It is, above all, a time for courage—we must be ready to forgo the comforts of this year to assure our safety in future years.

Only fourteen months remain till the next presidential campaign! When will we hear words of true statesmanship encouraging us to dispense with the crutches of paternalism and restore individual self-reliance?

Who will lead the citizens of the Republic away from the temptations of today's defeatism and inspire us all to make the sacrifices so necessary if, in a world of increasing slavery, we are to preserve our freedoms?

"THE POWER TO INTERPRET IS NOT THE POWER TO AMEND"

BY SENATOR SAM J. ERVIN, JR.

Former Associate Justice, North Carolina Supreme Court

MAY 11, 1959

TO BE SURE, all Americans should obey court decrees in cases to which they are parties, even though they may honestly and reasonably deem such decrees unwarranted. But it is sheer intellectual rubbish to contend that Americans are required to believe in the infallibility of judges, or to make mental obeisance to judicial aberrations. They have an inalienable right to think and speak their honest thoughts concerning all things under the sun, including the decisions of Supreme Court majorities.

The truth is that on many occasions during recent years the Supreme Court has usurped and exercised the power of the Congress and the States to amend the Constitution while professing to interpret it.

A study of the decisions invalidating State action and State legislation compels the conclusion that some Supreme Court Justices now deem themselves to be the final and infallible supervisors of the desirability or wisdom of all State action and all State legislation.

Congress is told by the Supreme Court that it really did not mean what it said in exceedingly plain English when it enacted statutes to regulate the naturalization of aliens and to punish criminal conspiracies to overthrow the Government by force.

Congress is told by the Court that its committees must conduct their investigations according to rules imposed by the Court which make it virtually certain that no information will ever be obtained from an unwilling witness.

California is told by the Court that it cannot punish its residents for criminal offenses committed within its borders if such residents are ignorant of the statutes creating such criminal offenses.

California and New Mexico are told by the Court that they cannot determine the fitness or qualifications of those who apply to them for licenses to practice law in their courts.

New Hampshire and Pennsylvania are told by the Court that they cannot investigate or punish seditious activities within their borders.

New York is told by the Court that it cannot prescribe standards of propriety and fitness for its teachers.

North Carolina is told by the Court that it cannot determine the status of its own citizens within its own borders.

Pennsylvania and the trustees of the will of Stephen Girard, who has slumbered "in the tongueless silence of the dreamless dust" for 126 years, are told by the Court that the Fourteenth Amendment empowers the Court to write a post-mortem codicil to the will which Stephen Girard made while he walked earth's surface and entertained the belief that disposing of private property by will is a matter for its owner rather than judges.

Let us consider and weigh the reasoning of those who seek to justify the proposition that it is permissible for the Supreme Court to amend the Constitution under the guise of interpreting it.

Their arguments rest upon a wholly fallacious premise, namely, that the power to interpret and the power to amend are identical. The power to interpret the Constitution is the power to ascertain its meaning, and the power to amend the Constitution is the power to change its meaning.

It seems at first blush that those who advance these arguments overlook the significant fact that Article V of the Constitution vests the power to amend the Constitution in the Congress and the States, and not in the Chief Justice and Associate Justices of the Supreme Court. But not so. They simply nullify Article V with these neat assertions:

"The method of amendment authorized by Article V is too cumbersome and slow. Consequently, the Supreme Court must do the amending. The alternative is to let the Constitution freeze in the pattern which one generation gave it."

To a country lawyer, this is merely a "highfalutin" way of saying that the oath of a Supreme Court Justice to support the Constitution does not obligate him to pay any attention to Article V or any other provision displeasing to him.

If the thesis that a majority of the members of the Supreme Court have the rightful power to change the meaning of the Constitution under the guise of interpreting it every time a sitting Justice wavers in mind or a newly appointed Justice ascends the bench should find permanent acceptance, the Constitution would become, to all practical intents and purposes, an uncertain and unstable document of no beneficial value to the country.

Yea, more than this, it would become a constant menace to sound government at all levels, and to the freedom of the millions of Americans who are not at liberty to join Supreme Court Justices in saying that Supreme Court decisions on constitutional questions are not binding on them.

"NEGOTIATION" FARCE

MAY 18, 1959

AT GENEVA

THE DICTATORIAL POWER wielded by one man in the Kremlin could hardly be portrayed more vividly than in the travesty now going on here in Geneva.

Two sides seeking seriously to negotiate an agreement do not do so in the public square, with hundreds of persons looking on.

Two sides presumably desiring to reach an agreement do not proclaim to the world that their authorized agents are powerless and say, in effect, that substitute negotiators on a higher level later will have to conduct the real negotiation.

But this is precisely what has been revealed as the purpose and the technique of the Geneva conference of Foreign Ministers. Almost everybody knows it is a transparent fraud, but nevertheless this is what the dictator in Moscow wants and it is considered expedient to bow to his whim.

Even when the "summit" conference takes place later in the year, there is no assurance of a sincere intention to negotiate.

Dictator Khrushchev feels he has all the trump cards. He is dealing with three governments—Great Britain, France and the United States—and they are not a single entity. There are divisive influences at work within their own ranks. The negotiating Ministers here give lip service to unity, but each is beholden to a political government which in turn is dominated to a large extent by fear of what the opposition party will say in criticism.

For today the wave of appeasement is worldwide. It says, in effect, "Don't do or say anything that could possibly involve us in war."

Yet a dictator who is convinced that his adversary will not fight plays a winning hand. He grabs a little now and later on a little more until a climax comes that is worse than anything that has gone before. Then war becomes almost inevitable.

The newspapers of Britain, France and the United States tell the Communists every day that major political ferment is at work in each country. While an outward showing of unity is made by the negotiators, there are weak spots in the armor of the West. One of these is the desire for a "deal" involving trade with the Communists by some of our European allies. Khrushchev is still hopeful that he can drive a wedge between the United States and Britain and that, when a showdown comes, even the Socialist opposition in West Germany will play ball with the Communists.

As for the United States, certain Senators in the Democratic Party are almost daily issuing statements to the press which give the Soviets the impression that the Democratic Party is the ruling power and that the President and the Secretary of State are mere figureheads. This erroneous interpretation probably is based on familiarity in Europe only with the parliamentary system of government. Most Europeans do not know the American constitutional system and feel, therefore, that the 1958 congressional elections represented a vote of a lack of confidence in the Executive by the American people. The outpouring of adverse criticism constantly from various Democrats on the Senate Foreign Relations Committee in recent months tends to strengthen this assumption.

While all these political circumstances are by no means an assurance of a Kremlin victory, they do play a vital part in the strategy which the Communist boss employs in dealing with the West in international conferences.

Next, and hardly less important, is the manner in which any statements by the military leaders of the West are treated in the press of Europe. If America insists, for instance, on her absolute right to fly cargo planes to West Berlin at a high altitude, this is promptly denounced in Britain's press as "provocative." What these manifestations of timidity really do is to give an impression of total defeatism.

Then there's the discussion of missile bases. The Kremlin is betting on the political opposition inside the democracies in Europe ultimately to prevent the use of any such bases. Similarly, the Soviet propaganda against nuclear tests has been so successful throughout the world that the Western governments have been compelled by an ill-informed public opinion to agree to suspend such tests. This could easily be the forerunner of a ban on the use of nuclear weapons altogether. If that happens, the West will then have to rely on conventional forces, and in this respect the Soviets have a vast superiority in numbers.

So Dictator Khrushchev, like Hitler in Nazi Germany, feels he is in complete command and that, without firing a shot, he can "negotiate" the gradual retreat of the West, if not its surrender to the principal demands of the Kremlin.

The tragedy is that perhaps the free nations in the next few years will have to fight a world war again to demonstrate anew the fallacies and miscalculations of a ruthless dictator.

THE INTERNATIONAL MYSTERY

MAY 25, 1959

AT GENEVA

FOR MORE THAN SIX MONTHS NOW an extraordinary conference has been going on here between the Soviet Union and representatives of the Western Powers for the avowed purpose of writing a treaty which all nations could sign and which would thereafter bar any further testing of nuclear weapons.

What gave rise to this meeting, and what are the motives of the Communists who have engaged in a mysterious and prolonged activity to focus world-wide attention on the whole subject of nuclear tests?

It is known that Soviet agents played a part in many Western countries in lining up scientists to raise an alarm about "fall-out" and the dangers to human health that supposedly result from the tests. Despite the testimony of competent scientists that radioactivity released by the tests has not approached danger levels, and despite authentic data that the human race has always been subject to even more radioactivity from natural causes than the tests have yielded, there has been waged a campaign of terror. This has gained momentum because the public is readily misled by dire prophecies of great injury, and nobody can, of course, disprove claims about what might happen fifty or a hundred years from now.

But why do the Soviets want a ban on testing? They reply by telling our representatives that they already have enough nuclear weapons to devastate America. They are aware, too, that the United States possesses the nuclear strength to destroy the Soviet Union three times over. So, the argument goes, why continue testing? It's an enormous expense and, besides, if some irresponsible nation gets nuclear secrets, no nation will be safe from sudden attack.

If this line of thought is accepted, the question arises as to why the Soviets seek to impose so many restrictions on the proposed systems of inspection. Certainly if all nations give up testing, there must be no cheating, and, if there is sincerity all around, why should there be so many objections raised by the Soviets to plans for effective inspection?

Prime Minister Macmillan, during his recent visit to Moscow, suggested to Premier Khrushchev that there might be a limited number of inspections a year, and, as usual, the Soviet leader accepted the idea "in principle." Later on, when the American delegation here sought details, no information was forthcoming from the Russians.

Also, a debate ensued as to whether foreigners were to be permitted on the inspection teams. It turned out that the Soviets wanted one of their own citizens to act as "umpire" in interpreting the data whenever a dispute would arise concerning an alleged violation. It's the same old story of Communist trickery such as developed when "neutral" teams were set up in 1953 to police the terms of the Korean armistice, which has since been violated many times.

What then is the Communist game? It's to bring about an agreement to abandon tests, which the West will certainly not violate but which Moscow will disregard at will if experiments, developed after months of laboratory work, are deemed worth the risk of a few days of condemnation by the Western press. For obviously the West isn't going to terminate such a treaty on the basis of vague reports from scientists which the public will not understand. So the Soviets are not risking much by signing a treaty.

The Communists will, of course, gain a victory in the world at large if tests are banned. For, logically, the same public opinion which has been developed to support the abandonment of tests will then find itself accepting the even more persuasive argument that says, "Why use nuclear weapons at all?"

If nuclear weapons are outlawed, the Soviets will rule the world. For they already have bigger "conventional" forces than any combination of their adversaries could quickly mobilize. Under such circumstances, Khrushchev will dictate to Western Europe just as Hitler had hoped to do. Without firing a shot, the Soviet regime will then have won its principal objective—world domination.

Pressed by political forces, some of the Allied governments are urging the United States to go along with the ban on testing. Our own scientists are divided as to the advisability of such a step. Communist influence has reached into every Allied country and into every national legislature to win support for the test ban. Yet nobody has ever explained satisfactorily how any such treaty could be absolutely safeguarded to detect violations, nor what is back of the extraordinary campaign of terror and deliberate confusion which has enveloped this controversy during the last few years.

Maybe when the treaty comes before the Senate for ratification, the American people will have their chance to get answers to some of the mysterious questions that surround the whole crusade for the ending of nuclear tests.

THE PERSISTENT POWER OF TRUTH

JUNE 1, 1959

AT GENEVA

WHY SHOULD THE SOVIETS "negotiate" any agreements here that are unsatisfactory from their point of view? They feel they have nothing to lose by disagreeing and that eventually they will gain their objectives by wearing out their adversaries at the diplomatic table.

Perhaps the most significant aspect of the four-power conference going on here is that there is virtually no pressure upon the Soviets. Conversely, there is unending pressure upon the West to be "realistic" and accept things as they are—to endow the murderers in the Kremlin with the prestige and respectability of "summit" conferences. How quickly some of us forget Hungary!

Throughout history international agreements have been consummated when it was to the interest of both parties to agree. In fact, in order to get an agreement, there has often been a recognition of the principle of reciprocal concessions. But at this conference the Soviets are firm in their demand that all the concessions of a substantial nature must be made by the Western Powers.

There is a major reason for this attitude. No military pressure, for instance, exists that could possibly influence the Communist rulers in Moscow. They know beyond any peradventure of a doubt that the West will not attack, will not use military force to gain its ends, and, indeed, will not even threaten war. The Communists, on the other hand, have no scruples about threatening to precipitate a war over the status of West Berlin. Coincident with the conference here, they arranged to intensify the bombardment by Red China of the off-shore islands near Formosa.

Nobody in the West is advocating the use of military pressure, and, of course, there can be no justification for such a policy. The Soviets, however, profess to believe that the mere presence of military bases in Western Europe is in itself evidence of hostile intent when, in fact, all measures taken by the North Atlantic Treaty Organization have been purely defensive.

If the stationing in Germany of Western troops, including American divisions, together with the building of missile bases in different parts of Europe, were really part of any Western plan to use military pressure, there is no evidence that the Soviets have been in the slightest degree influenced by it to agree to a reasonable settlement of current issues. On the contrary, while they pretend to be frightened by NATO, they nevertheless stirred up the military crisis over Berlin and issued an ultimatum demanding withdrawal of the Western Allies by May 27. The Soviets have laid aside this demand temporarily but have never abandoned it.

Thus the military pressure, coming wholly from the Communists, is upon the West, whereas the Western countries, possessing no counterbalancing factor of a military nature except to prepare their defenses, find themselves caught in deadlock after deadlock in the negotiations here.

What kind of pressure would be effective against the Kremlin? The answer lies in the use of moral rather than military force.

It was President Wilson who, in his message of April 1917 recognizing a state of war with the Imperial German Government, drew a distinction between the Kaiser's autocratic regime and the German people. We drew the same distinction in World War II, and the evidence today shows that the people of Germany during the war really had no more sympathy with Hitlerism than we did. The evidence also shows that the dictatorship in the Kremlin, by the alliance it made with Hitler in 1939, helped to bring on World War II. Millions of Russians died as a result of that diabolical plot.

Our quarrel today is not with the peoples of the Soviet Union. It is with their tyrannical masters. We can appeal over the heads of the men in the Kremlin to the peoples behind the Iron Curtain. Some propaganda efforts along this line have, to be sure, been made, but our own Government's policy in that respect is inadequate as well as timid. We do not use effectively the moral force at our disposal. Congress is penny-wise and pound-foolish in appropriating money in this field.

The true story of the Western position in world affairs can be carried every day to the peoples of the Soviet Union and of the enslaved "satellite" states. It can build up a pressure that goes far beyond anything that could be accomplished by military means. Inevitably, oppressed peoples, without any military help from the outside, do overthrow their unscrupulous rulers. When the time comes for the concerted will of a nation to be expressed, even the armed forces take their cue from the people.

The cause of freedom depends for its victories today, as always, on the persistent power of truth.

THE SPIRIT LIVES ON!

JUNE 8, 1959

THE ACCOLADES HAVE BEEN BESTOWED and the eulogies have been spoken. The tasks performed by the departed have been delegated to an able successor. What concerns us now is whether the eminent statesman who has been lost to the free world has left an enduring legacy.

The fame of John Foster Dulles spread to the four corners of the earth because he was an indomitable fighter for a great cause. He was brave in life and braver still as, with a full awareness of his fate, he approached the brink of death.

It is our duty now to examine carefully the legacy of moral principle which he bequeathed to us. For he strove indefatigably to spare the peoples of the world another big war. He was maligned as "inflexible" because he would not compromise with evil. He was denounced as too "rigid" because he refused to bow to the deceptive wiles of an unscrupulous adversary. But he invariably tried every resource of argument and every formula of honorable adjustment in order to achieve acceptance of a simple truth—that peoples must be free to work out their own destiny and that military force must be renounced as the sole means of settling international disputes.

Mr. Dulles believed in personal diplomacy. He tried with all the earnestness and sincerity of spoken words to overcome face to face the handicaps of long-range communication—the cumbersome language of instruction to faraway Ambassadors.

In an age of air travel, the American Secretary felt it would take relatively little of his time to maintain personal contact with high officials of other governments, and he didn't worry about the critics who said he was away from Washington too much. On accepting the post, Mr. Dulles explained to President Eisenhower why he believed in frequent missions overseas. He urged that he not be required to administer the details of his large department. As it turns out, a competent staff—from which the new Secretary of State was chosen—is still functioning today as it has in the past during the absences of Mr. Dulles.

But it is no criticism of the viewpoint which Mr. Dulles held to say that the multiple problems that he handled would appear to be too much for any one man. It would have been better if there could have been established, inside the Department of State, a council of five outstanding men to function without administrative duties but concerned primarily with the broad principles of foreign policy. Such a plan was outlined on this page on Nov. 14, 1952. The problem deserves anew the careful attention of the Congress and the Administration.

The world is fortunate that Mr. Dulles was able to carry the load so well. He could do so only because he derived added vigor from his unswerving confidence in the rightness of the principles he espoused. God gives inspired men extra strength to fight the battles of mankind.

The essence of the Dulles philosophy in foreign policy was that morality must triumph over unmorality, that a surrender to expediency can only lead to eventual disaster. He was ever mindful of how the paths of appeasement led to two world wars. He saw no merit in cringing before the enemy or in taking any steps that could be construed as weak or irresolute. He believed that, to avoid war, it is necessary to risk war. On this he never deviated, though the cynics ridiculed his willingness to take risks as mere "brinkmanship."

Nor did Mr. Dulles ever allow material considerations to sway him. His hardest decision undoubtedly was his recommendation that the United States publicly disapprove of the British-French policy in the attempted seizure of Suez by force in 1956. For this, he has never been forgiven in certain quarters in London and Paris where resentments still rankle. But the courageous application of a principle against friend and foe alike is a mark of true morality itself.

To withhold diplomatic recognition, moreover, from the regime in Peking required a heroic determination and an unflinching devotion to principle. Too many people have been ready to forgive Red China's aggression and accept criminal rulers into respectable society, endowing them with a prestige they do not deserve.

Are we who remain behind willing and ready to carry the banner that John Foster Dulles held aloft and, irrespective of political party, put moral values above the passion for material gain and ephemeral comforts that so often present such alluring alternatives in dealing with world affairs? Or are we to forsake ideals because that is seemingly the easier way?

The spirit of America has always been consecrated, on the battlefield and elsewhere, to the attainment of unselfish ends—that liberty and freedom might be enshrined throughout the world. This was the spirit that Mr. Dulles breathed throughout his whole career. This is the spirit which will live on because it was and is the spirit that from the birth of the Republic has guided the American people in war and in peace.

THE MIRACLE OF NATO

JUNE 15, 1959

AT LONDON

IT IS NOT JUST a political alliance known, because of its initials, as "NATO."

It is not merely a military bloc, though one of its objects is the common defense of its 15 member countries.

Its name—the North Atlantic Treaty Organization—covers not only the military objective but something far more important to the world. For here is an association of free nations, knit together by common interests, and yet not one of them is yielding its sovereignty or limiting the freedom of its own people.

The Atlantic Congress, which has been meeting here under the auspices of NATO, is an assembly of delegates from the various countries which are members. They gathered ostensibly to celebrate the tenth anniversary of NATO itself, but in reality to explore ways and means of promoting further benefits that can accrue when free peoples get together to discuss all kinds of problems affecting their daily lives.

But, it might be asked, wasn't this the original purpose of the League of Nations and of its successor, the United Nations? In a broad sense this was the theme of the founders of both those organizations. The open hostility of the Communist governments to the free nations made it necessary a decade ago for the countries threatened with attack to unite in a system of collective defense, which contingency was itself provided for in the Charter of the United Nations.

NATO has been an unexpected success. Whether it is the realization of the common danger or whether it is an awareness of the necessity for international co-operation even when war is not imminent, the fact remains that 15 countries, large and small, have bound themselves together without surrendering their sovereignty.

This is a time in the world, moreover, when nationalism has lost none of its fervor. Colony after colony has broken away from the mother country to assert its independence. Never before have there been so many autonomous entities as are inscribed now on the world map.

There are, at the same time, those who would curtail, if not wipe out, the last vestiges of sovereignty in a "one world" concept. There are others who argue for a union of major states in a governmental sense, and still others who, in their eagerness to remove trade barriers, would break down boundary lines and bring about actual mergers of governments. Something of this sort has developed in the Middle East in the United Arab Republic, and there are advocates of a United States of Europe who look ahead to a combination of states patterned after our own country.

But nationalism is deeply ingrained. Patriotism is an essential to national life. Tradition is dear to free peoples. So we see today a striking contradiction—at the very time when smaller nations are striving for independence, many other nations are finding a basis for more and more international co-operation.

Undoubtedly a merged military force tends to bring about a merger of other elements in the field of government, but the success of NATO emphasizes that it isn't at all necessary to yield any sovereignty or to subordinate one government to another or to create a supergovernment to which all the component parts pay homage. For NATO is an example of togetherness that need not be formal but which progresses because a common purpose actuates all the member countries.

Disputes there are between them from time to time on what might be termed local matters. These will doubtless arise in the future as they have in the past but, as long as the family spirit of today prevails, there is less and less chance of serious friction between the NATO countries.

Conferences of delegates such as have gathered here afford an opportunity for an exchange of ideas and a mingling of prominent individuals in all walks of life from every one of the member countries. Progress cannot always be recorded in a tangible sense because in international intercourse the intangibles play an even greater part.

An exchange of goods and services, for instance, by lowering tariff and quota barriers has come to be recognized inside Europe as essential to a prosperous economy for all countries. The fight against poverty and low standards of living is now coming to be understood as one that cannot be left wholly to the doctrine of the survival of the fittest. There must be co-operation between peoples on the economic as well as on the military and the political fronts.

NATO is a miracle primarily because it is a symbol of good feeling, of brotherhood among nations, and of successful collaboration through a sharing of skills and knowledge so that free nations may continue to live in independence, preserving all the advantages of autonomy but gaining also all the advantages that come from pooling their individual resources for the common good.

THE NEW EUROPE

JUNE 22, 1959

RETURNING FROM A FOURTH VISIT to Europe since the end of World War II, this writer brings back impressions of a new and invigorated West.

The strength of a nation or of a group of nations is an intangible and is not always measured by material things. Sometimes the spirit of a people is even more significant than its stock of worldly goods.

The truth is that Europe has not fully recovered from the effects of the last war but is definitely farther ahead, after 14 years of striving for an economic equilibrium, than it ever has been in a similar length of time following its other big wars.

This time America fortunately has not made the mistake of the 1920s, when we ignored Europe, and particularly Germany, and allowed the economic debacle there to bring on the dictatorship of Hitler. The Second World War, with its terrible losses, might not have occurred if we had projected then a "Marshall Plan" for Europe or if we had put the weight of our moral and physical power on the side of the democracies early enough to head off the Axis alliance.

But, lest it be thought that mere grants of money by the American Government in what has often been referred to as "foreign aid" have alone been responsible for Europe's present comeback, attention should be drawn to the vast amount of American private capital that has been boldly ventured overseas and has contributed so much to world recovery.

Thus, as revealed in an article in the June 1 issue of this magazine, nearly $300 billion have been sent abroad from the United States in the last ten years. American purchases of foreign goods account for $190 billion, while $27 billion have been invested overseas by American citizens. Government loans and gifts total approximately $75 billion. Private donations and organizations like CARE have provided $7 billion to help feed and clothe the destitute.

What has most of this money been used for? To purchase the latest American machinery and equipment, to rebuild industries and cities, and to create the necessary reserves in gold for the further development of business and trade.

Europe looks better, the people seem better dressed and happier than a decade ago. For Europe has hope and confidence now. It has a feeling of security in that its more fortunate partner, spared the devastation of bombings, has wisely come to the rescue.

America can be proud of its accomplishment. Our policy has been not merely one of good sense toward Europe but in our own self-interest. The world is more than ever interrelated on the economic side. A continuance of economic chaos in Western Europe following World War II would have imperiled America's own progress.

Perhaps the outstanding fact about the European situation today is that, despite the interminable threat generated by Communist imperialism, unity of spirit and mutuality of interest is strongly imbedded in the minds of Western peoples. There are, to be sure, debates over methods and formulas. There are differences of interpretation about current developments and a wide variety of plans on how to deal with the Soviets. But when the Kremlin makes the mistake of overstepping the bounds in any important controversy, there is in the West an instantaneous restoration of a common front.

In some respects the situation is like the 1930s. The voices of appeasement are often heard. The same old arguments are made that "summit" meetings and four-power conferences are desirable nowadays if only to get a clarification of the intentions of our potential adversary. Unfortunately, sometimes the West thereby puts itself in a cringing position, waiting for the aggressor to consummate his acts of aggression.

Infiltration of the Western countries by Communist propaganda continues as Moscow probes for the weak spot in the Western armor—political disintegration from within. But again the spirit of a free people seems somehow, through its free press and radio and its parliamentary debates, to maintain national resoluteness. On the whole, the public in all the Western countries is alert to the Soviet game.

The mood, moreover, is one of caution and restraint. There is patience and calmness. There is confidence that democracy will win out against totalitarianism, though the struggle may be long and at times exasperating. The partnership with America was never more important to the free peoples of Europe.

If war comes, the West is ready. We can, if necessary, inflict an incredible amount of destruction. The Soviets know this. So the struggle now is on the psychological and economic fronts—and the reconstruction of Europe on the economic side has given the peoples of the free countries the very confidence and strength they have needed to present a united front against those who threaten the peace of the world. Invulnerable unity among the free nations is the key to the prevention of another world war.

WHAT "WRITTEN CONSTITUTION"?

JUNE 29, 1959

JUSTICE BLACK two weeks ago wrote an opinion dissenting from the judgment of five other Justices of the Supreme Court on the subject of congressional power to interrogate a witness about his Communist connections.

Mr. Black spoke, also, for Chief Justice Warren and Justice Douglas. A brief opinion agreeing with Justice Black's basic conclusion was filed by Justice Brennan.

Thus, the high court divided 5 to 4. The majority and minority opinions, respectively, are significant, because of the reasoning of the Justices on both sides of the argument.

The issue in the case turned on whether anyone connected with the Communist Party can claim the right of protection under the First Amendment to the Constitution which says Congress shall make no law abridging "freedom of speech." Justice Black declared that for a congressional committee to attempt to investigate members of the Communist Party is to interfere with "freedom of speech," because, as he sees it, the Communists are simply another political party.

This view is refuted convincingly in the majority opinion, written by Justice Harlan in behalf also of Justices Frankfurter, Clark, Whittaker and Stewart. He avers that the interests of the people as a whole must be "balanced" against the rights claimed under the First Amendment. He calls attention to the avowed objective of the Communist Party which differs from other political parties in that the overthrow of the government of the United States by force is advocated. He might have added that the Communist Party is working directly in the interests of a foreign government which is engaged in a "cold war" with this country, and hence cannot by any means be put on an equal footing with the Republican, Democratic or Socialist Parties in America.

This "balancing of interests," however, seems to disturb Justice Black, who thinks "illegal aims" of a political party should not be the criterion. He writes:

"This is closely akin to the notion that neither the First Amendment nor any other provision of the Bill of Rights should be enforced unless the Court believes it is *reasonable* to do so. Not only does this violate the genius of our *written* Constitution, but it runs expressly counter to the injunction to Court and Congress made by Madison when he introduced the Bill of Rights. . . .

"Unless we return to this view of our judicial function, unless we once again accept the notion that the Bill of Rights means what it says and that this Court must enforce that meaning, I am of the opinion that our great charter of liberty will be more honored in the breach than in the observance."

What strange words these are to read today, in the light of that 1954 decision which told the country that it must accept a reversal of the "psychology of 1896" as set forth in the famous Plessy vs. Ferguson decision. This had upheld 20 years of State Supreme Court rulings in favor of "separate but equal" facilities.

There was no Communist menace when the First Amendment to the Constitution was ratified in 1791. Might it not be argued, therefore, that whatever the psychology of 1791, it should now be "reversed"?

Justice Black says the demands of the Government against protection from Communist activity and in favor of what is called "self-preservation" are exaggerated. Yet, would he and Chief Justice Warren, Justice Douglas and Justice Brennan wait till the Court decides some day, apparently after subversives have gained their point, that maybe the situation wasn't exaggerated after all? Can we ignore the "clear and present danger" doctrine enunciated by Judge Learned Hand, who wrote that it isn't necessary to wait for a plot to be consummated before the government takes action to prevent its own overthrow?

But the majority opinion which has been called a "change" from the famous Watkins case is in itself far from reassuring. For while it claims to distinguish between this and preceding cases, the fact remains that after reading both sides in the 5 to 4 decision, nobody can say positively whether we have today a "written" or an "unwritten" Constitution.

The argument of the majority is that Congress may, within limits, compel answers by witnesses from whom information is sought on which to base the writing of new laws. The minority says this is merely "exposure for its own sake." But how else, except by exposure of wrong doing, can public opinion be crystallized on the need for corrective laws? Would some of these Justices forbid congressional committees to expose racketeering in labor unions, just because this subjects certain witnesses to "humiliation and public shame?"

Clearly, the fact that the Justices divided 5 to 4 on whether the Republic can preserve itself against a group or party that aims to overthrow all our freedoms is not conducive to confidence in the wisdom of the present Supreme Court of the United States. Will the latest ruling be reversed as one Justice changes his mind? Is this a "written Constitution"?

A COMMUNIST VICTORY

JULY 6, 1959

NOBODY can feel happy about the rejection by the Senate of the nomination of Admiral Strauss to be Secretary of Commerce, unless, perhaps, it is the Communists here and abroad, and those Americans who satisfied their personal vengefulness.

Many of the Senators who voted against Mr. Strauss did so with the greatest reluctance and under a political pressure which caused them much uneasiness.

The nation does not yet know the full story of what happened. The American people ought to be told just why the upper house of Congress, on the flimsiest grounds, came to reject an appointment to the Cabinet.

There were several potential candidates for the Presidency who voted against Mr. Strauss. They were warned by their fellow-Senators that unless they played ball with the leadership it would hurt them next year at the Democratic National Convention.

There were Democratic Senators who were advised, in realistic language, that unless they voted with the group which was out to punish Admiral Strauss, they could not expect help reciprocally on their own legislative measures.

There were Democratic Senators in the public ownership group who were told that a vote for Strauss would be construed as a vote against public power.

There were Democratic Senators who teamed up with the ringleaders of the opposition to Mr. Strauss because they believed that party members should stick together. Whatever the reasons, 48 Democratic votes out of 64 were recorded against the nomination, while 32 out of 34 Republicans favored the confirmation of Mr. Strauss.

There were 15 Democrats who rose above the passions of partisanship to support Admiral Strauss. They deserve the thanks of the nation.

This was one of the rare instances in which a presidential appointment to the Cabinet was rejected by the Senate. But there is really no parallel. For in almost all the other cases, there was a serious defect, either in the character or record of the nominee, or a possible conflict of private interest with a government post.

Efforts were made to trump up charges against Admiral Strauss, to form some kind of basis for rejecting the nomination. The record shows the charges were transparently partisan and unproved.

Here is a man confirmed twice before by the Senate when both a Republican and a Democratic President appointed him to important posts.

Here is a man of unimpeachable character and honesty, who was elected annually for six years to be President of the Temple Emanuel, on Fifth Avenue in New York City, one of the most widely known Hebrew congregations in the world.

Here is a man who now is President of the Board of Trustees of the Institute for Advanced Studies at Princeton, a post he has held for several years.

Here is a man who fought the Communists inside government, and who was to no small extent responsible for the development of the hydrogen bomb during the Truman regime, when some scientists with Communist connections were trying to stop or retard our Government's study of that weapon, even as the Soviets were rushing their experiments with it.

Here is a man who in 1953 brought to the attention of the President serious charges against a well-known scientist. The latter was subsequently denied clearance for security reasons by an impartial board of which Mr. Strauss was not a member. This same scientist was revealed to have lied to his own government. He confessed his lie after three years, during which time he misled the security officers as they hunted a Soviet spy.

But for patriotically bringing this matter to the President's attention, Admiral Strauss won the undying enmity of many scientists who are "free thinkers" about such things as security. Some of these scientists helped to spur the movement that led to the Senate's action.

It would be wrong to infer that any Senators were consciously influenced by the Communist drive. But the effect is the same. The Communist broadcasts for months have been demanding that Strauss be fired. They feared that in his position as Secretary of Commerce he would effectively carry on an anti-Communist drive on the economic front. Since the rejection of the nomination by the Senate, the Moscow radio has been boldly exultant.

The world has been told, moreover, that the President of the United States cannot appoint a member of his own Cabinet and secure confirmation, unless he gets the consent of the opposition party. What a travesty on so-called democratic government!

What can the American people do about such things? They can vote at the polls against the kind of Democratic Party leadership that permits an insidious vendetta to transcend the public interest.

Admiral Strauss, whose record of public service is exemplary, cannot be injured in the eyes of those who have known his public service. The Democratic Party has made him a martyr. It has written a disgraceful chapter in the history of the United States Senate.

A SHOCKING DECISION

JULY 13, 1959

THE SUPREME COURT OF THE UNITED STATES has just rendered a ruling that comes as a shock to the churchgoing people of America. For the Court says the Federal Constitution "protects advocacy of the opinion that adultery may sometimes be proper, no less than advocacy of socialism or the single tax."

Yet, in many States of the Union, the Biblical Commandment—"Thou shalt not commit adultery"—is embodied in law and adultery is listed as a crime.

Does the Supreme Court mean that it is lawful now to teach or advocate the commission of a crime and that this is protected by the "free speech" clause of the Constitution?

The latest ruling would take away from the States the right to regulate in their own way the morals of the local communities. This is a far-reaching usurpation. It transforms the Supreme Court of the United States into what one of its own Justices calls a "Supreme Board of Censors."

The State of New York had passed laws saying that it was unlawful to exhibit any motion picture without a license, and declaring that licenses would be denied for any movies which are "immoral" in that they portray "acts of sexual immorality . . . as desirable, acceptable, or proper patterns of behavior."

Justice Stewart, speaking for the Court, said:

"What New York has done, therefore, is to prevent the exhibition of a motion picture because that picture advocates an idea—that adultery under certain circumstances may be proper behavior. Yet the First Amendment's basic guarantee is of freedom to advocate ideas. The State, quite simply, has thus struck at the very heart of constitutionally protected liberty.

"It is contended that the State's action was justified because the motion picture attractively portrays a relationship which is contrary to the moral standards, the religious precepts, and the legal code of its citizenry. This argument misconceives what it is that the Constitution protects. Its guarantee is not confined to the expression of ideas that are conventional or shared by a majority. It protects advocacy of the opinion that adultery may sometimes be proper, no less than advocacy of socialism or the single tax. And in the realm of ideas it protects expression which is eloquent no less than that which is unconvincing."

But is adultery really on a par with "socialism" or the "single tax"? Isn't there a confusion here between the field of economics and the field of morals?

While Justice Stewart spoke only for himself and Justice Brennan and Chief Justice Warren in the written opinion that is formally recorded as the Court's ruling, the other six Justices concurred in the result but for differing reasons. All but one of the Justices saw the film in question before deciding the case.

Justice Clark concurred in the result, but thought the New York court had denied a license, not because of what was portrayed in the picture itself, but "because of its 'espousal' of sexual immorality as 'desirable' or as 'proper conduct for the people of our State.'" He said the New York court placed "more emphasis on what the film teaches than on what it depicts."

Justices Harlan, Frankfurter and Whittaker concurred in the result, but in a separate opinion said the Supreme Court "has moved too swiftly in striking down a statute" and that the law could still be applied to plain cases of obscenity, pornography and immorality. These judges of the Supreme Court minimized this particular film as just depicting a "love triangle."

Justices Black and Douglas concurred in the result on the basis that no State law should be held valid which applies any restraint previous to the showing of the pictures, and that prosecutions could ensue afterwards if valid laws of the State were violated.

Justice Black, in a separate concurring opinion, said he didn't see the picture in question, but expressed a belief that the Supreme Court "is about the most inappropriate Supreme Board of Censors that could be found." He wrote also that, so far as he knew, judges possess no special expertness "providing exceptional competency to set standards and to supervise the private morals of the Nation." He continued:

"In addition, the Justices of this Court seem especially unsuited to make the kind of value judgments—as to what movies are good or bad for local communities—which the concurring opinions appear to require. . . .

"The end result of such decisions seems to me to be a purely personal determination by individual Justices as to whether a particular picture viewed is too bad to allow it to be seen by the public. Such an individualized determination cannot be guided by reasonably fixed and certain standards."

What's wrong, then, with letting the States themselves do it, as the Ninth and Tenth Amendments to the Constitution prescribe? These two Amendments —just as important as the First or the Fourteenth— specifically say that all powers and rights not delegated to the Federal Government "are reserved to the States respectively, or to the people."

IT'S THE PEOPLE'S VETO

JULY 20, 1959

POLITICAL DISCUSSION lately has centered on the presidential veto. The Democratic National Chairman has urged members of his party in Congress to exercise their power to force vetoes on the theory that it is politically advantageous to do so. President Eisenhower, on the other hand, has been accused of using his authority to negate the will of Congress, and there have been denunciations of this as "government by veto."

What we are witnessing today is the strange phenomenon of irresponsible government because there exists in both houses of Congress a two-thirds majority which is opposite to the party in control of the executive branch of the Government. There have been instances where, even when the same party controlled the White House and two thirds of both houses of Congress, a presidential veto has been overridden. This is a reflection of public opinion—it is, in a sense, the people's veto of a presidential action.

In the 1937 battle between President Roosevelt and Congress on legislation to increase the membership of the Supreme Court from nine to fifteen Justices, he could not muster even a 51 per cent majority, though the Democrats actually had elected in 1936 more than two thirds of both houses. The people said, "No."

The truth is, as Woodrow Wilson wrote in his book on "Constitutional Government" five years before he became President, the Chief Executive alone is in a position to represent the national interest, and he can derive substantial power and prestige from his hold on public opinion. This is why there is a fallacy in the oft-repeated comment that a President in his second term is a "lame duck" and that the Constitution should not have been amended to prohibit more than two terms in the Presidency.

This amendment was adopted in 1947 to some extent on the theory that a President leads by reason of the patronage or favors he can dispense and that, if eligible continually for re-election, he could win votes in Congress by virtually bribing members with promises of presidential beneficence. But this assumes that an unpopular President could thwart the public will. It ignores the fact that every two years all members of the House, along with a third of the Senate, must go before the electorate.

A President is as strong as the public opinion that he is able to mobilize. Mr. Eisenhower is in a powerful position today precisely because he is not a candidate for another term. The country feels he is not politically ambitious, and he has announced that he will not attempt to dictate the nominee of the 1960 Republican National Convention.

Whatever influence Mr. Eisenhower has over his own party or over the members of the Democratic Party in Congress comes from his accurate sensing of the national will. He himself, in discussing this point at last week's press conference, said:

"I am trying to do what will, I believe, be good for the country, and I don't enjoy vetoing bills. I don't believe that there is any validity in such expressions as 'government by veto.'

"I am part of the process of legislation and when I am the only official, along with the Vice President, who is voted into office by all the people, I think I have got a special responsibility to all the people. So, I try to tell them and explain to them what I am doing. If they approve, that ought to have some effect."

The argument is sometimes made that a majority of the people are in favor of the Democratic Party because in the 1958 election Democrats carried both the House and the Senate overwhelmingly. It is pointed out that even in 1956, when President Eisenhower was re-elected, the Democrats actually polled more votes for Congress than did the Republicans. The figures, however, present a statistical paradox. For, actually, the votes for Congress are cast in individual districts or States, and, where one congressional candidate is acknowledged to have preponderant support, many citizens do not take the trouble to vote.

Recently another paradox has been noted in the Gallup polls. They show Mr. Eisenhower to have made a gain in popularity from 52 to 62 per cent since last year's congressional elections. But the pollsters still find that more people label themselves as Democrats than as Republicans.

This has little bearing on what the nation wants at any particular moment by way of legislation or action by the Executive. Each proposal or national policy has to be judged on its merits. If the President vetoes a bill and public opinion generally is on his side, it would not be good politics for members of the opposite party or of his own party to override the veto.

The President is elected by all the people. He is not supposed to bow to sectional or pressure groups.

Mr. Eisenhower is singularly free from political entanglements. He has no political ambition. He has only a little more than 18 months to serve. If he refuses to sign a bill, it's because he thinks that is what the people want. This is indeed a people's veto.

THE RIGHT TO MANAGE

JULY 27, 1959

THE ISSUE IN THE STEEL STRIKE is not simply an increase in wages for the employes. If it were, the big plants would be going full blast now. It never has been a question of wage scales alone. It goes deeper—to the working rules that shall govern a day's work.

This is not something that concerns only the steel industry. It affects many other industries. It is the main reason for some of the other big strikes now being carried on by various labor unions.

When a new piece of machinery is introduced, should a labor union have the right to say that just as many men must be employed as before? Why should workers be permitted to stand idly by and get paid for watching the machine operate? Why should employes ever be paid for work not done?

This practice is called "featherbedding." It is one of the reasons that the railroads are in trouble. Their wage costs have risen because they have not always been able to take advantage of mechanical improvements.

Basically the issue is whether the owners or operators of a business have the right to manage it or whether a labor-union monopoly shall dictate what have come to be known as "working rules."

It is this fundamental issue which has caused the steel strike. It is affecting the economy of the nation.

Are the American people to be penalized by a retardation of their economic progress, and is the strike to be settled only after it has inflicted colossal damage?

The labor unions have abused their law-given right of collective bargaining. Each citizen has a right to work or not work as he pleases, but shall a concerted action throughout an entire industry, that interrupts production and restrains trade, be immunized from any penalty? We do not permit corporations to exercise any such economic power. Shall any labor union be allowed to exercise this monopoly "in restraint of trade" and escape any responsibility for its acts?

The steel strike brings into focus many questions that need to be resolved once and for all. Otherwise, our free-enterprise system will gradually disintegrate, and industry after industry will have to be taken over by the Government and given a subsidy. The initiative which enabled the American economic system to accomplish more than any other system on earth would then be stifled, and the results would be tragic.

Union labor has the right, of course, to bargain for better wages and working conditions. But employers should have the right to receive an honest day's work for the wages paid—which is not always the case today. The length of the workweek is a proper subject for bargaining but, in the final analysis, the employer must be the judge of the quality of the work done and of the number of persons he will employ on each job.

An examination of the existing contracts in the steel industry will reveal that management gradually has been deprived of its main prerogatives. There can be no fulfillment of the rights of investors when interference comes from outside bodies which have no obligation to see that a proper return shall be earned on the capital invested.

The wages of capital are as important as the wages of labor. Otherwise, investors will shy away from a company and decline to lend it the funds it needs for expansion, thus preventing the creation of new jobs.

Statesmanship in labor as well as in management is needed to make the private-enterprise system work. The pendulum has swung away from the days when employers operated "sweat shops" and conducted their businesses without regard to humane considerations. Today it is the labor-union monopoly which cruelly calls a strike and inflicts hardship on millions of innocent human beings with the same crass disregard for the people of the country as a whole as some employers used to show to their own employes.

Should government intervene? This gets the controversy into politics. Appeals urging mediation are proper, but for government to impose its will on either side would be wrong.

The existing law provides for an 80-day "cooling off" period while a strike is suspended. But, when this is over, there is no means of compelling a settlement. And there need not be. For then we would enter the realm of compulsory arbitration which depends on the individual caprice or judgment of arbitrators who have no responsibility for the consequences of their acts.

We must depend instead on the force of public opinion. When the American people learn all the facts about labor-union monopolies, they will want them prohibited, just as they did the trusts formed by "greedy corporations."

The right of an individual to work or quit work, and to join or refrain from joining a union, is basic in the American democratic system. So also must we uphold as inviolable the right of the employer to manage his property in behalf of those who have entrusted their life's savings to him. That's the way to industrial peace.

THE RIGHT OF ACCESS

AUGUST 3, 1959

A STRANGE PIECE OF NEWS came over the wires of the United Press International on July 21 to the newspapers of the United States and to the news ticker machines in the White House, the Capitol, and the Government departments. It read as follows:

"Pittsburgh—Agreement was reached tonight in a dispute concerning free passage of supervisory employes at the Pittsburgh and nearby Aliquippa works of Jones & Laughlin Steel Corporation.

"The company announced that two locals of the United Steelworkers Union agreed to permit supervisors and salaried employes to pass freely in and out of the works.

"The steel firm said it agreed to drop court injunction proceedings against the union. . . .

"More than 1,000 supervisory personnel have been in the plants since the nationwide steel strike started last Wednesday (July 15). They stayed in the plants because pickets would not allow them to re-enter.

"The company sought a court injunction that would have allowed the supervisors to enter and leave the plants at will. A joint statement issued by Jones & Laughlin and Districts 16 and 20 of the United Steelworkers Union said:

" 'The union and the corporation have agreed that all supervisory and salaried employes in the corporation having business in the Pittsburgh and Aliquippa works will pass freely in and out of the works. The corporation will promptly discontinue the injunction proceedings which it commenced against the union in the Courts of Common Pleas of Allegheny and Beaver Counties.' "

What a humiliating record! Although the local police are supposed to furnish protection to the citizens who wish to work, it appears that the governing power has been transferred to private hands.

This has happened before. Because there can be no assurance of police protection, the employer evidently must plead with the union to call off its strong-arm men and let the company at least operate its business office during a strike.

For years we have been told that "peaceful picketing," permitted under federal and State law, means merely "free speech" and that it does not include any right to coerce or to intimidate.

But in practice it would appear that the labor unions usually surround a plant during a strike and actually use threats of force or actual force to interfere with the entry into and departure from a plant of those employes who choose to stay at work. This is union custom, but it is, in fact, mob rule.

Apparently the local police, influenced to no small extent by the political power of the labor unions, look the other way in episodes of this kind or intervene only after there has been bloodshed. When will the Congress of the United States inquire into the breakdown of civil rights in labor disputes?

We have today a Civil Rights Commission with full subpoena powers investigating the alleged loss of voting rights by citizens in Southern States. Why not a similar commission to investigate the loss of civil rights by citizens in Northern States who are denied the protection of local or State police? Congress can at least establish the facts and determine later what legislation, if any, is needed.

For today Congress is becoming interested in interstate aspects of crime that presumably cannot be dealt with by the States alone. Thus, the "civil rights" bill being currently considered by the House Judiciary Committee would make it a federal crime to cross State lines to escape prosecution for bombing "any building, structure, facility, or vehicle" used for "religious or educational purposes." But why stop there? If the Federal Government is to step in to investigate and try fugitives in bombing cases, some members of Congress are asking why the proposed law shouldn't apply to the bombing of any building. Since when are certain groups of citizens to be protected against crime, while others go unprotected?

There are, indeed, interstate aspects of many crimes committed locally. When picketing by brute force, for example, is ordered, sometimes the instructions come from a national union headquarters. There have been many instances of damage to plants and injury to workers which have been committed by "goon" squads operating from State to State during big strikes.

Must the employers in America plead with the unions for permission to allow persons to go in to or out of offices and plants? Is this not a supergovernment conducted by union power? Why should it have been necessary for a company to get permission from a labor union to gain access to its own plant?

These are conditions which the Congress of the United States has an obligation to investigate. For it is a federal law that grants collective-bargaining monopolies to labor unions. It is the duty of Congress, therefore, to protect by law the citizen's right of access wherever there is a threat or an actual violation.

"ENTER, CZAR NIKITA!"

AUGUST 10, 1959

OFFICIALLY the Government of the United States cannot decline to permit any member of a foreign government to come to this country for a visit as a tourist. Nor can the Government in Washington deny our own citizens the right to say what they please to any visitor, whoever he may be. Freedom of speech is the rule in America.

If, therefore, as is being widely discussed, the Soviet Premier comes to the United States, our officials will have to be "courteous." But this does not require cheers of applause from the resentful among us who see in Nikita Khrushchev the man who has ordered the murder or exile of tens of thousands of men and women in Hungary, East Germany and the other "captive nations," as well as inside the Soviet Union itself.

A convict who returns to society rehabilitated in mind may or may not be received in his community as an equal. But Nikita Khrushchev would be coming to America unrepentant, arrogant, dictatorial and without abandoning a single one of his threats to our safety.

The hope of those Americans who favor his trip is that he will become "educated" about this country and its economic strength as well as its spirit of peacefulness. It is optimistically assumed that, when he gets to know America better, he will lose his misconception of our purposes and will be more flexible in negotiations.

This, however, is a fallacious theory. The leopard doesn't change his spots when he emerges from the jungle. Khrushchev is just another Hitler. He has gotten to be boss of the Soviet Union by trampling over his opposition and by distorting truth. He has threatened to "bury" the people of the United States under an avalanche of atomic missiles. He has issued an ultimatum to force us out of West Berlin. He has instructed his Foreign Minister to make no agreement at Geneva that substantially alters his previous position. He wants no reunification of Germany. He insists that our troops withdraw altogether from Europe and that we give up our plane and missile bases there.

Some misguided Westerners think there is logic in his demands—that we ought not to "encircle" the Soviet empire. But they forget that, once our forces withdraw from bases overseas, we cannot instantly get them back, whereas it would take the Soviets just a few hours to send their troops and planes to conquer Germany, France and Britain.

It is imperative that the United States and its allies maintain their psychological as well as their military position. To yield to Khrushchev means discouragement to the peoples of the "captive" countries and, indeed, to the hopes of freedom-seeking peoples everywhere.

Why should we yield? To make money out of trade? Khrushchev thinks we are addicted to materialism and that the businessmen of the West place the pursuit of money above all else.

But the Soviet leader is mistaken. While the Allies in the 1930s did allow trade in strategic materials to go on almost to the time of Hitler's attack in September, 1939, we shall not make that same error again.

Things have not changed too much with respect to autocratic rule in Russia over the years. In 1951 there was published a translation of a book originally written in 1839 by the Marquis de Custine entitled "Journey For Our Time." It is a journal of his travels in Russia 120 years ago. Walter Bedell Smith, former American Ambassador to Moscow, in an introduction says:

"A change in nomenclature has not altered the character of Russia's rulers or of its institutions. Whether it is Stalin or the Czar, it is still 'the little father' of the Russian people and it is still merciless despotism. . . .

"The privileged class is today as remote from the mass of citizens as was Nicholas' court. The rank and position of the individual derives from the new Soviet 'Czar' as surely as it did in the days of Nicholas I or in the days of Peter the Great. The ruler continues to be the most powerful and least accessible of all the world's sovereigns. . .

"But like his Czarist predecessors, he is omnipresent, dominating the lives and thoughts of his subjects in every city, village, and hamlet across one-sixth of the world's surface. In Custine's words: 'All must strive scrupulously to obey the thought of the sovereign; his mind alone determines the destiny of all.' "

Essentially, there is little difference between the Russian Czars of yesteryears and the Soviet "Premier" of today. Czar Nikita's rule is just as absolute. The people live under a reign of terror, and there is no limit to his tenure. He is the Czar of all the Russias—the Soviet empire. This now includes the neighboring countries in Eastern Europe, which are kept in a state of subjugation by the presence of Soviet troops.

Yes, if Czar Nikita wants to come to visit our shores, the United States Government can only say, "Welcome," in an official sense, but the American people reserve the right to say that no tyrant or murderer can ever be "welcome" in free America.

THE FALLACIES OF OUR TIMES

AUGUST 24, 1959

GEORGE SANTAYANA, the famous philosopher, once wrote: "Those who refuse to learn from history are condemned to repeat it."

There appeared on the editorial page of this publication on Oct. 3, 1938, just after the conference at Munich between British Prime Minister Chamberlain, French Premier Daladier and Chancellor Hitler of Germany, an editorial entitled "Heroes of Peace." This writer now ruefully reprints excerpts from it:

"They—the people—strewed flowers in the streets of Paris. They cheered madly in the streets of London.

"For whom? For heroes returning from the brave exploits of military and naval glory?

"Centuries of precedent in the chapters of history tell us of the triumphal return of conquerors amid the applause of multitudes—applause for the courage and fortitude of body which had won wars. But last week those for whom the people of the world cheered were not the heroes of war.

"They were new captains of the human spirit—the heroes of peace.

"The world cheers today a new kind of courage. It is the courage of reason which dares to assert justice even to those who in other respects might be undeserving.

"For none of us can even in passing condone the misguided course of a Hitler in the treatment of the minorities of Germany, and yet we can perceive the justice of the claims of the German people for the revision of a boundary which should long ago have been revised.

"We are concerned now not with the details of the settlement but with the natural and simple causes which led to that climax of last Friday. The events are of such transcendent significance that they may well mean the end of one epoch and the beginning of a new period of mutual tolerance and concession in international affairs.

"Should reason—moral force—replace brutishness and physical force, there are no problems, not even those of the oppressed minorities inside Germany itself, which will not ultimately yield to solutions of human brotherhood. . . .

"Force was really defeated, not triumphant at Munich. The force that mobilized armies was pushed finally to one side in an outburst of fraternal emotion which seems incredible to read about today as we contrast it with the newspaper headlines of only a few days before.

"It is well to note these quick changes for their epochal meaning. The German leaders now avow through their spokesmen a feeling of friendship for their erstwhile enemies, the French. The British and German heads of government announce that they desire never to see their respective peoples go to war again. Pacts to limit armaments are in process of development already.

"Do we not see in all this recognition of the principle that force really settles nothing and that the temptation to resort to force arises out of a sense of injustice and indignation which provokes aggression?"

Two weeks later this writer began to have misgivings about Munich, and wrote an open letter to Chancellor Hitler, printed in this publication on Oct. 17, 1938. Pertinent excerpts from that editorial follow:

"You, on the other hand, have rested your case on the theory that military force alone has obtained what negotiation and diplomacy could not obtain for Germany. This age-old philosophy obviously has its dangers, because there comes a time when force is met by force and when other proud nations, too, become ready to make supreme sacrifices in order that they may not be dominated by other nations.

"The Peace of Munich awakened a responsive chord throughout America insofar as it seemed to symbolize a willingness to settle at a round table that which had never before been settled for any appreciable length of time by bayonets or shells.

"But the address which you delivered last week at Saarbruecken has occasioned some puzzlement. Your words therein have been seized upon in America and elsewhere as a direct negation of all that was implied in the Peace of Munich. . . .

"In your hands is the decision whether the rest of the world takes literally the Peace of Munich as the beginning of an era of tranquility or the beginning of preparation for a terrible war in which the United States inevitably would become involved."

Ten and a half months later—in September 1939 —World War II broke out, as Hitler attacked Warsaw and as Britain and France decided to make good their treaty pledge guaranteeing the safety of a free Poland.

Will another paranoiac—Nikita Khrushchev—commanding vast military power now misconstrue democracy's concessions and conciliatory spirit as a sign of weakness when he sees so many Americans bowing obsequiously before him?

We should ponder well the fateful warning of Santayana: "Those who refuse to learn from history are condemned to repeat it."

UNCOMPROMISING IDEALISM

AUGUST 31, 1959

THE ISSUE PRESENTED by the visit of Nikita Khrushchev—so far as the Government is concerned—is not whether a visiting potentate shall be received with cheers or jeers. Obviously the contacts must be courteous, polite and, in a sense, surrounded with all the official pomp that ceremonious occasions of this kind require.

But the opposition to the Khrushchev visit and the protests being voiced throughout our land are based on fears that the result will be a glossing over of past misdeeds and crimes and a readiness by our Government to condone the acts of an aggressor government such as the Soviet Union has proved itself to be.

What the protests really say is that our governmental officials should not be taken in by specious cries of "peaceful co-existence" or begin to abandon the ideals for which America has stood so staunchly.

Appeasement never pays. It encourages the aggressor to misconstrue soft talk for cowardice and weakness. Irresoluteness has often been the precursor of war.

Whether or not one agrees with Mr. Eisenhower that the risk in inviting the Soviet Premier was worth taking as a diversionary tactic in the "cold war," the fact remains that the real battle is in the court of world opinion. The debate should not be recessed. It is more than ever important to restate our principles and to call attention to the violations of human rights and international obligations of which Khrushchev is guilty.

We must not forsake our ideals. Let us re-read the words of President Wilson spoken at San Diego, Calif., on Sept. 19, 1919, as he pleaded for ratification of the Versailles Treaty. This was the treaty drawn up at Paris to end World War I, and it included the League of Nations Covenant. He said:

"We went into this war not only to see that autocratic power never threatened the world again, but for even larger purposes than that. Other autocratic powers may spring up, but there is only one soil in which they can spring up, and that is the wrongs done to free peoples of the world. The heart and center of this treaty is that it sets at liberty people all over Europe and in Asia who had hitherto been enslaved by powers which were not their rightful sovereigns and masters.

"So long as wrongs like that exist in the world, you cannot bring permanent peace to the world. I go further than that. So long as wrongs of that sort exist, you ought not to bring permanent peace to the world, because those wrongs ought to be righted, and enslaved peoples ought to be free to right them.

"For my part, I will not take any part in composing difficulties that ought not to be composed, and a difficulty between an enslaved people and its autocratic rulers ought not to be composed.

"We in America have stood from the day of our birth for the emancipation of people throughout the world who were living unwillingly under governments which were not of their own choice. The thing which we have held more sacred than any other is that all just government rests upon the consent of the governed, and all over the world that principle has been disregarded, that principle has been flouted by the strong, and only the weak have suffered."

By "permanent peace," Wilson meant, of course, any set-up designed to last indefinitely without change. He believed in an international concert of free peoples to keep the peace, but this, he thought, could be done only by guaranteeing the right of self-determination of peoples. The famous Article Ten of the League of Nations Covenant, which was unhappily omitted from the Charter of the United Nations, reads in part:

"The high contracting parties undertake to respect and preserve as against external aggression the territorial integrity and existing political independence of all states members of the League."

This, indeed, is still the "heart and center" of the peace problem that faces the world 40 years after Article Ten and American entry into the League were rejected by the United States Senate. Yet it was primarily this principle that Britain and France were upholding in 1939 when they went to war to repel Hitler's attack on independent Poland. We ourselves, moreover, were drawn into the conflict when an autocratic government in Japan attacked the United States.

Today the Communist autocracy is encroaching on independent Laos, which is being attacked by Communist-led troops that come across the border from Communist-controlled North Vietnam.

Communist autocracy is reaching into Northern India and sending in bands of guerrilla fighters.

Communist autocracy is sowing the seeds of domestic friction by infiltrating the Middle East, Africa, the Caribbean area and South America.

To compromise with autocracy in any form is to abandon the ideals for which millions of soldiers and countless civilians in the free world have made the supreme sacrifice.

To prevent a third world war, we must maintain an uncompromising idealism.

THE ONE BIG DANGER

SEPTEMBER 7, 1959

MISSILES AND NUCLEAR BOMBS are in themselves no menace to mankind—nor are the "conventional" weapons which can inflict widespread destruction. The menace is the man who, in disregard of the wishes of his people, can order the trigger pulled.

The one big danger in the world, therefore, is one-man rule—autocratic government.

The head of such a government—Nikita Khrushchev —was accurately described by Vice President Nixon, in a speech just delivered before the American Legion, as "a man who holds in his hands the greatest power any one man has ever held in the history of civilization—who by his decision alone could press the button which could start a chain reaction which would destroy civilization as we know it."

We may toast and smile, we may reason and argue, we may show our forthcoming visitor evidences of our economic and military strength, but what ironclad assurance can we ever obtain that this man—given to drinking to excess—may not in a moment of anger suddenly order his missiles to be fired and his planes to bomb the peoples of the West?

How can we be certain that the Soviet dictator will be restrained, since he is plainly the monarch of all he surveys and actually wields more power than even the Czars of old?

There can be no safety for any democracy as long as there is in existence anywhere an armed autocracy which can, without warning, destroy us.

There can be no peace as long as the democracies face their biggest danger—the power of one man to control the destiny of the world.

The basic cause of World War I and World War II was the power of an autocratic one-man government to make war on other nations.

Despite public appeals in 1912 for a "naval holiday," one man—the Kaiser—started the war in 1914.

Despite the peace talk and appeasement at Munich in 1938, one man—Hitler—started the war in 1939.

What, then, are we doing to remove the menace of one-man government? Will we remove it merely by showing Khrushchev our might—a sort of veiled threat—or even by President Eisenhower's politeness in making a return visit to the Soviet Union?

We shall not make progress by enhancing the prestige of the dictatorship government in Moscow.

We shall not make progress by abandoning our position in West Berlin in favor of a "deal" that satisfies the material cravings of some of our allies for more trade with the Soviets but robs us of our self-respect and, indeed, reveals us as irresolute and faltering.

We shall not make progress by oversimplifying our dilemma with the Soviet Union as we give an impression that, by temporarily restraining the hand of the mad man, we have accomplished peace for the world.

There has been too much emphasis on the "one-man" idea as the answer to the current crisis. Personal diplomacy cannot be of avail against an autocratic system that rules only through intimidation and terror.

Nikita Khrushchev is accustomed to brutishness, to murders—"purges"—and to the exercise of whatever force seems necessary to him to gain his ends.

We must use the occasion of the Khrushchev visit to talk over his head to the peoples behind the Iron Curtain. The protests from groups of citizens in our midst will be made, but there must be forthcoming also from the Government of the United States a restatement of the case for democracy.

Warning must be given that democratic governments cannot "peacefully co-exist" alongside an autocratic government that keeps on threatening to destroy us.

This is not just an internal question—it is external in its global effects. The lives of free men everywhere are at stake. As long as an autocratic government is in power in Moscow, there can be no disarmament agreement, no treaty to bar aggression, no written pledge that will be worth the paper on which it is written.

Only when peoples are able, in free elections, to choose their leaders and to remove them at will can there be an assurance of peace in the world. Peoples don't make war—only dictators do.

Until the people of the Soviet Union and the peoples of the neighboring countries of Eastern Europe are free, there can be no relief from the burdens of armament. Tension cannot be relaxed anywhere while the murderous regime in Moscow keeps its conspiratorial agents in every part of the world and its troops quartered in supposedly independent countries.

The menace is one-man rule. We should be courageous enough to tell Nikita Khrushchev that we cannot feel safe as long as his people are enslaved and that we will feel secure only when the peoples of the many nationalities that make up the Soviet Union have successfully asserted their right to individual freedom. This may not happen soon, but we must not lose sight of the long-range goal—the removal of autocratic governments from a position that enables them to endanger the peace of the world.

KHRUSHCHEV'S OPENING BARRAGE

SEPTEMBER 14, 1959

NIKITA KHRUSHCHEV has let loose a barrage of propaganda designed to deceive the people of the United States as to the true intentions of the Soviet Government and the real purpose of his visit to the United States.

The Soviet Premier has written a lengthy article in the current issue of *Foreign Affairs,* a quarterly magazine published by the Council on Foreign Relations, Inc.—a private organization of citizens in New York City devoted to the study of international problems. He makes an argument ostensibly for "peaceful coexistence" of states with different social systems, but in reality he outlines his concept of world conquest by Soviet imperialism.

The whole discourse boldly disregards the facts as they actually exist throughout the world today. Mr. Khrushchev says:

"What, then, is the policy of peaceful coexistence? In its simplest expression it signifies the repudiation of war as a means of solving controversial issues. However, this does not cover the entire concept of peaceful coexistence. Apart from the commitment to nonaggression, it also presupposes an obligation on the part of all states to desist from violating each other's territorial integrity and sovereignty in any form and under any pretext whatsoever.

"The principle of peaceful coexistence signifies a renunciation of interference in the internal affairs of other countries with the object of altering their system of government or mode of life or for any other motives."

Yet the Soviet Government has violated every single precept contained in the above pronouncement.

Soviet imperialism has violated the territorial integrity and sovereignty of Latvia, Lithuania and Estonia.

Soviet imperialism has established a firm hold on the governments of the so-called satellite states in Eastern Europe and today maintains troops in those countries to uphold the Communist stooges who are stationed inside each government to see that the Communist point of view is the law of the land.

Soviet imperialism sent its troops and munitions into the mainland of China to help overthrow the Nationalist Government there.

Soviet imperialism has undermined the governments of independent nations in the Middle East.

Soviet imperialism shipped arms into North Africa to help stir up revolt.

Soviet imperialism sent munitions into North Korea in 1950, and direct assistance was given to North Korean armies despite the fact that the United Nations had called on the Soviet Union, as well as on all other U. N. members to repel the aggression in that area.

Soviet imperialism has given support to its ally—Red China—which has violated the territorial integrity of neighboring countries, first, by overthrowing the government of Tibet and now by marching troops into India as well as Laos.

The record of the Soviet Union since 1945 has been one of continuous aggression in different parts of the world.

No continent has been immune from Soviet infiltration. The latest examples include the operations of Communist agents in Cuba and in other Central American countries as well as in Latin America generally.

Nobody questions the right of a people to support theories of state socialism. There is really no important international issue at stake in so-called "ideological differences." The United States does not object to the social system that any other country in the world may choose to adopt for itself. It objects only when such a social system conspires to invade an independent country, violates its territorial integrity, or seeks to undermine its independence.

Mr. Khrushchev is disturbed about the resolution recently passed by the Congress of the United States expressing sympathy with the "captive nations." He says:

"It would be interesting to see, incidentally, how the authors of this resolution would have reacted if the parliament of Mexico, for instance, had passed a resolution demanding that Texas, Arizona and California be 'liberated from American slavery.' "

The answer to this is simple. Let Mr. Khrushchev agree to permit the people of the several states of the Soviet Union and of the satellite states in Eastern Europe to have the same right to vote in free elections as the people of Texas, Arizona and California have enjoyed in the century that has elapsed since the territory of these States was legally acquired by formal treaty. The United Nations would be glad indeed to furnish impartial supervision. Mr. Khrushchev goes on to say:

"The Soviet Union has liquidated its bases on the territories of other states."

Does not the head of the Soviet Government know

that the American people have a free press, that the American newspapers have reported repeatedly the presence of Soviet troops in Eastern European countries which are supposedly independent? Does he think we have forgotten what happened only three years ago in Hungary, when Soviet troops deprived the people of that country of the right to determine their own form of government?

As Mr. Khrushchev goes back to 1939, he unwittingly reminds us of the Soviet treachery that enabled Hitler to start World War II. The Soviet Premier declares:

"In the Second World War the Hitlerites occupied Western Europe before advancing against the Soviet Union."

But Mr. Khrushchev omits to say that it was the Soviet Union which made World War II possible when Stalin and Molotov in August 1939 entered into an alliance that protected the Nazis on their Eastern front, and thus gave Hitler free rein to attack France and Britain. That's how Western Europe came to be occupied.

The Soviet Premier prates a good deal about the importance of letting people decide their own fate, but he is unwilling to let the German people form a united republic today. He writes:

"It now seems that no sober-minded leader in the West is inclined any longer to advance the unrealistic demand for the so-called reunion of Germany before the conclusion of a peace treaty, inasmuch as more and more political leaders are becoming aware of the fact that reunion in the conditions now obtaining is a process which depends upon the Germans themselves and not upon any outside interference."

But does not the Soviet Premier realize that the whole world knows East Germany is occupied by Soviet troops today? How can there be any free elections in East Germany as long as Soviet military forces there keep the people under duress? He adds:

"We should start from the obvious fact that two German states exist, and that the Germans themselves must decide how they want to live."

But who is interfering with the right of the German people as a whole to decide "how they want to live"?

Only the Soviet armies are interfering. The free world is ready to see elections held in East Germany as well as in West Germany to establish a single government over both.

Again and again· proposals to that effect made by the West were rebuffed by the Soviets at the Geneva Conference last spring. Yet Mr. Khrushchev says:

"As for Germany's unity, I am convinced that Germany will be united sooner or later. However, before this moment comes—and no one can foretell when it will come—no attempts should be made to interfere

from outside in this internal process, to sustain the state of war which is fraught with many grave dangers and surprises for peace in Europe and throughout the world."

But at this very moment the Soviet Government is interfering "from outside" and is unwilling to let the peoples of the two Germanys determine their own form of government.

Not a single sentence in the article mentions the ultimatum issued last autumn by the Soviet Premier demanding that the West pull its forces out of West Berlin. Yet it was this demand which started the present crisis in the world. The ultimatum has never been withdrawn. Mr. Krushchev says:

"We resolutely reject any attempts to ascribe to the Soviet Union the intention of seizing West Berlin and infringing upon the right of the population in this part of the city to preserve its present way of life."

But the record of what has happened since last November, when the Soviet Government issued its first note demanding the departure from West Berlin of all Western troops, contains ample evidence that the Soviet Government did threaten to "seize" West Berlin. The words of the threat have been widely printed for all to read.

The Soviet Premier is demanding that the "status quo" be maintained throughout Eastern Europe. He wishes the past to be forgotten, the injustices of recent history to remain uncorrected, and the conquests by Soviet imperialism to be accepted now by the free world as an accomplished fact. He adds:

"It is necessary that everybody should understand the irrevocable fact that the historic process is irreversible. It is impossible to bring back yesterday. It is high time to understand that the world of the 20th century is not the world of the 19th century, that two diametrically opposed social and economic systems exist in the world today side by side, and that the Socialist system, in spite of all the attacks upon it, has grown so strong, has developed into such a force, as to make any return to the past impossible."

But the free world is not demanding the return to any social systems of the 19th century. It is protesting against the return to the despotism of the Middle Ages. It is demanding, indeed, a return to freedom and independence. There has never been any time in world history when freedom was considered outdated or liberty was regarded as outmoded.

The lessons of history teach us that peoples do not indefinitely acquiesce in enslavement. Sooner or later they do demand that dictators be removed and that the right of self-determination of peoples be recognized.

Mr. Khrushchev objects to discussion of the idea of "rolling back" Communism. But nobody is advocating the "rolling back" of Communism as an ideology or as a theory. What is being advocated by free men everywhere is the "rolling back" of Communist imperialism, which imposes its will by brute force and deprives people in Eastern Europe and Asia of the right to determine their own destiny.

The Soviet Premier evades the real issue and misrepresents it. He is trying to tell the American people that all that is wrong with the world is the existence of "two different social systems."

The American people, however, as well as the peoples of other countries, know the difference between tyranny and freedom. They will never acquiesce in the maintenance of a system of oppression, and they will always reserve the right to express their sympathy for other peoples who are unfortunately the victims of dictatorship and autocracy.

Mr. Khrushchev's plea for the "status quo" will not be accepted. The American people will never agree that "peaceful coexistence," as Soviet imperialism interprets it, shall be tolerated along with its far-flung process of infiltration, subversion and aggression in different parts of the world.

How ironical it is to read calls for more trade—the right to import strategic materials for the Soviet war machine—and hypocritical pleas that "no ideological differences should be an obstacle to the development and extension of mutually advantageous economic contacts." Mr. Khrushchev's emphasis is entirely on materialism. He says nothing about the cause of human freedom.

To fill this omission, Francis B. Stevens—who before retirement was in charge of the division of Russian affairs in the Department of State and now is on the Board of Editors of this magazine—offers an interesting plan. He suggests that the United States reply to the Soviet challenge of "peaceful competition" in industrial and agricultural productivity by proposing in return a "freedom competition." The purpose would be to see which nation could do most to assure liberty for its citizens and self-determination for other peoples.

Such a challenge to the Soviet Union would call upon the Moscow Government and its allies to join with the United States in a crusade to promote and advance in all countries of the world the following freedoms:

Freedom of worship.
Freedom of assembly.
Freedom of information.
Freedom from fear of arbitrary arrest.
Freedom from want.
Freedom of political activity by all opposition parties.
Freedom from external aggression.
Freedom from internal subversion by foreign agents.
Freedom of choice by every nation to determine its own political and economic system.

With reference to the last-mentioned freedom of choice, it is astounding to find Mr. Khrushchev now insisting that this principle has always been accepted by the Soviet Government. The Soviet Premier, in his article, gives vent to the following outburst of piety:

"As for the social system in some state or other, that is the domestic affair of the people of each country. We always have stood and we stand today for non-interference in the internal affairs of other countries. We have always abided, and we shall abide, by these positions."

What is disturbing is not only the effrontery of the Soviet Premier in making such an untrue statement, but his deliberate disregard of what the Soviet Government is doing today with troops and money and agents throughout the world. It is in itself significant that the Soviet Premier assumes an article containing such untruths will actually be accepted as truth by the people of the United States. What an insult, particularly to the intelligence of such a well-informed group of Americans as the members of the Council on Foreign Relations!

What possible motive could have induced Nikita Khrushchev to have such an article prepared for this audience? Does he really believe the American people will not perceive his hypocrisy?

The words in the article may be those of Nikita Khrushchev, but the concepts are those of Adolf Hitler and of all the other dictators in past history who have disturbed the peace of the world.

The forces of freedom sooner or later must arise to defend themselves against such dictators and to help all peoples to liberate themselves from the yoke of tyranny and autocratic government. Meanwhile, the organized deception and injustices perpetrated by despotic governments must be exposed to full view. For they offend truth and violate the right of all men to be free.

IRRESPONSIBLE GOVERNMENT

SEPTEMBER 21, 1959

BY OVERRIDING the President's veto of a bill to provide more than $1 billion for various "public works" projects, Congress in the last few days has dramatized for the nation the irresponsibility of our present-day Government.

Many meritorious provisions are contained in this particular bill, but 67 projects are included which have never been passed upon by the Bureau of the Budget or given the necessary study by the Army Engineers, who usually examine in advance all such proposals. The President pleaded in vain that these 67 projects be eliminated now and examined later.

Why, then, did more than two thirds of the members of both houses of Congress vote to enact the bill anyway?

Only because selfishness apparently reigned supreme, as considerations of local politics seemed to replace the courage that statesmen ought to exhibit in dealing with the national interest.

Worst of all, however, the country was given an exhibition of disorderly government—a species of legislative anarchy.

Time and again Congress has felt the "lure of the pork barrel" as members from one section are bludgeoned into voting for bills that benefit another section in order to get support for their own projects.

The remedy, of course, is to amend the Federal Constitution to permit the President to veto any item in an appropriation bill so that it would require a two-thirds vote to enact into law any single provision to which the Executive, as the representative of the national interest, takes exception. New Jersey, for example, has such an article in its Constitution, and it is working well.

This reform has long been advocated by Senator Harry Byrd of Virginia, Democrat, and many other experienced legislators. But it doesn't seem to catch the fancy of the "modernists" or the so-called "liberals" who prefer the reactionary practices of the past.

The record of the two parties, moreover, on the "public works" bill tells a story of the failure of the majority party in Congress. Thus, the Democrats in the House voted 260 to 5 in favor of the measure, while the Republicans voted 116 to 20 against it. In the Senate, the Democratic majority likewise voted to override the veto.

That's the way the two major parties lined up on the issue of fiscal responsibility and orderly government.

The Democratic Party has just refused also to grant to the Treasury Department the necessary authority to raise interest rates on Government securities.

Politics and selfishness again have deprived the nation of laws needed to preserve fiscal stability.

The public debt today is about $290 billion. The utmost care and the best financial judgment must be used in order to manage effectively a national debt of that size.

It is not a task for 537 members of Congress. It is a responsibility that must be delegated to the executive branch of the Government, with a certain amount of discretion granted in order to deal with rapidly changing conditions from day to day.

To interfere with the orderly refinancing of the debt owed by the Government to the people is the acme of irresponsibility. The consequences could be disastrous to the nation.

The Democratic Party in Congress has apparently decided to take the risk of financial chaos.

The President should, therefore, not hesitate now to carry the issue to the American people and explain what the recklessness of Congress means.

For the Treasury must be given the power to sell long-term as well as short-term securities and savings bonds at whatever interest rate the current market may require under the laws of supply and demand.

To handicap the Government in this field of financial operation is to weaken the whole structure of interest rates in the country and to cast doubt abroad on the stability of the American dollar.

A Congress which disregards the repeated warnings of the President about the dangers of inflation and an unbalanced budget, and which refuses to give the Treasury the necessary authority to manage the national debt, is an irresponsible Congress.

But the people, too, have a veto—they have the last word.

In the 1960 election, the American people will have an opportunity to remove from power the Democratic Party which has failed them in Congress. By fixing responsibility on a Republican majority in the new Congress, the people can order a start made toward responsible government. Perhaps then we can have assurance of fiscal stability. And this is essential if the purchasing power of the dollar within this country is to be kept from further decline and if the value of the dollar in world markets is to be maintained on a sound basis.

LAW OR ANARCHY?

SEPTEMBER 28, 1959

THE SPECTACLE of two heads of state striving in personal conversation to reach an understanding on problems of world peace, because normal channels have brought no solutions, is discouraging evidence of how far away we are from fundamentals.

For decades past, we and the people of other free nations have extolled law as the governing principle of human conduct.

Today we have turned the clock back. We have reverted to the days of the monarchs and the czars—to the mistaken theory that, if two chiefs of state will only smile at one another and wine and dine each other, all will be well between their countries.

The slavish praise recently bestowed, for instance, by statesmen in many countries on the formula of holding frequent "summit" conferences is an indication of how far afield we have strayed. For we have virtually ceased to champion the concept that the rule of law can as well be applied to nations as to individuals. Instead, we have become victims of the propaganda that says two "prime ministers" can settle by means of compromise, concession and surrender to expediency those international problems which involve the very essence of orderly progress in a civilized society.

Fifty years ago, eminent statesmen of many countries, including our own, urged that every "justiciable" question—issues involving purely judicial and legal matters—be submitted to an international court and that disputants should agree to abide by the decision. We rarely hear that doctrine expounded today.

A World Court has indeed been set up at The Hague, but there are very few people who know much about it. Governments hesitate to use it. For there is no world opinion behind the idea of submitting international disputes to the World Court.

We in America, after many years of debate in our Senate, ratified a resolution making America a participant in the World Court. We insisted on a "reservation" which specifically exempted domestic questions, and we felt that whether to submit such a case for settlement should be decided by our own Government.

Today it is being argued by the Administration that we should abandon this reservation altogether. Regardless of the merits of such a proposal, the fact is that we haven't even given the World Court itself the respect and support that it deserves.

What is needed is a Senate resolution of reassurance which would state affirmatively that the Court shall confine itself to consideration only of those cases involving "essentially international questions."

The intermittent debate over what kind of cases the World Court should decide has diverted attention from the basic issue—whether a tribunal shall be utilized to help make international law as powerful in the court of world opinion as statutory law is within a country that believes in the rule of law.

Most of the disputes that today threaten the peace of the world are international. They involve questions of fact that can be investigated and truths that can be established by impartial commissions.

The problems that have arisen in Hungary and East Germany are not internal. They are the direct result of a forcible prevention of free elections by an outside government. The exercise of sovereignty is only theoretical where military duress is applied from the outside and a puppet government is then hailed as having been chosen by its own people. Such interference is plainly an international action.

We have in the Middle East a potential source of possible war. Egypt contends she owns the Suez Canal and, alleging that she is in a state of war, argues that even vessels flying a Danish flag can be barred if they carry cargoes from Israel to non-Egyptian ports. But, by historic treaties and agreements, the Canal is an international waterway. Long ago international law set forth the rights of neutrals even in time of war. Surely here is an issue for the World Court to decide. Why isn't world opinion being mobilized today behind this rule of law?

Premier Khrushchev and President Eisenhower cannot substitute official communiqués or public exhortations for the rule of law. "Settlements" sought through the expediencies of personal conference cannot be lasting. We have yielded to the passion for exhibitionism in world politics. We cannot assure peace through the temporary blending of the minds of two individuals who happen to be heads of government. Nor can we be safe as long as a one-man government is in power in Moscow. The people must rule.

We are living in a state of international anarchy. We must instead build a firm foundation of law and order and be prepared, if necessary, to visit the condemnation of mankind on the guilty and to utilize all the instrumentalities of moral force to achieve respect for and obedience to a world system of law.

Leaders pass off the stage, but legal principles governing international behaviour can form an enduring code that will help to preserve world peace.

PRAYERS FOR KHRUSHCHEV

OCTOBER 5, 1959

WE HAVE JUST SEEN at close range the dictator of a huge empire who, forsaking the things of the spirit, glorifies materialism.

We have seen a ruler who wields immense power but who gives vent to tempers of anger and resentment as he scorns those debates among free men which seek to establish truth.

But Jesus told us not to suppress truth or to suspend our quest for justice. He said:

"Moreover if thy brother shall trespass against thee, go and tell him his fault between thee and him alone: if he shall hear thee, thou hast gained thy brother. But if he will not hear thee, then take with thee one or two more, that in the mouth of two or three witnesses every word may be established. And if he shall neglect to hear them, tell it unto the church: but if he neglect to hear the church, let him be unto thee as a heathen man and a publican."

We have tried to speak in the privacy of diplomatic conversations—at Geneva, at Moscow, at Washington, and, in fact, through every available channel of communication. But we have failed to turn our adversary from the paths of materialism to the paths of idealism.

We may well paraphrase: What is a ruler profited if he shall gain the moon, and he lose his own soul?

For the Scriptures remind us that man "cannot serve God and mammon." Man, moreover, cannot "live by bread alone" or by the rewards of trade or business. Man can find happiness only in the things of the spirit that give him faith in the immortality of the human soul. Jesus expressed this eternal truth: "God is a spirit: and they that worship Him must worship Him in spirit and in truth."

The whole world today lives amid the terrors spread by the ruler of the Soviet empire. As did Napoleon and Hitler, another follower of Satan ignores the precepts of a God-given Gospel and seeks more and more power over vast numbers of men, women and children in other lands. There come from him, to be sure, soft words of promise—but he insists that we must disarm first, while his empire must not be inspected closely to insure a similar disarmament.

We cannot compromise with evil. There can be no trust where pledges have been repeatedly dishonored.

What course, then, do we follow?

Jesus tells us to "love" our enemies and "do good" unto them. Surely this does not mean that we must surrender to evil men so that they may continue their evil acts against us. Does it mean perhaps that, in a spirit of compassion, we should ask the Almighty to change the evil men and make them good men? For we, as mortals, cannot perform that miracle. We cannot transform evil men into good men by mere exhortation or even by the polemics of angry debate. We can only state our case in prayers to the Ruler of us all and beg that He answer our prayers.

Nikita Khrushchev must some day face his Maker. How long beforehand will the Soviet tyrant come to see that Communism, in disregarding human liberty and rejecting God's word, faces the same punishment as was visited upon the people of Sodom and Gomorrah who, too, spurned God?

Nikita Khrushchev will not be in power always. Tyrants, of course, sometimes succeed tyrants, but the spirit of freedom is persistent and bides its time. It gives people the necessary courage to lift the yoke of tyranny. For it brings to bear eventually the strongest force known to us all—moral force.

It is a force born of the Judeo-Christian philosophy of fairness and justice.

It is a force that comes from the hearts of men as they turn for help to the God of our fathers who through the centuries has guided the destiny of man.

It is a force that can prompt us to pray to God to instill in the Soviet ruler an abiding faith in His power.

It is a force that can teach us to establish an enduring friendship with those who have once been our enemies but who repent and do penance.

All of us must come to learn that there is indeed a substitute for the hates and the passions that have led so often to "organized murder." It is human love. It can permeate nations as well as their rulers. And in that spirit, we pray for the transgressors in the Kremlin in the hope that they may be inspired to take to heart the words of the Gospel:

"The time is fulfilled, and the kingdom of heaven is at hand: repent ye, and believe the gospel. Repent: for the kingdom of God is at hand. . . .

"Blessed are the meek: for they shall inherit the earth.

"Blessed are they which do hunger and thirst after righteousness: for they shall be filled.

"Blessed are the merciful: for they shall obtain mercy.

"Blessed are the pure in heart: for they shall see God.

"Blessed are the peacemakers: for they shall be called the children of God."

"SOVIET PAPERS, PLEASE COPY!"

OCTOBER 12, 1959

NIKITA KHRUSHCHEV in his many speeches in this country repeatedly referred to the competition between "capitalism" and "socialism"—as if these words accurately describe the systems in America and in the Soviet Union, respectively.

Actually, the rivalry on the economic front is better described as the difference between the "private capitalism" of this country and the "state capitalism" of the Soviet Union.

As for the governmental systems, the difference is between a free republic and a dictatorship.

It is a difference between freedom and slavery, between volition and compulsion, between a system of private enterprise—in which the citizens are the owners of their homes and their enterprises—and a state-dominated monopoly in all business and production.

In the Soviet Union, the Government confiscates all capital and all wealth and apportions such compensation as it pleases to the individual. Here is how Mr. Khrushchev explained it in his nationwide television address from Washington on Sunday, September 27:

"Under socialism (Communism), a worker's remuneration is determined by the quantity and quality of his work for society. When we in our country expand our production still more and accumulate more wealth, we will go over to the Communist principle of distributing that wealth. Each will work according to his ability and receive according to his needs."

This means no labor unions and no trade associations except under government dictatorship, no private owners of any businesses whatsoever, no freedom of opportunity to the individual to advance—except with the political connivance of the Communist Party, which is a small minority of the total population. The majority is coerced into obedience—it's a case of obey or starve.

In the Soviet Union, they have high-sounding words in their Constitution, but the governing clique can do as it pleases anyway.

Under our free democratic system, the President and the Congress are elected by the votes of all the people. There are at least two political parties. Under the slavery system in the Soviet Union, the Government permits only one party. There is only one slate of candidates, and all votes must be cast for it.

Under our free democratic system, the legislative branch may differ with the Executive and enact laws over his veto. Under the slavery system, the legislators are told what to do by the Premier, who is the dictator.

Under our free democratic system, the courts are independent of any other branch of the Government, and the powers of each branch are limited. Under the slavery system, the courts enjoy no independence except in civil cases and the judges are the tools of the dictatorship government.

Under our free democratic system, the Government may not intrude on the rights of the individual as defined in the Constitution. Under the slavery system, the powers of government are concentrated in the hands of a small clique in the Kremlin, whose dictatorship reaches down into every community.

Under our free democratic system, there is freedom of the press, freedom of speech and freedom of religious worship. Under the slavery system, the Government tells writers what to write, broadcasters what to broadcast, editors what to print, painters what to paint, and preachers what to preach.

Under our free democratic system, the individual is protected against arbitrary arrest and against imprisonment without due process of law. Under the slavery system, the individual enjoys no such protection except on paper. For he is at the mercy of the dictatorship. Tens of thousands of Soviet citizens who have fled their country attest to this denial of liberty.

Under our free democratic system, the individual can work wherever he pleases and as long as he wishes. Under the slavery system, the Government assigns workers to jobs and tells them to what city or town or field they must go to work, irrespective of family considerations or needs.

Under our free democratic system, individuals with ability and ingenuity may use their earnings to become managers of their own enterprises, or they may invest their life savings in these private enterprises. Under the slavery system, there is no free market and the Government does all the planning. It decides what shall be produced and in what quantity, which industries shall go forward and which shall be retarded or suppressed altogether. This makes it possible to concentrate all effort on armament production.

Communism is "state socialism." It's a system of slavery in the political as well as in the economic field. The individual is at the mercy of the state.

Democracy means liberty and freedom—the absence of a dictatorship government. It still means to the American people what it meant in 1776—the inalienable right to "life, liberty, and the pursuit of happiness."

ECONOMIC ANARCHY

OCTOBER 19, 1959

BIG BUSINESS AND BIG LABOR are today engaged in a titanic struggle in America, and the innocent bystander—the public—is suffering.

Big Labor, with huge constituencies of members, is led by officers who owe their election to a platform which seeks higher wages each year irrespective of the effect on prices and on the inflationary trend.

Big Business, faced with rising costs and especially the competition of products made in foreign countries where labor is cheap, finds itself compelled to interrupt the series of wage raises it has been granting.

Strikes are numerous. They are hurting the workers as well as the businesses of the employers.

Isn't there some solution? This question has been asked for many decades. First the idea was advanced that there be established a court of labor relations. The unions, however, opposed it. They insisted that the issues were not judicial but economic.

Then came an era of voluntary arbitration, with each side choosing an arbitrator and the two then selecting a third. This meant, in effect, that one man became the umpire, and his decisions were regarded as fallible either due to lack of knowledge of the industry or to preconceptions that were often far from impartial in their application.

Finally, during wartime, Congress enacted the Smith-Connally law which permitted the President to seize an industry. Then the Government in reality fixed the wages and the prices.

When World War II was over, the seizure provisions were eliminated. In their place, a formula was adopted for an 80-day "cooling off" period. It was inserted in the Taft-Hartley Act and is the law of the land today.

But what happens after the 80-day period has ended? Some lawyers think that within a few days a new emergency would be created and the President could apply the rule again. The workers then would have to respond once more to a Government injunction ordering them to return to work for another 80 days.

Congress did not envisage that outcome. Instead, it provided that the President should report to both houses of Congress on what had occurred during the 80-day "cooling off" period, and should also present his recommendations.

What could a President recommend in such a contingency that he could not recommend before the strike?

Congress has too long neglected to answer this question. When labor unions demanded in 1935 that collective bargaining be made compulsory, labor-management relations were put under federal regulation in the Wagner Labor Relations Act.

Labor unions have toyed at times with the idea that federal intervention would be helpful to them. They have counted on their political influence at the polls to aid their cause. Unhappily, they persuaded President Truman in 1952 to seize the steel plants of the nation and impose a settlement, even though there was no provision of law at that time to legalize such a step. The Supreme Court of the United States promptly ruled the action to be a violation of the Constitution because no law existed to provide for it.

But there was nothing in that decision which said Congress lacked the constitutional power to provide in peacetime what it had imposed during wartime— namely, statutes which would authorize Government seizure of plants or the fixing of prices and wages.

Congress, therefore, now is obligated to take the next step—to prescribe what shall be done when collective-bargaining breaks down in industries that affect the public interest.

Congress should first abolish the present 80-day "cooling off" period altogether. It has turned out thus far to be merely a device that prolongs the agony of a labor dispute and postpones agreement. Each side withholds its best offer on the theory that it will be required later on to submit a new proposal anyway.

The responsibility to "bargain in good faith" should be clearly fixed upon the parties to the dispute. Before they are permitted to strike, both sides should be required by law to prove to a federal court that they have actually exhausted every opportunity for settlement by negotiation. When this is conclusively established, however, the President should be directed to ask the federal judiciary to choose three impartial arbitrators, who would report as soon as possible. No strike should be allowed in the interim.

Once the recommendations of the arbitrators were disclosed and were rejected by either party, a strike would be permitted, but collective bargaining meanwhile would be required. At any time during the strike, moreover, the Government would be empowered, if the public interest demanded it, to impose the terms of the arbitration.

Unless some such procedure is evolved, America faces an era of economic anarchy which could be fatal, especially during a "cold war" period such as we are passing through today.

THE BASIS FOR COMPROMISE

OCTOBER 26, 1959

SOONER OR LATER there has to be a negotiated settlement of every strike.

The longer a deadlock is continued, the more costly are the effects of the strike to all concerned.

When informal mediation in the steel strike was undertaken by the "fact-finding" board appointed by President Eisenhower, its efforts were immediately impeded by the nature of the stalemate.

Collective bargaining theoretically means constant negotiation in good faith. Why did this fail?

Something developed which was neither a violation of any law nor a deliberate effort to block a settlement.

Each side took the attitude that victory would come through persistence and that economic force would compel the other side to yield.

The public, as the innocent bystander, seems helpless in such circumstances. That's why calls usually arise for governmental compulsion—some way to force agreement.

But governmental coercion does not satisfy anybody. It only intensifies the bitterness and makes each side feel that the next time, through its own political influence, victory may come its way.

What then is the answer?

Certainly the first requirement is that the issues be defined by a competent tribunal appointed by the Government. This doesn't mean just an array of figures giving the respective claims of each side. There must be something more—a definition of the basic principles that motivate the unions and the employers.

Both sides might as well face it—the impression given to the public generally has been that in steel there were two antagonists with the same objective, namely, to win as much material gain as possible. This has sometimes been called "organized greed."

It has been well said in the pulpit that "there is enough in the world for everybody's need, but not enough for everybody's greed."

It would, however, be oversimplification to say that customarily only greed is involved. To a certain extent, we are dealing not alone with the facts in a strike but also with the psychological impression made by the way the facts are presented.

In the steel strike, union leaders have accused management of being hard-hearted and interested solely in profits. Management's reply has been that wages in the steel industry are today higher than in most other industries and that to let them rise still further means higher prices and an encouragement to inflation. It pointed also to the heavy inflow of steel imports recently from countries where labor is cheaper.

Basic principles cannot be put aside. For to do so is to invite even more perplexing difficulties later on. Private enterprise cannot survive if its prices are to be determined by wage costs that are constantly driven upward in disregard of all factors of competition. Nor can the purchasing power of the dollar be maintained if inflation is not repressed.

It would be ideal if labor and management could agree on a formula to govern wage increases and price rises. Neither side can afford to insist that it must get all that it demands, irrespective of the economic consequences to everybody else.

But do the rank and file of the union members know this? Have they been told the truth about the role of profit in our economy? Have they learned that if new tools and new plants are not to be provided for annually from profits—or from borrowed capital that is based on a fair return to the investor—fewer and fewer jobs will be created and eventually the Government will have to step in with some form of nationalization?

Is there a yardstick to measure a fair profit, a fair return to the investor, and a fair allocation of profits to a company's surplus each year to aid in technological improvement and job creation?

Such questions go to the heart of a negotiated settlement that applies not merely to a big strike today but to the whole future of the private-enterprise system—which we all prefer to a system of state capitalism such as Mr. Khrushchev thinks will beat us some day unless it is also introduced in America.

Principles should come first, and there need be no surrender of their tenets. But a barter is always possible. It is something that, while not wholly satisfying to both parties, nevertheless effects a transaction that each side can live with.

Why cannot reasonable men sit down together and in privacy consult not the politicians, not the demagogues, but their own consciences as trustees of the public interest, trustees of good unionism and sound management, respectively, and trustees of an economic system that must not be permitted to fail?

We must prove to the world that, amidst the free interplay of economic forces, there is in the American way a sense of individual responsibility—an honest belief in self-restraint. Organized selfishness must yield to organized unselfishness—in the public interest. This is the real basis for compromise.

WHAT PRINCIPLES?

NOVEMBER 2, 1959

WHENEVER THERE IS FRICTION between man and man, it is our tradition—our heritage—to rely on law or, in its absence, on ethics to find a basis for settlement.

Disputes between management and labor in our economic life are no longer confined to a relatively small number of individuals. Controversies of nation-wide scope have arisen affecting the lives and fortunes of millions of citizens.

Industry-wide bargaining is in itself a phenomenon of our expanding economy. Not only are the managements in an industry lined up in a group on one side, but a single union, on the other side, controls the lives and destinies of hundreds of thousands of employes even though they work in competing plants.

Thus what is denied employers by the antitrust laws—the right to combine and fix prices—is exercised by a national labor-union monopoly which, in a given industry, has control over the fixing of wage costs. This, in turn, determines prices and can force a decline in the purchasing power of the dollar.

Nobody can be compelled to work. But do a group of individuals have the right to conspire to prevent other citizens from working if they so desire?

Today many employers are required to fire any employe who refuses to join or to remain a member of a union. An employe who tries to cross a picket line subjects himself to threats of violence. Certainly, he runs the risk of union discipline.

Is all this in free America the sign of a growing totalitarianism? Has monopoly become so all-powerful now that the law must step in? Compulsory arbitration is being urged by some as a remedy if a strike is resumed upon the expiration of the 80-day injunction provided by the Taft-Hartley law. But is this the best answer?

What is needed is a declaration of principles and an acceptance by our society of the rights and equities proclaimed. Here are some suggestions:

1. Labor shall have the right to organize unions and to bargain collectively with employers, but must not impair free competition between the companies.

2. Labor is entitled to wages that are progressively improved, as economic conditions permit, and also to some share in the profits.

3. Labor is entitled to increasing benefits in the field of insurance, health and pensions—not as a matter of charity, but as a part of the total compensation for work done.

4. Executives and administrative employes usually not included in union membership are entitled to varying compensation, commensurate with their ability and their contribution to effective management.

5. Management is entitled to provide an adequate return to the investor of capital and to allocate annually to the company's surplus account a portion of profits sufficient to take care of future replacement and the improvement of plant and equipment.

6. Neither labor unions nor management shall engage in any concerted action to fix prices—which is the inevitable result of fixing wage costs for a whole industry. Neither employers nor labor unions shall be allowed to enter into agreements uniformly fixing wages in competing plants. Wages shall be determined on the basis of capacity to pay in each business.

7. Management shall have the exclusive right to manage. Working rules made by agreement between the unions and management shall be subject to revision in any future contract. A formula for the settlement of grievances is essential to good relations between management and the workers.

8. No citizen shall be coerced into joining a union or be penalized by a union or an employer for failing to join. No union shall interfere with the ingress or egress of workers at a plant at any time.

9. "Peaceful picketing" shall be confined to communications between the workers themselves. No "boycott" of any business shall be permitted. For it is a conspiracy to damage private property, which in common law is a punishable offense.

10. When automation is introduced or other changes made that diminish the number of employes required in any plant, it shall be the responsibility of management to provide adequate compensation until the workers to be released obtain substitute employment.

These are but a few of the principles that could help to establish a better relationship between management and labor.

Otherwise, we must succumb to a regimented society in which big unions and big industrial units assume wide powers, not only as between themselves but over our whole society.

Our economic progress as a nation has come largely because we have believed in private initiative, private enterprise and, above all, in recognizing the equities of the individual citizen—employer and employe alike.

We must not drift into a state of anarchy for which the only remedy will be a state-controlled economy.

THE END OF "NEUTRALISM"?

NOVEMBER 9, 1959

NOT SO LONG AGO "neutralism" as between the East and the West was hailed as a practical policy for small nations.

Throughout the world there were two views expressed. One was that each nation has a right to set its own course. The other was that morality cannot be disregarded and that there can be no neutrality as between right and wrong. Moral force, it was argued, would be sapped if such a doctrine were accepted.

In the background constantly was the prospect that sooner or later the Soviet government would regard "neutralism" as a sign of weakness and that, as has happened often before to weaker nations, appeasement would be misconstrued as a craven policy.

India was among the original champions of "neutralism." Nehru was quick to grasp the hands of the Red China leaders and give them diplomatic recognition. India, said the Prime Minister at New Delhi, must not take sides and, indeed, must embrace the doctrines of "peaceful co-existence." But today his country is on the verge of war as Red China's troops have committed act after act of aggression in the northern territories of India.

Most significant is the way public opinion itself inside India has directed more and more criticism against Nehru for his policy of vacillation and appeasement.

Perhaps the best comment on what has been happening to "neutralism" in the world appeared a few days ago in an editorial in the "London Times." It says in part:

"That Mr. Nehru should have to face a possibility of war with China—even though he has dismissed the idea as 'amazing folly'—is one of the strangest turns of the international wheel. India and China were the lawgivers for peaceful coexistence. Mr. Nehru and Marshal Tito and President Nasser became the high priests of the doctrine of neutralism. They have made up a formidable triumvirate, each representing a continent, and each having come by his own road to a firm intellectual conviction of the importance of being neutral. But the doctrine of neutralism has taken other hard knocks lately. It has never recovered the impetus of the peak years, 1955 and 1956, when, in the wake of the Bandung conference, neutralism seemed to be daily gaining fresh converts among Governments and individuals. At that time there were countries where to question neutralism—its virtues or practicability—was almost tabu. Now the position has changed. The high priests have come under fire from a quarter where, three or four years ago, they received most sympathy. China, whose Prime Minister, Mr. Chou En-lai, was one of the pacemakers at Bandung, has rounded on them all. Marshal Tito is accused of dangerous revisionism, President Nasser of playing imperialism's game in his quarrel with General Kassem, and Mr. Nehru of aggression.

"The neutralists are genuinely puzzled about what has gone wrong. They have not consciously changed any part of the doctrine of neutralism, in which, it must be emphasized, they still passionately believe. Nor, they would say, have they applied neutralism in any new way. But the doctrine has not saved them from those conflicts which they had hoped to avoid. . . .

"Neutralism was quickly and enthusiastically endorsed by Communist Governments, whereas in the west there was only grudging admission that it might be a possible policy.

"In consequence, for the past four years it has been a generally accepted axiom that on important questions of foreign policy neutralists and Communists speak with the same voice. Nuclear tests, disarmament, rights of colonial peoples, and so on—there was no disagreement between the two. Now this identity of viewpoints has been shown up as imperfect. Why? Partly, of course, because neutralism began to spread into the Communist world. The Hungarians' claim in November, 1956, for a neutral position has been neither forgiven nor forgotten. Yet if neutralism was morally sound as well as politically permissible, which the Communists were understood to have conceded, why should it not be allowed to spread? When Ceylon and Iraq switched from alliance with the west to neutralism there was no objection. If Russia's objection to Hungarian neutralism was that it would be only a stage to Hungary's absorption in the western alliance, was not the west justified in its fears about the outcome of Iraq's neutralism?

"The question which the neutralists have now to consider is whether Communism ever really meant to accept the half-way house of neutralism, except as a temporary expedient. . . .

"It may take some time before the cold wind from China makes a full impact on the neutralist world. There will be no stampede towards the west—and the west, having become used to the idea of neutralism, would not want one. But there may be more floating voters at the United Nations, and more understanding of the difficulties of mediation. To start with, it will be good for all concerned if neutralism ceases to be simply an international cliché."

A PURPOSEFUL TRIP

NOVEMBER 16, 1959

JUST WHY DID PRESIDENT EISENHOWER decide to take a trip to nine countries in Europe, Asia and Africa—something no other Chief Executive has ever done while in office?

Fifty years ago it was a novelty when President Taft stepped across the border into Mexico. When President Wilson in 1919 went to Paris for the peace conference after World War I, considerable opposition to the trip was expressed in Congress. A theory had gained ground that somehow a President should never leave the territory of the United States. Possibly this was because it was felt that he should be available at all times to perform any functions entrusted to him by law and that, under the Constitution, he could not do so unless on American territory. Then came the device of using American embassies and warships as places where documents could be lawfully signed by a President.

But, more than this, Mr. Eisenhower has made the Vice President a member of his official family and has familiarized the second highest man in the Government with the essential points of public policy. An unwritten rule which Mr. Eisenhower has adopted is that at no time would he be out of the country at the same time as the Vice President is away from our shores.

But what are the real reasons for such an extensive series of visits as the President will undertake in December of this year? One reason is that, if he goes to a certain area and doesn't visit all the countries therein with which we have close relationships, some nations will be offended. Another reason is that it is important to cement ties with all the countries in the free world.

So Mr. Eisenhower is planning to go to Italy, Turkey, Pakistan, Afghanistan, India, Iran, Greece and Morocco as well as to France, where the meeting of the NATO members will be held on his arrival in Paris. While in Rome, the President naturally will call on the new Pope. This will be regarded highly in the many Catholic countries of the world, particularly in Central and South America.

Just what can be accomplished by a brief visit to each of the nine capitals to which the President will go? Certainly no important public business can be transacted, and the visits will be mostly ceremonials and street parades. The real value will be in the publicity that will be given locally to every such stopover that Mr. Eisenhower makes.

To have a President of the United States visit any country in the Middle East, Asia or Africa is a big event to the peoples there. The news will be broadcast over the radio and prominently displayed, with photographs and long articles, in the press. Also, an opportunity is afforded to cultivate personal relations with the rulers in the different lands.

The average American isn't aware of how little is known abroad of American policies and ideals. The word "propaganda" has always had a tainted meaning in this country, and our Congress still hesitates to give the United States Information Agency enough funds to compete with Soviet propaganda throughout the world.

It is erroneously assumed in America that the newspapers abroad keep the peoples posted on what is happening in the United States and, especially, on its dealings with other countries. While the news agencies do transmit every day many thousands of words in brief dispatches, the newspapers in Europe, Asia and Africa have relatively little space to devote to foreign news. Consequently the American point of view rarely gets the attention it deserves in other countries.

When, however, a President of the United States arrives in a country and speaks there, this becomes "local" news. It is spread across the front pages and is given wide coverage on the air. Millions of persons then learn for the first time about the unselfish purposes of the policies of the United States.

Publicity of this kind is worth every sacrifice of time and energy that an American President can make. For it helps to achieve for the United States a position of strength in the world—a position before friendly peoples that is unattainable through years and years of effort in other ways. Ambassadors may come and go, but they cannot do in years what a President of the United States can do in a visit of a day or two. When he appears before the people, a chain reaction of international friendship and good will is initiated.

Mr. Eisenhower depended for a long time on the world-wide travels of the late Secretary of State John Foster Dulles and, brushing aside petty criticism, defended those journeys as essential to American policy. Now that Mr. Dulles is gone, the President himself is assuming the role of good-will Ambassador-at-large.

It is a commendable mission that Mr. Eisenhower is undertaking. It will help to emphasize the solidarity of the free nations. It comes at a critical time in world history when peace more than ever depends on the willingness of free peoples to make sacrifices for each other.

"COMMUNISTS, GO HOME!"

NOVEMBER 23, 1959

IN THE EARLY DAYS of the Republic, the United States proclaimed what has been known ever since as the "Monroe Doctrine." It declared that any attempt by any European power to interfere in the internal affairs of any country in this hemisphere will be considered by the United States to be an unfriendly act, "dangerous to our peace and safety."

Plainly there is a Communist menace in Central and South America. It threatens every government in this hemisphere. It operates through an apparatus directed and financed by the Soviet Government.

We know that Cuba is a hotbed of Communist activity. We know that riots and anti-American demonstrations have been fomented in other countries in the Caribbean area. The hostile reception given Vice President Nixon in Latin American countries was undoubtedly inspired by the Communists.

In recent days the American flag has been torn from our embassy in Panama City. For several months mischief-makers, instigated by the Communists, have been trying to stir up trouble between the United States and Panama.

The pattern is a familiar one. Ostensibly there is no connection with the Communist Party as such. Persons accused usually deny any Communist affiliation and argue that they are merely "nationalists." But truth-telling is not part of the Communists' code. Their technique calls rather for a concealment of their system of internal aggression.

The United States Government, however, and many of the governments to the south of us know the facts. And the facts establish clearly that the Soviet Government is flagrantly violating the Monroe Doctrine.

In recent years all the governments of Central and South America have embraced the Monroe Doctrine as an international principle for their guidance rather than as merely the responsibility of the United States alone. But some of the very governments, like Cuba, which would be expected to join in a demand that the Communists get out of this hemisphere are themselves involved now in the Communist conspiracy.

The entire plot, moreover, is aimed directly at the United States as the leader of the Western world. Hence it becomes the duty of our Government to assume this leadership and to invite as many of the other governments of this hemisphere as can do so to join in the crusade.

What can be done? A note of warning can be dispatched to Moscow notifying the Soviet Government that its activities in Latin America are becoming intolerable and that friendly relations cannot be maintained as long as Soviet agents of intrigue infest Latin-American capitals.

Also, the different governments of Central and South America can join with the United States in forming a commission to expose Communist operations in Latin America. Such a commission could visit each country and take testimony from interested citizens so that the entire world may get at firsthand the story of what has been and is going on.

What effect, it might be asked, would this have on the Soviets? It would at least force them to face openly the question of the sincerity of their allegedly peaceful purposes. It would expose the fakery in the claim that "tensions" in the "cold war" are being eased.

For Nikita Khrushchev, in his visits to Western countries, claims to be for "peaceful coexistence" and piously calls for an end to the "cold war." But his own regime is spending hundreds of millions of rubles annually to infiltrate not only Latin-American countries but also vast areas in Africa and Southeast Asia whose governments are not as yet banded together to break up the Communist game.

The Communists in Moscow say they don't want war and wish only to be let alone. But why don't they let other countries alone? Why is Moscow so busily engaged every day in a huge operation of radio propaganda, beamed to other countries, designed to stir up friction between the United States and its friends?

The technique of the Communists is not always discerned by the governments affected. The strategy is to employ nationals of other countries. Thus, Argentinians with a Communist background have been used to foment trouble in other countries. Also, Moscow now has the effrontery to arrange for Chinese agents to go to many Latin-American countries. There are some people to the south of us who are naive enough to believe that Red China is merely anxious to spread its philosophic doctrines in this hemisphere although it has problems galore of its own in India and Southeast Asia.

The Moscow and Peiping governments are joined together in a determined effort to use every resource of espionage to infiltrate civic and educational as well as governmental institutions in every country of this hemisphere. It is time to uncover the whole plot and blazon on signposts everywhere in North and South America the warning: "Communists, go home!"

THE RIGHT OF PETITION

NOVEMBER 30, 1959

THE FIRST AMENDMENT to the Constitution says that Congress shall make no law respecting the right of the people "to petition the Government for a redress of grievances."

Supposing, however, one political party in control of Congress passed a law placing barriers in the way of an opposition party so that it could not without financial penalty express its views, what would the American people say of such an act?

Supposing the Government decided to engage in business in competition with a private enterprise and took away the right of tax deductions from the private business in question so that it would be more expensive for it to appeal to the public for help, what would the American people say of such an act?

Yet the power to do some of these very things is contained in existing law and in proposed regulations by the Internal Revenue Service. Protests were made a few days ago in a public hearing, where various organizations warned against frustration of the right of petition.

This is not a partisan matter. It is a question of tolerance and of adherence to the fundamental precepts of the Constitution itself. Legislators who grow angry at their opposition are largely responsible for the insidious devices used to choke off expressions of criticism. But democratic government rests on the basic principle that everybody must have the right of free expression without being subject to financial or other penalties.

Congress has the right to legislate on improper methods of presenting a petition. If physical threats are used or if bribes are given to legislators, obviously existing law covers such crimes. But we are dealing here with open and above-board presentation of the views of the citizens.

Thus, the Congress many years ago denied tax-exempt status to organizations a substantial part of whose activities were "lobbying" for or against legislation. Oddly enough, in the cases that have arisen, the Supreme Court has never really defined "lobbying" but has said that Congress has the right to compel registration of lobbying representatives and the filing of a record of sums spent and their source.

There can be no logical objection to a requirement that the facts be disclosed. But when the executive branch of the Government puts out regulations that would penalize the expression of opinion by denying a tax deduction, even when the expense is "ordinary and necessary in carrying out any trade or business," the effect is the same as if a gag had been applied to the words of a citizen in a public assembly.

The Supreme Court of the United States in 1936 ruled that the State of Louisiana, in attempting to impose on newspapers of large circulation a special tax on gross receipts from which smaller newspapers were exempted, was plainly trying "under the guise of a tax to limit the circulation of information to which the public is entitled in virtue of the constitutional guaranties."

In other words, newspapers must pay the same taxes as any other business but a special tax of this kind is invalid because it abridges the freedom of the press.

Recently regulations have been proposed which would deny a tax deduction to workers for dues they have paid to unions if any such sums are used for "lobbying." Similarly, under the same regulations, businesses which may be engaged in a battle for survival against hostile legislation would not be permitted to deduct the expenses incurred either for trips to Washington or when they take space in the press to speak out against a specific piece of legislation.

The Internal Revenue Service is hardly to blame for the confused situation that has arisen. Nor has the Supreme Court had the constitutional issue squarely presented to it in a case involving the right of an individual business to speak out under its own name for or against legislative proposals affecting its future.

Basically, Congress is at fault for failing to wipe off the statute books the intolerable laws that today violate the spirit as well as the letter of the Constitution.

It ought to be possible to debate public issues without using legislative or taxing powers to punish critics.

We denounce the totalitarian mind as seeking to impose state control over our thoughts and acts.

True liberals have always fought the encroachment by government on individual liberty.

But today we look in vain to the so-called "liberal" side for the same vigor in opposing impediments to the right of petition as they are wont to exhibit in upholding other clauses of the First Amendment.

If government ownership or control of all business enterprises is to come to America, as Nikita Khrushchev predicts, let us at least have freedom of debate on this issue. Let no governmental power of a punitive nature, through either tax-deduction laws or rules, be used to squelch the freedom of expression which is guaranteed by our Constitution.

AN IMPOSSIBLE JOB

DECEMBER 14, 1959

NEIL MCELROY has just resigned as Secretary of Defense and Thomas S. Gates, Jr., has been appointed to succeed him. Both are able men, conscientious, energetic, fair-minded and meriting the praise bestowed on them for their respective records in public service.

But the job of Secretary of Defense today is an impossible one. It deserves to be completely re-examined.

The function of the office is to co-ordinate the planning and operation of the armed services. Actually, it includes many of the duties that under the Constitution belong only to the Commander in Chief. It covers also duties of planning for war that only the chiefs of the armed services themselves are competent to perform. We have, in effect, delegated by law to the Secretary of Defense the task of serving as a Deputy Commander in Chief of the armed services.

For years we have heard a hue and cry—and we still do—about "inter-service rivalries." This is an oversimplified explanation of the many differences of opinion as to how public moneys shall be spent in preparation for the contingency of war. In reality, while the Chiefs of Staff today do have pride in their respective services and want to see them maintained at a high degree of effectiveness, the basic problem is that nobody knows what kind of war to prepare for or when or where the next war will be fought.

Since nobody can be sure what the enemy will do under a given set of circumstances, the top commanders of our soldiers, our sailors and our aviators fundamentally desire to see maximum preparation made for any and all contingencies.

The customary compromise advanced is that a "calculated risk" must be taken. Because there isn't money enough to do everything, a choice must often be made between the lesser of two dangerous evils.

History tells us that new weapons have always been introduced faster than we can possibly learn the strategy that must govern their practical use. Hence, the transition period, as President Eisenhower sagely observed the other day, requires us not to let go of the old weapons before we concentrate on the new ones.

There are considerations, moreover, of psychological warfare which are important in molding the opinion of peoples everywhere. Officers of our military services are cautioned to speak in subdued tones or in innocuous phrases while Nikita Khrushchev barnstorms the capitals of Asia and Europe telling how his missiles can destroy America and how much ahead of us on rockets the Communists claim to be.

Then, too, we have the political medicine men who make campaign issues out of their nation's defense problems on the far-fetched theory that an Administration in power is so lacking in patriotism as to fail to maintain an effective defense or that it is being shortsighted in refusing to regard stunt trips to the moon as a "must"—even more pressing than the proper organization, for instance, of our conventional forces.

The new Secretary of Defense is reported to be interested in building up the prestige of the secretaries of the Army, the Navy and the Air Force so that they will at least not appear to be supernumeraries.

Even more important is to rebuild the structure of the Joint Chiefs of Staff so that military minds will have more chance, by collaboration, to develop proper military policies for the United States. Too much time has to be spent by the Chiefs in administering their own services. Nor do they have enough time to indoctrinate their subordinates in some of the over-all concepts that must govern our decisions in making diplomatic as well as military policies.

Today we happen to have in the Presidency a man of military experience, but in a little more than a year we shall have a President who has not been a professional soldier. The office of Secretary of Defense for the past seven years has had a backstop in the White House. Without an Eisenhower to lean upon, will there be as much confidence on the part of the general public in what the next Secretary of Defense in a new Administration may prescribe?

Clearly we need a re-emphasis on military planning by military men and a redefinition of the civilian's place in co-ordinating our armed services and keeping them equipped and trained to meet the demands of "limited" as well as unlimited war. For if nuclear weapons are to be banned, the danger of ground warfare of the conventional kind is not lessened but increased.

We cannot favor a single generalissimo to rule our military services, nor can we delegate to a civilian Secretary of Defense the responsibility of decision on questions that are purely military.

The answer lies in making better use of the military mind than we have been doing so that the civilian authority, in its final decisions, will have had the best kind of military advice. For on the wise collaboration and blending of both points of view depends the survival of the nation.

1960

1960—YEAR OF DESTINY?

JANUARY 4, 1960

Is 1960 a year in which the American people will vote to change administrations?

Is 1960 to see the die cast for an abandonment of the conservative fiscal policies that have steered the nation through the recent periods of economic crisis?

Is 1960 to record a decision in favor of policies that could result in a further devaluation of the dollar?

Is a new President to be chosen who believes in gambling on statistical prophecies of expected "growth" and in committing the Government to big spending programs, irrespective of the size of the deficit?

Or is 1960 to see a vote by the American people to continue the policies of restraint and moderation in economic affairs so effectively carried on by President Eisenhower?

Will the people say by their votes that they don't want a change for the worse—the risks and uncertainties that go with a grant of executive power to a party sharply divided between conservatives from the South and the radicals from the North?

The year 1960 can see a decision made to change the fundamental course of the nation. Or the people, by their votes, can confirm the sensible policies that have enabled the United States Government to maintain international leadership abroad and a stable economic position at home.

This is a critical time in the history of the world. The last two years have seen some especially significant events. A threat of war in Asia has been removed, temporarily, at least. A similar threat over the status of Berlin remains in the background. A new threat, however, to the stability of the world emerges now. It is of direct concern to our allies. Will the commitments made to them by President Eisenhower be maintained or forsaken by the next Administration?

It is most unfortunate that our election campaigns are so prolonged. For nearly ten months in 1960 the peoples of the world will be wondering what direction American policy will take. Then if a Democratic Administration is elected in November, a period of two and one-half months will ensue during which the most important negotiations on world problems will have to be suspended by our own Government. Our allies will be filled with anxiety, and our enemies will rejoice over the frustration within our ranks.

President Eisenhower's tour abroad has been hailed by both parties as a constructive mission that has truly reflected the spirit of America. Would that the same unanimity could be shown on foreign policy by the presidential candidates, so that the campaign might be fought out on domestic issues alone!

But it so happens that the whole economic position of the United States in the world depends on how we manage our internal affairs in relation to wages, prices, and interest rates, as well as trade movements. The economies of Europe and America are interrelated. If the United States decides to turn to more and more deficit spending, more and more public housing, more and more public ownership of electric power, and a gradual extension of socialistic principles on every side which can weaken and disrupt our free enterprise system, the prediction of Nikita Khrushchev, that our grandchildren will live under state socialism, will be nearer to fulfillment than he himself dreamed.

The current drive by pressure groups for bigger and bigger government subsidies involves commitments of many billions of dollars for future generations. There is, as has well been said, not enough in America for everybody's greed, but there is more than enough for everybody's needs.

Furthermore, to remove the experienced personnel of the Government at a critical time in the history of the United States, and to embark on programs of experimentation, foreign and domestic, while an entirely new group of persons seeks to become familiar with the complex questions of public policy, could be dangerous to the safety of the American people.

Under similar circumstances, the people of Great Britain decided against a change of administration.

Will the candidate of the Democratic Party give the nation assurances that if he is elected, there will be no fundamental change in foreign policy?

Will the candidate of the Republican Party pledge himself that, if elected, he will continue wholeheartedly the policies of the Eisenhower Administration?

The issue for the voters to decide in 1960 is the continuation or reversal of international policies that have opened the way to an era of peace with honor.

The issue for the voters to decide in 1960 on the domestic front is the continuation or reversal of policies that have insured a steady growth of the economy.

The year 1960 is a year of decision. It can alter American destiny—or it can conserve the sinews of strength that have made America so powerful.

Will the American people, by their votes, assure the world that the United States will continue to maintain economic stability at home, and will continue to exercise dynamic leadership abroad?

HOW NOT TO CHOOSE
A PRESIDENT

JANUARY 11, 1960

OUR PRESENT SYSTEM of choosing candidates for the Presidency relies on luck and chance.

Two men who happen to be popular personally but who have had no experience with the problems of administration in the executive departments of the Federal Government can be presented to the voters for their choice on Election Day.

Two men who have never had any experience in either house of Congress can be named as presidential candidates, and yet the functioning of the Presidency requires a familiarity with both the legislative and executive branches of the Federal Government.

America has been lucky, generally speaking, in her selection of Presidents, but the sad truth is that several Presidents have not been able to do in their first term as good a job as they have done in their second term.

This is because the first term is often taken up largely with learning procedures and the background of national and international problems.

Several of our Presidents have come to the White House from the office of Governor of a State. This is valuable experience, but it isn't federal experience.

Some of our Presidents, of course, have had legislative experience in Congress, but it is unfortunately true that no man who has been leader of his party in either the House or the Senate has been nominated for the Presidency in the last half-century.

President Eisenhower never served in any elective office in a State or the Federal Government. Though he has an absorptive mind, it takes time to learn the ropes. That's why sometimes a President, as in Mr. Eisenhower's case, can be more successful in his leadership in the second term than in the first term.

Wouldn't it be much better if we had a modified form of the parliamentary system, wherein a Prime Minister must earn his spurs in years of legislative combat? In most countries, like England and Canada, this means a day-by-day interrogation and response on every kind of problem of executive administration.

The two men in America who today are qualified for the Presidency by experience comparable to that of parliamentary leaders abroad are Vice President Richard Nixon, Republican, and Senator Lyndon Johnson of Texas, Democrat. Mr. Nixon had served two terms in the House of Representatives and two years as a Senator when he was elected Vice President. He has been an unofficial spokesman of his party in Congress during the last seven years, identifying the role of the Vice Presidency more with party leadership than ever before. In addition, Mr. Nixon not only has had frequent opportunities to sit with the President and his Cabinet and executive organizations like the National Security Council, but he has served effectively as liaison between the White House and Congress.

Senator Johnson has shown the kind of skill and masterful knowledge in handling controversial legislation that is exhibited by the parliamentary leaders in other countries. No one else being prominently mentioned today for the Democratic nomination has had similar training. Mr. Johnson, to be sure, lacks administrative experience, but, if America had adopted some form of parliamentary government, a Senate leader like Mr. Johnson would have had plenty of opportunity to become familiar with executive problems.

There's another advantage in the parliamentary system—it can provide for elections at two-year intervals or more frequently. President-elect Wilson touched on this point in a letter written in February, 1913, to the Majority Leader of the House of Representatives when it was considering a proposal in the 1912 Democratic platform for a single presidential term of six years. Mr. Wilson wrote:

"Four years is too long a term for a President who is not the true spokesman of the people, who is imposed upon and does not lead. It is too short a term for a President who is doing, or attempting a great work of reform, and who has not had time to finish it. . . .

"Sooner or later, it would seem, he must be made answerable to opinion in a somewhat more informal and intimate fashion—answerable, it may be, to the houses whom he seeks to lead, either personally or through a Cabinet, as well as to the people for whom they speak. But that is a matter to be worked out—as it inevitably will be—in some natural American way which we cannot yet even predict."

Our present system is woefully inadequate, and could give America for four years a President who, when a critical time arose in our history, ought not to be allowed to continue in office at all.

The existing system of choosing a President and the fixed tenure of office of the Chief Executive present a major problem with which the American people must some day come to grips, even if the politicians keep brushing it aside.

ORGANIZED GREED WINS

JANUARY 18, 1960

ORGANIZED GREED won out over self-restraint in the so-called "settlement" of the steel dispute.

Monopoly was the victor as a selfish minority rode roughshod over the interests of the majority.

The monopoly power of an industry-wide union extorted from a group of steel companies a billion-dollar wage increase. This expense will start next December—three weeks after the national elections—and will be passed on to the public in increased prices.

The American consumer, helpless against such monopoly, lost a crucial battle, as millions of unorganized citizens with fixed incomes now must face a steady loss of purchasing power.

Men in public life in both parties—who should have manifested the courage of their convictions—faltered. They succumbed to the doctrine that principle must be sacrificed to expediency.

A severe defeat, therefore, has come in the fight which has been waged for several months to maintain a stable dollar. The crusade to check inflation has been immeasurably weakened.

There is no ceiling in sight now for wages or for prices. The inexorable pressure of organized minorities, capable of inflicting economic damage on the whole people, will continue to be exerted irresponsibly.

Congress, beholden to such economic blocs for campaign contributions, does not dare to fight them.

Conscience has taken a holiday.

Thus has democracy failed in its greatest test of the century. Government, which is supposed to govern in the best interests of the whole people, did not stand up to the test.

The politicians permitted big unionism to achieve its biggest victory and allowed the American people to suffer their biggest defeat.

The managers of the steel companies stood up against a 116-day strike but had to yield in the end. They could not by themselves take the loss indefinitely, especially as Congress showed every sign of compelling a surrender to the union anyhow through Government-imposed pressure.

What now?

The wage-price spiral over the next five years will extend to other businesses and industries.

Since the steelworkers enjoy the highest wages ever paid in American industry, they could—in the interest of economic stability—have afforded at least a two-year suspension of the upward rise until national growth and efficiency at the workbench could justify further wage increases. The union nevertheless insisted on getting "all the traffic would bear" and resisted all changes in work rules.

The selfish slogan that "we must get ours no matter what happens" has triumphed. The innocent bystander will have to pay the bill through a devalued dollar.

The same greed now will motivate other unions. The drive for higher and higher wages, irrespective of the productivity of labor, has been won by the steel union. The other labor groups will demand a like result.

This flagrantly disregards the sense of responsibility that economic groups should exhibit toward society.

Nikita Khrushchev must be smiling. Our much-boasted system of voluntarism has proved to be irresponsible, and we face an era of economic chaos, the dreaded outcome of which may be state dictation through federal regulation of wages and prices.

Everything points now to the alliance of unsound economics with political expediency.

Under the circumstances, the purchasing power of the dollar, currently around 47 cents in terms of the 1939 dollar, may go down in the next decade to about 25 cents. It could go down faster than in the last ten years because the politicians have taken the lid off. There is nothing on the horizon that indicates any restraint upon the downward course of our monetary unit, unless perchance public opinion, when enlightened, becomes aroused and really demands stability.

Citizens who are trying to plan ahead for their families will struggle to find some way of meeting the financial hardships they may be expected to encounter in the coming years. But millions of people will be helpless to defend themselves.

Congress will naturally move to increase Social Security pensions and to raise the minimum-wage scales. States will endeavor to increase welfare payments. Something has to be done, to be sure, by Government to rescue the tens of millions of unorganized citizens who will have to pay the true cost of the steel "settlement" announced on January 4, 1960—a sad day in American history.

This is a presidential-election year. Demagoguery will thrive. Propaganda will mislead. Selfish ambition will rule the day. What a travesty on responsible government!

The new decade opens with a tragic defeat of the public interest by those politicians in labor and Government who preferred a temporary prosperity in 1960 to the sound measures that could have spared America a depression in 1961.

SHOULDN'T THE GOVERNMENT
PAY ITS DEBTS?

JANUARY 25, 1960

THE GOVERNMENT is what the people make it. Policies are what the people, through their chosen representatives, say they ought to be. The voters cannot avoid their responsibility.

Hence today, when there is a possibility of a surplus of 4.2 billion dollars in the coming fiscal year, it is pertinent to ask what should be done with that surplus.

Shall it be applied to our 291-billion-dollar debt, or shall it be spent?

This is the most important question before the Congress that has just assembled. It is the most important question before the whole country.

Shall we become "spenders" or "savers"?

It is easy enough to devise ways of spending 4.2 billion dollars. Already the proponents of some of the appropriations for special purposes who have been unsuccessful in the past see a chance to get the money now.

But shall the Government act like the man and his wife who go from window to window, convince themselves they "need" many an article they see, and then spend beyond their means, using borrowed money while failing to pay off any of their debts? Why is it that we frown on an individual who goes in debt over his head, and we don't frown on the Government when it does the same thing?

Certainly there is need for more money for school buildings and educational projects and for a variety of things that could easily eat up the 4.2-billion-dollar surplus, but the States and cities should provide most of these "improvements," as they are in the best position to judge how much the projects are really needed.

For the time does come when those who lend money to the Government begin to ask: When will the debts be paid? And as doubts arise, the value of Government bonds starts to drop on the markets of the world. The dollar itself immediately begins to be suspect. Fears are expressed that the dollar may not be adequately backed by gold or by assets sufficient to warrant further borrowings.

President Eisenhower made a significant reference to the expected surplus when he delivered his state-of-the-union message to Congress on January 7, but it was greeted with louder cheers from the "spenders" than from the "savers." Here is what he said:

"This budget will be a balanced one. Expenditures will be 79.8 billion dollars. The amount of income over outgo, described in the budget as a surplus to be applied against our national debt, is 4.2 billion.

"Personally, I do not feel that any amount can be properly called a surplus as long as the nation is in debt. I prefer to think of such an item as reduction on our children's inherited mortgage. And, once we have established such payments as normal practice, we can profitably make improvements in our tax structure and thereby truly reduce the heavy burdens of taxation. In any event, this one reduction will save taxpayers each year approximately 200 million dollars in interest costs.

"This favorable balance will ease pressures on our credit and capital markets. It will enhance the confidence of people all over the world in the strength of our economy and our currency."

It follows that, if we do not apply the surplus to debt reduction, it will not ease pressures on our credit and capital markets and that it will impair the confidence of people all over the world in the strength of our economy and our currency.

Our public debt increased during the depression in the 1930s from about 16 billion dollars to 55 billion, and rose to 263 billion by the close of World War II. Since then it has gone up another 28 billion, which includes a 12-billion-dollar deficit due to the 1957-58 recession. Wouldn't it be wiser to make at least a 4.2-billion reduction in the debt now that the "boom" has returned and tax receipts are rising?

Nobody expects the debt to be paid off within any given number of years, but investors do have a right to expect that the United States will live within its means and not further depreciate the value of the bonds already issued. To print paper money is easy for any government to do. To win the confidence of borrowers, it is necessary for a government to make a practice of applying the surplus each year to the payment of past debt.

Governments have gone bankrupt before, and it would be a calamity of indescribable proportions if the American dollar were to lose its value year after year as the "spenders" force the use of surpluses to obtain their extravagances, disregarding any obligation to repay the money already borrowed.

What presidential candidate will espouse the doctrine of paying off the public debt by annual contributions from surplus?

"WISDOM" IN A TROUBLED WORLD

FEBRUARY 8, 1960

IN MANY PARTS OF THE WORLD, there is turmoil, friction, fear—or else restlessness, discontent and a searching for the Utopia that is never found.

In France, there is a new crisis.

In Africa and Asia, seething masses of people clamor for a better life.

In the Middle East, deep-seated enmities show no signs of being resolved.

In China, hundreds of millions have become the pawns of dictators, even as tens of millions in the Soviet Union find themselves victims of the mad passion of their rulers for world conquest. Unscrupulous leaders turn away from individual betterment to the pursuit of more and more power over their fellow men. Human slavery is on the increase.

In Latin America, the crisis deepens. Cuba, the unhappy victim of Communist infiltration, now openly defies her long-time friend—the United States.

Throughout Central and South America, Communist intrigue carries its subversion into governments, universities, trade unions, the press and the church.

Amidst it all, the Soviet Union preaches hourly over the radio waves its own brand of hypocrisy. It claims to be for peace, for disarmament, for an abandonment of the use of nuclear weapons. But while its voice is the voice of Jacob, its hand is the hand of Esau.

Meanwhile, science is implored to make haste—to invent deadlier weapons.

International conferences seeking humane objectives proceed with external piety and inward distrust.

And what sort of spectacle does the United States itself present?

We see ambitious men belittling each other in a quest for political gain.

We see huge blocs, possessed of vast power over the economic life of our country, vying with each other in establishing their respective monopolies.

We see evidences of broken ethics in various fields.

We see a recrudescence of religious bigotry.

We see a contemptuous indifference to the lessons of history. Our boast is that this age—our age—is indeed the greatest of all. We ignore the Scriptural injunction: "For what shall it profit a man, if he shall gain the whole world, and lose his own soul?"

What, indeed, do we gain by going to the moon when we have forsaken our duty to each other on this planet? Where, to be sure, is the true key to peace? Is it in the weapons we have forged and in the missiles we shall build to protect ourselves against the madman who may press the button of world destruction or who, even foregoing war, will attempt conquest by threat?

What have we learned through history—that only war and brute force will gain victories for the strong over the weak? Or have we learned something of the spirit of man himself and of the incalculable power of human beings who, when they concert their will, can brush dictators aside as mere pygmies?

The writings of the great philosophers of the republics of ancient Greece bring uncomfortable reminders of our own inadequacy. We today criticize an emphasis on luxuries and an addiction to materialism. Yet we cry out for more and more subsidies to the individual and show less and less interest in the need for self-reliance. Unwittingly, we are building up the image of a totalitarian state in which the dependent citizen is taught to abide by the will of his omniscient masters.

What about the simple and elementary principles of human conduct that have brought happiness to many an individual and success to the pursuits of many an enterprising mind? Shall we regard as trite the doctrine of human love or the advocacy of a spirit of mutual helpfulness in all human relations?

We must have better communication—from group to group, from people to people. We must not give way to the egocentric illusion that other peoples have no wisdom to impart to us.

We must not look on history as the faded pages of some other generation's failures.

We must communicate to each other once more the wisdom of the ages—that friction among human beings is more often than not the product of selfishness and greed and that the need for co-operation between peoples is the greatest challenge of our times.

Science has its worthwhile objectives, but the constant effort to enlarge man's knowledge in any field of exploration must be put into proper perspective.

Shall we, ignoring the crises in human relations that beset us on earth, seek in outer space to gain an imaginary triumph in the competition for so-called "prestige"?

The answer comes from the books of faith. There can be no peace on earth until we have learned to respect the dignity of man and are willing to build on the foundation of human love the kind of world that the great teachers of mankind have portrayed to us from the time of the Ten Commandments and the Sermon on the Mount. These are the true lessons of mortal life.

ARE THE PEOPLE SO "DUMB"?

FEBRUARY 15, 1960

ARE THE CURRENT SPEECHES of some of the would-be presidential candidates an indication of how they size up the intelligence of the electorate?

Perhaps they are following the advice of the late Harry Hopkins of New Deal fame when he said: "The people are too damn dumb to understand."

Judging by the headlines, several of the candidates and their supporters in Congress are portraying America as helpless and "without leadership."

Presumably we are already licked by the Soviet Union—in science, in interplanetary travel, in education, in rocketry, in missiles, and in general "prestige" throughout the world.

Presumably we must spend more billions for defense, more billions for schools and education, more billions for housing, and more billions for "social needs."

Presumably the people aren't concerned at all about inflation and do not want to hear mention of such things as balancing the federal budget or paying off the national debt.

We read political speeches that talk of our "poverty" amidst plenty or of our lack of "economic growth."

The cry is for something called "positive leadership" and for what are termed "bold and imaginative ideas." The call is for an end to "budgetary considerations" in making national or international policy.

Some of these illusions stem from the isolated strata in which the modern intellectual travels. He worships at the altar of theory and abstraction. To him, for example, a Communist who conspires to overthrow our Government is just a man with a political belief different from our own.

Other illusions cherished by some of the political candidates are that the American people are lazy-minded, that they read newspapers superficially—mostly headlines—and don't keep up with what's going on. Much of the political strategy seems to be based on the theory that the people are easily aroused to vote against an Administration just because it doesn't spend money for pet projects envisaged by the "spenders."

Then there are other candidates who insist that America is losing her "leadership" in the world and that this can best be remedied by giving someone in the opposite party a chance to lead the world. What they seem to have quickly forgotten is that cheering crowds, unprecedented in numbers, greeted the President on his recent trip to Europe, Asia and Africa—everywhere Mr. Eisenhower was acclaimed as the champion of American freedom and democracy.

Yet we are told that American prestige is at a "low ebb" and that we are not winning friends throughout the world.

Lately the politicians have turned to another alleged weakness. They imply that the United States is about to be destroyed by enemy missiles—unless more and more billions are spent for defense. Or else it is asserted that, no matter what America does, it can't "catch up" with the Russians because they have a "big lead."

The average man is expected to believe that his high wages, his comforts—his high standard of living—are a sign of "softness," and that he must somehow deny himself all such things, pay higher taxes, and give the "spenders" a chance to spend more billions.

This isn't an alluring prospect for the voter, but some of the political "liberals" imply that, even if the American does enjoy a species of contentment, he now must be persuaded to give it up and accept a life of hardship and heavier taxation.

How will the voter size up the political candidates of 1960?

Is the average voter actually as much concerned as he is supposed to be with a photogenic smile or a new kind of haircut, or with the hand-shaking or baby-kissing propensities of the candidates?

What the voters basically want to find out is whether a candidate has integrity, and whether he has common sense plus courage.

The mere avowal by a candidate that he wishes to be President may satisfy his own ego, but it doesn't necessarily mean he has the judgment and the ability to deal objectively and sensibly with the vital questions that will surely confront the next President of the United States.

A candidate's record is important, but it isn't always indicative of what he will do if given full responsibility to direct the destiny of the nation.

A candidate is still a symbol of party government.

The American people, for the most part, judge a political party by its performance and, if it has been reasonably successful, it is continued in power. If it has made a "mess in Washington," the Administration is ousted from power.

But, in the final analysis, the people have sense enough to decide whether they are being led into war, or whether they are being led along the paths of peace and toward a steadily improving economic life. Most voters aren't as "dumb" as the politicians think.

THE COMMON SENSE "GAP"

FEBRUARY 22, 1960

JUDGING BY the sensational headlines and the political hysteria of the hour, America is in grave danger of being destroyed at any minute by 300 Soviet missiles.

We are supposed to be behind and cannot "catch up" for a couple of years or so—if then.

This is called the missile "gap."

But what is even more serious is the credulity of many people who have been led by Democratic Party politicians to believe that we are in dire peril.

It may suit the ambitions of the candidates for political office to play politics with our national defense. But what possible good can it do the cause of peace and understanding in the world for Americans to present the spectacle of a nation divided, leaderless and shivering with apprehension?

Even though as strong as our potential enemies, we run the risk of conveying the impression that we really are weak and hence must submit to their demands. What a tragic way to portray the United States at a critical time, when the President is about to go to a "summit" conference in Paris and then is to tour the Soviet Union!

Is Mr. Eisenhower to be presented before the world as the quivering messenger of a defeated people? Is this what the Democratic politicians want for their country?

None of the politicians, however extreme their statements, could really have been thinking of the impact of the recent barrage of criticism about our alleged weaknesses in defense. But it will be said that the politicians were, after all, just echoing the viewpoints of those generals who criticize the defense program on a professional basis, and that there could be no harm in bringing all this out into the open.

Nobody, of course, is objecting to discussion of our defense needs. We have had such debates since the founding of the Republic. But all of us will want to see some self-restraint imposed upon any public debate revealing vital facts about weapons of war, details of our military strength and secret data gathered from abroad.

Common sense tells us that if we are weak and are remedying the weaknesses, it is not wise from any standpoint to tell a potential enemy about it.

For the last two weeks there actually have been debates in Congress about our "intelligence estimates." This is the most confidential of all categories of governmental information. Yet we actually see would-be candidates for the Presidency and Democratic leaders publicly interpreting such "estimates" to the detriment not merely of the Administration, but of the position of their own country versus a potential enemy.

When General Power of the Strategic Air Command testified that the Soviets might, with 300 missiles, destroy our bases in this country, he was confining himself to a hypothetical situation that illustrated to him the importance of maintaining an airborne alert 24 hours a day, every day in the week. This would require a large and perhaps unnecessary expenditure. For when a crisis is on the horizon—and there are no signs of it in the immediate future—such an airborne alert can be ordered. The President has said that, the instant an airborne alert seems necessary, he will order it.

But is it true that 300 missiles could destroy America's retaliatory power just because bases in continental United States might be destroyed? First of all, those who know how far the development of rocketry has actually progressed say that it is impossible to fire a simultaneous salvo that would destroy all our bases at the same time. Since there necessarily would be a time lag between enemy firings, this would result in an opportunity for us to apply our retaliatory power.

Also, our Army has just revealed that, for the first time in history, a ballistic missile has been tracked down and destroyed in the air by another missile.

The Soviets, moreover, would have to do more than merely destroy our plane and missile bases in this country. There would have to be simultaneous destruction of all such bases in Britain and in Southern Europe, and of all our aircraft carriers and their bombers. Likewise, every single one of our missile-carrying submarines cruising under the seas in different parts of the world would have to be demolished at the same moment.

Our Polaris missiles, which are to be fired from submarines, are to be operational soon, and within the next two years we shall be building many more of them. They can approach unobserved within a few miles of an enemy's coast and fire missiles 1,200 miles inland.

The key to the controversy over defense is not how many missiles the Soviets possess but what our over-all power of massive retaliation happens to be.

There is need in America to apply common sense and close the "gap" between those who are engaging in flights of political fancy in an election year and the majority of the people, who believe the statements of the President of the United States—a military leader in his own right. He says unequivocally that we have the over-all power to deter attack.

TOWARD RESPONSIBLE GOVERNMENT

FEBRUARY 29, 1960

PRESIDENT EISENHOWER has proposed that the Constitution be amended to provide that members of the House of Representatives shall serve a four-year term, instead of two years as at present. But while the purpose—to achieve stability in government—is commendable, the objective can be better attained by a reform of the ballot. This could be done simply by the passage of a law by Congress.

For, under the Constitution, Congress has the power to regulate "the manner of holding elections for Senators and Representatives." What really is needed is to re-establish the system of party responsibility that was in effect in America for many decades but which began to disintegrate in recent years when several States, by law, ceased to permit a vote to be cast for both the presidential and congressional candidates by a single cross mark at the top of the ballot.

Instance after instance is recorded nowadays in which many citizens in a given State vote for a presidential nominee and then do not vote at all on the separate ballot containing the names of the nominees for Congress. In many States each candidate has to be voted for individually on a long list on different ballots, or else several levers in different columns have to be pulled on the voting machines. Certainly State, county and city elections should not be held at the same time as presidential elections. This clutters up the ballot and complicates the whole voting process.

A mistaken impression has prevailed that, when a President runs ahead of his congressional ticket, his own party is weaker. Actually, for the last half century, the total votes cast in each congressional district for the presidential nominees have, with few exceptions, topped the total vote for the congressional candidates. This margin has been steadily widening in recent years, irrespective of party. Back in 1896 and 1900, only about two per cent of the citizens who went to the polls would fail to vote for the nominees for Congress, whereas in the last few years the gap has become three times as large.

The reason is to be found in the increasing disadvantages of the separate ballot. Sometimes, when polling booths are crowded and the voters must wait in line for a long time, they tend to speed up the voting process and do not take the time to examine or mark separate ballots. Also, many citizens have been urged to split their ticket but, when they get into the polling booth, they do not know how to do it. They wind up voting only for the presidential and vice-presidential nominees. Splitting a ticket should, of course, always be permitted, but voting a "straight ticket" should not be made more and more difficult.

The election of a Congress is directly related to the election of a President. The two branches of Government together enact legislation. There is need, therefore, for some way to fix responsibility on one or the other of the political parties.

More and more in recent years we have had divided government. Until a few years ago, the number of occasions when a party elected a President but didn't elect a majority in Congress were few indeed. During the current 16-year period, the Democratic Party will have been in control of Congress for 12 years. During that same time, the Republicans will have been in control of the White House for eight years, in only two of which they have had a majority in Congress.

Under such a set-up there is no way for the people to fix party responsibility. The risk involved in divided government is growing. Important legislation is sidetracked, and the nation's progress is often retarded because of dissension between Congress and the President.

If the President and his party were elected by the people on a single ballot, we would have a much more orderly system of government. Even if in a congressional election a majority was chosen from the opposite party, this would be a proper expression of protest and could prove helpful in guiding a President in the remainder of his term. Divided government would at least not be in effect for more than two years.

The most salutary change, therefore, that could be made in our system is to require that all nominees for President and Vice President and for Congress in each district be voted for on a single ballot. This would enable the voter more readily to vote the "straight ticket." The party primaries would then come into their own as the real means of choosing nominees of each party for Congress, just as happens now in the South, where the primaries are even more important than the final election. The party platforms would again become meaningful.

Party responsibility would thus be restored. As we have seen in recent years, the absence of such responsibility and the growth of blocs within the political parties have weakened the legislative bodies in other lands as well as in our own.

Reform of the ballot is an important step toward party responsibility, and this, in turn, is essential to responsible government in America.

WARNING RUSSIA

MARCH 7, 1960

PRESIDENT EISENHOWER has opportunely reaffirmed the Monroe Doctrine. He has warned the Soviet Government and the Communist regimes that they must cease their attempts to subvert Latin America.

This is a desirable policy, as was pointed out on this page in the issue of November 23 last:

"In the early days of the Republic, the United States proclaimed what has been known ever since as the 'Monroe Doctrine.' It declared that any attempt by any European power to interfere in the internal affairs of any country in this hemisphere will be considered by the United States to be an unfriendly act, 'dangerous to our peace and safety.'

"Plainly there is a Communist menace in Central and South America. It threatens every government in this hemisphere. It operates through an apparatus directed and financed by the Soviet Government. . . .

"The United States Government and many of the governments to the south of us know the facts. And the facts establish clearly that the Soviet Government is flagrantly violating the Monroe Doctrine."

The President was urged to give warning to the Soviet Government that friendly relations cannot be maintained as long as Soviet agents of intrigue infest Latin-American capitals. It was suggested also that a commission of Central and South American states be organized to expose Communist operations there.

Mr. Eisenhower has wisely taken the first step to mobilize public opinion in Latin America against the Communist menace. In a speech to the Brazilian Congress on February 24, he said:

"But we would consider it intervention in the internal affairs of an American state if any power, whether by invasion, coercion or subversion, succeeded in denying freedom of choice to the people of any of our sister republics."

These are strong words—a timely warning. They follow the words of the Resolution adopted in 1954 at the 10th Inter-American Conference at Caracas, Venezuela, attended by the membership of the Organization of American States. It read in part as follows:

"(The conference) Declares: That the domination or control of the political institutions of any American state by the international Communist movement, extending to this hemisphere the political system of an extracontinental power, would constitute a threat to the sovereignty and political independence of the American states, endangering the peace of America, and would call for a meeting of consultation to consider the adoption of appropriate action in accordance with existing treaties."

This was what is known as the "Dulles Resolution," which the President has now repeated. Indeed, he has reaffirmed the historic Monroe Doctrine.

We have recently observed in the Middle East, and now in Cuba, how the Soviets start by infiltrating revolutionary movements and then, under the guise of carrying out "commercial agreements," send in "technicians" and agents to help bring about the bloodless conquest of an unsuspecting people.

The United States is actually confronted today with a Communist attempt to get a foothold in Cuba, which is only 90 miles away from our shores.

Back in June 1940, when there was a threat of Nazi conquest of the French, British and Dutch possessions in this hemisphere, President Franklin D. Roosevelt obtained from Congress a joint resolution which implemented a resolution adopted earlier that year by the foreign ministers of the American republics.

Congress served notice that no such transfer of sovereignty would be recognized and declared that, if such a transfer seemed likely, the United States "in addition to other measures" would consult with all the American republics "to determine on the steps which should be taken to safeguard their common interests."

The time has come for another resolution to be adopted by Congress, as suggested in an article in our issue of December 28 last by Samuel Flagg Bemis, professor of Diplomatic History and Inter-American Relations at Yale University. He pointed out that there might not be time to assemble a meeting of the Inter-American Organ of Consultation to provide for joint action by the Organization of American States. He proposed that Congress should state formally that "any one or more of the high contracting parties to the Inter-American Treaty of Reciprocal Assistance would be justified, in the exercise of individual or collective self-defense under Article 51 of the Charter of the United Nations, in taking steps to forestall intervention, domination, control and colonization by international Communism in the New World."

This precautionary step seems worth considering now. If in this way Congress reaffirms the Monroe Doctrine, while at the same time giving support to an inter-American instrument of defense, it would go far toward keeping the Communists from destroying the independence of the peoples to the south of us.

"THOU SHALT NOT KILL"

MARCH 14, 1960

LATELY THERE HAS BEEN a public agitation to abolish capital punishment.

The argument really is that the Commandment which says "thou shalt not kill" should be amended to read "thou shalt not kill the killer."

The case of Caryl Chessman, condemned by California law to die, has attracted world-wide attention.

Chessman didn't kill anybody. His sex crimes, however, are regarded by many citizens as worse than murder. Rape is looked upon as such a heinous offense that too often it has led to lynchings, primarily because angry citizens have feared that the law would be too lenient with the offender.

The Governor of California, in issuing a 60-day reprieve for Chessman, found himself compelled also to stay the sentences of four others convicted of murder.

To repeal the law that provides for capital punishment means, therefore, that actual murderers would also escape the death penalty.

The problem has many ramifications. Thus, in the District of Columbia, neither the judge nor the jury has any discretion—the death penalty is mandatory in all cases of first-degree murder. Certainly discretion should be permitted either the judge or jury.

But what we are dealing with now is the proposal that the death penalty be abandoned altogether. This raises a question that has its roots in religious as well as sociological controversy. From time immemorial, the injustice of arbitrary punishments has troubled the conscience of men. The Roman principle of justice, formulated by Emperors Maximilian and Diocletian, asserted that "the judge must not heed the clamor of the crowd, which often seeks to release the guilty and condemn the innocent."

We have had plenty of clamor over the Chessman case. In Britain, where proposals to abolish the death penalty have just been defeated in Parliament, the press gave big headlines to the Chessman affair. In Uruguay—headquarters of the Communist propaganda apparatus in Latin America—students in the universities were stimulated to make an uproar about the Chessman case and to threaten public demonstrations during President Eisenhower's visit.

But the criticism abroad was based on a fallacy. Even some of the British editorial writers knew so little about our dual sovereignty system in America that they thought the President could commute the sentence. It was not generally realized, moreover, that even the Governor of California has no power under present laws to commute the death sentence unless the State Supreme Court so recommends.

It is, therefore, natural that during the 60-day reprieve the State legislature should be asked by the Governor to repeal the capital-punishment law. At least this puts the question before the people.

In essence, the question is whether judges and juries should be permitted discretion to distinguish between the nature of the crimes and the extent to which irresponsible minds or those temporarily insane may have been guilty of premeditated murder.

Those who wish to abolish capital punishment argue, on the other hand, that the Commandment which says "thou shalt not kill" means that no one should be put to death even if he himself has killed another person.

The late Rabbi Solomon Goldman of Chicago, Biblical scholar, writing on this point in his book, "The Ten Commandments," says:

"Though the Commandment is a precept of civil law, it has often been used to great advantage by pacifists and opponents of capital punishment, thanks to the conciseness and absoluteness of its phrasing."

The Bible warns us pointedly that no one should be put to death without a fair trial. Plainly the doctrine throughout history has been one of simple defense by society against those who take the life of others.

The purpose of the death penalty is to deter those who might otherwise commit murder. It has been argued that this type of crime has not diminished and that the deterrent effect cannot be proved. It is a fact, however, that three States—Kansas, South Dakota and Oregon—have in recent years restored the death penalty after having once abandoned it. Eight States during the last two years have rejected and one has adopted proposals to abolish capital punishment. In all, 44 out of 50 States now use the death penalty for major crimes.

Great Britain, Canada, Australia, the Soviet Union and France have capital punishment. Most nations in Latin America, however, have abandoned its use except by military tribunals to punish revolutionaries.

One might hope that, in the progress of mankind toward higher standards of human behavior, even the worst criminal could be rehabilitated, if not restored to society. But just as pacifism often ignores the factual circumstances of life, so those who today would abolish capital punishment are dreaming of a theoretical Utopia in a far-off age.

HELP FOR THE CUBAN PEOPLE

MARCH 21, 1960

CUBA IS NOT just Castro and his clique. Cuba has 6,500,000 people—and they are in serious trouble.

Cuba is a nation in bondage. Relations with the outside world—especially with the United States—have been messed up by a dictator. He professes to be a friend of the Cuban people, but he is beginning to act as if he is their worst enemy.

How can the Cuban people get the truth? Almost without exception, the newspapers and the radio and television stations are controlled. The irrational outbursts of the Government—and little else—are broadcast inside Cuba. Communists are in positions of influence.

The Cuban people today do not know the dangers they face. The truth must be given them at once.

As President Eisenhower reiterated in speeches on his Latin-American tour, we champion the right of self-determination. The President said:

"We believe in the right of peoples to choose their own form of government, to build their own institutions, to abide by their own philosophy. But if a tyrannical form of government were imposed from the outside or with outside support—by force, threat or subversion—we would certainly deem this to be a violation of the policy of nonintervention and would expect the Organization of American States, acting under several solemn commitments, to take appropriate collective action."

This is a warning to the Communists in Moscow who have been fishing in Cuba's troubled waters. Already Communist propaganda is widely distributed inside Cuba. Fortunately, we, too, have access to the minds of the Cuban people.

If the friends of Cuba throughout this hemisphere were to organize and supply funds for radio broadcasts in the Spanish language directed to all residents of the island—which is only 90 miles away from us— something might be done to save the Cuban people.

It is important for the facts to be set forth. Cuba's biggest crop is sugar—it brings in about $500 million a year from sales abroad. Cuba imports much food that she herself could produce. But a balanced economy cannot be attained if unbalanced minds are allowed to run the country.

Many people in the United States are talking about "reprisals"—about cutting off the subsidy our Government pays now for Cuban sugar. This would be a mistake. The President, however, should be given a flexible power to handle the sugar problem.

If the Castro regime, on the other hand, by its tirades keeps on stirring up bad feeling in the United States, it may be difficult to prevent drastic reprisals by Congress. In such circumstances, while the Cuban people might for a little while live on the fat derived from confiscation of foreign-owned property, the net result might be an increase in our own sugar purchases from Peru, Mexico and Brazil. This could in a few years make us completely independent of Cuban sugar. Why should the American Government be forced into such a punitive policy?

Only the Cuban people can rescue themselves. They are an intelligent people. Their universities have turned out eminent men. They know the difference between dictatorship and democracy. They would concede that the past dictatorships have brought the present debacle. As President Eisenhower said in his report to the American people:

"Another persistent misunderstanding which I sought to correct wherever I traveled is that we sometimes support dictators. Of course we abhor all tyrannical forms of government, whether of the Left or Right."

But as long as we extend diplomatic recognition to a dictatorship government, we are accused of "supporting" such a regime.

There are, therefore, two steps we can take now to clear up such misunderstandings.

First, we can break off diplomatic relations with the Castro government. It obviously does not represent the Cuban people, and it has shown itself incapable of discharging international obligations—two requirements for the continuance of diplomatic recognition.

Second, we can appeal by radio to the Cuban people. This need not be an action of our Government, but a people-to-people expression of sympathy and concern.

We have throughout our history proclaimed our support for oppressed peoples. Our political parties in their national platforms have time and again expressed sympathy with groups striving for independence—the Boers in South Africa, the "home rule" groups in Ireland, the Armenians in the Near East, the Mexicans, and the Cubans themselves under Spanish rule.

If the facts were given now to the people of Cuba, they would insist on free elections. They would choose a sane leadership to rescue them from the economic and political chaos into which they have been plunged by selfish men who have been duped by Communist influences.

Let's help the Cuban people by giving them the whole truth.

"DISARMAMENT" BLACKMAIL

MARCH 28, 1960

THE SOVIET PLAN calls for "disarmament" within four years. During that time, the West is supposed to abolish all foreign bases, send American troops back home and trust to the "good faith" of the Communists thereafter to destroy their nuclear weapons.

The Soviets insist that they shall retain a free hand to do as they please after the West has given up its conventional forces and abandoned all foreign bases for troops, missiles and planes.

The Western plan calls for three stages without arbitrary time limits but demands initially a formula for compliance by the governments concerned.

Basically, the West wants a condition of mutual trust. It asks for immediate action aimed at "preventing aggression and preserving world peace and security, as national armaments are reduced," and declares that this can best be achieved "by an international organization, to be an organ of, or linked to, the United Nations."

The Western plan, in a nutshell, seeks to establish conditions of mutual confidence and good faith before either side is expected to give up its weapons.

The Soviets, on the other hand, brazenly ask that the West disarm at once, with all foreign bases and conventional forces eliminated in about three years. The first official statement made by the Soviet delegate at the Geneva Disarmament Conference says:

"During the same period it will also be possible to carry out such measures as the liquidation of alien bases on foreign territories, the withdrawal of foreign troops from these territories back within their national frontiers, and their disbandment as well as the cessation of the production of all types of conventional armaments."

Then, after the American missile pads and air bases for our bombers in Europe and Asia have been demolished and all American forces have gone home, the Soviets say that "all types of nuclear and rocket weapons should be destroyed and liquidation of entire machinery of states should be fully completed."

What is surprising about the plan is not that the Soviets propose such a procedure, but that they should believe the Western governments are naïve enough to accept it. No Trojan-horse scheme could be conceived with greater boldness or more transparent insincerity.

The world is asked to accept a disarmament plan which weakens its power of military retaliation while relying on an autocratic government in Moscow to carry out its pledge of disarmament. Actual experience, moreover, teaches us that the Soviet Government has violated virtually every important international agreement it has made in the last 25 years.

The British Minister of State, David Ormsby-Gore, touched on this same problem when he told the assembled delegates at the Geneva Disarmament Conference that the plan adopted must not at any stage give significant military advantage to one country or group of countries over others. He called for effective controls and remarked that there is no use "blinking at the fact that suspicion exists between nations and they will not be convinced that their neighbors have in fact reduced their forces until they have proof of it." He also warns that "it must be the object of a control system to furnish such proof."

The world has known for a long time that disarmament cannot be undertaken either immediately or in stages without foolproof measures of control, and that to permit one side to have a military advantage during any stage of the process opens the way to blackmail.

Really nothing new in principle has been developed by the disarmament discussions of recent years. They resemble many past efforts in history. They are either well-meaning attempts to stop the arms race temporarily for economic reasons and to preserve a "balance of power," or they are crafty and insidious schemes to accomplish a military supremacy for one side or the other by playing on the credulity of an adversary.

The Soviet objective of the moment is primarily to make propaganda—to give the appearance of peaceful intent and benevolent purpose. This is designed to allay unrest and fear inside Russia that the Kremlin is heading toward war. But the plain facts are that the "tensions" in the world are produced right along by the Soviet Government and its agents in foreign lands who are engaged in intensive campaigns of subversion.

The Communists are responsible for the tension in Korea and the Far East, the tension in the Middle East, the tension in Africa, the tension in Cuba and Latin America, and the tension over West Berlin.

How can there be any progress toward disarmament when there is so little faith in the word of the present Soviet Government? Only the peoples of the Soviet Union can assure world peace, and they can do so by ridding themselves of a tyrannical government that doesn't honor its agreements and by substituting a free government that the world can trust. That's the only sure road to a reduction of armaments.

HAS INFLATION BEEN CHECKED?

APRIL 4, 1960

FOR SEVERAL YEARS now many people in America who believe in a sound economy have been waging a battle against inflation. In simple terms, inflation means an artificial pressure to raise wages and consequently to raise prices. This causes the purchasing power of the dollar to go down and imposes hardships on pensioners and others who live on fixed incomes.

Some segments of the working force can get their wage scales moved up faster than others. Those who lag behind feel the pinch. Similarly, prices cannot be immediately raised by some businesses, and during the interval of transition they suffer losses.

The Eisenhower Administration—inheriting an inflation forced by World War II and then by the Korean War, which ended in 1953—was not able until after several years of readjustment and recession to begin its main fight against inflationary pressures. The demand of the President in December 1958 for a balanced budget won wide acclaim throughout the country as the nation started to realize that the time had come to get its finances in order.

Despite the predictions of disaster made during the 1957 recession by the "spenders" in Congress who advocated larger outlays by the Federal Government in the face of a $12-billion deficit in the budget, the Administration weathered the storm. A budget surplus now is in sight for the coming fiscal year, and the outlook is for a stabilized economy.

The word "stability" is little appreciated in the precincts of the politicians. The talk is either of a "big boom" or a "deep recession."

There is nothing static, however, about stability. Actually, it means an opportunity for a steady expansion and a widening of economic markets. It could mean enlarged profits through the sale of an increased volume of goods that the average man can afford to pay for out of his income.

"Stability" is not as familiar a term as "prosperity" in modern politics, but it can have a much more far-reaching effect on the nation's economy. A period of stability could be more lasting than a "boom" because it is built on a sounder foundation.

What are the prerequisites to a period of economic stability in America? Plainly, the most important requirement is a sense of restraint with respect to prices and wages.

Fortunately, the consumer has a veto power against higher prices. He merely refuses to buy what he can't afford now and what he cannot eventually pay for out of his income. Installment-buying may help certain sales temporarily, but inevitably, if incomes are not increased, the sales of products suffer and the consequences are widely felt.

It is, therefore, essential that, more than any other factor, the wages of the American worker should be given equitable consideration. He cannot be expected to work indefinitely at the same wage when profits continue to increase. He cannot be expected to pay the rising cost of medical care or live on a pension unless weight is given to what sometimes are called "fringe benefits."

American management has shown an enlightened attitude toward progressive increases in the workers' income. The tirades of the union leaders too often give a misleading impression that businessmen are all selfish individuals without human feeling.

But the facts show that this is a misguided and erroneous impression and that, while there are exceptions to all rules, the tendency of the businessmen of the country on the whole has been to go along with steady increases in wages as long as the public is able to absorb the higher wages as reflected in the cost of goods offered for sale.

Today, however, prices have risen to a point beyond which it may be dangerous to go in increasing wages without substantial increases in the productivity of labor. Foreign competition in several categories has begun to threaten American products in our markets.

Many analysts are saying that "inflation is over." What they really mean is that, logically and on the basis of sound economics, it ought to be over.

But has inflation really been checked? The answer must be sought not from economists but from the politicians and the labor-union leaders. Have they abandoned the drive they have been making for higher and higher wages without regard to what happens to prices and consumer resistance?

The kind of Congress elected next November means a great deal to the business future of America. Labor-union leaders do not hesitate to collect big sums to influence voters. They seek a majority in Congress to do their bidding—to increase the power of the labor monopoly and to increase Government spending.

Has inflation been checked? Will there be a period of economic stability? Or are we headed for a crash to be brought on by the reckless demands of the forces of organized greed?

These are questions still unanswered.

THE "RIGHT TO DEMONSTRATE"

APRIL 11, 1960

THE DIFFERENCE BETWEEN a "mobocracy" and a "democracy" is that in one there is no rule of law, while in the other there is respect for law and order—a willingness to submit to the wishes of the majority of the people as expressed in a system of representative government.

To determine what form of government shall prevail is the sovereign right of a community. Where self-government is denied, the right of revolt is recognized as the inalienable privilege of the people.

These are principles that we in America have espoused ever since the days when we rebelled against the tyranny of a king and established our own republic.

The whole world has accepted the doctrine of self-government and self-determination as a basic principle of human conduct, and, when we see it violated as it was in Hungary in 1956 and in Tibet in 1959, free men everywhere express their disapproval and horror. By doing so, we hope to encourage the downtrodden and the oppressed, though we may not feel an obligation to render them assistance by military force.

For a long time, international law has recognized the right of an outside government to demand respect for the lives and property of its citizens and, if necessary, to take forceful measures by military intervention to protect its own citizens.

To what extent, however, may nations express themselves on what appear to be purely internal matters? The United Nations has been debating lately, through the Security Council, the tragic situation in South Africa. The Government of the Union of South Africa objects to such a discussion on the ground that the recent riots are purely an internal matter relating to the preservation of law and order against mobs.

Our own Government has taken the position that, where a controversy exists as to whether an external or internal situation is involved, there should be full debate on that very point. Great Britain, France and Italy, while expressing regret over the developments in South Africa, appear to regard them as internal.

What is happening, of course, is that 29 Asian and African nations in the United Nations are expressing their "right to demonstrate." This is a proper expression of opinion and a rightful use of moral force. For, unless we are willing to debate in the court of public opinion any issue—including our own behavior—we cannot expect to make progress toward law and order and the establishment of human rights.

But what of the "right to demonstrate" when public officials are challenged? Did the mob of 20,000 which "marched" on the police station in South Africa—containing only 25 policemen—have the right to throw stones and taunt and threaten so that the police grew frightened and opened fire? This was an example not of a "peaceful assembly" but of a "mobocracy."

The net result has been the taking of severe measures of repression and the declaration of a national emergency by the South African Government so as to prevent further tragedies. The acts of lawlessness which have taken the form of burning the identity papers required of all citizens, irrespective of race, are indefensible. They are not in accord with the doctrines of "peaceful demonstration," but are a defiance of law.

In our own country, the "right to demonstrate" is likewise being abused. Negroes and whites have a right to gather in peaceful meetings to deplore the separation of the races at lunch counters, but they have no right to create disturbances inside stores which are private property.

Does the National Association for the Advancement of Colored People have the right to urge the public, by telephone call or handbills, to refrain from patronizing certain stores? "Secondary boycotts" by persons who are not parties to a labor dispute are prohibited by federal laws that have been upheld by the Supreme Court.

It may be questioned whether marching on police stations or State capitals in big numbers is a wise exercise of the "right to demonstrate." Cannot the same points be made and the same publicity obtained by smaller, well-behaved groups? When a large group is formed to "march" on a particular objective, the danger is that such a group can readily be converted into a mob by encouraging bystanders to join in demonstrations, which too often become lawless.

The Supreme Court of the United States has frequently upheld the right of free speech under our Constitution, but it has also ruled that it is not free speech to cry "Fire!" in a crowded theater. It is the impact of free speech and the circumstances surrounding otherwise peaceful gatherings which must be carefully considered. Certainly there is no right to form groups that defy the police in their efforts to maintain order, nor any right to invade private property or to conspire to destroy anyone's business if he is obeying the laws of the land.

There is only the right to "demonstrate" peacefully and with proper respect for the lawful rights of others in the community.

THE SPEECH WE HAVEN'T HEARD

APRIL 18, 1960

HOW REFRESHING IT WOULD BE this presidential-campaign year to hear from at least one of the candidates a speech that the voters could be sure came from the heart, a speech that eschewed the wiles of partisan politics and the insincerities of the demagogue!

Surely the American electorate would applaud enthusiastically a message that showed the presidential candidate to be seeking not just an office for himself but an opportunity really to serve all the people.

What might be said in such a speech? Here are a few thoughts the nation would be glad to hear expressed on the stump by a Democratic candidate:

"I want to say candidly that I do not think the Eisenhower Administration is a failure.

"I know that it is supposed to be good politics for an opposition candidate to condemn everything that has been done by the Administration in power when it is conducted by a party opposite from one's own.

"But I recognize that these are troublous times and that the problems are bewildering and complex. I attribute to the Administration good faith, high purpose and worthy effort. I shall make clear wherein I would differ from existing policies and programs.

"In international policy, the United States has continuously endeavored to stand for high ideals and to find ways to prevent war and maintain peace. If my approach to those problems differs from the Republican candidate's, I shall explain to you the why and the wherefore, but I do not promise to abandon all that has been done to forward the cause of international peace, even though politically, I presume, I should be attacking everything that my opponents have done.

"I shall do everything in my power to advance the prosperity of the United States and to prevent war. But I shall not be frightened by threats from any quarter of the globe. We should try to settle international disputes without resort to force, but I feel that life under slavery can be worse than death and that surrender to an enemy who would blackmail us is unthinkable. I do not favor 'peace at any price.'

"With respect to national defense, I deem it my duty to insist that national safety shall never be jeopardized. I am not a military man and shall have to rely on military men for technical advice. I shall seek out the best advice. Civilian responsibility will not be neglected.

"I cannot believe that any Administration, even though it is conducted by the party opposite from mine, would deliberately jeopardize the national safety.

I deplore the fact that candidates in a political campaign sometimes seek to convey that impression for partisan gain. I will not seek votes on the basis of a platform that questions the motives of loyal, faithful Americans in high office.

"I realize that overspending can ruin our economy and render us a target for attack as we struggle with a chaotic internal situation. There must be a balanced approach, and I promise it so far as I am concerned.

"I conceive it to be the duty of the Federal Government to promote the general welfare. But this must be consistent with fiscal strength and sound economics. I shall not be beholden to any group or class, irrespective of whether they have supported me or contributed funds to my election. I shall be, if elected, President of all the people, and I have made no commitments to any individuals or groups that supersede my commitment to the people as a whole."

What could a Republican candidate say in his own behalf? He could concede the value of the constructive criticism which comes from opponents. He could admit that some errors have been made over a period of seven years which will be corrected. He could disavow any obligation to particular groups or interests, as the national welfare supersedes all else. But he must be ready to express the fundamental principles on which his policies will be based and to explain the extent to which they will conform to or deviate from those of his predecessor.

No candidate is under obligation to defend what in his heart he knows was a wrong policy. He has every obligation to deal fairly and equitably with every issue that is today causing friction in our midst—as, for instance, the so-called "civil rights" issue. He must be ready to safeguard private rights as well as public rights and be willing to follow the Constitution as it is written, and not as some groups think it ought to be.

For the next President of the United States will be a success or a failure depending upon how carefully he sticks to his presidential function of adhering to the law, and how consistently he avoids the role of official or unofficial moralist.

Our Constitution enumerates certain rights that are delegated to the Federal Government and to the States, respectively. All other rights are reserved to the people themselves. What will the oath that the new President takes "to preserve, protect and defend" the Constitution really mean? The people are entitled to know.

A STORY OF COURAGE

APRIL 25, 1960

AUBREY STEEN MCLEOD passed away a few days ago. To the vast majority of the American people he is an "unknown soldier." For the epic of his courage is the untold story of a man who, at the age of 23, lost both his legs above the knees but managed in the 43 years thereafter to achieve a success in life.

"Mac," as he was called by his friends, was one of the first half-dozen Americans wounded in an air raid in France in World War I. He was a volunteer with a U. S. Army ambulance unit which reached France in May, 1917.

Here, in a letter written from a base hospital in France in October, 1917, to his parents in Indiana, is young McLeod's own description of his experience:

"Practically three weeks I have been lying on my back at the hospital and although it is very tiresome, I cannot complain, for I am exceedingly lucky to be alive.

"On the night of September 4, I was on guard with nine others and was sleeping in the reception tent when I was awakened by an explosion. No sooner was I on my feet than a bomb exploded across the street, and then one exploded just five feet from me. It shattered my left foot and filled both my legs with shrapnel, and a piece passed through the fleshy part of my side. Added to this, it was a poisonous shell.

"They amputated my left foot that night. Then gas poisoning set in, and they had to take off both my legs near the hips in order to save my life. If it had happened on the battlefield, I probably would not have lived. I was very fortunate being hit low, for five of our men were killed that night near here. I am receiving the best of care, and my legs are getting along splendidly.

"If everything progresses favorably, I should be home about November 1. Now please don't worry about me, for I am getting along fine. I shall be given artificial legs and will be able to get along O.K."

The wounded man was treated at Walter Reed Hospital in Washington for 11 months and then was transferred to a Boston hospital, where he was fitted with artificial legs. He decided to continue his studies. He graduated in 1921 from Massachusetts Institute of Technology as a chemical engineer, and then earned a Master of Arts degree in economics at Harvard in 1925. He attended classes in a wheel chair and took part in social activities as if he were as able-bodied as the rest of his classmates. He once said, as reported in the Boston "Globe" during his college days:

"The way I look at my case is this. There are numerous people who, in the excess of sympathy just at present for a wounded man, wish to do everything for him; but in the years to come, when the enthusiasm has dropped, the man has got to be able to make something for himself.

"So, as I lay in the hospital for so many months, I decided that I would gain the best education I could and not let my misfortune interfere in the continuation of my studies which were interrupted by the war. I made up my mind I would go on as though nothing had happened and to let nothing make me sour or discontented.

"I eat well, sleep well, and have all kinds of ambition and optimism. I want every wounded or disabled man back from the war to take note of my case. There could hardly be a more used-up man than I am, and yet I want the boys to take heart and go to work and make men of themselves.

"Why, a disabled man can do many things and, very often, can fit himself for a place in which he can earn more money than he ever earned when he was sound."

"Mac's" excellent judgment on investments enabled him to accumulate a small fortune. He became one of the most expert of forecasters of business conditions. He was appointed Actuary of the United States Treasury Department and served there from 1930 to 1937. He was noted for the accuracy of the estimates of future tax receipts which he annually gave to congressional committees.

Never did "Mac" falter. Never did he refer to his handicap as a barrier to anything he wanted to accomplish in life. Two years ago he lost his wife, the high school sweetheart who married him after his return from France. She, too, lived a life of courage. The parents, moreover, instilled courage in their only child, Norman Bruce McLeod, who volunteered in World War II for the hazardous duty of a U. S. Navy "frogman," and later was awarded the Silver Star.

Nearly 20 years ago, "Mac" joined the staff of this magazine as an economist. At the time of his death of a heart attack on April 9, 1960, in a Washington hospital, he was Chief of the Economic Unit of "U. S. News & World Report."

We salute an able economist, but we salute as well a man of unfailing courage. May his fortitude and determination always be an example to all who suffer physical handicaps. For, while the body may be maimed, the spirit of a man can be invincible.

WHAT'S THE ISSUE?

MAY 2, 1960

LOTS OF SPEECHES are being broadcast and lots of articles are appearing in the newspapers about the primary elections in various States. We hear about religious prejudice influencing voters, and we read about public opinion polls which in one month show a candidate's "popularity" rising, and in another month declining.

What's it all about? What, indeed, is the issue?

Is all the commotion just a means of putting one set of officials into Government to replace another?

Is one political party to turn things upside down to give us "a better America"? And who is to assure us that it will be better?

And when, indeed, are the real issues going to be outlined? There seems to be much emphasis on personalities and little stress on principles.

There are, of course, two concepts of Government today. The so-called "liberals" say the Government must use its power and expend the funds of all taxpayers to equalize differences in economic position. Wealth, we are told, must, in effect, be "redistributed," and Peter must be robbed to pay Paul. The Government, it is argued, owes everybody a living, irrespective of whether he wants to work. The Government, it is said, owes everybody a substantial pension and medical care. Nobody need provide for his own old age or that of his parents. The theory is that the Government must keep on spending for every social purpose, no matter if a Treasury deficit is continuously incurred. In fact, a "balanced budget" today is treated with contempt by our "intellectuals"—as if it were a sign of senility, a relic of bygone days, when bankruptcy used to be a disgrace, and runaway inflation inflicted untold hardships on the populace.

The new "philosophy" is that the Federal Government must be the master of everything. It must control education, must subsidize every group that has the votes to carry weight in politics, and must require a conformity of thought ranging from a denial of the right of an employer to hire whom he pleases to the right of the Government to tell broadcasters what kind of entertainment they must provide the public.

The trend in America of the socialistic-minded seems to be away from individual responsibility and self-reliance. Anyone who believes that a man should give a good day's work for the pay he receives is called a "labor baiter" or a "reactionary." Anybody who insists that the Federal Government remain solvent is charged with lacking a human heart.

Now what do we see opposed to all this? There is the anti-radical who doesn't want profligate spending nor collaboration between government and monopoly power in unions, or in any special group. There is the conservative who wants, for example, to see interest rates based on supply and demand, and not fixed by artificial factors in government that mean printing-press money in the end. Stability and a sound currency at home, and policies of conciliation abroad are basic in what is today scorned as "conservative."

Actually, conservatism is the only true liberalism because it seeks the maximum good for the maximum number.

What, therefore, is to be the issue in the coming campaign? Are the businessmen, the investors in bonds, the people with savings accounts, and those who want to build their own homes to be told it doesn't matter whether the purchasing power of the dollar declines further? Do the people want to turn out the present Administration and see a whole army of inexperienced appointees in executive posts? Can we afford such a gamble at this critical time in our history? Are these new officials to spend months and months getting acquainted with the facts on which the preceding administration based its action, and then will the new regime give the public an entirely different policy, or one that is only slightly modified?

Are we to change our foreign policy with a change of administration? Does this mean the whole world is to wait several months after next November to find out what the United States Government means to do? This is supposed to be a missile age, in which minutes count, and decisions cannot wait for freshmen to grow to be seniors.

Are the citizens generally to face a period of hesitation while one party insists that the time has come for a change, however undefined the word may be?

And what change? Will the voters really be told what they may expect? Will there be vague promises of a millennium, when everybody knows that growth of population and far-reaching factors of economic and political force over which we have no control in various parts of the world must inevitably influence American decisions, irrespective of what party is in power? If it is mere change the American people want, the presidential candidates should be telling us exactly what change they have in mind. And what makes them think the people are demanding a change? The big unanswered question still is: What's the issue?

"RENDER TO CAESAR THE THINGS THAT ARE CAESAR'S AND TO GOD THE THINGS THAT ARE GOD'S"

MAY 9, 1960

WE ARE CONFRONTED today with the so-called "religious issue" in American politics.

Presumably this means that some citizens believe the Church could unduly influence the policies or decisions of any Roman Catholic if he were elected President of the United States.

But what shall we say of the attempt by various churchmen of all faiths to use their positions and, indeed, their national church organizations as a means of engaging in the controversies of American politics?

Before we are ready to decide just how much influence the Catholic Church may exert on a man elected President, we must examine some of the pronouncements from Protestant churchmen who vigorously defend the right to issue through their national organizations statements on every conceivable question of governmental policy. These range from public comments on "integration" or "segregation," to denunciations of the Government of South Africa and proposals for diplomatic recognition of the Red China regime despite its record of inhumanity and aggression. Many churchmen justify their course by arguing that these are "moral" questions—a definition broad enough to include everything political.

In the May 2 issue of this magazine there were printed some excerpts from an address delivered at the Colgate-Rochester Divinity School by Eugene Carson Blake, chief executive officer of the United Presbyterian Church, U. S. A. He declared:

"I said further that the corporate church—like the preacher—must speak in love and hope. Despite the grounds for despair that appear all about us, I believe that the tone and substance of the corporate pronouncements of the National Council of Churches have been Biblically hopeful and spoken in Christian love.

"Next they must be competent. One must finally leave judgments of competence to those competent to make such judgments. But I can say that the procedures by which the churches and the National Council attempt to get competent advice and advisers—whether on a farm problem, or on international affairs, or housing, or public education, or race relations, or religious liberty—are procedures which anyone fair-minded among us might approve. It is again and again because the pronouncements reveal both knowledge and competence that those opposed to the conclusions reached have felt it necessary to attack not only the positions taken but the body taking the position.

"We have been charged with arrogance. Who are you to say, 'This is the Protestant position,' or, 'This is God's will'? It is interesting that the church's critics reveal themselves for what they are by attacking pronouncements first on the ground, 'You don't speak for me or any of the other 35 or 50 million of your constituents.' When it is replied that 'a church's task or a council's task is not to poll its members for their opinions but to try to speak God's will,' then the critics run to the charge of arrogance at our presuming to call them un-Christian for disagreeing.

"Let it be clearly understood that to try to preach or to speak in the name of God is in fact a dangerous business. Humility before God is a requisite. Churches and preachers do not always have and have not always had sufficient humility for their task. But historically the record will show that churches and preachers have usually been at their best when they have dared to speak out against all human premises as they believed God wanted them to speak."

There can be no quarrel with the right of any preacher as an individual to speak out on any question—political, legislative, moral, social or economic. But may he presume to speak for the members of his congregation? Or, in the case of a national church organization, does he speak even for all the clergymen in such an organization? And if there is to be an advisory council of laymen who are to serve as "competent advisers" in the matter of farm legislation or any other governmental problem, are we to assume that they, too, speak "in the name of God"?

Only a few days ago at Denver, Colo., the quadrennial General Conference of the Methodist Church heard a "state of the church" message bearing the signatures of the 74 members of the Methodist Council of Bishops. Some excerpts from the document are to be found on page 94 of this issue.

The Methodist statement reaffirmed that Church's opposition to discrimination on the basis of race, calling it "both unfair and un-Christian," and then said:

"The end of racial strife and discrimination in the world and in the Church has not been reached. In some sections of our Church the evils of racial discrimination and segregation have been significantly reduced. Yet there remains a wide divergence of social customs and conscience in the complex issue of race relations.

"No part of the problem will solve itself automatically. Much as we might like it, we cannot settle this matter forthwith by fiat."

Again, it may be asked, who speaks "in the name of God"? The Dutch Reformed Church in South Africa is in favor of separation of the races, while the Anglican Episcopal Church there emphatically disagrees.

Billy Graham, a Protestant evangelist, in an Easter message printed in our April 25 issue, wrote:

"The Bible most certainly approved of master and servant relationships, but not along racial lines. Paul told the young Christians of his day that masters are to be kind to their employes and that servants are to obey their masters faithfully as unto the Lord. Not once did he indicate that any particular race was to be a master and another to be a servant.

"The Bible also recognizes that each individual has the right to choose his own friendships and social relationships. I am convinced that forced integration will never work. You cannot make two races love each other and accept each other at the point of bayonets. It must come from the heart if it is to be successful. Otherwise, we can build walls of hatred and prejudice that will take generations to overcome.

"Christ said that our problems came from within: 'Out of the heart are the issues of life.' The Supreme Court can make all the decisions it feels are necessary; but, unless they are implemented by good will, love and understanding, great harm will be done. . . .

"The issue in America has moral, social and political implications. Sometimes these questions are extremely complicated—and equally devout men see them somewhat differently. The Christian life requires growth by education and communion with God. . . .

"I am also concerned about some clergymen of both races that have made the 'race issue' their gospel. This is not the Gospel! . . .

"Only the supernatural love of God through changed men can solve this burning question. This doesn't mean that the race problem is not to be preached and taught —but it is not to be our 'gospel' nor are we to judge a man's relationship to God solely on the basis of his attitude on the race question."

The other day the writer received a letter from Rev. C. Lewis Irwin, a native of Kansas, who was formerly a missionary to China and now is pastor of the Covenant Presbyterian Church in Indianapolis. He said:

"By no stretch of the imagination can I see Christ or the apostles placing the emphasis of the Gospel on social and political agitation. It is but a step from social and political agitation to legal action, and legal action must be backed by force and police action to be legal. Here is the trouble with present 'integration agitation'—it looks to agitation rather than a change of heart. Are we seeking to run the business of the Church without the inspiration and power of the Holy Spirit? The central truth of the Gospel is its power to transform human hearts by what Jesus did through His Cross, Resurrection, and outpouring of His Spirit at Pentecost.

"The greatness of St. Paul's theology is that his heart always stayed close to the Cross and therefore his mind stayed on the track of God's Truth. There is no guarantee that any theologian's mind will stay on the track of Truth if his heart is not ruled by the Holy Spirit.

"Communism is essentially 'man's mind in control' —and relying on force because it has not the secret of changing human nature. Social and political agitation tend to veer in this same direction because it no longer trusts in God's power to change the heart—and so it plays into the hands of Communism.

"If we really believe the Gospel's power to radically change the human heart and behavior—because it has done just that for us personally—we will not readily rush off on social and political agitation tangents. And I believe the battle must be fought here: not so much by argument, as by determined passion to raise up and demonstrate a force of Christian people who are committed to changing the world by changing human nature.

"The Gospel is God's property. We tamper with it at our peril. He will take in hand and correct or discredit those who try to change the Gospel that Jesus Christ bought for us all at such great cost."

May a layman write an addendum? Churchmen who engage in politics lose the confidence of laymen and tend to become partisans rather than objective instrumentalities of spiritual help. Unquestionably God's guidance to the individual is the inspiration we must depend upon for a solution to human problems. Guidance comes as we seek it, and the stimulus to individual communion with God is available to all of us through our respective faiths.

Church and state are separated by mandate of our Constitution. The collaboration, however, of churchmen and citizens in a community to improve the social welfare of the people is, of course, desirable and proper. But let us remember from the Book of Mark the advice that Jesus gave to the Pharisees:

"Render to Caesar the things that are Caesar's,
and to God the things that are God's."

THE WAVE OF DEFEATISM

MAY 16, 1960

A STRANGE WAVE OF DEFEATISM is sweeping the world. It becomes manifest in the public expressions of officials. It crops out in the comments, both here and abroad, on issues that relate to peace, disarmament and military defense.

Broadly speaking, the world has been effectively frightened. The idea is prevalent that at any moment all of humanity can be destroyed by a nuclear weapon. Just why any nation would want to demolish the whole world isn't clear. Certainly there would be no comfort to the victor in his devastating conquest.

We hear the word "stalemate" frequently used. The argument is that we have enough strength to deter an enemy from attacking us—perhaps even more than enough. But what happens in a world in which "a balance of terror" has been reached? Do we then accept the insults and threats of a would-be aggressor and appease him lest he go mad and attack us?

Cowardice in human relations has always led to disaster. Appeasement has brought us major wars in the past. We called it a "miscalculation" by the enemy, who was so sure we wouldn't fight that he took a chance—as Hitler did.

Attention has been focused lately on "summit" conferences. It is a significant device. It never was intended to be what the public has imagined—a conference to settle disputes. It is a forum for propaganda debate. It merely gives the would-be aggressor a chance to employ his propaganda tactics, as Premier Khrushchev has done by distorting the peaceful mission of an unarmed United States weather plane which he himself ordered to be shot down. Unless we face up resolutely to this latest challenge by Mr. Khrushchev and take issue firmly with his inflammatory actions and speeches, we shall find ourselves in worse trouble.

Obviously if an aggressor can get what he wants without going to war, he would be foolish not to press his advantage. The world has been told that "peaceful co-existence" is the desire of the Soviet Union. But, since the phrase was first proclaimed, we have no evidence that it is a policy of either peace or co-operation.

What do we see around the world? Mob violence in many countries. It is instigated largely by Communist agents. The free world is the victim of these plots of infiltration, yet behind the Iron Curtain the Soviets rule with a stern hand. There is no freedom of assembly, no freedom of speech, no freedom of the press. The Communist world has no "demonstrations."

But, on our side, we forget that young republics like Korea cannot overnight achieve perfection in democratic processes and that a nation with 600,000 troops of its own guarding an armistice line on its northern border cannot be operated in as orderly a manner as are the democracies of Britain and the United States.

So we throw our influence behind the agitators and topple the government of our ally in Korea. We seem to be active where we are powerful, and rather timid where we are not so influential, though a case could be made for "intervention" in Turkey or South Africa by employing the same "logic" as we used in interfering in Korea's internal affairs.

Our policy in the Department of State is, unfortunately, influenced by the theory that it is necessary for the United States to heed the criticisms which appear in the press of other countries about a government like that in Seoul. We were courageous enough to resist this type of well-meaning but shortsighted pronouncement when it was leveled against President Chiang Kai-shek of the Chinese Nationalist Government. But are we ready now to see our whole front line in the Far East crumble as the malcontents seek to disintegrate the governments of our allies there?

Criticism by the press of other countries is often based on material considerations—the desire for more trade or privileges in an economic sense. If we are guided by the waves of defeatism in the world, we will find ourselves surrendering country after country to the control of the Communists.

Are we really for "peace at any price"?

This is an election year, to be sure, but the American people do applaud a manifestation of courage when they observe it. Instead of being alarmed by positive action taken in support of major principles, the people welcome it.

It is right, of course, that President Eisenhower should attend the "summit" conference in deference to our allies, but he should cancel the planned trip to Russia. Until there is a better climate and until the Soviet Premier takes back the insults he has flung against the United States, there is no good reason why the President should regard himself as bound by the "courtesy" of returning the visit which Mr. Khrushchev paid to the United States last year.

The time has come to recognize realistically a malevolent influence in the world, and this can best be done by putting an end to the camouflaged ceremonials that hide from the world the true state of mind of the Communist aggressors.

HISTORY REPEATS

MAY 30, 1960

FIVE YEARS AGO the idea of a "summit" conference was being widely agitated. On all sides we heard the argument that went something like this:

"We cannot refuse to sit down and talk. If nothing comes of it, at least the air will be cleared and we shall know where we are."

In the Western countries, the opposition political parties particularly exerted pressure upon their governments to sit down with Khrushchev and "talk things over." Our own President yielded reluctantly to the supplications of many of our allies and agreed to "go to the summit" at Geneva in July 1955. The late John Foster Dulles, our eminent Secretary of State, was doubtful of the outcome. He stood steadfastly on principle—he could see no advantage in dealing with murderers. But he regretfully acquiesced, especially since it was argued that merely sitting down to talk could do no harm—and might do some good. While the "summit" conference was going on, Soviet arms were being sent to Nasser to stir up trouble in the Middle East. Nothing of substance came out of the conference.

We now can review the facts of history. We have another Hitler on the rampage. He talks wildly. He threatens. He is a dictator with the power to make war without notice.

The first reaction among many people in the West a few days ago when the second "summit" conference collapsed, was one of fright and shock. For what else was next, it was asked, except war?

This has been precisely the danger of "summit" conferences. When they fail, widespread fears arise that there's nothing else left but war.

On May 6, 1955, on this page, this writer said:

"If, to be sure, a four-power conference was to be a real negotiation such as diplomacy has many a time tried with useful results, it would not be conducted amid the fanfare of publicity which surrounds such occasions today. Ambassadors would canvass beforehand the possibilities and indeed lay the basis for mutual agreements. But the Soviets want to show their contempt for the West in public conferences to be reported by the press of the world. What better proof do we need of the insincerity of the Communist rulers? . . .

"The people of Soviet Russia and of China want freedom just as we do. We must not tighten the hold of their oppressors on them. We must open the way for their liberation by refusing to deal with gangster governments. For those governments constantly threaten the peace of the world, and there can be no safety for anybody as long as they remain in power.

"There is but one way to force the disintegration of the Communist empire. It is by forgetting four-power conferences and imposing a complete quarantine on the Communist regimes. This means extermination of their agents and conspirators from all free countries.

"These enemies must be driven from within our gates. It makes no sense to endeavor to negotiate with the master minds of world conspiracy."

On May 20, 1955, on this page appeared the following, written from Paris:

"The cynical quip heard here among diplomats is that the West desires peace at any price while the Communists want peace at no price at all. . . .

"Those in government, here and abroad, who know the inside story of all the futile efforts thus far to obtain from Moscow, through the customary diplomatic channels, some evidence of a sincere desire to negotiate peace must have a troubled conscience as they accept the enemy's propaganda trick—a spectacular meeting with Bulganin (at the 'summit')—and arouse false hopes everywhere about the prospects for peace. . . .

"A third world war must be avoided if it is humanly possible to do so, because the destruction of cities by atomic weapons is too horrible to contemplate. But it is precisely because a policy of weakness and craven surrender of basic principles invites attack that those who are crying for peace at any price can turn out to be the very ones who bring on a terrible war. . . .

"Whence comes this strange delusion that by a four-power conference good faith can be established where there has been none before? And when will we learn to take our stand on principle and adhere steadfastly to it no matter what the sacrifice? For there is only one way to deter any enemy government from aggression, and that is to persuade the people behind it that their rulers are endangering their lives—and, if this fails, then to make sure our force is adequate to defend ourselves against any attack that may come. . . .

"Governments that wish to preserve freedom must steer by the compass of basic principle. They cannot surrender to the whims of expediency now without risking the surrender of their liberties later on."

It is well to recall the comment of George Santayana, the famous philosopher, who once wrote: "Those who refuse to learn from history are· condemned to repeat it."

A KEY TO KHRUSHCHEV'S MIND?

MAY 23, 1960

BACK IN MAY, 1945, Joseph Stalin was chatting with Harry Hopkins in the Kremlin. The war in Europe was over, and the United States had suspended its "lend-lease" program. The head of the Soviet Union didn't like it—he wanted American financial aid to continue. Mr. Hopkins, who represented President Truman, explained why it couldn't be continued. Stalin was chagrined, and blurted out that it would hurt him with his "public opinion."

Noting Mr. Hopkins's smile, the Soviet dictator remarked: "Oh, yes, we have our public opinion, too."

This story, as told by Mr. Hopkins, sheds more light today on the shiftiness and adroitness of Nikita Khrushchev than any words he may use in his wide variety of statements at press interviews or in speeches before the Soviet parliament.

For there surely is a "public opinion" inside the Soviet Union. It may be misled by government propaganda and be kept from knowing the truth by the tactics of suppression and a controlled press, but human beings are the same the world over. They react to events in much the same way—they become suspicious.

Khrushchev took over a mess from his predecessors. The revolution had made some progress, but the horrible cost in human life exacted by World War II left a lasting impression on the mood and spirit of the people. They acquiesced in severe restrictions because they thought them unavoidable. They accepted dictatorship and austerity as Americans might accept wartime controls and the draft of our youth.

Since Khrushchev came to power in 1958, the Soviet Union has been partially successful in keeping down discontent by gradually improving the standard of living and by opening up the opportunities for education.

Today the educated population in Russia is relatively large. It constitutes a potential of trouble. It cannot be fooled as easily as was the uneducated mass before.

Nikita Khrushchev is a master politician. Europe hasn't seen anyone like him for generations. He has all the skill of some of the famous leaders of the British and French parliaments of the past and much of the astuteness of America's most successful politicians. He senses the public pulse at home and abroad.

Khrushchev's main preoccupation today is how to keep his people contented—or at least to limit their discontent so that revolution cannot be precipitated overnight by a protesting populace.

For revolutions are sudden affairs. They are not announced in advance. Tourists can't detect their symp-toms. Nor are the undercurrents always discernible to the most practiced diplomats.

Today Khrushchev is worried about his agricultural program. He is worried also about the army—an institution where trouble often starts in any dictatorship.

The most important task ahead of the Soviet Premier is to keep the peace with other nations. His regime carries enormous burdens, including that of Red China.

The slogans of "peaceful co-existence," therefore, are real to Khrushchev. He wants to put off war as long as humanly possible. He needs the time that an era of peace would give him—time to reconstruct his country and fulfill the theories and promises of Communism even in limited form.

Then why does the Soviet Premier magnify out of all proportion the recent incident of the spy plane? Because it helps to solidify internal opinion in Russia. It helps to divert attention when domestic dilemmas are building up. Recently there was a shake-up in the high command in the Kremlin. This is always a sign that something hasn't been going well.

The American plane episode came opportunely for Khrushchev. But he cannot let his tactics of defiance and provocative speeches go too far. He cannot afford to sabotage the whole series of "summit" meetings which are essential to him as a means of continuing over a period of years the era of "peaceful co-existence."

So one week the Soviet Premier is defiant, and another week he tries to exude a conciliatory spirit. Basically, he doesn't want a war with the United States and the rest of the free world. He wishes to appear as the man who achieved a suspension of nuclear tests, the abolition of huge armaments, and the economic advancement of his people.

America cannot, of course, rely on any ephemeral appraisals of the mood of Khrushchev. He may try to bluff too far and may miscalculate. Another dictator, more warlike, could supersede him.

Our defense, therefore, must go on, and our surveillance of an enemy that can pull off a surprise attack must continue because, from pad to target, a missile can destroy our cities in a half-hour's time.

Our policy, however, must not be confined to military preparations. We have every right to transcend boundaries in appealing directly to the Soviet people to overthrow their dictatorship and join the free world, where freedom of speech and information, freedom of worship, and all the privileges of free men are still the basis of true enjoyment of human life.

"THANKS, MR. KHRUSHCHEV!"

JUNE 6, 1960

SOMETIMES FROM UNEXPECTED QUARTERS we are handed a benefit. Hence we often say that "it is an ill wind that blows no good."

Nikita Khrushchev may be surprised to learn the true consequences of his reckless action in Paris recently as he torpedoed the "summit" conference and publicly insulted the President of the United States.

We are, indeed, indebted to the Soviet Premier for the following consequences:

1. The credulous, naive attitudes adopted by various groups among us in their advocacy of "summit" conferences were revealed as hopelessly impractical. No longer will we listen to the argument that these meetings can override the historic ways of diplomacy, supersede the United Nations and leave it to four men to settle the disputes which threaten the world with nuclear war.

2. The appeasers, who have thought that the way to get peace is by making concession after concession to the enemy, now have been proved illogical, misguided and without persuasive influence.

3. The leaders of thought who have urged that America maintain its strong defenses and place its reliance on the maintenance of deterrent strength have been vindicated and will now have an increasing influence with American public opinion.

4. The tactics of the Soviet Government, as it has sought to divide the Western allies, weaken NATO and cause a crumbling of morale in the West, have been successfully thwarted. The Western alliance today has a redoubled strength—it has faith in the rightness of its cause and in its military power to deter war.

5. The world has at last been told many unpublished facts in the story of Soviet espionage. The opportunity to do this might never have been forthcoming if a countermeasure, undertaken by the United States, had not been detected and exploited by Mr. Khrushchev when the U-2 was forced to land.

6. The knowledge of what really is going on in the "cold war" may have come as a shock at first to the peoples of the West, but slowly they are beginning to understand the realistic truth. They now will read and be influenced by the facts revealed about Communist infiltration as well as aggression.

7. Publication by the United States of the list of Soviet spies arrested within our own territory as they sought military information has exposed the hypocrisy of the Soviet protestations concerning the plane piloted by Francis Powers. For Powers was merely taking pictures. His plane was unarmed and clearly marked with the initials of the National Aeronautics and Space Administration, well known as a civilian agency of our Government. Is flying 12 miles or more above any country really a violation of international law? If so, then why have the Soviets launched space vehicles which can take photographs of United States territory?

8. Attention has been dramatically focused on picture-taking from the skies. In 1955 President Eisenhower made his "open skies" proposal to the Soviet Union as a means of providing "against the possibility of great surprise attack." He proposed that the two countries give each other a complete blueprint of their military establishments "from one end of our countries to the other," and then provide "ample facilities" for aerial reconnaissance and picture-taking of each other's territory. This plan was rejected out of hand by the Soviet Government and generally attracted little interest. Now, however, the world has been made aware of the importance of the plan and of the satellites already in orbit which can take pictures at great heights.

9. Emphasis has been placed on the "surprise attack" issue. It has been difficult for the Western governments to arouse world opinion on this contingency even though everyone knows the West would not strike the "first blow." The world now has had brought forcibly to its attention the vital necessity of preventing or intercepting "surprise attack." The House of Representatives, through one of its appropriation committees, has given formal sanction to such a policy.

10. The outcry of the Soviet Government about "aggression" and "spying" must inevitably cause the world to ask when the Soviets will withdraw their agents from Cuba and other Latin-American countries, as well as from Europe, Asia and Africa, and really cease their "aggression."

11. Last but not least, the Soviet chieftain has asserted a right to tell the American people the kind of Administration he wants to see elected in this country in November. Let's grant him that privilege on the condition that free elections be held in the Soviet Union and that our radio messages no longer be jammed as we exercise a similar right to tell the Soviet people whom they shall choose as their ruler.

Yes, we can say, "Thanks, Mr. Khrushchev!" for having opened not only our eyes but the eyes of free peoples everywhere to the simple fact that there can be no safety for any country as long as an arbitrary, autocratic regime, with the power to make sudden war, rules in Moscow.

THE TOTALITARIAN IMPULSE

JUNE 13, 1960

VISIONS OF A "PERFECT" SOCIETY are often presented to us in proposals for reform. They are usually characterized as "liberal." We are told that individualism is old-fashioned and that the state can bring us the millennium.

Even the private-enterprise system, which has built our nation's power to first rank, now is criticized as faulty because it is based on "self-interest."

Just what is this modern species of "intellectualism"?

Whether we examine its manifestations in the so-called socialistic society of the Soviet Union or come face to face with it in our own discussions of "national purpose," the fact remains that we are urged to ignore the past and grope for some magic reform designed to achieve Utopia.

On this point, David Sarnoff, who may be described as one of the statesmen of modern business, makes a significant comment. In an article on the theme "National Purpose," written for the New York "Times" and "Life" magazine, he says:

"The unfolding American debate on National Purpose carries the disquieting implication that our traditional purposes, though they served the nation well in the past, have somehow been outmoded if not wholly invalidated. This I do not believe to be true.

"I am convinced, on the contrary, that these time-tested purposes, rooted in the nation's whole history, are more compelling than ever before. More, they are indispensable in enabling the United States to meet the paramount challenge of this epoch: the struggle between Communism and freedom. If revitalized, re-defined for our times and translated into great decisions, they could turn the tides of conflict in our favor."

In truth, we are struggling against a strange defeatism—a loss of confidence in the power of a self-reliant individual or a self-supporting nation. We face, indeed, a misguided and naive "liberalism" which accepts a cruel Khrushchev abroad and the labor racketeer at home as practical necessities of our times.

The first tenet of present-day "liberalism" is that experience, as revealed by the past, is not to be taken seriously. We are asked to believe, in effect, that the human brain of yesteryears couldn't possibly compare with its counterpart of today.

Whether it be in the field of economic reform or in the much more perplexing role of diplomatic relations with other governments, history is tossed out the window and we are blandly advised that the lessons of bygone days are inapplicable because "things are different" now.

Yet, as we re-read the pages of history, whether it be of the days of the Greek republics or of the Roman empire, we see the same passion for autocratic power exerted always at the expense of the citizenry.

We find in intellectual circles today a growing sympathy with statism. Our universities abound in professors in all fields who feel that the abstract interests of the state must supersede individual freedom. Indeed, we are told that the state exists for the sole purpose of promoting the "general welfare," even at the expense of individual freedom.

Contradictions are plentiful. The same "liberal" who argues for more state power and authority over the individual becomes enraged if the state inquires, for example, into the individual associations of a citizen within subversive organizations. The right to consort with the enemies of our country, the right to subvert, the right to hide treasonable associations—hailed as individual privileges beyond the power of the state—are stanchly upheld by the "liberal." But when a citizen wishes his children to associate at school with children coming from a similar environment, this is deemed a violation of the law of "equality." If a private business wishes to serve customers at separate lunchrooms, this is denounced by "liberal" churchmen as a violation of "moral," if not legal, authority.

Conformity by coercion seems to be the basic concept of the modern intellectual. If the economy isn't providing prosperity for all, including the inefficient, the state presumably must step in with the equalizing factor.

If the other countries of the world lag behind and do not have an enterprising population of their own, the United States Government supposedly must provide what is deficient. The Government, in short, is expected to play the role of master patron.

Whether it be medical care for those who can already afford it or old-age security for the indolent, the Federal Government is urged to redistribute the wealth—to rob Peter to pay Paul—and to tax the efficient to take care of the inefficient.

There is only one ultimate result of this ideology. It is the establishment of a totalitarian state to tell the citizen what to do "from the cradle to the grave."

Is individual initiative really a fetish of the past? What else but a totalitarian impulse motivates such reasoning?

GOVERNOR ROCKEFELLER'S MISTAKE

JUNE 20, 1960

GOVERNOR ROCKEFELLER has every right to try to get the Republican presidential nomination, by forced "draft" or otherwise. He has every right to express his own views. He has every right to demand that all other spokesmen for the Republican Party explain their views.

But the New York Governor is not justified in calling, in effect, for the suicide of his own party. As a loyal Republican, he ought to avoid any action that could split his party, either before or after the national convention, and thus precipitate its defeat in November.

It is one thing to advocate improvements or extensions or amplifications of the Republican Administration's policies of the last seven and a half years. It is quite another to repudiate the leadership of President Eisenhower on national defense and other vital issues.

For the lessons of politics, as reflected in the behavior of the American electorate through many decades, tell us that the record of an Administration in power cannot be disavowed by the candidate of the same party and a national election won by those tactics.

Although Mr. Rockefeller's recent statement has words of praise for President Eisenhower's leadership, these are more than offset by his scathing criticism of the Administration's policies. If Adlai Stevenson himself had issued this very same statement, there would have been no surprise. But coming, as it does, from a Governor who was elected in 1958 on the Republican ticket, it creates an atmosphere of doubt as to which party Mr. Rockefeller really wants to lead. His statement would appear to make him a more logical contender for the Democratic presidential nomination.

While it is not unusual for rival candidates in the same party to express differing views about what ought to be done by the Government in the future, it is most unusual to take issue with the record of one's own party when it has been in office for seven and a half years.

If the Administration in power has been a success, it deserves to be supported. If it has been a failure, then the people logically should turn it out.

That's how the vast majority of the 70 million voters approach the subject and not by entrancement with glittering generalities about "national purpose" or "national output"—the kind of phrases that take up a large part of the Rockefeller statement.

Perhaps the reason why Governor Rockefeller's advisers misled him is that they do not understand the basic emotions of the electorate. The fetish that presidential elections turn on personalities alone has long been mistakenly held by those who really have not studied carefully the course of American campaigns.

One fact stands out. Theodore Roosevelt was perhaps the most popular individual in American politics in the last half-century, but he couldn't win in 1912 when he split the Republican Party.

The people in 1960 are going to be asked whether they believe the Eisenhower Administration has taken care of their economic interests. Aren't the people better off in wages and jobs than they were eight years ago—as their sons were being called to war? If not, the people will turn to the Democratic nominee. The Republican who starts out by condemning his own party will cause many millions of Republicans either to stay at home or to vote for the Democratic nominee. For if the Democrats have the right answers, it will be asked, why not elect a Democrat to carry out such a change?

Do the people really want a change of party in the White House, with all the risks that this entails—months and months of confusion in the executive branch of the Government? Or do the people desire continuity—a smooth transition from one Administration to another of the same party?

Vice President Nixon is an integral part of the Eisenhower Administration. He is committed to the maintenance of its principles, but he can, and no doubt will, propose some changes based on new circumstances or lessons learned by experience in the last several years. This, however, is a far cry from repudiating President Eisenhower's leadership and accepting the criticism that a military man who has been President of the United States for seven years and a half has failed to maintain the defense of his country.

Mr. Rockefeller's "egghead" advisers may not realize it yet, but Dwight Eisenhower still wields a powerful influence with the American people. It is difficult to picture him campaigning for a Republican nominee who says that the President has failed in national defense, failed in his handling of foreign policy, and failed in various fields of public endeavor, and that the opposition party's spokesmen and critics are right.

A vote for the Republican nominee naturally must be a vote of confidence in the Eisenhower Administration and an acceptance of the pledge to go forward on the basis of the principles approved by the people in 1952 and 1956. No other campaign strategy makes sense for the Republicans.

THE TRUE "SUMMIT"

JUNE 27, 1960

THE MOBS TAKE OVER. Just as in Korea a few weeks ago, now in Japan their wishes prevail. Law and order vanish as passions rise and governments crumble.

Is this mob spirit spontaneous that sometimes sweeps free countries and renders them helpless?

We know that Communist agents, financed by Communist gold and trained in the art of "demonstrations," have infiltrated many Western countries, including our own.

We hear in America the voices of the partisan and the defeatist. They tell us American "planning" is at fault because the mobs forced the Japanese Government to cancel President Eisenhower's visit to Tokyo. They tell us that American "prestige" is damaged because a Communist-led mob compels a weak government in Tokyo to withdraw its invitation to our President.

But can American prestige really be damaged by Communist-inspired demonstrations?

Is our prestige dependent upon Communist caprice? Is this what "peaceful coexistence" is supposed to be? Is this what the advocates of "summit" conferences— in Britain, in France and in America—have been pressing the Administration to accept as the basis of our policy?

We must brush aside the campaign oratory and the phrases of the partisan critics who see American policy at fault whenever the Communists perpetrate evil. We have doubtless made some mistakes. We have tried to be friendly to Khrushchev even as he was sabotaging us in other parts of the world and stimulating a movement to endanger our relations with Cuba.

We have tried to defend ourselves militarily by sending U-2 planes to detect Soviet preparations for surprise attack. Was it wrong for us to try to deter an attack by missiles that would carry nuclear weapons?

Clearly, we shall drift from crisis to crisis unless we make up our minds that the key to it all is in the hearts and minds of the peoples of the Soviet Union and of the other countries now under the domination of Communist imperialism.

We would not be worrying today over another world war if free governments were in control at Moscow and Peiping. Autocratic governments are nothing new in the world. They have disturbed the peace of mankind again and again.

President Woodrow Wilson taught us that it is not the people of a country but their autocratic government which becomes our enemy and makes the world unsafe for democratic institutions.

How do we get rid of autocratic governments? Only by military force, which, of course, means war? Surely the world can find a better answer. Humanity is certainly more resourceful now than ever before, especially since ways of communicating from people to people have been improved through scientific inventions and technological advances.

There is, of course, a valid approach through counterpropaganda—telling the story of freedom's cause by radio and otherwise. But there is an even more powerful influence which has never been fully exerted. It is the influence of the spirit of man himself. Jesus said: "God is a Spirit: and they that worship Him must worship Him in spirit and in truth."

Many of our clergymen and national church organizations, unfortunately, are so preoccupied with political and economic controversy on the domestic front that they have missed their opportunity to mobilize throughout the world the spiritual power of our nation and of other nations. Must laymen head up the new crusade?

It matters little from which source comes the inspiration of men and women everywhere to seek God's guidance in these hours of crisis.

How shall we convey to the people behind the Iron Curtain that we have for them the love that Jesus proclaimed as the true basis for human relationships?

It is not that we should strive to persuade others to adopt our system of government or our forms of worship. But we must try to meet the peoples of the Soviet Union at the altar of spiritual brotherhood.

We cannot undertake such a mission by proclaiming superior virtue—or by any "holier than thou" attitude. On the contrary, confession is good for the soul. As we concede our errors, we must try to extend the hand of sincere fellowship to those peoples who may wish to reveal their feelings to us. For it is under freedom rather than tyranny that the spirit of God can emancipate hundreds of millions of human beings who are the victims of totalitarianism.

We have worldly goods to share with our brethren. We can make unlimited sacrifices to gain world peace. For there is no crime like that of war in its massacre of the innocent.

We must reach out for God's guidance and seek the fellowship of the peoples of all countries as we turn to Him who presides over the destinies of all of us at the true "summit."

A "PERFECT" ADMINISTRATION?

JULY 4, 1960

JUDGING BY SOME SPEECHES, inside and outside Congress, that are getting headlines nowadays, there is a "perfect" way to run the foreign policy of the United States.

The critics have encouraged us to believe that the way to win the "cold war" is to elect a President next time who will know in advance what the Communist regime in Moscow is planning and will promptly take just the right action to defeat its purposes.

This, to be sure, is a very large order. It assumes that the President will always be in perfect health, that he will never need any time off for recreation—especially, that he will never play golf—and that, with a telephone at his bedside, he will be able at any hour of the night to issue orders to his thousands of subordinates. Indeed, it is asserted that the President should know what military pilots are taking off for any destination throughout the world every minute of the day and night. He should, it is said, be able to suspend any air-borne alert which our bombers occasionally fly in an attempt to get warning of the enemy's preparations for a surprise attack.

The President should also be tuned in—legitimately, of course, and not through any espionage device—on the deliberations at the Kremlin. He should be able to regulate his overseas trips so that he will not run into such a dilemma as he did in Paris or Tokyo. In fact, the President is to know in advance the temper of the mobs that are gathering in any foreign country to demonstrate against our "prestige." Above all, he is to be an expert in diagnosing the psychopathic aberrations of a Khrushchev.

More than this, the President must never fail to spend enough money to keep us "ahead of the Russians" in everything—from missiles to professors of science and all other categories of education. One ingenious way to accomplish all this supposedly is to use federal funds to increase the number of classrooms in the country and, of course, raise teachers' salaries.

If anyone so much as mentions the budget as a possible barrier to big spending programs, the President is to rise up to denounce "budget considerations" as old-fashioned or as thwarting our "national purpose."

Money, we will be told, grows on trees. Anyone who thinks that a perennially unbalanced budget will produce inflation and a 10-cent dollar is to be given a simple and pious lecture about the need for a 5 per cent increase annually in our "national growth." This presumably will at once dispel all fears of fiscal chaos.

Under the "perfect" Administration, to be sure, the chairman of the Senate Foreign Relations Committee will conduct our foreign policy, and the Secretary of State will take his instructions from Capitol Hill, despite the fact that the Constitution says this is solely an executive responsibility.

As for domestic problems, by waving a magic wand, we will have just the right wages, the right prices and adequate receipts from higher taxes. The Government would regulate all business.

The "perfect" Administration will regard as outmoded any protest decrying all this as destructive of private initiative. Instead, the slogan is to be "more spending for more growth, and more government in more business." Anyone who objects will be called a misguided disciple of "big business" or an old fogey who is far behind the times. The demand is for "bold and imaginative ideas" no matter what they cost. Taxpayers are to be dubbed "illiberal" if they object to paying more taxes while their dollars shrink in purchasing power.

As for money spent abroad, the foreign countries receiving it are to be given constant aid and yet do nothing for the United States in return. Our military bases there are to be regarded as superfluous and as annoying to the Communists—hence they would be withdrawn, as recommended by Moscow. If this brings us to a posture of "isolation," then it will be urged that we quickly get more missiles and intercontinental bombers, even if it costs many times what our allied bases cost us now. As for our allies, they are expected to enjoy these "disengagement" policies, comforted by the thought that all this is "peaceful coexistence."

What candidate can assure the "perfect" Administration? If any would-be nominee cannot do it, his campaign promises, whatever they are—even before the Conventions take place—must be held up to scorn. Only someone with the ability to awe Communists into immediate acquiescence in, if not submission to, our demands should theoretically be given serious consideration by the delegates of the two National Conventions.

Will the American people be misled into believing that Utopia is just around the corner and that, if only we will give up all our armament, including nuclear weapons, the lion and the lamb will lie down together? Fortunately, the average voter has plenty of common sense, and he will recognize that the "perfectionists" are really partisans who are overplaying their hand.

THE RIGHT TO FLY U-2'S

JULY 11, 1960

THE SENATE FOREIGN RELATIONS COMMITTEE, instead of voicing partisan innuendoes in its report to the Senate on the U-2 incident, might better have supported the position of the United States in its five-year-old crusade for freedom of the air.

For there is today no binding agreement between nations governing the use of airspace. The problem is still unresolved. This means that the United States has every justification for continuing to assert a right to fly unarmed planes or balloons for observation purposes high above the ground anywhere in the world.

This was the position taken by the late Secretary of State, John Foster Dulles, in February, 1956. Messrs. Krislov and Krylov, Soviet authorities on space law, disagreed with that view. Writing in an official publication in March, 1956, they charged that thousands of Western balloons had been dropped from airplanes. They claimed that the balloons had a diameter of 50 feet, carried a load of 1,500 pounds and contained "special apparatus for aerial reconnaissance, including cameras with large quantities of film and instruments for ascertaining the bearings of the areas photographed, radio equipment—receiving sets and transmitters—ensuring the following of the flight of the balloon and the automatic control of cameras."

The same article mentioned that the American press had reported that in January, 1956, alone "over 500 of these especially equipped balloons were launched, each costing approximately $50,000."

An exchange of notes between the United States and the Soviet Union ensued. Secretary Dulles, at a press conference on February 7, 1956, stated that "although there is no clear international law on the subject" of launching weather balloons, "the United States feels it has a right to send these balloons at a certain height anywhere around the globe." He added:

"We would be disposed to be respectful of the strong views of any country which was opposed to it. While one can never be sure of where a balloon is going to go when you put it up 50,000 feet in the air, we would be disposed to try to avoid the territory of any country which felt violent objection to it. We would do this, not as a matter of their right, but as a matter of decent, friendly relations."

This indubitably placed the issue in the field of direct negotiation between the two governments. The United States tried in vain to negotiate such an agreement. Then came, in 1957, an utter disregard of so-called "air sovereignty" by the Soviet Government when its series of "Sputniks," with cameras aboard, started flying over many countries.

The principle is just the same no matter at what height the air vehicle flies. A document issued in 1958 by the United States Senate Committee on Space and Astronautics quotes, in its leading article, a German authority on space law as follows:

"There are no provisions in positive law concerning the altitudes to which the complete and exclusive state sovereignty over airspace should extend."

America, therefore, has a right to fly her balloons or her unarmed U-2's anywhere in the world. The Soviet Union has a right to do likewise, and also to send her satellites around the globe.

We come, then, to the purpose of the flights high above the ground by unarmed vehicles. When their purpose is scientific, there is likely to be agreement on giving freedom of access. But are we to say that the cause of world peace is less important than experiments in science? Certainly the observation plane can be useful in testing the sincerity of governments which have signed disarmament agreements.

The United States has the inalienable right to defend its people against surprise attack. No principle is more deeply rooted in international law.

The Soviet Union is constantly issuing threats of attack. It insists on the right to strike the "first blow." In recent weeks it has openly threatened to attack Norway and Italy if unarmed American planes are allowed to fly from their bases across the Soviet Union. The United States is bound by the North Atlantic Treaty to come to the aid of any member country when attacked. A missile or bomber attack against Norway or Italy by the Soviet Union means instant retaliation by the United States. This could bring on World War III.

President Eisenhower made the issue plain in his "open skies" proposal which he laid before the "summit" conference at Geneva in 1955. The Soviets scorned it. In the absence of any agreement, America today has a right to enter any airspace to detect preparations for a surprise attack.

International law has long recognized the principle that a nation may take measures of self-defense, even though war has not actually occurred or diplomatic relations have not been severed.

The United States has the right to continue to fly U-2's. It is regrettable that in the forum of world opinion this point has not yet been emphasized.

"RITUALISTIC ORGY"?

JULY 18, 1960

IN A FRONT-PAGE EDITORIAL the other day, the "Daily Mail" of London, a conservative newspaper, characterized the presidential-election campaign in the United States as a "ritualistic orgy" that has enabled the Soviet Union to take the initiative in world affairs.

Our election system is, moreover, described as a "log-cabin pattern" and as "a throwback to the age of innocence and a form of self-indulgence."

The "Daily Mail" recalls Premier Khrushchev's refusal to negotiate with the West until there is a new man in the White House. The newspaper then adds:

"The United States can do nothing about this, nor can anyone else. For months the initiative belongs to Khrushchev and all because of this election hiatus. Yet America will not willingly relinquish one prancing drum-majorette, one toot of a trombone, in this ritualistic orgy."

The British editorial asks us to behave in a more adult manner because America "has become a great power and what she does affects mankind."

This is a pertinent, even if ill-informed, comment. For the truth is all the democracies, including Great Britain, insist on holding elections at most inopportune times. Only as recently as 1945, when Prime Minister Winston Churchill had been conducting foreign policy for his country at a critical time in world affairs, the British people put Clement Attlee and the Socialist Labor Government into power. In a matter of days Mr. Attlee exchanged places with Mr. Churchill at the conference table at Potsdam, where a scheming Stalin finally won concessions which have altered the history of mankind.

It must be conceded, however, that under a parliamentary system there is less chance of a change of government occurring at a time of crisis than under the American system. But even immediate succession is in itself no cure. For when Vice President Truman took over the Presidency in April, 1945, on the day of the death of President Roosevelt, the former was hardly prepared for the many vital decisions he soon had to make.

President Eisenhower, as a consequence, has from the start of his Administration taken special pains to acquaint Vice President Nixon with the most intimate details of national and international policies. Mr. Eisenhower has publicly promised to work with his successor, irrespective of who he is, so that in the period between Election Day on November 8 and Inauguration Day on January 20 there will be every opportunity for the closest co-operation between the outgoing and incoming Administrations.

No system of government devised by the democracies can assure against a crisis when there is a change of leadership. But this is one of the costs of freedom. It can be alleviated only by the suppression of partisanship and by the dedication of our leaders to the public interest as above all else.

The hiatus caused by the American election has not given Nikita Khrushchev any "initiative" he did not already possess. Nor is the present interval itself an unmixed evil. At least it has unified the free world against the Soviet Premier, who at Paris flung his insults at the head of our Government.

Plainly, Dictator Khrushchev had found he couldn't bluff the United States into surrendering West Berlin. He had found also that the United States would not disarm without a cheat-proof system of inspection. Under the circumstances, the Soviet Premier needed time. He did not want President Eisenhower to tour Russia and give the lie to Communist propaganda about America's alleged threats against the Soviet people.

So the Soviet chief evidently felt there was nothing else to do but to trump up an excuse that would push the whole series of negotiations into next year.

It is academic at the moment to discuss the merits of our governmental system as contrasted with that of Great Britain. This writer for many years has advocated the principle of a parliamentary system but recognizes the weaknesses in the British system, too, especially when the steady hand of a Churchill is withdrawn and the unsteady hand of an Attlee is substituted just a few days before Russia is to enter the war against Japan.

Our "ritualistic orgy" may not please other peoples, and there is much to be said in favor of a revision of the cumbersome process by which America chooses her Presidents. But, fortunately, with Vice President Nixon so intimately familiar with the inner workings of our Government, the American people now have an opportunity to confound Nikita Khrushchev.

Also, if either Senator Kennedy or Senator Johnson is elected, it can be taken for granted that the new President will accept the help of President Eisenhower and his Cabinet in the transition period.

The American election need not be a handicap to anyone except Nikita Khrushchev, who soon enough will find out that there is to be no change in the firmness of American policy toward the Soviet Union.

WHY NOT "QUARANTINE" THEM?

JULY 25, 1960

THERE IS A POWERFUL ALTERNATIVE to war with Khrushchev.

It doesn't require military demonstration or action.

It brings into play a greater force—the moral force of the free world.

It is what is known as the policy of "quarantine."

The concept was expressed in October 1937 in a speech in Chicago by President Franklin D. Roosevelt. It was aimed at Hitler's threats and aggressive acts. The policy was stated by Mr. Roosevelt as follows:

"It seems to be unfortunately true that the epidemic of world lawlessness is spreading.

"When an epidemic of physical disease starts to spread, the community approves and joins in a quarantine of the patients in order to protect the health of the community against the spread of the disease."

Unfortunately, our friends in Europe hesitated. Some were carrying on a profitable munitions trade with the very government that was two years later to attack them. The tragic fact is that economic weapons were not employed effectively as government after government declined to use the embargo as a means of isolating the aggressor.

The "quarantine" policy as it would be applied now, would be aimed not at the people of the Soviet Union but at their tyrannical rulers who are bent on dragging the nations of the world to the brink of a nuclear war.

The first step is to call on the Soviet Union to get out of the Western Hemisphere, where it has all but taken possession of the Cuban Government.

The next step is to demand that international Communism get out of all countries of the free world.

Unless the Soviets discontinue their hostile acts, the only recourse the United States has is to withdraw recognition from the Soviet Government and to sever diplomatic relations altogether.

This means that the Soviet Embassy in Washington would be abolished as the center of the most extensive apparatus of infiltration and espionage the world has ever known.

It means, of course, withdrawal of our Embassy and its staff from Moscow, but it also means, if it is to be effective, that diplomatic relations with the satellite governments must also be broken off.

This would create new problems for Premier Khrushchev and would help to stir up discontent inside those countries which are yearning for the time to arrive when they can throw off the Communist yoke.

By "quarantine," moreover, is meant the cutting off of commercial and financial intercourse with the Soviet Union and the closing of all our seaports and airports to the ships and planes of the Communist bloc.

Our allies in Europe may hesitate to go along with us, but sooner or later, as the gravity of the situation dawned on them, they, too, would find it necessary to help isolate the Soviets.

Certainly we should persuade as many Latin-American governments as possible to get rid of all Communist ties and to cut off diplomatic relations with Moscow. What the Soviets have done in Cuba, they can do in every country in this hemisphere from Canada to Argentina.

The Communist dynasty carries on its devilish work by the use of gold converted into American and European currencies. The time has come to block international exchange and disrupt the mechanism by which Moscow reaches into countries of this hemisphere as well as Europe, carrying on subversive acts in violation of every pledge given by the Soviet Government when it obtained diplomatic recognition from the United States in 1933.

Nearly every manifestation of so-called "nationalism," whether in Japan or Korea or Cuba or the Congo, has back of it to some extent the money and intrigue of international Communism.

The downing of 17 of our planes by the Soviets, with a loss of 91 lives, reveals a serious breach of international law by the Communist regime.

We entered World War I to assure freedom of the seas and to protect Americans traveling in international waters.

Just as the high seas are free to everybody, so is the air over the seas also free.

Shall there be no redress of the wrongs committed by the Soviets against American citizens traveling the airways?

A "quarantine" means isolating the virus of evil in the international situation and preventing the germs of an epidemic from spreading into the free world.

We don't want a nuclear war, but we also cannot tolerate the world-wide operations of the Communists in the "cold war" which is slowly dragging us to the precipice of a hot war. The "quarantine" offers us a course of peace with honor and enables us to call on the peoples of the free world to emulate our example in a crusade for human freedom.

THE RIGHTS OF WHAT MAN?

AUGUST 1, 1960

THE PLATFORM ADOPTED by the Democratic National Convention is entitled "The Rights of Man."

It is thousands of words long. Not many of the delegates read the document or heard it read.

Having promised financial benefits to various groups of voters—the sum total of which means an expenditure that could bankrupt the U. S. Treasury—the platform calls for a startling increase in the number of bureaus and governmental agencies. It also promises the States, cities and counties that virtually all their financial needs will be taken care of by the Federal Government.

After painting a rosy picture of all the handouts that the people are to receive, the platform soberly says:

"We believe, moreover, that except in periods of recessions or national emergency, these needs can be met with a balanced budget, with no increase in present tax rates, and with some surplus for the gradual reduction of our national debt."

Who is fooling whom? The outline of welfare proposals in the platform indicates clearly that it would take many billions of dollars above tax receipts to carry out even a small part of the extravagant program.

The rights of what man are being protected? Certainly not the rights of the savers, whose possessions would be decimated by inflation. Certainly not the rights of citizens generally, whose living costs would rise as the dollar shrinks in purchasing power.

There are a few passages on foreign policy addressed to the Communists which must be commended as being in harmony with the current policies of the United States. There are other passages, however, which bewilder any fair-minded reader. Thus, for instance, the platform says:

"Over the past 7½ years, our military power has steadily declined relative to that of the Russians and the Chinese and their satellites."

No member of the nonpartisan, nonpolitical agency of the Government known as the U. S. Joint Chiefs of Staff agrees with that gross disparagement of the power of our armed services today.

Platforms, to be sure, are mere catchalls, designed to attract votes. Something of a sense of guilt, however, must have crept into the minds of the platform writers, for, toward the end of the lengthy document, they make this naive confession:

"Much of the challenge of the 1960s, however, remains unforeseen and unforeseeable. If, therefore, the unfolding demands of the new decade at home or abroad should impose clear national responsibilities that cannot be fulfilled without higher taxes, we will not allow political disadvantage to deter us from doing what is required."

There is one section of the platform particularly which is bound to cost the Democrats many votes. It seeks to protect the "civil rights" of some groups but ignores "the rights of man" in the North as well as the South. This platform plank says:

"We will support whatever action is necessary to eliminate literacy tests and the payment of poll taxes as requirements for voting."

The minority report, signed by the delegations from ten Southern States, made an effective rebuttal as follows:

"Very recently the Supreme Court of the United States decided that the requirement by a State of literacy tests as a condition for voting was a proper exercise of its constitutional powers. Would you permit a man or a woman who did not know his or her a-b-c's, who could not add two and two, who did not know who was President of the United States, Governor of his State, or Mayor of his city, to vote for or against candidates for these offices?"

It might be asked also whether such a group of illiterate citizens should ever be permitted to exercise the balance of power in any State. Is this a protection of the "rights of man"—if so, what man? The platform continues:

"The time has come to assure equal access for all Americans to all areas of community life, including voting booths, schoolrooms, jobs, housing, and public facilities."

This can mean only that the platform advises a disregard of the right of the citizen to send his children to a private school and of the right of an employer to hire whom he pleases. Doesn't "equal access" to "all areas of community life" imply also that all private clubs and fraternal organizations must open their doors to everybody?

What happens then to the sacred right of privacy and the right of the individual to live his own life in freedom, unharassed by governmental despotism?

Isn't this "conformity by coercion"?

The rights of what man are going to be protected?

The American people are entitled to an answer from Senator Kennedy, the Democratic nominee, who has announced his wholehearted acceptance of the platform.

THE SCARE

AUGUST 8, 1960

BUSINESS IS IN an apprehensive mood.

The stock market has been fluctuating widely. Profits of corporations in the second quarter have fallen sharply. Fear is in the air.

What is the cause of this psychological crisis? A turn in the economic trend is usually not due to just one factor but to the interrelation of several factors. Basically, however, the mood of the business world affects the expansion of existing plants or the halting of such programs.

For today there is great uncertainty. One reason is the deep concern over the international situation. Any day, it is felt, can bring a climax that could force wage and price controls by government and a complete shift in our productive gears—from goods for private consumption to munitions of war.

The other factor, however, which is even more penetrating and more immediate in its impact, is domestic. Will there be a change in the national Administration —a removal from office next January of all the high officials now intimately familiar with national and international affairs, and the introduction of a new set of officials who must spend precious months learning the ropes while our "cold war" enemies precipitate crisis after crisis?

Do the people of this country, generally speaking, know what a change in Administration really involves?

Businessmen already are beginning to fear a Democratic victory. They are being told that there are more Democratic than Republican voters in the country and that recent elections have been showing a tide running toward the Democrats.

Nor are businessmen wishful thinkers. They are realists. If they become convinced there is going to be a change, they will adjust accordingly. They will postpone plans for new activities which otherwise would mean the creation of more and more job opportunities. They will wait to see which way the new Administration will go—toward socialism, as the New Deal did, or toward the maintenance of the private-enterprise system which has helped America to become so powerful in the economic world.

This system can be made to work only if there is a sense of responsibility on all sides. Management has been steadily giving in to demands for wage increases, not only to avoid strikes but to help sustain purchasing power. These objectives, however, have come into conflict with a tendency to let inflation go unrestrained. The Eisenhower Administration has suc-

ceeded in bringing a measure of stability to the dollar. But now comes again the threat of New Dealism and socialism and more and more inflation through more and more government spending.

Sure, inflation for a little while gives the appearance of prosperity and tends to send the stock market up. But American businessmen can see beneath the surface. They know that the coming election could mean another era of New Dealism, which was the most colossal failure, in an economic sense, the country has ever experienced. Relief measures and artificial projects were necessary, to be sure, as they always are in a depression. But the indifference exhibited for eight long years toward the production of heavy goods kept unemployment at the 8,000,000 mark. This condition was not relieved until World War II gave American factories orders for heavy goods. Wars are not the way to develop the American economy.

The Republican platform adopted at Chicago states the case succinctly:

"We therefore accord high priority to vigorous economic growth and recognize that its mainspring lies in the private sector of the economy. We must continue to foster a healthy climate in that sector. We reject the concept of artificial growth forced by massive new federal spending and loose money policies. The only effective way to accelerate economic growth is to increase the traditional strengths of our free economy—initiative and investment, productivity and efficiency."

Messrs. Kennedy and Johnson are committed by their platform to more and more spending of federal funds without regard to the impact this can have on the private-enterprise system.

Messrs. Nixon and Lodge are committed by their platform to the free-enterprise system, with a minimum of government intervention in the economic life of the nation.

The American people are asked to choose between these two doctrines. Small wonder businessmen hesitate and worry over whether there is to be an epochal change in the United States from a system of private enterprise to a system of state socialism! Shall Nikita Khrushchev's prophecy that our grandchildren will live under a socialistic system be fulfilled?

We are at the crossroads this autumn as we face a choice between two fundamentally different philosophies of government. That's the reason for the scare today.

THE FALSE GODS OF POLITICS

AUGUST 22, 1960

MANY MILLIONS OF AMERICANS watched the television or heard the radio broadcasts and read the newspapers during the two national political conventions. What impression did it all make? What information was really derived from the "speeches of acceptance" as to the real purposes of the candidates and the true significance of the platforms adopted?

Were the people able to detect the difference between sincerity and insincerity? Did they possibly get the feeling that the whole thing was a kind of game—a stratagem to convince the electorate that one's party or nominee, if successful at the polls, would achieve the millennium for all of us?

Politics is indeed a game. It is based on the assumption that the masses can be persuaded to accept promises and eloquent speeches as a guarantee of deeds to come. Platform planks are couched in ambiguous language. The art of using words that have a double meaning is accepted as the practical way to avoid being tied down too specifically to any proposal.

But what do the people think of such vague phrases as "national purpose" and "forward-looking programs" and "accelerated progress" and "national growth"? What does it all mean to the average man who is preoccupied with his own toil and struggle? Does he believe that by some magic device the central government will take care of all his needs and provide a livelihood with an ever-increasing income? Does he honestly feel that all this can be done without heavier taxes? Does he accept the fallacy that you can always rob Peter to pay Paul anyway, and that it doesn't matter much how many billions are spent for the "public welfare" or how far the dollar goes down in purchasing power as prices go up?

A New Deal politician once said: "We will spend and spend, tax and tax, and elect and elect." What a cynical appraisal of the intelligence of the electorate! Yet, upon reading the party platforms and the speeches at the conventions and the reports of the news conferences since, one is forced to the conclusion that the political leader of today tends to downgrade the perceptiveness of the voter.

What, after all, are the people seeking to learn from the candidates? Are they inquiring about the merits of spending in the "public sector" or the "private sector," as the intellectuals describe it? Are they worried about how much "foreign aid" we should extend or about our programs of financial assistance in "underdeveloped countries"?

It is true that the average man is concerned about the dangers of a nuclear war and is anxious for America to keep pace militarily with its potential enemies. But somehow, in conversations among voters, the whole question of foreign policy comes down to a simple proposition: Can the United States deter the Communists, and will the new President be able "to stand up to Khrushchev"?

Basically this is an expression of patriotism—of a desire not to see America "pushed around." But when you put the concrete question to the voter—whether he is willing to go to war, to fight for the American position—the answer becomes more pointed. If America is attacked, he will reply, there must naturally be retaliation. If, however, some faraway part of the world allied with us is attacked, it is not clear to him that America is justified in risking the lives of its soldiers even though our Government may be committed by treaty to such a course.

While the argument for international co-operation is logical and valid, the people as a whole have by no means been sold on the idea that they must risk everything in a conflict that might arise suddenly in a distant area of the globe.

It is significant that not a single speech from any candidate in either party has frankly warned the American people that they may at any moment have to make sacrifices of human life—that small wars as well as a big war may come and that the United States must not flinch from such tasks if the occasion arises.

Are the candidates telling the people the whole story—that we must be prepared to risk our lives? Or are we, by indifference, encouraging the enemy to assume we are afraid to fight? Will the nominees for President deal candidly with this issue?

We need experienced leaders at the helm, but we also need men of courage—men who are ready to speak in realistic terms, irrespective of so-called political consequences.

But who today will put aside ambition? Who will depart from the political hokum of campaigning—the hypocrisies of the hour?

Why do the candidates for public office give the impression that they will promise anything just to get votes? When will they stop worshiping the false gods of politics?

The Scriptures have put the case in a nutshell: "What shall it profit a man, if he shall gain the whole world, and he lose his own soul?"

THE BAROMETER OF "PRESTIGE"

AUGUST 29, 1960

THE SOVIETS LAUNCH a "Sputnik"—and our "prestige" presumably goes down.

The United States launches a series of air vehicles into space—so many that the public loses track of the number—and our "prestige" then goes up.

The Soviet Premier publicly insults the President of the United States, wrecks the "summit" conference, and a debate starts as to whose "prestige" is truly hurt.

Basically, the question relates to the standing of a country in the public opinion of the world. But whose public opinion? We cannot evaluate our "prestige" inside the Communist bloc because there is no free press there. Only one side—the Communist propaganda side—is presented.

How shall we appraise our "prestige" in the so-called "free world"? How many of the countries on our side of the Iron Curtain really have a free press? Government after government, either in the "neutralist" camp or in the "uncommitted" areas, is in control of the press. Hence the newspapers reflect only what the regime in power wants them to say.

But in Britain and France, at least, there is free expression. As these countries, allied with us, record their opinions on passing events, they sometimes are critical either of our method of handling a given question or of the broad position we take. The criticism of America comes largely from the "left wing" press, so called because it often reveals a sympathy for the socialistic approach in modern society. So it was interesting a few days ago to read in the London "Daily Mirror"—described in Reuters news service as a "left wing" newspaper—an article by the prominent columnist "Cassandra." He wrote:

"Mr. Khrushchev may roar that he will bury us, but whether he is able to put his threats into effect depends entirely on technicians who are quite likely to be pacifists at heart.

"The launching of the first Sputniks entirely changed the mood of the Soviet authorities and brought the prospect of a third—and final—world war sharply into focus.

"This week end the balance of technocratic powers has once again significantly shifted. The United States have had a resounding triumph in the space race—which is also the war race.

"Within a few hours they put a giant balloon into orbit a thousand miles above the earth. They recovered a space capsule in the sea after an orbital flight. They successfully launched an Atlas missile on target 5,000 miles away. They fired a Polaris missile on a test flight of 1,100 miles, and they got the famous X-15 rocket plane up to a height of 131,000 feet, at a speed of 2,196 miles an hour.

"These are tremendous achievements that will restore the confidence of the Americans to maintain the peace—and also that of their European allies."

Maybe the word "prestige" ought to be used to describe separate categories—military prestige, scientific prestige, economic prestige, and moral prestige.

Can it be doubted, however, that moral prestige is really the most important of all? Here are some of the tests:

Do we have individual freedom in America? Does the state tell us what we may think, what we may write in our publications, or what we may broadcast on the radio and television?

Do the American people uphold the rules of common honesty and demand integrity among public officials? Do we really give the citizens a chance to express at the polls their desires and their preferences?

Anyone who knows America can readily answer all these questions. But it often is discouraging to find that a different picture is painted abroad and by some petty politicians at home.

We are sometimes blamed for failing to appropriate more money for "foreign aid." But the truth is our prestige is not made by single events or by money alone or by the policies of a given Administration in Washington. It is built upon words and deeds as we conform to the spirit of the Declaration of Independence.

We have given generously, as citizens, to the sufferers from earthquakes in Japan and Chile and to the famine-stricken peoples of China. We have provided relief for homeless Belgians of World War I and twice for a vanquished Germany. Three times we have sent our young soldiers many thousands of miles away from our territory to fight for freedom's cause. We have repelled aggression in Korea. We have liberated the Philippines. We have saved France and Britain and Italy. We have also helped the peoples of the Soviet Union in their hour of greatest distress.

Surely our "prestige" is indelibly recorded in the humane acts of a free people.

If we can only remain dedicated for all time to human freedom and maintain our record of unselfishness, we shall not need to be concerned about the short-range readings on the barometer of "prestige."

INTERNATIONAL BANDITRY

SEPTEMBER 5, 1960

REALISM TODAY commands us to face up squarely to the fact that there can be no peace in the world, no "independence" for former colonial countries, and no safety for any free nations as long as international banditry is permitted to rove the earth.

"Self-determination" of peoples has long been a worthy ideal. America has proclaimed again and again its sympathy with the right of nations, large or small, to choose their own form of government.

But now we see the principle impaired everywhere. Whether it be in Latin America, or in Eastern Europe, or in the Middle East, or in the Far East, and indeed wherever we penetrate the chaos that currently prevails on the African continent, we find one culprit—one enemy of freedom.

The enemy is the Communist dictatorship in Moscow, allied with the Red regime in Peiping.

How long are the nations that are outside the Iron Curtain going to delude themselves with the idea that international rules and customs must be obeyed by only one side—the free world?

How long will the countries now invaded by subversive elements tolerate the presence of agents and provocateurs whose only mission is to stir up friction, thus preventing new nations from becoming democracies and undermining older nations even as they strive to maintain their traditions of tolerance for opposition parties?

The United Nations in its Charter adopted just 15 years ago says:

"All members shall refrain in their international relations from the threat or use of force against the territorial integrity or political independence of any member or state, or in any other manner inconsistent with the purposes of the United Nations."

How long, then, shall the Soviet Union and its stooges be permitted to violate the Charter of the U. N.? It would be better to dismantle the present organization and build a new one than to let defiance of the Charter go on. For while this document does not specifically provide for expulsion of a government which represents a permanent member of the Security Council, any group of members can always withdraw and form a new organization. This is what must be done if self-respect and the principles of freedom are to be maintained.

Every day that the Soviet Union is permitted to associate in the U. N. organization with the free nations, the world is, in effect, led to believe that the misdemeanors of the Moscow regime are tolerated.

Last year General De Gaulle made a heroic effort to help former French colonies in Africa to achieve their independence. In an address on December 13 at Dakar, capital of the new Mali Federation, the head of the French Republic said:

"The State of Mali is going to assume what some call the position of independence and which I prefer to call that of international sovereignty.

"I have said that I prefer the latter term, without, however, disputing the attractiveness and significance which the word 'independence' can and must have for any people, and especially for this people. Nevertheless, I prefer 'international sovereignty' because it seems to me to correspond better with the necessities that have always existed, and especially with the necessities of today. 'Independence' is a word which signifies a desire, an attitude, an intention; but the world being as it is—so small, so cramped, so interfering with itself—real independence, complete independence does not in reality belong to anyone.

"There is no state, however big or however powerful, which can get along without the others. No policy is possible without co-operation."

But in recent weeks, we have seen one of its two members—Senegal—withdrawing from that Federation.

What provoked the attempt at dissolution? What indeed is also behind the disintegration of the provinces of the former Belgian Congo and the civil war now raging there? Mainly the agents and saboteurs—native Africans trained in Moscow in recent years—who now stir up passions and prevent the new republics from achieving independence or maintaining any alliance with their former friends.

As a consequence, national economic structures are being ruined, and innocent people are being deprived of job opportunities. A dozen Marshall Plans will not rescue these ill-fated natives. It takes more than money. The answer is to rid Africa of the common enemy, the Communists.

What has happened in Africa has happened in Cuba. The Communist penetration of Latin America is also well under way.

How long will the free nations let the international banditry of the Communist regime continue? The time has come to isolate the Soviets—to withhold from them membership in any international organization, and to insist that every free country get rid of Communist agents and subversives as a qualification for membership in a new League of Freedom.

"DIVIDED GOVERNMENT"

SEPTEMBER 12, 1960

WE HAVE BEEN HEARING a good deal lately about "divided government." The phrase usually refers to the fact that, while the Republican Party controls the executive branch, the Democratic Party has virtually a two-thirds majority in the legislative branch of our Government.

But there is another type of division. For, even if the Democratic Party were to win the Presidency this year and retain control of both houses of Congress, a form of "divided government" would still remain.

This is because the Democratic Party is divided between conservatives and radicals, between spenders and savers, between adherents of States' rights and those who are striving constantly for more and more power to be centralized in the federal bureaucracy.

The Republicans have a small fringe of so-called "liberals" who go along with the radical Democrats once in a while, but the Republicans as a whole are closer to the conservative side of the argument, especially in trying to keep the purchasing power of the dollar from being depreciated still further.

This means that Mr. Nixon, if elected, can count on a working majority in Congress on basic economic issues and on fundamental questions involving the maintenance of States' rights.

If, on the other hand, Mr. Kennedy is elected, can he swing enough votes to get a majority of both houses on those issues where there is a cleavage involving conservative and radical viewpoints? It is being argued in his behalf that, when a measure was passed by Congress only to be vetoed by President Eisenhower, the bipartisan coalition of conservatives, with only one vote more than a third of either house, could uphold the veto. If Mr. Kennedy were in the White House, it is contended, such measures would again be passed by a majority vote of Congress, and he would sign them into law.

The flaw in this argument is that, in the recent session of Congress, there was every reason in politics why the Democrats should have supported the Kennedy effort to enact into law various provisions of the Democratic platform which was adopted at Los Angeles. But, with the aid of the Republican conservatives, an actual majority was mustered to frustrate the passage of such proposals.

Thus, the United Press International, in its dispatch the other day summarizing the accomplishments of the two houses of Congress, said:

"The 86th Congress, most Democratic in two decades, wound up today with a far more conservative record than anyone anticipated when it was elected 21 months ago.

"The final results were a bitter disappointment to liberal Democrats and union leaders who had expected passage of far-reaching new programs."

It is fallacious to believe that Mr. Kennedy's influence in Congress would increase just because he would be in a position to dispense favors from the White House to the Democrats. The conservatives aren't the kind who are influenced that way. Indeed the chances are that, as always happens when a party becomes a minority in a presidential election, the Republican "liberals" would tend to vote with their conservative brethren. Hence, some votes from the Republican side hitherto counted on by the Democratic "liberals" would be lost.

"Divided government" is unsatisfactory in many respects. For there is no way to fix responsibility on one or the other of the two major parties. The parliamentary system in vogue in Canada and many other English-speaking countries could cure this. But, in the absence of such a reform, it is well to understand that "divided government" in the United States means a coalition of conservatives versus a bloc of radicals, and that, in effect, if party names are disregarded, there are today two major political groups, and one of them—composed of conservatives, whatever their party affiliation—has really been in control of both houses of Congress as well as the White House for the last seven and a half years.

But with which of the two nominees for President would the conservatives in Congress work better? Obviously with Mr. Nixon, who—though anxious to forward the "liberal" cause in many ways—would owe his election largely to the preponderance of conservatives in the Republican Party.

If Senator Kennedy wins, he will find himself beholden to the AFL-CIO and the radical groups which sponsored his candidacy. He will be committed to a continuous fight against the Southern conservatives. The chances are he would not muster even as many Democratic votes on economic questions as he was able to get for his measures in the recent session of Congress.

So the country really faces in November a choice between another kind of "divided government" if Mr. Kennedy is elected and the continuance of a Congress co-operative with the President on basic economic issues if Mr. Nixon is victorious.

THE SOVIET'S TREASON
AGAINST THE U. N.

SEPTEMBER 19, 1960

BEFORE NIKITA KHRUSHCHEV is permitted to address the General Assembly of the United Nations, his credentials and record of deeds should be examined. For of what avail is it to listen to a hypocritical speech on "peace" by the head of a dictatorship government which is guilty of open treason against the United Nations itself?

The mutiny of the Soviet Union against the jurisdiction of the United Nations in the Congo speaks for itself. The President of the United States, in a formal statement, has said:

"The United States deplores the unilateral action of the Soviet Union in supplying aircraft and other equipment for military purposes to the Congo, thereby aggravating an already serious situation which finds Africans killing other Africans. If these planes are flown by Soviet military personnel this would be contrary to the principles so far applied regarding use in the Congo of military contingents from the larger powers. . . .

"The main responsibility in the case of the Congo has been thrown on the United Nations as the only organization able to act without adding to the risks of spreading the conflict. . . .

"I must repeat that the United States takes a most serious view of this action by the Soviet Union. In the interest of a peaceful solution in Africa, acceptable to all parties concerned, I urge the Soviet Union to desist from its unilateral activities and to lend its support instead to the practice of collective effort through the United Nations."

But the Soviet Union did precisely the same thing in Korea in 1950. It sent munitions and supplies to the armies of the Red Chinese and the North Koreans to fight the U. N. troops. America suffered 137,000 casualties in that war in behalf of the United Nations. Other nations also sacrificed their youth for the same objective. The U. N., by resolution, condemned Red China as an aggressor but took no action against the Moscow Government.

Now that the Soviet Union has again committed treason against the United Nations, the time has come to call a halt.

Unfortunately, there is no provision in the Charter whereby the Soviet Government can be expelled from the U. N., but the mechanism of formal inquiry is available.

The Soviet Government should, in effect, be tried for treason. The offenses in Korea as well as in the Congo should be fully investigated.

If the U. N. proves itself weak in this crisis, it will eventually compound its difficulties and increase the danger of world war. Certainly if this case of treason is overlooked or condoned, the U. N. is not going to be able to restrain other members hereafter. If, despite the formal action of the Security Council which authorized a U. N. Army to go into the Congo, the Soviet Union feels free to undermine that neutral project and assist one side in the civil war there, then the effectiveness of the U. N. as an international organization dedicated to maintaining world peace will be seriously impaired.

When the Soviet Premier comes to New York for the United Nations General Assembly meeting during the week of September 19, an opportunity is afforded to interrogate him formally on the treason charges which have been dramatized by the events of the last several days in the Congo and by President Eisenhower's comments.

Plainly Mr. Khrushchev wants to talk about "disarmament" and to carry on his propaganda of distortion. He will have an audience, to be sure, because the press, television and radio in the United States are free and believe in reporting the news. Why should the Soviet Premier be permitted to put on his own kind of show without a firm rebuttal?

Of what use is it to listen to speeches about "agreements" or "treaties" on disarmament when the Soviet Government violates the provisions of the United Nations Charter, one section of which says:

"All members shall give the United Nations every assistance in any action it takes in accordance with the provisions of the present Charter, and shall refrain from giving assistance to any state against which the United Nations is taking preventive or enforcement action."

The United States should press its charges of violation of the Charter. For if the Soviets get away with their present course, they will move into Cuba and into Latin America just as they have in Africa, claiming they are merely sending "food" planes and trucks for "peaceful" purposes, when the action is as plainly military as it was in Korea and as it now is in the Congo.

The time has come to deal courageously and forthrightly with the treason committed by the Soviet Union against the United Nations.

A TRIUMPH OF MORAL FORCE

OCTOBER 3, 1960

PRESIDENT EISENHOWER'S address before the General Assembly will be inscribed on the pages of history as a triumph of moral force.

Dignity was contrasted pointedly with the boorishness of some of the other heads of state at the New York scene. Unselfishness of purpose stood out clearly as a constructive program of aid was offered to a troubled world by the spokesman of the largest of the free nations.

It made one proud of the United States of America to hear the words of the President as he told the peoples of every continent that an awakened humanity must "make a renewed attack on poverty, illiteracy and disease," and that the United States is ready to help substantially toward that end.

In the face of baffling problems in Africa, the Middle East, Asia and Latin America, the President spoke hopefully, earnestly, co-operatively. He said:

"This is, indeed, a moment for honest appraisal and historic decision. We can strive to master these problems for narrow national advantage or we can begin at once to undertake a period of constructive action which will subordinate selfish interest to the general well being of the international community."

Mr. Eisenhower, in effect, asked his auditors to rise above the antics and erraticisms of Nikita Khrushchev and his group of stooges from Cuba and the so-called Communist bloc. The President called no names and engaged in no tirades—a demeanor strikingly different from the behavior of the Soviet Premier, who broke up the "summit" conference at Paris last May with emotional insults flung at the head of another state.

The President exhorted the thinking people of the world to come to grips with the dangers of a "war by miscalculation" and appealed for an effective system of disarmament as well as the resolution by peaceful means of all disputes—as, for instance, in West Berlin —that are dividing East and West.

But Mr. Eisenhower's address was notable, not alone because of its general statement of high purposes and worthy ideals, but because it proposed specific courses of action for all nations to follow.

The President dramatically called attention to the importance of supporting the efforts of the United Nations in Africa, and declared:

"Outside interference with these newly emerging nations, all eager to undertake the tasks of modernization, has created a serious challenge to the authority of the United Nations. . . .

"In response to the call of the Republic of the Congo, the United Nations, under its outstanding Secretary General, has recently mounted a large-scale effort to provide that new Republic with help. That effort has been flagrantly attacked by a few nations which wish to prolong strife in the Congo for their own purposes."

This was an indictment of the Soviet Union and its associates for a form of treason against the United Nations itself. Instead of calling, however, for condemnation of individual states, as might well have been done, the President preferred for the time being at least to demand a pledge from all members of the United Nations as follows:

"To refrain from intervening in these new nations' internal affairs—by subversion, force, propaganda, or any other means.

"To refrain from generating disputes between the states of this area or from encouraging them to wasteful and dangerous competition in armaments.

"And to refrain from any action to intensify or exploit present unsettled conditions in the Congo—by sending arms or forces into that troubled area, or by inciting its leaders and peoples to violence against each other.

"These actions my country—and many others—are now avoiding. I hope this Assembly will call upon all its members to do likewise, and that each speaker who follows me to this platform will solemnly pledge his country to honor this call."

This was no contest in invectives. This was no debate on the low level of personal abuse. It was an appeal by the head of a powerful nation conscious that moral force is a more persuasive influence in the long run than bluster or military threat.

"We must," said the President, "guard jealously against those who in alternating moods look upon the United Nations as an instrument for use or abuse."

Mr. Eisenhower described the United Nations as based on a "concept of unity in freedom," and "not a superstate above nations, but a world community embracing them all, rooted in law and justice."

What President Eisenhower, as the leader of the free world, has just proclaimed—even as did President Woodrow Wilson four decades ago—is the ideal of a peaceful union of nations, a "world of justice under law." This is the surest way to an enduring peace for humanity—a goal that can be achieved only as reason supersedes all else in the triumph of moral force.

THE GNAWING ISSUE

OCTOBER 10, 1960

DISCRIMINATION for reasons of race or religion or color involves a never-ending controversy.

Sometimes the pressures to discriminate are economic or competitive. Sometimes they are social. Sometimes they are the result of sheer emotion.

We are hearing much today about a so-called "religious issue." Some say the adherents of one presidential candidate are exploiting it to gain votes based on prejudice. Some say that the supporters of another candidate are bringing it up repeatedly to gain votes by sympathy from co-religionists.

But the issue is always there—a potential source of debate.

It is important, however, to keep the lines of jurisdiction clear in a controversy of this kind. Every individual has a right of association. The Supreme Court of the United States speaks of "freedom of association" as a derivative of our Constitution.

Individuals, therefore, can organize fraternal orders or clubs or associations and invite into their membership whomever they please. But this does not erase the fact that other individuals who believe themselves eligible for admission, either professionally or socially, often feel they are being discriminated against when denied entrance. This is in the domain of private rights, but it creates a gnawing issue.

Where we touch the public area, there is, of course, a different kind of controversy.

We come, for example, to the right of any citizen, irrespective of race or color or religion, to be President of the United States. Abstractly, and under constitutional provisions, there can be no such discrimination. But while national conventions may nominate, the people as a whole have the sole right to elect.

Citizens do vote their prejudices. No amount of debate on the highbrow side as to the nuances involved in the separation of church and state will be convincing to various persons at the grassroots level of discussion. Their viewpoint may be based less on reasoning than on emotion. They point to another religious group as holding itself apart from community activities or as claiming that only its own worshippers are true Christians. This stirs up a gnawing issue on both sides.

Nor will all persons concede they are "prejudiced" because they see danger in electing as President anyone from a particular church. They sincerely believe that a foreign government, combined with a certain church, can dictate to one of the same faith in this country who is elected to the Presidency.

Senator Kennedy said in his Houston speech that, if the time should ever come when the duties of his office would require him to either violate his conscience or violate the national interest, he would resign the office. One wishes that he hadn't spoken of such a contingency, however remote it may be.

It might be suggested by some that Mr. Kennedy is really implying that the Catholic Church would do better with a Protestant than a Catholic in the White House. For it was President Roosevelt, a Protestant, who unofficially recognized the Vatican during World War II by sending Myron Taylor there to be his personal representative and report to the United States Government. Also President Truman, a Protestant, kept Mr. Taylor at the same post after the war and recommended to Congress that formal diplomatic recognition be accorded to the Vatican by the United States.

The politician might contend that neither of these steps would, in view of Mr. Kennedy's statement at Houston, ever be taken by him if he were President. It could be cynically argued, therefore, that it would be better to elect a Catholic as Chief Executive because he would lean over backwards to do what the advocates of a strict separation of church and state have always urged. Merely to cite these contradictions is to illustrate the artificiality of the issue so far as politics is concerned.

We should be glad that two men of conscience have been nominated for the Presidency. We cannot be glad that the gnawing issue persists. Yet we cannot make human beings over and force them to conform to a pattern in their acts or their thinking when they have been told since the days of the founding of the Republic that not only are all men "created equal" but that they are "endowed by their Creator with certain unalienable rights." This means to them a right to associate with whomever they please and to vote for whomever they please without being required to account even for deplorable prejudices or other errors in appraising the virtues of particular candidates or the views they expound in a campaign.

The gnawing issue will persist, and maybe eventually the discussion will gradually diminish the pangs of torment suffered by those who feel they have been the victims of discrimination. Let us hope that pride of race or pride of religion or pride of color will some day enable those same persons to treat the whole debate with disdain.

WHOSE VICTORY

OCTOBER 17, 1960

LET US ASSUME it is the day after our presidential election—how do peoples throughout the world size up the result? What, for instance, is Moscow saying as Kennedy is elected or as Nixon is declared the winner? What is the reaction in Britain and France and among our allies on the other continents?

The basic principle involved is a simple one. Peoples in foreign lands, especially where there are parliamentary or legislative systems of government, have always assumed that a vote for the party in power means a "vote of confidence" in the administration or party that is continued in office. Conversely, a defeat for the party in power is always regarded as a "vote of no confidence" in that same party.

Applying this principle to the American election, a defeat for the Nixon-Lodge ticket would be construed throughout the world to mean a definite repudiation of the policies of President Eisenhower and his Administration during the previous seven years and nine months.

Nikita Khrushchev would doubtless rejoice at this verdict. For to him it would mean that the American people did not stand back of their President in the dispute with the Soviet ruler. The leader of international Communism would say that the American people have confirmed what he has been saying all along—namely, that they do not support their Government's policies. This could encourage him to embark recklessly on a dangerous course that might bring to the world a grave crisis.

Naturally, the Soviet Premier in his public utterances has been careful to denounce both nominees. But the Soviet radio stations, which broadcast around the clock to every part of the world, would nevertheless joyfully record a defeat for the Eisenhower Administration as a victory for the Soviets.

Americans know that no such inference is justified. Yet the Soviet interpretation—that the Eisenhower policies have been repudiated at the polls—will be shared in the press of Britain and France and elsewhere in the free world.

How can such a contingency be averted? Only by a statement, repeated day in and day out during the present campaign, by Senator Kennedy that he intends, if elected, to maintain the basic principles of American foreign policy and that a defeat for his opponents will not mean that the policies in effect heretofore will be materially changed.

Unhappily, from a reading of pronouncements already made by the Democratic Party's standard bearer and by Adlai Stevenson and other prominent Democrats, especially the Chairman of the Senate Foreign Relations Committee, Senator J. W. Fulbright, the impression has been conveyed that these policies will be changed in vital respects.

For several months now the argument has been hammered home by the Democrats that the "prestige" of the United States has sunk to a low point and that America is militarily weaker than the Soviets, especially in missiles. The whole thesis of the Democratic Party, as set forth in the platform adopted at the National Convention in Los Angeles, is that American foreign policy under the Eisenhower Administration has been a failure and that a Democratic Administration "will present a new face to the world."

The newspapers of Europe, Asia, Africa and Latin America have been publishing in recent weeks extracts from the speeches of Senator Kennedy. These all point up his plea to the voters to say by their ballots that the American people have "no confidence" in the Administration in power in Washington.

In the event of a change in party control of our executive branch, foreign governments would have to wait nearly three months—from November 8 to January 20—before a Democratic Administration, with an entirely new personnel in the top positions of Government, would take office. After the inauguration, a new Administration would doubtless need several months to read up on all the confidential data that have been gathered about the background of the world situation in the previous eight years. Some incumbent officials would perhaps be asked to stay on to help overcome the transition "gap." But what would the Communists be doing in the meantime to take advantage of such a critical situation as they intensify their subversive activities around the globe?

How, on the other hand, would a victory for the Nixon-Lodge ticket be interpreted abroad?

It would be construed as a "vote of confidence" by the American people in the international policies of the Eisenhower Administration. The rest of the world would be plainly assured that the United States will remain steadfast in its support of the principles of freedom and liberty and that the fight against Communist imperialism will not be diminished in vigor.

The people of the United States are confronted with a decision that will be of fateful significance in the history not only of America but of the whole world.

TO THE PEOPLES OF
THE SOVIET UNION—

OCTOBER 24, 1960

WE CAN SAY earnestly and sincerely to the peoples of the Soviet Union that we have the highest respect for them.

We can say to them also, with equal vehemence, that we in the United States have no desire at any time to shed the blood of a single human being in the Soviet Union or anywhere else.

We can say to the peoples of the whole world that we believe that war would be terrible and would solve nothing.

But how can war be prevented if the ruler of another nation shows recklessness and gives the impression that at any moment—without consulting anybody else—he may pull the trigger and start a war?

We in America have no desire to tell the people of any other country whom they should choose as a ruler or what form of government they shall maintain. But the time has come to say to the peoples of the Soviet Union that they have a man in charge of their government who has just given to the American people an exhibition of erratic behavior that is both startling and menacing.

Certainly there can be no negotiations leading to disarmament or the relief of tension unless there is mutual faith. Nikita Khrushchev now has destroyed all vestiges of that faith. No matter who is inaugurated President of the United States on January 20 next, the American people would never have confidence in any negotiations with Nikita Khrushchev. He is looked upon by the American people as a man who has not only insulted them but has completely misjudged them and who violates the fine traditions of decency and courtesy of the Russian people by taking off a shoe and flaunting it defiantly at a meeting of the General Assembly of the United Nations.

Such boorishness is tragic—not because the antics are in themselves dangerous, but because they symbolize irresponsibility, arbitrariness, lack of judgment, and the possibility that at some fateful moment they will bring a loss of temper and a missile-rattling adventure which could lead to war.

There is such a thing as fair play—not only at the Olympic sports tournament but also in the relations between great nations. The Soviet Premier comes to the United States, and what he says is reported everywhere in the press and on the regular news broadcasts throughout the United States. But what representatives of this country said at the same Assembly has not been told to the peoples of the Soviet Union.

How, then, can the people behind the Iron Curtain that separates us ever know the truth?

Certainly there are broadcasting stations whose messages can be beamed across international boundaries. Our own "Voice of America," operated by the U. S. Information Agency, can transmit thoughts like those expressed on this page to the peoples of other lands. There will be jamming of such broadcasts and interference, but the messages can get through to various locations from which word-of-mouth communication can spread them still farther.

The message is a simple one: Nikita Khrushchev has hurt the cause of peace. He has brought nearer the war that neither people wants. He has astonished the diplomats of the world by his crudeness and boorishness. He has made of himself an exhibitionist without scruple or manners.

Why should the people of Russia and the peoples of the other Communist-dominated countries be the victims of such behavior? Where is the dignity of high office, and where is the fair play that requires each side to give the other full opportunity to present its own arguments on every international issue?

We in America are deeply concerned about the possibility of a nuclear war. Many of our people are frightened. They are convinced now that Nikita Khrushchev is cruel enough to start a nuclear war. Why should the peoples of the Soviet Union be saddled with the burden of Nikita Khrushchev's mistakes? Must they be subjected to such humiliation as we have just witnessed in the General Assembly of the United Nations?

Plainly it is essential that the peoples of the Soviet Union select someone to represent them who will win back the prestige that has been lost for them by the unmoral Communist spokesman who defames his own country, even as he tries to defame the peoples of the other countries of the world.

Neither side wants war. But a crazy man can start one. And the American people are forced to conclude that only a man with an unbalanced mind could have done what Nikita Khrushchev did in New York City at the sessions of the General Assembly of the United Nations. Let us have in the U. N. a Soviet Premier who keeps his shoes on—and both feet on the ground.

CHANGE NOW?

OCTOBER 31, 1960

NEARLY EVERY CHANGE in the White House in the last half-century involving the defeat of the party in power has been followed by serious consequences in the nation's economic condition or in its international relations.

Was this a mere coincidence due to circumstances beyond our control? Or was our adversity related to some extent to the complete turnover of personnel in our own Government? Did other governments take advantage of our weakness in a transition period?

The historical record is startling in its implications.

In March 1913, the Democrats took over after 16 years of Republican rule. Soon we were involved in a protracted dispute with Mexico and our military forces were occupying Vera Cruz. Not long afterward World War I was disrupting American export trade and causing widespread unemployment. We were totally unprepared for the emergency.

In March 1921, when the Republicans took over the White House, the postwar readjustment that had begun after the armistice in November 1918 was complicated by a new Administration, which found itself almost immediately in the throes of a depression.

In November 1932, when the Democrats won, the worldwide depression that began in 1929 was on the mend, according to reports published that summer by the economic bureaus of the League of Nations. The outgoing President, Herbert Hoover, made a valiant effort to secure co-operation from President-elect Franklin D. Roosevelt in order to avert a catastrophe in this country. But this effort failed, and the bank holiday—the closing of all banks throughout the country—occurred almost coincidentally with the inauguration. The economic setback resulted in the loss of billions of dollars to the American people. Yet nearly all the banks later were revealed to have been solvent. Had there been co-operation, the panic might have been avoided.

It will be recalled that in July 1933, just a few months after President Roosevelt was inaugurated, he virtually abandoned America's delegation at the London Economic Conference because he really wasn't as familiar with the background of the world situation as he should have been. He called Secretary of State Hull back home, thus breaking up a meeting which, if continued, could have taken steps to bolster the European economy. This would have furnished the sinews for armament against the Hitler threat and might have helped to avert World War II.

In January 1953, as Dwight Eisenhower, Republican, was inaugurated, a serious loss in momentum occurred. It took the new team more than a year to get its bearings. The sharp cut in defense spending, due to the ending of the Korean War, upset the economy, and a recession developed in 1954.

Now, it will be suggested that perhaps this is an argument against a change in party at any time in the executive branch of the Government. On the contrary, it is an argument against the faulty method we follow in a transition from one party to the other.

Certainly, if there is a change in party in the White House next January, many important posts will have to be filled. The incumbents usually stay on until the new appointees actually take office. The new executives, while in the process of learning the confidential background of public affairs, must make important decisions almost every day.

Plainly our system of elections at fixed intervals is at fault.

Can, therefore, the adverse impact of a change of party in the White House ever be lessened? Should Congress be called into extra session at once if an election brings a change in the party in power in the White House? Should a law be passed authorizing the extension of the terms of service of certain officials who serve at the pleasure of the President? While new appointees would immediately assume official responsibility, they would have beside them experienced officials, as consultants, who could be urged for patriotic reasons to stay on temporarily.

But do the American people want a change in party in the White House at this critical stage of the "cold war"? Is this really the time for change—in the midst of an economic readjustment and world crisis? The American people twice in the 1940s, during World War II, refused to "change horses in midstream."

Rumors of a possible devaluation of gold by the United States are already affecting European stock markets, where the price of gold abroad is fluctuating widely. Press dispatches say this is in part due to a belief that the Democrats, with "easy money" policies and an inflationary situation caused by large budgetary deficits, will find themselves compelled to revalue gold, as Roosevelt did in 1933.

It is to be hoped that the electorate will give due weight to the risks. If, however, a change is desired, the people should demand a better formula for the transition than has been applied in the past.

THE CROSSROADS

NOVEMBER 7, 1960

THE COMING ELECTION in the United States can mean a crisis, not only for the world but for the American system of free enterprise.

Personalities are not as important as are the forces behind the respective candidates for the Presidency. These forces can readily effect a change in the whole direction of America's course as a free nation.

Shall we take the road to state socialism, or shall we continue on the road that has made us the richest and most powerful economic force in the world?

Merely to look at two faces on the television and to attempt to judge by the glibness of speech or the adroitness of the repartee which man will make the better President is to exalt the superficial and to ignore the fundamental issue of our times: What are the forces behind the two nominees?

It is not the John F. Kennedy of the campaign whose views will be reflected in the Presidency if the Democratic nominee wins. It will be the views of the powerful labor-union bosses, of the powerful "liberal" bloc, and of the powerful groups which are ready to trust Khrushchev and his Communist allies on disarmament and nuclear tests. There are hints, too, of the possible relinquishment of our bases in Western Europe.

It is not the Richard M. Nixon of the campaign whose views will be reflected in the Presidency if the Republican nominee wins. His own expressions, which have leaned now and then to the so-called "liberal" side in government spending, will be superseded by the principles dominant today in the Eisenhower Administration, which, despite a few deviations, has dedicated itself unflinchingly to fiscal soundness domestically and firmness in foreign policy.

Let us face the facts. America is at the crossroads. One road leads to more and more intervention by the Federal Government in the management and control of the business enterprises of the nation, large and small. The other road continues the course of free enterprise.

One road leads to the development of the "public sector" instead of the "private sector," as the terms are used by the Kennedy advisers—the "brain trust" which helped to draft the Democratic platform and will take over if Mr. Kennedy wins.

The "public sector" already is hailed as the enemy or rival of the "private sector." The idea that free enterprise shall be dominant is denounced as the Kennedy campaigners urge that the Government shall become master of the destiny of our business enterprises.

Already it is urged by the Kennedy side that the budget shall go unbalanced, if necessary, to finance social reforms, no matter what they cost and no matter how high go the taxes.

Already we observe Europe worrying about the effect of the American election on the future of the dollar.

But this is merely a symptom of the fundamental change that faces America if the Eisenhower policies, both domestic and foreign, are repudiated by a Kennedy victory at the polls on November 8. We shall see the turn toward the left in domestic policies—the same impulsive and impetuous acceptance of ill-founded theories and unwise economic doctrines that gave America a period of heavy unemployment and suffering from 1933 to 1941. Only our entry into the European war in the latter year restored the development of the heavy-goods industries in the United States. They had been sadly neglected because of government barriers, as more than 8,000,000 persons remained unemployed in every previous year except one during the Roosevelt Administrations.

America's population is growing rapidly. The experts predict we shall have a billion people 90 years hence, and presumably a half-billion people in 50 years. Certainly as population expands, the problem of governing such a mass of persons grows more and more complex. Shall freedom, however, be swept aside as we get a form of neo-fascism or neo-Communism? Mr. Khrushchev is convinced that we in America will be fellow travelers in his direction.

The American people—if not misled by false prophets and misguided crusaders—will not vote to destroy individual liberty as the Communists have done. But if the system of free enterprise is weakened and it disintegrates under the flag of "national purpose" and phony "liberalism," we will certainly be confronted with a strong central government whose totalitarian impulses will be manifested in a controlled press, radio and television, and in a dictatorship by labor bosses who will periodically get out the necessary vote to continue a program of "spend and spend, tax and tax, elect and elect."

This political refrain of New Deal days is already being enthusiastically chanted in the Kennedy camp, as the campaign comes to a close.

Will America, now at the crossroads, take the "left turn"?

THE ONLY HOPE NOW

NOVEMBER 14, 1960

WHAT IS THE REAL DIFFERENCE between a conservative and a radical—sometimes called a "liberal"? Let us assume sincerity of purpose, yet the fact is that the radical wants to experiment with what he calls "new ideas," while the conservative knows from bitter experience that most of them won't work.

As this is written, the outcome of the election is not known. But one thing is certain—the crucial battle between the unsound experimenters and the advocates of fiscal soundness is just beginning.

The conservative steadfastly adheres to the principle that a written Constitution with specified powers is better than an improvised Constitution in which the words "general welfare" are construed to mean license to impose anything from a managed economy to a totalitarian regime. Mr. Khrushchev, anticipating such flexibility, predicts that in a few generations we will succumb anyhow to state socialism.

The tendency of many writers of the current generation is to characterize a conservative as just a "reactionary"—someone who doesn't believe in progress, someone who wants to keep things as they are and doesn't want to change anything. Yet the largest number of true conservatives are to be found among the dynamic executives of modern business. They are not hard-hearted men who are opposed to human progress. They are not persons who wish to stunt America's growth. After all, as America grows, so grows the business community and the consumption of products.

The truth is that businessmen are conservative primarily because they deal with other people's money. To say that the so-called "liberal" is careless in his thinking about other people's money is not to impute to him any improper motives, but merely to emphasize his lack of experience with borrowed money.

The best self-education a "liberal" could get, whether he is a Republican or a Democrat, would be to take the risk of being responsible for the repayment of borrowed money through the earnings of a business that he himself operates. He cannot lean on the Government for a subsidy to pay all losses. Nor will his troubled conscience find refuge in bankruptcy. There is no way for him to get more sales except by making a product better than his competitor's. Smooth phrases will not maintain sales for an unsatisfactory commodity, despite all the satire about "Madison Avenue" techniques. It's easy enough to bring out a new idea with someone else's money—if you don't have to pay it back.

As the nation turns its eyes now to the so-called "liberals" who will take command of our national councils to a greater degree than ever before, it is important for the conservatives to close ranks. The ultraconservative who really is against social reforms and wants no governmental intervention of an economic nature, even when there are national emergencies, should not impede the movement of sensible conservatives to attain a constructive program of public policies.

In Congress, the conservatives of the South are Democrats and the conservatives of the North are Republicans. This coalition already has saved America from economic and financial disaster. It can do so again. It must rise against the experimentalists, with their emotional appeals based on the "general welfare." It must oppose the fuzzy thinking of those who say the way to win the "Sputnik" race is to increase teachers' salaries.

All the talk about "economic growth" and "care for the aged" comes down to a simple fact—that we can have growth unlimited if we encourage self-reliance. We can prepare for old age if we are thrifty or raise thrifty children. The unfortunate indigent and the unsuccessful, of course, must become a public charge on the rest of the people. But pride alone will keep the number down unless "liberalism" succeeds in making it honorable for everybody to live on "handouts."

As for our military position, it will not be strengthened merely by spending more money for gadgets. It can be weakened if we go bankrupt financially and cannot raise enough revenues by taxes to keep the budget balanced. Our power in the world can deteriorate overnight if we have a runaway inflation, such as weakened Germany, virtually wiped out its middle classes and ultimately forced a frustrated people in 1933 to acquiesce in the autocracy of Hitlerism.

Partisan differences among us must be put aside as we approach now the real crisis in American history—the struggle for survival against those in our midst who would lead us down the road to bankruptcy, even as they broadcast their illusory platitudes about the need for "moving ahead" by artificial "growth" to achieve "national purpose."

Words and phrases uttered in the campaign that have promised us Utopia will, by the time these lines are read, have served their purpose of political expediency.

The only hope now is that the conservatives of both parties in Congress, supported by the conservative majority in the nation, will work together to save America from financial chaos and defeat in the "cold war."

A MINORITY PRESIDENT

NOVEMBER 21, 1960

A NUMERICAL PLURALITY of a few thousand votes—about one half of one per cent of more than 67,000,000—does not by any means constitute an expression of the will of the majority of the American people on basic issues of domestic or world policy.

Senator John F. Kennedy won this election to the Presidency by a combination of minority blocs and groups influenced by reasons of religion, economic conditions and political expediency.

Ironically enough, the Negro voters in the North gave heavy majorities to the Democrats, as the "civil rights" crusade of the Republicans failed to pay off politically for them. Nor did the Republican following in various other minority groups turn out to be as numerous as that of the Democrats.

But the political expediency which caused the Democratic politicians in the South to go counter to the courageous stand on principle taken by so many hitherto Democratic newspapers—which openly supported the Republican ticket—cannot erase the fact that the people of the South are basically conservative. Their votes, if polled in a referendum solely on the merits or demerits of the Democratic national platform, would have been cast overwhelmingly for the conservative nominee—Vice President Nixon.

Similarly, whether it was pride of religion or resentment against the outbursts of some Protestant clergymen which caused so many Catholics to desert the Republican Party this time, there were millions of conservative Catholics who voted for Mr. Kennedy though actually preferring the non-radical policies and platform of his opponent.

In this sense, Mr. Kennedy's speeches did not represent the views of the majority. His election was due to a momentary coalition of minority groups. He owes his victory in large part to the work done by the labor unions in almost every precinct in the big Northern States. Contributing to his election were the resentments of many voters in areas where unemployment not only had brought distress to workers, but had had an adverse impact on the business of the communities.

Apart from the discontent, however, occasioned by the "readjustment" or "recession" now going on in the national economy, can there be said to have been in general a verdict of disapproval of the policies of the Eisenhower Administration? The closeness of the vote shows that the nation is fundamentally conservative in the sense that no sanction for radical experiments in either the domestic or foreign field can really

be inferred as having been given.

Naturally Nikita Khrushchev is rejoicing, and the controlled Soviet press is already claiming that the election proves that the American people "expect Washington to pursue a reasonable course in international affairs"—which presumably reflects a belief that the new Administration will make concessions to the Soviets. This is an erroneous interpretation, but the Moscow radio has for several days now been beaming all over the world comments to the effect that America has "repudiated" the Eisenhower policies.

Mr. Kennedy is not going to be "soft on Communism" unless he becomes the victim of advisers who are appeasers at heart. His Catholic environment would seem to belie any tendency to bow to the Communists. The Catholic Church has been a bulwark of opposition to Communism throughout the world. Mr. Kennedy shares the convictions of Catholics and non-Catholics that the triumph of Communism would end religious freedom and other freedoms as well.

There may, therefore, be a distinct plus in Mr. Kennedy's religious background. Indeed it is to be hoped that the religious issue in our politics will be less important hereafter than it has been in the past. A Roman Catholic has been elected to the White House for the first time. This should tell the world that there is really no religious test for office in America.

It is unfortunate, however, that, as this precedent is established, the election should have turned out to be so close. A landslide for a candidate whose basic policies won overwhelming approval by the vast majority of the people, and who happened at the same time to be a Catholic, would have better demonstrated that the people of the United States voted for or against a particular person, not on the basis of religious prejudice, but solely on the merits of the issues and the candidates. As it is, many observers, noting the big shift of votes in areas with a large Catholic population—with no parallel anywhere else in the country—contend that a Catholic bloc decided the election.

This is the time when we are all exhorted to let bygones be bygones and to give our new leader the wholehearted support of all the people. But it is a time for more than mere exhortation to the populace. It is a time to remind the successful party and the victorious candidates for all offices that elections do not settle fundamental issues but merely serve as vivid reminders of the diversity of interests and pressures that make up the modern political struggle.

THE PENALTY OF LEADERSHIP

NOVEMBER 28, 1960

NEARLY A HALF-CENTURY AGO widespread comment was occasioned by an advertisement about an automobile which had at that time won a position of leadership throughout the country. The ad was entitled "The Penalty of Leadership." It was an essay on the dilemma of the leader whose very achievement of the top position—whether in literature or the arts or industry—has often brought criticism, detraction and the "shafts of the envious few."

The leadership which is under attack today is that of our own nation—our own Government and its relations with the other peoples of the world.

We are criticized often in the foreign press, even as we are envied. We are accused of selfish motives. We are sniped at and even harassed—as, for instance, when our properties are confiscated in Cuba.

Our leadership also has been assailed as a partisan issue in our own country. During the recent political campaign, a severe indictment was filed by the subsequently victorious candidate for the Presidency. He insisted that he was not disparaging his own country but was merely pointing up the inadequacies of its "leadership."

This is no occasion for reviewing a political campaign, with its demagoguery and customary exaggerations. But now the shoe is on the other foot. It becomes the duty and responsibility of the new Administration to raise the "prestige" of the United States by official action. Exercises in campaign rhetoric will no longer be of avail.

Americans of all parties must co-operate to make effective the policies of our own Government abroad. But to do so we ourselves must face up to some important facts which unhappily many of the critics, however well-meaning they may be, have been inclined to overlook.

For, paradoxical as it may seem, we do not hold the reins of leadership in the world. We are not masters of the destiny of our allies. We are not the dictator of the Western alliance. The United States is simply one partner in the enterprise of maintaining the independence of nations that seek to be saved from conquest.

We are not the guardians of the underprivileged, though we desire to extend our benevolence to them if they show signs of self-reliance and self-sacrifice.

We have military strength, to be sure, but we cannot ever build up enough power to safeguard by ourselves the many nations which seek our aid.

What America aspires to do is to contribute to the strength of an alliance, but not to dominate it.

The concept of America as "the leader of the free world" is flattering, but it is also inappropriate. For America cannot lead unless others wish voluntarily to follow our initiative or our advice.

What the free world needs is a virile association and not an absolute monarch to boss the show.

To maintain peace in the world today, it is necessary to mobilize economic as well as military force to deter a common enemy.

But what kind of battle is it which sees members of one side condoning separate intercourse and even negotiation with members of an enemy group? We are supposed, for instance, to help various countries in Africa, in the Middle East and in Southeast Asia. But they, in turn, seem to feel free to adopt what they call a "neutralist" position—which means in plain terms that they reserve the right to play the two sides against each other for benefits they can derive from both.

How can there be mutual trust and good faith and, indeed, sacrifice if those nations which look upon us as saviours of their freedoms nevertheless permit the enemy to infiltrate their political institutions and to carry on insidious warfare against the United States?

We observe, for example, Communist activities in Central and South America and, in fact, on every continent. We adhere to the doctrine of non-interference in the internal affairs of other countries, but the Communists do not obey that rule.

We must never assume the role of "leadership" if dominance is implied. We must instead win concurrence only by persuasion and by relying on the rightness of our proposals.

Conversely, our allies must not expect us to bear the entire burden of defense—financial or economic or military. They cannot justly isolate themselves and decline to give us bases or refuse to permit nuclear weapons to be stored on their territory. How can we defend our lives and the lives of those who claim to be our friends and partners if they feel they can dissociate themselves at will from the responsibilities of a common defense?

There is, indeed, today a penalty on leadership, but it is imperative that there be no penalty inflicted on all of us because of the isolationist viewpoints of opposition parties in Great Britain or in France or elsewhere in the free world. It is time to face facts and take steps to strengthen the alliance. Only by the action of a united group of governments can there be a triumph over the common enemy.

"THE BEST AVAILABLE TALENT"

DECEMBER 5, 1960

THE NATION EXPECTS the new Administration to keep its main promise—to establish a Government that will not stand still but will "move ahead."

Miracles cannot be performed, nor can changes be made overnight that will give us prosperity at home and restore abroad the "prestige" we were told during the campaign America had allegedly lost through a lack of "bold and imaginative" ideas. But the nation does expect that, in the choosing of a Cabinet, the best minds of the country will be selected and not just the best political henchmen.

The New York "Times," which supported Senator Kennedy in his campaign for the Presidency, is apparently concerned about the outlook. It is disturbed by the newspaper stories emanating from the headquarters of the President-elect saying he is considering certain persons for his Cabinet whose chief claim to such posts seems to be more political than anything else. The "Times" reminds Mr. Kennedy that he said during the campaign:

"Should I be elected President, it would be my intention to ask the ablest men in the country to make whatever sacrifice is required to bring to the Government a ministry of the best available talent. . . . For no Government is better than the men who compose it— and I want the best. . . . All appointments, both high and low, will be made on the basis of ability—without regard to race, creed, national origin, sex, section or occupation."

The "Times" points out that "the promise could not be clearer, the pledge more solemn," and adds that, if this pledge means anything, it "means that political gratitude will be a totally insufficient reason for appointment to major federal office."

This important newspaper, which helped elect the new President, says it expects "better things of Senator Kennedy." So do the American people.

But in the same "Times" editorial we read these words of warning:

"It is simply not good enough to name a bright young political manager, no matter how bright or how young or how personally loyal, to a major post in government that by rights—if not by precedent—ought to be kept completely out of the political arena. It is simply not good enough to talk about seats on the Supreme Court of the United States as if they were political handouts. We do not say that Mr. Kennedy has done these things—and if he had, we would have to admit while criticizing him that most of his predecessors have committed similar faults. But we hope and believe that Mr. Kennedy will remain above this level of political thinking."

Undoubtedly these comments were occasioned by newspaper reports a few days earlier that Mr. Kennedy had in mind the appointment of his younger brother to head the Department of Justice, and by other dispatches which said that Governor Ribicoff of Connecticut, previously mentioned for the place, doesn't want to be Attorney General after all but would prefer a nomination to the next vacancy on the Supreme Court of the United States.

Now Robert Kennedy is an able young man, and he ought not to be penalized just because he is the brother of the President-elect. He might make a better Attorney General than some we have had in the past.

Also, Abraham Ribicoff is an able public servant, and he ought not to be pushed aside just because he happens to have been among the first Governors to advance the preconvention candidacy of the President-elect.

The real question, however, is whether in the entire United States, irrespective of race or creed or section or political service, there are not other persons better qualified for these posts. This is the crux of the problem that faces the man who has promised the American people a higher standard of service than presumably his predecessor has given them.

Cabinet posts, to be sure, have sometimes been awarded in the past on the basis of both political service and campaign contributions by either the appointees or their friends. This is not a time, however, to rake over the faults of the past. Mr. Kennedy himself has said he would look forward rather than backward. So the real obligation is to turn over a new leaf in Government—to get a Cabinet of outstanding men and let them become the highest council in the Federal Government in fact as well as in name.

It may well be that the newsmen covering the President-elect's headquarters have been doing a bit of speculating on their own based on what some of the politicians may be telling them.

Until Mr. Kennedy has announced his Cabinet, it is the duty of all of us to assume he will be faithful to his campaign pledge. For the nation expects the new President to fulfill his promise even though he may disappoint some of those ambitious politicians who helped him triumph at the national convention and in the election itself.

IRRESPONSIBLE GOVERNMENT

DECEMBER 12, 1960

THE NATION IS ACCEPTING with a strange complacency the conduct of the recent election for the Presidency.

Charges of fraud and irregularity in the counting of the ballots have been serious enough to require official investigations. But, distressing as it is for the world to be reading of such imputations of dishonesty, the real shame is that in the United States our elections are conducted under a provision of the Constitution which has long outlived its usefulness.

For, under Article II and the Twelfth Amendment, we are told that a President and Vice President are to be elected by the "electors" chosen in each State. But there is not a word in the Constitution that binds those electors to vote for the party nominees who have received the highest number of votes in their respective States.

We observed in the South this year tickets of electors in certain States described as "unpledged." Some were elected on that basis.

What most people today do not realize, however, is that no elector is constitutionally bound to vote for the candidates for President and Vice President who have, respectively, received the highest number of votes in his State. Only an "unwritten Amendment," as it has sometimes been called, has given us the present system whereby the electors usually pay heed to the wishes of the voters themselves. Six States have passed laws instructing electors to vote for the candidates of their political parties.

Since the early 1800s the electors have customarily been pledged by the party organizations to vote for the nominees of the party whether chosen by national convention or otherwise. But this is an unofficial action by a political party. Nowhere in the Constitution are political parties or organizations or the convention system even mentioned.

The Constitution does provide for a vote by the House of Representatives in the event that the electors do not give a majority to any candidate. When this happens, the members of the House from each State must decide for themselves which candidate to support. Each State delegation has a single vote and casts one ballot. Whoever got a majority of these 50 votes would today be elected President, and the Senate, using the same method, would select the Vice President.

It is always possible for enough electors to cast or withhold their votes so that no candidate has a majority in the Electoral College, and thus throw the election into the House of Representatives.

What a travesty this is on so-called democracy! How can the wishes of the people be recognized when an irresponsible faction in a few States can override or ignore the votes of the people?

What is needed is a constitutional amendment that requires the electors to vote in the Electoral College for the candidates of the party they represent.

There have been various reforms suggested from time to time which would permit the electoral vote in each State to be split so that each elector would represent only the majority in a congressional district, with two electors "at large" representing the State as a whole.

Certainly such a system would strengthen the position of the political parties and tend to emphasize party responsibility.

But even such a reform would not achieve the desired goal—responsible government. Under the parliamentary system, each district elects a member of the national legislature and each party selects its own leader from among those members. The "opposition" picks its own "shadow Cabinet" which, through day-by-day contact with the existing government, is kept constantly informed. Within 48 hours after an election the new government, which has already set up its entire Cabinet, usually takes over the whole executive machinery. Continuity is assured—something of transcendent importance in a nuclear age.

The Prime Minister is a member of both the executive and the legislative branches. His removal can be demanded at any time by a majority vote of the parliament. If he refuses to resign and asks for a general election, then the people decide whether he is right or wrong by electing new members or re-electing the incumbents. The leader of the party in control of the new parliament is the Prime Minister.

This is responsible government. The people at any time can express themselves on the issues and on the man they wish to lead them. There are some defects in the system, as, for instance, the lack of safeguards against the excessive power of the minority through "splinter" parties, a factor that caused the French recently to revamp their system.

But whether we should adopt a modified form of the parliamentary system or modernize our electoral system, certainly there is need for a thorough examination by Congress of this whole question so that by constitutional amendment we may be relieved of our present system of irresponsible government.

THE DIS-UNITED NATIONS

DECEMBER 19, 1960

EVERY DAY we speak of or read about the United Nations organization as wielding the power of a superstate.

But it isn't a superstate. It isn't even an alliance. It is a loosely organized association whose will can be thwarted at any time by a single "permanent" member of the so-called Security Council.

Originally the U. N. was designed to keep the peace in the world by using conciliation, mediation or military force to forestall or repel aggression as between states. What has thus far given the U. N. the moral support of mankind is the fear that in a nuclear age a small war might develop into a big war.

But today it is civil war within countries that the U. N. has tried to police. Troops have been dispatched by the U. N. to the Congo, for instance, to preserve order. The U. N. Charter says:

"Nothing contained in the present Charter shall authorize the United Nations to intervene in matters which are essentially within the domestic jurisdiction of any state . . ."

It is speciously argued that the request of a constituted government for military aid can be properly granted by the U. N.

Actually, there are no "constituted governments" in areas where rebellion or the military coup d'état is the instrument of factionalism and dissident elements.

The imperialistic regime in Moscow is, to be sure, seeking conquest by infiltration and by supplying military technicians to assist one party against another within troubled states. Action should be taken against the Soviets—and not against peoples struggling for independence.

Despite the pious protestations of the Soviet Union that it does not interfere with the sovereignty of any state, the fact is that the Moscow authorities are constantly invading and violating the sovereignty of nations everywhere—in Asia, Africa and Latin America as well as in Eastern Europe.

What we are witnessing is a gigantic operation by the Soviet Union to obtain by so-called peaceful conquest control of a vast territory.

Arrayed against the Soviet military bloc is the North Atlantic Treaty Organization, which has the disadvantage of being an alliance of sovereign governments each of which marks out its own course and decides for itself what aid it will give or withhold. This is a weak alliance, and the Soviet Union's progress is involuntarily assisted by the vacillation of the Western European governments which cannot even agree on what bases shall be allotted to the common defense or who shall fire the guns or missiles that are supposed to be ready at an instant's notice to ward off attack.

The opposing alliances of the East and the West are, of course, authorized by the Charter of the U. N. under Article 51. This enables any group of governments to consolidate their military strength for purposes of "collective self-defense" against a potential enemy.

So what does the "United Nations" really mean? It is a forum for debate, and in that respect it can be helpful. But when, in the guise of preserving peace in the world, the U. N. authorizes its Secretary-General to take charge of an allied military force to carry out broad instructions—theoretically approved by all—there is friction and dissension.

There may, indeed, be a bigger chance of a world war developing as a consequence of the U. N.'s well-intentioned efforts to police an area than might be the case if nature were allowed to take its course by the device of revolution. Certainly one of the ideals of freedom-loving countries is the right of revolution. It is a painful form of evolution, but it is wiser for the U. N. to block outside interference than to permit its own police force to meddle in internal affairs.

The U. N.'s venture in the Congo has been expensive. The Soviet Union refuses to pay its share. This is proof that there is no allegiance to the Charter by the Moscow regime and that, for all practical purposes, it might be more accurate to refer to the Dis-United Nations than to make a mockery of the present name.

For the members are not united. Some recognize the Charter's obligations, and some do not. The Soviet Union wouldn't let even a U. N. commission of inquiry go into Hungary in 1956 or 1957, and to this day keeps on ruling that country with a tyrannical hand. If the U. N. is expected to solve internal problems, why hasn't it sent an army into the captive countries in Europe?

Also, why should so-called independent countries be rushed into U. N. membership when they haven't even set up orderly governments or conducted free elections?

The sooner the people of the free world recognize that the Dis-United Nations is ignoring its own Charter and the high purposes for which it was established, the sooner will the alliance against Soviet imperialism be strengthened. For only when the peoples of the Soviet-Asian bloc have attained their freedom and set up free governments can there be an organization of truly united nations.

A "GOOD" CABINET?

DECEMBER 26, 1960

WHAT IS A "GOOD" CABINET? The average man reads about prominent personalities, and if the names are either well known or held in esteem by the press, then the consensus is that a good set of selections has been made.

Little thought is given to the functions to be performed by these new Cabinet officers. Even less is known of the system that actually prevails in Cabinet meetings.

The public thinks of the Cabinet as a group of intelligent advisers who sit in judgment on public questions and render a solemn verdict in which the President usually concurs.

But that is not what happens. Rarely does the head of one department attempt to give advice about another Cabinet member's department. It isn't timidity but lack of background.

Under our system, the President is boss. He can ignore the advice of his entire Cabinet if he likes. Often he does this not because he considers his own judgment superior but because he actually knows more of the intimate details of a problem than do his advisers as a whole. The tendency is to run a two-man government—the President and the Cabinet officer in charge of a particular field of operations.

Obviously, as a President constantly gets confidential reports from abroad and talks on the telephone perhaps two or three times a day with his Secretary of State or confers with him separately, much information becomes available, and there isn't time before making decisions to transmit all this to the other members of the Cabinet —or hours enough in the day for them to absorb it and do their own jobs.

The same thing is true of other fields of governmental action. How much time can the Secretary of State, for example, give to the study of agricultural problems or to the delicate question of whether interest rates should be higher or lower on government bonds?

Not a single member of the proposed Cabinet, moreover, owes his selection to any expression of the popular will. Out of the men selected for the new Cabinet, only two have ever run for Congress.

Some have been chosen merely as a political reward. Some have been picked because they have bright minds and can bring to the President some of those "bold and imaginative ideas" which have been promised in glowing phrases during the last few years of campaigning against the Administration in power.

This is not a new situation but one that has plagued our Government for many years. Before Dwight Eisenhower took office the following appeared on this page on February 29, 1952:

"The people generally think, of course, that the Cabinet sits with the President, gives him advice and helps him administer the Government. But the Cabinet officers are merely the operating heads of the Government departments. They are not familiar with the policies of departments other than their own. . . .

"The American Government needs to be streamlined. The American people should be able to hold the executive as well as the legislative branch accountable at the polls every two years or even more frequently if there is a major issue requiring an election. The entire Cabinet, as well as the leaders of the majority party in Congress, should share with the President the responsibility for policy-making. The people should be able at will to remove the Cabinet, the President, or Congress.

"Such a system would mean better men in the executive group and an operating set-up which would be administered primarily by career men who are not beholden to political influences."

Also, on January 28, 1955, an editorial on this page said in part:

"The Presidency today is, of course, too big for any one man. We shall not overcome the defects in our present system until the Cabinet of ten or more persons gives all of its time to the Chief Executive. This should be his 'staff.' Each of the major departments could be managed by a deputy, but the Cabinet members themselves should have offices alongside the President and meet with him at least once a day."

The foregoing ideas have been expressed repeatedly since February 1913, when the then President-elect Woodrow Wilson predicted in a letter to congressional leaders that America would some day have to amend its Constitution and provide for some system of Cabinet government accountable to the people. He wrote also that four years is sometimes too long a period for a President to be in that office and that sometimes it is too short.

When the two-term limitation on presidential tenure by constitutional amendment was submitted by Congress in 1947, this writer contended that it was a mistake. The people should be trusted to keep in office a good public servant and to oust him if he fails to respond to the public will.

What we need is accountability and stability, and we do not get either under our present system.

1961

THE COMING CLIMAX

JANUARY 9, 1961

THE CYCLE OF EVENTS that inevitably precedes a war is beginning to emerge.

The free world is tormented by a desire to pay almost any price to avoid a catastrophe. Yet bitter experience tells us that this is the very thing that can plunge us into bloody conflict.

We are being threatened today in every continent of the world.

Soviet imperialism is subverting government after government—in Latin America, in Africa, in Asia, and in Europe.

Even in our own country, there are some misguided newspaper editors, some misguided businessmen and some misguided intellectuals who pooh-pooh the menace. They raise smokescreens about the need for trade or to defend Communist activity as a right of "free speech."

It was Justice Oliver Wendell Holmes who, in a famous decision, said that free speech does not include the right to cry "Fire!" in a crowded theater. Nor is there in our Constitution any guarantee of protection for a Communist Party which organizes demonstrations and tries to infiltrate the churches and the colleges, the radio and the press—all at the behest of an enemy government.

This technique of infiltration is being applied throughout the free world—in Britain and in France and in Italy, as well as in North America.

When will we wake up to the fact that we are engaged in a world war—Communist style?

We call it a "cold war" as if this makes it remote from a "hot war" and hence a mere routine of modern diplomacy.

The tragic story of what is happening in Latin America is revealed in the article on page 60 of this issue. No country in this hemisphere apparently is free from the Soviet invasion.

We have placed our hopes in the Organization of American States, but its members are themselves weak because their own governments are threatened from within by Communist-inspired opposition.

We read of the troubles in Laos and in the Congo, and we are misled into believing that they are just part of the process of evolution from colonialism to independence. But the truth is that Western democracies are being fooled by the argument that all that's needed is economic help to remove poverty and illiteracy.

Something sinister has been introduced which must be faced squarely if the holocaust is to be averted.

The simple fact is that the Soviet Union, which spends billions of dollars annually on the "cold war," is convinced that the free world will not fight—that its alliances are weak and that it is disunited. That's what Hitler, too, believed, especially after the "summit" conference at Munich in 1938.

Every day there are signs that the Munich philosophy of appeasement pervades many of the free governments. Why should Moscow change its policy if it can make headway toward complete conquest by "peacefully" taking over government after government?

Nikita Khrushchev rants against "colonialism," but hypocritically maintains a system of tyranny that has made colonies for the Soviets out of several countries in Eastern Europe which once enjoyed independence.

What shall the free world do about all this? Shall it continue to hand out hundreds of millions of dollars every year and have no real voice in what happens to those funds? The propaganda against making grants with "strings" attached is of Soviet origin. So is the much-vaunted "neutralism," the whole object of which has been to put strings on America's policies and to prevent us from making our funds effective.

The time has come to stop fooling ourselves.

Not a dollar of "foreign aid" ought to be appropriated for use by any government which tolerates Communist agents or intrigue or a political party with affiliations in Moscow or Peiping.

If the countries which we are to help will rid themselves of Communist influence, we can support them to a certain extent, but we must not be expected to do that job alone. The nations aided must show some signs of a capacity to establish and maintain their own independence and self-governing system.

A showdown in Latin America is due.

The Monroe Doctrine warned European governments in 1823 to stay out of this hemisphere. It is still a valid doctrine today.

The Soviets have established a base in Cuba and are invading other Latin-American countries.

A warning should be issued to the Soviet Government to get its agents, spy rings and munitions depots out of Latin America.

If necessary, an armed blockade must be imposed—as was done recently along the coasts of Nicaragua and Guatemala—to enforce our position. Unless we show we are ready to fight, there will be no peace in the world.

The Soviets can't afford a war. They are bluffing. It is time to call their bluff, or soon we will face a tragic climax—the big war.

A NEW LAW OF NATIONS

JANUARY 16, 1961

WE ARE WITNESSING a momentous change in human behavior in the world—a deterioration of both law and order.

Organized governments hitherto have sought to formulate a set of principles that would govern the relations of peoples to one another. These principles have often been referred to as "international law" even though no central organization has existed to secure their enforcement.

As humanity has progressed in the fields of education and science, there has been a groping for some universal system of law.

Control of armament, for instance, is not a novel idea. It has often been suggested—even as far back as the 1890s and indeed by a Czar of Russia. Just after the turn of the century, the most significant events were the conferences at The Hague at which international conventions on a variety of subjects were signed. As a sequel came the League of Nations in 1919 and the United Nations in 1945.

But the cardinal weakness has been the inability of nations to agree on fundamental principles or to define the responsibilities of nations.

Actually, an International Court of Justice exists today at The Hague. But it suffers from a lack of definition of its true scope. Its method of selecting the judges is unsatisfactory. For they represent only themselves, and their decisions can be ignored by the parties at interest without really incurring any penalty.

From time to time, advocates of a supernational authority have pleaded for either a community system for specific regions or for the whole world. Opposition has been voiced on the ground that national sovereignty would thereby be violated and that independence and self-government would be sacrificed.

World government may be theoretically defensible in a perfect society, but it is questionable whether even the threat of a nuclear holocaust will diminish the passion for self-determination of international policy.

We are faced these days with a condition and not a theory. What can be done now that is practical? What course is realistic?

To get a remedy for a chronic ailment in government, man has often been compelled to re-read history —to reach back to fundamental principles of human law and morality. For these never grow obsolete. They are rooted in the principle that what's right is more important than who is right.

Perhaps a first step is to restore to use some definitions for which international law has managed to gain acceptance over a long period of time.

First and foremost is the right of a people to choose their own form of government. This means that the people are enabled freely to elect or remove their administrative or legislative representatives.

Second is the right of a people to rebel, if necessary, and, by force of arms, to remove from office anyone who abuses the powers of government delegated to him.

Third is the right of a people to maintain their sovereignty as against external attack and the right to seek allies to help protect the independence of a state.

But today there is need for agreement on another principle born out of recent experience. It is that what happens internally cannot be disregarded by other nations when there is an impact on the lives and properties of foreigners.

Certainly a threat to the peace of a whole area or to the peace of the world is not something that is beyond the reach of outside nations just because local sovereignty or independence may be involved.

If the nations of the world had acted in time, they could have disciplined Nazi Germany in the 1930s, by commercial embargoes or otherwise, and warded off a second world war. Instead, they actually sold munitions of war to Hitler and helped him to prepare for the very conflict they all dreaded.

What is urgently needed is the acceptance of a simple principle—that in a nuclear age preparations for war by any nation are the immediate concern of every other nation, and that sovereignty must be forfeited if a so-called independent nation violates those international rules which are designed to give the community protection against attack.

While all nations would not voluntarily agree to such a principle, the logical next step is to bind together as many governments as will abide by this formula of self-protection.

If the world is divided between those governments that respect equitable and fair principles of international law, and those which prefer to operate in a state of lawlessness, the chances for an effective defense or alliance against the outlaws are at least improved.

Likewise, the crusade for an international system of self-discipline which avoids the superstate, and yet guards against any misuse of the cloak of sovereignty, can be advanced as the world eventually agrees to a new law of nations. It's a logical way to try to put an end to the present era of international anarchy.

Index